THE COMPLETE WORKS OF

WILLIAM SHAKESPEARE

THE   COMPLETE   WORKS   OF

WILLIAM

SHAKESPEARE

ARRANGED   IN   THEIR   CHRONOLOGICAL   ORDER

Edited by

W. G. CLARK AND W. ALDIS WRIGHT

WITH AN INTRODUCTION TO EACH PLAY,
ADAPTED FROM THE SHAKESPEAREAN
PRIMER OF PROFESSOR DOWDEN

Volume Two

NELSON DOUBLEDAY, INC.
Garden City   *New York*

CONTENTS.

Volume One.

Volume Two.

vi

JULIUS CÆSAR.

(WRITTEN ABOUT 1601.)

INTRODUCTION.

This tragedy was produced as early as 1601; so we infer from a passage in Weaver's *Mirror of Martyrs* (1601) in which reference is made to the speeches of Brutus and Antony. The style of the versification, the diction, the characterization, all bear out the opinion that 1600 or 1601 is the date of *Julius Cæsar*. The historical materials of the play were found by the dramatist in the lives of Cæsar, of Brutus, and of Antony, as given in North's translation of Plutarch. Hints for the speeches of Brutus and Antony seem to have been obtained from Appian's *Civil Wars* (B. II., ch. 137–147) translated into English in 1578. Every thing is wrought out in the play with great care and completeness; it is well planned and well proportioned; there is no tempestuousness of passion, and no artistic mystery. The style is full, but not overburdened with thought or imagery; this is one of the most perfect of Shakespeare's plays; greater tragedies are less perfect, perhaps for the very reason that they try to grasp greater, more terrible, or more piteous themes. In *King Henry V.* Shakespeare had represented a great and heroic man of action. In the serious plays, which come next in chronological order, *Julius Cæsar* and *Hamlet*, the poet represents two men who were forced to act—to act in public affairs, and affairs of life and death—yet who were singularly disqualified for playing the part of men of action. Hamlet cannot act because his moral energy is sapped by a kind of skepticism and sterile despair about life, because his own ideas are more to him than deeds, because his will is diseased. Brutus does act, but he acts as an idealist and theorizer might, with no eye for the actual bearing of facts, and no sense of the true importance of persons. Intellectual doctrines and moral ideas rule the life of Brutus; and his life is most noble, high, and stainless, but his public action is a series of practical mistakes. Yet even while he errs we admire him, for all his errors are those of a pure and lofty spirit. In his wife—Cato's daughter, Portia—Brutus has found one who is equal to and worthy of himself. Shakespeare has shown her as perfectly a woman—sensitive, finely-tempered, tender—yet a woman who by her devotion to moral ideas might stand beside such a father and such a husband. And Brutus, with all his Stoicism, is gentle and tender: he can strike down Cæsar if Cæsar be a tyrant, but he cannot roughly rouse a sleeping boy (Act IV., Sc. iii., L. 270). Antony is a man of genius, with many splendid and some generous qualities, but self-indulgent, pleasure-loving, and a daring adventurer rather than a great leader of the State. The character of Cæsar is conceived in a curious and almost irritating manner. Shakespeare (as passages in other plays show) was certainly not ignorant of the greatness of one of the world's greatest men. But here it is his weaknesses that are insisted on. He is failing in body and mind, influenced by superstition, yields to flattery, thinks of himself as almost superhuman, has lost some of his insight into character, and his sureness and swiftness of action. Yet the play is rightly named *Julius Cæsar*. His bodily presence is weak, but his spirit rules throughout the play, and rises after his death in all its might, towering over the little band of conspirators, who at length fall before the spirit of Cæsar as it ranges for revenge.

DRAMATIS PERSONÆ.

JULIUS CÆSAR.
OCTAVIUS CÆSAR,
MARCUS ANTONIUS, } triumvirs after death of Julius Cæsar.
M. ÆMILIUS LEPIDUS,

CICERO,
PUBLIUS, } senators.
POPILIUS LENA,

MARCUS BRUTUS,
CASSIUS,
CASCA,
TREBONIUS, } conspirators against Julius Cæsar.
LIGARIUS,
DECIUS BRUTUS,
METELLUS CIMBER,
CINNA,

FLAVIUS and MARULLUS, tribunes.
ARTEMIDORUS of Cnidos, a teacher of rhetoric.
A Soothsayer.
CINNA, a poet. Another Poet.

LUCILIUS,
TITINIUS,
MESSALA, } friends to Brutus and Cassius.
Young CATO,
VOLUMNIUS,

VARRO,
CLITUS,
CLAUDIUS, } servants to Brutus.
STRATO,
LUCIUS,
DARDANIUS,

PINDARUS, servant to Cassius.

CALPURNIA, wife to Cæsar.
PORTIA, wife to Brutus.

Senators, Citizens, Guards, Attendants, &c.

SCENE: *Rome: the neighborhood of Sardis: the neighborhood of Philippi.*

ACT I.

SCENE I. *Rome. A street.*

Enter FLAVIUS, MARULLUS, *and certain*
Commoners.

Flav. Hence! home, you idle creatures get
  you home:
Is this a holiday? what! know you not,
Being mechanical, you ought not walk
Upon a laboring day without the sign
Of your profession? Speak, what trade art
  thou?
First Com. Why, sir, a carpenter.
Mar. Where is thy leather apron and thy
  rule?
What dost thou with thy best apparel on?
You, sir, what trade are you?
Sec. Com. Truly, sir, in respect of a fine
workman, I am but, as you would say, a cob-
bler.   11
Mar. But what trade art thou? answer me
directly.
Sec. Com. A trade, sir, that, I hope, I may
use with a safe conscience; which is, indeed,
sir, a mender of bad soles.
Mar. What trade, thou knave? thou
naughty knave, what trade?
Sec. Com. Nay, I beseech you, sir, be not
out with me: yet, if you be out, sir, I can
mend you.
Mar. What meanest thou by that? mend
me, thou saucy fellow?   21
Sec. Com. Why, sir, cobble you.
Flav. Thou art a cobbler, art thou?
Sec. Com. Truly, sir, all that I live by is
with the awl: I meddle with no tradesman's
matters, nor women's matters, but with awl. I
am, indeed, sir, a surgeon to old shoes; when
they are in great danger, I recover them. As
proper men as ever trod upon neat's leather
have gone upon my handiwork.   30
Flav. But wherefore art not in thy shop to-
day?
Why dost thou lead these men about the
  streets?
Sec. Com. Truly, sir, to wear out their
shoes, to get myself into more work. But, indeed, sir, we make holiday, to see Cæsar and
to rejoice in his triumph.
Mar. Wherefore rejoice? What conquest
  brings he home?
What tributaries follow him to Rome,
To grace in captive bonds his chariot-wheels?
You blocks, you stones, you worse than sense-
  less things!   40
O you hard hearts, you cruel men of Rome,
Knew you not Pompey? Many a time and oft
Have you climb'd up to walls and battlements,
To towers and windows, yea, to chimney-tops,
Your infants in your arms, and there have sat
The live-long day, with patient expectation,
To see great Pompey pass the streets of Rome:
And when you saw his chariot but appear,
Have you not made an universal shout,
That Tiber trembled underneath her banks, 50
To hear the replication of your sounds
Made in her concave shores?
And do you now put on your best attire?
And do you now cull out a holiday?
And do you now strew flowers in his way

That comes in triumph over Pompey's blood?
Be gone!
Run to your houses, fall upon your knees,
Pray to the gods to intermit the plague
That needs must light on this ingratitude.   60
Flav. Go, go, good countrymen, and, for
  this fault,
Assemble all the poor men of your sort;
Draw them to Tiber banks, and weep your
  tears
Into the channel, till the lowest stream
Do kiss the most exalted shores of all.
          [*Exeunt all the Commoners.*
See whether their basest metal be not moved;
They vanish tongue-tied in their guiltiness.
Go you down that way towards the Capitol;
This way will I: disrobe the images,
If you do find them deck'd with ceremonies.
Mar. May we do so?
You know it is the feast of Lupercal.
Flav. It is no matter; let no images
Be hung with Cæsar's trophies. I'll about,
And drive away the vulgar from the streets:
So do you too, where you perceive them thick.
These growing feathers pluck'd from Cæsar's
  wing
Will make him fly an ordinary pitch,
Who else would soar above the view of men
And keep us all in servile fearfulness.
                              [*Exeunt.*

SCENE II. *A public place.*

Flourish. Enter CÆSAR; ANTONY, *for the
  course;* CALPURNIA, PORTIA, DECIUS, CIC-
  ERO, BRUTUS, CASSIUS, *and* CASCA; *a great
  crowd following, among them a* Soothsayer.

Cæs. Calpurnia!
Casca.   Peace, ho! Cæsar speaks.
Cæs.   Calpurnia!
Cal. Here, my lord.
Cæs. Stand you directly in Antonius' way,
When he doth run his course. Antonius!
Ant. Cæsar, my lord?
Cæs. Forget not, in your speed, Antonius,
To touch Calpurnia; for our elders say,
The barren, touched in this holy chase,
Shake off their sterile curse.
Ant.   I shall remember:
When Cæsar says 'do this,' it is perform'd. 10
Cæs. Set on; and leave no ceremony out.
                              [*Flourish.*

Sooth. Cæsar!
Cæs. Ha! who calls?
Casca. Bid every noise be still: peace yet
  again!
Cæs. Who is it in the press that calls on
  me?
I hear a tongue, shriller than all the music,
Cry 'Cæsar!' Speak; Cæsar is turn'd to
  hear.
Sooth. Beware the ides of March.
Cæs.   What man is that?
Bru. A soothsayer bids you beware the ides
  of March.
Cæs. Set him before me; let me see his
  face.   20
Cas. Fellow, come from the throng; look
  upon Cæsar.
Cæs. What say'st thou to me now? speak
  once again.
Sooth. Beware the ides of March.

Cæs. He is a dreamer ; let us leave him :
pass.   [*Sennet. Exeunt all except
Brutus and Cassius.*
Cas. Will you go see the order of the
course ?
Bru. Not I.
Cas. I pray you, do.
Bru. I am not gamesome : I do lack some
part
Of that quick spirit that is in Antony.
Let me not hinder, Cassius, your desires ;   30
I'll leave you.
Cas. Brutus, I do observe you now of late :
I have not from your eyes that gentleness
And show of love as I was wont to have :
You bear too stubborn and too strange a hand
Over your friend that loves you.
Bru.   Cassius,
Be not deceived : if I have veil'd my look,
I turn the trouble of my countenance
Merely upon myself. Vexed I am
Of late with passions of some difference,   40
Conceptions only proper to myself,
Which give some soil perhaps to my behav-
iors ;
But let not therefore my good friends be
grieved—
Among which number, Cassius, be you one—
Nor construe any further my neglect,
Than that poor Brutus, with himself at war,
Forgets the shows of love to other men.
Cas. Then, Brutus, I have much mistook
your passion ;
By means whereof this breast of mine hath
buried   49
Thoughts of great value, worthy cogitations.
Tell me, good Brutus, can you see your face ?
Bru. No, Cassius ; for the eye sees not it-
self,
But by reflection, by some other things.
Cas. 'Tis just :
And it is very much lamented, Brutus,
That you have no such mirrors as will turn
Your hidden worthiness into your eye,
That you might see your shadow. I have heard,
Where many of the best respect in Rome,
Except immortal Cæsar, speaking of Brutus
And groaning underneath this age's yoke,   61
Have wish'd that noble Brutus had his eyes.
Bru. Into what dangers would you lead me,
Cassius,
That you would have me seek into myself
For that which is not in me ?
Cas. Therefore, good Brutus, be prepared
to hear :
And since you know you cannot see yourself
So well as by reflection, I, your glass,
Will modestly discover to yourself
That of yourself which you yet know not of.
And be not jealous on me, gentle Brutus :   71
Were I a common laugher, or did use
To stale with ordinary oaths my love
To every new protester ; if you know
That I do fawn on men and hug them hard
And after scandal them, or if you know
That I profess myself in banqueting
To all the rout, then hold me dangerous.
                  [*Flourish, and shout.*
Bru. What means this shouting ? I do fear,
the people
Choose Cæsar for their king.
Cas.   Ay, do you fear it ?   80
Then must I think you would not have it so.

Bru. I would not, Cassius ; yet I love him
well.
But wherefore do you hold me here so long ?
What is it that you would impart to me ?
If it be aught toward the general good,
Set honor in one eye and death i' the other,
And I will look on both indifferently,
For let the gods so speed me as I love
The name of honor more than I fear death.
Cas. I know that virtue to be in you, Bru-
tus,   90
As well as I do know your outward favor.
Well, honor is the subject of my story.
I cannot tell what you and other men
Think of this life ; but, for my single self,
I had as lief not be as live to be
In awe of such a thing as I myself.
I was born free as Cæsar ; so were you :
We both have fed as well, and we can both
Endure the winter's cold as well as he :
For once, upon a raw and gusty day,   100
The troubled Tiber chafing with her shores,
Cæsar said to me ' Darest thou, Cassius, now
Leap in with me into this angry flood,
And swim to yonder point ?' Upon the word,
Accoutred as I was, I plunged in
And bade him follow ; so indeed he did.
The torrent roar'd, and we did buffet it
With lusty sinews, throwing it aside
And stemming it with hearts of controversy ;
But ere we could arrive the point proposed,
Cæsar cried ' Help me, Cassius, or I sink !'
I, as Æneas, our great ancestor,   112
Did from the flames of Troy upon his shoulder
The old Anchises bear, so from the waves of
Tiber
Did I the tired Cæsar. And this man
Is now become a god, and Cassius is
A wretched creature and must bend his body,
If Cæsar carelessly but nod on him.
He had a fever when he was in Spain,
And when the fit was on him, I did mark   120
How he did shake : 'tis true, this god did
shake ;
His coward lips did from their color fly,
And that same eye whose bend doth awe the
world
Did lose his lustre : I did hear him groan :
Ay, and that tongue of his that bade the Ro-
mans
Mark him and write his speeches in their
books,
Alas, it cried ' Give me some drink, Titinius,'
As a sick girl. Ye gods, it doth amaze me
A man of such a feeble temper should
So get the start of the majestic world   130
And bear the palm alone. [*Shout. Flourish.*
Bru. Another general shout !
I do believe that these applauses are
For some new honors that are heap'd on
Cæsar.
Cas. Why, man, he doth bestride the nar-
row world
Like a Colossus, and we petty men
Walk under his huge legs and peep about
To find ourselves dishonorable graves.
Men at some time are masters of their fates :
The fault, dear Brutus, is not in our stars, 140
But in ourselves, that we are underlings.
Brutus and Cæsar : what should be in that
' Cæsar ' ?
Why should that name be sounded more than
yours ?

Write them together, yours is as fair a name ;
Sound them, it doth become the mouth as
　　well ;
Weigh them, it is as heavy ; conjure with 'em,
Brutus will start a spirit as soon as Cæsar.
Now, in the names of all the gods at once,
Upon what meat doth this our Cæsar feed,
That he is grown so great ? Age, thou art
　　shamed !　　　　　　　　　　　　　150
Rome, thou hast lost the breed of noble
　　bloods !
When went there by an age, since the great
　　flood,
But it was famed with more than with one
　　man ?
When could they say till now, that talk'd of
　　Rome,
That her wide walls encompass'd but one
　　man ?
Now is it Rome indeed and room enough,
When there is in it but one only man.
O, you and I have heard our fathers say,
There was a Brutus once that would have
　　brook'd
The eternal devil to keep his state in Rome
As easily as a king.　　　　　　　　161
　　Bru. That you do love me, I am nothing
　　　　jealous ;
What you would work me to, I have some
　　　　aim :
How I have thought of this and of these times,
I shall recount hereafter ; for this present,
I would not, so with love I might entreat you,
Be any further moved. What you have said
I will consider ; what you have to say
I will with patience hear, and find a time　169
Both meet to hear and answer such high
　　things.
Till then, my noble friend, chew upon this :
Brutus had rather be a villager
Than to repute himself a son of Rome
Under these hard conditions as this time
Is like to lay upon us.
　　Cas. I am glad that my weak words
Have struck but thus much show of fire from
　　Brutus.
　　Bru. The games are done and Cæsar is re-
　　turning.
　　Cas. As they pass by, pluck Casca by the
　　sleeve ;
And he will, after his sour fashion, tell you
What hath proceeded worthy note to-day.

　　　　Re-enter Cæsar *and his Train.*

　　Bru. I will do so. But, look you, Cassius,
The angry spot doth glow on Cæsar's brow,
And all the rest look like a chidden train :
Calpurnia's cheek is pale ; and Cicero
Looks with such ferret and such fiery eyes
As we have seen him in the Capitol,
Being cross'd in conference by some senators.
　　Cas. Casca will tell us what the matter is.
　　Cæs. Antonius !　　　　　　　　190
　　Ant. Cæsar ?
　　Cæs. Let me have men about me that are
　　fat ;
Sleek-headed men and such as sleep o' nights :
Yond Cassius has a lean and hungry look ;
He thinks too much : such men are dangerous.
　　Ant. Fear him not, Cæsar ; he's not dan-
　　gerous ;
He is a noble Roman and well given.

　　Cæs. Would he were fatter ! But I fear
　　him not :
Yet if my name were liable to fear,
I do not know the man I should avoid　　200
So soon as that spare Cassius. He reads much ;
He is a great observer and he looks
Quite through the deeds of men : he loves
　　no plays,
As thou dost, Antony ; he hears no music ;
Seldom he smiles, and smiles in such a sort
As if he mock'd himself and scorn'd his spirit
That could be moved to smile at any thing
Such men as he be never at heart's ease
Whiles they behold a greater than themselves,
And therefore are they very dangerous.　210
I rather tell thee what is to be fear'd
Than what I fear ; for always I am Cæsar.
Come on my right hand, for this ear is deaf,
And tell me truly what thou think'st of him.
　　[*Sennet. Exeunt Cæsar and all his
　　　　　　　　Train, but Casca.*
　　Casca. You pull'd me by the cloak ; would
　　you speak with me ?
　　Bru. Ay, Casca ; tell us what hath chanced
　　to-day,
That Cæsar looks so sad.
　　Casca. Why, you were with him, were you
　　not ?
　　Bru. I should not then ask Casca what
　　had chanced.　　　　　　　　　　219
　　Casca. Why, there was a crown offered
him : and being offered him, he put it by with
the back of his hand, thus ; and then the peo-
ple fell a-shouting.
　　Bru. What was the second noise for ?
　　Casca. Why, for that too.
　　Cas. They shouted thrice : what was the
　　last cry for ?
　　Casca. Why, for that too.
　　Bru. Was the crown offered him thrice ?
　　Casca. Ay, marry, was't, and he put it by
thrice, every time gentler than other, and at
every putting-by mine honest neighbors
shouted.
　　Cas. Who offered him the crown ?
　　Casca. Why, Antony.
　　Bru. Tell us the manner of it, gentle
　　Casca.
　　Casca. I can as well be hanged as tell the
manner of it : it was mere foolery ; I did not
mark it. I saw Mark Antony offer him a
crown ;—yet 'twas not a crown neither, 'twas
one of these coronets ;—and, as I told you, he
put it by once : but, for all that, to my thinking, he would fain have had it. Then he offered
it to him again ; then he put it by again : but,
to my thinking, he was very loath to lay his
fingers off it. And then he offered it the third
time ; he put it the third time by : and still as
he refused it, the rabblement hooted and
clapped their chapped hands and threw up
their sweaty night-caps and uttered such a
deal of stinking breath because Cæsar refused the crown that it had almost choked
Cæsar ; for he swounded and fell down at
it : and for mine own part, I durst not laugh,
for fear of opening my lips and receiving the
bad air.
　　Cas. But, soft, I pray you : what, did
　　Cæsar swound ?
　　Casca. He fell down in the market-place,
and foamed at mouth, and was speechless.

Bru. 'Tis very like : he hath the falling sickness.

Cas. No, Cæsar hath it not ; but you and I,
And honest Casca, we have the falling sickness.

Casca. I know not what you mean by that ; but, I am sure, Cæsar fell down. If the tag-rag people did not clap him and hiss him, according as he pleased and displeased them, as they use to do the players in the theatre, I am no true man.

Bru. What said he when he came unto himself ?

Casca. Marry, before he fell down, when he perceived the common herd was glad he refused the crown, he plucked me ope his doublet and offered them his throat to cut. An I had been a man of any occupation, if I would not have taken him at a word, I would I might go to hell among the rogues. And so he fell. When he came to himself again, he said, If he had done or said any thing amiss, he desired their worships to think it was his infirmity. Three or four wenches, where I stood, cried ' Alas, good soul ! ' and forgave him with all their hearts : but there's no heed to be taken of them ; if Cæsar had stabbed their mothers, they would have done no less.

Bru. And after that, he came, thus sad, away ?

Casca. Ay.   280

Cas. Did Cicero say any thing ?

Casca. Ay, he spoke Greek.

Cas. To what effect ?

Casca. Nay, an I tell you that, I'll ne'er look you i' the face again : but those that understood him smiled at one another and shook their heads ; but, for mine own part, it was Greek to me. I could tell you more news too : Marullus and Flavius, for pulling scarfs off Cæsar's images, are put to silence. Fare you well. There was more foolery yet, if I could remember it.   291

Cas. Will you sup with me to-night, Casca ?

Casca. No, I am promised forth.

Cas. Will you dine with me to-morrow ?

Casca. Ay, if I be alive and your mind hold and your dinner worth the eating.

Cas. Good : I will expect you.

Casca. Do so. Farewell, both.   [*Exit.*

Bru. What a blunt fellow is this grown to be !

He was quick mettle when he went to school.

Cas. So is he now in execution   301
Of any bold or noble enterprise,
However he puts on this tardy form.
This rudeness is a sauce to his good wit,
Which gives men stomach to digest his words
With better appetite.

Bru. And so it is. For this time I will leave you :
To-morrow, if you please to speak with me,
I will come home to you ; or, if you will,
Come home to me, and I will wait for you.

Cas. I will do so : till then, think of the world.   [*Exit Brutus.* 311
Well, Brutus, thou art noble ; yet, I see,
Thy honorable metal may be wrought
From that it is disposed : therefore it is meet

That noble minds keep ever with their likes ;
For who so firm that cannot be seduced ?
Cæsar doth bear me hard ; but he loves Brutus :
If I were Brutus now and he were Cassius,
He should not humor me. I will this night,
In several hands, in at his windows throw,
As if they came from several citizens,   321
Writings all tending to the great opinion
That Rome holds of his name ; wherein obscurely
Cæsar's ambition shall be glanced at :
And after this let Cæsar seat him sure ;
For we will shake him, or worse days endure.
[*Exit.*

SCENE III. *The same. A street.*

Thunder and lightning. Enter from opposite sides, CASCA, *with his sword drawn, and* CICERO.

Cic. Good even, Casca : brought you Cæsar home ?
Why are you breathless ? and why stare you so ?

Casca. Are not you moved, when all the sway of earth
Shakes like a thing unfirm ? O Cicero,
I have seen tempests, when the scolding winds
Have rived the knotty oaks, and I have seen
The ambitious ocean swell and rage and foam,
To be exalted with the threatening clouds :
But never till to-night, never till now,
Did I go through a tempest dropping fire. 10
Either there is a civil strife in heaven,
Or else the world, too saucy with the gods,
Incenses them to send destruction.

Cic. Why, saw you any thing more wonderful ?

Casca. A common slave—you know him well by sight—
Held up his left hand, which did flame and burn
Like twenty torches join'd, and yet his hand,
Not sensible of fire, remain'd unscorch'd.
Besides—I ha' not since put up my sword—
Against the Capitol I met a lion,   20
Who glared upon me, and went surly by,
Without annoying me : and there were drawn
Upon a heap a hundred ghastly women,
Transformed with their fear ; who swore they saw
Men all in fire walk up and down the streets.
And yesterday the bird of night did sit
Even at noon-day upon the market-place,
Hooting and shrieking. When these prodigies
Do so conjointly meet, let not men say
' These are their reasons ; they are natural ; '
For, I believe, they are portentous things 31
Unto the climate that they point upon.

Cic. Indeed, it is a strange-disposed time :
But men may construe things after their fashion,
Clean from the purpose of the things themselves.
Come Cæsar to the Capitol to-morrow ?

Casca. He doth ; for he did bid Antonius
Send word to you he would be there to-morrow.

Cic. Good night then, Casca : this disturbed sky
Is not to walk in.

Casca. Farewell, Cicero.   [*Exit Cicero.* 40

Enter CASSIUS.

Cas. Who's there?

Casca.   A Roman.

Cas.   Casca, by your voice.

Casca. Your ear is good. Cassius, what
night is this!

Cas. A very pleasing night to honest men.

Casca. Who ever knew the heavens men-
ace so?

Cas. Those that have known the earth so
full of faults.

For my part, I have walk'd about the streets,
Submitting me unto the perilous night,
And, thus unbraced, Casca, as you see,
Have bared my bosom to the thunder-stone;
And when the cross blue lightning seem'd to
open   50
The breast of heaven, I did present myself
Even in the aim and very flash of it.

Casca. But wherefore did you so much
tempt the heavens?

It is the part of men to fear and tremble,
When the most mighty gods by tokens send
Such dreadful heralds to astonish us.

Cas. You are dull, Casca, and those sparks
of life

That should be in a Roman you do want,
Or else you use not. You look pale and gaze
And put on fear and cast yourself in wonder,
To see the strange impatience of the heavens:
But if you would consider the true cause
Why all these fires, why all these gliding
ghosts,
Why birds and beasts from quality and kind,
Why old men fool and children calculate,
Why all these things change from their ordi-
nance
Their natures and preformed faculties
To monstrous quality,—why, you shall find
That heaven hath infused them with these
spirits,
To make them instruments of fear and warn-
ing   70
Unto some monstrous state.
Now could I, Casca, name to thee a man
Most like this dreadful night,
That thunders, lightens, opens graves, and
roars
As doth the lion in the Capitol,
A man no mightier than thyself or me
In personal action, yet prodigious grown
And fearful, as these strange eruptions are.

Casca. 'Tis Cæsar that you mean; is it
not, Cassius?   79

Cas. Let it be who it is: for Romans now
Have thews and limbs like to their ancestors;
But, woe the while! our fathers' minds are
dead,
And we are govern'd with our mothers' spir-
its;
Our yoke and sufferance show us womanish.

Casca. Indeed, they say the senators to-
morrow
Mean to establish Cæsar as a king;
And he shall wear his crown by sea and land,
In every place, save here in Italy.

Cas. I know where I will wear this dagger
then;
Cassius from bondage will deliver Cassius;
Therein, ye gods, you make the weak most
strong;   91
Therein, ye gods, you tyrants do defeat:

Nor stony tower, nor walls of beaten brass,
Nor airless dungeon, nor strong links of iron,
Can be retentive to the strength of spirit;
But life, being weary of these worldly bars,
Never lacks power to dismiss itself.
If I know this, know all the world besides,
That part of tyranny that I do bear
I can shake off at pleasure.   [*Thunder still.*

Casca.   So can I: 100
So every bondman in his own hand bears
The power to cancel his captivity.

Cas. And why should Cæsar be a tyrant
then?
Poor man! I know he would not be a wolf,
But that he sees the Romans are but sheep:
He were no lion, were not Romans hinds.
Those that with haste will make a mighty fire
Begin it with weak straws: what trash is
Rome,
What rubbish and what offal, when it serves
For the base matter to illuminate   110
So vile a thing as Cæsar! But, O grief,
Where hast thou led me? I perhaps speak
this
Before a willing bondman; then I know
My answer must be made. But I am arm'd,
And dangers are to me indifferent.

Casca. You speak to Casca, and to such a
man
That is no fleering tell-tale. Hold, my hand:
Be factious for redress of all these griefs,
And I will set this foot of mine as far
As who goes farthest.

Cas.   There's a bargain made. 120
Now know you, Casca, I have moved already
Some certain of the noblest-minded Romans
To undergo with me an enterprise
Of honorable-dangerous consequence;
And I do know, by this, they stay for me
In Pompey's porch: for now, this fearful
night,
There is no stir or walking in the streets;
And the complexion of the element
In favor's like the work we have in hand,
Most bloody, fiery, and most terrible.   130

Casca. Stand close awhile, for here comes
one in haste.

Cas. 'Tis Cinna; I do know him by his
gait;
He is a friend.

Enter CINNA.

    Cinna, where haste you so?

Cin. To find out you. Who's that? Metellus Cimber?

Cas. No, it is Casca; one incorporate
To our attempts. Am I not stay'd for, Cinna?

Cin. I am glad on 't. What a fearful night
is this!
There's two or three of us have seen strange
sights.

Cas. Am I not stay'd for? tell me.

Cin.   Yes, you are.
O Cassius, if you could   140
But win the noble Brutus to our party—

Cas. Be you content: good Cinna, take
this paper,
And look you lay it in the prætor's chair,
Where Brutus may but find it; and throw
this
In at his window; set this up with wax
Upon old Brutus' statue: all this done,

Repair to Pompey's porch, where you shall
find us.
Is Decius Brutus and Trebonius there ?
Cin. All but Metellus Cimber ; and he's
gone   149
To seek you at your house. Well, I will hie,
And so bestow these papers as you bade me.
Cas. That done, repair to Pompey's
theatre.   *[Exit Cinna.*
Come, Casca, you and I will yet ere day
See Brutus at his house : three parts of him
Is ours already, and the man entire
Upon the next encounter yields him ours.
Casca. O, he sits high in all the people's
hearts ;
And that which would appear offence in us,
His countenance, like richest alchemy,
Will change to virtue and to worthiness. 160
Cas. Him and his worth and our great
need of him
You have right well conceited. Let us go,
For it is after midnight ; and ere day
We will awake him and be sure of him.
                                              [Exeunt.

ACT II.

SCENE I. *Rome. Brutus's orchard.*

Enter BRUTUS.

Bru. What, Lucius, ho !
I cannot, by the progress of the stars,
Give guess how near to day. Lucius, I say !
I would it were my fault to sleep so soundly.
When, Lucius, when ? awake, I say ! what,
Lucius !

Enter LUCIUS.

Luc. Call'd you, my lord ?
Bru. Get me a taper in my study, Lucius :
When it is lighted, come and call me here.
Luc. I will, my lord.   *[Exit.*
Bru. It must be by his death : and for my
part,
I know no personal cause to spurn at him, 11
But for the general. He would be crown'd :
How that might change his nature, there's the
question.
It is the bright day that brings forth the
adder ;
And that craves wary walking. Crown him ?
—that ;—
And then, I grant, we put a sting in him,
That at his will he may do danger with.
The abuse of greatness is, when it disjoins
Remorse from power : and, to speak truth of
Cæsar,   19
I have not known when his affections sway'd
More than his reason. But 'tis a common
proof,
That lowliness is young ambition's ladder,
Whereto the climber-upward turns his face ;
But when he once attains the upmost round,
He then unto the ladder turns his back,
Looks in the clouds, scorning the base degrees
By which he did ascend. So Cæsar may.
Then, lest he may, prevent. And, since the
quarrel
Will bear no color for the thing he is,
Fashion it thus ; that what he is, augmented,
Would run to these and these extremities : 31
And therefore think him as a serpent's egg

Which, hatch'd, would, as his kind, grow mischievous,
And kill him in the shell.

Re-enter LUCIUS.

Luc. The taper burneth in your closet, sir.
Searching the window for a flint, I found
This paper, thus seal'd up ; and, I am sure,
It did not lie there when I went to bed.
                          [Gives him the letter.
Bru. Get you to bed again ; it is not day.
Is not to-morrow, boy, the ides of March ?
Luc. I know not, sir.   41
Bru. Look in the calendar, and bring me
word.
Luc. I will, sir.   *[Exit.*
Bru. The exhalations whizzing in the air
Give so much light that I may read by them.
                    [Opens the letter and reads.
' Brutus, thou sleep'st : awake, and see thy-
self.
Shall Rome, &c. Speak, strike, redress !
Brutus, thou sleep'st : awake ! '
Such instigations have been often dropp'd
Where I have took them up.   50
' Shall Rome, &c.' Thus must I piece it out :
Shall Rome stand under one man's awe ?
What, Rome ?
My ancestors did from the streets of Rome
The Tarquin drive, when he was call'd a king.
' Speak, strike, redress !' Am I entreated
To speak and strike ? O Rome, I make thee
promise :
If the redress will follow, thou receivest
Thy full petition at the hand of Brutus !

Re-enter LUCIUS.

Luc. Sir, March is wasted fourteen days.
                          [Knocking within.
Bru. 'Tis good. Go to the gate ; somebody
knocks.   *[Exit Lucius.* 60
Since Cassius first did whet me against Cæsar,
I have not slept.
Between the acting of a dreadful thing
And the first motion, all the interim is
Like a phantasma, or a hideous dream :
The Genius and the mortal instruments
Are then in council ; and the state of man,
Like to a little kingdom, suffers then
The nature of an insurrection.

Re-enter LUCIUS.

Luc. Sir, 'tis your brother Cassius at the
door,
Who doth desire to see you.
Bru.   Is he alone ?   71
Luc. No, sir, there are moe with him.
Bru.   Do you know them ?
Luc. No, sir ; their hats are pluck'd about
their ears,
And half their faces buried in their cloaks,
That by no means I may discover them
By any mark of favor.
Bru.   Let 'em enter. *[Exit Lucius.*
They are the faction. O conspiracy,
Shamest thou to show thy dangerous brow by
night,
When evils are most free ? O, then by day
Where wilt thou find a cavern dark enough 80
To mask thy monstrous visage ? Seek none,
conspiracy ;
Hide it in smiles and affability :
For if thou path, thy native semblance on,

Not Erebus itself were dim enough
To hide thee from prevention.

Enter the conspirators, CASSIUS, CASCA,
DECIUS, CINNA, METELLUS CIMBER, *and*
TREBONIUS.

Cas. I think we are too bold upon your
rest :
Good morrow, Brutus ; do we trouble you ?
Bru. I have been up this hour, awake all
night.
Know I these men that come along with you ?
Cas. Yes, every man of them, and no man
here   90
But honors you ; and every one doth wish
You had but that opinion of yourself
Which every noble Roman bears of you.
This is Trebonius.
Bru.   He is welcome hither.
Cas. This, Decius Brutus.
Bru.   He is welcome too.
Cas. This, Casca ; this, Cinna ; and this,
Metellus Cimber.
Bru. They are all welcome.
What watchful cares do interpose themselves
Betwixt your eyes and night ?
Cas. Shall I entreat a word ?   100
          [*Brutus and Cassius whisper.*
Dec. Here lies the east : doth not the day
break here ?
Casca. No.
Cin. O, pardon, sir, it doth ; and yon
gray lines
That fret the clouds are messengers of day.
Casca. You shall confess that you are both
deceived.
Here, as I point my sword, the sun arises,
Which is a great way growing on the south,
Weighing the youthful season of the year.
Some two months hence up higher toward the
north
He first presents his fire ; and the high east
Stands, as the Capitol, directly here.   111
Bru. Give me your hands all over, one by
one.
Cas. And let us swear our resolution.
Bru. No, not an oath : if not the face of
men,
The sufferance of our souls, the time's abuse,—
If these be motives weak, break off betimes,
And every man hence to his idle bed ;
So let high-sighted tyranny range on,
Till each man drop by lottery. But if these,
As I am sure they do, bear fire enough   120
To kindle cowards and to steel with valor
The melting spirits of women, then, country-
men,
What need we any spur but our own cause,
To prick us to redress ? what other bond
Than secret Romans, that have spoke the
word,
And will not palter ? and what other oath
Than honesty to honesty engaged,
That this shall be, or we will fall for it ?
Swear priests and cowards and men cautelous,
Old feeble carrions and such suffering souls
That welcome wrongs ; unto bad causes swear
Such creatures as men doubt ; but do not
stain
The even virtue of our enterprise,
Nor the insuppressive mettle of our spirits,
To think that or our cause or our performance
Did need an oath ; when every drop of blood

That every Roman bears, and nobly bears,
Is guilty of a several bastardy,
If he do break the smallest particle
Of any promise that hath pass'd from him.
Cas. But what of Cicero ? shall we
sound him ?   141
I think he will stand very strong with us.
Casca. Let us not leave him out.
Cin.   No, by no means.
Met. O, let us have him, for his silver hairs
Will purchase us a good opinion
And buy men's voices to commend our deeds :
It shall be said, his judgment ruled our hands ;
Our youths and wildness shall no whit appear,
But all be buried in his gravity.
Bru. O, name him not : let us not break
with him ;   150
For he will never follow any thing
That other men begin.
Cas.   Then leave him out.
Casca. Indeed he is not fit.
Dec. Shall no man else be touch'd but
only Cæsar ?
Cas. Decius, well urged : I think it is not
meet,
Mark Antony, so well beloved of Cæsar,
Should outlive Cæsar : we shall find of him
A shrewd contriver ; and, you know, his
means,
If he improve them, may well stretch so far
As to annoy us all : which to prevent,   160
Let Antony and Cæsar fall together.
Bru. Our course will seem too bloody,
Caius Cassius,
To cut the head off and then hack the limbs,
Like wrath in death and envy afterwards ;
For Antony is but a limb of Cæsar :
Let us be sacrificers, but not butchers, Caius.
We all stand up against the spirit of Cæsar ;
And in the spirit of men there is no blood :
O, that we then could come by Cæsar's
spirit,
And not dismember Cæsar ! But, alas,   170
Cæsar must bleed for it ! And, gentle friends,
Let's kill him boldly, but not wrathfully ;
Let's carve him as a dish fit for the gods,
Not hew him as a carcass fit for hounds :
And let our hearts, as subtle masters do,
Stir up their servants to an act of rage,
And after seem to chide 'em. This shall make
Our purpose necessary and not envious :
Which so appearing to the common eyes,
We shall be call'd purgers, not murderers. 180
And for Mark Antony, think not of him ;
For he can do no more than Cæsar's arm
When Cæsar's head is off.
Cas.   Yet I fear him ;
For in the ingrafted love he bears to Cæsar—
Bru. Alas, good Cassius, do not think of
him :
If he love Cæsar, all that he can do
Is to himself, take thought and die for Cæsar :
And that were much he should ; for he is
given
To sports, to wildness and much company.
Treb. There is no fear in him ; let him not
die ;   190
For he will live, and laugh at this hereafter.
                                    [*Clock strikes.*
Bru. Peace ! count the clock.
Cas.   The clock hath stricken three.
Treb. 'Tis time to part.

Cas. But it is doubtful yet,
Whether Cæsar will come forth to-day, or
no;
For he is superstitious grown of late,
Quite from the main opinion he held once
Of fantasy, of dreams and ceremonies:
It may be, these apparent prodigies,
The unaccustom'd terror of this night,
And the persuasion of his augurers, 200
May hold him from the Capitol to-day.

Dec. Never fear that: if he be so resolved,
I can o'ersway him; for he loves to hear
That unicorns may be betray'd with trees,
And bears with glasses, elephants with holes,
Lions with toils and men with flatterers;
But when I tell him he hates flatterers,
He says he does, being then most flattered.
Let me work;
For I can give his humor the true bent, 210
And I will bring him to the Capitol.

Cas. Nay, we will all of us be there to
fetch him.

Bru. By the eighth hour: is that the uttermost?

Cin. Be that the uttermost, and fail not
then.

Met. Caius Ligarius doth bear Cæsar
hard,
Who rated him for speaking well of Pompey:
I wonder none of you have thought of him.

Bru. Now, good Metellus, go along by
him:
He loves me well, and I have given him reasons;
Send him but hither, and I'll fashion him. 220

Cas. The morning comes upon 's: we'll
leave you, Brutus.
And, friends, disperse yourselves; but all re-
member
What you have said, and show yourselves true
Romans.

Bru. Good gentlemen, look fresh and mer-
rily;
Let not our looks put on our purposes,
But bear it as our Roman actors do,
With untired spirits and formal constancy:
And so good morrow to you every one.
[*Exeunt all but Brutus.*
Boy! Lucius! Fast asleep? It is no matter;
Enjoy the honey-heavy dew of slumber: 230
Thou hast no figures nor no fantasies,
Which busy care draws in the brains of men;
Therefore thou sleep'st so sound.

Enter PORTIA.

Por. Brutus, my lord!
Bru. Portia, what mean you? wherefore
rise you now?
It is not for your health thus to commit
Your weak condition to the raw cold morning.

Por. Nor for yours neither. You've un-
gently, Brutus,
Stole from my bed: and yesternight, at sup-
per,
You suddenly arose, and walk'd about, 239
Musing and sighing, with your arms across,
And when I ask'd you what the matter was,
You stared upon me with ungentle looks;
I urged you further; then you scratch'd your
head,
And too impatiently stamp'd with your foot;
Yet I insisted, yet you answer'd not,
But, with an angry wafture of your hand,

Gave sign for me to leave you: so I did;
Fearing to strengthen that impatience
Which seem'd too much enkindled, and withal
Hoping it was but an effect of humor, 250
Which sometime hath his hour with every
man.
It will not let you eat, nor talk, nor sleep,
And could it work so much upon your shape
As it hath much prevail'd on your condition,
I should not know you, Brutus. Dear my lord,
Make me acquainted with your cause of grief.

Bru. I am not well in health, and that is
all.

Por. Brutus is wise, and, were he not in
health,
He would embrace the means to come by it.

Bru. Why, so I do. Good Portia, go to
bed. 260

Por. Is Brutus sick? and is it physical
To walk unbraced and suck up the humors
Of the dank morning? What, is Brutus sick,
And will he steal out of his wholesome bed,
To dare the vile contagion of the night
And tempt the rheumy and unpurged air
To add unto his sickness? No, my Brutus;
You have some sick offence within your mind,
Which, by the right and virtue of my place,
I ought to know of: and, upon my knees, 270
I charm you, by my once-commended beauty,
By all your vows of love and that great vow
Which did incorporate and make us one,
That you unfold to me, yourself, your half,
Why you are heavy, and what men to-night
Have had resort to you: for here have been
Some six or seven, who did hide their faces
Even from darkness.

Bru. Kneel not, gentle Portia.

Por. I should not need, if you were gentle
Brutus.
Within the bond of marriage, tell me, Brutus,
Is it excepted I should know no secrets 281
That appertain to you? Am I yourself
But, as it were, in sort or limitation,
To keep with you at meals, comfort your bed,
And talk to you sometimes? Dwell I but in
the suburbs
Of your good pleasure? If it be no more,
Portia is Brutus' harlot, not his wife.

Bru. You are my true and honorable wife,
As dear to me as are the ruddy drops
That visit my sad heart. 290

Por. If this were true, then should I know
this secret.
I grant I am a woman; but withal
A woman that Lord Brutus took to wife:
I grant I am a woman; but withal
A woman well-reputed, Cato's daughter.
Think you I am no stronger than my sex,
Being so father'd and so husbanded?
Tell me your counsels, I will not disclose 'em:
I have made strong proof of my constancy,
Giving myself a voluntary wound 300
Here, in the thigh: can I bear that with pa-
tience,
And not my husband's secrets?

Bru. O ye gods,
Render me worthy of this noble wife!
[*Knocking within.*
Hark, hark! one knocks: Portia, go in
awhile;
And by and by thy bosom shall partake
The secrets of my heart.
All my engagements I will construe to thee,

All the charactery of my sad brows :
Leave me with haste. [*Exit Portia.*] Lucius,
　　who's that knocks ?

Re-enter LUCIUS *with* LIGARIUS.

　Luc. He is a sick man that would speak
　　with you.　　　　　　　　　　　310
　Bru. Caius Ligarius, that Metellus spake
of.
Boy, stand aside. Caius Ligarius ! how ?
　Lig. Vouchsafe good morrow from a
　　feeble tongue.
　Bru. O, what a time have you chose out,
　　brave Caius,
To wear a kerchief ! Would you were not
　　sick !
　Lig. I am not sick, if Brutus have in hand
Any exploit worthy the name of honor.
　Bru. Such an exploit have I in hand, Li-
　　garius,
Had you a healthful ear to hear of it.
　Lig. By all the gods that Romans bow be-
　　fore,　　　　　　　　　　　　320
I here discard my sickness ! Soul of Rome !
Brave son, derived from honorable loins !
Thou, like an exorcist, hast conjured up
My mortified spirit. Now bid me run,
And I will strive with things impossible ;
Yea, get the better of them. What's to do ?
　Bru. A piece of work that will make sick
　　men whole.
　Lig. But are not some whole that we must
　　make sick ?
　Bru. That must we also. What it is, my
　　Caius,
I shall unfold to thee, as we are going　　330
To whom it must be done.
　Lig.　　　　　　　Set on your foot,
And with a heart new-fired I follow you,
To do I know not what : but it sufficeth
That Brutus leads me on.
　Bru.　　　　　Follow me, then. [*Exeunt.*

SCENE II. *Cæsar's house.*

Thunder and lightning. Enter CÆSAR, *in his
night-gown.*

　Cæs. Nor heaven nor earth have been at
　　peace to-night :
Thrice hath Calpurnia in her sleep cried out,
' Help, ho ! they murder Cæsar ! ' Who's
　　within ?

Enter a Servant.

　Serv. My lord ?
　Cæs. Go bid the priests do present sacri-
fice
And bring me their opinions of success.
　Serv. I will, my lord.　　　　　　[*Exit.*

Enter CALPURNIA.

　Cal. What mean you, Cæsar ? think you
　　to walk forth ?
You shall not stir out of your house to-day.
　Cæs. Cæsar shall forth : the things that
　　threaten'd me　　　　　　　　10
Ne'er look'd but on my back ; when they shall
　　see
The face of Cæsar, they are vanished.
　Cal. Cæsar, I never stood on ceremonies,
Yet now they fright me. There is one within,
Besides the things that we have heard and
　　seen,

Recounts most horrid sights seen by the watch.
A lioness hath whelped in the streets ;
And graves have yawn'd, and yielded up their
　　dead ;
Fierce fiery warriors fought upon the clouds,
In ranks and squadrons and right form of war,
Which drizzled blood upon the Capitol ;　　21
The noise of battle hurtled in the air,
Horses did neigh, and dying men did groan,
And ghosts did shriek and squeal about the
　　streets.
O Cæsar ! these things are beyond all use,
And I do fear them.
　Cæs.　　　　　What can be avoided
Whose end is purposed by the mighty gods ?
Yet Cæsar shall go forth ; for these predic-
　　tions
Are to the world in general as to Cæsar.
　Cal. When beggars die, there are no
　　comets seen ;　　　　　　　　30
The heavens themselves blaze forth the death
　　of princes.
　Cæs. Cowards die many times before their
　　deaths :
The valiant never taste of death but once.
Of all the wonders that I yet have heard,
It seems to me most strange that men should
　　fear ;
Seeing that death, a necessary end,
Will come when it will come.

Re-enter Servant.

　　　　　　　What say the augurers ?
　Serv. They would not have you to stir
　　forth to-day.
Plucking the entrails of an offering forth,
They could not find a heart within the beast.
　Cæs. The gods do this in shame of cow-
　　ardice :　　　　　　　　　　41
Cæsar should be a beast without a heart,
If he should stay at home to-day for fear.
No, Cæsar shall not : danger knows full well
That Cæsar is more dangerous than he :
We are two lions litter'd in one day,
And I the elder and more terrible :
And Cæsar shall go forth.
　Cal.　　　　　　Alas, my lord,
Your wisdom is consumed in confidence.
Do not go forth to-day : call it my fear　　50
That keeps you in the house, and not your
　　own.
We'll send Mark Antony to the senate-house :
And he shall say you are not well to-day :
Let me, upon my knee, prevail in this.
　Cæs. Mark Antony shall say I am not
　　well,
And, for thy humor, I will stay at home.

Enter DECIUS.

Here's Decius Brutus, he shall tell them so.
　Dec. Cæsar, all hail ! good morrow,
　　worthy Cæsar !
I come to fetch you to the senate-house.
　Cæs. And you are come in very happy
　　time,　　　　　　　　　　　60
To bear my greeting to the senators
And tell them that I will not come to-day :
Cannot, is false, and that I dare not, falser :
I will not come to-day : tell them so, Decius.
　Cal. Say he is sick.
　Cæs.　　　　　Shall Cæsar send a lie ?
Have I in conquest stretch'd mine arm so far,
To be afraid to tell graybeards the truth ?

Decius, go tell them Cæsar will not come.

Dec. Most mighty Cæsar, let me know
    some cause,
Lest I be laugh'd at when I tell them so.   70
    Cæs. The cause is in my will : I will not
    come ;
That is enough to satisfy the senate.
But for your private satisfaction,
Because I love you, I will let you know :
Calpurnia here, my wife, stays me at home :
She dreamt to-night she saw my statua,
Which, like a fountain with an hundred spouts,
Did run pure blood : and many lusty Romans
Came smiling, and did bathe their hands in it :
And these does she apply for warnings, and
    portents,   80
And evils imminent ; and on her knee
Hath begg'd that I will stay at home to-day.

Dec. This dream is all amiss interpreted ;
It was a vision fair and fortunate :
Your statue spouting blood in many pipes,
In which so many smiling Romans bathed,
Signifies that from you great Rome shall suck
Reviving blood, and that great men shall press
For tinctures, stains, relics and cognizance.
This by Calpurnia's dream is signified.   90

Cæs. And this way have you well ex-
    pounded it.

Dec. I have, when you have heard what I
    can say :
And know it now : the senate have concluded
To give this day a crown to mighty Cæsar.
If you shall send them word you will not
    come,
Their minds may change. Besides, it were a
    mock
Apt to be render'd, for some one to say
' Break up the senate till another time,
When Cæsar's wife shall meet with better
    dreams.'
If Cæsar hide himself, shall they not whisper
' Lo, Cæsar is afraid ' ?   101
Pardon me, Cæsar ; for my dear dear love
To your proceeding bids me tell you this ;
And reason to my love is liable.

Cæs. How foolish do your fears seem now,
    Calpurnia !
I am ashamed I did yield to them.
Give me my robe, for I will go.

Enter PUBLIUS, BRUTUS, LIGARIUS, METEL-
    LUS, CASCA, TREBONIUS, *and* CINNA.

And look where Publius is come to fetch me.

Pub. Good morrow, Cæsar.

Cæs.   Welcome, Publius.
What, Brutus, are you stirr'd so early too ?
Good morrow, Casca. Caius Ligarius,   111
Cæsar was ne'er so much your enemy
As that same ague which hath made you lean.
What is 't o'clock ?

Bru.   Cæsar, 'tis strucken eight.

Cæs. I thank you for your pains and cour-
    tesy.

Enter ANTONY.

See ! Antony, that revels long o' nights,
Is notwithstanding up. Good morrow, Antony.

Ant. So to most noble Cæsar.

Cæs.   Bid them prepare within :
I am to blame to be thus waited for.
Now, Cinna : now, Metellus : what, Tre-
    bonius !
I have an hour's talk in store for you ;

Remember that you call on me to-day :
Be near me, that I may remember you.

Treb. Cæsar, I will : [*Aside*] and so near
    will I be,
That your best friends shall wish I had been
    further.

Cæs. Good friends, go in, and taste some
    wine with me ;
And we, like friends, will straightway go to-
    gether.

Bru. [*Aside*] That every like is not the
    same, O Cæsar,
The heart of Brutus yearns to think upon !
                       [*Exeunt.*

SCENE III. *A street near the Capitol.*

Enter ARTEMIDORUS, *reading a paper.*

Art. ' Cæsar, beware of Brutus ; take heed
of Cassius ; come not near Casca ; have an eye
to Cinna, trust not Trebonius : mark well
Metellus Cimber : Decius Brutus loves thee
not : thou hast wronged Caius Ligarius. There
is but one mind in all these men, and it is bent
against Cæsar. If thou beest not immortal,
look about you : security gives way to conspiracy. The mighty gods defend thee ! Thy
lover,
                      ' ARTEMIDORUS.'
Here will I stand till Cæsar pass along,   11
And as a suitor will I give him this.
My heart laments that virtue cannot live
Out of the teeth of emulation.
If thou read this, O Cæsar, thou mayst live ;
If not, the Fates with traitors do contrive.
                         [*Exit.*

SCENE IV. *Another part of the same street,
    before the house of Brutus.*

Enter PORTIA *and* LUCIUS.

Por. I prithee, boy, run to the senate-
    house ;
Stay not to answer me, but get thee gone :
Why dost thou stay ?

Luc.   To know my errand, madam.

Por. I would have had thee there, and here
    again,
Ere I can tell thee what thou shouldst do there.
O constancy, be strong upon my side,
Set a huge mountain 'tween my heart and
    tongue !
I have a man's mind, but a woman's might.
How hard it is for women to keep counsel !
Art thou here yet ?

Luc.   Madam, what should I do ? 10
Run to the Capitol, and nothing else ?
And so return to you, and nothing else ?

Por. Yes, bring me word, boy, if thy lord
    look well,
For he went sickly forth : and take good note
What Cæsar doth, what suitors press to him.
Hark, boy ! what noise is that ?

Luc. I hear none, madam.

Por.   Prithee, listen well ;
I heard a bustling rumor, like a fray,
And the wind brings it from the Capitol.

Luc. Sooth, madam, I hear nothing.   20

Enter the Soothsayer.

Por. Come hither, fellow : which way hast
    thou been ?

Sooth. At mine own house, good lady.

Por. What is't o'clock ?

Sooth.　　　　About the ninth hour, lady.
Por. Is Cæsar yet gone to the Capitol ?
Sooth. Madam, not yet : I go to take my
　　stand,
To see him pass on to the Capitol.
Por. Thou hast some suit to Cæsar, hast
　　thou not ?
Sooth. That I have, lady : if it will please
　　Cæsar
To be so good to Cæsar as to hear me,
I shall beseech him to befriend himself.　30
Por. Why, know'st thou any harm's in-
　　tended towards him ?
Sooth. None that I know will be, much
　　that I fear may chance.
Good morrow to you. Here the street is nar-
　　row :
The throng that follows Cæsar at the heels,
Of senators, of prætors, common suitors,
Will crowd a feeble man almost to death :
I'll get me to a place more void, and there
Speak to great Cæsar as he comes along.
　　　　　　　　　　　　　　　　　[Exit.
Por. I must go in. Ay me, how weak a
　　thing
The heart of woman is ! O Brutus,　　40
The heavens speed thee in thine enterprise !
Sure, the boy heard me : Brutus hath a suit
That Cæsar will not grant. O, I grow faint.
Run, Lucius, and commend me to my lord ;
Say I am merry : come to me again,
And bring me word what he doth say to thee.
　　　　　　　　　　　　　[Exeunt severally.

ACT III.

SCENE I. *Rome. Before the Capitol ; the
　　Senate sitting above.*

A crowd of people ; among them ARTEMIDO-
RUS *and the* Soothsayer. *Flourish. Enter* CÆ-
SAR, BRUTUS, CASSIUS, CASCA, DECIUS,
METULLUS, TREBONIUS, CINNA, ANTONY,
LEPIDUS, POPILIUS, PUBLIUS, *and others.*

Cæs. [*To the Soothsayer*] The ides of
　　March are come.
Sooth. Ay, Cæsar ; but not gone.
Art. Hail, Cæsar ! read this schedule.
Dec. Trebonius doth desire you to o'er-
　　read,
At your best leisure, this his humble suit.
Art. O Cæsar, read mine first ; for mine's
　　a suit
That touches Cæsar nearer : read it, great
　　Cæsar.
Cæs. What touches us ourself shall be last
　　served.
Art. Delay not, Cæsar ; read it instantly.
Cæs. What, is the fellow mad ?
Pub.　　　　　　　Sirrah, give place.　10
Cas. What, urge you your petitions in the
　　street ?
Come to the Capitol.

CÆSAR *goes up to the Senate-House, the rest
　　following.*

Pop. I wish your enterprise to-day may
　　thrive.
Cas. What enterprise, Popilius ?
Pop.　　　　　　　　　Fare you well.
　　　　　　　　　　　　[Advances to Cæsar.
Bru. What said Popilius Lena ?

Cas. He wish'd to-day our enterprise might
　　thrive.
I fear our purpose is discovered.
Bru. Look, how he makes to Cæsar ; mark
　　him.
Cas. Casca, be sudden, for we fear preven-
　　tion.
Brutus, what shall be done ? If this be known,
Cassius or Cæsar never shall turn back,　21
For I will slay myself.
Bru.　　　　　　Cassius, be constant :
Popilius Lena speaks not of our purposes ;
For, look, he smiles, and Cæsar doth not
　　change.
Cas. Trebonius knows his time ; for, look
　　you, Brutus.
He draws Mark Antony out of the way.
　　　　　　　[Exeunt Antony and Trebonius.
Dec. Where is Metellus Cimber ? Let him
　　go,
And presently prefer his suit to Cæsar.
Bru. He is address'd : press near and sec-
　　ond him.
Cin. Casca, you are the first that rears
　　your hand.　　　　　　　　　　30
Cæs. Are we all ready ? What is now
　　amiss
That Cæsar and his senate must redress ?
Met. Most high, most mighty, and most
　　puissant Cæsar,
Metellus Cimber throws before thy seat
An humble heart,—　　　　　*[Kneeling.*
Cæs.　　　　　I must prevent thee, Cimber.
These couchings and these lowly courtesies
Might fire the blood of ordinary men,
And turn pre-ordinance and first decree
Into the law of children. Be not fond,
To think that Cæsar bears such rebel blood 40
That will be thaw'd from the true quality
With that which melteth fools ; I mean, sweet
　　words,
Low-crooked court'sies and base spaniel-
　　fawning.
Thy brother by decree is banished :
If thou dost bend and pray and fawn for him,
I spurn thee like a cur out of my way.
Know, Cæsar doth not wrong, nor without
　　cause
Will he be satisfied.
Met. Is there no voice more worthy than
　　my own
To sound more sweetly in great Cæsar's ear
For the repealing of my banish'd brother ?　51
Bru. I kiss thy hand, but not in flattery,
　　Cæsar ;
Desiring thee that Publius Cimber may
Have an immediate freedom of repeal.
Cæs. What, Brutus !
Cas.　　　　Pardon, Cæsar ; Cæsar, pardon :
As low as to thy foot doth Cassius fall,
To beg enfranchisement for Publius Cimber.
Cæs. I could be well moved, if I were as
　　you :
If I could pray to move, prayers would move
　　me :
But I am constant as the northern star,　60
Of whose true-fix'd and resting quality
There is no fellow in the firmament.
The skies are painted with unnumber'd sparks,
They are all fire and every one doth shine,
But there's but one in all doth hold his place :
So in the world ; 'tis furnish'd well with men,

And men are flesh and blood, and apprehen-
sive ;
Yet in the number I do know but one
That unassailable holds on his rank,
Unshaked of motion : and that I am he,   70
Let me a little show it, even in this ;
That I was constant Cimber should be ban-
ish'd,
And constant do remain to keep him so.
   Cin.   O Cæsar,—
   Cæs.   Hence ! wilt thou lift up Olympus ?
   Dec.   Great Cæsar,—
   Cæs.   Doth not Brutus bootless kneel ?
   Casca.   Speak, hands, for me !
   [*Casca first, then the other Conspirators
       and Marcus Brutus stab Cæsar.*
   Cæs.   Et tu, Brute ! Then fall, Cæsar.
                      [*Dies.*
   Cin.   Liberty ! Freedom ! Tyranny is dead !
Run hence, proclaim, cry it about the streets.
   Cas.   Some to the common pulpits, and cry
out   80
'Liberty, freedom, and enfranchisement !'
   Bru.   People and senators, be not af-
frighted ;
Fly not ; stand still : ambition's debt is paid.
   Casca.   Go to the pulpit, Brutus.
   Dec.   And Cassius too.
   Bru.   Where's Publius ?
   Cin.   Here, quite confounded with this mu-
tiny.
   Met.   Stand fast together, lest some friend
of Cæsar's
Should chance—
   Bru.   Talk not of standing. Publius, good
cheer ;
There is no harm intended to your person, 90
Nor to no Roman else : so tell them, Publius.
   Cas.   And leave us, Publius ; lest that the
people,
Rushing on us, should do your age some mis-
chief.
   Bru.   Do so : and let no man abide this
deed,
But we the doers.

Re-enter Trebonius.

   Cas.   Where is Antony ?
   Treb.   Fled to his house amazed :
Men, wives and children stare, cry out and run
As it were doomsday.
   Bru.   Fates, we will know your pleasures :
That we shall die, we know ; 'tis but the time
And drawing days out, that men stand upon.
   Cas.   Why, he that cuts off twenty years of
life   101
Cuts off so many years of fearing death.
   Bru.   Grant that, and then is death a bene-
fit :
So are we Cæsar's friends, that have abridged
His time of fearing death. Stoop, Romans,
stoop,
And let us bathe our hands in Cæsar's blood
Up to the elbows, and besmear our swords :
Then walk we forth, even to the market-place,
And, waving our red weapons o'er our heads,
Let's all cry ' Peace, freedom and liberty !'
   Cas.   Stoop, then, and wash. How many
ages hence   111
Shall this our lofty scene be acted over
In states unborn and accents yet unknown !
   Bru.   How many times shall Cæsar bleed
in sport,

That now on Pompey's basis lies along
No worthier than the dust !
   Cas.   So oft as that shall be,
So often shall the knot of us be call'd
The men that gave their country liberty.
   Dec.   What, shall we forth ?
   Cas.   Ay, every man away :
Brutus shall lead ; and we will grace his heels
With the most boldest and best hearts of
Rome.   121

Enter a Servant.

   Bru.   Soft ! who comes here ? A friend of
Antony's.
   Serv.   Thus, Brutus, did my master bid me
kneel :
Thus did Mark Antony bid me fall down ;
And, being prostrate, thus he bade me say :
Brutus is noble, wise, valiant, and honest ;
Cæsar was mighty, bold, royal, and loving :
Say I love Brutus, and I honor him ;
Say I fear'd Cæsar, honor'd him and loved
him.
If Brutus will vouchsafe that Antony   130
May safely come to him, and be resolved
How Cæsar hath deserved to lie in death,
Mark Antony shall not love Cæsar dead
So well as Brutus living ; but will follow
The fortunes and affairs of noble Brutus
Thorough the hazards of this untrod state
With all true faith. So says my master Antony.
   Bru.   Thy master is a wise and valiant Ro-
man ;
I never thought him worse.
Tell him, so please him come unto this place,
He shall be satisfied ; and, by my honor,   141
Depart untouch'd.
   Serv.   I'll fetch him presently. [*Exit.*
   Bru.   I know that we shall have him well to
friend.
   Cas.   I wish we may : but yet have I a mind
That fears him much ; and my misgiving still
Falls shrewdly to the purpose.
   Bru.   But here comes Antony.

Re-enter Antony.

              Welcome, Mark Antony.
   Ant.   O mighty Cæsar ! dost thou lie so
low ?
Are all thy conquests, glories, triumphs, spoils,
Shrunk to this little measure ? Fare thee well.
I know not, gentlemen, what you intend,   151
Who else must be let blood, who else is rank :
If I myself, there is no hour so fit
As Cæsar's death hour, nor no instrument
Of half that worth as those your swords, made
rich
With the most noble blood of all this world.
I do beseech ye, if you bear me hard,
Now, whilst your purpled hands do reek and
smoke,
Fulfil your pleasure. Live a thousand years,
I shall not find myself so apt to die :   160
No place will please me so, no mean of death,
As here by Cæsar, and by you cut off,
The choice and master spirits of this age.
   Bru.   O Antony, beg not your death of us.
Though now we must appear bloody and cruel,
As, by our hands and this our present act,
You see we do, yet see you but our hands
And this bleeding business they have done :
Our hearts you see not ; they are pitiful ;
And pity to the general wrong of Rome—   170

As fire drives out fire, so pity pity—
Hath done this deed on Cæsar. For your part,
To you our swords have leaden points, Mark
   Antony :
Our arms, in strength of malice, and our hearts
Of brothers' temper, do receive you in
With all kind love, good thoughts, and rever-
   ence.
   Cas. Your voice shall be as strong as any
   man's
In the disposing of new dignities.
   Bru. Only be patient till we have appeased
The multitude, beside themselves with fear,
And then we will deliver you the cause,   181
Why I, that did love Cæsar when I struck him,
Have thus proceeded.
   Ant.   I doubt not of your wisdom.
Let each man render me his bloody hand :
First, Marcus Brutus, will I shake with you ;
Next, Caius Cassius, do I take your hand ;
Now, Decius Brutus, yours : now yours, Me-
   tellus ;
Yours, Cinna ; and, my valiant Casca, yours ;
Though last, not least in love, yours, good
   Trebonius.
Gentlemen all,—alas, what shall I say ?   190
My credit now stands on such slippery ground,
That one of two bad ways you must conceit
   me,
Either a coward or a flatterer.
That I did love thee, Cæsar, O, 'tis true :
If then thy spirit look upon us now,
Shall it not grieve thee dearer than thy death,
To see thy Antony making his peace,
Shaking the bloody fingers of thy foes,
Most noble ! in the presence of thy corse ?
Had I as many eyes as thou hast wounds, 200
Weeping as fast as they stream forth thy
   blood,
It would become me better than to close
In terms of friendship with thine enemies.
Pardon me, Julius ! Here wast thou bay'd,
   brave hart ;
Here didst thou fall ; and here thy hunters
   stand,
Sign'd in thy spoil, and crimson'd in thy lethe.
O world, thou wast the forest to this hart ;
And this, indeed, O world, the heart of thee.
How like a deer, strucken by many princes,
Dost thou here lie !   210
   Cas. Mark Antony,—
   Ant.   Pardon me, Caius Cassius :
The enemies of Cæsar shall say this ;
Then, in a friend, it is cold modesty.
   Cas. I blame you not for praising Cæsar
   so ;
But what compact mean you to have with us ?
Will you be prick'd in number of our friends ;
Or shall we on, and not depend on you ?
   Ant. Therefore I took your hands, but was,
   indeed,
Sway'd from the point, by looking down on
   Cæsar.   219
Friends am I with you all and love you all,
Upon this hope, that you shall give me reasons
Why and wherein Cæsar was dangerous.
   Bru. Or else were this a savage spectacle :
Our reasons are so full of good regard
That were you, Antony, the son of Cæsar,
You should be satisfied.
   Ant.   That's all I seek :
And am moreover suitor that I may

Produce his body to the market-place ;
And in the pulpit, as becomes a friend,
Speak in the order of his funeral.   230
   Bru. You shall, Mark Antony.
   Cas.   Brutus, a word with you.
[*Aside to Bru.*] You know not what you do :
   do not consent
That Antony speak in his funeral :
Know you how much the people may be moved
By that which he will utter ?
   Bru.   By your pardon ;
I will myself into the pulpit first,
And show the reason of our Cæsar's death :
What Antony shall speak, I will protest
He speaks by leave and by permission,
And that we are contented Cæsar shall   240
Have all true rites and lawful ceremonies.
It shall advantage more than do us wrong.
   Cas. I know not what may fall ; I like it
   not.
   Bru. Mark Antony, here, take you Cæsar's
   body.
You shall not in your funeral speech blame us,
But speak all good you can devise of Cæsar,
And say you do't by our permission ;
Else shall you not have any hand at all
About his funeral : and you shall speak
In the same pulpit whereto I am going,   250
After my speech is ended.
   Ant.   Be it so ;
I do desire no more.
   Bru. Prepare the body then, and follow us.
              [*Exeunt all but Antony.*
   Ant. O, pardon me, thou bleeding piece of
   earth,
That I am meek and gentle with these butch-
   ers !
Thou art the ruins of the noblest man
That ever lived in the tide of times.
Woe to the hand that shed this costly blood !
Over thy wounds now do I prophesy,—
Which, like dumb mouths, do ope their ruby
   lips,   260
To beg the voice and utterance of my tongue—
A curse shall light upon the limbs of men ;
Domestic fury and fierce civil strife
Shall cumber all the parts of Italy ;
Blood and destruction shall be so in use
And dreadful objects so familiar
That mothers shall but smile when they behold
Their infants quarter'd with the hands of war ;
All pity choked with custom of fell deeds :
And Cæsar's spirit, ranging for revenge,   270
With Ate by his side come hot from hell,
Shall in these confines with a monarch's voice
Cry ' Havoc,' and let slip the dogs of war ;
That this foul deed shall smell above the earth
With carrion men, groaning for burial.

Enter a *Servant.*

You serve Octavius Cæsar, do you not ?
   Serv. I do, Mark Antony.
   Ant. Cæsar did write for him to come to
   Rome.
   Serv. He did receive his letters, and is
   coming ;
And bid me say to you by word of mouth—
O Cæsar !—   [*Seeing the body.*   281
   Ant. Thy heart is big, get thee apart and
   weep.
Passion, I see, is catching ; for mine eyes,
Seeing those beads of sorrow stand in thine,
Began to water. Is thy master coming ?

Serv. He lies to-night within seven leagues
    of Rome.
    Ant. Post back with speed, and tell him
    what hath chanced :
Here is a mourning Rome, a dangerous Rome,
No Rome of safety for Octavius yet ;   289
Hie hence, and tell him so. Yet, stay awhile ;
Thou shalt not back till I have borne this corse
Into the market-place : there shall I try
In my oration, how the people take
The cruel issue of these bloody men ;
According to the which, thou shalt discourse
To young Octavius of the state of things.
Lend me your hand.
         [Exeunt with Cæsar's body.

SCENE II. *The Forum.*

Enter BRUTUS *and* CASSIUS, *and a throng of*
Citizens.

    Citizens. We will be satisfied ; let us be
    satisfied.
    Bru. Then follow me, and give me audi-
    ence, friends.
Cassius, go you into the other street,
And part the numbers.
Those that will hear me speak, let 'em stay
here ;
Those that will follow Cassius, go with him ;
And public reasons shall be rendered
Of Cæsar's death.
    First Cit.   I will hear Brutus speak.
    Sec. Cit. I will hear Cassius ; and compare
    their reasons,
When severally we hear them rendered.   10
    [Exit Cassius, with some of the Citizens.
    Brutus goes into the pulpit.
    Third Cit. The noble Brutus is ascended :
    silence !
    Bru. Be patient till the last.
Romans, countrymen, and lovers ! hear me for
my cause, and be silent, that you may hear :
believe me for mine honor, and have respect
to mine honor, that you may believe : censure
me in your wisdom, and awake your senses,
that you may the better judge. If there be any
in this assembly, any dear friend of Cæsar's,
to him I say, that Brutus' love to Cæsar was
no less than his. If then that friend demand
why Brutus rose against Cæsar, this is my answer :—Not that I loved Cæsar less, but that
I loved Rome more. Had you rather Cæsar
were living and die all slaves, than that Cæsar
were dead, to live all free men ? As Cæsar
loved me, I weep for him ; as he was fortunate, I rejoice at it ; as he was valiant, I honor
him : but, as he was ambitious, I slew him.
There is tears for his love ; joy for his fortune ;
honor for his valor ; and death for his ambition. Who is here so base that would be a
bondman ? If any, speak ; for him have I offended. Who is here so rude that would not be
a Roman ? If any, speak ; for him have I offended. Who is here so vile that will not love
his country ? If any, speak ; for him have I
offended. I pause for a reply.
    All. None, Brutus, none.
    Bru. Then none have I offended. I have
done no more to Cæsar than you shall do to
Brutus. The question of his death is enrolled
in the Capitol ; his glory not extenuated,
wherein he was worthy, nor his offences enforced, for which he suffered death.

Enter ANTONY *and others, with* CÆSAR'S *body.*

Here comes his body, mourned by Mark Antony : who, though he had no hand in his
death, shall receive the benefit of his dying, a
place in the commonwealth ; as which of you
shall not ? With this I depart,—that, as I slew
my best lover for the good of Rome, I have the
same dagger for myself, when it shall please
my country to need my death.
    All. Live, Brutus ! live, live !
    First Cit. Bring him with triumph home
    unto his house.
    Sec. Cit. Give him a statue with his ances-
    tors.
    Third Cit. Let him be Cæsar.
    Fourth Cit.   Cæsar's better parts
Shall be crown'd in Brutus.
    First Cit.   We'll bring him to his house
With shouts and clamors.
    Bru.   My countrymen,—
    Sec. Cit. Peace, silence ! Brutus speaks.
    First Cit.   Peace, ho !
    Bru. Good countrymen, let me depart
alone,
And, for my sake, stay here with Antony :   61
Do grace to Cæsar's corpse, and grace his
speech
Tending to Cæsar's glories ; which Mark An-
tony,
By our permission, is allow'd to make.
I do entreat you, not a man depart,
Save I alone, till Antony have spoke.   *[Exit.*
    First Cit. Stay, ho ! and let us hear Mark
    Antony.
    Third Cit. Let him go up into the public
    chair ;
We'll hear him. Noble Antony, go up.
    Ant. For Brutus' sake, I am beholding to
    you.   *[Goes into the pulpit.* 70
    Fourth Cit. What does he say of Brutus ?
    Third Cit.   He says, for Brutus' sake,
He finds himself beholding to us all.
    Fourth Cit. 'Twere best he speak no harm
    of Brutus here.
    First Cit. This Cæsar was a tyrant.
    Third Cit.   Nay, that's certain :
We are blest that Rome is rid of him.
    Sec. Cit. Peace ! let us hear what Antony
    can say.
    Ant. You gentle Romans,—
    Citizens.   Peace, ho ! let us hear him.
    Ant. Friends, Romans, countrymen, lend
    me your ears ;
I come to bury Cæsar, not to praise him.
The evil that men do lives after them ;   80
The good is oft interred with their bones ;
So let it be with Cæsar. The noble Brutus
Hath told you Cæsar was ambitious :
If it were so, it was a grievous fault,
And grievously hath Cæsar answer'd it.
Here, under leave of Brutus and the rest—
For Brutus is an honorable man ;
So are they all, all honorable men—
Come I to speak in Cæsar's funeral.
He was my friend, faithful and just to me :   90
But Brutus says he was ambitious ;
And Brutus is an honorable man.
He hath brought many captives home to Rome
Whose ransoms did the general coffers fill :
Did this in Cæsar seem ambitious ?
When that the poor have cried, Cæsar hath
wept :

Ambition should be made of sterner stuff :
Yet Brutus says he was ambitious ;
And Brutus is an honorable man.
You all did see that on the Lupercal   100
I thrice presented him a kingly crown,
Which he did thrice refuse : was this ambi-
  tion ?
Yet Brutus says he was ambitious ;
And, sure, he is an honorable man.
I speak not to disprove what Brutus spoke,
But here I am to speak what I do know.
You all did love him once, not without cause :
What cause withholds you then, to mourn for
  him ?
O judgment ! thou art fled to brutish beasts,
And men have lost their reason. Bear with
  me ;   110
My heart is in the coffin there with Cæsar,
And I must pause till it come back to me.
  First Cit. Methinks there is much reason
    in his sayings.
  Sec. Cit. If thou consider rightly of the
    matter,
Cæsar has had great wrong.
  Third Cit.   Has he, masters ?
I fear there will a worse come in his place.
  Fourth Cit. Mark'd ye his words ? He
    would not take the crown ;
Therefore 'tis certain he was not ambitious.
  First Cit. If it be found so, some will dear
    abide it.
  Sec. Cit. Poor soul ! his eyes are red as fire
    with weeping.   120
  Third Cit. There's not a nobler man in
    Rome than Antony.
  Fourth Cit. Now mark him, he begins
    again to speak.
  Ant. But yesterday the word of Cæsar
    might
Have stood against the world ; now lies he
  there.
And none so poor to do him reverence.
O masters, if I were disposed to stir
Your hearts and minds to mutiny and rage,
I should do Brutus wrong, and Cassius wrong,
Who, you all know, are honorable men :
I will not do them wrong ; I rather choose 130
To wrong the dead, to wrong myself and you,
Than I will wrong such honorable men.
But here's a parchment with the seal of Cæ-
  sar ;
I found it in his closet, 'tis his will :
Let but the commons hear this testament—
Which, pardon me, I do not mean to read—
And they would go and kiss dead Cæsar's
  wounds
And dip their napkins in his sacred blood,
Yea, beg a hair of him for memory,
And, dying, mention it within their wills, 140
Bequeathing it as a rich legacy
Unto their issue.
  Fourth Cit. We'll hear the will : read it,
    Mark Antony.
  All. The will, the will ! we will hear Cæ-
    sar's will.
  Ant. Have patience, gentle friends, I must
    not read it ;
It is not meet you know how Cæsar loved you.
You are not wood, you are not stones, but
  men ;
And, being men, hearing the will of Cæsar,
It will inflame you, it will make you mad : 149

'Tis good you know not that you are his heirs ;
For, if you should, O, what would come of it !
  Fourth Cit. Read the will ; we'll hear it,
    Antony ;
You shall read us the will, Cæsar's will.
  Ant. Will you be patient ? will you stay
    awhile ?
I have o'ershot myself to tell you of it :
I fear I wrong the honorable men
Whose daggers have stabb'd Cæsar ; I do fear
  it.
  Fourth Cit. They were traitors : honorable
    men !
  All. The will ! the testament !
  Sec. Cit. They were villains, murderers :
the will ! read the will.   160
  Ant. You will compel me, then, to read the
    will ?
Then make a ring about the corpse of Cæsar,
And let me show you him that made the will.
Shall I descend ? and will you give me leave ?
  Several Cit. Come down.
  Sec. Cit. Descend.
  Third Cit. You shall have leave.
                       [*Antony comes down.*
  Fourth Cit. A ring ; stand round.
  First Cit. Stand from the hearse, stand
    from the body.
  Sec. Cit. Room for Antony, most noble
    Antony.   170
  Ant. Nay, press not so upon me ; stand far
    off.
  Several Cit. Stand back ; room ; bear back.
  Ant. If you have tears, prepare to shed
    them now.
You all do know this mantle : I remember
The first time ever Cæsar put it on ;
'Twas on a summer's evening, in his tent,
That day he overcame the Nervii :
Look, in this place ran Cassius' dagger
  through :
See what a rent the envious Casca made :
Through this the well-beloved Brutus stabb'd ;
And as he pluck'd his cursed steel away,   181
Mark how the blood of Cæsar follow'd it,
As rushing out of doors, to be resolved
If Brutus so unkindly knock'd, or no ;
For Brutus, as you know, was Cæsar's angel :
Judge, O you gods, how dearly Cæsar loved
  him !
This was the most unkindest cut of all ;
For when the noble Cæsar saw him stab,
Ingratitude, more strong than traitors' arms,
Quite vanquish'd him : then burst his mighty
  heart ;   190
And, in his mantle muffling up his face,
Even at the base of Pompey's statua,
Which all the while ran blood, great Cæsar
  fell.
O, what a fall was there, my countrymen !
Then I, and you, and all of us fell down,
Whilst bloody treason flourish'd over us.
O, now you weep ; and, I perceive, you feel
The dint of pity : these are gracious drops.
Kind souls, what, weep you when you but be-
  hold
Our Cæsar's vesture wounded ? Look you
  here,   200
Here is himself, marr'd, as you see, with trai-
  tors.
  First Cit. O piteous spectacle !
  Sec. Cit. O noble Cæsar !

Third Cit. O woful day !
Fourth Cit. O traitors, villains !
First Cit. O most bloody sight !
Sec. Cit. We will be revenged.
All. Revenge ! About ! Seek ! Burn !
Fire ! Kill ! Slay ! Let not a traitor live !
Ant. Stay, countrymen.   210
First Cit. Peace there ! hear the noble Antony.
Sec. Cit. We'll hear him, we'll follow him, we'll die with him.
Ant. Good friends, sweet friends, let me not stir you up
To such a sudden flood of mutiny.
They that have done this deed are honorable :
What private griefs they have, alas, I know not,
That made them do it : they are wise and honorable,
And will, no doubt, with reasons answer you.
I come not, friends, to steal away your hearts :
I am no orator, as Brutus is ;   221
But, as you know me all, a plain blunt man,
That love my friend ; and that they know full well
That gave me public leave to speak of him :
For I have neither wit, nor words, nor worth,
Action, nor utterance, nor the power of speech,
To stir men's blood : I only speak right on ;
I tell you that which you yourselves do know ;
Show you sweet Cæsar's wounds, poor poor dumb mouths,
And bid them speak for me : but were I Brutus,   230
And Brutus Antony, there were an Antony
Would ruffle up your spirits and put a tongue
In every wound of Cæsar that should move
The stones of Rome to rise and mutiny.
All. We'll mutiny.
First Cit. We'll burn the house of Brutus.
Third Cit. Away, then ! come, seek the conspirators.
Ant. Yet hear me, countrymen ; yet hear me speak.
All. Peace, ho ! Hear Antony. Most noble Antony !
Ant. Why, friends, you go to do you know not what :   240
Wherein hath Cæsar thus deserved your loves ?
Alas, you know not : I must tell you, then :
You have forgot the will I told you of.
All. Most true. The will ! Let's stay and hear the will.
Ant. Here is the will, and under Cæsar's seal.
To every Roman citizen he gives,
To every several man, seventy-five drachmas.
Sec. Cit. Most noble Cæsar ! We'll revenge his death.
Third Cit. O royal Cæsar !
Ant. Hear me with patience.   250
All. Peace, ho !
Ant. Moreover, he hath left you all his walks,
His private arbors and new-planted orchards,
On this side Tiber ; he hath left them you,
And to your heirs for ever, common pleasures,
To walk abroad, and recreate yourselves.
Here was a Cæsar ! when comes such another ?

First Cit. Never, never. Come, away, away !
We'll burn his body in the holy place,
And with the brands fire the traitors' houses.
Take up the body.   261
Sec. Cit. Go fetch fire.
Third Cit. Pluck down benches.
Fourth Cit. Pluck down forms, windows, any thing.
        [*Exeunt Citizens with the body.*
Ant. Now let it work. Mischief, thou art afoot,
Take thou what course thou wilt !

Enter a Servant.

                        How now, fellow !
Serv. Sir, Octavius is already come to Rome.
Ant. Where is he ?
Serv. He and Lepidus are at Cæsar's house.
Ant. And thither will I straight to visit him :
He comes upon a wish. Fortune is merry, 271
And in this mood will give us any thing.
Serv. I heard him say, Brutus and Cassius
Are rid like madmen through the gates of Rome.
Ant. Belike they had some notice of the people,
How I had moved them. Bring me to Octavius.   [*Exeunt.*

Scene III. *A street.*

Enter Cinna *the poet.*

Cin. I dreamt to-night that I did feast with Cæsar,
And things unlucky charge my fantasy :
I have no will to wander forth of doors,
Yet something leads me forth.

Enter Citizens.

First Cit. What is your name ?
Sec. Cit. Whither are you going ?
Third Cit. Where do you dwell ?
Fourth Cit. Are you a married man or a bachelor ?
Sec. Cit. Answer every man directly. 10
First Cit. Ay, and briefly.
Fourth Cit. Ay, and wisely.
Third Cit. Ay, and truly, you were best.
Cin. What is my name ? Whither am I going ? Where do I dwell ? Am I a married man or a bachelor ? Then, to answer every man directly and briefly, wisely and truly : wisely I say, I am a bachelor.
Sec. Cit. That's as much as to say, they are fools that marry : you'll bear me a bang for that, I fear. Proceed ; directly.   21
Cin. Directly, I am going to Cæsar's funeral.
First Cit. As a friend or an enemy ?
Cin. As a friend.
Sec. Cit. That matter is answered directly.
Fourth Cit. For your dwelling,—briefly.
Cin. Briefly, I dwell by the Capitol.
Third Cit. Your name, sir, truly.
Cin. Truly, my name is Cinna.
First Cit. Tear him to pieces ; he's a conspirator.   31
Cin. I am Cinna the poet, I am Cinna the poet.

Fourth Cit. Tear him for his bad verses,
tear him for his bad verses.

Cin. I am not Cinna the conspirator.

Fourth Cit. It is no matter, his name's
Cinna ; pluck but his name out of his heart,
and turn him going.

Third Cit. Tear him, tear him ! Come,
brands, ho ! fire-brands : to Brutus', to Cassius'; burn all : some to Decius' house, and
some to Casca's ; some to Ligarius' : away,
go !   [*Exeunt.*

ACT IV.

SCENE I. *A house in Rome.*

ANTONY, OCTAVIUS, *and* LEPIDUS, *seated at a
table.*

Ant. These many, then, shall die ; their
names are prick'd.

Oct. Your brother too must die ; consent
you, Lepidus ?

Lep. I do consent—

Oct.   Prick him down, Antony.

Lep. Upon condition Publius shall not live,
Who is your sister's son, Mark Antony.

Ant. He shall not live ; look, with a spot I
damn him.
But, Lepidus, go you to Cæsar's house ;
Fetch the will hither, and we shall determine
How to cut off some charge in legacies.

Lep. What, shall I find you here ?   10

Oct. Or here, or at the Capitol.
                                [*Exit Lepidus.*

Ant. This is a slight unmeritable man,
Meet to be sent on errands : is it fit,
The three-fold world divided, he should stand
One of the three to share it ?

Oct.   So you thought him ;
And took his voice who should be prick'd to
die,
In our black sentence and proscription.

Ant. Octavius, I have seen more days than
you :
And though we lay these honors on this man,
To ease ourselves of divers slanderous loads,
He shall but bear them as the ass bears gold,
To groan and sweat under the business,   22
Either led or driven, as we point the way ;
And having brought our treasure where we
will,
Then take we down his load, and turn him off,
Like to the empty ass, to shake his ears,
And graze in commons.

Oct.   You may do your will ;
But he's a tried and valiant soldier.

Ant. So is my horse, Octavius ; and for
that
I do appoint him store of provender :   30
It is a creature that I teach to fight,
To wind, to stop, to run directly on,
His corporal motion govern'd by my spirit.
And, in some taste, is Lepidus but so ;
He must be taught and train'd and bid go
forth ;
A barren-spirited fellow ; one that feeds
On abjects, orts and imitations,
Which, out of use and staled by other men,
Begin his fashion : do not talk of him,
But as a property. And now, Octavius,   40
Listen great things :—Brutus and Cassius

Are levying powers : we must straight make
head :
Therefore let our alliance be combined,
Our best friends made, our means stretch'd ;
And let us presently go sit in council,
How covert matters may be best disclosed,
And open perils surest answered.

Oct. Let us do so : for we are at the stake,
And bay'd about with many enemies ;
And some that smile have in their hearts, I
fear,   50
Millions of mischiefs.   [*Exeunt.*

SCENE II. *Camp near Sardis. Before Bru-
tus's tent.*

Drum. Enter BRUTUS, LUCILIUS, LUCIUS, *and
Soldiers ;* TITINIUS *and* PINDARUS *meeting
them.*

Bru. Stand, ho !

Lucil. Give the word, ho ! and stand.

Bru. What now, Lucilius ! is Cassius near ?

Lucil. He is at hand ; and Pindarus is
come
To do you salutation from his master.

Bru. He greets me well. Your master,
Pindarus,
In his own change, or by ill officers,
Hath given me some worthy cause to wish
Things done, undone : but, if he be at hand,
I shall be satisfied.

Pin.   I do not doubt   10
But that my noble master will appear
Such as he is, full of regard and honor.

Bru. He is not doubted. A word, Lucilius ;
How he received you, let me be resolved.

Lucil. With courtesy and with respect
enough ;
But not with such familiar instances,
Nor with such free and friendly conference,
As he hath used of old.

Bru.   Thou hast described
A hot friend cooling : ever note, Lucilius,
When love begins to sicken and decay,   20
It useth an enforced ceremony.
There are no tricks in plain and simple faith ;
But hollow men, like horses hot at hand,
Make gallant show and promise of their met-
tle ;
But when they should endure the bloody spur,
They fall their crests, and, like deceitful jades,
Sink in the trial. Comes his army on ?

Lucil. They mean this night in Sardis to be
quarter'd ;
The greater part, the horse in general,
Are come with Cassius.

Bru.   Hark ! he is arrived. 30
                        [*Low march within.*
March gently on to meet him.

Enter CASSIUS *and his powers.*

Cas. Stand, ho !

Bru. Stand, ho ! Speak the word along.

First Sol. Stand !

Sec. Sol. Stand !

Third Sol. Stand !

Cas. Most noble brother, you have done
me wrong.

Bru. Judge me, you gods ! wrong I mine
enemies ?
And, if not so, how should I wrong a brother ?

Cas. Brutus, this sober form of yours hides
wrongs ;   40

And when you do them—
Bru.   Cassius, be content;
Speak your griefs softly : I do know you well.
Before the eyes of both our armies here,
Which should perceive nothing but love from
    us,
Let us not wrangle : bid them move away ;
Then in my tent, Cassius, enlarge your griefs,
And I will give you audience.
Cas.   Pindarus,
Bid our commanders lead their charges off
A little from this ground.
Bru.   Lucilius, do you the like ; and let no
    man   50
Come to our tent till we have done our con-
    ference.
Let Lucius and Titinius guard our door.
                                    [*Exeunt.*

SCENE III. *Brutus's tent.*

Enter BRUTUS *and* CASSIUS.

Cas.   That you have wrong'd me doth ap-
    pear in this :
You have condemn'd and noted Lucius Pella
For taking bribes here of the Sardians ;
Wherein my letters, praying on his side,
Because I knew the man, were slighted off.
Bru.   You wronged yourself to write in
    such a case.
Cas.   In such a time as this it is not meet
That every nice offence should bear his com-
    ment.
Bru.   Let me tell you, Cassius, you yourself
Are much condemn'd to have an itching
    palm ;
To sell and mart your offices for gold   11
To undeservers.
Cas.   I an itching palm !
You know that you are Brutus that speak
    this,
Or, by the gods, this speech were else your last.
Bru.   The name of Cassius honors this cor-
    ruption,
And chastisement doth therefore hide his head,
Cas.   Chastisement !
Bru.   Remember March, the ides of March
    remember :
Did not great Julius bleed for justice' sake ?
What villain touch'd his body, that did stab,
And not for justice ? What, shall one of us,
That struck the foremost man of all this world
But for supporting robbers, shall we now
Contaminate our fingers with base bribes,
And sell the mighty space of our large honors
For so much trash as may be grasped thus ?
I had rather be a dog, and bay the moon,
Than such a Roman.
Cas.   Brutus, bay not me ;
I'll not endure it : you forget yourself,
To hedge me in ; I am a soldier, I,   30
Older in practice, abler than yourself
To make conditions.
Bru.   Go to ; you are not, Cassius.
Cas.   I am.
Bru.   I say you are not.
Cas.   Urge me no more, I shall forget my-
    self :
Have mind upon your health, tempt me no
    further.
Bru.   Away, slight man !
Cas.   Is't possible ?

Bru.   Hear me, for I will speak.
Must I give way and room to your rash
    choler ?
Shall I be frighted when a madman stares ? 40
Cas.   O ye gods, ye gods ! must I endure
    all this ?
Bru.   All this ! ay, more : fret till your
    proud heart break ;
Go show your slaves how choleric you are,
And make your bondmen tremble. Must I
    budge ?
Must I observe you ? must I stand and crouch
Under your testy humor ? By the gods
You shall digest the venom of your spleen,
Though it do split you ; for, from this day
    forth,
I'll use you for my mirth, yea, for my laughter,
When you are waspish.
Cas.   Is it come to this ?   50
Bru.   You say you are a better soldier :
Let it appear so ; make your vaunting true,
And it shall please me well : for mine own
    part,
I shall be glad to learn of noble men.
Cas.   You wrong me every way ; you wrong
    me, Brutus ;
I said, an elder soldier, not a better :
Did I say ' better ' ?
Bru.   If you did, I care not.
Cas.   When Cæsar lived, he durst not thus
    have moved me.
Bru.   Peace, peace ! you durst not so have
    tempted him.
Cas.   I durst not !   60
Bru.   No.
Cas.   What, durst not tempt him !
Bru.   For your life you durst not.
Cas.   Do not presume too much upon my
    love ;
I may do that I shall be sorry for.
Bru.   You have done that you should be
    sorry for.
There is no terror, Cassius, in your threats,
For I am arm'd so strong in honesty
That they pass by me as the idle wind,
Which I respect not. I did send to you
For certain sums of gold, which you denied
    me :   70
For I can raise no money by vile means :
By heaven, I had rather coin my heart,
And drop my blood for drachmas, than to
    wring
From the hard hands of peasants their vile
    trash
By any indirection : I did send
To you for gold to pay my legions,
Which you denied me : was that done like
    Cassius ?
Should I have answer'd Caius Cassius so ?
When Marcus Brutus grows so covetous,   79
To lock such rascal counters from his friends,
Be ready, gods, with all your thunderbolts ;
Dash him to pieces !
Cas.   I denied you not.
Bru.   You did.
Cas.   I did not : he was but a fool that
    brought
My answer back. Brutus hath rived my heart :
A friend should bear his friend's infirmities,
But Brutus makes mine greater than they are.
Bru.   I do not, till you practice them on
    me.

Cas. You love me not.
Bru. I do not like your faults.
Cas. A friendly eye could never see such
faults. 90
Bru. A flatterer's would not, though they
do appear
As huge as high Olympus.
Cas. Come, Antony, and young Octavius,
come,
Revenge yourselves alone on Cassius,
For Cassius is aweary of the world;
Hated by one he loves; braved by his brother;
Check'd like a bondman; all his faults ob-
served,
Set in a note-book, learn'd, and conn'd by
rote,
To cast into my teeth. O, I could weep
My spirit from mine eyes! There is my dag-
ger, 100
And here my naked breast; within, a heart
Dearer than Plutus' mine, richer than gold:
If that thou be'st a Roman, take it forth;
I, that denied thee gold, will give my heart:
Strike, as thou didst at Cæsar; for, I know,
When thou didst hate him worst, thou lovedst
him better
Than ever thou lovedst Cassius.
Bru. Sheathe your dagger:
Be angry when you will, it shall have scope;
Do what you will, dishonor shall be humor.
O Cassius, you are yoked with a lamb 110
That carries anger as the flint bears fire;
Who, much enforced, shows a hasty spark,
And straight is cold again.
Cas. Hath Cassius lived
To be but mirth and laughter to his Brutus,
When grief, and blood ill-temper'd, vexeth
him?
Bru. When I spoke that, I was ill-temper'd
too.
Cas. Do you confess so much? Give me
your hand.
Bru. And my heart too.
Cas. O Brutus! 120
Bru. What's the matter?
Cas. Have not you love enough to bear
with me,
When that rash humor which my mother gave
me
Makes me forgetful?
Bru. Yes, Cassius; and, from henceforth,
When you are over-earnest with your Brutus,
He'll think your mother chides, and leave you
so.
Poet. [*Within*] Let me go in to see the
generals;
There is some grudge between 'em, 'tis not
meet
They be alone.
Lucil. [*Within*] You shall not come to
them.
Poet. [*Within*] Nothing but death shall
stay me.

Enter Poet, *followed by* Lucilius, Titinius,
and Lucius.

Cas. How now! what's the matter?
Poet. For shame, you generals! what do
you mean? 130
Love, and be friends, as two such men should
be;
For I have seen more years, I'm sure, than ye.

Cas. Ha, ha! how vilely doth this cynic
rhyme!
Bru. Get you hence, sirrah; saucy fellow,
hence!
Cas. Bear with him, Brutus; 'tis his fash-
ion.
Bru. I'll know his humor, when he knows
his time:
What should the wars do with these jigging
fools?
Companion, hence!
Cas. Away, away, be gone.
[*Exit Poet.*
Bru. Lucilius and Titinius, bid the com-
manders
Prepare to lodge their companies to-night. 140
Cas. And come yourselves, and bring Mes-
sala with you
Immediately to us.
[*Exeunt Lucilius and Titinius.*
Bru. Lucius, a bowl of wine! [*Exit Lucius.*
Cas. I did not think you could have been
so angry.
Bru. O Cassius, I am sick of many griefs.
Cas. Of your philosophy you make no use,
If you give place to accidental evils.
Bru. No man bears sorrow better. Portia
is dead.
Cas. Ha! Portia!
Bru. She is dead.
Cas. How 'scaped I killing when I cross'd
you so? 150
O insupportable and touching loss!
Upon what sickness?
Bru. Impatient of my absence,
And grief that young Octavius with Mark
Antony
Have made themselves so strong:—for with
her death
That tidings came;—with this she fell distract,
And, her attendants absent, swallow'd fire.
Cas. And died so?
Bru. Even so.
Cas. O ye immortal gods!

Re-enter Lucius, *with wine and taper.*

Bru. Speak no more of her. Give me a
bowl of wine.
In this I bury all unkindness, Cassius.
Cas. My heart is thirsty for that noble
pledge. 160
Fill, Lucius, till the wine o'erswell the cup;
I cannot drink too much of Brutus' love.
Bru. Come in, Titinius! [*Exit Lucius.*

Re-enter Titinius, *with* Messala.

Welcome, good Messala.
Now sit we close about this taper here,
And call in question our necessities.
Cas. Portia, art thou gone?
Bru. No more, I pray you.
Messala, I have here received letters,
That young Octavius and Mark Antony
Come down upon us with a mighty power,
Bending their expedition toward Philippi. 170
Mes. Myself have letters of the selfsame
tenor.
Bru. With what addition?
Mes. That by proscription and bills of out-
lawry,
Octavius, Antony, and Lepidus,
Have put to death an hundred senators.

Bru. Therein our letters do not well agree ;
Mine speak of seventy senators that died
By their proscriptions, Cicero being one.
  Cas. Cicero one !
  Mes.   Cicero is dead,
And by that order of proscription.   180
Had you your letters from your wife, my
    lord ?
  Bru. No, Messala.
  Mes. Nor nothing in your letters writ of
    her ?
  Bru. Nothing, Messala.
  Mes.   That, methinks, is strange.
  Bru. Why ask you ? hear you aught of her
    in yours ?
  Mes. No, my lord.
  Bru. Now, as you are a Roman, tell me
    true.
  Mes. Then like a Roman bear the truth I
    tell :
For certain she is dead, and by strange man-
    ner.
  Bru. Why, farewell, Portia. We must die,
    Messala :   190
With meditating that she must die once,
I have the patience to endure it now.
  Mes. Even so great men great losses should
    endure.
  Cas. I have as much of this in art as you,
But yet my nature could not bear it so.
  Bru. Well, to our work alive. What do you
    think
Of marching to Philippi presently ?
  Cas. I do not think it good.
  Bru.   Your reason ?
  Cas.   This it is :
'Tis better that the enemy seek us :
So shall he waste his means, weary his sol-
    diers,   200
Doing himself offence ; whilst we, lying still,
Are full of rest, defence, and nimbleness.
  Bru. Good reasons must, of force, give
    place to better.
The people 'twixt Philippi and this ground
Do stand but in a forced affection ;
For they have grudged us contribution :
The enemy, marching along by them,
By them shall make a fuller number up,
Come on refresh'd, new-added, and encour-
    aged ;
From which advantage shall we cut him off,
If at Philippi we do face him there,   211
These people at our back.
  Cas.   Hear me, good brother.
  Bru. Under your pardon. You must note
    beside,
That we have tried the utmost of our friends,
Our legions are brim-full, our cause is ripe :
The enemy increaseth every day ;
We, at the height, are ready to decline.
There is a tide in the affairs of men,
Which, taken at the flood, leads on to fortune ;
Omitted, all the voyage of their life   220
Is bound in shallows and in miseries.
On such a full sea are we now afloat ;
And we must take the current when it serves,
Or lose our ventures.
  Cas.   Then, with your will, go on ;
We'll along ourselves, and meet them at
    Philippi.
  Bru. The deep of night is crept upon our
    talk,

And nature must obey necessity ;
Which we will niggard with a little rest.
There is no more to say ?
  Cas.   No more. Good night :
Early to-morrow will we rise, and hence.   230
  Bru. Lucius ! [*Enter Lucius.*] My gown.
        [*Exit Lucius.*] Farewell, good Messala :
Good night, Titinius. Noble, noble Cassius,
Good night, and good repose.
  Cas.   O my dear brother !
This was an ill beginning of the night :
Never come such division 'tween our souls !
Let it not, Brutus.
  Bru.   Every thing is well.
  Cas. Good night, my lord.
  Bru.   Good night, good brother.
  Tit. Mess. Good night, Lord Brutus.
  Bru.   Farewell, every one.
        [*Exeunt all but Brutus.*

        Re-enter Lucius, *with the gown.*
Give me the gown. Where is thy instrument ?
  Luc. Here in the tent.
  Bru. What, thou speak'st drowsily ?   240
Poor knave, I blame thee not ; thou art o'er-
    watch'd.
Call Claudius and some other of my men :
I'll have them sleep on cushions in my tent.
  Luc. Varro and Claudius !

        Enter Varro *and* Claudius.
  Var. Calls my lord ?
  Bru. I pray you, sirs, lie in my tent and
    sleep ;
It may be I shall raise you by and by
On business to my brother Cassius.
  Var. So please you, we will stand and
    watch your pleasure.
  Bru. I will not have it so : lie down, good
    sirs ;   250
It may be I shall otherwise bethink me.
Look, Lucius, here's the book I sought for so ;
I put it in the pocket of my gown.
        [*Var. and Clau. lie down.*
  Luc. I was sure your lordship did not give
    it me.
  Bru. Bear with me, good boy, I am much
    forgetful.
Canst thou hold up thy heavy eyes awhile,
And touch thy instrument a strain or two ?
  Luc. Ay, my lord, an't please you.
  Bru.   It does, my boy :
I trouble thee too much, but thou art willing.
  Luc. It is my duty, sir.   260
  Bru. I should not urge thy duty past thy
    might ;
I know young bloods look for a time of rest.
  Luc. I have slept, my lord, already.
  Bru. It was well done ; and thou shalt
    sleep again ;
I will not hold thee long : if I do live,
I will be good to thee.   [*Music, and a song.*
This is a sleepy tune. O murderous slumber,
Lay'st thou thy leaden mace upon my boy,
That plays thee music ? Gentle knave, good
    night ;   269
I will not do thee so much wrong to wake
    thee :
If thou dost nod, thou break'st thy instru-
    ment ;
I'll take it from thee ; and, good boy, good
    night.

Let me see, let me see ; is not the leaf turn'd
    down
Where I left reading ? Here it is, I think.

Enter the Ghost of CÆSAR.

How ill this taper burns ! Ha ! who comes
    here ?
I think it is the weakness of mine eyes
That shapes this monstrous apparition.
It comes upon me. Art thou any thing ?
Art thou some god, some angel, or some devil,
That makest my blood cold and my hair to
    stare ?   280
Speak to me what thou art.
    Ghost. Thy evil spirit, Brutus.
    Bru. Why comest thou ?
    Ghost. To tell thee thou shalt see me at
    Philippi.
    Bru. Well ; then I shall see thee again ?
    Ghost. Ay, at Philippi.
    Bru. Why, I will see thee at Philippi, then.
                                    [*Exit Ghost.*
Now I have taken heart thou vanishest :
Ill spirit, I would hold more talk with thee.
Boy, Lucius ! Varro ! Claudius ! Sirs, awake !
Claudius !   291
    Luc. The strings, my lord, are false.
    Bru. He thinks he still is at his instrument.
Lucius, awake !
    Luc. My lord ?
    Bru. Didst thou dream, Lucius, that thou
    so criedst out ?
    Luc. My lord, I do not know that I did
    cry.
    Bru. Yes, that thou didst : didst thou see
    any thing ?
    Luc. Nothing, my lord.
    Bru. Sleep again, Lucius. Sirrah Clau-
    dius !   300
[*To Var.*] Fellow thou, awake !
    Var. My lord ?
    Clau. My lord ?
    Bru. Why did you so cry out, sirs, in your
    sleep ?
    Var. Clau. Did we, my lord ?
    Bru.   Ay : saw you any thing ?
    Var. No, my lord, I saw nothing.
    Clau.   Nor I, my lord.
    Bru. Go and commend me to my brother
    Cassius ;
Bid him set on his powers betimes before,
And we will follow.
    Var. Clau. It shall be done, my lord. 309
                                        [*Exeunt.*

ACT V.

SCENE I. *The plains of Philippi.*

Enter OCTAVIUS, ANTONY, *and their* army.

    Oct. Now, Antony, our hopes are an-
    swered :
You said the enemy would not come down,
But keep the hills and upper regions ;
It proves not so : their battles are at hand ;
They mean to warn us at Philippi here,
Answering before we do demand of them.
    Ant. Tut, I am in their bosoms, and I
    know
Wherefore they do it : they could be content
To visit other places ; and come down

With fearful bravery, thinking by this face 10
To fasten in our thoughts that they have cour-
    age ;
But 'tis not so.

Enter a Messenger.

    Mess.   Prepare you, generals :
The enemy comes on in gallant show ;
Their bloody sign of battle is hung out,
And something to be done immediately.
    Ant. Octavius, lead your battle softly on,
Upon the left hand of the even field.
    Oct. Upon the right hand I ; keep thou the
    left.
    Ant. Why do you cross me in this exigent ?
    Oct. I do not cross you ; but I will do so.
                                     [*March.* 20

Drum. Enter BRUTUS, CASSIUS, *and their*
    Army ; LUCILIUS, TITINIUS, MESSALA, *and
    others.*

    Bru. They stand, and would have parley.
    Cas. Stand fast, Titinius : we must out and
    talk.
    Oct. Mark Antony, shall we give sign of
    battle ?
    Ant. No, Cæsar, we will answer on their
    charge.
Make forth ; the generals would have some
    words.
    Oct. Stir not until the signal.
    Bru. Words before blows : is it so, coun-
    trymen ?
    Oct. Not that we love words better, as you
    do.
    Bru. Good words are better than bad
    strokes, Octavius.
    Ant. In your bad strokes, Brutus, you give
    good words :   30
Witness the hole you made in Cæsar's heart,
Crying ' Long live ! hail, Cæsar ! '
    Cas.   Antony,
The posture of your blows are yet unknown ;
But for your words, they rob the Hybla bees,
And leave them honeyless.
    Ant.   Not stingless too.
    Bru. O, yes, and soundless too ;
For you have stol'n their buzzing, Antony,
And very wisely threat before you sting.
    Ant. Villains, you did not so, when your
    vile daggers
Hack'd one another in the sides of Cæsar : 40
You show'd your teeth like apes, and fawn'd
    like hounds,
And bow'd like bondmen, kissing Cæsar's
    feet ;
Whilst damned Casca, like a cur, behind
Struck Cæsar on the neck. O you flatterers !
    Cas. Flatterers ! Now, Brutus, thank your-
    self :
This tongue had not offended so to-day,
If Cassius might have ruled.
    Oct. Come, come, the cause : if arguing
    make us sweat,
The proof of it will turn to redder drops.
Look !   50
I draw a sword against conspirators ;
When think you that the sword goes up again ?
Never, till Cæsar's three and thirty wounds
Be well avenged ; or till another Cæsar
Have added slaughter to the sword of traitors.

Bru. Cæsar, thou canst not die by traitors'
hands,
Unless thou bring'st them with thee.
Oct.   So I hope ;
I was not born to die on Brutus' sword.
Bru. O, if thou wert the noblest of thy
strain,
Young man, thou couldst not die more honor-
able.   60
Cas. A peevish schoolboy, worthless of
such honor,
Join'd with a masker and a reveller !
Ant. Old Cassius still !
Oct.   Come, Antony, away !
Defiance, traitors, hurl we in your teeth :
If you dare fight to-day, come to the field ;
If not, when you have stomachs.
        [*Exeunt Octavius, Antony, and their army.*
Cas. Why, now, blow wind, swell billow
and swim bark !
The storm is up, and all is on the hazard.
Bru. Ho, Lucilius ! hark, a word with you.
Lucil.   [*Standing forth*] My lord ?
        [*Brutus and Lucilius converse apart.*
Cas. Messala !
Mes. [*Standing forth*] What says my gen-
eral ?   70
Cas. Messala,
This is my birth-day ; as this very day
Was Cassius born. Give me thy hand, Mes-
sala :
Be thou my witness that against my will,
As Pompey was, am I compell'd to set
Upon one battle all our liberties.
You know that I held Epicurus strong
And his opinion : now I change my mind,
And partly credit things that do presage.
Coming from Sardis, on our former ensign 80
Two mighty eagles fell, and there they perch'd,
Gorging and feeding from our soldiers' hands ;
Who to Philippi here consorted us :
This morning are they fled away and gone ;
And in their steads do ravens, crows and kites,
Fly o'er our heads and downward look on us,
As we were sickly prey : their shadows seem
A canopy most fatal, under which
Our army lies, ready to give up the ghost.
Mes. Believe not so.
Cas.   I but believe it partly ; 90
For I am fresh of spirit and resolved
To meet all perils very constantly.
Bru. Even so, Lucilius.
Cas.   Now, most noble Brutus,
The gods to-day stand friendly, that we may,
Lovers in peace, lead on our days to age !
But since the affairs of men rest still incertain,
Let's reason with the worst that may befall.
If we do lose this battle, then is this
The very last time we shall speak together :
What are you then determined to do ?   100
Bru. Even by the rule of that philosophy
By which I did blame Cato for the death
Which he did give himself, I know not how,
But I do find it cowardly and vile,
For fear of what might fall, so to prevent
The time of life : arming myself with patience
To stay the providence of some high powers
That govern us below.
Cas.   Then, if we lose this battle,
You are contented to be led in triumph
Thorough the streets of Rome ?   110

Bru. No, Cassius, no : think not, thou no-
ble Roman,
That ever Brutus will go bound to Rome ;
He bears too great a mind. But this same day
Must end that work the ides of March begun ;
And whether we shall meet again I know not.
Therefore our everlasting farewell take :
For ever, and for ever, farewell, Cassius !
If we do meet again, why, we shall smile ;
If not, why then, this parting was well made.
Cas. For ever, and for ever, farewell, Bru-
tus !
If we do meet again, we'll smile indeed ;   121
If not, 'tis true this parting was well made.
Bru. Why, then, lead on. O, that a man
might know
The end of this day's business ere it come !
But it sufficeth that the day will end,
And then the end is known. Come, ho ! away !
                                                [*Exeunt.*

SCENE II. *The same. The field of battle.*

Alarum. Enter Brutus *and* Messala.

Bru. Ride, ride, Messala, ride, and give
these bills
Unto the legions on the other side.
                                        [*Loud alarum.*
Let them set on at once ; for I perceive
But cold demeanor in Octavius' wing,
And sudden push gives them the overthrow.
Ride, ride, Messala : let them all come down.
                                                [*Exeunt.*

SCENE III. *Another part of the field.*

Alarums. Enter Cassius *and* Titinius.

Cas. O, look, Titinius, look, the villains
fly !
Myself have to mine own turn'd enemy :
This ensign here of mine was turning back ;
I slew the coward, and did take it from him.
Tit. O Cassius, Brutus gave the word too
early ;
Who, having some advantage on Octavius,
Took it too eagerly : his soldiers fell to spoil,
Whilst we by Antony are all enclosed.

Enter Pindarus.

Pin. Fly further off, my lord, fly further
off ;
Mark Antony is in your tents, my lord :   10
Fly, therefore, noble Cassius, fly far off.
Cas. This hill is far enough. Look, look,
Titinius ;
Are those my tents where I perceive the fire ?
Tit. They are, my lord.
Cas.   Titinius, if thou lovest me,
Mount thou my horse, and hide thy spurs in
him,
Till he have brought thee up to yonder troops,
And here again ; that I may rest assured
Whether yond troops are friend or enemy.
Tit. I will be here again, even with a
thought.   [*Exit.* 19
Cas. Go, Pindarus, get higher on that hill ;
My sight was ever thick ; regard Titinius,
And tell me what thou notest about the field.
                        [*Pindarus ascends the hill.*
This day I breathed first : time is come round,
And where I did begin, there shall I end ;
My life is run his compass. Sirrah, what
news ?

Pin. [*Above*] O my lord !
Cas. What news ?
Pin. [*Above*] Titinius is enclosed round
     about
With horsemen, that make to him on the spur ;
Yet he spurs on. Now they are almost on
     him.   30
Now, Titinius ! Now some light. O, he lights
     too.
He's ta'en. [*Shout*.] And, hark ! they shout for
     joy.
Cas. Come down, behold no more.
O, coward that I am, to live so long,
To see my best friend ta'en before my face !

         PINDARUS *descends*.

Come hither, sirrah :
In Parthia did I take thee prisoner ;
And then I swore thee, saving of thy life,
That whatsoever I did bid thee do,
Thou shouldst attempt it. Come now, keep
     thine oath ;   40
Now be a freeman : and with this good sword,
That ran through Cæsar's bowels, search this
     bosom.
Stand not to answer : here, take thou the
     hilts ;
And, when my face is cover'd, as 'tis now,
Guide thou the sword. [*Pindarus stabs him.*]
     Cæsar, thou art revenged,
Even with the sword that kill'd thee. [*Dies.*
Pin. So, I am free; yet would not so have
     been,
Durst I have done my will. O Cassius,
Far from this country Pindarus shall run,
Where never Roman shall take note of him. 50
                                          [*Exit.*

     Re-enter TITINIUS *with* MESSALA.

Mes. It is but change, Titinius ; for Octa-
     vius
Is overthrown by noble Brutus' power,
As Cassius' legions are by Antony.
Tit. These tidings will well comfort Cas-
     sius.
Mes. Where did you leave him ?
Tit.   All disconsolate,
With Pindarus his bondman, on this hill.
Mes. Is not that he that lies upon the
     ground ?
Tit. He lies not like the living. O my
     heart !
Mes. Is not that he ?
Tit.   No, this was he, Messala,
But Cassius is no more. O setting sun,   60
As in thy red rays thou dost sink to-night,
So in his red blood Cassius' day is set ;
The sun of Rome is set ! Our day is gone ;
Clouds, dews, and dangers come ; our deeds
     are done !
Mistrust of my success hath done this deed.
Mes. Mistrust of good success hath done
     this deed.
O hateful error, melancholy's child,
Why dost thou show to the apt thoughts of
     men
The things that are not? O error, soon con-
     ceived,
Thou never comest unto a happy birth,   70
But kill'st the mother that engender'd thee !
Tit. What, Pindarus ! where art thou, Pin-
     darus ?

Mes. Seek him, Titinius, whilst I go to
     meet
The noble Brutus, thrusting this report
Into his ears ; I may say, thrusting it ;
For piercing steel and darts envenomed
Shall be as welcome to the ears of Brutus
As tidings of this sight.
Tit.   Hie you, Messala,
And I will seek for Pindarus the while.
                              [*Exit Messala.*
Why didst thou send me forth, brave Cassius ?
Did I not meet thy friends ? and did not they
Put on my brows this wreath of victory,
And bid me give it thee ? Didst thou not hear
     their shouts ?
Alas, thou hast misconstrued every thing !
But, hold thee, take this garland on thy brow ;
Thy Brutus bid me give it thee, and I
Will do his bidding. Brutus, come apace,
And see how I regarded Caius Cassius.
By your leave, gods :—this is a Roman's part :
Come, Cassius' sword, and find Titinius' heart.
                              [*Kills himself.* 90

Alarum. Re-enter MESSALA, *with* BRUTUS,
young CATO, STRATO, VOLUMNIUS, *and* LU-
CILIUS.

Bru. Where, where, Messala, doth his body
     lie ?
Mes. Lo, yonder, and Titinius mourning it.
Bru. Titinius' face is upward.
Cato.   He is slain.
Bru. O Julius Cæsar, thou art mighty yet !
Thy spirit walks abroad, and turns our swords
In our own proper entrails.   [*Low alarums.*
Cato.   Brave Titinius !
Look, whether he have not crown'd dead Cas-
     sius !
Bru. Are yet two Romans living such as
     these ?
The last of all the Romans, fare thee well !
It is impossible that ever Rome   100
Should breed thy fellow. Friends, I owe more
     tears
To this dead man than you shall see me pay.
I shall find time, Cassius, I shall find time.
Come, therefore, and to Thasos send his body :
His funerals shall not be in our camp,
Lest it discomfort us. Lucilius, come ;
And come, young Cato ; let us to the field.
Labeo and Flavius, set our battles on :
'Tis three o'clock ; and, Romans, yet ere
     night
We shall try fortune in a second fight.
                              [*Exeunt.*

     SCENE IV. *Another part of the field.*

Alarum. Enter fighting, Soldiers *of both armies ; then* BRUTUS, *young* CATO, LUCILIUS,
and others.

Bru. Yet, countrymen, O, yet hold up your
     heads !
Cato. What bastard doth not ? Who will
     go with me ?
I will proclaim my name about the field :
I am the son of Marcus Cato, ho !
A foe to tyrants, and my country's friend ;
I am the son of Marcus Cato, ho !
Bru. And I am Brutus, Marcus Brutus, I ;
Brutus, my country's friend ; know me for
     Brutus !   [*Exit.*

Lucil. O young and noble Cato, art thou
   down ?
Why, now thou diest as bravely as Titinius ;
And mayst be honor'd, being Cato's son.   11
   First Sold. Yield, or thou diest.
   Lucil.   Only I yield to die :
There is so much that thou wilt kill me
   straight ;   [*Offering money.*
Kill Brutus, and be honor'd in his death.
   First Sold. We must not. A noble prisoner !
   Sec. Sold. Room, ho ! Tell Antony, Brutus
   is ta'en.
   First Sold. I'll tell the news. Here comes
   the general.

Enter ANTONY.

Brutus is ta'en, Brutus is ta'en, my lord.
   Ant. Where is he ?
   Lucil. Safe, Antony ; Brutus is safe
   enough :
I dare assure thee that no enemy   21
Shall ever take alive the noble Brutus :
The gods defend him from so great a shame !
When you do find him, or alive or dead,
He will be found like Brutus, like himself.
   Ant. This is not Brutus, friend ; but, I as-
   sure you,
A prize no less in worth : keep this man safe ;
Give him all kindness : I had rather have
Such men my friends than enemies. Go on,
And see whether Brutus be alive or dead ;   30
And bring us word unto Octavius' tent
How every thing is chanced.   [*Exeunt.*

SCENE V. *Another part of the field.*

Enter BRUTUS, DARDANIUS, CLITUS, STRATO,
   and VOLUMNIUS.

   Bru. Come, poor remains of friends, rest
   on this rock.
   Cli. Statilius show'd the torch-light, but,
   my lord,
He came not back : he is or ta'en or slain.
   Bru. Sit thee down, Clitus : slaying is the
   word ;
It is a deed in fashion. Hark thee, Clitus.
                    [*Whispers.*
   Cli. What, I, my lord ? No, not for all the
   world.
   Bru. Peace then ! no words.
   Cli.   I'll rather kill myself.
   Bru. Hark thee, Dardanius.   [*Whispers.*
   Dar.   Shall I do such a deed ?
   Cli. O Dardanius !
   Dar. O Clitus !   10
   Cli. What ill request did Brutus make to
   thee ?
   Dar. To kill him, Clitus. Look, he medi-
   tates.
   Cli. Now is that noble vessel full of grief,
That it runs over even at his eyes.
   Bru. Come hither, good Volumnius ; list a
   word.
   Vol. What says my lord ?
   Bru. Why, this, Volumnius :
The ghost of Cæsar hath appear'd to me
Two several times by night ; at Sardis once,
And, this last night, here in Philippi fields :
I know my hour is come.
   Vol.   Not so, my lord.   20
   Bru. Nay, I am sure it is, Volumnius.
Thou seest the world, Volumnius, how it goes ;

Our enemies have beat us to the pit :
                    [*Low alarums.*
It is more worthy to leap in ourselves,
Than tarry till they push us. Good Volumnius,
Thou know'st that we two went to school to-
   gether :
Even for that our love of old, I prithee,
Hold thou my sword-hilts, whilst I run on it.
   Vol. That's not an office for a friend, my
   lord.   [*Alarum still.*
   Cli. Fly, fly, my lord ; there is no tarrying
   here.   30
   Bru. Farewell to you ; and you ; and you,
   Volumnius.
Strato, thou hast been all this while asleep ;
Farewell to thee too, Strato. Countrymen,
My heart doth joy that yet in all my life
I found no man but he was true to me.
I shall have glory by this losing day
More than Octavius and Mark Antony
By this vile conquest shall attain unto.
So fare you well at once ; for Brutus' tongue
Hath almost ended his life's history :   40
Night hangs upon mine eyes ; my bones would
   rest,
That have but labor'd to attain this hour.
   [*Alarum. Cry within,* ' Fly, fly, fly ! '
   Cli. Fly, my lord, fly.
   Bru.   Hence ! I will follow.
   [*Exeunt Clitus, Dardanius, and Volumnius.*
I prithee, Strato, stay thou by thy lord :
Thou art a fellow of a good respect ;
Thy life hath had some smatch of honor in it :
Hold then my sword, and turn away thy face,
While I do run upon it. Wilt thou, Strato ?
   Stra. Give me your hand first. Fare you
   well, my lord.
   Bru. Farewell, good Strato. [*Runs on his
   sword.*] Cæsar, now be still :   50
I kill'd not thee with half so good a will.
                    [*Dies.*

Alarum. Retreat. Enter OCTAVIUS, ANTONY,
   MESSALA, LUCILIUS, *and the army.*

   Oct. What man is that ?
   Mes. My master's man. Strato, where is
   thy master ?
   Stra. Free from the bondage you are in,
   Messala :
The conquerors can but make a fire of him ;
For Brutus only overcame himself,
And no man else hath honor by his death.
   Lucil. So Brutus should be found. I thank
   thee, Brutus,
That thou hast proved Lucilius' saying true.
   Oct. All that served Brutus, I will entertain
   them.   60
Fellow, wilt thou bestow thy time with me ?
   Stra. Ay, if Messala will prefer me to you.
   Oct. Do so, good Messala.
   Mes. How died my master, Strato ?
   Stra. I held the sword, and he did run on
   it.
   Mes. Octavius, then take him to follow
   thee,
That did the latest service to my master.
   Ant. This was the noblest Roman of them
   all :
All the conspirators save only he
Did that they did in envy of great Cæsar ;   70
He only, in a general honest thought
And common good to all, made one of them.

His life was gentle, and the elements
So mix'd in him that Nature might stand up
And say to all the world ' This was a man ! '
   Oct. According to his virtue let us use him,
With all respect and rites of burial.

Within my tent his bones to-night shall lie,
Most like a soldier, order'd honorably.
So call the field to rest ; and let's away,   80
To part the glories of this happy day.
                               [Exeunt.

HAMLET.

(WRITTEN ABOUT 1602.)

INTRODUCTION.

Hamlet represents the mid period of the growth of Shakespeare's genius, when comedy and history ceased to be adequate for the expression of his deeper thoughts and sadder feelings about life, and when he was just entering upon his great series of tragic writings. In July, 1602, the printer Roberts entered in the Stationers' register, "The Revenge of Hamlett, Prince of Denmark, as y latelie was acted by the Lord Chamberlain his servantes," and in the next year the play was printed. The true relation of this first quarto of *Hamlet* to the second quarto, published in 1604—" newly imprinted, and enlarged to almost as much againe as it was "—is a matter in dispute. It is believed by some critics that the quarto of 1603 is merely an imperfect report of the play as we find it in the edition of the year after ; but there are some material differences which cannot thus be explained. In the earlier quarto, instead of Polonius and Reynaldo, we find the names Corambis and Montano ; the order of certain scenes varies from that of the later quarto ; "the madness of Hamlet is much more pronounced, and the Queen's innocence of her husband's murder much more explicitly stated." We are forced to believe either that the earlier quarto contains portions of an old play by some other writer than Shakespeare—an opinion adopted on apparently insufficient grounds by some recent editor—or that it represents imperfectly Shakespeare's first draught of the play, and that the difference between it and the second quarto is due to Shakespeare's revision of his own work. This last opinion seems to be the true one, but the value of any comparison between the two quartos, with a view to understand Shakespeare's manner of rehandling his work, is greatly diminished by the fact that numerous gaps of the imperfect report given in the earlier quarto seem to have been filled in by a stupid stage hack. That an old play on the subject of Hamlet existed there can be no doubt ; it is referred to in 1589 (perhaps in 1587) by Nash, in his *Epistle* prefixed to Greene's *Menaphon*, and again in 1596 by Lodge (*Wit's Miserie and the World's Madnesse*), where he alludes to "the vizard of the Ghost which cried so miserably at the Theator, like an oister wife, 'Hamlet, revenge'." A German play on the subject of Hamlet exists which is supposed to have been acted by English players in Germany in 1603 ; the name Corambus appears in it ; and it is possible that portions of the old pre-Shakespearean drama are contained in the German *Hamlet*. The old play may have been one of the bloody tragedies of revenge among which we find *Titus Andronicus* and *The Spanish Tragedy*, and it would be characteristic of Shakespeare that he should refine the motives and spirit of the drama, so as to make the duty of vengeance laid upon Hamlet a painful burden which he is hardly able to support. Besides the old play of Hamlet, Shakespeare had probably before him the prose *Hystorie of Hamblet* (though no edition exists earlier than 1608), translated from Belleforest's *Histoires Tragiques*. The story had been told some hundreds of years previously in the *Historia Danica* of Saxo Grammaticus (about 1180–1208). The Hamlet of the *Hystorie*, after a fierce revenge, becomes King of Denmark, marries two wives, and finally dies in battle.

No play of Shakespeare's has had a higher power of interesting spectators and readers, and none has given rise to a greater variety of conflicting interpretations. It has been rightly named a tragedy of thought, and in this respect, as well as others, takes its place beside *Julius Cæsar*. Neither Brutus nor Hamlet is the victim of an overmastering passion as are the chief persons of the later tragedies—*e.g.* Othello, Macbeth, Coriolanus. The burden of a terrible duty is laid upon each of them, and neither is fitted for bearing such a burden. Brutus is disqualified for action by his moral idealism, his student-like habits, his capacity for dealing with abstractions rather than with men and things. Hamlet is disqualified for action by his excess of the reflective tendency, and by his unstable will, which alternates between complete inactivity and fits of excited energy. Naturally sensitive, he receives a painful shock from the hasty second marriage of his mother ; already the springs of faith and joy in his nature are embittered ; then follows the terrible discovery of his father's murder, with the injunction laid upon him to revenge the crime ; upon this again follow the repulses which he receives from Ophelia. A deep melancholy lays hold of his spirit, and all of life grows dark and sad to his vision. Although hating his father's murderer, he has little heart to push on his revenge. He is aware that he is suspected and surrounded by spies. Partly to baffle them, partly to create a veil behind which to seclude his true self, partly because his whole moral nature is indeed deeply disordered, he assumes the part of one whose wits have gone astray. Except for one loyal friend, he is alone among enemies or supposed traitors. Ophelia he regards as no more loyal or honest to him than his mother had been to her dead husband. The ascertainment of Claudius's guilt by means of the play still leaves him incapable of the last decisive act of vengeance. Not so, however, with the king, who now recognizing his foe in Hamlet, does not delay to despatch him to a bloody death in England. But there is in Hamlet a terrible power of sudden and desperate action. From the melancholy which broods over him after the burial of Ophelia he rouses himself to the play of swords with Laertes, and at the last, with strength which leaps up before its final extinction, he accomplishes the punishment of the malefactor. Horatio, with his fortitude, his self-possession, his strong equanimity is a contrast to the Prince. And Laertes, who takes violent measures at the shortest notice to revenge *his* father's murder, is in another way a contrast ; but Laertes is the young gallant of the period, and his capacity for action arises in part from the absence of those moral checks of which Hamlet is sensible. Polonius is owner of the shallow wisdom of this world, and exhibits this grotesquely while now on the brink of dotage ; he sees, but cannot see through Hamlet's ironical mockery of him. Ophelia is tender, sensitive, affectionate, but the reverse of heroic ; she fails Hamlet in his need, and then in her turn becoming the sufferer, gives way under the pressure of her afflictions. We do not honor, we only commiserate her.

DRAMATIS PERSONÆ.

CLAUDIUS, king of Denmark.
HAMLET, son to the late, and nephew to the present king.
POLONIUS, lord chamberlain.
HORATIO, friend to Hamlet.
LAERTES, son to Polonius.
VOLTIMAND,
CORNELIUS,
ROSENCRANTZ,
GUILDENSTERN, } courtiers.
OSRIC,
A Gentleman,
A Priest.
MARCELLUS, } officers.
BERNARDO,

FRANCISCO, a soldier.
REYNALDO, servant to Polonius.
Players.
Two Clowns, grave-diggers.
FORTINBRAS, prince of Norway.
A Captain.
English Ambassadors.

GERTRUDE, queen of Denmark, and mother to Hamlet.
OPHELIA, daughter to Polonius.
Lords, Ladies, Officers, Soldiers, Sailors, Messengers, and other Attendants.
Ghost of Hamlet's Father.
SCENE : *Denmark.*

ACT I.

SCENE I. *Elsinore. A platform before the castle.*

FRANCISCO *at his post. Enter to him* BERNARDO.

Ber. Who's there ?
Fran. Nay, answer me : stand, and unfold yourself.
Ber. Long live the king !
Fran. Bernardo ?
Ber. He.
Fran. You come most carefully upon your hour.
Ber. 'Tis now struck twelve ; get thee to bed, Francisco.
Fran. For this relief much thanks : 'tis bitter cold,
And I am sick at heart.
Ber. Have you had quiet guard ?
Fran. Not a mouse stirring. 10
Ber. Well, good night.
If you do meet Horatio and Marcellus,
The rivals of my watch, bid them make haste.
Fran. I think I hear them. Stand, ho ! Who's there ?

Enter HORATIO *and* MARCELLUS.

Hor. Friends to this ground.
Mar. And liegemen to the Dane.
Fran. Give you good night.
Mar. O, farewell, honest soldier :

Who hath relieved you ?
Fran. Bernardo has my place.
Give you good night. [*Exit.*
Mar. Holla ! Bernardo !
Ber. Say,
What, is Horatio there ?
Hor. A piece of him.
Ber. Welcome, Horatio : welcome, good Marcellus. 20
Mar. What, has this thing appear'd again to-night ?
Ber. I have seen nothing.
Mar. Horatio says 'tis but our fantasy,
And will not let belief take hold of him
Touching this dreaded sight, twice seen of us :
Therefore I have entreated him along
With us to watch the minutes of this night ;
That if again this apparition come,
He may approve our eyes and speak to it.
Hor. Tush, tush, 'twill not appear.
Ber. Sit down awhile ; 30
And let us once again assail your ears,
That are so fortified against our story
What we have two nights seen.
Hor. Well, sit we down,
And let us hear Bernardo speak of this.
Ber. Last night of all,
When yond same star that's westward from the pole
Had made his course to illume that part of heaven
Where now it burns, Marcellus and myself,
The bell then beating one,—

Enter Ghost.

Mar. Peace, break thee off; look, where it
comes again! 40
Ber. In the same figure, like the king that's
dead.
Mar. Thou art a scholar; speak to it, Horatio.
Ber. Looks it not like the king? mark it,
Horatio.
Hor. Most like: it harrows me with fear
and wonder.
Ber. It would be spoke to.
Mar. Question it, Horatio.
Hor. What art thou that usurp'st this time
of night,
Together with that fair and warlike form
In which the majesty of buried Denmark
Did sometimes march? by heaven I charge
thee, speak!
Mar. It is offended.
Ber. See, it stalks away! 50
Hor. Stay! speak, speak! I charge thee,
speak! [*Exit Ghost.*
Mar. 'Tis gone, and will not answer.
Ber. How now, Horatio! you tremble and
look pale!
Is not this something more than fantasy?
What think you on't?
Hor. Before my God, I might not this believe
Without the sensible and true avouch
Of mine own eyes.
Mar. Is it not like the king?
Hor. As thou art to thyself:
Such was the very armor he had on 60
When he the ambitious Norway combated;
So frown'd he once, when, in an angry parle,
He smote the sledded Polacks on the ice.
'Tis strange.
Mar. Thus twice before, and jump at this
dead hour,
With martial stalk hath he gone by our watch.
Hor. In what particular thought to work I
know not;
But in the gross and scope of my opinion,
This bodes some strange eruption to our state.
Mar. Good now, sit down, and tell me, he
that knows, 70
Why this same strict and most observant watch
So nightly toils the subject of the land,
And why such daily cast of brazen cannon,
And foreign mart for implements of war;
Why such impress of shipwrights, whose sore
task
Does not divide the Sunday from the week;
What might be toward, that this sweaty haste
Doth make the night joint-laborer with the
day:
Who is't that can inform me?
Hor. That can I;
At least, the whisper goes so. Our last king,
Whose image even but now appear'd to us, 81
Was, as you know, by Fortinbras of Norway,
Thereto prick'd on by a most emulate pride,
Dared to the combat; in which our valiant
Hamlet—
For so this side of our known world esteem'd
him—
Did slay this Fortinbras; who by a seal'd compact,
Well ratified by law and heraldry,

Did forfeit, with his life, all those his lands
Which he stood seized of, to the conqueror:
Against the which, a moiety competent 90
Was gaged by our king; which had return'd
To the inheritance of Fortinbras,
Had he been vanquisher; as, by the same
covenant,
And carriage of the article design'd,
His fell to Hamlet. Now, sir, young Fortinbras,
Of unimproved mettle hot and full,
Hath in the skirts of Norway here and there
Shark'd up a list of lawless resolutes,
For food and diet, to some enterprise
That hath a stomach in't; which is no other—
As it doth well appear unto our state— 101
But to recover of us, by strong hand
And terms compulsatory, those foresaid lands
So by his father lost: and this, I take it,
Is the main motive of our preparations,
The source of this our watch and the chief
head
Of this post-haste and romage in the land.
Ber. I think it be no other but e'en so:
Well may it sort that this portentous figure
Comes armed through our watch; so like the
king 110
That was and is the question of these wars.
Hor. A mote it is to trouble the mind's eye.
In the most high and palmy state of Rome,
A little ere the mightiest Julius fell,
The graves stood tenantless and the sheeted
dead
Did squeak and gibber in the Roman streets:
As stars with trains of fire and dews of blood,
Disasters in the sun; and the moist star
Upon whose influence Neptune's empire stands
Was sick almost to doomsday with eclipse:
And even the like precurse of fierce events, 121
As harbingers preceding still the fates
And prologue to the omen coming on,
Have heaven and earth together demonstrated
Unto our climatures and countrymen.—
But soft, behold! lo, where it comes again!

Re-enter Ghost.

I'll cross it, though it blast me. Stay, illusion!
If thou hast any sound, or use of voice,
Speak to me:
If there be any good thing to be done, 130
That may to thee do ease and grace to me,
Speak to me: [*Cock crows.*
If thou art privy to thy country's fate,
Which, happily, foreknowing may avoid,
O, speak!
Or if thou hast uphoarded in thy life
Extorted treasure in the womb of earth,
For which, they say, you spirits oft walk in
death,
Speak of it: stay, and speak! Stop it, Marcellus.
Mar. Shall I strike at it with my partisan?
Hor. Do, if it will not stand. 141
Ber. 'Tis here!
Hor. 'Tis here!
Mar. 'Tis gone! [*Exit Ghost.*
We do it wrong, being so majestical,
To offer it the show of violence;
For it is, as the air, invulnerable,
And our vain blows malicious mockery.
Ber. It was about to speak, when the cock
crew.
Hor. And then it started like a guilty thing

Upon a fearful summons. I have heard,
The cock, that is the trumpet to the morn, 150
Doth with his lofty and shrill-sounding throat
Awake the god of day ; and, at his warning,
Whether in sea or fire, in earth or air,
The extravagant and erring spirit hies
To his confine : and of the truth herein
This present object made probation.
   Mar. It faded on the crowing of the cock.
Some say that ever 'gainst that season comes
Wherein our Saviour's birth is celebrated, 159
The bird of dawning singeth all night long :
And then, they say, no spirit dares stir abroad ;
The nights are wholesome ; then no planets
   strike,
No fairy takes, nor witch hath power to charm,
So hallow'd and so gracious is the time.
   Hor. So have I heard and do in part be-
   lieve it.
But, look, the morn, in russet mantle clad,
Walks o'er the dew of yon high eastward hill :
Break we our watch up ; and by my advice,
Let us impart what we have seen to-night
Unto young Hamlet ; for, upon my life, 170
This spirit, dumb to us, will speak to him.
Do you consent we shall acquaint him with it,
As needful in our loves, fitting our duty ?
   Mar. Let's do't, I pray ; and I this morn-
   ing know
Where we shall find him most conveniently.
                       [*Exeunt.*

SCENE II. *A room of state in the castle.*

Enter the KING, QUEEN, HAMLET, POLONIUS,
LAERTES, VOLTIMAND, CORNELIUS, Lords,
and Attendants.

   King. Though yet of Hamlet our dear
   brother's death
The memory be green, and that it us befitted
To bear our hearts in grief and our whole
   kingdom
To be contracted in one brow of woe,
Yet so far hath discretion fought with nature
That we with wisest sorrow think on him,
Together with remembrance of ourselves.
Therefore our sometime sister, now our queen,
The imperial jointress to this warlike state,
Have we, as 'twere with a defeated joy,— 10
With an auspicious and a dropping eye,
With mirth in funeral and with dirge in mar-
   riage,
In equal scale weighing delight and dole,—
Taken to wife : nor have we herein barr'd
Your better wisdoms, which have freely gone
With this affair along. For all, our thanks.
Now follows, that you know, young Fortin-
   bras,
Holding a weak supposal of our worth,
Or thinking by our late dear brother's death
Our state to be disjoint and out of frame, 20
Colleagued with the dream of his advantage,
He hath not fail'd to pester us with message,
Importing the surrender of those lands
Lost by his father, with all bonds of law,
To our most valiant brother. So much for him.
Now for ourself and for this time of meeting :
Thus much the business is : we have here writ
To Norway, uncle of young Fortinbras,—
Who, impotent and bed-rid, scarcely hears
Of this his nephew's purpose,—to suppress 30
His further gait herein ; in that the levies,
The lists and full proportions, are all made

Out of his subject : and we here dispatch
You, good Cornelius, and you, Voltimand,
For bearers of this greeting to old Norway ;
Giving to you no further personal power
To business with the king, more than the scope
Of these delated articles allow.
Farewell, and let your haste commend your
   duty.
   Cor. } In that and all things will we show
   Vol. }   our duty.   40
   King. We doubt it nothing : heartily fare-
   well.
         [*Exeunt Voltimand and Cornelius.*
And now, Laertes, what's the news with you ?
You told us of some suit ; what is't, Laertes ?
You cannot speak of reason to the Dane,
And loose your voice : what wouldst thou beg,
   Laertes,
That shall not be my offer, not thy asking ?
The head is not more native to the heart,
The hand more instrumental to the mouth,
Than is the throne of Denmark to thy father.
What wouldst thou have, Laertes ?
   Laer.   My dread lord, 50
Your leave and favor to return to France ;
From whence though willingly I came to Den-
   mark,
To show my duty in your coronation,
Yet now, I must confess, that duty done,
My thoughts and wishes bend again toward
   France
And bow them to your gracious leave and
   pardon.
   King. Have you your father's leave ? What
   says Polonius ?
   Pol. He hath, my lord, wrung from me my
   slow leave
By laborsome petition, and at last
Upon his will I seal'd my hard consent :   60
I do beseech you, give him leave to go.
   King. Take thy fair hour, Laertes ; time be
   thine,
And thy best graces spend it at thy will !
But now, my cousin Hamlet, and my son,—
   Ham. [*Aside*] A little more than kin, and
   less than kind.
   King. How is it that the clouds still hang
   on you ?
   Ham. Not so, my lord ; I am too much i'
   the sun.
   Queen. Good Hamlet, cast thy nighted
   color off,
And let thine eye look like a friend on Den-
   mark.
Do not for ever with thy vailed lids   70
Seek for thy noble father in the dust :
Thou know'st 'tis common ; all that lives must
   die,
Passing through nature to eternity.
   Ham. Ay, madam, it is common.
   Queen.   If it be,
Why seems it so particular with thee ?
   Ham. Seems, madam ! nay it is ; I know
   not ' seems.'
'Tis not alone my inky cloak, good mother,
Nor customary suits of solemn black,
Nor windy suspiration of forced breath,
No, nor the fruitful river in the eye,   80
Nor the dejected 'havior of the visage,
Together with all forms, moods, shapes of
   grief,
That can denote me truly : these indeed seem,

For they are actions that a man might play :
But I have that within which passeth show ;
These but the trappings and the suits of woe.
  King. 'Tis sweet and commendable in your
    nature, Hamlet,
To give these mourning duties to your father :
But, you must know, your father lost a father ;
That father lost, lost his, and the survivor
    bound   90
In filial obligation for some term
To do obsequious sorrow : but to persever
In obstinate condolement is a course
Of impious stubbornness ; 'tis unmanly grief ;
It shows a will most incorrect to heaven,
A heart unfortified, a mind impatient,
An understanding simple and unschool'd :
For what we know must be and is as common
As any the most vulgar thing to sense,
Why should we in our peevish opposition 100
Take it to heart ? Fie ! 'tis a fault to heaven,
A fault against the dead, a fault to nature,
To reason most absurd : whose common theme
Is death of fathers, and who still hath cried,
From the first corse till he that died to-day,
' This must be so.' We pray you, throw to
    earth
This unprevailing woe, and think of us
As of a father : for let the world take note,
You are the most immediate to our throne ;
And with no less nobility of love   110
Than that which dearest father bears his son,
Do I impart toward you. For your intent
In going back to school in Wittenberg,
It is most retrograde to our desire :
And we beseech you, bend you to remain
Here, in the cheer and comfort of our eye,
Our chiefest courtier, cousin, and our son.
  Queen. Let not thy mother lose her
    prayers, Hamlet :
I pray thee, stay with us ; go not to Witten-
    berg.
  Ham. I shall in all my best obey you,
    madam.
  King. Why, 'tis a loving and a fair reply :
Be as ourself in Denmark. Madam, come ;
This gentle and unforced accord of Hamlet
Sits smiling to my heart : in grace whereof,
No jocund health that Denmark drinks to-day,
But the great cannon to the clouds shall tell,
And the king's rouse the heavens shall bruit
    again,
Re-speaking earthly thunder. Come away.
                    [*Exeunt all but Hamlet.*
  Ham. O, that this too too solid flesh would
    melt
Thaw and resolve itself into a dew !   130
Or that the Everlasting had not fix'd
His canon 'gainst self-slaughter ! O God !
    God !
How weary, stale, flat and unprofitable,
Seem to me all the uses of this world !
Fie on't ! ah fie ! 'tis an unweeded garden,
That grows to seed ; things rank and gross in
    nature
Possess it merely. That it should come to this !
But two months dead : nay, not so much, not
    two :
So excellent a king ; that was, to this,   139
Hyperion to a satyr ; so loving to my mother
That he might not beteem the winds of heaven
Visit her face too roughly. Heaven and earth !

Must I remember ? why, she would hang on
    him,
As if increase of appetite had grown
By what it fed on : and yet, within a month—
Let me not think on't—Frailty, thy name is
    woman !—
A little month, or ere those shoes were old
With which she follow'd my poor father's
    body,
Like Niobe, all tears :—why she, even she—
O God ! a beast, that wants discourse of rea-
    son,   150
Would have mourn'd longer—married with my
    uncle,
My father's brother, but no more like my fa-
    ther
Than I to Hercules : within a month :
Ere yet the salt of most unrighteous tears
Had left the flushing in her galled eyes,
She married. O, most wicked speed, to post
With such dexterity to incestuous sheets !
It is not nor it cannot come to good :
But break, my heart ; for I must hold my
    tongue.

Enter HORATIO, MARCELLUS, *and* BERNARDO.

  Hor. Hail to your lordship !
  Ham.   I am glad to see you well : 160
Horatio,—or I do forget myself.
  Hor. The same, my lord, and your poor
    servant ever.
  Ham. Sir, my good friend ; I'll change that
    name with you :
And what make you from Wittenberg, Hora-
    tio ?
Marcellus ?
  Mar. My good lord—
  Ham. I am very glad to see you. Good
    even, sir.
But what, in faith, make you from Witten-
    berg ?
  Hor. A truant disposition, good my lord.
  Ham. I would not hear your enemy say so,
Nor shall you do mine ear that violence,   171
To make it truster of your own report
Against yourself : I know you are no truant.
But what is your affair in Elsinore ?
We'll teach you to drink deep ere you depart.
  Hor. My lord, I came to see your father's
    funeral.
  Ham. I pray thee, do not mock me, fellow-
    student ;
I think it was to see my mother's wedding.
  Hor. Indeed, my lord, it follow'd hard
    upon.
  Ham. Thrift, thrift, Horatio ! the funeral
    baked meats   180
Did coldly furnish forth the marriage tables.
Would I had met my dearest foe in heaven
Or ever I had seen that day, Horatio !
My father !—methinks I see my father.
  Hor. Where, my lord ?
  Ham.   In my mind's eye, Horatio.
  Hor. I saw him once ; he was a goodly
    king.
  Ham. He was a man, take him for all in
    all,
I shall not look upon his like again.
  Hor. My lord, I think I saw him yester-
    night.
  Ham. Saw ? who ?   190
  Hor. My lord, the king your father.

Ham. The king my father !
Hor. Season your admiration for awhile
With an attent ear, till I may deliver,
Upon the witness of these gentlemen,
This marvel to you.
Ham. For God's love, let me hear.
Hor. Two nights together had these gentle-
men,
Marcellus and Bernardo, on their watch,
In the dead vast and middle of the night,
Been thus encounter'd. A figure like your fa-
ther,
Armed at point exactly, cap-a-pe, 200
Appears before them, and with solemn march
Goes slow and stately by them : thrice he
walk'd
By their oppress'd and fear-surprised eyes,
Within his truncheon's length ; whilst they, dis-
tilled
Almost to jelly with the act of fear,
Stand dumb and speak not to him. This to me
In dreadful secrecy impart they did ;
And I with them the third night kept the
watch ;
Where, as they had deliver'd, both in time,
Form of the thing, each word made true and
good, 210
The apparition comes : I knew your father ;
These hands are not more like.
Ham. But where was this ?
Mar. My lord, upon the platform where
we watch'd.
Ham. Did you not speak to it ?
Hor. My lord, I did ;
But answer made it none : yet once methought
It lifted up its head and did address
Itself to motion, like as it would speak ;
But even then the morning cock crew loud,
And at the sound it shrunk in haste away,
And vanish'd from our sight.
Ham. 'Tis very strange. 220
Hor. As I do live, my honor'd lord, 'tis
true ;
And we did think it writ down in our duty
To let you know of it.
Ham. Indeed, indeed, sirs, but this trou-
bles me.
Hold you the watch to-night ?
Mar. }
Ber. } We do, my lord.
Ham. Arm'd, say you ?
Mar. }
Ber. } Arm'd, my lord.
Ham. From top to toe ?
Mar. }
Ber. } My lord, from head to foot.
Ham. Then saw you not his face ?
Hor. O, yes, my lord ; he wore his beaver
up. 230
Ham. What, look'd he frowningly ?
Hor. A countenance more in sorrow than
in anger.
Ham. Pale or red ?
Hor. Nay, very pale.
Ham. And fix'd his eyes upon you ?
Hor. Most constantly.
Ham. I would I had been there.
Hor. It would have much amazed you.
Ham. Very like, very like. Stay'd it long ?
Hor. While one with moderate haste might
tell a hundred.

Mar. }
Ber. } Longer, longer.
Hor. Not when I saw't.
Ham. His beard was grizzled,—no ? 240
Hor. It was, as I have seen it in his life,
A sable silver'd.
Ham. I will watch to-night ;
Perchance 'twill walk again.
Hor. I warrant it will.
Ham. If it assume my noble father's per-
son,
I'll speak to it, though hell itself should gape
And bid me hold my peace. I pray you all,
If you have hitherto conceal'd this sight,
Let it be tenable in your silence still ;
And whatsoever else shall hap to-night,
Give it an understanding, but no tongue : 250
I will requite your loves. So, fare you well :
Upon the platform, 'twixt eleven and twelve,
I'll visit you.
All. Our duty to your honor.
Ham. Your loves, as mine to you : fare-
well. [*Exeunt all but Hamlet.*
My father's spirit in arms ! all is not well ;
I doubt some foul play : would the night were
come !
Till then sit still, my soul : foul deeds will rise,
Though all the earth o'erwhelm them, to men's
eyes. [*Exit.*

Scene III. *A room in Polonius' house.*

Enter Laertes *and* Ophelia.

Laer. My necessaries are embark'd : fare-
well :
And, sister, as the winds give benefit
And convoy is assistant, do not sleep,
But let me hear from you.
Oph. Do you doubt that ?
Laer. For Hamlet and the trifling of his
favor,
Hold it a fashion and a toy in blood,
A violet in the youth of primy nature,
Forward, not permanent, sweet, not lasting,
The perfume and suppliance of a minute ;
No more.
Oph. No more but so ?
Laer. Think it no more : 10
For nature, crescent, does not grow alone
In thews and bulk, but, as this temple waxes,
The inward service of the mind and soul
Grows wide withal. Perhaps he loves you now,
And now no soil nor cautel doth besmirch
The virtue of his will : but you must fear,
His greatness weigh'd, his will is not his own ;
For he himself is subject to his birth :
He may not, as unvalued persons do,
Carve for himself ; for on his choice depends
The safety and health of this whole state ; 21
And therefore must his choice be circum-
scribed
Unto the voice and yielding of that body
Whereof he is the head. Then if he says he
loves you,
It fits your wisdom so far to believe it
As he in his particular act and place
May give his saying deed ; which is no fur-
ther
Than the main voice of Denmark goes withal.
Then weigh what loss your honor may sus-
tain,

If with too credent ear you list his songs, 30
Or lose your heart, or your chaste treasure open
To his unmaster'd importunity.
Fear it, Ophelia, fear it, my dear sister,
And keep you in the rear of your affection,
Out of the shot and danger of desire.
The chariest maid is prodigal enough,
If she unmask her beauty to the moon :
Virtue itself 'scapes not calumnious strokes :
The canker galls the infants of the spring,
Too oft before their buttons be disclosed, 40
And in the morn and liquid dew of youth
Contagious blastments are most imminent.
Be wary then ; best safety lies in fear :
Youth to itself rebels, though none else near.
 Oph. I shall the effect of this good lesson keep,
As watchman to my heart. But, good my brother,
Do not, as some ungracious pastors do,
Show me the steep and thorny way to heaven ;
Whiles, like a puff'd and reckless libertine,
Himself the primrose path of dalliance treads,
And recks not his own rede. 51
 Laer.   O, fear me not.
I stay too long : but here my father comes.

    Enter POLONIUS.

A double blessing is a double grace,
Occasion smiles upon a second leave.
 Pol. Yet here, Laertes ! aboard, aboard, for shame !
The wind sits in the shoulder of your sail,
And you are stay'd for. There ; my blessing with thee !
And these few precepts in thy memory
See thou character. Give thy thoughts no tongue,
Nor any unproportioned thought his act. 60
Be thou familiar, but by no means vulgar.
Those friends thou hast, and their adoption tried,
Grapple them to thy soul with hoops of steel ;
But do not dull thy palm with entertainment
Of each new-hatch'd, unfledged comrade. Beware
Of entrance to a quarrel, but being in,
Bear't that the opposed may beware of thee.
Give every man thy ear, but few thy voice ;
Take each man's censure, but reserve thy judgment.
Costly thy habit as thy purse can buy, 70
But not express'd in fancy ; rich, not gaudy ;
For the apparel oft proclaims the man,
And they in France of the best rank and station
Are of a most select and generous chief in that.
Neither a borrower nor a lender be ;
For loan oft loses both itself and friend,
And borrowing dulls the edge of husbandry.
This above all : to thine ownself be true,
And it must follow, as the night the day,
Thou canst not then be false to any man. 80
Farewell : my blessing season this in thee !
 Laer. Most humbly do I take my leave, my lord.
 Pol. The time invites you ; go ; your servants tend.

 Laer. Farewell, Ophelia ; and remember well
What I have said to you.
 Oph.   'Tis in my memory lock'd,
And you yourself shall keep the key of it.
 Laer. Farewell.   [*Exit.*
 Pol. What is't, Ophelia, he hath said to you ?
 Oph. So please you, something touching the Lord Hamlet.
 Pol. Marry, well bethought : 90
'Tis told me, he hath very oft of late
Given private time to you ; and you yourself
Have of your audience been most free and bounteous :
If it be so, as so 'tis put on me,
And that in way of caution, I must tell you,
You do not understand yourself so clearly
As it behoves my daughter and your honor.
What is between you ? give me up the truth.
 Oph. He hath, my lord, of late made many tenders
Of his affection to me. 100
 Pol. Affection ! pooh ! you speak like a green girl,
Unsifted in such perilous circumstance.
Do you believe his tenders, as you call them ?
 Oph. I do not know, my lord, what I should think.
 Pol. Marry, I'll teach you : think yourself a baby ;
That you have ta'en these tenders for true pay,
Which are not sterling. Tender yourself more dearly ;
Or—not to crack the wind of the poor phrase,
Running it thus—you'll tender me a fool.
 Oph. My lord, he hath importuned me with love 110
In honorable fashion.
 Pol. Ay, fashion you may call it ; go to, go to.
 Oph. And hath given countenance to his speech, my lord,
With almost all the holy vows of heaven.
 Pol. Ay, springes to catch woodcocks. I do know,
When the blood burns, how prodigal the soul
Lends the tongue vows : these blazes, daughter,
Giving more light than heat, extinct in both,
Even in their promise, as it is a-making,
You must not take for fire. From this time
Be somewhat scanter of your maiden presence ; 121
Set your entreatments at a higher rate
Than a command to parley. For Lord Hamlet,
Believe so much in him, that he is young
And with a larger tether may he walk
Than may be given you : in few, Ophelia,
Do not believe his vows ; for they are brokers,
Not of that dye which their investments show,
But mere implorators of unholy suits,
Breathing like sanctified and pious bawds,
The better to beguile. This is for all : 131
I would not, in plain terms, from this time forth,
Have you so slander any moment leisure,
As to give words or talk with the Lord Hamlet.
Look to't, I charge you : come your ways.
 Oph. I shall obey, my lord. [*Exeunt.*

SCENE IV. *The platform.*

Enter HAMLET, HORATIO, *and* MARCELLUS.

Ham. The air bites shrewdly; it is very cold.

Hor. It is a nipping and an eager air.

Ham. What hour now?

Hor.　　　　　　　I think it lacks of twelve.

Ham. No, it is struck.

Hor. Indeed? I heard it not: then it draws near the season
Wherein the spirit held his wont to walk.

[*A flourish of trumpets, and ordnance shot off, within.*

What does this mean, my lord?

Ham. The king doth wake to-night and takes his rouse,
Keeps wassail, and the swaggering up-spring reels;
And, as he drains his draughts of Rhenish down,　　　　　10
The kettle-drum and trumpet thus bray out
The triumph of his pledge.

Hor.　　　　　Is it a custom?

Ham. Ay, marry, is't:
But to my mind, though I am native here
And to the manner born, it is a custom
More honor'd in the breach than the observance.
This heavy-headed revel east and west
Makes us traduced and tax'd of other nations:
They clepe us drunkards, and with swinish phrase
Soil our addition; and indeed it takes　　20
From our achievements, though perform'd at height,
The pith and marrow of our attribute.
So, oft it chances in particular men,
That for some vicious mole of nature in them,
As, in their birth—wherein they are not guilty,
Since nature cannot choose his origin—
By the o'ergrowth of some complexion,
Oft breaking down the pales and forts of reason,
Or by some habit that too much o'er-leavens
The form of plausive manners, that these men,
Carrying, I say, the stamp of one defect,　　31
Being nature's livery, or fortune's star,—
Their virtues else—be they as pure as grace,
As infinite as man may undergo—
Shall in the general censure take corruption
From that particular fault: the dram of eale
Doth all the noble substance of a doubt
To his own scandal.

Hor.　　　　Look, my lord, it comes!

Enter Ghost.

Ham. Angels and ministers of grace defend us!
Be thou a spirit of health or goblin damn'd,
Bring with thee airs from heaven or blasts from hell,　　41
Be thy intents wicked or charitable,
Thou comest in such a questionable shape
That I will speak to thee: I'll call thee Hamlet,
King, father, royal Dane: O, answer me!
Let me not burst in ignorance; but tell
Why thy canonized bones, hearsed in death,
Have burst their cerements; why the sepulchre,
Wherein we saw thee quietly inurn'd,

Hath oped his ponderous and marble jaws, 50
To cast thee up again. What may this mean,
That thou, dead corse, again in complete steel
Revisit'st thus the glimpses of the moon,
Making night hideous; and we fools of nature
So horridly to shake our disposition
With thoughts beyond the reaches of our souls?
Say, why is this? wherefore? what should we do?　　[*Ghost beckons Hamlet.*

Hor. It beckons you to go away with it,
As if it some impartment did desire
To you alone.

Mar. Look, with what courteous action 60
It waves you to a more removed ground:
But do not go with it.

Hor.　　　　　No, by no means.

Ham. It will not speak; then I will follow it.

Hor. Do not, my lord.

Ham.　　　Why, what should be the fear?
I do not set my life at a pin's fee;
And for my soul, what can it do to that,
Being a thing immortal as itself?
It waves me forth again: I'll follow it.

Hor. What if it tempt you toward the flood, my lord,
Or to the dreadful summit of the cliff　　70
That beetles o'er his base into the sea,
And there assume some other horrible form,
Which might deprive your sovereignty of reason
And draw you into madness? think of it:
The very place puts toys of desperation,
Without more motive, into every brain
That looks so many fathoms to the sea
And hears it roar beneath.

Ham.　　　　　It waves me still.
Go on; I'll follow thee.

Mar. You shall not go, my lord.

Ham.　　　　Hold off your hands. 80

Hor. Be ruled; you shall not go.

Ham.　　　　My fate cries out,
And makes each petty artery in this body
As hardy as the Nemean lion's nerve.
Still am I call'd. Unhand me, gentlemen.
By heaven, I'll make a ghost of him that lets me!
I say, away! Go on; I'll follow thee.

　　　　　[*Exeunt Ghost and Hamlet.*

Hor. He waxes desperate with imagination.

Mar. Let's follow; 'tis not fit thus to obey him.

Hor. Have after. To what issue will this come?

Mar. Something is rotten in the state of Denmark.　　90

Hor. Heaven will direct it.

Mar.　　　　Nay, let's follow him. [*Exeunt.*

SCENE V. *Another part of the platform.*

Enter GHOST *and* HAMLET.

Ham. Where wilt thou lead me? speak; I'll go no further.

Ghost. Mark me.

Ham.　　　　I will.

Ghost.　　　My hour is almost come,
When I to sulphurous and tormenting flames
Must render up myself.

Ham.　　　Alas, poor ghost!

Ghost. Pity me not, but lend thy serious hearing

To what I shall unfold.
　Ham.　　　　　Speak; I am bound to hear.
　Ghost.　So art thou to revenge, when thou
　　shalt hear.
　Ham.　What?
　Ghost.　I am thy father's spirit,
Doom'd for a certain term to walk the night,
And for the day confined to fast in fires,　11
Till the foul crimes done in my days of nature
Are burnt and purged away. But that I am
　　forbid
To tell the secrets of my prison-house,
I could a tale unfold whose lightest word
Would harrow up thy soul, freeze thy young
　　blood,
Make thy two eyes, like stars, start from their
　　spheres,
Thy knotted and combined locks to part
And each particular hair to stand on end,
Like quills upon the fretful porpentine :　20
But this eternal blazon must not be
To ears of flesh and blood. List, list, O, list !
If thou didst ever thy dear father love—
　Ham.　O God !
　Ghost.　Revenge his foul and most unnatu-
　　ral murder.
　Ham.　Murder !
　Ghost.　Murder most foul, as in the best it
　　is ;
But this most foul, strange and unnatural.
　Ham.　Haste me to know't, that I, with
　　wings as swift
As meditation or the thoughts of love,　30
May sweep to my revenge.
　Ghost.　　　　　I find thee apt ;
And duller shouldst thou be than the fat weed
That roots itself in ease on Lethe wharf,
Wouldst thou not stir in this. Now, Hamlet,
　　hear :
'Tis given out that, sleeping in my orchard,
A serpent stung me ; so the whole ear of Den-
　　mark
Is by a forged process of my death
Rankly abused : but know, thou noble youth,
The serpent that did sting thy father's life
Now wears his crown.
　Ham.　　　　　O my prophetic soul ! 40
My uncle !
　Ghost.　Ay, that incestuous, that adulterate
　　beast,
With witchcraft of his wit, with traitorous
　　gifts,—
O wicked wit and gifts, that have the power
So to seduce !—won to his shameful lust
The will of my most seeming-virtuous queen :
O Hamlet, what a falling-off was there !
From me, whose love was of that dignity
That it went hand in hand even with the vow
I made to her in marriage, and to decline　50
Upon a wretch whose natural gifts were poor
To those of mine !
But virtue, as it never will be moved,
Though lewdness court it in a shape of heaven,
So lust, though to a radiant angel link'd,
Will sate itself in a celestial bed,
And prey on garbage.
But, soft ! methinks I scent the morning air ;
Brief let me be. Sleeping within my orchard,
My custom always of the afternoon,　60
Upon my secure hour thy uncle stole,
With juice of cursed hebenon in a vial,
And in the porches of my ears did pour

The leperous distilment ; whose effect
Holds such an enmity with blood of man
That swift as quicksilver it courses through
The natural gates and alleys of the body,
And with a sudden vigor it doth posset
And curd, like eager droppings into milk,
The thin and wholesome blood : so did it mine;
And a most instant tetter bark'd about,　71
Most lazar-like, with vile and loathsome crust,
All my smooth body.
Thus was I, sleeping, by a brother's hand
Of life, of crown, of queen, at once dis-
　　patch'd :
Cut off even in the blossoms of my sin,
Unhousel'd, disappointed, unanel'd,
No reckoning made, but sent to my account
With all my imperfections on my head :
O, horrible ! O, horrible ! most horrible !　80
If thou hast nature in thee, bear it not ;
Let not the royal bed of Denmark be
A couch for luxury and damned incest.
But, howsoever thou pursuest this act,
Taint not thy mind, nor let thy soul contrive
Against thy mother aught : leave her to heaven
And to those thorns that in her bosom lodge,
To prick and sting her. Fare thee well at
　　once !
The glow-worm shows the matin to be near,
And 'gins to pale his uneffectual fire :　90
Adieu, adieu ! Hamlet, remember me. [*Exit.*
　Ham.　O all you host of heaven ! O earth !
　　what else ?
And shall I couple hell ? O, fie ! Hold, hold,
　　my heart ;
And you, my sinews, grow not instant old,
But bear me stiffly up. Remember thee !
Ay, thou poor ghost, while memory holds a
　　seat
In this distracted globe. Remember thee !
Yea, from the table of my memory
I'll wipe away all trivial fond records,
All saws of books, all forms, all pressures past,
That youth and observation copied there ;　101
And thy commandment all alone shall live
Within the book and volume of my brain,
Unmix'd with baser matter : yes, by heaven !
O most pernicious woman !
O villain, villain, smiling, damned villain !
My tables,—meet it is I set it down,
That one may smile, and smile, and be a vil-
　　lain ;
At least I'm sure it may be so in Denmark :
　　　　　　　　　　　　　　　　　[*Writing.*
So, uncle, there you are. Now to my word ;
It is ' Adieu, adieu ! remember me.'　111
I have sworn 't.
　Mar. ⎫　[*Within*] My lord, my lord,—
　Hor. ⎭
　Mar.　　　　　[*Within*] Lord Hamlet,—
　Hor.　　　　　[*Within*] Heaven secure him !
　Ham.　So be it !
　Hor.　[*Within*] Hillo, ho, ho, my lord !
　Ham.　Hillo, ho, ho, boy ! come, bird,
　　come.

　　Enter Horatio *and* Marcellus.

　Mar.　How is't, my noble lord ?
　Hor.　　　　　What news, my lord ?
　Ham.　O, wonderful !
　Hor.　　　　　Good my lord, tell it.
　Ham.　No ; you'll reveal it.
　Hor.　Not I, my lord, by heaven.

Mar. Nor I, my lord. 120
Ham. How say you, then ; would heart of
man once think it ?
But you'll be secret ?
Hor. ⎱ Ay, by heaven, my lord.
Mar. ⎰
Ham. There's ne'er a villain dwelling in
all Denmark
But he's an arrant knave.
Hor. There needs no ghost, my lord, come
from the grave
To tell us this.
Ham. Why, right ; you are i' the right ;
And so, without more circumstance at all,
I hold it fit that we shake hands and part :
You, as your business and desire shall point
you ;
For every man has business and desire, 130
Such as it is ; and for mine own poor part,
Look you, I'll go pray.
Hor. These are but wild and whirling
words, my lord.
Ham. I'm sorry they offend you, heartily ;
Yes, 'faith heartily.
Hor. There's no offence, my lord.
Ham. Yes, by Saint Patrick, but there is,
Horatio,
And much offence too. Touching this vision
here,
It is an honest ghost, that let me tell you :
For your desire to know what is between us,
O'ermaster 't as you may. And now, good
friends, 140
As you are friends, scholars and soldiers,
Give me one poor request.
Hor. What is't, my lord ? we will.
Ham. Never make known what you have
seen to-night.
Hor. ⎱ My lord, we will not.
Mar. ⎰
Ham. Nay, but swear't.
Hor. In faith,
My lord, not I.
Mar. Nor I, my lord, in faith.
Ham. Upon my sword.
Mar. We have sworn, my lord, already.
Ham. Indeed, upon my sword, indeed.
Ghost. [*Beneath*] Swear.
Ham. Ah, ha, boy ! say'st thou so ? art
thou there, truepenny ? 150
Come on—you hear this fellow in the cel-
larage—
Consent to swear.
Hor. Propose the oath, my lord.
Ham. Never to speak of this that you have
seen,
Swear by my sword.
Ghost. [*Beneath*] Swear.
Ham. Hic et ubique ? then we'll shift our
ground.
Come hither, gentlemen,
And lay your hands again upon my sword :
Never to speak of this that you have heard,
Swear by my sword. 160
Ghost. [*Beneath*] Swear.
Ham. Well said, old mole ! canst work i'
the earth so fast ?
A worthy pioner ! Once more remove, good
friends.
Hor. O day and night, but this is wondrous
strange !

Ham. And therefore as a stranger give it
welcome.
There are more things in heaven and earth,
Horatio,
Than are dreamt of in your philosophy.
But come ;
Here, as before, never, so help you mercy,
How strange or odd soe'er I bear myself, 170
As I perchance hereafter shall think meet
To put an antic disposition on,
That you, at such times seeing me, never shall,
With arms encumber'd thus, or this head-
shake,
Or by pronouncing of some doubtful phrase,
As ' Well, well, we know,' or ' We could, an
if we would,'
Or ' If we list to speak,' or ' There be, an if
they might,'
Or such ambiguous giving out, to note
That you know aught of me : this not to do,
So grace and mercy at your most need help
you, 180
Swear.
Ghost. [*Beneath*] Swear.
Ham. Rest, rest, perturbed spirit ! [*They
swear.*] So, gentlemen,
With all my love I do commend me to you :
And what so poor a man as Hamlet is
May do, to express his love and friending to
you,
God willing, shall not lack. Let us go in to-
gether ;
And still your fingers on your lips, I pray.
The time is out of joint : O cursed spite,
That ever I was born to set it right !
Nay, come, let's go together. [*Exeunt.* 190

ACT II.

SCENE I. *A room in Polonius' house.*

Enter POLONIUS *and* REYNALDO.

Pol. Give him this money and these notes,
Reynaldo.
Rey. I will, my lord.
Pol. You shall do marvellous wisely, good
Reynaldo,
Before you visit him, to make inquire
Of his behavior.
Rey. My lord, I did intend it.
Pol. Marry, well said ; very well said.
Look you, sir,
Inquire me first what Danskers are in Paris ;
And how, and who, what means, and where
they keep,
What company, at what expense ; and finding
By this encompassment and drift of question
That they do know my son, come you more
nearer 11
Than your particular demands will touch it :
Take you, as 'twere, some distant knowledge
of him ;
As thus, ' I know his father and his friends,
And in part him : ' do you mark this, Rey-
naldo ?
Rey. Ay, very well, my lord.
Pol. ' And in part him ; but ' you may say
' not well :
But, if 't be he I mean, he's very wild ;
Addicted so and so : ' and there put on him

What forgeries you please; marry, none so
　　rank　　　　　　　　　　　　　　　20
As may dishonor him; take heed of that;
But, sir, such wanton, wild and usual slips
As are companions noted and most known
To youth and liberty.
　　Rey.　　　　　As gaming, my lord.
　　Pol.　Ay, or drinking, fencing, swearing,
　　quarrelling,
Drabbing : you may go so far.
　　Rey.　My lord, that would dishonor him.
　　Pol.　'Faith, no ; as you may season it in
　　the charge
You must not put another scandal on him,
That he is open to incontinency ;　　　30
That's not my meaning : but breathe his faults
　　so quaintly
That they may seem the taints of liberty,
The flash and outbreak of a fiery mind,
A savageness in unreclaimed blood,
Of general assault.
　　Rey.　　　　　But, my good lord,—
　　Pol.　Wherefore should you do this ?
　　Rey.　　　　　　　Ay, my lord,
I would know that.
　　Pol.　　　　Marry, sir, here's my drift ;
And, I believe, it is a fetch of wit :
You laying these slight sullies on my son,
As 'twere a thing a little soil'd i' the working,
Mark you,　　　　　　　　　　　41
Your party in converse, him you would sound,
Having ever seen in the prenominate crimes
The youth you breathe of guilty, be assured
He closes with you in this consequence ;
' Good sir,' or so, or ' friend,' or ' gentle-
　man,'
According to the phrase or the addition
Of man and country.
　　Rey.　　　　　Very good, my lord.
　　Pol.　And then, sir, does he this—he does—
what was I about to say ? By the mass, I was
about to say something : where did I leave ?
　　Rey.　At ' closes in the consequence,' at
' friend or so,' and ' gentleman.'
　　Pol.　At ' closes in the consequence,' ay,
　marry ;
He closes thus : ' I know the gentleman ;
I saw him yesterday, or t' other day,
Or then, or then ; with such, or such ; and, as
　you say,
There was a' gaming ; there o'ertook in's
　rouse ;
There falling out at tennis : ' or perchance,
' I saw him enter such a house of sale,'　60
Videlicet, a brothel, or so forth.
See you now ;
Your bait of falsehood takes this carp of
　truth :
And thus do we of wisdom and of reach,
With windlasses and with assays of bias,
By indirections find directions out :
So by my former lecture and advice,
Shall you my son. You have me, have you
　not ?
　　Rey.　My lord, I have.
　　Pol.　　　God be wi' you ; fare you well.
　　Rey.　Good my lord !　　　　　70
　　Pol.　Observe his inclination in yourself.
　　Rey.　I shall, my lord.
　　Pol.　And let him ply his music.
　　Rey.　　　　　Well, my lord.
　　Pol.　Farewell !　　　[*Exit Reynaldo.*

Enter OPHELIA.

How now, Ophelia ! what's the matter ?
　　Oph.　O, my lord, my lord, I have been so
affrighted !
　　Pol.　With what, i' the name of God ?
　　Oph.　My lord, as I was sewing in my
closet,
Lord Hamlet, with his doublet all unbraced ;
No hat upon his head ; his stockings foul'd,
Ungarter'd, and down-gyved to his ancle ;　80
Pale as his shirt ; his knees knocking each
　other ;
And with a look so piteous in purport
As if he had been loosed out of hell
To speak of horrors,—he comes before me.
　　Pol.　Mad for thy love ?
　　Oph.　　　　My lord, I do not know ;
But truly, I do fear it.
　　Pol.　　　　　What said he?
　　Oph.　He took me by the wrist and held me
　hard ;
Then goes he to the length of all his arm ;
And, with his other hand thus o'er his brow,
He falls to such perusal of my face　　90
As he would draw it. Long stay'd he so ;
At last, a little shaking of mine arm
And thrice his head thus waving up and down,
He raised a sigh so piteous and profound
As it did seem to shatter all his bulk
And end his being : that done, he lets me go :
And, with his head over his shoulder turn'd,
He seem'd to find his way without his eyes ;
For out o'doors he went without their helps,
And, to the last, bended their light on me. 100
　　Pol.　Come, go with me : I will go seek the
　king.
This is the very ecstasy of love,
Whose violent property fordoes itself
And leads the will to desperate undertakings
As oft as any passion under heaven
That does afflict our natures. I am sorry.
What, have you given him any hard words of
　late ?
　　Oph.　No, my good lord, but, as you did
　command,
I did repel his letters and denied
His access to me.
　　Pol.　　　　That hath made him mad.　110
I am sorry that with better heed and judg-
　ment
I had not quoted him : I fear'd he did but
　trifle,
And meant to wreck thee ; but, beshrew my
　jealousy !
By heaven, it is as proper to our age
To cast beyond ourselves in our opinions
As it is common for the younger sort
To lack discretion. Come, go we to the king :
This must be known ; which, being kept close,
　might move
More grief to hide than hate to utter love.
　　　　　　　　　　　　　　　[*Exeunt.*

SCENE II.　*A room in the castle.*

Enter KING, QUEEN, ROSENCRANTZ, GUIL-
　DENSTERN, *and* Attendants.

　　King.　Welcome, dear Rosencrantz and
　Guildenstern !
Moreover that we much did long to see you,
The need we have to use you did provoke
Our hasty sending. Something have you heard

Of Hamlet's transformation; so call it,
Sith nor the exterior nor the inward man
Resembles that it was. What it should be,
More than his father's death, that thus hath
    put him
So much from the understanding of himself,
I cannot dream of : I entreat you both,   10
That, being of so young days brought up with
    him,
And sith so neighbor'd to his youth and ha-
    vior,
That you vouchsafe your rest here in our court
Some little time : so by your companies
To draw him on to pleasures, and to gather,
So much as from occasion you may glean,
Whether aught, to us unknown, afflicts him
    thus,
That, open'd, lies within our remedy.
    Queen. Good gentlemen, he hath much
    talk'd of you ;
And sure I am two men there are not living
To whom he more adheres. If it will please
    you   21
To show us so much gentry and good will
As to expend your time with us awhile,
For the supply and profit of our hope,
Your visitation shall receive such thanks
As fits a king's remembrance.
    Ros.   Both your majesties
Might, by the sovereign power you have of us,
Put your dread pleasures more into command
Than to entreaty.
    Guil.   But we both obey,
And here give up ourselves, in the full bent
To lay our service freely at your feet,   31
To be commanded.
    King. Thanks, Rosencrantz and gentle
    Guildenstern.
    Queen. Thanks, Guildenstern and gentle
    Rosencrantz :
And I beseech you instantly to visit
My too much changed son. Go, some of you,
And bring these gentlemen where Hamlet is.
    Guil. Heavens make our presence and our
    practices
Pleasant and helpful to him !
    Queen.   Ay, amen !
        [*Exeunt Rosencrantz, Guildenstern, and
                some Attendants.*

    Enter POLONIUS.

    Pol. The ambassadors from Norway, my
    good lord,   40
Are joyfully return'd.
    King. Thou still hast been the father of
    good news.
    Pol. Have I, my lord ? I assure my good
liege,
I hold my duty, as I hold my soul,
Both to my God and to my gracious king :
And I do think, or else this brain of mine
Hunts not the trail of policy so sure
As it hath used to do, that I have found
The very cause of Hamlet's lunacy.
    King. O, speak of that ; that do I long to
    hear.   50
    Pol. Give first admittance to the ambas-
    sadors ;
My news shall be the fruit to that great feast.
    King. Thyself do grace to them, and bring
    them in.   [*Exit Polonius.*
He tells me, my dear Gertrude, he hath found

The head and source of all your son's dis-
    temper.
    Queen. I doubt it is no other but the main ;
His father's death, and our o'erhasty mar-
    riage.
    King. Well, we shall sift him.

    Re-enter POLONIUS, *with* VOLTIMAND *and*
                CORNELIUS.

            Welcome, my good friends !
Say, Voltimand, what from our brother Nor-
    way ?
    Volt. Most fair return of greetings and
    desires.   60
Upon our first, he sent out to suppress
His nephew's levies ; which to him appear'd
To be a preparation 'gainst the Polack ;
But, better look'd into, he truly found
It was against your highness : whereat grieved,
That so his sickness, age and impotence
Was falsely borne in hand, sends out arrests
On Fortinbras ; which he, in brief, obeys ;
Receives rebuke from Norway, and in fine
Makes vow before his uncle never more   70
To give the assay of arms against your maj-
    esty.
Whereon old Norway, overcome with joy,
Gives him three thousand crowns in annual
    fee,
And his commission to employ those soldiers,
So levied as before, against the Polack :
With an entreaty, herein further shown,
                [*Giving a paper.*
That it might please you to give quiet pass
Through your dominions for this enterprise,
On such regards of safety and allowance
As therein are set down.
    King.   It likes us well ;   80
And at our more consider'd time we'll read,
Answer, and think upon this business.
Meantime we thank you for your well-took
    labor :
Go to your rest ; at night we'll feast together :
Most welcome home !
        [*Exeunt Voltimand and Cornelius.*
    Pol.   This business is well ended.
My liege, and madam, to expostulate
What majesty should be, what duty is,
Why day is day, night night, and time is time,
Were nothing but to waste night, day and time.
Therefore, since brevity is the soul of wit,   90
And tediousness the limbs and outward flour-
    ishes,
I will be brief : your noble son is mad :
Mad call I it ; for, to define true madness,
What is't but to be nothing else but mad ?
But let that go.
    Queen.   More matter, with less art.
    Pol. Madam, I swear I use no art at all.
That he is mad, 'tis true : 'tis true 'tis pity ;
And pity 'tis 'tis true : a foolish figure ;
But farewell it, for I will use no art.
Mad let us grant him, then : and now remains
That we find out the cause of this effect,   101
Or rather say, the cause of this defect,
For this effect defective comes by cause :
Thus it remains, and the remainder thus.
Perpend.
I have a daughter—have while she is mine—
Who, in her duty and obedience, mark,
Hath given me this : now gather, and surmise.
                      [*Reads.*

' To the celestial and my soul's idol, the most
beautified Ophelia,'—   110
That's an ill phrase, a vile phrase ; ' beauti-
fied ' is a vile phrase : but you shall hear.
Thus :   [*Reads.*
' In her excellent white bosom, these, &c.'
   Queen. Came this from Hamlet to her ?
   Pol. Good madam, stay awhile ; I will be
faithful.   [*Reads.*
   ' Doubt thou the stars are fire ;
      Doubt that the sun doth move ;
   Doubt truth to be a liar ;
      But never doubt I love.   119
' O dear Ophelia, I am ill at these numbers ;
I have not art to reckon my groans : but that
I love thee best, O most best, believe it. Adieu.
   ' Thine evermore, most dear lady, whilst
      this machine is to him, HAMLET.'
This, in obedience, hath my daughter shown
   me,
And more above, hath his solicitings,
As they fell out by time, by means and place,
All given to mine ear.
   King.   But how hath she
Received his love ?
   Pol.   What do you think of me?
   King. As of a man faithful and honorable.
   Pol. I would fain prove so. But what might
   you think,   131
When I had seen this hot love on the wing—
As I perceived it, I must tell you that,
Before my daughter told me—what might you,
Or my dear majesty your queen here, think,
If I had play'd the desk or table-book,
Or given my heart a winking, mute and dumb,
Or look'd upon this love with idle sight ;
What might you think ? No, I went round to
   work,
And my young mistress thus I did bespeak :
' Lord Hamlet is a prince, out of thy star ; 141
This must not be : ' and then I precepts gave
   her,
That she should lock herself from his resort,
Admit no messengers, receive no tokens.
Which done, she took the fruits of my advice ;
And he, repulsed—a short tale to make—
Fell into a sadness, then into a fast,
Thence to a watch, thence into a weakness,
Thence to a lightness, and, by this declension,
Into the madness wherein now he raves,   150
And all we mourn for.
   King.   Do you think 'tis this ?
   Queen. It may be, very likely.
   Pol. Hath there been such a time—I'd fain
know that—
That I have positively said ' 'Tis so,'
When it proved otherwise ?
   King.   Not that I know.
   Pol. [*Pointing to his head and shoulder*]
   Take this from this, if this be otherwise :
If circumstances lead me, I will find
Where truth is hid, though it were hid indeed
Within the centre.
   King.   How may we try it further ?
   Pol. You know, sometimes he walks four
   hours together   160
Here in the lobby.
   Queen.   So he does indeed.
   Pol. At such a time I'll loose my daughter
to him :
Be you and I behind an arras then ;
Mark the encounter : if he love her not

And be not from his reason fall'n thereon,
Let me be no assistant for a state,
But keep a farm and carters.
   King.   We will try it.
   Queen. But, look, where sadly the poor
   wretch comes reading.
   Pol. Away, I do beseech you, both away :
I'll board him presently.

   [*Exeunt King, Queen, and Attendants.*

   Enter HAMLET, *reading.*

      O, give me leave :   170
How does my good Lord Hamlet ?
   Ham. Well, God-a-mercy.
   Pol. Do you know me, my lord ?
   Ham. Excellent well ; you are a fish-
monger.
   Pol. Not I, my lord.
   Ham. Then I would you were so honest a
man.
   Pol. Honest, my lord !
   Ham. Ay, sir ; to be honest, as this world
goes, is to be one man picked out of ten thou-
sand.
   Pol. That's very true, my lord.   180
   Ham. For if the sun breed maggots in a
dead dog, being a god kissing carrion,—Have
you a daughter ?
   Pol. I have, my lord.
   Ham. Let her not walk i' the sun : concep-
tion is a blessing : but not as your daughter
may conceive. Friend, look to 't.
   Pol. [*Aside*] How say you by that ? Still
harping on my daughter : yet he knew me
not at first ; he said I was a fishmonger : he
is far gone, far gone : and truly in my youth
I suffered much extremity for love ; very near
this. I'll speak to him again. What do you
read, my lord ?
   Ham. Words, words, words.
   Pol. What is the matter, my lord ?
   Ham. Between who ?
   Pol. I mean, the matter that you read, my
lord.
   Ham. Slanders, sir : for the satirical rogue
says here that old men have grey beards, that
their faces are wrinkled, their eyes purging
thick amber and plum-tree gum and that they
have a plentiful lack of wit, together with
most weak hams : all which, sir, though I
most powerfully and potently believe, yet I
hold it not honesty to have it thus set down,
for yourself, sir, should be old as I am, if like
a crab you could go backward.
   Pol. [*Aside*] Though this be madness, yet
there is method in 't. Will you walk out of
the air, my lord ?
   Ham. Into my grave.   210
   Pol. Indeed, that is out o' the air. [*Aside*]
How pregnant sometimes his replies are ! a
happiness that often madness hits on, which
reason and sanity could not so prosperously be
delivered of. I will leave him, and suddenly
contrive the means of meeting between him
and my daughter.—My honorable lord, I will
most humbly take my leave of you.
   Ham. You cannot, sir, take from me any
thing that I will more willingly part withal :
except my life, except my life, except my life.
   Pol. Fare you well, my lord.
   Ham. These tedious old fools !

Enter ROSENCRANTZ *and* GUILDENSTERN.

Pol. You go to seek the Lord Hamlet; there he is.

Ros. [*To Polonius*] God save you, sir!

[*Exit Polonius.*

Guil. My honored lord!

Ros. My most dear lord!

Ham. My excellent good friends! How dost thou, Guildenstern? Ah, Rosencrantz! Good lads, how do ye both?　230

Ros. As the indifferent children of the earth.

Guil. Happy, in that we are not over-happy;

On fortune's cap we are not the very button.

Ham. Nor the soles of her shoe?

Ros. Neither, my lord.

Ham. Then you live about her waist, or in the middle of her favors?

Guil. 'Faith, her privates we.

Ham. In the secret parts of fortune? O, most true; she is a strumpet. What's the news?

Ros. None, my lord, but that the world's grown honest.　241

Ham. Then is doomsday near: but your news is not true. Let me question more in particular: what have you, my good friends, deserved at the hands of fortune, that she sends you to prison hither?

Guil. Prison, my lord!

Ham. Denmark's a prison.

Ros. Then is the world one.　250

Ham. A goodly one; in which there are many confines, wards and dungeons, Denmark being one o' the worst.

Ros. We think not so, my lord.

Ham. Why, then, 'tis none to you; for there is nothing either good or bad, but thinking makes it so: to me it is a prison.

Ros. Why then, your ambition makes it one; 'tis too narrow for your mind.　259

Ham. O God, I could be bounded in a nutshell and count myself a king of infinite space, were it not that I have bad dreams.

Guil. Which dreams indeed are ambition, for the very substance of the ambitious is merely the shadow of a dream.

Ham. A dream itself is but a shadow.

Ros. Truly, and I hold ambition of so airy and light a quality that it is but a shadow's shadow.

Ham. Then are our beggars bodies, and our monarchs and outstretched heroes the beggars' shadows. Shall we to the court? for, by my fay, I cannot reason.

Ros.
Guil. } We'll wait upon you.

Ham. No such matter: I will not sort you with the rest of my servants, for, to speak to you like an honest man, I am most dreadfully attended. But, in the beaten way of friendship, what make you at Elsinore?

Ros. To visit you, my lord; no other occasion.

Ham. Beggar that I am, I am even poor in thanks; but I thank you: and sure, dear friends, my thanks are too dear a halfpenny. Were you not sent for? Is it your own inclining? Is it a free visitation? Come, deal justly with me: come, come; nay, speak.

Guil. What should we say, my lord?

Ham. Why, any thing, but to the purpose. You were sent for; and there is a kind of confession in your looks which your modesties have not craft enough to color: I know the good king and queen have sent for you.　291

Ros. To what end, my lord?

Ham. That you must teach me. But let me conjure you, by the rights of our fellowship, by the consonancy of our youth, by the obligation of our ever-preserved love, and by what more dear a better proposer could charge you withal, be even and direct with me, whether you were sent for, or no?

Ros. [*Aside to Guil.*] What say you?　300

Ham. [*Aside*] Nay, then, I have an eye of you.—If you love me, hold not off.

Guil. My lord, we were sent for.

Ham. I will tell you why; so shall my anticipation prevent your discovery, and your secrecy to the king and queen moult no feather. I have of late—but wherefore I know not—lost all my mirth, forgone all custom of exercises; and indeed it goes so heavily with my disposition that this goodly frame, the earth, seems to me a sterile promontory, this most excellent canopy, the air, look you, this brave o'erhanging firmament, this majestical roof fretted with golden fire, why, it appears no other thing to me than a foul and pestilent congregation of vapors. What a piece of work is a man! how noble in reason! how infinite in faculty! in form and moving how express and admirable! in action how like an angel! in apprehension how like a god! the beauty of the world! the paragon of animals! And yet, to me, what is this quintessence of dust? man delights not me: no, nor woman neither, though by your smiling you seem to say so.

Ros. My lord, there was no such stuff in my thoughts.

Ham. Why did you laugh then, when I said 'man delights not me'?

Ros. To think, my lord, if you delight not in man, what lenten entertainment the players shall receive from you: we coted them on the way; and hither are they coming, to offer you service.

Ham. He that plays the king shall be welcome; his majesty shall have tribute of me; the adventurous knight shall use his foil and target; the lover shall not sigh gratis; the humorous man shall end his part in peace; the clown shall make those laugh whose lungs are tickled o' the sere; and the lady shall say her mind freely, or the blank verse shall halt for't. What players are they?　340

Ros. Even those you were wont to take delight in, the tragedians of the city.

Ham. How chances it they travel? their residence, both in reputation and profit, was better both ways.

Ros. I think their inhibition comes by the means of the late innovation.

Ham. Do they hold the same estimation they did when I was in the city? are they so followed?　350

Ros. No, indeed, are they not.

Ham. How comes it? do they grow rusty?

Ros. Nay, their endeavor keeps in the wonted pace: but there is, sir, an aery of children, little eyases, that cry out on the top of question, and are most tyrannically clapped for't : these are now the fashion, and so be-rattle the common stages—so they call them—that many wearing rapiers are afraid of goose-quills and dare scarce come thither. 360

Ham. What, are they children ? who main-tains 'em ? how are they escoted ? Will they pursue the quality no longer than they can sing ? will they not say afterwards, if they should grow themselves to common players—as it is most like, if their means are no better —their writers do them wrong, to make them exclaim against their own succession ?

Ros. 'Faith, there has been much to do on both sides ; and the nation holds it no sin to tarre them to controversy : there was, for a while, no money bid for argument, unless the poet and the player went to cuffs in the ques-tion.

Ham. Is 't possible ?

Guil. O, there has been much throwing about of brains.

Ham. Do the boys carry it away ?

Ros. Ay, that they do, my lord ; Hercules and his load too. 379

Ham. It is not very strange ; for mine uncle is king of Denmark, and those that would make mows at him while my father lived, give twenty, forty, fifty, an hundred duc-ats a-piece for his picture in little. 'Sblood, there is something in this more than natural, if philosophy could find it out.

[*Flourish of trumpets within.*

Guil. There are the players.

Ham. Gentlemen, you are welcome to Elsi-nore. Your hands, come then : the appurte-nance of welcome is fashion and ceremony : let me comply with you in this garb, lest my extent to the players, which, I tell you, must show fairly outward, should more appear like entertainment than yours. You are welcome : but my uncle-father and aunt-mother are de-ceived.

Guil. In what, my dear lord ?

Ham. I am but mad north-north-west : when the wind is southerly I know a hawk from a handsaw.

Enter POLONIUS.

Pol. Well be with you, gentlemen !

Ham. Hark you, Guildenstern ; and you too : at each ear a hearer : that great baby you see there is not yet out of his swaddling-clouts.

Ros. Happily he's the second time come to them ; for they say an old man is twice a child.

Ham. I will prophesy he comes to tell me of the players ; mark it. You say right, sir : o'Monday morning ; 'twas so indeed.

Pol. My lord, I have news to tell you.

Ham. My lord, I have news to tell you. When Roscius was an actor in Rome,— 410

Pol. The actors are come hither, my lord.

Ham. Buz, buz !

Pol. Upon mine honor,—

Ham. Then came each actor on his ass,—

Pol. The best actors in the world, either for tragedy, comedy, history, pastoral, pas-toral-comical, historical-pastoral, tragical-his-torical, tragical - comical - historical - pastoral, scene individable, or poem unlimited : Seneca cannot be too heavy, nor Plautus too light. For

the law of writ and the liberty, these are the only men. 421

Ham. O Jephthah, judge of Israel, what a treasure hadst thou !

Pol. What a treasure had he, my lord ?

Ham. Why,

'One fair daughter and no more,
The which he loved passing well.'

Pol. [*Aside*] Still on my daughter.

Ham. Am I not i' the right, old Jephthah ?

Pol. If you call me Jephthah, my lord, I have a daughter that I love passing well. 431

Ham. Nay, that follows not.

Pol. What follows, then, my lord ?

Ham. Why,

'As by lot, God wot,'

and then, you know,

'It came to pass, as most like it was,'—

the first row of the pious chanson will show you more ; for look, where my abridgement comes.

Enter four or five Players.

You are welcome, masters ; welcome, all. I am glad to see thee well. Welcome, good friends. O, my old friend ! thy face is valanced since I saw thee last : comest thou to beard me in Denmark ? What, my young lady and mis-tress ! By'r lady, your ladyship is nearer to heaven than when I saw you last, by the alti-tude of a chopine. Pray God, your voice, like a piece of uncurrent gold, be not cracked within the ring. Masters, you are all welcome. We'll e'en to't like French falconers, fly at any thing we see : we'll have a speech straight : come, give us a taste of your quality ; come, a passionate speech.

First Play. What speech, my lord ?

Ham. I heard thee speak me a speech once, but it was never acted ; or, if it was, not above once ; for the play, I remember, pleased not the million ; 'twas caviare to the general : but it was—as I received it, and others, whose judgments in such matters cried in the top of mine—an excellent play, well digested in the scenes, set down with as much modesty as cun-ning. I remember, one said there were no sal-lets in the lines to make the matter savory, nor no matter in the phrase that might indict the author of affectation ; but called it an honest method, as wholesome as sweet, and by very much more handsome than fine. One speech in it I chiefly loved : 'twas Æneas' tale to Dido ; and thereabout of it especially, where he speaks of Priam's slaughter : if it live in your memory, begin at this line : let me see, let me see— 471

'The rugged Pyrrhus, like the Hyrcanian beast,'—

it is not so :—it begins with Pyrrhus :—

'The rugged Pyrrhus, he whose sable arms,
Black as his purpose, did the night resemble
When he lay couched in the ominous horse,
Hath now this dread and black complexion smear'd
With heraldry more dismal ; head to foot
Now is he total gules ; horridly trick'd
With blood of fathers, mothers, daughters, sons,
Baked and impasted with the parching streets,
That lend a tyrannous and damned light

To their lord's murder : roasted in wrath
    and fire,
And thus o'er-sized with coagulate gore,
With eyes like carbuncles, the hellish Pyr-
    rhus
Old grandsire Priam seeks.'
So, proceed you.
    Pol. 'Fore God, my lord, well spoken, with
good accent and good discretion.
    First Play.   ' Anon he finds him
Striking too short at Greeks ; his antique
    sword,
Rebellious to his arm, lies where it falls,
Repugnant to command : unequal match'd,
Pyrrhus at Priam drives ; in rage strikes
    wide ;
But with the whiff and wind of his fell
    sword
The unnerved father falls. Then senseless
    Ilium,
Seeming to feel this blow, with flaming top
Stoops to his base, and with a hideous crash
Takes prisoner Pyrrhus' ear : for, lo ! his
    sword,
Which was declining on the milky head 500
Of reverend Priam, seem'd i' the air to
    stick :
So, as a painted tyrant, Pyrrhus stood,
And like a neutral to his will and matter,
Did nothing.
But, as we often see, against some storm,
A silence in the heavens, the rack stand still,
The bold winds speechless and the orb be-
    low
As hush as death, anon the dreadful thun-
    der
Doth rend the region, so, after Pyrrhus'
    pause,   509
Aroused vengeance sets him new a-work ;
And never did the Cyclops' hammers fall
On Mars's armor forged for proof eterne
With less remorse than Pyrrhus' bleeding
    sword
Now falls on Priam.
Out, out, thou strumpet, Fortune ! All you
    gods,
In general synod, take away her power ;
Break all the spokes and fellies from her
    wheel,
And bowl the round nave down the hill of
    heaven,
As low as to the fiends ! '
    Pol. This is too long.   520
    Ham. It shall to the barber's, with your
beard. Prithee, say on : he's for a jig or a tale
of bawdry, or he sleeps : say on : come to
Hecuba.
    First Play. ' But who, O, who had seen the
mobled queen—'
    Ham. ' The mobled queen ? '
    Pol. That's good ; ' mobled queen ' is good.
    First Play. ' Run barefoot up and down,
    threatening the flames
With bisson rheum ; a clout upon that head
Where late the diadem stood, and for a
    robe,
About her lank and all o'er-teemed loins,
A blanket, in the alarm of fear caught up ;
Who this had seen, with tongue in venom
    steep'd,
'Gainst Fortune's state would treason have
    pronounced :

But if the gods themselves did see her then
When she saw Pyrrhus make malicious sport
In mincing with his sword her husband's
    limbs,
The instant burst of clamor that she made,
Unless things mortal move them not at all,
Would have made milch the burning eyes of
    heaven,   540
And passion in the gods.'
    Pol. Look, whether he has not turned his
color and has tears in's eyes. Pray you, no
more.
    Ham. 'Tis well ; I'll have thee speak out
the rest soon. Good my lord, will you see the
players well bestowed ? Do you hear, let them
be well used ; for they are the abstract and
brief chronicles of the time : after your death
you were better have a bad epitaph than their
ill report while you live.   551
    Pol. My lord, I will use them according to
their desert.
    Ham. God's bodykins, man, much better :
use every man after his desert, and who should
'scape whipping ? Use them after your own
honor and dignity : the less they deserve, the
more merit is in your bounty. Take them in.
    Pol. Come, sirs.   559
    Ham. Follow him, friends : we'll hear a
play to-morrow. [*Exit Polonius with all the
Players but the First.*] Dost thou hear me, old
friend ; can you play the Murder of Gonzago ?
    First Play. Ay, my lord.
    Ham. We'll ha't to-morrow night. You
could, for a need, study a speech of some
dozen or sixteen lines, which I would set down
and insert in't, could you not ?
    First Play. Ay, my lord.   569
    Ham. Very well. Follow that lord ; and
look you mock him not. [*Exit First Player.*]
My good friends, I'll leave you till night : you
are welcome to Elsinore.
    Ros. Good my lord !
    Ham. Ay, so, God be wi' ye ; [*Exeunt
Rosencrantz and Guildenstern.*] Now I am
alone.
O, what a rogue and peasant slave am I !
Is it not monstrous that this player here,
But in a fiction, in a dream of passion,
Could force his soul so to his own conceit
That from her working all his visage wann'd,
Tears in his eyes, distraction in's aspect, 581
A broken voice, and his whole function suiting
With forms to his conceit ? and all for noth-
    ing !
For Hecuba !
What's Hecuba to him, or he to Hecuba,
That he should weep for her ? What would he
    do,
Had he the motive and the cue for passion
That I have ? He would drown the stage with
    tears
And cleave the general ear with horrid speech,
Make mad the guilty and appal the free, 590
Confound the ignorant, and amaze indeed
The very faculties of eyes and ears.
Yet I,
A dull and muddy-mettled rascal, peak,
Like John-a-dreams, unpregnant of my cause,
And can say nothing ; no, not for a king,
Upon whose property and most dear life
A damn'd defeat was made. Am I a coward ?
Who calls me villain ? breaks my pate across ?

Plucks off my beard, and blows it in my face ?
Tweaks me by the nose ? gives me the lie i' the
   throat,   600
As deep as to the lungs ? who does me this ?
   Ha !
'Swounds, I should take it : for it cannot be
But I am pigeon-liver'd and lack gall
To make oppression bitter, or ere this
I should have fatted all the region kites
With this slave's offal : bloody, bawdy villain !
Remorseless, treacherous, lecherous, kindless
   villain !
O, vengeance !   610
Why, what an ass am I ! This is most brave,
That I, the son of a dear father murder'd,
Prompted to my revenge by heaven and hell,
Must, like a whore, unpack my heart with
   words,
And fall a-cursing, like a very drab,
A scullion !
Fie upon't ! foh ! About, my brain ! I have
   heard
That guilty creatures sitting at a play
Have by the very cunning of the scene
Been struck so to the soul that presently   620
They have proclaim'd their malefactions ;
For murder, though it have no tongue, will
   speak
With most miraculous organ. I'll have these
   players
Play something like the murder of my father
Before mine uncle : I'll observe his looks ;
I'll tent him to the quick : if he but blench,
I know my course. The spirit that I have seen
May be the devil : and the devil hath power
To assume a pleasing shape ; yea, and perhaps   630
As he is very potent with such spirits,
Abuses me to damn me : I'll have grounds
More relative than this : the play 's the thing
Wherein I'll catch the conscience of the king.
                          [*Exit.*

ACT III.

Scene I. *A room in the castle.*

Enter King, Queen, Polonius, Ophelia,
   Rosencrantz, *and* Guildenstern.

King. And can you, by no drift of circum-
   stance,
Get from him why he puts on this confusion,
Grating so harshly all his days of quiet
With turbulent and dangerous lunacy ?
  Ros. He does confess he feels himself dis-
   tracted ;
But from what cause he will by no means
   speak.
  Guil. Nor do we find him forward to be
   sounded,
But, with a crafty madness, keeps aloof,
When we would bring him on to some confes-
   sion
Of his true state.
  Queen.   Did he receive you well ?   10
  Ros. Most like a gentleman.
  Guil. But with much forcing of his dispo-
   sition.
  Ros. Niggard of question ; but, of our de-
   mands,
Most free in his reply.

  Queen.   Did you assay him
To any pastime ?
  Ros. Madam, it so fell out, that certain
   players
We o'er-raught on the way : of these we told
   him ;
And there did seem in him a kind of joy
To hear of it : they are about the court,
And, as I think, they have already order   20
This night to play before him.
  Pol.   'Tis most true :
And he beseech'd me to entreat your majesties
To hear and see the matter.
  King. With all my heart ; and it doth much
   content me
To hear him so inclined.
Good gentlemen, give him a further edge,
And drive his purpose on to these delights.
  Ros. We shall, my lord.
         [*Exeunt Rosencrantz and Guildenstern.*
  King.   Sweet Gertrude, leave us too ;
For we have closely sent for Hamlet hither,
That he, as 'twere by accident, may here   30
Affront Ophelia :
Her father and myself, lawful espials,
Will so bestow ourselves that, seeing, unseen,
We may of their encounter frankly judge,
And gather by him, as he is behaved,
If 't be the affliction of his love or no
That thus he suffers for.
  Queen.   I shall obey you.
And for your part, Ophelia, I do wish
That your good beauties be the happy cause
Of Hamlet's wildness : so shall I hope your
   virtues   40
Will bring him to his wonted way again,
To both your honors.
  Oph. Madam, I wish it may. [*Exit Queen.*
  Pol. Ophelia, walk you here. Gracious, so
   please you,
We will bestow ourselves. [*To Ophelia*] Read
   on this book ;
That show of such an exercise may color
Your loneliness. We are oft to blame in this,—
'Tis too much proved—that with devotion's
   visage
And pious action we do sugar o'er
The devil himself.
  King. [*Aside*] O, 'tis too true !
How smart a lash that speech doth give my
   conscience !   50
The harlot's cheek, beautied with plastering
   art,
Is not more ugly to the thing that helps it
Than is my deed to my most painted word :
O heavy burthen !
  Pol. I hear him coming : let's withdraw,
   my lord.   [*Exeunt King and Polonius.*

Enter Hamlet.

  Ham. To be, or not to be : that is the ques-
   tion :
Whether 'tis nobler in the mind to suffer
The slings and arrows of outrageous fortune,
Or to take arms against a sea of troubles,
And by opposing end them ? To die : to sleep ;
No more ; and by a sleep to say we end   61
The heart-ache and the thousand natural
   shocks
That flesh is heir to, 'tis a consummation
Devoutly to be wish'd. To die, to sleep ;

To sleep : perchance to dream : ay, there's the
    rub ;
For in that sleep of death what dreams may
    come
When we have shuffled off this mortal coil,
Must give us pause : there's the respect
That makes calamity of so long life ;
For who would bear the whips and scorns of
    time,   70
The oppressor's wrong, the proud man's con-
    tumely,
The pangs of despised love, the law's delay,
The insolence of office and the spurns
That patient merit of the unworthy takes,
When he himself might his quietus make
With a bare bodkin ? who would fardels bear,
To grunt and sweat under a weary life,
But that the dread of something after death,
The undiscover'd country from whose bourn
No traveller returns, puzzles the will   80
And makes us rather bear those ills we have
Than fly to others that we know not of ?
Thus conscience does make cowards of us all ;
And thus the native hue of resolution
Is sicklied o'er with the pale cast of thought,
And enterprises of great pith and moment
With this regard their currents turn awry,
And lose the name of action.—Soft you now !
The fair Ophelia ! Nymph, in thy orisons
Be all my sins remember'd.
    Oph.   Good my lord,   90
How does your honor for this many a day ?
    Ham.   I humbly thank you ; well, well, well.
    Oph.   My lord, I have remembrances of
    yours,
That I have longed long to re-deliver ;
I pray you, now receive them.
    Ham.   No, not I ;
I never gave you aught.
    Oph.   My honor'd lord, you know right
    well you did ;
And, with them, words of so sweet breath com-
    posed
As made the things more rich : their perfume
    lost,
Take these again ; for to the noble mind   100
Rich gifts wax poor when givers prove unkind.
There, my lord.
    Ham.   Ha, ha ! are you honest ?
    Oph.   My lord ?
    Ham.   Are you fair ?
    Oph.   What means your lordship ?
    Ham.   That if you be honest and fair, your
honesty should admit no discourse to your
beauty.
    Oph.   Could beauty, my lord, have better
commerce than with honesty ?   110
    Ham.   Ay, truly ; for the power of beauty
will sooner transform honesty from what it is
to a bawd than the force of honesty can translate beauty into his likeness : this was sometime a paradox, but now the time gives it
proof. I did love you once.
    Oph.   Indeed, my lord, you made me be-
lieve so.
    Ham.   You should not have believed me ;
for virtue cannot so inoculate our old stock
but we shall relish of it : I loved you not.   120
    Oph.   I was the more deceived.
    Ham.   Get thee to a nunnery : why wouldst
thou be a breeder of sinners ? I am myself indifferent honest ; but yet I could accuse me of

such things that it were better my mother had
not borne me : I am very proud, revengeful,
ambitious, with more offences at my beck than
I have thoughts to put them in, imagination to
give them shape, or time to act them in. What
should such fellows as I do crawling between
earth and heaven ? We are arrant knaves, all ;
believe none of us. Go thy ways to a nunnery.
Where's your father ?
    Oph.   At home, my lord.
    Ham.   Let the doors be shut upon him, that
he may play the fool no where but in's own
house. Farewell.
    Oph.   O, help him, you sweet heavens !
    Ham.   If thou dost marry, I'll give thee this
plague for thy dowry : be thou as chaste as
ice, as pure as snow, thou shalt not escape
calumny. Get thee to a nunnery, go : farewell.
Or, if thou wilt needs marry, marry a fool ;
for wise men know well enough what monsters
you make of them. To a nunnery, go, and
quickly too. Farewell.
    Oph.   O heavenly powers, restore him !
    Ham.   I have heard of your paintings too,
well enough ; God has given you one face, and
you make yourselves another : you jig, you
amble, and you lisp, and nick-name God's
creatures, and make your wantonness your ignorance. Go to, I'll no more on't ; it hath
made me mad. I say, we will have no more
marriages : those that are married already, all
but one, shall live ; the rest shall keep as they
are. To a nunnery, go.   [*Exit.*
    Oph.   O, what a noble mind is here o'er-
    thrown !
The courtier's, soldier's, scholar's, eye, tongue,
    sword ;
The expectancy and rose of the fair state,   160
The glass of fashion and the mould of form,
The observed of all observers, quite, quite
    down !
And I, of ladies most deject and wretched,
That suck'd the honey of his music vows,
Now see that noble and most sovereign reason,
Like sweet bells jangled, out of tune and
    harsh ;
That unmatch'd form and feature of blown
    youth
Blasted with ecstasy : O, woe is me,
To have seen what I have seen, see what I see !

    Re-enter KING *and* POLONIUS.

    King.   Love ! his affections do not that way
    tend ;   170
Nor what he spake, though it lack'd form a
    little,
Was not like madness. There's something in
    his soul,
O'er which his melancholy sits on brood ;
And I do doubt the hatch and the disclose
Will be some danger : which for to prevent,
I have in quick determination
Thus set it down : he shall with speed to Eng-
    land,
For the demand of our neglected tribute :
Haply the seas and countries different
With variable objects shall expel   180
This something-settled matter in his heart,
Whereon his brains still beating puts him thus
From fashion of himself. What think you
    on't ?
    Pol.   It shall do well : but yet do I believe

The origin and commencement of his grief
Sprung from neglected love. How now, Ophe-
　　lia !
You need not tell us what Lord Hamlet said ;
We heard it all. My lord, do as you please ;
But, if you hold it fit, after the play　　　189
Let his queen mother all alone entreat him
To show his grief : let her be round with him ;
And I'll be placed, so please you, in the ear
Of all their conference. If she find him not,
To England send him, or confine him where
Your wisdom best shall think.

King.　　　　　　　　It shall be so :
Madness in great ones must not unwatch'd go.
　　　　　　　　　　　　　　　　[Exeunt.

SCENE II.　*A hall in the castle.*

Enter HAMLET *and* Players.

Ham.　Speak the speech, I pray you, as I
pronounced it to you, trippingly on the
tongue : but if you mouth it, as many of your
players do, I had as lief the town-crier spoke
my lines. Nor do not saw the air too much
with your hand, thus, but use all gently ; for
in the very torrent, tempest, and, as I may say,
the whirlwind of passion, you must acquire
and beget a temperance that may give it
smoothness. O, it offends me to the soul to
hear a robustious periwig-pated fellow tear a
passion to tatters, to very rags, to split the ears
of the groundlings, who for the most part are
capable of nothing but inexplicable dumb-
shows and noise : I would have such a fellow
whipped for o'erdoing Termagant ; it out-
herods Herod : pray you, avoid it.

First Play.　I warrant your honor.

Ham.　Be not too tame neither, but let your
own discretion be your tutor : suit the action
to the word, the word to the action ; with this
special observance, that you o'erstep not the
modesty of nature : for any thing so overdone
is from the purpose of playing, whose end,
both at the first and now, was and is, to hold,
as 'twere, the mirror up to nature ; to show
virtue her own feature, scorn her own image,
and the very age and body of the time his form
and pressure. Now this overdone, or come
tardy off, though it make the unskilful laugh,
cannot but make the judicious grieve ; the censure of the which one must in your allowance
o'erweigh a whole theatre of others. O, there
be players that I have seen play, and heard
others praise, and that highly, not to speak it
profanely, that, neither having the accent of
Christians nor the gait of Christian, pagan, nor
man, have so strutted and bellowed that I have
thought some of nature's journeymen had
made men and not made them well, they imitated humanity so abominably.

First Play.　I hope we have reformed that
indifferently with us, sir.　　　　　41

Ham.　O, reform it altogether. And let
those that play your clowns speak no more
than is set down for them ; for there be of
them that will themselves laugh, to set on some
quantity of barren spectators to laugh too ;
though, in the mean time, some necessary question of the play be then to be considered :
that's villanous, and shows a most pitiful ambition in the fool that uses it. Go, make you
ready.　　　　　　　　　　　*[Exeunt Players.*

Enter POLONIUS, ROSENCRANTZ, *and* GUIL-
DENSTERN.

How now, my lord ! will the king hear this
piece of work ?

Pol.　And the queen too, and that presently.

Ham.　Bid the players make haste. *[Exit
Polonius.]* Will you two help to hasten them ?

Ros. }
Guil. }　We will, my lord.

　　　　[Exeunt Rosencrantz and Guildenstern.
Ham.　What ho ! Horatio !

Enter HORATIO.

Hor.　Here, sweet lord, at your service.

Ham.　Horatio, thou art e'en as just a man
As e'er my conversation coped withal.　　60

Hor.　O, my dear lord,—

Ham.　　　　　　Nay, do not think I flatter ;
For what advancement may I hope from thee
That no revenue hast but thy good spirits,
To feed and clothe thee ? Why should the poor
　　be flatter'd ?
No, let the candied tongue lick absurd pomp,
And crook the pregnant hinges of the knee
Where thrift may follow fawning. Dost thou
　　hear ?
Since my dear soul was mistress of her choice
And could of men distinguish, her election　69
Hath seal'd thee for herself ; for thou hast
　　been
As one, in suffering all, that suffers nothing,
A man that fortune's buffets and rewards
Hast ta'en with equal thanks : and blest are
　　those
Whose blood and judgment are so well com-
　　mingled,
That they are not a pipe for fortune's finger
To sound what stop she please. Give me that
　　man
That is not passion's slave, and I will wear him
In my heart's core, ay, in my heart of heart,
As I do thee.—Something too much of this.—
There is a play to-night before the king ;　80
One scene of it comes near the circumstance
Which I have told thee of my father's death :
I prithee, when thou seest that act afoot,
Even with the very comment of thy soul
Observe mine uncle : if his occulted guilt
Do not itself unkennel in one speech,
It is a damned ghost that we have seen,
And my imaginations are as foul
As Vulcan's stithy. Give him heedful note ;
For I mine eyes will rivet to his face,　　90
And after we will both our judgments join
In censure of his seeming.

Hor.　　　　　　Well, my lord :
If he steal aught the whilst this play is playing,
And 'scape detecting, I will pay the theft.

Ham.　They are coming to the play ; I must
　　be idle :
Get you a place.

Danish march. A flourish. Enter KING,
QUEEN, POLONIUS, OPHELIA, ROSENCRANTZ,
GUILDENSTERN, *and others.*

King.　How fares our cousin Hamlet ?

Ham.　Excellent, i' faith ; of the chame-
leon's dish : I eat the air, promise-crammed :
you cannot feed capons so.　　　　100

King.　I have nothing with this answer,
Hamlet ; these words are not mine.

Ham. No, nor mine now. [*To Polonius*]
My lord, you played once i' the university, you
say ?

Pol. That did I, my lord ; and was accounted a good actor.

Ham. What did you enact ?

Pol. I did enact Julius Cæsar : I was killed
i' the Capitol ; Brutus killed me.   110

Ham. It was a brute part of him to kill so
capital a calf there. Be the players ready ?

Ros. Ay, my lord ; they stay upon your patience.

Queen. Come hither, my dear Hamlet, sit
by me.

Ham. No, good mother, here's metal more
attractive.

Pol. [*To the King*] O, ho ! do you mark
that ?

Ham. Lady, shall I lie in your lap ?
          [*Lying down at Ophelia's feet.*

Oph. No, my lord.   120

Ham. I mean, my head upon your lap ?

Oph. Ay, my lord.

Ham. Do you think I meant country matters ?

Oph. I think nothing, my lord.

Ham. That's a fair thought to lie between
maids' legs.

Oph. What is, my lord ?

Ham. Nothing.

Oph. You are merry, my lord.

Ham. Who, I ?

Oph. Ay, my lord.   130

Ham. O God, your only jig-maker. What
should a man do but be merry ? for, look you,
how cheerfully my mother looks, and my father died within these two hours.

Oph. Nay, 'tis twice two months, my lord.

Ham. So long ? Nay then, let the devil
wear black, for I'll have a suit of sables. O
heavens ! die two months ago, and not forgotten yet ? Then there's hope a great man's
memory may outlive his life half a year : but,
by'r lady, he must build churches, then ; or
else shall he suffer not thinking on, with the
hobby-horse, whose epitaph is ' For, O, for, O,
the hobby-horse is forgot.'

Hautboys play. The dumb-show enters.

Enter a King *and a* Queen *very lovingly ; the*
Queen *embracing him, and he her. She*
kneels, and makes show of protestation unto
him. He takes her up, and declines his head
upon her neck : lays him down upon a bank
of flowers : she, seeing him asleep, leaves
him. Anon comes in a fellow, takes off his
crown, kisses it, and pours poison in the
King's *ears, and exit. The* Queen *returns ;*
finds the King *dead, and makes passionate*
action. The Poisoner, *with some two or*
three Mutes, *comes in again, seeming to la-*
ment with her. The dead body is carried
away. The Poisoner *wooes the* Queen *with*
gifts : she seems loath and unwilling awhile,
but in the end accepts his love. [*Exeunt.*

Oph. What means this, my lord ?

Ham. Marry, this is miching mallecho ; it
means mischief.

Oph. Belike this show imports the argument of the play.   150

Enter Prologue.

Ham. We shall know by this fellow : the
players cannot keep counsel ; they'll tell all.

Oph. Will he tell us what this show meant ?

Ham. Ay, or any show that you'll show
him : be not you ashamed to show, he'll not
shame to tell you what it means.

Oph. You are naught, you are naught : I'll
mark the play.

Pro. For us, and for our tragedy,
     Here stooping to your clemency,   160
     We beg your hearing patiently. [*Exit.*

Ham. Is this a prologue, or the posy of a
ring ?

Oph. 'Tis brief, my lord.

Ham. As woman's love.

Enter two Players, King *and* Queen.

P. King. Full thirty times hath Phœbus'
          cart gone round
Neptune's salt wash and Tellus' orbed
          ground,
And thirty dozen moons with borrow'd
          sheen
About the world have times twelve thirties
          been,
Since love our hearts and Hymen did our
          hands
Unite commutual in most sacred bands. 170

P. Queen. So many journeys may the
          sun and moon
Make us again count o'er ere love be done !
But, woe is me, you are so sick of late,
So far from cheer and from your former
          state,
That I distrust you. Yet, though I distrust,
Discomfort you, my lord, it nothing must :
For women's fear and love holds quantity ;
In neither aught, or in extremity.
Now, what my love is, proof hath made you
          know ;
And as my love is sized, my fear is so : 180
Where love is great, the littlest doubts are
          fear ;
Where little fears grow great, great love
          grows there.

P. King. 'Faith, I must leave thee, love,
          and shortly too ;
My operant powers their functions leave to
          do :
And thou shalt live in this fair world be-
          hind,
Honor'd, beloved ; and haply one as kind
For husband shalt thou—

P. Queen.   O, confound the rest !
Such love must needs be treason in my
          breast :
In second husband let me be accurst !   189
None wed the second but who kill'd the first.

Ham. [*Aside*] Wormwood, wormwood.

P. Queen. The instances that second
          marriage move
Are base respects of thrift, but none of
          love :
A second time I kill my husband dead,
When second husband kisses me in bed.

P. King. I do believe you think what
          now you speak ;
But what we do determine oft we break.
Purpose is but the slave to memory,
Of violent birth, but poor validity ;
Which now, like fruit unripe, sticks on the
          tree ;   200

But fall, unshaken, when they mellow be.
Most necessary 'tis that we forget
To pay ourselves what to ourselves is debt :
What to ourselves in passion we propose,
The passion ending, doth the purpose lose.
The violence of either grief or joy
Their own enactures with themselves destroy :
Where joy most revels, grief doth most lament ;
Grief joys, joy grieves, on slender accident.
This world is not for aye, nor 'tis not strange
That even our loves should with our fortunes change ;
For 'tis a question left us yet to prove,
Whether love lead fortune, or else fortune love.
The great man down, you mark his favorite flies ;
The poor advanced makes friends of enemies.
And hitherto doth love on fortune tend ;
For who not needs shall never lack a friend,
And who in want a hollow friend doth try,
Directly seasons him his enemy.
But, orderly to end where I begun,　　220
Our wills and fates do so contrary run
That our devices still are overthrown ;
Our thoughts are ours, their ends none of our own :
So think thou wilt no second husband wed ;
But die thy thoughts when thy first lord is dead.
　P. Queen. Nor earth to me give food, nor heaven light !
Sport and repose lock from me day and night !
To desperation turn my trust and hope !
An anchor's cheer in prison be my scope !
Each opposite that blanks the face of joy　230
Meet what I would have well and it destroy !
Both here and hence pursue me lasting strife,
If, once a widow, ever I be wife !
　Ham. If she should break it now !
　P. King. 'Tis deeply sworn. Sweet, leave me here awhile ;
My spirits grow dull, and fain I would beguile
The tedious day with sleep.　　　[*Sleeps.*
　P. Queen.　　　　　Sleep rock thy brain ;
And never come mischance between us twain !　　　　　　　　[*Exit.*
　Ham. Madam, how like you this play ? 239
　Queen. The lady protests too much, methinks.
　Ham. O, but she'll keep her word.
　King. Have you heard the argument ? Is there no offence in 't ?
　Ham. No, no, they do but jest, poison in jest ; no offence i' the world.
　King. What do you call the play ?
　Ham. The Mouse-trap. Marry, how ? Tropically. This play is the image of a murder done in Vienna : Gonzago is the duke's name ; his wife, Baptista : you shall see anon ; 'tis a knavish piece of work : but what o' that ? your majesty and we that have free souls, it touches us not : let the galled jade wince, our withers are unwrung.

　　　　　Enter LUCIANUS.

This is one Lucianus, nephew to the king.
　Oph. You are as good as a chorus, my lord.
　Ham. I could interpret between you and your love, if I could see the puppets dallying.
　Oph. You are keen, my lord, you are keen.
　Ham. It would cost you a groaning to take off my edge.　　　　　　　260
　Oph. Still better, and worse.
　Ham. So you must take your husbands. Begin, murderer ; pox, leave thy damnable faces, and begin. Come : ' the croaking raven doth bellow for revenge.'
　Luc. Thoughts black, hands apt, drugs fit, and time agreeing ;
Confederate season, else no creature seeing ;
Thou mixture rank, of midnight weeds collected,
With Hecate's ban thrice blasted, thrice infected,
Thy natural magic and dire property,　270
On wholesome life usurp immediately.
　　[*Pours the poison into the sleeper's ears.*
　Ham. He poisons him i' the garden for's estate. His name's Gonzago : the story is extant, and writ in choice Italian : you shall see anon how the murderer gets the love of Gonzago's wife.
　Oph. The king rises.
　Ham. What, frighted with false fire !
　Queen. How fares my lord ?
　Pol. Give o'er the play.
　King. Give me some light : away !　280
　All. Lights, lights, lights !
　　[*Exeunt all but Hamlet and Horatio.*
　Ham. Why, let the stricken deer go weep,
　　　The hart ungalled play ;
　　For some must watch, while some must sleep :
　　　So runs the world away.
Would not this, sir, and a forest of feathers—
if the rest of my fortunes turn Turk with me—
with two Provincial roses on my razed shoes,
get me a fellowship in a cry of players, sir ?
　Hor. Half a share.　　　　　290
　Ham. A whole one, I.
　　For thou dost know, O Damon dear,
　　　This realm dismantled was
　　Of Jove himself ; and now reigns here
　　　A very, very—pajock.
　Hor. You might have rhymed.
　Ham. O good Horatio, I'll take the ghost's word for a thousand pound. Didst perceive ?
　Hor. Very well, my lord.
　Ham. Upon the talk of the poisoning ? 300
　Hor. I did very well note him.
　Ham. Ah, ha ! Come, some music ! come, the recorders !
　　For if the king like not the comedy,
　　Why then, belike, he likes it not, perdy.
Come, some music !

　Re-enter ROSENCRANTZ *and* GUILDENSTERN.

　Guil. Good my lord, vouchsafe me a word with you.
　Ham. Sir, a whole history.
　Guil. The king, sir,—　　　　310
　Ham. Ay, sir, what of him ?
　Guil. Is in his retirement marvellous distempered.
　Ham. With drink, sir ?
　Guil. No, my lord, rather with choler.

Ham. Your wisdom should show itself more richer to signify this to his doctor ; for, for me to put him to his purgation would perhaps plunge him into far more choler. 319

Guil. Good my lord, put your discourse into some frame and start not so wildly from my affair.

Ham. I am tame, sir : pronounce.

Guil. The queen, your mother, in most great affliction of spirit, hath sent me to you.

Ham. You are welcome.

Guil. Nay, good my lord, this courtesy is not of the right breed. If it shall please you to make me a wholesome answer, I will do your mother's commandment : if not, your pardon and my return shall be the end of my business.

Ham. Sir, I cannot. 331

Guil. What, my lord ?

Ham. Make you a wholesome answer ; my wit's diseased : but, sir, such answer as I can make, you shall command ; or, rather, as you say, my mother : therefore no more, but to the matter : my mother, you say,—

Ros. Then thus she says ; your behavior hath struck her into amazement and admiration. 339

Ham. O wonderful son, that can so astonish a mother ! But is there no sequel at the heels of this mother's admiration ? Impart.

Ros. She desires to speak with you in her closet, ere you go to bed.

Ham. We shall obey, were she ten times our mother. Have you any further trade with us ?

Ros. My lord, you once did love me.

Ham. So I do still, by these pickers and stealers. 349

Ros. Good my lord, what is your cause of distemper ? you do, surely, bar the door upon your own liberty, if you deny your griefs to your friend.

Ham. Sir, I lack advancement.

Ros. How can that be, when you have the voice of the king himself for your succession in Denmark ?

Ham. Ay, but sir, ' While the grass grows,' —the proverb is something musty. 359

Re-enter Players *with recorders.*

O, the recorders ! let me see one. To withdraw with you :—why do you go about to recover the wind of me, as if you would drive me into a toil ?

Guil. O, my lord, if my duty be too bold, my love is too unmannerly.

Ham. I do not well understand that. Will you play upon this pipe ?

Guil. My lord, I cannot.

Ham. I pray you.

Guil. Believe me, I cannot.

Ham. I do beseech you. 370

Guil. I know no touch of it, my lord.

Ham. 'Tis as easy as lying : govern these ventages with your fingers and thumb, give it breath with your mouth, and it will discourse most eloquent music. Look you, these are the stops.

Guil. But these cannot I command to any utterance of harmony ; I have not the skill.

Ham. Why, look you now, how unworthy a thing you make of me ! You would play upon me ; you would seem to know my stops ; you would pluck out the heart of my mystery ; you would sound me from my lowest note to the top of my compass : and there is much music, excellent voice, in this little organ ; yet cannot you make it speak. 'Sblood, do you think I am easier to be played on than a pipe ? Call me what instrument you will, though you can fret me, yet you cannot play upon me.

Enter POLONIUS.

God bless you, sir ! 390

Pol. My lord, the queen would speak with you, and presently.

Ham. Do you see yonder cloud that's almost in shape of a camel ?

Pol. By the mass, and 'tis like a camel, indeed.

Ham. Methinks it is like a weasel.

Pol. It is backed like a weasel.

Ham. Or like a whale ?

Pol. Very like a whale. 399

Ham. Then I will come to my mother by and by. They fool me to the top of my bent. I will come by and by.

Pol. I will say so.

Ham. By and by is easily said. [*Exit Polonius.*] Leave me, friends.

[*Exeunt all but Hamlet.*

'Tis now the very witching time of night, When churchyards yawn and hell itself breathes out

Contagion to this world : now could I drink hot blood,

And do such bitter business as the day

Would quake to look on. Soft ! now to my mother. 410

O heart, lose not thy nature ; let not ever

The soul of Nero enter this firm bosom :

Let me be cruel, not unnatural :

I will speak daggers to her, but use none ;

My tongue and soul in this be hypocrites ;

How in my words soever she be shent,

To give them seals never, my soul, consent !

[*Exit.*

SCENE III. *A room in the castle.*

Enter KING, ROSENCRANTZ, *and* GUILDENSTERN.

King. I like him not, nor stands it safe with us

To let his madness range. Therefore prepare you ;

I your commission will forthwith dispatch,

And he to England shall along with you :

The terms of our estate may not endure

Hazard so dangerous as doth hourly grow

Out of his lunacies.

Guil. We will ourselves provide :

Most holy and religious fear it is

To keep those many many bodies safe

That live and feed upon your majesty. 10

Ros. The single and peculiar life is bound,

With all the strength and armor of the mind,

To keep itself from noyance ; but much more

That spirit upon whose weal depend and rest

The lives of many. The cease of majesty

Dies not alone ; but, like a gulf, doth draw

What's near it with it : it is a massy wheel,

Fix'd on the summit of the highest mount,

To whose huge spokes ten thousand lesser things

Are mortised and adjoin'd ; which, when it
    falls,   20
Each small annexment, petty consequence,
Attends the boisterous ruin. Never alone
Did the king sigh, but with a general groan.
   King. Arm you, I pray you, to this speedy
    voyage ;
For we will fetters put upon this fear,
Which now goes too free-footed.
   Ros. }
   Guil. }   We will haste us.
      [*Exeunt Rosencrantz and Guildenstern.*

          Enter POLONIUS.

   Pol. My lord, he's going to his mother's
    closet :
Behind the arras I'll convey myself,
To hear the process ; I'll warrant she'll tax
    him home :
And, as you said, and wisely was it said,   30
'Tis meet that some more audience than a
    mother,
Since nature makes them partial, should o'er-
    hear
The speech, of vantage. Fare you well, my
    liege :
I'll call upon you ere you go to bed,
And tell you what I know.
   King.   Thanks, dear my lord.
                      [*Exit Polonius.*
O, my offence is rank, it smells to heaven ;
It hath the primal eldest curse upon't,
A brother's murder. Pray can I not,
Though inclination be as sharp as will :   39
My stronger guilt defeats my strong intent ;
And, like a man to double business bound,
I stand in pause where I shall first begin,
And both neglect. What if this cursed hand
Were thicker than itself with brother's blood,
Is there not rain enough in the sweet heavens
To wash it white as snow ? Whereto serves
    mercy
But to confront the visage of offence ?
And what's in prayer but this two-fold force,
To be forestalled ere we come to fall,   49
Or pardon'd being down ? Then I'll look up ;
My fault is past. But, O, what form of prayer
Can serve my turn ? ' Forgive me my foul mur-
    der ' ?
That cannot be ; since I am still possess'd
Of those effects for which I did the murder,
My crown, mine own ambition and my queen.
May one be pardon'd and retain the offence ?
In the corrupted currents of this world
Offence's gilded hand may shove by justice,
And oft 'tis seen the wicked prize itself
Buys out the law : but 'tis not so above ;   60
There is no shuffling, there the action lies
In his true nature ; and we ourselves com-
    pell'd,
Even to the teeth and forehead of our faults,
To give in evidence. What then ? what rests ?
Try what repentance can : what can it not ?
Yet what can it when one can not repent ?
O wretched state ! O bosom black as death !
O limed soul, that, struggling to be free,
Art more engaged ! Help, angels ! Make
    assay !
Bow, stubborn knees ; and, heart with strings
    of steel,   70
Be soft as sinews of the new-born babe !
All may be well.   [*Retires and kneels.*

           Enter HAMLET.

   Ham. Now might I do it pat, now he is
    praying ;
And now I'll do't. And so he goes to heaven ;
And so am I revenged. That would be
    scann'd :
A villain kills my father ; and for that,
I, his sole son, do this same villain send
To heaven.
O, this is hire and salary, not revenge.
He took my father grossly, full of bread ;   80
With all his crimes broad blown, as flush as
    May ;
And how his audit stands who knows save
    heaven ?
But in our circumstance and course of
    thought,
'Tis heavy with him : and am I then revenged,
To take him in the purging of his soul,
When he is fit and season'd for his passage ?
No !
Up, sword ; and know thou a more horrid
    hent :
When he is drunk asleep, or in his rage,
Or in the incestuous pleasure of his bed ;   90
At gaming, swearing, or about some act
That has no relish of salvation in't ;
Then trip him, that his heels may kick at
    heaven,
And that his soul may be as damn'd and black
As hell, whereto it goes. My mother stays :
This physic but prolongs thy sickly days.
                         [*Exit.*
   King. [*Rising*] My words fly up, my
    thoughts remain below :
Words without thoughts never to heaven go.
                         [*Exit.*

    SCENE IV. *The Queen's closet.*
    Enter QUEEN *and* POLONIUS.

   Pol. He will come straight. Look you lay
    home to him :
Tell him his pranks have been too broad to
    bear with,
And that your grace hath screen'd and stood
    between
Much heat and him. I'll sconce me even here.
Pray you, be round with him.
   Ham. [*Within*] Mother, mother, mother !
   Queen.   I'll warrant you,
Fear me not : withdraw, I hear him coming.
      [*Polonius hides behind the arras.*

           Enter HAMLET.

   Ham. Now, mother, what's the matter ?
   Queen. Hamlet, thou hast thy father much
    offended.
   Ham. Mother, you have my father much
    offended.   10
   Queen. Come, come, you answer with an
    idle tongue.
   Ham. Go, go, you question with a wicked
    tongue.
   Queen. Why, how now, Hamlet !
   Ham.   What's the matter now ?
   Queen. Have you forgot me ?
   Ham.   No, by the rood, not so :
You are the queen, your husband's brother's
    wife ;
And—would it were not so !—you are my
    mother.

Queen. Nay, then, I'll set those to you that
    can speak.
Ham. Come, come, and sit you down ; you
    shall not budge ;
You go not till I set you up a glass
Where you may see the inmost part of you. 20
Queen. What wilt thou do ? thou wilt not
    murder me ?
Help, help, ho !
Pol. [*Behind*] What, ho ! help, help, help !
Ham. [*Drawing*] How now ! a rat ? Dead,
    for a ducat, dead !
          [*Makes a pass through the arras.*
Pol. [*Behind*] O, I am slain !
                 [*Falls and dies.*
Queen. O me, what hast thou done ?
Ham.   Nay, I know not :
Is it the king ?
Queen. O, what a rash and bloody deed is
    this !
Ham. A bloody deed ! almost as bad, good
    mother,
As kill a king, and marry with his brother.
Queen. As kill a king !
Ham.   Ay, lady, 'twas my word. 30
[*Lifts up the arras and discovers Polonius.*
Thou wretched, rash, intruding fool, farewell !
I took thee for thy better : take thy fortune ;
Thou find'st to be too busy is some danger.
Leave wringing of your hands : peace ! sit you
    down,
And let me wring your heart ; for so I shall,
If it be made of penetrable stuff,
If damned custom have not brass'd it so
That it is proof and bulwark against sense.
Queen. What have I done, that thou darest
    wag thy tongue
In noise so rude against me ?
Ham.   Such an act 40
That blurs the grace and blush of modesty,
Calls virtue hypocrite, takes off the rose
From the fair forehead of an innocent love
And sets a blister there, makes marriage-vows
As false as dicers' oaths : O, such a deed
As from the body of contraction plucks
The very soul, and sweet religion makes
A rhapsody of words : heaven's face doth
    glow :
Yea, this solidity and compound mass,
With tristful visage, as against the doom,   50
Is thought-sick at the act.
Queen.   Ay me, what act,
That roars so loud, and thunders in the index ?
Ham. Look here, upon this picture, and on
    this,
The counterfeit presentment of two brothers.
See, what a grace was seated on this brow ;
Hyperion's curls ; the front of Jove himself ;
An eye like Mars, to threaten and command ;
A station like the herald Mercury
New-lighted on a heaven-kissing hill ;
A combination and a form indeed,   60
Where every god did seem to set his seal,
To give the world assurance of a man :
This was your husband. Look you now, what
    follows :
Here is your husband ; like a mildew'd ear,
Blasting his wholesome brother. Have you
    eyes ?
Could you on this fair mountain leave to feed,
And batten on this moor ? Ha ! have you eyes ?
You cannot call it love ; for at your age

The hey-day in the blood is tame, it's humble,
And waits upon the judgment : and what judg-
    ment   70
Would step from this to this ? Sense, sure, you
    have,
Else could you not have motion ; but sure, that
    sense
Is apoplex'd ; for madness would not err,
Nor sense to ecstasy was ne'er so thrall'd
But it reserved some quantity of choice,
To serve in such a difference. What devil was't
That thus hath cozen'd you at hoodman-blind ?
Eyes without feeling, feeling without sight,
Ears without hands or eyes, smelling sans all,
Or but a sickly part of one true sense   80
Could not so mope.
O shame ! where is thy blush ? Rebellious hell,
If thou canst mutine in a matron's bones,
To flaming youth let virtue be as wax,
And melt in her own fire : proclaim no shame
When the compulsive ardor gives the charge,
Since frost itself as actively doth burn
And reason panders will.
Queen.   O Hamlet, speak no more :
Thou turn'st mine eyes into my very soul ;
And there I see such black and grained spots
As will not leave their tinct.   91
Ham.   Nay, but to live
In the rank sweat of an enseamed bed,
Stew'd in corruption, honeying and making
    love
Over the nasty sty,—
Queen.   O, speak to me no more ;
These words, like daggers, enter in mine ears ;
No more, sweet Hamlet !
Ham.   A murderer and a villain ;
A slave that is not twentieth part the tithe
Of your precedent lord ; a vice of kings ;
A cutpurse of the empire and the rule,
That from a shelf the precious diadem stole,
And put it in his pocket !   101
Queen.   No more !
Ham. A king of shreds and patches,—

Enter Ghost.

Save me, and hover o'er me with your wings,
You heavenly guards ! What would your gra-
    cious figure ?
Queen. Alas, he's mad !
Ham. Do you not come your tardy son to
    chide,
That, lapsed in time and passion, lets go by
The important acting of your dread com-
    mand ?
O, say !
Ghost. Do not forget : this visitation   110
Is but to whet thy almost blunted purpose.
But, look, amazement on thy mother sits :
O, step between her and her fighting soul :
Conceit in weakest bodies strongest works :
Speak to her, Hamlet.
Ham.   How is it with you, lady ?
Queen. Alas, how is't with you,
That you do bend your eye on vacancy
And with the incorporal air do hold dis-
    course ?
Forth at your eyes your spirits wildly peep ;
And, as the sleeping soldiers in the alarm, 120
Your bedded hair, like life in excrements,
Starts up, and stands on end. O gentle son,
Upon the heat and flame of thy distemper
Sprinkle cool patience. Whereon do you look ?

Ham. On him, on him! Look you, how
    pale he glares!
His form and cause conjoin'd, preaching to
    stones,
Would make them capable. Do not look upon
    me;
Lest with this piteous action you convert
My stern effects: then what I have to do
Will want true color; tears perchance for
    blood.   130
    Queen. To whom do you speak this?
    Ham.   Do you see nothing there?
    Queen. Nothing at all; yet all that is I see.
    Ham. Nor did you nothing hear?
    Queen.   No, nothing but ourselves.
    Ham. Why, look you there! look, how it
    steals away!
My father, in his habit as he lived!
Look, where he goes, even now, out at the
    portal!   [*Exit Ghost*.
    Queen. This is the very coinage of your
    brain:
This bodiless creation ecstasy
Is very cunning in.
    Ham.   Ectasy!
My pulse, as yours, doth temperately keep
    time,   140
And makes as healthful music: it is not mad-
    ness
That I have utter'd: bring me to the test,
And I the matter will re-word; which madness
Would gambol from. Mother, for love of
    grace,
Lay not that flattering unction to your soul,
That not your trespass, but my madness
    speaks:
It will but skin and film the ulcerous place,
Whilst rank corruption, mining all within,
Infects unseen. Confess yourself to heaven;
Repent what's past; avoid what is to come;
And do not spread the compost on the weeds,
To make them ranker. Forgive me this my
    virtue;
For in the fatness of these pursy times
Virtue itself of vice must pardon beg,
Yea, curb and woo for leave to do him good.
    Queen. O Hamlet, thou hast cleft my heart
    in twain.
    Ham. O, throw away the worser part of it,
And live the purer with the other half.
Good night: but go not to mine uncle's bed;
Assume a virtue, if you have it not.   160
That monster, custom, who all sense doth eat,
Of habits devil, is angel yet in this,
That to the use of actions fair and good
He likewise gives a frock or livery,
That aptly is put on. Refrain to-night,
And that shall lend a kind of easiness
To the next abstinence: the next more easy;
For use almost can change the stamp of na-
    ture,
And either . . . . the devil, or throw him out
With wondrous potency. Once more, good
    night: 170
And when you are desirous to be bless'd,
I'll blessing beg of you. For this same lord,
                [*Pointing to Polonius*.
I do repent: but heaven hath pleased it so,
To punish me with this and this with me,
That I must be their scourge and minister.
I will bestow him, and will answer well
The death I gave him. So, again, good night.

I must be cruel, only to be kind:
Thus bad begins and worse remains behind.
One word more, good lady.
    Queen.   What shall I do? 180
    Ham. Not this, by no means, that I bid
    you do:
Let the bloat king tempt you again to bed;
Pinch wanton on your cheek; call you his
    mouse;
And let him, for a pair of reechy kisses,
Or paddling in your neck with his damn'd
    fingers,
Make you to ravel all this matter out,
That I essentially am not in madness,
But mad in craft. 'Twere good you let him
    know;
For who, that's but a queen, fair, sober, wise,
Would from a paddock, from a bat, a gib, 190
Such dear concernings hide? who would do
    so?
No, in despite of sense and secrecy,
Unpeg the basket on the house's top,
Let the birds fly, and, like the famous ape,
To try conclusions, in the basket creep,
And break your own neck down.
    Queen. Be thou assured, if words be made
    of breath,
And breath of life, I have no life to breathe
What thou hast said to me.
    Ham. I must to England; you know that?
    Queen.   Alack, 200
I had forgot: 'tis so concluded on.
    Ham. There's letters seal'd: and my two
    schoolfellows,
Whom I will trust as I will adders fang'd,
They bear the mandate; they must sweep my
    way,
And marshal me to knavery. Let it work;
For 'tis the sport to have the enginer
Hoist with his own petar: and 't shall go hard
But I will delve one yard below their mines,
And blow them at the moon: O, 'tis most
    sweet,
When in one line two crafts directly meet. 210
This man shall set me packing:
I'll lug the guts into the neighbor room.
Mother, good night. Indeed this counsellor
Is now most still, most secret and most grave,
Who was in life a foolish prating knave.
Come, sir, to draw toward an end with you.
Good night, mother.
             [*Exeunt severally; Hamlet dragging
                        in Polonius*.

ACT IV.

Scene I. *A room in the castle.*

Enter King, Queen, Rosencrantz, *and*
             Guildenstern.

    King. There's matter in these sighs, these
    profound heaves:
You must translate: 'tis fit we understand
    them.
Where is your son?
    Queen. Bestow this place on us a little
    while.
        [*Exeunt Rosencrantz and Guildenstern*.
Ah, my good lord, what have I seen to-night!
    King. What, Gertrude? How does Ham-
    let?

Queen. Mad as the sea and wind, when
both contend
Which is the mightier : in his lawless fit,
Behind the arras hearing something stir,
Whips out his rapier, cries, 'A rat, a rat!'
And, in this brainish apprehension, kills   11
The unseen good old man.
King.   O heavy deed !
It had been so with us, had we been there :
His liberty is full of threats to all ;
To you yourself, to us, to every one.
Alas, how shall this bloody deed be answer'd ?
It will be laid to us, whose providence
Should have kept short, restrain'd and out of
haunt,
This mad young man : but so much was our
love,
We would not understand what was most fit ;
But, like the owner of a foul disease,   21
To keep it from divulging, let it feed
Even on the pith of life. Where is he gone ?
Queen. To draw apart the body he hath
kill'd :
O'er whom his very madness, like some ore
Among a mineral of metals base,
Shows itself pure ; he weeps for what is done.
King. O Gertrude, come away !
The sun no sooner shall the mountains touch,
But we will ship him hence : and this vile
deed   30
We must, with all our majesty and skill,
Both countenance and excuse. Ho, Guilden-
stern !

Re-enter ROSENCRANTZ *and* GUILDENSTERN.

Friends both, go join you with some further
aid :
Hamlet in madness hath Polonius slain,
And from his mother's closet hath he dragg'd
him :
Go seek him out ; speak fair, and bring the
body
Into the chapel. I pray you, haste in this.
                    [*Exeunt Rosencrantz and Guildenstern.*
Come, Gertrude, we'll call up our wisest
friends ;
And let them know, both what we mean to do,
And what's untimely done   40
Whose whisper o'er the world's diameter,
As level as the cannon to his blank,
Transports his poison'd shot, may miss our
name,
And hit the woundless air. O, come away !
My soul is full of discord and dismay.
                    [*Exeunt.*

SCENE II.   *Another room in the castle.*
Enter HAMLET.

Ham. Safely stowed.
Ros. } [*Within*] Hamlet ! Lord Hamlet !
Guil. }
Ham. What noise ? who calls on Hamlet ?
O, here they come.

Enter ROSENCRANTZ *and* GUILDENSTERN.

Ros. What have you done, my lord, with
the dead body ?
Ham. Compounded it with dust, whereto
'tis kin.
Ros. Tell us where 'tis, that we may take
it thence
And bear it to the chapel.

Ham. Do not believe it.
Ros. Believe what ?   10
Ham. That I can keep your counsel and
not mine own. Besides, to be demanded of a
sponge ! what replication should be made by
the son of a king ?
Ros. Take you me for a sponge, my lord ?
Ham. Ay, sir, that soaks up the king's
countenance, his rewards, his authorities. But
such officers do the king best service in the
end : he keeps them, like an ape, in the corner
of his jaw ; first mouthed, to be last swallowed : when he needs what you have gleaned,
it is but squeezing you, and, sponge, you shall
be dry again.
Ros. I understand you not, my lord.
Ham. I am glad of it : a knavish speech
sleeps in a foolish ear.
Ros. My lord, you must tell us where the
body is, and go with us to the king.
Ham. The body is with the king, but the
king is not with the body. The king is a
thing—   30
Guil. A thing, my lord !
Ham. Of nothing : bring me to him. Hide
fox, and all after.   [*Exeunt.*

SCENE III.   *Another room in the castle.*

Enter KING, *attended.*

King. I have sent to seek him, and to find
the body.
How dangerous is it that this man goes loose !
Yet must not we put the strong law on him :
He's loved of the distracted multitude,
Who like not in their judgment, but their
eyes ;
And where 'tis so, the offender's scourge is
weigh'd,
But never the offence. To bear all smooth and
even,
This sudden sending him away must seem
Deliberate pause : diseases desperate grown
By desperate appliance are relieved,   10
Or not at all.

Enter ROSENCRANTZ.

                    How now ! what hath befall'n ?
Ros. Where the dead body is bestow'd, my
lord,
We cannot get from him.
King.   But where is he ?
Ros. Without, my lord ; guarded, to know
your pleasure.
King. Bring him before us.
Ros. Ho, Guildenstern ! bring in my lord.

Enter HAMLET *and* GUILDENSTERN.

King. Now, Hamlet, where's Polonius ?
Ham. At supper.
King. At supper ! where ?   19
Ham. Not where he eats, but where he is
eaten : a certain convocation of politic worms
are e'en at him. Your worm is your only emperor for diet : we fat all creatures else to fat
us, and we fat ourselves for maggots : your
fat king and your lean beggar is but variable
service, two dishes, but to one table : that's the
end.
King. Alas, alas !
Ham. A man may fish with the worm that
hath eat of a king, and eat of the fish that
hath fed of that worm.   30

King. What dost you mean by this ?
Ham. Nothing but to show you how a king may go a progress through the guts of a beggar.
King. Where is Polonius ?
Ham. In heaven ; send hither to see : if your messenger find him not there, seek him i' the other place yourself. But indeed, if you find him not within this month, you shall nose him as you go up the stairs into the lobby.
King. Go seek him there.   40
                              [*To some Attendants.*
Ham. He will stay till ye come.
                              [*Exeunt Attendants.*
King. Hamlet, this deed, for thine especial
          safety,—
Which we do tender, as we dearly grieve
For that which thou hast done,—must send
          thee hence
With fiery quickness : therefore prepare thy-
          self ;
The bark is ready, and the wind at help,
The associates tend, and every thing is bent
For England.
Ham.   For England !
King.   Ay, Hamlet.
Ham.   Good.
King. So is it, if thou knew'st our purposes.
Ham. I see a cherub that sees them. But, come ; for England ! Farewell, dear mother.
King. Thy loving father, Hamlet.
Ham. My mother : father and mother is man and wife ; man and wife is one flesh ; and so, my mother. Come, for England !
                              [*Exit.*
King. Follow him at foot ; tempt him with
          speed aboard ;
Delay it not ; I'll have him hence to-night :
Away ! for every thing is seal'd and done
That else leans on the affair : pray you, make
          haste.
          [*Exeunt Rosencrantz and Guildenstern.*
And, England, if my love thou hold'st at
          aught—
As my great power thereof may give thee
          sense,
Since yet thy cicatrice looks raw and red
After the Danish sword, and thy free awe
Pays homage to us—thou mayst not coldly set
Our sovereign process ; which imports at full,
By letters congruing to that effect,
The present death of Hamlet. Do it, England ;
For like the hectic in my blood he rages,
And thou must cure me : till I know 'tis done,
Howe'er my haps, my joys were ne'er begun.
                              [*Exit.* 70

SCENE IV. *A plain in Denmark.*

Enter FORTINBRAS, *a* Captain, *and* Soldiers,
          marching.

For. Go, captain, from me greet the Dan-
          ish king ;
Tell him that, by his license, Fortinbras
Craves the conveyance of a promised march
Over his kingdom. You know the rendezvous.
If that his majesty would aught with us,
We shall express our duty in his eye ;
And let him know so.
Cap.   I will do't, my lord.
For. Go softly on.
                              [*Exeunt Fortinbras and Soldiers.*

Enter HAMLET, ROSENCRANTZ, GUILDEN-
          STERN, *and others.*

Ham. Good sir, whose powers are these ?
Cap. They are of Norway, sir.   10
Ham. How purposed, sir, I pray you ?
Cap. Against some part of Poland.
Ham. Who commands them, sir ?
Cap. The nephews to old Norway, Fortin-
          bras.
Ham. Goes it against the main of Poland,
          sir,
Or for some frontier ?
Cap. Truly to speak, and with no addition,
We go to gain a little patch of ground
That hath in it no profit but the name.
To pay five ducats, five, I would not farm it ;
Nor will it yield to Norway or the Pole   21
A ranker rate, should it be sold in fee.
Ham. Why, then the Polack never will de-
          fend it.
Cap. Yes, it is already garrison'd.
Ham. Two thousand souls and twenty
          thousand ducats
Will not debate the question of this straw :
This is the imposthume of much wealth and
          peace,
That inward breaks, and shows no cause with-
          out
Why the man dies. I humbly thank you, sir.
Cap. God be wi' you, sir.   [*Exit.*
Ros. Wil't please you go, my lord ?   30
Ham. I'll be with you straight. Go a little
          before.   [*Exeunt all except Hamlet.*
How all occasions do inform against me,
And spur my dull revenge ! What is a man,
If his chief good and market of his time
Be but to sleep and feed ? a beast, no more.
Sure, he that made us with such large dis-
          course,
Looking before and after, gave us not
That capability and god-like reason
To fust in us unused. Now, whether it be
Bestial oblivion, or some craven scruple   40
Of thinking too precisely on the event,
A thought which, quarter'd, hath but one part
          wisdom
And ever three parts coward, I do not know
Why yet I live to say ' This thing's to do ; '
Sith I have cause and will and strength and
          means
To do't. Examples gross as earth exhort me :
Witness this army of such mass and charge
Led by a delicate and tender prince,
Whose spirit with divine ambition puff'd
Makes mouths at the invisible event,   50
Exposing what is mortal and unsure
To all that fortune, death and danger dare,
Even for an egg-shell. Rightly to be great
Is not to stir without great argument,
But greatly to find quarrel in a straw
When honor's at the stake. How stand I then,
That have a father kill'd, a mother stain'd,
Excitements of my reason and my blood,
And let all sleep ? while, to my shame, I see
The imminent death of twenty thousand men,
That, for a fantasy and trick of fame,   61
Go to their graves like beds, fight for a plot
Whereon the numbers cannot try the cause,
Which is not tomb enough and continent
To hide the slain ? O, from this time forth,

My thoughts be bloody, or be nothing worth !
            [*Exit.*

SCENE V. *Elsinore. A room in the castle.*

Enter QUEEN, HORATIO, *and a* Gentleman.

Queen. I will not speak with her.
Gent. She is importunate, indeed distract :
Her mood will needs be pitied.
Queen.   What would she have ?
Gent. She speaks much of her father ; says
    she hears
There's tricks i' the world ; and hems, and
    beats her heart ;
Spurns enviously at straws ; speaks things in
    doubt,
That carry but half sense : her speech is noth-
    ing,
Yet the unshaped use of it doth move
The hearers to collection ; they aim at it,
And botch the words up fit to their own
    thoughts ;   10
Which, as her winks, and nods, and gestures
    yield them,
Indeed would make one think there might be
    thought,
Though nothing sure, yet much unhappily.
Hor. 'Twere good she were spoken with ;
    for she may strew
Dangerous conjectures in ill-breeding minds.
Queen. Let her come in.   [*Exit Horatio.*
To my sick soul, as sin's true nature is,
Each toy seems prologue to some great amiss :
So full of artless jealousy is guilt,
It spills itself in fearing to be spilt.   20

    Re-enter HORATIO, *with* OPHELIA.

Oph. Where is the beauteous majesty of
    Denmark ?
Queen. How now, Ophelia !
Oph. [*Sings*] How should I your true love
    know
       From another one ?
    By his cockle hat and staff,
       And his sandal shoon.
Queen. Alas, sweet lady, what imports this
    song ?
Oph. Say you ? nay, pray you, mark.
[*Sings*] He is dead and gone, lady,
       He is dead and gone ;   30
    At his head a grass-green turf,
       At his heels a stone.
Queen. Nay, but, Ophelia,—
Oph. Pray you, mark.
[*Sings*] White his shroud as the mountain
    snow,—

       Enter KING.

Queen. Alas, look here, my lord.
Oph. [*Sings*] Larded with sweet flowers ;
    Which bewept to the grave did go
       With true-love showers.
King. How do you, pretty lady ?   40
Oph. Well, God 'ild you ! They say the owl
was a baker's daughter. Lord, we know what
we are, but know not what we may be. God
be at your table !
King. Conceit upon her father.
Oph. Pray you, let's have no words of
this ; but when they ask you what it means,
say you this :
[*Sings*] To-morrow is Saint Valentine's day,

       All in the morning betime,
And I a maid at your window,   50
       To be your Valentine.
Then up he rose, and donn'd his
    clothes,
       And dupp'd the chamber-door ;
Let in the maid, that out a maid
       Never departed more.
King. Pretty Ophelia !
Oph. Indeed, la, without an oath, I'll make
an end on't :
[*Sings*] By Gis and by Saint Charity,
       Alack, and fie for shame !
Young men will do't, if they come to't ;
       By cock, they are to blame.   61
Quoth she, before you tumbled me,
       You promised me to wed.
So would I ha' done, by yonder sun,
       An thou hadst not come to my bed.
King. How long hath she been thus ?
Oph. I hope all will be well. We must be
patient : but I cannot choose but weep, to
think they should lay him i' the cold ground.
My brother shall know of it : and so I thank
you for your good counsel. Come, my coach !
Good night, ladies ; good night, sweet ladies ;
good night, good night.   [*Exit.*
King. Follow her close ; give her good
    watch,
I pray you.   [*Exit Horatio.*
O, this is the poison of deep grief ; it springs
All from her father's death. O Gertrude,
    Gertrude,
When sorrows come, they come not single
    spies,
But in battalions. First, her father slain :
Next, your son gone ; and he most violent
    author   80
Of his own just remove : the people muddied,
Thick and unwholesome in their thoughts and
    whispers,
For good Polonius' death ; and we have done
    but greenly,
In hugger-mugger to inter him : poor Ophelia
Divided from herself and her fair judgment,
Without the which we are pictures, or mere
    beasts :
Last, and as much containing as all these,
Her brother is in secret come from France ;
Feeds on his wonder, keeps himself in clouds,
And wants not buzzers to infect his ear   90
With pestilent speeches of his father's death ;
Wherein necessity, of matter beggar'd,
Will nothing stick our person to arraign
In ear and ear. O my dear Gertrude, this,
Like to a murdering-piece, in many places
Gives me superfluous death. [*A noise within.*
Queen.   Alack, what noise is this ?
King. Where are my Switzers ? Let them
    guard the door.

       Enter another Gentleman.

What is the matter ?
Gent.   Save yourself, my lord :
The ocean, overpeering of his list,
Eats not the flats with more impetuous haste
Than young Laertes, in a riotous head,   101
O'erbears your officers. The rabble call him
    lord ;
And, as the world were now but to begin,
Antiquity forgot, custom not known,
The ratifiers and props of every word,

They cry ' Choose we : Laertes shall be king : '
Caps, hands, and tongues, applaud it to the
    clouds :
' Laertes shall be king, Laertes king ! '
  Queen. How cheerfully on the false trail
    they cry !
O, this is counter, you false Danish dogs ! 110
  King. The doors are broke. [*Noise within.*

  Enter LAERTES, *armed ;* Danes *following.*

  Laer. Where is this king ? Sirs, stand you
    all without.
  Danes. No, let's come in.
  Laer.   I pray you, give me leave.
  Danes. We will, we will.
          [*They retire without the door.*
  Laer. I thank you : keep the door. O thou
    vile king,
Give me my father !
  Queen.   Calmly, good Laertes.
  Laer. That drop of blood that's calm pro-
    claims me bastard,
Cries cuckold to my father, brands the harlot
Even here, between the chaste unsmirched
    brow
Of my true mother.
  King.   What is the cause, Laertes,   120
That thy rebellion looks so giant-like ?
Let him go, Gertrude ; do not fear our person :
There's such divinity doth hedge a king,
That treason can but peep to what it would,
Acts little of his will. Tell me, Laertes,
Why thou art thus incensed. Let him go,
    Gertrude.
Speak, man.
  Laer. Where is my father ?
  King.   Dead.
  Queen.   But not by him.
  King. Let him demand his fill.
  Laer. How came he dead ? I'll not be jug-
    gled with :   130
To hell, allegiance ! vows, to the blackest
    devil !
Conscience and grace, to the profoundest pit !
I dare damnation. To this point I stand,
That both the worlds I give to negligence,
Let come what comes ; only I'll be revenged
Most thoroughly for my father.
  King.   Who shall stay you ?
  Laer. My will, not all the world :
And for my means, I'll husband them so well,
They shall go far with little.
  King.   Good Laertes,
If you desire to know the certainty   140
Of your dear father's death, is't writ in your
    revenge,
That, swoopstake, you will draw both friend
    and foe,
Winner and loser ?
  Laer. None but his enemies.
  King.   Will you know them then ?
  Laer. To his good friends thus wide I'll
    ope my arms ;
And like the kind life-rendering pelican,
Repast them with my blood.
  King.   Why, now you speak
Like a good child and a true gentleman.
That I am guiltless of your father's death,
And am most sensible in grief for it,   150
It shall as level to your judgment pierce
As day does to your eye.
  Danes. [*Within*] Let her come in.

  Laer. How now ! what noise is that ?

      Re-enter OPHELIA.

O heat, dry up my brains ! tears seven times
    salt,
Burn out the sense and virtue of mine eye !
By heaven, thy madness shall be paid by
    weight,
Till our scale turn the beam. O rose of May !
Dear maid, kind sister, sweet Ophelia !
O heavens ! is't possible, a young maid's wits
Should be as moral as an old man's life ?   160
Nature is fine in love, and where 'tis fine,
It sends some precious instance of itself
After the thing it loves.
  Oph. [*Sings*]
    They bore him barefaced on the bier ;
    Hey non nonny, nonny, hey nonny ;
    And in his grave rain'd many a tear :—
Fare you well, my dove !
  Laer. Hadst thou thy wits, and didst per-
    suade revenge,
It could not move thus.
  Oph. [*Sings*] You must sing a-down a-down,
    An you call him a-down-a.   171
O, how the wheel becomes it ! It is the false
steward, that stole his master's daughter.
  Laer. This nothing's more than matter.
  Oph. There's rosemary, that's for remem-
brance ; pray, love, remember : and there is
pansies, that's for thoughts.
  Laer. A document in madness, thoughts
and remembrance fitted.   179
  Oph. There's fennel for you, and colum-
bines : there's rue for you ; and here's some
for me : we may call it herb-grace o' Sundays :
O, you must wear your rue with a difference.
There's a daisy : I would give you some vio-
lets, but they withered all when my father
died : they say he made a good end,—
    [*Sings*] For bonny sweet Robin is all my
    joy.
  Laer. Thought and affliction, passion, hell
    itself,
She turns to favor and to prettiness.
  Oph. [*Sings*] And will he not come again ?
    And will he not come again ?
    No, no, he is dead :
    Go to thy death-bed :
    He never will come again.

    His beard was as white as snow,
    All flaxen was his poll :
    He is gone, he is gone,
    And we cast away moan :
    God ha' mercy on his soul !
And of all Christian souls, I pray God. God
    be wi' ye.   [*Exit.* 200
  Laer. Do you see this, O God ?
  King. Laertes, I must commune with your
    grief,
Or you deny me right. Go but apart,
Make choice of whom your wisest friends you
    will.
And they shall hear and judge 'twixt you and
    me :
If by direct or by collateral hand
They find us touch'd, we will our kingdom
    give,
Our crown, our life, and all that we call ours,
To you in satisfaction ; but if not,
Be you content to lend your patience to us,

And we shall jointly labor with your soul 211
To give it due content.
    Laer.   Let this be so;
His means of death, his obscure funeral—
No trophy, sword, nor hatchment o'er his
    bones,
No noble rite nor formal ostentation—
Cry to be heard, as 'twere from heaven to
    earth,
That I must call't in question.
    King.   So you shall;
And where the offence is let the great axe fall.
I pray you, go with me.   [*Exeunt.*

SCENE VI. *Another room in the castle.*

Enter HORATIO *and a* Servant.

    Hor. What are they that would speak with
    me?
    Serv. Sailors, sir: they say they have let-
    ters for you.
    Hor. Let them come in.   [*Exit Servant.*
I do not know from what part of the world
I should be greeted, if not from Lord Hamlet.

Enter Sailors.

    First Sail. God bless you, sir.
    Hor. Let him bless thee too.
    First Sail. He shall, sir, an't please him.
There's a letter for you, sir; it comes from the
ambassador that was bound for England; if
your name be Horatio, as I am let to know it
is.   11
    Hor. [*Reads*] 'Horatio, when thou shalt
have overlooked this, give these fellows some
means to the king: they have letters for him.
Ere we were two days old at sea, a pirate of
very warlike appointment gave us chase.
Finding ourselves too slow of sail, we put on a
compelled valor, and in the grapple I boarded
them: on the instant they got clear of our
ship; so I alone became their prisoner. They
have dealt with me like thieves of mercy: but
they knew what they did; I am to do a good
turn for them. Let the king have the letters
I have sent; and repair thou to me with as
much speed as thou wouldst fly death. I have
words to speak in thine ear will make thee
dumb; yet are they much too light for the
bore of the matter. These good fellows will
bring thee where I am. Rosencrantz and
Guildenstern hold their course for England:
of them I have much to tell thee. Farewell. 30
    'He that thou knowest thine, HAMLET.'
Come, I will make you way for these your
    letters;
And do't the speedier, that you may direct me
To him from whom you brought them.
                                      [*Exeunt.*

SCENE VII. *Another room in the castle.*

Enter KING *and* LAERTES.

    King. Now must your conscience my ac-
    quaintance seal,
And you must put me in your heart for friend,
Sith you have heard, and with a knowing ear,
That he which hath your noble father slain
Pursued my life.
    Laer.   It well appears: but tell me
Why you proceeded not against these feats,
So crimeful and so capital in nature,
As by your safety, wisdom, all things else,
You mainly were stirr'd up.
    King.   O, for two special reasons;
Which may to you, perhaps, seem much un-
    sinew'd,   10
But yet to me they are strong. The queen his
    mother
Lives almost by his looks; and for myself—
My virtue or my plague, be it either which—
She's so conjunctive to my life and soul,
That, as the star moves not but in his sphere,
I could not but by her. The other motive,
Why to a public count I might not go,
Is the great love the general gender bear him;
Who, dipping all his faults in their affection,
Would, like the spring that turneth wood to
    stone,
Convert his gyves to graces; so that my ar-
    rows,
Too slightly timber'd for so loud a wind,
Would have reverted to my bow again,
And not where I had aim'd them.
    Laer. And so have I a noble father lost;
A sister driven into desperate terms,
Whose worth, if praises may go back again,
Stood challenger on mount of all the age
For her perfections: but my revenge will
    come.
    King. Break not your sleeps for that: you
    must not think   30
That we are made of stuff so flat and dull
That we can let our beard be shook with
    danger
And think it pastime. You shortly shall hear
    more:
I loved your father, and we love ourself;
And that, I hope, will teach you to imagine—

Enter a Messenger.

How now! what news?
    Mess.   Letters, my lord, from Hamlet;
This to your majesty; this to the queen.
    King. From Hamlet! who brought them?
    Mess. Sailors, my lord, they say; I saw
    them not:
They were given me by Claudio; he received
    them   40
Of him that brought them.
    King.   Laertes, you shall hear them.
Leave us.   [*Exit Messenger.*
    [*Reads*] 'High and mighty, You shall know
I am set naked on your kingdom. To-morrow
shall I beg leave to see your kingly eyes: when
I shall, first asking your pardon thereunto, re-
count the occasion of my sudden and more
strange return.   'HAMLET.'
What should this mean? Are all the rest
    come back?   50
Or is it some abuse, and no such thing?
    Laer. Know you the hand?
    King. 'Tis Hamlet's character. 'Naked!'
And in a postscript here, he says 'alone.'
Can you advise me?
    Laer. I'm lost in it, my lord. But let him
    come;
It warms the very sickness in my heart,
That I shall live and tell him to his teeth,
'Thus didest thou.'
    King.   If it be so, Laertes—
As how should it be so? how otherwise?—
Will you be ruled by me?
    Laer.   Ay, my lord;   60
So you will not o'errule me to a peace.

King. To thine own peace. If he be now
    return'd,
As checking at his voyage, and that he means
No more to undertake it, I will work him
To an exploit, now ripe in my device,
Under the which he shall not choose but fall :
And for his death no wind of blame shall
    breathe,
But even his mother shall uncharge the prac-
    tice
And call it accident.
    Laer.   My lord, I will be ruled ;
The rather, if you could devise it so   70
That I might be the organ.
    King.   It falls right.
You have been talk'd of since your travel
    much,
And that in Hamlet's hearing, for a quality
Wherein, they say, you shine : your sum of
    parts
Did not together pluck such envy from him
As did that one, and that, in my regard,
Of the unworthiest siege.
    Laer.   What part is that, my lord ?
    King. A very riband in the cap of youth,
Yet needful too ; for youth no less becomes
The light and careless livery that it wears   80
Than settled age his sables and his weeds,
Importing health and graveness. Two months
    since,
Here was a gentleman of Normandy :—
I've seen myself, and served against, the
    French,
And they can well on horseback : but this gal-
    lant
Had witchcraft in't ; he grew unto his seat ;
And to such wondrous doing brought his
    horse,
As he had been incorpsed and demi-natured
With the brave beast : so far he topp'd my
    thought,
That I, in forgery of shapes and tricks,   90
Come short of what he did.
    Laer.   A Norman was't ?
    King. A Norman.
    Laer. Upon my life, Lamond.
    King.   The very same.
    Laer. I know him well : he is the brooch
    indeed
And gem of all the nation.
    King. He made confession of you,
And gave you such a masterly report
For art and exercise in your defence
And for your rapier most especially,
That he cried out, 'twould be a sight indeed,
If one could match you : the scrimers of their
    nation,   101
He swore, had had neither motion, guard, nor
    eye,
If you opposed them. Sir, this report of his
Did Hamlet so envenom with his envy
That he could nothing do but wish and beg
Your sudden coming o'er, to play with him.
Now, out of this,—
    Laer.   What out of this, my lord ?
    King. Laertes, was your father dear to
    you ?
Or are you like the painting of a sorrow,
A face without a heart ?
    Laer.   Why ask you this ?   110
    King. Not that I think you did not love
    your father ;

But that I know love is begun by time ;
And that I see, in passages of proof,
Time qualifies the spark and fire of it.
There lives within the very flame of love
A kind of wick or snuff that will abate it ;
And nothing is at a like goodness still ;
For goodness, growing to a plurisy,
Dies in his own too much : that we would do
We should do when we would ; for this
    ' would ' changes   120
And hath abatements and delays as many
As there are tongues, are hands, are acci-
    dents ;
And then this ' should ' is like a spendthrift
    sigh,
That hurts by easing. But, to the quick o' the
    ulcer :—
Hamlet comes back : what would you under-
    take,
To show yourself your father's son in deed
More than in words ?
    Laer.   To cut his throat i' the church.
    King. No place, indeed, should murder
    sanctuarize ;
Revenge should have no bounds. But, good
    Laertes,
Will you do this, keep close within your cham-
    ber.   130
Hamlet return'd shall know you are come
    home :
We'll put on those shall praise your excellence
And set a double varnish on the fame
The Frenchman gave you, bring you in fine to-
    gether
And wager on your heads : he, being remiss,
Most generous and free from all contriving,
Will not peruse the foils ; so that, with ease,
Or with a little shuffling, you may choose
A sword unbated, and in a pass of practice
Requite him for your father.
    Laer.   I will do't : 140
And, for that purpose, I'll anoint my sword.
I bought an unction of a mountebank,
So mortal that, but dip a knife in it,
Where it draws blood no cataplasm so rare,
Collected from all simples that have virtue
Under the moon, can save the thing from death
That is but scratch'd withal : I'll touch my
    point
With this contagion, that, if I gall him slightly,
It may be death.
    King.   Let's further think of this ;
Weigh what convenience both of time and
    means   150
May fit us to our shape : if this should fail,
And that our drift look through our bad per-
    formance,
'Twere better not assay'd : therefore this proj-
    ect
Should have a back or second, that might hold,
If this should blast in proof. Soft ! let me see :
We'll make a solemn wager on your cunnings :
I ha't.
When in your motion you are hot and dry—
As make your bouts more violent to that end—
And that he calls for drink, I'll have prepared
    him   160
A chalice for the nonce, whereon but sipping,
If he by chance escape your venom'd stuck,
Our purpose may hold there.

Enter QUEEN.

How now, sweet queen !

Queen. One woe doth tread upon another's heel,
So fast they follow ; your sister's drown'd, Laertes.

Laer. Drown'd ! O, where ?

Queen. There is a willow grows aslant a brook,
That shows his hoar leaves in the glassy stream ;
There with fantastic garlands did she come
Of crow-flowers, nettles, daisies, and long pur-
ples   170
That liberal shepherds give a grosser name,
But our cold maids do dead men's fingers call them :
There, on the pendent boughs her coronet weeds
Clambering to hang, an envious sliver broke ;
When down her weedy trophies and herself
Fell in the weeping brook. Her clothes spread wide ;
And, mermaid-like, awhile they bore her up :
Which time she chanted snatches of old tunes ;
As one incapable of her own distress,
Or like a creature native and indued   180
Unto that element : but long it could not be
Till that her garments, heavy with their drink,
Pull'd the poor wretch from her melodious lay
To muddy death.

Laer.   Alas, then, she is drown'd ?

Queen. Drown'd, drown'd.

Laer. Too much of water hast thou, poor Ophelia,
And therefore I forbid my tears : but yet
It is our trick ; nature her custom holds,
Let shame say what it will : when these are gone,   189
The woman will be out. Adieu, my lord :
I have a speech of fire, that fain would blaze,
But that this folly douts it.   [*Exit.*

King.   Let's follow, Gertrude !
How much I had to do to calm his rage !
Now fear I this will give it start again ;
Therefore let's follow.   [*Exeunt.*

ACT V.

SCENE I. *A churchyard.*

Enter two Clowns, *with spades, &c.*

First Clo. Is she to be buried in Christian burial that wilfully seeks her own salvation ?

Sec. Clo. I tell thee she is : and therefore make her grave straight : the crowner hath sat on her, and finds it Christian burial.

First Clo. How can that be, unless she drowned herself in her own defence ?

Sec. Clo. Why, 'tis found so.

First Clo. It must be ' se offendendo ; ' it cannot be else. For here lies the point : if I drown myself wittingly, it argues an act : and an act hath three branches : it is, to act, to do, to perform : argal, she drowned herself wittingly.

Sec. Clo. Nay, but hear you, goodman delver,—

First Clo. Give me leave. Here lies the water ; good : here stands the man ; good ; if the man go to this water, and drown himself, it is, will he, nill he, he goes,—mark you that ; but if the water come to him and drown him, he drowns not himself : argal, he that is not guilty of his own death shortens not his own life.

Sec. Clo. But is this law ?

First Clo. Ay, marry, is't ; crowner's quest law.

Sec. Clo. Will you ha' the truth on't ? If this had not been a gentlewoman, she should have been buried out o' Christian burial.

First Clo. Why, there thou say'st : and the more pity that great folk should have counte-nance in this world to drown or hang them-selves, more than their even Christian. Come, my spade. There is no ancient gentleman but gardeners, ditchers, and grave-makers : they hold up Adam's profession.

Sec. Clo. Was he a gentleman ?

First Clo. He was the first that ever bore arms.

Sec. Clo. Why, he had none.   39

First Clo. What, art a heathen ? How dost thou understand the Scripture ? The Scrip-ture says ' Adam digged : ' could he dig with-out arms ? I'll put another question to thee : if thou answerest me not to the purpose, con-fess thyself—

Sec. Clo. Go to.

First Clo. What is he that builds stronger than either the mason, the shipwright, or the carpenter ?

Sec. Clo. The gallows-maker ; for that frame outlives a thousand tenants.   50

First Clo. I like thy wit well, in good faith : the gallows does well ; but how does it well ? it does well to those that do ill : now thou dost ill to say the gallows is built stronger than the church : argal, the gallows may do well to thee. To't again, come.

Sec. Clo. ' Who builds stronger than a ma-son, a shipwright, or a carpenter ? '

First Clo. Ay, tell me that, and unyoke.

Sec. Clo. Marry, now I can tell.   60

First Clo. To't.

Sec. Clo. Mass, I cannot tell.

Enter HAMLET *and* HORATIO, *at a distance.*

First Clo. Cudgel thy brains no more about it, for your dull ass will not mend his pace with beating ; and, when you are asked this question next, say ' a grave-maker : ' the houses that he makes last till doomsday. Go, get thee to Yaughan : fetch me a stoup of liquor.   [*Exit Sec. Clown.*
                [*He digs and sings.*
In youth, when I did love, did love,
        Methought it was very sweet,   70
To contract, O, the time, for, ah, my behove,
        O, methought, there was nothing meet.

Ham. Has this fellow no feeling of his business, that he sings at grave-making ?

Hor. Custom hath made it in him a prop-erty of easiness.

Ham. 'Tis e'en so : the hand of little em-ployment hath the daintier sense.

First Clo. [*Sings*]
        But age, with his stealing steps,
        Hath claw'd me in his clutch,   80
And hath shipped me intil the land,
        As if I had never been such.
                [*Throws up a skull.*

Ham. That skull had a tongue in it, and could sing once : how the knave jowls it to the ground, as if it were Cain's jaw-bone, that did the first murder ! It might be the pate of a politician, which this ass now o'er-reaches ; one that would circumvent God, might it not ?

Hor. It might, my lord.   89

Ham. Or of a courtier ; which could say ' Good morrow, sweet lord ! How dost thou, good lord ? ' This might be my lord such-a-one, that praised my lord such-a-one's horse, when he meant to beg it ; might it not ?

Hor. Ay, my lord.

Ham. Why, e'en so : and now my Lady Worm's ; chapless, and knocked about the mazzard with a sexton's spade : here's fine revolution, an we had the trick to see't. Did these bones cost no more the breeding, but to play at loggats with 'em ? mine ache to think on't.   101

First Clo. [*Sings*]

A pick-axe, and a spade, a spade,
    For and a shrouding sheet :
O, a pit of clay for to be made
    For such a guest is meet.

[*Throws up another skull.*

Ham. There's another : why may not that be the skull of a lawyer ? Where be his quiddities now, his quillets, his cases, his tenures, and his tricks ? why does he suffer this rude knave now to knock him about the sconce with a dirty shovel, and will not tell him of his action of battery ? Hum ! This fellow might be in's time a great buyer of land, with his statutes, his recognizances, his fines, his double vouchers, his recoveries : is this the fine of his fines, and the recovery of his recoveries, to have his fine pate full of fine dirt ? will his vouchers vouch him no more of his purchases, and double ones too, than the length and breadth of a pair of indentures ? The very conveyances of his lands will hardly lie in this box ; and must the inheritor himself have no more, ha ?

Hor. Not a jot more, my lord.

Ham. Is not parchment made of sheepskins ?

Hor. Ay, my lord, and of calf-skins too.

Ham. They are sheep and calves which seek out assurance in that. I will speak to this fellow. Whose grave's this, sirrah ?

First Clo. Mine, sir.

[*Sings*] O, a pit of clay for to be made
    For such a guest is meet.   130

Ham. I think it be thine, indeed ; for thou liest in't.

First Clo. You lie out on't, sir, and therefore it is not yours : for my part, I do not lie in't, and yet it is mine.

Ham. Thou dost lie in't, to be in't and say it is thine : 'tis for the dead, not for the quick ; therefore thou liest.

First Clo. 'Tis a quick lie, sir ; 'twill away again, from me to you.   140

Ham. What man dost thou dig it for ?

First Clo. For no man, sir.

Ham. What woman, then ?

First Clo. For none, neither.

Ham. Who is to be buried in't ?

First Clo. One that was a woman, sir ; but, rest her soul, she's dead.

Ham. How absolute the knave is ! we must speak by the card, or equivocation will undo us. By the Lord, Horatio, these three years I have taken a note of it ; the age is grown so picked that the toe of the peasant comes so near the heel of the courtier, he galls his kibe. How long hast thou been a grave-maker ?

First Clo. Of all the days i' the year, I came to't that day that our last king Hamlet overcame Fortinbras.

Ham. How long is that since ?

First Clo. Cannot you tell that ? every fool can tell that : it was the very day that young Hamlet was born ; he that is mad, and sent into England.

Ham. Ay, marry, why was he sent into England ?

First Clo. Why, because he was mad : he shall recover his wits there ; or, if he do not, it's no great matter there.

Ham. Why ?

First Clo. 'Twill not be seen in him there ; there the men are as mad as he.   170

Ham. How came he mad ?

First Clo. Very strangely, they say.

Ham. How strangely ?

First Clo. Faith, e'en with losing his wits.

Ham. Upon what ground ?

First Clo. Why, here in Denmark : I have been sexton here, man and boy, thirty years.

Ham. How long will a man lie i' the earth ere he rot ?   179

First Clo. I' faith, if he be not rotten before he die—as we have many pocky corses now-a-days, that will scarce hold the laying in —he will last you some eight year or nine year : a tanner will last you nine year.

Ham. Why he more than another ?

First Clo. Why, sir, his hide is so tanned with his trade, that he will keep out water a great while ; and your water is a sore decayer of your whoreson dead body. Here's a skull now ; this skull has lain in the earth three and twenty years.   191

Ham. Whose was it ?

First Clo. A whoreson mad fellow's it was : whose do you think it was ?

Ham. Nay, I know not.

First Clo. A pestilence on him for a mad rogue ! a' poured a flagon of Rhenish on my head once. This same skull, sir, was Yorick's skull, the king's jester.

Ham. This ?   200

First Clo. E'en that.

Ham. Let me see. [*Takes the skull.*] Alas, poor Yorick ! I knew him, Horatio : a fellow of infinite jest, of most excellent fancy : he hath borne me on his back a thousand times ; and now, how abhorred in my imagination it is ! my gorge rises at it. Here hung those lips that I have kissed I know not how oft. Where be your gibes now ? your gambols ? your songs ? your flashes of merriment, that were wont to set the table on a roar ? Not one now, to mock your own grinning ? quite chapfallen ? Now get you to my lady's chamber, and tell her, let her paint an inch thick, to this favor she must come ; make her laugh at that. Prithee, Horatio, tell me one thing.

Hor. What's that, my lord ?

Ham. Dost thou think Alexander looked o' this fashion i' the earth ?

Hor. E'en so.   220

Ham. And smelt so ? pah !

[*Puts down the skull.*

Hor. E'en so, my lord.

Ham. To what base uses we may return, Horatio ! Why may not imagination trace the noble dust of Alexander, till he find it stopping a bung-hole ?

Hor. 'Twere to consider too curiously, to consider so.

Ham. No, faith, not a jot ; but to follow him thither with modesty enough, and likelihood to lead it : as thus : Alexander died, Alexander was buried, Alexander returneth into dust ; the dust is earth ; of earth we make loam; and why of that loam, whereto he was converted, might they not stop a beer-barrel ?
Imperious Cæsar, dead and turn'd to clay,
Might stop a hole to keep the wind away :
O, that that earth, which kept the world in awe,
Should patch a wall to expel the winter's flaw !
But soft ! but soft ! aside : here comes the king.

Enter Priest, *&c. in procession ; the Corpse of* OPHELIA, LAERTES *and* Mourners *following ;* KING, QUEEN, *their trains, &c.*

The queen, the courtiers : who is this they follow ?
And with such maimed rites ? This doth betoken
The corse they follow did with desperate hand
Fordo its own life : 'twas of some estate.
Couch we awhile, and mark.
[*Retiring with Horatio.*

Laer. What ceremony else ?

Ham. That is Laertes,
A very noble youth : mark.

Laer. What ceremony else ?

First Priest. Her obsequies have been as far enlarged
As we have warrantise : her death was doubtful ; 250
And, but that great command o'ersways the order,
She should in ground unsanctified have lodged
Till the last trumpet : for charitable prayers,
Shards, flints and pebbles should be thrown on her ;
Yet here she is allow'd her virgin crants,
Her maiden strewments and the bringing home
Of bell and burial.

Laer. Must there no more be done ?

First Priest. No more be done :
We should profane the service of the dead
To sing a requiem and such rest to her 260
As to peace-parted souls.

Laer. Lay her i' the earth :
And from her fair and unpolluted flesh
May violets spring ! I tell thee, churlish priest,
A ministering angel shall my sister be,
When thou liest howling.

Ham. What, the fair Ophelia !

Queen. Sweets to the sweet : farewell !
[*Scattering flowers.*
I hoped thou shouldst have been my Hamlet's wife ;
I thought thy bride-bed to have deck'd, sweet maid,
And not have strew'd thy grave.

Laer. O, treble woe
Fall ten times treble on that cursed head, 270
Whose wicked deed thy most ingenious sense

Deprived thee of ! Hold off the earth awhile,
Till I have caught her once more in mine arms : [*Leaps into the grave.*
Now pile your dust upon the quick and dead,
Till of this flat a mountain you have made,
To o'ertop old Pelion, or the skyish head
Of blue Olympus.

Ham. [*Advancing*] What is he whose grief
Bears such an emphasis ? whose phrase of sorrow
Conjures the wandering stars, and makes them stand
Like wonder-wounded hearers ? This is I, 280
Hamlet the Dane. [*Leaps into the grave.*

Laer. The devil take thy soul !
[*Grappling with him.*

Ham. Thou pray'st not well.
I prithee, take thy fingers from my throat ;
For, though I am not splenitive and rash,
Yet have I something in me dangerous,
Which let thy wiseness fear : hold off thy hand.

King. Pluck them a sunder.

Queen. Hamlet, Hamlet !

All. Gentlemen,—

Hor. Good my lord, be quiet.
[*The Attendants part them, and they come out of the grave.*

Ham. Why I will fight with him upon this theme
Until my eyelids will no longer wag. 290

Queen. O my son, what theme ?

Ham. I loved Ophelia : forty thousand brothers
Could not, with all their quantity of love,
Make up my sum. What wilt thou do for her ?

King. O, he is mad, Laertes.

Queen. For love of God, forbear him.

Ham. 'Swounds, show me what thou'lt do :
Woo't weep ? woo't fight ? woo't fast ? woo't tear thyself ?
Woo't drink up eisel ? eat a crocodile ?
I'll do't. Dost thou come here to whine ? 300
To outface me with leaping in her grave ?
Be buried quick with her, and so will I :
And, if thou prate of mountains, let them throw
Millions of acres on us, till our ground,
Singeing his pate against the burning zone,
Make Ossa like a wart ! Nay, an thou'lt mouth,
I'll rant as well as thou.

Queen. This is mere madness :
And thus awhile the fit will work on him ;
Anon, as patient as the female dove,
When that her golden couplets are disclosed,
His silence will sit drooping.

Ham. Hear you, sir ;
What is the reason that you use me thus ?
I loved you ever : but it is no matter :
Let Hercules himself do what he may,
The cat will mew and dog will have his day.
[*Exit.*

King. I pray you, good Horatio, wait upon him. [*Exit Horatio.*
[*To Laertes*] Strengthen your patience in our last night's speech ;
We'll put the matter to the present push.
Good Gertrude, set some watch over your son.
This grave shall have a living monument : 320
An hour of quiet shortly shall we see ;
Till then, in patience our proceeding be.
[*Exeunt.*

Scene II. *A hall in the castle.*

Enter Hamlet *and* Horatio.

Ham. So much for this, sir : now shall you
see the other ;
You do remember all the circumstance ?
Hor. Remember it, my lord ?
Ham. Sir, in my heart there was a kind of
fighting,
That would not let me sleep : methought I lay
Worse than the mutines in the bilboes. Rashly,
And praised be rashness for it, let us know,
Our indiscretion sometimes serves us well,
When our deep plots do pall : and that should
teach us
There's a divinity that shapes our ends,   10
Rough-hew them how we will,—
Hor.   That is most certain.
Ham. Up from my cabin,
My sea-gown scarf'd about me, in the dark
Groped I to find out them ; had my desire,
Finger'd their packet, and in fine withdrew
To mine own room again ; making so bold,
My fears forgetting manners, to unseal
Their grand commission ; where I found, Ho-
ratio,—
O royal knavery !—an exact command,
Larded with many several sorts of reasons   20
Importing Denmark's health and England's
too,
With, ho ! such bugs and goblins in my life,
That, on the supervise, no leisure bated,
No, not to stay the grinding of the axe,
My head should be struck off.
Hor.   Is't possible ?
Ham. Here's the commission : read it at
more leisure.
But wilt thou hear me how I did proceed ?
Hor. I beseech you.
Ham. Being thus be-netted round with vil-
lanies,—
Ere I could make a prologue to my brains,   30
They had begun the play—I sat me down,
Devised a new commission, wrote it fair :
I once did hold it, as our statists do,
A baseness to write fair and labor'd much
How to forget that learning, but, sir, now
It did me yeoman's service : wilt thou know
The effect of what I wrote ?
Hor.   Ay, good my lord.
Ham. An earnest conjuration from the
king,
As England was his faithful tributary,
As love between them like the palm might
flourish,   40
As peace should still her wheaten garland wear
And stand a comma 'tween their amities,
And many such-like ' As'es of great charge,
That, on the view and knowing of these con-
tents,
Without debatement further, more or less,
He should the bearers put to sudden death,
Not shriving-time allow'd.
Hor.   How was this seal'd ?
Ham. Why, even in that was heaven or-
dinant.
I had my father's signet in my purse,
Which was the model of that Danish seal ;   50
Folded the writ up in form of the other,
Subscribed it, gave't the impression, placed it
safely,
The changeling never known. Now, the next
day

Was our sea-fight ; and what to this was se-
quent
Thou know'st already.
Hor. So Guildenstern and Rosencrantz go
to't.
Ham. Why, man, they did make love to
this employment ;
They are not near my conscience ; their defeat
Does by their own insinuation grow :
'Tis dangerous when the baser nature comes
Between the pass and fell incensed points   61
Of mighty opposites.
Hor.   Why, what a king is this !
Ham. Does it not, think'st thee, stand me
now upon—
He that hath kill'd my king and whored my
mother,
Popp'd in between the election and my hopes,
Thrown out his angle for my proper life,
And with such cozenage—is't not perfect con-
science,
To quit him with this arm ? and is't not to be
damn'd,
To let this canker of our nature come
In further evil ?   70
Hor. It must be shortly known to him from
England
What is the issue of the business there.
Ham. It will be short : the interim is
mine ;
And a man's life's no more than to say ' One.'
But I am very sorry, good Horatio,
That to Laertes I forgot myself ;
For, by the image of my cause, I see
The portraiture of his : I'll court his favors.
But, sure, the bravery of his grief did put me
Into a towering passion.
Hor.   Peace ! who comes here ?   80

Enter Osric.

Osr. Your lordship is right welcome back
to Denmark.
Ham. I humbly thank you, sir. Dost know
this water-fly ?
Hor. No, my good lord.
Ham. Thy state is the more gracious ; for
'tis a vice to know him. He hath much land,
and fertile : let a beast be lord of beasts, and
his crib shall stand at the king's mess : 'tis a
chough ; but, as I say, spacious in the possession of dirt.   90
Osr. Sweet lord, if your lordship were at
leisure, I should impart a thing to you from
his majesty.
Ham. I will receive it, sir, with all diligence
of spirit. Put your bonnet to his right use ; 'tis
for the head.
Osr. I thank your lordship, it is very hot.
Ham. No, believe me, 'tis very cold ; the
wind is northerly.   99
Osr. It is indifferent cold, my lord, indeed.
Ham. But yet methinks it is very sultry and
hot for my complexion.
Osr. Exceedingly, my lord ; it is very sultry,—as 'twere,—I cannot tell how. But, my
lord, his majesty bade me signify to you that
he has laid a great wager on your head : sir,
this is the matter,—
Ham. I beseech you, remember—
[*Hamlet moves him to put on his hat.*
Osr. Nay, good my lord ; for mine ease, in
good faith. Sir, here is newly come to court
Laertes ; believe me, an absolute gentleman,

full of most excellent differences, of very soft society and great showing : indeed, to speak feelingly of him, he is the card or calendar of gentry, for you shall find in him the continent of what part a gentleman would see.

Ham. Sir, his definement suffers no perdition in you ; though, I know, to divide him inventorially would dizzy the arithmetic of memory, and yet but yaw neither, in respect of his quick sail. But, in the verity of extolment, I take him to be a soul of great article ; and his infusion of such dearth and rareness, as, to make true diction of him, his semblable is his mirror ; and who else would trace him, his umbrage, nothing more.

Osr. Your lordship speaks most infallibly of him.

Ham. The concernancy, sir ? why do we wrap the gentleman in our more rawer breath ?
Osr. Sir ?　　　　　　　　　　　　　　　130
Hor. Is't not possible to understand in another tongue ? You will do't, sir, really.
Ham. What imports the nomination of this gentleman ?
Osr. Of Laertes ?
Hor. His purse is empty already ; all's golden words are spent.
Ham. Of him, sir.
Osr. I know you are not ignorant—
Ham. I would you did, sir ; yet, in faith, if you did, it would not much approve me. Well, sir ?
Osr. You are not ignorant of what excellence Laertes is—
Ham. I dare not confess that, lest I should compare with him in excellence ; but, to know a man well, were to know himself.
Osr. I mean, sir, for his weapon ; but in the imputation laid on him by them, in his meed he's unfellowed.　　　　　　　　150
Ham. What's his weapon ?
Osr. Rapier and dagger.
Ham. That's two of his weapons : but, well.
Osr. The king, sir, hath wagered with him six Barbary horses : against the which he has imponed, as I take it, six French rapiers and poniards, with their assigns, as girdle, hangers, and so : three of the carriages, in faith, are very dear to fancy, very responsive to the hilts, most delicate carriages, and of very liberal conceit.
Ham. What call you the carriages ?
Hor. I knew you must be edified by the margent ere you had done.
Osr. The carriages, sir, are the hangers.
Ham. The phrase would be more german to the matter, if we could carry cannon by our sides : I would it might be hangers till then. But, on : six Barbary horses against six French swords, their assigns, and three liberal-conceited carriages ; that's the French bet against the Danish. Why is this ' imponed,' as you call it ?　　　　　　　　　　　　　171
Osr. The king, sir, hath laid, that in a dozen passes between yourself and him, he shall not exceed you three hits : he hath laid on twelve for nine ; and it would come to immediate trial, if your lordship would vouchsafe the answer.
Ham. How if I answer ' no ' ?
Osr. I mean, my lord, the opposition of your person in trial.　　　　　　　　　179

Ham. Sir, I will walk here in the hall : if it please his majesty, 'tis the breathing time of day with me ; let the foils be brought, the gentleman willing, and the king hold his purpose, I will win for him an I can ; if not, I will gain nothing but my shame and the odd hits.
Osr. Shall I re-deliver you e'en so ?
Ham. To this effect, sir ; after what flourish your nature will.
Osr. I commend my duty to your lordship.
Ham. Yours, yours. [*Exit Osric.*] He does well to commend it himself ; there are no tongues else for's turn.
Hor. This lapwing runs away with the shell on his head.
Ham. He did comply with his dug, before he sucked it. Thus has he—and many more of the same bevy that I know the drossy age dotes on—only got the tune of the time and outward habit of encounter ; a kind of yesty collection, which carries them through and through the most fond and winnowed opinions ; and do but blow them to their trial, the bubbles are out.

Enter a Lord.

Lord. My lord, his majesty commended him to you by young Osric, who brings back to him, that you attend him in the hall : he sends to know if your pleasure hold to play with Laertes, or that you will take longer time.
Ham. I am constant to my purposes ; they follow the king's pleasure : if his fitness speaks, mine is ready ; now or whensoever, provided I be so able as now.　　　　　　　　211
Lord. The king and queen and all are coming down.
Ham. In happy time.
Lord. The queen desires you to use some gentle entertainment to Laertes before you fall to play.
Ham. She well instructs me. [*Exit Lord.*
Hor. You will lose this wager, my lord.
Ham. I do not think so : since he went into France, I have been in continual practice : I shall win at the odds. But thou wouldst not think how ill all's here about my heart : but it is no matter.
Hor. Nay, good my lord,—
Ham. It is but foolery ; but it is such a kind of gain-giving, as would perhaps trouble a woman.
Hor. If your mind dislike any thing, obey it : I will forestal their repair hither, and say you are not fit.　　　　　　　　　　229
Ham. Not a whit, we defy augury : there's a special providence in the fall of a sparrow. If it be now, 'tis not to come ; if it be not to come, it will be now ; if it be not now, yet it will come : the readiness is all : since no man has aught of what he leaves, what is't to leave betimes ?

Enter KING, QUEEN, LAERTES, Lords, OSRIC, *and* Attendants *with foils, &c.*

King. Come, Hamlet, come, and take this hand from me.

[*The King puts Laertes' hand into Hamlet's.*
Ham. Give me your pardon, sir : I've done you wrong ;
But pardon't, as you are a gentleman.
This presence knows,

And you must needs have heard, how I am
    punish'd   240
With sore distraction. What I have done,
That might your nature, honor and exception
Roughly awake, I here proclaim was madness.
Was't Hamlet wrong'd Laertes ? Never Ham-
    let :
If Hamlet from himself be ta'en away,
And when he's not himself does wrong Laertes,
Then Hamlet does it not, Hamlet denies it.
Who does it, then ? His madness : if't be so,
Hamlet is of the faction that is wrong'd ;
His madness is poor Hamlet's enemy.   250
Sir, in this audience,
Let my disclaiming from a purposed evil
Free me so far in your most generous thoughts,
That I have shot mine arrow o'er the house,
And hurt my brother.

Laer.   I am satisfied in nature,
Whose motive, in this case, should stir me
    most
To my revenge : but in my terms of honor
I stand aloof ; and will no reconcilement,
Till by some elder masters, of known honor,
I have a voice and precedent of peace,   260
To keep my name ungored. But till that time,
I do receive your offer'd love like love,
And will not wrong it.

Ham.   I embrace it freely ;
And will this brother's wager frankly play.
Give us the foils. Come on.

Laer.   Come, one for me.

Ham. I'll be your foil, Laertes : in mine ig-
    norance
Your skill shall, like a star i' the darkest night,
Stick fiery off indeed.

Laer.   You mock me, sir.

Ham. No, by this hand.

King. Give them the foils, young Osric.
    Cousin Hamlet,   270
You know the wager ?

Ham.   Very well, my lord ;
Your grace hath laid the odds o' the weaker
    side.

King. I do not fear it ; I have seen you
    both :
But since he is better'd, we have therefore
    odds.

Laer. This is too heavy, let me see another.

Ham. This likes me well. These foils have
    all a length ?   [*They prepare to play.*

Osr. Ay, my good lord.

King. Set me the stoups of wine upon that
    table.
If Hamlet give the first or second hit,
Or quit in answer of the third exchange,   280
Let all the battlements their ordnance fire :
The king shall drink to Hamlet's better breath ;
And in the cup an union shall he throw,
Richer than that which four successive kings
In Denmark's crown have worn. Give me the
    cups ;
And let the kettle to the trumpet speak,
The trumpet to the cannoneer without,
The cannons to the heavens, the heavens to
    earth,
' Now the king drinks to Hamlet.' Come, be-
    gin :
And you, the judges, bear a wary eye.   290

Ham. Come on, sir.

Laer.   Come, my lord. [*They play.*

Ham.   One.

Laer.   No.

Ham.   Judgment.

Osr. A hit, a very palpable hit.

Laer.   Well ; again.

King. Stay ; give me drink. Hamlet, this
    pearl is thine ;
Here's to thy health.
        [*Trumpets sound, and cannon shot off
                                    within.*
                Give him the cup.

Ham. I'll play this bout first ; set it by
    awhile.
Come. [*They play.*] Another hit ; what say
    you ?

Laer. A touch, a touch, I do confess.

King. Our son shall win.

Queen. He's fat, and scant of breath.
Here, Hamlet, take my napkin, rub thy brows ;
The queen carouses to thy fortune, Hamlet.

Ham. Good madam !   301

King. Gertrude, do not drink.

Queen. I will, my lord ; I pray you, pardon
    me.

King. [*Aside*] It is the poison'd cup : it is
    too late.

Ham. I dare not drink yet, madam ; by
    and by.

Queen. Come, let me wipe thy face.

Laer. My lord, I'll hit him now.

King.   I do not think't.

Laer. [*Aside*] And yet 'tis almost 'gainst
    my conscience.

Ham. Come, for the third, Laertes : you
    but dally ;
I pray you, pass with your best violence ;
I am afeard you make a wanton of me.   310

Laer. Say you so ? come on. [*They play.*

Osr. Nothing, neither way.

Laer. Have at you now !
[*Laertes wounds Hamlet ; then in scuffling,
    they change rapiers, and Hamlet wounds
    Laertes.*

King. Part them ; they are incensed.

Ham. Nay, come, again. [*The Queen falls.*

Osr.   Look to the queen there, ho !

Hor. They bleed on both sides. How is it,
    my lord ?

Osr. How is't, Laertes ?

Laer. Why, as a woodcock to mine own
    springe, Osric ;
I am justly kill'd with mine own treachery.

Ham. How does the queen ?

King. She swounds to see them bleed.

Queen. No, no, the drink, the drink,—O
    my dear Hamlet,—   320
The drink, the drink ! I am poison'd. [*Dies.*

Ham. O villany ! Ho ! let the door be
    lock'd :
Treachery ! Seek it out.

Laer. It is here, Hamlet : Hamlet, thou art
    slain ;
No medicine in the world can do thee good ;
In thee there is not half an hour of life ;
The treacherous instrument is in thy hand,
Unbated and envenom'd : the foul practice
Hath turn'd itself on me ; lo, here I lie,   329
Never to rise again : thy mother's poison'd :
I can no more : the king, the king's to blame.

Ham. The point !—envenom'd too !
Then, venom, to thy work. [*Stabs the King.*

All. Treason ! treason !

King. O, yet defend me, friends ; I am but
    hurt.

Ham. Here, thou incestuous, murderous, damned Dane,
Drink off this potion. Is thy union here ?
Follow my mother.   [*King dies.*
    Laer.   He is justly served ;
It is a poison temper'd by himself.   339
Exchange forgiveness with me, noble Hamlet :
Mine and my father's death come not upon thee,
Nor thine on me.   [*Dies.*
    Ham. Heaven make thee free of it ! I follow thee.
I am dead, Horatio. Wretched queen, adieu !
You that look pale and tremble at this chance,
That are but mutes or audience to this act,
Had I but time—as this fell sergeant, death,
Is strict in his arrest—O, I could tell you—
But let it be. Horatio, I am dead ;
Thou livest ; report me and my cause aright
To the unsatisfied.
    Hor.   Never believe it :   351
I am more an antique Roman than a Dane :
Here's yet some liquor left.
    Ham.   As thou'rt a man,
Give me the cup : let go ; by heaven, I'll have't.
O good Horatio, what a wounded name,
Things standing thus unknown, shall live behind me !
If thou didst ever hold me in thy heart
Absent thee from felicity awhile,
And in this harsh world draw thy breath in pain,
To tell my story.
        [*March afar off, and shot within.*
            What warlike noise is this ?   360
    Osr. Young Fortinbras, with conquest come from Poland,
To the ambassadors of England gives
This warlike volley.
    Ham.   O, I die, Horatio ;
The potent poison quite o'er-crows my spirit :
I cannot live to hear the news from England ;
But I do prophesy the election lights
On Fortinbras : he has my dying voice ;
So tell him, with the occurrents, more and less,
Which have solicited. The rest is silence. [*Dies.*
    Hor. Now cracks a noble heart. Good night, sweet prince :   370
And flights of angels sing thee to thy rest !
Why does the drum come hither ?
                    [*March within.*

Enter FORTINBRAS, *the* English Ambassadors, *and others.*

    Fort. Where is this sight ?
    Hor.   What is it ye would see ?

If aught of woe or wonder, cease your search.
    Fort. This quarry cries on havoc. O proud death,
What feast is toward in thine eternal cell,
That thou so many princes at a shot
So bloodily hast struck ?
    First Amb.   The sight is dismal ;
And our affairs from England come too late :
The ears are senseless that should give us hearing,
To tell him his commandment is fulfill'd,   381
That Rosencrantz and Guildenstern are dead :
Where should we have our thanks ?
    Hor.   Not from his mouth,
Had it the ability of life to thank you :
He never gave commandment for their death.
But since, so jump upon this bloody question,
You from the Polack wars, and you from England,
Are here arrived, give order that these bodies
High on a stage be placed to the view ;   389
And let me speak to the yet unknowing world
How these things came about : so shall you hear
Of carnal, bloody, and unnatural acts,
Of accidental judgments, casual slaughters,
Of deaths put on by cunning and forced cause,
And, in this upshot, purposes mistook
Fall'n on the inventors' heads : all this can I
Truly deliver.
    Fort.   Let us haste to hear it,
And call the noblest to the audience.
For me, with sorrow I embrace my fortune :
I have some rights of memory in this kingdom,
Which now to claim my vantage doth invite me.
    Hor. Of that I shall have also cause to speak,
And from his mouth whose voice will draw on more ;
But let this same be presently perform'd,
Even while men's minds are wild ; lest more mischance
On plots and errors, happen.
    Fort.   Let four captains
Bear Hamlet, like a soldier, to the stage ;
For he was likely, had he been put on,
To have proved most royally : and, for his passage,
The soldiers' music and the rites of war   410
Speak loudly for him.
Take up the bodies : such a sight as this
Becomes the field, but here shows much amiss.
Go, bid the soldiers shoot.
        [*A dead march. Exeunt, bearing off the
        dead bodies ; after which a peal of ordnance is shot off.*

ALL'S WELL THAT ENDS WELL.

(WRITTEN ABOUT 1602.)

INTRODUCTION.

Among the plays of Shakespeare mentioned by Meres in his *Palladis Tamia* (1598) occurs the name of *Love's Labour's Won*. This has been identified by some critics with *The Taming of the Shrew* and by others with *Much Ado About Nothing;* but the weight of authority inclines to the opinion that under this title Meres spoke of the play known to us as *All's Well that Ends Well*. It seems not improbable that *All's Well*, as we possess it in the First Folio—and no earlier edition exists—is a rehandling, very thoroughly carried out, of an earlier version of this comedy. Coleridge believed that two styles were discernible in it ; and there is certainly a larger proportion of rhyming lines in it than in any other play written after the year 1600. It is, however, far from certain that any portion of the play is of early origin, and assigning conjecturally the date about 1602 as that of the completion of the whole, we may view it as belonging to the later group of the second cycle of Shakespeare's comedies, not so early, therefore, as *Twelfth Night* or *As You Like It*, and certainly earlier than *Measure for Measure*. The story of Helena and Bertram was found by Shakespeare in Paynter's *Palace of Pleasure* (1566), Paynter having translated it from the *Decameron* of Boccacio (Novel 9, Third day). Shakespeare added the characters of the Countess, Lafeu, Parolles, and the Clown. What interested the poet's imagination in Boccacio's story was evidently the position and person of the heroine. In Boccacio, Giletta, the physician's daughter, is inferior in rank to the young Count, Beltramo, but she is rich. Shakespeare's Helena is of humbler birth than his Bertram, and she is also poor. Yet poor, and comparatively low-born, she aspires to be the young Count's wife, she pursues him to Paris, and wins him against his will. To show Helena thus reversing in a measure the ordinary relations of man and woman, and yet to show her neither self-seeking nor unwomanly, was the task which the dramatist attempted. On the one hand he insists much on Bertram's youth, and gives him the faults and vices of youth, making the reader or spectator of the play feel that his hero has great need of such a finely-tempered, right-willed and loyal nature to stand by his side as that of Helena. On the other hand he shows us Helena's enthusiastic attachment to Bertram, her fears and cares on his behalf, her adhesion to him rather than to herself, when her husband seems to set their interests in opposition to one another, until we come to feel that the imperious need which makes Helena overstep social conventions is the need of perfect service to the man she loves. Bertram's beauty and courage must bear part of the blame for Helena's loving him better than he deserves. With the youthful desire for independence which makes him break away from her, she can intelligently sympathize. In the last Act she appears—when he has entangled himself in falsehood and shame—to save him, and rescue him from his baser self. We feel that when he has at last really found Helena, he is safe, and all ends well. Parolles, the incarnation of bragging meanness, is the counterfoil of Helena—she, the doer of virtuous deeds ; he, the utterer of vain and swelling words ; she, all brave womanliness ; he, too cowardly for manhood. Parolles has been compared to Falstaff, but they ought rather to be contrasted ; for Sir John is a man of genius, with real wit and power of fascination, and no ridicule can destroy him, but the exposure of Parolles makes him dwindle into his native pitifulness. The Countess is a charming creation of Shakespeare ; in no play, unless it be some of his latest romantic dramas, is old age made more beautiful and dignified.

DRAMATIS PERSONÆ.

KING OF FRANCE.
DUKE OF FLORENCE.
BERTRAM, Count of Rousillon.
LAFEU, an old lord.
PAROLLES, a follower of Bertram.
Steward, ⎫ servants to the Countess of
Clown, ⎭ Rousillon.
A Page.

COUNTESS OF ROUSILLON, mother to Bertram.

HELENA, a gentlewoman protected by the Countess.
An old Widow of Florence.
DIANA, daughter to the Widow.
VIOLENTA, ⎫ neighbors and friends to the
MARIANA, ⎭ Widow.
Lords, Officers, Soldiers, &c., French and Florentine.

SCENE : *Rousillon ; Paris ; Florence ; Marseilles.*

ACT I.

SCENE I. *Rousillon. The* COUNT'S *palace.*

Enter BERTRAM, *the* COUNTESS *of* ROUSILLON, HELENA, *and* LAFEU, *all in black.*

Count. In delivering my son from me, I bury a second husband.

Ber. And I in going, madam, weep o'er my father's death anew : but I must attend his majesty's command, to whom I am now in ward, evermore in subjection.

Laf. You shall find of the king a husband, madam ; you, sir, a father : he that so generally is at all times good must of necessity hold his virtue to you ; whose worthiness would stir it up where it wanted rather than lack it where there is such abundance.

Count. What hope is there of his majesty's amendment ?

Laf. He hath abandoned his physicians, madam ; under whose practices he hath persecuted time with hope, and finds no other advantage in the process but only the losing of hope by time.

Count. This young gentlewoman had a father,—O, that 'had' ! how sad a passage 'tis ! —whose skill was almost as great as his honesty ; had it stretched so far, would have made nature immortal, and death should have play for lack of work. Would, for the king's sake, he were living ! I think it would be the death of the king's disease.

Laf. How called you the man you speak of, madam ?

Count. He was famous, sir, in his profession, and it was his great right to be so : Gerard de Narbon. 31

Laf. He was excellent indeed, madam : the king very lately spoke of him admiringly and mourningly : he was skilful enough to have lived still, if knowledge could be set up against mortality.

Ber. What is it, my good lord, the king languishes of ?

Laf. A fistula, my lord.

Ber. I heard not of it before.

Laf. I would it were not notorious. Was this gentlewoman the daughter of Gerard de Narbon ?

Count. His sole child, my lord, and bequeathed to my overlooking. I have those hopes of her good that her education promises ; her dispositions she inherits, which makes fair gifts fairer ; for where an unclean mind carries virtuous qualities, there commendations go with pity ; they are virtues and traitors too ; in her they are the better for their simpleness ; she derives her honesty and achieves her goodness.

Laf. Your commendations, madam, get from her tears.

Count. 'Tis the best brine a maiden can season her praise in. The remembrance of her father never approaches her heart but the tyranny of her sorrows takes all livelihood from her cheek. No more of this, Helena ; go to, no more ; lest it be rather thought you affect a sorrow than have it. 61

Hel. I do affect a sorrow indeed, but I have it too.

Laf. Moderate lamentation is the right of the dead, excessive grief the enemy to the living.

Count. If the living be enemy to the grief, the excess makes it soon mortal.

Ber. Madam, I desire your holy wishes.

Laf. How understand we that ?

Count. Be thou blest, Bertram, and succeed thy father 70
In manners, as in shape ! thy blood and virtue
Contend for empire in thee, and thy goodness
Share with thy birthright ! Love all, trust a few,
Do wrong to none : be able for thine enemy
Rather in power than use, and keep thy friend
Under thy own life's key : be check'd for silence,
But never tax'd for speech. What heaven more will,
That thee may furnish and my prayers pluck down,
Fall on thy head ! Farewell, my lord ;
'Tis an unseason'd courtier ; good my lord, 80
Advise him.

Laf. He cannot want the best
That shall attend his love.

Count. Heaven bless him ! Farewell, Bertram.   [*Exit.*

Ber. [*To Helena*] The best wishes that can be forged in your thoughts be servants to you ! Be comfortable to my mother, your mistress, and make much of her.

Laf. Farewell, pretty lady : you must hold the credit of your father.

      [*Exeunt Bertram and Lafeu.*

Hel. O, were that all ! I think not on my father ; 90
And these great tears grace his remembrance more
Than those I shed for him. What was he like ?
I have forgot him : my imagination
Carries no favor in't but Bertram's.
I am undone : there is no living, none,
If Bertram be away. 'Twere all one
That I should love a bright particular star
And think to wed it, he is so above me :
In his bright radiance and collateral light
Must I be comforted, not in his sphere. 100
The ambition in my love thus plagues itself :
The hind that would be mated by the lion
Must die for love. 'Twas pretty, though plague,
To see him every hour ; to sit and draw
His arched brows, his hawking eye, his curls,
In our heart's table ; heart too capable
Of every line and trick of his sweet favor :
But now he's gone, and my idolatrous fancy
Must sanctify his reliques. Who comes here ?

Enter PAROLLES.

[*Aside*] One that goes with him : I love him for his sake ; 110
And yet I know him a notorious liar,
Think him a great way fool, solely a coward ;
Yet these fixed evils sit so fit in him,
That they take place, when virtue's steely bones
Look bleak i' the cold wind : withal, full oft we see
Cold wisdom waiting on superfluous folly.

Par. Save you, fair queen !

Hel. And you, monarch !

Par. No.

Hel. And no. 120

Par. Are you meditating on virginity ?

Hel. Ay. You have some stain of soldier in you : let me ask you a question. Man is enemy to virginity ; how may we barricado it against him ?

Par. Keep him out.

Hel. But he assails ; and our virginity, though valiant, in the defence yet is weak : unfold to us some warlike resistance.

Par. There is none : man, sitting down before you, will undermine you and blow you up.

Hel. Bless our poor virginity from underminers and blowers up ! Is there no military policy, how virgins might blow up men ? 133

Par. Virginity being blown down, man will quicklier be blown up : marry, in blowing him down again, with the breach yourselves made, you lose your city. It is not politic in the commonwealth of nature to preserve virginity. Loss of virginity is rational increase and there was never virgin got till virginity was first lost. That you were made of is metal to make virgins. Virginity by being once lost may be ten times found ; by being ever kept, it is ever lost : 'tis too cold a companion ; away with 't !

Hel. I will stand for 't a little, though therefore I die a virgin.

Par. There's little can be said in 't ; 'tis against the rule of nature. To speak on the part of virginity, is to accuse your mothers ; which is most infallible disobedience. He that hangs himself is a virgin : virginity murders itself and should be buried in highways out of all sanctified limit, as a desperate offendress against nature. Virginity breeds mites, much like a cheese ; consumes itself to the very paring, and so dies with feeding his own stomach. Besides, virginity is peevish, proud, idle, made of self-love, which is the most inhibited sin in the canon. Keep it not ; you cannot choose but loose by't : out with 't ! within ten year it will make itself ten, which is a goodly increase ; and the principal itself not much the worse : away with 't !

Hel. How might one do, sir, to lose it to her own liking ?

Par. Let me see : marry, ill, to like him that ne'er it likes. 'Tis a commodity will lose the gloss with lying ; the longer kept, the less worth : off with 't while 'tis vendible ; answer the time of request. Virginity, like an old courtier, wears her cap out of fashion : richly suited, but unsuitable : just like the brooch and the tooth-pick, which wear not now. Your date is better in your pie and your porridge than in your cheek ; and your virginity, your old virginity, is like one of our French withered pears, it looks ill, it eats drily ; marry, 'tis a withered pear ; it was formerly better ; marry, yet 'tis a withered pear : will you anything with it ?

Hel. Not my virginity yet. . . .

There shall your master have a thousand loves,
A mother and a mistress and a friend, 181
A phœnix, captain and an enemy,
A guide, a goddess, and a sovereign,
A counsellor, a traitress, and a dear ;
His humble ambition, proud humility,
His jarring concord, and his discord dulcet,

His faith, his sweet disaster ; with a world
Of pretty, fond, adoptious christendoms,
That blinking Cupid gossips. Now shall he—
I know not what he shall. God send him well !
The court's a learning place, and he is one—

Par. What one, i' faith ?

Hel. That I wish well. 'Tis pity—

Par. What's pity ?

Hel. That wishing well had not a body in't,
Which might be felt ; that we, the poorer born,
Whose baser stars do shut us up in wishes,
Might with effects of them follow our friends,
And show what we alone must think, which never
Return us thanks. 200

Enter Page.

Page. Monsieur Parolles, my lord calls for you. [*Exit.*

Par. Little Helen, farewell ; if I can remember thee, I will think of thee at court.

Hel. Monsieur Parolles, you were born under a charitable star.

Par. Under Mars, I.

Hel. I especially think, under Mars.

Par. Why under Mars ?

Hel. The wars have so kept you under that you must needs be born under Mars. 210

Par. When he was predominant.

Hel. When he was retrograde, I think, rather.

Par. Why think you so ?

Hel. You go so much backward when you fight.

Par. That's for advantage.

Hel. So is running away, when fear proposes the safety ; but the composition that your valor and fear makes in you is a virtue of a good wing, and I like the wear well. 219

Par. I am so full of businesses, I cannot answer thee acutely. I will return perfect courtier ; in the which, my instruction shall serve to naturalize thee, so thou wilt be capable of a courtier's counsel and understand what advice shall thrust upon thee ; else thou diest in thine unthankfulness, and thine ignorance makes thee away : farewell. When thou hast leisure, say thy prayers ; when thou hast none, remember thy friends ; get thee a good husband, and use him as he uses thee ; so, farewell. [*Exit.* 230

Hel. Our remedies oft in ourselves do lie,
Which we ascribe to heaven : the fated sky
Gives us free scope, only doth backward pull
Our slow designs when we ourselves are dull.
What power is it which mounts my love so high,
That makes me see, and cannot feed mine eye ?
The mightiest space in fortune nature brings
To join like likes and kiss like native things.
Impossible be strange attempts to those
That weigh their pains in sense and do suppose 240
What hath been cannot be : who ever strove
So show her merit, that did miss her love ?
The king's disease—my project may deceive me,
But my intents are fix'd and will not leave me. [*Exit.*

SCENE II. *Paris. The* KING'S *palace.*

Flourish of cornets. Enter the KING OF FRANCE, *with letters, and divers Attendants.*

King. The Florentines and Senoys are by
   the ears ;
Have fought with equal fortune and continue
A braving war.

First Lord.   So 'tis reported, sir.

King. Nay, 'tis most credible ; we here re-
   ceive it
A certainty, vouch'd from our cousin Austria,
With caution that the Florentine will move us
For speedy aid ; wherein our dearest friend
Prejudicates the business and would seem
To have us make denial.

First Lord.   His love and wisdom,
Approved so to your majesty, may plead   10
For amplest credence.

King.   He hath arm'd our answer,
And Florence is denied before he comes :
Yet, for our gentlemen that mean to see
The Tuscan service, freely have they leave
To stand on either part.

Sec. Lord.   It well may serve
A nursery to our gentry, who are sick
For breathing and exploit.

King.   What's he comes here ?

Enter BERTRAM, LAFEU, *and* PAROLLES.

First Lord. It is the Count Rousillon, my
   good lord,
Young Bertram.

King. Youth, thou bear'st thy father's
   face ;
Frank nature, rather curious than in haste, 20
Hath well composed thee. Thy father's moral
   parts
Mayst thou inherit too ! Welcome to Paris.

Ber. My thanks and duty are your majesty's.

King. I would I had that corporal sound-
   ness now,
As when thy father and myself in friendship
First tried our soldiership ! He did look far
Into the service of the time and was
Discipled of the bravest : he lasted long ;
But on us both did haggish age steal on
And wore us out of act. It much repairs me
To talk of your good father. In his youth   31
He had the wit which I can well observe
To-day in our young lords ; but they may jest
Till their own scorn return to them unnoted
Ere they can hide their levity in honor ;
So like a courtier, contempt nor bitterness
Were in his pride or sharpness ; if they were,
His equal had awaked them, and his honor,
Clock to itself, knew the true minute when
Exception bid him speak, and at this time   40
His tongue obey'd his hand : who were below
   him
He used as creatures of another place
And bow'd his eminent top to their low ranks,
Making them proud of his humility,
In their poor praise he humbled. Such a man
Might be a copy to these younger times ;
Which, follow'd well, would demonstrate them
   now
But goers backward.

Ber.   His good remembrance, sir,
Lies richer in your thoughts than on his tomb ;
So in approof lives not his epitaph   50
As in your royal speech.

King. Would I were with him ! He would
   always say—
Methinks I hear him now ; his plausive words
He scatter'd not in ears, but grafted them,
To grow there and to bear,—' Let me not
   live,'—
This his good melancholy oft began,
On the catastrophe and heel of pastime,
When it was out,—' Let me not live,' quoth he,
' After my flame lacks oil, to be the snuff   59
Of younger spirits, whose apprehensive senses
All but new things disdain ; whose judgments
   are
Mere fathers of their garments ; whose con-
   stancies
Expire before their fashions.' This he wish'd ;
I after him do after him wish too,
Since I nor wax nor honey can bring home,
I quickly were dissolved from my hive,
To give some laborers room.

Sec. Lord.   You are loved, sir :
They that least lend it you shall lack you first.

King. I fill a place, I know't. How long
   is't, count,
Since the physician at your father's died ?   70
He was much famed.

Ber.   Some six months since, my lord.

King. If he were living, I would try him
   yet.
Lend me an arm ; the rest have worn me out
With several applications ; nature and sickness
Debate it at their leisure. Welcome, count ;
My son's no dearer.

Ber.   Thank your majesty.
                    [*Exeunt. Flourish.*

SCENE III. *Rousillon. The* COUNT'S *palace.*

Enter COUNTESS, Steward, *and* Clown.

Count. I will now hear ; what say you of
this gentlewoman ?

Stew. Madam, the care I have had to even
your content, I wish might be found in the calendar of my past endeavors ; for then we
wound our modesty and make foul the clearness of our deservings, when of ourselves we
publish them.

Count. What does this knave here ? Get
you gone, sirrah : the complaints I have heard
of you I do not all believe : 'tis my slowness
that I do not ; for I know you lack not folly
to commit them, and have ability enough to
make such knaveries yours.

Clo. 'Tis not unknown to you, madam, I
am a poor fellow.

Count. Well, sir.

Clo. No, madam, 'tis not so well that I am
poor, though many of the rich are damned :
but, if I may have your ladyship's good will to
go to the world, Isbel the woman and I will
do as we may.   21

Count. Wilt thou needs be a beggar ?

Clo. I do beg your good will in this case.

Count. In what case ?

Clo. In Isbel's case and mine own. Service
is no heritage : and I think I shall never have
the blessing of God till I have issue o' my
body ; for they say barnes are blessings.

Count. Tell me thy reason why thou wilt
marry.

Clo. My poor body, madam, requires it : I
am driven on by the flesh ; and he must needs
go that the devil drives.

Count. Is this all your worship's reason ?

Clo. Faith, madam, I have other holy reasons, such as they are.

Count. May the world know them ?

Clo. I have been, madam, a wicked creature, as you and all flesh and blood are ; and, indeed, I do marry that I may repent.

Count. Thy marriage, sooner than thy wickedness.   41

Clo. I am out o' friends, madam ; and I hope to have friends for my wife's sake.

Count. Such friends are thine enemies, knave.

Clo. You're shallow, madam, in great friends ; for the knaves come to do that for me which I am aweary of. He that ears my land spares my team and gives me leave to in the crop ; if I be his cuckold, he's my drudge : he that comforts my wife is the cherisher of my flesh and blood ; he that cherishes my flesh and blood loves my flesh and blood ; he that loves my flesh and blood is my friend : ergo, he that kisses my wife is my friend. If men could be contented to be what they are, there were no fear in marriage ; for young Charbon the Puritan and old Poysam the Papist, howsome'er their hearts are severed in religion, their heads are both one ; they may joul horns together, like any deer i' the herd.

Count. Wilt thou ever be a foul-mouthed and calumnious knave ?   61

Clo. A prophet I, madam ; and I speak the truth the next way :

For I the ballad will repeat,
   Which men full true shall find ;
Your marriage comes by destiny,
   Your cuckoo sings by kind.

Count. Get you gone, sir ; I'll talk with you more anon.

Stew. May it please you, madam, that he bid Helen come to you : of her I am to speak.

Count. Sirrah, tell my gentlewoman I would speak with her ; Helen, I mean.

Clo. Was this fair face the cause, quoth she,
   Why the Grecians sacked Troy ?
Fond done, done fond,
   Was this King Priam's joy ?
With that she sighed as she stood,
With that she sighed as she stood,
   And gave this sentence then ;   80
Among nine bad if one be good,
Among nine bad if one be good,
   There's yet one good in ten.

Count. What, one good in ten ? you corrupt the song, sirrah.

Clo. One good woman in ten, madam ; which is a purifying o' the song : would God would serve the world so all the year ! we'ld find no fault with the tithe-woman, if I were the parson. One in ten, quoth a' ! An we might have a good woman born but one every blazing star, or at an earthquake, 'twould mend the lottery well : a man may draw his heart out, ere a' pluck one.

Count. You'll be gone, sir knave, and do as I command you.

Clo. That man should be at woman's command, and yet no hurt done ! Though honesty be no puritan, yet it will do no hurt ; it will wear the surplice of humility over the black gown of a big heart. I am going, forsooth : the business is for Helen to come hither. [*Exit.*

Count. Well, now.

Stew. I know, madam, you love your gentlewoman entirely.

Count. Faith, I do : her father bequeathed her to me ; and she herself, without other advantage, may lawfully make title to as much love as she finds : there is more owing her than is paid ; and more shall be paid her than she'll demand.

Stew. Madam, I was very late more near her than I think she wished me : alone she was, and did communicate to herself her own words to her own ears ; she thought, I dare vow for her, they touched not any stranger sense. Her matter was, she loved your son : Fortune, she said, was no goddess, that had put such difference betwixt their two estates ; Love no god, that would not extend his might, only where qualities were level ; Dian no queen of virgins, that would suffer her poor knight surprised, without rescue in the first assault or ransom afterward. This she delivered in the most bitter touch of sorrow that e'er I heard virgin exclaim in : which I held my duty speedily to acquaint you withal ; sithence, in the loss that may happen, it concerns you something to know it.

Count. You have discharged this honestly ; keep it to yourself : many likelihoods informed me of this before, which hung so tottering in the balance that I could neither believe nor misdoubt. Pray you, leave me : stall this in your bosom ; and I thank you for your honest care : I will speak with you further anon.

[*Exit Steward.*

Enter Helena.

Even so it was with me when I was young :
   If ever we are nature's, these are ours ; this
      thorn
Doth to our rose of youth rightly belong ;
   Our blood to us, this to our blood is born ;
It is the show and seal of nature's truth,
   Where love's strong passion is impress'd in
      youth :
By our remembrances of days foregone,   140
Such were our faults, or then we thought them
      none.
Her eye is sick on't : I observe her now.

Hel. What is your pleasure, madam ?

Count.   You know, Helen,
I am a mother to you.

Hel. Mine honorable mistress.

Count.   Nay, a mother :
Why not a mother ? When I said ' a mother,'
Methought you saw a serpent : what's in
      ' mother,'
That you start at it ? I say, I am your mother ;
And put you in the catalogue of those
That were enwombed mine : 'tis often seen 150
Adoption strives with nature and choice breeds
A native slip to us from foreign seeds :
You ne'er oppress'd me with a mother's groan,
Yet I express to you a mother's care :
God's mercy, maiden ! does it curd thy blood
To say I am thy mother ? What's the matter,
That this distemper'd messenger of wet,
The many-color'd Iris, rounds thine eye ?
Why ? that you are my daughter ?

Hel.   That I am not.

Count. I say, I am your mother.

Hel.   Pardon, madam ; 160
The Count Rousillon cannot be my brother :
I am from humble, he from honor'd name ;

No note upon my parents, his all noble :
My master, my dear lord he is ; and I
His servant live, and will his vassal die :
He must not be my brother.
 Count.   Nor I your mother ?
 Hel. You are my mother, madam ; would
  you were,—
So that my lord your son were not my
 brother,—
Indeed my mother ! or were you both our
 mothers,
I care no more for than I do for heaven, 170
So I were not his sister. Can't no other,
But, I your daughter, he must be my brother ?
 Count. Yes, Helen, you might be my
  daughter-in-law :
God shield you mean it not ! daughter and
 mother
So strive upon your pulse. What, pale again ?
My fear hath catch'd your fondness : now I
 see
The mystery of your loneliness, and find
Your salt tears' head : now to all sense 'tis
 gross
You love my son ; invention is ashamed,
Against the proclamation of thy passion, 180
To say thou dost not : therefore tell me true ;
But tell me then, 'tis so ; for, look, thy cheeks
Confess it, th' one to th' other ; and thine eyes
See it so grossly shown in thy behaviors
That in their kind they speak it : only sin
And hellish obstinacy tie thy tongue,
That truth should be suspected. Speak, is't so ?
If it be so, you have wound a goodly clew ;
If it be not, forswear't : howe'er, I charge thee,
As heaven shall work in me for thine avail,
Tell me truly.   191
 Hel.   Good madam, pardon me !
 Count. Do you love my son ?
 Hel.   Your pardon, noble mistress !
 Count. Love you my son ?
 Hel.   Do not you love him, madam ?
 Count. Go not about ; my love hath in't a
  bond,
Whereof the world takes note : come, come,
 disclose
The state of your affection ; for your passions
Have to the full appeach'd.
 Hel.   Then, I confess,
Here on my knee, before high heaven and you,
That before you, and next unto high heaven,
I love your son.   200
My friends were poor, but honest ; so's my
 love :
Be not offended ; for it hurts not him
That he is loved of me : I follow him not
By any token of presumptuous suit ;
Nor would I have him till I do deserve him ;
Yet never know how that desert should be.
I know I love in vain, strive against hope ;
Yet in this captious and intenible sieve
I still pour in the waters of my love
And lack not to lose still : thus, Indian-like,
Religious in mine error, I adore 211
The sun, that looks upon his worshipper,
But knows of him no more. My dearest
 madam,
Let not your hate encounter with my love
For loving where you do : but if yourself,
Whose aged honor cites a virtuous youth,
Did ever in so true a flame of liking
Wish chastely and love dearly, that your Dian
Was both herself and love : O, then, give pity

To her, whose state is such that cannot choose
But lend and give where she is sure to lose ;
That seeks not to find that her search implies,
But riddle-like lives sweetly where she dies !
 Count. Had you not lately an intent,—
  speak truly,—
To go to Paris ?
 Hel.   Madam, I had.
 Count.   Wherefore ? tell true.
 Hel. I will tell truth ; by grace itself I
  swear.
You know my father left me some prescrip-
 tions
Of rare and proved effects, such as his reading
And manifest experience had collected
For general sovereignty ; and that he will'd me
In heedfull'st reservation to bestow them, 231
As notes whose faculties inclusive were
More than they were in note : amongst the
 rest,
There is a remedy, approved, set down,
To cure the desperate languishings whereof
The king is render'd lost.
 Count.   This was your motive
For Paris, was it ? speak.
 Hel. My lord your son made me to think
  of this ;
Else Paris and the medicine and the king
Had from the conversation of my thoughts
Haply been absent then.   241
 Count.   But think you, Helen,
If you should tender your supposed aid,
He would receive it ? he and his physicians
Are of a mind ; he, that they cannot help him,
They, that they cannot help : how shall they
 credit
A poor unlearned virgin, when the schools,
Embowell'd of their doctrine, have left off
The danger to itself ?
 Hel.   There's something in't,
More than my father's skill, which was the
 greatest
Of his profession, that his good receipt 250
Shall for my legacy be sanctified
By the luckiest stars in heaven : and, would
 your honor
But give me leave to try success, I'ld venture
The well-lost life of mine on his grace's cure
By such a day and hour.
 Count.   Dost thou believe't ?
 Hel. Ay, madam, knowingly.
 Count. Why, Helen, thou shalt have my
  leave and love,
Means and attendants and my loving greetings
To those of mine in court : I'll stay at home
And pray God's blessing into thy attempt : 260
Be gone to-morrow ; and be sure of this,
What I can help thee to thou shalt not miss.
           [*Exeunt.*

ACT II.

SCENE I. *Paris. The* KING'S *palace.*

Flourish of cornets. Enter the KING, *attended
with divers young* Lords *taking leave for the
Florentine war ;* BERTRAM, *and* PAROLLES.

 King. Farewell, young lords ; these warlike
  principles
Do not throw from you : and you, my lords,
 farewell :
Share the advice betwixt you ; if both gain, all

The gift doth stretch itself as 'tis received,
And is enough for both.
  First Lord.   'Tis our hope, sir,
After well enter'd soldiers, to return
And find your grace in health.
  King. No, no, it cannot be ; and yet my
    heart
Will not confess he owes the malady
That doth my life besiege. Farewell, young
    lords ;   . 10
Whether I live or die, be you the sons
Of worthy Frenchmen : let higher Italy,—
Those bated that inherit but the fall
Of the last monarchy,—see that you come
Not to woo honor, but to wed it ; when
The bravest questant shrinks, find what you
    seek,
That fame may cry you loud : I say, farewell.
  Sec. Lord. Health, at your bidding, serve
    your majesty !
  King. Those girls of Italy, take heed of
    them :
They say, our French lack language to deny,
If they demand : beware of being captives, 21
Before you serve.
  Both.   Our hearts receive your warnings.
  King. Farewell. Come hither to me.
               [Exit, attended.
  First Lord. O my sweet lord, that you will
    stay behind us !
  Par. 'Tis not his fault, the spark.
  Sec. Lord.   O, 'tis brave wars !
  Par. Most admirable : I have seen those
    wars.
  Ber. I am commanded here, and kept a
    coil with
' Too young ' and ' the next year ' and ' 'tis too
    early.'
  Par. An thy mind stand to't, boy, steal
    away bravely.
  Ber. I shall stay here the forehorse to a
    smock,   30
Creaking my shoes on the plain masonry,
Till honor be bought up and no sword worn
But one to dance with ! By heaven, I'll steal
    away.
  First Lord. There's honor in the theft.
  Par.   Commit it, count.
  Sec. Lord. I am your accessary ; and so,
    farewell.
  Ber. I grow to you, and our parting is a
tortured body.
  First Lord. Farewell, captain.
  Sec. Lord. Sweet Monsieur Parolles !
  Par. Noble heroes, my sword and yours are
kin. Good sparks and lustrous, a word, good
metals : you shall find in the regiment of the
Spinii one Captain Spurio, with his cicatrice,
an emblem of war, here on his sinister cheek ;
it was this very sword entrenched it : say to
him, I live ; and observe his reports for me.
  First Lord. We shall, noble captain.
               [Exeunt Lords.
  Par. Mars dote on you for his novices !
what will ye do ?
  Ber. Stay : the king.   50

Re-enter King. Bertram *and* Parolles
retire.

  Par. [*To Ber*] Use a more spacious ceremony to the noble lords ; you have restrained
yourself within the list of too cold an adieu :
be more expressive to them : for they wear
themselves in the cap of the time, there do
muster true gait, eat, speak, and move under
the influence of the most received star ; and
though the devil lead the measure, such are to
be followed : after them, and take a more dilated farewell.
  Ber. And I will do so.   60
  Par. Worthy fellows ; and like to prove
most sinewy sword-men.
        [Exeunt Bertram and Parolles.

Enter Lafeu.

  Laf. [*Kneeling*] Pardon, my lord, for me
    and for my tidings.
  King. I'll fee thee to stand up.
  Laf. Then here's a man stands, that has
    brought his pardon.
I would you had kneel'd, my lord, to ask me
    mercy,
And that at my bidding you could so stand up.
  King. I would I had ; so I had broke thy
    pate,
And ask'd thee mercy for't.
  Laf. Good faith, across : but, my good
    lord 'tis thus ;   70
Will you be cured of your infirmity ?
  King. No.
  Laf. O, will you eat no grapes, my royal
    fox ?
Yes, but you will my noble grapes, an if
My royal fox could reach them : I have seen
    a medicine
That's able to breathe life into a stone,
Quicken a rock, and make you dance canary
With spritely fire and motion ; whose simple
    touch,
Is powerful to araise King Pepin, nay,
To give great Charlemain a pen in's hand, 80
And write to her a love-line.
  King.   What ' her ' is this ?
  Laf. Why, Doctor She : my lord, there's
    one arrived,
If you will see her : now, by my faith and
    honor,
If seriously I may convey my thoughts
In this my light deliverance, I have spoke
With one that, in her sex, her years, profes-
    sion,
Wisdom and constancy, hath amazed me more
Than I dare blame my weakness : will you see
    her,
For that is her demand, and know her busi-
    ness ?
That done, laugh well at me.
  King.   Now, good Lafeu, 90
Bring in the admiration ; that we with thee
May spend our wonder too, or take off thine
By wondering how thou took'st it.
  Laf.   Nay, I'll fit you,
And not be all day neither.   *[Exit.*
  King. Thus he his special nothing ever pro-
    logues.

Re-enter Lafeu, *with* Helena.

  Laf. Nay, come your ways.
  King.   This haste hath wings indeed.
  Laf. Nay, come your ways :
This is his majesty ; say your mind to him :
A traitor you do look like ; but such traitors
His majesty seldom fears : I am Cressid's
    uncle,   100
That dare leave two together ; fare you well.
               [Exit.

King. Now, fair one, does your business
 follow us ?
Hel. Ay, my good lord.
Gerard de Narbon was my father;
In what he did profess, well found.
King.   I knew him.
Hel. The rather will I spare my praises to-
 wards him :
Knowing him is enough. On's bed of death
Many receipts he gave me : chiefly one,
Which, as the dearest issue of his practice,
And of his old experience the only darling, 110
He bade me store up, as a triple eye,
Safer than mine own two, more dear ; I have
 so ;
And hearing your high majesty is touch'd
With that malignant cause wherein the honor
Of my dear father's gift stands chief in power,
I come to tender it and my appliance
With all bound humbleness.
King.   We thank you, maiden ;
But may not be so credulous of cure,
When our most learned doctors leave us and
The congregated college have concluded   120
That laboring art can never ransom nature
From her inaidible estate ; I say we must not
So stain our judgment, or corrupt our hope,
To prostitute our past-cure malady
To empirics, or to dissever so
Our great self and our credit, to esteem
A senseless help when help past sense we deem.
Hel. My duty then shall pay me for my
 pains :
I will no more enforce mine office on you ;
Humbly entreating from your royal thoughts
A modest one, to bear me back again.   131
King. I cannot give thee less, to be call'd
 grateful :
Thou thought'st to help me ; and such thanks
 I give
As one near death to those that wish him live :
But what at full I know, thou know'st no part,
I knowing all my peril, thou no art.
Hel. What I can do can do no hurt to try,
Since you set up your rest 'gainst remedy.
He that of greatest works is finisher
Oft does them by the weakest minister :   140
So holy writ in babes hath judgment shown,
When judges have been babes ; great floods
 have flown
From simple sources, and great seas have dried
When miracles have by the greatest been de-
 nied.
Oft expectation fails and most oft there
Where most it promises, and oft it hits
Where hope is coldest and despair most fits.
King. I must not hear thee ; fare thee well,
 kind maid ;
Thy pains not used must by thyself be paid :
Proffers not took reap thanks for their reward.
Hel. Inspired merit so by breath is barr'd :
It is not so with Him that all things knows
As 'tis with us that square our guess by shows ;
But most it is presumption in us when
The help of heaven we count the act of men.
Dear sir, to my endeavors give consent ;
Of heaven, not me, make an experiment.
I am not an impostor that proclaim
Myself against the level of mine aim ;
But know I think and think I know most sure
My art is not past power nor you past cure.
King. Art thou so confident ? within what
 space

Hopest thou my cure ?
Hel.   The great'st grace lending grace
Ere twice the horses of the sun shall bring
Their fiery torcher his diurnal ring,
Ere twice in murk and occidental damp
Moist Hesperus hath quench'd his sleepy lamp,
Or four and twenty times the pilot's glass
Hath told the thievish minutes how they pass,
What is infirm from your sound parts shall fly,
Health shall live free and sickness freely die.
King. Upon thy certainty and confidence
What darest thou venture ?
Hel.   Tax of impudence,
A strumpet's boldness, a divulged shame
Traduced by odious ballads : my maiden's
 name
Sear'd otherwise ; nay, worse—if worse—ex-
 tended
With vilest torture let my life be ended.
King. Methinks in thee some blessed spirit
 doth speak
His powerful sound within an organ weak :
And what impossibility would slay   180
In common sense, sense saves another way.
Thy life is dear ; for all that life can rate
Worth name of life in thee hath estimate,
Youth, beauty, wisdom, courage, all
That happiness and prime can happy call :
Thou this to hazard needs must intimate
Skill infinite or monstrous desperate.
Sweet practiser, thy physic I will try,
That ministers thine own death if I die.
Hel. If I break time, or flinch in property
Of what I spoke, unpitied let me die,
And well deserved : not helping, death's my
 fee ;
But, if I help, what do you promise me ?
King. Make thy demand.
Hel.   But will you make it even ?
King. Ay, by my sceptre and my hopes of
 heaven.
Hel. Then shalt thou give me with thy
 kingly hand
What husband in thy power I will command :
Exempted be from me the arrogance
To choose from forth the royal blood of
 France,
My low and humble name to propagate   200
With any branch or image of thy state ;
But such a one, thy vassal, whom I know
Is free for me to ask, thee to bestow.
King. Here is my hand ; the premises ob-
 served,
Thy will by my performance shall be served :
So make the choice of thy own time, for I,
Thy resolved patient, on thee still rely.
More should I question thee, and more I must,
Though more to know could not be more to
 trust,
From whence thou camest, how tended on :
 but rest   210
Unquestion'd welcome and undoubted blest.
Give me some help here, ho ! If thou proceed
As high as word, my deed shall match thy
 meed.   [*Flourish. Exeunt.*

SCENE II. *Rousillon. The* COUNT'S *palace.*

Enter COUNTESS *and* CLOWN.

Count. Come on, sir ; I shall now put you
to the height of your breeding.
Clo. I will show myself highly fed and
lowly taught : I know my business is but to
the court.

Count. To the court! why, what place make you special, when you put off that with such contempt? But to the court!

Clo. Truly, madam, if God have lent a man any manners, he may easily put it off at court: he that cannot make a leg, put off's cap, kiss his hand and say nothing, has neither leg, hands, lip, nor cap; and indeed such a fellow, to say precisely, were not for the court; but for me, I have an answer will serve all men.

Count. Marry, that's a bountiful answer that fits all questions.

Clo. It is like a barber's chair that fits all buttocks, the pin-buttock, the quatch-buttock, the brawn buttock, or any buttock.

Count. Will your answer serve fit to all questions? 21

Clo. As fit as ten groats is for the hand of an attorney, as your French crown for your taffeta punk, as Tib's rush for Tom's forefinger, as a pancake for Shrove Tuesday, a morris for May-day, as the nail to his hole, the cuckold to his horn, as a scolding queen to a wrangling knave, as the nun's lip to the friar's mouth, nay, as the pudding to his skin.

Count. Have you, I say, an answer of such fitness for all questions? 31

Clo. From below your duke to beneath your constable, it will fit any question.

Count. It must be an answer of most monstrous size that must fit all demands.

Clo. But a trifle neither, in good faith, if the learned should speak truth of it: here it is, and all that belongs to't. Ask me if I am a courtier: it shall do you no harm to learn.

Count. To be young again, if we could: I will be a fool in question, hoping to be the wiser by your answer. I pray you, sir, are you a courtier?

Clo. O Lord, sir! There's a simple putting off. More, more, a hundred of them.

Count. Sir, I am a poor friend of yours, that loves you.

Clo. O Lord, sir! Thick, thick, spare not me.

Count. I think, sir, you can eat none of this homely meat.

Clo. O Lord, sir! Nay, put me to't, I warrant you. 51

Count. You were lately whipped, sir, as I think.

Clo. O Lord, sir! spare not me.

Count. Do you cry, ' O Lord, sir ! ' at your whipping, and ' spare not me ? ' Indeed your ' O Lord, sir ! ' is very sequent to your whipping : you would answer very well to a whipping, if you were but bound to't.

Clo. I ne'er had worse luck in my life in my ' O Lord, sir ! ' I see things may serve long, but not serve ever. 61

Count. I play the noble housewife with the time,
To entertain't so merrily with a fool.

Clo. O Lord, sir! why, there't serves well again.

Count. An end, sir; to your business. Give Helen this,
And urge her to a present answer back :
Commend me to my kinsmen and my son :
This is not much.

Clo. Not much commendation to them. 70

Count. Not much employment for you : you understand me ?

Clo. Most fruitfully : I am there before my legs.

Count. Haste you again. [*Exeunt severally.*

SCENE III. *Paris. The* KING'S *palace.*

Enter BERTRAM, LAFEU, *and* PAROLLES.

Laf. They say miracles are past ; and we have our philosophical persons, to make modern and familiar, things supernatural and causeless. Hence is it that we make trifles of terrors, ensconcing ourselves into seeming knowledge, when we should submit ourselves to an unknown fear.

Par. Why, 'tis the rarest argument of wonder that hath shot out in our latter times.

Ber. And so 'tis.

Laf. To be relinquish'd of the artists,— 10

Par. So I say.

Laf. Both of Galen and Paracelsus.

Par. So I say.

Laf. Of all the learned and authentic fellows,—

Par. Right ; so I say.

Laf. That gave him out incurable,—

Par. Why, there 'tis ; so say I too.

Laf. Not to be helped,—

Par. Right ; as 'twere, a man assured of a—

Laf. Uncertain life, and sure death. 20

Par. Just, you say well ; so would I have said.

Laf. I may truly say, it is a novelty to the world.

Par. It is, indeed : if you will have it in showing, you shall read it in—what do you call there ?

Laf. A showing of a heavenly effect in an earthly actor.

Par. That's it ; I would have said the very same. 30

Laf. Why, your dolphin is not lustier : 'fore me, I speak in respect—

Par. Nay, 'tis strange, 'tis very strange, that is the brief and the tedious of it ; and he's of a most facinerious spirit that will not acknowledge it to be the—

Laf. Very hand of heaven.

Par. Ay, so I say.

Laf. In a most weak—[*pausing*] and debile minister, great power, great transcendence : which should, indeed, give us a further use to be made than alone the recovery of the king, as to be—[*pausing*] generally thankful.

Par. I would have said it ; you say well. Here comes the king.

Enter KING, HELENA, *and* Attendants.
LAFEU *and* PAROLLES *retire.*

Laf. Lustig, as the Dutchman says : I'll like a maid the better, whilst I have a tooth in my head : why, he's able to lead her a coranto.

Par. Mort du vinaigre ! is not this Helen ?

Laf. 'Fore God, I think so. 51

King. Go, call before me all the lords in court.

Sit, my preserver, by thy patient's side ;
And with this healthful hand, whose banish'd sense
Thou hast repeal'd, a second time receive
The confirmation of my promised gift,
Which but attends thy naming.

Enter three or four Lords.

Fair maid, send forth thine eye : this youthful
    parcel
Of noble bachelors stand at my bestowing,
O'er whom both sovereign power and father's
    voice   60
I have to use : thy frank election make ;
Thou hast power to choose, and they none to
    forsake.
    Hel. To each of you one fair and virtuous
    mistress
Fall, when Love please ! marry, to each, but
    one !
    Laf. I'd give bay Curtal and his furniture,
My mouth no more were broken than these
    boys',
And writ as little beard.
    King.   Peruse them well :
Not one of those but had a noble father.
    Hel. Gentlemen,
Heaven hath through me restored the king to
    health.   70
    All. We understand it, and thank heaven
    for you.
    Hel. I am a simple maid, and therein
    wealthiest,
That I protest I simply am a maid.
Please it your majesty, I have done already :
The blushes in my cheeks thus whisper me,
' We blush that thou shouldst choose ; but, be
    refused,
Let the white death sit on thy cheek for ever ;
We'll ne'er come there again.'
    King.   Make choice ; and, see,
Who shuns thy love shuns all his love in me.
    Hel. Now, Dian, from thy altar do I fly, 80
And to imperial Love, that god most high,
Do my sighs stream. Sir, will you hear my
    suit ?
    First Lord. And grant it.
    Hel.   Thanks, sir ; all the
    rest is mute.
    Laf. I had rather be in this choice than
throw ames-ace for my life.
    Hel. The honor, sir, that flames in your
    fair eyes,
Before I speak, too threateningly replies :
Love make your fortunes twenty times above
Her that so wishes and her humble love !
    Sec. Lord. No better, if you please.
    Hel.   My wish receive, 90
Which great Love grant ! and so, I take my
    leave.
    Laf. Do all they deny her ? An they were
sons of mine, I'd have them whipped ; or I
would send them to the Turk, to make eunuchs
of.
    Hel. Be not afraid that I your hand should
take ;
I'll never do you wrong for your own sake :
Blessing upon your vows ! and in your bed
Find fairer fortune, if you ever wed !
    Laf. These boys are boys of ice, they'll
none have her : sure, they are bastards to the
English ; the French ne'er got 'em.   101
    Hel. You are too young, too happy, and
    too good,
To make yourself a son out of my blood.
    Fourth Lord. Fair one, I think not so.
    Laf. There's one grape yet ; I am sure thy
father drunk wine : but if thou be'st not an

ass, I am a youth of fourteen ; I have known
thee already.
    Hel. [*To Bertram*] I dare not say I take
    you ; but I give
Me and my service, ever whilst I live,   110
Into your guiding power. This is the man.
    King. Why, then, young Bertram, take her ;
    she's thy wife.
    Ber. My wife, my liege ! I shall beseech
    your highness,
In such a business give me leave to use
The help of mine own eyes.
    King.   Know'st thou not, Bertram,
What she has done for me ?
    Ber.   Yes, my good lord ;
But never hope to know why I should marry
    her.
    King. Thou know'st she has raised me
    from my sickly bed.
    Ber. But follows it, my lord, to bring me
    down
Must answer for your raising ? I know her
    well :   120
She had her breeding at my father's charge.
A poor physician's daughter my wife ! Disdain
Rather corrupt me ever !
    King.   'Tis only title thou disdain'st in her,
    the which
I can build up. Strange is it that our bloods,
Of color, weight, and heat, pour'd all together,
Would quite confound distinction, yet stand off
In differences so mighty. If she be
All that is virtuous, save what thou dislikest,
A poor physician's daughter, thou dislikest 130
Of virtue for the name : but do not so :
From lowest place when virtuous things pro-
    ceed,
The place is dignified by the doer's deed :
Where great additions swell's, and virtue none,
It is a dropsied honor. Good alone
Is good without a name. Vileness is so :
The property by what it is should go,
Not by the title. She is young, wise, fair ;
In these to nature she's immediate heir,
And these breed honor : that is honor's scorn,
Which challenges itself as honor's born 141
And is not like the sire : honors thrive,
When rather from our acts we them derive
Than our foregoers : the mere word's a slave
Debosh'd on every tomb, on every grave
A lying trophy, and as oft is dumb
Where dust and damn'd oblivion is the tomb
Of honor'd bones indeed. What should be
    said ?
If thou canst like this creature as a maid,
I can create the rest : virtue and she   150
Is her own dower ; honor and wealth from
    me.
    Ber. I cannot love her, nor will strive to
    do't.
    King. Thou wrong'st thyself, if thou
    shouldst strive to choose.
    Hel. That you are well restored, my lord,
    I'm glad :
Let the rest go.
    King. My honor's at the stake ; which to
    defeat,
I must produce my power. Here, take her
    hand,
Proud scornful boy, unworthy this good gift ;
That dost in vile misprision shackle up
My love and her desert ; that canst not dream,
We, poising us in her defective scale,   161

Shall weigh thee to the beam; that wilt not
    know,
It is in us to plant thine honor where
We please to have it grow. Check thy con-
    tempt :
Obey our will, which travails in thy good :
Believe not thy disdain, but presently
Do thine own fortunes that obedient right
Which both thy duty owes and our power
    claims ;
Or I will throw thee from my care for ever
Into the staggers and the careless lapse 170
Of youth and ignorance ; both my revenge
    and hate
Loosing upon thee, in the name of justice,
Without all terms of pity. Speak ; thine an-
    swer.
  Ber. Pardon, my gracious lord ; for I
    submit
My fancy to your eyes : when I consider
What great creation and what dole of honor
Flies where you bid it, I find that she, which
    late
Was in my nobler thoughts most base, is now
The praised of the king ; who, so ennobled,
Is as 'twere born so.
  King.   Take her by the hand, 180
And tell her she is thine : to whom I promise
A counterpoise, if not to thy estate
A balance more replete.
  Ber.   I take her hand.
  King. Good fortune and the favor of the
    king
Smile upon this contract ; whose ceremony
Shall seem expedient on the now-born brief,
And be perform'd to-night : the solemn feast
Shall more attend upon the coming space,
Expecting absent friends. As thou lovest her,
Thy love's to me religious ; else, does err. 190
    [Exeunt all but Lafeu and Parolles.
  Laf. *[Advancing]* Do you hear, mon-
sieur? a word with you.
  Par. Your pleasure, sir ?
  Laf. Your lord and master did well to
make his recantation.
  Par. Recantation ! My lord ! my master !
  Laf. Ay ; is it not a language I speak ?
  Par. A most harsh one, and not to be un-
derstood without bloody succeeding. My mas-
ter !   200
  Laf. Are you companion to the Count
Rousillon ?
  Par. To any count, to all counts, to what
is man.
  Laf. To what is count's man : count's master is of another style.
  Par. You are too old, sir ; let it satisfy
you, you are too old.
  Laf. I must tell thee, sirrah, I write man ;
to which title age cannot bring thee.
  Par. What I dare too well do, I dare not
do.   210
  Laf. I did think thee, for two ordinaries,
to be a pretty wise fellow ; thou didst make
tolerable vent of thy travel ; it might pass :
yet the scarfs and the bannerets about thee did
manifoldly dissuade me from believing thee a
vessel of too great a burthen. I have now
found thee ; when I lose thee again, I care
not : yet art thou good for nothing but taking
up ; and that thou't scarce worth.
  Par. Hadst thou not the privilege of antiquity upon thee,—   221

  Laf. Do not plunge thyself too far in anger, lest thou hasten thy trial ; which if—Lord
have mercy on thee for a hen ! So, my good
window of lattice, fare thee well : thy casement I need not open, for I look through
thee. Give me thy hand.
  Par. My lord, you give me most egregious
indignity.
  Laf. Ay, with all my heart ; and thou art
worthy of it.   231
  Par. I have not, my lord, deserved it.
  Laf. Yes, good faith, every dram of it ;
and I will not bate thee a scruple.
  Par. Well, I shall be wiser.
  Laf. Even as soon as thou canst, for thou
hast to pull at a smack o' the contrary. If
ever thou be'st bound in thy scarf and beaten,
thou shalt find what it is to be proud of thy
bondage. I have a desire to hold my acquaintance with thee, or rather my knowledge, that
I may say in the default, he is a man I know.
  Par. My lord, you do me most insupportable vexation.
  Laf. I would it were hell-pains for thy
sake, and my poor doing eternal : for doing I
am past : as I will by thee, in what motion
age will give me leave.   *[Exit.*
  Par. Well, thou hast a son shall take this
disgrace off me ; scurvy, old, filthy, scurvy
lord ! Well, I must be patient ; there is no fet-
tering of authority. I'll beat him, by my life,
if I can meet him with any convenience, an
he were double and double a lord. I'll have
no more pity of his age than I would of—
I'll beat him, an if I could but meet him again.

    Re-enter LAFEU.

  Laf. Sirrah, your lord and master's married ; there's news for you : you have a new
mistress.
  Par. I most unfeignedly beseech your lordship to make some reservation of your
wrongs : he is my good lord : whom I serve
above is my master.
  Laf. Who ? God ?
  Par. Ay, sir.
  Laf. The devil it is that's thy master. Why
dost thou garter up thy arms o' this fashion ?
dost make hose of thy sleeves ? do other servants so ? Thou wert best set thy lower part
where thy nose stands. By mine honor, if I
were but two hours younger, I'ld beat thee :
methinks, thou art a general offence, and every man should beat thee : I think thou wast
created for men to breathe themselves upon
thee.
  Par. This is hard and undeserved measure,
my lord.
  Laf. Go to, sir ; you were beaten in Italy
for picking a kernel out of a pomegranate ;
you are a vagabond and no true traveller : you
are more saucy with lords and honorable personages than the commission of your birth and
virtue gives you heraldry. You are not worth
another word, else I'ld call you knave. I leave
you.   *[Exit.* 281
  Par. Good, very good ; it is so then : good,
very good ; let it be concealed awhile.

    Re-enter BERTRAM.

  Ber. Undone, and forfeited to cares for
    ever !
  Par. What's the matter, sweet-heart ?

Ber. Although before the solemn priest I
have sworn,
I will not bed her.
Par. What, what, sweet-heart ?
Ber. O my Parolles, they have married
me !
I'll to the Tuscan wars, and never bed her. 290
Par. France is a dog-hole, and it no more
merits
The tread of a man's foot : to the wars !
Ber. There's letters from my mother :
what the import is, I know not yet.
Par. Ay, that would be known. To the
wars, my boy, to the wars !
He wears his honor in a box unseen,
That hugs his kicky-wicky here at home,
Spending his manly marrow in her arms,
Which should sustain the bound and high
curvet
Of Mars's fiery steed. To other regions   300
France is a stable ; we that dwell in't jades ;
Therefore, to the war !
Ber. It shall be so : I'll send her to my
house,
Acquaint my mother with my hate to her,
And wherefore I am fled ; write to the king
That which I durst not speak ; his present
gift
Shall furnish me to those Italian fields,
Where noble fellows strike : war is no strife
To the dark house and the detested wife.
Par. Will this capriccio hold in thee ? art
sure ?   310
Ber. Go with me to my chamber, and ad-
vise me.
I'll send her straight away : to-morrow
I'll to the wars, she to her single sorrow.
Par. Why, these balls bound ; there's noise
in it. 'Tis hard :
A young man married is a man that's marr'd :
Therefore away, and leave her bravely ; go :
The king has done you wrong : but, hush, 'tis
so.   [*Exeunt.*

SCENE IV. *Paris. The* KING'S *palace.*

Enter HELENA *and* CLOWN.

Hel. My mother greets me kindly ; is she
well ?
Clo. She is not well ; but yet she has her
health : she's very merry ; but yet she is not
well : but thanks be given, she's very well and
wants nothing i' the world ; but yet she is not
well.
Hel. If she be very well, what does she ail,
that she's not very well ?
Clo. Truly, she's very well indeed, but for
two things.
Hel. What two things ?   10
Clo. One, that she's not in heaven, whither
God send her quickly ! the other that she's in
earth, from whence God send her quickly !

Enter PAROLLES.

Par. Bless you, my fortunate lady !
Hel. I hope, sir, I have your good will to
have mine own good fortunes.
Par. You had my prayers to lead them
on ; and to keep them on, have them still. O,
my knave, how does my old lady ?
Clo. So that you had her wrinkles and I
her money, I would she did as you say.   21
Par. Why, I say nothing.
Clo. Marry, you are the wiser man ; for

many a man's tongue shakes out his master's
undoing : to say nothing, to do nothing, to
know nothing, and to have nothing, is to be a
great part of your title ; which is within a very
little of nothing.
Par. Away ! thou'rt a knave.
Clo. You should have said, sir, before a
knave thou'rt a knave ; that's, before me
thou'rt a knave : this had been truth, sir.   31
Par. Go to, thou art a witty fool ; I have
found thee.
Clo. Did you find me in yourself, sir ? or
were you taught to find me ? The search, sir,
was profitable ; and much fool may you find
in you, even to the world's pleasure and the
increase of laughter.
Par. A good knave, i' faith, and well fed.
Madam, my lord will go away to-night ;   40
A very serious business calls on him.
The great prerogative and rite of love,
Which, as your due, time claims, he does ac-
knowledge ;
But puts it off to a compell'd restraint ;
Whose want, and whose delay, is strew'd with
sweets,
Which they distil now in the curbed time,
To make the coming hour o'erflow with joy
And pleasure drown the brim.
Hel.   What's his will else ?
Par. That you will take your instant leave
o' the king,
And make this haste as your own good pro-
ceeding,   50
Strengthen'd with what apology you think
May make it probable need.
Hel.   What more commands he ?
Par. That, having this obtain'd, you pres-
ently
Attend his further pleasure.
Hel. In every thing I wait upon his will.
Par. I shall report it so.
Hel.   I pray you. [*Exit Parolles.*]
Come, sirrah.   [*Exeunt.*

SCENE V. *Paris. The* KING'S *palace.*

Enter LAFEU *and* BERTRAM.

Laf. But I hope your lordship thinks not
him a soldier.
Ber. Yes, my lord, and of very valiant
approof.
Laf. You have it from his own deliverance.
Ber. And by other warranted testimony.
Laf. Then my dial goes not true : I took
this lark for a bunting.
Ber. I do assure you, my lord, he is very
great in knowledge and accordingly valiant.
Laf. I have then sinned against his experience and transgressed against his valor ; and
my state that way is dangerous, since I cannot yet find in my heart to repent. Here he
comes : I pray you, make us friends ; I will
pursue the amity.

Enter PAROLLES.

Par. [*To Bertram*] These things shall be
done, sir.
Laf. Pray you, sir, who's his tailor ?
Par. Sir ?
Laf. O, I know him well, I, sir ; he, sir, 's
a good workman, a very good tailor.   21
Ber. [*Aside to Par.*] Is she gone to the
king ?
Par. She is.

Ber. Will she away to-night?
Par. As you'll have her.
Ber. I have writ my letters, casketed my
treasure,
Given order for our horses; and to-night,
When I should take possession of the bride,
End ere I do begin.   29
Laf. A good traveller is something at the
latter end of a dinner; but one that lies three
thirds and uses a known truth to pass a thousand nothings with, should be once heard and
thrice beaten. God save you, captain.
Ber. Is there any unkindness between my
lord and you, monsieur?
Par. I know not how I have deserved to
run into my lord's displeasure.
Laf. You have made shift to run into 't,
boots and spurs and all, like him that leaped
into the custard; and out of it you'll run
again, rather than suffer question for your
residence.
Ber. It may be you have mistaken him, my
lord.
Laf. And shall do so ever, though I took
him at 's prayers. Fare you well, my lord;
and believe this of me, there can be no kernel
in this light nut; the soul of this man is his
clothes. Trust him not in matter of heavy consequence; I have kept of them tame, and
know their natures. Farewell, monsieur: I
have spoken better of you than you have or
will to deserve at my hand; but we must do
good against evil.   [*Exit.*
Par. An idle lord, I swear.
Ber. I think so.
Par. Why, do you not know him?
Ber. Yes, I do know him well, and common speech
Gives him a worthy pass. Here comes my
clog.

Enter Helena.

Hel. I have, sir, as I was commanded from
you,
Spoke with the king and have procured his
leave   60
For present parting; only he desires
Some private speech with you.
Ber.   I shall obey his will.
You must not marvel, Helen, at my course,
Which holds not color with the time, nor does
The ministration and required office
On my particular. Prepared I was not
For such a business; therefore am I found
So much unsettled: this drives me to entreat
you
That presently you take your way for home;
And rather muse than ask why I entreat you,
For my respects are better than they seem   71
And my appointments have in them a need
Greater than shows itself at the first view
To you that know them not. This to my
mother: [*Giving a letter.*
'Twill be two days ere I shall see you, so
I leave you to your wisdom.
Hel.   Sir, I can nothing say,
But that I am your most obedient servant.
Ber. Come, come, no more of that.
Hel.   And ever shall
With true observance seek to eke out that
Wherein toward me my homely stars have
fail'd
To equal my great fortune.

Ber.   Let that go: 81
My haste is very great: farewell; hie home.
Hel. Pray, sir, your pardon.
Ber.   Well, what would you say?
Hel. I am not worthy of the wealth I owe,
Nor dare I say 'tis mine, and yet it is;
But, like a timorous thief, most fain would
steal
What law does vouch mine own.
Ber.   What would you have?
Hel. Something; and scarce so much:
nothing, indeed.
I would not tell you what I would, my lord:
Faith, yes;   90
Strangers and foes do sunder, and not kiss.
Ber. I pray you, stay not, but in haste to
horse.
Hel. I shall not break your bidding, good
my lord.
Ber. Where are my other men, monsieur?
Farewell.   [*Exit Helena.*
Go thou toward home; where I will never
come
Whilst I can shake my sword or hear the
drum.
Away, and for our flight.
Par.   Bravely, coragio!
                                    [*Exeunt.*

ACT III.

Scene I. *Florence. The* Duke's *palace.*

Flourish. Enter the Duke *of Florence at-
tended; the two Frenchmen, with a troop
of soldiers.*
Duke. So that from point to point now
have you heard
The fundamental reasons of this war,
Whose great decision hath much blood let
forth
And more thirsts after.
First Lord.   Holy seems the quarrel
Upon your grace's part; black and fearful
On the opposer.
Duke. Therefore we marvel much our
cousin France
Would in so just a business shut his bosom
Against our borrowing prayers.
Sec. Lord.   Good my lord,
The reasons of our state I cannot yield,   10
But like a common and an outward man,
That the great figure of a council frames
By self-unable motion: therefore dare not
Say what I think of it, since I have found
Myself in my incertain grounds to fail
As often as I guess'd.
Duke.   Be it his pleasure.
First Lord. But I am sure the younger of
our nature,
That surfeit on their ease, will day by day
Come here for physic.
Duke.   Welcome shall they be;
And all the honors that can fly from us   20
Shall on them settle. You know your places
well;
When better fall, for your avails they fell:
To-morrow to the field.   [*Flourish. Exeunt.*

Scene II. *Rousillon. The* Count's *palace.*
Enter Countess *and* Clown.
Count. It hath happened all as I would

have had it, save that he comes not along with her.

Clo. By my troth, I take my young lord to be a very melancholy man.

Count. By what observance, I pray you ?

Clo. Why, he will look upon his boot and sing ; mend the ruff and sing ; ask questions and sing ; pick his teeth and sing. I know a man that had this trick of melancholy sold a goodly manor for a song.   10

Count. Let me see what he writes, and when he means to come.   [*Opening a letter.*

Clo. I have no mind to Isbel since I was at court : our old ling and our Isbels o' the country are nothing like your old ling and your Isbels o' the court : the brains of my Cupid's knocked out, and I begin to love, as an old man loves money, with no stomach.

Count. What have we here ?

Clo. E'en that you have there. [*Exit.* 20

Count. [*Reads*] I have sent you a daughter-in-law : she hath recovered the king, and undone me. I have wedded her, not bedded her ; and sworn to make the 'not' eternal. You shall hear I am run away : know it before the report come. If there be breadth enough in the world, I will hold a long distance. My duty to you.   Your unfortunate son,
              BERTRAM.

This is not well, rash and unbridled boy,   30
To fly the favors of so good a king ;
To pluck his indignation on thy head
By the misprising of a maid too virtuous
For the contempt of empire.

      Re-enter CLOWN.

Clo. O madam, yonder is heavy news within between two soldiers and my young lady !

Count. What is the matter ?

Clo. Nay, there is some comfort in the news, some comfort ; your son will not be killed so soon as I thought he would.   40

Count. Why should he be killed ?

Clo. So say I, madam, if he run away, as I hear he does : the danger is in standing to't ; that's the loss of men, though it be the getting of children. Here they come will tell you more : for my part, I only hear your son was run away.   [*Exit.*

    Enter HELENA, *and two* Gentlemen.

First Gent. Save you, good madam.

Hel. Madam, my lord is gone, for ever gone.

Sec. Gent. Do not say so.

Count. Think upon patience. Pray you, gentlemen,   50
I have felt so many quirks of joy and grief,
That the first face of neither, on the start,
Can woman me unto't : where is my son, I pray you ?

Sec. Gent. Madam, he's gone to serve the duke of Florence :
We met him thitherward ; for thence we came,
And, after some dispatch in hand at court,
Thither we bend again.

Hel. Look on his letter, madam ; here's my passport.

[*Reads*] When thou canst get the ring upon my finger which never shall come off, and show me a child begotten of thy body that I

am father to, then call me husband : but in such a ' then ' I write a ' never.'

This is a dreadful sentence.

Count. Brought you this letter, gentlemen ?

First Gent.   Ay, madam ;
And for the contents' sake are sorry for our pains.

Count. I prithee, lady, have a better cheer ;
If thou engrossest all the griefs are thine,
Thou robb'st me of a moiety : he was my son ;
But I do wash his name out of my blood,   70
And thou art all my child. Towards Florence is he ?

Sec. Gent. Ay, madam.

Count.   And to be a soldier ?

Sec. Gent. Such is his noble purpose ; and believe 't,
The duke will lay upon him all the honor
That good convenience claims.

Count.   Return you thither ?

First Gent. Ay, madam, with the swiftest wing of speed.

Hel. [*Reads*] Till I have no wife I have nothing in France.

'Tis bitter.

Count. Find you that there ?

Hel.   Ay, madam.

First Gent. 'Tis but the boldness of his hand, haply, which his heart was not consenting to.   80

Count. Nothing in France, until he have no wife !
There's nothing here that is too good for him
But only she ; and she deserves a lord
That twenty such rude boys might tend upon
And call her hourly mistress. Who was with him ?

First Gent. A servant only, and a gentleman
Which I have sometime known.

Count. Parolles, was it not ?

First Gent. Ay, my good lady, he.

Count. A very tainted fellow, and full of wickedness.
My son corrupts a well-derived nature   90
With his inducement.

First Gent.   Indeed, good lady,
The fellow has a deal of that too much,
Which holds him much to have.

Count. You're welcome, gentlemen.
I will entreat you, when you see my son,
To tell him that his sword can never win
The honor that he loses : more I'll entreat you
Written to bear along.

Sec. Gent.   We serve you, madam,
In that and all your worthiest affairs.

Count. Not so, but as we change our courtesies.   100
Will you draw near !

    [*Exeunt Countess and Gentlemen.*

Hel. ' Till I have no wife, I have nothing in France.'
Nothing in France, until he has no wife !
Thou shalt have none, Rousillon, none in France ;
Then hast thou all again. Poor lord ! is't I
That chase thee from thy country and expose
Those tender limbs of thine to the event
Of the none-sparing war ? and is it I
That drive thee from the sportive court, where thou
Wast shot at with fair eyes, to be the mark

Of smoky muskets ? O you leaden messen-
gers,   111
That ride upon the violent speed of fire,
Fly with false aim ; move the still-peering air,
That sings with piercing ; do not touch my
lord.
Whoever shoots at him, I set him there ;
Whoever charges on his forward breast,
I am the caitiff that do hold him to't ;
And, though I kill him not, I am the cause
His death was so effected : better 'twere
I met the ravin lion when he roar'd   120
With sharp constraint of hunger ; better 'twere
That all the miseries which nature owes
Were mine at once. No, come thou home,
Rousillon,
Whence honor but of danger wins a scar,
As oft it loses all : I will be gone ;
My being here it is that holds thee hence :
Shall I stay here to do't ? no, no, although
The air of paradise did fan the house
And angels officed all : I will be gone,
That pitiful rumor may report my flight,   130
To consolate thine ear. Come, night ; end,
day !
For with the dark, poor thief, I'll steal away.
                                                [*Exit.*

SCENE III. *Florence. Before the* DUKE'S
palace.

Flourish. Enter the DUKE *of Florence,* BER-
TRAM, PAROLLES, Soldiers, Drum, *and* Trumpets.

Duke. The general of our horse thou art ;
and we,
Great in our hope, lay our best love and cre-
dence
Upon thy promising fortune.
Ber.   Sir, it is
A charge too heavy for my strength, but yet
We'll strive to bear it for your worthy sake
To the extreme edge of hazard.
Duke.   Then go thou forth ;
And fortune play upon thy prosperous helm,
As thy auspicious mistress !
Ber.   This very day,
Great Mars, I put myself into thy file :
Make me but like my thoughts, and I shall
prove   10
A lover of thy drum, hater of love. [*Exeunt.*

SCENE IV. *Rousillon. The* COUNT'S *palace.*

Enter COUNTESS *and* Steward.

Count. Alas ! and would you take the let-
ter of her ?
Might you not know she would do as she has
done,
By sending me a letter ? Read it again.
Stew. [*Reads*]
I am Saint Jaques' pilgrim, thither gone :
Ambitious love hath so in me offended,
That barefoot plod I the cold ground upon,
   With sainted vow my faults to have
   amended.
Write, write, that from the bloody course of
war
My dearest master, your dear son, may hie :
Bless him at home in peace, whilst I from far
His name with zealous fervor sanctify :   11
His taken labors bid him me forgive ;
I, his despiteful Juno, sent him forth
From courtly friends, with camping foes to
live,

Where death and danger dogs the heels of
worth :
He is too good and fair for death and me :
   Whom I myself embrace, to set him free.
Count. Ah, what sharp stings are in her
mildest words !
Rinaldo, you did never lack advice so much,
As letting her pass so : had I spoke with her,
I could have well diverted her intents,   21
Which thus she hath prevented.
Stew.   Pardon me, madam :
If I had given you this at over-night,
She might have been o'erta'en ; and yet she
writes,
Pursuit would be but vain.
Count.   What angel shall
Bless this unworthy husband ? he cannot
thrive,
Unless her prayers, whom heaven delights to
hear
And loves to grant, reprieve him from the
wrath
Of greatest justice. Write, write, Rinaldo,
To this unworthy husband of his wife ;   30
Let every word weigh heavy of her worth
That he does weigh too light : my greatest
grief,
Though little he do feel it, set down sharply.
Dispatch the most convenient messenger :
When haply he shall hear that she is gone,
He will return ; and hope I may that she,
Hearing so much, will speed her foot again,
Led hither by pure love : which of them both
Is dearest to me, I have no skill in sense
To make distinction : provide this messenger :   41
My heart is heavy and mine age is weak ;
Grief would have tears, and sorrow bids me
speak.   [*Exeunt.*

SCENE V. *Florence. Without the walls. A
tucket afar off.*

Enter an old Widow *of Florence,* DIANA, VIO-
LENTA, *and* MARIANA, *with other* Citizens.

Wid. Nay, come ; for if they do approach
the city, we shall lose all the sight.
Dia. They say the French count has done
most honorable service.
Wid. It is reported that he has taken their
greatest commander ; and that with his own
hand he slew the duke's brother. [*Tucket.*] We
have lost our labor ; they are gone a contrary way : hark ! you may know by their
trumpets.   9
Mar. Come, let's return again, and suffice
ourselves with the report of it. Well, Diana,
take heed of this French earl : the honor of
a maid is her name ; and no legacy is so rich
as honesty.
Wid. I have told my neighbor how you
have been solicited by a gentleman his companion.
Mar. I know that knave ; hang him ! one
Parolles : a filthy officer he is in those suggestions for the young earl. Beware of them,
Diana ; their promises, enticements, oaths, tokens, and all these engines of lust, are not the
things they go under : many a maid hath been
seduced by them ; and the misery is, example,
that so terrible shows in the wreck of maiden-
hood, cannot for all that dissuade succession,
but that they are limed with the twigs that
threaten them. I hope I need not to advise you
further ; but I hope your own grace will keep

you where you are, though there were no further danger known but the modesty which is so lost.   30

Dia. You shall not need to fear me.

Wid. I hope so.

Enter HELENA, *disguised like a Pilgrim.*

Look, here comes a pilgrim : I know she will lie at my house ; thither they send one another : I'll question her. God save you, pilgrim ! whither are you bound ?

Hel. To Saint Jaques le Grand.

Where do the palmers lodge, I do beseech you ?

Wid. At the Saint Francis here beside the port.

Hel. Is this the way ?   40

Wid. Ay, marry, is't. [*A march afar.*]
   Hark you ! they come this way.
If you will tarry, holy pilgrim,
But till the troops come by,
I will conduct you where you shall be lodged ;
The rather, for I think I know your hostess
As ample as myself.

Hel. Is it yourself ?

Wid. If you shall please so, pilgrim.

Hel. I thank you, and will stay upon your leisure.

Wid. You came, I think, from France ?

Hel. I did so.

Wid. Here you shall see a countryman of yours   50
That has done worthy service.

Hel. His name, I pray you.

Dia. The Count Rousillon : know you such a one ?

Hel. But by the ear, that hears most nobly of him :
His face I know not.

Dia. Whatsome'er he is,
He's bravely taken here. He stole from France,
As 'tis reported, for the king had married him
Against his liking : think you it is so ?

Hel. Ay, surely, mere the truth : I know his lady.

Dia. There is a gentleman that serves the count
Reports but coarsely of her.

Hel. What's his name ? 60

Dia. Monsieur Parolles.

Hel. O, I believe with him,
In argument of praise, or to the worth
Of the great count himself, she is too mean
To have her name repeated : all her deserving
Is a reserved honesty, and that
I have not heard examined.

Dia. Alas, poor lady !
'Tis a hard bondage to become the wife
Of a detesting lord.

Wid. I warrant, good creature, wheresoe'er she is,
Her heart weighs sadly : this young maid might do her   70
A shrewd turn, if she pleased.

Hel. How do you mean ?
May be the amorous count solicits her
In the unlawful purpose.

Wid. He does indeed ;
And brokes with all that can in such a suit
Corrupt the tender honor of a maid :
But she is arm'd for him and keeps her guard
In honestest defence.

Mar. The gods forbid else !

Wid. So, now they come :

Drum and Colors.

Enter BERTRAM, PAROLLES, *and the whole army.*

That is Antonio, the duke's eldest son ;
That, Escalus.

Hel. Which is the Frenchman ?

Dia. He ; 80
That with the plume : 'tis a most gallant fellow.
I would he loved his wife : if he were honester
He were much goodlier : is't not a handsome gentleman ?

Hel. I like him well.

Dia. 'Tis pity he is not honest : yond's that same knave
That leads him to these places : were I his lady,
I would poison that vile rascal.

Hel. Which is he ?

Dia. That jack-an-apes with scarfs : why is he melancholy ?

Hel. Perchance he's hurt i' the battle.   90

Par. Lose our drum ! well.

Mar. He's shrewdly vexed at something : look, he has spied us.

Wid. Marry, hang you !

Mar. And your courtesy, for a ring-carrier !   [*Exeunt Bertram, Parolles, and army.*

Wid. The troop is past. Come, pilgrim, I will bring you
Where you shall host : of enjoin'd penitents
There's four or five, to great Saint Jaques bound,
Already at my house.

Hel. I humbly thank you :
Please it this matron and this gentle maid 100
To eat with us to-night, the charge and thanking
Shall be for me ; and, to requite you further,
I will bestow some precepts of this virgin
Worthy the note.

Both. We'll take your offer kindly.
                                           [*Exeunt.*

SCENE VI. *Camp before Florence.*

Enter BERTRAM *and the two French* Lords.

Sec. Lord. Nay, good my lord, put him to't ; let him have his way.

First Lord. If your lordship find him not a hilding, hold me no more in your respect.

Sec. Lord. On my life, my lord, a bubble.

Ber. Do you think I am so far deceived in him ?

Sec. Lord. Believe it, my lord, in mine own direct knowledge, without any malice, but to speak of him as my kinsman, he's a most notable coward, an infinite and endless liar, an hourly promise-breaker, the owner of no one good quality worthy your lordship's entertainment.

First Lord. It were fit you knew him ; lest, reposing too far in his virtue, which he hath not, he might at some great and trusty business in a main danger fail you.

Ber. I would I knew in what particular action to try him.   19

First Lord. None better than to let him fetch off his drum, which you hear him so confidently undertake to do.

Sec. Lord. I, with a troop of Florentines, will suddenly surprise him ; such I will have, whom I am sure he knows not from the enemy : we will bind and hoodwink him so, that he shall suppose no other but that he is carried into the leaguer of the adversaries, when we bring him to our own tents. Be but your lordship present at his examination : if he do not, for the promise of his life and in the highest compulsion of base fear, offer to betray you and deliver all the intelligence in his power against you, and that with the divine forfeit of his soul upon oath, never trust my judgment in any thing.

First Lord. O, for the love of laughter, let him fetch his drum ; he says he has a stratagem for't : when your lordship sees the bottom of his success in't, and to what metal this counterfeit lump of ore will be melted, if you give him not John Drum's entertainment, your inclining cannot be removed. Here he comes.

Enter PAROLLES.

Sec. Lord. [*Aside to Ber.*] O, for the love of laughter, hinder not the honor of his design : let him fetch off his drum in any hand.

Ber. How now, monsieur ! this drum sticks sorely in your disposition.

First Lord. A pox on't, let it go ; 'tis but a drum.   49

Par. 'But a drum' ! is't 'but a drum' ? A drum so lost ! There was excellent command, —to charge in with our horse upon our own wings, and to rend our own soldiers !

First Lord. That was not to be blamed in the command of the service : it was a disaster of war that Cæsar himself could not have prevented, if he had been there to command.

Ber. Well, we cannot greatly condemn our success : some dishonor we had in the loss of that drum ; but it is not to be recovered.   60

Par. It might have been recovered.

Ber. It might ; but it is not now.

Par. It is to be recovered : but that the merit of service is seldom attributed to the true and exact performer, I would have that drum or another, or ' hic jacet.'

Ber. Why, if you have a stomach, to't, monsieur : if you think your mystery in stratagem can bring this instrument of honor again into his native quarter, be magnanimous in the enterprise and go on ; I will grace the attempt for a worthy exploit : if you speed well in it, the duke shall both speak of it, and extend to you what further becomes your greatness, even to the utmost syllable of your worthiness.

Par. By the hand of a soldier, I will undertake it.

Ber. But you must not now slumber in it.

Par. I'll about it this evening : and I will presently pen down my dilemmas, encourage myself in my certainty, put myself into my mortal preparation ; and by midnight look to hear further from me.

Ber. May I be bold to acquaint his grace you are gone about it ?

Par. I know not what the success will be, my lord ; but the attempt I vow.

Ber. I know thou'rt valiant ; and, to the possibility of thy soldiership, will subscribe for thee. Farewell.   90

Par. I love not many words. [*Exit.*

Sec. Lord. No more than a fish loves water. Is not this a strange fellow, my lord, that so confidently seems to undertake this business,

which he knows is not to be done ; damns himself to do and dares better be damned than to do't ?

First Lord. You do not know him, my lord, as we do : certain it is that he will steal himself into a man's favor and for a week escape a great deal of discoveries ; but when you find him out, you have him ever after.   101

Ber. Why, do you think he will make no deed at all of this that so seriously he does address himself unto ?

Sec. Lord. None in the world ; but return with an invention and clap upon you two or three probable lies : but we have almost embossed him ; you shall see his fall to-night ; for indeed he is not for your lordship's respect.   109

First Lord. We'll make you some sport with the fox ere we case him. He was first smoked by the old lord Lafeu : when his disguise and he is parted, tell me what a sprat you shall find him ; which you shall see this very night.

Sec. Lord. I must go look my twigs : he shall be caught.

Ber. Your brother he shall go along with me.

Sec. Lord. As't please your lordship : I'll leave you.   [*Exit.*

Ber. Now will I lead you to the house, and show you
The lass I spoke of.

First Lord.   But you say she's honest.

Ber. That's all the fault : I spoke with her
   but once   120
And found her wondrous cold ; but I sent to
   her,
By this same coxcomb that we have i' the wind,
Tokens and letters which she did re-send ;
And this is all I have done. She's a fair creature :
Will you go see her ?

First Lord.   With all my heart, my lord.
                                                            [*Exeunt.*

SCENE VII. *Florence. The* Widow's *house.*

Enter HELENA *and* Widow.

Hel. If you misdoubt me that I am not she,
I know not how I shall assure you further,
But I shall lose the grounds I work upon.

Wid. Though my estate be fallen, I was
   well born,
Nothing acquainted with these businesses ;
And would not put my reputation now
In any staining act.

Hel.   Nor would I wish you.
First, give me trust, the count he is my husband,
And what to your sworn counsel I have spoken
Is so from word to word ; and then you cannot,   10
By the good aid that I of you shall borrow,
Err in bestowing it.

Wid.   I should believe you :
For you have show'd me that which well approves
You're great in fortune.

Hel.   Take this purse of gold,
And let me buy your friendly help thus far,
Which I will over-pay and pay again
When I have found it. The count he wooes
   your daughter,
Lays down his wanton siege before her beauty,

Resolved to carry her : let her in fine consent,
As we'll direct her how 'tis best to bear it.   20
Now my important blood will nought deny
That she'll demand : a ring the county wears,
That downward hath succeeded in his house
From son to son, some four or five descents
Since the first father wore it : this ring he
holds
In most rich choice ; yet in his idle fire,
To buy his will, it would not seem too dear,
Howe'er repented after.
   Wid.   Now I see
The bottom of your purpose.
   Hel. You see it lawful, then : it is no more,
But that your daughter, ere she seems as
won,   31
Desires this ring ; appoints him an encounter ;
In fine, delivers me to fill the time,
Herself most chastely absent : after this,
To marry her, I'll add three thousand crowns
To what is passed already.
   Wid.   I have yielded :
Instruct my daughter how she shall persever,
That time and place with this deceit so lawful
May prove coherent. Every night he comes
With musics of all sorts and songs composed
To her unworthiness : it nothing steads us   41
To chide him from our eaves ; for he persists
As if his life lay on't.
   Hel.   Why then to-night
Let us assay our plot ; which, if it speed,
Is wicked meaning in a lawful deed
And lawful meaning in a lawful act,
Where both not sin, and yet a sinful fact :
But let's about it.   [*Exeunt.*

ACT IV.

Scene I. *Without the Florentine camp.*

Enter Second French Lord, *with five or six
other Soldiers in ambush.*

   Sec. Lord. He can come no other way but
by this hedge-corner. When you sally upon
him, speak what terrible language you will :
though you understand it not yourselves, no
matter ; for we must not seem to understand
him, unless when one among us whom we must
produce for an interpreter.
   First Sold. Good captain, let me be the interpreter.
   Sec. Lord. Art not acquainted with him ?
knows he not thy voice ?   11
   First Sold. No, sir, I warrant you.
   Sec. Lord. But what linsey-woolsey hast
thou to speak to us again ?
   First Sold. E'en such as you speak to me.
   Sec. Lord. He must think us some band of
strangers i' the adversary's entertainment. Now
he hath a smack of all neighboring languages ;
therefore we must every one be a man of his
own fancy, not to know what we speak one to
another ; so we seem to know, is to know
straight our purpose : choughs' language, gabble enough, and good enough. As for you, interpreter, you must seem very politic. But
couch, ho ! here he comes, to beguile two
hours in a sleep, and then to return and swear
the lies he forges.

Enter Parolles.

   Par. Ten o'clock : within these three hours
'twill be time enough to go home. What shall
I say I have done ? It must be a very plausive
invention that carries it : they begin to smoke
me ; and disgraces have of late knocked too
often at my door. I find my tongue is too fool-
hardy ; but my heart hath the fear of Mars
before it and of his creatures, not daring the
reports of my tongue.
   Sec. Lord. This is the first truth that e'er
thine own tongue was guilty of.
   Par. What the devil should move me to undertake the recovery of this drum, being not
ignorant of the impossibility, and knowing I
had no such purpose ? I must give myself some
hurts, and say I got them in exploit : yet slight
ones will not carry it ; they will say, 'Came
you off with so little ? ' and great ones I dare
not give. Wherefore, what's the instance ?
Tongue, I must put you into a butter-woman's
mouth and buy myself another of Bajazet's
mule, if you prattle me into these perils.
   Sec. Lord. Is it possible he should know
what he is, and be that he is ?   49
   Par. I would the cutting of my garments
would serve the turn, or the breaking of my
Spanish sword.
   Sec. Lord. We cannot afford you so.
   Par. Or the baring of my beard ; and to
say it was in stratagem.
   Sec. Lord. 'Twould not do.
   Par. Or to drown my clothes, and say I
was stripped.
   Sec. Lord. Hardly serve.
   Par. Though I swore I leaped from the
window of the citadel.   61
   Sec. Lord. How deep ?
   Par. Thirty fathom.
   Sec. Lord. Three great oaths would scarce
make that be believed.
   Par. I would I had any drum of the ene-
my's : I would swear I recovered it.
   Sec. Lord. You shall hear one anon.
   Par. A drum now of the enemy's,—
                     [*Alarum within.*
   Sec. Lord. Throca movousus, cargo, cargo,
cargo.   71
   All. Cargo, cargo, cargo, villiando par
corbo, cargo.
   Par. O, ransom, ransom ! do not hide mine
eyes.   [*They seize and blindfold him.*
   First Sold. Boskos thromuldo boskos.
   Par. I know you are the Muskos' regi-
ment :
And I shall lose my life for want of language ;
If there be here German, or Dane, low Dutch,
Italian, or French, let him speak to me ; I'll
Discover that which shall undo the Florentine.
   First Sold. Boskos vauvado : I understand
thee, and can speak thy tongue. Kerely bonto,
sir, betake thee to thy faith, for seventeen
poniards are at thy bosom.
   Par. O !
   First Sold. O, pray, pray, pray ! Manka
revania dulche.
   Sec. Lord. Oscorbidulchos volivorco.
   First Sold. The general is content to spare
thee yet ;
And, hoodwink'd as thou art, will lead thee
on   90
To gather from thee : haply thou mayst inform
Something to save thy life.
   Par.   O, let me live !
And all the secrets of our camp I'll show,

Their force, their purposes; nay, I'll speak
 that
Which you will wonder at.
 First Sold.   But wilt thou faithfully?
 Par. If I do not, damn me.
 First Sold. Acordo linta.
Come on; thou art granted space.
   [*Exit, with Parolles guarded. A short
      alarum within.*
 Sec. Lord. Go, tell the Count Rousillon,
  and my brother,
We have caught the woodcock, and will keep
 him muffled   100
Till we do hear from them.
 Sec. Sold.   Captain, I will.
 Sec. Lord. A' will betray us all unto our-
 selves :
Inform on that.
 Sec. Sold. So I will, sir.
 Sec. Lord. Till then I'll keep him dark and
 safely lock'd.   [*Exeunt.*

SCENE II. *Florence. The* Widow's *house.*

Enter BERTRAM *and* DIANA.

 Ber. They told me that your name was
Fontibell.
 Dia. No, my good lord, Diana.
 Ber.   Titled goddess ;
And worth it, with addition ! But, fair soul,
In your fine frame hath love no quality ?
If the quick fire of youth light not your mind,
You are no maiden, but a monument :
When you are dead, you should be such a one
As you are now, for you are cold and stern ;
And now you should be as your mother was
When your sweet self was got.   10
 Dia. She then was honest.
 Ber.   So should you be.
 Dia.   No :
My mother did but duty ; such, my lord,
As you owe to your wife.
 Ber.   No more o' that ;
I prithee, do not strive against my vows :
I was compell'd to her ; but I love thee
By love's own sweet constraint, and will for
 ever
Do thee all rights of service.
 Dia.   Ay, so you serve us
Till we serve you ; but when you have our
 roses,
You barely leave our thorns to prick ourselves
And mock us with our bareness.
 Ber.   How have I sworn ! 20
 Dia. 'Tis not the many oaths that makes
 the truth,
But the plain single vow that is vow'd true.
What is not holy, that we swear not by,
But take the High'st to witness : then, pray
 you, tell me,
If I should swear by God's great attributes,
I loved you dearly, would you believe my
 oaths,
When I did love you ill ? This has no holding,
To swear by him whom I protest to love,
That I will work against him : therefore your
 oaths
Are words and poor conditions, but unseal'd,
At least in my opinion.   31
 Ber.   Change it, change it ;
Be not so holy-cruel : love is holy ;
And my integrity ne'er knew the crafts
That you do charge men with. Stand no more
 off,

But give thyself unto my sick desires,
Who then recover : say thou art mine, and
 ever
My love as it begins shall so persever.
 Dia. I see that men make ropes in such a
 scarre
That we'll forsake ourselves. Give me that ring.
 Ber. I'll lend it thee, my dear ; but have no
 power   40
To give it from me.
 Dia.   Will you not, my lord ?
 Ber. It is an honor 'longing to our house,
Bequeathed down from many ancestors ;
Which were the greatest obloquy i' the world
In me to lose.
 Dia.   Mine honor's such a ring :
My chastity's the jewel of our house,
Bequeathed down from many ancestors ;
Which were the greatest obloquy i' the world
In me to lose : thus your own proper wisdom
Brings in the champion Honor on my part, 50
Against your vain assault.
 Ber.   Here, take my ring :
My house, mine honor, yea, my life, be thine,
And I'll be bid by thee.
 Dia. When midnight comes, knock at my
 chamber-window :
I'll order take my mother shall not hear.
Now will I charge you in the band of truth,
When you have conquer'd my yet maiden bed,
Remain there but an hour, nor speak to me :
My reasons are most strong ; and you shall
 know them
When back again this ring shall be deliver'd :
And on your finger in the night I'll put 61
Another ring, that what in time proceeds
May token to the future our past deeds.
Adieu, till then ; then, fail not. You have won
A wife of me, though there my hope be done.
 Ber. A heaven on earth I have won by
 wooing thee.   [*Exit.*
 Dia. For which live long to thank both
 heaven and me !
You may so in the end.
My mother told me just how he would woo,
As if she sat in 's heart ; she says all men 70
Have the like oaths : he had sworn to marry
 me
When his wife's dead ; therefore I'll lie with
 him
When I am buried. Since Frenchmen are so
 braid,
Marry that will, I live and die a maid :
Only in this disguise I think't no sin
To cozen him that would unjustly win. [*Exit.*

SCENE III. *The Florentine camp.*

Enter the two French Lords *and some two or
three* Soldiers.

 First Lord. You have not given him his
mother's letter ?
 Sec. Lord. I have delivered it an hour
since : there is something in't that stings his
nature ; for on the reading it he changed almost into another man.
 First Lord. He has much worthy blame
laid upon him for shaking off so good a wife
and so sweet a lady.   9
 Sec. Lord. Especially he hath incurred the
everlasting displeasure of the king, who had
even tuned his bounty to sing happiness to him.
I will tell you a thing, but you shall let it dwell
darkly with you.

First Lord. When you have spoken it, 'tis dead, and I am the grave of it.

Sec. Lord. He hath perverted a young gentlewoman here in Florence, of a most chaste renown ; and this night he fleshes his will in the spoil of her honor : he hath given her his monumental ring, and thinks himself made in the unchaste composition.

First Lord. Now, God delay our rebellion ! as we are ourselves, what things are we !

Sec. Lord. Merely our own traitors. And as in the common course of all treasons, we still see them reveal themselves, till they attain to their abhorred ends, so he that in this action contrives against his own nobility, in his proper stream o'erflows himself. 30

First Lord. Is it not meant damnable in us, to be trumpeters of our unlawful intents ? We shall not then have his company to-night ?

Sec. Lord. Not till after midnight ; for he is dieted to his hour.

First Lord. That approaches apace ; I would gladly have him see his company anatomized, that he might take a measure of his own judgments, wherein so curiously he had set this counterfeit. 40

Sec. Lord. We will not meddle with him till he come ; for his presence must be the whip of the other.

First Lord. In the mean time, what hear you of these wars ?

Sec. Lord. I hear there is an overture of peace.

First Lord. Nay, I assure you, a peace concluded.

Sec. Lord. What will Count Rousillon do then ? will he travel higher, or return again into France ? 51

First Lord. I perceive, by this demand, you are not altogether of his council.

Sec. Lord. Let it be forbid, sir ; so should I be a great deal of his act.

First Lord. Sir, his wife some two months since fled from his house : her pretence is a pilgrimage to Saint Jaques le Grand ; which holy undertaking with most austere sanctimony she accomplished ; and, there residing, the tenderness of her nature became as a prey to her grief ; in fine, made a groan of her last breath, and now she sings in heaven.

Sec. Lord. How is this justified ?

First Lord. The stronger part of it by her own letters, which makes her story true, even to the point of her death : her death itself, which could not be her office to say is come, was faithfully confirmed by the rector of the place. 60

Sec. Lord. Hath the count all this intelligence ?

First Lord. Ay, and the particular confirmations, point from point, so to the full arming of the verity.

Sec. Lord. I am heartily sorry that he'll be glad of this.

First Lord. How mightily sometimes we make us comforts of our losses !

Sec. Lord. And how mightily some other times we drown our gain in tears ! The great dignity that his valor hath here acquired for him shall at home be encountered with a shame as ample.

First Lord. The web of our life is of a mingled yarn, good and ill together : our virtues would be proud, if our faults whipped them not ; and our crimes would despair, if they were not cherished by our virtues.

Enter a Messenger.

How now ! where's your master ?

Serv. He met the duke in the street, sir, of whom he hath taken a solemn leave : his lordship will next morning for France. The duke hath offered him letters of commendations to the king.

Sec. Lord. They shall be no more than needful there, if they were more than they can commend.

First Lord. They cannot be too sweet for the king's tartness. Here's his lordship now.

Enter BERTRAM.

How now, my lord ! is't not after midnight ?

Ber. I have to-night dispatched sixteen businesses, a month's length a-piece, by an abstract of success : I have congied with the duke, done my adieu with his nearest ; buried a wife, mourned for her ; writ to my lady mother I am returning; entertained my convoy ; and between these main parcels of dispatch effected many nicer needs ; the last was the greatest, but that I have not ended yet.

Sec. Lord. If the business be of any difficulty, and this morning your departure hence, it requires haste of your lordship. 109

Ber. I mean, the business is not ended, as fearing to hear of it hereafter. But shall we have this dialogue between the fool and the soldier ? Come, bring forth this counterfeit module, he has deceived me, like a double-meaning prophesier.

Sec. Lord. Bring him forth : has sat i' the stocks all night, poor gallant knave.

Ber. No matter ; his heels have deserved it, in usurping his spurs so long. How does he carry himself ? 120

Sec. Lord. I have told your lordship already, the stocks carry him. But to answer you as you would be understood ; he weeps like a wench that had shed her milk : he hath confessed himself to Morgan, whom he supposes to be a friar, from the time of his remembrance to this very instant disaster of his setting i' the stocks : and what think you he hath confessed ?

Ber. Nothing of me, has a' ? 129

Sec. Lord. His confession is taken, and it shall be read to his face : if your lordship be in't, as I believe you are, you must have the patience to hear it.

Enter PAROLLES *guarded, and* First Soldier.

Ber. A plague upon him ! muffled ! he can say nothing of me : hush, hush !

First Lord. Hoodman comes ! Portotartarosa.

First Sold. He calls for the tortures : what will you say without 'em ?

Par. I will confess what I know without constraint : if ye pinch me like a pasty, I can say no more. 141

First Sold. Bosko chimurcho.

First Lord. Boblibindo chicurmurco.

First Sold. You are a merciful general. Our general bids you answer to what I shall ask you out of a note.

Par. And truly, as I hope to live.

First Sold. [*Reads*] 'First demand of him how many horse the duke is strong.' What say you to that ?   150

Par. Five or six thousand ; but very weak and unserviceable : the troops are all scattered, and the commanders very poor rogues, upon my reputation and credit and as I hope to live.

First Sold. Shall I set down your answer so ?

Par. Do : I'll take the sacrament on't, how and which way you will.

Ber. All's one to him. What a past-saving slave is this !   159

First Lord. You're deceived, my lord : this is Monsieur Parolles, the gallant militarist,— that was his own phrase,—that had the whole theoric of war in the knot of his scarf, and the practice in the chape of his dagger.

Sec. Lord. I will never trust a man again for keeping his sword clean, nor believe he can have every thing in him by wearing his apparel neatly.

First Sold. Well, that's set down.   169

Par. Five or six thousand horse, I said,— I will say true,—or thereabouts, set down, for I'll speak truth.

First Lord. He's very near the truth in this.

Ber. But I con him no thanks for't, in the nature he delivers it.

Par. Poor rogues, I pray you, say.

First Sold. Well, that's set down.

Par. I humbly thank you, sir : a truth's a truth, the rogues are marvellous poor.   179

First Sold. [*Reads*] 'Demand of him, of what strength they are a-foot.' What say you to that ?

Par. By my troth, sir, if I were to live this present hour, I will tell true. Let me see : Spurio, a hundred and fifty ; Sebastian, so many ; Corambus, so many ; Jaques, so many ; Guiltian, Cosmo, Lodowick, and Gratii, two hundred and fifty each ; mine own company, Chitopher, Vaumond, Bentii, two hundred and fifty each : so that the muster-file, rotten and sound, upon my life, amounts not to fifteen thousand poll ; half of the which dare not shake the snow from off their cassocks, lest they shake themselves to pieces.

Ber. What shall be done to him ?

First Lord. Nothing, but let him have thanks. Demand of him my condition, and what credit I have with the duke.

First Sold. Well, that's set down. [*Reads*] 'You shall demand of him, whether one Captain Dumain be i' the camp, a Frenchman ; what his reputation is with the duke ; what his valor, honesty, and expertness in wars ; or whether he thinks it were not possible, with well-weighing sums of gold, to corrupt him to a revolt.' What say you to this ? what do you know of it ?

Par. I beseech you, let me answer to the particular of the inter'gatories : demand them singly.

First Sold. Do you know this Captain Dumain ?   210

Par. I know him : a' was a botcher's 'prentice in Paris, from whence he was whipped for getting the shrieve's fool with child,—a dumb innocent, that could not say him nay.

Ber. Nay, by your leave, hold your hands ; though I know his brains are forfeit to the next tile that falls.

First Sold. Well, is this captain in the duke of Florence's camp ?   219

Par. Upon my knowledge, he is, and lousy.

First Lord. Nay, look not so upon me ; we shall hear of your lordship anon.

First Sold. What is his reputation with the duke ?

Par. The duke knows him for no other but a poor officer of mine ; and writ to me this other day to turn him out o' the band : I think I have his letter in my pocket.

First Sold. Marry, we'll search.   229

Par. In good sadness, I do not know ; either it is there, or it is upon a file with the duke's other letters in my tent.

First Sold. Here 'tis ; here's a paper : shall I read it to you ?

Par. I do not know if it be it or no.

Ber. Our interpreter does it well.

First Lord. Excellently.

First Sold. [*Reads*] 'Dian, the count's a fool, and full of gold,'—

Par. That is not the duke's letter, sir ; that is an advertisement to a proper maid in Florence, one Diana, to take heed of the allurement of one Count Rousillon, a foolish idle boy, but for all that very ruttish : I pray you, sir, put it up again.

First Sold. Nay, I'll read it first, by your favor.

Par. My meaning in't, I protest, was very honest in the behalf of the maid ; for I knew the young count to be a dangerous and lascivious boy, who is a whale to virginity and devours up all the fry it finds.   250

Ber. Damnable both-sides rogue !

First Sold. [*Reads*] 'When he swears oaths, bid him drop gold, and take it ;

After he scores, he never pays the score :
Half won is match well made ; match, and well make it ;

He ne'er pays after-debts, take it before ;
And say a soldier, Dian, told thee this,
Men are to mell with, boys are not to kiss :
For count of this, the count's a fool, I know it,
Who pays before, but not when he does owe it.

Thine, as he vowed to thee in thine ear, 260
PAROLLES.'

Ber. He shall be whipped through the army with this rhyme in's forehead.

Sec. Lord. This is your devoted friend, sir, the manifold linguist and the armipotent soldier.

Ber. I could endure any thing before but a cat, and now he's a cat to me.

First Sold. I perceive, sir, by the general's looks, we shall be fain to hang you.   269

Par. My life, sir, in any case : not that I am afraid to die ; but that, my offences being many, I would repent out the remainder of nature : let me live, sir, in a dungeon, i' the stocks, or any where, so I may live.

First Sold. We'll see what may be done, so you confess freely ; therefore, once more to this Captain Dumain : you have answered to his reputation with the duke and to his valor : what is his honesty ?   279

Par. He will steal, sir, an egg out of a cloister : for rapes and ravishments he parallels Nessus : he professes not keeping of oaths ; in breaking 'em he is stronger than

Hercules : he will lie, sir, with such volubility, that you would think truth were a fool : drunkenness is his best virtue, for he will be swine-drunk ; and in his sleep he does little harm, save to his bed-clothes about him ; but they know his conditions and lay him in straw. I have but little more to say, sir, of his honesty : he has every thing that an honest man should not have ; what an honest man should have, he has nothing.

First Lord. I begin to love him for this.

Ber. For this description of thine honesty ? A pox upon him for me, he's more and more a cat.

First Sold. What say you to his expertness in war ?

Par. Faith, sir, he has led the drum before the English tragedians ; to belie him, I will not, and more of his soldiership I know not ; except, in that country he had the honor to be the officer at a place there called Mile-end, to instruct for the doubling of files : I would do the man what honor I can, but of this I am not certain.

First Lord. He hath out-villained villany so far, that the rarity redeems him.

Ber. A pox on him, he's a cat still.

First Sold. His qualities being at this poor price, I need not to ask you if gold will corrupt him to revolt.   310

Par. Sir, for a quart d'écu he will sell the fee-simple of his salvation, the inheritance of it ; and cut the entail from all remainders, and a perpetual succession for it perpetually.

First Sold. What's his brother, the other Captain Dumain ?

Sec. Lord. Why does he ask him of me ?

First Sold. What's he ?

Par. E'en a crow o' the same nest ; not altogether so great as the first in goodness, but greater a great deal in evil : he excels his brother for a coward, yet his brother is reputed one of the best that is : in a retreat he outruns any lackey ; marry, in coming on he has the cramp.

First Sold. If your life be saved, will you undertake to betray the Florentine ?

Par. Ay, and the captain of his horse, Count Rousillon.

First Sold. I'll whisper with the general, and know his pleasure.   330

Par. [*Aside*] I'll no more drumming ; a plague of all drums ! Only to seem to deserve well, and to beguile the supposition of that lascivious young boy the count, have I run into this danger. Yet who would have suspected an ambush where I was taken ?

First Sold. There is no remedy, sir, but you must die : the general says, you that have so traitorously discovered the secrets of your army and made such pestiferous reports of men very nobly held, can serve the world for no honest use ; therefore you must die. Come, headsman, off with his head.

Par. O Lord, sir, let me live, or let me see my death !

First Lord. That shall you, and take your leave of all your friends. [*Unblinding him.* So, look about you : know you any here ?

Ber. Good morrow, noble captain.   349

Sec. Lord. God bless you, Captain Parolles.

First Lord. God save you, noble captain.

Sec. Lord. Captain, what greeting will you to my Lord Lafeu ? I am for France.

First Lord. Good captain, will you give me a copy of the sonnet you writ to Diana in behalf of the Count Rousillon ? an I were not a very coward, I'ld compel it of you : but fare you well.   [*Exeunt Bertram and Lords.*

First Sold. You are undone, captain, all but your scarf ; that has a knot on't yet.   359

Par. Who cannot be crushed with a plot ?

First Sold. If you could find out a country where but women were that had received so much shame, you might begin an impudent nation. Fare ye well, sir ; I am for France too : we shall speak of you there.
                    [*Exit with Soldiers.*

Par. Yet am I thankful : if my heart were great,
'Twould burst at this. Captain I'll be no more ;
But I will eat and drink, and sleep as soft
As captain shall : simply the thing I am
Shall make me live. Who knows himself a braggart,   370
Let him fear this, for it will come to pass
That every braggart shall be found an ass.
Rust, sword ! cool, blushes ! and, Parolles, live
Safest in shame ! being fool'd, by foolery thrive !
There's place and means for every man alive.
I'll after them.   [*Exit.*

SCENE IV. *Florence. The* Widow's *house.*

Enter HELENA, Widow, *and* DIANA.

Hel. That you may well perceive I have not wrong'd you,
One of the greatest in the Christian world
Shall be my surety ; 'fore whose throne 'tis needful,
Ere I can perfect mine intents, to kneel :
Time was, I did him a desired office,
Dear almost as his life ; which gratitude
Through flinty Tartar's bosom would peep forth,
And answer, thanks : I duly am inform'd
His grace is at Marseilles ; to which place
We have convenient convoy. You must know,
I am supposed dead : the army breaking,   11
My husband hies him home ; where, heaven aiding,
And by the leave of my good lord the king,
We'll be before our welcome.

Wid.   Gentle madam,
You never had a servant to whose trust
Your business was more welcome.

Hel.   Nor you, mistress,
Ever a friend whose thoughts more truly labor
To recompense your love : doubt not but heaven
Hath brought me up to be your daughter's dower,
As it hath fated her to be my motive   20
And helper to a husband. But, O strange men !
That can such sweet use make of what they hate,
When saucy trusting of the cozen'd thoughts
Defiles the pitchy night : so lust doth play
With what it loathes for that which is away.
But more of this hereafter. You, Diana,
Under my poor instructions yet must suffer
Something in my behalf.

Dia.   Let death and honesty
Go with your impositions, I am yours
Upon your will to suffer.

Hel.   Yet, I pray you :   30
But with the word the time will bring on sum-
      mer,
When briers shall have leaves as well as
      thorns,
And be as sweet as sharp. We must away ;
Our wagon is prepared, and time revives us :
ALL'S WELL THAT ENDS WELL : still the fine's
      the crown ;
Whate'er the course, the end is the renown.
                                    [*Exeunt.*

SCENE V. *Rousillon. The* COUNT'S *palace.*

Enter COUNTESS, LAFEU, *and* CLOWN.

Laf.   No, no, no, your son was misled with
a snipt-taffeta fellow there, whose villanous
saffron would have made all the unbaked and
doughy youth of a nation in his color : your
daughter-in-law had been alive at this hour,
and your son here at home, more advanced by
the king than by that red-tailed humble-bee I
speak of.

Count.   I would I had not known him ; it
was the death of the most virtuous gentlewoman that ever nature had praise for creating. If she had partaken of my flesh, and cost
me the dearest groans of a mother, I could
not have owed her a more rooted love.

Laf.   'Twas a good lady, 'twas a good lady :
we may pick a thousand salads ere we light on
such another herb.

Clo.   Indeed, sir, she was the sweet marjoram of the salad, or rather, the herb of grace.

Laf.   They are not herbs, you knave ; they
are nose-herbs.   20

Clo.   I am no great Nebuchadnezzar, sir ;
I have not much skill in grass.

Laf.   Whether dost thou profess thyself, a
knave or a fool ?

Clo.   A fool, sir, at a woman's service, and
a knave at a man's.

Laf.   Your distinction ?

Clo.   I would cozen the man of his wife and
do his service.

Laf.   So you were a knave at his service,
indeed.   31

Clo.   And I would give his wife my bauble,
sir, to do her service.

Laf.   I will subscribe for thee, thou art
both knave and fool.

Clo.   At your service.

Laf.   No, no, no.

Clo.   Why, sir, if I cannot serve you, I can
serve as great a prince as you are.

Laf.   Who's that ? a Frenchman ?   40

Clo.   Faith, sir, a' has an English name ;
but his fisnomy is more hotter in France than
there.

Laf.   What prince is that ?

Clo.   The black prince, sir ; alias, the
prince of darkness ; alias, the devil.

Laf.   Hold thee, there's my purse : I give
thee not this to suggest thee from thy master
thou talkest of ; serve him still.

Clo.   I am a woodland fellow, sir, that always loved a great fire ; and the master I
speak of ever keeps a good fire. But, sure, he
is the prince of the world ; let his nobility remain in's court. I am for the house with the
narrow gate, which I take to be too little for
pomp to enter : some that humble themselves
may ; but the many will be too chill and tender, and they'll be for the flowery way that
leads to the broad gate and the great fire.

Laf.   Go thy ways, I begin to be aweary of
thee ; and I tell thee so before, because I
would not fall out with thee. Go thy ways : let
my horses be well looked to, without any
tricks.

Clo.   If I put any tricks upon 'em, sir, they
shall be jades' tricks ; which are their own
right by the law of nature.   [*Exit.*

Laf.   A shrewd knave and an unhappy.

Count.   So he is. My lord that's gone made
himself much sport out of him : by his authority he remains here, which he thinks is a
patent for his sauciness ; and, indeed, he has
no pace, but runs where he will.   71

Laf.   I like him well ; 'tis not amiss. And
I was about to tell you, since I heard of the
good lady's death and that my lord your son
was upon his return home, I moved the king
my master to speak in the behalf of my daughter ; which, in the minority of them both, his
majesty, out of a self-gracious remembrance,
did first propose : his highness hath promised
me to do it ; and, to stop up the displeasure
he hath conceived against your son, there is
no fitter matter. How does your ladyship like
it ?

Count.   With very much content, my lord ;
and I wish it happily effected.

Laf.   His highness comes post from Marseilles, of as able body as when he numbered
thirty : he will be here to-morrow, or I am deceived by him that in such intelligence hath
seldom failed.

Count.   It rejoices me, that I hope I shall
see him ere I die. I have letters that my son
will be here to-night : I shall beseech your
lordship to remain with me till they meet together.

Laf.   Madam, I was thinking with what
manners I might safely be admitted.

Count.   You need but plead your honorable
privilege.

Laf.   Lady, of that I have made a bold
charter ; but I thank my God it holds yet.

Re-enter CLOWN.

Clo.   O madam, yonder's my lord your son
with a patch of velvet on's face : whether
there be a scar under't or no, the velvet
knows ; but 'tis a goodly patch of velvet : his
left cheek is a cheek of two pile and a half,
but his right cheek is worn bare.

Laf.   A scar nobly got, or a noble scar, is
a good livery of honor ; so belike is that.

Clo.   But it is your carbonadoed face.

Laf.   Let us go see your son, I pray you : I
long to talk with the young noble soldier. 109

Clo.   Faith there's a dozen of 'em, with
delicate fine hats and most courteous feathers,
which bow the head and nod at every man.
                                    [*Exeunt.*

ACT V.

SCENE I. *Marseilles. A street.*

Enter HELENA, Widow, *and* DIANA, *with two
Attendants.*

Hel.   But this exceeding posting day and
night

Must wear your spirits low; we cannot help
   it :
But since you have made the days and nights
   as one,
To wear your gentle limbs in my affairs,
Be bold you do so grow in my requital
As nothing can unroot you. In happy time ;

Enter a Gentleman.

This man may help me to his majesty's ear,
If he would spend his power. God save you,
   sir.
   Gent.   And you.
   Hel.   Sir, I have seen you in the court of
France.   10
   Gent.   I have been sometimes there.
   Hel.   I do presume, sir, that you are not
   fallen
From the report that goes upon your good-
   ness ;
An therefore, goaded with most sharp oc-
   casions,
Which lay nice manners by, I put you to
The use of your own virtues, for the which
I shall continue thankful.
   Gent.   What's your will ?
   Hel.   That it will please you
To give this poor petition to the king,
And aid me with that store of power you have
To come into his presence.   21
   Gent.   The king's not here.
   Hel.   Not here, sir !
   Gent.   Not, indeed :
He hence removed last night and with more
   haste
Than is his use.
   Wid.   Lord, how we lose our pains !
   Hel.   ALL'S WELL THAT ENDS WELL yet,
Though time seem so adverse and means unfit.
I do beseech you, whither is he gone ?
   Gent.   Marry, as I take it, to Rousillon ;
Whither I am going.
   Hel.   I do beseech you, sir,
Since you are like to see the king before me,
Commend the paper to his gracious hand,   31
Which I presume shall render you no blame
But rather make you thank your pains for it.
I will come after you with what good speed
Our means will make us means.
   Gent.   This I'll do for you.
   Hel.   And you shall find yourself to be well
   thank'd,
Whate'er falls more. We must to horse again.
Go, go, provide.   [*Exeunt.*

SCENE II.   *Rousillon. Before the* COUNT'S
         palace.

Enter CLOWN, *and* PAROLLES, *following.*

   Par.   Good Monsieur Lavache, give my
Lord Lefeu this letter : I have ere now, sir,
been better known to you, when I have held
familiarity with fresher clothes ; but I am now,
sir, muddied in fortune's mood, and smell
somewhat strong of her strong displeasure.
   Clo.   Truly, fortune's displeasure is but
sluttish, if it smell so strongly as thou speakest of : I will henceforth eat no fish of fortune's buttering. Prithee, allow the wind. 10
   Par.   Nay, you need not to stop your nose,
sir ; I spake but by a metaphor.
   Clo.   Indeed, sir, if your metaphor stink, I
will stop my nose ; or against any man's metaphor. Prithee, get thee further.

   Par.   Pray you, sir, deliver me this paper.
   Clo.   Foh ! prithee, stand away : a paper
from fortune's close-stool to give to a nobleman ! Look, here he comes himself.   19

Enter LAFEU.

Here is a purr of fortune's, sir, or of fortune's
cat,—but not a musk-cat,—that has fallen into
the unclean fishpond of her displeasure, and,
as he says, is muddied withal : pray you, sir,
use the carp as you may ; for he looks like
a poor, decayed, ingenious, foolish, rascally
knave. I do pity his distress in my similes of
comfort and leave him to your lordship. [*Exit.*
   Par.   My lord, I am a man whom fortune
hath cruelly scratched.   29
   Laf.   And what would you have me to do ?
'Tis too late to pare her nails now. Wherein
have you played the knave with fortune, that
she should scratch you, who of herself is a
good lady and would not have knaves thrive
long under her ? There's a quart d'écu for
you : let the justices make you and fortune
friends : I am for other business.
   Par.   I beseech your honor to hear me one
single word.
   Laf.   You beg a single penny more : come,
you shall ha't ; save your word.   40
   Par.   My name, my good lord, is Parolles.
   Laf.   You beg more than 'word,' then.
Cox my passion ! give me your hand. How
does your drum ?
   Par.   O my good lord, you were the first
that found me !
   Laf.   Was I, in sooth ? and I was the first
that lost thee.
   Par.   It lies in you, my lord, to bring me
in some grace, for you did bring me out.   50
   Laf.   Out upon thee, knave ! dost thou put
upon me at once both the office of God and
the devil ? One brings thee in grace and the
other brings thee out. [*Trumpets sound.*] The
king's coming ; I know by his trumpets. Sirrah, inquire further after me ; I had talk of
you last night : though you are a fool and a
knave, you shall eat ; go to, follow.
   Par.   I praise God for you.   [*Exeunt.*

SCENE III.   *Rousillon. The* COUNT'S *palace.*

Flourish. Enter KING, COUNTESS, LAFEU, *the
      two* French Lords, *with* Attendants.

   King.   We lost a jewel of her ; and our es-
      teem
Was made much poorer by it : but your son,
As mad in folly, lack'd the sense to know
Her estimation home.
   Count.   'Tis past, my liege ;
And I beseech your majesty to make it
Natural rebellion, done i' the blaze of youth ;
When oil and fire, too strong for reason's
      force,
O'erbears it and burns on.
   King.   My honor'd lady,
I have forgiven and forgotten all ;
Though my revenges were high bent upon him,
And watch'd the time to shoot.
   Laf.   This I must say,   11
But first I beg my pardon, the young lord
Did to his majesty, his mother and his lady
Offence of mighty note ; but to himself
The greatest wrong of all. He lost a wife
Whose beauty did astonish the survey

Of richest eyes, whose words all ears took
captive,
Whose dear perfection hearts that scorn'd to
serve
Humbly call'd mistress.
  King.   Praising what is lost
Makes the remembrance dear. Well, call him
  hither ;   20
We are reconciled, and the first view shall kill
All repetition : let him not ask our pardon ;
The nature of his great offence is dead,
And deeper than oblivion we do bury
The incensing relics of it : let him approach,
A stranger, no offender ; and inform him
So 'tis our will he should.
  Gent.   I shall, my liege. [*Exit.*
  King. What says he to your daughter ?
  have you spoke ?
  Laf. All that he is hath reference to your
  highness.
  King. Then shall we have a match. I have
  letters sent me   30
That set him high in fame.

Enter BERTRAM.

  Laf.   He looks well on't.
  King. I am not a day of season,
For thou mayst see a sunshine and a hail
In me at once : but to the brightest beams
Distracted clouds give way ; so stand thou
  forth ;
The time is fair again.
  Ber.   My high-repented blames,
Dear sovereign, pardon to me.
  King.   All is whole ;
Not one word more of the consumed time.
Let's take the instant by the forward top ;
For we are old, and on our quick'st decrees 40
The inaudible and noiseless foot of Time
Steals ere we can effect them. You remember
The daughter of this lord ?
  Ber. Admiringly, my liege, at first
I stuck my choice upon her, ere my heart
Durst make too bold a herald of my tongue
Where the impression of mine eye infixing,
Contempt his scornful perspective did lend
  me,
Which warp'd the line of every other favor ;
Scorn'd a fair color, or express'd it stolen ; 50
Extended or contracted all proportions
To a most hideous object : thence it came
That she whom all men praised and whom
  myself,
Since I have lost, have loved, was in mine eye
The dust that did offend it.
  King.   Well excused :
That thou didst love her, strikes some scores
  away
From the great compt : but love that comes
  too late,
Like a remorseful pardon slowly carried,
To the great sender turns a sour offence,
Crying, 'That's good that's gone.' Our rash
  faults   60
Make trivial price of serious things we have,
Not knowing them until we know their grave :
Oft our displeasures, to ourselves unjust,
Destroy our friends and after weep their dust :
Our own love waking cries to see what's
  done,
While shame full late sleeps out the after-
  noon.

Be this sweet Helen's knell, and now forget
  her.
Send forth your amorous token for fair Maud-
  lin :
The main consents are had ; and here we'll
  stay
To see our widower's second marriage-day. 70
  Count. Which better than the first, O dear
  heaven, bless !
Or, ere they meet, in me, O nature, cesse !
  Laf. Come on, my son, in whom my
  house's name
Must be digested, give a favor from you
To sparkle in the spirits of my daughter,
That she may quickly come. [*Bertram gives
  a ring.*] By my old beard,
And every hair that's on't, Helen, that's dead,
Was a sweet creature : such a ring as this,
The last that e'er I took her leave at court,
I saw upon her finger.
  Ber.   Hers it was not.   80
  King. Now, pray you, let me see it ; for
  mine eye,
While I was speaking, oft was fasten'd to't.
This ring was mine ; and, when I gave it
  Helen,
I bade her, if her fortunes ever stood
Necessitied to help, that by this token
I would relieve her. Had you that craft, to
  reave her
Of what should stead her most ?
  Ber.   My gracious sovereign,
Howe'er it pleases you to take it so,
The ring was never hers.
  Count.   Son, on my life,
I have seen her wear it ; and she reckon'd it
At her life's rate.   91
  Laf.   I am sure I saw her wear it.
  Ber. You are deceived, my lord ; she never
  saw it :
In Florence was it from a casement thrown
  me,
Wrapp'd in a paper, which contain'd the name
Of her that threw it : noble she was, and
  thought
I stood engaged : but when I had subscribed
To mine own fortune and inform'd her fully
I could not answer in that course of honor
As she had made the overture, she ceased
In heavy satisfaction and would never   100
Receive the ring again.
  King.   Plutus himself,
That knows the tinct and multiplying medi-
  cine,
Hath not in nature's mystery more science
Than I have in this ring : 'twas mine, 'twas
  Helen's,
Whoever gave it you. Then, if you know
That you are well acquainted with yourself,
Confess 'twas hers, and by what rough en-
  forcement
You got it from her : she call'd the saints to
  surety
That she would never put it from her finger,
Unless she gave it to yourself in bed,   110
Where you have never come, or sent it us
Upon her great disaster.
  Ber.   She never saw it.
  King. Thou speak'st it falsely, as I love
  mine honor ;
And makest conjectural fears to come into
  me

Which I would fain shut out. If it should
    prove
That thou art so inhuman,—'twill not prove
    so ;—
And yet I know not : thou didst hate her
    deadly,
And she is dead ; which nothing, but to close
Her eyes myself, could win me to believe,
More than to see this ring. Take him away.
                [*Guards seize* Bertram.
My fore-past proofs, howe'er the matter fall,
Shall tax my fears of little vanity,
Having vainly fear'd too little. Away with
    him !
We'll sift this matter further.
  Ber.   If you shall prove
This ring was ever hers, you shall as easy
Prove that I husbanded her bed in Florence,
Where yet she never was. [*Exit, guarded.*
  King. I am wrapp'd in dismal thinkings.

        Enter a Gentleman.

  Gent.   Gracious sovereign,
Whether I have been to blame or no, I know
    not :
Here's a petition from a Florentine,   130
Who hath for four or five removes come short
To tender it herself. I undertook it,
Vanquish'd thereto by the fair grace and
    speech
Of the poor suppliant, who by this I know
Is here attending : her business looks in her
With an importing visage ; and she told me,
In a sweet verbal brief, it did concern
Your highness with herself.
  King. [*Reads*] Upon his many protesta-
tions to marry me when his wife was dead, I
blush to say it, he won me. Now is the Count
Rousillon a widower : his vows are forfeited
to me, and my honor's paid to him. He stole
from Florence, taking no leave, and I follow
him to his country for justice : grant it me, O
king ! in you it best lies ; otherwise a seducer
flourishes, and a poor maid is undone.
                DIANA CAPILET.
  Laf. I will buy me a son-in-law in a fair,
and toll for this : I'll none of him.
  King. The heavens have thought well on
    thee, Lafeu,   150
To bring forth this discovery. Seek these
    suitors :
Go speedily and bring again the count.
I am afeard the life of Helen, lady,
Was foully snatch'd.
  Count.   Now, justice on the doers !

    Re-enter BERTRAM, *guarded.*

  King. I wonder, sir, sith wives are mon-
    sters to you,
And that you fly them as you swear them
    lordship,
Yet you desire to marry.

    Enter Widow *and* DIANA.

              What woman's that ?
  Dia. I am, my lord, a wretched Florentine,
Derived from the ancient Capilet :
My suit, as I do understand, you know, 160
And therefore know how far I may be pitied.
  Wid. I am her mother, sir, whose age and
    honor
Both suffer under this complaint we bring,
And both shall cease, without your remedy.

  King. Come hither, count ; do you know
    these women ?
  Ber. My lord, I neither can nor will deny
But that I know them : do they charge me
    further ?
  Dia. Why do you look so strange upon
    your wife ?
  Ber. She's none of mine, my lord.
  Dia.   If you shall marry,
You give away this hand, and that is mine ;
You give away heaven's vows, and those are
    mine ;   171
You give away myself, which is known mine ;
For I by vow am so embodied yours,
That she which marries you must marry me,
Either both or none.
  Laf. Your reputation comes too short for
my daughter ; you are no husband for her.
  Ber. My lord, this is a fond and desperate
    creature,
Whom sometime I have laugh'd with : let your
    highness   179
Lay a more noble thought upon mine honor
Than for to think that I would sink it here.
  King. Sir, for my thoughts, you have them
    ill to friend
Till your deeds gain them : fairer prove your
    honor
Than in my thought it lies.
  Dia.   Good my lord,
Ask him upon his oath, if he does think
He had not my virginity.
  King. What say'st thou to her ?
  Ber.   She's impudent, my lord,
And was a common gamester to the camp.
  Dia. He does me wrong, my lord ; if I
    were so,
He might have bought me at a common
    price :
Do not believe him. O, behold this ring,
Whose high respect and rich validity
Did lack a parallel ; yet for all that
He gave it to a commoner o' the camp,
If I be one.
  Count. He blushes, and 'tis it :
Of six preceding ancestors, that gem,
Conferr'd by testament to the sequent issue,
Hath it been owed and worn. This is his wife ;
That ring's a thousand proofs.
  King.   Methought you said
You saw one here in court could witness it.
  Dia. I did, my lord, but loath am to pro-
    duce   201
So bad an instrument : his name's Parolles.
  Laf. I saw the man to-day, if man he be.
  King. Find him, and bring him hither.
                [*Exit an Attendant.*
  Ber.   What of him ?
He's quoted for a most perfidious slave,
With all the spots o' the world tax'd and de-
    bosh'd ;
Whose nature sickens but to speak a truth.
Am I or that or this for what he'll utter,
That will speak any thing ?
  King.   She hath that ring of yours.
  Ber. I think she has : certain it is I liked
    her,   210
And boarded her i' the wanton way of youth :
She knew her distance and did angle for me,
Madding my eagerness with her restraint,
As all impediments in fancy's course
Are motives of more fancy ; and, in fine,
Her infinite cunning, with her modern grace,

Subdued me to her rate : she got the ring ;
And I had that which any inferior might
At market-price have bought.
 Dia.   I must be patient :
You, that have turn'd off a first so noble
  wife,   220
May justly diet me. I pray you yet ;
Since you lack virtue, I will lose a husband ;
Send for your ring, I will return it home,
And give me mine again.
 Ber.   I have it not.
 King. What ring was yours, I pray you ?
 Dia.   Sir, much like
The same upon your finger.
 King. Know you this ring ? this ring was
  his of late.
 Dia. And this was it I gave him, being
  abed.
 King. The story then goes false, you threw
  it him
Out of a casement.
 Dia.   I have spoke the truth. 230

    Enter PAROLLES.

 Ber. My lord, I do confess the ring was
  hers.
 King. You boggle shrewdly, every feather
  starts you.
Is this the man you speak of ?
 Dia.   Ay, my lord.
 King. Tell me, sirrah, but tell me true, I
  charge you,
Not fearing the displeasure of your master,
Which on your just proceeding I'll keep off,
By him and by this woman here what know
  you ?
 Par. So please your majesty, my master
hath been an honorable gentleman : tricks he
hath had in him, which gentlemen have. 240
 King. Come, come, to the purpose : did he
love this woman ?
 Par. Faith, sir, he did love her ; but how ?
 King. How, I pray you ?
 Par. He did love her, sir, as a gentleman
loves a woman.
 King. How is that ?
 Par. He loved her, sir, and loved her not.
 King. As thou art a knave, and no knave.
What an equivocal companion is this ! 250
 Par. I am a poor man, and at your maj-
esty's command.
 Laf. He's a good drum, my lord, but a
naughty orator.
 Dia. Do you know he promised me mar-
riage ?
 Par. Faith, I know more than I'll speak.
 King. But wilt thou not speak all thou
knowest ?
 Par. Yes, so please your majesty. I did
go between them, as I said ; but more than
that, he loved her : for indeed he was mad for
her, and talked of Satan and of Limbo and of
Furies and I know not what : yet I was in that
credit with them at that time that I knew of
their going to bed, and of other motions, as
promising her marriage, and things which
would derive me ill will to speak of ; therefore
I will not speak what I know.
 King. Thou hast spoken all already, unless
thou canst say they are married : but thou art
too fine in thy evidence ; therefore stand aside.
This ring, you say, was yours ?   271
 Dia.   Ay, my good lord.

 King. Where did you buy it ? or who gave
  it you ?
 Dia. It was not given me, nor I did not buy
  it.
 King. Who lent it you ?
 Dia.   It was not lent me neither.
 King. Where did you find it, then ?
 Dia.   I found it not.
 King. If it were yours by none of all these
  ways,
How could you give it him ?
 Dia.   I never gave it him.
 Laf. This woman's an easy glove, my lord ;
she goes off and on at pleasure.
 King. This ring was mine ; I gave it his
  first wife.   280
 Dia. It might be yours or hers, for aught I
  know.
 King. Take her away ; I do not like her
  now ;
To prison with her : and away with him.
Unless thou tell'st me where thou hadst this
  ring,
Thou diest within this hour.
 Dia.   I'll never tell you.
 King. Take her away.
 Dia.   I'll put in bail, my liege.
 King. I think thee now some common cus-
tomer.
 Dia. By Jove, if ever I knew man, 'twas
  you.
 King. Wherefore hast thou accused him all
  this while ?
 Dia. Because he's guilty, and he is not
  guilty :   290
He knows I am no maid, and he'll swear to't ;
I'll swear I am a maid, and he knows not.
Great king, I am no strumpet, by my life ;
I am either maid, or else this old man's wife.
 King. She does abuse our ears : to prison
  with her.
 Dia. Good mother, fetch my bail. Stay,
  royal sir :   [*Exit Widow.*
The jeweller that owes the ring is sent for,
And he shall surety me. But for this lord,
Who hath abused me, as he knows himself,
Though yet he never harm'd me, here I quit
  him :   300
He knows himself my bed he hath defiled ;
And at that time he got his wife with child :
Dead though she be, she feels her young one
  kick :
So there's my riddle : one that's dead is quick :
And now behold the meaning.

  Re-enter Widow, *with* HELENA.

 King.   Is there no exorcist
Beguiles the truer office of mine eyes ?
Is't real that I see ?
 Hel.   No, my good lord ;
'Tis but the shadow of a wife you see,
The name and not the thing.
 Ber.   Both, both. O, pardon !
 Hel. O my good lord, when I was like this
  maid,   310
I found you wondrous kind. There is your
  ring ;
And, look you, here's your letter ; this it says :
' When from my finger you can get this ring
And are by me with child,' &c. This is done :
Will you be mine, now you are doubly won ?
 Ber. If she, my liege, can make me know
  this clearly,

I'll love her dearly, ever, ever dearly.
 Hel. If it appear not plain and prove un-
  true,
Deadly divorce step between me and you !
O my dear mother, do I see you living ? 320
 Laf. Mine eyes smell onions ; I shall weep
  anon :
[*To Parolles*] Good Tom Drum, lend me a
  handkercher : so,
I thank thee : wait on me home, I'll make
  sport with thee :
Let thy courtesies alone, they are scurvy ones.
 King. Let us from point to point this story
  know,
To make the even truth in pleasure flow.
[*To Diana*] If thou be'st yet a fresh uncropped
  flower,
Choose thou thy husband, and I'll pay thy
  dower ;

For I can guess that by thy honest aid
Thou keep'st a wife herself, thyself a maid.
Of that and all the progress, more or less, 331
Resolvedly more leisure shall express :
All yet seems well ; and if it end so meet,
The bitter past, more welcome is the sweet.
         [*Flourish.*

EPILOGUE.

 King. The king's a beggar, now the play is
  done :
All is well ended, if this suit be won,
That you express content ; which we will pay,
With strife to please you, day exceeding day :
Ours be your patience then, and yours our
  parts ;
Your gentle hands lend us, and take our hearts.
        [*Exeunt.* 340

MEASURE FOR MEASURE.

(WRITTEN ABOUT 1603.)

INTRODUCTION.

This is one of the darkest and most painful of the comedies of Shakespeare, but its darkness is lit by the central figure of Isabella, with her white passion of purity and of indignation against sin. The play deals with deep things of our humanity—with righteousness and charity, with self-deceit, and moral weakness and strength, even with life and death themselves. All that is soft, melodious, romantic, has disappeared from the style ; it shows a fearless vigor, penetrating imagination, and much intellectual force and boldness. Its date is uncertain. Two passages (Act I., Sc. I, L. 68–73, and Act II., Sc. IV., L. 24–29) have been conjectured to contain " a courtly apology for King James I.'s stately and ungracious demeanor on his entry into England ; " and possibly the revival in 1604 of a statute which punished with death any divorced person who married again while his or her former husband or wife was living, may have added point to one chief incident in the play. Shakespeare took the story from Whetstone's play *Promos and Cassandra* (1578), and the prose telling of the tale by the same author in his *Heptameron of Civil Discourses* (1582). Whetstone's original was a story in the *Hecatomithi* of Giraldi Cinthio. Shakespeare alters some of the incidents, making the Duke present in disguise throughout, preserving the honor of the heroine, and introducing the character of Mariana to take her wifely place by Angelo as a substitute for Isabella. *Measure for Measure*, like *The Merchant of Venice*, is remarkable for its great pleading scenes ; and to Portia's ardor and intellectual force Isabella adds a noble severity of character, a devotion to an ideal of rectitude and purity, and a religious enthusiasm. In Vienna, " where corruption boils and bubbles," appears this figure of virginal strength and uprightness ; at the last she is to preside over the sinful city and perhaps to save it. She is almost " a thing ensky'd and sainted," yet she returns from the cloister to the world, there to fill her place as wife and Duchess. Angelo, at the outset, though he must be conscious of the wrong he has done to his betrothed, is more self-deceived than a deceiver. He does not know his own heart, and is severe against others in his imagined superiority to every possible temptation. A terrible abyss is opened to him in the evil passion of his own nature. The unmasking of the self-deceiver is not here, as in the happy comedies, a piece of the mirth of the play ; it is painful and stern. The Duke acts throughout as a kind of overruling providence ; he has the wisdom of the serpent, which he uses for good ends, and he looks through life with a steady gaze, which results in a justice and even tenderness towards others. Claudio is made chiefly to be saved by his sister, but he has a grace of youth and a clinging enjoyment of life and love, which interest us in him sufficiently for pity if not for admiration. The minor characters possess each his characteristic feature, but are less important individually than as representatives of the wide-spread social corruption and degradation which surround the chief characters, and form the soil on which they move and the air they breathe. " We never throughout the play get into the free open joyous atmosphere, so invigorating in other works of Shakespeare ; the oppressive gloom of the prison, the foul breath of the house of shame, are only exchanged for the chilly damp of conventual walls, or the oppressive retirement of the monastery."

DRAMATIS PERSONÆ.

VINCENTIO, the Duke.
ANGELO, Deputy.
ESCALUS, an ancient Lord.
CLAUDIO, a young gentleman.
LUCIO, a fantastic.
Two other gentlemen.
PROVOST.
PETER, } two friars.
THOMAS, }
A Justice.
VARRIUS.
ELBOW, a simple constable.

FROTH, a foolish gentleman.
POMPEY, servant to Mistress Overdone.
ABHORSON, an executioner.
BARNARDINE, a dissolute prisoner.

ISABELLA, sister to Claudio.
MARIANA, betrothed to Angelo.
JULIET, beloved of Claudio.
FRANCISCA, a nun.
MISTRESS OVERDONE, a bawd.

Lords, Officers, Citizens, Boy, and Attendants.

SCENE : *Vienna.*

ACT I.

Scene I. *An apartment in the* Duke's *palace.*

Enter Duke, Escalus, Lords *and* Attendants.

Duke. Escalus.

Escal. My lord.

Duke. Of government the properties to unfold,
Would seem in me to affect speech and discourse ;
Since I am put to know that your own science
Exceeds, in that, the lists of all advice
My strength can give you : then no more remains,
But that to your sufficiency........
...................as your worth is able,
And let them work. The nature of our people,
Our city's institutions, and the terms   11
For common justice, you're as pregnant in
As art and practice hath enriched any
That we remember. There is our commission,
From which we would not have you warp.
Call hither,
I say, bid come before us Angelo.
                              [*Exit an Attendant.*
What figure of us think you he will bear ?
For you must know, we have with special soul
Elected him our absence to supply,
Lent him our terror, dress'd him with our love,
And given his deputation all the organs   21
Of our own power : what think you of it ?

Escal. If any in Vienna be of worth
To undergo such ample grace and honor,
It is Lord Angelo.

Duke.   Look where he comes.

Enter Angelo.

Ang. Always obedient to your grace's will,
I come to know your pleasure.

Duke.   Angelo,
There is a kind of character in thy life,
That to the observer doth thy history
Fully unfold. Thyself and thy belongings   30
Are not thine own so proper as to waste
Thyself upon thy virtues, they on thee.
Heaven doth with us as we with torches do,
Not light them for themselves ; for if our virtues
Did not go forth of us, 'twere all alike
As if we had them not. Spirits are not finely
touch'd
But to fine issues, nor Nature never lends
The smallest scruple of her excellence
But, like a thrifty goddess, she determines
Herself the glory of a creditor,   40
Both thanks and use. But I do bend my speech
To one that can my part in him advertise ;
Hold therefore, Angelo :—
In our remove be thou at full ourself ;
Mortality and mercy in Vienna
Live in thy tongue and heart : old Escalus,
Though first in question, is thy secondary.
Take thy commission.

Ang.   Now, good my lord,
Let there be some more test made of my metal,
Before so noble and so great a figure   50
Be stamp'd upon it.

Duke.   No more evasion :
We have with a leaven'd and prepared choice
Proceeded to you ; therefore take your honors.
Our haste from hence is of so quick condition
That it prefers itself and leaves unquestion'd
Matters of needful value. We shall write to you,
As time and our concernings shall importune,
How it goes with us, and do look to know
What doth befall you here. So, fare you well :
To the hopeful execution do I leave you   60
Of your commissions.

Ang.   Yet give leave, my lord,
That we may bring you something on the way.

Duke. My haste may not admit it ;
Nor need you, on mine honor, have to do
With any scruple ; your scope is as mine own
So to enforce or qualify the laws
As to your soul seems good. Give me your hand :
I'll privily away. I love the people,
But do not like to stage me to their eyes :
Though it do well, I do not relish well   70
Their loud applause and Aves vehement ;
Nor do I think the man of safe discretion
That does affect it. Once more, fare you well.

Ang. The heavens give safety to your purposes !

Escal. Lead forth and bring you back in happiness !

Duke. I thank you. Fare you well. [*Exit.*

Escal. I shall desire you, sir, to give me leave
To have free speech with you ; and it concerns me
To look into the bottom of my place :
A power I have, but of what strength and nature   80
I am not yet instructed.

Ang. 'Tis so with me. Let us withdraw together,
And we may soon our satisfaction have
Touching that point.

Escal. I'll wait upon your honor.   [*Exeunt.*

Scene II. *A street.*

Enter Lucio *and two* Gentlemen.

Lucio. If the duke with the other dukes come not to composition with the King of Hungary, why then all the dukes fall upon the king.

First Gent. Heaven grant us its peace, but not the King of Hungary's !

Sec. Gent. Amen.

Lucio. Thou concludest like the sanctimonious pirate, that went to sea with the Ten Commandments, but scraped one out of the table.

Sec. Gent. 'Thou shalt not steal ' ?   10

Lucio. Ay, that he razed.

First Gent. Why, 'twas a commandment to command the captain and all the rest from their functions : they put forth to steal. There's not a soldier of us all, that, in the thanksgiving before meat, do relish the petition well that prays for peace.

Sec. Gent. I never heard any soldier dislike it.

Lucio. I believe thee ; for I think thou never wast where grace was said.   20

Sec. Gent. No ? a dozen times at least.

First Gent. What, in metre ?

Lucio. In any proportion or in any language.

First Gent. I think, or in any religion.

Lucio. Ay, why not ? Grace is grace, despite of all controversy : as, for example, thou thyself art a wicked villain, despite of all grace.

First Gent. Well, there went but a pair of shears between us.

Lucio. I grant; as there may between the lists and the velvet. Thou art the list. 31

First Gent. And thou the velvet: thou art good velvet; thou'rt a three-piled piece, I warrant thee: I had as lief be a list of an English kersey as be piled, as thou art piled, for a French velvet. Do I speak feelingly now?

Lucio. I think thou dost; and, indeed, with most painful feeling of thy speech: I will, out of thine own confession, learn to begin thy health; but, whilst I live, forget to drink after thee. 40

First Gent. I think I have done myself wrong, have I not?

Sec. Gent. Yes, that thou hast, whether thou art tainted or free.

Lucio. Behold, behold, where Madam Mitigation comes! I have purchased as many diseases under her roof as come to—

Sec. Gent. To what, I pray?

Lucio. Judge.

Sec. Gent. To three thousand dolors a year.

First Gent. Ay, and more. 51

Lucio. A French crown more.

First Gent. Thou art always figuring diseases in me; but thou art full of error; I am sound.

Lucio. Nay, not as one would say, healthy; but so sound as things that are hollow: thy bones are hollow; impiety has made a feast of thee.

Enter MISTRESS OVERDONE.

First Gent. How now! which of your hips has the most profound sciatica?

Mrs. Ov. Well, well; there's one yonder arrested and carried to prison was worth five thousand of you all.

Sec. Gent. Who's that, I pray thee?

Mrs. Ov. Marry, sir, that's Claudio, Signior Claudio.

First Gent. Claudio to prison? 'tis not so.

Mrs. Ov. Nay, but I know 'tis so: I saw him arrested, saw him carried away; and, which is more, within these three days his head to be chopped off. 70

Lucio. But, after all this fooling, I would not have it so. Art thou sure of this?

Mrs. Ov. I am too sure of it: and it is for getting Madam Julietta with child.

Lucio. Believe me, this may be: he promised to meet me two hours since, and he was ever precise in promise-keeping.

Sec. Gent. Besides, you know, it draws something near to the speech we had to such a purpose.

First Gent. But, most of all, agreeing with the proclamation. 81

Lucio. Away! let's go learn the truth of it.
[*Exeunt Lucio and Gentlemen.*

Mrs. Ov. Thus, what with the war, what with the sweat, what with the gallows and what with poverty, I am custom-shrunk.

Enter POMPEY.

How now! what's the news with you?

Pom. Yonder man is carried to prison.

Mrs. Ov. Well; what has he done?

Pom. A woman.

Mrs. Ov. But what's his offence? 90

Pom. Groping for trouts in a peculiar river.

Mrs. Ov. What, is there a maid with child by him?

Pom. No, but there's a woman with maid by him. You have not heard of the proclamation, have you?

Mrs. Ov. What proclamation, man?

Pom. All houses in the suburbs of Vienna must be plucked down.

Mrs. Ov. And what shall become of those in the city? 101

Pom. They shall stand for seed: they had gone down too, but that a wise burgher put in for them.

Mrs. Ov. But shall all our houses of resort in the suburbs be pulled down?

Pom. To the ground, mistress.

Mrs. Ov. Why, here's a change indeed in the commonwealth! What shall become of me?

Pom. Come; fear you not: good counsellors lack no clients: though you change your place, you need not change your trade; I'll be your tapster still. Courage! there will be pity taken on you: you that have worn your eyes almost out in the service, you will be considered.

Mrs. Ov. What's to do here, Thomas tapster? let's withdraw.

Pom. Here comes Signior Claudio, led by the provost to prison; and there's Madam Juliet. [*Exeunt.*

Enter PROVOST, CLAUDIO, JULIET, *and* Officers.

Claud. Fellow, why dost thou show me thus to the world? 120
Bear me to prison, where I am committed.

Prov. I do it not in evil disposition,
But from Lord Angelo by special charge.

Claud. Thus can the demigod Authority
Make us pay down for our offence by weight
The words of heaven; on whom it will, it will;
On whom it will not, so; yet still 'tis just.

Re-enter LUCIO *and two* Gentlemen.

Lucio. Why, how now, Claudio! whence comes this restraint?

Claud. From too much liberty, my Lucio, liberty:
As surfeit is the father of much fast, 130
So every scope by the immoderate use
Turns to restraint. Our natures do pursue,
Like rats that ravin down their proper bane,
A thirsty evil; and when we drink we die.

Lucio. If I could speak so wisely under an arrest, I would send for certain of my creditors: and yet, to say the truth, I had as lief have the foppery of freedom as the morality of imprisonment. What's thy offence, Claudio?

Claud. What but to speak of would offend again. 140

Lucio. What, is't murder?

Claud. No.

Lucio. Lechery?

Claud. Call it so.

Prov. Away, sir! you must go.

Claud. One word, good friend. Lucio, a word with you.

Lucio. A hundred, if they'll do you any good.
Is lechery so look'd after?

Claud. Thus stands it with me : upon a
   true contract
I got possession of Julietta's bed :   150
You know the lady ; she is fast my wife,
Save that we do the denunciation lack
Of outward order : this we came not to,
Only for propagation of a dower
Remaining in the coffer of her friends,
From whom we thought it meet to hide our
   love
Till time had made them for us. But it chances
The stealth of our most mutual entertainment
With character too gross is writ on Juliet.
   Lucio. With child, perhaps ?
   Claud.   Unhappily, even so. 160
And the new deputy now for the duke—
Whether it be the fault and glimpse of new-
   ness,
Or whether that the body public be
A horse whereon the governor doth ride,
Who, newly in the seat, that it may know
He can command, lets it straight feel the spur ;
Whether the tyranny be in his place,
Or in his eminence that fills it up,
I stagger in :—but this new governor
Awakes me all the enrolled penalties   170
Which have, like unscour'd armor, hung by
   the wall
So long that nineteen zodiacs have gone round
And none of them been worn ; and, for a
   name,
Now puts the drowsy and neglected act
Freshly on me : 'tis surely for a name.
   Lucio. I warrant it is : and thy head stands
so tickle on thy shoulders that a milkmaid,
if she be in love, may sigh it off. Send after
the duke and appeal to him.
   Claud. I have done so, but he's not to be
   found.   180
I prithee, Lucio, do me this kind service :
This day my sister should the cloister enter
And there receive her approbation :
Acquaint her with the danger of my state :
Implore her, in my voice, that she make
   friends
To the strict deputy ; bid herself assay him :
I have great hope in that ; for in her youth
There is a prone and speechless dialect,
Such as move men ; beside, she hath prosper-
   ous art
When she will play with reason and discourse,
And well she can persuade.   191
   Lucio. I pray she may ; as well for the
encouragement of the like, which else would
stand under grievous imposition, as for the
enjoying of thy life, who I would be sorry
should be thus foolishly lost at a game of tick-
tack. I'll to her.
   Claud. I thank you, good friend Lucio.
   Lucio. Within two hours.
   Claud.   Come, officer, away !
                                    [*Exeunt.*

SCENE III. *A monastery.*

Enter Duke *and* FRIAR THOMAS.

   Duke. No, holy father ; throw away that
   thought ;
Believe not that the dribbling dart of love
Can pierce a complete bosom. Why I desire
   thee
To give me secret harbor, hath a purpose
More grave and wrinkled than the aims and
   ends

Of burning youth.
   Fri. T.   May your grace speak of it ?
   Duke. My holy sir, none better knows than
   you
How I have ever loved the life removed
And held in idle price to haunt assemblies
Where youth, and cost, and witless bravery
   keeps.   10
I have deliver'd to Lord Angelo,
A man of stricture and firm abstinence,
My absolute power and place here in Vienna,
And he supposes me travell'd to Poland ;
For so I have strew'd it in the common ear,
And so it is received. Now, pious sir,
You will demand of me why I do this ?
   Fri. T. Gladly, my lord.
   Duke. We have strict statutes and most
   biting laws,
The needful bits and curbs to headstrong
   weeds,   20
Which for this nineteen years we have let slip ;
Even like an o'ergrown lion in a cave,
That goes not out to prey. Now, as fond
   fathers,
Having bound up the threatening twigs of
   birch,
Only to stick it in their children's sight
For terror, not to use, in time the rod
Becomes more mock'd than fear'd ; so our
   decrees,
Dead to infliction, to themselves are dead ;
And liberty plucks justice by the nose ;
The baby beats the nurse, and quite athwart
Goes all decorum.   31
   Fri. T.   It rested in your grace
To unloose this tied-up justice when you
   pleased :
And it in you more dreadful would have
   seem'd
Than in Lord Angelo.
   Duke.   I do fear, too dreadful :
Sith 'twas my fault to give the people scope,
'Twould be my tyranny to strike and gall them
For what I bid them do : for we bid this be
   done,
When evil deeds have their permissive pass
And not the punishment. Therefore indeed,
   my father,
I have on Angelo imposed the office ;   40
Who may, in the ambush of my name, strike
   home,
And yet my nature never in the fight
To do in slander. And to behold his sway,
I will, as 'twere a brother of your order,
Visit both prince and people : therefore, I
   prithee,
Supply me with the habit and instruct me
How I may formally in person bear me
Like a true friar. More reasons for this action
At our more leisure shall I render you ;
Only, this one : Lord Angelo is precise ;   50
Stands at a guard with envy ; scarce confesses
That his blood flows, or that his appetite
Is more to bread than stone : hence shall we
   see,
If power change purpose, what our seemers be.
                                    [*Exeunt.*

SCENE IV. *A nunnery.*

Enter ISABELLA *and* FRANCISCA.

   Isab. And have you nuns no farther priv-
ileges ?
   Fran. Are not these large enough ?

Isab. Yes, truly; I speak not as desiring
    more;
But rather wishing a more strict restraint
Upon the sisterhood, the votarists of Saint
    Clare.
Lucio. [*Within*] Ho! Peace be in this
    place!
Isab.   Who's that which calls?
Fran. It is a man's voice. Gentle Isabella,
Turn you the key, and know his business of
    him;
You may, I may not; you are yet unsworn.
When you have vow'd, you must not speak
    with men   10
But in the presence of the prioress:
Then, if you speak, you must not show your
    face,
Or, if you show your face, you must not speak.
He calls again; I pray you, answer him. [*Exit.*
    Isab. Peace and prosperity! Who is't that
        calls?

Enter Lucio.

Lucio. Hail, virgin, if you be, as those
    cheek-roses
Proclaim you are no less! Can you so stead
    me
As bring me to the sight of Isabella,
A novice of this place and the fair sister
To her unhappy brother Claudio?   20
    Isab. Why 'her unhappy brother'? let me
        ask,
The rather for I now must make you know
I am that Isabella and his sister.
    Lucio. Gentle and fair, your brother kindly
        greets you:
Not to be weary with you, he's in prison.
    Isab. Woe me! for what?
    Lucio. For that which, if myself might be
        his judge,
He should receive his punishment in thanks:
He hath got his friend with child.
    Isab. Sir, make me not your story.
    Lucio.   It is true.   30
I would not—though 'tis my familiar sin
With maids to seem the lapwing and to jest,
Tongue far from heart—play with all virgins
    so:
I hold you as a thing ensky'd and sainted,
By your renouncement an immortal spirit,
And to be talk'd with in sincerity,
As with a saint.
    Isab. You do blaspheme the good in mock-
        ing me.
    Lucio. Do not believe it. Fewness and
        truth, 'tis thus:
Your brother and his lover have embraced:
As those that feed grow full, as blossoming
    time   41
That from the seedness the bare fallow brings
To teeming foison, even so her plenteous womb
Expresseth his full tilth and husbandry.
    Isab. Some one with child by him? My
        cousin Juliet?
    Lucio. Is she your cousin?
    Isab. Adoptedly; as school-maids change
        their names
By vain though apt affection.
    Lucio.   She it is.
    Isab. O, let him marry her.
    Lucio.   This is the point.
The duke is very strangely gone from hence;
Bore many gentlemen, myself being one,   51

In hand and hope of action: but we do learn
By those that know the very nerves of state,
His givings-out were of an infinite distance
From his true-meant design. Upon his place,
And with full line of his authority,
Governs Lord Angelo; a man whose blood
Is very snow-broth; one who never feels
The wanton stings and motions of the sense,
But doth rebate and blunt his natural edge   60
With profits of the mind, study and fast.
He—to give fear to use and liberty,
Which have for long run by the hideous law,
As mice by lions—hath pick'd out an act,
Under whose heavy sense your brother's life
Falls into forfeit: he arrests him on it;
And follows close the rigor of the statute,
To make him an example. All hope is gone,
Unless you have the grace by your fair prayer
To soften Angelo: and that's my pith of busi-
    ness   70
'Twixt you and your poor brother.
    Isab. Doth he so seek his life?
    Lucio.   Has censured him
Already; and, as I hear, the provost hath
A warrant for his execution.
    Isab. Alas! what poor ability's in me
To do him good?
    Lucio.   Assay the power you have.
    Isab. My power? Alas, I doubt—
    Lucio.   Our doubts are traitors
And make us lose the good we oft might win
By fearing to attempt. Go to Lord Angelo,
And let him learn to know, when maidens sue,
Men give like gods; but when they weep and
    kneel,
All their petitions are as freely theirs
As they themselves would owe them.
    Isab. I'll see what I can do.
    Lucio.   But speedily.
    Isab. I will about it straight;
No longer staying but to give the mother
Notice of my affair. I humbly thank you:
Commend me to my brother: soon at night
I'll send him certain word of my success.
    Lucio. I take my leave of you.
    Isab.   Good sir, adieu.   90
                                        [*Exeunt.*

ACT II.

Scene I. *A hall in* Angelo's *house.*

Enter Angelo, Escalus, *and a* Justice, Prov-
    ost, Officers, *and other* Attendants, *behind.*

    Ang. We must not make a scarecrow of
        the law,
Setting it up to fear the birds of prey,
And let it keep one shape, till custom make it
Their perch and not their terror.
    Escal.   Ay, but yet
Let us be keen, and rather cut a little,
Than fall, and bruise to death. Alas, this gen-
    tleman,
Whom I would save, had a most noble father!
Let but your honor know,
Whom I believe to be most strait in virtue,
That, in the working of your own affections,
Had time cohered with place or place with
    wishing,   11
Or that the resolute acting of your blood
Could have attain'd the effect of your own
    purpose,

Whether you had not sometime in your life
Err'd in this point which now you censure
him,
And pull'd the law upon you.

Ang. 'Tis one thing to be tempted, Escalus,
Another thing to fall. I not deny,
The jury, passing on the prisoner's life,
May in the sworn twelve have a thief or two
Guiltier than him they try. What's open made
   to justice,   21
That justice seizes : what know the laws
That thieves do pass on thieves ? 'Tis very
   pregnant,
The jewel that we find, we stoop and take't
Because we see it ; but what we do not see
We tread upon, and never think of it.
You may not so extenuate his offence
For I have had such faults ; but rather tell
   me,
When I, that censure him, do so offend,
Let mine own judgment pattern out my death,
And nothing come in partial. Sir, he must die.

Escal. Be it as your wisdom will.

Ang.   Where is the provost ?

Prov. Here, if it like your honor.

Ang.   See that Claudio
Be executed by nine to-morrow morning :
Bring him his confessor, let him be prepared ;
For that's the utmost of his pilgrimage.
                      [*Exit Provost.*

Escal. [*Aside*] Well, heaven forgive him !
   and forgive us all !
Some rise by sin, and some by virtue fall :
Some run from brakes of ice, and answer
   none :
And some condemned for a fault alone.   40

Enter ELBOW, *and* Officers *with* FROTH *and*
        POMPEY.

Elb. Come, bring them away : if these be
good people in a commonweal that do nothing
but use their abuses in common houses, I know
no law : bring them away.

Ang. How now, sir ! What's your name ?
and what's the matter ?

Elb. If it please your honor, I am the poor
duke's constable, and my name is Elbow : I do
lean upon justice, sir, and do bring in here
before your good honor two notorious benefactors.   50

Ang. Benefactors ? Well ; what benefactors
are they ? are they not malefactors ?

Elb. If it please your honor, I know not
well what they are : but precise villains they
are, that I am sure of ; and void of all profanation in the world that good Christians ought
to have.

Escal. This comes off well ; here's a wise
officer.

Ang. Go to : what quality are they of ?
Elbow is your name ? why dost thou not speak,
Elbow ?   60

Pom. He cannot, sir ; he's out at elbow.

Ang. What are you, sir ?

Elb. He, sir ! a tapster, sir ; parcel-bawd ;
one that serves a bad woman ; whose house,
sir, was, as they say, plucked down in the
suburbs ; and now she professes a hot-house,
which, I think, is a very ill house too.

Escal. How know you that ?

Elb. My wife, sir, whom I detest before
heaven and your honor,—   70

Escal. How ? thy wife ?

Elb. Ay, sir ; whom, I thank heaven, is
an honest woman,—

Escal. Dost thou detest her therefore ?

Elb. I say, sir, I will detest myself also, as
well as she, that this house, if it be not a
bawd's house, it is pity of her life, for it is
a naughty house.

Escal. How dost thou know that, constable ?

Elb. Marry, sir, by my wife ; who, if she
had been a woman cardinally given, might
have been accused in fornication, adultery,
and all uncleanliness there.

Escal. By the woman's means ?

Elb. Ay, sir, by Mistress Overdone's
means : but as she spit in his face, so she defied him.

Pom. Sir, if it please your honor, this is
not so.

Elb. Prove it before these varlets here,
thou honorable man ; prove it.

Escal. Do you hear how he misplaces ?   90

Pom. Sir, she came in great with child ; and
longing, saving your honor's reverence, for
stewed prunes ; sir, we had but two in the
house, which at that very distant time stood,
as it were, in a fruit-dish, a dish of some
three-pence ; your honors have seen such
dishes ; they are not China dishes, but very
good dishes,—

Escal. Go to, go to : no matter for the dish,
sir.

Pom. No, indeed, sir, not of a pin ; you
are therein in the right : but to the point. As
I say, this Mistress Elbow, being, as I say,
with child, and being great-bellied, and longing, as I said, for prunes ; and having but two
in the dish, as I said, Master Froth here, this
very man, having eaten the rest, as I said,
and, as I say, paying for them very honestly ;
for, as you know, Master Froth, I could not
give you three-pence again.

Froth. No, indeed.

Pom. Very well ; you being then, if you
be remembered, cracking the stones of the
foresaid prunes,—   111

Froth. Ay, so I did indeed.

Pom. Why, very well ; I telling you then,
if you be remembered, that such a one and
such a one were past cure of the thing you
wot of, unless they kept very good diet, as I
told you,—

Froth. All this is true.

Pom. Why, very well, then,—

Escal. Come, you are a tedious fool : to
the purpose. What was done to Elbow's wife,
that he hath cause to complain of ? Come
me to what was done to her.

Pom. Sir, your honor cannot come to that
yet.

Escal. No, sir, nor I mean it not.

Pom. Sir, but you shall come to it, by
your honor's leave. And, I beseech you, look
into Master Froth here, sir ; a man of fourscore pound a year ; whose father died at Hallowmas : was't not at Hallowmas, Master
Froth ?

Froth. All-hallond eve.   130

Pom. Why, very well ; I hope here be
truths. He, sir, sitting, as I say, in a lower
chair, sir ; 'twas in the Bunch of Grapes,
where indeed you have a delight to sit, have
you not?

Froth. I have so; because it is an open room and good for winter.

Pom. Why, very well, then; I hope here be truths.

Ang. This will last out a night in Russia, When nights are longest there : I'll take my leave.   140
And leave you to the hearing of the cause ; Hoping you'll find good cause to whip them all.

Escal. I think no less. Good morrow to your lordship.   [*Exit Angelo.*
Now, sir, come on : what was done to Elbow's wife, once more ?

Pom. Once, sir ? there was nothing done to her once.

Elb. I beseech you, sir, ask him what this man did to my wife.

Pom. I beseech your honor, ask me.   150

Escal. Well, sir ; what did this gentleman to her ?

Pom. I beseech you, sir, look in this gentleman's face. Good Master Froth, look upon his honor ; 'tis for a good purpose. Doth your honor mark his face ?

Escal. Ay, sir, very well.

Pom. Nay, I beseech you, mark it well.

Escal. Well, I do so.

Pom. Doth your honor see any harm in his face ?   160

Escal. Why, no.

Pom. I'll be supposed upon a book, his face is the worst thing about him. Good, then ; if his face be the worst thing about him, how could Master Froth do the constable's wife any harm ? I would know that of your honor.

Escal. He's in the right. Constable, what say you to it ?

Elb. First, an it like you, the house is a respected house ; next, this is a respected fellow ; and his mistress is a respected woman.

Pom. By this hand, sir, his wife is a more respected person than any of us all.

Elb. Varlet, thou liest ; thou liest, wicked varlet ! the time has yet to come that she was ever respected with man, woman, or child.

Pom. Sir, she was respected with him before he married with her.

Escal. Which is the wiser here ? Justice or Iniquity ? Is this true ?   181

Elb. O thou caitiff ! O thou varlet ! O thou wicked Hannibal ! I respected with her before I was married to her ! If ever I was respected with her, or she with me, let not your worship think me the poor duke's officer. Prove this, thou wicked Hannibal, or I'll have mine action of battery on thee.

Escal. If he took you a box o' the ear, you might have your action of slander too. 190

Elb. Marry, I thank your good worship for it. What is't your worship's pleasure I shall do with this wicked caitiff ?

Escal. Truly, officer, because he hath some offences in him that thou wouldst discover if thou couldst, let him continue in his courses till thou knowest what they are.

Elb. Marry, I thank your worship for it. Thou seest, thou wicked varlet, now, what's come upon thee : thou art to continue now, thou varlet ; thou art to continue.   201

Escal. Where were you born, friend ?

Froth. Here in Vienna, sir.

Escal. Are you of fourscore pounds a year ?

Froth. Yes, an't please you, sir.

Escal. So. What trade are you of, sir ?

Pom. A tapster ; a poor widow's tapster.

Escal. Your mistress' name ?

Pom. Mistress Overdone.

Escal. Hath she had any more than one husband ?   211

Pom. Nine, sir ; Overdone by the last.

Escal. Nine ! Come hither to me, Master Froth. Master Froth, I would not have you acquainted with tapsters : they will draw you, Master Froth, and you will hang them. Get you gone, and let me hear no more of you.

Froth. I thank your worship. For mine own part, I never come into any room in a tap-house, but I am drawn in.   220

Escal. Well, no more of it, Master Froth : farewell. [*Exit Froth.*] Come you hither to me, Master tapster. What's your name, Master tapster ?

Pom. Pompey.

Escal. What else ?

Pom. Bum, sir.

Escal. Troth, and your bum is the greatest thing about you ; so that in the beastliest sense you are Pompey the Great. Pompey, you are partly a bawd, Pompey, howsoever you color it in being a tapster, are you not ? come, tell me true : it shall be the better for you.

Pom. Truly, sir, I am a poor fellow that would live.

Escal. How would you live, Pompey ? by being a bawd ? What do you think of the trade, Pompey ? is it a lawful trade ?

Pom. If the law would allow it, sir.

Escal. But the law will not allow it, Pompey ; nor it shall not be allowed in Vienna. 241

Pom. Does your worship mean to geld and splay all the youth of the city ?

Escal. No, Pompey.

Pom. Truly, sir, in my poor opinion, they will to't then. If your worship will take order for the drabs and the knaves, you need not to fear the bawds.

Escal. There are pretty orders beginning, I can tell you : it is but heading and hanging.

Pom. If you head and hang all that offend that way but for ten year together, you'll be glad to give out a commission for more heads : if this law hold in Vienna ten year, I'll rent the fairest house in it after three-pence a bay : if you live to see this come to pass, say Pompey told you so.

Escal. Thank you, good Pompey ; and, in requital of your prophecy, hark you : I advise you, let me not find you before me again upon any complaint whatsoever ; no, not for dwelling where you do : if I do, Pompey, I shall beat you to your tent, and prove a shrewd Cæsar to you ; in plain dealing, Pompey, I shall have you whipt : so, for this time, Pompey, fare you well.

Pom. I thank your worship for your good counsel : [*Aside*] but I shall follow it as the flesh and fortune shall better determine. Whip me ? No, no ; let carman whip his jade : The valiant heart is not whipt out of his trade.
                                        [*Exit.* 270

Escal. Come hither to me, Master Elbow ; come hither, Master constable. How long have you been in this place of constable ?

Elb. Seven year and a half, sir.

Escal. I thought, by your readiness in the office, you had continued in it some time. You say, seven years together?

Elb. And a half, sir.

Escal. Alas, it hath been great pains to you. They do you wrong to put you so oft upon 't : are there not men in your ward sufficient to serve it?

Elb. Faith, sir, few of any wit in such matters : as they are chosen, they are glad to choose me for them; I do it for some piece of money, and go through with all.

Escal. Look you bring me in the names of some six or seven, the most sufficient of your parish.

Elb. To your worship's house, sir?

Escal. To my house. Fare you well.

[*Exit Elbow.*

What's o'clock, think you? 280

Just. Eleven, sir.

Escal. I pray you home to dinner with me.

Just. I humbly thank you.

Escal. It grieves me for the death of Claudio;
But there's no remedy.

Just. Lord Angelo is severe.

Escal. It is but needful :
Mercy is not itself, that oft looks so;
Pardon is still the nurse of second woe :
But yet,—poor Claudio! There is no remedy. Come, sir. [*Exeunt.* 290

SCENE II. *Another room in the same.*

Enter PROVOST *and a* Servant.

Serv. He's hearing of a cause; he will come straight :
I'll tell him of you.

Prov. Pray you, do. [*Exit Servant.*]
I'll know
His pleasure; may be he will relent. Alas,
He hath but as offended in a dream!
All sects, all ages smack of this vice; and he
To die for't!

Enter ANGELO.

Ang. Now, what's the matter, provost?

Prov. Is it your will Claudio shall die to-morrow?

Ang. Did not I tell thee yea? hadst thou not order?
Why dost thou ask again?

Prov. Lest I might be too rash :
Under your good correction, I have seen, 10
When, after execution, judgment hath
Repented o'er his doom.

Ang. Go to; let that be mine :
Do you your office, or give up your place,
And you shall well be spared.

Prov. I crave your honor's pardon.
What shall be done, sir, with the groaning Juliet?
She's very near her hour.

Ang. Dispose of her
To some more fitter place, and that with speed.

Re-enter Servant.

Serv. Here is the sister of the man condemn'd
Desires access to you.

Ang. Hath he a sister?

Prov. Ay, my good lord; a very virtuous maid, 20

And to be shortly of a sisterhood,
If not already.

Ang. Well, let her be admitted.

[*Exit Servant.*

See you the fornicatress be removed :
Let her have needful, but not lavish, means;
There shall be order for't.

Enter ISABELLA *and* LUCIO.

Prov. God save your honor!

Ang. Stay a little while. [*To Isab.*] You're welcome : what's your will?

Isab. I am a woeful suitor to your honor,
Please but your honor hear me.

Ang. Well; what's your suit?

Isab. There is a vice that most I do abhor,
And most desire should meet the blow of justice;
For which I would not plead, but that I must;
For which I must not plead, but that I am
At war 'twixt will and will not.

Ang. Well; the matter?

Isab. I have a brother is condemn'd to die :
I do beseech you, let it be his fault,
And not my brother.

Prov. [*Aside*] Heaven give thee moving graces!

Ang. Condemn the fault and not the actor of it?
Why, every fault's condemn'd ere it be done :
Mine were the very cipher of a function,
To fine the faults whose fine stands in record,
And let go by the actor. 41

Isab. O just but severe law!
I had a brother, then. Heaven keep your honor!

Lucio. [*Aside to Isab.*] Give't not o'er so :
to him again, entreat him;
Kneel down before him, hang upon his gown :
You are too cold; if you should need a pin,
You could not with more tame a tongue desire it :
To him, I say!

Isab. Must he needs die?

Ang. Maiden, no remedy.

Isab. Yes; I do think that you might pardon him,
And neither heaven nor man grieve at the mercy.

Ang. I will not do't.

Isab. But can you, if you would? 51

Ang. Look, what I will not, that I cannot do.

Isab. But might you do't, and do the world no wrong,
If so your heart were touch'd with that remorse
As mine is to him?

Ang. He's sentenced; 'tis too late.

Lucio. [*Aside to Isab.*] You are too cold.

Isab. Too late? why, no; I, that do speak a word,
May call it back again. Well, believe this,
No ceremony that to great ones 'longs,
Not the king's crown, nor the deputed sword,
The marshal's truncheon, nor the judge's robe,
Become them with one half so good a grace 62
As mercy does.
If he had been as you and you as he,
You would have slipt like him; but he, like you,
Would not have been so stern.

Ang.   Pray you, be gone.
Isab. I would to heaven I had your potency,
And you were Isabel ! should it then be thus ?
No ; I would tell what 'twere to be a judge,
And what a prisoner.
Lucio. [*Aside to Isab.*] Ay, touch him ;
there's the vein.   70
Ang. Your brother is a forfeit of the law,
And you but waste your words.
Isab.   Alas, alas !
Why, all the souls that were were forfeit once ;
And He that might the vantage best have took
Found out the remedy. How would you be,
If He, which is the top of judgment, should
But judge you as you are ? O, think on that ;
And mercy then will breathe within your lips,
Like man new made.
Ang.   Be you content, fair maid ;
It is the law, not I condemn your brother :   80
Were he my kinsman, brother, or my son,
It should be thus with him : he must die to-morrow.
Isab. To-morrow ! O, that's sudden ! Spare
him, spare him !
He's not prepared for death. Even for our kitchens
We kill the fowl of season : shall we serve heaven
With less respect than we do minister
To our gross selves ? Good, good my lord, be-think you ;
Who is it that hath died for this offence ?
There's many have committed it.
Lucio.   [*Aside to Isab.*] Ay, well said.
Ang. The law hath not been dead, though
it hath slept :   90
Those many had not dared to do that evil,
If the first that did the edict infringe
Had answer'd for his deed : now 'tis awake
Takes note of what is done ; and, like a prophet,
Looks in a glass, that shows what future evils,
Either new, or by remissness new-conceived,
And so in progress to be hatch'd and born,
Are now to have no successive degrees,
But, ere they live, to end.
Isab.   Yet show some pity.
Ang. I show it most of all when I show
justice ;   100
For then I pity those I do not know,
Which a dismiss'd offence would after gall ;
And do him right that, answering one foul wrong,
Lives not to act another. Be satisfied ;
Your brother dies to-morrow ; be content.
Isab. So you must be the first that gives
this sentence,
And he, that suffers. O, it is excellent
To have a giant's strength ; but it is tyrannous
To use it like a giant.
Lucio. [*Aside to Isab.*] That's well said.
Isab. Could great men thunder   110
As Jove himself does, Jove would ne'er be quiet,
For every pelting, petty officer
Would use his heaven for thunder ;
Nothing but thunder ! Merciful Heaven,
Thou rather with thy sharp and sulphurous bolt
Split'st the unwedgeable and gnarled oak
Than the soft myrtle : but man, proud man,
Drest in a little brief authority,

Most ignorant of what he's most assured,
His glassy essence, like an angry ape,   120
Plays such fantastic tricks before high heaven
As make the angels weep ; who, with our spleens,
Would all themselves laugh mortal.
Lucio. [*Aside to Isab.*] O, to him, to him,
wench ! he will relent ;
He's coming ; I perceive 't.
Prov. [*Aside*] Pray heaven she win him !
Isab. We cannot weigh our brother with ourself :
Great men may jest with saints ; 'tis wit in them,
But in the less foul profanation.
Lucio. Thou'rt i' the right, girl ; more o' that.
Isab. That in the captain's but a choleric
word,   130
Which in the soldier is flat blasphemy.
Lucio. [*Aside to Isab.*] Art advised o' that ?
more on 't.
Ang. Why do you put these sayings upon me ?
Isab. Because authority, though it err like others,
Hath yet a kind of medicine in itself,
That skins the vice o' the top. Go to your bosom ;
Knock there, and ask your heart what it doth know
That's like my brother's fault : if it confess
A natural guiltiness such as is his,
Let it not sound a thought upon your tongue
Against my brother's life.
Ang.   [*Aside.*] She speaks, and 'tis
Such sense, that my sense breeds with it. Fare
you well.
Isab. Gentle my lord, turn back.
Ang. I will bethink me : come again to-morrow.
Isab. Hark how I'll bribe you : good my
lord, turn back.
Ang. How ! bribe me ?
Isab. Ay, with such gifts that heaven shall
share with you.
Lucio. [*Aside to Isab.*] You had marr'd all else.
Isab. Not with fond shekels of the tested gold,
Or stones whose rates are either rich or poor
As fancy values them ; but with true prayers
That shall be up at heaven and enter there
Ere sun-rise, prayers from preserved souls,
From fasting maids whose minds are dedicate
To nothing temporal.
Ang.   Well ; come to me to-morrow.
Lucio. [*Aside to Isab.*] Go to ; 'tis well ;
away !
Isab. Heaven keep your honor safe !
Ang.   [*Aside*] Amen :
For I am that way going to temptation,
Where prayers cross.
Isab.   At what hour to-morrow
Shall I attend your lordship ?
Ang.   At any time 'fore noon. 160
Isab. 'Save your honor !
[*Exeunt Isabella, Lucio, and Provost.*
Ang.   From thee, even from thy virtue !
What's this, what's this ? Is this her fault or mine ?
The tempter or the tempted, who sins most ?
Ha !

Not she : nor doth she tempt : but it is I
That, lying by the violet in the sun,
Do as the carrion does, not as the flower,
Corrupt with virtuous season. Can it be
That modesty may more betray our sense
Than woman's lightness ? Having waste ground
 enough,   170
Shall we desire to raze the sanctuary
And pitch our evils there ? O, fie, fie, fie !
What dost thou, or what art thou, Angelo ?
Dost thou desire her foully for those things
That make her good ? O, let her brother live !
Thieves for their robbery have authority
When judges steal themselves. What, do I love
 her,
That I desire to hear her speak again,
And feast upon her eyes ? What is't I dream
 on ?
O cunning enemy, that, to catch a saint, 180
With saints dost bait thy hook ! Most danger-
 ous
Is that temptation that doth goad us on
To sin in loving virtue : never could the
 strumpet,
With all her double vigor, art and nature,
Once stir my temper ; but this virtuous maid
Subdues me quite. Ever till now,
When men were fond, I smiled and wonder'd
 how.   [*Exit.*

SCENE III. *A room in a prison.*

Enter, severally, DUKE *disguised as a friar,
and* PROVOST.

 Duke. Hail to you, provost ! so I think you
are.
 Prov. I am the provost. What's your will,
good friar ?
 Duke. Bound by my charity and my blest
order,
I come to visit the afflicted spirits
Here in the prison. Do me the common right
To let me see them and to make me know
The nature of their crimes, that I may minister
To them accordingly.
 Prov. I would do more than that, if more
 were needful.

Enter JULIET.

Look, here comes one : a gentlewoman of
 mine,   10
Who, falling in the flaws of her own youth,
Hath blister'd her report : she is with child ;
And he that got it, sentenced ; a young man
More fit to do another such offence
Than die for this.
 Duke. When must he die ?
 Prov.   As I do think, to-morrow.
I have provided for you : stay awhile,
         [*To Juliet.*
And you shall be conducted.
 Duke. Repent you, fair one, of the sin you
 carry ?
 Jul. I do ; and bear the shame most pa-
 tiently.   20
 Duke. I'll teach you how you shall arraign
 your conscience,
And try your penitence, if it be sound,
Or hollowly put on.
 Jul.   I'll gladly learn.
 Duke. Love you the man that wrong'd
 you ?
 Jul. Yes, as I love the woman that wrong'd
 him.

 Duke. So then it seems your most offence-
 ful act
Was mutually committed ?
 Jul.   Mutually.
 Duke. Then was your sin of heavier kind
 than his.
 Jul. I do confess it, and repent it, father.
 Duke. 'Tis meet so, daughter : but lest you
 do repent,   30
As that the sin hath brought you to this shame,
Which sorrow is always towards ourselves, not
 heaven,
Showing we would not spare heaven as we love
 it,
But as we stand in fear,—
 Jul. I do repent me, as it is an evil,
And take the shame with joy.
 Duke.   There rest.
Your partner, as I hear, must die to-morrow,
And I am going with instruction to him.
Grace go with you, Benedicite ! [*Exit.*
 Jul. Must die to-morrow ! O injurious love,
That respites me a life, whose very comfort
Is still a dying horror !
 Prov.   'Tis pity of him. [*Exeunt.*

SCENE IV. *A room in* ANGELO'S *house.*

Enter ANGELO.

 Ang. When I would pray and think, I think
 and pray
To several subjects. Heaven hath my empty
 words ;
Whilst my invention, hearing not my tongue,
Anchors on Isabel : Heaven in my mouth,
As if I did but only chew his name ;
And in my heart the strong and swelling evil
Of my conception. The state, whereon I stud-
 ied,
Is like a good thing, being often read,
Grown fear'd and tedious ; yea, my gravity,
Wherein—let no man hear me—I take pride,
Could I with boot change for an idle plume, 11
Which the air beats for vain. O place, O form,
How often dost thou with thy case, thy habit,
Wrench awe from fools and tie the wiser souls
To thy false seeming ! Blood, thou art blood :
Let's write good angel on the devil's horn :
'Tis not the devil's crest.

Enter a Servant.

       How now ! who's there ?
 Serv. One Isabel, a sister, desires access to
you.
 Ang. Teach her the way. [*Exit Serv.*] O
 heavens !
Why does my blood thus muster to my heart,
Making both it unable for itself,   21
And dispossessing all my other parts
Of necessary fitness ?
So play the foolish throngs with one that
 swoons ;
Come all to help him, and so stop the air
By which he should revive : and even so
The general, subject to a well-wish'd king,
Quit their own part, and in obsequious fond-
 ness
Crowd to his presence, where their untaught
 love
Must needs appear offence.

Enter ISABELLA.

      How now, fair maid ? 30
 Isab. I am come to know your pleasure.

Ang. That you might know it, would much
   better please me
Than to demand what 'tis. Your brother can-
   not live.
Isab. Even so. Heaven keep your honor !
Ang. Yet may he live awhile ; and, it may
   be,
As long as you or I : yet he must die.
Isab. Under your sentence ?
Ang. Yea.
Isab. When, I beseech you ? that in his re-
   prieve,
Longer or shorter, he may be so fitted   40
That his soul sicken not.
Ang. Ha ! fie, these filthy vices ! It were as
   good
To pardon him that hath from nature stolen
A man already made, as to remit
Their saucy sweetness that do coin heaven's
   image
In stamps that are forbid : 'tis all as easy
Falsely to take away a life true made
As to put metal in restrained means
To make a false one.
Isab. 'Tis set down so in heaven, but not
   in earth.   50
Ang. Say you so ? then I shall pose you
   quickly.
Which had you rather, that the most just law
Now took your brother's life ; or, to redeem
   him,
Give up your body to such sweet uncleanness
As she that he hath stain'd ?
Isab.   Sir, believe this,
I had rather give my body than my soul.
Ang. I talk not of your soul : our com-
   pell'd sins
Stand more for number than for accompt.
Isab.   How say you ?
Ang. Nay, I'll not warrant that ; for I can
   speak
Against the thing I say. Answer to this :   60
I, now the voice of the recorded law,
Pronounce a sentence on your brother's life :
Might there not be a charity in sin
To save this brother's life ?
Isab.   Please you to do't,
I'll take it as a peril to my soul,
It is no sin at all, but charity.
Ang. Pleased you to do't at peril of your
   soul,
Were equal poise of sin and charity.
Isab. That I do beg his life, if it be sin,
Heaven let me bear it ! you granting of my
   suit,
If that be sin, I'll make it my morn prayer 71
To have it added to the faults of mine,
And nothing of your answer.
Ang.   Nay, but hear me.
Your sense pursues not mine : either you are
   ignorant,
Or seem so craftily ; and that's not good.
Isab. Let me be ignorant, and in nothing
   good,
But graciously to know I am no better.
Ang. Thus wisdom wishes to appear most
   bright
When it doth tax itself ; as these black masks
Proclaim an enshield beauty ten times louder
Than beauty could, display'd. But mark me ;
To be received plain, I'll speak more gross :
Your brother is to die.
Isab. So.

Ang. And his offence is so, as it appears,
Accountant to the law upon that pain.
Isab. True.
Ang. Admit no other way to save his life,—
As I subscribe not that, nor any other,
But in the loss of question,—that you, his sis-
   ter,   90
Finding yourself desired of such a person,
Whose credit with the judge, or own great
   place,
Could fetch your brother from the manacles
Of the all-building law ; and that there were
No earthly mean to save him, but that either
You must lay down the treasures of your body
To this supposed, or else to let him suffer ;
What would you do ?
Isab. As much for my poor brother as my-
   self :   100
That is, were I under the terms of death,
The impression of keen whips I'ld wear as
   rubies,
And strip myself to death, as to a bed
That longing have been sick for, ere I'ld yield
My body up to shame.
Ang.   Then must your brother die.
Isab. And 'twere the cheaper way :
Better it were a brother died at once,
Than that a sister, by redeeming him,
Should die for ever.
Ang. Were not you then as cruel as the
   sentence
That you have slander'd so ?   110
Isab. Ignomy in ransom and free pardon
Are of two houses : lawful mercy
Is nothing kin to foul redemption.
Ang. You seem'd of late to make the law
   a tyrant ;
And rather proved the sliding of your brother
A merriment than a vice.
Isab. O, pardon me, my lord ; it oft falls
   out,
To have what we would have, we speak not
   what we mean :
I something do excuse the thing I hate,
For his advantage that I dearly love.   120
Ang. We are all frail.
Isab.   Else let my brother die,
If not a feodary, but only he
Owe and succeed thy weakness.
Ang. Nay, women are frail too.
Isab. Ay, as the glasses where they view
   themselves ;
Which are as easy broke as they make forms.
Women ! Help Heaven ! men their creation
   mar
In profiting by them. Nay, call us ten times
   frail ;
For we are soft as our complexions are,
And credulous to false prints.
Ang.   I think it well :   130
And from this testimony of your own sex,—
Since I suppose we are made to be no stronger
Than faults may shake our frames,—let me be
   bold ;
I do arrest your words. Be that you are,
That is, a woman ; if you be more, you're
   none ;
If you be one, as you are well express'd
By all external warrants, show it now,
By putting on the destined livery.
Isab. I have no tongue but one : gentle my
   lord,
Let me entreat you speak the former language.

Ang.   Plainly conceive, I love you.   141
Isab.   My brother did love Juliet,
And you tell me that he shall die for it.
Ang.   He shall not, Isabel, if you give me
love.
Isab.   I know your virtue hath a license in't,
Which seems a little fouler than it is,
To pluck on others.
Ang.   Believe me, on mine honor,
My words express my purpose.
Isab.   Ha ! little honor to be much be-
lieved,
And most pernicious purpose ! Seeming, seem-
ing !   150
I will proclaim thee, Angelo ; look for't :
Sign me a present pardon for my brother,
Or with an outstretch'd throat I'll tell the
world aloud
What man thou art.
Ang.   Who will believe thee, Isabel ?
My unsoil'd name, the austereness of my life,
My vouch against you, and my place i' the
state,
Will so your accusation overweigh,
That you shall stifle in your own report
And smell of calumny. I have begun,
And now I give my sensual race the rein : 160
Fit thy consent to my sharp appetite ;
Lay by all nicety and prolixious blushes,
That banish what they sue for ; redeem thy
brother
By yielding up thy body to my will ;
Or else he must not only die the death,
But thy unkindness shall his death draw out
To lingering sufferance. Answer me to-morrow,
Or, by the affection that now guides me most,
I'll prove a tyrant to him. As for you,
Say what you can, my false o'erweighs your
true.   [*Exit.* 170
Isab.   To whom should I complain ? Did I
tell this,
Who would believe me ? O perilous mouths,
That bear in them one and the self-same
tongue,
Either of condemnation or approof ;
Bidding the law make court'sy to their will :
Hooking both right and wrong to the appetite,
To follow as it draws ! I'll to my brother :
Though he hath fallen by prompture of the
blood,
Yet hath he in him such a mind of honor,
That, had he twenty heads to tender down 180
On twenty bloody blocks, he'ld yield them up,
Before his sister should her body stoop
To such abhorr'd pollution.
Then, Isabel, live chaste, and, brother, die :
More than our brother is our chastity.
I'll tell him yet of Angelo's request,
And fit his mind to death, for his soul's rest.
[*Exit.*

ACT III.

SCENE I.   *A room in the prison.*

Enter DUKE *disguised as before,* CLAUDIO,
and PROVOST.

Duke.   So then you hope of pardon from
Lord Angelo ?
Claud.   The miserable have no other medi-
cine

But only hope :
I've hope to live, and am prepared to die.
Duke.   Be absolute for death ; either death
or life
Shall thereby be the sweeter. Reason thus with
life :
If I do lose thee, I do lose a thing
That none but fools would keep : a breath
thou art,
Servile to all the skyey influences,   9
That dost this habitation, where thou keep'st,
Hourly afflict : merely, thou art death's fool ;
For him thou labor'st by thy flight to shun
And yet runn'st toward him still. Thou art not
noble ;
For all the accommodations that thou bear'st
Are nursed by baseness. Thou'rt by no means
valiant ;
For thou dost fear the soft and tender fork
Of a poor worm. Thy best of rest is sleep,
And that thou oft provokest ; yet grossly
fear'st
Thy death, which is no more. Thou art not
thyself ;   19
For thou exist'st on many a thousand grains
That issue out of dust. Happy thou art not ;
For what thou hast not, still thou strivest to
get,
And what thou hast, forget'st. Thou art not
certain ;
For thy complexion shifts to strange effects,
After the moon. If thou art rich, thou'rt poor ;
For, like an ass whose back with ingots bows,
Thou bear's thy heavy riches but a journey,
And death unloads thee. Friend hast thou
none ;
For thine own bowels, which do call thee sire,
The mere effusion of thy proper loins,   30
Do curse the gout, serpigo, and the rheum,
For ending thee no sooner. Thou hast nor
youth nor age,
But, as it were, an after-dinner's sleep,
Dreaming on both ; for all thy blessed youth
Becomes as aged, and doth beg the alms
Of palsied eld ; and when thou art old and
rich,
Thou hast neither heat, affection, limb, nor
beauty,
To make thy riches pleasant. What's yet in
this
That bears the name of life ? Yet in this life
Lie hid moe thousand deaths : yet death we
fear,
That makes these odds all even.   41
Claud.   I humbly thank you.
To sue to live, I find I seek to die ;
And, seeking death, find life : let it come on.
Isab.   [*Within*] What, ho ! Peace here ;
grace and good company !
Prov.   Who's there ? come in : the wish de-
serves a welcome.
Duke.   Dear sir, ere long I'll visit you
again.
Claud.   Most holy sir, I thank you.

Enter ISABELLA.

Isab.   My business is a word or two with
Claudio.
Prov.   And very welcome. Look, signior,
here's your sister.
Duke.   Provost, a word with you.   50
Prov.   As many as you please.

Duke. Bring me to hear them speak, where
I may be concealed.
                    [*Exeunt Duke and Provost.*
Claud. Now, sister, what's the comfort?
Isab.   Why,
As all comforts are; most good, most good
indeed.
Lord Angelo, having affairs to heaven,
Intends you for his swift ambassador,
Where you shall be an everlasting leiger :
Therefore your best appointment make with
    speed ;   60
To-morrow you set on.
Claud.   Is there no remedy?
Isab. None, but such remedy as, to save a
    head,
To cleave a heart in twain.
Claud.   But is there any?
Isab. Yes, brother, you may live :
There is a devilish mercy in the judge,
If you'll implore it, that will free your life,
But fetter you till death.
Claud.   Perpetual durance?
Isab. Ay, just; perpetual durance, a re-
    straint,
Though all the world's vastidity you had,
To a determined scope.
Claud.   But in what nature? 70
Isab. In such a one as, you consenting to't,
Would bark your honor from that trunk you
    bear,
And leave you naked.
Claud.   Let me know the point.
Isab. O, I do fear thee, Claudio ; and I
    quake,
Lest thou a feverous life shouldst entertain,
And six or seven winters more respect
Than a perpetual honor. Darest thou die?
The sense of death is most in apprehension ;
And the poor beetle, that we tread upon,
In corporal sufferance finds a pang as great 80
As when a giant dies.
Claud.   Why give you me this shame?
Think you I can a resolution fetch
From flowery tenderness? If I must die,
I will encounter darkness as a bride,
And hug it in mine arms.
Isab. There spake my brother ; there my
    father's grave
Did utter forth a voice. Yes, thou must die :
Thou art too noble to conserve a life
In base appliances. This outward-sainted
    deputy,   90
Whose settled visage and deliberate word
Nips youth i' the head and follies doth emmew
As falcon doth the fowl, is yet a devil
His filth within being cast, he would appear
A pond as deep as hell.
Claud.   The prenzie Angelo !
Isab. O, 'tis the cunning livery of hell,
The damned'st body to invest and cover
In prenzie guards ! Dost thou think, Claudio ?
If I would yield him my virginity,
Thou mightst be freed.
Claud.   O heavens ! it cannot be.
Isab. Yes, he would give 't thee, from this
    rank offence,   100
So to offend him still. This night's the time
That I should do what I abhor to name,
Or else thou diest to-morrow.
Claud.   Thou shalt not do't.
Isab. O, were it but my life,
I'ld throw it down for your deliverance

As frankly as a pin.
Claud.   Thanks, dear Isabel.
Isab. Be ready, Claudio, for your death to-
    morrow.
Claud. Yes. Has he affections in him,
That thus can make him bite the law by the
    nose,
When he would force it ? Sure, it is no sin, 110
Or of the deadly seven, it is the least.
Isab. Which is the least ?
Claud. If it were damnable, he being so
    wise,
Why would he for the momentary trick
Be perdurably fined ? O Isabel !
Isab. What says my brother ?
Claud.   Death is a fearful thing.
Isab. And shamed life a hateful.
Claud. Ay, but to die, and go we know not
    where ;
To lie in cold obstruction and to rot ;
This sensible warm motion to become   120
A kneaded clod ; and the delighted spirit
To bathe in fiery floods, or to reside
In thrilling region of thick-ribbed ice ;
To be imprison'd in the viewless winds,
And blown with restless violence round about
The pendent world ; or to be worse than worst
Of those that lawless and incertain thought
Imagine howling : 'tis too horrible !
The weariest and most loathed worldly life
That age, ache, penury and imprisonment 130
Can lay on nature is a paradise
To what we fear of death.
Isab. Alas, alas !
Claud.   Sweet sister, let me live :
What sin you do to save a brother's life,
Nature dispenses with the deed so far
That it becomes a virtue.
Isab.   O you beast !
O faithless coward ! O dishonest wretch !
Wilt thou be made a man out of my vice ?
Is't not a kind of incest, to take life
From thine own sister's shame ? What should
    I think ?   140
Heaven shield my mother play'd my father
    fair !
For such a warped slip of wilderness
Ne'er issued from his blood. Take my de-
    fiance !
Die, perish ! Might but my bending down
Reprieve thee from thy fate, it should pro-
    ceed :
I'll pray a thousand prayers for thy death,
No word to save thee.
Claud. Nay, hear me, Isabel.
Isab.   O, fie, fie, fie !
Thy sin's not accidental, but a trade.
Mercy to thee would prove itself a bawd : 150
'Tis best thou diest quickly.
Claud.   O hear me, Isabella !

Re-enter Duke.

Duke. Vouchsafe a word, young sister, but
    one word.
Isab. What is your will ?
Duke. Might you dispense with your leisure, I would by and by have some speech with
you : the satisfaction I would require is likewise your own benefit.
Isab. I have no superfluous leisure ; my
stay must be stolen out of other affairs ; but I
will attend you awhile.   [*Walks apart.*
Duke. Son, I have overheard what hath

passed between you and your sister. Angelo
had never the purpose to corrupt her; only
he hath made an essay of her virtue to practise his judgment with the disposition of natures: she, having the truth of honor in her,
hath made him that gracious denial which he
is most glad to receive. I am confessor to Angelo, and I know this to be true; therefore
prepare yourself to death: do not satisfy your
resolution with hopes that are fallible: to-
morrow you must die; go to your knees and
make ready.

Claud. Let me ask my sister pardon. I am
so out of love with life that I will sue to be rid
of it.

Duke. Hold you there: farewell. [*Exit
Claudio.*] Provost, a word with you!

Re-enter PROVOST.

Prov. What's your will, father?

Duke. That now you are come, you will be
gone. Leave me awhile with the maid: my
mind promises with my habit no loss shall
touch her by my company.

Prov. In good time.

[*Exit Provost. Isabella comes forward.*

Duke. The hand that hath made you fair
hath made you good: the goodness that is
cheap in beauty makes beauty brief in goodness; but grace, being the soul of your complexion, shall keep the body of it ever fair.
The assault that Angelo hath made to you,
fortune hath conveyed to my understanding;
and, but that frailty hath examples for his falling, I should wonder at Angelo. How will you
do to content this substitute, and to save your
brother?

Isab. I am now going to resolve him: I had
rather my brother die by the law than my son
should be unlawfully born. But, O, how much
is the good duke deceived in Angelo! If ever
he return and I can speak to him, I will open
my lips in vain, or discover his government.

Duke. That shall not be much amiss: yet,
as the matter now stands, he will avoid your
accusation; he made trial of you only. Therefore fasten your ear on my advisings: to the
love I have in doing good a remedy presents
itself. I do make myself believe that you may
most uprighteously do a poor wronged lady a
merited benefit; redeem your brother from the
angry law; do no stain to your own gracious
person; and much please the absent duke, if
peradventure he shall ever return to have hearing of this business.   211

Isab. Let me hear you speak farther. I
have spirit to do anything that appears not
foul in the truth of my spirit.

Duke. Virtue is bold, and goodness never
fearful. Have you not heard speak of Mariana,
the sister of Frederick the great soldier who
miscarried at sea?

Isab. I have heard of the lady, and good
words went with her name.   220

Duke. She should this Angelo have married; was affianced to her by oath, and the
nuptial appointed: between which time of the
contract and limit of the solemnity, her
brother Frederick was wrecked at sea, having
in that perished vessel the dowry of his sister.
But mark how heavily this befell to the poor
gentlewoman: there she lost a noble and renowned brother, in his love toward her ever

most kind and natural; with him, the portion
and sinew of her fortune, her marriage-dowry;
with both, her combinate husband, this well-
seeming Angelo.

Isab. Can this be so? did Angelo so leave
her?

Duke. Left her in her tears, and dried not
one of them with his comfort; swallowed his
vows whole, pretending in her discoveries of
dishonor: in few, bestowed her on her own
lamentation, which she yet wears for his sake;
and he, a marble to her tears, is washed with
them, but relents not.

Isab. What a merit were it in death to take
this poor maid from the world! What corruption in this life, that it will let this man live!
But how out of this can she avail?

Duke. It is a rupture that you may easily
heal: and the cure of it not only saves your
brother, but keeps you from dishonor in doing
it.

Isab. Show me how, good father.

Duke. This forenamed maid hath yet in
her the continuance of her first affection: his
unjust unkindness, that in all reason should
have quenched her love, hath, like an impediment in the current, made it more violent and
unruly. Go you to Angelo; answer his requiring with a plausible obedience; agree with his
demands to the point; only refer yourself to
this advantage, first, that your stay with him
may not be long; that the time may have all
shadow and silence in it; and the place answer
to convenience. This being granted in course,
—and now follows all,—we shall advise this
wronged maid to stead up your appointment,
go in your place; if the encounter acknowledge itself hereafter, it may compel him to her
recompense: and here, by this, is your brother
saved, your honor untainted, the poor Mariana
advantaged, and the corrupt deputy scaled.
The maid will I frame and make fit for his
attempt. If you think well to carry this as you
may, the doubleness of the benefit defends the
deceit from reproof. What think you of it?

Isab. The image of it gives me content already; and I trust it will grow to a most prosperous perfection.

Duke. It lies much in your holding up.
Haste you speedily to Angelo: if for this night
he entreat you to his bed, give him promise of
satisfaction. I will presently to Saint Luke's:
there, at the moated grange, resides this dejected Mariana. At that place call upon me;
and dispatch with Angelo, that it may be
quickly.

Isab. I thank you for this comfort. Fare
you well, good father. [*Exeunt severally.*   281

SCENE II. *The street before the prison.*

Enter, on one side, DUKE *disguised as before; on the other,* ELBOW, *and* Officers
with POMPEY.

Elb. Nay, if there be no remedy for it, but
that you will needs buy and sell men and
women like beasts, we shall have all the world
drink brown and white bastard.

Duke. O heavens! what stuff is here?

Pom. 'Twas never merry world since, of
two usuries, the merriest was put down, and
the worser allowed by order of law a furred
gown to keep him warm; and furred with fox
and lamb-skins too, to signify, that craft, be-

ing richer than innocency, stands for the fac-
ing. 11

Elb. Come your way, sir. 'Bless you, good
father friar.

Duke. And you, good brother father. What
offence hath this man made you, sir?

Elb. Marry, sir, he hath offended the law:
and, sir, we take him to be a thief too, sir;
for we have found upon him, sir, a strange
picklock, which we have sent to the deputy.

Duke. Fie, sirrah! a bawd, a wicked
bawd!
The evil that thou causest to be done, 21
That is thy means to live. Do thou but think
What 'tis to cram a maw or clothe a back
From such a filthy vice: say to thyself,
From their abominable and beastly touches
I drink, I eat, array myself, and live.
Canst thou believe thy living is a life,
So stinkingly depending? Go mend, go mend.

Pom. Indeed, it does stink in some sort,
sir; but yet, sir, I would prove— 30

Duke. Nay, if the devil have given thee
proofs for sin,
Thou wilt prove his. Take him to prison, of-
ficer:
Correction and instruction must both work
Ere this rude beast will profit.

Elb. He must before the deputy, sir; he
has given him warning: the deputy cannot
abide a whoremaster: if he be a whore-
monger, and comes before him, he were as
good go a mile on his errand.

Duke. That we were all, as some would
seem to be, 40
From our faults, as faults from seeming, free!

Elb. His neck will come to your waist,—a
cord, sir.

Pom. I spy comfort; I cry bail. Here's a
gentleman and a friend of mine.

Enter Lucio.

Lucio. How now, noble Pompey! What,
at the wheels of Cæsar? art thou led in triumph? What, is there none of Pygmalion's
images, newly made woman, to be had now,
for putting the hand in the pocket and extracting it clutched? What reply, ha? What sayest
thou to this tune, matter and method? Is't not
drowned i' the last rain, ha? What sayest thou,
Trot? Is the world as it was, man? Which is
the way? Is it sad, and few words? or how?
The trick of it?

Duke. Still thus, and thus; still worse!

Lucio. How doth my dear morsel, thy mistress? Procures she still, ha?

Pom. Troth, sir, she hath eaten up all her
beef, and she is herself in the tub.

Lucio. Why, 'tis good; it is the right of it;
it must be so: ever your fresh whore and your
powdered bawd: an unshunned consequence;
it must be so. Art going to prison, Pompey?

Pom. Yes, faith, sir.

Lucio. Why, 'tis not amiss, Pompey. Farewell: go, say I sent thee thither. For debt,
Pompey? or how?

Elb. For being a bawd, for being a bawd.

Lucio. Well, then, imprison him: if imprisonment be the due of a bawd, why, 'tis his
right: bawd is he doubtless, and of antiquity
too; bawd-born. Farewell, good Pompey.
Commend me to the prison, Pompey: you will

turn good husband now, Pompey; you will
keep the house.

Pom. I hope, sir, your good worship will
be my bail.

Lucio. No, indeed, will I not, Pompey; it
is not the wear. I will pray, Pompey, to increase your bondage: if you take it not patiently, why, your mettle is the more. Adieu,
trusty Pompey. 'Bless you, friar. 81

Duke. And you.

Lucio. Does Bridget paint still, Pompey,
ha?

Elb. Come your ways, sir; come.

Pom. You will not bail me, then, sir?

Lucio. Then, Pompey, nor now. What
news abroad, friar? what news?

Elb. Come your ways, sir; come.

Lucio. Go to kennel, Pompey; go. [*Exeunt
Elbow, Pompey and Officers.*] What news,
friar, of the duke? 91

Duke. I know none. Can you tell me of
any?

Lucio. Some say he is with the Emperor of
Russia; other some, he is in Rome: but where
is he, think you?

Duke. I know not where; but wheresoever,
I wish him well.

Lucio. It was a mad fantastical trick of
him to steal from the state, and usurp the beggary he was never born to. Lord Angelo dukes
it well in his absence; he puts transgression
to 't. 101

Duke. He does well in 't.

Lucio. A little more lenity to lechery would
do no harm in him: something too crabbed
that way, friar.

Duke. It is too general a vice, and severity
must cure it.

Lucio. Yes, in good sooth, the vice is of a
great kindred; it is well allied: but it is impossible to extirp it quite, friar, till eating and
drinking be put down. They say this Angelo
was not made by man and woman after this
downright way of creation: is it true, think
you?

Duke. How should he be made, then?

Lucio. Some report a sea-maid spawned
him; some, that he was begot between two
stock-fishes. But it is certain that when he
makes water his urine is congealed ice; that
I know to be true: and he is a motion gen-
erative; that's infallible.

Duke. You are pleasant, sir, and speak
apace.

Lucio. Why, what a ruthless thing is this
in him, for the rebellion of a codpiece to take
away the life of a man! Would the duke that
is absent have done this? Ere he would have
hanged a man for the getting a hundred bastards, he would have paid for the nursing a
thousand: he had some feeling of the sport:
he knew the service, and that instructed him
to mercy.

Duke. I never heard the absent duke much
detected for women; he was not inclined that
way.

Lucio. O, sir, you are deceived. 131

Duke. 'Tis not possible.

Lucio. Who, not the duke? yes, your beggar of fifty; and his use was to put a ducat in
her clack-dish: the duke had crotchets in him.
He would be drunk too; that let me inform
you.

Duke. You do him wrong, surely.

Lucio. Sir, I was an inward of his. A shy fellow was the duke : and I believe I know the cause of his withdrawing. 140

Duke. What, I prithee, might be the cause ?

Lucio. No, pardon ; 'tis a secret must be locked within the teeth and the lips : but this I can let you understand, the greater file of the subject held the duke to be wise.

Duke. Wise ! why, no quesion but he was.

Lucio. A very superficial, ignorant, unweighing fellow.

Duke. Either this is envy in you, folly, or mistaking : the very stream of his life and the business he hath helmed must upon a warranted need give him a better proclamation. Let him be but testimonied in his own bringings-forth, and he shall appear to the envious a scholar, a statesman and a soldier. Therefore you speak unskilfully ; or if your knowledge be more it is much darkened in your malice.

Lucio. Sir, I know him, and I love him.

Duke. Love talks with better knowledge, and knowledge with dearer love. 160

Lucio. Come, sir, I know what I know.

Duke. I can hardly believe that, since you know not what you speak. But, if ever the duke return, as our prayers are he may, let me desire you to make your answer before him. If it be honest you have spoke, you have courage to maintain it : I am bound to call upon you ; and, I pray you, your name ?

Lucio. Sir, my name is Lucio ; well known to the duke. 170

Duke. He shall know you better, sir, if I may live to report you.

Lucio. I fear you not.

Duke. O, you hope the duke will return no more ; or you imagine me too unhurtful an opposite. But indeed I can do you little harm ; you'll forswear this again.

Lucio. I'll be hanged first : thou art deceived in me, friar. But no more of this. Canst thou tell if Claudio die to-morrow or no ? 180

Duke. Why should he die, sir ?

Lucio. Why ? For filling a bottle with a tundish. I would the duke we talk of were returned again : the ungenitured agent will unpeople the province with continency ; sparrows must not build in his house-eaves, because they are lecherous. The duke yet would have dark deeds darkly answered ; he would never bring them to light : would he were returned ! Marry, this Claudio is condemned for untrussing. Farewell, good friar : I prithee, pray for me. The duke, I say to thee again, would eat mutton on Fridays. He's not past it yet, and I say to thee, he would mouth with a beggar, though she smelt brown bread and garlic : say that I said so. Farewell. [*Exit.*

Duke. No might nor greatness in mortality Can censure 'scape ; back-wounding calumny The whitest virtue strikes. What king so strong Can tie the gall up in the slanderous tongue ? But who comes here ? 200

Enter ESCALUS, PROVOST, *and* Officers *with* MISTRESS OVERDONE.

Escal. Go ; away with her to prison !

Mrs. Ov. Good my lord, be good to me ;

your honor is accounted a merciful man ; good my lord.

Escal. Double and treble admonition, and still forfeit in the same kind ! This would make mercy swear and play the tyrant.

Prov. A bawd of eleven years' continuance, may it please your honor.

Mrs. Ov. My lord, this is one Lucio's information against me. Mistress Kate Keepdown was with child by him in the duke's time ; he promised her marriage : his child is a year and a quarter old, come Philip and Jacob : I have kept it myself ; and see how he goes about to abuse me !

Escal. That fellow is a fellow of much license : let him be called before us. Away with her to prison ! Go to ; no more words. [*Exeunt Officers with Mistress Ov.*] Provost, my brother Angelo will not be altered ; Claudio must die to-morrow : let him be furnished with divines, and have all charitable preparation. If my brother wrought by my pity, it should not be so with him.

Prov. So please you, this friar hath been with him, and advised him for the entertainment of death.

Escal. Good even, good father.

Duke. Bliss and goodness on you !

Escal. Of whence are you ?

Duke. Not of this country, though my chance is now 230
To use it for my time : I am a brother Of gracious order, late come from the See In special business from his holiness.

Escal. What news abroad i' the world ?

Duke. None, but that there is so great a fever on goodness, that the dissolution of it must cure it : novelty is only in request ; and it is as dangerous to be aged in any kind of course, as it is virtuous to be constant in any undertaking. There is scarce truth enough alive to make societies secure ; but security enough to make fellowships accurst : much upon this riddle runs the wisdom of the world. This news is old enough, yet it is every day's news. I pray you, sir, of what disposition was the duke ?

Escal. One that, above all other strifes, contended especially to know himself.

Duke. What pleasure was he given to ?

Escal. Rather rejoicing to see another merry, than merry at any thing which professed to make him rejoice : a gentleman of all temperance. But leave we him to his events, with a prayer they may prove prosperous ; and let me desire to know how you find Claudio prepared. I am made to understand that you have lent him visitation.

Duke. He professes to have received no sinister measure from his judge, but most willingly humbles himself to the determination of justice : yet had he framed to himself, by the instruction of his frailty, many deceiving promises of life ; which I by my good leisure have discredited to him, and now is he resolved to die.

Escal. You have paid the heavens your function, and the prisoner the very debt of your calling. I have labored for the poor gentleman to the extremest shore of my modesty : but my brother justice have I found so severe, that he hath forced me to tell him he is indeed Justice.

Duke. If his own life answer the straitness

of his proceeding, it shall become him well ;
wherein if he chance to fail, he hath sentenced
himself.

Escal. I am going to visit the prisoner.
Fare you well.

Duke. Peace be with you !

        [*Exeunt Escalus and Provost.*

He who the sword of heaven will bear
Should be as holy as severe ;
Pattern in himself to know,
Grace to stand, and virtue go ;
More nor less to others paying
Than by self-offences weighing.   280
Shame to him whose cruel striking
Kills for faults of his own liking !
Twice treble shame on Angelo,
To weed my vice and let his grow !
O, what may man within him hide,
Though angel on the outward side !
How may likeness made in crimes,
Making practice on the times,
To draw with idle spiders' strings
Most ponderous and substantial things ! 290
Craft against vice I must apply :
With Angelo to-night shall lie
His old betrothed but despised ;
So disguise shall, by the disguised,
Pay with falsehood false exacting,
And perform an old contracting.   [*Exit.*

ACT IV.

Scene I. *The moated grange at* St. Luke's.

Enter Mariana *and a* Boy.

Boy *sings.*

Take, O, take those lips away,
    That so sweetly were forsworn ;
And those eyes, the break of day,
    Lights that do mislead the morn ;
But my kisses bring again, bring again ;
    Seals of love, but sealed in vain, sealed in
        vain.

Mari. Break off thy song, and haste thee
    quick away :
Here comes a man of comfort, whose advice
Hath often still'd my brawling discontent.

           [*Exit Boy.*

Enter Duke *disguised as before.*

I cry you mercy, sir ; and well could wish 10
You had not found me here so musical :
Let me excuse me, and believe me so,
My mirth it much displeased, but pleased my
    woe.

Duke. 'Tis good ; though music oft hath
    such a charm
To make bad good, and good provoke to harm.
I pray you, tell me, hath any body inquired
for me here to-day ? much upon this time have
I promised here to meet.

Mari. You have not been inquired after :
I have sat here all day.   20

Enter Isabella.

Duke. I do constantly believe you. The
time is come even now. I shall crave your forbearance a little : may be I will call upon you
anon, for some advantage to yourself.

Mari. I am always bound to you. [*Exit.*

Duke. Very well met, and well come.
What is the news from this good deputy ?

Isab. He hath a garden circummured with
    brick,
Whose western side is with a vineyard back'd ;
And to that vineyard is a planched gate, 30
That makes his opening with this bigger key :
This other doth command a little door
Which from the vineyard to the garden leads ;
There have I made my promise
Upon the heavy middle of the night
To call upon him.

Duke. But shall you on your knowledge
    find this way ?

Isab. I have ta'en a due and wary note
    upon't :
With whispering and most guilty diligence,
In action all of precept, he did show me 40
The way twice o'er.

Duke. Are there no other tokens
Between you 'greed concerning her observ-
    ance ?

Isab. No, none, but only a repair i' the
    dark ;
And that I have possess'd him my most stay
Can be but brief ; for I have made him know
I have a servant comes with me along,
That stays upon me, whose persuasion is
I come about my brother.

Duke.   'Tis well borne up.
I have not yet made known to Mariana
A word of this. What, ho ! within ! come
    forth !   50

Re-enter Mariana.

I pray you, be acquainted with this maid ;
She comes to do you good.

Isab.   I do desire the like.

Duke. Do you persuade yourself that I re-
    spect you ?

Mari. Good friar, I know you do, and have
    found it.

Duke. Take, then, this your companion by
    the hand,
Who hath a story ready for your ear.
I shall attend your leisure : but make haste ;
The vaporous night approaches.

Mari. Will't please you walk aside ?

    [*Exeunt Mariana and Isabella.*

Duke. O place and greatness ! millions of
    false eyes   60
Are stuck upon thee : volumes of report
Run with these false and most contrarious
    quests
Upon thy doings : thousand escapes of wit
Make thee the father of their idle dreams
And rack thee in their fancies.

Re-enter Mariana *and* Isabella.

           Welcome, how agreed ?

Isab. She'll take the enterprise upon her,
    father,
If you advise it.

Duke.   It is not my consent,
But my entreaty too.

Isab.   Little have you to say
When you depart from him, but, soft and low,
' Remember now my brother.'

Mari.   Fear me not. 70

Duke. Nor, gentle daughter, fear you not
    at all.
He is your husband on a pre-contract :
To bring you thus together, 'tis no sin,
Sith that the justice of your title to him
Doth flourish the deceit. Come, let us go :

Our corn's to reap, for yet our tithe's to sow.
[*Exeunt.*

SCENE II.   *A room in the prison.*

Enter PROVOST *and* POMPEY.

Prov. Come hither, sirrah. Can you cut off
a man's head ?

Pom. If the man be a bachelor, sir, I can ;
but if he be a married man, he's his wife's
head, and I can never cut off a woman's head.

Prov. Come, sir, leave me your snatches,
and yield me a direct answer. To-morrow
morning are to die Claudio and Barnardine.
Here is in our prison a common executioner,
who in his office lacks a helper : if you will
take it on you to assist him, it shall redeem
you from your gyves ; if not, you shall have
your full time of imprisonment and your deliverance with an unpitied whipping, for you
have been a notorious bawd.

Pom. Sir, I have been an unlawful bawd
time out of mind ; but yet I will be content to
be a lawful hangman. I would be glad to receive some instruction from my fellow partner.

Prov. What, ho ! Abhorson ! Where's Abhorson, there ?   21

Enter ABHORSON.

Abhor. Do you call, sir ?

Prov. Sirrah, here's a fellow will help you
to-morrow in your execution. If you think it
meet, compound with him by the year, and
let him abide here with you ; if not, use him
for the present and dismiss him. He cannot
plead his estimation with you ; he hath been
a bawd.

Abhor. A bawd, sir ? fie upon him ! he will
discredit our mystery.   30

Prov. Go to, sir ; you weigh equally ; a
feather will turn the scale.   [*Exit.*

Pom. Pray, sir, by your good favor,—for
surely, sir, a good favor you have, but that
you have a hanging look,—do you call, sir,
your occupation a mystery ?

Abhor. Ay, sir ; a mystery.

Pom. Painting, sir, I have heard say, is a
mystery ; and your whores, sir, being members
of my occupation, using painting, do prove my
occupation a mystery : but what mystery there
should be in hanging, if I should be hanged, I
cannot imagine.

Abhor. Sir, it is a mystery.

Pom. Proof ?

Abhor. Every true man's apparel fits your
thief : if it be too little for your thief, your
true man thinks it big enough ; if it be too
big for your thief, your thief thinks it little
enough : so every true man's apparel fits your
thief.   50

Re-enter PROVOST.

Prov. Are you agreed ?

Pom. Sir, I will serve him ; for I do find
your hangman is a more penitent trade than
your bawd ; he doth oftener ask forgiveness.

Prov. You, sirrah, provide your block and
your axe to-morrow four o'clock.

Abhor. Come on, bawd ; I will instruct
thee in my trade ; follow.

Pom. I do desire to learn, sir : and I hope,
if you have occasion to use me for your own
turn, you shall find me yare ; for truly, sir, for
your kindness I owe you a good turn.

Prov. Call hither Barnardine and Claudio :
[*Exeunt Pompey and Abhorson.*
The one has my pity ; not a jot the other,
Being a murderer, though he were my brother.

Enter CLAUDIO.

Look, here's the warrant, Claudio, for thy
death :
'Tis now dead midnight, and by eight to-morrow
Thou must be made immortal. Where's Barnardine ?

Claud. As fast lock'd up in sleep as guilt-
less labor
When it lies starkly in the traveller's bones :
He will not wake.   71

Prov.   Who can do good on him ?
Well, go, prepare yourself. [*Knocking within.*]
But, hark, what noise ?
Heaven give your spirits comfort ! [*Exit
Claudio.*] By and by.
I hope it is some pardon or reprieve
For the most gentle Claudio.

Enter DUKE *disguised as before.*

Welcome, father.

Duke. The best and wholesomest spirits of
the night
Envelope you, good Provost ! Who call'd here
of late ?

Prov. None, since the curfew rung.

Duke. Not Isabel ?

Prov.   No.

Duke.   They will, then, ere't be long.

Prov. What comfort is for Claudio ?   80

Duke. There's some in hope.

Prov.   It is a bitter deputy.

Duke. Not so, not so ; his life is parallel'd
Even with the stroke and line of his great
justice :
He doth with holy abstinence subdue
That in himself which he spurs on his power
To qualify in others : were he meal'd with that
Which he corrects, then were he tyrannous ;
But this being so, he's just. [*Knocking within.*
Now are they come.
[*Exit Provost.*
This is a gentle provost : seldom when
The steeled gaoler is the friend of men.
[*Knocking within.*   90
How now ! what noise ? That spirit's possessed
with haste
That wounds the unsisting postern with these
strokes.

Re-enter PROVOST.

Prov. There he must stay until the officer
Arise to let him in : he is call'd up.

Duke. Have you no countermand for Claudio yet,
But he must die to-morrow ?

Prov.   None, sir, none.

Duke. As near the dawning, provost, as it
is,
You shall hear more ere morning.

Prov.   Happily
You something know ; yet I believe there
comes
No countermand ; no such example have we :
Besides, upon the very siege of justice   101
Lord Angelo hath to the public ear
Profess'd the contrary.

Enter a MESSENGER.

This is his lordship's man.

Duke. And here comes Claudio's pardon.

Mes. [*Giving a paper.*] My lord hath sent you this note; and by me this further charge, that you swerve not from the smallest article of it, neither in time, matter, or other circumstance. Good morrow; for, as I take it, it is almost day.

Prov. I shall obey him. [*Exit Messenger.*

Duke. [*Aside*] This is his pardon, purchased by such sin
For which the pardoner himself is in.
Hence hath offence his quick celerity,
When it is borne in high authority:
When vice makes mercy, mercy's so extended,
That for the fault's love is the offender friended.
Now, sir, what news?

Prov. I told you. Lord Angelo, belike thinking me remiss in mine office, awakens me with this unwonted putting-on; methinks strangely, for he hath not used it before.   121

Duke. Pray you, let's hear.

Prov. [*Reads*]
'Whatsoever you may hear to the contrary, let Claudio be executed by four of the clock; and in the afternoon Barnardine: for my better satisfaction, let me have Claudio's head sent me by five. Let this be duly performed; with a thought that more depends on it than we must yet deliver. Thus fail not to do your office, as you will answer it at your peril.'   130
What say you to this, sir?

Duke. What is that Barnardine who is to be executed in the afternoon?

Prov. A Bohemian born, but here nursed up and bred; one that is a prisoner nine years old.

Duke. How came it that the absent duke had not either delivered him to his liberty or executed him? I have heard it was ever his manner to do so.

Prov. His friends still wrought reprieves for him: and, indeed, his fact, till now in the government of Lord Angelo, came not to an undoubtful proof.

Duke. It is now apparent?

Prov. Most manifest, and not denied by himself.

Duke. Hath he borne himself penitently in prison? how seems he to be touched?

Prov. A man that apprehends death no more dreadfully but as a drunken sleep; careless, reckless, and fearless of what's past, present, or to come; insensible of mortality, and desperately mortal.

Duke. He wants advice.

Prov. He will hear none: he hath evermore had the liberty of the prison; give him leave to escape hence, he would not: drunk many times a day, if not many days entirely drunk. We have very oft awaked him, as if to carry him to execution, and showed him a seeming warrant for it: it hath not moved him at all.

Duke. More of him anon. There is written in your brow, provost, honesty and constancy: if I read it not truly, my ancient skill beguiles me; but, in the boldness of my cunning, I will lay myself in hazard. Claudio, whom here you have warrant to execute, is no greater forfeit to the law than Angelo who hath sentenced him. To make you understand this in a manifested effect, I crave but four days' respite; for the which you are to do me both a present and a dangerous courtesy.

Prov. Pray, sir, in what?

Duke. In the delaying death.

Prov. Alack, how may I do it, having the hour limited, and an express command, under penalty, to deliver his head in the view of Angelo? I may make my case as Claudio's, to cross this in the smallest.

Duke. By the vow of mine order I warrant you, if my instructions may be your guide. Let this Barnardine be this morning executed, and his head borne to Angelo.

Prov. Angelo hath seen them both, and will discover the favor.

Duke. O, death's a great disguiser; and you may add to it. Shave the head, and tie the beard; and say it was the desire of the penitent to be so bared before his death: you know the course is common. If any thing fall to you upon this, more than thanks and good fortune, by the saint whom I profess, I will plead against it with my life.

Prov. Pardon me, good father; it is against my oath.

Duke. Were you sworn to the duke, or to the deputy?

Prov. To him, and to his substitutes.

Duke. You will think you have made no offence, if the duke avouch the justice of your dealing?   201

Prov. But what likelihood is in that?

Duke. Not a resemblance, but a certainty. Yet since I see you fearful, that neither my coat, integrity, nor persuasion can with ease attempt you, I will go further than I meant, to pluck all fears out of you. Look you, sir, here is the hand and seal of the duke: you know the character, I doubt not; and the signet is not strange to you.

Prov. I know them both.   210

Duke. The contents of this is the return of the duke: you shall anon over-read it at your pleasure; where you shall find, within these two days he will be here. This is a thing that Angelo knows not; for he this very day receives letters of strange tenor; perchance of the duke's death; perchance entering into some monastery; but, by chance, nothing of what is writ. Look, the unfolding star calls up the shepherd. Put not yourself into amazement how these things should be: all difficulties are but easy when they are known. Call your executioner, and off with Barnardine's head: I will give him a present shrift and advise him for a better place. Yet you are amazed; but this shall absolutely resolve you. Come away; it is almost clear dawn.   [*Exeunt.*

SCENE III. *Another room in the same.*

Enter POMPEY.

Pom. I am as well acquainted here as I was in our house of profession: one would think it were Mistress Overdone's own house, for here be many of her old customers. First, here's young Master Rash; he's in for a commodity of brown paper and old ginger, nine-score and seventeen pounds; of which he made five marks, ready money: marry, then ginger was not much in request, for the old

women were all dead. Then is there here one
Master Caper, at the suit of Master Three-pile
the mercer, for some four suits of peach-col-
ored satin, which now peaches him a beggar.
Then have we here young Dizy, and young
Master Deep-vow, and Master Copperspur,
and Master Starve-lackey the rapier and dagger man, and young Drop-heir that killed lusty
Pudding, and Master Forthlight the tilter, and
brave Master Shooty the great traveller, and
wild Half-can that stabbed Pots, and, I think,
forty more ; all great doers in our trade, and
are now ' for the Lord's sake.'

Enter ABHORSON.

Abhor. Sirrah, bring Barnardine hither.

Pom. Master Barnardine ! you must rise
and be hanged, Master Barnardine !

Abhor. What, ho, Barnardine !

Bar. [*Within*] A pox o' your throats ! Who
makes that noise there ? What are you ?

Pom. Your friends, sir ; the hangman. You
must be so good, sir, to rise and be put to
death.

Bar. [*Within*] Away, you rogue, away ! I
am sleepy.　　　　　　　　　　　　　31

Abhor. Tell him he must awake, and that
quickly too.

Pom. Pray, Master Barnardine, awake till
you are executed, and sleep afterwards.

Abhor. Go in to him, and fetch him out.

Pom. He is coming, sir, he is coming ; I
hear his straw rustle.

Abhor. Is the axe upon the block, sirrah ?

Pom. Very ready, sir.　　　　　　　40

Enter BARNARDINE.

Bar. How now, Abhorson ? what's the
news with you ?

Abhor. Truly, sir, I would desire you to
clap into your prayers ; for, look you, the
warrant's come.

Bar. You rogue, I have been drinking all
night ; I am not fitted for 't.

Pom. O, the better, sir ; for he that drinks
all night, and is hanged betimes in the morning, may sleep the sounder all the next day.

Abhor. Look you, sir ; here comes your
ghostly father : do we jest now, think you ?

Enter DUKE *disguised as before.*

Duke. Sir, induced by my charity, and
hearing how hastily you are to depart, I am
come to advise you, comfort you and pray with
you.

Bar. Friar, not I : I have been drinking
hard all night, and I will have more time to
prepare me, or they shall beat out my brains
with billets : I will not consent to die this day,
that's certain.

Duke. O, sir, you must : and therefore I
beseech you　　　　　　　　　　　　60
Look forward on the journey you shall go.

Bar. I swear I will not die to-day for any
man's persuasion.

Duke. But hear you.

Bar. Not a word : if you have any thing to
say to me, come to my ward ; for thence will
not I to-day.　　　　　　　　　　[*Exit.*

Duke. Unfit to live or die : O gravel heart !
After him, fellows ; bring him to the block.

　　　　　　[*Exeunt Abhorson and Pompey.*

Re-enter PROVOST.

Prov. Now, sir, how do you find the prisoner ?　　　　　　　　　　　　　70

Duke. A creature unprepared, unmeet for
death ;
And to transport him in the mind he is
Were damnable.

Prov.　　　　　Here in the prison, father,
There died this morning of a cruel fever
One Ragozine, a most notorious pirate,
A man of Claudio's years ; his beard and head
Just of his color. What if we do omit
This reprobate till he were well inclined ;
And satisfy the deputy with the visage
Of Ragozine, more like to Claudio ?　　80

Duke. O, 'tis an accident that heaven pro-
vides !
Dispatch it presently ; the hour draws on
Prefix'd by Angelo : see this be done,
And sent according to command ; whiles I
Persuade this rude wretch willingly to die.

Prov. This shall be done, good father, pres-
ently.
But Barnardine must die this afternoon :
And how shall we continue Claudio,
To save me from the danger that might come
If he were known alive ?

Duke.　　　　Let this be done.　　90
Put them in secret holds, both Barnardine and
Claudio :
Ere twice the sun hath made his journal greet-
ing
To the under generation, you shall find
Your safety manifested.

Prov. I am your free dependant.

Duke. Quick, dispatch, and send the head
to Angelo.　　　　　　　　　[*Exit Provost.*
Now will I write letters to Angelo,—
The provost, he shall bear them,—whose con-
tents
Shall witness to him I am near at home,
And that, by great injunctions, I am bound 100
To enter publicly : him I'll desire
To meet me at the consecrated fount
A league below the city ; and from thence,
By cold gradation and well-balanced form,
We shall proceed with Angelo.

Re-enter PROVOST.

Prov. Here is the head ; I'll carry it myself.

Duke. Convenient is it. Make a swift re-
turn ;
For I would commune with you of such things
That want no ear but yours.

Prov.　　　　I'll make all speed. [*Exit.*

Isab. [*Within*] Peace, ho, be here !　110

Duke. The tongue of Isabel. She's come to
know
If yet her brother's pardon be come hither :
But I will keep her ignorant of her good,
To make her heavenly comforts of despair,
When it is least expected.

Enter ISABELLA.

Isab.　　　　　　Ho, by your leave !

Duke. Good morning to you, fair and gracious daughter.

Isab. The better, given me by so holy a
man.
Hath yet the deputy sent my brother's pardon ?

Duke. He hath released him, Isabel, from
the world :

His head is off and sent to Angelo.   120
Isab. Nay, but it is not so.
Duke. It is no other : show your wisdom, daughter,
In your close patience.
Isab. O, I will to him and pluck out his eyes !
Duke. You shall not be admitted to his sight.
Isab. Unhappy Claudio ! wretched Isabel !
Injurious world ! most damned Angelo !
Duke. This nor hurts him nor profits you a jot ;
Forbear it therefore ; give your cause to heaven.
Mark what I say, which you shall find   130
By every syllable a faithful verity :
The duke comes home to-morrow ; nay, dry your eyes ;
One of our convent, and his confessor,
Gives me this instance : already he hath carried
Notice to Escalus and Angelo,
Who do prepare to meet him at the gates,
There to give up their power. If you can, pace your wisdom
In that good path that I would wish it go,
And you shall have your bosom on this wretch,
Grace of the duke, revenges to your heart,   140
And general honor.
Isab.   I am directed by you.
Duke. This letter, then, to Friar Peter give ;
'Tis that he sent me of the duke's return :
Say, by this token, I desire his company
At Mariana's house to-night. Her cause and yours
I'll perfect him withal, and he shall bring you
Before the duke, and to the head of Angelo
Accuse him home and home. For my poor self,
I am combined by a sacred vow
And shall be absent. Wend you with this letter :
Command these fretting waters from your eyes
With a light heart ; trust not my holy order,
If I pervert your course. Who's here ?

Enter Lucio.

Lucio. Good even. Friar, where's the provost ?
Duke. Not within, sir.
Lucio. O pretty Isabella, I am pale at mine heart to see thine eyes so red : thou must be patient. I am fain to dine and sup with water and bran ; I dare not for my head fill my belly ; one fruitful meal would set me to 't. But they say the duke will be here to-morrow. By my troth, Isabel, I loved thy brother : if the old fantastical duke of dark corners had been at home, he had lived.   [*Exit Isabella.*
Duke. Sir, the duke is marvellous little beholding to your reports ; but the best is, he lives not in them.
Lucio. Friar, thou knowest not the duke so well as I do : he's a better woodman than thou takest him for.   171
Duke. Well, you'll answer this one day. Fare ye well.
Lucio. Nay, tarry ; I'll go along with thee : I can tell thee pretty tales of the duke.
Duke. You have told me too many of him already, sir, if they be true ; if not true, none were enough.
Lucio. I was once before him for getting a wench with child.   180

Duke. Did you such a thing ?
Lucio. Yes, marry, did I : but I was fain to forswear it ; they would else have married me to the rotten medlar.
Duke. Sir, your company is fairer than honest. Rest you well.
Lucio. By my troth, I'll go with thee to the lane's end : if bawdy talk offend you, we'll have very little of it. Nay, friar, I am a kind of burr ; I shall stick.   [*Exeunt.*   190

SCENE IV. *A room in* Angelo's *house.*

Enter Angelo *and* Escalus.

Escal. Every letter he hath writ hath disvouched other.
Ang. In most uneven and distracted manner. His actions show much like to madness : pray heaven his wisdom be not tainted ! And why meet him at the gates, and redeliver our authorities there ?
Escal. I guess not.
Ang. And why should we proclaim it in an hour before his entering, that if any crave redress of injustice, they should exhibit their petitions in the street ?
Escal. He shows his reason for that : to have a dispatch of complaints, and to deliver us from devices hereafter, which shall then have no power to stand against us.
Ang. Well, I beseech you, let it be proclaimed betimes i' the morn ; I'll call you at your house : give notice to such men of sort and suit as are to meet him.   20
Escal. I shall, sir. Fare you well.
Ang. Good night.   [*Exit Escalus.*
This deed unshapes me quite, makes me unpregnant
And dull to all proceedings. A deflower'd maid !
And by an eminent body that enforced
The law against it ! But that her tender shame
Will not proclaim against her maiden loss,
How might she tongue me ! Yet reason dares her no ;
For my authority bears of a credent bulk,
That no particular scandal once can touch   30
But it confounds the breather. He should have lived,
Save that his riotous youth, with dangerous sense,
Might in the times to come have ta'en revenge,
By so receiving a dishonor'd life
With ransom of such shame. Would yet he had lived !
Alack, when once our grace we have forgot,
Nothing goes right : we would, and we would not.   [*Exit.*

SCENE V. *Fields without the town.*

Enter Duke *in his own habit, and* Friar
Peter.

Duke. These letters at fit time deliver me :
                              [*Giving letters.*
The provost knows our purpose and our plot.
The matter being afoot, keep your instruction,
And hold you ever to our special drift ;
Though sometimes you do blench from this to that,
As cause doth minister. Go call at Flavius' house,
And tell him where I stay : give the like notice

To Valentinus, Rowland, and to Crassus,
And bid them bring the trumpets to the gate;
But send me Flavius first.
　Fri. P.　It shall be speeded well. [*Exit.* 10

　　　　　Enter VARRIUS.

　Duke. I thank thee, Varrius; thou hast
　　made good haste :
Come, we will walk. There's other of our
　　friends
Will greet us here anon, my gentle Varrius.
　　　　　　　　　　　　　　　[*Exeunt.*

SCENE VI. *Street near the city gate.*

　　Enter ISABELLA *and* MARIANA.

　Isab. To speak so indirectly I am loath :
I would say the truth ; but to accuse him so,
That is your part : yet I am advised to do it ;
He says, to veil full purpose.
　Mari.　　　　Be ruled by him.
　Isab. Besides, he tells me that, if perad-
　　venture
He speak against me on the adverse side,
I should not think it strange ; for 'tis a physic
That's bitter to sweet end.
　Mari.　I would Friar Peter—
　Isab.　　　O, peace ! the friar is come.

　　　　　Enter FRIAR PETER.

　Fri. P. Come, I have found you out a
　　stand most fit,　　　　　　　　10
Where you may have such vantage on the
　　duke,
He shall not pass you. Twice have the trum-
　　pets sounded ;
The generous and gravest citizens
Have hent the gates, and very near upon
The duke is entering : therefore, hence, away !
　　　　　　　　　　　　　　[*Exeunt.*

────────

ACT V.

SCENE I. *The city gate.*

MARIANA *veiled,* ISABELLA, *and* FRIAR PETER,
at their stand. Enter DUKE, VARRIUS,
LORDS, ANGELO, ESCALUS, LUCIO, PROVOST,
OFFICERS, *and* CITIZENS, *at several doors.*

　Duke. My very worthy cousin, fairly met !
Our old and faithful friend, we are glad to see
　　you.
　Ang. ⎱ Happy return be to your royal
　Escal. ⎰　　grace !
　Duke. Many and hearty thankings to you
　　both.
We have made inquiry of you ; and we hear
Such goodness of your justice, that our soul
Cannot but yield you forth to public thanks,
Forerunning more requital.
　Ang.　　You make my bonds still greater.
　Duke. O, your desert speaks loud ; and I
　　should wrong it,
To lock it in the wards of covert bosom,　10
When it deserves, with characters of brass,
A forted residence 'gainst the tooth of time
And razure of oblivion. Give me your hand,
And let the subject see, to make them know
That outward courtesies would fain proclaim
Favors that keep within. Come, Escalus,
You must walk by us on our other hand ;
And good supporters are you.

　FRIAR PETER *and* ISABELLA *come forward.*

　Fri. P. Now is your time : speak loud and
　　kneel before him.
　Isab.　Justice, O royal duke ! Vail your re-
　　gard　　　　　　　　　　　　20
Upon a wrong'd, I would fain have said, a
　　maid !
O worthy prince, dishonor not your eye
By throwing it on any other object
Till you have heard me in my true complaint
And given me justice, justice, justice, justice !
　Duke. Relate your wrongs ; in what ? by
　　whom ? be brief.
Here is Lord Angelo shall give you justice :
Reveal yourself to him.
　Isab.　　　　O worthy duke,
You bid me seek redemption of the devil :
Hear me yourself ; for that which I must
　　speak　　　　　　　　　　30
Must either punish me, not being believed,
Or wring redress from you. Hear me, O hear
　　me, here !
　Ang. My lord, her wits, I fear me, are not
　　firm :
She hath been a suitor to me for her brother
Cut off by course of justice,—
　Isab.　　　　By course of justice !
　Ang. And she will speak most bitterly and
　　strange.
　Isab.　Most strange, but yet most truly, will
　　I speak :
That Angelo's forsworn ; is it not strange ?
That Angelo's a murderer ; is 't not strange ?
That Angelo is an adulterous thief,　　40
An hypocrite, a virgin-violator ;
Is it not strange and strange ?
　Duke.　　　Nay, it is ten times strange.
　Isab. It is not truer he is Angelo
Than this is all as true as it is strange :
Nay, it is ten times true ; for truth is truth
To the end of reckoning.
　Duke.　　　Away with her ! Poor soul,
She speaks this in the infirmity of sense.
　Isab. O prince, I conjure thee, as thou be-
　　lievest
There is another comfort than this world,
That thou neglect me not, with that opinion
That I am touch'd with madness ! Make not
　　impossible　　　　　　　　.51
That which but seems unlike : 'tis not im-
　　possible
But one, the wicked'st caitiff on the ground,
May seem as shy, as grave, as just, as ab-
　　solute
As Angelo ; even so may Angelo,
In all his dressings, characts, titles, forms,
Be an arch-villain ; believe it, royal prince :
If he be less, he's nothing ; but he's more,
Had I more name for badness.
　Duke.　　　By mine honesty,
If she be mad,—as I believe no other,—　60
Her madness hath the oddest frame of sense,
Such a dependency of thing on thing,
As e'er I heard in madness.
　Isab.　　　O gracious duke,
Harp not on that, nor do not banish reason
For inequality ; but let your reason serve
To make the truth appear where it seems hid,
And hide the false seems true.
　Duke.　　　Many that are not mad
Have, sure, more lack of reason. What would
　　you say ?

Isab. I am the sister of one Claudio,
Condemn'd upon the act of fornication   70
To lose his head; condemn'd by Angelo:
I, in probation of a sisterhood,
Was sent to by my brother; one Lucio
As then the messenger,—
   Lucio.   That's I, an't like your grace:
I came to her from Claudio, and desired her
To try her gracious fortune with Lord Angelo
For her poor brother's pardon.
   Isab.   That's he indeed.
   Duke. You were not bid to speak.
   Lucio.   No, my good lord;
Nor wish'd to hold my peace.
   Duke.   I wish you now, then;
Pray you, take note of it: and when you have
A business for yourself, pray heaven you then
Be perfect.
   Lucio. I warrant your honor.
   Duke. The warrant's for yourself; take
   heed to't.
   Isab. This gentleman told somewhat of my
   tale,—
   Lucio. Right.
   Duke. It may be right; but you are i' the
   wrong
To speak before your time. Proceed.
   Isab.   I went
To this pernicious caitiff deputy,—
   Duke. That's somewhat madly spoken.
   Isab.   Pardon it;   90
The phrase is to the matter.
   Duke. Mended again. The matter; pro-
   ceed.
   Isab. In brief, to set the needless process
   by,
How I persuaded, how I pray'd, and kneel'd,
How he refell'd me, and how I replied,—
For this was of much length,—the vile con-
   clusion
I now begin with grief and shame to utter:
He would not, but by gift of my chaste body
To his concupiscible intemperate lust,
Release my brother; and, after much debate-
   ment,
My sisterly remorse confutes mine honor,   100
And I did yield to him: but the next morn
   betimes,
His purpose surfeiting, he sends a warrant
For my poor brother's head.
   Duke.   This is most likely!
   Isab. O, that it were as like as it is true!
   Duke. By heaven, fond wretch, thou
   know'st not what thou speak'st,
Or else thou art suborn'd against his honor
In hateful practice. First, his integrity
Stands without blemish. Next, it imports no
   reason
That with such vehemency he should pursue
Faults proper to himself: if he had so
   offended,
He would have weigh'd thy brother by himself
And not have cut him off. Some one hath set
   you on:
Confess the truth, and say by whose advice
Thou camest here to complain.
   Isab.   And is this all?
Then, O you blessed ministers above,
Keep me in patience, and with ripen'd time
Unfold the evil which is here wrapt up
In countenance! Heaven shield your grace
   from woe,
As I, thus wrong'd, hence unbelieved go!

   Duke. I know you'ld fain be gone. An
   officer!   120
To prison with her! Shall we thus permit
A blasting and a scandalous breath to fall
On him so near us? This needs must be a
   practice.
Who knew of your intent and coming hither?
   Isab. One that I would were here, Friar
   Lodowick.
   Duke. A ghostly father, belike. Who
   knows that Lodowick?
   Lucio. My lord, I know him; 'tis a med-
   dling friar;
I do not like the man: had he been lay, my
   lord,
For certain words he spake against your
   grace
In your retirement, I had swinged him
   soundly.   130
   Duke. Words against me! this is a good
   friar, belike!
And to set on this wretched woman here
Against our substitute! Let this friar be
   found.
   Lucio. But yesternight, my lord, she and
   that friar,
I saw them at the prison: a saucy friar,
A very scurvy fellow.
   Fri. P. Blessed be your royal grace!
I have stood by, my lord, and I have heard
Your royal ear abused. First, hath this woman
Most wrongfully accused your substitute,   140
Who is as free from touch or soil with her
As she from one ungot.
   Duke.   We did believe no less.
Know you that Friar Lodowick that she
   speaks of?
   Fri. P. I know him for a man divine and
   holy;
Not scurvy, nor a temporary meddler,
As he's reported by this gentleman;
And, on my trust, a man that never yet
Did, as he vouches, misreport your grace.
   Lucio. My lord, most villanously; believe
   it.
   Fri. P. Well, he in time may come to clear
   himself;   150
But at this instant he is sick, my lord,
Of a strange fever. Upon his mere request,
Being come to knowledge that there was com-
   plaint
Intended 'gainst Lord Angelo, came I hither,
To speak, as from his mouth, what he doth
   know
Is true and false; and what he with his oath
And all probation will make up full clear,
Whensoever he's convented. First, for this
   woman,
To justify this worthy nobleman,
So vulgarly and personally accused,   160
Her shall you hear disproved to her eyes,
Till she herself confess it.
   Duke.   Good friar, let's hear it.
   [*Isabella is carried off guarded; and
          Mariana comes forward.*
Do you not smile at this, Lord Angelo?
O heaven, the vanity of wretched fools!
Give us some seats. Come, cousin Angelo;
In this I'll be impartial; be you judge
Of your own cause. Is this the witness, friar?
First, let her show her face, and after speak.
   Mari. Pardon, my lord; I will not show
   my face

Until my husband bid me.   170
  Duke. What, are you married ?
  Mari. No, my lord.
  Duke. Are you a maid ?
  Mari. No, my lord.
  Duke. A widow, then ?
  Mari. Neither, my lord.
  Duke. Why, you are nothing then : neither
maid, widow, nor wife ?
  Lucio. My lord, she may be a punk ; for
many of them are neither maid, widow, nor
wife.   180
  Duke. Silence that fellow : I would he had
         some cause
To prattle for himself.
  Lucio. Well, my lord.
  Mari. My lord, I do confess I ne'er was
married :
And I confess besides I am no maid :
I have known my husband ; yet my husband
Knows not that ever he knew me.
  Lucio. He was drunk then, my lord : it
can be no better.
  Duke. For the benefit of silence, would
thou wert so too !   191
  Lucio. Well, my lord.
  Duke. This is no witness for Lord Angelo.
  Mari. Now I come to't, my lord :
She that accuses him of fornication,
In self-same manner doth accuse my husband,
And charges him, my lord, with such a time
When I'll depose I had him in mine arms
With all the effect of love.
  Ang. Charges she more than me ?
  Mari.   Not that I know. 200
  Duke. No ? you say your husband.
  Mari. Why, just, my lord, and that is An-
         gelo,
Who thinks he knows that he ne'er knew my
         body,
But knows he thinks that he knows Isabel's.
  Ang. This is a strange abuse. Let's see thy
         face.
  Mari. My husband bids me ; now I will
unmask.   [*Unveiling.*
This is that face, thou cruel Angelo,
Which once thou sworest was worth the look-
         ing on ;
This is the hand which, with a vow'd contract,
Was fast belock'd in thine ; this is the body
That took away the match from Isabel,   211
And did supply thee at thy garden-house
In her imagined person.
  Duke.   Know you this woman ?
  Lucio. Carnally, she says.
  Duke.   Sirrah, no more !
  Lucio. Enough, my lord.
  Ang. My lord, I must confess I know this
         woman :
And five years since there was some speech of
         marriage
Betwixt myself and her ; which was broke off,
Partly for that her promised proportions
Came short of composition, but in chief   220
For that her reputation was disvalued
In levity : since which time of five years
I never spake with her, saw her, nor heard
         from her,
Upon my faith and honor.
  Mari.   Noble prince,
As there comes light from heaven and words
         from breath,

As there is sense in truth and truth in virtue,
I am affianced this man's wife as strongly
As words could make up vows : and, my good
         lord,
But Tuesday night last gone in's garden-house
He knew me as a wife. As this is true,   230
Let me in safety raise me from my knees ;
Or else for ever be confixed here,
A marble monument !
  Ang.   I did but smile till now :
Now, good my lord, give me the scope of jus-
         tice ;
My patience here is touch'd. I do perceive
These poor informal women are no more
But instruments of some more mightier mem-
         ber
That sets them on : let me have way, my lord,
To find this practice out.
  Duke.   Ay, with my heart ;
And punish them to your height of pleasure.
Thou foolish friar, and thou pernicious
         woman,
Compact with her that's gone, think'st thou
         thy oaths,
Though they would swear down each partic-
         ular saint,
Were testimonies against his worth and credit
That's seal'd in approbation ? You, Lord Es-
         calus,
Sit with my cousin ; lend him your kind pains
To find out this abuse, whence 'tis derived.
There is another friar that set them on ;
Let him be sent for.
  Fri. P. Would he were here, my lord ! for
         he indeed   250
Hath set the women on to this complaint :
Your provost knows the place where he abides
And he may fetch him.
  Duke. Go do it instantly. [*Exit Provost.*
And you, my noble and well-warranted cousin,
Whom it concerns to hear this matter forth,
Do with your injuries as seems you best,
In any chastisement : I for a while will leave
         you ;
But stir not you till you have well determined
Upon these slanderers.
  Escal. My lord, we'll do it throughly. 260
                                 [*Exit Duke.*
Signior Lucio, did not you say you knew that
Friar Lodowick to be a dishonest person ?
  Lucio. 'Cucullus non facit monachum : '
honest in nothing but in his clothes ; and one
that hath spoke most villanous speeches of the
duke.
  Escal. We shall entreat you to abide here
till he come and enforce them against him :
we shall find this friar a notable fellow.
  Lucio. As any in Vienna, on my word.
  Escal. Call that same Isabel here once
again ; I would speak with her.
                           [*Exit an Attendant.*]
Pray you, my lord, give me leave to question ;
you shall see how I'll handle her.
  Lucio. Not better than he, by her own report.
  Escal. Say you ?
  Lucio. Marry, sir, I think, if you handled
her privately, she would sooner confess : per-
chance, publicly, she'll be ashamed.
  Escal. I will go darkly to work with her.
  Lucio. That's the way ; for women are
light at midnight.   281

Re-enter OFFICERS *with* ISABELLA ; *and* PROV-
OST *with the* DUKE *in his friar's habit.*

Escal. Come on, mistress : here's a gentlewoman denies all that you have said.

Lucio. My lord, here comes the rascal I
spoke of ; here with the provost.

Escal. In very good time : speak not you
to him till we call upon you.

Lucio. Mum.

Escal. Come, sir : did you set these women
on to slander Lord Angelo ? they have confessed you did.   291

Duke. 'Tis false.

Escal. How ! know you where you are ?

Duke. Respect to your great place ! and
let the devil
Be sometime honor'd for his burning throne !
Where is the duke ? 'tis he should hear me
speak.

Escal. The duke's in us ; and we will hear
you speak :
Look you speak justly.

Duke. Boldly, at least. But, O, poor souls,
Come you to seek the lamb here of the fox ?
Good night to your redress ! Is the duke
gone ?
Then is your cause gone too. The duke's un-
just,
Thus to retort your manifest appeal,
And put your trial in the villain's mouth
Which here you come to accuse.

Lucio. This is the rascal ; this is he I
spoke of.

Escal. Why, thou unreverend and unhal-
low'd friar,
Is't not enough thou hast suborn'd these
women
To accuse this worthy man, but, in foul mouth
And in the witness of his proper ear,   310
To call him villain ? and then to glance from
him
To the duke himself, to tax him with injus-
tice ?
Take him hence ; to the rack with him ! We'll
touse you
Joint by joint, but we will know his purpose.
What, 'unjust' !

Duke.   Be not so hot ; the duke
Dare no more stretch this finger of mine than
he
Dare rack his own : his subject am I not,
Nor here provincial. My business in this state
Made me a looker on here in Vienna,   319
Where I have seen corruption boil and bubble
Till it o'er-run the stew ; laws for all faults,
But faults so countenanced, that the strong
statutes
Stand like the forfeits in a barber's shop,
As much in mock as mark.

Escal. Slander to the state ! Away with
him to prison !

Ang. What can you vouch against him,
Signior Lucio ?
Is this the man that you did tell us of ?

Lucio. 'Tis he, my lord. Come hither,
goodman baldpate : do you know me ?

Duke. I remember you, sir, by the sound
of your voice : I met you at the prison, in the
absence of the duke.

Lucio. O, did you so ? And do you remember what you said of the duke ?

Duke. Most notedly, sir.

Lucio. Do you so, sir ? And was the duke
a fleshmonger, a fool, and a coward, as you
then reported him to be ?

Duke. You must, sir, change persons with
me, ere you make that my report : you, indeed, spoke so of him ; and much more, much
worse.   341

Lucio. O thou damnable fellow ! Did not
I pluck thee by the nose for thy speeches ?

Duke. I protest I love the duke as I love
myself.

Ang. Hark, how the villain would close
now, after his treasonable abuses !

Escal. Such a fellow is not to be talked
withal. Away with him to prison ! Where is
the provost ? Away with him to prison ! lay
bolts enough upon him : let him speak no
more. Away with those giglots too, and with
the other confederate companion !

Duke. [*To Provost.*] Stay, sir ; stay awhile.

Ang. What, resists he ? Help him, Lucio.

Lucio. Come, sir ; come, sir ; come, sir ;
foh, sir ! Why, you bald-pated, lying rascal,
you must be hooded, must you ? Show your
knave's visage, with a pox to you ! show your
sheep-biting face, and be hanged an hour !
Will't not off ?   360
[*Pulls off the friar's hood, and discovers
the Duke.*

Duke. Thou art the first knave that e'er
madest a duke.
First, provost, let me bail these gentle three.
[*To Lucio*] Sneak not away, sir ; for the friar
and you
Must have a word anon. Lay hold on him.

Lucio. This may prove worse than hanging.

Duke. [*To Escalus*] What you have spoke
I pardon : sit you down :
We'll borrow place of him. [*To Angelo*] Sir,
by your leave.
Hast thou or word, or wit, or impudence,
That yet can do thee office ? If thou hast,
Rely upon it till my tale be heard,   370
And hold no longer out.

Ang.   O my dread lord,
I should be guiltier than my guiltiness,
To think I can be undiscernible,
When I perceive your grace, like power divine,
Hath look'd upon my passes. Then, good
prince,
No longer session hold upon my shame,
But let my trial be mine own confession :
Immediate sentence then and sequent death
Is all the grace I beg.

Duke.   Come hither, Mariana.
Say, wast thou e'er contracted to this woman ?

Ang. I was, my lord.   381

Duke. Go take her hence, and marry her
instantly.
Do you the office, friar ; which consummate,
Return him here again. Go with him, provost.
[*Exeunt Angelo, Mariana, Friar Peter
and Provost.*

Escal. My lord, I am more amazed at his
dishonor
Than at the strangeness of it.

Duke.   Come hither, Isabel.
Your friar is now your prince : as I was then
Advertising and holy to your business,
Not changing heart with habit, I am still
Attorney'd at your service.

Isab.   O, give me pardon, 390
That I, your vassal, have employ'd and pain'd

Your unknown sovereignty!
Duke.   You are pardon'd, Isabel:
And now, dear maid, be you as free to us.
Your brother's death, I know, sits at your
            heart;
And you may marvel why I obscured myself,
Laboring to save his life, and would not rather
Make rash remonstrance of my hidden power
Than let him so be lost. O most kind maid,
It was the swift celerity of his death,
Which I did think with slower foot came on,
That brain'd my purpose. But, peace be with
            him!   401
That life is better life, past fearing death,
Than that which lives to fear: make it your
            comfort,
So happy is your brother.
Isab.   I do, my lord.

Re-enter ANGELO, MARIANA, FRIAR PETER,
            and PROVOST.

Duke. For this new-married man ap-
            proaching here,
Whose salt imagination yet hath wrong'd
Your well defended honor, you must pardon
For Mariana's sake: but as he adjudged your
            brother,—
Being criminal, in double violation
Of sacred chastity and of promise-breach 410
Thereon dependent, for your brother's life,—
The very mercy of the law cries out
Most audible, even from his proper tongue,
'An Angelo for Claudio, death for death!'
Haste still pays haste, and leisure answers
            leisure;
Like doth quit like, and MEASURE still FOR
            MEASURE.
Then, Angelo, thy fault's thus manifested;
Which, though thou wouldst deny, denies thee
            vantage.
We do condemn thee to the very block
Where Claudio stoop'd to death, and with like
            haste.   420
Away with him!
Mari.   O my most gracious lord,
I hope you will not mock me with a husband.
Duke. It is your husband mock'd you with
            a husband.
Consenting to the safeguard of your honor,
I thought your marriage fit; else imputation,
For that he knew you, might reproach your
            life
And choke your good to come; for his pos-
            sessions,
Although by confiscation they are ours,
We do instate and widow you withal,
To buy you a better husband.
Mari.   O my dear lord, 430
I crave no other, nor no better man.
Duke. Never crave him; we are definitive.
Mari. Gentle my liege,—   [*Kneeling.*
Duke.   You do but lose your labor.
Away with him to death! [*To Lucio*] Now,
            sir, to you.
Mari. O my good lord! Sweet Isabel, take
            my part;
Lend me your knees, and all my life to come
I'll lend you all my life to do you service.
Duke. Against all sense you do importune
            her:
Should she kneel down in mercy of this fact,
Her brother's ghost his paved bed would
            break,

And take her hence in horror.
Mari.   Isabel,   441
Sweet Isabel, do yet but kneel by me;
Hold up your hands, say nothing; I'll speak
            all.
They say, best men are moulded out of faults;
And, for the most, become much more the
            better
For being a little bad: so may my husband.
O Isabel, will you not lend a knee?
Duke. He dies for Claudio's death.
Isab.   Most bounteous sir,
Look, if it please you, on this man condemn'd,
As if my brother lived: I partly think   450
A due sincerity govern'd his deeds,
Till he did look on me: since it is so,
Let him not die. My brother had but justice,
In that he did the thing for which he died:
For Angelo,
His act did not o'ertake his bad intent,
And must be buried but as an intent
That perish'd by the way: thoughts are no
            subjects;
Intents but merely thoughts.
Mari.   Merely, my lord.
Duke. Your suit's unprofitable; stand up,
            I say.   460
I have bethought me of another fault.
Provost, how came it Claudio was beheaded
At an unusual hour?
Prov.   It was commanded so.
Duke. Had you a special warrant for the
            deed?
Prov. No, my good lord; it was by private
            message.
Duke. For which I do discharge you of
            your office:
Give up your keys.
Prov.   Pardon me, noble lord:
I thought it was a fault, but knew it not;
Yet did repent me, after more advice;
For testimony whereof, one in the prison, 470
That should by private order else have died,
I have reserved alive.
Duke.   What's he?
Prov.   His name is Barnardine.
Duke. I would thou hadst done so by
            Claudio.
Go fetch him hither; let me look upon him.
            [*Exit Provost.*
Escal. I am sorry, one so learned and so
            wise
As you, Lord Angelo, have still appear'd,
Should slip so grossly, both in the heat of
            blood,
And lack of temper'd judgment afterward.
Ang. I am sorry that such sorrow I pro-
            cure:
And so deep sticks it in my penitent heart 480
That I crave death more willingly than mercy;
'Tis my deserving, and I do entreat it.

Re-enter PROVOST, *with* BARNARDINE,
            CLAUDIO *muffled, and* JULIET.

Duke. Which is that Barnardine?
Prov.   This, my lord.
Duke. There was a friar told me of this
            man.
Sirrah, thou art said to have a stubborn soul,
That apprehends no further than this world,
And squarest thy life according. Thou'rt con-
            demn'd:
But, for those earthly faults, I quit them all;

And pray thee take this mercy to provide   489
For better times to come. Friar, advise him;
I leave him to your hand. What muffled fel-
    low's that?
    Prov.   This is another prisoner that I saved,
Who should have died when Claudio lost his
    head;
As like almost to Claudio as himself.
                                [*Unmuffles Claudio.*
    Duke. [*To Isabella*] If he be like your
        brother, for his sake
Is he pardon'd; and, for your lovely sake,
Give me your hand and say you will be mine.
He is my brother too: but fitter time for that.
By this Lord Angelo perceives he's safe;
Methinks I see a quickening in his eye.   500
Well, Angelo, your evil quits you well:
Look that you love your wife; her worth
    worth yours.
I find an apt remission in myself;
And yet here's one in place I cannot pardon.
[*To Lucio*] You, sirrah, that knew me for a
    fool, a coward,
One all of luxury, an ass, a madman;
Wherein have I so deserved of you,
That you extol me thus?
    Lucio.   'Faith, my lord, I spoke it but ac-
cording to the trick. If you will hang me for it,
you may; but I had rather it would please you
I might be whipt.
    Duke.   Whipt first, sir, and hanged after.
Proclaim it, provost, round about the city,
Is any woman wrong'd by this lewd fellow,
As I have heard him swear himself there's one
Whom he begot with child, let her appear,

And he shall marry her: the nuptial finish'd,
Let him be whipt and hang'd.
    Lucio.   I beseech your highness, do not
marry me to a whore. Your highness said
even now, I made you a duke: good my lord,
do not recompense me in making me a cuck-
old.
    Duke.   Upon mine honor, thou shalt marry
        her.
Thy slanders I forgive; and therewithal
Remit thy other forfeits. Take him to prison;
And see our pleasure herein executed.
    Lucio.   Marrying a punk, my lord, is press-
ing to death, whipping, and hanging.
    Duke.   Slandering a prince deserves it.   530
                        [*Exeunt Officers with Lucio.*
She, Claudio, that you wrong'd, look you re-
    store.
Joy to you, Mariana! Love her, Angelo;
I have confess'd her and I know her virtue.
Thanks, good friend Escalus, for thy much
    goodness:
There's more behind that is more gratulate.
Thanks, provost, for thy care and secrecy:
We shall employ thee in a worthier place.
Forgive him, Angelo, that brought you home
The head of Ragozine for Claudio's:
The offence pardons itself. Dear Isabel,   540
I have a motion much imports your good;
Whereto if you'll a willing ear incline,
What's mine is yours and what is yours is
    mine.
So, bring us to our palace; where we'll show
What's yet behind, that's meet you all should
    know.   [*Exeunt.*

TROILUS AND CRESSIDA.

(WRITTEN ABOUT 1603 ?)

INTRODUCTION.

This play appeared in two quarto editions in the year 1609 ; on the title-page of the earlier of the two it is stated to have been acted at the Globe ; the later contains a singular preface in which the play is spoken of as " never stal'd with the stage, never clapper-clawed with the palmes of the vulgar," and as having been published against the will of " the grand possessors." Perhaps the play was printed at first for the use of the theatre, with the intention of being published after having been represented, and the printers, against the known wishes of the proprietors of Shakespeare's manuscript, anticipated the first representation and issued the quarto with the attractive announcement that it was an absolute novelty. The editors of the folio, after having decided that *Troilus and Cressida* should follow *Romeo and Juliet* among the tragedies, changed their minds, apparently uncertain how the play should be classed, and placed it between the Histories and Tragedies ; this led to the cancelling of a leaf, and the filling up of a blank space left by the alteration, with the Prologue to *Troilus and Cressida*—a prologue which is believed by several critics not to have come from Shakespeare's hand. There is extreme uncertainty with respect to the date of the play. Dekker and Chettle were engaged in 1599 upon a play on this subject, and, from an entry in the Stationers' register, February 7, 1602–1603, it appears that a *Troilus and Cressida* had been acted by Shakespeare's company, the Lord Chamberlain's Servants. Was this Shakespeare's play ? We are thrown back upon internal evidence to decide this question, and the internal evidence is itself of a conflicting kind, and has led to opposite conclusions. The massive worldly wisdom of Ulysses argues, it is supposed, in favor of a late date, and the general tone of the play has been compared with that of *Timon of Athens*. The fact that it does not contain a single weak ending, and only six light endings, is, however, almost decisive evidence against our placing it after either *Timon* or *Macbeth ;* and the other metrical characteristics are considered, by the most careful student of this class of evidence in the case of the present play (Hertzberg), to point to a date about 1603. Other authorities place it as late as 1608 or 1609 ; while a third theory (that of Verplanck and Grant White) attempts to solve the difficulties by supposing that it was first written in 1603, and revised and enlarged shortly before the publication of the quarto. Parts of the play—notably the last battle of Hector—appear not to be by Shakespeare. The interpretation of the play itself is as difficult as the ascertainment of the external facts of its history. With what intention, and in what spirit did Shakespeare write this strange comedy ? All the Greek heroes who fought against Troy are pitilessly exposed to ridicule ; Helen and Cressida are light, sensual, and heartless, for whose sake it seems infatuated folly to strike a blow ; Troilus is an enthusiastic young fool ; and even Hector, though valiant and generous, spends his life in a cause which he knows to be unprofitable, if not evil. All this is seen and said by Thersites, whose mind is made up of the scum of the foulness of human life. But can Shakespeare's view of things have been the same as that of Thersites ? The central theme, the young love and faith of Troilus given to one who was false and fickle, and his discovery of his error, lends its color to the whole play. It is the comedy of disillusion. And as Troilus passed through the illusion of his first love for woman, so by middle life the world itself often appears like one that has not kept her promises, and who is a poor deceiver. We come to see the seamy side of life ; and from this mood of disillusion it is a deliverance to pass on even to a dark and tragic view of life, to which beauty and virtue reappear, even though human weakness or human vice may do them bitter wrong. Now such a mood of contemptuous depreciation of life may have come over Shakespeare, and spoilt him, at that time, for a writer of comedy. But for Isabella we should find the coming on of this mood in *Measure for Measure ;* there is perhaps a touch of it in *Hamlet*. At this time *Troilus and Cressida* may have been written, and soon afterwards Shakespeare, rousing himself to a deeper inquest into things, may have passed on to his great series of tragedies. The materials for *Troilus and Cressida* were found by Shakespeare in Chaucer's *Troilus and Creseide*, Caxton's translation from the French, *Remyles, or Destruction of Troy,* and perhaps also Lydgate's *Troye Boke*.

DRAMATIS PERSONÆ.

PRIAM, king of Troy.

HECTOR,
TROILUS,
PARIS,　} his sons.
DEIPHOBUS,
HELENUS,

MARGARELON, a bastard son of Priam.

ÆNEAS,
ANTENOR,　} Trojan commanders.

CALCHAS, a Trojan priest, taking part with the Greeks.

PANDARUS, uncle to Cressida.

AGAMEMNON, the Grecian general.

MENELAUS, his brother.

ACHILLES,
AJAX,
ULYSSES,　} Grecian princes.
NESTOR,
DIOMEDES,
PATROCLUS,

THERSITES, a deformed and scurrilous Grecian.

ALEXANDER, servant to Cressida.

Servant to Troilus.
Servant to Paris.
Servant to Diomedes.

HELEN, wife to Menelaus.
ANDROMACHE, wife to Hector.
CASSANDRA, daughter to Priam, a prophetess.
CRESSIDA, daughter to Calchas.

Trojan and Greek Soldiers, and Attendants.

SCENE : *Troy, and the Grecian camp before it.*

PROLOGUE.

IN Troy, there lies the scene. From isles of Greece
The princes orgulous, their high blood chafed,
Have to the port of Athens sent their ships,
Fraught with the ministers and instruments
Of cruel war : sixty and nine, that wore
Their crownets regal, from the Athenian bay
Put forth toward Phrygia ; and their vow is made
To ransack Troy, within whose strong immures
The ravish'd Helen, Menelaus' queen,
With wanton Paris sleeps ; and that's the quarrel.　　10
To Tenedos they come ;
And the deep-drawing barks do there disgorge
Their warlike fraughtage : now on Dardan plains
The fresh and yet unbruised Greeks do pitch
Their brave pavilions : Priam's six-gated city,
Dardan and Tymbria, Helias, Chetas, Troien,
And Antenorides, with massy staples
And corresponsive and fulfilling bolts,
Sperr up the sons of Troy.
Now expectation, tickling skittish spirits,　　20
On one and other side, Trojan and Greek,
Sets all on hazard : and hither am I come
A prologue arm'd, but not in confidence
Of author's pen or actor's voice, but suited
In like conditions as our argument,
To tell you, fair beholders, that our play
Leaps o'er the vaunt and firstlings of those broils,
Beginning in the middle, starting thence away
To what may be digested in a play.　　29
Like or find fault ; do as your pleasures are :
Now good or bad, 'tis but the chance of war.

ACT I.

SCENE I. *Troy. Before Priam's palace.*

Enter TROILUS *armed, and* PANDARUS.

Tro. Call here my varlet ; I'll unarm again :

Why should I war without the walls of Troy,
That find such cruel battle here within ?
Each Trojan that is master of his heart,
Let him to field ; Troilus, alas ! hath none.
Pan. Will this gear ne'er be mended ?
Tro. The Greeks are strong and skilful to their strength,
Fierce to their skill and to their fierceness valiant ;
But I am weaker than a woman's tear,
Tamer than sleep, fonder than ignorance,　　10
Less valiant than the virgin in the night
And skilless as unpractised infancy.
Pan. Well, I have told you enough of this : for my part, I'll not meddle nor make no further. He that will have a cake out of the wheat must needs tarry the grinding.
Tro. Have I not tarried ?
Pan. Ay, the grinding ; but you must tarry the bolting.
Tro. Have I not tarried ?
Pan. Ay, the bolting, but you must tarry the leavening.　　20
Tro. Still have I tarried.
Pan. Ay, to the leavening ; but here's yet in the word ' hereafter ' the kneading, the making of the cake, the heating of the oven and the baking ; nay, you must stay the cooling too, or you may chance to burn your lips.
Tro. Patience herself, what goddess e'er she be,
Doth lesser blench at sufferance than I do.
At Priam's royal table do I sit ;
And when fair Cressid comes into my thoughts,—　　30
So, traitor ! ' When she comes ! ' When is she thence ?
Pan. Well, she looked yesternight fairer than ever I saw her look, or any woman else.
Tro. I was about to tell thee :—when my heart,
As wedged with a sigh, would rive in twain,
Lest Hector or my father should perceive me,
I have, as when the sun doth light a storm,
Buried this sigh in wrinkle of a smile :
But sorrow, that is couch'd in seeming gladness,

Is like that mirth fate turns to sudden sadness. 40
Pan. An her hair were not somewhat
darker than Helen's—well, go to—there were
no more comparison between the women : but,
for my part, she is my kinswoman ; I would
not, as they term it, praise her : but I would
somebody had heard her talk yesterday, as I
did. I will not dispraise your sister Cassandra's
wit, but—
Tro. O Pandarus ! I tell thee, Pandarus,—
When I do tell thee, there my hopes lie
drown'd,
Reply not in how many fathoms deep 50
They lie indrench'd. I tell thee I am mad
In Cressid's love : thou answer'st ' she is fair ; '
Pour'st in the open ulcer of my heart
Her eyes, her hair, her cheek, her gait, her
voice,
Handlest in thy discourse, O, that her hand,
In whose comparison all whites are ink,
Writing their own reproach, to whose soft
seizure
The cygnet's down is harsh and spirit of sense
Hard as the palm of ploughman : this thou
tell'st me,
As true thou tell'st me, when I say I love
her ; 60
But, saying thus, instead of oil and balm,
Thou lay'st in every gash that love hath given
me
The knife that made it.
Pan. I speak no more than truth.
Tro. Thou dost not speak so much.
Pan. Faith, I'll not meddle in't. Let her be
as she is : if she be fair, 'tis the better for her ;
an she be not, she has the mends in her own
hands.
Tro. Good Pandarus, how now, Pandarus !
Pan. I have had my labor for my travail ;
ill-thought on of her and ill-thought on of
you ; gone between and between, but small
thanks for my labor.
Tro. What, art thou angry, Pandarus ?
what, with me ?
Pan. Because she's kin to me, therefore
she's not so fair as Helen : an she were not
kin to me, she would be as fair on Friday as
Helen is on Sunday. But what care I ? I care
not an she were a black-a-moor ; 'tis all one
to me. 80
Tro. Say I she is not fair ?
Pan. I do not care whether you do or no.
She's a fool to stay behind her father ; let her
to the Greeks ; and so I'll tell her the next
time I see her : for my part, I'll meddle nor
make no more i' the matter.
Tro. Pandarus,—
Pan. Not I.
Tro. Sweet Pandarus,—
Pan. Pray you, speak no more to me : I
will leave all as I found it, and there an end.
[*Exit Pandarus. An alarum.* 91
Tro. Peace, you ungracious clamors ! peace,
peace, rude sounds !
Fools on both sides ! Helen must needs be
fair,
When with your blood you daily paint her
thus.
I cannot fight upon this argument ;
It is too starved a subject for my sword.
But Pandarus,—O gods, how do you plague
me !

I cannot come to Cressid but by Pandar ;
And he's as tetchy to be woo'd to woo,
As she is stubborn-chaste against all suit. 100
Tell me, Apollo, for thy Daphne's love,
What Cressid is, what Pandar, and what we ?
Her bed is India ; there she lies, a pearl :
Between our Ilium and where she resides,
Let it be call'd the wild and wandering flood,
Ourself the merchant, and this sailing Pandar
Our doubtful hope, our convoy and our bark.

Alarum. Enter ÆNEAS.

Æne. How now, Prince Troilus ! where-
fore not afield ?
Tro. Because not there : this woman's an-
swer sorts,
For womanish it is to be from thence. 110
What news, Æneas, from the field to-day ?
Æne. That Paris is returned home and
hurt.
Tro. By whom, Æneas ?
Æne. Troilus, by Menelaus.
Tro. Let Paris bleed ; 'tis but a scar to
scorn ;
Paris is gored with Menelaus' horn. [*Alarum.*
Æne. Hark, what good sport is out of
town to-day !
Tro. Better at home, if ' would I might '
were ' may.'
But to the sport abroad : are you bound
thither ?
Æne. In all swift haste.
Tro. Come, go we then together.
[*Exeunt.*

SCENE II. *The same. A street.*

Enter CRESSIDA *and* ALEXANDER.

Cres. Who were those went by ?
Alex. Queen Hecuba and Helen.
Cres. And whither go they ?
Alex. Up to the eastern tower,
Whose height commands as subject all the
vale,
To see the battle. Hector, whose patience
Is, as a virtue, fix'd, to-day was moved :
He chid Andromache and struck his armorer,
And, like as there were husbandry in war,
Before the sun rose he was harness'd light,
And to the field goes he ; where every flower
Did, as a prophet, weep what it foresaw 10
In Hector's wrath.
Cres. What was his cause of anger ?
Alex. The noise goes, this : there is among
the Greeks
A lord of Trojan blood, nephew to Hector ;
They call him Ajax.
Cres. Good ; and what of him ?
Alex. They say he is a very man per se,
And stands alone.
Cres. So do all men, unless they are drunk,
sick, or have no legs.
Alex. This man, lady, hath robbed many
beasts of their particular additions ; he is as
valiant as the lion, churlish as the bear, slow
as the elephant : a man into whom nature hath
so crowded humors that his valor is crushed
into folly, his folly sauced with discretion :
there is no man hath a virtue that he hath not
a glimpse of, nor any man an attaint but he
carries some stain of it : he is melancholy
without cause, and merry against the hair : he
hath the joints of every thing, but everything
so out of joint that he is a gouty Briareus,

many hands and no use, or purblind Argus,
all eyes and no sight.   31
Cres. But how should this man, that makes
me smile, make Hector angry ?
Alex. They say he yesterday coped Hector
in the battle and struck him down, the disdain
and shame whereof hath ever since kept Hector fasting and waking.
Cres. Who comes here ?
Alex. Madam, your uncle Pandarus.

Enter PANDARUS.

Cres. Hector's a gallant man.   40
Alex. As may be in the world, lady.
Pan. What's that ? what's that ?
Cres. Good morrow, uncle Pandarus.
Pan. Good morrow, cousin Cressid : what
do you talk of ? Good morrow, Alexander.
How do you, cousin ? When were you at
Ilium ?
Cres. This morning, uncle.
Pan. What were you talking of when I
came ? Was Hector armed and gone ere ye
came to Ilium ? Helen was not up, was she ?
Cres. Hector was gone, but Helen was not
up.
Pan. Even so : Hector was stirring early.
Cres. That were we talking of, and of his
anger.
Pan. Was he angry ?
Cres. So he says here.
Pan. True, he was so : I know the cause
too : he'll lay about him to-day, I can tell them
that : and there's Troilus will not come far
behind him ; let them take heed of Troilus, I
can tell them that too.   61
Cres. What, is he angry too ?
Pan. Who, Troilus ? Troilus is the better
man of the two.
Cres. O Jupiter ! there's no comparison.
Pan. What, not between Troilus and Hector ? Do you know a man if you see him ?
Cres. Ay, if I ever saw him before and
knew him.
Pan. Well, I say Troilus is Troilus.   70
Cres. Then you say as I say ; for, I am
sure, he is not Hector.
Pan. No, nor Hector is not Troilus in some
degrees.
Cres. 'Tis just to each of them ; he is himself.
Pan. Himself ! Alas, poor Troilus ! I would
he were.
Cres. So he is.
Pan. Condition, I had gone barefoot to
India.   80
Cres. He is not Hector.
Pan. Himself ! no, he's not himself : would
a' were himself ! Well, the gods are above ;
time must friend or end : well, Troilus, well :
I would my heart were in her body. No, Hector is not a better man than Troilus.
Cres. Excuse me.
Pan. He is elder.
Cres. Pardon me, pardon me.   89
Pan. Th' other's not come to't ; you shall
tell me another tale, when th' other's come to't.
Hector shall not have his wit this year.
Cres. He shall not need it, if he have his
own.
Pan. Nor his qualities.
Cres. No matter.
Pan. Nor his beauty.

Cres. 'Twould not become him ; his own's
better.
Pan. You have no judgment, niece : Helen
herself swore th' other day, that Troilus, for
a brown favor—for so 'tis, I must confess,—
not brown neither,—
Cres. No, but brown.
Pan. 'Faith, to say truth, brown and not
brown.
Cres. To say the truth, true and not true.
Pan. She praised his complexion above
Paris.
Cres. Why, Paris hath color enough.
Pan. So he has.   109
Cres. Then Troilus should have too much :
if she praised him above, his complexion is
higher than his ; he having color enough, and
the other higher, is too flaming a praise for a
good complexion. I had as lief Helen's golden
tongue had commended Troilus for a copper
nose.
Pan. I swear to you, I think Helen loves
him better than Paris.
Cres. Then she's a merry Greek indeed.
Pan. Nay, I am sure she does. She came
to him th' other day into the compassed window,—and, you know, he has not past three
or four hairs on his chin,—
Cres. Indeed, a tapster's arithmetic may
soon bring his particulars therein to a total.
Pan. Why, he is very young : and yet will
he, within three pound, lift as much as his
brother Hector.
Cres. Is he so young a man and so old a
lifter ?   129
Pan. But to prove to you that Helen loves
him : she came and puts me her white hand
to his cloven chin—
Cres. Juno have mercy ! how came it
cloven ?
Pan. Why, you know, 'tis dimpled : I think
his smiling becomes him better than any man
in all Phrygia.
Cres. O, he smiles valiantly.
Pan. Does he not ?
Cres. O yes, an 'twere a cloud in autumn.
Pan. Why, go to, then : but to prove to
you that Helen loves Troilus,—   141
Cres. Troilus will stand to the proof, if
you'll prove it so.
Pan. Troilus ! why, he esteems her no more
than I esteem an addle egg.
Cres. If you love an addle egg as well as
you love an idle head, you would eat chickens
i' the shell.
Pan. I cannot choose but laugh, to think
how she tickled his chin : indeed, she has a
marvellous white hand, I must needs confess,—   151
Cres. Without the rack.
Pan. And she takes upon her to spy a white
hair on his chin.
Cres. Alas, poor chin ! many a wart is
richer.
Pan. But there was such laughing ! Queen
Hecuba laughed that her eyes ran o'er.
Cres. With mill-stones.
Pan. And Cassandra laughed.
Cres. But there was more temperate fire
under the pot of her eyes : did her eyes run
o'er too ?   161
Pan. And Hector laughed.
Cres. At what was all this laughing ?

Pan. Marry, at the white hair that Helen spied on Troilus' chin.

Cres. An't had been a green hair, I should have laughed too.

Pan. They laughed not so much at the hair as at his pretty answer.

Cres. What was his answer ?   170

Pan. Quoth she, ' Here's but two and fifty hairs on your chin, and one of them is white.'

Cres. This is her question.

Pan. That's true ; make no question of that. ' Two and fifty hairs,' quoth he, ' and one white : that white hair is my father, and all the rest are his sons.' ' Jupiter ! ' quoth she, ' which of these hairs is Paris, my husband ? ' ' The forked one,' quoth he, ' pluck't out, and give it him.' But there was such laughing ! and Helen so blushed, and Paris so chafed, and all the rest so laughed, that it passed.

Cres. So let it now ; for it has been a great while going by.

Pan. Well, cousin, I told you a thing yesterday ; think on't.

Cres. So I do.

Pan. I'll be sworn 'tis true ; he will weep you, an 'twere a man born in April.   189

Cres. And I'll spring up in his tears, an 'twere a nettle against May.

                              [*A retreat sounded.*

Pan. Hark ! they are coming from the field : shall we stand up here, and see them as they pass toward Ilium ? good niece, do, sweet niece Cressida.

Cres. At your pleasure.

Pan. Here, here, here's an excellent place ; here we may see most bravely : I'll tell you them all by their names as they pass by ; but mark Troilus above the rest.   200

Cres. Speak not so loud.

ÆNEAS passes.

Pan. That's Æneas : is not that a brave man ? he's one of the flowers of Troy, I can tell you : but mark Troilus ; you shall see anon.

ANTENOR passes.

Cres. Who's that ?

Pan. That's Antenor : he has a shrewd wit, I can tell you ; and he's a man good enough ; he's one o' the soundest judgments in Troy, whosoever, and a proper man of person. When comes Troilus ? I'll show you Troilus anon : if he see me, you shall see him nod at me.

Cres. Will he give you the nod ?

Pan. You shall see.

Cres. If he do, the rich shall have more.

HECTOR passes.

Pan. That's Hector, that, that, look you, that ; there's a fellow ! Go thy way, Hector ! There's a brave man, niece. O brave Hector ! Look how he looks ! there's a countenance ! is't not a brave man ?

Cres. O, a brave man !   220

Pan. Is a' not ? it does a man's heart good. Look you what hacks are on his helmet ! look you yonder, do you see ? look you there : there's no jesting ; there's laying on, take't off who will, as they say : there be hacks !

Cres. Be those with swords ?

Pan. Swords ! any thing, he cares not ; an the devil come to him, it's all one : by God's lid, it does one's heart good. Yonder comes Paris, yonder comes Paris.   230

PARIS passes.

Look ye yonder, niece ; is't not a gallant man too, is't not ? Why, this is brave now. Who said he came hurt home to-day ? he's not hurt : why, this will do Helen's heart good now, ha ! Would I could see Troilus now ! You shall see Troilus anon.

HELENUS passes.

Cres. Who's that ?

Pan. That's Helenus. I marvel where Troilus is. That's Helenus. I think he went not forth to-day. That's Helenus.   240

Cres. Can Helenus fight, uncle ?

Pan. Helenus ? no. Yes, he'll fight indifferent well. I marvel where Troilus is. Hark ! do you not hear the people cry ' Troilus ' ? Helenus is a priest.

Cres. What sneaking fellow comes yonder ?

TROILUS passes.

Pan. Where ? yonder ? that's Deiphobus. 'Tis Troilus ! there's a man, niece ! Hem ! Brave Troilus ! the prince of chivalry !

Cres. Peace, for shame, peace !   250

Pan. Mark him ; note him. O brave Troilus ! Look well upon him, niece : look you how his sword is bloodied, and his helm more hacked than Hector's, and how he looks, and how he goes ! O admirable youth ! he ne'er saw three and twenty. Go thy way, Troilus, go thy way ! Had I a sister were a grace, or a daughter a goddess, he should take his choice. O admirable man ! Paris ? Paris is dirt to him ; and, I warrant, Helen, to change, would give an eye to boot.   260

Cres. Here come more.

Forces pass.

Pan. Asses, fools, dolts ! chaff and bran, chaff and bran ! porridge after meat ! I could live and die i' the eyes of Troilus. Ne'er look, ne'er look : the eagles are gone : crows and daws, crows and daws ! I had rather be such a man as Troilus than Agamemnon and all Greece.

Cres. There is among the Greeks Achilles, a better man than Troilus.   269

Pan. Achilles ! a drayman, a porter, a very camel.

Cres. Well, well.

Pan. ' Well, well ! ' why, have you any discretion ? have you any eyes ? Do you know what a man is ? Is not birth, beauty, good shape, discourse, manhood, learning, gentleness, virtue, youth, liberality, and such like, the spice and salt that season a man ?

Cres. Ay, a minced man : and then to be baked with no date in the pie, for then the man's date's out.   281

Pan. You are such a woman ! one knows not at what ward you lie.

Cres. Upon my back, to defend my belly ; upon my wit, to defend my wiles ; upon my secrecy, to defend mine honesty ; my mask, to defend my beauty ; and you, to defend all these : and at all these wards I lie, at a thousand watches.

Pan. Say one of your watches.   290

Cres. Nay, I'll watch you for that ; and

that's one of the chiefest of them too : if I
cannot ward what I would not have hit, I can
watch you for telling how I took the blow ;
unless it swell past hiding, and then it's past
watching.

Pan. You are such another !

Enter Troilus's Boy.

Boy. Sir, my lord would instantly speak
with you.

Pan. Where ?

Boy. At your own house ; there he unarms
him.   300

Pan. Good boy, tell him I come. [*Exit boy.*]
I doubt he be hurt. Fare ye well, good niece.

Cres. Adieu, uncle.

Pan. I'll be with you, niece, by and by.

Cres. To bring, uncle ?

Pan. Ay, a token from Troilus.

Cres. By the same token, you are a bawd.
                                              [*Exit Pandarus.*
Words, vows, gifts, tears, and love's full sac-
      rifice,
He offers in another's enterprise :
But more in Troilus thousand fold I see   310
Than in the glass of Pandar's praise may be ;
Yet hold I off. Women are angels, wooing :
Things won are done ; joy's soul lies in the
      doing.
That she beloved knows nought that knows not
      this :
Men prize the thing ungain'd more than it is :
That she was never yet that ever knew
Love got so sweet as when desire did sue.
Therefore this maxim out of love I teach :
Achievement is command ; ungain'd, beseech :
Then though my heart's content firm love doth
      bear,   320
Nothing of that shall from mine eyes appear.
                                              [*Exeunt.*

Scene III. *The Grecian camp. Before
      Agamemnon's tent.*

Sennet. Enter Agamemnon, Nestor, Ulysses,
      Menelaus, *and others.*

Agam. Princes,
What grief hath set the jaundice on your
      cheeks ?
The ample proposition that hope makes
In all designs begun on earth below
Fails in the promised largeness : checks and
      disasters
Grow in the veins of actions highest rear'd,
As knots, by the conflux of meeting sap,
Infect the sound pine and divert his grain
Tortive and errant from his course of growth.
Nor, princes, is it matter new to us   10
That we come short of our suppose so far
That after seven years' siege yet Troy walls
      stand ;
Sith every action that hath gone before,
Whereof we have record, trial did draw
Bias and thwart, not answering the aim,
And that unbodied figure of the thought
That gave't surmised shape. Why then, you
      princes,
Do you with cheeks abashed behold our works,
And call them shames ? which are indeed
      nought else
But the protractive trials of great Jove   20
To find persistive constancy in men :
The fineness of which metal is not found

In fortune's love ; for then the bold and cow-
      ard,
The wise and fool, the artist and unread,
The hard and soft seem all affined and kin :
But, in the wind and tempest of her frown,
Distinction, with a broad and powerful fan,
Puffing at all, winnows the light away ;
And what hath mass or matter, by itself
Lies rich in virtue and unmingled.   30

Nest. With due observance of thy godlike
      seat,
Great Agamemnon, Nestor shall apply
Thy latest words. In the reproof of chance
Lies the true proof of men : the sea being
      smooth,
How many shallow bauble boats dare sail
Upon her patient breast, making their way
With those of nobler bulk !
But let the ruffian Boreas once enrage
The gentle Thetis, and anon behold
The strong-ribb'd bark through liquid moun-
      tains cut,   40
Bounding between the two moist elements,
Like Perseus' horse : where's then the saucy
      boat
Whose weak untimber'd sides but even now
Co-rivall'd greatness ? Either to harbor fled,
Or made a toast for Neptune. Even so
Doth valor's show and valor's worth divide
In storms of fortune ; for in her ray and
      brightness
The herd hath more annoyance by the breeze
Than by the tiger ; but when the splitting wind
Makes flexible the knees of knotted oaks,   50
And flies fled under shade, why, then the thing
      of courage
As roused with rage with rage doth sympa-
      thize,
And with an accent tuned in selfsame key
Retorts to chiding fortune.

Ulyss.   Agamemnon,
Thou great commander, nerve and bone of
      Greece,
Heart of our numbers, soul and only spirit,
In whom the tempers and the minds of all
Should be shut up, hear what Ulysses speaks.
Besides the applause and approbation
To which, [*To Agamemnon*] most mighty for
      thy place and sway,   60
[*To Nestor*] And thou most reverend for thy
      stretch'd-out life
I give to both your speeches, which were such
As Agamemnon and the hand of Greece
Should hold up high in brass, and such again
As venerable Nestor, hatch'd in silver,
Should with a bond of air, strong as the axle-
      tree
On which heaven rides, knit all the Greekish
      ears
To his experienced tongue, yet let it please
      both,
Thou great, and wise, to hear Ulysses speak.

Agam. Speak, prince of Ithaca ; and be't
      of less expect   70
That matter needless, of importless burden,
Divide thy lips, than we are confident,
When rank Thersites opes his mastic jaws,
We shall hear music, wit and oracle.

Ulyss. Troy, yet upon his basis, had been
      down,
And the great Hector's sword had lack'd a
      master,
But for these instances.

The specialty of rule hath been neglected :
And, look, how many Grecian tents do stand
Hollow upon this plain, so many hollow fac-
    tions.   80
When that the general is not like the hive
To whom the foragers shall all repair,
What honey is expected ? Degree being viz-
    arded,
The unworthiest shows as fairly in the mask.
The heavens themselves, the planets and this
    centre
Observe degree, priority and place,
Insisture, course, proportion, season, form,
Office and custom, in all line of order ;
And therefore is the glorious planet Sol
In noble eminence enthroned and sphered 90
Amidst the other ; whose medicinable eye
Corrects the ill aspects of planets evil,
And posts, like the commandment of a king,
Sans check to good and bad : but when the
    planets
In evil mixture to disorder wander,
What plagues and what portents ! what mu-
    tiny !
What raging of the sea ! shaking of earth !
Commotion in the winds ! frights, changes,
    horrors,
Divert and crack, rend and deracinate
The unity and married calm of states   100
Quite from their fixure ! O, when degree is
    shaked,
Which is the ladder to all high designs,
Then enterprise is sick ! How could commu-
    nities,
Degrees in schools and brotherhoods in cities,
Peaceful commerce from dividable shores,
The primogenitive and due of birth,
Prerogative of age, crowns, sceptres, laurels,
But by degree, stand in authentic place ?
Take but degree away, untune that string,
And, hark, what discord follows ! each thing
    meets   110
In mere oppugnancy : the bounded waters
Should lift their bosoms higher than the shores
And make a sop of all this solid globe :
Strength should be lord of imbecility,
And the rude son should strike his father
    dead :
Force should be right ; or rather, right and
    wrong,
Between whose endless jar justice resides,
Should lose their names, and so should justice
    too.
Then every thing includes itself in power,
Power into will, will into appetite ;   120
And appetite, an universal wolf,
So doubly seconded with will and power,
Must make perforce an universal prey,
And last eat up himself. Great Agamemnon,
This chaos, when degree is suffocate,
Follows the choking.
And this neglection of degree it is
That by a pace goes backward, with a purpose
It hath to climb. The general's disdain'd
By him one step below, he by the next,   130
That next by him beneath ; so every step,
Exampled by the first pace that is sick
Of his superior, grows to an envious fever
Of pale and bloodless emulation :
And 'tis this fever that keeps Troy on foot,
Not her own sinews. To end a tale of length,
Troy in our weakness stands, not in her
    strength.

Nest. Most wisely hath Ulysses here dis-
    cover'd
The fever whereof all our power is sick.
    Agam. The nature of the sickness found,
        Ulysses,   140
What is the remedy ?
    Ulyss. The great Achilles, whom opinion
        crowns
The sinew and the forehand of our host,
Having his ear full of his airy fame,
Grows dainty of his worth, and in his tent
Lies mocking our designs : with him Patroclus
Upon a lazy bed the livelong day
Breaks scurril jests ;
And with ridiculous and awkward action,
Which, slanderer, he imitation calls,   150
He pageants us. Sometime, great Agamemnon,
Thy topless deputation he puts on,
And, like a strutting player, whose conceit
Lies in his hamstring, and doth think it rich
To hear the wooden dialogue and sound
'Twixt his stretch'd footing and the scaffold-
    age,—
Such to-be-pitied and o'er-wrested seeming
He acts thy greatness in : and when he speaks,
'Tis like a chime a-mending ; with terms un-
    squared,
Which, from the tongue of roaring Typhon
    dropp'd,   160
Would seem hyperboles. At this fusty stuff
The large Achilles, on his press'd bed lolling,
From his deep chest laughs out a loud ap-
    plause ;
Cries ' Excellent ! 'tis Agamemnon just.
Now play me Nestor ; hem, and stroke thy
    beard,
As he being drest to some oration.'
That's done, as near as the extremest ends
Of parallels, as like as Vulcan and his wife :
Yet god Achilles still cries ' Excellent !
'Tis Nestor right. Now play him me, Patroclus,
Arming to answer in a night alarm.'   171
And then, forsooth, the faint defects of age
Must be the scene of mirth ; to cough and spit,
And, with a palsy-fumbling on his gorget,
Shake in and out the rivet : and at this sport
Sir Valor dies ; cries ' O, enough, Patroclus ;
Or give me ribs of steel ! I shall split all
In pleasure of my spleen.' And in this fashion,
All our abilities, gifts, natures, shapes,
Severals and generals of grace exact,   180
Achievements, plots, orders, preventions,
Excitements to the field, or speech for truce,
Success or loss, what is or is not, serves
As stuff for these two to make paradoxes.
    Nest. And in the imitation of these twain—
Who, as Ulysses says, opinion crowns
With an imperial voice—many are infect.
Ajax is grown self-will'd, and bears his head
In such a rein, in full as proud a place
As broad Achilles ; keeps his tent like him ;
Makes factious feasts ; rails on our state of
    war,   191
Bold as an oracle, and sets Thersites,
A slave whose gall coins slanders like a mint,
To match us in comparisons with dirt,
To weaken and discredit our exposure,
How rank soever rounded in with danger.
    Ulyss. They tax our policy, and call it cow-
        ardice,
Count wisdom as no member of the war,
Forestall prescience, and esteem no act   199
But that of hand : the still and mental parts,

That do contrive how many hands shall strike,
When fitness calls them on, and know by
　　measure
Of their observant toil the enemies' weight,—
Why, this hath not a finger's dignity :
They call this bed-work, mappery, closet-war ;
So that the ram that batters down the wall,
For the great swing and rudeness of his poise,
They place before his hand that made the en-
　　gine,
Or those that with the fineness of their souls
By reason guide his execution.　　　　　210
　Nest. Let this be granted, and Achilles'
　　horse
Makes many Thetis' sons.　　　[*A tucket.*
　Agam. What trumpet ? look, Menelaus.
　Men. From Troy.

Enter ÆNEAS.

　Agam. What would you 'fore our tent ?
　Æne. Is this great Agamemnon's tent, I
　　pray you ?
　Agam. Even this.
　Æne. May one, that is a herald and a
　　prince,
Do a fair message to his kingly ears ?
　Agam. With surety stronger than Achilles'
　　arm　　　　　　　　　　　　　　　　220
'Fore all the Greekish heads, which with one
　　voice
Call Agamemnon head and general.
　Æne. Fair leave and large security. How
　　may
A stranger to those most imperial looks
Know them from eyes of other mortals ?
　Agam.　　　　　　　　　　　　How !
　Æne. Ay ;
I ask, that I might waken reverence,
And bid the cheek be ready with a blush
Modest as morning when she coldly eyes
The youthful Phœbus :　　　　　　　　230
Which is that god in office, guiding men ?
Which is the high and mighty Agamemnon ?
　Agam. This Trojan scorns us ; or the men
　　of Troy
Are ceremonious courtiers.
　Æne. Courtiers as free, as debonair, un-
　　arm'd,
As bending angels ; that's their fame in peace :
But when they would seem soldiers, they have
　　galls,
Good arms, strong joints, true swords ; and,
　　Jove's accord,
Nothing so full of heart. But peace, Æneas,
Peace, Trojan ; lay thy finger on thy lips ! 240
The worthiness of praise distains his worth,
If that the praised himself bring the praise
　　forth :
But what the repining enemy commends,
That breath fame blows ; that praise, sole pure,
　　transcends.
　Agam. Sir, you of Troy, call you yourself
　　Æneas ?
　Æne. Ay, Greek, that is my name.
　Agam. What's your affair, I pray you ?
　Æne. Sir, pardon ; 'tis for Agamemnon's
　　ears.
　Agam. He hears naught privately that
　　comes from Troy.
　Æne. Nor I from Troy come not to
　　whisper him :　　　　　　　　　　　250
I bring a trumpet to awake his ear,
To set his sense on the attentive bent,

And then to speak.
　Agam.　　　　　Speak frankly as the wind ;
It is not Agamemnon's sleeping hour :
That thou shalt know. Trojan, he is awake,
He tells thee so himself.
　Æne.　　　　　　　　Trumpet, blow loud,
Send thy brass voice through all these lazy
　　tents ;
And every Greek of mettle, let him know,
What Troy means fairly shall be spoke aloud.
　　　　　　　　　　　　[*Trumpet sounds.*
We have, great Agamemnon, here in Troy 260
A prince call'd Hector,—Priam is his father,—
Who in this dull and long-continued truce
Is rusty grown : he bade me take a trumpet,
And to this purpose speak. Kings, princes,
　　lords !
If there be one among the fair'st of Greece
That holds his honor higher than his ease,
That seeks his praise more than he fears his
　　peril,
That knows his valor, and knows not his fear,
That loves his mistress more than in con-
　　fession,
With truant vows to her own lips he loves,
And dare avow her beauty and her worth 271
In other arms than hers,—to him this chal-
　　lenge.
Hector, in view of Trojans and of Greeks,
Shall make it good, or do his best to do it,
He hath a lady, wiser, fairer, truer,
Than ever Greek did compass in his arms,
And will to-morrow with his trumpet call
Midway between your tents and walls of Troy,
To rouse a Grecian that is true in love :
If any come, Hector shall honor him ;　　280
If none, he'll say in Troy when he retires,
The Grecian dames are sunburnt and not
　　worth
The splinter of a lance. Even so much.
　Agam. This shall be told our lovers, Lord
　　Æneas ;
If none of them have soul in such a kind,
We left them all at home : but we are soldiers ;
And may that soldier a mere recreant prove,
That means not, hath not, or is not in love !
If then one is, or hath, or means to be,
That one meets Hector ; if none else, I am he.
　Nest. Tell him of Nestor, one that was a
　　man　　　　　　　　　　　　　　　291
When Hector's grandsire suck'd : he is old
　　now ;
But if there be not in our Grecian host
One noble man that hath one spark of fire,
To answer for his love, tell him from me
I'll hide my silver beard in a gold beaver
And in my vantbrace put this wither'd brawn,
And meeting him will tell him that my lady
Was fairer than his grandam and as chaste
As may be in the world : his youth in flood,
I'll prove this truth with my three drops of
　　blood.　　　　　　　　　　　　　301
　Æne. Now heavens forbid such scarcity
　　of youth !
　Ulyss. Amen.
　Agam. Fair Lord Æneas, let me touch
　　your hand ;
To our pavilion shall I lead you, sir.
Achilles shall have word of this intent ;
So shall each lord of Greece, from tent to
　　tent :
Yourself shall feast with us before you go

And find the welcome of a noble foe.
    [*Exeunt all but Ulysses and Nestor.*
Ulyss. Nestor!   310
Nest. What says Ulysses?
Ulyss. I have a young conception in my
  brain;
Be you my time to bring it to some shape.
Nest. What is't?
Ulyss. This 'tis:
Blunt wedges rive hard knots: the seeded
  pride
That hath to this maturity blown up
In rank Achilles must or now be cropp'd,
Or, shedding, breed a nursery of like evil,
To overbulk us all.
Nest.   Well, and how?   320
Ulyss. This challenge that the gallant Hec-
  tor sends,
However it is spread in general name,
Relates in purpose only to Achilles.
Nest. The purpose is perspicuous even as
  substance,
Whose grossness little characters sum up:
And, in the publication, make no strain,
But that Achilles, were his brain as barren
As banks of Libya,—though, Apollo knows,
'Tis dry enough,—will, with great speed of
  judgment,
Ay, with celerity, find Hector's purpose 330
Pointing on him.
Ulyss. And wake him to the answer, think
  you?
Nest. Yes, 'tis most meet: whom may you
  else oppose,
That can from Hector bring his honor off,
If not Achilles? Though 't be a sportful com-
  bat,
Yet in the trial much opinion dwells;
For here the Trojans taste our dear'st repute
With their finest palate: and trust to me,
  Ulysses,
Our imputation shall be oddly poised
In this wild action; for the success, 340
Although particular, shall give a scantling
Of good or bad unto the general;
And in such indexes, although small pricks
To their subsequent volumes, there is seen
The baby figure of the giant mass
Of things to come at large. It is supposed
He that meets Hector issues from our choice
And choice, being mutual act of all our souls,
Makes merit her election, and doth boil,
As 'twere from us all, a man distill'd 350
Out of our virtues; who miscarrying,
What heart receives from hence the conquer-
  ing part,
To steel a strong opinion to themselves?
Which entertain'd, limbs are his instruments,
In no less working than are swords and bows
Directive by the limbs.
Ulyss. Give pardon to my speech:
Therefore 'tis meet Achilles meet not Hector.
Let us, like merchants, show our foulest wares,
And think, perchance, they'll sell; if not, 360
The lustre of the better yet to show,
Shall show the better. Do not consent
That ever Hector and Achilles meet;
For both our honor and our shame in this
Are dogg'd with two strange followers.
Nest. I see them not with my old eyes:
  what are they?
Ulyss. What glory our Achilles shares
  from Hector,

Were he not proud, we all should share with
  him:
But he already is too insolent;
And we were better parch in Afric sun 370
Than in the pride and salt scorn of his eyes,
Should he 'scape Hector fair: if he were foil'd,
Why then, we did our main opinion crush
In taint of our best man. No, make a lottery;
And, by device, let blockish Ajax draw
The sort to fight with Hector: among our-
  selves
Give him allowance for the better man;
For that will physic the great Myrmidon
Who broils in loud applause, and make him
  fall
His crest that prouder than blue Iris bends.
If the dull brainless Ajax come safe off, 381
We'll dress him up in voices: if he fail,
Yet go we under our opinion still
That we have better men. But, hit or miss,
Our project's life this shape of sense assumes:
Ajax employ'd plucks down Achilles' plumes.
Nest. Ulysses,
Now I begin to relish thy advice;
And I will give a taste of it forthwith
To Agamemnon: go we to him straight. 390
Two curs shall tame each other: pride alone
Must tarre the mastiffs on, as 'twere their
  bone.   [*Exeunt.*

ACT II.

SCENE I. *A part of the Grecian camp.*

Enter AJAX *and* THERSITES.

Ajax. Thersites!
Ther. Agamemnon, how if he had boils?
full, all over, generally?
Ajax. Thersites!
Ther. And those boils did run? say so:
did not the general run then? were not that a
botchy core?
Ajax. Dog!
Ther. Then would come some matter from
him; I see none now. 10
Ajax. Thou bitch-wolf's son, canst thou
not hear? [*Beating him*] Feel, then.
Ther. The plague of Greece upon thee,
thou mongrel beef-witted lord!
Ajax. Speak then, thou vinewedst leaven,
speak: I will beat thee into handsomeness.
Ther. I shall sooner rail thee into wit and
holiness: but, I think, thy horse will sooner
con an oration than thou learn a prayer without book. Thou canst strike, canst thou? a
red murrain o' thy jade's tricks! 21
Ajax. Toadstool, learn me the proclamation.
Ther. Dost thou think I have no sense,
thou strikest me thus?
Ajax. The proclamation!
Ther. Thou art proclaimed a fool, I think.
Ajax. Do not, porpentine, do not: my
fingers itch.
Ther. I would thou didst itch from head to
foot and I had the scratching of thee; I would
make thee the loathsomest scab in Greece.
When thou art forth in the incursions, thou
strikest as slow as another.
Ajax. I say, the proclamation!
Ther. Thou grumblest and railest every
hour on Achilles, and thou art as full of envy

at his greatness as Cerberus is at Proserpina's
beauty, ay, that thou barkest at him.

Ajax.　Mistress Thersites!

Ther.　Thou shouldest strike him.　　　40

Ajax.　Cobloaf!

Ther.　He would pun thee into shivers with
his fist, as a sailor breaks a biscuit.

Ajax.　[*Beating him*] You whoreson cur!

Ther.　Do, do.

Ajax.　Thou stool for a witch!

Ther.　Ay, do, do; thou sodden-witted
lord! thou hast no more brain than I have in
mine elbows; an assinego may tutor thee:
thou scurvy-valiant ass! thou art here but to
thrash Trojans; and thou art bought and sold
among those of any wit, like a barbarian slave.
If thou use to beat me, I will begin at thy
heel, and tell what thou art by inches, thou
thing of no bowels, thou!

Ajax.　You dog!

Ther.　You scurvy lord!

Ajax.　[*Beating him*] You cur!

Ther.　Mars his idiot! do, rudeness; do,
camel; do, do.　　　　　59

　　　Enter ACHILLES *and* PATROCLUS.

Achil.　Why, how now, Ajax! wherefore
do you thus? How now, Thersites! what's
the matter, man?

Ther.　You see him there, do you?

Achil.　Ay; what's the matter?

Ther.　Nay, look upon him.

Achil.　So I do: what's the matter?

Ther.　Nay, but regard him well.

Achil.　'Well!' why, I do so.

Ther.　But yet you look not well upon him;
for whosoever you take him to be, he is Ajax.

Achil.　I know that, fool.　　　71

Ther.　Ay, but that fool knows not himself.

Ajax.　Therefore I beat thee.

Ther.　Lo, lo, lo, lo, what modicums of wit
he utters! his evasions have ears thus long. I
have bobbed his brain more than he has beat
my bones: I will buy nine sparrows for a
penny, and his pia mater is not worth the
nineth part of a sparrow. This lord, Achilles,
Ajax, who wears his wit in his belly and his
guts in his head, I'll tell you what I say of
him.　　　　　81

Achil.　What?

Ther.　I say, this Ajax—
　　　　　　　[*Ajax offers to beat him.*

Achil.　Nay, good Ajax.

Ther.　Has not so much wit—

Achil.　Nay, I must hold you.

Ther.　As will stop the eye of Helen's needle, for whom he comes to fight.

Achil.　Peace, fool!

Ther.　I would have peace and quietness,
but the fool will not: he there: that he: look
you there.

Ajax.　O thou damned cur! I shall—

Achil.　Will you set your wit to a fool's?

Ther.　No, I warrant you; for a fool's will
shame it.

Patr.　Good words, Thersites.

Achil.　What's the quarrel?

Ajax.　I bade the vile owl go learn me the
tenor of the proclamation, and he rails upon
me.　　　　　100

Ther.　I serve thee not.

Ajax.　Well, go to, go to.

Ther.　I serve here voluntarily.

Achil.　Your last service was sufferance,
'twas not voluntary: no man is beaten voluntary: Ajax was here the voluntary, and you
as under an impress.

Ther.　E'en so; a great deal of your wit,
too, lies in your sinews, or else there be liars.
Hector shall have a great catch, if he knock
out either of your brains: a' were as good
crack a fusty nut with no kernel.

Achil.　What, with me too, Thersites?

Ther.　There's Ulysses and old Nestor,
whose wit was mouldy ere your grandsires
had nails on their toes, yoke you like draught-
oxen and make you plough up the wars.

Achil.　What, what?

Ther.　Yes, good sooth: to, Achilles! to,
Ajax! to!　　　　　120

Ajax.　I shall cut out your tongue.

Ther.　'Tis no matter; I shall speak as
much as thou afterwards.

Patr.　No more words, Thersites; peace!

Ther.　I will hold my peace when Achilles'
brach bids me, shall I?

Achil.　There's for you, Patroclus.

Ther.　I will see you hanged, like clotpoles,
ere I come any more to your tents: I will keep
where there is wit stirring and leave the faction of fools.　　　　　[*Exit.*

Patr.　A good riddance.

Achil.　Marry, this, sir, is proclaim'd
　　through all our host:
That Hector, by the fifth hour of the sun,
Will with a trumpet 'twixt our tents and Troy
To-morrow morning call some knight to arms
That hath a stomach; and such a one that
　　dare
Maintain—I know not what: 'tis trash. Fare-
　　well.

Ajax.　Farewell. Who shall answer him?

Achil.　I know not: 'tis put to lottery; oth-
　　erwise　　　　　140
He knew his man.

Ajax.　O, meaning you. I will go learn
　　more of it.　　　　　[*Exeunt.*

SCENE II.　*Troy. A room in Priam's palace.*

Enter PRIAM, HECTOR, TROILUS, PARIS, *and*
　　　　　HELENUS.

Pri.　After so many hours, lives, speeches
　　spent,
Thus once again says Nestor from the Greeks:
'Deliver Helen, and all damage else—
As honor, loss of time, travail, expense,
Wounds, friends, and what else dear that is
　　consumed
In hot digestion of this cormorant war—
Shall be struck off.' Hector, what say you
　　to 't?

Hect.　Though no man lesser fears the
　　Greeks than I
As far as toucheth my particular,
Yet, dread Priam,　　　　　10
There is no lady of more softer bowels,
More spongy to suck in the sense of fear,
More ready to cry out 'Who knows what fol-
　　lows?'
Than Hector is: the wound of peace is surety,
Surety secure; but modest doubt is call'd
The beacon of the wise, the tent that searches
To the bottom of the worst. Let Helen go:
Since the first sword was drawn about this
　　question,

Every tithe soul, 'mongst many thousand
    dismes,
Hath been as dear as Helen ; I mean, of ours :
If we have lost so many tenths of ours,   21
To guard a thing not ours nor worth to us,
Had it our name, the value of one ten,
What merit's in that reason which denies
The yielding of her up ?
    Tro.   Fie, fie, my brother !
Weigh you the worth and honor of a king
So great as our dread father in a scale
Of common ounces ? will you with counters
    sum
The past proportion of his infinite ?
And buckle in a waist most fathomless   30
With spans and inches so diminutive
As fears and reasons ? fie, for godly shame !
    Hel.   No marvel, though you bite so sharp
    at reasons,
You are so empty of them. Should not our
    father
Bear the great sway of his affairs with reasons,
Because your speech hath none that tells him
    so ?
    Tro.   You are for dreams and slumbers,
    brother priest ;
You fur your gloves with reason. Here are
    your reasons :
You know an enemy intends you harm ;
You know a sword employ'd is perilous,   40
And reason flies the object of all harm :
Who marvels then, when Helenus beholds
A Grecian and his sword, if he do set
The very wings of reason to his heels
And fly like chidden Mercury from Jove,
Or like a star disorb'd ? Nay, if we talk of
    reason,
Let's shut our gates and sleep : manhood and
    honor
Should have hare-hearts, would they but fat
    their thoughts
With this cramm'd reason : reason and respect
Make livers pale and lustihood deject.   50
    Hect.   Brother, she is not worth what she
    doth cost
The holding.
    Tro.   What is aught, but as 'tis valued ?
    Hect.   But value dwells not in particular
    will ;
It holds his estimate and dignity
As well wherein 'tis precious of itself
As in the prizer : 'tis mad idolatry
To make the service greater than the god
And the will dotes that is attributive
To what infectiously itself affects,
Without some image of the affected merit.   60
    Tro.   I take to-day a wife, and my election
Is led on in the conduct of my will ;
My will enkindled by mine eyes and ears,
Two traded pilots 'twixt the dangerous shores
Of will and judgment : how may I avoid,
Although my will distaste what it elected,
The wife I chose ? there can be no evasion
To blench from this and to stand firm by
    honor :
We turn not back the silks upon the merchant,
When we have soil'd them, nor the remainder
    viands   70
We do not throw in unrespective sieve,
Because we now are full. It was thought meet
Paris should do some vengeance on the
    Greeks :
Your breath of full consent bellied his sails ;

The seas and winds, old wranglers, took a
    truce
And did him service : he touch'd the ports de-
    sired,
And for an old aunt whom the Greeks held
    captive,
He brought a Grecian queen, whose youth and
    freshness
Wrinkles Apollo's, and makes stale the morn-
    ing.
Why keep we her ? the Grecians keep our
    aunt :   80
Is she worth keeping ? why, she is a pearl,
Whose price hath launch'd above a thousand
    ships,
And turn'd crown'd kings to merchants.
If you'll avouch 'twas wisdom Paris went—
As you must needs, for you all cried ' Go,
    go,'—
If you'll confess he brought home noble
    prize—
As you must needs, for you all clapp'd your
    hands
And cried ' Inestimable ! '—why do you now
The issue of your proper wisdoms rate,
And do a deed that fortune never did,   90
Beggar the estimation which you prized
Richer than sea and land ? O, theft most base,
That we have stol'n what we do fear to keep !
But, thieves, unworthy of a thing so stol'n,
That in their country did them that disgrace,
We fear to warrant in our native place !
    Cas.   [*Within*] Cry, Trojans, cry !
    Pri.   What noise ? what shriek is this ?
    Tro.   'Tis our mad sister, I do know her
    voice.
    Cas.   [*Within*] Cry, Trojans !
    Hect.   It is Cassandra.

Enter CASSANDRA, *raving.*

    Cas.   Cry, Trojans, cry ! lend me ten thou-
    sand eyes,
And I will fill them with prophetic tears.
    Hect.   Peace, sister, peace !
    Cas.   Virgins and boys, mid-age and wrin-
    kled eld,
Soft infancy, that nothing canst but cry,
Add to my clamors ! let us pay betimes
A moiety of that mass of moan to come.
Cry, Trojans, cry ! practice your eyes with
    tears !
Troy must not be, nor goodly Ilion stand ;
Our firebrand brother, Paris, burns us all.   110
Cry, Trojans, cry ! a Helen and a woe :
Cry, cry ! Troy burns, or else let Helen go.
                                    [*Exit.*
    Hect.   Now, youthful Troilus, do not these
    high strains
Of divination in our sister work
Some touches of remorse ? or is your blood
So madly hot that no discourse of reason,
Nor fear of bad success in a bad cause,
Can qualify the same ?
    Tro.   Why, brother Hector,
We may not think the justness of each act
Such and no other than event doth form it,
Nor once deject the courage of our minds,   121
Because Cassandra's mad : her brain-sick rap-
    tures
Cannot distaste the goodness of a quarrel
Which hath our several honors all engaged
To make it gracious. For my private part,
I am no more touch'd than all Priam's sons :

And Jove forbid there should be done amongst us
Such things as might offend the weakest spleen
To fight for and maintain!   129
  Par. Else might the world convince of levity
As well my undertakings as your counsels:
But I attest the gods, your full consent
Gave wings to my propension and cut off
All fears attending on so dire a project.
For what, alas, can these my single arms?
What Propugnation is in one man's valor,
To stand the push and enmity of those
This quarrel would excite? Yet, I protest,
Were I alone to pass the difficulties
And had as ample power as I have will, 140
Paris should ne'er retract what he hath done,
Nor faint in the pursuit.
  Pri.   Paris, you speak
Like one besotted on your sweet delights:
You have the honey still, but these the gall;
So to be valiant is no praise at all.
  Par. Sir, I propose not merely to myself
The pleasures such a beauty brings with it;
But I would have the soil of her fair rape
Wiped off, in honorable keeping her.
What treason were it to the ransack'd queen,
Disgrace to your great worths and shame to me,   151
Now to deliver her possession up
On terms of base compulsion! Can it be
That so degenerate a strain as this
Should once set footing in your generous bosoms?
There's not the meanest spirit on our party
Without a heart to dare or sword to draw
When Helen is defended, nor none so noble
Whose life were ill bestow'd or death unfamed
Where Helen is the subject; then, I say,
Well may we fight for her whom, we know well,
The world's large spaces cannot parallel.
  Hect. Paris and Troilus, you have both said well,
And on the cause and question now in hand
Have glozed, but superficially: not much
Unlike young men, whom Aristotle thought
Unfit to hear moral philosophy:
The reasons you allege do more conduce
To the hot passion of distemper'd blood
Than to make up a free determination 170
'Twixt right and wrong, for pleasure and revenge
Have ears more deaf than adders to the voice
Of any true decision. Nature craves
All dues be render'd to their owners: now,
What nearer debt in all humanity
Than wife is to the husband? If this law
Of nature be corrupted through affection,
And that great minds, of partial indulgence
To their benumbed wills, resist the same,
There is a law in each well-order'd nation 180
To curb those raging appetites that are
Most disobedient and refractory.
If Helen then be wife to Sparta's king,
As it is known she is, these moral laws
Of nature and of nations speak aloud
To have her back return'd: thus to persist
In doing wrong extenuates not wrong,
But makes it much more heavy. Hector's opinion
Is this in way of truth; yet ne'ertheless,
My spritely brethren, I propend to you 190

In resolution to keep Helen still,
For 'tis a cause that hath no mean dependance
Upon our joint and several dignities.
  Tro. Why, there you touch'd the life of our design:
Were it not glory that we more affected
Than the performance of our heaving spleens,
I would not wish a drop of Trojan blood
Spent more in her defence. But, worthy Hector,
She is a theme of honor and renown,
A spur to valiant and magnanimous deeds,
Whose present courage may beat down our foes,   201
And fame in time to come canonize us;
For, I presume, brave Hector would not lose
So rich advantage of a promised glory
As smiles upon the forehead of this action
For the wide world's revenue.
  Hect.   I am yours,
You valiant offspring of great Priamus.
I have a roisting challenge sent amongst
The dull and factious nobles of the Greeks
Will strike amazement to their drowsy spirits:
I was advertised their great general slept, 211
Whilst emulation in the army crept:
This, I presume, will wake him.   [*Exeunt.*

SCENE III. *The Grecian camp. Before Achilles' tent.*

Enter THERSITES, *solus.*

  Ther. How now, Thersites! what, lost in the labyrinth of thy fury! Shall the elephant Ajax carry it thus? he beats me, and I rail at him: O, worthy satisfaction! would it were otherwise; that I could beat him, whilst he railed at me. 'Sfoot, I'll learn to conjure and raise devils, but I'll see some issue of my spiteful execrations. Then there's Achilles, a rare enginer! If Troy be not taken till these two undermine it, the walls will stand till they fall of themselves. O thou great thunder-darter of Olympus, forget that thou art Jove, the king of gods, and, Mercury, lose all the serpentine craft of thy caduceus, if ye take not that little little less than little wit from them that they have! which short-armed ignorance itself knows is so abundant scarce, it will not in circumvention deliver a fly from a spider, without drawing their massy irons and cutting the web. After this, the vengeance on the whole camp! or rather, the bone-ache! for that, methinks, is the curse dependant on those that war for a placket. I have said my prayers and devil Envy say Amen. What ho! my Lord Achilles!

Enter PATROCLUS.

  Patr. Who's there? Thersites! Good Thersites, come in and rail.
  Ther. If I could have remembered a gilt counterfeit, thou wouldst not have slipped out of my contemplation: but it is no matter; thyself upon thyself! The common curse of mankind, folly and ignorance, be thine in great revenue! heaven bless thee from a tutor, and discipline come not near thee! Let thy blood be thy direction till thy death! then if she that lays thee out says thou art a fair corse, I'll be sworn and sworn upon't she never shrouded any but lazars. Amen. Where's Achilles?

Patr. What, art thou devout ? wast thou in prayer ?
Ther. Ay : the heavens hear me !   40

Enter ACHILLES.

Achil. Who's there ?
Patr. Thersites, my lord.
Achil. Where, where ? Art thou come ? why, my cheese, my digestion, why hast thou not served thyself in to my table so many meals ? Come, what's Agamemnon ?
Ther. Thy commander, Achilles. Then tell me, Patroclus, what's Achilles ?
Patr. Thy lord, Thersites : then tell me, I pray thee, what's thyself ?   50
Ther. Thy knower, Patroclus : then tell me, Patroclus, what art thou ?
Patr. Thou mayst tell that knowest.
Achil. O, tell, tell.
Ther. I'll decline the whole question. Agamemnon commands Achilles ; Achilles is my lord ; I am Patroclus' knower, and Patroclus is a fool.
Patr. You rascal !
Ther. Peace, fool ! I have not done.   60
Achil. He is a privileged man. Proceed, Thersites.
Ther. Agamemnon is a fool ; Achilles is a fool ; Thersites is a fool, and, as aforesaid, Patroclus is a fool.
Achil. Derive this ; come.
Ther. Agamemnon is a fool to offer to command Achilles ; Achilles is a fool to be commanded of Agamemnon ; Thersites is a fool to serve such a fool, and Patroclus is a fool positive.   70
Patr. Why am I a fool ?
Ther. Make that demand of the prover. It suffices me thou art. Look you, who comes here ?
Achil. Patroclus, I'll speak with nobody. Come in with me, Thersites.   [*Exit.*
Ther. Here is such patchery, such juggling and such knavery ! all the argument is a cuckold and a whore ; a good quarrel to draw emulous factions and bleed to death upon. Now, the dry serpigo on the subject ! and war and lechery confound all !   [*Exit.*

Enter AGAMEMNON, ULYSSES, NESTOR, DIOMEDES, *and* AJAX.

Agam. Where is Achilles ?
Patr. Within his tent ; but ill disposed, my lord.
Agam. Let it be known to him that we are here.
He shent our messengers ; and we lay by
Our appertainments, visiting of him :
Let him be told so ; lest perchance he think
We dare not move the question of our place,
Or know not what we are.   90
Patr.   I shall say so to him. [*Exit.*
Ulyss. We saw him at the opening of his tent :
He is not sick.
Ajax. Yes, lion-sick, sick of proud heart : you may call it melancholy, if you will favor the man ; but, by my head, 'tis pride : but why, why ? let him show us the cause. A word, my lord.   [*Takes Agamemnon aside.*
Nest. What moves Ajax thus to bay at him ?

Ulyss. Achilles hath inveigled his fool from him.   100
Nest. Who, Thersites ?
Ulyss. He.
Nest. Then will Ajax lack matter, if he have lost his argument.
Ulyss. No, you see, he is his argument that has his argument, Achilles.
Nest. All the better ; their fraction is more our wish than their faction : but it was a strong composure a fool could disunite.   109
Ulyss. The amity that wisdom knits not, folly may easily untie. Here comes Patroclus.

Re-enter PATROCLUS.

Nest. No Achilles with him.
Ulyss. The elephant hath joints, but none for courtesy : his legs are legs for necessity, not for flexure.
Patr. Achilles bids me say, he is much sorry,
If any thing more than your sport and pleasure
Did move your greatness and this noble state
To call upon him ; he hopes it is no other
But for your health and your digestion sake,
And after-dinner's breath.   121
Agam.   Hear you, Patroclus :
We are too well acquainted with these answers :
But his evasion, wing'd thus swift with scorn,
Cannot outfly our apprehensions.
Much attribute he hath, and much the reason
Why we ascribe it to him ; yet all his virtues,
Not virtuously on his own part beheld,
Do in our eyes begin to lose their gloss,
Yea, like fair fruit in an unwholesome dish,
Are like to rot untasted. Go and tell him, 130
We come to speak with him ; and you shall not sin,
If you do say we think him over-proud
And under-honest, in self-assumption greater
Than in the note of judgment ; and worthier than himself
Here tend the savage strangeness he puts on,
Disguise the holy strength of their command,
And underwrite in an observing kind
His humorous predominance ; yea, watch
His pettish lunes, his ebbs, his flows, as if   139
The passage and whole carriage of this action
Rode on his tide. Go tell him this, and add,
That if he overhold his price so much,
We'll none of him ; but let him, like an engine
Not portable, lie under this report :
'Bring action hither, this cannot go to war :
A stirring dwarf we do allowance give
Before a sleeping giant.' Tell him so.
Patr. I shall ; and bring his answer presently.   [*Exit.*
Agam. In second voice we'll not be satisfied ;
We come to speak with him. Ulysses, enter you.   [*Exit Ulysses.* 150
Ajax. What is he more than another ?
Agam. No more than what he thinks he is.
Ajax. Is he so much ? Do you not think he thinks himself a better man than I am ?
Agam. No question.
Ajax. Will you subscribe his thought, and say he is ?
Agam. No, noble Ajax ; you are as strong, as valiant, as wise, no less noble, much more gentle, and altogether more tractable.   160

Ajax. Why should a man be proud ? How doth pride grow ? I know not what pride is.

Agam. Your mind is the clearer, Ajax, and your virtues the fairer. He that is proud eats up himself : pride is his own glass, his own trumpet, his own chronicle ; and whatever praises itself but in the deed, devours the deed in the praise.

Ajax. I do hate a proud man, as I hate the engendering of toads.   170

Nest. Yet he loves himself : is 't not strange ?   [*Aside.*

Re-enter ULYSSES.

Ulyss. Achilles will not to the field to-morrow.

Agam. What's his excuse ?

Ulyss.   He doth rely on none,
But carries on the stream of his dispose
Without observance or respect of any,
In will peculiar and in self-admission.

Agam. Why will he not upon our fair request
Untent his person and share the air with us ?

Ulyss. Things small as nothing, for request's sake only,
He makes important : possess'd he is with greatness,   180
And speaks not to himself but with a pride
That quarrels at self-breath : imagined worth
Holds in his blood such swoln and hot discourse
That 'twixt his mental and his active parts
Kingdom'd Achilles in commotion rages
And batters down himself : what should I say ?
He is so plaguy proud that the death-tokens of it
Cry ' No recovery.'

Agam.   Let Ajax go to him.
Dear lord, go you and greet him in his tent :
'Tis said he holds you well, and will be led
At your request a little from himself.   191

Ulyss. O Agamemnon, let it not be so !
We'll consecrate the steps that Ajax makes
When they go from Achilles : shall the proud lord
That bastes his arrogance with his own seam
And never suffers matter of the world
Enter his thoughts, save such as do revolve
And ruminate himself, shall he be worshipp'd
Of that we hold an idol more than he ?   199
No, this thrice worthy and right valiant lord
Must not so stale his palm, nobly acquired ;
Nor, by my will, assubjugate his merit,
As amply titled as Achilles is,
By going to Achilles :
That were to enlard his fat already pride
And add more coals to Cancer when he burns
With entertaining great Hyperion.
This lord go to him ! Jupiter forbid,
And say in thunder ' Achilles go to him.'

Nest. [*Aside to Dio.*] O, this is well ; he rubs the vein of him.   210

Dio. [*Aside to Nest.*] And how his silence drinks up this applause !

Ajax. If I go to him, with my armed fist I'll pash him o'er the face.

Agam. O, no, you shall not go.

Ajax. An a' be proud with me, I'll pheeze his pride :
Let me go to him.

Ulyss. Not for the worth that hangs upon our quarrel.

Ajax. A paltry, insolent fellow !

Nest. How he describes himself !

Ajax. Can he not be sociable ?   220

Ulyss. The raven chides blackness.

Ajax. I'll let his humors blood.

Agam. He will be the physician that should be the patient.

Ajax. An all men were o' my mind,—

Ulyss. Wit would be out of fashion.

Ajax. A' should not bear it so, a' should eat swords first : shall pride carry it ?

Nest. An 'twould, you'ld carry half.

Ulyss. A' would have ten shares.   230

Ajax. I will knead him ; I'll make him supple.

Nest. He's not yet through warm : force him with praises : pour in, pour in ; his ambition is dry.

Ulyss. [*To Agam.*] My lord, you feed too much on this dislike.

Nest. Our noble general, do not do so.

Dio. You must prepare to fight without Achilles.

Ulyss. Why, 'tis this naming of him does him harm.
Here is a man—but 'tis before his face ;   240
I will be silent.

Nest.   Wherefore should you so ?
He is not emulous, as Achilles is.

Ulyss. Know the whole world, he is as valiant.

Ajax. A whoreson dog, that shall palter thus with us !
Would he were a Trojan !

Nest. What a vice were it in Ajax now,—

Ulyss. If he were proud,—

Dio. Or covetous of praise,—

Ulyss. Ay, or surly borne,—

Dio. Or strange, or self-affected !   250

Ulyss. Thank the heavens, lord, thou art of sweet composure ;
Praise him that got thee, she that gave thee suck :
Famed be thy tutor, and thy parts of nature
Thrice famed, beyond all erudition :
But he that disciplined thy arms to fight,
Let Mars divide eternity in twain,
And give him half : and, for thy vigor,
Bull-bearing Milo his addition yield
To sinewy Ajax. I will not praise thy wisdom,
Which, like a bourn, a pale, a shore, confines
Thy spacious and dilated parts : here's Nestor ;   261
Instructed by the antiquary times,
He must, he is, he cannot but be wise :
But pardon, father Nestor, were your days
As green as Ajax' and your brain so temper'd,
You should not have the eminence of him,
But be as Ajax.

Ajax.   Shall I call you father ?

Nest. Ay, my good son.

Dio.   Be ruled by him, Lord Ajax.

Ulyss. There is no tarrying here ; the hart Achilles
Keeps thicket. Please it our great general
To call together all his state of war :   271
Fresh kings are come to Troy : to-morrow
We must with all our main of power stand fast :
And here's a lord,—come knights from east to west,

And cull their flower, Ajax shall cope the best.

Agam. Go we to council. Let Achilles
     sleep :
Light boats sail swift, though greater hulks
     draw deep.   [*Exeunt.*

ACT III.

SCENE I. *Troy. Priam's palace.*

Enter a Servant *and* PANDARUS.

Pan. Friend, you ! pray you, a word : do
not you follow the young Lord Paris ?

Serv. Ay, sir, when he goes before me.

Pan. You depend upon him, I mean ?

Serv. Sir, I do depend upon the lord.

Pan. You depend upon a noble gentleman ;
I must needs praise him.

Serv. The lord be praised !

Pan. You know me, do you not ?

Serv. Faith, sir, superficially.   10

Pan. Friend, know me better ; I am the
Lord Pandarus.

Serv. I hope I shall know your honor
better.

Pan. I do desire it.

Serv. You are in the state of grace.

Pan. Grace ! not so, friend : honor and
lordship are my titles. [*Music within.*] What
music is this ?

Serv. I do but partly know, sir : it is music
in parts.   20

Pan. Know you the musicians ?

Serv. Wholly, sir.

Pan. Who play they to ?

Serv. To the hearers, sir.

Pan. At whose pleasure, friend ?

Serv. At mine, sir, and theirs that love
music.

Pan. Command, I mean, friend.

Serv. Who shall I command, sir ?

Pan. Friend, we understand not one another : I am too courtly and thou art too cunning. At whose request do these men play ?

Serv. That's to 't indeed, sir : marry, sir,
at the request of Paris my lord, who's there in
person ; with him, the mortal Venus, the heart-
blood of beauty, love's invisible soul,—

Pan. Who, my cousin Cressida ?

Serv. No, sir, Helen : could you not find
out that by her attributes ?

Pan. It should seem, fellow, that thou hast
not seen the Lady Cressida. I come to speak
with Paris from the Prince Troilus : I will
make a complimental assault upon him, for
my business seethes.

Serv. Sodden business ! there's a stewed
phrase indeed !

Enter PARIS *and* HELEN, *attended.*

Pan. Fair be to you, my lord, and to all
this fair company ! fair desires, in all fair
measure, fairly guide them ! especially to you,
fair queen ! fair thoughts be your fair pillow !

Helen. Dear lord, you are full of fair
words.   50

Pan. You speak your fair pleasure, sweet
queen. Fair prince, here is good broken music.

Par. You have broke it, cousin : and, by
my life, you shall make it whole again ; you
shall piece it out with a piece of your performance. Nell, he is full of harmony.

Pan. Truly, lady, no.

Helen. O, sir,—

Pan. Rude, in sooth ; in good sooth, very
rude.   60

Par. Well said, my lord ! well, you say so
in fits.

Pan. I have business to my lord, dear
queen. My lord, will you vouchsafe me a
word ?

Helen. Nay, this shall not hedge us out :
we'll hear you sing, certainly.

Pan. Well, sweet queen, you are pleasant
with me. But, marry, thus, my lord : my dear
lord and most esteemed friend, your brother
Troilus,—   70

Helen. My Lord Pandarus ; honey-sweet
lord,—

Pan. Go to, sweet queen, to go :—commends himself most affectionately to you,—

Helen. You shall not bob us out of our
melody : if you do, our melancholy upon your
head !

Pan. Sweet queen, sweet queen ! that's a
sweet queen, i' faith.

Helen. And to make a sweet lady sad is a
sour offence.   80

Pan. Nay, that shall not serve your turn ;
that shall not, in truth, la. Nay, I care not
for such words ; no, no. And, my lord, he
desires you, that if the king call for him at
supper, you will make his excuse.

Helen. My Lord Pandarus,—

Pan. What says my sweet queen, my very
very sweet queen ?

Par. What exploit's in hand ? where sups
he to-night ?   90

Helen. Nay, but, my lord,—

Pan. What says my sweet queen ? My
cousin will fall out with you. You must not
know where he sups.

Par. I'll lay my life, with my disposer Cressida.

Pan. No, no, no such matter ; you are
wide : come, your disposer is sick.

Par. Well, I'll make excuse.

Pan. Ay, good my lord. Why should you
say Cressida ? no, your poor disposer's sick.

Par. I spy.

Pan. You spy ! what do you spy ? Come,
give me an instrument. Now, sweet queen.

Helen. Why, this is kindly done.

Pan. My niece is horribly in love with a
thing you have, sweet queen.

Helen. She shall have it, my lord, if it be
not my lord Paris.

Pan. He ! no, she'll none of him ; they two
are twain.   111

Helen. Falling in, after falling out, may
make them three.

Pan. Come, come, I'll hear no more of
this ; I'll sing you a song now.

Helen. Ay, ay, prithee now. By my troth,
sweet lord, thou hast a fine forehead.

Pan. Ay, you may, you may.

Helen. Let thy song be love : this love will
undo us all. O Cupid, Cupid, Cupid !   120

Pan. Love ! ay, that it shall, i' faith.

Par. Ay, good now, love, love, nothing but
love.

Pan. In good troth, it begins so. [*Sings.*
Love, love, nothing but love, still more !
 For, O, love's bow
  Shoots buck and doe :
  The shaft confounds,
  Not that it wounds,
 But tickles still the sore.   130
These lovers cry Oh ! oh ! they die !
 Yet that which seems the wound to
   kill,
Doth turn oh ! oh ! to ha ! ha ! he !
So dying love lives still :
Oh ! oh ! a while, but ha ! ha ! ha !
Oh ! oh ! groans out for ha ! ha ! ha !
Heigh-ho !

Helen. In love, i' faith, to the very tip of
the nose.   139

Par. He eats nothing but doves, love, and
that breeds hot blood, and hot blood begets
hot thoughts, and hot thoughts beget hot
deeds, and hot deeds is love.

Pan. Is this the generation of love ? hot
blood, hot thoughts, and hot deeds ? Why,
they are vipers : is love a generation of vipers ?
Sweet lord, who's a-field to-day ?

Par. Hector, Deiphobus, Helenus, Antenor,
and all the gallantry of Troy : I would fain
have armed to-day, but my Nell would not
have it so. How chance my brother Troilus
went not ?   151

Helen. He hangs the lip at something : you
know all, Lord Pandarus.

Pan. Not I, honey-sweet queen. I long to
hear how they sped to-day. You'll remember
your brother's excuse ?

Par. To a hair.

Pan. Farewell, sweet queen.

Helen. Commend me to your niece.

Pan. I will, sweet queen.   [*Exit.* 160
       [*A retreat sounded.*

Par. They're come from field : let us to
   Priam's hall,
To greet the warriors. Sweet Helen, I must
   woo you
To help unarm our Hector : his stubborn
   buckles,
With these your white enchanting fingers
   touch'd,
Shall more obey than to the edge of steel
Or force of Greekish sinews ; you shall do
   more
Than all the island kings,—disarm great
   Hector.

Helen. 'Twill make us proud to be his
   servant, Paris ;
Yea, what he shall receive of us in duty
Gives us more palm in beauty than we have,
Yea, overshines ourself.   171

Par. Sweet, above thought I love thee.
       [*Exeunt.*

SCENE II. *The same. Pandarus' orchard.*

Enter PANDARUS *and* TROILUS' *Boy, meeting.*

Pan. How now ! where's thy master ? at
my cousin Cressida's ?

Boy. No, sir ; he stays for you to conduct
him thither.

Pan. O, here he comes.

Enter TROILUS.

How now, how now !

Tro. Sirrah, walk off.   [*Exit Boy.*

Pan. Have you seen my cousin ?

Tro. No, Pandarus : I stalk about her
   door,
Like a strange soul upon the Stygian banks 10
Staying for waftage. O, be thou my Charon,
And give me swift transportation to those fields
Where I may wallow in the lily-beds
Proposed for the deserver ! O gentle Pandarus,
From Cupid's shoulder pluck his painted wings
And fly with me to Cressid !

Pan. Walk here i' the orchard, I'll bring
her straight.   [*Exit.*

Tro. I am giddy ; expectation whirls me
   round.
The imaginary relish is so sweet   20
That it enchants my sense : what will it be,
When that the watery palate tastes indeed
Love's thrice repured nectar ? death, I fear me,
Swooning destruction, or some joy too fine,
Too subtle-potent, tuned too sharp in sweet-
   ness,
For the capacity of my ruder powers :
I fear it much ; and I do fear besides,
That I shall lose distinction in my joys ;
As doth a battle, when they charge on heaps
The enemy flying.   30

Re-enter PANDARUS.

Pan. She's making her ready, she'll come
straight : you must be witty now. She does so
blush, and fetches her wind so short, as if she
were frayed with a sprite : I'll fetch her. It is
the prettiest villain : she fetches her breath as
short as a new-ta'en sparrow.   [*Exit.*

Tro. Even such a passion doth embrace my
   bosom :
My heart beats thicker than a feverous pulse ;
And all my powers do their bestowing lose,
Like vassalage at unawares encountering   40
The eye of majesty.

Re-enter PANDARUS *with* CRESSIDA.

Pan. Come, come, what need you blush ?
shame's a baby. Here she is now : swear the
oaths now to her that you have sworn to me.
What, are you gone again ? you must be
watched ere you be made tame, must you ?
Come your ways, come your ways ; an you
draw backward, we'll put you i' the fills. Why
do you not speak to her ? Come, draw this
curtain, and let's see your picture. Alas the
day, how loath you are to offend daylight ! an
'twere dark, you'ld close sooner. So, so ; rub
on, and kiss the mistress. How now ! a kiss in
fee-farm ! build there, carpenter ; the air is
sweet. Nay, you shall fight your hearts out ere
I part you. The falcon as the tercel, for all
the ducks i' the river : go to, go to.

Tro. You have bereft me of all words, lady.

Pan. Words pay no debts, give her deeds :
but she'll bereave you o' the deeds too, if she
call your activity in question. What, billing
again ? Here's ' In witness whereof the parties
interchangeably '—Come in, come in : I'll go
get a fire.   [*Exit.*

Cres. Will you walk in, my lord ?

Tro. O Cressida, how often have I wished
me thus !

Cres. Wished, my lord ! The gods grant,—
O my lord !

Tro. What should they grant ? what makes
this pretty abruption ? What too curious dreg
espies my sweet lady in the fountain of our
love ?

Cres. More dregs than water, if my fears have eyes.

Tro. Fears make devils of cherubins; they never see truly.

Cres. Blind fear, that seeing reason leads, finds safer footing than blind reason stumbling without fear : to fear the worst oft cures the worse. 79

Tro. O, let my lady apprehend no fear : in all Cupid's pageant there is presented no monster.

Cres. Nor nothing monstrous neither ?

Tro. Nothing, but our undertakings ; when we vow to weep seas, live in fire, eat rocks, tame tigers ; thinking it harder for our mistress to devise imposition enough than for us to undergo any difficulty imposed. This is the monstruosity in love, lady, that the will is infinite and the execution confined, that the desire is boundless and the act a slave to limit.

Cres. They say all lovers swear more performance than they are able and yet reserve an ability that they never perform, vowing more than the perfection of ten and discharging less than the tenth part of one. They that have the voice of lions and the act of hares, are they not monsters ?

Tro. Are there such ? such are not we : praise us as we are tasted, allow us as we prove ; our head shall go bare till merit crown it : no perfection in reversion shall have a praise in present : we will not name desert before his birth, and, being born, his addition shall be humble. Few words to fair faith : Troilus shall be such to Cressid as what envy can say worst shall be a mock for his truth, and what truth can speak truest not truer than Troilus.

Cres. Will you walk in, my lord ?

Re-enter PANDARUS.

Pan. What, blushing still ? have you not done talking yet ? 109

Cres. Well, uncle, what folly I commit, I dedicate to you.

Pan. I thank you for that : if my lord get a boy of you, you'll give him me. Be true to my lord : if he flinch, chide me for it.

Tro. You know now your hostages ; your uncle's word and my firm faith.

Pan. Nay, I'll give my word for her too : our kindred, though they be long ere they are wooed, they are constant being won : they are burs, I can tell you ; they'll stick where they are thrown.

Cres. Boldness comes to me now, and brings me heart. 121

Prince Troilus, I have loved you night and day

For many weary months.

Tro. Why was my Cressid then so hard to win ?

Cres. Hard to seem won : but I was won, my lord,

With the first glance that ever—pardon me—

If I confess much, you will play the tyrant.

I love you now ; but not, till now, so much

But I might master it : in faith, I lie ; 129

My thoughts were like unbridled children, grown

Too headstrong for their mother. See, we fools !

Why have I blabb'd ? who shall be true to us,

When we are so unsecret to ourselves ?

But, though I loved you well, I woo'd you not ;

And yet, good faith, I wish'd myself a man,

Or that we women had men's privilege

Of speaking first. Sweet, bid me hold my tongue,

For in this rapture I shall surely speak

The thing I shall repent. See, see, your silence,

Cunning in dumbness, from my weakness draws

My very soul of counsel ! stop my mouth. 141

Tro. And shall, albeit sweet music issues thence.

Pan. Pretty, i' faith.

Cres. My lord, I do beseech you, pardon me ;

'Twas not my purpose, thus to beg a kiss :

I am ashamed. O heavens ! what have I done ?

For this time will I take my leave, my lord.

Tro. Your leave, sweet Cressid !

Pan. Leave ! an you take leave till to-morrow morning,— 150

Cres. Pray you, content you.

Tro.   What offends you, lady ?

Cres. Sir, mine own company.

Tro.   You cannot shun Yourself.

Cres. Let me go and try :

I have a kind of self resides with you ;

But an unkind self, that itself will leave,

To be another's fool. I would be gone :

Where is my wit ? I know not what I speak.

Tro. Well know they what they speak that speak so wisely.

Cres. Perchance, my lord, I show more craft than love ; 160

And fell so roundly to a large confession,

To angle for your thoughts : but you are wise,

Or else you love not, for to be wise and love

Exceeds man's might ; that dwells with gods above.

Tro. O that I thought it could be in a woman—

As, if it can, I will presume in you—

To feed for aye her lamp and flames of love ;

To keep her constancy in plight and youth,

Outliving beauty's outward, with a mind 169

That doth renew swifter than blood decays !

Or that persuasion could but thus convince me,

That my integrity and truth to you

Might be affronted with the match and weight

Of such a winnow'd purity in love ;

How were I then uplifted ! but, alas !

I am as true as truth's simplicity

And simpler than the infancy of truth.

Cres. In that I'll war with you.

Tro.   O virtuous fight,

When right with right wars who shall be most right ! 179

True swains in love shall in the world to come

Approve their truths by Troilus : when their rhymes,

Full of protest, of oath and big compare,

Want similes, truth tired with iteration,

As true as steel, as plantage to the moon,

As sun to day, as turtle to her mate,

As iron to adamant, as earth to the centre,

Yet, after all comparisons of truth,

As truth's authentic author to be cited,

' As true as Troilus ' shall crown up the verse,

And sanctify the numbers.

Cres.   Prophet may you be ! 190

If I be false, or swerve a hair from truth,

When time is old and hath forgot itself,
When waterdrops have worn the stones of
  Troy,
And blind oblivion swallow'd cities up,
And mighty states characterless are grated
To dusty nothing, yet let memory,
From false to false, among false maids in love,
Upbraid my falsehood! when they've said 'as
  false
As air, as water, wind, or sandy earth,
As fox to lamb, as wolf to heifer's calf,   200
Pard to the hind, or stepdame to her son,'
'Yea,' let them say, to stick the heart of
  falsehood,
'As false as Cressid.'
  Pan. Go to, a bargain made: seal it, seal
it; I'll be the witness. Here I hold your hand,
here my cousin's. If ever you prove false one
to another, since I have taken such pains to
bring you together, let all pitiful goers-between
be called to the world's end after my name;
call them all Pandars; let all constant men be
Troiluses, all false women Cressids, and all
brokers-between Pandars! say, amen.
  Tro. Amen.
  Cres. Amen.
  Pan. Amen. Whereupon I will show you a
chamber with a bed; which bed, because it
shall not speak of your pretty encounters, press
it to death: away!
And Cupid grant all tongue-tied maidens here
Bed, chamber, Pandar to provide this gear!
                                      [*Exeunt.* 221

SCENE III.   *The Grecian camp. Before
              Achilles' tent.*

Enter AGAMEMNON, ULYSSES, DIOMEDES,
NESTOR, AJAX, MENELAUS, *and* CALCHAS.

  Cal. Now, princes, for the service I have
    done you,
The advantage of the time prompts me aloud
To call for recompense. Appear it to your
    mind
That, through the sight I bear in things to
    love,
I have abandon'd Troy, left my possession,
Incurr'd a traitor's name; exposed myself,
From certain and possess'd conveniences,
To doubtful fortunes; sequestering from me
    all
That time, acquaintance, custom and condition
Made tame and most familiar to my nature,
And here, to do you service, am become   11
As new into the world, strange, unacquainted:
I do beseech you, as in way of taste,
To give me now a little benefit,
Out of those many register'd in promise,
Which, you say, live to come in my behalf.
  Agam. What wouldst thou of us, Trojan?
    make demand.
  Cal. You have a Trojan prisoner, call'd
    Antenor,
Yesterday took: Troy holds him very dear.
Oft have you—often have you thanks there-
    fore—   20
Desired my Cressid in right great exchange,
Whom Troy hath still denied: but this An-
    tenor,
I know, is such a wrest in their affairs
That their negotiations all must slack,
Wanting his manage; and they will almost
Give us a prince of blood, a son of Priam,

In change of him: let him be sent, great
    princes,
And he shall buy my daughter; and her pres-
    ence
Shall quite strike off all service I have done,
In most accepted pain.
  Agam.   Let Diomedes bear him, 30
And bring us Cressid hither: Calchas shall
    have
What he requests of us. Good Diomed,
Furnish you fairly for this interchange:
Withal bring word if Hector will to-morrow
Be answer'd in his challenge: Ajax is ready.
  Dio. This shall I undertake; and 'tis a bur-
    den
Which I am proud to bear.
                    [*Exeunt Diomedes and Calchas.*

Enter ACHILLES *and* PATROCLUS, *before their
  tent.*

  Ulyss. Achilles stands i' the entrance of his
    tent:
Please it our general to pass strangely by him,
As if he were forgot; and, princes all,   40
Lay negligent and loose regard upon him:
I will come last. 'Tis like he'll question me
Why such unplausive eyes are bent on him:
If so, I have derision medicinable,
To use between your strangeness and his pride,
Which his own will shall have desire to drink:
It may be good: pride hath no other glass
To show itself but pride, for supple knees
Feed arrogance and are the proud man's fees.
  Agam. We'll execute your purpose, and
    put on   50
A form of strangeness as we pass along:
So do each lord, and either greet him not,
Or else disdainfully, which shall shake him
    more
Than if not look'd on. I will lead the way.
  Achil. What, comes the general to speak
    with me?
You know my mind, I'll fight no more 'gainst
    Troy.
  Agam. What says Achilles? would he
    aught with us?
  Nest. Would you, my lord, aught with the
    general?
  Achil. No.
  Nest. Nothing, my lord.   60
  Agam. The better.
                    [*Exeunt Agamemnon and Nestor.*
  Achil. Good day, good day.
  Men. How do you? how do you?   [*Exit.*
  Achil. What, does the cuckold scorn me?
  Ajax. How now, Patroclus?
  Achil. Good morrow, Ajax.
  Ajax. Ha?
  Achil. Good morrow.
  Ajax. Ay, and good next day too.   [*Exit.*
  Achil. What mean these fellows? Know
    they not Achilles?   70
  Patr. They pass by strangely: they were
    used to bend,
To send their smiles before them to Achilles;
To come as humbly as they used to creep
To holy altars.
  Achil.   What, am I poor of late?
'Tis certain, greatness, once fall'n out with
    fortune,
Must fall out with men too: what the declined
    is
He shall as soon read in the eyes of others

As feel in his own fall ; for men, like butter-
flies,
Show not their mealy wings but to the sum-
mer,
And not a man, for being simply man,   80
Hath any honor, but honor for those honors
That are without him, as place, riches, favor,
Prizes of accident as oft as merit :
Which when they fall, as being slippery stand-
ers,
The love that lean'd on them as slippery too,
Do one pluck down another and together
Die in the fall. But 'tis not so with me :
Fortune and I are friends : I do enjoy
At ample point all that I did possess,
Save these men's looks ; who do, methinks, find
out   90
Something not worth in me such rich behold-
ing
As they have often given. Here is Ulysses ;
I'll interrupt his reading.
How now Ulysses !
Ulyss.   Now, great Thetis' son !
Achil. What are you reading ?
Ulyss.   A strange fellow here
Writes me : ' That man, how dearly ever
parted,
How much in having, or without or in,
Cannot make boast to have that which he
hath,
Nor feels not what he owes, but by reflection ;
As when his virtues shining upon others   100
Heat them and they retort that heat again
To the first giver.'
Achil.   This is not strange, Ulysses.
The beauty that is borne here in the face
The bearer knows not, but commends itself
To others' eyes ; nor doth the eye itself,
That most pure spirit of sense, behold itself,
Not going from itself ; but eye to eye opposed
Salutes each other with each other's form ;
For speculation turns not to itself,
Till it hath travell'd and is mirror'd there   110
Where it may see itself. This is not strange at
all.
Ulyss. I do not strain at the position,—
It is familiar,—but at the author's drift ;
Who, in his circumstance, expressly proves
That no man is the lord of any thing,
Though in and of him there be much con-
sisting,
Till he communicate his parts to others :
Nor doth he of himself know them for aught
Till he behold them form'd in the applause
Where they're extended ; who, like an arch,
reverberates   120
The voice again, or, like a gate of steel
Fronting the sun, receives and renders back
His figure and his heat. I was much wrapt in
this ;
And apprehended here immediately
The unknown Ajax.
Heavens, what a man is there ! a very horse,
That has he knows not what. Nature, what
things there are
Most abject in regard and dear in use !
What things again most dear in the esteem
And poor in worth ! Now shall we see to-
morrow—   130
An act that very chance doth throw upon
him—
Ajax renown'd. O heavens, what some men do,
While some men leave to do !

How some men creep in skittish fortune's hall,
Whiles others play the idiots in her eyes !
How one man eats into another's pride,
While pride is fasting in his wantonness !
To see these Grecian lords !—why, even al-
ready
They clap the lubber Ajax on the shoulder,
As if his foot were on brave Hector's breast
And great Troy shrieking.   141
Achil. I do believe it ; for they pass'd by
me
As misers do by beggars, neither gave to me
Good word nor look : what, are my deeds for-
got ?
Ulyss. Time hath, my lord, a wallet at his
back,
Wherein he puts alms for oblivion,
A great-sized monster of ingratitudes :
Those scraps are good deeds past ; which are
devour'd
As fast as they are made, forgot as soon
As done : perseverance, dear my lord,   150
Keeps honor bright : to have done is to hang
Quite out of fashion, like a rusty mail
In monumental mockery. Take the instant
way ;
For honor travels in a strait so narrow,
Where one but goes abreast : keep then the
path ;
For emulation hath a thousand sons
That one by one pursue : if you give way,
Or hedge aside from the direct forthright,
Like to an enter'd tide, they all rush by
And leave you hindmost ;   160
Or, like a gallant horse fall'n in first rank,
Lie there for pavement to the abject rear,
O'er-run and trampled on : then what they do
in present,
Though less than yours in past, must o'ertop
yours ;
For time is like a fashionable host
That slightly shakes his parting guest by the
hand,
And with his arms outstretch'd, as he would
fly,
Grasps in the comer : welcome ever smiles,
And farewell goes out sighing. O, let not virtue
seek
Remuneration for the thing it was ;   170
For beauty, wit,
High birth, vigor of bone, desert in service,
Love, friendship, charity, are subjects all
To envious and calumniating time.
One touch of nature makes the whole world
kin,
That all with one consent praise new-born
gawds,
Though they are made and moulded of things
past,
And give to dust that is a little gilt
More laud than gilt o'er-dusted.
The present eye praises the present object.
Then marvel not, thou great and complete
man,   181
That all the Greeks begin to worship Ajax ;
Since things in motion sooner catch the eye
Than what not stirs. The cry went once on
thee,
And still it might, and yet it may again,
If thou wouldst not entomb thyself alive
And case thy reputation in thy tent ;
Whose glorious deeds, but in these fields of
late,

Made emulous missions 'mongst the gods
    themselves
And drave great Mars to faction.
Achil.   Of this my privacy 190
I have strong reasons.
Ulyss.   But 'gainst your privacy
The reasons are more potent and heroical :
'Tis known, Achilles, that you are in love
With one of Priam's daughters.
Achil.   Ha ! known !
Ulyss. Is that a wonder ?
The providence that's in a watchful state
Knows almost every grain of Plutus' gold,
Finds bottom in the uncomprehensive deeps,
Keeps place with thought and almost, like the
    gods,
Does thoughts unveil in their dumb cradles.
There is a mystery—with whom relation 201
Durst never meddle—in the soul of state ;
Which hath an operation more divine
Than breath or pen can give expressure to :
All the commerce that you have had with Troy
As perfectly is ours as yours, my lord ;
And better would it fit Achilles much
To throw down Hector than Polyxena ;
But it must grieve young Pyrrhus now at home,
When fame shall in our islands sound her
    trump, 211
And all the Greekish girls shall tripping sing,
' Great Hector's sister did Achilles win,
But our great Ajax bravely beat down him.'
Farewell, my lord : I as your lover speak ;
The fool slides o'er the ice that you should
    break.   [*Exit.*
    Patr. To this effect, Achilles, have I moved
    you :
A woman impudent and mannish grown
Is not more loathed than an effeminate man
In time of action. I stand condemn'd for this ;
They think my little stomach to the war 220
And your great love to me restrains you thus :
Sweet, rouse yourself ; and the weak wanton
    Cupid
Shall from your neck unloose his amorous
    fold,
And, like a dew-drop from the lion's mane,
Be shook to air.
    Achil.   Shall Ajax fight with Hector ?
    Patr. Ay, and perhaps receive much honor
    by him.
    Achil. I see my reputation is at stake ;
My fame is shrewdly gored.
    Patr.   O, then, beware ;
Those wounds heal ill that men do give them-
    selves :
Omission to do what is necessary 230
Seals a commission to a blank of danger ;
And danger, like an ague, subtly taints
Even then when we sit idly in the sun.
    Achil. Go call Thersites hither, sweet Pa-
    troclus :
I'll send the fool to Ajax and desire him
To invite the Trojan lords after the combat
To see us here unarm'd : I have a woman's
    longing,
An appetite that I am sick withal,
To see great Hector in his weeds of peace,
To talk with him and to behold his visage,
Even to my full of view. 241

Enter THERSITES.

                 A labor saved !
    Ther. A wonder !

    Achil. What ?
    Ther. Ajax goes up and down the field,
asking for himself.
    Achil. How so ?
    Ther. He must fight singly to-morrow with
Hector, and is so prophetically proud of an
heroical cudgelling that he raves in saying
nothing.
    Achil. How can that be ? 250
    Ther. Why, he stalks up and down like a
peacock,—a stride and a stand : ruminates
like an hostess that hath no arithmetic but her
brain to set down her reckoning : bites his lip
with a politic regard, as who should say
' There were wit in this head, an 'twould out ; '
and so there is, but it lies as coldly in him as
fire in a flint, which will not show without
knocking. The man's undone forever ; for if
Hector break not his neck i' the combat, he'll
break 't himself in vain-glory. He knows not
me : I said ' Good morrow, Ajax ; ' and he
replies ' Thanks, Agamemnon.' What think
you of this man that takes me for the general ? He's grown a very land-fish, language-
less, a monster. A plague of opinion ! a man
may wear it on both sides, like a leather jerkin.
    Achil. Thou must be my ambassador to
him, Thersites.
    Ther. Who, I ? why, he'll answer nobody ;
he professes not answering : speaking is for
beggars ; he wears his tongue in's arms. I will
put on his presence : let Patroclus make demands to me, you shall see the pageant of
Ajax.
    Achil. To him, Patroclus ; tell him I hum-
bly desire the valiant Ajax to invite the most
valorous Hector to come unarmed to my tent,
and to procure safe-conduct for his person of
the magnanimous and most illustrious six-or-
seven-times-honored captain-general of the
Grecian army, Agamemnon, et cetera. Do
this. 280
    Patr. Jove bless great Ajax !
    Ther. Hum !
    Patr. I come from the worthy Achilles,—
    Ther. Ha !
    Patr. Who most humbly desires you to in-
vite Hector to his tent,—
    Ther. Hum !
    Patr. And to procure safe-conduct from
Agamemnon.
    Ther. Agamemnon ! 290
    Patr. Ay, my lord.
    Ther. Ha !
    Patr. What say you to 't ?
    Ther. God b' wi' you, with all my heart.
    Patr. Your answer, sir.
    Ther. If to-morrow be a fair day, by eleven
o'clock it will go one way or other : howsoever, he shall pay for me ere he has me.
    Patr. Your answer, sir.
    Ther. Fare you well, with all my heart.
    Achil. Why, but he is not in this tune, is
he ? 301
    Ther. No, but he's out o' tune thus. What
music will be in him when Hector has knocked
out his brains, I know not ; but, I am sure,
none, unless the fiddler Apollo get his sinews
to make catlings on.
    Achil. Come, thou shalt bear a letter to
him straight.
    Ther. Let me bear another to his horse ;
for that's the more capable creature. 310

Achil. My mind is troubled, like a fountain stirr'd ;
And I myself see not the bottom of it.

[*Exeunt Achilles and Patroclus.*

Ther. Would the fountain of your mind
were clear again, that I might water an ass at
it ! I had rather be a tick in a sheep than such
a valiant ignorance. [*Exit.*

ACT IV.

SCENE I. *Troy. A street.*

Enter, from one side, ÆNEAS, *and* Servant
with a torch ; from the other, PARIS, DEI-
PHOBUS, ANTENOR, DIOMEDES, *and others,
with torches.*

Par. See, ho ! who is that there ?
Dei.   It is the Lord Æneas.
Æne. Is the prince there in person ?
Had I so good occasion to lie long
As you, Prince Paris, nothing but heavenly
business
Should rob my bed-mate of my company.
Dio. That's my mind too. Good morrow,
Lord Æneas.
Par. A valiant Greek, Æneas,—take his
hand,—
Witness the process of your speech, wherein
You told how Diomed, a whole week by days,
Did haunt you in the field.
Æne.   Health to you, valiant sir, 10
During all question of the gentle truce ;
But when I meet you arm'd, as black defiance
As heart can think or courage execute.
Dio. The one and other Diomed embraces.
Our bloods are now in calm ; and, so long,
health !
But when contention and occasion meet,
By Jove, I'll play the hunter for thy life
With all my force, pursuit and policy.
Æne. And thou shalt hunt a lion, that will
fly
With his face backward. In humane gentle-
ness,   20
Welcome to Troy ! now, by Anchises' life,
Welcome, indeed ! By Venus' hand I swear,
No man alive can love in such a sort
The thing he means to kill more excellently.
Dio. We sympathize : Jove, let Æneas
live,
If to my sword his fate be not the glory,
A thousand complete courses of the sun !
But, in mine emulous honor, let him die,
With every joint a wound, and that to-mor-
row !
Æne. We know each other well.   30
Dio. We do ; and long to know each other
worse.
Par. This is the most despiteful gentle
greeting,
The noblest hateful love, that e'er I heard of.
What business, lord, so early ?
Æne. I was sent for to the king ; but why,
I know not.
Par. His purpose meets you : 'twas to
bring this Greek
To Calchas' house, and there to render him,
For the enfreed Antenor, the fair Cressid :
Let's have your company, or, if you please,
Haste there before us : I constantly do
think—   40

Or rather, call my thought a certain knowl-
edge—
My brother Troilus lodges there to-night :
Rouse him and give him note of our ap-
proach,
With the whole quality wherefore : I fear
We shall be much unwelcome.
Æne.   That I assure you :
Troilus had rather Troy were borne to Greece
Than Cressid borne from Troy.
Par.   There is no help ;
The bitter disposition of the time
Will have it so. On, lord ; we'll follow you.
Æne. Good morrow, all.   50

[*Exit with Servant.*

Par. And tell me, noble Diomed, faith, tell
me true,
Even in the soul of sound good-fellowship,
Who, in your thoughts, merits fair Helen best,
Myself or Menelaus ?
Dio.   Both alike :
He merits well to have her, that doth seek her,
Not making any scruple of her soilure,
With such a hell of pain and world of charge,
And you as well to keep her, that defend her,
Not palating the taste of her dishonor,
With such a costly loss of wealth and friends :
He, like a puling cuckold, would drink up 61
The lees and dregs of a flat tamed piece ;
You, like a lecher, out of whorish loins
Are pleased to breed out your inheritors :
Both merits poised, each weighs nor less nor
more ;
But he as he, the heavier for a whore.
Par. You are too bitter to your country-
woman.
Dio. She's bitter to her country : hear me,
Paris :
For every false drop in her bawdy veins
A Grecian's life hath sunk ; for every scruple
Of her contaminated carrion weight,   71
A Trojan hath been slain : since she could
speak,
She hath not given so many good words
breath
As for her Greeks and Trojans suffer'd death.
Par. Fair Diomed, you do as chapmen do,
Dispraise the thing that you desire to buy :
But we in silence hold this virtue well,
We'll but commend what we intend to sell.
Here lies our way.   [*Exeunt.*

SCENE II. *The same. Court of Pandarus'
house.*

Enter TROILUS *and* CRESSIDA.

Tro. Dear, trouble not yourself : the morn
is cold.
Cres. Then, sweet my lord, I'll call mine
uncle down ;
He shall unbolt the gates.
Tro.   Trouble him not ;
To bed, to bed : sleep kill those pretty eyes,
And give as soft attachment to thy senses
As infants' empty of all thought !
Cres.   Good morrow, then.
Tro. I prithee now, to bed.
Cres.   Are you a-weary of me ?
Tro. O Cressida ! but that the busy day,
Waked by the lark, hath roused the ribald
crows,
And dreaming night will hide our joys no
longer,
I would not from thee.

Cres.   Night hath been too brief.
Tro. Beshrew the witch! with venomous
    wights she stays
As tediously as hell, but flies the grasps of
    love
With wings more momentary-swift than
    thought.
You will catch cold, and curse me.
Cres.   Prithee, tarry:
You men will never tarry.
O foolish Cressid! I might have still held off,
And then you would have tarried. Hark!
    there's one up.
Pan. [*Within*] What, 's all the doors open
    here?
Tro. It is your uncle.   20
Cres. A pestilence on him! now will he be
    mocking:
I shall have such a life!

Enter PANDARUS.

Pan. How now, how now! how go maiden-
    heads? Here, you maid! where's my cousin
    Cressid?
Cres. Go hang yourself, you naughty
    mocking uncle!
You bring me to do, and then you flout me
    too.
Pan. To do what? to do what? let her say
what: what have I brought you to do?
Cres. Come, come, beshrew your heart!
    you'll ne'er be good,   30
Nor suffer others.
Pan. Ha, ha! Alas, poor wretch! ah, poor
capocchia! hast not slept to-night? would he
not, a naughty man, let it sleep? a bugbear
take him!
Cres. Did not I tell you? Would he were
    knock'd i' the head! [*Knocking within.*
Who's that at door? good uncle, go and see.
My lord, come you again into my chamber:
You smile and mock me, as if I meant
    naughtily.
Tro. Ha, ha!   39
Cres. Come, you are deceived, I think of
    no such thing.   [*Knocking within.*
How earnestly they knock! Pray you, come
    in:
I would not for half Troy have you seen here.
              [*Exeunt Troilus and Cressida.*
Pan. Who's there? what's the matter?
will you beat down the door? How now!
what's the matter?

Enter ÆNEAS.

Æne. Good morrow, lord, good morrow.
Pan. Who's there? my Lord Æneas! By
    my troth,
I knew you not: what news with you so
    early?
Æne. Is not Prince Troilus here?
Pan. Here! what should he do here?   50
Æne. Come, he is here, my lord; do not
    deny him:
It doth import him much to speak with me.
Pan. Is he here, say you? 'tis more than
I know, I'll be sworn: for my own part, I
came in late. What should he do here?
Æne. Who!—nay, then: come, come,
you'll do him wrong ere you're ware: you'll
be so true to him, to be false to him: do not
you know of him, but yet go fetch him hither;
go.

Re-enter TROILUS.

Tro. How now! what's the matter?   60
Æne. My lord, I scarce have leisure to
    salute you,
My matter is so rash: there is at hand
Paris your brother, and Deiphobus,
The Grecian Diomed, and our Antenor
Deliver'd to us; and for him forthwith,
Ere the first sacrifice, within this hour,
We must give up to Diomedes' hand
The Lady Cressida.
Tro.   Is it so concluded?
Æne. By Priam and the general state of
    Troy:
They are at hand and ready to effect it.   70
Tro. How my achievements mock me!
I will go meet them: and, my Lord Æneas,
We met by chance; you did not find me here.
Æne. Good, good, my lord; the secrets of
    nature
Have not more gift in taciturnity.
              [*Exeunt Troilus and Æneas.*
Pan. Is't possible? no sooner got but lost?
The devil take Antenor! the young prince
will go mad: a plague upon Antenor! I
would they had broke 's neck!

Re-enter CRESSIDA.

Cres. How now! what's the matter? who
was here?   81
Pan. Ah, ah!
Cres. Why sigh you so profoundly?
where's my lord? gone! Tell me, sweet uncle,
what's the matter?
Pan. Would I were as deep under the
earth as I am above!
Cres. O the gods! what's the matter?
Pan. Prithee, get thee in: would thou
hadst ne'er been born! I knew thou wouldst
be his death. O, poor gentleman! A plague
upon Antenor!
Cres. Good uncle, I beseech you, on my
knees I beseech you, what's the matter?
Pan. Thou must be gone, wench, thou
must be gone; thou art changed for Antenor:
thou must to thy father, and be gone from
Troilus: 'twill be his death; 'twill be his
bane; he cannot bear it.
Cres. O you immortal gods! I will not go.
Pan. Thou must.   101
Cres. I will not, uncle: I have forgot my
    father;
I know no touch of consanguinity;
No kin, no love, no blood, no soul so near me
As the sweet Troilus. O you gods divine!
Make Cressid's name the very crown of false-
    hood,
If ever she leave Troilus! Time, force, and
    death,
Do to this body what extremes you can;
But the strong base and building of my love
Is as the very centre of the earth,   110
Drawing all things to it. I'll go in and
    weep,—
Pan. Do, do.
Cres. Tear my bright hair and scratch my
    praised cheeks,
Crack my clear voice with sobs and break my
    heart
With sounding Troilus. I will not go from
    Troy.   [*Exeunt.*

SCENE III. *The same. Street before Pandarus' house.*

Enter PARIS, TROILUS, ÆNEAS, DEIPHOBUS, ANTENOR, *and* DIOMEDES.

Par. It is great morning, and the hour prefix'd
Of her delivery to this valiant Greek
Comes fast upon. Good my brother Troilus,
Tell you the lady what she is to do,
And haste her to the purpose.

Tro.   Walk into her house ;
I'll bring her to the Grecian presently :
And to his hand when I deliver her,
Think it an altar, and thy brother Troilus
A priest there offering to it his own heart.
            [*Exit.*

Par. I know what 'tis to love ;
And would, as I shall pity, I could help !
Please you walk in, my lords.   [*Exeunt.*

SCENE IV. *The same. Pandarus' house.*

Enter PANDARUS *and* CRESSIDA.

Pan. Be moderate, be moderate.
Cres. Why tell you me of moderation ?
The grief is fine, full, perfect, that I taste,
And violenteth in a sense as strong
As that which causeth it : how can I moder-
  ate it ?
If I could temporize with my affection,
Or brew it to a weak and colder palate,
The like allayment could I give my grief.
My love admits no qualifying dross ;
No more my grief, in such a precious loss. 10
Pan. Here, here, here he comes.

Enter TROILUS.

Ah, sweet ducks !
Cres. O Troilus ! Troilus !
        [*Embracing him.*
Pan. What a pair of spectacles is here !
Let me embrace too. ' O heart,' as the goodly saying is,
 '—— O heart, heavy heart,
 Why sigh'st thou without breaking ?'
where he answers again,
 ' Because thou canst not ease thy smart 20
 By friendship nor by speaking.'
There was never a truer rhyme. Let us cast
away nothing, for we may live to have need
of such a verse : we see it, we see it. How
now, lambs ?
Tro. Cressid, I love thee in so strain'd a
  purity,
That the bless'd gods, as angry with my
  fancy,
More bright in zeal than the devotion which
Cold lips blow to their deities, take thee from
  me.
Cres. Have the gods envy ?   30
Pan. Ay, ay, ay, ay ; 'tis too plain a case.
Cres. And is it true that I must go from
  Troy ?
Tro. A hateful truth.
Cres.   What, and from Troilus too ?
Tro. From Troy and Troilus.
Cres.   Is it possible ?
Tro. And suddenly ; where injury of
  chance
Puts back leave-taking, justles roughly by
All time of pause, rudely beguiles our lips
Of all rejoindure, forcibly prevents

Our lock'd embrasures, strangles our dear
  vows   39
Even in the birth of our own laboring breath :
We two, that with so many thousand sighs
Did buy each other, must poorly sell our-
  selves
With the rude brevity and discharge of one.
Injurious time now with a robber's haste
Crams his rich thievery up, he knows not
  how :
As many farewells as be stars in heaven,
With distinct breath and consign'd kisses to
  them,
He fumbles up into a lose adieu,
And scants us with a single famish'd kiss,
Distasted with the salt of broken tears.   50
Æne. [*Within*] My lord, is the lady
  ready ?
Tro. Hark ! you are call'd : some say the
  Genius so
Cries ' come ' to him that instantly must die.
Bid them have patience ; she shall come anon.
Pan. Where are my tears ? rain, to lay this
wind, or my heart will be blown up by the
root.   [*Exit.*
Cres. I must then to the Grecians ?
Tro.   No remedy.
Cres. A woful Cressid 'mongst the merry
  Greeks !
When shall we see again ?
Tro. Hear me, my love : be thou but true
  of heart,—   60
Cres. I true ! how now ! what wicked
  deem is this ?
Tro. Nay, we must use expostulation
  kindly,
For it is parting from us :
I speak not ' be thou true,' as fearing thee,
For I will throw my glove to Death himself,
That there's no maculation in thy heart :
But ' be thou true,' say I, to fashion in
My sequent protestation ; be thou true,
And I will see thee.
Cres. O, you shall be exposed, my lord, to
  dangers   70
As infinite as imminent ! but I'll be true.
Tro. And I'll grow friend with danger.
  Wear this sleeve.
Cres. And you this glove. When shall I see
  you ?
Tro. I will corrupt the Grecian sentinels,
To give thee nightly visitation.
But yet be true.
Cres.   O heavens ! ' be true ' again !
Tro. Hear while I speak it, love :
The Grecian youths are full of quality ;
They're loving, well composed with gifts of
  nature,
Flowing and swelling o'er with arts and ex-
  ercise :   80
How novelty may move, and parts with per-
  son,
Alas, a kind of godly jealousy—
Which, I beseech you, call a virtuous sin—
Makes me afeard.
Cres.   O heavens ! you love me not.
Tro. Die I a villain, then !
In this I do not call your faith in question
So mainly as my merit : I cannot sing,
Nor heel the high lavolt, nor sweeten talk,
Nor play at subtle games ; fair virtues all,
To which the Grecians are most prompt and
  pregnant :   90

But I can tell that in each grace of these
There lurks a still and dumb-discoursive devil
That tempts most cunningly : but be not
    tempted.
  Cres. Do you think I will ?
  Tro. No.
But something may be done that we will not :
And sometimes we are devils to ourselves,
When we will tempt the frailty of our powers,
Presuming on their changeful potency.
  Æne. [*Within*] Nay, good my lord,—
  Tro.   Come, kiss ; and let us part.   100
  Par. [*Within*] Brother Troilus !
  Tro.   Good brother, come you hither ;
And bring Æneas and the Grecian with you.
  Cres. My lord, will you be true ?
  Tro. Who, I ? alas, it is my vice, my fault :
Whiles others fish with craft for great opinion,
I with great truth catch mere simplicity ;
Whilst some with cunning gild their copper
    crowns,
With truth and plainness I do wear mine bare.
Fear not my truth : the moral of my wit   109
Is ' plain and true ; ' there's all the reach of it.

Enter ÆNEAS, PARIS, ANTENOR, DEIPHOBUS,
    and DIOMEDES.

Welcome, Sir Diomed ! here is the lady
Which for Antenor we deliver you :
At the port, lord, I'll give her to thy hand,
And by the way possess thee what she is.
Entreat her fair ; and, by my soul, fair Greek,
If e'er thou stand at mercy of my sword,
Name Cressid, and thy life shall be as safe
As Priam is in Ilion.
  Dio.   Fair Lady Cressid,
So please you, save the thanks this prince ex-
    pects :
The lustre in your eye, heaven in your cheek,
Pleads your fair usage ; and to Diomed   121
You shall be mistress, and command him
    wholly.
  Tro. Grecian, thou dost not use me cour-
    teously,
To shame the zeal of my petition to thee
In praising her : I tell thee, lord of Greece,
She is as far high-soaring o'er thy praises
As thou unworthy to be call'd her servant.
I charge thee use her well, even for my
    charge ;
For, by the dreadful Pluto, if thou dost not,
Though the great bulk Achilles be thy guard,
I'll cut thy throat.   131
  Dio. O, be not moved, Prince Troilus :
Let me be privileged by my place and message,
To be a speaker free ; when I am hence,
I'll answer to my lust : and know you, lord,
I'll nothing do on charge : to her own worth
She shall be prized ; but that you say ' be't so,'
I'll speak it in my spirit and honor, ' no.'
  Tro. Come, to the port. I'll tell thee, Dio-
    med,
This brave shall oft make thee to hide thy
    head.   139
Lady, give me your hand, and, as we walk,
To our own selves bend we our needful talk.
    [*Exeunt Troilus, Cressida, and Diomedes.*
                        [*Trumpet within.*
  Par. Hark ! Hector's trumpet.
  Æne.   How have we spent this morning !
The prince must think me tardy and remiss,
That sore to ride before him to the field.

  Par. 'Tis Troilus' fault : come, come, to
    field with him.
  Dei. Let us make ready straight.
  Æne.   Yea, with a bridegroom's fresh
    alacrity,
Let us address to tend on Hector's heels :
The glory of our Troy doth this day lie
On his fair worth and single chivalry.   150
                        [*Exeunt.*

SCENE V. *The Grecian camp. Lists set out.*

Enter AJAX, *armed ;* AGAMEMNON, ACHIL-
LES, PATROCLUS, MENELAUS, ULYSSES, NES-
TOR, *and others.*

  Agam. Here art thou in appointment fresh
    and fair,
Anticipating time with starting courage.
Give with thy trumpet a loud note to Troy,
Thou dreadful Ajax ; that the appalled air
May pierce the head of the great combatant
And hale him hither.
  Ajax.   Thou, trumpet, there's my purse.
Now crack thy lungs, and split thy brazen
    pipe :
Blow, villain, till thy sphered bias cheek
Outswell the colic of puff'd Aquilon :
Come, stretch thy chest, and let thy eyes spout
    blood ;   10
Thou blow'st for Hector. [*Trumpet sounds.*
  Ulyss. No trumpet answers.
  Achil.   'Tis but early days.
  Agam. Is not yond Diomed, with Calchas'
    daughter ?
  Ulyss. 'Tis he, I ken the manner of his
    gait ;
He rises on the toe : that spirit of his
In aspiration lifts him from the earth.

    Enter DIOMEDES, *with* CRESSIDA.

  Agam. Is this the Lady Cressid ?
  Dio.   Even she.
  Agam. Most dearly welcome to the Greeks,
    sweet lady.
  Nest. Our general doth salute you with a
    kiss.
  Ulyss. Yet is the kindness but particular ;
'Twere better she were kiss'd in general.   21
  Nest. And very courtly counsel : I'll begin.
So much for Nestor.
  Achil. I'll take what winter from your lips,
    fair lady :
Achilles bids you welcome.
  Men. I had good argument for kissing
    once.
  Patr. But that's no argument for kissing
    now ;
For this popp'd Paris in his hardiment,
And parted thus you and your argument.
  Ulyss. O deadly gall, and theme of all our
    scorns !   30
For which we lose our heads to gild his horns.
  Patr. The first was Menelaus' kiss ; this,
    mine :
Patroclus kisses you.
  Men.   O, this is trim !
  Patr. Paris and I kiss evermore for him.
  Men. I'll have my kiss, sir. Lady, by your
    leave.
  Cres. In kissing, do you render or receive ?
  Patr. Both take and give.
  Cres.   I'll make my match to live,
The kiss you take is better than you give ;
Therefore no kiss.

Men. I'll give you boot, I'll give you three
 for one. 40
Cres. You're an odd man ; give even or
 give none.
Men. An odd man, lady ! every man is
 odd.
Cres. No, Paris is not ; for you know 'tis
 true,
That you are odd, and he is even with you.
Men. You fillip me o' the head.
Cres.   No, I'll be sworn.
Ulyss. It were no match, your nail against
 his horn.
May I, sweet lady, beg a kiss of you ?
Cres. You may.
Ulyss.   I do desire it.
Cres.   Why, beg, then.
Ulyss. Why then for Venus' sake, give me
 a kiss,
When Helen is a maid again, and his. 50
Cres. I am your debtor, claim it when 'tis
 due.
Ulyss. Never's my day, and then a kiss of
 you.
Dio. Lady, a word : I'll bring you to your
 father.   [*Exit with Cressida.*
Nest. A woman of quick sense.
Ulyss.   Fie, fie upon her !
There's language in her eye, her cheek, her lip,
Nay, her foot speaks ; her wanton spirits look
 out
At every joint and motive of her body.
O, these encounterers, so glib of tongue,
That give accosting welcome ere it comes,
And wide unclasp the tables of their thoughts
To every ticklish reader ! set them down 61
For sluttish spoils of opportunity
And daughters of the game. [*Trumpet within.*
All. The Trojans' trumpet.
Agam.   Yonder comes the troop.

Enter HECTOR, *armed ;* ÆNEAS, TROILUS, *and
other* Trojans, *with* Attendants.

Æne. Hail, all you state of Greece ! what
 shall be done
To him that victory commands ? or do you
 purpose
A victor shall be known ? will you the knights
Shall to the edge of all extremity
Pursue each other, or shall be divided
By any voice or order of the field ? 70
Hector bade ask.
Agam. Which way would Hector have it ?
Æne. He cares not ; he'll obey conditions.
Achil. 'Tis done like Hector ; but securely
 done,
A little proudly, and great deal misprizing
The knight opposed.
Æne.   If not Achilles, sir,
What is your name ?
Achil.   If not Achilles, nothing.
Æne. Therefore Achilles : but, whate'er,
 know this :
In the extremity of great and little,
Valor and pride excel themselves in Hector ;
The one almost as infinite as all, 80
The other blank as nothing. Weigh him well,
And that which looks like pride is courtesy.
This Ajax is half made of Hector's blood :
In love whereof, half Hector stays at home ;
Half heart, half hand, half Hector comes to
 seek

This blended knight, half Trojan and half
 Greek.
Achil. A maiden battle, then ? O, I per-
 ceive you.

Re-enter DIOMEDES.

Agam. Here is Sir Diomed. Go, gentle
 knight,
Stand by our Ajax : as you and Lord Æneas
Consent upon the order of their fight, 90
So be it ; either to the uttermost,
Or else a breath : the combatants being kin
Half stints their strife before their strokes be-
 gin. [*Ajax and Hector enter the lists.*
Ulyss. They are opposed already.
Agam. What Trojan is that same that
 looks so heavy ?
Ulyss. The youngest son of Priam, a true
 knight,
Not yet mature, yet matchless, firm of word,
Speaking in deeds and deedless in his tongue ;
Not soon provoked nor being provoked soon
 calm'd :
His heart and hand both open and both free ;
For what he has he gives, what thinks he
 shows ; 101
Yet gives he not till judgment guide his
 bounty,
Nor dignifies an impure thought with breath ;
Manly as Hector, but more dangerous ;
For Hector in his blaze of wrath subscribes
To tender objects, but he in heat of action
Is more vindicative than jealous love :
They call him Troilus, and on him erect
A second hope, as fairly built as Hector.
Thus says Æneas ; one that knows the youth
Even to his inches, and with private soul 111
Did in great Ilion thus translate him to me.
   [*Alarum. Hector and Ajax fight.*
Agam. They are in action.
Nest. Now, Ajax, hold thine own !
Tro.   Hector, thou sleep'st ;
Awake thee !
Agam. His blows are well disposed : there,
 Ajax !
Dio. You must no more. [*Trumpets cease.*
Æne. Princes, enough, so please you.
Ajax. I am not warm yet ; let us fight
 again.
Dio. As Hector pleases.
Hect.   Why, then will I no more :
Thou art, great lord, my father's sister's son,
A cousin-german to great Priam's seed ; 121
The obligation of our blood forbids
A gory emulation 'twixt us twain :
Were thy commixtion Greek and Trojan so
That thou couldst say ' This hand is Grecian
 all,
And this is Trojan ; the sinews of this leg
All Greek, and this all Troy ; my mother's
 blood
Runs on the dexter cheek, and this sinister
Bounds in my father's ; ' by Jove multipotent,
Thou shouldst not bear from me a Greekish
 member 130
Wherein my sword had not impressure made
Of our rank feud : but the just gods gainsay
That any drop thou borrow'dst from thy
 mother,
My sacred aunt, should by my mortal sword
Be drain'd ! Let me embrace thee, Ajax :
By him that thunders, thou hast lusty arms ;

Hector would have them fall upon him thus :
Cousin, all honor to thee !
  Ajax.   I thank thee, Hector :
Thou art too gentle and too free a man :
I came to kill thee, cousin, and bear hence 140
A great addition earned in thy death.
  Hect. Not Neoptolemus so mirable,
On whose bright crest Fame with her loud'st
  Oyes
Cries ' This is he,' could promise to himself
A thought of added honor torn from Hector.
  Æne. There is expectance here from both
  the sides,
What further you will do.
  Hect.   We'll answer it ;
The issue is embracement : Ajax, farewell.
  Ajax. If I might in entreaties find suc-
  cess—
As seld I have the chance—I would desire 150
My famous cousin to our Grecian tents.
  Dio. 'Tis Agamemnon's wish, and great
  Achilles
Doth long to see unarm'd the valiant Hector.
  Hect. Æneas, call my brother Troilus to
  me,
And signify this loving interview
To the expecters of our Trojan part ;
Desire them home. Give me thy hand, my
  cousin ;
I will go eat with thee and see your knights.
  Ajax. Great Agamemnon comes to meet
  us here.
  Hect. The worthiest of them tell me name
  by name ;   160
But for Achilles, mine own searching eyes
Shall find him by his large and portly size.
  Agam. Worthy of arms ! as welcome as to
  one
That would be rid of such an enemy ;
But that's no welcome : understand more
  clear,
What's past and what's to come is strew'd
  with husks
And formless ruin of oblivion ;
But in this extant moment, faith and troth,
Strain'd purely from all hollow bias-drawing,
Bids thee, with most divine integrity,   170
From heart of very heart, great Hector, wel-
  come.
  Hect. I thank thee, most imperious Aga-
  memnon.
  Agam. [*To Troilus*] My well-famed lord
of Troy, no less to you.
  Men. Let me confirm my princely broth-
er's greeting :
You brace of warlike brothers, welcome
hither.
  Hect. Who must we answer?
  Æne.   The noble Menelaus.
  Hect. O, you, my lord ? by Mars his
gauntlet, thanks !
Mock not, that I affect the untraded oath ;
Your quondam wife swears still by Venus'
glove :
She's well, but bade me not commend her to
you.   180
  Men. Name her not now, sir ; she's a
deadly theme.
  Hect. O, pardon ; I offend.
  Nest. I have, thou gallant Trojan, seen
thee oft
Laboring for destiny make cruel way

Through ranks of Greekish youth, and I have
  seen thee,
As hot as Perseus, spur thy Phrygian steed,
Despising many forfeits and subduements,
When thou hast hung thy advanced sword i'
  the air,
Not letting it decline on the declined,
That I have said to some my standers by 190
' Lo, Jupiter is yonder, dealing life ! '
And I have seen thee pause and take thy
  breath,
When that a ring of Greeks have hemm'd thee
  in,
Like an Olympian wrestling : this have I seen ;
But this thy countenance, still lock'd in steel,
I never saw till now. I knew thy grandsire,
And once fought with him : he was a soldier
  good ;
But, by great Mars, the captain of us all,
Never like thee. Let an old man embrace
  thee ;
And, worthy warrior, welcome to our tents.
  Æne. 'Tis the old Nestor.   201
  Hect. Let me enbrace thee, good old
chronicle,
That hast so long walk'd hand in hand with
  time :
Most reverend Nestor, I am glad to clasp thee.
  Nest. I would my arms could match thee
  in contention,
As they contend with thee in courtesy.
  Hect. I would they could.
  Nest. Ha !
By this white beard, I'ld fight with thee to-
  morrow.
Well, welcome, welcome !—I have seen the
  time.   210
  Ulyss. I wonder now how yonder city
  stands
When we have here her base and pillar by us.
  Hect. I know your favor, Lord Ulysses,
  well.
Ah, sir, there's many a Greek and Trojan
  dead,
Since first I saw yourself and Diomed
In Ilion, on your Greekish embassy.
  Ulyss. Sir, I foretold you then what would
  ensue :
My prophecy is but half his journey yet ;
For yonder walls, that pertly front your town,
Yond towers, whose wanton tops do buss the
  clouds,   220
Must kiss their own feet.
  Hect.   I must not believe you :
There they stand yet, and modestly I think,
The fall of every Phrygian stone will cost
A drop of Grecian blood : the end crowns all,
And that old common arbitrator, Time,
Will one day end it.
  Ulyss.   So to him we leave it.
Most gentle and most valiant Hector, wel-
  come :
After the general, I beseech you next
To feast with me and see me at my tent.
  Achil. I shall forestall thee, Lord Ulysses,
  thou !   230
Now, Hector, I have fed mine eyes on thee ;
I have with exact view perused thee, Hector,
And quoted joint by joint.
  Hect.   Is this Achilles ?
  Achil. I am Achilles.
  Hect. Stand fair, I pray thee : let me look
  on thee.

Achil. Behold thy fill.

Hect. Nay, I have done already.

Achil. Thou art too brief : I will the second time,
As I would buy thee, view thee limb by limb.

Hect. O, like a book of sport thou'lt read
me o'er ; 240
But there's more in me than thou understand'st.
Why dost thou so oppress me with thine eye ?

Achil. Tell me, you heavens, in which part
of his body
Shall I destroy him ? whether there, or there,
or there ?
That I may give the local wound a name
And make distinct the very breach whereout
Hector's great spirit flew : answer me,
heavens !

Hect. It would discredit the blest gods,
proud man,
To answer such a question: stand again :
Think'st thou to catch my life so pleasantly
As to prenominate in nice conjecture 250
Where thou wilt hit me dead ?

Achil. I tell thee, yea.

Hect. Wert thou an oracle to tell me so,
I'ld not believe thee. Henceforth guard thee
well ;
For I'll not kill thee there, nor there, nor
there ;
But, by the forge that stithied Mars his helm,
I'll kill thee every where, yea, o'er and o'er.
You wisest Grecians, pardon me this brag ;
His insolence draws folly from my lips ;
But I'll endeavor deeds to match these words,
Or may I never—

Ajax. Do not chafe thee, cousin : 260
And you, Achilles, let these threats alone,
Till accident or purpose bring you to't :
You may have every day enough of Hector,
If you have stomach ; the general state, I fear,
Can scarce entreat you to be odd with him.

Hect. I pray you, let us see you in the
field :
We have had pelting wars, since you refused
The Grecians' cause.

Achil. Dost thou entreat me, Hector ?
To-morrow do I meet thee, fell as death ;
To-night all friends.

Hect. Thy hand upon that match. 270

Agam. First, all you peers of Greece, go
to my tent ;
There in the full convive we : afterwards,
As Hector's leisure and your bounties shall
Concur together, severally entreat him.
Beat loud the tabourines, let the trumpets
blow,
That this great soldier may his welcome know.
[*Exeunt all except Troilus and Ulysses.*

Tro. My Lord Ulysses, tell me, I beseech
you,
In what place of the field doth Calchas keep ?

Ulyss. At Menelaus' tent, most princely
Troilus : 279
There Diomed doth feast with him to-night ;
Who neither looks upon the heaven nor earth,
But gives all gaze and bent of amorous view
On the fair Cressid.

Tro. Shall I, sweet lord, be bound to you
so much,
After we part from Agamemnon's tent,
To bring me thither ?

Ulyss. You shall command me, sir.

As gentle tell me, of what honor was
This Cressida in Troy ? Had she no lover
there
That wails her absence ?

Tro. O, sir, to such as boasting show their
scars 290
A mock is due. Will you walk on, my lord ?
She was beloved, she loved ; she is, and
doth :
But still sweet love is food for fortune's tooth.
[*Exeunt.*

ACT V.

SCENE I. *The Grecian camp. Before
Achilles' tent.*

Enter ACHILLES *and* PATROCLUS.

Achil. I'll heat his blood with Greekish
wine to-night,
Which with my scimitar I'll cool to-morrow.
Patroclus, let us feast him to the height.

Patr. Here comes Thersites.

Enter THERSITES.

Achil. How now, thou core of envy !
Thou crusty batch of nature, what's the news ?

Ther. Why, thou picture of what thou
seemest, and idol of idiot worshippers, here's
a letter for thee.

Achil. From whence, fragment ?

Ther. Why, thou full dish of fool, from
Troy. 10

Patr. Who keeps the tent now ?

Ther. The surgeon's box, or the patient's
wound.

Patr. Well said, adversity ! and what need
these tricks ?

Ther. Prithee, be silent, boy ; I profit not
by thy talk : thou art thought to be Achilles'
male varlet.

Patr. Male varlet, you rogue ! what's that ?

Ther. Why, his masculine whore. Now,
the rotten diseases of the south, the guts-griping, ruptures, catarrhs, loads o' gravel i' the
back, lethargies, cold palsies, raw eyes, dirt-
rotten livers, wheezing lungs, bladders full of
imposthume, sciaticas, limekilns i' the palm,
incurable bone-ache, and the rivelled fee-simple of the tetter, take and take again such preposterous discoveries !

Patr. Why thou damnable box of envy,
thou, what meanest thou to curse thus ? 30

Ther. Do I curse thee ?

Patr. Why, no, you ruinous butt, you
whoreson indistinguishable cur, no.

Ther. No ! why art thou then exasperate,
thou idle immaterial skein of sleave-silk, thou
green sarcenet flap for a sore eye, thou tas-
sel of a prodigal's purse, thou ? Ah, how the
poor world is pestered with such waterflies,
diminutives of nature !

Patr. Out, gall ! 40

Ther. Finch-egg !

Achil. My sweet Patroclus, I am thwarted
quite
From my great purpose in to-morrow's battle.
Here is a letter from Queen Hecuba,
A token from her daughter, my fair love,
Both taxing me and gaging me to keep
An oath that I have sworn. I will not break
it :

Fall Greeks ; fail fame ; honor or go or stay ;
My major vow lies here, this I'll obey.
Come, come, Thersites, help to trim my tent :
This night in banqueting must all be spent. 51
Away, Patroclus !

            [Exeunt Achilles and Patroclus.

Ther. With too much blood and too little
brain, these two may run mad ; but, if with
too much brain and too little blood they do,
I'll be a curer of madmen. Here's Agamemnon, an honest fellow enough and one that
loves quails ; but he has not so much brain
as earwax : and the goodly transformation of
Jupiter there, his brother, the bull,—the primi-
tive statue, and oblique memorial of cuckolds ; a thrifty shoeing-horn in a chain, hanging at his brother's leg,—to what form but
that he is, should wit larded with malice and
malice forced with wit turn him to ? To an
ass, were nothing ; he is both ass and ox : to
an ox, were nothing ; he is both ox and ass.
To be a dog, a mule, a cat, a fitchew, a toad,
a lizard, an owl, a puttock, or a herring without a roe, I would not care ; but to be Menelaus, I would conspire against destiny. Ask
me not what I would be, if I were not Thersites ; for I care not to be the louse of a lazar,
so I were not Menelaus ! Hey-day ! spirits and
fires !

Enter Hector, Troilus, Ajax, Agamemnon,
  Ulysses, Nestor, Menelaus, *and* Diomedes, *with lights.*

Agam. We go wrong, we go wrong.
Ajax.   No, yonder 'tis ;
There, where we see the lights.
Hect.   I trouble you.
Ajax. No, not a whit.
Ulyss.   Here comes himself to guide you.

        Re-enter Achilles.

Achil. Welcome, brave Hector ; welcome,
  princes all.
Agam. So now, fair prince of Troy, I bid
  good night.
Ajax commands the guard to tend on you.
Hect. Thanks and good night to the
  Greeks' general.   80
Men. Good night, my lord.
Hect.   Good night, sweet lord Menelaus.
Ther. Sweet draught : ' sweet ' quoth 'a !
sweet sink, sweet sewer.
Achil. Good night and welcome, both at
  once, to those
That go or tarry.
Agam.   Good night.

      [Exeunt Agamemnon and Menelaus.

Achil. Old Nestor tarries ; and you too,
  Diomed,
Keep Hector company an hour or two.
Dio. I cannot, lord ; I have important
  business,
The tide whereof is now. Good night, great
  Hector.   90
Hect. Give me your hand.
Ulyss. [*Aside to Troilus*] Follow his
  torch ; he goes to Calchas' tent :
I'll keep you company.
Tro.   Sweet sir, you honor me.
Hect. And so, good night.

        [Exit Diomedes ; Ulysses and Troilus
                    following.
Achil.   Come, come, enter my tent.

    [Exeunt Achilles, Hector, Ajax, and Nestor.

Ther. That same Diomed's a false-hearted
rogue, a most unjust knave ; I will no more
trust him when he leers than I will a serpent
when he hisses : he will spend his mouth, and
promise, like Brabbler the hound : but when
he performs, astronomers foretell it ; it is prodigious, there will come some change ; the sun
borrows of the moon, when Diomed keeps his
word. I will rather leave to see Hector, than
not to dog him : they say he keeps a Trojan
drab, and uses the traitor Calchas' tent : I'll
after. Nothing but lechery ! all incontinent
varlets !   *[Exit.*

Scene II.   *The same. Before Calchas' tent.*

           Enter Diomedes.

Dio. What, are you up here, ho ? speak.
Cal. [*Within*] Who calls ?
Dio. Diomed. Calchas, I think. Where's
  your daughter ?
Cal. [*Within*] She comes to you.

Enter Troilus *and* Ulysses, *at a distance ;*
      after them, Thersites.

Ulyss. Stand where the torch may not discover us.

           Enter Cressida.

Tro. Cressid comes forth to him.
Dio.   How now, my charge !
Cres. Now, my sweet guardian ! Hark, a
  word with you.   *[Whispers.*
Tro. Yea, so familiar !
Ulyss. She will sing any man at first sight.
Ther. And any man may sing her, if he can
take her cliff ; she's noted.   11
Dio. Will you remember ?
Cres. Remember ! yes.
Dio. Nay, but do, then ;
And let your mind be coupled with your words.
Tro. What should she remember ?
Ulyss. List.
Cres. Sweet honey Greek, tempt me no
  more to folly.
Ther. Roguery !
Dio. Nay, then,—   20
Cres. I'll tell you what,—
Dio. Foh, foh ! come, tell a pin : you are
  forsworn.
Cres. In faith, I cannot : what would you
  have me do ?
Ther. A juggling trick,—to be secretly
  open.
Dio. What did you swear you would be-
  stow on me ?
Cres. I prithee, do not hold me to mine
  oath ;
Bid me do any thing but that, sweet Greek.
Dio. Good night.
Tro. Hold, patience !
Ulyss. How now, Trojan !   30
Cres. Diomed,—
Dio. No, no, good night : I'll be your fool
  no more.
Tro. Thy better must.
Cres. Hark, one word in your ear.
Tro. O plague and madness !
Ulyss. You are moved, prince ; let us de-
  part, I pray you,
Lest your displeasure should enlarge itself
To wrathful terms : this place is dangerous ;
The time right deadly ; I beseech you, go.

Tro. Behold, I pray you !   39
Ulyss.   Nay, good my lord, go off :
You flow to great distraction ; come, my lord.
Tro. I pray thee, stay.
Ulyss.   You have not patience ; come.
Tro. I pray you, stay ; by hell and all hell's
     torments,
I will not speak a word !
Dio.   And so, good night.
Cres. Nay, but you part in anger.
Tro.   Doth that grieve thee ?
O wither'd truth !
Ulyss.   Why, how now, lord !
Tro.   By Jove,
I will be patient.
Cres. Guardian !—why, Greek !
Dio. Foh, foh ! adieu ; you palter.
Cres. In faith, I do not : come hither once
     again.
Ulyss. You shake, my lord, at something :
     will you go ?   50
You will break out.
Tro.   She strokes his cheek !
Ulyss.   Come, come.
Tro. Nay, stay ; by Jove, I will not speak
     a word :
There is between my will and all offences
A guard of patience : stay a little while.
Ther. How the devil Luxury, with his fat
rump and potato-finger, tickles these together !
Fry, lechery, fry !
Dio. But will you, then ?
Cres. In faith, I will, la ; never trust me
     else.
Dio. Give me some token for the surety of
     it.   60
Cres. I'll fetch you one.   [*Exit.*
Ulyss. You have sworn patience.
Tro.   Fear me not, sweet lord ;
I will not be myself, nor have cognition
Of what I feel : I am all patience.

          Re-enter CRESSIDA.

Ther. Now the pledge ; now, now, now !
Cres. Here, Diomed, keep this sleeve.
Tro. O beauty ! where is thy faith ?
Ulyss.   My lord,—
Tro. I will be patient ; outwardly I will.
Cres. You look upon that sleeve ; behold it
     well.
He loved me—O false wench !—Give't me
     again.   70
Dio. Whose was't ?
Cres. It is no matter, now I have't again.
I will not meet with you to-morrow night :
I prithee, Diomed, visit me no more.
Ther. Now she sharpens : well said, whet-
     stone !
Dio. I shall have it.
Cres.   What, this ?
Dio.   Ay, that.
Cres. O, all you gods ! O pretty, pretty
     pledge !
Thy master now lies thinking in his bed
Of thee and me, and sighs, and takes my glove,
And gives memorial dainty kisses to it,   80
As I kiss thee. Nay, do not snatch it from me ;
He that takes that doth take my heart withal.
Dio. I had your heart before, this follows
     it.
Tro. I did swear patience.
Cres. You shall not have it, Diomed ; faith,
     you shall not ;

I'll give you something else.
Dio. I will have this : whose was it ?
Cres.   It is no matter.
Dio. Come, tell me whose it was.
Cres. 'Twas one's that loved me better
     than you will.
But, now you have it, take it.
Dio.   Whose was it ?   90
Cres. By all Diana's waiting-women yond,
And by herself, I will not tell you whose.
Dio. To-morrow will I wear it on my helm,
And grieve his spirit that dares not challenge
     it.
Tro. Wert thou the devil, and worest it on
     thy horn,
It should be challenged.
Cres. Well, well, 'tis done, 'tis past : and
     yet it is not ;
I will not keep my word.
Dio.   Why, then, farewell ;
Thou never shalt mock Diomed again.
Cres. You shall not go : one cannot speak
     a word,   100
But it straight starts you.
Dio.   I do not like this fooling.
Ther. Nor I, by Pluto : but that that likes
not you pleases me best.
Dio. What, shall I come ? the hour ?
Cres. Ay, come :—O Jove !—do come :—I
     shall be plagued.
Dio. Farewell till then.
Cres.   Good night : I prithee, come.
                              [*Exit Diomedes.*
Troilus, farewell ! one eye yet looks on thee ;
But with my heart the other eye doth see.
Ah, poor our sex ! this fault in us I find,
The error of our eye directs our mind :   110
What error leads must err ; O, then conclude
Minds sway'd by eyes are full of turpitude.
                                        [*Exit.*
Ther. A proof of strength she could not
     publish more,
Unless she said ' My mind is now turn'd
     whore.'
Ulyss. All's done, my lord.
Tro.   It is.
Ulyss.   Why stay we, then ?
Tro. To make a recordation to my soul
Of every syllable that here was spoke.
But if I tell how these two did co-act,
Shall I not lie in publishing a truth ?
Sith yet there is a credence in my heart,   120
An esperance so obstinately strong,
That doth invert the attest of eyes and ears,
As if those organs had deceptious functions,
Created only to calumniate.
Was Cressid here ?
Ulyss.   I cannot conjure, Trojan.
Tro. She was not, sure.
Ulyss.   Most sure she was.
Tro. Why, my negation hath no taste of
     madness.
Ulyss. Nor mine, my lord : Cressid was
     here but now.
Tro. Let it not be believed for woman-
     hood !
Think, we had mothers ; do not give advantage
To stubborn critics, apt, without a theme, 131
For depravation, to square the general sex
By Cressid's rule : rather think this not Cres-
     sid.
Ulyss. What hath she done, prince, that
     can soil our mothers ?

Tro. Nothing at all, unless that this were
she.

Ther. Will he swagger himself out on 's
own eyes ?

Tro. This she ? no, this is Diomed's Cres-
sida :
If beauty have a soul, this is not she ;
If souls guide vows, if vows be sanctimonies,
If sanctimony be the gods' delight,   140
If there be rule in unity itself,
This is not she. O madness of discourse,
That cause sets up with and against itself !
Bi-fold authority ! where reason can revolt
Without perdition, and loss assume all reason
Without revolt : this is, and is not, Cressid.
Within my soul there doth conduce a fight
Of this strange nature that a thing inseparate
Divides more wider than the sky and earth,
And yet the spacious breadth of this division
Admits no orifex for a point as subtle   151
As Ariachne's broken woof to enter.
Instance, O instance ! strong as Pluto's gates ;
Cressid is mine, tied with the bonds of heaven :
Instance, O instance ! strong as heaven itself ;
The bonds of heaven are slipp'd, dissolved, and
loosed ;
And with another knot, five-finger-tied,
The fractions of her faith, orts of her love,
The fragments, scraps, the bits and greasy
relics   159
Of her o'er-eaten faith, are bound to Diomed.
Ulyss. May worthy Troilus be half attach'd
With that which here his passion doth ex-
press ?
Tro. Ay, Greek ; and that shall be divulged
well
In characters as red as Mars his heart
Inflamed with Venus : never did young man
fancy
With so eternal and so fix'd a soul.
Hark, Greek : as much as I do Cressid love,
So much by weight hate I her Diomed :
That sleeve is mine that he'll bear on his
helm ;
Were it a casque composed by Vulcan's skill,
My sword should bite it : not the dreadful
spout   171
Which shipmen do the hurricano call,
Constringed in mass by the almighty sun,
Shall dizzy with more clamor Neptune's ear
In his descent than shall my prompted sword
Falling on Diomed.
Ther. He'll tickle it for his concupy.
Tro. O Cressid ! O false Cressid ! false,
false, false !
Let all untruths stand by thy stained name,
And they'll seem glorious.
Ulyss.   O, contain yourself ;
Your passion draws ears hither.   181

Enter ÆNEAS.

Æne. I have been seeking you this hour,
my lord :
Hector, by this, is arming him in Troy ;
Ajax, your guard, stays to conduct you home.
Tro. Have with you, prince. My courteous
lord, adieu.
Farewell, revolted fair ! and, Diomed,
Stand fast, and wear a castle on thy head !
Ulyss. I'll bring you to the gates.
Tro. Accept distracted thanks.
        [*Exeunt Troilus, Æneas, and Ulysses.*
Ther. Would I could meet that rogue Dio-

med ! I would croak like a raven ; I would
bode, I would bode. Patroclus will give me any
thing for the intelligence of this whore : the
parrot will not do more for an almond than
he for a commodious drab. Lechery, lechery ;
still, wars and lechery ; nothing else holds fashion : a burning devil take them !   [*Exit.*

SCENE III.   *Troy.   Before Priam's palace.*

Enter HECTOR *and* ANDROMACHE.

And. When was my lord so much ungently
temper'd,
To stop his ears against admonishment ?
Unarm, unarm, and do not fight to-day.
Hect. You train me to offend you ; get you
in :
By all the everlasting gods, I'll go !
And. My dreams will, sure, prove ominous
to the day.
Hect. No more, I say.

Enter CASSANDRA.

Cas.   Where is my brother Hector ?
And. Here, sister ; arm'd, and bloody in
intent.
Consort with me in loud and dear petition,   9
Pursue we him on knees ; for I have dream'd
Of bloody turbulence, and this whole night
Hath nothing been but shapes and forms of
slaughter.
Cas. O, 'tis true.
Hect.   Ho ! bid my trumpet sound !
Cas. No notes of sally, for the heavens,
sweet brother.
Hect. Be gone, I say : the gods have heard
me swear.
Cas. The gods are deaf to hot and peevish
vows :
They are polluted offerings, more abhorr'd
Than spotted livers in the sacrifice.
And. O, be persuaded ! do not count it
holy
To hurt by being just : it is as lawful,   20
For we would give much, to use violent thefts,
And rob in the behalf of charity.
Cas. It is the purpose that makes strong
the vow ;
But vows to every purpose must not hold :
Unarm, sweet Hector.
Hect.   Hold you still, I say ;
Mine honor keeps the weather of my fate :
Life every man holds dear ; but the brave man
Holds honor far more precious-dear than life.

Enter TROILUS.

How now, young man ! mean'st thou to fight
to-day ?
And. Cassandra, call my father to per-
suade.   [*Exit Cassandra.* 30
Hect. No, faith, young Troilus ; doff thy
harness, youth ;
I am to-day i' the vein of chivalry :
Let grow thy sinews till their knots be strong,
And tempt not yet the brushes of the war.
Unarm thee, go, and doubt thou not, brave
boy,
I'll stand to-day for thee and me and Troy.
Tro. Brother, you have a vice of mercy in
you,
Which better fits a lion than a man.
Hect. What vice is that, good Troilus ?
chide me for it.

Tro. When many times the captive Grecian
  falls,   40
Even in the fan and wind of your fair sword,
You bid them rise, and live.
Hect.   O, 'tis fair play.
Tro.   Fool's play, by heaven, Hector.
Hect. How now ! how now !
Tro.   For the love of all the gods,
Let's leave the hermit pity with our mothers,
And when we have our armors buckled on,
The venom'd vengeance ride upon our swords,
Spur them to ruthful work, rein them from
  ruth.
Hect. Fie, savage, fie !
Tro.   Hector, then 'tis wars.
Hect. Troilus, I would not have you fight
  to-day.   50
Tro. Who should withhold me ?
Not fate, obedience, nor the hand of Mars
Beckoning with fiery truncheon my retire ;
Not Priamus and Hecuba on knees,
Their eyes o'ergalled with recourse of tears ;
Nor you, my brother, with your true sword
  drawn,
Opposed to hinder me, should stop my way,
But by my ruin.

Re-enter CASSANDRA, *with* PRIAM.

Cas. Lay hold upon him, Priam, hold him
  fast !
He is thy crutch ; now if thou lose thy stay,
Thou on him leaning, and all Troy on thee, 61
Fall all together.
Pri.   Come, Hector, come, go back :
Thy wife hath dream'd ; thy mother hath had
  visions ;
Cassandra doth foresee ; and I myself
Am like a prophet suddenly enrapt
To tell thee that this day is ominous :
Therefore, come back.
Hect.   Æneas is a-field ;
And I do stand engaged to many Greeks,
Even in the faith of valor, to appear
This morning to them.
Pri.   Ay, but thou shalt not go.
Hect. I must not break my faith.   71
You know me dutiful ; therefore, dear sir,
Let me not shame respect ; but give me leave
To take that course by your consent and voice,
Which you do here forbid me, royal Priam.
Cas. O Priam, yield not to him !
And.   Do not, dear father.
Hect. Andromache, I am offended with
  you :
Upon the love you bear me, get you in.
            [*Exit Andromache.*
Tro. This foolish, dreaming, superstitious
  girl
Makes all these bodements.
Cas.   O, farewell, dear Hector !
Look, how thou diest ! look, how thy eye turns
  pale !   81
Look, how thy wounds do bleed at many
  vents !
Hark, how Troy roars ! how Hecuba cries out !
How poor Andromache shrills her dolors
  forth !
Behold, distraction, frenzy and amazement,
Like witless antics, one another meet,
And all cry, Hector ! Hector's dead ! O Hec-
  tor !
Tro. Away ! away !

Cas. Farewell : yet, soft ! Hector, I take
  my leave :
Thou dost thyself and all our Troy deceive.
            [*Exit.*
Hect. You are amazed, my liege, at her ex-
  claim :   91
Go in and cheer the town : we'll forth and
  fight,
Do deeds worth praise and tell you them at
  night.
Pri. Farewell : the gods with safety stand
  about thee !
[*Exeunt severally Priam and Hector. Alarums.*
Tro. They are at it, hark ! Proud Diomed,
  believe,
I come to lose my arm, or win my sleeve.

Enter PANDARUS.

Pan. Do you hear, my lord ? do you hear ?
Tro. What now ?
Pan. Here's a letter come from yond poor
  girl.
Tro. Let me read.   100
Pan. A whoreson tisick, a whoreson rascally tisick so troubles me, and the foolish fortune of this girl ; and what one thing, what
another, that I shall leave you one o' these
days : and I have a rheum in mine eyes too,
and such an ache in my bones that, unless a
man were cursed, I cannot tell what to think
on 't. What says she there ?
Tro. Words, words, mere words, no matter
  from the heart :
The effect doth operate another way.   109
            [*Tearing the letter.*
Go, wind, to wind, there turn and change together.
My love with words and errors still she feeds ;
But edifies another with her deeds.
            [*Exeunt severally.*

SCENE IV. *Plains between Troy and the Grecian camp.*

Alarums : excursions. Enter THERSITES.

Ther. Now they are clapper-clawing one
another ; I'll go look on. That dissembling
abominable varlet, Diomed, has got that same
scurvy doting foolish young knave's sleeve of
Troy there in his helm : I would fain see them
meet ; that that same young Trojan ass, that
loves the whore there, might send that Greekish whore-masterly villain, with the sleeve,
back to the dissembling luxurious drab, of a
sleeveless errand. O' the t'other side, the policy of those crafty swearing rascals, that stale
old mouse-eaten dry cheese, Nestor, and that
same dog-fox, Ulysses, is not proved worthy
a blackberry : they set me up, in policy, that
mongrel cur, Ajax, against that dog of as bad
a kind, Achilles : and now is the cur Ajax
prouder than the cur Achilles, and will not
arm to-day ; whereupon the Grecians begin to
proclaim barbarism, and policy grows into
an ill opinion. Soft ! here comes sleeve, and
t'other.

Enter DIOMEDES, TROILUS *following.*

Tro. Fly not ; for shouldst thou take the
  river Styx,   20
I would swim after.
Dio.   Thou dost miscall retire :
I do not fly, but advantageous care

Withdrew me from the odds of multitude :
Have at thee !

Ther. Hold thy whore, Grecian !—now for
thy whore, Trojan !—now the sleeve, now the
sleeve !

    [*Exeunt Troilus and Diomedes, fighting.*

        Enter HECTOR.

Hect. What art thou, Greek ? art thou for
    Hector's match ?
Art thou of blood and honor ?

Ther. No, no, I am a rascal ; a scurvy rail-
ing knave : a very filthy rogue.   31

Hect. I do believe thee : live.   [*Exit.*

Ther. God-a-mercy, that thou wilt believe
me ; but a plague break thy neck for frighting
me ! What's become of the wenching rogues ?
I think they have swallowed one another : I
would laugh at that miracle : yet, in a sort,
lechery eats itself. I'll seek them.   [*Exit.*

    SCENE V. *Another part of the plains.*

    Enter DIOMEDES *and a* Servant.

Dio. Go, go, my servant, take thou Troilus'
    horse ;
Present the fair steed to my lady Cressid :
Fellow, commend my service to her beauty ;
Tell her I have chastised the amorous Trojan,
And am her knight by proof.

Serv.   I go, my lord. [*Exit.*

      Enter AGAMEMNON.

Agam. Renew, renew ! The fierce Poly-
    damas
Hath beat down Menon : bastard Margarelon
Hath Doreus prisoner,
And stands colossus-wise, waving his beam,
Upon the pashed corses of the kings   10
Epistrophus and Cedius : Polyxenes is slain,
Amphimachus and Thoas deadly hurt,
Patroclus ta'en or slain, and Palamedes
Sore hurt and bruised : the dreadful Sagittary
Appals our numbers : haste we, Diomed,
To reinforcement, or we perish all.

       Enter NESTOR.

Nest. Go, bear Patroclus' body to Achilles ;
And bid the snail-paced Ajax arm for shame.
There is a thousand Hectors in the field :
Now here he fights on Galathe his horse,   20
And there lacks work ; anon he's there afoot,
And there they fly or die, like scaled sculls
Before the belching whale ; then is he yonder,
And there the strawy Greeks, ripe for his edge,
Fall down before him, like the mower's swath :
Here, there, and every where, he leaves and
    takes,
Dexterity so obeying appetite
That what he will he does, and does so much
That proof is call'd impossibility.

       Enter ULYSSES.

Ulyss. O, courage, courage, princes ! great
    Achilles   30
Is arming, weeping, cursing, vowing venge-
    ance :
Patroclus' wounds have roused his drowsy
    blood,
Together with his mangled Myrmidons,
That noseless, handless, hack'd and chipp'd,
    come to him,
Crying on Hector. Ajax hath lost a friend
And foams at mouth, and he is arm'd and at it,

Roaring for Troilus, who hath done to-day
Mad and fantastic execution,
Engaging and redeeming of himself
With such a careless force and forceless care
As if that luck, in very spite of cunning,   41
Bade him win all.

        Enter AJAX.

Ajax. Troilus ! thou coward Troilus ! [*Exit.*
Dio.   Ay, there, there.
Nest. So, so, we draw together.

      Enter ACHILLES.

Achil.   Where is this Hector ?
Come, come, thou boy-queller, show thy face ;
Know what it is to meet Achilles angry :
Hector ! where's Hector ? I will none but
    Hector.   [*Exeunt.*

    SCENE VI. *Another part of the plains.*

        Enter AJAX.

Ajax. Troilus, thou coward Troilus, show
    thy head !

      Enter DIOMEDES.

Dio. Troilus, I say ! where's Troilus ?
Ajax.   What wouldst thou ?
Dio. I would correct him.
Ajax. Were I the general, thou shouldst
    have my office
Ere that correction. Troilus, I say ! what,
    Troilus !

        Enter TROILUS.

Tro. O traitor Diomed ! turn thy false
    face, thou traitor,
And pay thy life thou owest me for my horse !
Dio. Ha, art thou there ?
Ajax. I'll fight with him alone : stand,
    Diomed.   9
Dio. He is my prize ; I will not look upon.
Tro. Come, both you cogging Greeks ;
    have at you both !   [*Exeunt, fighting.*

      Enter HECTOR.

Hect. Yea, Troilus ? O, well fought, my
    youngest brother !

      Enter ACHILLES.

Achil. Now do I see thee, ha ! have at thee,
    Hector !
Hect. Pause, if thou wilt.
Achil. I do disdain thy courtesy, proud
    Trojan :
Be happy that my arms are out of use :
My rest and negligence befriends thee now,
But thou anon shalt hear of me again ;
Till when, go seek thy fortune.   [*Exit.*
Hect.   Fare thee well : 19
I would have been much more a fresher man,
Had I expected thee. How now, my brother !

      Re-enter TROILUS.

Tro. Ajax hath ta'en Æneas : shall it be ?
No, by the flame of yonder glorious heaven,
He shall not carry him : I'll be ta'en too,
Or bring him off : fate, hear me what I say !
I reck not though I end my life to-day. [*Exit.*

    Enter one in sumptuous armor.

Hect. Stand, stand, thou Greek ; thou art a
    goodly mark :
No ? wilt thou not ? I like thy armor well ;
I'll frush it and unlock the rivets all,

But I'll be master of it : wilt thou not, beast,
    abide ?   30
Why, then fly on, I'll hunt thee for thy hide.
                                       [*Exeunt.*

SCENE VII. *Another part of the plains.*

    Enter ACHILLES, *with* Myrmidons.

Achil. Come here about me, you my Myr-
    midons ;
Mark what I say. Attend me where I wheel :
Strike not a stroke, but keep yourselves in
    breath :
And when I have the bloody Hector found,
Empale him with your weapons round about ;
In fellest manner execute your aims.
Follow me, sirs, and my proceedings eye :
It is decreed Hector the great must die.
                                      [*Exeunt.*

    Enter MENELAUS *and* PARIS, *fighting : then*
              THERSITES.

Ther. The cuckold and the cuckold-maker
are at it. Now, bull ! now, dog ! 'Loo, Paris,
'loo ! now my double-henned sparrow ! 'loo,
Paris, 'loo ! The bull has the game : ware
horns, ho ! [*Exeunt Paris and Menelaus.*

      Enter MARGARELON.

Mar. Turn, slave, and fight.
Ther. What art thou ?
Mar. A bastard son of Priam's.
Ther. I am a bastard too ; I love bastards :
I am a bastard begot, bastard instructed, bastard in mind, bastard in valor, in every thing
illegitimate. One bear will not bite another,
and wherefore should one bastard ? Take heed,
the quarrel's most ominous to us : if the son
of a whore fight for a whore, he tempts judgment : farewell, bastard. [*Exit.*
Mar. The devil take thee, coward ! [*Exit.*

SCENE VIII. *Another part of the plains.*

      Enter HECTOR.

Hect. Most putrefied core, so fair without,
Thy goodly armor thus hath cost thy life.
Now is my day's work done ; I'll take good
    breath :
Rest, sword ; thou hast thy fill of blood and
    death.
    [*Puts off his helmet and hangs his shield
                      behind him.*

    Enter ACHILLES *and* Myrmidons.

Achil. Look, Hector, how the sun begins to
    set ;
How ugly night comes breathing at his heels :
Even with the vail and darking of the sun,
To close the day up, Hector's life is done.
Hect. I am unarm'd ; forego this vantage,
    Greek.
Achil. Strike, fellows, strike ; this is the
    man I seek. [*Hector falls.* 10
So, Ilion, fall thou next ! now, Troy, sink
    down !
Here lies thy heart, thy sinews, and thy bone.
On, Myrmidons, and cry you all amain,
' Achilles hath the mighty Hector slain.'
                    [*A retreat sounded.*
Hark ! a retire upon our Grecian part.
Myr. The Trojan trumpets sound the like,
    my lord.
Achil. The dragon wing of night o'er-
    spreads the earth,

And, stickler-like, the armies separates.
My half-supp'd sword, that frankly would have
    fed,
Pleased with this dainty bait, thus goes to bed.
                  [*Sheathes his sword.*
Come, tie his body to my horse's tail ;
Along the field I will the Trojan trail. [*Exeunt.*

SCENE IX. *Another part of the plains.*

    Enter AGAMEMNON, AJAX, MENELAUS, NES-
    TOR, DIOMEDES, *and others, marching.*
    Shouts within.

Agam. Hark ! hark ! what shout is that ?
Nest. Peace, drums !
[*Within*] Achilles ! Achilles ! Hector's slain !
    Achilles.
Dio. The bruit is, Hector's slain, and by
    Achilles.
Ajax. If it be so, yet bragless let it be ;
Great Hector was a man as good as he.
Agam. March patiently along : let one be
    sent
To pray Achilles see us at our tent.
If in his death the gods have us befriended, 9
Great Troy is ours, and our sharp wars are
    ended. [*Exeunt, marching.*

SCENE X. *Another part of the plains.*

    Enter ÆNEAS *and* Trojans.

Æne. Stand, ho ! yet are we masters of the
    field :
Never go home ; here starve we out the night.

      Enter TROILUS.

Tro. Hector is slain.
All.   Hector ! the gods forbid !
Tro. He's dead ; and at the murderer's
    horse's tail,
In beastly sort, dragg'd through the shameful
    field.
Frown on, you heavens, effect your rage with
    speed !
Sit, gods, upon your thrones, and smile at
    Troy !
I say, at once let your brief plagues be mercy,
And linger not our sure destructions on !
Æne. My lord, you do discomfort all the
    host. 10
Tro. You understand me not that tell me
    so :
I do not speak of flight, of fear, of death,
But dare all imminence that gods and men
Address their dangers in. Hector is gone :
Who shall tell Priam so, or Hecuba ?
Let him that will a screech-owl aye be call'd,
Go in to Troy, and say there, Hector's dead :
There is a word will Priam turn to stone ;
Make wells and Niobes of the maids and wives,
Cold statues of the youth, and, in a word, 20
Scare Troy out of itself. But, march away :
Hector is dead ; there is no more to say.
Stay yet. You vile abominable tents,
Thus proudly pight upon our Phrygian plains,
Let Titan rise as early as he dare,
I'll through and through you ! and, thou great-
    sized coward,
No space of earth shall sunder our two hates :
I'll haunt thee like a wicked conscience still,
That mouldeth goblins swift as frenzy's
    thoughts.
Strike a free march to Troy ! with comfort
    go :

Hope of revenge shall hide our inward woe. 31
[*Exeunt Æneas and Trojans.*

As TROILUS *is going out, enter, from the other
side,* PANDARUS.

Pan. But hear you, hear you!
Tro. Hence, broker-lackey! ignomy and
shame
Pursue thy life, and live aye with thy name!
[*Exit.*

Pan. A goodly medicine for my aching
bones! O world! world! world! thus is the
poor agent despised! O traitors and bawds,
how earnestly are you set a-work, and how ill
requited! why should our endeavor be so
loved and the performance so loathed? what
verse for it? what instance for it? Let me
see: 41

Full merrily the humble-bee doth sing,
Till he hath lost his honey and his sting;
And being once subdued in armed tail,
Sweet honey and sweet notes together fail.
Good traders in the flesh, set this in your
painted cloths.
As many as be here of pander's hall,
Your eyes, half out, weep out at Pandar's fall;
Or if you cannot weep, yet give some groans,
Though not for me, yet for your aching bones.
Brethren and sisters of the hold-door trade,
Some two months hence my will shall here be
made:
It should be now, but that my fear is this,
Some galled goose of Winchester would hiss:
Till then I'll sweat and seek about for eases,
And at that time bequeathe you my diseases.
[*Exit.*

OTHELLO.

(WRITTEN ABOUT 1604.)

INTRODUCTION.

Othello is the only play which appeared in quarto (in 1622) in the interval between Shakespeare's death and the publication of the first folio. We have no means, except by internal evidence, of ascertaining the date at which the play was written. Upon the strength of a supposed allusion to the armorial bearings of the new order of Baronets, instituted in 1611 (Act III., Sc. IV. L. 46–47), the play has been referred to a year not earlier than 1611 ; but the metrical tests confirm the impression produced by the general character and spirit of the tragedy, that it cannot belong to the same period as *The Tempest, Cymbeline,* and *The Winter's Tale.* It is evidently one of the group of tragedies of passion which includes *Macbeth* and *Lear.* The year 1604 has been accepted by several critics as a not improbable date for *Othello.* The original of the story is found in Cinthio's *Hecatomithi,* but it has been in a marvellous manner elevated and re-created by Shakespeare. Coleridge has justly said that the agonized doubt which lays hold of the Moor is not the jealousy of a man of naturally jealous temper, and he contrasts Othello with Leontes in *The Winter's Tale,* and Leonatus in *Cymbeline.* A mean watchfulness or prying suspicion is the last thing that Othello could be guilty of. He is of a free and noble nature, naturally trustful, with a kind of grand innocence, retaining some of his barbaric simpleness of soul in midst of the subtle and astute politicians of Venice. He is great in simple heroic action, but unversed in the complex affairs of life, and a stranger to the malignant deceits of the debased Italian character. Nothing is more chivalrous, more romantic, than the love of Othello and Desdemona. The beautiful Italian girl is fascinated by the real strength and grandeur, and the tender protectiveness of the Moor. He is charmed by the sweetness, the sympathy, the gentle disposition, the gracious womanliness of Desdemona. But neither quite rightly knows the other ; there is none of that perfect equality and perfect knowledge between them which unite so flawlessly Brutus and Portia. There is no character in Shakespeare's plays so full of serpentine power and serpentine poison as Iago. He is envious of Cassio, and suspects that the Moor may have wronged his honor ; but his malignancy is out of all proportion to even its alleged motives. Cassio, notwithstanding his moral weaknesses, is a chivalrous nature, possessed by enthusiastic admiration of his great general and the beautiful lady who is his wife. But Iago can see neither human virtue nor greatness. All things to him are common and unclean, and he is content that they should be so. He is not the sly, sneaking, and too manifest villain of some of the actors of his part. He is " honest Iago," and passes for a rough yet shrewd critic of life, who is himself frank and candid. To ensnare the nobly guileless Othello was, therefore, no impossible task. Shakespeare does not allow Iago to triumph ; his end is wretched as his life has been. And Othello, restored to love through such tragic calamity, dies once more reunited to his wife, and loyal, in spite of all his wrongs, to the city of his adoption. It is he who has sinned, and not she who was dearer to him than himself, and of his own wrongs and griefs he can make a sudden end.

DRAMATIS PERSONÆ.

DUKE OF VENICE.
BRABANTIO, a senator.
Other Senators.
GRATIANO, brother to Brabantio.
LODOVICO, kinsman to Brabantio.
OTHELLO, a noble Moor in the service of the Venetian state.
CASSIO, his lieutenant.
IAGO, his ancient.
RODERIGO, a Venetian gentleman.
MONTANO, Othello's predecessor in the government of Cyprus.

Clown, servant to Othello.

DESDEMONA, daughter to Brabantio and wife to Othello.
EMILIA, wife to Iago.
BIANCA, mistress to Cassio.

Sailor, Messenger, Herald, Officers, Gentlemen, Musicians, and Attendants.

SCENE : *Venice : a Sea-port in Cyprus.*

ACT I.

Scene I. *Venice. A street.*

Enter Roderigo *and* Iago.

Rod. Tush! never tell me; I take it much
    unkindly
That thou, Iago, who hast had my purse
As if the strings were thine, shouldst know of
    this.
Iago. 'Sblood, but you will not hear me:
If ever I did dream of such a matter,
Abhor me.
Rod. Thou told'st me thou didst hold him
    in thy hate.
Iago. Despise me, if I do not. Three great
    ones of the city,
In personal suit to make me his lieutenant,
Off-capp'd to him: and, by the faith of man,
I know my price, I am worth no worse a
    place   11
But he, as loving his own pride and purposes,
Evades them, with a bombast circumstance
Horribly stuff'd with epithets of war;
And, in conclusion,
Nonsuits my mediators; for, 'Certes,' says
    he,
'I have already chose my officer.'
And what was he?
Forsooth, a great arithmetician,
One Michael Cassio, a Florentine,   20
A fellow almost damn'd in a fair wife;
That never set a squadron in the field,
Nor the division of a battle knows
More than a spinster; unless the bookish
    theoric,
Wherein the toged consuls can propose
As masterly as he: mere prattle, without
    practice,
Is all his soldiership. But he, sir, had the
    election:
And I, of whom his eyes had seen the proof
At Rhodes, at Cyprus and on other grounds
Christian and heathen, must be be-lee'd and
    calm'd   30
By debitor and creditor: this counter-caster,
He, in good time, must his lieutenant be,
And I—God bless the mark!—his Moorship's
    ancient.
Rod. By heaven, I rather would have been
    his hangman.
Iago. Why, there's no remedy; 'tis the
    curse of service,
Preferment goes by letter and affection,
And not by old gradation, where each second
Stood heir to the first. Now, sir, be judge
    yourself,
Whether I in any just term am affined
To love the Moor.
Rod.   I would not follow him then. 40
Iago. O, sir, content you;
I follow him to serve my turn upon him:
We cannot all be masters, nor all masters
Cannot be truly follow'd. You shall mark
Many a duteous and knee-crooking knave,
That, doting on his own obsequious bondage,
Wears out his time, much like his master's ass,
For nought but provender, and when he's old,
    cashier'd:
Whip me such honest knaves. Others there are
Who, trimm'd in forms and visages of duty,
Keep yet their hearts attending on them-
    selves,   51
And, throwing but shows of service on their
    lords,
Do well thrive by them and when they have
    lined their coats
Do themselves homage: these fellows have
    some soul;
And such a one do I profess myself. For, sir,
It is as sure as you are Roderigo,
Were I the Moor, I would not be Iago:
In following him, I follow but myself;
Heaven is my judge, not I for love and duty,
But seeming so, for my peculiar end: 60
For when my outward action doth demon-
    strate
The native act and figure of my heart
In compliment extern, 'tis not long after
But I will wear my heart upon my sleeve
For daws to peck at: I am not what I am.
Rod. What a full fortune does the thick-
    lips owe,
If he can carry't thus!
Iago.   Call up her father,
Rouse him: make after him, poison his de-
    light,
Proclaim him in the streets; incense her kins-
    men,
And, though he in a fertile climate dwell, 70
Plague him with flies: though that his joy be
    joy,
Yet throw such changes of vexation on't,
As it may lose some color.
Rod. Here is her father's house; I'll call
    aloud.
Iago. Do, with like timorous accent and
    dire yell
As when, by night and negligence, the fire
Is spied in populous cities.
Rod. What, ho, Brabantio! Signior Bra-
    bantio, ho!
Iago. Awake! what, ho, Brabantio!
    thieves! thieves! thieves!
Look to your house, your daughter and your
    bags!   80
Thieves! thieves!

Brabantio *appears above, at a window.*

Bra. What is the reason of this terrible
    summons?
What is the matter there?
Rod. Signior, is all your family within?
Iago. Are your doors lock'd?
Bra.   Why, wherefore ask you this?
Iago. 'Zounds, sir, you're robb'd; for
    shame, put on your gown;
Your heart is burst, you have lost half your
    soul;
Even now, now, very now, an old black ram
Is tupping your white ewe. Arise, arise;
Awake the snorting citizens with the bell, 90
Or else the devil will make a grandsire of
    you:
Arise, I say.
Bra.   What, have you lost your wits?
Rod. Most reverend signior, do you know
    my voice?
Bra. Not I: what are you?
Rod. My name is Roderigo.
Bra.   The worser welcome:
I have charged thee not to haunt about my
    doors:
In honest plainness thou hast heard me say

My daughter is not for thee ; and now, in
    madness,
Being full of supper and distempering
    draughts,
Upon malicious bravery, dost thou come 100
To start my quiet.
    Rod. Sir, sir, sir,—
    Bra.   But thou must needs be sure
My spirit and my place have in them power
To make this bitter to thee.
    Rod.   Patience, good sir.
    Bra. What tell'st thou me of robbing ?
    this is Venice ;
My house is not a grange.
    Rod.   Most grave Brabantio,
In simple and pure soul I come to you.
    Iago. 'Zounds, sir, you are one of those
that will not serve God, if the devil bid you.
Because we come to do you service and you
think we are ruffians, you'll have your daughter covered with a Barbary horse ; you'll
have your nephews neigh to you ; you'll have
coursers for cousins and gennets for germans.
    Bra. What profane wretch art thou ?
    Iago. I am one, sir, that comes to tell you
your daughter and the Moor are now making
the beast with two backs.
    Bra. Thou art a villain.
    Iago.   You are—a senator.
    Bra. This thou shalt answer ; I know thee,
    Roderigo.   120
    Rod. Sir, I will answer any thing. But, I
    beseech you,
If 't be your pleasure and most wise consent,
As partly I find it is, that your fair daughter,
At this odd-even and dull watch o' the night,
Transported, with no worse nor better guard
But with a knave of common hire, a gon-
    dolier,
To the gross clasps of a lascivious Moor,—
If this be known to you and your allowance,
We then have done you bold and saucy
    wrongs ;
But if you know not this, my manners tell
    me   130
We have your wrong rebuke. Do not believe
That, from the sense of all civility,
I thus would play and trifle with your rever-
    ence :
Your daughter, if you have not given her
    leave,
I say again, hath made a gross revolt ;
Tying her duty, beauty, wit and fortunes
In an extravagant and wheeling stranger
Of here and every where. Straight satisfy your-
    self :
If she be in her chamber or your house,
Let loose on me the justice of the state   140
For thus deluding you.
    Bra.   Strike on the tinder, ho !
Give me a taper ! call up all my people !
This accident is not unlike my dream :
Belief of it oppresses me already.
Light, I say ! light !   [*Exit above.*
    Iago.   Farewell ; for I must leave you :
It seems not meet, nor wholesome to my
    place,
To be produced—as, if I stay, I shall—
Against the Moor : for, I do know, the state,
However this may gall him with some check,
Cannot with safety cast him, for he's em-
    bark'd   150
With such loud reason to the Cyprus wars,

Which even now stand in act, that, for their
    souls,
Another of his fathom they have none,
To lead their business : in which regard,
Though I do hate him as I do hell-pains,
Yet, for necessity of present life,
I must show out a flag and sign of love,
Which is indeed but sign. That you shall
    surely find him,
Lead to the Sagittary the raised search ;
And there will I be with him. So, farewell.
                      [*Exit.* 160

Enter, below, BRABANTIO, *and* Servants *with
torches.*

    Bra. It is too true an evil : gone she is ;
And what's to come of my despised time
Is nought but bitterness. Now, Roderigo,
Where didst thou see her ? O unhappy girl !
With the Moor, say'st thou ? Who would be
    a father !
How didst thou know 'twas she ? O, she de-
    ceives me
Past thought ! What said she to you ? Get
    more tapers :
Raise all my kindred. Are they married, think
    you ?
    Rod. Truly, I think they are.
    Bra. O heaven ! How got she out ? O
    treason of the blood !   170
Fathers, from hence trust not your daugh-
    ters' minds
By what you see them act. Is there not charms
By which the property of youth and maidhood
May be abused ? Have you not read, Rod-
    erigo,
Of some such thing ?
    Rod.   Yes, sir, I have indeed.
    Bra. Call up my brother. O, would you
    had had her !
Some one way, some another. Do you know
Where we may apprehend her and the Moor ?
    Rod. I think I can discover him, if you
    please,
To get good guard and go along with me. 180
    Bra. Pray you, lead on. At every house
    I'll call ;
I may command at most. Get weapons, ho !
And raise some special officers of night.
On, good Roderigo : I'll deserve your pains.
                      [*Exeunt.*

    SCENE II. *Another street.*
Enter OTHELLO, IAGO, *and* Attendants *with
torches.*

    Iago. Though in the trade of war I have
    slain men,
Yet do I hold it very stuff o' the conscience
To do no contrived murder : I lack iniquity
Sometimes to do me service : nine or ten
    times
I had thought to have yerk'd him here under
    the ribs.
    Oth. 'Tis better as it is.
    Iago.   Nay, but he prated,
And spoke such scurvy and provoking terms
Against your honor
That, with the little godliness I have,
I did full hard forbear him. But, I pray you,
    sir,   10
Are you fast married ? Be assured of this,
That the magnifico is much beloved,
And hath in his effect a voice potential

As double as the duke's : he will divorce you ;
Or put upon you what restraint and griev-
    ance
The law, with all his might to enforce it on,
Will give him cable.
    Oth.   Let him do his spite :
My services which I have done the signiory
Shall out-tongue his complaints. 'Tis yet to
    know,—   19
Which, when I know that boasting is an honor,
I shall promulgate—I fetch my life and being
From men of royal siege, and my demerits
May speak unbonneted to as proud a fortune
As this that I have reach'd : for know, Iago,
But that I love the gentle Desdemona,
I would not my unhoused free condition
Put into circumscription and confine
For the sea's worth. But, look ! what lights
    come yond ?
    Iago. Those are the raised father and his
        friends :
You were best go in.
    Oth.   Not I : I must be found : 30
My parts, my title and my perfect soul
Shall manifest me rightly. Is it they ?
    Iago. By Janus, I think no.

Enter CASSIO, *and certain* Officers *with torches.*

    Oth. The servants of the duke, and my
        lieutenant.
The goodness of the night upon you, friends !
What is the news ?
    Cas.   The duke does greet you, general,
And he requires your haste-post-haste appear-
    ance,
Even on the instant.
    Oth.   What is the matter, think you ?
    Cas. Something from Cyprus, as I may
        divine :
It is a business of some heat : the galleys   40
Have sent a dozen sequent messengers
This very night at one another's heels,
And many of the consuls, raised and met,
Are at the duke's already : you have been
    hotly call'd for ;
When, being not at your lodging to be found,
The senate hath sent about three several
    quests
To search you out.
    Oth.   'Tis well I am found by you.
I will but spend a word here in the house,
And go with you.   [*Exit.*
    Cas.   Ancient, what makes he here ?
    Iago. 'Faith, he to-night hath boarded a
        land carack :   50
If it prove lawful prize, he's made for ever.
    Cas. I do not understand.
    Iago.   He's married.
    Cas.   To who?

Re-enter OTHELLO.

    Iago. Marry, to—Come, captain, will you
        go ?
    Oth.   Have with you.
    Cas. Here comes another troop to seek for
        you.
    Iago. It is Brabantio. General, be advised ;
He comes to bad intent.

Enter BRABANTIO, RODERIGO, *and* Officers
    with torches and weapons.

    Oth.   Holla ! stand there !
    Rod. Signior, it is the Moor.

    Bra.   Down with him, thief !
        [*They draw on both sides.*
    Iago. You, Roderigo ! come, sir, I am for
        you.
    Oth. Keep up your bright swords, for the
        dew will rust them.
Good signior, you shall more command with
    years   60
Than with your weapons.
    Bra. O thou foul thief, where hast thou
        stow'd my daughter ?
Damn'd as thou art, thou hast enchanted her ;
For I'll refer me to all things of sense,
If she in chains of magic were not bound,
Whether a maid so tender, fair and happy,
So opposite to marriage that she shunn'd
The wealthy curled darlings of our nation,
Would ever have, to incur a general mock,
Run from her guardage to the sooty bosom 70
Of such a thing as thou, to fear, not to delight.
Judge me the world, if 'tis not gross in sense
That thou hast practised on her with foul
    charms,
Abused her delicate youth with drugs or min-
    erals
That weaken motion : I'll have 't disputed on ;
'Tis probable and palpable to thinking.
I therefore apprehend and do attach thee
For an abuser of the world, a practiser
Of arts inhibited and out of warrant.
Lay hold upon him : if he do resist,   80
Subdue him at his peril.
    Oth.   Hold your hands,
Both you of my inclining, and the rest :
Were it my cue to fight, I should have known
    it
Without a prompter. Where will you that I
    go
To answer this your charge ?
    Bra.   To prison, till fit time
Of law and course of direct session
Call thee to answer.
    Oth.   What if I do obey ?
How may the duke be therewith satisfied,
Whose messengers are here about my side,
Upon some present business of the state   90
To bring me to him ?
    First Off. 'Tis true, most worthy signior ;
The duke's in council, and your noble self,
I am sure, is sent for.
    Bra.   How ! the duke in council !
In this time of the night ! Bring him away :
Mine's not an idle cause : the duke himself,
Or any of my brothers of the state,
Cannot but feel this wrong as 'twere their
    own ;
For if such actions may have passage free,
Bond-slaves and pagans shall our statesmen
    be.   [*Exeunt.*

SCENE III. A council-chamber.

The DUKE *and* Senators *sitting at a table ;*
    Officers *attending.*

    Duke. There is no composition in these
        news
That gives them credit.
    First Sen. Indeed, they are disproportion'd ;
My letters say a hundred and seven galleys.
    Duke. And mine, a hundred and forty.
    Sec. Sen.   And mine, two hundred :
But though they jump not on a just account,—
As in these cases, where the aim reports,

'Tis oft with difference—yet do they all con-
firm
A Turkish fleet, and bearing up to Cyprus.
  Duke. Nay, it is possible enough to judg-
      ment :
I do not so secure me in the error,   10
But the main article I do approve
In fearful sense.
  Sailor. [*Within*] What, ho ! what, ho !
      what, ho !
  First Off. A messenger from the galleys.

        Enter a Sailor.

  Duke.   Now, what's the business ?
  Sail. The Turkish preparation makes for
      Rhodes ;
So was I bid report here to the state
By Signior Angelo.
  Duke. How say you by this change ?
  First Sen.   This cannot be,
By no assay of reason : 'tis a pageant,
To keep us in false gaze. When we consider
The importance of Cyprus to the Turk,   20
And let ourselves again but understand,
That as it more concerns the Turk than
      Rhodes,
So may he with more facile question bear it,
For that it stands not in such warlike brace,
But altogether lacks the abilities
That Rhodes is dress'd in : if we make thought
      of this,
We must not think the Turk is so unskilful
To leave that latest which concerns him first,
Neglecting an attempt of ease and gain,
To wake and wage a danger profitless.   30
  Duke. Nay, in all confidence, he's not for
      Rhodes.
  First Off. Here is more news.

        Enter a Messenger.

  Mess. The Ottomites, reverend and gra-
      cious,
Steering with due course towards the isle of
      Rhodes,
Have there injointed them with an after fleet.
  First Sen. Ay, so I thought. How many,
      as you guess ?
  Mess. Of thirty sail : and now they do re-
      stem
Their backward course, bearing with frank ap-
      pearance
Their purposes toward Cyprus. Signior Mon-
      tano,
Your trusty and most valiant servitor,   40
With his free duty recommends you thus,
And prays you to believe him.
  Duke. 'Tis certain, then, for Cyprus.
Marcus Luccicos, is not he in town ?
  First Sen. He's now in Florence.
  Duke. Write from us to him ; post-post-
      haste dispatch.
  First Sen. Here comes Brabantio and the
      valiant Moor.

  Enter BRABANTIO, OTHELLO, IAGO,
      RODERIGO, *and* Officers.

  Duke. Valiant Othello, we must straight
      employ you
Against the general enemy Ottoman.
[*To Brabantio*] I did not see you ; welcome,
      gentle signior ;   50
We lack'd your counsel and your help to-
      night.

  Bra. So did I yours. Good your grace,
      pardon me ;
Neither my place nor aught I heard of busi-
      ness
Hath raised me from my bed, nor doth the
      general care
Take hold on me, for my particular grief
Is of so flood-gate and o'erbearing nature
That it engluts and swallows other sorrows
And it is still itself.
  Duke.   Why, what's the matter ?
  Bra. My daughter ! O, my daughter !
  Duke and Sen.   Dead ?
  Bra.   Ay, to me ;
She is abused, stol'n from me, and corrupted
By spells and medicines bought of mounte-
      banks ;   61
For nature so preposterously to err,
Being not deficient, blind, or lame of sense,
Sans witchcraft could not.
  Duke. Whoe'er he be that in this foul pro-
      ceeding
Hath thus beguiled your daughter of herself
And you of her, the bloody book of law
You shall yourself read in the bitter letter
After your own sense, yea, though our proper
      son
Stood in your action.
  Bra.   Humbly I thank your grace.   70
Here is the man, this Moor, whom now, it
      seems,
Your special mandate for the state-affairs
Hath hither brought.
  Duke and Sen.   We are very sorry for't.
  Duke. [*To Othello*] What, in your own
      part, can you say to this ?
  Bra. Nothing, but this is so.
  Oth. Most potent, grave, and reverend si-
      gniors,
My very noble and approved good masters,
That I have ta'en away this old man's daugh-
      ter,
It is most true ; true, I have married her :
The very head and front of my offending   80
Hath this extent, no more. Rude am I in my
      speech,
And little bless'd with the soft phrase of
      peace :
For since these arms of mine had seven years'
      pith,
Till now some nine moons wasted, they have
      used
Their dearest action in the tented field,
And little of this great world can I speak,
More than pertains to feats of broil and battle,
And therefore little shall I grace my cause
In speaking for myself. Yet, by your gracious
      patience,
I will a round unvarnish'd tale deliver   90
Of my whole course of love ; what drugs, what
      charms,
What conjuration and what mighty magic,
For such proceeding I am charged withal,
I won his daughter.
  Bra.   A maiden never bold ;
Of spirit so still and quiet, that her motion
Blush'd at herself ; and she, in spite of nature,
Of years, of country, credit, every thing,
To fall in love with what she fear'd to look on !
It is a judgment maim'd and most imperfect
That will confess perfection so could err   100
Against all rules of nature, and must be driven
To find out practices of cunning hell,

Why this should be. I therefore vouch again
That with some mixtures powerful o'er the
    blood,
Or with some dram conjured to this effect,
He wrought upon her.
  Duke.   To vouch this, is no proof,
Without more wider and more overt test
Than these thin habits and poor likelihoods
Of modern seeming do prefer against him.
  First Sen. But, Othello, speak :   110
Did you by indirect and forced courses
Subdue and poison this young maid's affec-
    tions ?
Or came it by request and such fair question
As soul to soul affordeth ?
  Oth.   I do beseech you,
Send for the lady to the Sagittary,
And let her speak of me before her father :
If you do find me foul in her report,
The trust, the office I do hold of you,
Not only take away, but let your sentence
Even fall upon my life.
  Duke.   Fetch Desdemona hither. 120
  Oth. Ancient, conduct them : you best
    know the place. [*Exeunt Iago and At-
                tendants.*
And, till she come, as truly as to heaven
I do confess the vices of my blood,
So justly to your grave ears I'll present
How I did thrive in this fair lady's love,
And she in mine.
  Duke. Say it, Othello.
  Oth. Her father loved me ; oft invited me ;
Still question'd me the story of my life,
From year to year, the battles, sieges, fortunes,
That I have pass'd.   131
I ran it through, even from my boyish days,
To the very moment that he bade me tell it ;
Wherein I spake of most disastrous chances,
Of moving accidents by flood and field,
Of hair-breadth scapes i' the imminent deadly
    breach,
Of being taken by the insolent foe
And sold to slavery, of my redemption thence
And portance in my travels' history :
Wherein of antres vast and deserts idle, 140
Rough quarries, rocks and hills whose heads
    touch heaven,
It was my hint to speak,—such was the proc-
    ess ;
And of the Cannibals that each other eat,
The Anthropophagi and men whose heads
Do grow beneath their shoulders. This to hear
Would Desdemona seriously incline :
But still the house-affairs would draw her
    thence :
Which ever as she could with haste dispatch,
She'ld come again, and with a greedy ear
Devour up my discourse : which I observing,
Took once a pliant hour, and found good
    means   151
To draw from her a prayer of earnest heart
That I would all my pilgrimage dilate,
Whereof by parcels she had something heard,
But not intentively : I did consent,
And often did beguile her of her tears,
When I did speak of some distressful stroke
That my youth suffer'd. My story being done,
She gave me for my pains a world of sighs :
She swore, in faith, 'twas strange, 'twas pass-
    ing strange,   160
'Twas pitiful, 'twas wondrous pitiful :
She wish'd she had not heard it, yet she wish'd

That heaven had made her such a man : she
    thank'd me,
And bade me, if I had a friend that loved her,
I should but teach him how to tell my story,
And that would woo her. Upon this hint I
    spake :
She loved me for the dangers I had pass'd,
And I loved her that she did pity them.
This only is the witchcraft I have used :
Here comes the lady ; let her witness it. 170

  Enter DESDEMONA, IAGO, *and* Attendants.

  Duke. I think this tale would win my
    daughter too.
Good Brabantio,
Take up this mangled matter at the best :
Men do their broken weapons rather use
Than their bare hands.
  Bra.   I pray you, hear her speak :
If she confess that she was half the wooer,
Destruction on my head, if my bad blame
Light on the man ! Come hither, gentle mis-
    tress :
Do you perceive in all this noble company
Where most you owe obedience ?
  Des.   My noble father, 180
I do perceive here a divided duty :
To you I am bound for life and education ;
My life and education both do learn me
How to respect you ; you are the lord of duty ;
I am hitherto your daughter : but here's my
    husband,
And so much duty as my mother show'd
To you, preferring you before her father,
So much I challenge that I may profess
Due to the Moor my lord.
  Bra.   God be wi' you ! I have done.
Please it your grace, on to the state-affairs :
I had rather to adopt a child than get it. 191
Come hither, Moor :
I here do give thee that with all my heart
Which, but thou hast already, with all my
    heart
I would keep from thee. For your sake, jewel,
I am glad at soul I have no other child :
For thy escape would teach me tyranny,
To hang clogs on them. I have done, my lord.
  Duke. Let me speak like yourself, and lay
    a sentence,   199
Which, as a grise or step, may help these lovers
Into your favor.
When remedies are past, the griefs are ended
By seeing the worst, which late on hopes de-
    pended.
To mourn a mischief that is past and gone
Is the next way to draw new mischief on.
What cannot be preserved when fortune takes
Patience her injury a mockery makes.
The robb'd that smiles steals something from
    the thief ;
He robs himself that spends a bootless grief.
  Bra. So let the Turk of Cyprus us beguile ;
We lose it not, so long as we can smile. 211
He bears the sentence well that nothing bears
But the free comfort which from thence he
    hears,
But he bears both the sentence and the sorrow
That, to pay grief, must of poor patience bor-
    row.
These sentences, to sugar, or to gall,
Being strong on both sides, are equivocal :
But words are words ; I never yet did hear

That the bruised heart was pierced through
the ear.
I humbly beseech you, proceed to the affairs
of state.   220
Duke. The Turk with a most mighty preparation makes for Cyprus. Othello, the fortitude of the place is best known to you ; and
though we have there a substitute of most
allowed sufficiency, yet opinion, a sovereign
mistress of effects, throws a more safer voice
on you : you must therefore be content to
slubber the gloss of your new fortunes with
this more stubborn and boisterous expedition.
Oth. The tyrant custom, most grave sena-
tors,   230
Hath made the flinty and steel couch of war
My thrice-driven bed of down : I do agnize
A natural and prompt alacrity
I find in hardness, and do undertake
These present wars against the Ottomites.
Most humbly therefore bending to your state,
I crave fit disposition for my wife,
Due reference of place and exhibition,
With such accommodation and besort
As levels with her breeding.
Duke.   If you please,   240
Be't at her father's.
Bra.   I'll not have it so.
Oth. Nor I.
Des.   Nor I ; I would not there reside,
To put my father in impatient thoughts
By being in his eye. Most gracious duke,
To my unfolding lend your prosperous ear ;
And let me find a charter in your voice,
To assist my simpleness.
Duke. What would you, Desdemona ?
Des. That I did love the Moor to live with
him,   249
My downright violence and storm of fortunes
May trumpet to the world : my heart's subdued
Even to the very quality of my lord :
I saw Othello's visage in his mind,
And to his honor and his valiant parts
Did I my soul and fortunes consecrate.
So that, dear lords, if I be left behind,
A moth of peace, and he go to the war,
The rites for which I love him are bereft me,
And I a heavy interim shall support
By his dear absence. Let me go with him. 260
Oth. Let her have your voices.
Vouch with me, heaven, I therefore beg it not,
To please the palate of my appetite,
Nor to comply with heat—the young affects
In me defunct—and proper satisfaction,
But to be free and bounteous to her mind :
And heaven defend your good souls, that you
think
I will your serious and great business scant
For she is with me : no, when light-wing'd toys
Of feather'd Cupid seal with wanton dullness
My speculative and officed instruments,   271
That my disports corrupt and taint my busi-
ness,
Let housewives make a skillet of my helm,
And all indign and base adversities
Make head against my estimation !
Duke. Be it as you shall privately deter-
mine,
Either for her stay or going : the affair cries
haste,
And speed must answer it.
First Sen. You must away to-night.
Oth.   With all my heart.

Duke. At nine i' the morning here we'll
meet again.   280
Othello, leave some officer behind,
And he shall our commission bring to you ;
With such things else of quality and respect
As doth import you.
Oth.   So please your grace, my ancient ;
A man he is of honesty and trust :
To his conveyance I assign my wife,
With what else needful your good grace shall
think
To be sent after me.
Duke.   Let it be so.
Good night to every one. [*To Bra.*] And, no-
ble signior,
If virtue no delighted beauty lack,   290
Your son-in-law is far more fair than black.
First Sen. Adieu, brave Moor, use Desde-
mona well.
Bra. Look to her, Moor, if thou hast eyes
to see :
She has deceived her father, and may thee.
[*Exeunt Duke, Senators, Officers, &c.*
Oth. My life upon her faith ! Honest Iago,
My Desdemona must I leave to thee :
I prithee, let thy wife attend on her :
And bring them after in the best advantage.
Come, Desdemona : I have but an hour
Of love, of worldly matters and direction, 300
To spend with thee : we must obey the time.
[*Exeunt Othello and Desdemona.*
Rod. Iago,—
Iago. What say'st thou, noble heart ?
Rod. What will I do, thinkest thou ?
Iago. Why, go to bed, and sleep.
Rod. I will incontinently drown myself.
Iago. If thou dost, I shall never love thee
after. Why, thou silly gentleman !
Rod. It is silliness to live when to live is
torment ; and then have we a prescription to
die when death is our physician.   311
Iago. O villanous ! I have looked upon the
world for four times seven years ; and since I
could distinguish betwixt a benefit and an injury, I never found man that knew how to
love himself. Ere I would say, I would drown
myself for the love of a guinea-hen, I would
change my humanity with a baboon.
Rod. What should I do ? I confess it is my
shame to be so fond ; but it is not in my virtue to amend it.   321
Iago. Virtue ! a fig ! 'tis in ourselves that
we are thus or thus. Our bodies are our gardens, to the which our wills are gardeners : so
that if we will plant nettles, or sow lettuce, set
hyssop and weed up thyme, supply it with one
gender of herbs, or distract it with many, either to have it sterile with idleness, or manured
with industry, why, the power and corrigible
authority of this lies in our wills. If the balance of our lives had not one scale of reason
to poise another of sensuality, the blood and
baseness of our natures would conduct us to
most preposterous conclusions : but we have
reason to cool our raging motions, our carnal
stings, our unbitted lusts, whereof I take this
that you call love to be a sect or scion.
Rod. It cannot be.
Iago. It is merely a lust of the blood and
a permission of the will. Come, be a man.
Drown thyself ! drown cats and blind puppies. I have professed me thy friend and I
confess me knit to thy deserving with cables

of perdurable toughness; I could never better
stead thee than now. Put money in thy purse;
follow thou the wars; defeat thy favor with an
usurped beard; I say, put money in thy purse.
It cannot be that Desdemona should long continue her love to the Moor,—put money in
thy purse,—nor he his to her: it was a violent
commencement, and thou shalt see an answer-
able sequestration :—put but money in thy
purse. These Moors are changeable in their
wills :—fill thy purse with money :—the food
that to him now is as luscious as locusts, shall
be to him shortly as bitter as coloquintida.
She must change for youth : when she is sated
with his body, she will find the error of her
choice : she must have change, she must :
therefore put money in thy purse. If thou wilt
needs damn thyself, do it a more delicate way
than drowning. Make all the money thou
canst : if sanctimony and a frail vow betwixt
an erring barbarian and a supersubtle Venetian be not too hard for my wits and all the
tribe of hell, thou shalt enjoy her; therefore
make money. A pox of drowning thyself! it is
clean out of the way : seek thou rather to be
hanged in compassing thy joy than to be
drowned and go without her.

Rod. Wilt thou be fast to my hopes, if I
depend on the issue ?   370

Iago. Thou art sure of me :—go, make
money :—I have told thee often, and I re-tell
thee again and again, I hate the Moor : my
cause is hearted; thine hath no less reason.
Let us be conjunctive in our revenge against
him : if thou canst cuckold him, thou dost thyself a pleasure, me a sport. There are many
events in the womb of time which will be delivered. Traverse ! go, provide thy money. We
will have more of this to-morrow. Adieu.

Rod. Where shall we meet i' the morn-
ing ?   381

Iago. At my lodging.

Rod. I'll be with thee betimes.

Iago. Go to; farewell. Do you hear, Roderigo ?

Rod. What say you ?

Iago. No more of drowning, do you hear ?

Rod. I am changed : I'll go sell all my
land.   [*Exit.*

Iago. Thus do I ever make my fool my
purse :
For I mine own gain'd knowledge should pro-
fane,
If I would time expend with such a snipe,
But for my sport and profit. I hate the Moor :
And it is thought abroad, that 'twixt my sheets
He has done my office : I know not if't be
true :
But I, for mere suspicion in that kind,
Will do as if for surety. He holds me well;
The better shall my purpose work on him.
Cassio's a proper man : let me see now :
To get his place and to plume up my will   399
In double knavery—How, how ? Let's see :—
After some time, to abuse Othello's ear
That he is too familiar with his wife.
He hath a person and a smooth dispose
To be suspected, framed to make women false.
The Moor is of a free and open nature,
That thinks men honest that but seem to be
so,
And will as tenderly be led by the nose
As asses are.

I have't. It is engender'd. Hell and night
Must bring this monstrous birth to the world's
light.   [*Exit.* 410

ACT II.

SCENE I. *A Sea-port in Cyprus. An open
place near the quay.*

Enter MONTANO *and two* Gentlemen.

Mon. What from the cape can you discern
at sea ?

First Gent. Nothing at all : it is a high-
wrought flood;
I cannot, 'twixt the heaven and the main,
Descry a sail.

Mon.   Methinks the wind hath spoke aloud
at land;
A fuller blast ne'er shook our battlements :
If it hath ruffian'd so upon the sea,
What ribs of oak, when mountains melt on
them,
Can hold the mortise ? What shall we hear of
this ?

Sec. Gent. A segregation of the Turkish
fleet :   10
For do but stand upon the foaming shore,
The chidden billow seems to pelt the clouds;
The wind-shaked surge, with high and mon-
strous mane,
Seems to cast water on the burning bear,
And quench the guards of the ever-fixed pole :
I never did like molestation view
On the enchafed flood.

Mon.   If that the Turkish fleet
Be not enshelter'd and embay'd, they are
drown'd :
It is impossible they bear it out.

Enter a third Gentleman.

Third Gent. News, lads ! our wars are
done.   20
The desperate tempest hath so bang'd the
Turks,
That their designment halts : a noble ship of
Venice
Hath seen a grievous wreck and sufferance
On most part of their fleet.

Mon. How ! is this true ?

Third Gent.   The ship is here put in,
A Veronesa; Michael Cassio,
Lieutenant to the warlike Moor Othello,
Is come on shore : the Moor himself at sea,
And is in full commission here for Cyprus.

Mon. I am glad on't; 'tis a worthy gov-
ernor.   30
Third Gent. But this same Cassio, though
he speak of comfort
Touching the Turkish loss, yet he looks sadly,
And prays the Moor be safe; for they were
parted
With foul and violent tempest.

Mon.   Pray heavens he be;
For I have served him, and the man com-
mands
Like a full soldier. Let's to the seaside, ho !
As well to see the vessel that's come in
As to throw out our eyes for brave Othello,
Even till we make the main and the aerial
blue
An indistinct regard.

Third Gent.   Come, let's do so :   40

For every minute is expectancy
Of more arrivance.

Enter CASSIO.

Cas. Thanks, you the valiant of this war-
like isle,
That so approve the Moor! O, let the heavens
Give him defence against the elements,
For I have lost him on a dangerous sea.
    Mon. Is he well shipp'd?
    Cas. His bark is stoutly timber'd, and his
pilot
Of very expert and approved allowance;
Therefore my hopes, not surfeited to death,
Stand in bold cure.   51
    [*A cry within* ' A sail, a sail, a sail!']

Enter a fourth Gentleman.

Cas. What noise?
Fourth Gent. The town is empty; on the
brow o' the sea
Stand ranks of people, and they cry ' A sail!'
    Cas. My hopes do shape him for the gover-
nor.   [*Guns heard.*
    Sec. Gent. They do discharge their shot of
courtesy:
Our friends at least.
    Cas.   I pray you, sir, go forth,
And give us truth who 'tis that is arrived.
    Sec. Gent. I shall.   [*Exit.*
    Mon. But, good lieutenant, is your general
wived?   60
    Cas. Most fortunately: he hath achieved a
maid
That paragons description and wild fame;
One that excels the quirks of blazoning pens,
And in the essential vesture of creation
Does tire the ingener.

Re-enter second Gentleman.

              How now! who has put in?
    Sec. Gent. 'Tis one Iago, ancient to the
general.
    Cas. Has had most favorable and happy
speed:
Tempests themselves, high seas, and howling
winds,
The gutter'd rocks and congregated sands,—
Traitors ensteep'd to clog the guiltless keel,—
As having sense of beauty, do omit   71
Their mortal natures, letting go safely by
The divine Desdemona.
    Mon.   What is she?
    Cas. She that I spake of, our great cap-
tain's captain,
Left in the conduct of the bold Iago,
Whose footing here anticipates our thoughts
A se'nnight's speed. Great Jove, Othello guard,
And swell his sail with thine own powerful
breath,
That he may bless this bay with his tall ship,
Make love's quick pants in Desdemona's
arms,   80
Give renew'd fire to our extinguished spirits
And bring all Cyprus comfort!

Enter DESDEMONA, EMILIA, IAGO, RODERIGO,
and Attendants.

              O, behold,
The riches of the ship is come on shore!
Ye men of Cyprus, let her have your knees.
Hail to thee, lady! and the grace of heaven,
Before, behind thee, and on every hand,

Enwheel thee round!
    Des.   I thank you, valiant Cassio.
What tidings can you tell me of my lord?
    Cas. He is not yet arrived: nor know I
aught
But that he's well and will be shortly here. 90
    Des. O, but I fear—How lost you com-
pany?
    Cas. The great contention of the sea and
skies
Parted our fellowship—But, hark! a sail.
    [*Within* ' A sail, a sail!'   *Guns heard.*
    Sec. Gent. They give their greeting to the
citadel;
This likewise is a friend.
    Cas. See for the news. [*Exit Gentleman.*
Good ancient, you are welcome.   [*To Emilia.*]
        Welcome, mistress.
Let it not gall your patience, good Iago,
That I extend my manners; 'tis my breeding
That gives me this bold show of courtesy. 100
                    [*Kissing her.*
    Iago. Sir, would she give you so much of
her lips
As of her tongue she oft bestows on me,
You'ld have enough.
    Des.   Alas, she has no speech.
    Iago. In faith, too much;
I find it still, when I have list to sleep:
Marry, before your ladyship, I grant,
She puts her tongue a little in her heart,
And chides with thinking.
    Emil. You have little cause to say so.
    Iago. Come on, come on; you are pictures
out of doors,   110
Bells in your parlors, wild-cats in your kitch-
ens,
Saints in your injuries, devils being offended,
Players in your housewifery, and housewives
in your beds.
    Des. O, fie upon thee, slanderer!
    Iago. Nay, it is true, or else I am a Turk:
You rise to play and go to bed to work.
    Emil. You shall not write my praise.
    Iago.   No, let me not.
    Des. What wouldst thou write of me, if
thou shouldst praise me?
    Iago. O gentle lady, do not put me to't;
For I am nothing, if not critical.   120
    Des. Come on, assay. There's one gone to
the harbor?
    Iago. Ay, madam.
    Des. I am not merry; but I do beguile
The thing I am, by seeming otherwise.
Come, how wouldst thou praise me?
    Iago. I am about it; but indeed my inven-
tion
Comes from my pate as birdlime does from
frize;
It plucks out brains and all: but my Muse
labors,
And thus she is deliver'd.
If she be fair and wise, fairness and wit, 130
The one's for use, the other useth it.
    Des. Well praised! How if she be black
and witty?
    Iago. If she be black, and thereto have a
wit,
She'll find a white that shall her blackness fit.
    Des. Worse and worse.
    Emil. How if fair and foolish?

Iago. She never yet was foolish that was
fair ;
For even her fólly help'd her to an heir.

Des. These are old fond paradoxes to make
fools laugh i' the alehouse. What miserable
praise hast thou for her that's foul and foolish?　　　　　　　　　　　　　　　　　141

Iago. There's none so foul and foolish
thereunto,
But does foul pranks which fair and wise ones
do.

Des. O heavy ignorance ! thou praisest the
worst best. But what praise couldst thou bestow on a deserving woman indeed, one that,
in the authority of her merit, did justly put on
the vouch of very malice itself ?

Iago. She that was ever fair and never
proud,
Had tongue at will and yet was never loud, 151
Never lack'd gold and yet went never gay,
Fled from her wish and yet said ' Now I may,'
She that being anger'd, her revenge being nigh,
Bade her wrong stay and her displeasure fly,
She that in wisdom never was so frail
To change the cod's head for the salmon's tail ;
She that could think and ne'er disclose her
mind,
See suitors following and not look behind,
She was a wight, if ever such wight were,—

Des. To do what ?　　　　　　　　　160

Iago. To suckle fools and chronicle small
beer.

Des. O most lame and impotent conclusion ! Do not learn of him, Emilia, though he
be thy husband. How say you, Cassio ? is he
not a most profane and liberal counsellor ?

Cas. He speaks home, madam : you may
relish him more in the soldier than in the
scholar.

Iago. [*Aside*] He takes her by the palm :
ay, well said, whisper : with as little a web as
this will I ensnare as great a fly as Cassio. Ay,
smile upon her, do ; I will gyve thee in thine
own courtship. You say true ; 'tis so, indeed :
if such tricks as these strip you out of your
lieutenantry, it had been better you had not
kissed your three fingers so oft, which now
again you are most apt to play the sir in. Very
good ; well kissed ! an excellent courtesy !
'tis so, indeed. Yet again your fingers to your
lips ? would they were clyster-pipes for your
sake ! [*Trumpet within.*] The Moor ! I know
his trumpet.　　　　　　　　　　　　180

Cas. 'Tis truly so.

Des. Let's meet him and receive him.

Cas. Lo, where he comes !

Enter OTHELLO *and* Attendants.

Oth. O my fair warrior !

Des. 　　　　　　　　My dear Othello !

Oth. It gives me wonder great as my con-
tent
To see you here before me. O my soul's joy !
If after every tempest come such calms,
May the winds blow till they have waken'd
death !
And let the laboring bark climb hills of seas
Olympus-high and duck again as low　　190
As hell's from heaven ! If it were now to die,
'Twere now to be most happy ; for, I fear,
My soul hath her content so absolute
That not another comfort like to this

Succeeds in unknown fate.

Des. 　　　　　　　The heavens forbid
But that our loves and comforts should in-
crease,
Even as our days do grow !

Oth. 　　　　　　　Amen to that, sweet powers !
I cannot speak enough of this content ;
It stops me here ; it is too much of joy :
And this, and this, the greatest discords be
　　　　　　　　　　　[*Kissing her.* 200
That e'er our hearts shall make !

Iago. [*Aside*] O, you are well tuned now !
But I'll set down the pegs that make this
music,
As honest as I am.

Oth. 　　　　　Come, let us to the castle.
News, friends ; our wars are done, the Turks
are drown'd.
How does my old acquaintance of this isle ?
Honey, you shall be well desired in Cyprus ;
I have found great love amongst them. O my
sweet,
I prattle out of fashion, and I dote
In mine own comforts. I prithee, good Iago,
Go to the bay and disembark my coffers : 210
Bring thou the master to the citadel ;
He is a good one, and his worthiness
Does challenge much respect. Come, Desde-
mona,
Once more, well met at Cyprus.

[*Exeunt Othello, Desdemona, and Attendants.*

Iago. Do thou meet me presently at the
harbor. Come hither. If thou be'st valiant,—
as, they say, base men being in love have then
a nobility in their natures more than is native
to them,—list me. The lieutenant to-night
watches on the court of guard :—first, I must
tell thee this—Desdemona is directly in love
with him.　　　　　　　　　　　　　221

Rod. With him ! why, 'tis not possible.

Iago. Lay thy finger thus, and let thy soul
be instructed. Mark me with what violence
she first loved the Moor, but for bragging and
telling her fantastical lies : and will she love
him still for prating ? let not thy discreet
heart think it. Her eye must be fed ; and what
delight shall she have to look on the devil ?
When the blood is made dull with the act of
sport, there should be, again to inflame it and
to give satiety a fresh appetite, loveliness in
favor, sympathy in years, manners and beauties ; all which the Moor is defective in : now,
for want of these required conveniences, her
delicate tenderness will find itself abused, begin to heave the gorge, disrelish and abhor the
Moor ; very nature will instruct her in it and
compel her to some second choice. Now, sir,
this granted,—as it is a most pregnant and
unforced position—who stands so eminent in
the degree of this fortune as Cassio does ? a
knave very voluble ; no further conscionable
than in putting on the mere form of civil and
humane seeming, for the better compassing of
his salt and most hidden loose affection ? why,
none ; why, none : a slipper and subtle knave,
a finder of occasions, that has an eye can
stamp and counterfeit advantages, though true
advantage never present itself ; a devilish
knave. Besides, the knave is handsome, young,
and hath all those requisites in him that folly
and green minds look after : a pestilent com-

plete knave ; and the woman hath found him
already.

Rod. I cannot believe that in her ; she's
full of most blessed condition.

Iago. Blessed fig's-end ! the wine she drinks
is made of grapes : if she had been blessed,
she would never have loved the Moor. Blessed
pudding ! Didst thou not see her paddle with
the palm of his hand ? didst not mark that ?

Rod. Yes, that I did ; but that was but
courtesy.

Iago. Lechery, by this hand ; an index and
obscure prologue to the history of lust and
foul thoughts. They met so near with their
lips that their breaths embraced together. Villanous thoughts, Roderigo ! when these mu-
tualities so marshal the way, hard at hand
comes the master and main exercise, the incorporate conclusion, Pish ! But, sir, be you
ruled by me : I have brought you from Venice. Watch you to-night ; for the command,
I'll lay't upon you. Cassio knows you not. I'll
not be far from you : do you find some occasion to anger Cassio, either by speaking too
loud, or tainting his discipline ; or from what
other course you please, which the time shall
more favorably minister.

Rod. Well.

Iago. Sir, he is rash and very sudden in
choler, and haply may strike at you : provoke
him, that he may ; for even out of that will I
cause these of Cyprus to mutiny ; whose quali-
fication shall come into no true taste again
but by the displanting of Cassio. So shall you
have a shorter journey to your desires by the
means I shall then have to prefer them ; and
the impediment most profitably removed, without the which there were no expectation of
our prosperity.

Rod. I will do this, if I can bring it to any
opportunity.   290

Iago. I warrant thee. Meet me by and by
at the citadel : I must fetch his necessaries
ashore. Farewell.

Rod. Adieu.   [*Exit*

Iago. That Cassio loves her, I do well be-
    lieve it ;
That she loves him, 'tis apt and of great
    credit :
The Moor, howbeit that I endure him not,
Is of a constant, loving, noble nature,
And I dare think he'll prove to Desdemona
A most dear husband. Now, I do love her
    too ;   300
Not out of absolute lust, though peradventure
I stand accountant for as great a sin,
But partly led to diet my revenge,
For that I do suspect the lusty Moor
Hath leap'd into my seat ; the thought whereof
Doth, like a poisonous mineral, gnaw my in-
    wards ;
And nothing can or shall content my soul
Till I am even'd with him, wife for wife,
Or failing so, yet that I put the Moor
At least into a jealousy so strong   310
That judgment cannot cure. Which thing to
    do,
If this poor trash of Venice, whom I trash
For his quick hunting, stand the putting on,
I'll have our Michael Cassio on the hip,
Abuse him to the Moor in the rank garb—
For I fear Cassio with my night-cap too—

Make the Moor thank me, love me and re-
    ward me,
For making him egregiously an ass
And practising upon his peace and quiet 319
Even to madness. 'Tis here, but yet confused :
Knavery's plain face is never seen till used.
                                              [*Exit.*

SCENE II. *A street.*

Enter a Herald *with a proclamation;* People
    following.

Her. It is Othello's pleasure, our noble and
valiant general, that, upon certain tidings now
arrived, importing the mere perdition of the
Turkish fleet, every man put himself into triumph ; some to dance, some to make bonfires,
each man to what sport and revels his addic-
tion leads him : for, besides these beneficial
news, it is the celebration of his nuptial. So
much was his pleasure should be proclaimed.
All offices are open, and there is full liberty of
feasting from this present hour of five till the
bell have told eleven. Heaven bless the isle of
Cyprus and our noble general Othello !
                                             [*Exeunt.*

SCENE III. *A hall in the castle.*

Enter OTHELLO, DESDEMONA, CASSIO, *and*
    Attendants.

Oth. Good Michael, look you to the guard
    to-night :
Let's teach ourselves that honorable stop,
Not to outsport discretion.

Cas.   Iago hath direction what to do ;
But, notwithstanding, with my personal eye
Will I look to't.

Oth.   Iago is most honest.
Michael, good night : to-morrow with your
    earliest
Let me have speech with you. [*To Desdemona*]
    Come, my dear love,
The purchase made, the fruits are to ensue ;
That profit 's yet to come 'tween me and you.
Good night.   11
[*Exeunt Othello, Desdemona, and Attendants.*

Enter IAGO.

Cas. Welcome, Iago ; we must to the
watch.

Iago. Not this hour, lieutenant ; 'tis not
yet ten o' the clock. Our general cast us thus
early for the love of his Desdemona ; who let
us not therefore blame : he hath not yet made
wanton the night with her ; and she is sport
for Jove.

Cas. She's a most exquisite lady.

Iago. And, I'll warrant her, full of game.

Cas. Indeed, she's a most fresh and delicate creature.   21

Iago. What an eye she has ! methinks it
sounds a parley of provocation.

Cas. An inviting eye ; and yet methinks
right modest.

Iago. And when she speaks, is it not an
alarum to love ?

Cas. She is indeed perfection.

Iago. Well, happiness to their sheets !
Come, lieutenant, I have a stoup of wine ; and
here without are a brace of Cyprus gallants
that would fain have a measure to the health
of black Othello.

Cas. Not to-night, good Iago : I have very

poor and unhappy brains for drinking : I could
well wish courtesy would invent some other
custom of entertainment.

Iago. O, they are our friends; but one cup :
I'll drink for you.   39

Cas. I have drunk but one cup to-night,
and that was craftily qualified too, and, behold, what innovation it makes here : I am
unfortunate in the infirmity, and dare not task
my weakness with any more.

Iago. What, man ! 'tis a night of revels :
the gallants desire it.

Cas. Where are they ?

Iago. Here at the door ; I pray you, call
them in.

Cas. I'll do't ; but it dislikes me.   [*Exit.*

Iago. If I can drink but one cup upon him,
With that which he hath drunk to-night al-
    ready,   51
He'll be as full of quarrel and offence
As my young mistress' dog. Now, my sick fool
    Roderigo,
Whom love hath turn'd almost the wrong side
    out,
To Desdemona hath to-night caroused
Potations pottle-deep ; and he's to watch :
Three lads of Cyprus, noble swelling spirits,
That hold their honors in a wary distance,
The very elements of this warlike isle,
Have I to-night fluster'd with flowing cups, 60
And they watch too. Now, 'mongst this flock
    of drunkards,
Am I to put our Cassio in some action
That may offend the isle.—But here they
    come :
If consequence do but approve my dream,
My boat sails freely, both with wind and
    stream.

Re-enter Cassio ; *with him* Montano *and*
Gentlemen ; *servants following with wine.*

Cas. 'Fore God, they have given me a rouse
already.

Mon. Good faith, a little one ; not past a
pint, as I am a soldier.

Iago. Some wine, ho !   70
[*Sings*] And let me the canakin clink, clink ;
    And let me the canakin clink :
    A soldier's a man ;
    A life's but a span ;
    Why, then, let a soldier drink.
Some wine, boys !

Cas. 'Fore God, an excellent song.

Iago. I learned it in England, where, in-
deed, they are most potent in potting : your
Dane, your German, and your swag-bellied
Hollander—Drink, ho !—are nothing to your
English.   81

Cas. Is your Englishman so expert in his
drinking ?

Iago. Why, he drinks you, with facility,
your Dane dead drunk ; he sweats not to overthrow your Almain ; he gives your Hollander
a vomit, ere the next pottle can be filled.

Cas. To the health of our general !

Mon. I am for it, lieutenant ; and I'll do
you justice.   90

Iago. O sweet England !
King Stephen was a worthy peer,
    His breeches cost him but a crown ;
He held them sixpence all too dear,
    With that he call'd the tailor lown.

He was a wight of high renown,
    And thou art but of low degree :
'Tis pride that pulls the country down ;
    Then take thine auld cloak about thee.
Some wine, ho !   100

Cas. Why, this is a more exquisite song
than the other.

Iago. Will you hear't again ?

Cas. No ; for I hold him to be unworthy
of his place that does those things. Well,
God's above all ; and there be souls must be
saved, and there be souls must not be saved.

Iago. It's true, good lieutenant.

Cas. For mine own part,—no offence to
the general, nor any man of quality,—I hope
to be saved.   111

Iago. And so do I too, lieutenant.

Cas. Ay, but, by your leave, not before
me ; the lieutenant is to be saved before the
ancient. Let's have no more of this ; let's to
our affairs.—Forgive us our sins !—Gentlemen, let's look to our business. Do not think,
gentlemen, I am drunk : this is my ancient ;
this is my right hand, and this is my left : I
am not drunk now ; I can stand well enough,
and speak well enough.   120

All. Excellent well.

Cas. Why, very well then ; you must not
think then that I am drunk.   [*Exit.*

Mon. To the platform, masters ; come,
let's set the watch.

Iago. You see this fellow that is gone be-
    fore ;
He is a soldier fit to stand by Cæsar
And give direction : and do but see his vice ;
'Tis to his virtue a just equinox,
The one as long as the other : 'tis pity of him.
I fear the trust Othello puts him in,   131
On some odd time of his infirmity,
Will shake this island.

Mon.   But is he often thus ?

Iago. 'Tis evermore the prologue to his
    sleep :
He'll watch the horologe a double set,
If drink rock not his cradle.

Mon.   It were well
The general were put in mind of it.
Perhaps he sees it not ; or his good nature
Prizes the virtue that appears in Cassio, 139
And looks not on his evils : is not this true ?

Enter Roderigo.

Iago. [*Aside to him*] How now, Rod-
    erigo !
I pray you, after the lieutenant ; go.
                                      [*Exit Roderigo.*

Mon. And 'tis great pity that the noble
    Moor
Should hazard such a place as his own second
With one of an ingraft infirmity :
It were an honest action to say
So to the Moor.

Iago.   Not I, for this fair island :
I do love Cassio well ; and would do much
To cure him of this evil—But, hark ! what
    noise ?
          [*Cry within : '* Help ! help ! *'*

Re-enter Cassio, *driving in* Roderigo.

Cas. You rogue ! you rascal !

Mon.   What's the matter, lieutenant ?

Cas. A knave teach me my duty !   151

I'll beat the knave into a twiggen bottle.
Rod. Beat me!
Cas. Dost thou prate, rogue?
[*Striking Roderigo.*
Mon. Nay, good lieutenant;
[*Staying him.*
I pray you, sir, hold your hand.
Cas. Let me go, sir,
Or I'll knock you o'er the mazzard.
Mon. Come, come, you're drunk.
Cas. Drunk! [*They fight.*
Iago. [*Aside to Roderigo*] Away, I say;
go out, and cry a mutiny.
[*Exit Roderigo.*
Nay, good lieutenant,—alas, gentlemen;—
Help, ho!—Lieutenant,—sir,—Montano,—sir;
Help, masters!—Here's a goodly watch in-
deed! [*Bell rings.*
Who's that which rings the bell?—Diablo, ho!
The town will rise: God's will, lieutenant,
hold!
You will be shamed for ever.

Re-enter OTHELLO *and* Attendants.

Oth. What is the matter here?
Mon. 'Zounds, I bleed still; I am hurt to
the death. [*Faints.*
Oth. Hold, for your lives!
Iago. Hold, ho! Lieutenant,—sir,—Mon-
tano,—gentlemen,—
Have you forgot all sense of place and duty?
Hold! the general speaks to you; hold, hold,
for shame!
Oth. Why, how now, ho! from whence
ariseth this?
Are we turn'd Turks, and to ourselves do that
Which heaven hath forbid the Ottomites? 171
For Christian shame, put by this barbarous
brawl:
He that stirs next to carve for his own rage
Holds his soul light; he dies upon his motion.
Silence that dreadful bell: it frights the isle
From her propriety. What is the matter, mas-
ters?
Honest Iago, that look'st dead with grieving,
Speak, who began this? on thy love, I charge
thee.
Iago. I do not know: friends all but now,
even now, 179
In quarter, and in terms like bride and groom
Devesting them for bed; and then, but now—
As if some planet had unwitted men—
Swords out, and tilting one at other's breast,
In opposition bloody. I cannot speak
Any beginning to this peevish odds;
And would in action glorious I had lost
Those legs that brought me to a part of it!
Oth. How comes it, Michael, you are thus
forgot?
Cas. I pray you, pardon me; I cannot
speak.
Oth. Worthy Montano, you were wont to be
civil; 190
The gravity and stillness of your youth
The world hath noted, and your name is great
In mouths of wisest censure: what's the mat-
ter,
That you unlace your reputation thus
And spend your rich opinion for the name
Of a night-brawler? give me answer to it.
Mon. Worthy Othello, I am hurt to dan-
ger:

Your officer, Iago, can inform you,—
While I spare speech, which something now
offends me,—
Of all that I do know: nor know I aught 200
By me that's said or done amiss this night;
Unless self-charity be sometimes a vice,
And to defend ourselves it be a sin
When violence assails us.
Oth. Now, by heaven,
My blood begins my safer guides to rule;
And passion, having my best judgment collied,
Assays to lead the way: if I once stir,
Or do but lift this arm, the best of you
Shall sink in my rebuke. Give me to know
How this foul rout began, who set it on; 210
And he that is approved in this offence,
Though he had twinn'd with me, both at a
birth,
Shall lose me. What! in a town of war,
Yet wild, the people's hearts brimful of fear,
To manage private and domestic quarrel,
In night, and on the court and guard of
safety!
'Tis monstrous. Iago, who began't?
Mon. If partially affined, or leagued in
office,
Thou dost deliver more or less than truth,
Thou art no soldier.
Iago. Touch me not so near: 220
I had rather have this tongue cut from my
mouth
Than it should do offence to Michael Cassio;
Yet, I persuade myself, to speak the truth
Shall nothing wrong him. Thus it is, general.
Montano and myself being in speech,
There comes a fellow crying out for help:
And Cassio following him with determined
sword,
To execute upon him. Sir, this gentleman
Steps in to Cassio, and entreats his pause:
Myself the crying fellow did pursue, 230
Lest by his clamor—as it so fell out—
The town might fall in fright: he, swift of
foot,
Outran my purpose; and I return'd the rather
For that I heard the clink and fall of swords,
And Cassio high in oath; which till to-night
I ne'er might say before. When I came back—
For this was brief—I found them close to-
gether,
At blow and thrust; even as again they were
When you yourself did part them.
More of this matter cannot I report: 240
But men are men; the best sometimes forget:
Though Cassio did some little wrong to him,
As men in rage strike those that wish them
best,
Yet surely Cassio, I believe, received
From him that fled some strange indignity,
Which patience could not pass.
Oth. I know, Iago,
Thy honesty and love doth mince this matter,
Making it light to Cassio. Cassio, I love thee;
But never more be officer of mine.

Re-enter DESDEMONA, *attended.*

Look, if my gentle love be not raised up! 250
I'll make thee an example.
Des. What's the matter?
Oth. All's well now, sweeting; come away
to bed.

Sir, for your hurts, myself will be your sur-
    geon :
Lead him off.   [*To Montano, who is led off.*
Iago, look with care about the town,
And silence those whom this vile brawl dis-
    tracted.
Come, Desdemona : 'tis the soldiers' life
To have their balmy slumbers waked with
    strife. [*Exeunt all but Iago and Cassio.*
Iago. What, are you hurt, lieutenant ?
Cas. Ay, past all surgery.   260
Iago. Marry, heaven forbid !
Cas. Reputation, reputation, reputation !
O, I have lost my reputation ! I have lost the
immortal part of myself, and what remains is
bestial. My reputation, Iago, my reputation !
Iago. As I am an honest man, I thought
you had received some bodily wound ; there
is more sense in that than in reputation.
Reputation is an idle and most false imposition : oft got without merit, and lost without
deserving : you have lost no reputation at all,
unless you repute yourself such a loser.
What, man ! there are ways to recover the
general again : you are but now cast in his
mood, a punishment more in policy than in
malice, even so as one would beat his of-
fenceless dog to affright an imperious lion :
sue to him again, and he's yours.
Cas. I will rather sue to be despised than
to deceive so good a commander with so
slight, so drunken, and so indiscreet an officer. Drunk ? and speak parrot ? and squab-
ble ? swagger ? swear ? and discourse fustian
with one's own shadow ? O thou invisible
spirit of wine, if thou hast no name to be
known by, let us call thee devil !
Iago. What was he that you followed with
your sword ? What had he done to you ?
Cas. I know not.
Iago. Is't possible ?
Cas. I remember a mass of things, but
nothing distinctly ; a quarrel, but nothing
wherefore. O God, that men should put an
enemy in their mouths to steal away their
brains ! that we should, with joy, pleasance,
revel and applause, transform ourselves into
beasts !
Iago. Why, but you are now well enough :
how came you thus recovered ?
Cas. It hath pleased the devil drunkenness
to give place to the devil wrath ; one unper-
fectness shows me another, to make me
frankly despise myself.   300
Iago. Come, you are too severe a mor-
aler : as the time, the place, and the condition
of this country stands, I could heartily wish
this had not befallen ; but, since it is as it is,
mend it for your own good.
Cas. I will ask him for my place again ;
he shall tell me I am a drunkard ! Had I as
many mouths as Hydra, such an answer
would stop them all. To be now a sensible
man, by and by a fool, and presently a beast !
O strange ! Every inordinate cup is unblessed
and the ingredient is a devil.
Iago. Come, come, good wine is a good
familiar creature, if it be well used : exclaim
no more against it. And, good lieutenant, I
think you think I love you.
Cas. I have well approved it, sir. I drunk !
Iago. You or any man living may be drunk

at a time, man. I'll tell you what you shall
do. Our general's wife is now the general : I
may say so in this respect, for that he hath
devoted and given up himself to the contemplation, mark, and denotement of her parts
and graces : confess yourself freely to her ;
importune her help to put you in your place
again : she is of so free, so kind, so apt, so
blessed a disposition, she holds it a vice in
her goodness not to do more than she is requested : this broken joint between you and
her husband entreat her to splinter ; and, my
fortunes against any lay worth naming, this
crack of your love shall grow stronger than it
was before.   331
Cas. You advise me well.
Iago. I protest, in the sincerity of love and
honest kindness.
Cas. I think it freely ; and betimes in the
morning I will beseech the virtuous Desde-
mona to undertake for me : I am desperate
of my fortunes if they check me here.
Iago. You are in the right. Good night,
lieutenant ; I must to the watch.   340
Cas. Good night, honest Iago.   [*Exit.*
Iago. And what's he then that says I play
    the villain ?
When this advice is free I give and honest,
Probal to thinking and indeed the course
To win the Moor again ? For 'tis most easy
The inclining Desdemona to subdue
In any honest suit : she's framed as fruitful
As the free elements. And then for her
To win the Moor—were't to renounce his
    baptism,
All seals and symbols of redeemed sin,   350
His soul is so enfetter'd to her love,
That she may make, unmake, do what she
    list,
Even as her appetite shall play the god
With his weak function. How am I then a
    villain
To counsel Cassio to this parallel course,
Directly to his good ? Divinity of hell !
When devils will the blackest sins put on,
They do suggest at first with heavenly shows,
As I do now : for whiles this honest fool
Plies Desdemona to repair his fortunes   360
And she for him pleads strongly to the Moor,
I'll pour this pestilence into his ear,
That she repeals him for her body's lust ;
And by how much she strives to do him good,
She shall undo her credit with the Moor.
So will I turn her virtue into pitch,
And out of her own goodness make the net
That shall enmesh them all.

Re-enter RODERIGO.

                        How now, Roderigo !
Rod. I do follow here in the chase, not
like a hound that hunts, but one that fills up
the cry. My money is almost spent ; I have
been to-night exceedingly well cudgelled ; and
I think the issue will be, I shall have so much
experience for my pains, and so, with no
money at all and a little more wit, return
again to Venice.
Iago. How poor are they that have not
    patience !
What wound did ever heal but by degrees ?
Thou know'st we work by wit, and not by
    witchcraft ;

And wit depends on dilatory time.
Does't not go well ? Cassio hath beaten thee,
And thou, by that small hurt, hast cashier'd
 Cassio :   381
Though other things grow fair against the
 sun,
Yet fruits that blossom first will first be ripe :
Content thyself awhile. By the mass, 'tis
 morning ;
Pleasure and action make the hours seem
 short.
Retire thee ; go where thou art billeted :
Away, I say ; thou shalt know more here-
 after :
Nay, get thee gone. [*Exit Roderigo.*] Two
 things are to be done :
My wife must move for Cassio to her mis-
 tress ;
I'll set her on ;   390
Myself the while to draw the Moor apart,
And bring him jump when he may Cassio
 find
Soliciting his wife : ay, that's the way :
Dull not device by coldness and delay. [*Exit.*

ACT III.

SCENE I. *Before the castle.*

Enter CASSIO *and some* Musicians.

Cas. Masters, play here ; I will content
 your pains ;
Something that's brief ; and bid ' Good morrow, general.'   [*Music.*

Enter Clown.

Clo. Why, masters, have your instruments
been in Naples, that they speak i' the nose
thus ?
First Mus. How, sir, how !
Clo. Are these, I pray you, wind-instru-
ments ?
First Mus. Ay, marry, are they, sir.
Clo. O, thereby hangs a tail.
First Mus. Whereby hangs a tale, sir ? 9
Clo. Marry, sir, by many a wind-instru-
ment that I know. But, masters, here's money
for you : and the general so likes your music,
that he desires you, for love's sake, to make
no more noise with it.
First Mus. Well, sir, we will not.
Clo. If you have any music that may not
be heard, to't again : but, as they say, to
hear music the general does not greatly care.
First Mus. We have none such, sir.
Clo. Then put up your pipes in your bag,
for I'll away : go ; vanish into air ; away ! 21
      [*Exeunt Musicians.*
Cas. Dost thou hear, my honest friend ?
Clo. No, I hear not your honest friend ; I
hear you.
Cas. Prithee, keep up thy quillets. There's
a poor piece of gold for thee : if the gentlewoman that attends the general's wife be stirring, tell her there's one Cassio entreats her a
little favor of speech : wilt thou do this ?
Clo. She is stirring, sir : if she will stir
hither, I shall seem to notify unto her. 31
Cas. Do, good my friend. [*Exit Clown.*

Enter IAGO.

In happy time, Iago.

Iago. You have not been a-bed, then ?
Cas. Why, no ; the day had broke
Before we parted. I have made bold, Iago,
To send in to your wife : my suit to her
Is, that she will to virtuous Desdemona
Procure me some access.
Iago.   I'll send her to you presently ;
And I'll devise a mean to draw the Moor
Out of the way, that your converse and busi-
 ness
May be more free.   41
Cas. I humbly thank you for't. [*Exit
 Iago.*] I never knew
A Florentine more kind and honest.

Enter EMILIA.

Emil. Good morrow, good lieutenant : I
 am sorry
For your displeasure ; but all will sure be
 well.
The general and his wife are talking of it ;
And she speaks for you stoutly : the Moor
 replies,
That he you hurt is of great fame in Cyprus,
And great affinity, and that in wholesome
 wisdom
He might not but refuse you ; but he protests
 he loves you   50
And needs no other suitor but his likings
To take the safest occasion by the front
To bring you in again.
Cas.   Yet, I beseech you,
If you think fit, or that it may be done,
Give me advantage of some brief discourse
With Desdemona alone.
Emil.   Pray you, come in ;
I will bestow you where you shall have time
To speak your bosom freely.
Cas. I am much bound to you. [*Exeunt.*

SCENE II. *A room in the castle.*

Enter OTHELLO, IAGO, *and* Gentlemen.

Oth. These letters give, Iago, to the pilot ;
And by him do my duties to the senate :
That done, I will be walking on the works ;
Repair there to me.
Iago.   Well, my good lord, I'll do't.
Oth. This fortification, gentlemen, shall we
 see't ?
Gent. We'll wait upon your lordship.
          [*Exeunt.*

SCENE III. *The garden of the castle.*

Enter DESDEMONA, CASSIO, *and* EMILIA.

Des. Be thou assured, good Cassio, I will
 do
All my abilities in thy behalf.
Emil. Good madam, do : I warrant it
 grieves my husband,
As if the case were his.
Des. O, that's an honest fellow. Do not
 doubt, Cassio,
But I will have my lord and you again
As friendly as you were.
Cas.   Bounteous madam,
Whatever shall become of Michael Cassio,
He's never any thing but your true servant.
Des. I know't ; I thank you. You do love
 my lord :   10
You have known him long ; and be you well
 assured

He shall in strangeness stand no further off
Than in a polite distance.

Cas.   Ay, but, lady,
That policy may either last so long,
Or feed upon such nice and waterish diet,
Or breed itself so out of circumstance,
That, I being absent and my place supplied,
My general will forget my love and service.

Des. Do not doubt that; before Emilia
here
I give thee warrant of thy place : assure thee,
If I do vow a friendship, I'll perform it   21
To the last article : my lord shall never rest ;
I'll watch him tame and talk him out of pa-
tience ;
His bed shall seem a school, his board a
shrift ;
I'll intermingle every thing he does
With Cassio's suit : therefore be merry, Cas-
sio ;
For thy solicitor shall rather die
Than give thy cause away.

Emil. Madam, here comes my lord.

Cas. Madam, I'll take my leave.   30

Des. Why, stay, and hear me speak.

Cas. Madam, not now : I am very ill at
ease,
Unfit for mine own purposes.

Des. Well, do your discretion.
                              [*Exit Cassio.*

                Enter OTHELLO *and* IAGO.

Iago. Ha ! I like not that.

Oth.   What dost thou say ?

Iago. Nothing, my lord : or if—I know not
what.

Oth. Was not that Cassio parted from my
wife ?

Iago. Cassio, my lord ! No, sure, I cannot
think it,
That he would steal away so guilty-like,
Seeing you coming.

Oth.   I do believe 'twas he.   40

Des. How now, my lord !
I have been talking with a suitor here,
A man that languishes in your displeasure.

Oth. Who is't you mean ?

Des. Why, your lieutenant, Cassio. Good
my lord,
If I have any grace or power to move you,
His present reconciliation take ;
For if he be not one that truly loves you,
That errs in ignorance and not in cunning,
I have no judgment in an honest face :   50
I prithee, call him back.

Oth.   Went he hence now ?

Des. Ay, sooth ; so humbled
That he hath left part of his grief with me,
To suffer with him. Good love, call him back.

Oth. Not now, sweet Desdemona ; some
other time.

Des. But shall't be shortly ?

Oth.   The sooner, sweet, for you.

Des. Shall't be to-night at supper ?

Oth.   No, not to-night.

Des. To-morrow dinner, then ?

Oth.   I shall not dine at home ;
I meet the captains at the citadel.

Des. Why, then, to-morrow night ; or Tuesday morn ;   60
On Tuesday noon, or night ; on Wednesday
morn :

I prithee, name the time, but let it not
Exceed three days : in faith, he's penitent ;
And yet his trespass, in our common reason—
Save that, they say, the wars must make ex-
amples
Out of their best—is not almost a fault
To incur a private check. When shall he
come ?
Tell me, Othello : I wonder in my soul,
What you would ask me, that I should deny,
Or stand so mammering on. What ! Michael
Cassio,   70
That came a-wooing with you, and so many a
time,
When I have spoke of you dispraisingly,
Hath ta'en your part ; to have so much to do
To bring him in ! Trust me, I could do
much,—

Oth. Prithee, no more : let him come
when he will ;
I will deny thee nothing.

Des.   Why, this is not a boon ;
'Tis as I should entreat you wear your gloves,
Or feed on nourishing dishes, or keep you
warm,
Or sue to you to do a peculiar profit
To your own person : nay, when I have a suit
Wherein I mean to touch your love indeed, 81
It shall be full of poise and difficult weight
And fearful to be granted.

Oth.   I will deny thee nothing :
Whereon, I do beseech thee, grant me this,
To leave me but a little to myself.

Des. Shall I deny you ? no : farewell, my
lord.

Oth. Farewell, my Desdemona : I'll come
to thee straight.

Des. Emilia, come. Be as your fancies
teach you ;
Whate'er you be, I am obedient.
                [*Exeunt Desdemona and Emilia.*

Oth. Excellent wretch ! Perdition catch my
soul,   90
But I do love thee ! and when I love thee not,
Chaos is come again.

Iago. My noble lord,—

Oth.   What dost thou say, Iago ?

Iago. Did Michael Cassio, when you woo'd
my lady,
Know of your love ?

Oth. He did, from first to last : why dost
thou ask ?

Iago. But for a satisfaction of my thought ;
No further harm.

Oth.   Why of thy thought, Iago ?

Iago. I did not think he had been acquainted with her.

Oth. O, yes ; and went between us very oft.

Iago. Indeed !   101

Oth. Indeed ! ay, indeed : discern'st thou
aught in that ?
Is he not honest ?

Iago.   Honest, my lord !

Oth.   Honest ! ay, honest.

Iago. My lord, for aught I know.

Oth. What dost thou think ?

Iago.   Think, my lord !

Oth.   Think, my lord !
By heaven, he echoes me,
As if there were some monster in his thought
Too hideous to be shown. Thou dost mean
something :

I heard thee say even now, thou likedst not
    that,
When Cassio left my wife : what didst not
    like ?   110
And when I told thee he was of my counsel
In my whole course of wooing, thou criedst
    ' Indeed ! '
And didst contract and purse thy brow to-
    gether,
As if thou then hadst shut up in thy brain
Some horrible conceit : if thou dost love me,
Show me thy thought.
    Iago.   My lord, you know I love you.
    Oth.   I think thou dost ;
And, for I know thou 'rt full of love and hon-
    esty,
And weigh'st thy words before thou givest
    them breath,
Therefore these stops of thine fright me the
    more :   120
For such things in a false disloyal knave
Are tricks of custom, but in a man that's just
They are close delations, working from the
    heart
That passion cannot rule.
    Iago.   For Michael Cassio,
I dare be sworn I think that he is honest.
    Oth.   I think so too.
    Iago.   Men should be what they seem ;
Or those that be not, would they might seem
    none !
    Oth.   Certain, men should be what they
    seem.
    Iago.   Why, then, I think Cassio's an hon-
    est man.
    Oth.   Nay, yet there's more in this :   130
I prithee, speak to me as to thy thinkings,
As thou dost ruminate, and give thy worst of
    thoughts
The worst of words.
    Iago.   Good my lord, pardon me :
Though I am bound to every act of duty,
I am not bound to that all slaves are free to.
Utter my thoughts ? Why, say they are vile
    and false ;
As where's that palace whereinto foul things
Sometimes intrude not ? who has a breast so
    pure,
But some uncleanly apprehensions
Keep leets and law-days and in session sit 140
With meditations lawful ?
    Oth.   Thou dost conspire against thy friend,
    Iago,
If thou but think'st him wrong'd and makest
    his ear
A stranger to thy thoughts.
    Iago.   I do beseech you—
Though I perchance am vicious in my guess,
As, I confess, it is my nature's plague
To spy into abuses, and oft my jealousy
Shapes faults that are not—that your wisdom
    yet,
From one that so imperfectly conceits,
Would take no notice, nor build yourself a
    trouble   150
Out of his scattering and unsure observance.
It were not for your quiet nor your good,
Nor for my manhood, honesty, or wisdom,
To let you know my thoughts.
    Oth.   What dost thou mean ?
    Iago.   Good name in man and woman, dear
    my lord,

Is the immediate jewel of their souls :
Who steals my purse steals trash ; 'tis some-
    thing, nothing ;
'Twas mine, 'tis his, and has been slave to
    thousands ;
But he that filches from me my good name
Robs me of that which not enriches him   160
And makes me poor indeed.
    Oth.   By heaven, I'll know thy thoughts.
    Iago.   You cannot, if my heart were in
    your hand ;
Nor shall not, whilst 'tis in my custody.
    Oth.   Ha !
    Iago.   O, beware, my lord, of jealousy ;
It is the green-eyed monster which doth mock
The meat it feeds on ; that cuckold lives in
    bliss
Who, certain of his fate, loves not his
    wronger;
But, O, what damned minutes tells he o'er
Who dotes, yet doubts, suspects, yet strongly
    loves !   170
    Oth.   O misery !
    Iago.   Poor and content is rich and rich
    enough,
But riches fineless is as poor as winter
To him that ever fears he shall be poor.
Good heaven, the souls of all my tribe defend
From jealousy !
    Oth.   Why, why is this ?
Think'st thou I'ld make a life of jealousy,
To follow still the changes of the moon
With fresh suspicions ? No ; to be once in
    doubt
Is once to be resolved : exchange me for a
    goat,
When I shall turn the business of my soul 181
To such exsufflicate and blown surmises,
Matching thy inference. 'Tis not to make me
    jealous
To say my wife is fair, feeds well, loves com-
    pany,
Is free of speech, sings, plays and dances well ;
Where virtue is, these are more virtuous :
Nor from mine own weak merits will I draw
The smallest fear or doubt of her revolt ;
For she had eyes, and chose me. No, Iago ;
I'll see before I doubt ; when I doubt, prove ;
And on the proof, there is no more but this,—
Away at once with love or jealousy !
    Iago.   I am glad of it ; for now I shall have
    reason
To show the love and duty that I bear you
With franker spirit : therefore, as I am bound,
Receive it from me. I speak not yet of proof.
Look to your wife ; observe her well with
    Cassio ;
Wear your eye thus, not jealous nor secure :
I would not have your free and noble nature,
Out of self-bounty, be abused ; look to't : 200
I know our country disposition well ;
In Venice they do let heaven see the pranks
They dare not show their husbands ; their best
    conscience
Is not to leave't undone, but keep't unknown.
    Oth.   Dost thou say so ?
    Iago.   She did deceive her father, marrying
    you ;
And when she seem'd to shake and fear your
    looks,
She loved them most.
    Oth.   And so she did.

Iago.   Why, go to then ;
She that, so young, could give out such a
    seeming,
To seal her father's eyes up close as oak— 210
He thought 'twas witchcraft—but I am much
    to blame ;
I humbly do beseech you of your pardon
For too much loving you.
    Oth.   I am bound to thee for ever.
    Iago. I see this hath a little dash'd your
        spirits.
    Oth. Not a jot, not a jot.
    Iago.   I' faith, I fear it has.
I hope you will consider what is spoke
Comes from my love. But I do see you're
        moved :
I am to pray you not to strain my speech
To grosser issues nor to larger reach
Than to suspicion.   220
    Oth. I will not.
    Iago.   Should you do so, my lord,
My speech should fall into such vile success
As my thoughts aim not at. Cassio's my
        worthy friend—
My lord, I see you're moved.
    Oth.   No, not much moved :
I do not think but Desdemona's honest.
    Iago. Long live she so ! and long live you
        to think so !
    Oth. And yet, how nature erring from it-
        self,—
    Iago. Ay, there's the point : as—to be bold
        with you—
Not to affect many proposed matches   229
Of her own clime, complexion, and degree,
Whereto we see in all things nature tends—
Foh ! one may smell in such a will most rank,
Foul disproportion, thoughts unnatural.
But pardon me ; I do not in position
Distinctly speak of her ; though I may fear
Her will, recoiling to her better judgment,
May fall to match you with her country forms
And happily repent.
    Oth.   Farewell, farewell :
If more thou dost perceive, let me know more ;
Set on thy wife to observe : leave me, Iago.
    Iago. [*Going*] My lord, I take my leave.
    Oth. Why did I marry ? This honest crea-
        ture doubtless
Sees and knows more, much more, than he
    unfolds.
    Iago. [*Returning*] My lord, I would I
        might entreat your honor
To scan this thing no further ; leave it to
    time :
Though it be fit that Cassio have his place,
For sure, he fills it up with great ability,
Yet, if you please to hold him off awhile,
You shall by that perceive him and his
    means :
Note, if your lady strain his entertainment 250
With any strong or vehement importunity ;
Much will be seen in that. In the mean time,
Let me be thought too busy in my fears—
As worthy cause I have to fear I am—
And hold her free, I do beseech your honor.
    Oth. Fear not my government.
    Iago. I once more take my leave.   [*Exit.*
    Oth. This fellow's of exceeding honesty,
And knows all qualities, with a learned spirit,
Of human dealings. If I do prove her hag-
    gard,   260

Though that her jesses were my dear heart-
    strings,
I'ld whistle her off and let her down the wind,
To pray at fortune. Haply, for I am black
And have not those soft parts of conversation
That chamberers have, or for I am declined
Into the vale of years,—yet that's not much—
She's gone. I am abused ; and my relief
Must be to loathe her. O curse of marriage,
That we can call these delicate creatures ours,
And not their appetites ! I had rather be a
    toad,   270
And live upon the vapor of a dungeon,
Than keep a corner in the thing I love
For others' uses. Yet, 'tis the plague of great
    ones ;
Prerogatived are they less than the base ;
'Tis destiny unshunnable, like death :
Even then this forked plague is fated to us
When we do quicken. Desdemona comes :

Re-enter DESDEMONA *and* EMILIA.

If she be false, O, then heaven mocks itself !
I'll not believe 't.
    Des.   How now, my dear Othello !
Your dinner, and the generous islanders 280
By you invited, do attend your presence.
    Oth. I am to blame.
    Des.   Why do you speak so faintly ?
Are you not well ?
    Oth. I have a pain upon my forehead here.
    Des. 'Faith, that's with watching ; 'twill
        away again :
Let me but bind it hard, within this hour
It will be well.
    Oth.   Your napkin is too little :
        [*He puts the handkerchief from him ; and
                                    it drops.*
Let it alone. Come, I'll go in with you.
    Des. I am very sorry that you are not well.
                [*Exeunt Othello and Desdemona.*
    Emil. I am glad I have found this napkin :
This was her first remembrance from the
    Moor :
My wayward husband hath a hundred times
Woo'd me to steal it ; but she so loves the
    token,
For he conjured her she should ever keep it,
That she reserves it evermore about her
To kiss and talk to. I'll have the work ta'en
    out,
And give 't Iago : what he will do with it
Heaven knows, not I ;
I nothing but to please his fantasy.

Re-enter IAGO.

    Iago. How now ! what do you here alone ?
    Emil. Do not you chide ; I have a thing for
        you.   301
    Iago. A thing for me ? it is a common
        thing—
    Emil. Ha !
    Iago. To have a foolish wife.
    Emil. O, is that all ? What will you give
        me now
For the same handkerchief ?
    Iago.   What handkerchief ?
    Emil. What handkerchief ?
Why, that the Moor first gave to Desdemona ;
That which so often you did bid me steal.
    Iago. Hast stol'n it from her ?   310

Emil. No, 'faith ; she let it drop by negli-
gence.
And, to the advantage, I, being here, took 't
up.
Look, here it is.
   Iago.   A good wench ; give it me.
   Emil. What will you do with 't, that you
have been so earnest
To have me filch it ?
   Iago. [*Snatching it*] Why, what's that to
you ?
   Emil. If it be not for some purpose of im-
port,
Give 't me again : poor lady, she'll run mad
When she shall lack it.
   Iago. Be not acknown on 't ; I have use
for it.
Go, leave me.   [*Exit Emilia.* 320
I will in Cassio's lodging lose this napkin,
And let him find it. Trifles light as air
Are to the jealous confirmations strong
As proofs of holy writ : this may do something.
The Moor already changes with my poison :
Dangerous conceits are, in their natures, poi-
sons,
Which at the first are scarce found to distaste,
But with a little act upon the blood,
Burn like the mines of sulphur. I did say so :
Look, where he comes !

Re-enter OTHELLO.

              Not poppy, nor mandragora, 330
Nor all the drowsy syrups of the world,
Shall ever medicine thee to that sweet sleep
Which thou owedst yesterday.
   Oth.   Ha ! ha ! false to me ?
   Iago. Why, how now, general ! no more of
that.
   Oth. Avaunt ! be gone ! thou hast set me
on the rack :
I swear 'tis better to be much abused
Than but to know 't a little.
   Iago.   How now, my lord !
   Oth. What sense had I of her stol'n hours
of lust ?
I saw 't not, thought it not, it harm'd not me :
I slept the next night well, was free and
merry ;
I found not Cassio's kisses on her lips : 341
He that is robb'd, not wanting what is stol'n,
Let him not know 't, and he's not robb'd at all.
   Iago. I am sorry to hear this.
   Oth. I had been happy, if the general
camp,
Pioners and all, had tasted her sweet body,
So I had nothing known. O, now, for ever
Farewell the tranquil mind ! farewell content !
Farewell the plumed troop, and the big wars,
That make ambition virtue ! O, farewell ! 350
Farewell the neighing steed, and the shrill
trump,
The spirit-stirring drum, the ear-piercing fife,
The royal banner, and all quality,
Pride, pomp and circumstance of glorious
war !
And, O you mortal engines, whose rude
throats
The immortal Jove's dead clamors counterfeit,
Farewell ! Othello's occupation 's gone !
   Iago. Is 't possible, my lord ?
   Oth. Villain, be sure thou prove my love a
whore,

Be sure of it ; give me the ocular proof : 360
Or by the worth of man's eternal soul,
Thou hadst been better have been born a dog
Than answer my waked wrath !
   Iago.   Is't come to this ?
   Oth. Make me to see't ; or, at the least, so
prove it,
That the probation bear no hinge nor loop
To hang a doubt on ; or woe upon thy life !
   Iago. My noble lord,—
   Oth. If thou dost slander her and torture
me,
Never pray more ; abandon all remorse ;
On horror's head horrors accumulate ; 370
Do deeds to make heaven weep, all earth
amazed ;
For nothing canst thou to damnation add
Greater than that.
   Iago.   O grace ! O heaven forgive me !
Are you a man ? have you a soul or sense ?
God be wi' you ; take mine office. O wretched
fool,
That livest to make thine honesty a vice !
O monstrous world ! Take note, take note, O
world,
To be direct and honest is not safe.
I thank you for this profit ; and from hence
I'll love no friend, sith love breeds such of-
fence.
   Oth. Nay, stay : thou shouldst be honest.
   Iago. I should be wise, for honesty's a fool
And loses that it works for.
   Oth.   By the world,
I think my wife be honest and think she is not ;
I think that thou art just and think thou art
not.
I'll have some proof. Her name, that was as
fresh
As Dian's visage, is now begrimed and black
As mine own face. If there be cords, or knives,
Poison, or fire, or suffocating streams,
I'll not endure it. Would I were satisfied ! 390
   Iago. I see, sir, you are eaten up with pas-
sion :
I do repent me that I put it to you.
You would be satisfied ?
   Oth.   Would ! nay, I will.
   Iago. And may : but, how ? how satisfied,
my lord ?
Would you, the supervisor, grossly gape on—
Behold her topp'd ?
   Oth.   Death and damnation ! O !
   Iago. It were a tedious difficulty, I think,
To bring them to that prospect : damn them
then,
If ever mortal eyes do see them bolster
More than their own ! What then ? how then ?
What shall I say ? Where's satisfaction ? 401
It is impossible you should see this,
Were they as prime as goats, as hot as mon-
keys,
As salt as wolves in pride, and fools as gross
As ignorance made drunk. But yet, I say,
If imputation and strong circumstances,
Which lead directly to the door of truth,
Will give you satisfaction, you may have 't.
   Oth. Give me a living reason she's disloyal.
   Iago. I do not like the office :   410
But, sith I am enter'd in this cause so far,
Prick'd to 't by foolish honesty and love,
I will go on. I lay with Cassio lately ;
And, being troubled with a raging tooth,

I could not sleep.
There are a kind of men so loose of soul,
That in their sleeps will mutter their affairs :
One of this kind is Cassio :
In sleep I heard him say ' Sweet Desdemona,
Let us be wary, let us hide our loves ; ' 420
And then, sir, would he gripe and wring my
    hand,
Cry ' O sweet creature ! ' and then kiss me
    hard,
As if he pluck'd up kisses by the roots
That grew upon my lips : then laid his leg
Over my thigh, and sigh'd, and kiss'd ; and
    then
Cried ' Cursed fate that gave thee to the
    Moor ! '
    Oth. O monstrous ! monstrous !
    Iago. Nay, this was but his dream.
    Oth. But this denoted a foregone con-
    clusion :
'Tis a shrewd doubt, though it be but a dream.
    Iago. And this may help to thicken other
    proofs 430
That do demonstrate thinly.
    Oth. I'll tear her all to pieces.
    Iago. Nay, but be wise : yet we see noth-
    ing done ;
She may be honest yet. Tell me but this,
Have you not sometimes seen a handkerchief
Spotted with strawberries in your wife's hand ?
    Oth. I gave her such a one ; 'twas my first
    gift.
    Iago. I know not that ; but such a hand-
    kerchief—
I am sure it was your wife's—did I to-day
See Cassio wipe his beard with.
    Oth. If it be that,— 439
    Iago. If it be that, or any that was hers,
It speaks against her with the other proofs.
    Oth. O, that the slave had forty thousand
    lives !
One is too poor, too weak for my revenge.
Now do I see 'tis true. Look here, Iago ;
All my fond love thus do I blow to heaven.
'Tis gone.
Arise, black vengeance, from thy hollow cell !
Yield up, O love, thy crown and hearted
    throne
To tyrannous hate ! Swell, bosom, with thy
    fraught,
For 'tis of aspics' tongues !
    Iago. Yet be content. 450
    Oth. O, blood, blood, blood !
    Iago. Patience, I say ; your mind perhaps
    may change.
    Oth. Never, Iago. Like to the Pontic sea,
Whose icy current and compulsive course
Ne'er feels retiring ebb, but keeps due on
To the Propontic and the Hellespont,
Even so my bloody thoughts, with violent
    pace,
Shall ne'er look back, ne'er ebb to humble
    love,
Till that a capable and wide revenge
Swallow them up. Now, by yond marble
    heaven, 460
[*Kneels*] In the due reverence of a sacred vow
I here engage my words.
    Iago. Do not rise yet.
[*Kneels*] Witness, you ever-burning lights
    above,
You elements that clip us round about,

Witness that here Iago doth give up
The execution of his wit, hands, heart,
To wrong'd Othello's service ! Let him com-
    mand,
And to obey shall be in me remorse,
What bloody business ever. [*They rise.*
    Oth. I greet thy love,
Not with vain thanks, but with acceptance
    bounteous, 470
And will upon the instant put thee to't :
Within these three days let me hear thee say
That Cassio's not alive.
    Iago. My friend is dead ; 'tis done at your
    request :
But let her live.
    Oth. Damn her, lewd minx ! O, damn her !
Come, go with me apart ; I will withdraw,
To furnish me with some swift means of death
For the fair devil. Now art thou my lieuten-
    ant.
    Iago. I am your own for ever. [*Exeunt.*

SCENE IV. *Before the castle.*

Enter DESDEMONA, EMILIA, *and* Clown.

    Des. Do you know, sirrah, where Lieuten-
ant Cassio lies ?
    Clo. I dare not say he lies any where.
    Des. Why, man ?
    Clo. He's a soldier, and for one to say a
soldier lies, is stabbing.
    Des. Go to : where lodges he ?
    Clo. To tell you where he lodges, is to tell
you where I lie.
    Des. Can any thing be made of this ? 10
    Clo. I know not where he lodges, and for
me to devise a lodging and say he lies here or
he lies there, were to lie in mine own throat.
    Des. Can you inquire him out, and be edi-
fied by report ?
    Clo. I will catechize the world for him ;
that is, make questions, and by them answer.
    Des. Seek him, bid him come hither : tell
him I have moved my lord on his behalf, and
hope all will be well. 20
    Clo. To do this is within the compass of
man's wit : and therefore I will attempt the
doing it. [*Exit.*
    Des. Where should I lose that handker-
chief, Emilia ?
    Emil. I know not, madam.
    Des. Believe me, I had rather have lost my
purse
Full of crusadoes : and, but my noble Moor
Is true of mind and made of no such base-
    ness
As jealous creatures are, it were enough
To put him to ill thinking.
    Emil. Is he not jealous ?
    Des. Who, he ? I think the sun where he
    was born 30
Drew all such humors from him.
    Emil. Look, where he comes.
    Des. I will not leave him now till Cassio
Be call'd to him.

Enter OTHELLO.

            How is't with you, my lord ?
    Oth. Well, my good lady. [*Aside*] O, hard-
    ness to dissemble !—
How do you, Desdemona ?
    Des.   Well, my good lord.

Oth. Give me your hand : this hand is
    moist, my lady.
Des. It yet hath felt no age nor known no
    sorrow.
Oth. This argues fruitfulness and liberal
    heart :
Hot, hot, and moist : this hand of yours re-
    quires
A sequester from liberty, fasting and prayer,
Much castigation, exercise devout ;   41
For here's a young and sweating devil here,
That commonly rebels. 'Tis a good hand,
A frank one.
Des.   You may, indeed, say so ;
For 'twas that hand that gave away my heart.
Oth. A liberal hand : the hearts of old
    gave hands ;
But our new heraldry is hands, not hearts.
Des. I cannot speak of this. Come now,
    your promise.
Oth. What promise, chuck ?
Des. I have sent to bid Cassio come speak
    with you.   50
Oth. I have a salt and sorry rheum offends
    me ;
Lend me thy handkerchief.
Des.   Here, my lord.
Oth. That which I gave you.
Des.   I have it not about me.
Oth. Not ?
Des.   No, indeed, my lord.
Oth.   That is a fault.
That handkerchief
Did an Egyptian to my mother give ;
She was a charmer, and could almost read
The thoughts of people : she told her, while
    she kept it,
'Twould make her amiable and subdue my
    father
Entirely to her love, but if she lost it   60
Or made a gift of it, my father's eye
Should hold her loathed and his spirits should
    hunt
After new fancies : she, dying, gave it me ;
And bid me, when my fate would have me
    wive,
To give it her. I did so : and take heed on't ;
Make it a darling like your precious eye ;
To lose 't or give 't away were such perdition
As nothing else could match.
Des.   Is 't possible ?
Oth. 'Tis true : there's magic in the web of
    it :
A sibyl, that had number'd in the world   70
The sun to course two hundred compasses,
In her prophetic fury sew'd the work ;
The worms were hallow'd that did breed the
    silk ;
And it was dyed in mummy which the skilful
Conserved of maidens' hearts.
Des.   Indeed ! is't true ?
Oth. Most veritable ; therefore look to 't
    well.
Des. Then would to God that I had never
    seen 't !
Oth. Ha ! wherefore ?
Des. Why do you speak so startingly and
    rash ?
Oth. Is 't lost ? is 't gone ? speak, is it out
    o' the way ?   80
Des. Heaven bless us !
Oth. Say you ?

Des. It is not lost ; but what an if it were ?
Oth. How !
Des. I say, it is not lost.
Oth.   Fetch 't, let me see 't.
Des. Why, so I can, sir, but I will not now.
This is a trick to put me from my suit :
Pray you, let Cassio be received again :
Oth. Fetch me the handkerchief : my mind
    misgives.
Des. Come, come ;   90
You'll never meet a more sufficient man.
Oth. The handkerchief !
Des.   I pray, talk me of Cassio.
Oth. The handkerchief !
Des.   A man that all his time
Hath founded his good fortunes on your love,
Shared dangers with you,—
Oth. The handkerchief !
Des. In sooth, you are to blame.
Oth. Away !   [*Exit.*
Emil. Is not this man jealous ?
Des. I ne'er saw this before.   100
Sure, there's some wonder in this handker-
    chief :
I am most unhappy in the loss of it.
Emil. 'Tis not a year or two shows us a
    man :
They are all but stomachs, and we all but
    food ;
To eat us hungerly, and when they are full,
They belch us. Look you, Cassio and my
    husband !

Enter CASSIO *and* IAGO.

Iago. There is no other way ; 'tis she must
    do 't :
And, lo, the happiness ! go, and importune her.
Des. How now, good Cassio ! what 's the
    news with you ?
Cas. Madam, my former suit : I do be-
    seech you   110
That by your virtuous means I may again
Exist, and be a member of his love
Whom I with all the office of my heart
Entirely honor : I would not be delay'd.
If my offence be of such mortal kind
That nor my service past, nor present sorrows,
Nor purposed merit in futurity,
Can ransom me into his love again,
But to know so must be my benefit ;
So shall I clothe me in a forced content, 120
And shut myself up in some other course,
To fortune's alms.
Des.   Alas, thrice-gentle Cassio !
My advocation is not now in tune ;
My lord is not my lord ; nor should I know
    him,
Were he in favor as in humor alter'd.
So help me every spirit sanctified,
As I have spoken for you all my best
And stood within the blank of his displeasure
For my free speech ! you must awhile be pa-
    tient :
What I can do I will ; and more I will   130
Than for myself I dare : let that suffice you.
Iago. Is my lord angry ?
Emil.   He went hence but now,
And certainly in strange unquietness.
Iago. Can he be angry ? I have seen the
    cannon,
When it hath blown his ranks into the air,
And, like the devil, from his very arm

Puff'd his own brother :—and can he be an-
  gry ?
Something of moment then : I will go meet
  him :
There's matter in 't indeed, if he be angry.
  Des. I prithee, do so.   [*Exit Iago.*
        Something, sure, of state, 140
Either from Venice, or some unhatch'd prac-
  tice
Made demonstrable here in Cyprus to him,
Hath puddled his clear spirit : and in such
  cases
Men's natures wrangle with inferior things,
Though great ones are their object. 'Tis even
  so ;
For let our finger ache, and it indues
Our other healthful members even to that
  sense
Of pain : nay, we must think men are not gods,
Nor of them look for such observances
As fit the bridal. Beshrew me much, Emilia,
I was, unhandsome warrior as I am,   151
Arraigning his unkindness with my soul ;
But now I find I had suborn'd the witness,
And he's indicted falsely.
  Emil.   Pray heaven it be state-matters, as
    you think,
And no conception nor no jealous toy
Concerning you.
  Des.   Alas the day ! I never gave him cause.
  Emil.   But jealous souls will not be an-
    swer'd so ;
They are not ever jealous for the cause, 160
But jealous for they are jealous : 'tis a mon-
  ster
Begot upon itself, born on itself.
  Des.   Heaven keep that monster from
    Othello's mind !
  Emil.   Lady, amen.
  Des.   I will go seek him. Cassio, walk here-
    about :
If I do find him fit, I'll move your suit
And seek to effect it to my uttermost.
  Cas.   I humbly thank your ladyship.
    [*Exeunt Desdemona and Emilia.*

        Enter BIANCA.

  Bian.   Save you, friend Cassio !
  Cas.   What make you from home ?
How is it with you, my most fair Bianca ? 170
I' faith, sweet love, I was coming to your
  house.
  Bian.   And I was going to your lodging,
    Cassio.
What, keep a week away ? seven days and
  nights ?
Eight score eight hours ? and lovers' absent
  hours,
More tedious than the dial eight score times ?
O weary reckoning !
  Cas.   Pardon me, Bianca :
I have this while with leaden thoughts been
  press'd :
But I shall, in a more continuate time,
Strike off this score of absence. Sweet Bianca,
  [*Giving her Desdemona's handkerchief.*
Take me this work out.
  Bian.   O Cassio, whence came this ? 180
This is some token from a newer friend :
To the felt absence now I feel a cause :
Is 't come to this ? Well, well.
  Cas.   Go to, woman !

Throw your vile guesses in the devil's teeth,
From whence you have them. You are jealous
  now
That this is from some mistress, some remem-
  brance :
No, in good troth, Bianca.
  Bian.   Why, whose is it ?
  Cas.   I know not, sweet : I found it in my
    chamber.   188
I like the work well : ere it be demanded—
As like enough it will—I'd have it copied :
Take it, and do 't ; and leave me for this time.
  Bian.   Leave you ! wherefore ?
  Cas.   I do attend here on the general ;
And think it no addition, nor my wish,
To have him see me woman'd.
  Bian.   Why, I pray you ?
  Cas.   Not that I love you not.
  Bian.   But that you do not love me.
I pray you, bring me on the way a little,
And say if I shall see you soon at night.
  Cas.   'Tis but a little way that I can bring
    you ;
For I attend here : but I'll see you soon. 200
  Bian.   'Tis very good ; I must be circum-
    stanced.   [*Exeunt.*

          ——————

ACT IV.

  Scene I. *Cyprus. Before the castle.*

    Enter OTHELLO *and* IAGO.
  Iago.   Will you think so ?
  Oth.   Think so, Iago !
  Iago.   What,
To kiss in private ?
  Oth.   An unauthorized kiss.
  Iago.   Or to be naked with her friend in
    bed
An hour or more, not meaning any harm ?
  Oth.   Naked in bed, Iago, and not mean
    harm !
It is hypocrisy against the devil :
They that mean virtuously, and yet do so,
The devil their virtue tempts, and they tempt
  heaven.
  Iago.   So they do nothing, 'tis a venial slip :
But if I give my wife a handkerchief,—   10
  Oth.   What then ?
  Iago.   Why, then, 'tis hers, my lord ; and,
    being hers,
She may, I think, bestow't on any man.
  Oth.   She is protectress of her honor too :
May she give that ?
  Iago.   Her honor is an essence that's not
    seen ;
They have it very oft that have it not :
But, for the handkerchief,—
  Oth.   By heaven, I would most gladly have
    forgot it.
Thou said'st—O, it comes o'er my memory, 20
As doth the raven o'er the infected house,
Boding to all—he had my handkerchief.
  Iago.   Ay, what of that ?
  Oth.   That's not so good now.
  Iago.   What,
If I had said I had seen him do you wrong ?
Or heard him say,—as knaves be such abroad,
Who having, by their own importunate suit,
Or voluntary dotage of some mistress,

Convinced or supplied them, cannot choose
But they must blab—

Oth.   Hath he said any thing?
Iago. He hath, my lord; but be you well
    assured,   30
No more than he'll unswear.

Oth.   What hath he said?
Iago. 'Faith, that he did—I know not what
    he did.

Oth. What? what?
Iago. Lie—
Oth.   With her?
Iago.   With her, on her; what you will.
Oth. Lie with her! lie on her! We say lie
on her, when they belie her. Lie with her!
that's fulsome.—Handkerchief—confessions—
handkerchief!—To confess, and be hanged for
his labor;—first, to be hanged, and then to
confess.—I tremble at it. Nature would not
invest herself in such shadowing passion without some instruction. It is not words that
shake me thus. Pish! Noses, ears, and lips.
—Is't possible?—Confess—handkerchief!—O
devil!   [*Falls in a trance.*

Iago. Work on,
My medicine, work! Thus credulous fools are
    caught;
And many worthy and chaste dames even thus,
All guiltless, meet reproach. What, ho! my
    lord!
My lord, I say! Othello!

Enter CASSIO.

                          How now, Cassio!
Cas. What's the matter?   50
Iago. My lord is fall'n into an epilepsy:
This is his second fit; he had one yesterday.
Cas. Rub him about the temples.
Iago.   No, forbear;
The lethargy must have his quiet course:
If not, he foams at mouth and by and by
Breaks out to savage madness. Look, he stirs:
Do you withdraw yourself a little while,
He will recover straight: when he is gone,
I would on great occasion speak with you.   59
                          [*Exit Cassio.*
How is it, general? have you not hurt your
    head?
Oth. Dost thou mock me?
Iago.   I mock you! no, by heaven.
Would you would bear your fortune like a
    man!
Oth. A horned man's a monster and a
    beast.
Iago. There's many a beast then in a popu-
    lous city,
And many a civil monster.
Oth. Did he confess it?
Iago.   Good sir, be a man;
Think every bearded fellow that's but yoked
May draw with you: there's millions now alive
That nightly lie in those unproper beds
Which they dare swear peculiar: your case is
    better.   70
O, 'tis the spite of hell, the fiend's arch-mock,
To lip a wanton in a secure couch,
And to suppose her chaste! No, let me know;
And knowing what I am, I know what she
    shall be.
Oth. O, thou art wise; 'tis certain.
Iago.   Stand you awhile apart;
Confine yourself but in a patient list.

Whilst you were here o'erwhelmed with your
    grief—
A passion most unsuiting such a man—
Cassio came hither: I shifted him away,
And laid good 'scuse upon your ecstasy,   80
Bade him anon return and here speak with me;
The which he promised. Do but encave your-
    self,
And mark the fleers, the gibes, and notable
    scorns,
That dwell in every region of his face;
For I will make him tell the tale anew,
Where, how, how oft, how long ago, and when
He hath, and is again to cope your wife:
I say, but mark his gesture. Marry, patience;
Or I shall say you are all in all in spleen,
And nothing of a man.
Oth.   Dost thou hear, Iago?   90
I will be found most cunning in my patience;
But—dost thou hear?—most bloody.
Iago.   That's not amiss;
But yet keep time in all. Will you withdraw?
                          [*Othello retires.*
Now will I question Cassio of Bianca,
A housewife that by selling her desires
Buys herself bread and clothes: it is a creature
That dotes on Cassio; as 'tis the strumpet's
    plague
To beguile many and be beguiled by one:
He, when he hears of her, cannot refrain   99
From the excess of laughter. Here he comes:

Re-enter CASSIO.

As he shall smile, Othello shall go mad;
And his unbookish jealousy must construe
Poor Cassio's smiles, gestures and light be-
    havior,
Quite in the wrong. How do you now, lieu-
    tenant?
Cas. The worser that you give me the ad-
    dition
Whose want even kills me.
Iago. Ply Desdemona well, and you are
    sure on't.
[*Speaking lower*] Now, if this suit lay in
    Bianca's power,
How quickly should you speed!
Cas.   Alas, poor caitiff!
Oth. Look, how he laughs already!   110
Iago. I never knew woman love man so.
Cas. Alas, poor rogue! I think, i' faith, she
    loves me.
Oth. Now he denies it faintly, and laughs
    it out.
Iago. Do you hear, Cassio?
Oth.   Now he importunes him
To tell it o'er: go to; well said, well said.
Iago. She gives it out that you shall marry
    her:
Do you intend it?
Cas. Ha, ha, ha!   120
Oth. Do you triumph, Roman? do you
    triumph?
Cas. I marry her! what? a customer!
Prithee, bear some charity to my wit: do not
think it so unwholesome. Ha, ha, ha!
Oth. So, so, so, so: they laugh that win.
Iago. 'Faith, the cry goes that you shall
    marry her.
Cas. Prithee, say true.
Iago. I am a very villain else.
Oth. Have you scored me? Well.   130

Cas. This is the monkey's own giving out : she is persuaded I will marry her, out of her own love and flattery, not out of my promise.

Oth. Iago beckons me ; now he begins the story.

Cas. She was here even now ; she haunts me in every place. I was the other day talking on the sea-bank with certain Venetians ; and thither comes the bauble, and, by this hand, she falls me thus about my neck— 140

Oth. Crying ' O dear Cassio ! ' as it were : his gesture imports it.

Cas. So hangs, and lolls, and weeps upon me ; so hales, and pulls me : ha, ha, ha !

Oth. Now he tells how she plucked him to my chamber. O, I see that nose of yours, but not that dog I shall throw it to.

Cas. Well, I must leave her company.

Iago. Before me ! look, where she comes.

Cas. 'Tis such another fitchew ! marry, a perfumed one. 151

Enter BIANCA.

What do you mean by this haunting of me ?

Bian. Let the devil and his dam haunt you ! What do you mean by that same handkerchief you gave me even now ? I was a fine fool to take it. I must take out the work ?—A likely piece of work, that you should find it in your chamber, and not know who left it there ! This is some minx's token, and I must take out the work ? There ; give it your hobby-horse : wheresoever you had it, I'll take out no work on 't. 161

Cas. How now, my sweet Bianca ! how now ! how now !

Oth. By heaven, that should be my handkerchief !

Bian. An you'll come to supper to-night, you may ; an you will not, come when you are next prepared for. [*Exit.*

Iago. After her, after her.

Cas. 'Faith, I must ; she'll rail in the street else. 171

Iago. Will you sup there ?

Cas. 'Faith, I intend so.

Iago. Well, I may chance to see you ; for I would very fain speak with you.

Cas. Prithee, come ; will you ?

Iago. Go to ; say no more. [*Exit Cassio.*

Oth. [*Advancing*] How shall I murder him, Iago ?

Iago. Did you perceive how he laughed at his vice ? 181

Oth. O Iago !

Iago. And did you see the handkerchief ?

Oth. Was that mine ?

Iago. Yours by this hand : and to see how he prizes the foolish woman your wife ! she gave it him, and he hath given it his whore.

Oth. I would have him nine years a-killing. A fine woman ! a fair woman ! a sweet woman !

Iago. Nay, you must forget that. 190

Oth. Ay, let her rot, and perish, and be damned to-night ; for she shall not live : no, my heart is turned to stone ; I strike it, and it hurts my hand. O, the world hath not a sweeter creature : she might lie by an emperor's side and command him tasks.

Iago. Nay, that's not your way.

Oth. Hang her ! I do but say what she is : so delicate with her needle : an admirable

musician : O ! she will sing the savageness out of a bear : of so high and plenteous wit and invention :— 201

Iago. She's the worse for all this.

Oth. O, a thousand thousand times : and then, of so gentle a condition !

Iago. Ay, too gentle.

Oth. Nay, that's certain : but yet the pity of it, Iago ! O Iago, the pity of it, Iago !

Iago. If you are so fond over her iniquity, give her patent to offend ; for, if it touch not you, it comes near nobody. 210

Oth. I will chop her into messes : cuckold me !

Iago. O, 'tis foul in her.

Oth. With mine officer !

Iago. That's fouler.

Oth. Get me some poison, Iago ; this night : I'll not expostulate with her, lest her body and beauty unprovide my mind again : this night, Iago. 219

Iago. Do it not with poison, strangle her in her bed, even the bed she hath contaminated.

Oth. Good, good : the justice of it pleases : very good.

Iago. And for Cassio, let me be his undertaker : you shall hear more by midnight.

Oth. Excellent good. [*A trumpet within.*] What trumpet is that same ?

Iago. Something from Venice, sure. 'Tis Lodovico

Come from the duke : and, see, your wife is with him.

Enter LODOVICO, DESDEMONA, *and* Attendants.

Lod. Save you, worthy general !

Oth.   With all my heart, sir.

Lod. The duke and senators of Venice greet you.   [*Gives him a letter.*

Oth. I kiss the instrument of their pleasures.   [*Opens the letter, and reads.*

Des. And what's the news, good cousin Lodovico ?

Iago. I am very glad to see you, signior ; Welcome to Cyprus.

Lod. I thank you. How does Lieutenant Cassio ?

Iago. Lives, sir.

Des. Cousin, there's fall'n between him and my lord

An unkind breach : but you shall make all well.

Oth. Are you sure of that ?

Des. My lord ?

Oth. [*Reads*] ' This fail you not to do, as you will—' 240

Lod. He did not call ; he's busy in the paper.

Is there division 'twixt my lord and Cassio ?

Des. A most unhappy one : I would do much

To atone them, for the love I bear to Cassio.

Oth. Fire and brimstone !

Des.   My lord ?

Oth.   Are you wise ?

Des. What, is he angry ?

Lod.   May be the letter moved him ;

For, as I think, they do command him home, Deputing Cassio in his government.

Des. Trust me, I am glad on't.

Oth.   Indeed !

Des.　　　　　　　　　　My lord ?
Oth. I am glad to see you mad.
Des.　　　　Why, sweet Othello,— 250
Oth. [*Striking her*] Devil !
Des. I have not deserved this.
Lod. My lord, this would not be believed in Venice,
Though I should swear I saw't : 'tis very much :
Make her amends ; she weeps.
Oth.　　　　　　　　O devil, devil !
If that the earth could teem with woman's tears,
Each drop she falls would prove a crocodile.
Out of my sight !
　Des. I will not stay to offend you. [*Going.*
Lod. Truly, an obedient lady :
I do beseech your lordship, call her back. 260
Oth. Mistress !
Des.　　　　　　　　My lord ?
Oth.　　　　What would you with her, sir ?
Lod. Who, I, my lord ?
Oth. Ay ; you did wish that I would make her turn :
Sir, she can turn, and turn, and yet go on,
And turn again ; and she can weep, sir, weep ;
And she's obedient, as you say, obedient,
Very obedient. Proceed you in your tears.
Concerning this, sir,—O well-painted passion !—
I am commanded home. Get you away ;
I'll send for you anon. Sir, I obey the mandate,　　　　　　　　　　　　270
And will return to Venice. Hence, avaunt !
　　　　　　　　　　　[*Exit Desdemona.*
Cassio shall have my place. And, sir, tonight,
I do entreat that we may sup together :
You are welcome, sir, to Cyprus.—Goats and monkeys !　　　　　　　　　[*Exit.*
Lod. Is this the noble Moor whom our full senate
Call all in all sufficient ? Is this the nature
Whom passion could not shake ? whose solid virtue
The shot of accident, nor dart of chance,
Could neither graze nor pierce ?
Iago.　　　　　He is much changed.
Lod. Are his wits safe ? is he not light of brain ?　　　　　　　　　　　280
Iago. He's that he is : I may not breathe my censure
What he might be : if what he might he is not,
I would to heaven he were !
Lod.　　　　What, strike his wife !
Iago. 'Faith, that was not so well ; yet would I knew
That stroke would prove the worst !
Lod.　　　　　　　　Is it his use ?
Or did the letters work upon his blood,
And new-create this fault ?
Iago.　　　　　　　　Alas, alas !
It is not honesty in me to speak
What I have seen and known. You shall observe him,
And his own courses will denote him so 290
That I may save my speech : do but go after,
And mark how he continues.
Lod. I am sorry that I am deceived in him.
　　　　　　　　　　　　　[*Exeunt.*

SCENE II. *A room in the castle.*
Enter OTHELLO *and* EMILIA.

Oth. You have seen nothing then ?
Emil. Nor ever heard, nor ever did suspect.
Oth. Yes, you have seen Cassio and she together.
Emil. But then I saw no harm, and then I heard
Each syllable that breath made up between them.
Oth. What, did they never whisper ?
Emil.　　　　　　　　Never, my lord.
Oth. Nor send you out o' the way ?
Emil. Never.
Oth. To fetch her fan, her gloves, her mask, nor nothing ?
Emil. Never, my lord.　　　　　　　10
Oth. That's strange.
Emil. I durst, my lord, to wager she is honest,
Lay down my soul at stake : if you think other,
Remove your thought ; it doth abuse your bosom.
If any wretch have put this in your head,
Let heaven requite it with the serpent's curse !
For, if she be not honest, chaste, and true,
There's no man happy ; the purest of their wives
Is foul as slander.
Oth.　　　Bid her come hither : go.
　　　　　　　　　　　[*Exit Emilia.*
She says enough ; yet she's a simple bawd 20
That cannot say as much. This is a subtle whore,
A closet lock and key of villanous secrets :
And yet she'll kneel and pray ; I have seen her do 't.

Enter DESDEMONA *with* EMILIA.

Des. My lord, what is your will ?
Oth.　　　　Pray, chuck, come hither.
Des. What is your pleasure ?
Oth.　　　　Let me see your eyes ;
Look in my face.
Des.　　　What horrible fancy 's this ?
Oth. [*To Emilia*] Some of your function, mistress ;
Leave procreants alone and shut the door ;
Cough, or cry ' hem,' if any body come :
Your mystery, your mystery : nay, dispatch.
　　　　　　　　　　[*Exit Emilia.* 30
Des. Upon my knees, what doth your speech import ?
I understand a fury in your words.
But not the words.
Oth. Why, what art thou ?
Des.　　　Your wife, my lord ; your true
And loyal wife.
Oth.　　　Come, swear it, damn thyself ;
Lest, being like one of heaven, the devils themselves
Should fear to seize thee : therefore be double damn'd :
Swear thou art honest.
Des.　　　Heaven doth truly know it.
Oth. Heaven truly knows that thou art false as hell.
Des. To whom, my lord ? with whom ? how am I false ?　　　　　　　40
Oth. O Desdemona ! away ! away ! away !
Des. Alas the heavy day ! Why do you weep ?
Am I the motive of these tears, my lord ?
If haply you my father do suspect

An instrument of this your calling back,
Lay not your blame on me : if you have lost
    him,
Why, I have lost him too.
   Oth.   Had it pleased heaven
To try me with affliction ; had they rain'd
All kinds of sores and shames on my bare
    head.
Steep'd me in poverty to the very lips,   50
Given to captivity me and my utmost hopes,
I should have found in some place of my soul
A drop of patience : but, alas, to make me
A fixed figure for the time of scorn
To point his slow unmoving finger at !
Yet could I bear that too ; well, very well :
But there, where I have garner'd up my heart,
Where either I must live, or bear no life ;
The fountain from the which my current runs,
Or else dries up ; to be discarded thence ! 60
Or keep it as a cistern for foul toads
To knot and gender in ! Turn thy complexion
    there,
Patience, thou young and rose-lipp'd cheru-
    bin,—
Ay, there, look grim as hell !
   Des. I hope my noble lord esteems me
    honest.
   Oth. O, ay ; as summer flies are in the
    shambles,
That quicken even with blowing. O thou weed,
Who art so lovely fair and smell'st so sweet
That the sense aches at thee, would thou hadst
    ne'er been born !
   Des. Alas, what ignorant sin have I com-
    mitted ?   70
   Oth. Was this fair paper, this most goodly
    book,
Made to write ' whore ' upon ? What com-
    mitted !
Committed ! O thou public commoner !
I should make very forges of my cheeks,
That would to cinders burn up modesty,
Did I but speak thy deeds. What committed !
Heaven stops the nose at it and the moon
    winks,
The bawdy wind that kisses all it meets
Is hush'd within the hollow mine of earth,
And will not hear it. What committed ! 80
Impudent strumpet !
   Des.   By heaven, you do me wrong.
   Oth. Are you not a strumpet ?
   Des.   No, as I am a Christian :
If to preserve this vessel for my lord
From any other foul unlawful touch
Be not to be a strumpet, I am none.
   Oth. What, not a whore ?
   Des.   No, as I shall be saved.
   Oth. Is't possible ?
   Des. O, heaven forgive us !
   Oth.   I cry you mercy, then :
I took you for that cunning whore of Venice
That married with Othello. [*Raising his voice*]
      You, mistress,   90
That have the office opposite to Saint Peter,
And keep the gate of hell !

            Re-enter Emilia.

            You, you, ay, you !
We have done our course ; there's money for
    your pains :
I pray you, turn the key and keep our counsel.
                           [*Exit.*

   Emil. Alas, what does this gentleman con-
    ceive ?
How do you, madam ? how do you, my good
    lady ?
   Des. 'Faith, half asleep.
   Emil. Good madam, what's the matter
    with my lord ?
   Des. With who ?
   Emil. Why, with my lord, madam.   100
   Des. Who is thy lord ?
   Emil.   He that is yours, sweet lady.
   Des. I have none : do not talk to me,
    Emilia ;
I cannot weep ; nor answer have I none,
But what should go by water. Prithee, to-
    night
Lay on my bed my wedding sheets : remem-
    ber ;
And call thy husband hither.
   Emil.   Here's a change indeed ! [*Exit.*
   Des. 'Tis meet I should be used so, very
    meet.
How have I been behaved, that he might stick
The small'st opinion on my least misuse ?

      Re-enter Emilia *with* Iago.

   Iago. What is your pleasure, madam ?
    How is't with you ?   110
   Des. I cannot tell. Those that do teach
    young babes
Do it with gentle means and easy tasks :
He might have chid me so ; for, in good faith,
I am a child to chiding.
   Iago.   What's the matter, lady ?
   Emil. Alas, Iago, my lord hath so bewhored
    her.
Thrown such despite and heavy terms upon
    her,
As true hearts cannot bear.
   Des. Am I that name, Iago ?
   Iago.   What name, fair lady ?
   Des. Such as she says my lord did say I
    was.
   Emil. He call'd her whore : a beggar in his
    drink   120
Could not have laid such terms upon his callat.
   Iago. Why did he so ?
   Des. I do not know ; I am sure I am none
    such.
   Iago. Do not weep, do not weep. Alas the
    day !
   Emil. Hath she forsook so many noble
    matches,
Her father and her country and her friends,
To be call'd whore ? would it not make one
    weep ?
   Des. It is my wretched fortune.
   Iago.   Beshrew him for't !
How comes this trick upon him ?
   Des.   Nay, heaven doth know.
   Emil. I will be hang'd, if some eternal vil-
    lain,   130
Some busy and insinuating rogue,
Some cogging, cozening slave, to get some
    office,
Have not devised this slander ; I'll be hang'd
    else.
   Iago. Fie, there is no such man ; it is im-
    possible.
   Des. If any such there be, heaven pardon
    him !
   Emil. A halter pardon him ! and hell gnaw
    his bones !

Why should he call her whore ? who keeps her
    company ?
What place ? what time ? what form ? what
    likelihood ?
The Moor's abused by some most villanous
    knave,
Some base notorious knave, some scurvy fel-
    low. 140
O heaven, that such companions thou'ldst un-
    fold,
And put in every honest hand a whip
To lash the rascals naked through the world
Even from the east to the west !
Iago.   Speak within door.
Emil.   O, fie upon them ! Some such squire
    he was
That turn'd your wit the seamy side without,
And made you to suspect me with the Moor.
Iago. You are a fool ; go to.
Des.   O good Iago,
What shall I do to win my lord again ?
Good friend, go to him ; for, by this light of
    heaven, 150
I know not how I lost him. Here I kneel :
If e'er my will did trespass 'gainst his love,
Either in discourse of thought or actual deed,
Or that mine eyes, mine ears, or any sense,
Delighted them in any other form ;
Or that I do not yet, and ever did,
And ever will—though he do shake me off
To beggarly divorcement—love him dearly,
Comfort forswear me ! Unkindness may do
    much ;
And his unkindness may defeat my life, 160
But never taint my love. I cannot say ' whore : '
It does abhor me now I speak the word ;
To do the act that might the addition earn
Not the world's mass of vanity could make me.
Iago. I pray you, be content ; 'tis but his
    humor :
The business of the state does him offence,
And he does chide with you.
Des. If 'twere no other,—
Iago.   'Tis but so, I warrant.
    [*Trumpets within.*
Hark, how these instruments summon to sup-
    per !
The messengers of Venice stay the meat ; 170
Go in, and weep not; all things shall be well.
    [*Exeunt Desdemona and Emilia.*

    Enter RODERIGO.

How now, Roderigo !
Rod. I do not find that thou dealest justly
with me.
Iago. What in the contrary ?
Rod. Every day thou daffest me with some
device, Iago ; and rather, as it seems to me
now, keepest from me all conveniency than
suppliest me with the least advantage of hope.
I will indeed no longer endure it, nor am I yet
persuaded to put up in peace what already I
have foolishly suffered.
Iago. Will you hear me, Roderigo ?
Rod. 'Faith, I have heard too much, for
your words and performances are no kin together.
Iago. You charge me most unjustly.
Rod. With nought but truth. I have wasted
myself out of my means. The jewels you have
had from me to deliver to Desdemona would
half have corrupted a votarist : you have told
me she hath received them and returned me

expectations and comforts of sudden respect
and acquaintance, but I find none.
Iago. Well ; go to ; very well.
Rod. Very well ! go to ! I cannot go to,
man ; nor 'tis not very well : nay, I think it
is scurvy, and begin to find myself fobbed in
it.
Iago. Very well.
Rod. I tell you 'tis not very well. I will
make myself known to Desdemona : if she
will return me my jewels, I will give over my
suit and repent my unlawful solicitation ; if
not, assure yourself I will seek satisfaction of
you.
Iago. You have said now.
Rod. Ay, and said nothing but what I protest intendment of doing.
Iago. Why, now I see there's mettle in
thee, and even from this instant to build on
thee a better opinion than ever before. Give
me thy hand, Roderigo : thou hast taken
against me a most just exception ; but yet, I
protest, I have dealt most directly in thy affair.
Rod. It hath not appeared.
Iago. I grant indeed it hath not appeared,
and your suspicion is not without wit and
judgment. But, Roderigo, if thou hast that in
thee indeed, which I have greater reason to
believe now than ever, I mean purpose, courage and valor, this night show it : if thou the
next night following enjoy not Desdemona,
take me from this world with treachery and
devise engines for my life.
Rod. Well, what is it ? is it within reason
and compass ?
Iago. Sir, there is especial commission
come from Venice to depute Cassio in Othello's place.
Rod. Is that true ? why, then Othello and
Desdemona return again to Venice.
Iago. O, no ; he goes into Mauritania and
takes away with him the fair Desdemona, unless his abode be lingered here by some accident : wherein none can be so determinate as
the removing of Cassio.
Rod. How do you mean, removing of him ?
Iago. Why, by making him uncapable of
Othello's place ; knocking out his brains.
Rod. And that you would have me to do ?
Iago. Ay, if you dare do yourself a profit
and a right. He sups to-night with a harlotry,
and thither will I go to him : he knows not
yet of his honorable fortune. If you will watch
his going thence, which I will fashion to fall
out between twelve and one, you may take
him at your pleasure : I will be near to second
your attempt, and he shall fall between us.
Come, stand not amazed at it, but go along
with me ; I will show you such a necessity
in his death that you shall think yourself
bound to put it on him. It is now high supper-
time, and the night grows to waste : about it.
Rod. I will hear further reason for this.
Iago. And you shall be satisfied. [*Exeunt.*

SCENE III. *Another room in the castle.*

Enter OTHELLO, LODOVICO, DESDEMONA,
    EMILIA, *and* Attendants.

Lod. I do beseech you, sir, trouble yourself no further.
Oth. O, pardon me : 'twill do me good to
walk.

Lod. Madam, good night; I humbly thank
your ladyship.

Des. Your honor is most welcome.

Oth.   Will you walk, sir?
O,—Desdemona,—

Des. My lord?

Oth. Get you to bed on the instant; I will
be returned forthwith: dismiss your attendant
there: look it be done.

Des. I will, my lord.   10

[*Exeunt Othello, Lodovico, and Attendants.*

Emil. How goes it now? he looks gentler
than he did.

Des. He says he will return incontinent:
He hath commanded me to go to bed,
And bade me to dismiss you.

Emil.   Dismiss me!

Des. It was his bidding: therefore, good
Emilia,
Give me my nightly wearing, and adieu:
We must not now displease him.

Emil. I would you had never seen him!

Des. So would not I: my love doth so approve him,
That even his stubbornness, his checks, his
frowns,—   20
Prithee, unpin me,—have grace and favor in
them.

Emil. I have laid those sheets you bade me
on the bed.

Des. All's one. Good faith, how foolish
are our minds!
If I do die before thee, prithee, shroud me
In one of those same sheets.

Emil.   Come, come, you talk.

Des. My mother had a maid call'd Bar-
bara:
She was in love, and he she loved proved mad
And did forsake her: she had a song of 'wil-
low;'
An old thing 'twas, but it express'd her fortune,
And she died singing it: that song to-night
Will not go from my mind; I have much to do,
But to go hang my head all at one side,
And sing it like poor Barbara. Prithee, dis-
patch.

Emil. Shall I go fetch your night-gown?

Des.   No, unpin me here.
This Lodovico is a proper man.

Emil. A very handsome man.

Des. He speaks well.

Emil. I know a lady in Venice would have
walked barefoot to Palestine for a touch of his
nether lip.   40

Des. [*Singing*] The poor soul sat sighing
by a sycamore tree,
Sing all a green willow:
Her hand on her bosom, her head on her knee,
Sing willow, willow, willow:
The fresh streams ran by her, and murmur'd
her moans;
Sing willow, willow, willow;
Her salt tears fell from her, and soften'd the
stones;—
Lay by these:—
[*Singing*] Sing willow, willow, willow;
Prithee, hie thee; he'll come anon:—   50
[*Singing*] Sing all a green willow must be my
garland.
Let nobody blame him; his scorn I ap-
prove,—
Nay, that's not next.—Hark! who is't that
knocks?

Emil. It's the wind.

Des. [*Singing*] I call'd my love false love;
but what said he then?
Sing willow, willow, willow:
If I court moe women, you'll couch with
moe men.—
So, get thee gone; good night. Mine eyes do
itch;
Doth that bode weeping?

Emil.   'Tis neither here nor there.

Des. I have heard it said so. O, these men,
these men!   60
Dost thou in conscience think,—tell me, Emi-
lia,—
That there be women do abuse their husbands
In such gross kind?

Emil.   There be some such, no question.

Des. Wouldst thou do such a deed for all
the world?

Emil. Why, would not you?

Des.   No, by this heavenly light!

Emil. Nor I neither by this heavenly light;
I might do't as well i' the dark.

Des. Wouldst thou do such a deed for all
the world?

Emil. The world's a huge thing: it is a
great price
For a small vice.

Des. In troth, I think thou wouldst not.   70

Emil. In troth, I think I should; and undo't when I had done. Marry, I would not do
such a thing for a joint-ring, nor for measures
of lawn, nor for gowns, petticoats, nor caps,
nor any petty exhibition; but, for the whole
world,—why, who would not make her husband a cuckold to make him a monarch? I
should venture purgatory for't.

Des. Beshrew me, if I would do such a
wrong
For the whole world.   79

Emil. Why the wrong is but a wrong i' the
world: and having the world for your labor,
'tis a wrong in your own world, and you might
quickly make it right.

Des. I do not think there is any such
woman.

Emil. Yes, a dozen; and as many to the
vantage as would store the world they played
for.
But I do think it is their husbands' faults
If wives do fall: say that they slack their du-
ties,
And pour our treasures into foreign laps,
Or else break out in peevish jealousies,   90
Throwing restraint upon us; or say they strike
us,
Or scant our former having in despite;
Why, we have galls, and though we have some
grace,
Yet have we some revenge. Let husbands know
Their wives have sense like them: they see
and smell
And have their palates both for sweet and sour,
As husbands have. What is it that they do
When they change us for others? Is it sport?
I think it is: and doth affection breed it?
I think it doth: is't frailty that thus errs?   100
It is so too: and have not we affections,
Desires for sport, and frailty, as men have?
Then let them use us well: else let them know,
The ills we do, their ills instruct us so.

Des. Good night, good night : heaven me
 such uses send,
Not to pick bad from bad, but by bad mend !
          [*Exeunt.*

ACT V.

SCENE I. *Cyprus. A street.*

Enter IAGO *and* RODERIGO.

Iago. Here, stand behind this bulk ; straight
 will he come :
Wear thy good rapier bare, and put it home :
Quick, quick ; fear nothing ; I'll be at thy el-
 bow :
It makes us, or it mars us ; think on that,
And fix most firm thy resolution.
 Rod. Be near at hand ; I may miscarry in't.
 Iago. Here, at thy hand : be bold, and take
 thy stand.   [*Retires.*
 Rod. I have no great devotion to the deed ;
And yet he hath given me satisfying reasons :
'Tis but a man gone. Forth, my sword : he
 dies.   10
 Iago. I have rubb'd this young quat almost
 to the sense,
And he grows angry. Now, whether he kill
 Cassio,
Or Cassio him, or each do kill the other,
Every way makes my gain : live Roderigo,
He calls me to a restitution large
Of gold and jewels that I bobb'd from him,
As gifts to Desdemona ;
It must not be : if Cassio do remain,
He hath a daily beauty in his life
That makes me ugly ; and, besides, the Moor
May unfold me to him ; there stand I in much
 peril :   21
No, he must die. But so : I hear him coming.

Enter CASSIO.

 Rod. I know his gait, 'tis he.—Villain, thou
 diest !   [*Makes a pass at Cassio.*
 Cas. That thrust had been mine enemy in-
 deed,
But that my coat is better than thou know'st
I will make proof of thine.
    [*Draws, and wounds Roderigo.*
 Rod.   O, I am slain !
 [*Iago from behind wounds Cassio in the
       leg, and exit.*
 Cas. I am maim'd for ever. Help, ho !
 murder ! murder !   [*Falls.*

Enter OTHELLO.

 Oth. The voice of Cassio : Iago keeps his
 word.
 Rod. O, villain that I am !
 Oth.   It is even so.
 Cas. O, help, ho ! light ! a surgeon ! 30
 Oth. 'Tis he :—O brave Iago, honest and
 just,
That hast such noble sense of thy friend's
 wrong !
Thou teachest me. Minion, your dear lies dead,
And your unblest fate hies : strumpet, I come.
Forth of my heart those charms, thine eyes,
 are blotted ;
Thy bed, lust-stain'd, shall with lust's blood
 be spotted.   [*Exit.*

Enter LODOVICO *and* GRATIANO.

 Cas. What, ho ! no watch ? no passage ?
 murder ! murder !
 Gra. 'Tis some mischance ; the cry is very
 direful.
 Cas. O, help !
 Lod. Hark !   40
 Rod. O wretched villain !
 Lod. Two or three groan : it is a heavy
 night :
These may be counterfeits : let's think't un-
 safe
To come in to the cry without more help.
 Rod. Nobody come ? then shall I bleed to
 death.
 Lod. Hark !

Re-enter IAGO, *with a light.*

 Gra. Here's one comes in his shirt, with
 light and weapons.
 Iago. Who's there ? whose noise is this that
 cries on murder ?
 Lod. We do not know.
 Iago.   Did not you hear a cry ?
 Cas. Here, here ! for heaven's sake, help
 me !
 Iago.   What's the matter ? 50
 Gra. This is Othello's ancient, as I take it.
 Lod. The same indeed ; a very valiant fel-
 low.
 Iago. What are you here that cry so griev-
 ously ?
 Cas. Iago ? O, I am spoil'd, undone by
 villains !
Give me some help.
 Iago. O me, lieutenant ! what villains have
 done this ?
 Cas. I think that one of them is hereabout,
And cannot make away.
 Iago.   O treacherous villains !
What are you there ? come in, and give some
 help.   [*To Lodovico and Gratiano.*
 Rod. O, help me here !   60
 Cas. That's one of them.
 Iago.   O murderous slave ! O villain !
         [*Stabs Roderigo.*
 Rod. O damn'd Iago ! O inhuman dog !
 Iago. Kill men i' the dark !—Where be
 these bloody thieves ?—
How silent is this town !—Ho ! murder !
 murder !—
What may you be ? are you of good or evil ?
 Lod. As you shall prove us, praise us.
 Iago. Signior Lodovico ?
 Lod. He, sir.
 Iago. I cry you mercy. Here's Cassio hurt
 by villains.
 Gra. Cassio !   70
 Iago. How is't, brother !
 Cas. My leg is cut in two.
 Iago.   Marry, heaven forbid !
Light, gentlemen ; I'll bind it with my shirt.

Enter BIANCA.

 Bian. What is the matter, ho ? who is't
 that cried ?
 Iago. Who is't that cried !
 Bian. O my dear Cassio ! my sweet Cas-
 sio ! O Cassio, Cassio, Cassio !
 Iago. O notable strumpet ! Cassio, may
 you suspect
Who they should be that have thus mangled
 you ?
 Cas. No.   80

Gra. I am sorry to find you thus : I have
    been to seek you.

Iago. Lend me a garter. So. O, for a chair,
To bear him easily hence !

Bian. Alas, he faints ! O Cassio, Cassio,
    Cassio !

Iago. Gentlemen all, I do suspect this trash
To be a party in this injury.
Patience awhile, good Cassio. Come, come ;
Lend me a light. Know we this face or no ?
Alas my friend and my dear countryman
Roderigo ! no :—yes, sure :—O heaven ! Rod-
    erigo !   90

Gra. What, of Venice ?

Iago. Even he, sir ; did you know him ?

Gra.   Know him ! ay.

Iago. Signior Gratiano ? I cry you gentle
    pardon ;
These bloody accidents must excuse my man-
    ners,
That so neglected you.

Gra.   I am glad to see you.

Iago. How do you, Cassio ? O, a chair, a
    chair !

Gra. Roderigo !

Iago. He, he, 'tis he. [*A chair brought in.*]
O, that's well said ; the chair.
Some good man bear him carefully from
    hence ;
I'll fetch the general's surgeon. [*To Bianca*]
For you, mistress,   100
Save you your labor. He that lies slain here,
    Cassio,
Was my dear friend : what malice was between
    you ?

Cas. None in the world ; nor do I know
    the man.

Iago. [*To Bian.*] What, look you pale ? O,
    bear him out o' the air.
    [*Cassio and Roderigo are borne off.*
Stay you, good gentlemen. Look you pale, mis-
    tress ?
Do you perceive the gastness of her eye ?
Nay, if you stare, we shall hear more anon.
Behold her well ; I pray you, look upon her :
Do you see, gentlemen ? nay, guiltiness will
    speak,
Though tongues were out of use.   110

Enter EMILIA.

Emil. 'Las, what's the matter ? what's the
    matter, husband ?

Iago. Cassio hath here been set on in the
    dark
By Roderigo and fellows that are scaped :
He's almost slain, and Roderigo dead.

Emil. Alas, good gentleman ! alas, good
    Cassio !

Iago. This is the fruit of whoring. Prithee,
    Emilia,
Go know of Cassio where he supp'd to-night.
[*To Bianca*] What, do you shake at that ?

Bian. He supp'd at my house ; but I there-
    fore shake not.

Iago. O, did he so ? I charge you, go with
    me.   120

Emil. Fie, fie upon thee, strumpet !

Bian. I am no strumpet ; but of life as
    honest
As you that thus abuse me.

Emil.   As I ! foh ! fie upon thee !

Iago. Kind gentlemen, let's go see poor
    Cassio dress'd

Come, mistress, you must tell's another tale.
Emilia, run you to the citadel,
And tell my lord and lady what hath happ'd.
Will you go on ? I pray. [*Aside*] This is the
    night
That either makes me or fordoes me quite.
    [*Exeunt.*

SCENE II. *A bedchamber in the castle:* DES-
DEMONA *in bed asleep ; a light burning.*

Enter OTHELLO.

Oth. It is the cause, it is the cause, my
    soul,—
Let me not name it to you, you chaste stars !—
It is the cause. Yet I'll not shed her blood ;
Nor scar that whiter skin of hers than snow,
And smooth as monumental alabaster.
Yet she must die, else she'll betray more men.
Put out the light, and then put out the light :
If I quench thee, thou flaming minister,
I can again thy former light restore,   9
Should I repent me : but once put out thy light,
Thou cunning'st pattern of excelling nature,
I know not where is that Promethean heat
That can thy light relume. When I have
    pluck'd the rose,
I cannot give it vital growth again,
It must needs wither : I'll smell it on the tree.
    [*Kissing her.*
Ah, balmy breath, that dost almost persuade
Justice to break her sword ! One more, one
    more.
Be thus when thou art dead, and I will kill
    thee,
And love thee after. One more, and this the
    last :
So sweet was ne'er so fatal. I must weep, 20
But they are cruel tears : this sorrow's heav-
    enly ;
It strikes where it doth love. She wakes.

Des. Who's there ? Othello ?

Oth.   Ay, Desdemona.

Des. Will you come to bed, my lord ?

Oth. Have you pray'd to-night, Desde-
    mona ?

Des.   Ay, my lord.

Oth. If you bethink yourself of any crime
Unreconciled as yet to heaven and grace,
Solicit for it straight.

Des. Alas, my lord, what do you mean by
    that ?

Oth. Well, do it, and be brief ; I will walk
    by :   30
I would not kill thy unprepared spirit ;
No ; heaven forfend ! I would not kill thy soul.

Des. Talk you of killing ?

Oth.   Ay, I do.

Des.   Then heaven
Have mercy on me !

Oth.   Amen, with all my heart !

Des. If you say so, I hope you will not kill
    me.

Oth. Hum !

Des. And yet I fear you ; for you are fatal
    then
When your eyes roll so : why I should fear I
    know not,
Since guiltiness I know not ; but yet I feel I
    fear.

Oth. Think on thy sins.

Des.   They are loves I bear to you. 40

Oth. Ay, and for that thou diest.

Des. That death's unnatural that kills for
  loving.
Alas, why gnaw you so your nether lip ?
Some bloody passion shakes your very frame :
These are portents ; but yet I hope, I hope,
They do not point on me.
  Oth.   Peace, and be still !
Des. I will so. What's the matter ?
Oth. That handkerchief which I so loved
  and gave thee
Thou gavest to Cassio.
  Des.   No, by my life and soul !
Send for the man, and ask him.
  Oth.   Sweet soul, take heed, 50
Take heed of perjury ; thou art on thy death-
  bed.
Des. Ay, but not yet to die.
Oth.   Yes, presently :
Therefore confess thee freely of thy sin ;
For to deny each article with oath
Cannot remove nor choke the strong concep-
  tion
That I do groan withal. Thou art to die.
  Des. Then Lord have mercy on me !
Oth.   I say, amen.
Des. And have you mercy too ! I never did
Offend you in my life ; never loved Cassio
But with such general warranty of heaven 60
As I might love ; I never gave him token.
  Oth. By heaven, I saw my handkerchief
  in's hand.
O perjured woman ! thou dost stone my heart,
And makest me call what I intend to do
A murder, which I thought a sacrifice :
I saw the handkerchief.
  Des.   He found it then ;
I never gave it him : send for him hither ;
Let him confess a truth.
  Oth.   He hath confess'd.
Des. What, my lord ?
Oth. That he hath used thee.
Des.   How ? unlawfully ?
Oth.   Ay. 70
Des. He will not say so.
Oth.   No, his mouth is stopp'd ;
Honest Iago hath ta'en order for't.
  Des. O ! my fear interprets : what, is he
  dead ?
Oth. Had all his hairs been lives, my great
  revenge
Had stomach for them all.
  Des. Alas ! he is betray'd and I undone.
Oth. Out, strumpet ! weep'st thou for him
  to my face ?
Des. O, banish me, my lord, but kill me
  not !
Oth. Down, strumpet !
Des. Kill me to-morrow : let me live to-
  night ! 80
Oth. Nay, if you strive,—
Des. But half an hour !
Oth.   Being done, there is no pause.
Des. But while I say one prayer !
Oth.   It is too late.
                        [*He stifles her.*
Emil. [*Within*] My lord, my lord ! what,
  ho ! my lord, my lord !
Oth. What noise is this ? Not dead ? not
  yet quite dead ?
I that am cruel am yet merciful ;
I would not have thee linger in thy pain :
So, so.

Emil. [*Within*] What, ho ! my lord, my
  lord !
Oth.   Who's there ?
Emil. [*Within*] O, good my lord, I would
  speak a word with you ! 90
Oth. Yes : 'tis Emilia. By and by. She's
  dead.
'Tis like she comes to speak of Cassio's
  death.—
The noise was here. Ha ! no more moving ?
Still as the grave. Shall she come in ? were't
  good ?—
I think she stirs again :—no. What's best to
  do ?
If she come in, she'll sure speak to my wife :
My wife ! my wife ! what wife ? I have no wife.
O, insupportable ! O heavy hour !
Methinks it should be now a huge eclipse
Of sun and moon, and that the affrighted
  globe
Should yawn at alteration.
  Emil. [*Within*] I do beseech you 101
That I may speak with you, O, good my lord !
  Oth. I had forgot thee : O, come in, Emi-
  lia ;
Soft ; by and by. Let me the curtains draw.
Where art thou ?   [*Unlocks the door.*

                Enter EMILIA.

                What's the matter with thee now ?
Emil. O, my good lord, yonder's foul mur-
  ders done !
Oth. What, now ?
Emil. But now, my lord.
Oth. It is the very error of the moon ;
She comes more nearer earth than she was
  wont, 110
And makes men mad.
  Emil. Cassio, my lord, hath kill'd a young
  Venetian
Call'd Roderigo.
  Oth.   Roderigo kill'd !
And Cassio kill'd !
  Emil.   No, Cassio is not kill'd.
Oth. Not Cassio kill'd ! then murder's out
  of tune,
And sweet revenge grows harsh.
  Des. O, falsely, falsely murder'd !
Emil.   Alas, what cry is that ?
Oth. That ! what ?
Emil. Out, and alas ! that was my lady's
  voice. 119
Help ! help, ho ! help ! O lady, speak again !
Sweet Desdemona ! O sweet mistress, speak !
Des. A guiltless death I die.
Emil. O, who hath done this deed ?
Des. Nobody ; I myself. Farewell :
Commend me to my kind lord : O, farewell !
                        [*Dies.*
Oth. Why, how should she be murder'd ?
Emil.   Alas, who knows ?
Oth. You heard her say herself, it was not
  I.
Emil. She said so : I must needs report the
  truth.
Oth. She's, like a liar, gone to burning
  hell :
'Twas I that kill'd her.
Emil.   O, the more angel she, 130
And you the blacker devil !
  Oth. She turn'd to folly, and she was a
  whore.

Emil. Thou dost belie her, and thou art a
    devil.

Oth. She was false as water.

Emil.   Thou art rash as fire, to say
That she was false : O, she was heavenly
    true !

Oth. Cassio did top her ; ask thy husband
    else.
O, I were damn'd beneath all depth in hell,
But that I did proceed upon just grounds
To this extremity. Thy husband knew it all.

Emil. My husband !   140

Oth. Thy husband.

Emil. That she was false to wedlock ?

Oth. Ay, with Cassio. Nay, had she been
    true,
If heaven would make me such another world
Of one entire and perfect chrysolite,
I'ld not have sold her for it.

Emil. My husband !

Oth.   Ay, 'twas he that told me first :
An honest man he is, and hates the slime
That sticks on filthy deeds.

Emil.   My husband !

Oth. What needs this iteration, woman ? I
    say thy husband.   150

Emil. O mistress, villany hath made mocks
    with love,
My husband say that she was false !

Oth.   He, woman ;
I say thy husband : dost understand the
    word ?
My friend, thy husband, honest, honest Iago.

Emil. If he say so, may his pernicious soul
Rot half a grain a day ! he lies to the heart :
She was too fond of her most filthy bargain.

Oth. Ha !

Emil. Do thy worst :
This deed of thine is no more worthy heaven
Than thou wast worthy her.   161

Oth.   Peace, you were best.

Emil. Thou hast not half that power to do
    me harm
As I have to be hurt. O gull ! O dolt !
As ignorant as dirt ! thou hast done a deed—
I care not for thy sword ; I'll make thee
    known,
Though I lost twenty lives.—Help ! help, ho !
    help !
The Moor hath kill'd my mistress ! Murder !
    murder !

Enter MONTANO, GRATIANO, IAGO, *and
others.*

Mon. What is the matter ? How now, gen-
    eral !

Emil. O, are you come, Iago ? you have
    done well,
That men must lay their murders on your
    neck.   170

Gra. What is the matter ?

Emil. Disprove this villain, if thou be'st a
    man :
He says thou told'st him that his wife was
    false :
I know thou didst not, thou'rt not such a
    villain :
Speak, for my heart is full.

Iago. I told him what I thought, and told
    no more
Than what he found himself was apt and
    true.

Emil. But did you ever tell him she was
    false ?

Iago. I did.

Emil. You told a lie, an odious, damned
    lie ;   180
Upon my soul, a lie, a wicked lie.
She false with Cassio !—did you say with
    Cassio ?

Iago. With Cassio, mistress. Go to, charm
    your tongue.

Emil. I will not charm my tongue ; I am
    bound to speak :
My mistress here lies murder'd in her bed,—

All. O heavens forfend !

Emil. And your reports have set the mur-
    der on.

Oth. Nay, stare not, masters : it is true,
    indeed.

Gra. 'Tis a strange truth.

Mon. O monstrous act !

Emil.   Villany, villany, villany ! 190
I think upon't, I think : I smell't : O vil-
    lany !—
I thought so then :—I'll kill myself for
    grief :—
O villany, villany !

Iago. What, are you mad ? I charge you,
    get you home.

Emil. Good gentlemen, let me have leave
    to speak :
'Tis proper I obey him, but not now.
Perchance, Iago, I will ne'er go home.

Oth. O ! O ! O !   [*He falls on the bed.*

Emil. Nay, lay thee down and roar ;
For thou hast kill'd the sweetest innocent
That e'er did lift up eye.

Oth.   [*Rising*] O, she was foul ! 200
I scarce did know you, uncle : there lies your
    niece,
Whose breath, indeed, these hands have newly
    stopp'd :
I know this act shows horrible and grim.

Gra. Poor Desdemona ! I am glad thy fa-
    ther's dead :
Thy match was mortal to him, and pure grief
Shore his old thread in twain : did he live
    now,
This sight would make him do a desperate
    turn,
Yea, curse his better angel from his side,
And fall to reprobation.

Oth. 'Tis pitiful ; but yet Iago knows 210
That she with Cassio hath the act of shame
A thousand times committed ; Cassio con-
    fess'd it :
And she did gratify his amorous works
With that recognizance and pledge of love
Which I first gave her ; I saw it in his hand :
It was a handkerchief, an antique token
My father gave my mother.

Emil. O heaven ! O heavenly powers !

Iago. Come, hold your peace.

Emil.   'Twill out, 'twill out : I peace !
No, I will speak as liberal as the north : 220
Let heaven and men and devils, let them all,
All, all, cry shame against me, yet I'll speak.

Iago. Be wise, and get you home.

Emil.   I will not.
    [*Iago offers to stab Emilia.*

Gra.   Fie !
Your sword upon a woman ?

Emil. O thou dull Moor! that handker-
chief thou speak'st of
I found by fortune and did give my husband;
For often, with a solemn earnestness,
More than indeed belong'd to such a trifle,
He begg'd of me to steal it.
Iago. Villanous whore!
Emil. She give it Cassio! no, alas! I found
it, 230
And I did give't my husband.
Iago. Filth, thou liest!
Emil. By heaven, I do not, I do not, gen-
tlemen.
O murderous coxcomb! what should such a
fool
Do with so good a woman?
Oth. Are there no stones in heaven
But what serve for the thunder?—Precious
villain!
[*He runs at Iago: Iago, from behind,
stabs Emilia, and exit.*
Gra. The woman falls; sure, he hath kill'd
his wife.
Emil. Ay, ay: O, lay me by my mistress'
side.
Gra. He's gone, but his wife's kill'd.
Mon. 'Tis a notorious villain. Take you
this weapon,
Which I have here recover'd from the Moor:
Come, guard the door without; let him not
pass, 241
But kill him rather. I'll after that same vil-
lain,
For 'tis a damned slave.
[*Exeunt Montano and Gratiano.*
Oth. I am not valiant neither,
But every puny whipster gets my sword:
But why should honor outlive honesty?
Let it go all.
Emil. What did thy song bode, lady?
Hark, canst thou hear me? I will play the
swan,
And die in music. [*Singing*] Willow, willow,
willow,—
Moor, she was chaste; she loved thee, cruel
Moor:
So come my soul to bliss, as I speak true; 250
So speaking as I think, I die, I die. [*Dies.*
Oth. I have another weapon in this cham-
ber:
It is a sword of Spain, the ice-brook's tem-
per:—
O, here it is. Uncle, I must come forth.
Gra. [*Within*] If thou attempt it, it will
cost thee dear:
Thou hast no weapon, and perforce must
suffer.
Oth. Look in upon me then and speak
with me,
Or, naked as I am, I will assault thee.

Re-enter GRATIANO.

Gra. What is the matter?
Oth. Behold, I have a weapon;
A better never did itself sustain 260
Upon a soldier's thigh: I have seen the day,
That, with this little arm and this good sword,
I have made my way through more impedi-
ments
Than twenty times your stop: but, O vain
boast!
Who can control his fate? 'tis not so now.

Be not afraid, though you do see me weap-
on'd;
Here is my journey's end, here is my butt,
And very sea-mark of my utmost sail.
Do you go back dismay'd? 'tis a lost fear;
Man but a rush against Othello's breast, 270
And he retires. Where should Othello go?
Now, how dost thou look now? O ill-starr'd
wench!
Pale as thy smock! when we shall meet at
compt,
This look of thine will hurl my soul from
heaven,
And fiends will snatch at it. Cold, cold, my
girl!
Even like thy chastity. O cursed slave!
Whip me, ye devils,
From the possession of this heavenly sight!
Blow me about in winds! roast me in sul-
phur!
Wash me in steep-down gulfs of liquid fire!
O Desdemona! Desdemona! dead! 281
Oh! Oh! Oh!

Enter LODOVICO, MONTANO, CASSIO *carried in
a chair, and* Officers *with* IAGO, *prisoner.*

Lod. Where is this rash and most unfor-
tunate man?
Oth. That's he that was Othello: here I
am.
Lod. Where is that viper? bring the villain
forth.
Oth. I look down towards his feet; but
that's a fable.
If that thou be'st a devil, I cannot kill thee.
[*Wounds Iago.*
Lod. Wrench his sword from him.
Iago. I bleed, sir; but not kill'd.
Oth. I am not sorry neither: I'ld have
thee live;
For, in my sense, 'tis happiness to die. 290
Lod. O thou Othello, thou wert once so
good,
Fall'n in the practice of a damned slave,
What shall be said to thee?
Oth. Why, any thing:
An honorable murderer, if you will;
For nought I did in hate, but all in honor.
Lod. This wretch hath part confess'd his
villany:
Did you and he consent in Cassio's death?
Oth. Ay.
Cas. Dear general, I never gave you cause.
Oth. I do believe it, and I ask your par-
don.
Will you, I pray, demand that demi-devil 301
Why he hath thus ensnared my soul and
body?
Iago. Demand me nothing: what you
know, you know:
From this time forth I never will speak word.
Lod. What, not to pray?
Gra. Torments will ope your lips.
Oth. Well, thou dost best.
Lod. Sir, you shall understand what hath
befall'n,
Which, as I think, you know not. Here is a
letter
Found in the pocket of the slain Roderigo;
And here another: the one of them imports
The death of Cassio to be undertook 311
By Roderigo.
Oth. O villain!

Cas. Most heathenish and most gross !
Lod. Now here's another discontented paper,
Found in his pocket too; and this, it seems,
Roderigo meant to have sent this damned villain ;
But that belike Iago in the interim
Came in and satisfied him.
Oth. O the pernicious caitiff !
How came you, Cassio, by that handkerchief
That was my wife's ?
Cas. I found it in my chamber : 320
And he himself confess'd but even now
That there he dropp'd it for a special purpose
Which wrought to his desire.
Oth. O fool ! fool ! fool !
Cas. There is besides in Roderigo's letter,
How he upbraids Iago, that he made him
Brave me upon the watch ; whereon it came
That I was cast : and even but now he spake,
After long seeming dead, Iago hurt him,
Iago set him on.
Lod. You must forsake this room, and go
with us : 330
Your power and your command is taken off,
And Cassio rules in Cyprus. For this slave,
If there be any cunning cruelty
That can torment him much and hold him
long,
It shall be his. You shall close prisoner rest,
Till that the nature of your fault be known
To the Venetian state. Come, bring him away.
Oth. Soft you ; a word or two before you
go.
I have done the state some service, and they
know't.
No more of that. I pray you, in your letters,
When you shall these unlucky deeds relate,
Speak of me as I am ; nothing extenuate,

Nor set down aught in malice : then must you
speak
Of one that loved not wisely but too well ;
Of one not easily jealous, but being wrought
Perplex'd in the extreme ; of one whose hand,
Like the base Indian, threw a pearl away
Richer than all his tribe ; of one whose subdued eyes,
Albeit unused to the melting mood,
Drop tears as fast as the Arabian trees 350
Their medicinal gum. Set you down this ;
And say besides, that in Aleppo once,
Where a malignant and a turban'd Turk
Beat a Venetian and traduced the state,
I took by the throat the circumcised dog,
And smote him, thus. [*Stabs himself.*
Lod. O bloody period !
Gra. All that's spoke is marr'd.
Oth. I kiss'd thee ere I kill'd thee : no way
but this ;
Killing myself, to die upon a kiss.
[*Falls on the bed, and dies.*
Cas. This did I fear, but thought he had
no weapon ; 360
For he was great of heart.
Lod. [*To Iago*] O Spartan dog,
More fell than anguish, hunger, or the sea !
Look on the tragic loading of this bed ;
This is thy work : the object poisons sight ;
Let it be hid. Gratiano, keep the house,
And seize upon the fortunes of the Moor,
For they succeed on you. To you, lord governor,
Remains the censure of this hellish villain ;
The time, the place, the torture : O, enforce
it !
Myself will straight aboard : and to the state
This heavy act with heavy heart relate. 371
[*Exeunt.*

KING LEAR.

(WRITTEN ABOUT 1605.)

INTRODUCTION.

Among the tragedies of passion *King Lear* is the one in which passions assume the largest proportions, act upon the widest theatre, and attain their absolute extremes. The story of Lear and his daughters was found by Shakespeare in Holinshed, and he may have taken a few hints from an old play, *The True Chronicle History of King Leir*. In both Holinshed's version and that of the True Chronicle, the army of Lear and his French allies is victorious ; Lear is reinstated in his kingdom ; but Holinshed relates how, after Lear's death, her sister's sons warred against Cordelia and took her prisoner, when " being a woman of a manly courage and despairing to recover liberty," she slew herself. With the story of Lear Shakespeare connects that of Gloucester and his two sons. An episode in Sir Philip Sidney's *Arcadia* supplied characters and incidents for this portion of the play, Sidney's blind king of Paphlagonia corresponding to the Gloucester of Shakespeare. But here, too, the story had in the dramatist's original a happy ending : the Paphlagonian king is restored to his throne, and the brothers are reconciled. The date of the play is probably 1605 or 1606. It was entered on the Stationers' register, Nov. 26, 1607, and the entry states that it had been acted " upon St. Stephen's day at Christmas last," *i.e.* Dec. 26, 1606. It was printed in quarto in 1608. Shakespeare cares little to give the opening incidents of his play a look of prosaic, historical probability. The spectator or reader is asked, as it were, to grant the dramatist certain data, and then to observe what the imagination can make of them. Good and evil in this play are clearly severed from one another—(more so than in *Macbeth* or in *Othello*)—and at the last, goodness, if we judge merely by external fortune, would seem to be, if not defeated, at least not triumphant. Shakespeare has dared, while paying little regard to mere historical verisimilitude, to represent the most solemn and awful mysteries of life as they actually are, without attempting to offer a ready-made explanation of them. Cordelia dies strangled in prison ; yet we know that her devotion of love was not misspent. Lear expires in an agony of grief ; but he has been delivered from his pride and passionate wilfulness : he has found that instead of being a master, at whose nod all things must bow, he is weak and helpless, a sport even of the wind and the rain ; his ignorance of true love, and pleasure in false professions of love, have given place to an agonized clinging to the love which is real, deep, and tranquil because of its fulness. Lear is the greatest sufferer in Shakespeare's plays ; though so old, he has strength which makes him a subject for prolonged and vast agony ; and patience is unknown to him. The elements seem to have conspired against him with his unnatural daughters ; the upheaval of the moral world, and the rage of tempest in the air seem to be parts of the same gigantic convulsion. In the midst of this tempest wanders unhoused the white-haired Lear ; while his fool—most pathetic of all the minor characters of Shakespeare— jests half-wildly, half-coherently, half-bitterly, half-tenderly, and always with a sad remembrance of the happier past. The poor boy's heart has been sore ever since his " young mistress went to France." If Cordelia is pure love, tender and faithful, and Kent is unmingled loyalty, the monsters Goneril and Regan are gorgons rather than women, such as Shakespeare has nowhere else conceived. The aspect of Goneril can almost turn to stone ; in Regan's tongue there is a viperous hiss. The story of Gloucester enlarges the basis of the tragedy. Lear's affliction is no mere private incident ; there is a breaking of the bonds of nature and society all around us. But Gloucester is suffering for a former sin of self-indulgence, Lear is " more sinned against than sinning." Yet Gloucester is granted a death which is half joyful. His affliction serves as a measure of the longer affliction of the king. Edgar and Edmund are a contrasted pair—both are men of penetration, energy, and skill, one on the side of evil, the other on the side of good. Everywhere throughout the play Shakespeare's imaginative daring impresses us. Nothing in poetry is bolder or more wonderful than the scene on the night of the tempest in the hovel where the king, whose intellect has now given way, is in company with Edgar, assuming madness, the Fool, with his forced pathetic mirth, and Kent.

DRAMATIS PERSONÆ.

LEAR, king of Britain.
KING OF FRANCE.
DUKE OF BURGUNDY.
DUKE OF CORNWALL.

DUKE OF ALBANY.
EARL OF KENT.
EARL OF GLOUCESTER.
EDGAR, son to Gloucester.

EDMUND, bastard son to Gloucester.
CURAN, a courtier.
Old man, tenant to Gloucester.
Doctor.
Fool.
OSWALD, steward to Goneril.
A Captain employed by Edmund.
Gentleman attendant on Cordelia.
A Herald.

Servants to Cornwall.

GONERIL,
REGAN,   } daughters to Lear.
CORDELIA,

Knights of Lear's train, Captains, Messengers,
    Soldiers, and Attendants.

SCENE : *Britain.*

ACT I.

SCENE I. *King Lear's palace.*

Enter KENT, GLOUCESTER, *and* EDMUND.

Kent. I thought the king had more affected
the Duke of Albany than Cornwall.

Glou. It did always seem so to us : but
now, in the division of the kingdom, it appears
not which of the dukes he values most ; for
equalities are so weighed, that curiosity in neither can make choice of either's moiety.

Kent. Is not this your son, my lord ?

Glou. His breeding, sir, hath been at my
charge : I have so often blushed to acknowledge him, that now I am brazed to it.   11

Kent. I cannot conceive you.

Glou. Sir, this young fellow's mother
could : whereupon she grew round-wombed,
and had, indeed, sir, a son for her cradle ere
she had a husband for her bed. Do you smell
a fault ?

Kent. I cannot wish the fault undone, the
issue of it being so proper.

Glou. But I have, sir, a son by order of
law, some year elder than this, who yet is no
dearer in my account : though this knave came
something saucily into the world before he was
sent for, yet was his mother fair ; there was
good sport at his making, and the whoreson
must be acknowledged. Do you know this noble gentleman, Edmund ?

Edm. No, my lord.

Glou. My lord of Kent : remember him
hereafter as my honorable friend.

Edm. My services to your lordship.

Kent. I must love you, and sue to know
you better.   31

Edm. Sir, I shall study deserving.

Glou. He hath been out nine years, and
away he shall again. The king is coming.

Sennet. Enter KING LEAR, CORNWALL, AL-
BANY, GONERIL, REGAN, CORDELIA, *and*
Attendants.

Lear. Attend the lords of France and Burgundy, Gloucester.

Glou. I shall, my liege.
      [*Exeunt Gloucester and Edmund.*

Lear. Meantime we shall express our
darker purpose.
Give me the map there. Know that we have
    divided
In three our kingdom : and 'tis our fast intent
To shake all cares and business from our age ;
Conferring them on younger strengths, while
    we   41
Unburthen'd crawl toward death. Our son of
    Cornwall,
And you, our no less loving son of Albany,
We have this hour a constant will to publish
Our daughters' several dowers, that future
    strife
May be prevented now. The princes, France
    and Burgundy,
Great rivals in our youngest daughter's love,
Long in our court have made their amorous
    sojourn,
And here are to be answer'd. Tell me, my
    daughters,—
Since now we will divest us, both of rule,   50
Interest of territory, cares of state,—
Which of you shall we say doth love us most ?
That we our largest bounty may extend
Where nature doth with merit challenge. Gon-
    eril,
Our eldest-born, speak first.

Gon. Sir, I love you more than words can
    wield the matter ;
Dearer than eye-sight, space, and liberty ;
Beyond what can be valued, rich or rare ;
No less than life, with grace, health, beauty,
    honor ;
As much as child e'er loved, or father found ;
A love that makes breath poor, and speech un-
    able ;   61
Beyond all manner of so much I love you.

Cor. [*Aside*] What shall Cordelia do ?
    Love, and be silent.

Lear. Of all these bounds, even from this
    line to this,
With shadowy forests and with champains
    rich'd,
With plenteous rivers and wide-skirted meads,
We make thee lady : to thine and Albany's
    issue
Be this perpetual. What says our second daugh-
    ter,
Our dearest Regan, wife to Cornwall ? Speak.

Reg. Sir, I am made   70
Of the self-same metal that my sister is,
And prize me at her worth. In my true heart
I find she names my very deed of love ;
Only she comes too short : that I profess
Myself an enemy to all other joys,
Which the most precious square of sense pos-
    sesses ;
And find I am alone felicitate
In your dear highness' love.

Cor.   [*Aside*] Then poor Cordelia !
And yet not so ; since, I am sure, my love's
More richer than my tongue.   80

Lear. To thee and thine hereditary ever
Remain this ample third of our fair kingdom ;
No less in space, validity, and pleasure,
Than that conferr'd on Goneril. Now, our joy,
Although the last, not least ; to whose young
    love
The vines of France and milk of Burgundy

Strive to be interess'd ; what can you say to
　　draw
A third more opulent than your sisters ? Speak.
　Cor. Nothing, my lord.
　Lear. Nothing !　　　　　　　　　　　90
　Cor. Nothing.
　Lear. Nothing will come of nothing : speak
　　again.
　Cor. Unhappy that I am, I cannot heave
My heart into my mouth : I love your majesty
According to my bond ; nor more nor less.
　Lear. How, how, Cordelia ! mend your
　　speech a little,
Lest it may mar your fortunes.
　Cor.　　　　　　　　　　　　Good my lord,
You have begot me, bred me, loved me : I
Return those duties back as are right fit,
Obey you, love you, and most honor you.　100
Why have my sisters husbands, if they say
They love you all ? Haply, when I shall wed,
That lord whose hand must take my plight
　　shall carry
Half my love with him, half my care and duty :
Sure, I shall never marry like my sisters,
To love my father all.
　Lear. But goes thy heart with this ?
　Cor.　　　　　　　　Ay, good my lord.
　Lear. So young, and so untender ?
　Cor. So young, my lord, and true.
　Lear. Let it be so ; thy truth, then, be thy
　　dower :　　　　　　　　　　　　110
For, by the sacred radiance of the sun,
The mysteries of Hecate, and the night ;
By all the operation of the orbs
From whom we do exist, and cease to be ;
Here I disclaim all my paternal care,
Propinquity and property of blood,
And as a stranger to my heart and me
Hold thee, from this, for ever. The barbarous
　　Scythian,
Or he that makes his generation messes
To gorge his appetite, shall to my bosom　120
Be as well neighbor'd, pitied, and relieved,
As thou my sometime daughter.
　Kent.　　　　　　　　Good my liege,—
　Lear. Peace, Kent !
Come not between the dragon and his wrath.
I loved her most, and thought to set my rest
On her kind nursery. Hence, and avoid my
　　sight !
So be my grave my peace, as here I give
Her father's heart from her ! Call France ;
　　who stirs ?
Call Burgundy. Cornwall and Albany,
With my two daughters' dowers digest this
　　third :　　　　　　　　　　　　130
Let pride, which she calls plainness, marry her.
I do invest you jointly with my power,
Pre-eminence, and all the large effects
That troop with majesty. Ourself, by monthly
　　course,
With reservation of an hundred knights,
By you to be sustain'd, shall our abode
Make with you by due turns. Only we still re-
　　tain
The name, and all the additions to a king ;
The sway, revenue, execution of the rest,
Beloved sons, be yours : which to confirm, 140
This coronet part betwixt you.
　　　　　　　　　　　　[*Giving the crown.*
　Kent.　　　　　　　　　Royal Lear,
Whom I have ever honor'd as my king,
Loved as my father, as my master follow'd,

As my great patron thought on in my
　　prayers,—
　Lear. The bow is bent and drawn, make
　　from the shaft.
　Kent. Let it fall rather, though the fork in-
　　vade
The region of my heart : be Kent unmannerly,
When Lear is mad. What wilt thou do, old
　　man ?
Think'st thou that duty shall have dread to
　　speak,
When power to flattery bows ? To plainness
　　honor's bound,　　　　　　　　150
When majesty stoops to folly. Reverse thy
　　doom ;
And, in thy best consideration, check
This hideous rashness : answer my life my
　　judgment,
Thy youngest daughter does not love thee
　　least ;
Nor are those empty-hearted whose low sound
Reverbs no hollowness.
　Lear.　　　　　　　Kent, on thy life, no more.
　Kent. My life I never held but as a pawn
To wage against thy enemies ; nor fear to lose
　　it,
Thy safety being the motive.
　Lear.　　　　　　　　　Out of my sight !
　Kent. See better, Lear ; and let me still re-
　　main　　　　　　　　　　　　160
The true blank of thine eye.
　Lear. Now, by Apollo,—
　Kent.　　　　　　　Now, by Apollo, king,
Thou swear'st thy gods in vain.
　Lear.　　　　　　　　O, vassal ! miscreant !
　　　　　　　[*Laying his hand on his sword.*
　Alb. ⎫ Dear sir, forbear.
　Corn. ⎭
　Kent. Do :
Kill thy physician, and the fee bestow
Upon thy foul disease. Revoke thy doom ;
Or, whilst I can vent clamor from my throat,
I'll tell thee thou dost evil.
　Lear.　　　　　　　　Hear me, recreant !
On thine allegiance, hear me !　　　　170
Since thou hast sought to make us break our
　　vow,
Which we durst never yet, and with strain'd
　　pride
To come between our sentence and our power,
Which nor our nature nor our place can bear,
Our potency made good, take thy reward.
Five days we do allot thee, for provision
To shield thee from diseases of the world ;
And on the sixth to turn thy hated back
Upon our kingdom : if, on the tenth day fol-
　　lowing,　　　　　　　　　　　179
Thy banish'd trunk be found in our dominions,
The moment is thy death. Away ! by Jupiter,
This shall not be revoked.
　Kent. Fare thee well, king : sith thus thou
　　wilt appear,
Freedom lives hence, and banishment is here.
[*To Cordelia*] The gods to their dear shelter
　　take thee, maid,
That justly think'st, and hast most rightly said !
[*To Regan and Goneril*] And your large
　　speeches may your deeds approve,
That good effects may spring from words of
　　love.
Thus Kent, O princes, bids you all adieu ;
He'll shape his old course in a country new.
　　　　　　　　　　　　　　[*Exit.*

Flourish. Re-enter Gloucester, *with* France, Burgundy, *and* Attendants.

Glou. Here's France and Burgundy, my noble lord.   191

Lear. My lord of Burgundy.
We first address towards you, who with this king
Hath rivall'd for our daughter : what, in the least,
Will you require in present dower with her,
Or cease your quest of love ?

Bur.   Most royal majesty,
I crave no more than what your highness offer'd,
Nor will you tender less.

Lear.   Right noble Burgundy,
When she was dear to us, we did hold her so ;
But now her price is fall'n. Sir, there she stands :   200
If aught within that little seeming substance,
Or all of it, with our displeasure pieced,
And nothing more, may fitly like your grace,
She's there, and she is yours.

Bur.   I know no answer.

Lear. Will you, with those infirmities she owes,
Unfriended, new-adopted to our hate,
Dower'd with our curse, and stranger'd with our oath,
Take her, or leave her ?

Bur.   Pardon me, royal sir ;
Election makes not up on such conditions.

Lear. Then leave her, sir ; for, by the power that made me,   210
I tell you all her wealth. [*To France*] For you, great king,
I would not from your love make such a stray,
To match you where I hate ; therefore beseech you
To avert your liking a more worthier way
Than on a wretch whom nature is ashamed
Almost to acknowledge hers.

France.   This is most strange,
That she, that even but now was your best object,
The argument of your praise, balm of your age,
Most best, most dearest, should in this trice of time   219
Commit a thing so monstrous, to dismantle
So many folds of favor. Sure, her offence
Must be of such unnatural degree,
That monsters it, or your fore-vouch'd affection
Fall'n into taint : which to believe of her,
Must be a faith that reason without miracle
Could never plant in me.

Cor.   I yet beseech your majesty,—
If for I want that glib and oily art,
To speak and purpose not ; since what I well intend,
I'll do't before I speak,—that you make known
It is no vicious blot, murder, or foulness,   230
No unchaste action, or dishonor'd step,
That hath deprived me of your grace and favor ;
But even for want of that for which I am richer,
A still-soliciting eye, and such a tongue
As I am glad I have not, though not to have it
Hath lost me in your liking.

Lear.   Better thou

Hadst not been born than not to have pleased me better.

France. Is it but this,—a tardiness in nature
Which often leaves the history unspoke   239
That it intends to do ? My lord of Burgundy,
What say you to the lady ? Love's not love
When it is mingled with regards that stand
Aloof from the entire point. Will you have her ?
She is herself a dowry.

Bur.   Royal Lear,
Give but that portion which yourself proposed,
And here I take Cordelia by the hand,
Duchess of Burgundy.

Lear. Nothing : I have sworn ; I am firm.

Bur. I am sorry, then, you have so lost a father
That you must lose a husband.

Cor.   Peace be with Burgundy !   250
Since that respects of fortune are his love,
I shall not be his wife.

France. Fairest Cordelia, that art most rich, being poor ;
Most choice, forsaken ; and most loved, despised !
Thee and thy virtues here I seize upon :
Be it lawful I take up what's cast away.
Gods, gods ! 'tis strange that from their cold'st neglect
My love should kindle to inflamed respect.
Thy dowerless daughter, king, thrown to my chance,
Is queen of us, of ours, and our fair France :
Not all the dukes of waterish Burgundy   261
Can buy this unprized precious maid of me.
Bid them farewell, Cordelia, though unkind :
Thou losest here, a better where to find.

Lear. Thou hast her, France : let her be thine ; for we
Have no such daughter, nor shall ever see
That face of hers again. Therefore be gone
Without our grace, our love, our benison.
Come, noble Burgundy.

          [*Flourish. Exeunt all but France,
            Goneril, Regan, and Cordelia.*

France. Bid farewell to your sisters.   270

Cor. The jewels of our father, with wash'd eyes
Cordelia leaves you : I know you what you are ;
And like a sister am most loath to call
Your faults as they are named. Use well our father :
To your professed bosoms I commit him
But yet, alas, stood I within his grace,
I would prefer him to a better place.
So, farewell to you both.

Reg. Prescribe not us our duties.

Gon.   Let your study
Be to content your lord, who hath received you   280
At fortune's alms. You have obedience scanted,
And well are worth the want that you have wanted.

Cor. Time shall unfold what plaited cunning hides :
Who cover faults, at last shame them derides.
Well may you prosper !

France.   Come, my fair Cordelia.
            [*Exeunt France and Cordelia.*

Gon. Sister, it is not a little I have to say

of what most nearly appertains to us both. I
think our father will hence to-night.

Reg. That's most certain, and with you;
next month with us.　　　　　　290

Gon. You see how full of changes his age
is ; the observation we have made of it hath
not been little : he always loved our sister
most ; and with what poor judgment he hath
now cast her off appears too grossly.

Reg. 'Tis the infirmity of his age : yet he
hath ever but slenderly known himself.

Gon. The best and soundest of his time
hath been but rash ; then must we look to receive from his age, not alone the imperfections
of long-engraffed condition, but therewithal
the unruly waywardness that infirm and choleric years bring with them.

Reg. Such unconstant starts are we like to
have from him as this of Kent's banishment.

Gon. There is further compliment of leave-
taking between France and him. Pray you, let's
hit together : if our father carry authority with
such dispositions as he bears, this last surrender of his will but offend us.　　　　310

Reg. We shall further think on't.

Gon. We must do something, and i' the
heat.　　　　　　　　　　　　[*Exeunt.*

SCENE II. *The Earl of Gloucester's castle.*

Enter EDMUND, *with a letter.*

Edm. Thou, nature, art my goddess ; to
　　thy law
My services are bound. Wherefore should I
Stand in the plague of custom, and permit
The curiosity of nations to deprive me,
For that I am some twelve or fourteen moon-
　　shines
Lag of a brother ? Why bastard ? wherefore
　　base ?
When my dimensions are as well compact,
My mind as generous, and my shape as true,
As honest madam's issue ? Why brand they us
With base ? with baseness ? bastardy ? base,
　　base ?　　　　　　　　　　　10
Who, in the lusty stealth of nature, take
More composition and fierce quality
Than doth, within a dull, stale, tired bed,
Go to the creating a whole tribe of fops,
Got 'tween asleep and wake ? Well, then,
Legitimate Edgar, I must have your land :
Our father's love is to the bastard Edmund
As to the legitimate : fine word,—legitimate !
Well, my legitimate, if this letter speed,
And my invention thrive, Edmund the base 20
Shall top the legitimate. I grow ; I prosper :
Now, gods, stand up for bastards !

Enter GLOUCESTER.

Glou. Kent banish'd thus ! and France in
　　choler parted !
And the king gone to-night ! subscribed his
　　power !
Confined to exhibition ! All this done
Upon the gad ! Edmund, how now ! what
　　news ?

Edm. So please your lordship, none.
　　　　　　[*Putting up the letter.*

Glou. Why so earnestly seek you to put up
that letter ?

Edm. I know no news, my lord.

Glou. What paper were you reading ?　30

Edm. Nothing, my lord.

Glou. No ? What needed, then, that terrible dispatch of it into your pocket ? the quality of nothing hath not such need to hide itself. Let's see : come, if it be nothing, I shall
not need spectacles.

Edm. I beseech you, sir, pardon me : it is
a letter from my brother, that I have not all
o'er-read ; and for so much as I have perused,
I find it not fit for your o'er-looking.　40

Glou. Give me the letter, sir.

Edm. I shall offend, either to detain or
give it. The contents, as in part I understand
them, are to blame.

Glou. Let's see, let's see.

Edm. I hope, for my brother's justification,
he wrote this but as an essay or taste of my
virtue.

Glou. [*Reads*] ' This policy and reverence
of age makes the world bitter to the best of
our times ; keeps our fortunes from us till our
oldness cannot relish them. I begin to find an
idle and fond bondage in the oppression of
aged tyranny ; who sways, not as it hath
power, but as it is suffered. Come to me, that
of this I may speak more. If our father would
sleep till I waked him, you should enjoy half
his revenue for ever, and live the beloved of
your brother,　　　　　　　　EDGAR.'
Hum—conspiracy !—' Sleep till I waked him,
—you should enjoy half his revenue,'—My son
Edgar ! Had he a hand to write this ? a heart
and brain to breed it in ?—When came this to
you ? who brought it ?

Edm. It was not brought me, my lord ;
there's the cunning of it ; I found it thrown in
at the casement of my closet.

Glou. You know the character to be your
brother's ?

Edm. If the matter were good, my lord, I
durst swear it were his ; but, in respect of that,
I would fain think it were not.　　　70

Glou. It is his.

Edm. It is his hand, my lord ; but I hope
his heart is not in the contents.

Glou. Hath he never heretofore sounded
you in this business ?

Edm. Never, my lord : but I have heard
him oft maintain it to be fit, that, sons at
perfect age, and fathers declining, the father
should be as ward to the son, and the son
manage his revenue.

Glou. O villain, villain ! His very opinion
in the letter ! Abhorred villain ! Unnatural, detested, brutish villain ! worse than brutish !
Go, sirrah, seek him ; I'll apprehend him :
abominable villain ! Where is he ?

Edm. I do not well know, my lord. If it
shall please you to suspend your indignation
against my brother till you can derive from
him better testimony of his intent, you shall
run a certain course ; where, if you violently
proceed against him, mistaking his purpose, it
would make a great gap in your own honor,
and shake in pieces the heart of his obedience.
I dare pawn down my life for him, that he
hath wrote this to feel my affection to your
honor, and to no further pretence of danger.

Glou. Think you so ?

Edm. If your honor judge it meet, I will
place you where you shall hear us confer of
this, and by an auricular assurance have your

satisfaction; and that without any further delay than this very evening. 101

Glou. He cannot be such a monster—

Edm. Nor is not, sure.

Glou. To his father, that so tenderly and entirely loves him. Heaven and earth! Edmund, seek him out: wind me into him, I pray you: frame the business after your own wisdom. I would unstate myself, to be in a due resolution.

Edm. I will seek him, sir, presently: convey the business as I shall find means and acquaint you withal. 111

Glou. These late eclipses in the sun and moon portend no good to us: though the wisdom of nature can reason it thus and thus, yet nature finds itself scourged by the sequent effects: love cools, friendship falls off, brothers divide: in cities, mutinies; in countries, discord; in palaces, treason; and the bond cracked 'twixt son and father. This villain of mine comes under the prediction; there's son against father: the king falls from bias of nature; there's father against child. We have seen the best of our time: machinations, hollowness, treachery, and all ruinous disorders, follow us disquietly to our graves. Find out this villain, Edmund; it shall lose thee nothing; do it carefully. And the noble and true-hearted Kent banished! his offence, honesty! 'Tis strange.   [*Exit.*

Edm. This is the excellent foppery of the world, that, when we are sick in fortune,—often the surfeit of our own behavior,—we make guilty of our disasters the sun, the moon, and the stars: as if we were villains by necessity; fools by heavenly compulsion; knaves, thieves, and treachers, by spherical predominance; drunkards, liars, and adulterers, by an enforced obedience of planetary influence; and all that we are evil in, by a divine thrusting on: an admirable evasion of whoremaster man, to lay his goatish disposition to the charge of a star! My father compounded with my mother under the dragon's tail; and my nativity was under Ursa major; so that it follows, I am rough and lecherous. Tut, I should have been that I am, had the maidenliest star in the firmament twinkled on my bastardizing. Edgar—

Enter EDGAR.

And pat he comes like the catastrophe of the old comedy: my cue is villanous melancholy, with a sigh like Tom o' Bedlam. O, these eclipses do portend these divisions! fa, sol, la, mi.

Edg. How now, brother Edmund! what serious contemplation are you in? 151

Edm. I am thinking, brother, of a prediction I read this other day, what should follow these eclipses.

Edg. Do you busy yourself about that?

Edm. I promise you, the effects he writes of succeed unhappily; as of unnaturalness between the child and the parent; death, dearth, dissolutions of ancient amities; divisions in state, menaces and maledictions against king and nobles; needless diffidences, banishment of friends, dissipation of cohorts, nuptial breaches, and I know not what.

Edg. How long have you been a sectary astronomical?

Edm. Come, come; when saw you my father last?

Edg. Why, the night gone by.

Edm. Spake you with him?

Edg. Ay, two hours together. 170

Edm. Parted you in good terms? Found you no displeasure in him by word or countenance?

Edg. None at all.

Edm. Bethink yourself wherein you may have offended him: and at my entreaty forbear his presence till some little time hath qualified the heat of his displeasure; which at this instant so rageth in him, that with the mischief of your person it would scarcely allay.

Edg. Some villain hath done me wrong.

Edm. That's my fear. I pray you, have a continent forbearance till the speed of his rage goes slower; and, as I say, retire with me to my lodging, from whence I will fitly bring you to hear my lord speak: pray ye, go; there's my key: if you do stir abroad, go armed.

Edg. Armed, brother!

Edm. Brother, I advise you to the best; go armed: I am no honest man if there be any good meaning towards you: I have told you what I have seen and heard; but faintly, nothing like the image and horror of it: pray you, away.

Edg. Shall I hear from you anon?

Edm. I do serve you in this business.

         [*Exit Edgar.*

A credulous father! and a brother noble,
Whose nature is so far from doing harms,
That he suspects none: on whose foolish honesty
My practices ride easy! I see the business.
Let me, if not by birth, have lands by wit: 199
All with me's meet that I can fashion fit.

         [*Exit.*

SCENE III. *The Duke of Albany's palace.*

Enter GONERIL, *and* OSWALD, *her steward.*

Gon. Did my father strike my gentleman for chiding of his fool?

Osw. Yes, madam.

Gon. By day and night he wrongs me; every hour
He flashes into one gross crime or other,
That sets us all at odds: I'll not endure it:
His knights grow riotous, and himself upbraids us
On every trifle. When he returns from hunting,
I will not speak with him; say I am sick:
If you come slack of former services, 9
You shall do well; the fault of it I'll answer.

Osw. He's coming, madam; I hear him.

         [*Horns within.*

Gon. Put on what weary negligence you please,
You and your fellows; I'll have it come to question:
If he dislike it, let him to our sister,
Whose mind and mine, I know, in that are one,
Not to be over-ruled. Idle old man,
That still would manage those authorities
That he hath given away! Now, by my life,
Old fools are babes again; and must be used
With checks as flatteries,—when they are seen abused. 20
Remember what I tell you.

Osw.   Well, madam.

Gon. And let his knights have colder looks
among you ;
What grows of it, no matter ; advise your fellows so :
I would breed from hence occasions, and I
shall,
That I may speak : I'll write straight to my
sister,
To hold my very course. Prepare for dinner.
                                    [*Exeunt.*

Scene IV. *A hall in the same.*

Enter Kent, *disguised.*

Kent. If but as well I other accents bor-
row,
That can my speech defuse, my good intent
May carry through itself to that full issue
For which I razed my likeness. Now, banish'd
Kent,
If thou canst serve where thou dost stand con-
demn'd,
So may it come, thy master, whom thou lovest,
Shall find thee full of labors.

Horns within. Enter Lear, Knights,
and Attendants.

Lear. Let me not stay a jot for dinner ; go
get it ready. [*Exit an Attendant.*] How now !
what art thou ?   10
Kent. A man, sir.
Lear. What dost thou profess ? what
wouldst thou with us ?
Kent. I do profess to be no less than I
seem ; to serve him truly that will put me in
trust : to love him that is honest ; to converse
with him that is wise, and says little ; to fear
judgment ; to fight when I cannot choose ; and
to eat no fish.
Lear. What art thou ?
Kent. A very honest-hearted fellow, and as
poor as the king.   21
Lear. If thou be as poor for a subject as he
is for a king, thou art poor enough. What
wouldst thou ?
Kent. Service.
Lear. Who wouldst thou serve ?
Kent. You.
Lear. Dost thou know me, fellow ?
Kent. No, sir ; but you have that in your
countenance which I would fain call master.
Lear. What's that ?   31
Kent. Authority.
Lear. What services canst thou do ?
Kent. I can keep honest counsel, ride, run,
mar a curious tale in telling it, and deliver a
plain message bluntly : that which ordinary
men are fit for, I am qualified in ; and the best
of me is diligence.
Lear. How old art thou ?   39
Kent. Not so young, sir, to love a woman
for singing, nor so old to dote on her for any
thing : I have years on my back forty eight.
Lear. Follow me ; thou shalt serve me :
if I like thee no worse after dinner, I will
not part from thee yet. Dinner, ho, dinner !
Where's my knave ? my fool ? Go you, and
call my fool hither.   [*Exit an Attendant.*

Enter Oswald.

You, you, sirrah, where's my daughter ?
Osw. So please you,—   [*Exit.*
Lear. What says the fellow there ? Call the

clotpoll back. [*Exit a Knight.*] Where's my
fool, ho ? I think the world's asleep.

Re-enter Knight.

How now ! where's that mongrel ?
Knight. He says, my lord, your daughter
is not well.
Lear. Why came not the slave back to me
when I called him.
Knight. Sir, he answered me in the round-
est manner, he would not.
Lear. He would not !   60
Knight. My lord, I know not what the matter is ; but, to my judgment, your highness is
not entertained with that ceremonious affection as you were wont ; there's a great abatement of kindness appears as well in the general dependants as in the duke himself also
and your daughter.
Lear. Ha ! sayest thou so ?
Knight. I beseech you, pardon me, my
lord, if I be mistaken ; for my duty cannot be
silent when I think your highness wronged. 71
Lear. Thou but rememberest me of mine
own conception : I have perceived a most faint
neglect of late ; which I have rather blamed
as mine own jealous curiosity than as a very
pretence and purpose of unkindness : I will
look further into't. But where's my fool ? I
have not seen him this two days.
Knight. Since my young lady's going into
France, sir, the fool hath much pined away.
Lear. No more of that ; I have noted it
well. Go you, and tell my daughter I would
speak with her. [*Exit an Attendant.*] Go you,
call hither my fool.   [*Exit an Attendant.*

Re-enter Oswald.

O, you sir, you, come you hither, sir : who am
I, sir ?
Osw. My lady's father.
Lear. 'My lady's father' ! my lord's
knave : your whoreson dog ! you slave ! you
cur !
Osw. I am none of these, my lord ; I beseech your pardon.   91
Lear. Do you bandy looks with me, you
rascal ?   [*Striking him.*
Osw. I'll not be struck, my lord.
Kent. Nor tripped neither, you base foot-
ball player.   [*Tripping up his heels.*
Lear. I thank thee, fellow ; thou servest
me, and I'll love thee.
Kent. Come, sir, arise, away ! I'll teach
you differences : away, away ! If you will
measure your lubber's length again, tarry : but
away ! go to ; have you wisdom ? so.
                          [*Pushes Oswald out.*
Lear. Now, my friendly knave, I thank
thee : there's earnest of thy service.
                          [*Giving Kent money.*

Enter Fool.

Fool. Let me hire him too : here's my coxcomb.   [*Offering Kent his cap.*
Lear. How now, my pretty knave ! how
dost thou ?
Fool. Sirrah, you were best take my coxcomb.
Kent. Why, fool ?   110
Fool. Why, for taking one's part that's out
of favor : nay, an thou canst not smile as the

wind sits, thou'lt catch cold shortly : there,
take my coxcomb : why, this fellow has banished two on's daughters, and did the third a
blessing against his will ; if thou follow him,
thou must needs wear my coxcomb. How now,
nuncle ! Would I had two coxcombs and two
daughters !

Lear. Why, my boy ?   119

Fool. If I gave them all my living, I'ld
keep my coxcombs myself. There's mine ; beg
another of thy daughters.

Lear. Take heed, sirrah ; the whip.

Fool. Truth's a dog must to kennel ; he
must be whipped out, when Lady the brach
may stand by the fire and stink.

Lear. A pestilent gall to me !

Fool. Sirrah, I'll teach thee a speech.

Lear. Do.

Fool. Mark it, nuncle :   130
  Have more than thou showest,
  Speak less than thou knowest,
  Lend less than thou owest,
  Ride more than thou goest,
  Learn more than thou trowest,
  Set less than thou throwest ;
  Leave thy drink and thy whore,
  And keep in-a-door,
  And thou shalt have more
  Than two tens to a score.   140

Kent. This is nothing, fool.

Fool. Then 'tis like the breath of an un-
fee'd lawyer ; you gave me nothing for't. Can
you make no use of nothing, nuncle ?

Lear. Why, no, boy ; nothing can be made
out of nothing.

Fool. [*To Kent*] Prithee, tell him, so much
the rent of his land comes to : he will not believe a fool.

Lear. A bitter fool !   150

Fool. Dost thou know the difference, my
boy, between a bitter fool and a sweet fool ?

Lear. No, lad ; teach me.

Fool. That lord that counsell'd thee
  To give away thy land,
  Come place him here by me,
  Do thou for him stand :
  The sweet and bitter fool
  Will presently appear ;
  The one in motley here,   160
    The other found out there.

Lear. Dost thou call me fool, boy ?

Fool. All thy other titles thou hast given
away ; that thou wast born with.

Kent. This is not altogether fool, my lord.

Fool. No, faith, lords and great men will
not let me ; if I had a monopoly out, they
would have part on't : and ladies too, they
will not let me have all fool to myself ; they'll
be snatching. Give me an egg, nuncle, and I'll
give thee two crowns.   171

Lear. What two crowns shall they be ?

Fool. Why, after I have cut the egg i' the
middle, and eat up the meat, the two crowns
of the egg. When thou clovest thy crown i'
the middle, and gavest away both parts, thou
borest thy ass on thy back o'er the dirt : thou
hadst little wit in thy bald crown, when thou
gavest thy golden one away. If I speak like
myself in this, let him be whipped that first
finds it so.   180

[*Singing*] Fools had ne'er less wit in a year ;
  For wise men are grown foppish,
  They know not how their wits to wear,
    Their manners are so apish.

Lear. When were you wont to be so full of
songs, sirrah ?

Fool. I have used it, nuncle, ever since
thou madest thy daughters thy mothers : for
when thou gavest them the rod, and put'st
down thine own breeches,   190
[*Singing*] Then they for sudden joy did weep,
  And I for sorrow sung,
  That such a king should play bo-peep,
    And go the fools among.
Prithee, nuncle, keep a schoolmaster that can
teach thy fool to lie : I would fain learn to
lie.

Lear. An you lie, sirrah, we'll have you
whipped.

Fool. I marvel what kin thou and thy
daughters are : they'll have me whipped for
speaking true, thou'lt have me whipped for
lying ; and sometimes I am whipped for holding my peace. I had rather be any kind o'
thing than a fool : and yet I would not be
thee, nuncle ; thou hast pared thy wit o' both
sides, and left nothing i' the middle : here
comes one o' the parings.

Enter Goneril.

Lear. How now, daughter ! what makes
that frontlet on ? Methinks you are too much
of late i' the frown.   209

Fool. Thou wast a pretty fellow when thou
hadst no need to care for her frowning ; now
thou art an O without a figure : I am better
than thou art now ; I am a fool, thou art
nothing. [*To Gon.*] Yes, forsooth, I will hold
my tongue ; so your face bids me, though
you say nothing. Mum, mum,
  He that keeps nor crust nor crum,
    Weary of all, shall want some.
[*Pointing to Lear*] That's a shealed peascod.

Gon. Not only, sir, this your all-licensed
fool,   220
But other of your insolent retinue
Do hourly carp and quarrel ; breaking forth
In rank and not-to-be endured riots. Sir,
I had thought, by making this well known
    unto you,
To have found a safe redress ; but now grow
    fearful,
By what yourself too late have spoke and
    done.
That you protect this course, and put it on
By your allowance ; which if you should, the
    fault
Would not 'scape censure, nor the redresses
    sleep,   229
Which, in the tender of a wholesome weal,
Might in their working do you that offence,
Which else were shame, that then necessity
Will call discreet proceeding.

Fool. For, you trow, nuncle,
  The hedge-sparrow fed the cuckoo so
    long,
  That it's had it head bit off by it young.
So, out went the candle, and we were left
    darkling.

Lear. Are you our daughter ?

Gon. Come, sir,
I would you would make use of that good
    wisdom,   240

Whereof I know you are fraught; and put away
These dispositions, that of late transform you
From what you rightly are.

Fool. May not an ass know when the cart draws the horse? Whoop, Jug! I love thee.

Lear. Doth any here know me? This is not Lear:
Doth Lear walk thus? speak thus? Where are his eyes?
Either his notion weakens, his discernings
Are lethargied—Ha! waking? 'tis not so.
Who is it that can tell me who I am?   250

Fool. Lear's shadow.

Lear. I would learn that; for, by the marks of sovereignty, knowledge, and reason,
I should be false persuaded I had daughters.

Fool. Which they will make an obedient father.

Lear. Your name, fair gentlewoman?

Gon. This admiration, sir, is much o' the savor
Of other your new pranks. I do beseech you
To understand my purposes aright: 260
As you are old and reverend, you should be wise.
Here do you keep a hundred knights and squires;
Men so disorder'd, so debosh'd and bold,
That this our court, infected with their manners,
Shows like a riotous inn: epicurism and lust
Make it more like a tavern or a brothel
Than a graced palace. The shame itself doth speak
For instant remedy: be then desired
By her, that else will take the thing she begs,
A little to disquantity your train;   270
And the remainder, that shall still depend,
To be such men as may besort your age,
And know themselves and you.

Lear.   Darkness and devils!
Saddle my horses; call my train together:
Degenerate bastard! I'll not trouble thee.
Yet have I left a daughter.

Gon. You strike my people; and your disorder'd rabble
Make servants of their betters.

Enter ALBANY.

Lear. Woe, that too late repents,—[*To Alb.*] O, sir, are you come?
Is it your will? Speak, sir. Prepare my horses.
Ingratitude, thou marble-hearted fiend,   281
More hideous when thou show'st thee in a child
Than the sea-monster!

Alb.   Pray, sir, be patient.

Lear. [*To Gon.*] Detested kite! thou liest.
My train are men of choice and rarest parts,
That all particulars of duty know,
And in the most exact regard support
The worships of their name. O most small fault,
How ugly didst thou in Cordelia show!
That, like an engine, wrench'd my frame of nature   290
From the fix'd place; drew from heart all love,
And added to the gall. O Lear, Lear, Lear!
Beat at this gate, that let thy folly in,
                 [*Striking his head.*

And thy dear judgment out! Go, go, my people.

Alb. My lord, I am guiltless, as I am ignorant
Of what hath moved you.

Lear.   It may be so, my lord.
Hear, nature, hear; dear goddess, hear!
Suspend thy purpose, if thou didst intend
To make this creature fruitful!
Into her womb convey sterility!   300
Dry up in her the organs of increase;
And from her derogate body never spring
A babe to honor her! If she must teem,
Create her child of spleen; that it may live,
And be a thwart disnatured torment to her!
Let it stamp wrinkles in her brow of youth;
With cadent tears fret channels in her cheeks;
Turn all her mother's pains and benefits
To laughter and contempt; that she may feel
How sharper than a serpent's tooth it is   310
To have a thankless child! Away, away!
                 [*Exit.*

Alb. Now, gods that we adore, whereof comes this?

Gon. Never afflict yourself to know the cause;
But let his disposition have that scope
That dotage gives it.

Re-enter LEAR.

Lear. What, fifty of my followers at a clap!
Within a fortnight!

Alb.   What's the matter, sir?

Lear. I'll tell thee: [*To Gon.*] Life and death! I am ashamed
That thou hast power to shake my manhood thus;
That these hot tears, which break from me perforce,   320
Should make thee worth them. Blasts and fogs upon thee!
The untented woundings of a father's curse
Pierce every sense about thee! Old fond eyes,
Beweep this cause again, I'll pluck ye out,
And cast you, with the waters that you lose,
To temper clay. Yea, is it come to this?
Let it be so: yet have I left a daughter,
Who, I am sure, is kind and comfortable:
When she shall hear this of thee, with her nails   329
She'll flay thy wolvish visage. Thou shalt find
That I'll resume the shape which thou dost think
I have cast off for ever: thou shalt, I warrant thee.
                 [*Exeunt Lear, Kent, and Attendants.*

Gon. Do you mark that, my lord?

Alb. I cannot be so partial, Goneril,
To the great love I bear you,—

Gon. Pray you, content. What, Oswald, ho!
[*To the Fool*] You, sir, more knave than fool, after your master.

Fool. Nuncle Lear, nuncle Lear, tarry and take the fool with thee.
        A fox, when one has caught her,   340
        And such a daughter,
        Should sure to the slaughter,
        If my cap would buy a halter:
        So the fool follows after.   [*Exit.*

Gon. This man hath had good counsel :—
a hundred knights !
'Tis politic and safe to let him keep
At point a hundred knights : yes, that, on ev-
ery dream,
Each buzz, each fancy, each complaint, dis-
like,
He may enguard his dotage with their powers,
And hold our lives in mercy. Oswald, I say ! 350
Alb. Well, you may fear too far.
Gon.   Safer than trust too far :
Let me still take away the harms I fear,
Not fear still to be taken : I know his heart.
What he hath utter'd I have writ my sister
If she sustain him and his hundred knights
When I have show'd the unfitness,—

Re-enter OSWALD.

          How now, Oswald !
What, have you writ that letter to my sister ?
Osw. Yes, madam.
Gon. Take you some company, and away
to horse :
Inform her full of my particular fear ; 360
And thereto add such reasons of your own
As may compact it more. Get you gone ;
And hasten your return. [*Exit Oswald.*] No,
no, my lord,
This milky gentleness and course of yours
Though I condemn not, yet, under pardon,
You are much more attask'd for want of wis-
dom
Than praised for harmful mildness.
Alb. How far your eyes may pierce I can-
not tell :
Striving to better, oft we mar what's well.
Gon. Nay, then— 370
Alb. Well, well ; the event. [*Exeunt.*

SCENE V. *Court before the same.*

Enter LEAR, KENT, *and* Fool.

Lear. Go you before to Gloucester with
these letters. Acquaint my daughter no further with any thing you know than comes
from her demand out of the letter. If your
diligence be not speedy, I shall be there afore
you.
Kent. I will not sleep, my lord, till I have
delivered your letter. [*Exit.*
Fool. If a man's brains were in's heels,
were't not in danger of kibes ?
Lear. Ay, boy. 10
Fool. Then, I prithee, be merry ; thy wit
shall ne'er go slip-shod.
Lear. Ha, ha, ha !
Fool. Shalt see thy other daughter will use
thee kindly ; for though she's as like this as a
crab's like an apple, yet I can tell what I can
tell.
Lear. Why, what canst thou tell, my boy ?
Fool. She will taste as like this as a crab
does to a crab. Thou canst tell why one's nose
stands i' the middle on's face ? 20
Lear. No.
Fool. Why, to keep one's eyes of either
side's nose ; that what a man cannot smell out,
he may spy into.
Lear. I did her wrong—
Fool. Canst tell how an oyster makes his
shell ?
Lear. No.
Fool. Nor I neither ; but I can tell why a
snail has a house. 30

Lear. Why ?
Fool. Why, to put his head in ; not to give
it away to his daughters, and leave his horns
without a case.
Lear. I will forget my nature. So kind a
father ! Be my horses ready ?
Fool. Thy asses are gone about 'em. The
reason why the seven stars are no more than
seven is a pretty reason.
Lear. Because they are not eight ? 40
Fool. Yes, indeed : thou wouldst make a
good fool.
Lear. To take 't again perforce ! Monster
ingratitude !
Fool. If thou wert my fool, nuncle, I'ld
have thee beaten for being old before thy time.
Lear. How 's that ?
Fool. Thou shouldst not have been old till
thou hadst been wise.
Lear. O, let me not be mad, not mad,
sweet heaven 50
Keep me in temper : I would not be mad !

Enter Gentleman.

How now ! are the horses ready ?
Gent. Ready, my lord.
Lear. Come, boy.
Fool. She that's a maid now, and laughs
at my departure,
Shall not be a maid long, unless things be cut
shorter. [*Exeunt.*

ACT II.

SCENE I. *The Earl of Gloucester's castle.*

Enter EDMUND, *and* CURAN *meets him.*

Edm. Save thee, Curan.
Cur. And you, sir. I have been with your
father, and given him notice that the Duke of
Cornwall and Regan his duchess will be here
with him this night.
Edm. How comes that ?
Cur. Nay, I know not. You have heard of
the news abroad ; I mean the whispered ones,
for they are yet but ear-kissing arguments ?
Edm. Not I : pray you, what are they ? 10
Cur. Have you heard of no likely wars to-
ward, 'twixt the Dukes of Cornwall and Al-
bany ?
Edm. Not a word.
Cur. You may do, then, in time. Fare you
well, sir. [*Exit.*
Edm. The duke be here to-night ? The
better ! best !
This weaves itself perforce into my business.
My father hath set guard to take my brother ;
And I have one thing, of a queasy question,
Which I must act : briefness and fortune,
work ! 20
Brother, a word ; descend : brother, I say !

Enter EDGAR.

My father watches : O sir, fly this place ;
Intelligence is given where you are hid ;
You have now the good advantage of the
night :
Have you not spoken 'gainst the Duke of
Cornwall ?
He's coming hither : now, i' the night, i' the
haste,
And Regan with him : have you nothing said

Upon his party 'gainst the Duke of Albany?
Advise yourself.

Edg.　　　I am sure on't, not a word　29

Edm. I hear my father coming : pardon
me :
In cunning I must draw my sword upon you :
Draw ; seem to defend yourself ; now quit you
　　well.
Yield : come before my father. Light, ho,
　　here !
Fly, brother. Torches, torches ! So, farewell.
　　　　　　　　　　　　　　[Exit Edgar.
Some blood drawn on me would beget opinion
　　　　　　　　　　　　[Wounds his arm.
Of my more fierce endeavor : I have seen
　　drunkards
Do more than this in sport. Father, father !
Stop, stop ! No help ?

Enter GLOUCESTER, *and* Servants *with torches.*

Glou. Now, Edmund, where's the villain ?

Edm. Here stood he in the dark, his sharp
　　sword out,　　　　　　　　　　　　40
Mumbling of wicked charms, conjuring the
　　moon
To stand auspicious mistress,—

Glou.　　　　　　　　But where is he ?

Edm. Look, sir, I bleed.

Glou.　　　Where is the villain, Edmund ?

Edm. Fled this way, sir. When by no
　　means he could—

Glou. Pursue him, ho ! Go after. [*Exeunt
some Servants.*] By no means what ?

Edm. Persuade me to the murder of your
　　lordship ;
But that I told him, the revenging gods
'Gainst parricides did all their thunders bend ;
Spoke, with how manifold and strong a bond
The child was bound to the father ; sir, in fine,
Seeing how loathly opposite I stood　　　51
To his unnatural purpose, in fell motion,
With his prepared sword, he charges home
My unprovided body, lanced mine arm :
But when he saw my best alarum'd spirits,
Bold in the quarrel's right, roused to the en-
　　counter,
Or whether gasted by the noise I made,
Full suddenly he fled.

Glou.　　　　　Let him fly far :
Not in this land shall he remain uncaught ;
And found—dispatch. The noble duke my
　　master,　　　　　　　　　　　　60
My worthy arch and patron, comes to-night :
By his authority I will proclaim it,
That he which finds him shall deserve our
　　thanks,
Bringing the murderous coward to the stake ;
He that conceals him, death.

Edm. When I dissuaded him from his in-
　　tent,
And found him pight to do it, with curst
　　speech
I threaten'd to discover him : he replied,
' Thou unpossessing bastard ! dost thou think,
If I would stand against thee, would the re-
　　posal　　　　　　　　　　　　70
Of any trust, virtue, or worth in thee
Make thy words faith'd ? No : what I should
　　deny,—
As this I would : ay, though thou didst pro-
　　duce
My very character,—I'ld turn it all
To thy suggestion, plot, and damned practice :

And thou must make a dullard of the world,
If they not thought the profits of my death
Were very pregnant and potential spurs
To make thee seek it.'

Glou.　　　　Strong and fasten'd villain !
Would he deny his letter ? I never got him.
　　　　　　　　　　　[Tucket within. 81
Hark, the duke's trumpets ! I know not why
　　he comes.
All ports I'll bar ; the villain shall not 'scape ;
The duke must grant me that : besides, his
　　picture
I will send far and near, that all the kingdom
May have the due note of him ; and of my
　　land,
Loyal and natural boy, I'll work the means
To make thee capable.

Enter CORNWALL, REGAN, *and* Attendants.

Corn. How now, my noble friend ! since I
　　came hither,
Which I can call but now, I have heard
　　strange news.

Reg. If it be true, all vengeance comes too
　　short　　　　　　　　　　　　90
Which can pursue the offender. How dost, my
　　lord ?

Glou. O, madam, my old heart is crack'd,
　　it's crack'd !

Reg. What, did my father's godson seek
　　your life ?
He whom my father named ? your Edgar ?

Glou. O, lady, lady, shame would have it
　　hid !

Reg. Was he not companion with the
　　riotous knights
That tend upon my father ?

Glou. I know not, madam : 'tis too bad,
　　too bad.

Edm. Yes, madam, he was of that consort.

Reg. No marvel, then, though he were ill
　　affected :　　　　　　　　　　　100
'Tis they have put him on the old man's death,
To have the expense and waste of his revenues.
I have this present evening from my sister
Been well inform'd of them ; and with such
　　cautions,
That if they come to sojourn at my house,
I'll not be there.

Corn.　　　Nor I, assure thee, Regan.
Edmund, I hear that you have shown your fa-
　　ther
A child-like office.

Edm.　　　　'Twas my duty, sir.

Glou. He did bewray his practice ; and
　　received
This hurt you see, striving to apprehend him.

Corn. Is he pursued ?　　　　　　111

Glou.　　　　　Ay, my good lord.

Corn. If he be taken, he shall never more
Be fear'd of doing harm : make your own
　　purpose,
How in my strength you please. For you,
　　Edmund,
Whose virtue and obedience doth this instant
So much commend itself, you shall be ours :
Natures of such deep trust we shall much
　　need ;
You we first seize on.

Edm.　　　　I shall serve you, sir,
Truly, however else.

Glou.　　　　For him I thank your grace.

Corn. You know not why we came to visit
    you,—   120
Reg. Thus out of season, threading dark-
    eyed night :
Occasions, noble Gloucester, of some poise,
Wherein we must have use of your advice :
Our father he hath writ, so hath our sister,
Of differences, which I least thought it fit
To answer from our home ; the several mes-
    sengers
From hence attend dispatch. Our good old
    friend,
Lay comforts to your bosom ; and bestow
Your needful counsel to our business,
Which craves the instant use.
Glou.   I serve you, madam :   130
Your graces are right welcome.   [*Exeunt.*

Scene II. *Before Gloucester's castle.*

Enter Kent *and* Oswald, *severally.*

Osw. Good dawning to thee, friend : art of
this house ?
Kent. Ay.
Osw. Where may we set our horses ?
Kent. I' the mire.
Osw. Prithee, if thou lovest me, tell me.
Kent. I love thee not.
Osw. Why, then, I care not for thee.
Kent. If I had thee in Lipsbury pinfold, I
would make thee care for me.   10
Osw. Why dost thou use me thus ? I know
thee not.
Kent. Fellow, I know thee.
Osw. What dost thou know me for ?
Kent. A knave ; a rascal ; an eater of
broken meats ; a base, proud, shallow, beggarly, three-suited, hundred-pound, filthy,
worsted-stocking knave ; a lily-livered, action-
taking knave, a whoreson, glass-gazing, super-
serviceable, finical rogue ; one-trunk-inheriting
slave ; one that wouldst be a bawd, in way of
good service, and art nothing but the composition of a knave, beggar, coward, pandar, and
the son and heir of a mongrel bitch : one
whom I will beat into clamorous whining, if
thou deniest the least syllable of thy addition.
Osw. Why, what a monstrous fellow art
thou, thus to rail on one that is neither known
of thee nor knows thee !   29
Kent. What a brazen-faced varlet art thou,
to deny thou knowest me ! Is it two days ago
since I tripped up thy heels, and beat thee before the king ? Draw, you rogue : for, though
it be night, yet the moon shines ; I'll make a
sop o' the moonshine of you : draw, you
whoreson cullionly barber-monger, draw.
                [*Drawing his sword.*
Osw. Away ! I have nothing to do with
thee.
Kent. Draw, you rascal : you come with
letters against the king ; and take vanity the
puppet's part against the royalty of her father : draw, you rogue, or I'll so carbonado
your shanks : draw, you rascal ; come your
ways.
Osw. Help, ho ! murder ! help !
Kent. Strike, you slave ; stand, rogue,
stand ; you neat slave, strike.   [*Beating him.*
Osw. Help, ho ! murder ! murder !

Enter Edmund, *with his rapier drawn,* Cornwall, Regan, Gloucester, *and* Servants.

Edm. How now ! What's the matter ?
Kent. With you, goodman boy, an you
please : come, I'll flesh ye ; come on, young
master.
Glou. Weapons ! arms ! What 's the mat-
ter here ?   51
Corn. Keep peace, upon your lives :
He dies that strikes again. What is the matter ?
Reg. The messengers from our sister and
the king.
Corn. What is your difference ? speak.
Osw. I am scarce in breath, my lord.
Kent. No marvel, you have so bestirred
your valor. You cowardly rascal, nature dis-
claims in thee : a tailor made thee.   60
Corn. Thou art a strange fellow : a tailor
make a man ?
Kent. Ay, a tailor, sir : a stone-cutter or
a painter could not have made him so ill,
though he had been but two hours at the trade.
Corn. Speak yet, how grew your quarrel ?
Osw. This ancient ruffian, sir, whose life I
have spared at suit of his gray beard,—
Kent. Thou whoreson zed ! thou unneces-
sary letter ! My lord, if you will give me
leave, I will tread this unbolted villain into
mortar, and daub the wall of a jakes with
him. Spare my gray beard, you wagtail ?
Corn. Peace, sirrah !
You beastly knave, know you no reverence ?
Kent. Yes, sir ; but anger hath a privilege.
Corn. Why art thou angry ?
Kent. That such a slave as this should
    wear a sword,
Who wears no honesty. Such smiling rogues
    as these,
Like rats, oft bite the holy cords a-twain   80
Which are too intrinse t' unloose ; smooth ev-
    ery passion
That in the natures of their lords rebel ;
Bring oil to fire, snow to their colder moods ;
Renege, affirm, and turn their halcyon beaks
With every gale and vary of their masters,
Knowing nought, like dogs, but following.
A plague upon your epileptic visage !
Smile you my speeches, as I were a fool ?
Goose, if I had you upon Sarum plain,
I'ld drive ye cackling home to Camelot.   90
Corn. What, art thou mad, old fellow ?
Glou. How fell you out ? say that.
Kent. No contraries hold more antipathy
Than I and such a knave.
Corn. Why dost thou call him knave ?
    What's his offence ?
Kent. His countenance likes me not.
Corn. No more, perchance, does mine, nor
    his, nor hers.
Kent. Sir, 'tis my occupation to be plain :
I have seen better faces in my time
Than stands on any shoulder that I see   100
Before me at this instant.
Corn.   This is some fellow,
Who, having been praised for bluntness, doth
    affect
A saucy roughness, and constrains the garb
Quite from his nature : he cannot flatter, he,
An honest mind and plain, he must speak
    truth !
An they will take it, so ; if not, he's plain.
These kind of knaves I know, which in this
    plainness
Harbor more craft and more corrupter ends
Than twenty silly ducking observants

That stretch their duties nicely.   110
     Kent. Sir, in good sooth, in sincere verity,
Under the allowance of your great aspect,
Whose influence, like the wreath of radiant
     fire
On flickering Phœbus' front,—
     Corn.   What mean'st by this ?
     Kent. To go out of my dialect, which you
discommend so much. I know, sir, I am no
flatterer : he that beguiled you in a plain ac-
cent was a plain knave ; which for my part
I will not be, though I should win your dis-
pleasure to entreat me to 't.   120
     Corn. What was the offence you gave
     him ?
     Osw. I never gave him any :
It pleased the king his master very late
To strike at me, upon his misconstruction ;
When he, conjunct, and flattering his dis-
     pleasure,
Tripp'd me behind ; being down, insulted,
     rail'd,
And put upon him such a deal of man,
That worthied him, got praises of the king
For him attempting who was self-subdued ;
And, in the fleshment of this dread exploit,
Drew on me here again.   131
     Kent. None of these rogues and cowards
But Ajax is their fool.
     Corn.   Fetch forth the stocks !
You stubborn ancient knave, you reverend
     braggart,
We'll teach you—
     Kent.   Sir, I am too old to learn :
Call not your stocks for me : I serve the king ;
On whose employment I was sent to you :
You shall do small respect, show too bold
     malice
Against the grace and person of my master,
Stocking his messenger.
     Corn. Fetch forth the stocks ! As I have
     life and honor,   140
There shall he sit till noon.
     Reg. Till noon ! till night, my lord ; and
     all night too.
     Kent. Why, madam, if I were your father's
     dog,
You should not use me so.
     Reg.   Sir, being his knave, I will.
     Corn. This is a fellow of the self-same
     color
Our sister speaks of. Come, bring away the
     stocks !   [*Stocks brought out.*
     Glou. Let me beseech your grace not to
     do so :
His fault is much, and the good king his
     master
Will check him for 't : your purposed low
     correction
Is such as basest and contemned'st wretches
For pilferings and most common trespasses
Are punish'd with : the king must take it ill,
That he 's so slightly valued in his messenger,
Should have him thus restrain'd.
     Corn.   I'll answer that.
     Reg. My sister may receive it much more
     worse,
To have her gentleman abused, assaulted,
For following her affairs. Put in his legs.
          [*Kent is put in the stocks.*
Come, my good lord, away.
     [*Exeunt all but Gloucester and Kent.*

     Glou. I am sorry for thee, friend ; 'tis the
     duke's pleasure,
Whose disposition, all the world well knows,
Will not be rubb'd nor stopp'd : I'll entreat
     for thee.   161
     Kent. Pray, do not, sir : I have watched
     and travell'd hard ;
Some time I shall sleep out, the rest I'll whistle.
A good man's fortune may grow out at heels :
Give you good morrow !
     Glou. The duke 's to blame in this ; 'twill
     be ill taken.   [*Exit.*
     Kent. Good king, that must approve the
     common saw,
Thou out of heaven's benediction comest
To the warm sun !
Approach, thou beacon to this under globe,
That by thy comfortable beams I may   171
Peruse this letter ! Nothing almost sees mira-
     cles
But misery : I know 'tis from Cordelia,
Who hath most fortunately been inform'd
Of my obscured course ; and shall find time
From this enormous state, seeking to give
Losses their remedies. All weary and o'er-
     watch'd,
Take vantage, heavy eyes, not to behold
This shameful lodging.
Fortune, good night : smile once more : turn
     thy wheel !   [*Sleeps.* 180

SCENE III. *A wood.*

Enter EDGAR.

     Edg. I heard myself proclaim'd ;
And by the happy hollow of a tree
Escaped the hunt. No port is free ; no place,
That guard, and most unusual vigilance,
Does not attend my taking. Whiles I may
     'scape,
I will preserve myself : and am bethought
To take the basest and most poorest shape
That ever penury, in contempt of man,
Brought near to beast : my face I'll grime
     with filth ;
Blanket my loins : elf all my hair in knots ;
And with presented nakedness out-face   11
The winds and persecutions of the sky.
The country gives me proof and precedent
Of Bedlam beggars, who, with roaring voices,
Strike in their numb'd and mortified bare arms
Pins, wooden pricks, nails, sprigs of rosemary ;
And with this horrible object, from low farms,
Poor pelting villages, sheep-cotes, and mills,
Sometime with lunatic bans, sometime with
     prayers,
Enforce their charity. Poor Turlygod ! poor
     Tom !   20
That 's something yet : Edgar I nothing am.
          [*Exit.*

SCENE IV. *Before Gloucester's castle. Kent in the stocks.*

Enter LEAR, *Fool, and* Gentleman.

     Lear. 'Tis strange that they should so de-
     part from home,
And not send back my messenger.
     Gent.   As I learn'd,
The night before there was no purpose in them
Of this remove.
     Kent.   Hail to thee, noble master !
     Lear. Ha !
Makest thou this shame thy pastime ?

Kent.   No, my lord.
Fool. Ha, ha! he wears cruel garters.
Horses are tied by the heads, dogs and bears
by the neck, monkeys by the loins, and men
by the legs: when a man's over-lusty at legs,
then he wears wooden nether-stocks.   11
Lear. What 's he that hath so much thy
    place mistook
To set thee here?
Kent.   It is both he and she;
Your son and daughter.
Lear. No.
Kent. Yes.
Lear. No, I say.
Kent. I say, yea.
Lear. No, no, they would not.
Kent. Yes, they have.   20
Lear. By Jupiter, I swear, no.
Kent. By Juno, I swear, ay.
Lear.   They durst not do 't;
They could not, would not do 't; 'tis worse
    than murder,
To do upon respect such violent outrage:
Resolve me, with all modest haste, which way
Thou mightst deserve, or they impose, this
    usage,
Coming from us.
Kent.   My lord, when at their home
I did commend your highness' letters to them,
Ere I was risen from the place that show'd
My duty kneeling, came there a reeking post,
Stew'd in his haste, half breathless, panting
    forth   31
From Goneril his mistress salutations;
Deliver'd letters, spite of intermission,
Which presently they read: on whose contents,
They summon'd up their meiny, straight took
    horse;
Commanded me to follow, and attend
The leisure of their answer; gave me cold
    looks:
And meeting here the other messenger,
Whose welcome, I perceived, had poison'd
    mine,—
Being the very fellow that of late   40
Display'd so saucily against your highness,—
Having more man than wit about me, drew:
He raised the house with loud and coward
    cries.
Your son and daughter found this trespass
    worth
The shame which here it suffers.
Fool. Winter's not gone yet, if the wild-
geese fly that way.
        Fathers that wear rags
          Do make their children blind;
        But fathers that bear bags   50
          Shall see their children kind.
        Fortune, that arrant whore,
          Ne'er turns the key to the poor.
But, for all this, thou shalt have as many do-
lours for thy daughters as thou canst tell in a
year.
Lear. O, how this mother swells up toward
    my heart!
Hysterica passio, down, thou climbing sorrow,
Thy element's below! Where is this daughter?
Kent. With the earl, sir, here within.
Lear.   Follow me not;
Stay here.   [*Exit.* 60
Gent. Made you no more offence but what
you speak of?
Kent. None.

How chance the king comes with so small a
    train?
Fool. And thou hadst been set i' the stocks
for that question, thou hadst well deserved it.
Kent. Why, fool?
Fool. We'll set thee to school to an ant, to
teach thee there's no laboring i' the winter.
All that follow their noses are led by their
eyes but blind men; and there's not a nose
among twenty but can smell him that's stinking. Let go thy hold when a great wheel runs
down a hill, lest it break thy neck with following it: but the great one that goes up the
hill, let him draw thee after. When a wise
man gives thee better counsel, give me mine
again: I would have none but knaves follow
it, since a fool gives it.
        That sir which serves and seeks for gain,
          And follows but for form,   80
        Will pack when it begins to rain,
          And leave thee in the storm,
        But I will tarry; the fool will stay,
          And let the wise man fly:
        The knave turns fool that runs away;
          The fool no knave, perdy.
Kent. Where learned you this, fool?
Fool. Not i' the stocks, fool.

Re-enter Lear, *with* Gloucester.

Lear. Deny to speak with me? They are
    sick? they are weary?
They have travell'd all the night? Mere
    fetches;   90
The images of revolt and flying off.
Fetch me a better answer.
Glou.   My dear lord,
You know the fiery quality of the duke;
How unremoveable and fix'd he is
In his own course.
Lear. Vengeance! plague! death! con-
    fusion!
Fiery? what quality? Why, Gloucester,
    Gloucester,
I'ld speak with the Duke of Cornwall and his
    wife.
Glou. Well, my good lord, I have inform'd
    them so.
Lear. Inform'd them! Dost thou under-
    stand me, man?   100
Glou. Ay, my good lord.
Lear. The king would speak with Corn-
    wall; the dear father
Would with his daughter speak, commands
    her service:
Are they inform'd of this? My breath and
    blood!
Fiery? the fiery duke? Tell the hot duke
    that—
No, but not yet: may be he is not well:
Infirmity doth still neglect all office
Whereto our health is bound; we are not
    ourselves
When nature, being oppress'd, commands the
    mind
To suffer with the body: I'll forbear;   110
And am fall'n out with my more headier will,
To take the indisposed and sickly fit
For the sound man. Death on my state!
    wherefore   [*Looking on* Kent.
Should he sit here? This act persuades me
That this remotion of the duke and her
Is practice only. Give me my servant forth.

Go tell the duke and 's wife I'ld speak with
　　them,
Now, presently : bid them come forth and
　　hear me,
Or at their chamber-door I'll beat the drum
Till it cry sleep to death.　　　　　　120
　　Glou. I would have all well betwixt you.
　　　　　　　　　　　　　　　　[*Exit.*
　　Lear. O me, my heart, my rising heart !
　　but, down !
　　Fool. Cry to it, nuncle, as the cockney did
to the eels when she put 'em i' the paste alive ;
she knapped 'em o' the coxcombs with a stick,
and cried ' Down, wantons, down ! ' 'Twas her
brother that, in pure kindness to his horse,
buttered his hay.

Enter CORNWALL, REGAN, GLOUCESTER, *and*
　　　　　　Servants.

　　Lear. Good morrow to you both.
　　Corn.　　　　　　Hail to your grace !
　　　　　　　　　　[*Kent is set at liberty.* 130
　　Reg. I am glad to see your highness.
　　Lear. Regan, I think you are ; I know
　　what reason
I have to think so : if thou shouldst not be
　　glad,
I would divorce me from thy mother's tomb,
Sepulchring an adultress. [*To Kent*] O, are
　　you free ?
Some other time for that. Beloved Regan,
Thy sister's naught : O Regan, she hath tied
Sharp-tooth'd unkindness, like a vulture, here :
　　　　　　　　　　[*Points to his heart.*
I can scarce speak to thee ; thou'lt not believe
With how depraved a quality—O Regan !
　　Reg. I pray you, sir, take patience : I have
　　hope.　　　　　　　　　　　　140
You less know how to value her desert
Than she to scant her duty.
　　Lear.　　　　　　Say, how is that ?
　　Reg. I cannot think my sister in the least
Would fail her obligation : if, sir, perchance
She have restrain'd the riots of your followers,
'Tis on such ground, and to such wholesome
　　end,
As clears her from all blame.
　　Lear. My curses on her !
　　Reg.　　　　　O, sir, you are old,
Nature in you stands on the very verge　149
Of her confine : you should be ruled and led
By some discretion, that discerns your state
Better than you yourself. Therefore, I pray
　　you,
That to our sister you do make return ;
Say you have wrong'd her, sir.
　　Lear.　　　　　Ask her forgiveness ?
Do you but mark how this becomes the
　　house :
' Dear daughter, I confess that I am old ;
　　　　　　　　　　　　[*Kneeling.*
Age is unnecessary : on my knees I beg
That you'll vouchsafe me raiment, bed, and
　　food.'
　　Reg. Good sir, no more ; these are un-
　　sightly tricks :
Return you to my sister.
　　Lear. [*Rising*] Never, Regan :　　　160
She hath abated me of half my train ;
Look'd black upon me ; struck me with her
　　tongue,
Most serpent-like, upon the very heart :
All the stored vengeances of heaven fall

On her ingrateful top ! Strike her young
　　bones,
You taking airs, with lameness !
　　Corn.　　　　　　Fie, sir, fie !
　　Lear. You nimble lightnings, dart your
　　blinding flames
Into her scornful eyes ! Infect her beauty,
You fen-suck'd fogs, drawn by the powerful
　　sun,
To fall and blast her pride !　　　　170
　　Reg. O the blest gods ! so will you wish on
　　me,
When the rash mood is on.
　　Lear. No, Regan, thou shalt never have
　　my curse :
Thy tender-hefted nature shall not give
Thee o'er to harshness : her eyes are fierce ;
　　but thine
Do comfort and not burn. 'Tis not in thee
To grudge my pleasures, to cut off my train,
To bandy hasty words, to scant my sizes,
And in conclusion to oppose the bolt
Against my coming in : thou better know'st
The offices of nature, bond of childhood, 181
Effects of courtesy, dues of gratitude ;
Thy half o' the kingdom hast thou not forgot,
Wherein I thee endow'd.
　　Reg.　　　　Good sir, to the purpose.
　　Lear. Who put my man i' the stocks ?
　　　　　　　　　　　　[*Tucket within.*
　　Corn.　　　　What trumpet's that ?
　　Reg. I know't, my sister's : this approves
　　her letter,
That she would soon be here.

　　　　　　Enter OSWALD.

　　　　　　　　　　Is your lady come ?
　　Lear. This is a slave, whose easy-borrow'd
　　pride
Dwells in the fickle grace of her he follows.
Out, varlet, from my sight !
　　Corn.　　　What means your grace ? 190
　　Lear. Who stock'd my servant ? Regan, I
　　have good hope
Thou didst not know on't. Who comes here ?
　　O heavens,

　　　　　　Enter GONERIL.

If you do love old men, if your sweet sway
Allow obedience, if yourselves are old,
Make it your cause ; send down, and take my
　　part !
[*To Gon.*] Art not ashamed to look upon
　　this beard ?
O Regan, wilt thou take her by the hand ?
　　Gon. Why not by the hand, sir ? How have
　　I offended ?
All's not offence that indiscretion finds
And dotage terms so.
　　Lear.　　　O sides, you are too tough ; 200
Will you yet hold ? How came my man i' the
　　stocks ?
　　Corn. I set him there, sir : but his own dis-
　　orders
Deserved much less advancement.
　　Lear.　　　　　You ! did you ?
　　Reg. I pray you, father, being weak, seem
　　so.
If, till the expiration of your month,
You will return and sojourn with my sister,
Dismissing half your train, come then to me :
I am now from home, and out of that provi-
　　sion

Which shall be needful for your entertainment.

Lear. Return to her, and fifty men dismiss'd ? 210
No, rather I abjure all roofs, and choose
To wage against the enmity o' the air ;
To be a comrade with the wolf and owl,—
Necessity's sharp pinch ! Return with her ?
Why, the hot-blooded France, that dowerless took
Our youngest born, I could as well be brought
To knee his throne, and, squire-like ; pension beg
To keep base life afoot. Return with her ?
Persuade me rather to be slave and sumpter
To this detested groom. [*Pointing at Oswald.*

Gon. At your choice, sir. 220

Lear. I prithee, daughter, do not make me mad :
I will not trouble thee, my child ; farewell :
We'll no more meet, no more see one another :
But yet thou art my flesh, my blood, my daughter ;
Or rather a disease that's in my flesh,
Which I must needs call mine : thou art a boil,
A plague-sore, an embossed carbuncle,
In my corrupted blood. But I'll not chide thee ;
Let shame come when it will, I do not call it :
I do not bid the thunder-bearer shoot, 230
Nor tell tales of thee to high-judging Jove :
Mend when thou canst ; be better at thy leisure :
I can be patient ; I can stay with Regan,
I and my hundred knights.

Reg. Not altogether so :
I look'd not for you yet, nor am provided
For your fit welcome. Give ear, sir, to my sister ;
For those that mingle reason with your passion
Must be content to think you old, and so—
But she knows what she does.

Lear. Is this well spoken ?

Reg. I dare avouch it, sir : what, fifty followers ? 240
Is it not well ? What should you need of more ?
Yea, or so many, sith that both charge and danger
Speak 'gainst so great a number ? How, in one house,
Should many people, under two commands,
Hold amity ? 'Tis hard ; almost impossible.

Gon. Why might not you, my lord, receive attendance
From those that she calls servants or from mine ?

Reg. Why not, my lord ? If then they chanced to slack you,
We could control them. If you will come to me,—
For now I spy a danger,—I entreat you 250
To bring but five and twenty : to no more
Will I give place or notice.

Lear. I gave you all—

Reg. And in good time you gave it.

Lear. Made you my guardians, my depositaries ;
But kept a reservation to be follow'd
With such a number. What, must I come to you
With five and twenty, Regan ? said you so ?

Reg. And speak't again, my lord ; no more with me.

Lear. Those wicked creatures yet do look well-favor'd,
When others are more wicked : not being the worst 260
Stands in some rank of praise. [*To Gon.*] I'll go with thee :
Thy fifty yet doth double five and twenty,
And thou art twice her love.

Gon. Hear me, my lord ;
What need you five and twenty, ten, or five,
To follow in a house where twice so many
Have a command to tend you ?

Reg. What need one ?

Lear. O, reason not the need : our basest beggars
Are in the poorest thing superfluous :
Allow not nature more than nature needs,
Man's life's as cheap as beast's : thou art a lady ; 270
If only to go warm were gorgeous,
Why, nature needs not what thou gorgeous wear'st,
Which scarcely keeps thee warm. But, for true need,—
You heavens, give me that patience, patience I need !
You see me here, you gods, a poor old man,
As full of grief as age ; wretched in both !
If it be you that stir these daughters' hearts
Against their father, fool me not so much
To bear it tamely ; touch me with noble anger,
And let not women's weapons, water-drops,
Stain my man's cheeks ! No, you unnatural hags, 281
I will have such revenges on you both,
That all the world shall—I will do such things,—
What they are, yet I know not : but they shall be
The terrors of the earth. You think I'll weep ;
No, I'll not weep :
I have full cause of weeping ; but this heart
Shall break into a hundred thousand flaws,
Or ere I'll weep. O fool, I shall go mad !
[*Exeunt Lear, Gloucester, Kent, and Fool.
Storm and tempest.*

Corn. Let us withdraw ; 'twill be a storm.

Reg. This house is little : the old man and his people 291
Cannot be well bestow'd.

Gon. 'Tis his own blame ; hath put himself from rest,
And must needs taste his folly.

Reg. For his particular, I'll receive him gladly,
But not one follower.

Gon. So am I purposed.
Where is my lord of Gloucester ?

Corn. Follow'd the old man forth : he is return'd.

Re-enter GLOUCESTER.

Glou. The king is in high rage.

Corn. Whither is he going ?

Glou. He calls to horse ; but will I know not whither. 300

Corn. 'Tis best to give him way ; he leads himself.

Gon. My lord, entreat him by no means to stay.

Glou. Alack, the night comes on, and the bleak winds
Do sorely ruffle ; for many miles about

There's scarce a bush.
  Reg.   O, sir, to wilful men,
The injuries that they themselves procure
Must be their schoolmasters. Shut up your
    doors :
He is attended with a desperate train ;
And what they may incense him to, being apt
To have his ear abused, wisdom bids fear. 310
  Corn.   Shut up your doors, my lord ; 'tis a
    wild night :
My Regan counsels well ; come out o' the
    storm.   [*Exeunt.*

ACT III.

SCENE I. *A heath.*

Storm still. Enter KENT *and a* Gentleman,
    meeting.

  Kent.   Who's there, besides foul weather ?
  Gent.   One minded like the weather, most
    unquietly.
  Kent.   I know you. Where's the king ?
  Gent.   Contending with the fretful element :
Bids the winds blow the earth into the sea,
Or swell the curled water 'bove the main,
That things might change or cease ; tears his
    white hair,
Which the impetuous blasts, with eyeless rage,
Catch in their fury, and make nothing of ;
Strives in his little world of man to out-scorn
The to-and-fro-conflicting wind and rain.   11
This night, wherein the cub-drawn bear would
    couch,
The lion and the belly-pinched wolf
Keep their fur dry, unbonneted he runs,
And bids what will take all.
  Kent.   But who is with him ?
  Gent.   None but the fool ; who labors to
    out-jest
His heart-struck injuries.
  Kent.   Sir, I do know you ;
And dare, upon the warrant of my note,
Commend a dear thing to you. There is di-
    vision,
Although as yet the face of it be cover'd   20
With mutual cunning, 'twixt Albany and Corn-
    wall ;
Who have—as who have not, that their great
    stars
Throned and set high ?—servants, who seem
    no less,
Which are to France the spies and specula-
    tions
Intelligent of our state ; what hath been seen,
Either in snuffs and packings of the dukes,
Or the hard rein which both of them have
    borne
Against the old kind king ; or something
    deeper,
Whereof perchance these are but furnishings ;
But, true it is, from France there comes a
    power   30
Into this scatter'd kingdom ; who already,
Wise in our negligence, have secret feet
In some of our best ports, and are at point
To show their open banner. Now to you :
If on my credit you dare build so far
To make your speed to Dover, you shall find
Some that will thank you, making just report
Of how unnatural and bemadding sorrow
The king hath cause to plain.

I am a gentleman of blood and breeding ;   40
And, from some knowledge and assurance,
    offer
This office to you.
  Gent.   I will talk further with you.
  Kent.   No, do not.
For confirmation that I am much more
Than my out-wall, open this purse, and take
What it contains. If you shall see Cordelia,—
As fear not but you shall,—show her this ring ;
And she will tell you who your fellow is
That yet you do not know. Fie on this storm !
I will go seek the king.   50
  Gent.   Give me your hand : have you no
    more to say ?
  Kent.   Few words, but, to effect, more than
    all yet ;
That, when we have found the king,—in which
    your pain
That way, I'll this,—he that first lights on him
Holla the other.   [*Exeunt severally.*

SCENE II. *Another part of the heath. Storm*
    still.

Enter LEAR *and* Fool.

  Lear.   Blow, winds, and crack your cheeks !
    rage ! blow !
You cataracts and hurricanoes, spout
Till you have drench'd our steeples, drown'd
    the cocks !
You sulphurous and thought-executing fires,
Vaunt-couriers to oak-cleaving thunderbolts,
Singe my white head ! And thou, all-shaking
    thunder,
Smite flat the thick rotundity o' the world !
Crack nature's moulds, all germens spill at
    once,
That make ingrateful man !   9
  Fool.   O nuncle, court holy-water in a dry
house is better than this rain-water out o' door.
Good nuncle, in, and ask thy daughters' bless-
ing : here's a night pities neither wise man nor
fool.
  Lear.   Rumble thy bellyful ! Spit, fire !
    spout, rain !
Nor rain, wind, thunder, fire, are my daugh-
    ters :
I tax not you, you elements, with unkindness ;
I never gave you kingdom, call'd you children,
You owe me no subscription : then let fall
Your horrible pleasure : here I stand, your
    slave,
A poor, infirm, weak, and despised old man :
But yet I call you servile ministers,   21
That have with two pernicious daughters join'd
Your high engender'd battles 'gainst a head
So old and white as this. O ! O ! 'tis foul !
  Fool.   He that has a house to put's head in
has a good head-piece.
        The cod-piece that will house
            Before the head has any,
        The head and he shall louse ;
            So beggars marry many.   30
        The man that makes his toe
            What he his heart should make
        Shall of a corn cry woe,
            And turn his sleep to wake.
For there was never yet fair woman but she
made mouths in a glass.
  Lear.   No, I will be the pattern of all pa-
    tience ;
I will say nothing.

Enter Kent.

Kent. Who's there ?

Fool. Marry, here's grace and a cod-piece ;
that's a wise man and a fool.

Kent. Alas, sir, are you here ? things that
love night
Love not such nights as these ; the wrathful
skies
Gallow the very wanderers of the dark,
And make them keep their caves : since I was
man,
Such sheets of fire, such bursts of horrid
thunder,
Such groans of roaring wind and rain, I never
Remember to have heard : man's nature can-
not carry
The affliction nor the fear.

Lear.   Let the great gods,
That keep this dreadful pother o'er our heads,
Find out their enemies now. Tremble, thou
wretch,   51
That hast within thee undivulged crimes,
Unwhipp'd of justice : hide thee, thou bloody
hand ;
Thou perjured, and thou simular man of virtue
That art incestuous : caitiff, to pieces shake,
That under covert and convenient seeming
Hast practised on man's life : close pent-up
guilts,
Rive your concealing continents, and cry
These dreadful summoners grace. I am a man
More sinn'd against than sinning.

Kent.   Alack, bare-headed ! 60
Gracious my lord, hard by here is a hovel ;
Some friendship will it lend you 'gainst the
tempest :
Repose you there ; while I to this hard house—
More harder than the stones whereof 'tis
raised ;
Which even but now, demanding after you,
Denied me to come in—return, and force
Their scanted courtesy.

Lear.   My wits begin to turn.
Come on, my boy : how dost, my boy ? art
cold ?
I am cold myself. Where is this straw, my
fellow ?
The art of our necessities is strange,   70
That can make vile things precious. Come,
your hovel.
Poor fool and knave, I have one part in my
heart
That's sorry yet for thee.

Fool. [*Singing*] He that has and a little
tiny wit—
With hey, ho, the wind and the rain,—
Must make content with his fortunes fit,
For the rain it raineth every day.

Lear. True, my good boy. Come, bring us
to this hovel. [*Exeunt Lear and Kent.*

Fool. This is a brave night to cool a courtezan.

I'll speak a prophecy ere I go :   80
When priests are more in word than matter ;
When brewers mar their malt with water ;
When nobles are their tailors' tutors ;
No heretics burn'd, but wenches' suitors ;
When every case in law is right ;
No squire in debt, nor no poor knight ;
When slanders do not live in tongues ;
Nor cutpurses come not to throngs ;
When usurers tell their gold i' the field ;

And bawds and whores do churches build ;
Then shall the realm of Albion   91
Come to great confusion :
Then comes the time, who lives to see't,
That going shall be used with feet.
This prophecy Merlin shall make ; for I live
before his time.   [*Exit.*

Scene III. *Gloucester's castle.*

Enter Gloucester *and* Edmund.

Glou. Alack, alack, Edmund, I like not
this unnatural dealing. When I desire their
leave that I might pity him, they took from me
the use of mine own house ; charged me, on
pain of their perpetual displeasure, neither to
speak of him, entreat for him, nor any way
sustain him.

Edm. Most savage and unnatural !

Glou. Go to ; say you nothing. There's a
division betwixt the dukes ; and a worse matter than that : I have received a letter this
night ; 'tis dangerous to be spoken ; I have
locked the letter in my closet : these injuries
the king now bears will be revenged home ;
there's part of a power already footed : we
must incline to the king. I will seek him, and
privily relieve him : go you and maintain talk
with the duke, that my charity be not of him
perceived : if he ask for me, I am ill, and gone
to bed. Though I die for it, as no less is threat-
ened me, the king my old master must be relieved. There is some strange thing toward, Edmund ; pray you, be careful.   [*Exit.* 21

Edm. This courtesy, forbid thee, shall the
duke
Instantly know ; and of that letter too :
This seems a fair deserving, and must draw
me
That which my father loses ; no less than all :
The younger rises when the old doth fall.
                                       [*Exit.*

Scene IV. *The heath. Before a hovel.*

Enter Lear, Kent, *and* Fool.

Kent. Here is the place, my lord ; good my
lord, enter :
The tyranny of the open night's too rough
For nature to endure.   [*Storm still.*

Lear.   Let me alone.

Kent. Good my lord, enter here.

Lear.   Wilt break my heart ?

Kent. I had rather break mine own. Good
my lord, enter.

Lear. Thou think'st 'tis much that this con-
tentious storm
Invades us to the skin : so 'tis to thee ;
But where the greater malady is fix'd,
The lesser is scarce felt. Thou'ldst shun a
bear ;
But if thy flight lay toward the raging sea, 10
Thou'ldst meet the bear i' the mouth. When
the mind's free,
The body's delicate : the tempest in my mind
Doth from my senses take all feeling else
Save what beats there. Filial ingratitude !
Is it not as this mouth should tear this hand
For lifting food to't ? But I will punish home :
No, I will weep no more. In such a night
To shut me out ! Pour on ; I will endure.
In such a night as this ! O Regan, Goneril !
Your old kind father, whose frank heart gave
all,—   20

O, that way madness lies ; let me shun that ;
No more of that.

Kent. Good my lord, enter here.

Lear. Prithee, go in thyself : seek thine
own ease :
This tempest will not give me leave to ponder
On things would hurt me more. But I'll go in.
[*To the Fool*] In, boy ; go first. You house-
less poverty,—
Nay, get thee in. I'll pray, and then I'll sleep.
　　　　　　　　　　　　　　[Fool goes in.
Poor naked wretches, whereso'er you are,
That bide the pelting of this pitiless storm,
How shall your houseless heads and unfed
　　sides,　　　　　　　　　　　　　　30
Your loop'd and window'd raggedness, defend
　you
From seasons such as these ? O, I have ta'en
Too little care of this ! Take physic, pomp ;
Expose thyself to feel what wretches feel,
That thou mayst shake the superflux to them,
And show the heavens more just.

Edg. [*Within*] Fathom and half, fathom
and half ! Poor Tom !
　　　　　[The Fool runs out from the hovel.
Fool. Come not in here, nuncle, here's a
　spirit
Help me, help me !　　　　　　　　40
Kent. Give me thy hand. Who's there ?
Fool. A spirit, a spirit : he says his name's
poor Tom.
Kent. What art thou that dost grumble
there i' the straw ? Come forth.

　　　Enter EDGAR *disguised as a mad man.*

Edg. Away ! the foul fiend follows me !
Through the sharp hawthorn blows the cold
　wind.
Hum ! go to thy cold bed, and warm thee.
Lear. Hast thou given all to thy two
daughters ?
And art thou come to this ?　　　　　50
Edg. Who gives any thing to poor Tom ?
whom the foul fiend hath led through fire and
through flame, and through ford and whirli-
pool e'er bog and quagmire ; that hath laid
knives under his pillow, and halters in his
pew ; set ratsbane by his porridge ; made him
proud of heart, to ride on a bay trotting-horse
over four-inched bridges, to course his own
shadow for a traitor. Bless thy five wits !
Tom's a-cold,—O, do de, do de, do de. Bless
thee from whirlwinds, star-blasting, and taking ! Do poor Tom some charity, whom the
foul fiend vexes : there could I have him now,
—and there,—and there again, and there.
　　　　　　　　　　　　　[Storm still.
Lear. What, have his daughters brought
　him to this pass ?
Couldst thou save nothing ? Didst thou give
　them all ?
Fool. Nay, he reserved a blanket, else we
had been all shamed.
Lear. Now, all the plagues that in the pen-
dulous air
Hang fated o'er men's faults light on thy
　daughters !　　　　　　　　　　　70
Kent. He hath no daughters, sir.
Lear. Death, traitor ! nothing could have
subdued nature
To such a lowness but his unkind daughters.
Is it the fashion, that discarded fathers
Should have thus little mercy on their flesh ?

Judicious punishment ! 'twas this flesh begot
Those pelican daughters.
Edg. Pillicock sat on Pillicock-hill :
Halloo, halloo, loo, loo !
Fool. This cold night will turn us all to
fools and madmen.　　　　　　　　81
Edg. Take heed o' the foul fiend : obey
thy parents ; keep thy word justly ; swear not ;
commit not with man's sworn spouse ; set not
thy sweet heart on proud array. Tom's a-cold.
Lear. What hast thou been ?
Edg. A serving-man, proud in heart and
mind ; that curled my hair ; wore gloves in
my cap ; served the lust of my mistress' heart,
and did the act of darkness with her ; swore
as many oaths as I spake words, and broke
them in the sweet face of heaven : one that
slept in the contriving of lust, and waked to
do it : wine loved I deeply, dice dearly : and
in woman out-paramoured the Turk : false of
heart, light of ear, bloody of hand ; hog in
sloth, fox in stealth, wolf in greediness, dog in
madness, lion in prey. Let not the creaking
of shoes nor the rustling of silks betray thy
poor heart to woman : keep thy foot out of
brothels, thy hand out of plackets, thy pen
from lenders' books, and defy the foul fiend.
Still through the hawthorn blows the cold
　wind :
Says suum, mun, ha, no, nonny.
Dolphin my boy, my boy, sessa ! let him trot
by.　　　　　　　　　　　　*[Storm still.*
Lear. Why, thou wert better in thy grave
than to answer with thy uncovered body this
extremity of the skies. Is man no more than
this ? Consider him well. Thou owest the worm
no silk, the beast no hide, the sheep no wool,
the cat no perfume. Ha ! here's three on 's
are sophisticated ! Thou art the thing itself :
unaccommodated man is no more but such a
poor, bare, forked animal as thou art. Off, off,
you lendings ! come unbutton here.
　　　　　　　　　[Tearing off his clothes.
Fool. Prithee, nuncle, be contented ; 'tis a
naughty night to swim in. Now a little fire in
a wild field were like an old lecher's heart ;
a small spark, all the rest on's body cold.
Look, here comes a walking fire.　　　119

　　　Enter GLOUCESTER, *with a torch.*

Edg. This is the foul fiend Flibbertigibbet :
he begins at curfew, and walks till the first
cock ; he gives the web and the pin, squints
the eye, and makes the hare-lip ; mildews the
white wheat, and hurts the poor creature of
earth.
S. Withold footed thrice the old ;
He met the night-mare, and her nine-fold ;
　　Bid her alight,
　　And her troth plight,
And, aroint thee, witch, aroint thee !
Kent. How fares your grace ?　　　130
Lear. What's he ?
Kent. Who's there ? What is't you seek ?
Glou. What are you there ? Your names ?
Edg. Poor Tom ; that eats the swimming
frog, the toad, the tadpole, the wall-newt and
the water ; that in the fury of his heart, when
the foul fiend rages, eats cow-dung for sallets ;
swallows the old rat and the ditch-dog ; drinks
the green mantle of the standing pool ; who is
whipped from tithing to tithing, and stock-
punished, and imprisoned ; who hath had three

suits to his back, six shirts to his body, horse
to ride, and weapon to wear ;
  But mice and rats, and such small deer,
  Have been Tom's food for seven long year.
Beware my follower. Peace, Smulkin ; peace,
  thou fiend !
  Glou. What, hath your grace no better
  company ?
  Edg. The prince of darkness is a gentle-
  man :
Modo he's call'd, and Mahu.
  Glou. Our flesh and blood is grown so vile,
  my lord,   150
That it doth hate what gets it.
  Edg. Poor Tom's a-cold.
  Glou. Go in with me : my duty cannot
  suffer
To obey in all your daughters' hard com-
  mands :
Though their injunction be to bar my doors,
And let this tyrannous night take hold upon
  you,
Yet have I ventured to come seek you out,
And bring you where both fire and food is
  ready.
  Lear. First let me talk with this philoso-
  pher.
What is the cause of thunder ?   160
  Kent. Good my lord, take his offer ; go
into the house.
  Lear. I'll talk a word with this same
learned Theban.
What is your study ?
  Edg. How to prevent the fiend, and to kill
vermin.
  Lear. Let me ask you one word in private.
  Kent. Importune him once more to go, my
  lord ;
His wits begin to unsettle.
  Glou. Canst thou blame him ? [*Storm still.*
His daughters seek his death : ah, that good
  Kent !
He said it would be thus, poor banish'd man !
Thou say'st the king grows mad ; I'll tell thee,
  friend,   170
I am almost mad myself : I had a son,
Now outlaw'd from my blood ; he sought my
  life,
But lately, very late : I loved him, friend ;
No father his son dearer : truth to tell thee,
The grief hath crazed my wits. What a night's
  this !
I do beseech your grace,—
  Lear.   O, cry your mercy, sir.
Noble philosopher, your company.
  Edg. Tom's a-cold.
  Glou. In, fellow, there, into the hovel :
keep thee warm.
  Lear. Come let's in all.
  Kent.   This way, my lord.
  Lear.   With him ; 180
I will keep still with my philosopher.
  Kent. Good my lord, soothe him ; let him
take the fellow.
  Glou. Take him you on.
  Kent. Sirrah, come on ; go along with us.
  Lear. Come, good Athenian.
  Glou. No words, no words : hush.
  Edg. Child Rowland to the dark tower
  came,
    His word was still,—Fie, foh, and fum,
    I smell the blood of a British man.
                          [*Exeunt.*

SCENE V. *Gloucester's castle.*

Enter CORNWALL *and* EDMUND.

  Corn. I will have my revenge ere I depart
his house.
  Edm. How, my lord, I may be censured,
that nature thus gives way to loyalty, something fears me to think of.
  Corn. I now perceive, it was not altogether
your brother's evil disposition made him seek
his death ; but a provoking merit, set a-work
by a reprovable badness in himself.   9
  Edm. How malicious is my fortune, that I
must repent to be just ! This is the letter he
spoke of, which approves him an intelligent
party to the advantages of France. O heavens !
that this treason were not, or not I the de-
tector !
  Corn. Go with me to the duchess.
  Edm. If the matter of this paper be certain, you have mighty business in hand.
  Corn. True or false, it hath made thee earl
of Gloucester. Seek out where thy father is,
that he may be ready for our apprehension. 20
  Edm. [*Aside*] If I find him comforting the
king, it will stuff his suspicion more fully.—I
will persevere in my course of loyalty, though
the conflict be sore between that and my
blood.
  Corn. I will lay trust upon thee ; and thou
shalt find a dearer father in my love. [*Exeunt.*

SCENE VI. *A chamber in a farmhouse ad-
        joining the castle.*

Enter GLOUCESTER, LEAR, KENT, FOOL, *and*
           EDGAR.

  Glou. Here is better than the open air ;
take it thankfully. I will piece out the comfort
with what addition I can : I will not be long
from you.
  Kent. All the power of his wits have given
way to his impatience : the gods reward your
kindness !   [*Exit Gloucester.*
  Edg. Fratteretto calls me ; and tells me
Nero is an angler in the lake of darkness.
Pray, innocent, and beware the foul fiend.
  Fool. Prithee, nuncle, tell me whether a
madman be a gentleman or a yeoman ?   11
  Lear. A king, a king !
  Fool. No, he's a yeoman that has a gentle-
man to his son ; for he's a mad yeoman that
sees his son a gentleman before him.
  Lear. To have a thousand with red burn-
  ing spits
Come hissing in upon 'em,—
  Edg. The foul fiend bites my back.
  Fool. He's mad that trusts in the tameness
of a wolf, a horse's health, a boy's love, or a
whore's oath.   21
  Lear. It shall be done ; I will arraign them
  straight.
[*To Edgar*] Come, sit thou here, most
  learned justicer ;
[*To the Fool*] Thou, sapient sir, sit here.
Now, you she foxes !
  Edg. Look, where he stands and glares !
Wantest thou eyes at trial, madam ?
    Come o'er the bourn, Bessy, to me,—
  Fool.   Her boat hath a leak,
    And she must not speak
    Why she dares not come over to thee.
  Edg. The foul fiend haunts poor Tom in

the voice of a nightingale. Hopdance cries in
Tom's belly for two white herring. Croak not,
black angel; I have no food for thee.

Kent. How do you, sir? Stand you not so
amazed:
Will you lie down and rest upon the cushions?

Lear. I'll see their trial first. Bring in the
evidence.
[*To Edgar*] Thou robed man of justice, take
thy place;
[*To the Fool*] And thou, his yoke-fellow of
equity,
Bench by his side: [*To Kent*] you are o' the
commission, 40
Sit you too.

Edg. Let us deal justly.
    Sleepest or wakest thou, jolly shepherd?
      Thy sheep be in the corn;
    And for one blast of thy minikin mouth,
      Thy sheep shall take no harm.
Pur! the cat is gray.

Lear. Arraign her first; 'tis Goneril. I here
take my oath before this honorable assembly,
she kicked the poor king her father. 50

Fool. Come hither, mistress. Is your name
Goneril?

Lear. She cannot deny it.

Fool. Cry you mercy, I took you for a
joint-stool.

Lear. And here's another, whose warp'd
looks proclaim
What store her heart is made on. Stop her
there!
Arms, arms, sword, fire! Corruption in the
place!
False justicer, why hast thou let her 'scape?

Edg. Bless thy five wits! 60

Kent. O pity! Sir, where is the patience
now,
That thou so oft have boasted to retain?

Edg. [*Aside*] My tears begin to take his
part so much,
They'll mar my counterfeiting.

Lear. The little dogs and all,
Tray, Blanch, and Sweet-heart, see, they bark
at me.

Edg. Tom will throw his head at them.
Avaunt, you curs!
    Be thy mouth or black or white,
    Tooth that poisons if it bite; 70
    Mastiff, greyhound, mongrel grim,
    Hound or spaniel, brach or lym,
    Or bobtail tike or trundle-tail,
    Tom will make them weep and wail:
    For, with throwing thus my head,
    Dogs leap the hatch, and all are fled.
Do de, de, de. Sessa! Come, march to wakes
and fairs and market-towns. Poor Tom, thy
horn is dry. 79

Lear. Then let them anatomize Regan; see
what breeds about her heart. Is there any
cause in nature that makes these hard hearts?
[*To Edgar*] You, sir, I entertain for one of
my hundred; only I do not like the fashion of
your garments: you will say they are Persian
attire: but let them be changed.

Kent. Now, good my lord, lie here and
rest awhile.

Lear. Make no noise, make no noise; draw
the curtains: so, so, so. We'll go to supper i'
the morning. So, so, so. 91

Fool. And I'll go to bed at noon.

Re-enter GLOUCESTER.

Glou. Come hither, friend: where is the
king my master?

Kent. Here, sir; but trouble him not, his
wits are gone.

Glou. Good friend, I prithee, take him in
thy arms;
I have o'erheard a plot of death upon him:
There is a litter ready; lay him in 't,
And drive towards Dover, friend, where thou
shalt meet
Both welcome and protection. Take up thy
master: 99
If thou shouldst dally half an hour, his life,
With thine, and all that offer to defend him,
Stand in assured loss: take up, take up;
And follow me, that will to some provision
Give thee quick conduct.

Kent. Oppressed nature sleeps:
This rest might yet have balm'd thy broken
senses,
Which, if convenience will not allow,
Stand in hard cure. [*To the Fool*] Come, help
to bear thy master;
Thou must not stay behind.

Glou. Come, come, away.
        [*Exeunt all but Edgar.*

Edg. When we our betters see bearing our
woes,
We scarcely think our miseries our foes. 110
Who alone suffers suffers most i' the mind,
Leaving free things and happy shows behind:
But then the mind much sufferance doth o'er-
skip,
When grief hath mates, and bearing fellow-
ship.
How light and portable my pain seems now,
When that which makes me bend makes the
king bow,
He childed as I father'd! Tom, away!
Mark the high noises; and thyself bewray,
When false opinion, whose wrong thought de-
files thee,
In thy just proof, repeals and reconciles thee.
What will hap more to-night, safe 'scape the
king! 121
Lurk, lurk.   [*Exit.*

SCENE VII. *Gloucester's castle.*

Enter CORNWALL, REGAN, GONERIL, EDMUND,
and Servants.

Corn. Post speedily to my lord your husband; show him this letter: the army of
France is landed. Seek out the villain Gloucester.   [*Exeunt some of the Servants.*

Reg. Hang him instantly.

Gon. Pluck out his eyes.

Corn. Leave him to my displeasure. Edmund, keep you our sister company: the revenges we are bound to take upon your traitorous father are not fit for your beholding.
Advise the duke, where you are going, to a
most festinate preparation: we are bound to
the like. Our posts shall be swift and intelligent betwixt us. Farewell, dear sister: farewell, my lord of Gloucester.

Enter OSWALD.

How now! where's the king?

Osw. My lord of Gloucester hath convey'd
him hence:
Some five or six and thirty of his knights,

Hot questrists after him, met him at gate ;
Who, with some other of the lords dependants,
Are gone with him towards Dover ; where
      they boast
To have well-armed friends.
      Corn.   Get horses for your mistress.
      Gon. Farewell, sweet lord, and sister.   21
      Corn. Edmund, farewell.
            [*Exeunt Goneril, Edmund, and Oswald.*
            Go seek the traitor Gloucester,
Pinion him like a thief, bring him before us.
            [*Exeunt other Servants.*
Though well we may not pass upon his life
Without the form of justice, yet our power
Shall do a courtesy to our wrath, which men
May blame, but not control. Who's there ?
      the traitor ?

Enter GLOUCESTER, *brought in by two or
      three.*

      Reg. Ingrateful fox ! 'tis he.
      Corn. Bind fast his corky arms.
      Glou. What mean your graces ? Good my
      friends, consider   30
You are my guests : do me no foul play,
      friends.
      Corn. Bind him, I say. [*Servants bind him.*
      Reg.   Hard, hard. O filthy traitor !
      Glou. Unmerciful lady as you are, I'm
      none.
      Corn. To this chair bind him. Villain,
      thou shalt find—
            [*Regan plucks his beard.*
      Glou. By the kind gods, 'tis most ignobly
      done
To pluck me by the beard.
      Reg. So white, and such a traitor !
      Glou.   Naughty lady,
These hairs, which thou dost ravish from my
      chin,
Will quicken, and accuse thee : I am your
      host :
With robbers' hands my hospitable favors   40
You should not ruffle thus. What will you
      do ?
      Corn. Come, sir, what letters had you late
      from France ?
      Reg. Be simple answerer, for we know the
      truth.
      Corn. And what confederacy have you
      with the traitors
Late footed in the kingdom ?
      Reg. To whose hands have you sent the
      lunatic king ?
Speak.
      Glou. I have a letter guessingly set down,
Which came from one that's of a neutral
      heart,
And not from one opposed.
      Corn.   Cunning.
      Reg.   And false.
      Corn. Where hast thou sent the king ? 50
      Glou. To Dover.
      Reg. Wherefore to Dover ? Wast thou not
      charged at peril—
      Corn. Wherefore to Dover ? Let him first
      answer that.
      Glou. I am tied to the stake, and I must
      stand the course.
      Reg. Wherefore to Dover, sir ?
      Glou. Because I would not see thy cruel
      nails

Pluck out his poor old eyes ; nor thy fierce
      sister
In his anointed flesh stick boarish fangs.
The sea, with such a storm as his bare head
In hell-black night endured, would have buoy'd
      up,   60
And quench'd the stelled fires :
Yet, poor old heart, he holp the heavens to
      rain.
If wolves had at thy gate howl'd that stern
      time,
Thou shouldst have said ' Good porter, turn
      the key,'
All cruels else subscribed : but I shall see
The winged vengeance overtake such children.
      Corn. See't shalt thou never. Fellows, hold
      the chair.
Upon these eyes of thine I'll set my foot.
      Glou. He that will think to live till he be
      old,
Give me some help ! O cruel ! O you gods !
      Reg. One side will mock another ; the
      other too.   71
      Corn. If you see vengeance,—
      First Serv.   Hold your hand, my lord :
I have served you ever since I was a child ;
But better service have I never done you
Than now to bid you hold.
      Reg.   How now, you dog !
      First Serv. If you did wear a beard upon
      your chin,
I'd shake it on this quarrel. What do you
      mean ?
      Corn. My villain ! [*They draw and fight.*
      First Serv. Nay, then, come on, and take
      the chance of anger.
      Reg. Give me thy sword. A peasant stand
      up thus !   80
      [*Takes a sword, and runs at him behind.*
      First Serv. O, I am slain ! My lord, you
      have one eye left
To see some mischief on him. O !   [*Dies.*
      Corn. Lest it see more, prevent it. Out,
      vile jelly !
Where is thy lustre now ?
      Glou. All dark and comfortless. Where's
      my son Edmund ?
Edmund, enkindle all the sparks of nature,
To quit this horrid act.
      Reg.   Out, treacherous villain !
Thou call'st on him that hates thee : it was he
That made the overture of thy treasons to us ;
Who is too good to pity thee.   90
      Glou. O my follies ! then Edgar was
      abused.
Kind gods, forgive me that, and prosper him !
      Reg. Go thrust him out at gates, and let
      him smell
His way to Dover. [*Exit one with Gloucester.*
      How is't, my lord ? how look you ?
      Corn. I have received a hurt : follow me,
      lady.
Turn out that eyeless villain ; throw this slave
Upon the dunghill. Regan, I bleed apace :
Untimely comes this hurt : give me your arm.
            [*Exit Cornwall, led by Regan.*
      Sec. Serv. I'll never care what wickedness
      I do,
If this man come to good.
      Third Serv.   If she live long,   100
And in the end meet the old course of death,
Women will all turn monsters.

Sec. Serv. Let's follow the old earl, and
get the Bedlam
To lead him where he would : his roguish
madness
Allows itself to any thing.
Third Serv. Go thou : I'll fetch some flax
and whites of eggs
To apply to his bleeding face. Now, heaven
help him !   [*Exeunt severally.*

ACT IV.

Scene I. *The heath.*

Enter Edgar.

Edg. Yet better thus, and known to be
contemn'd,
Than still contemn'd and flatter'd. To be
worst,
The lowest and most dejected thing of for-
tune,
Stands still in esperance, lives not in fear :
The lamentable change is from the best ;
The worst returns to laughter. Welcome, then,
Thou unsubstantial air that I embrace !
The wretch that thou hast blown unto the
worst
Owes nothing to thy blasts. But who comes
here ?

Enter Gloucester, *led by an* Old Man.

My father, poorly led ? World, world, O
world !   10
But that thy strange mutations make us hate
thee,
Life would not yield to age.
  Old Man. O, my good lord, I have been
your tenant, and your father's tenant, these
fourscore years.
  Glou. Away, get thee away ; good friend,
be gone :
Thy comforts can do me no good at all ;
Thee they may hurt.
  Old Man. Alack, sir, you cannot see your
way.
  Glou. I have no way, and therefore want
no eyes ;   20
I stumbled when I saw : full oft 'tis seen,
Our means secure us, and our mere defects
Prove our commodities. O dear son Edgar,
The food of thy abused father's wrath !
Might I but live to see thee in my touch,
I'ld say I had eyes again !
  Old Man.   How now ! Who's there ?
  Edg. [*Aside*] O gods ! Who is't can say ' I
am at the worst ' ?
I am worse than e'er I was.
  Old Man.   'Tis poor mad Tom.
  Edg. [*Aside*] And worse I may be yet : the
worst is not
So long as we can say ' This is the worst.'   30
  Old Man. Fellow, where goest ?
  Glou.   Is it a beggar-man ?
  Old Man. Madman and beggar too.
  Glou. He has some reason, else he could
not beg.
I' the last night's storm I such a fellow saw ;
Which made me think a man a worm : my
son
Came then into my mind ; and yet my mind
Was then scarce friends with him : I have
heard more since.

As flies to wanton boys, are we to the gods,
They kill us for their sport.
  Edg.   [*Aside*] How should this be ?
Bad is the trade that must play fool to sor-
row,   40
Angering itself and others.—Bless thee, mas-
ter !
  Glou. Is that the naked fellow ?
  Old Man.   Ay, my lord.
  Glou. Then, prithee, get thee gone : if, for
my sake,
Thou wilt o'ertake us, hence a mile or twain,
I' the way toward Dover, do it for ancient
love ;
And bring some covering for this naked soul,
Who I'll entreat to lead me.
  Old Man.   Alack, sir, he is mad.
  Glou. 'Tis the times' plague, when mad-
men lead the blind.
Do as I bid thee, or rather do thy pleasure ;
Above the rest, be gone.   50
  Old Man. I'll bring him the best 'parel that
I have,
Come on't what will.   [*Exit.*
  Glou. Sirrah, naked fellow,—
  Edg. Poor Tom's a-cold. [*Aside*] I cannot
daub it further.
  Glou. Come hither, fellow.
  Edg. [*Aside*] And yet I must.—Bless thy
sweet eyes, they bleed.
  Glou. Know'st thou the way to Dover ?
  Edg. Both stile and gate, horse-way and
foot-path. Poor Tom hath been scared out of
his good wits : bless thee, good man's son,
from the foul fiend ! five fiends have been in
poor Tom at once ; of lust, as Obidicut ; Hob-
bididance, prince of dumbness ; Mahu, of
stealing ; Modo, of murder ; Flibbertigibbet,
of mopping and mowing, who since possesses
chambermaids and waiting-women. So, bless
thee, master !
  Glou. Here, take this purse, thou whom
the heavens' plagues
Have humbled to all strokes : that I am
wretched
Makes thee the happier : heavens, deal so
still !
Let the superfluous and lust-dieted man,   70
That slaves your ordinance, that will not see
Because he doth not feel, feel your power
quickly ;
So distribution should undo excess,
And each man have enough. Dost thou know
Dover ?
  Edg. Ay, master.
  Glou. There is a cliff, whose high and
bending head
Looks fearfully in the confined deep :
Bring me but to the very brim of it,
And I'll repair the misery thou dost bear
With something rich about me : from that
place
I shall no leading need.
  Edg.   Give me thy arm :   81
Poor Tom shall lead thee.   [*Exeunt.*

Scene II. *Before the Duke of Albany's
palace.*

Enter Goneril *and* Edmund.

Gon. Welcome, my lord : I marvel our
mild husband
Not met us on the way.

Enter OSWALD.

Now, where's your master ?
Osw. Madam, within ; but never man so
    changed.
I told him of the army that was landed ;
He smiled at it : I told you were coming :
His answer was ' The worse : ' of Glouces-
    ter's treachery,
And of the loyal service of his son,
When I inform'd him, then he call'd me sot,
And told me I had turn'd the wrong side out :
What most he should dislike seems pleasant
    to him ;   10
What like, offensive.
Gon. [*To Edm.*] Then shall you go no
    further.
It is the cowish terror of his spirit,
That dares not undertake : he'll not feel
    wrongs
Which tie him to an answer. Our wishes on
    the way
May prove effects. Back, Edmund, to my
    brother ;
Hasten his musters and conduct his powers :
I must change arms at home, and give the
    distaff
Into my husband's hands. This trusty servant
Shall pass between us : ere long you are like
    to hear,
If you dare venture in your own behalf,   20
A mistress's command. Wear this ; spare
    speech ;   [*Giving a favor.*
Decline your head : this kiss, if it durst speak,
Would stretch thy spirits up into the air :
Conceive, and fare thee well.
Edm. Yours in the ranks of death.
Gon.   My most dear Gloucester !
                    [*Exit Edmund.*
O, the difference of man and man !
To thee a woman's services are due :
My fool usurps my body.
Osw.   Madam, here comes my lord.
                          [*Exit.*

Enter the DUKE OF ALBANY.

Gon. I have been worth the whistle.
Alb.   O Goneril !
You are not worth the dust which the rude
    wind   30
Blows in your face. I fear your disposition :
That nature, which contemns its origin,
Cannot be border'd certain in itself ;
She that herself will sliver and disbranch
From her material sap, perforce must wither
And come to deadly use.
Gon. No more ; the text is foolish.
Alb. Wisdom and goodness to the vile
    seem vile :
Filths savor but themselves. What have you
    done ?
Tigers, not daughters, what have you per-
    form'd ?   40
A father, and a gracious aged man,
Whose reverence even the head-lugg'd bear
    would lick,
Most barbarous, most degenerate ! have you
    madded.
Could my good brother suffer you to do it ?
A man, a prince, by him so benefited !
If that the heavens do not their visible spirits
Send quickly down to tame these vile of-
    fences,

It will come,
Humanity must perforce prey on itself,
Like monsters of the deep.
Gon.   Milk-liver'd man ! 50
That bear'st a cheek for blows, a head for
    wrongs ;
Who hast not in thy brows an eye discerning
Thine honor from thy suffering ; that not
    know'st
Fools do those villains pity who are punish'd
Ere they have done their mischief. Where's
    thy drum ?
France spreads his banners in our noiseless
    land ;
With plumed helm thy slayer begins threats ;
Whiles thou, a moral fool, sit'st still, and
    criest
' Alack, why does he so ? '
Alb.   See thyself, devil !
Proper deformity seems not in the fiend   60
So horrid as in woman.
Gon.   O vain fool !
Alb. Thou changed and self-cover'd thing,
    for shame,
Be-monster not thy feature. Were't my fitness
To let these hands obey my blood,
They are apt enough to dislocate and tear
Thy flesh and bones : howe'er thou art a fiend,
A woman's shape doth shield thee.
Gon. Marry, your manhood now—

Enter a Messenger.

Alb. What news ?
Mess. O, my good lord, the Duke of Corn-
    wall 's dead :   70
Slain by his servant, going to put out
The other eye of Gloucester.
Alb.   Gloucester's eyes !
Mess. A servant that he bred, thrill'd with
    remorse,
Opposed against the act, bending his sword
To his great master ; who, thereat enraged,
Flew on him, and amongst them fell'd him
    dead ;
But not without that harmful stroke, which
    since
Hath pluck'd him after.
Alb.   This shows you are above,
You justicers, that these our nether crimes
So speedily can venge ! But, O poor Glouces-
    ter !
Lost he his other eye ?
Mess.   Both, both, my lord. 81
This letter, madam, craves a speedy answer ;
'Tis from your sister.
Gon. [*Aside*] One way I like this well ;
But being widow, and my Gloucester with her,
May all the building in my fancy pluck
Upon my hateful life : another way,
The news is not so tart.—I'll read, and answer.
                            [*Exit.*
Alb. Where was his son when they did take
    his eyes ?
Mess. Come with my lady hither.
Alb.   He is not here. 90
Mess. No, my good lord ; I met him back
    again.
Alb. Knows he the wickedness ?
Mess. Ay, my good lord ; 'twas he inform'd
    against him ;
And quit the house on purpose, that their pun-
    ishment
Might have the freer course.

Alb.   Gloucester, I live
To thank thee for the love thou show'dst the
          king,
And to revenge thine eyes. Come hither,
          friend :
Tell me what more thou know'st.   [*Exeunt.*

SCENE III. *The French camp near Dover.*

Enter KENT *and a* Gentleman.

Kent. Why the King of France is so suddenly gone back know you the reason ?

Gent. Something he left imperfect in the
state, which since his coming forth is thought
of ; which imports to the kingdom so much
fear and danger, that his personal return was
most required and necessary.

Kent. Who hath he left behind him general ?

Gent. The Marshal of France, Monsieur
La Far.   10

Kent. Did your letters pierce the queen to
any demonstration of grief ?

Gent. Ay, sir ; she took them, read them
          in my presence ;
And now and then an ample tear trill'd down
Her delicate cheek : it seem'd she was a queen
Over her passion ; who, most rebel-like,
Sought to be king o'er her.

Kent.   O, then it moved her.

Gent. Not to a rage : patience and sorrow
          strove
Who should express her goodliest. You have
          seen
Sunshine and rain at once : her smiles and
          tears
Were like a better way : those happy smilets,
That play'd on her ripe lip, seem'd not to know
What guests were in her eyes ; which parted
          thence,
As pearls from diamonds dropp'd. In brief,
Sorrow would be a rarity most beloved,
If all could so become it.

Kent.   Made she no verbal question ?

Gent. 'Faith, once or twice she heaved the
          name of ' father '
Pantingly forth, as if it press'd her heart :
Cried ' Sisters ! sisters ! Shame of ladies !
          sisters !
Kent ! father ! sisters ! What, i' the storm ?
          i' the night ?   30
Let pity not be believed ! ' There she shook
The holy water from her heavenly eyes,
And clamor moisten'd : then away she started
To deal with grief alone.

Kent.   It is the stars,
The stars above us, govern our conditions ;
Else one self mate and mate could not beget
Such different issues. You spoke not with her
          since ?

Gent. No.

Kent. Was this before the king return'd ?

Gent.   No, since.

Kent. Well, sir, the poor distressed Lear's
          i' the town ;   40
Who sometime, in his better tune, remembers
What we are come about, and by no means
Will yield to see his daughter.

Gent.   Why, good sir ?

Kent. A sovereign shame so elbows him :
          his own unkindness,
That stripp'd her from his benediction, turn'd
          her
To foreign casualties, gave her dear rights

To his dog-hearted daughters, these things sting
His mind so venomously, that burning shame
Detains him from Cordelia.

Gent.   Alack, poor gentleman !

Kent. Of Albany's and Cornwall's powers
          you heard not ?   50

Gent. 'Tis so, they are afoot.

Kent. Well, sir, I'll bring you to our mas-
          ter Lear,
And leave you to attend him : some dear cause
Will in concealment wrap me up awhile ;
When I am known aright, you shall not grieve
Lending me this acquaintance. I pray you, go
Along with me.   [*Exeunt.*

SCENE IV. *The same. A tent.*

Enter, with drum and colors, CORDELIA,
          Doctor, *and* Soldiers.

Cor. Alack, 'tis he : why, he was met even
          now
As mad as the vex'd sea ; singing aloud ;
Crown'd with rank fumiter and furrow-weeds,
With bur-docks, hemlock, nettles, cuckoo-
          flowers,
Darnel, and all the idle weeds that grow
In our sustaining corn. A century send forth ;
Search every acre in the high-grown field,
And bring him to our eye. [*Exit an Officer.*]
          What can man's wisdom
In the restoring his bereaved sense ?
He that helps him take all my outward worth.

Doct. There is means, madam :   11
Our foster-nurse of nature is repose,
The which he lacks ; that to provoke in him,
Are many simples operative, whose power
Will close the eye of anguish.

Cor.   All blest secrets,
All you unpublish'd virtues of the earth,
Spring with my tears ! be aidant and remediate
In the good man's distress ! Seek, seek for
          him ;
Lest his ungovern'd rage dissolve the life
That wants the means to lead it.

Enter a Messenger.

Mess.   News, madam ;   20
The British powers are marching hitherward.

Cor. 'Tis known before ; our preparation
          stands
In expectation of them. O dear father,
It is thy business that I go about ;
Therefore great France
My mourning and important tears hath pitied.
No blown ambition doth our arms incite,
But love, dear love, and our aged father's
          right :
Soon may I hear and see him !   [*Exeunt.*

SCENE V. *Gloucester's castle.*

Enter REGAN *and* OSWALD.

Reg. But are my brother's powers set
          forth ?

Osw.   Ay, madam.

Reg. Himself in person there ?

Osw.   Madam, with much ado :
Your sister is the better soldier.

Reg. Lord Edmund spake not with your
          lord at home ?

Osw. No, madam.

Reg. What might import my sister's letter
          to him ?

Osw. I know not, lady.

Reg. 'Faith, he is posted hence on serious
matter.
It was great ignorance, Gloucester's eyes being
out,
To let him live : where he arrives he moves 10
All hearts against us : Edmund, I think, is
gone,
In pity of his misery, to dispatch
His nighted life : moreover, to descry
The strength o' the enemy.
  Osw. I must needs after him, madam, with
    my letter.
  Reg. Our troops set forth to-morrow : stay
    with us ;
The ways are dangerous.
  Osw.   I may not, madam :
My lady charged my duty in this business.
  Reg. Why should she write to Edmund ?
    Might not you
Transport her purposes by word ? Belike, 20
Something—I know not what : I'll love thee
    much,
Let me unseal the letter.
  Osw.   Madam, I had rather—
  Reg. I know your lady does not love her
    husband ;
I am sure of that : and at her late being here
She gave strange œillades and most speaking
    looks
To noble Edmund. I know you are of her
    bosom.
  Osw. I, madam ?
  Reg. I speak in understanding ; you are ; I
    know't :
Therefore I do advise you, take this note :
My lord is dead ; Edmund and I have talk'd ;
And more convenient is he for my hand 31
Than for your lady's : you may gather more.
If you do find him, pray you, give him this ;
And when your mistress hears thus much from
    you,
I pray, desire her call her wisdom to her.
So, fare you well.
If you do chance to hear of that blind traitor,
Preferment falls on him that cuts him off.
  Osw. Would I could meet him, madam ! I
    should show
What party I do follow.
  Reg.   Fare thee well. [*Exeunt.* 40

    SCENE VI. *Fields near Dover.*

Enter GLOUCESTER, *and* EDGAR *dressed like a
    peasant.*

  Glou. When shall we come to the top of
    that same hill ?
  Edg. You do climb up it now : look, how
    we labor.
  Glou. Methinks the ground is even.
  Edg.   Horrible steep.
Hark, do you hear the sea ?
  Glou.   No, truly.
  Edg. Why, then, your other senses grow
    imperfect
By your eyes' anguish.
  Glou.   So may it be, indeed :
Methinks thy voice is alter'd ; and thou
    speak'st
In better phrase and matter than thou didst.
  Edg. You're much deceived : in nothing
    am I changed
But in my garments.
  Glou.   Methinks you're better spoken. 10

  Edg. Come on, sir ; here's the place : stand
    still. How fearful
And dizzy 'tis, to cast one's eyes so low !
The crows and choughs that wing the midway
    air
Show scarce so gross as beetles : half way
    down
Hangs one that gathers samphire, dreadful
    trade !
Methinks he seems no bigger than his head :
The fishermen, that walk upon the beach,
Appear like mice ; and yond tall anchoring
    bark,
Diminish'd to her cock ; her cock, a buoy
Almost too small for sight : the murmuring
    surge,   20
That on the unnumber'd idle pebbles chafes,
Cannot be heard so high. I'll look no more ;
Lest my brain turn, and the deficient sight
Topple down headlong.
  Glou.   Set me where you stand.
  Edg. Give me your hand : you are now
    within a foot
Of the extreme verge : for all beneath the
    moon
Would I not leap upright.
  Glou.   Let go my hand.
Here, friend, 's another purse ; in it a jewel
Well worth a poor man's taking : fairies and
    gods
Prosper it with thee ! Go thou farther off ; 30
Bid me farewell, and let me hear thee going.
  Edg. Now fare you well, good sir.
  Glou.   With all my heart.
  Edg. Why I do trifle thus with his despair
Is done to cure it.
  Glou. [*Kneeling*] O you mighty gods !
This world I do renounce, and, in your sights,
Shake patiently my great affliction off :
If I could bear it longer, and not fall
To quarrel with your great opposeless wills,
My snuff and loathed part of nature should
Burn itself out. If Edgar live, O, bless him !
Now, fellow, fare thee well. [*He falls forward.*
  Edg.   Gone, sir : farewell.
And yet I know not how conceit may rob
The treasury of life, when life itself
Yields to the theft : had he been where he
    thought,
By this, had thought been past. Alive or dead ?
Ho, you sir ! friend ! Hear you, sir ! speak !
Thus might he pass indeed : yet he revives.
What are you, sir ?
  Glou.   Away, and let me die.
  Edg. Hadst thou been aught but gossamer,
    feathers, air,
So many fathom down precipitating,   50
Thou'dst shiver'd like an egg : but thou dost
    breathe ;
Hast heavy substance ; bleed'st not ; speak'st ;
    art sound.
Ten masts at each make not the altitude
Which thou hast perpendicularly fell :
Thy life's a miracle. Speak yet again.
  Glou. But have I fall'n, or no ?
  Edg. From the dread summit of this chalky
    bourn.
Look up a-height ; the shrill-gorged lark so
    far
Cannot be seen or heard : do but look up.
  Glou. Alack, I have no eyes.   60
Is wretchedness deprived that benefit,

To end itself by death ? 'Twas yet some comfort,
When misery could beguile the tyrant's rage,
And frustrate his proud will.

Edg. Give me your arm :
Up : so. How is 't ? Feel you your legs ? You stand.

Glou. Too well, too well.

Edg. This is above all strangeness.
Upon the crown o' the cliff, what thing was that
Which parted from you ?

Glou. A poor unfortunate beggar.

Edg. As I stood here below, methought his eyes
Were two full moons ; he had a thousand noses, 70
Horns whelk'd and waved like the enridged sea :
It was some fiend ; therefore, thou happy father,
Think that the clearest gods, who make them honors
Of men's impossibilities, have preserved thee.

Glou. I do remember now : henceforth I'll bear
Affliction till it do cry out itself
' Enough, enough,' and die. That thing you speak of,
I took it for a man ; often 'twould say
' The fiend, the fiend : ' he led me to that place.

Edg. Bear free and patient thoughts. But who comes here ? 80

Enter LEAR, *fantastically dressed with wild flowers.*

The safer sense will ne'er accommodate
His master thus.

Lear. No, they cannot touch me for coining ; I am the king himself.

Edg. O thou side-piercing sight !

Lear. Nature's above art in that respect.
There's your press-money. That fellow handles his bow like a crow-keeper : draw me a clothier's yard. Look, look, a mouse ! Peace, peace ; this piece of toasted cheese will do 't. There's my gauntlet ; I'll prove it on a giant. Bring up the brown bills. O, well flown, bird ! i' the clout, i' the clout : hewgh ! Give the word.

Edg. Sweet marjoram.

Lear. Pass.

Glou. I know that voice.

Lear. Ha ! Goneril, with a white beard ! They flattered me like a dog ; and told me I had white hairs in my beard ere the black ones were there. To say ' ay ' and ' no ' to every thing that I said !—' Ay ' and ' no ' too was no good divinity. When the rain came to wet me once, and the wind to make me chatter ; when the thunder would not peace at my bidding ; there I found 'em, there I smelt 'em out. Go to, they are not men o' their words : they told me I was every thing ; 'tis a lie, I am not ague-proof.

Glou. The trick of that voice I do well remember :
Is 't not the king ?

Lear. Ay, every inch a king :
When I do stare, see how the subject quakes.
I pardon that man's life. What was thy cause ?
Adultery ?
Thou shalt not die : die for adultery ! No :

The wren goes to 't, and the small gilded fly
Does lecher in my sight.
Let copulation thrive ; for Gloucester's bastard son
Was kinder to his father than my daughters
Got 'tween the lawful sheets.
To 't, luxury, pell-mell ! for I lack soldiers.
Behold yond simpering dame, 120
Whose face between her forks presages snow ;
That minces virtue, and does shake the head
To hear of pleasure's name ;
The fitchew, nor the soiled horse, goes to 't
With a more riotous appetite.
Down from the waist they are Centaurs,
Though women all above :
But to the girdle do the gods inherit,
Beneath is all the fiends' ;
There's hell, there's darkness, there's the sulphurous pit, 130
Burning, scalding, stench, consumption ; fie,
fie, fie ! pah, pah ! Give me an ounce of civet,
good apothecary, to sweeten my imagination :
there's money for thee.

Glou. O, let me kiss that hand !

Lear. Let me wipe it first ; it smells of mortality.

Glou. O ruin'd piece of nature ! This great world
Shall so wear out to nought. Dost thou know me ?

Lear. I remember thine eyes well enough.
Dost thou squiny at me ? No, do thy worst,
blind Cupid ; I'll not love. Read thou this
challenge ; mark but the penning of it.

Glou. Were all the letters suns, I could not see one.

Edg. I would not take this from report ; it is,
And my heart breaks at it.

Lear. Read.

Glou. What, with the case of eyes ?

Lear. O, ho, are you there with me ? No
eyes in your head, nor no money in your
purse ? Your eyes are in a heavy case, your
purse in a light ; yet you see how this world
goes. 151

Glou. I see it feelingly.

Lear. What, art mad ? A man may see
how this world goes with no eyes. Look with
thine ears : see how yond justice rails upon
yond simple thief. Hark, in thine ear : change
places ; and, handy-dandy, which is the justice,
which is the thief ? Thou hast seen a
farmer's dog bark at a beggar ?

Glou. Ay, sir. 160

Lear. And the creature run from the cur ?
There thou mightst behold the great image of
authority : a dog 's obeyed in office.
Thou rascal beadle, hold thy bloody hand !
Why dost thou lash that whore ? Strip thine own back ;
Thou hotly lust'st to use her in that kind
For which thou whipp'st her. The usurer hangs the cozener.
Through tatter'd clothes small vices do appear ;
Robes and furr'd gowns hide all. Plate sin with gold, 169
And the strong lance of justice hurtless breaks :
Arm it in rags, a pigmy's straw does pierce it.
None does offend, none, I say, none ; I'll able 'em :

Take that of me, my friend, who have the
      power
To seal the accuser's lips. Get thee glass eyes;
And, like a scurvy politician, seem
To see the things thou dost not. Now, now,
      now, now :
Pull off my boots : harder, harder : so.
      Edg. O, matter and impertinency mix'd !
Reason in madness !
      Lear. If thou wilt weep my fortunes, take
      my eyes.   180
I know thee well enough ; thy name is Glouces-
      ter :
Thou must be patient ; we came crying hither :
Thou know'st, the first time that we smell the
      air,
We wawl and cry. I will preach to thee :
      mark.
      Glou. Alack, alack the day !
      Lear. When we are born, we cry that we
      are come
To this great stage of fools : this a good
      block !
It were a delicate stratagem, to shoe
A troop of horse with felt : I'll put 't in proof ;
And when I have stol'n upon these sons-in-
      law,   190
Then, kill, kill, kill, kill, kill, kill !

      Enter a Gentleman, *with* Attendants.

      Gent. O, here he is : lay hand upon him.
      Sir,
Your most dear daughter—
      Lear. No rescue ? What, a prisoner ? I
      am even
The natural fool of fortune. Use me well ;
You shall have ransom. Let me have sur-
      geons ;
I am cut to the brains.
      Gent.   You shall have any thing.
      Lear. No seconds ? all myself ?
Why, this would make a man a man of salt,
To use his eyes for garden water-pots,   200
Ay, and laying autumn's dust.
      Gent.   Good sir,—
      Lear. I will die bravely, like a bridegroom.
      What !
I will be jovial : come, come ; I am a king,
My masters, know you that.
      Gent. You are a royal one, and we obey
      you.
      Lear. Then there's life in't. Nay, if you
get it, you shall get it with running. Sa, sa,
sa, sa.   [*Exit running ; Attendants follow.*
      Gent. A sight most pitiful in the meanest
      wretch,
Past speaking of in a king ! Thou hast one
      daughter,
Who redeems nature from the general curse
Which twain have brought her to.   211
      Edg. Hail, gentle sir.
      Gent.   Sir, speed you : what 's your will ?
      Edg. Do you hear aught, sir, of a battle
      toward ?
      Gent. Most sure and vulgar : every one
      hears that,
Which can distinguish sound.
      Edg.   But, by your favor,
How near 's the other army ?
      Gent. Near and on speedy foot ; the main
      descry
Stands on the hourly thought.
      Edg.   I thank you, sir : that's all.

      Gent. Though that the queen on special
      cause is here,
Her army is moved on.
      Edg.   I thank you, sir. 220
                                          [*Exit Gent.*
      Glou. You ever-gentle gods, take my
      breath from me :
Let not my worser spirit tempt me again
To die before you please !
      Edg.   Well pray you, father.
      Glou. Now, good sir, what are you ?
      Edg. A most poor man, made tame to for-
      tune's blows ;
Who, by the art of known and feeling sorrows,
Am pregnant to good pity. Give me your hand,
I'll lead you to some biding.
      Glou.   Hearty thanks :
The bounty and the benison of heaven
To boot, and boot !

                  Enter OSWALD.

      Osw. A proclaim'd prize ! Most happy !
That eyeless head of thine was first framed
      flesh   231
To raise my fortunes. Thou old unhappy
      traitor,
Briefly thyself remember : the sword is out
That must destroy thee.
      Glou.   Now let thy friendly hand
Put strength enough to't. [*Edgar interposes.*
      Osw.   Wherefore, bold peasant,
Darest thou support a publish'd traitor ?
      Hence ;
Lest that the infection of his fortune take
Like hold on thee. Let go his arm.
      Edg. Chill not let go, zir, without vurther
'casion.   240
      Osw. Let go, slave, or thou diest !
      Edg. Good gentleman, go your gait, and
let poor volk pass. An chud ha' bin zwaggered
out of my life, 'twould not ha' bin zo long as
'tis by a vortnight. Nay, come not near th' old
man ; keep out, che vor ye, or ise try whether
your costard or my ballow be the harder :
chill be plain with you.
      Osw. Out, dunghill !
      Edg. Chill pick your teeth, zir : come ; no
matter vor your foins.   251
      [*They fight, and Edgar knocks him down.*
      Osw. Slave, thou hast slain me : villain,
      take my purse :
If ever thou wilt thrive, bury my body ;
And give the letters which thou find'st about
      me
To Edmund earl of Gloucester ; seek him out
Upon the British party : O, untimely death !
                                               [*Dies.*
      Edg. I know thee well : a serviceable vil-
      lain ;
As duteous to the vices of thy mistress
As badness would desire.
      Glou.   What, is he dead ?
      Edg. Sit you down, father ; rest you   260
Let's see these pockets : the letters that he
      speaks of
May be my friends. He's dead ; I am only
      sorry
He had no other death's-man. Let us see :
Leave, gentle wax ; and, manners, blame us
      not :
To know our enemies' minds, we'ld rip their
      hearts ;
Their papers, is more lawful.

[Reads] ' Let our reciprocal vows be remembered. You have many opportunities to cut him off : if your will want not, time and place will be fruitfully offered. There is nothing done, if he return the conqueror : then am I the prisoner, and his bed my goal ; from the loathed warmth whereof deliver me, and supply the place for your labor.

' Your—wife, so I would say—
     ' Affectionate servant,
       ' GONERIL.'

O undistinguish'd space of woman's will !
A plot upon her virtuous husband's life ;
And the exchange my brother ! Here, in the
  sands,   280
Thee I'll rake up, the post unsanctified
Of murderous lechers : and in the mature
  time
With this ungracious paper strike the sight
Of the death practised duke : for him 'tis well
That of thy death and business I can tell.

Glou. The king is mad : how stiff is my
  vile sense,
That I stand up, and have ingenious feeling
Of my huge sorrows ! Better I were distract :
So should my thoughts be sever'd from my
  griefs,
And woes by wrong imaginations lose   290
The knowledge of themselves.

Edg.   Give me your hand :
        [Drum afar off.
Far off, methinks, I hear the beaten drum :
Come, father, I'll bestow you with a friend.
          [Exeunt.

SCENE VII. *A tent in the French camp.* LEAR
on a bed asleep, soft music playing ; Gentleman, *and others attending.*

  Enter CORDELIA, KENT, *and* Doctor.

Cor. O thou good Kent, how shall I live
  and work,
To match thy goodness ? My life will be too
  short,
And every measure fail me.

Kent. To be acknowledged, madam, is
  o'erpaid.
All my reports go with the modest truth ;
Nor more nor clipp'd, but so.

Cor.   Be better suited :
These weeds are memories of those worser
  hours :
I prithee, put them off.

Kent.   Pardon me, dear madam ;
Yet to be known shortens my made intent :
My boon I make it, that you know me not   10
Till time and I think meet.

Cor. Then be't so, my good lord. [*To the
Doctor*] How does the king ?

Doct. Madam, sleeps still.

Cor. O you kind gods,
Cure this great breach in his abused nature !
The untuned and jarring senses, O, wind up
Of this child-changed father !

Doct.   So please your majesty
That we may wake the king : he hath slept
  long.

Cor. Be govern'd by your knowledge, and
  proceed
I' the sway of your own will. Is he array'd ?

Gent. Ay, madam ; in the heaviness of his
  sleep   21
We put fresh garments on him.

Doct. Be by, good madam, when we do
  awake him ;
I doubt not of his temperance.

Cor.   Very well.

Doct. Please you, draw near. Louder the
  music there !

Cor. O my dear father ! Restoration hang
Thy medicine on my lips ; and let this kiss
Repair those violent harms that my two sisters
Have in thy reverence made !

Kent.   Kind and dear princess !

Cor. Had you not been their father, these
  white flakes   30
Had challenged pity of them. Was this a face
To be opposed against the warring winds ?
To stand against the deep dread-bolted thun-
  der ?
In the most terrible and nimble stroke
Of quick, cross lightning ? to watch—poor
  perdu !—
With this thin helm ? Mine enemy's dog,
Though he had bit me, should have stood that
  night
Against my fire ; and wast thou fain, poor fa-
  ther,
To hovel thee with swine, and rogues forlorn,
In short and musty straw ? Alack, alack !   40
'Tis wonder that thy life and wits at once
Had not concluded all. He wakes ; speak to
  him.

Doct. Madam, do you ; 'tis fittest.

Cor. How does my royal lord ? How fares
  your majesty ?

Lear. You do me wrong to take me out o'
  the grave :
Thou art a soul in bliss ; but I am bound
Upon a wheel of fire, that mine own tears
Do scald like molten lead.

Cor.   Sir, do you know me ?

Lear. You are a spirit, I know : when did
  you die ?

Cor. Still, still, far wide !   50

Doct. He's scarce awake : let him alone
  awhile.

Lear. Where have I been ? Where am I ?
  Fair daylight ?
I am mightily abused. I should e'en die with
  pity,
To see another thus. I know not what to say.
I will not swear these are my hands : let's see ;
I feel this pin prick. Would I were assured
Of my condition !

Cor.   O, look upon me, sir,
And hold your hands in benediction o'er me :
No, sir, you must not kneel.

Lear.   Pray, do not mock me :
I am a very foolish fond old man,   60
Fourscore and upward, not an hour more nor
  less ;
And, to deal plainly,
I fear I am not in my perfect mind.
Methinks I should know you, and know this
  man ;
Yet I am doubtful : for I am mainly ignorant
What place this is ; and all the skill I have
Remembers not these garments ; nor I know
  not
Where I did lodge last night. Do not laugh at
  me ;
For, as I am a man, I think this lady
To be my child Cordelia.

Cor.   And so I am, I am. 70

Lear. Be your tears wet? yes, 'faith. I
   pray, weep not:
If you have poison for me, I will drink it.
I know you do not love me; for your sisters
Have, as I do remember, done me wrong:
You have some cause, they have not.
   Cor.   No cause, no cause.
   Lear. Am I in France?
   Kent.   In your own kingdom, sir.
   Lear. Do not abuse me.
   Doct. Be comforted, good madam: the
      great rage,
You see, is kill'd in him: and yet it is danger
To make him even o'er the time he has lost.
Desire him to go in; trouble him no more 81
Till further settling.
   Cor. Will't please your highness walk?
   Lear.   You must bear with me:
Pray you now, forget and forgive: I am old
   and foolish.
      [*Exeunt all but Kent and Gentleman.*
   Gent. Holds it true, sir, that the Duke of
Cornwall was so slain?
   Kent. Most certain, sir.
   Gent. Who is conductor of his people?
   Kent. As 'tis said, the bastard son of
      Gloucester.   90
   Gent. They say Edgar, his banished son, is
with the Earl of Kent in Germany.
   Kent. Report is changeable. 'Tis time to
look about; the powers of the kingdom ap-
proach apace.
   Gent. The arbitrement is like to be bloody.
Fare you well, sir.   [*Exit.*
   Kent. My point and period will be
      throughly wrought,
Or well or ill, as this day's battle's fought.
                                           [*Exit.*

ACT V.

SCENE I. *The British camp, near Dover.*

Enter, with drum and colors, EDMUND,
   REGAN, *Gentlemen, and* Soldiers.

   Edm. Know of the duke if his last purpose
hold,
Or whether since he is advised by aught
To change the course: he's full of alteration
And self-reproving: bring his constant pleas-
   ure.   [*To a Gentleman, who goes out.*
   Reg. Our sister's man is certainly miscar-
ried.
   Edm. 'Tis to be doubted, madam.
   Reg.   Now, sweet lord,
You know the goodness I intend upon you:
Tell me—but truly—but then speak the truth,
Do you not love my sister?
   Edm.   In honor'd love.
   Reg. But have you never found my broth-
      er's way   10
To the forfended place?
   Edm.   That thought abuses you.
   Reg. I am doubtful that you have been
      conjunct
And bosom'd with her, as far as we call hers.
   Edm. No, by mine honor, madam.
   Reg. I never shall endure her: dear my
      lord,
Be not familiar with her.
   Edm.   Fear me not:
She and the duke her husband!

Enter, with drum and colors, ALBANY,
   GONERIL, *and* Soldiers.

   Gon. [*Aside*] I had rather lose the battle
      than that sister
Should loosen him and me.
   Alb. Our very loving sister, well be-met.
Sir, this I hear; the king is come to his daugh-
      ter,   21
With others whom the rigor of our state
Forced to cry out. Where I could not be hon-
      est,
I never yet was valiant: for this business,
It toucheth us, as France invades our land,
Not bolds the king, with others, whom, I fear,
Most just and heavy causes make oppose.
   Edm. Sir, you speak nobly.
   Reg.   Why is this reason'd?
   Gon. Combine together 'gainst the enemy;
For these domestic and particular broils 30
Are not the question here.
   Alb.   Let's then determine
With the ancient of war on our proceedings.
   Edm. I shall attend you presently at your
      tent.
   Reg. Sister, you'll go with us?
   Gon. No.
   Reg. 'Tis most convenient; pray you, go
with us.
   Gon. [*Aside*] O, ho, I know the riddle.—I
will go.

As they are going out, enter EDGAR *disguised.*

   Edg. If e'er your grace had speech with
      man so poor,
Hear me one word.
   Alb.   I'll overtake you. Speak.
      [*Exeunt all but Albany and Edgar.*
   Edg. Before you fight the battle, ope this
      letter.   40
If you have victory, let the trumpet sound
For him that brought it: wretched though I
      seem,
I can produce a champion that will prove
What is avouched there. If you miscarry,
Your business of the world hath so an end,
And machination ceases. Fortune love you.
   Alb. Stay till I have read the letter.
   Edg.   I was forbid it.
When time shall serve, let but the herald cry,
And I'll appear again.   49
   Alb. Why, fare thee well: I will o'erlook
      thy paper.   [*Exit Edgar.*

Re-enter EDMUND.

   Edm. The enemy's in view; draw up your
      powers.
Here is the guess of their true strength and
      forces
By diligent discovery; but your haste
Is now urged on you.
   Alb.   We will greet the time. [*Exit.*
   Edm. To both these sisters have I sworn
      my love;
Each jealous of the other, as the stung
Are of the adder. Which of them shall I take?
Both? one? or neither? Neither can be en-
      joy'd,
If both remain alive: to take the widow
Exasperates, makes mad her sister Goneril; 60
And hardly shall I carry out my side,
Her husband being alive. Now then we'll use

His countenance for the battle ; which being done,
Let her who would be rid of him devise
His speedy taking off. As for the mercy
Which he intends to Lear and to Cordelia,
The battle done, and they within our power,
Shall never see his pardon ; for my state
Stands on me to defend, not to debate. [*Exit.*

SCENE II. *A field between the two camps.*

Alarum within. Enter, with drum and colors,
LEAR, CORDELIA, *and* Soldiers, *over the stage ; and exeunt.*

Enter EDGAR *and* GLOUCESTER.

Edg. Here, father, take the shadow of this tree
For your good host ; pray that the right may thrive :
If ever I return to you again,
I'll bring you comfort.
 Glou.   Grace go with you, sir !
            [*Exit Edgar.*

Alarum and retreat within. Re-enter EDGAR.

 Edg. Away, old man ; give me thy hand ; away !
King Lear hath lost, he and his daughter ta'en :
Give me thy hand ; come on.
 Glou. No farther, sir ; a man may rot even here.
 Edg. What, in ill thoughts again ? Men must endure
Their going hence, even as their coming hither :
Ripeness is all : come on.   11
 Glou.   And that's true too. [*Exeunt.*

SCENE III. *The British camp near Dover.*

Enter, in conquest, with drum and colors, ED-
MUND : LEAR *and* CORDELIA, *prisoners ;*
Captain, Soldiers, &c.

 Edm. Some officers take them away : good guard,
Until their greater pleasures first be known
That are to censure them.
 Cor.   We are not the first
Who, with best meaning, have incurr'd the worst.
For thee, oppressed king, am I cast down ;
Myself could else out-frown false fortune's frown.
Shall we not see these daughters and these sisters ?
 Lear. No, no, no, no ! Come, let's away to prison :
We two alone will sing like birds i' the cage :
When thou dost ask me blessing, I'll kneel down,   10
And ask of thee forgiveness : so we'll live,
And pray, and sing, and tell old tales, and laugh
At gilded butterflies, and hear poor rogues
Talk of court news ; and we'll talk with them too,
Who loses and who wins ; who's in, who's out ;
And take upon's the mystery of things,
As if we were God's spies : and we'll wear out,
In a wall'd prison, packs and sects of great ones,
That ebb and flow by the moon.
 Edm.   Take them away.

 Lear. Upon such sacrifices, my Cordelia,
The gods themselves throw incense. Have I caught thee ?   21
He that parts us shall bring a brand from heaven,
And fire us hence like foxes. Wipe thine eyes ;
The good-years shall devour them, flesh and fell,
Ere they shall make us weep : we'll see 'em starve first.
Come. [*Exeunt Lear and Cordelia, guarded.*
 Edm. Come hither, captain ; hark.
Take thou this note [*giving a paper*] ; go follow them to prison :
One step I have advanced thee ; if thou dost
As this instructs thee, thou dost make thy way
To noble fortunes : know thou this, that men
Are as the time is : to be tender-minded   31
Does not become a sword : thy great employment
Will not bear question ; either say thou'lt do 't,
Or thrive by other means.
 Capt.   I'll do 't, my lord.
 Edm. About it ; and write happy when thou hast done.
Mark, I say, instantly ; and carry it so
As I have set it down.
 Capt. I cannot draw a cart, nor eat dried oats ;
If it be man's work, I'll do 't.   [*Exit.*

Flourish. Enter ALBANY, GONERIL, REGAN, *another* Captain, *and* Soldiers.

 Alb. Sir, you have shown to-day your valiant strain,   40
And fortune led you well : you have the captives
That were the opposites of this day's strife ;
We do require them of you, so to use them
As we shall find their merits and our safety
May equally determine.
 Edm.   Sir, I thought it fit
To send the old and miserable king
To some retention and appointed guard ;
Whose age has charms in it, whose title more,
To pluck the common bosom on his side,
And turn our impress'd lances in our eyes   50
Which do command them. With him I sent the queen ;
My reason all the same ; and they are ready
To-morrow, or at further space, to appear
Where you shall hold your session. At this time
We sweat and bleed : the friend hath lost his friend ;
And the best quarrels, in the heat, are cursed
By those that feel their sharpness :
The question of Cordelia and her father
Requires a fitter place.
 Alb.   Sir, by your patience,
I hold you but a subject of this war,   60
Not as a brother.
 Reg.   That's as we list to grace him.
Methinks our pleasure might have been demanded,
Ere you had spoke so far. He led our powers ;
Bore the commission of my place and person ;
The which immediacy may well stand up,
And call itself your brother.
 Gon.   Not so hot :
In his own grace he doth exalt himself,
More than in your addition.

Reg.   In my rights,
By me invested, he compeers the best.
   Gon.   That were the most, if he should hus-
band you.   70
   Reg.   Jesters do oft prove prophets.
   Gon.   Holla, holla !
That eye that told you so look'd but a-squint.
   Reg.   Lady, I am not well ; else I should
      answer
From a full-flowing stomach. General,
Take thou my soldiers, prisoners, patrimony ;
Dispose of them, of me ; the walls are thine :
Witness the world, that I create thee here
My lord and master.
   Gon.   Mean you to enjoy him ?
   Alb.   The let-alone lies not in your good
      will.
   Edm.   Nor in thine, lord.
   Alb.   Half-blooded fellow, yes.   80
   Reg.   [*To Edmund*] Let the drum strike,
      and prove my title thine.
   Alb.   Stay yet ; hear reason. Edmund, I ar-
      rest thee
On capital treason ; and, in thine attaint,
This gilded serpent [*pointing to Gon.*]. For
      your claim, fair sister,
I bar it in the interest of my wife :
'Tis she is sub-contracted to this lord,
And I, her husband, contradict your bans.
If you will marry, make your loves to me,
My lady is bespoke.
   Gon.   An interlude !
   Alb.   Thou art arm'd, Gloucester : let the
      trumpet sound :   90
If none appear to prove upon thy head
Thy heinous, manifest, and many treasons,
There is my pledge [*throwing down a glove*] ;
      I'll prove it on thy heart,
Ere I taste bread, thou art in nothing less
Than I have here proclaim'd thee.
   Reg.   Sick, O, sick !
   Gon.   [*Aside*] If not, I'll ne'er trust medi-
      cine.
   Edm.   There's my exchange [*throwing down
      a glove*] : what in the world he is
That names me traitor, villain-like he lies :
Call by thy trumpet : he that dares approach,
On him, on you, who not ? I will maintain 100
My truth and honor firmly.
   Alb.   A herald, ho !
   Edm.   A herald, ho, a herald !
   Alb.   Trust to thy single virtue ; for thy sol-
      diers,
All levied in my name, have in my name
Took their discharge.
   Reg.   My sickness grows upon me.
   Alb.   She is not well ; convey her to my
      tent.   [*Exit Regan, led.*

                Enter a Herald.

Come hither, herald,—Let the trumpet sound,
And read out this.
   Capt.   Sound, trumpet ! [*A trumpet sounds.*
   Her.   [*Reads*] ' If any man of quality or de-
gree within the lists of the army will maintain
upon Edmund, supposed Earl of Gloucester,
that he is a manifold traitor, let him appear
by the third sound of the trumpet : he is bold
in his defence.'
   Edm.   Sound !   [*First trumpet.*
   Her.   Again !   [*Second trumpet.*
   Her.   Again !   [*Third trumpet.*
                        [*Trumpet answers within.*

Enter EDGAR, *at the third sound, armed, with*
            a trumpet before him.

   Alb.   Ask him his purposes, why he appears
Upon this call o' the trumpet.
   Her.   What are you ?   119
Your name, your quality ? and why you an-
      swer
This present summons ?
   Edg.   Know, my name is lost ;
By treason's tooth bare-gnawn and canker-bit :
Yet am I noble as the adversary
I come to cope.
   Alb.   Which is that adversary ?
   Edg.   What's he that speaks for Edmund
      Earl of Gloucester ?
   Edm.   Himself : what say'st thou to him ?
   Edg.   Draw thy sword,
That, if my speech offend a noble heart,
Thy arm may do thee justice : here is mine.
Behold, it is the privilege of mine honors,
My oath, and my profession : I protest,   130
Maugre thy strength, youth, place, and emi-
      nence,
Despite thy victor sword and fire-new fortune,
Thy valor and thy heart, thou art a traitor ;
False to thy gods, thy brother, and thy father ;
Conspirant 'gainst this high-illustrious prince ;
And, from the extremest upward of thy head
To the descent and dust below thy foot,
A most toad-spotted traitor. Say thou ' No,'
This sword, this arm, and my best spirits, are
      bent
To prove upon thy heart, whereto I speak, 140
Thou liest.
   Edm.   In wisdom I should ask thy name ;
But, since thy outside looks so fair and war-
      like,
And that thy tongue some say of breeding
      breathes,
What safe and nicely I might well delay
By rule of knighthood, I disdain and spurn :
Back do I toss these treasons to thy head ;
With the hell-hated lie o'erwhelm thy heart ;
Which, for they yet glance by and scarcely
      bruise,
This sword of mine shall give them instant
      way,
Where they shall rest for ever. Trumpets,
      speak !
         [*Alarums. They fight. Edmund falls.*
   Alb.   Save him, save him !
   Gon.   This is practice, Gloucester :   151
By the law of arms thou wast not bound to
      answer
An unknown opposite ; thou art not van-
      quish'd,
But cozen'd and beguiled.
   Alb.   Shut your mouth, dame,
Or with this paper shall I stop it : Hold, sir :
Thou worse than any name, read thine own
      evil :
No tearing, lady : I perceive you know it.
               [*Gives the letter to Edmund.*
   Gon.   Say, if I do, the laws are mine, not
      thine :
Who can arraign me for't.
   Alb.   Most monstrous ! oh !   159
Know'st thou this paper ?
   Gon.   Ask me not what I know. [*Exit.*
   Alb.   Go after her : she's desperate ; govern
      her.

Edm. What you have charged me with,
         that have I done ;
And more, much more ; the time will bring it
         out :
'Tis past, and so am I. But what art thou
That hast this fortune on me ? If thou'rt noble,
I do forgive thee.
     Edg.   Let's exchange charity.
I am no less in blood than thou art, Edmund ;
If more, the more thou hast wrong'd me.
My name is Edgar, and thy father's son.
The gods are just, and of our pleasant vices
Make instruments to plague us :   171
The dark and vicious place where thee he got
Cost him his eyes.
     Edm.   Thou hast spoken right, 'tis true ;
The wheel is come full circle : I am here.
     Alb. Methought thy very gait did prophesy
A royal nobleness : I must embrace thee :
Let sorrow split my heart, if ever I
Did hate thee or thy father !
     Edg.   Worthy prince, I know't.
     Alb. Where have you hid yourself ?
How have you known the miseries of your
         father ?   180
     Edg. By nursing them, my lord. List a brief
         tale ;
And when 'tis told, O, that my heart would
         burst !
The bloody proclamation to escape,
That follow'd me so near,—O, our lives' sweet-
         ness !
That we the pain of death would hourly die
Rather than die at once !—taught me to shift
Into a madman's rags ; to assume a semblance
That very dogs disdain'd : and in this habit
Met I my father with his bleeding rings,
Their precious stones new lost : became his
         guide,   190
Led him, begg'd for him, saved him from de-
         spair ;
Never,—O fault !—reveal'd myself unto him,
Until some half-hour past, when I was arm'd :
Not sure, though hoping, of this good success,
I ask'd his blessing, and from first to last
Told him my pilgrimage : but his flaw'd heart,
Alack, too weak the conflict to support !
'Twixt two extremes of passion, joy and grief,
Burst smilingly.
     Edm. This speech of yours hath moved me,
And shall perchance do good : but speak you
         on ;   200
You look as you had something more to say.
     Alb. If there be more, more woeful, hold
         it in ;
For I am almost ready to dissolve,
Hearing of this.
     Edg.   This would have seem'd a period
To such as love not sorrow ; but another,
To amplify too much, would make much more,
And top extremity.
Whilst I was big in clamor came there in a
         man,
Who, having seen me in my worst estate,
Shunn'd my abhorr'd society ; but then, find-
         ing   210
Who 'twas that so endured, with his strong
         arms
He fastened on my neck, and bellow'd out
As he'ld burst heaven ; threw him on my fa-
         ther ;
Told the most piteous tale of Lear and him

That ever ear received : which in recounting
His grief grew puissant and the strings of life
Began to crack : twice then the trumpets
         sounded,
And there I left him tranced.
     Alb.   But who was this ?
     Edg. Kent, sir, the banish'd Kent ; who in
         disguise
Follow'd his enemy king, and did him service
Improper for a slave.   221

Enter a Gentleman, *with a bloody knife.*

     Gent. Help, help, O, help !
     Edg.   What kind of help ?
     Alb.   Speak, man.
     Edg. What means that bloody knife ?
     Gent.   'Tis hot, it smokes ;
It came even from the heart of—O, she's
         dead !
     Alb. Who dead ? speak, man.
     Gent. Your lady, sir, your lady : and her
         sister
By her is poisoned ; she hath confess'd it.
     Edm. I was contracted to them both : all
         three
Now marry in an instant.
     Edg.   Here comes Kent.
     Alb. Produce their bodies, be they alive or
         dead :   230
This judgment of the heavens, that makes us
         tremble,
Touches us not with pity.   [*Exit Gentleman.*

Enter KENT.

         O, is this he ?
The time will not allow the compliment
Which very manners urges.
     Kent.   I am come
To bid my king and master aye good night :
Is he not here ?
     Alb.   Great thing of us forgot !
Speak, Edmund, where's the king ? and
         where's Cordelia ?
See'st thou this object, Kent ?
[*The bodies of Goneril and Regan are brought
         in.*

     Kent. Alack, why thus ?
     Edm.   Yet Edmund was beloved :
The one the other poison'd for my sake,   240
And after slew herself.
     Alb. Even so. Cover their faces.
     Edm. I pant for life : some good I mean
         to do,
Despite of mine own nature. Quickly send,
Be brief in it, to the castle ; for my writ
Is on the life of Lear and on Cordelia :
Nay, send in time.
     Alb.   Run, run, O, run !
     Edg. To who, my lord ? Who hath the of-
         fice ? send
Thy token of reprieve.
     Edm. Well thought on : take my sword,
Give it the captain.   251
     Alb. Haste thee, for thy life. [*Exit Edgar.*
     Edm. He hath commission from thy wife
         and me
To hang Cordelia in the prison, and
To lay the blame upon her own despair,
That she fordid herself.
     Alb. The gods defend her ! Bear him hence
         awhile.   [*Edmund is borne off.*

Re-enter LEAR, *with* CORDELIA *dead in his arms;* EDGAR, *Captain, and others following.*

Lear. Howl, howl, howl, howl! O, you are men of stones:
Had I your tongues and eyes, I'ld use them so
That heaven's vault should crack. She's gone for ever!   259
I know when one is dead, and when one lives;
She's dead as earth. Lend me a looking-glass;
If that her breath will mist or stain the stone,
Why, then she lives.
Kent.   Is this the promised end?
Edg. Or image of that horror?
Alb.   Fall, and cease!
Lear. This feather stirs; she lives! if it be so,
It is a chance which does redeem all sorrows
That ever I have felt.
Kent. [*Kneeling*] O my good master!
Lear. Prithee, away.
Edg. 'Tis noble Kent, your friend.
Lear. A plague upon you, murderers, traitors all!
I might have saved her; now she's gone for ever!   270
Cordelia, Cordelia! stay a little. Ha!
What is't thou say'st? Her voice was ever soft,
Gentle, and low, an excellent thing in woman.
I kill'd the slave that was a-hanging thee.
Capt. 'Tis true, my lords, he did.
Lear.   Did I not, fellow?
I have seen the day, with my good biting falchion
I would have made them skip: I am old now,
And these same crosses spoil me. Who are you?
Mine eyes are not o' the best: I'll tell you straight.
Kent. If fortune brag of two she loved and hated,   280
One of them we behold.
Lear. This is a dull sight. Are you not Kent?
Kent.   The same,
Your servant Kent. Where is your servant Caius?
Lear. He's a good fellow, I can tell you that;
He'll strike, and quickly too: he's dead and rotten.
Kent. No, my good lord; I am the very man,—
Lear. I'll see that straight.
Kent. That, from your first of difference and decay,
Have follow'd your sad steps.
Lear.   You are welcome hither.

Kent. Nor no man else: all's cheerless, dark, and deadly.   290
Your eldest daughters have fordone themselves,
And desperately are dead.
Lear.   Ay, so I think.
Alb. He knows not what he says: and vain it is
That we present us to him.
Edg.   Very bootless.

Enter a Captain.

Capt. Edmund is dead, my lord.
Alb.   That's but a trifle here.
You lords and noble friends, know our intent.
What comfort to this great decay may come
Shall be applied: for us, we will resign,
During the life of this old majesty,
To him our absolute power: [*To Edgar and Kent*] you, to your rights: 300
With boot, and such addition as your honors
Have more than merited. All friends shall taste
The wages of their virtue, and all foes
The cup of their deservings. O, see, see!
Lear. And my poor fool is hang'd! No, no, no life!
Why should a dog, a horse, a rat, have life,
And thou no breath at all? Thou'lt come no more,
Never, never, never, never, never!
Pray you, undo this button: thank you, sir.
Do you see this? Look on her, look, her lips,
Look there, look there!   [*Dies.* 311
Edg.   He faints! My lord, my lord!
Kent. Break, heart; I prithee, break!
Edg.   Look up, my lord.
Kent. Vex not his ghost: O, let him pass! he hates him much
That would upon the rack of this tough world
Stretch him out longer.
Edg.   He is gone, indeed.
Kent. The wonder is, he hath endured so long:
He but usurp'd his life.
Alb. Bear them from hence. Our present business
Is general woe. [*To Kent and Edgar*] Friends of my soul, you twain   319
Rule in this realm, and the gored state sustain.
Kent. I have a journey, sir, shortly to go;
My master calls me, I must not say no.
Alb. The weight of this sad time we must obey;
Speak what we feel, not what we ought to say.
The oldest hath borne most: we that are young
Shall never see so much, nor live so long.
          [*Exeunt, with a dead march.*

MACBETH.

(WRITTEN ABOUT 1606.)

INTRODUCTION.

Macbeth was seen acted by Dr. Forman—who gives a detailed sketch of the play—on April 20, 1610; but the characteristics of versification forbid us to place it after *Pericles* and *Antony and Cleopatra*, or very near *The Tempest*. Upon the whole, the internal evidence supports the opinion of Malone, that the play was written about 1606. The materials for his play Shakespeare found in Holinshed's *Chronicle*, connecting the portion which treats of Duncan and Macbeth with Holinshed's account of the murder of King Duffe by Donwald. The appearance of Banquo's ghost and the sleep-walking of Lady Macbeth appear to be inventions of the dramatist. The Cambridge editors, Messrs. Clark and Wright, are of opinion that *Macbeth* was interpolated with passages by Middleton, but this theory is in a high degree doubtful. While in *Hamlet* and others of Shakespeare's plays we feel that Shakespeare refined upon or brooded over his thoughts, *Macbeth* seems as if struck out at a heat and imagined from first to last with unabated fervor. It is like a sketch by a great master in which every thing is executed with rapidity and power, and a subtlety of workmanship which has become instructive. The theme of the drama is the gradual ruin through yielding to evil within and evil without, of a man, who, though from the first tainted by base and ambitious thoughts, yet possessed elements in his nature of possible honor and loyalty. The contrast between Macbeth and Lady Macbeth, united by their affections, their fortunes and their crime, is made to illustrate and light up the character of each. Macbeth has physical courage, but moral weakness, and is subject to excited imaginative fears. His faint and intermittent loyalty embarrasses him—he would have the gains of crime without its pains. But when once his hands are dyed with blood, he hardly cares to withdraw them, and the same fears which had tended to hold him back from murder now urge him on to double and treble murders until slaughter, almost reckless, becomes the habit of his reign. At last the gallant soldier of the opening of the play fights for his life with a wild and brutelike force. His whole existence has become joyless and loveless, and yet he clings to existence. Lady Macbeth is of a finer and more delicate nature. Having fixed her eye upon an end—the attainment for her husband of Duncan's crown—she accepts the inevitable means; she nerves herself for the terrible night's work by artificial stimulants; yet she cannot strike the sleeping king who resembles her father. Having sustained her weaker husband, her own strength gives way; and in sleep, when her will cannot control her thoughts, she is piteously afflicted by the memory of one stain of blood upon her little hand. At last her thread of life snaps suddenly. Macbeth, whose affection for her was real, has sunk too far in the apathy of joyless crime to feel deeply her loss. Banquo, the loyal soldier, praying for restraint against evil thoughts which enter his mind as they had entered Macbeth's, but which work no evil there, is set over against Macbeth, as virtue is set over against disloyalty. The witches are the supernatural beings of terror, in harmony with Shakespeare's tragic period, as the fairies of the *Midsummer Night's Dream* are the supernatural beings of his days of fancy and frolic, and as Ariel is the supernatural genius of his latest period. There is at once a grossness, a horrible reality about the witches, and a mystery and grandeur of evil influence.

DRAMATIS PERSONÆ.

DUNCAN, king of Scotland.

MALCOLM,
DONALBAIN, } his sons.

MACBETH,
BANQUO, } generals of the king's army.

MACDUFF,
LENNOX,
ROSS,
MENTEITH, } noblemen of Scotland.
ANGUS,
CAITHNESS,

FLEANCE, son to Banquo.

SIWARD, Earl of Northumberland, general of the English forces.

Young SIWARD, his son.

SEYTON, an officer attending on Macbeth.

Boy, son to Macduff.
An English Doctor.
A Scotch Doctor.
A Soldier.
A Porter.
An Old Man.

LADY MACBETH.
LADY MACDUFF.
Gentlewoman attending on Lady Macbeth.

HECATE.
Three Witches.
Apparitions.

Lords, Gentlemen, Officers, Soldiers, Murderers, Attendants, and Messengers.

SCENE : *Scotland : England.*

ACT I.

Scene I.   *A desert place.*

Thunder and lightning.   Enter three Witches.

First Witch.   When shall we three meet
again
In thunder, lightning, or in rain ?
Sec. Witch.   When the hurlyburly's done,
When the battle's lost and won.
Third Witch.   That will be ere the set of
sun.
First Witch.   Where the place ?
Sec. Witch.   Upon the heath.
Third Witch.   There to meet with Macbeth.
First Witch.   I come, Graymalkin !
Sec. Witch.   Paddock calls.
Third Witch.   Anon.   10
All.   Fair is foul, and foul is fair :
Hover through the fog and filthy air.
                                        [*Exeunt.*

Scene II.   *A camp near Forres.*

Alarum within.   Enter Duncan, Malcolm,
Donalbain, Lennox, *with* Attendants,
meeting a bleeding Sergeant.

Dun.   What bloody man is that ? He can
report,
As seemeth by his plight, of the revolt
The newest state.
Mal.   This is the sergeant
Who like a good and hardy soldier fought
'Gainst my captivity. Hail, brave friend !
Say to the king the knowledge of the broil
As thou didst leave it.
Ser.   Doubtful it stood ;
As two spent swimmers, that do cling together
And choke their art. The merciless Macdon-
wald—
Worthy to be a rebel, for to that   10
The multiplying villanies of nature
Do swarm upon him—from the western isles
Of kerns and gallowglasses is supplied ;
And fortune, on his damned quarrel smiling,
Show'd like a rebel's whore : but all's too
weak :
For brave Macbeth—well he deserves that
name—
Disdaining fortune, with his brandish'd steel,
Which smoked with bloody execution,
Like valor's minion carved out his passage
Till he faced the slave ;   20
Which ne'er shook hands, nor bade farewell
to him,
Till he unseam'd him from the nave to the
chaps,
And fix'd his head upon our battlements.
Dun.   O valiant cousin ! worthy gentleman !
Ser.   As whence the sun 'gins his reflection
Shipwrecking storms and direful thunders
break,
So from that spring whence comfort seem'd
to come
Discomfort swells. Mark, king of Scotland,
mark :
No sooner justice had with valor arm'd
Compell'd these skipping kerns to trust their
heels,   30
But the Norweyan lord surveying vantage,
With furbish'd arms and new supplies of men
Began a fresh assault.
Dun.   Dismay'd not this

Our captains, Macbeth and Banquo ?
Ser.   Yes ;
As sparrows eagles, or the hare the lion.
If I say sooth, I must report they were
As cannons overcharged with double cracks,
so they
Doubly redoubled strokes upon the foe :
Except they meant to bathe in reeking wounds,
Or memorize another Golgotha,   40
I cannot tell.
But I am faint, my gashes cry for help.
Dun.   So well thy words become thee as
thy wounds ;
They smack of honor both. Go get him sur-
geons.   [*Exit Sergeant, attended.*
Who comes here ?

Enter Ross.

Mal.   The worthy thane of Ross.
Len.   What a haste looks through his eyes !
So should he look
That seems to speak things strange.
Ross.   God save the king !
Dun.   Whence camest thou, worthy thane ?
Ross.   From Fife, great king ;
Where the Norweyan banners flout the sky
And fan our people cold. Norway himself,   50
With terrible numbers,
Assisted by that most disloyal traitor
The thane of Cawdor, began a dismal conflict ;
Till that Bellona's bridegroom, lapp'd in proof,
Confronted him with self-comparisons,
Point against point rebellious, arm 'gainst arm.
Curbing his lavish spirit : and, to conclude,
The victory fell on us.
Dun.   Great happiness !
Ross.   That now
Sweno, the Norways' king, craves composi-
tion :
Nor would we deign him burial of his men 60
Till he disbursed at Saint Colme's inch
Ten thousand dollars to our general use.
Dun.   No more that thane of Cawdor shall
deceive
Our bosom interest : go pronounce his present
death,
And with his former title greet Macbeth.
Ross.   I'll see it done.
Dun.   What he hath lost noble Macbeth
hath won.   [*Exeunt.*

Scene III.   *A heath near Forres.*

Thunder.   Enter the three Witches.

First Witch.   Where hast thou been, sister ?
Sec. Witch.   Killing swine.
Third Witch.   Sister, where thou ?
First Witch.   A sailor's wife had chestnuts
in her lap,
And munch'd, and munch'd, and munch'd :—
'Give me,' quoth I :
'Aroint thee, witch !' the rump-fed ronyon
cries.
Her husband's to Aleppo gone, master o' the
Tiger :
But in a sieve I'll thither sail,
And, like a rat without a tail,
I'll do, I'll do, and I'll do.   10
Sec. Witch.   I'll give thee a wind.
First Witch.   Thou'rt kind.
Third Witch.   And I another.
First Witch.   I myself have all the other,
And the very ports they blow,
All the quarters that they know

I' the shipman's card.
I will drain him dry as hay :
Sleep shall neither night nor day
Hang upon his pent-house lid ;   20
He shall live a man forbid :
Weary se'nnights nine times nine
Shall he dwindle, peak and pine :
Though his bark cannot be lost,
Yet it shall be tempest-tost.
Look what I have.

 Sec. Witch. Show me, show me.

 First Witch. Here I have a pilot's thumb,
Wreck'd as homeward he did come.
       [*Drum within.*

 Third Witch. A drum, a drum !   30
Macbeth doth come.

 All. The weird sisters, hand in hand,
Posters of the sea and land,
Thus do go about, about :
Thrice to thine and thrice to mine
And thrice again, to make up nine.
Peace ! the charm's wound up.

  Enter Macbeth *and* Banquo.

 Macb. So foul and fair a day I have not
seen.

 Ban. How far is't call'd to Forres ? What
are these
So wither'd and so wild in their attire,   40
That look not like the inhabitants o' the earth,
And yet are on't ? Live you ? or are you aught
That man may question ? You seem to under-
stand me,
By each at once her chappy finger laying
Upon her skinny lips : you should be women,
And yet your beards forbid me to interpret
That you are so.

 Macb. Speak, if you can : what are you ?

 First Witch. All hail, Macbeth ! hail to
thee, thane of Glamis !

 Sec. Witch. All hail, Macbeth, hail to thee,
thane of Cawdor !

 Third Witch. All hail, Macbeth, thou shalt
be king hereafter !   50

 Ban. Good sir, why do you start ; and seem
to fear
Things that do sound so fair ? I' the name of
truth,
Are ye fantastical, or that indeed
Which outwardly ye show ? My noble partner
You greet with present grace and great predic-
tion
Of noble having and of royal hope,
That he seems rapt withal : to me you speak
not.
If you can look into the seeds of time,
And say which grain will grow and which will
not,
Speak then to me, who neither beg nor fear   60
Your favors nor your hate.

 First Witch. Hail !

 Sec. Witch. Hail !

 Third Witch. Hail !

 First Witch. Lesser than Macbeth, and
greater.

 Sec. Witch. Not so happy, yet much happier.

 Third Witch. Thou shalt get kings, though
thou be none :
So all hail, Macbeth and Banquo !

 First Witch. Banquo and Macbeth, all hail !

 Macb. Stay, you imperfect speakers, tell
me more :   70

By Sinel's death I know I am thane of Glamis ;
But how of Cawdor ? the thane of Cawdor
lives,
A prosperous gentleman ; and to be king
Stands not within the prospect of belief,
No more than to be Cawdor. Say from whence
You owe this strange intelligence ? or why
Upon this blasted heath you stop our way
With such prophetic greeting ? Speak, I charge
you.   [*Witches vanish.*

 Ban. The earth hath bubbles, as the water
has,
And these are of them. Whither are they vanish'd ?   80

 Macb. Into the air ; and what seem'd corporal melted
As breath into the wind. Would they had
stay'd !

 Ban. Were such things here as we do speak
about ?
Or have we eaten on the insane root
That takes the reason prisoner ?

 Macb. Your children shall be kings.

 Ban.   You shall be king.

 Macb. And thane of Cawdor too : went it
not so ?

 Ban. To the selfsame tune and words.
Who's here ?

  Enter Ross *and* Angus.

 Ross. The king hath happily received, Mac-
beth,
The news of thy success ; and when he reads
Thy personal venture in the rebels' fight,   91
His wonders and his praises do contend
Which should be thine or his : silenced with
that,
In viewing o'er the rest o' the selfsame day,
He finds thee in the stout Norweyan ranks,
Nothing afeard of what thyself didst make,
Strange images of death. As thick as hail
Came post with post ; and every one did bear
Thy praises in his kingdom's great defence,
And pour'd them down before him.

 Ang.   We are sent   100
To give thee from our royal master thanks ;
Only to herald thee into his sight,
Not pay thee.

 Ross. And, for an earnest of a greater
honor,
He bade me, from him, call thee thane of
Cawdor :
In which addition, hail, most worthy thane !
For it is thine.

 Ban. What, can the devil speak true ?

 Macb. The thane of Cawdor lives : why do
you dress me
In borrow'd robes ?

 Ang. Who was the thane lives yet ;
But under heavy judgment bears that life   110
Which he deserves to lose. Whether he was
combined
With those of Norway, or did line the rebel
With hidden help and vantage, or that with
both
He labor'd in his country's wreck, I know not ;
But treasons capital, confess'd and proved,
Have overthrown him.

 Macb. [*Aside*] Glamis, and thane of Caw-
dor !
The greatest is behind. [*To Ross and Angus*]
Thanks for your pains.

[*To Ban.*] Do you not hope your children
  shall be kings,
When those that gave the thane of Cawdor
  to me
Promised no less to them ?
  Ban.   That trusted home 120
Might yet enkindle you unto the crown,
Besides the thane of Cawdor. But 'tis strange :
And oftentimes, to win us to our harm,
The instruments of darkness tell us truths,
Win us with honest trifles, to betray's
In deepest consequence.
Cousins, a word, I pray you.
  Macb.   [*Aside*] Two truths are told,
As happy prologues to the swelling act
Of the imperial theme.—I thank you, gentle-
  men.
[*Aside*] This supernatural soliciting   130
Cannot be ill, cannot be good : if ill,
Why hath it given me earnest of success,
Commencing in a truth ? I am thane of Caw-
  dor :
If good, why do I yield to that suggestion
Whose horrid image doth unfix my hair
And make my seated heart knock at my ribs,
Against the use of nature ? Present fears
Are less than horrible imaginings :
My thought, whose murder yet is but fantas-
  tical,
Shakes so my single state of man that function
Is smother'd in surmise, and nothing is   141
But what is not.
  Ban.   Look, how our partner's rapt.
  Macb. [*Aside*] If chance will have me
    king, why, chance may crown me,
Without my stir.
  Ban.   New honors come upon him,
Like our strange garments, cleave not to their
  mould
But with the aid of use.
  Macb.   [*Aside*] Come what come may,
Time and the hour runs through the roughest
  day.
  Ban. Worthy Macbeth, we stay upon your
    leisure.
  Macb. Give me your favor : my dull brain
    was wrought
With things forgotten. Kind gentlemen, your
  pains   150
Are register'd where every day I turn
The leaf to read them. Let us toward the king.
Think upon what hath chanced, and, at more
  time,
The interim having weigh'd it, let us speak
Our free hearts each to other.
  Ban.   Very gladly.
  Macb. Till then, enough. Come, friends.
                                        [*Exeunt.*

SCENE IV. *Forres. The palace.*

Flourish. Enter DUNCAN, MALCOLM, DONAL-
  BAIN, LENNOX, *and* Attendants.

  Dun. Is execution done on Cawdor ? Are
    not
Those in commission yet return'd ?
  Mal.   My liege,
They are not yet come back. But I have spoke
With one that saw him die : who did report
That very frankly he confess'd his treasons,
Implored your highness' pardon and set forth
A deep repentance : nothing in his life
Became him like the leaving it ; he died

As one that had been studied in his death
To throw away the dearest thing he owed,   10
As 'twere a careless trifle.
  Dun.   There's no art
To find the mind's construction in the face :
He was a gentleman on whom I built
An absolute trust.

Enter MACBETH, BANQUO, ROSS, *and* ANGUS.
                              O worthiest cousin !
The sin of my ingratitude even now
Was heavy on me : thou art so far before
That swiftest wing of recompense is slow
To overtake thee. Would thou hadst less de-
  served,
That the proportion both of thanks and pay-
  ment   19
Might have been mine ! only I have left to say,
More is thy due than more than all can pay.
  Macb. The service and the loyalty I owe,
In doing it, pays itself. Your highness' part
Is to receive our duties ; and our duties
Are to your throne and state children and
  servants,
Which do but what they should, by doing
  every thing
Safe toward your love and honor.
  Dun.   Welcome hither :
I have begun to plant thee, and will labor
To make thee full of growing. Noble Ban-
  quo,
That hast no less deserved, nor must be
  known   30
No less to have done so, let me infold thee
And hold thee to my heart.
  Ban.   There if I grow,
The harvest is your own.
  Dun.   My plenteous joys,
Wanton in fulness, seek to hide themselves
In drops of sorrow. Sons, kinsmen, thanes,
And you whose places are the nearest, know
We will establish our estate upon
Our eldest, Malcolm, whom we name here-
  after
The Prince of Cumberland ; which honor must
Not unaccompanied invest him only,   40
But signs of nobleness, like stars, shall shine
On all deservers. From hence to Inverness,
And bind us further to you.
  Macb. The rest is labor, which is not used
    for you :
I'll be myself the harbinger and make joyful
The hearing of my wife with your approach ;
So humbly take my leave.
  Dun.   My worthy Cawdor !
  Macb. [*Aside*] The Prince of Cumber-
    land ! that is a step
On which I must fall down, or else o'erleap,
For in my way it lies. Stars, hide your fires ;
Let not light see my black and deep desires :
The eye wink at the hand ; yet let that be,
Which the eye fears, when it is done, to see.
                                        [*Exit.*
  Dun. True, worthy Banquo ; he is full so
    valiant,
And in his commendations I am fed ;
It is a banquet to me. Let's after him,
Whose care is gone before to bid us welcome :
It is a peerless kinsman. [*Flourish. Exeunt.*

SCENE V. *Inverness. Macbeth's castle.*

Enter LADY MACBETH, *reading a letter.*

  Lady M. 'They met me in the day of suc-

cess : and I have learned by the perfectest report, they have more in them than mortal
knowledge. When I burned in desire to question them further, they made themselves air,
into which they vanished. Whiles I stood rapt
in the wonder of it, came missives from the
king, who all-hailed me " Thane of Cawdor ; "
by which title, before, these weird sisters sa-
luted me, and referred me to the coming on
of time, with " Hail, king that shalt be ! " This
have I thought good to deliver thee, my dearest partner of greatness, that thou mightst not
lose the dues of rejoicing, by being ignorant
of what greatness is promised thee. Lay it to
thy heart, and farewell.'
Glamis thou art, and Cawdor ; and shalt be
What thou art promised : yet do I fear thy
    nature ;
It is too full o' the milk of human kindness
To catch the nearest way : thou wouldst be
    great ;
Art not without ambition, but without   20
The illness should attend it : what thou
    wouldst highly,
That wouldst thou holily ; wouldst not play
    false,
And yet wouldst wrongly win : thou'ldst have,
    great Glamis,
That which cries ' Thus thou must do, if thou
    have it ;
And that which rather thou dost fear to do
Than wishest should be undone.' Hie thee
    hither,
That I may pour my spirits in thine ear ;
And chastise with the valor of my tongue
All that impedes thee from the golden round,
Which fate and metaphysical aid doth seem 30
To have thee crown'd withal.

    Enter a Messenger.

           What is your tidings ?
  Mess. The king comes here to-night.
  Lady M.   Thou'rt mad to say it :
Is not thy master with him ? who, were't so,
Would have inform'd for preparation.
  Mess. So please you, it is true : our thane
    is coming :
One of my fellows had the speed of him,
Who, almost dead for breath, had scarcely
    more
Than would make up his message.
  Lady M.   Give him tending ;
He brings great news.   *[Exit Messenger.*
        The raven himself is hoarse
That croaks the fatal entrance of Duncan 40
Under my battlements. Come, you spirits
That tend on mortal thoughts, unsex me here,
And fill me from the crown to the toe top-full
Of direst cruelty ! make thick my blood ;
Stop up the access and passage to remorse,
That no compunctious visitings of nature
Shake my fell purpose, nor keep peace be-
    tween
The effect and it ! Come to my woman's
    breasts,
And take my milk for gall, you murdering
    ministers,
Wherever in your sightless substances   50
You wait on nature's mischief ! Come, thick
    night,
And pall thee in the dunnest smoke of hell,
That my keen knife see not the wound it
    makes,

Nor heaven peep through the blanket of the
    dark,
To cry ' Hold, hold ! '

    Enter MACBETH.

        Great Glamis ! worthy Cawdor !
Greater than both, by the all-hail hereafter !
Thy letters have transported me beyond
This ignorant present, and I feel now
The future in the instant.
  Macb.   My dearest love,
Duncan comes here to-night.
  Lady M.   And when goes hence ? 60
  Macb. To-morrow, as he purposes.
  Lady M.   O, never
Shall sun that morrow see !
Your face, my thane, is as a book where men
May read strange matters. To beguile the
    time,
Look like the time ; bear welcome in your
    eye,
Your hand, your tongue : look like the inno-
    cent flower,
But be the serpent under't. He that's coming
Must be provided for : and you shall put
This night's great business into my dispatch ;
Which shall to all our nights and days to
    come   70
Give solely sovereign sway and masterdom.
  Macb. We will speak further.
  Lady M.   Only look up clear ;
To alter favor ever is to fear :
Leave all the rest to me.   *[Exeunt.*

  SCENE VI. *Before Macbeth's castle.*

Hautboys and torches. Enter DUNCAN, MAL-
  COLM, DONALBAIN, BANQUO, LENNOX,
  MACDUFF, ROSS, ANGUS, *and* Attendants.

  Dun. This castle hath a pleasant seat ; the
    air
Nimbly and sweetly recommends itself
Unto our gentle senses.
  Ban.   This guest of summer,
The temple-haunting martlet, does approve,
By his loved mansionry, that the heaven's
    breath
Smells wooingly here : no jutty, frieze,
Buttress, nor coign of vantage, but this bird
Hath made his pendent bed and procreant
    cradle :
Where they most breed and haunt, I have
    observed,
The air is delicate.

    Enter LADY MACBETH.

  Dun. See, see, our honor'd hostess !   10
The love that follows us sometime is our
    trouble,
Which still we thank as love. Herein I teach
    you
How you shall bid God 'ild us for your pains,
And thank us for your trouble.
  Lady M.   All our service
In every point twice done and then done
    double
Were poor and single business to contend
Against those honors deep and broad where-
    with
Your majesty loads our house : for those of
    old,
And the late dignities heap'd up to them,
We rest your hermits.

Dun. Where's the thane of Cawdor ?   20
We coursed him at the heels, and had a purpose
To be his purveyor : but he rides well ;
And his great love, sharp as his spur, hath help him
To his home before us. Fair and noble hostess,
We are your guest to-night.
Lady M.   Your servants ever
Have theirs, themselves and what is theirs, in compt,
To make their audit at your highness' pleasure,
Still to return your own.
Dun.   Give me your hand ;
Conduct me to mine host : we love him highly,
And shall continue our graces towards him.
By your leave, hostess.   [*Exeunt.*   31

SCENE VII. *Macbeth's castle.*

Hautboys and torches. Enter a Sewer, *and divers* Servants *with dishes and service, and pass over the stage. Then enter* MACBETH.

Macb. If it were done when 'tis done, then 'twere well
It were done quickly : if the assassination
Could trammel up the consequence, and catch
With his surcease success ; that but this blow
Might be the be-all and the end-all here,
But here, upon this bank and shoal of time,
We'ld jump the life to come. But in these cases
We still have judgment here ; that we but teach
Bloody instructions, which, being taught, return
To plague the inventor : this even-handed justice   10
Commends the ingredients of our poison'd chalice
To our own lips. He's here in double trust ;
First, as I am his kinsman and his subject,
Strong both against the deed ; then, as his host,
Who should against his murderer shut the door,
Not bear the knife myself. Besides, this Duncan
Hath borne his faculties so meek, hath been
So clear in his great office, that his virtues
Will plead like angels, trumpet-tongued, against
The deep damnation of his taking-off ;   20
And pity, like a naked new-born babe,
Striding the blast, or heaven's cherubim, horsed
Upon the sightless couriers of the air,
Shall blow the horrid deed in every eye,
That tears shall drown the wind. I have no spur
To prick the sides of my intent, but only
Vaulting ambition, which o'erleaps itself
And falls on the other.

Enter LADY MACBETH.

                    How now ! what news ?
Lady M. He has almost supp'd : why have you left the chamber ?
Macb. Hath he ask'd for me ?
Lady M.   Know you not he has ?   30
Macb. We will proceed no further in this business :

He hath honor'd me of late ; and I have bought
Golden opinions from all sorts of people,
Which would be worn now in their newest gloss,
Not cast aside so soon.
Lady M.   Was the hope drunk
Wherein you dress'd yourself ? hath it slept since ?
And wakes it now, to look so green and pale
At what it did so freely ? From this time
Such I account thy love. Art thou afeard
To be the same in thine own act and valor   40
As thou art in desire ? Wouldst thou have that
Which thou esteem'st the ornament of life,
And live a coward in thine own esteem,
Letting ' I dare not ' wait upon ' I would,'
Like the poor cat i' the adage ?
Macb.   Prithee, peace :
I dare do all that may become a man ;
Who dares do more is none.
Lady M.   What beast was't, then,
That made you break this enterprise to me ?
When you durst do it, then you were a man ;
And, to be more than what you were, you would   50
Be so much more the man. Nor time nor place
Did then adhere, and yet you would make both :
They have made themselves, and that their fitness now
Does unmake you. I have given suck, and know
How tender 'tis to love the babe that milks me :
I would, while it was smiling in my face,
Have pluck'd my nipple from his boneless gums,
And dash'd the brains out, had I so sworn as you
Have done to this.
Macb.   If we should fail ?
Lady M.   We fail !
But screw your courage to the sticking-place,
And we'll not fail. When Duncan is asleep—
Whereto the rather shall his day's hard journey
Soundly invite him—his two chamberlains
Will I with wine and wassail so convince
That memory, the warder of the brain,
Shall be a fume, and the receipt of reason
A limbeck only : when in swinish sleep
Their drenched natures lie as in a death,
What cannot you and I perform upon
The unguarded Duncan ? what not put upon   70
His spongy officers, who shall bear the guilt
Of our great quell ?
Macb.   Bring forth men-children only ;
For thy undaunted mettle should compose
Nothing but males. Will it not be received,
When we have mark'd with blood those sleepy two
Of his own chamber and used their very daggers,
That they have done't ?
Lady M.   Who dares receive it other,
As we shall make our griefs and clamor roar
Upon his death ?
Macb.   I am settled, and bend up
Each corporal agent to this terrible feat.   80
Away, and mock the time with fairest show :

False face must hide what the false heart doth
    know.   [*Exeunt.*

ACT II.

SCENE I. *Court of Macbeth's castle.*

Enter BANQUO, *and* FLEANCE *bearing a torch
before him.*

Ban. How goes the night, boy ?
Fle.   The moon is down ; I have not heard
    the clock.
Ban. And she goes down at twelve.
Fle.   I take't, 'tis later, sir.
Ban. Hold, take my sword. There's hus-
    bandry in heaven ;
Their candles are all out. Take thee that too.
A heavy summons lies like lead upon me,
And yet I would not sleep : merciful powers,
Restrain in me the cursed thoughts that nature
Gives way to in repose !

Enter MACBETH, *and a* Servant *with a torch.*
              Give me my sword.
Who's there ?   10
  Macb. A friend.
  Ban. What, sir, not yet at rest ? The king's
    a-bed :
He hath been in unusual pleasure, and
Sent forth great largess to your offices.
This diamond he greets your wife withal,
By the name of most kind hostess ; and shut
    up
In measureless content.
  Macb.   Being unprepared,
Our will became the servant to defect ;
Which else should free have wrought.
  Ban.   All's well.
I dreamt last night of the three weird sisters :
To you they have show'd some truth.   21
  Macb.   I think not of them :
Yet, when we can entreat an hour to serve,
We would spend it in some words upon that
    business,
If you would grant the time.
  Ban.   At your kind'st leisure.
  Macb. If you shall cleave to my consent,
    when 'tis,
It shall make honor for you.
  Ban.   So I lose none
In seeking to augment it, but still keep
My bosom franchised and allegiance clear,
I shall be counsell'd.
  Macb.   Good repose the while !
  Ban. Thanks, sir : the like to you !   30
           [*Exeunt Banquo and Fleance.*
  Macb. Go bid thy mistress, when my drink
    is ready,
She strike upon the bell. Get thee to bed.
                [*Exit Servant.*
Is this a dagger which I see before me,
The handle toward my hand ? Come, let me
    clutch thee.
I have thee not, and yet I see thee still.
Art thou not, fatal vision, sensible
To feeling as to sight ? or art thou but
A dagger of the mind, a false creation,
Proceeding from the heat-oppressed brain ?
I see thee yet, in form as palpable   40
As this which now I draw.
Thou marshall'st me the way that I was going ;
And such an instrument I was to use.

Mine eyes are made the fools o' the other
    senses,
Or else worth all the rest ; I see thee still,
And on thy blade and dudgeon gouts of blood,
Which was not so before. There's no such
    thing :
It is the bloody business which informs
Thus to mine eyes. Now o'er the one half-
    world
Nature seems dead, and wicked dreams abuse
The curtain'd sleep ; witchcraft celebrates   51
Pale Hecate's offerings, and wither'd murder,
Alarum'd by his sentinel, the wolf,
Whose howl's his watch, thus with his stealthy
    pace,
With Tarquin's ravishing strides, towards his
    design
Moves like a ghost. Thou sure and firm-set
    earth,
Hear not my steps, which way they walk, for
    fear
Thy very stones prate of my whereabout,
And take the present horror from the time,
Which now suits with it. Whiles I threat, he
    lives :   60
Words to the heat of deeds too cold breath
    gives.   [*A bell rings.*
I go, and it is done ; the bell invites me.
Hear it not, Duncan ; for it is a knell
That summons thee to heaven or to hell.
                     [*Exit.*

SCENE II. *The same.*
Enter LADY MACBETH.

Lady M. That which hath made them
    drunk hath made me bold ;
What hath quench'd them hath given me fire.
    Hark ! Peace !
It was the owl that shriek'd, the fatal bellman,
Which gives the stern'st good-night. He is
    about it :
The doors are open ; and the surfeited grooms
Do mock their charge with snores : I have
    drugg'd their possets,
That death and nature do contend about them,
Whether they live or die.
  Macb. [*Within*] Who's there ? what, ho !   9
  Lady M. Alack, I am afraid they have
    awaked,
And 'tis not done. The attempt and not the
    deed
Confounds us. Hark ! I laid their daggers
    ready ;
He could not miss 'em. Had he not resembled
My father as he slept, I had done't.

Enter MACBETH.
                  My husband !
  Macb. I have done the deed. Didst thou
    not hear a noise ?
  Lady M. I heard the owl scream and the
    crickets cry.
Did not you speak ?
  Macb.   When ?
  Lady M.   Now.
  Macb.   As I descended ?
  Lady M. Ay.
  Macb. Hark !
Who lies i' the second chamber ?
  Lady M.   Donalbain.   20
  Macb. This is a sorry sight.
             [*Looking on his hands.*

Lady M. A foolish thought, to say a sorry sight.

Macb. There's one did laugh in's sleep, and one cried 'Murder!'
That they did wake each other: I stood and heard them:
But they did say their prayers, and address'd them
Again to sleep.

Lady M. There are two lodged together.

Macb. One cried 'God bless us!' and 'Amen' the other;
As they had seen me with these hangman's hands.
Listening their fear, I could not say 'Amen,'
When they did say 'God bless us!'

Lady M.   Consider it not so deeply. 30

Macb. But wherefore could not I pronounce 'Amen'?
I had most need of blessing, and 'Amen'
Stuck in my throat.

Lady M. These deeds must not be thought
After these ways; so, it will make us mad.

Macb. Methought I heard a voice cry 'Sleep no more!
Macbeth does murder sleep', the innocent sleep,
Sleep that knits up the ravell'd sleave of care,
The death of each day's life, sore labor's bath,
Balm of hurt minds, great nature's second course,
Chief nourisher in life's feast,—

Lady M.   What do you mean?

Macb. Still it cried 'Sleep no more!' to all the house: 41
'Glamis hath murder'd sleep, and therefore Cawdor
Shall sleep no more; Macbeth shall sleep no more.'

Lady M. Who was it that thus cried? Why, worthy thane,
You do unbend your noble strength, to think
So brainsickly of things. Go get some water,
And wash this filthy witness from your hand.
Why did you bring these daggers from the place?
They must lie there: go carry them; and smear
The sleepy grooms with blood.

Macb.   I'll go no more: 50
I am afraid to think what I have done;
Look on't again I dare not.

Lady M.   Infirm of purpose!
Give me the daggers: the sleeping and the dead
Are but as pictures: 'tis the eye of childhood
That fears a painted devil. If he do bleed,
I'll gild the faces of the grooms withal;
For it must seem their guilt.

                    [*Exit. Knocking within.*

Macb.   Whence is that knocking?
How is't with me, when every noise appals me?
What hands are here? ha! they pluck out mine eyes.
Will all great Neptune's ocean wash this blood
Clean from my hand? No, this my hand will rather   61
The multitudinous seas in incarnadine,
Making the green one red.

        Re-enter Lady Macbeth.

Lady M. My hands are of your color; but I shame
To wear a heart so white. [*Knocking within.*]
    I hear a knocking
At the south entry: retire we to our chamber;
A little water clears us of this deed:
How easy is it, then! Your constancy
Hath left you unattended. [*Knocking within.*]
    Hark! more knocking.
Get on your nightgown, lest occasion call us,
And show us to be watchers. Be not lost   71
So poorly in your thoughts.

Macb. To know my deed, 'twere best not know myself. [*Knocking within.*
Wake Duncan with thy knocking! I would thou couldst!   [*Exeunt.*

SCENE III. *The same.*

Knocking within. Enter a Porter.

Porter. Here's a knocking indeed! If a man were porter of hell-gate, he should have old turning the key. [*Knocking within.*] Knock, knock, knock! Who's there, i' the name of Beelzebub? Here's a farmer, that hanged himself on the expectation of plenty: come in time; have napkins enow about you; here you'll sweat for't. [*Knocking within.*] Knock, knock! Who's there, in the other devil's name? Faith, here's an equivocator, that could swear in both the scales against either scale; who committed treason enough for God's sake, yet could not equivocate to heaven: O, come in, equivocator. [*Knocking within.*] Knock, knock, knock! Who's there? Faith, here's an English tailor come hither, for stealing out of a French hose: come in, tailor; here you may roast your goose. [*Knocking within.*] Knock, knock; never at quiet! What are you? But this place is too cold for hell. I'll devil-porter it no further: I had thought to have let in some of all professions that go the primrose way to the everlasting bonfire. [*Knocking within.*] Anon, anon! I pray you, remember the porter.   [*Opens the gate.*

Enter Macduff *and* Lennox.

Macd. Was it so late, friend, ere you went to bed,
That you do lie so late?

Port. 'Faith sir, we were carousing till the second cock: and drink, sir, is a great provoker of three things.

Macd. What three things does drink especially provoke?   30

Port. Marry, sir, nose-painting, sleep, and urine. Lechery, sir, it provokes, and unprovokes; it provokes the desire, but it takes away the performance: therefore, much drink may be said to be an equivocator with lechery: it makes him, and it mars him; it sets him on, and it takes him off; it persuades him, and disheartens him; makes him stand to, and not stand to; in conclusion, equivocates him in a sleep, and, giving him the lie, leaves him.

Macd. I believe drink gave thee the lie last night.   41

Port. That it did, sir, i' the very throat on me: but I requited him for his lie; and, I think, being too strong for him, though he took up my legs sometime, yet I made a shift to cast him.

Macd. Is thy master stirring?

Enter MACBETH.

Our knocking has awaked him; here he
　comes.

Len. Good morrow, noble sir.
Macb. 　　　　　　　Good morrow, both.
Macd. Is the king stirring, worthy thane?
Macb. 　　　　　　　Not yet. 50
Macd. He did command me to call timely
　on him:
I have almost slipp'd the hour.
Macb. 　　　　　　I'll bring you to him.
Macd. I know this is a joyful trouble to
　you;
But yet 'tis one.
Macb. 　　The labor we delight in physics
　pain.
This is the door.
Macd. 　　　　　I'll make so bold to call,
For 'tis my limited service. 　　　　　[*Exit.*
Len. Goes the king hence to-day?
Macb. 　　　　　　He does: he did appoint so.
Len. The night has been unruly: where we
　lay,
Our chimneys were blown down; and, as they
　say, 　　　　　　　　　　　　　　60
Lamentings heard i' the air; strange screams
　of death,
And prophesying with accents terrible
Of dire combustion and confused events
New hatch'd to the woeful time: the obscure
　bird
Clamor'd the livelong night: some say, the
　earth
Was feverous and did shake.
Macb. 　　　　　　　'Twas a rough night.
Len. My young remembrance cannot par-
　allel
A fellow to it.

Re-enter MACDUFF.

Macd. O horror, horror, horror! Tongue
　nor heart
Cannot conceive nor name thee!
Macb. ⎫
Len. 　⎬ 　　　　　What's the matter. 70
Macd. Confusion now hath made his mas-
　terpiece!
Most sacrilegious murder hath broke ope
The Lord's anointed temple, and stole thence
The life o' the building!
Macb. 　　　　　What is 't you say? the life?
Len. Mean you his majesty?
Macd. Approach the chamber, and destroy
　your sight
With a new Gorgon: do not bid me speak;
See, and then speak yourselves.
　　　　　[*Exeunt Macbeth and Lennox.*
　　　　　　　　　　　Awake, awake!
Ring the alarum-bell. Murder and treason!
Banquo and Donalbain! Malcolm! awake!
Shake off this downy sleep, death's counterfeit,
And look on death itself! up, up, and see 82
The great doom's image! Malcolm! Banquo!
As from your graves rise up, and walk like
　sprites,
To countenance this horror! Ring the bell.
　　　　　　　　　　　　　　[*Bell rings.*

Enter LADY MACBETH.

Lady M. What's the business,
That such a hideous trumpet calls to parley
The sleepers of the house? speak, speak!

Macd. 　　　　　　　O gentle lady,
'Tis not for you to hear what I can speak:
The repetition, in a woman's ear, 　　　　90
Would murder as it fell.

Enter BANQUO.

　　　　　　O Banquo, Banquo,
Our royal master 's murder'd!
Lady M. 　　　　　　　Woe, alas!
What, in our house?
Ban. 　　　　　　Too cruel any where.
Dear Duff, I prithee, contradict thyself,
And say it is not so.

Re-enter MACBETH *and* LENNOX, *with* ROSS.

Macb. Had I but died an hour before this
　chance,
I had lived a blessed time; for, from this in-
　stant,
There 's nothing serious in mortality:
All is but toys: renown and grace is dead;
The wine of life is drawn, and the mere lees
Is left this vault to brag of. 　　　　　101

Enter MALCOLM *and* DONALBAIN.

Don. What is amiss?
Macb. 　　　　　You are, and do not know't:
The spring, the head, the fountain of your
　blood
Is stopp'd; the very source of it is stopp'd.
Macd. Your royal father 's murder'd.
Mal. 　　　　　　　O, by whom?
Len. Those of his chamber, as it seem'd,
　had done 't:
Their hands and faces were all badged with
　blood;
So were their daggers, which unwiped we
　found
Upon their pillows:
They stared, and were distracted; no man's
　life 　　　　　　　　　　　　　110
Was to be trusted with them.
Macb. O, yet I do repent me of my fury,
That I did kill them.
Macd. 　　　　　Wherefore did you so?
Macb. Who can be wise, amazed, tem-
　perate and furious,
Loyal and neutral, in a moment? No man:
The expedition of my violent love
Outrun the pauser, reason. Here lay Duncan,
His silver skin laced with his golden blood;
And his gash'd stabs look'd like a breach in
　nature
For ruin's wasteful entrance: there, the mur-
　derers,
Steep'd in the colors of their trade, their dag-
　gers
Unmannerly breech'd with gore: who could
　refrain,
That had a heart to love, and in that heart
Courage to make 's love known?
Lady M. 　　　　　Help me hence, ho!
Macd. Look to the lady.
Mal. [*Aside to Don.*] Why do we hold our
　tongues,
That most may claim this argument for ours?
Don. [*Aside to Mal.*] What should be
　spoken here, where our fate,
Hid in an auger-hole, may rush, and seize us?
Let 's away; 　　　　　　　　　129
Our tears are not yet brew'd.
Mal. [*Aside to Don.*] Nor our strong sor-
　row

Upon the foot of motion.
Ban.   Look to the lady :
      [*Lady Macbeth is carried out.*
And when we have our naked frailties hid,
That suffer in exposure, let us meet,
And question this most bloody piece of work,
To know it further. Fears and scruples shake
      us :
In the great hand of God I stand ; and thence
Against the undivulged pretence I fight
Of treasonous malice.
  Macd.   And so do I.
  All.   So all.
  Macb. Let's briefly put on manly readiness,
And meet i' the hall together.
  All.   Well contented. 140
      [*Exeunt all but Malcolm and Donalbain.*
  Mal. What will you do ? Let's not consort
      with them :
To show an unfelt sorrow is an office
Which the false man does easy. I'll to England.
  Don. To Ireland, I ; our separated fortune
Shall keep us both the safer : where we are,
There's daggers in men's smiles : the near in
      blood,
The nearer bloody.
  Mal.   This murderous shaft that's shot
Hath not yet lighted, and our safest way
Is to avoid the aim. Therefore, to horse ;
And let us not be dainty of leave-taking,   150
But shift away : there's warrant in that theft
Which steals itself, when there's no mercy left.
                                      [*Exeunt.*

Scene IV. *Outside Macbeth's castle.*

Enter Ross *and an* old Man.

  Old M. Threescore and ten I can remem-
      ber well :
Within the volume of which time I have seen
Hours dreadful and things strange ; but this
      sore night
Hath trifled former knowings.
  Ross.   Ah, good father,
Thou seest, the heavens, as troubled with man's
      act,
Threaten his bloody stage : by the clock, 'tis
      day,
And yet dark night strangles the travelling
      lamp :
Is't night's predominance, or the day's shame,
That darkness does the face of earth entomb,
When living light should kiss it ?
  Old M.   'Tis unnatural, 10
Even like the deed that's done. On Tuesday
      last,
A falcon, towering in her pride of place,
Was by a mousing owl hawk'd at and kill'd.
  Ross. And Duncan's horses—a thing most
      strange and certain—
Beauteous and swift, the minions of their race,
Turn'd wild in nature, broke their stalls, flung
      out,
Contending 'gainst obedience, as they would
      make
War with mankind.
  Old M.   'Tis said they eat each other.
  Ross. They did so, to the amazement of
      mine eyes
That look'd upon't. Here comes the good Mac-
      duff.   20

Enter MACDUFF.

How goes the world, sir, now ?

  Macd.   Why, see you not ?
  Ross. Is't known who did this more than
      bloody deed ?
  Macd. Those that Macbeth hath slain.
  Ross.   Alas, the day !
What good could they pretend ?
  Macd.   They were suborn'd :
Malcolm and Donalbain, the king's two sons,
Are stol'n away and fled ; which puts upon
      them
Suspicion of the deed.
  Ross.   'Gainst nature still !
Thriftless ambition, that wilt ravin up
Thine own life's means ! Then 'tis most like
The sovereignty will fall upon Macbeth.   30
  Macd. He is already named, and gone to
      Scone
To be invested.
  Ross.   Where is Duncan's body ?
  Macd. Carried to Colmekill,
The sacred storehouse of his predecessors,
And guardian of their bones.
  Ross.   Will you to Scone ?
  Macd. No, cousin, I'll to Fife.
  Ross.   Well, I will thither.
  Macd. Well, may you see things well done
      there : adieu !
Lest our old robes sit easier than our new !
  Ross. Farewell, father.
  Old M. God's benison go with you ; and
      with those   40
That would make good of bad, and friends of
      foes !   [*Exeunt.*

ACT III.

Scene I. *Forres. The palace.*

Enter BANQUO.

  Ban. Thou hast it now : king, Cawdor,
      Glamis, all,
As the weird women promised, and, I fear,
Thou play'dst most foully for't : yet it was
      said
It should not stand in thy posterity,
But that myself should be the root and father
Of many kings. If there come truth from
      them—
As upon thee, Macbeth, their speeches shine—
Why, by the verities on thee made good,
May they not be my oracles as well,   9
And set me up in hope ? But hush ! no more.

Sennet sounded. Enter MACBETH, *as king,*
  LADY MACBETH, *as queen,* LENNOX, ROSS,
  Lords, Ladies, *and* Attendants.

  Macb. Here's our chief guest.
  Lady M.   If he had been forgotten,
It had been as a gap in our great feast,
And all-thing unbecoming.
  Macb. To-night we hold a solemn supper
      sir,
And I'll request your presence.
  Ban.   Let your highness
Command upon me ; to the which my duties
Are with a most indissoluble tie
For ever knit.
  Macb. Ride you this afternoon ?
  Ban. Ay, my good lord.   20
  Macb. We should have else desired your
      good advice,

Which still hath been both grave and prosper-
  ous,
In this day's council; but we'll take to-mor-
  row.
Is't far you ride?
  Ban. As far, my lord, as will fill up the
    time
'Twixt this and supper: go not my horse the
    better,
I must become a borrower of the night
For a dark hour or twain.
  Macb.   Fail not our feast.
  Ban. My lord, I will not.
  Macb. We hear, our bloody cousins are
    bestow'd   30
In England and in Ireland, not confessing
Their cruel parricide, filling their hearers
With strange invention: but of that to-mor-
  row,
When therewithal we shall have cause of state
Craving us jointly. Hie you to horse: adieu,
Till you return at night. Goes Fleance with
  you?
  Ban. Ay, my good lord: our time does call
    upon 's.
  Macb. I wish your horses swift and sure of
    foot;
And so I do commend you to their backs.
Farewell.   *[Exit Banquo.* 40
Let every man be master of his time
Till seven at night: to make society
The sweeter welcome, we will keep ourself
Till supper-time alone: while then, God be
  with you!
  [Exeunt all but Macbeth, and an attendant.
Sirrah, a word with you: attend those men
Our pleasure?
  Atten. They are, my lord, without the pal-
    ace gate.
  Macb. Bring them before us.
                 [Exit Attendant.
           To be thus is nothing;
But to be safely thus.—Our fears in Banquo
Stick deep; and in his royalty of nature 50
Reigns that which would be fear'd: 'tis much
  he dares;
And, to that dauntless temper of his mind,
He hath a wisdom that doth guide his valor
To act in safety. There is none but he
Whose being I do fear: and, under him,
My Genius is rebuked; as, it is said,
Mark Antony's was by Cæsar. He chid the
  sisters
When first they put the name of king upon me,
And bade them speak to him: then prophet-
  like
They hail'd him father to a line of kings: 60
Upon my head they placed a fruitless crown,
And put a barren sceptre in my gripe,
Thence to be wrench'd with an unlineal hand,
No son of mine succeeding. If 't be so,
For Banquo's issue have I filed my mind;
For them the gracious Duncan have I mur-
  der'd;
Put rancors in the vessel of my peace
Only for them; and mine eternal jewel
Given to the common enemy of man,
To make them kings, the seed of Banquo
  kings!   70
Rather than so, come fate into the list.
And champion me to the utterance! Who's
  there!

  Re-enter Attendant, *with two* Murderers.
Now go to the door, and stay there till we call.
                 [Exit Attendant.
Was it not yesterday we spoke together?
  First Mur. It was, so please your highness.
  Macb.   Well then, now
Have you consider'd of my speeches? Know
That it was he in the times past which held
  you
So under fortune, which you thought had been
Our innocent self: this I made good to you
In our last conference, pass'd in probation
  with you,   80
How you were borne in hand, how cross'd, the
  instruments,
Who wrought with them, and all things else
  that might
To half a soul and to a notion crazed
Say 'Thus did Banquo.'
  First Mur.   You made it known to us.
  Macb. I did so, and went further, which
    is now
Our point of second meeting. Do you find
Your patience so predominant in your nature
That you can let this go? Are you so gos-
  pell'd
To pray for this good man and for his issue,
Whose heavy hand hath bow'd you to the
  grave
And beggar'd yours for ever?
  First Mur.   We are men, my liege. 91
  Macb. Ay, in the catalogue ye go for men;
As hounds and greyhounds, mongrels, spaniels,
  curs,
Shoughs, water-rugs and demi-wolves, are clept
All by the name of dogs: the valued file
Distinguishes the swift, the slow, the subtle,
The housekeeper, the hunter, every one
According to the gift which bounteous nature
Hath in him closed; whereby he does receive
Particular addition, from the bill   100
That writes them all alike: and so of men.
Now, if you have a station in the file,
Not i' the worst rank of manhood, say 't;
And I will put that business in your bosoms,
Whose execution takes your enemy off,
Grapples you to the heart and love of us,
Who wear our health but sickly in his life,
Which in his death were perfect.
  Sec. Mur.   I am one, my liege,
Whom the vile blows and buffets of the world
Have so incensed that I am reckless what 110
I do to spite the world.
  First Mur.   And I another
So weary with disasters, tugg'd with fortune,
That I would set my life on any chance,
To mend it, or be rid on't.
  Macb.   Both of you
Know Banquo was your enemy.
  Both Mur.   True, my lord.
  Macb. So is he mine; and in such bloody
    distance,
That every minute of his being thrusts
Against my near'st of life: and though I could
With barefaced power sweep him from my
  sight
And bid my will avouch it, yet I must not, 120
For certain friends that are both his and mine,
Whose loves I may not drop, but wail his fall
Who I myself struck down; and thence it is,
That I to your assistance do make love,
Masking the business from the common eye

For sundry weighty reasons.
Sec. Mur. We shall, my lord,
Perform what you command us.
First Mur. Though our lives—
Macb. Your spirits shine through you.
Within this hour at most
I will advise you where to plant yourselves ;
Acquaint you with the perfect spy o' the time,
The moment on't ; for't must be done to-night,
And something from the palace ; always
thought 132
That I require a clearness : and with him—
To leave no rubs nor botches in the work—
Fleance his son, that keeps him company,
Whose absence is no less material to me
Than is his father's, must embrace the fate
Of that dark hour. Resolve yourselves apart :
I'll come to you anon.
Both Mur. We are resolved, my lord.
Macb. I'll call upon you straight : abide
within. [*Exeunt Murderers.* 140
It is concluded. Banquo, thy soul's flight,
If it find heaven, must find it out to-night.
[*Exit.*

SCENE II. *The palace.*

Enter LADY MACBETH *and a* Servant.

Lady M. Is Banquo gone from court ?
Serv. Ay, madam, but returns again to-
night.
Lady M. Say to the king, I would attend
his leisure
For a few words.
Serv. Madam, I will. [*Exit.*
Lady M. Nought's had, all's spent,
Where our desire is got without content :
'Tis safer to be that which we destroy
Than by destruction dwell in doubtful joy.

Enter MACBETH.

How now, my lord ! why do you keep alone,
Of sorriest fancies your companions making,
Using those thoughts which should indeed have
died 10
With them they think on ? Things without all
remedy
Should be without regard : what's done is
done.
Macb. We have scotch'd the snake, not
kill'd it :
She'll close and be herself, whilst our poor
malice
Remains in danger of her former tooth.
But let the frame of things disjoint, both the
worlds suffer,
Ere we will eat our meal in fear and sleep
In the affliction of these terrible dreams
That shake us nightly : better be with the dead,
Whom we, to gain our peace, have sent to
peace, 20
Than on the torture of the mind to lie
In restless ecstasy. Duncan is in his grave ;
After life's fitful fever he sleeps well ;
Treason has done his worst : nor steel, nor
poison,
Malice domestic, foreign levy, nothing,
Can touch him further.
Lady M. Come on ;
Gentle my lord, sleek o'er your rugged looks ;
Be bright and jovial among your guests to-
night.
Macb. So shall I, love ; and so, I pray, be
you :

Let your remembrance apply to Banquo ; 30
Present him eminence, both with eye and
tongue :
Unsafe the while, that we
Must lave our honors in these flattering
streams,
And make our faces vizards to our hearts,
Disguising what they are.
Lady M. You must leave this.
Macb. O, full of scorpions is my mind,
dear wife !
Thou know'st that Banquo, and his Fleance,
lives.
Lady M. But in them nature's copy's not
eterne.
Macb. There's comfort yet ; they are as-
sailable ;
Then be thou jocund : ere the bat hath flown
His cloister'd flight, ere to black Hecate's sum-
mons 41
The shard-borne beetle with his drowsy hums
Hath rung night's yawning peal, there shall be
done
A deed of dreadful note.
Lady M. What's to be done ?
Macb. Be innocent of the knowledge, dear-
est chuck,
Till thou applaud the deed. Come, seeling
night,
Scarf up the tender eye of pitiful day ;
And with thy bloody and invisible hand
Cancel and tear to pieces that great bond
Which keeps me pale ! Light thickens ; and
the crow 50
Makes wing to the rooky wood :
Good things of day begin to droop and
drowse ;
While night's black agents to their preys do
rouse.
Thou marvell'st at my words : but hold thee
still ;
Things bad begun make strong themselves by
ill.
So, prithee, go with me. [*Exeunt.*

SCENE III. *A park near the palace.*

Enter three Murderers.

First Mur. But who did bid thee join with
us ?
Third Mur. Macbeth.
Sec. Mur. He needs not our mistrust, since
he delivers
Our offices and what we have to do
To the direction just.
First Mur. Then stand with us.
The west yet glimmers with some streaks of
day :
Now spurs the lated traveller apace
To gain the timely inn ; and near approaches
The subject of our watch.
Third Mur. Hark ! I hear horses.
Ban. [*Within*] Give us a light there, ho !
Sec. Mur. Then 'tis he : the rest
That are within the note of expectation 10
Already are i' the court.
First Mur. His horses go about.
Third Mur. Almost a mile : but he does
usually,
So all men do, from hence to the palace gate
Make it their walk.
Sec. Mur. A light, a light !

Enter BANQUO, *and* FLEANCE *with a torch.*

Third Mur.   'Tis he.
First Mur. Stand to't.
Ban. It will be rain to-night.
First Mur.   Let it come down.
                    [*They set upon Banquo.*
Ban. O, treachery! Fly, good Fleance, fly,
    fly, fly!
Thou mayst revenge. O slave!
            [*Dies. Fleance escapes.*
Third Mur. Who did strike out the light?
First Mur.   Was't not the way?
Third Mur. There's but one down; the son
    is fled.
Sec. Mur.   We have lost 20
Best half of our affair.
First Mur. Well, let's away, and say how
    much is done.   [*Exeunt.*

SCENE IV. *The same. Hall in the palace.*

A banquet prepared. Enter MACBETH, LADY
MACBETH, ROSS, LENNOX, Lords, *and* Attendants.

Macb. You know your own degrees; sit
    down: at first
And last the hearty welcome.
Lords.   Thanks to your majesty.
Macb. Ourself will mingle with society,
And play the humble host.
Our hostess keeps her state, but in best time
We will require her welcome.
Lady M. Pronounce it for me, sir, to all
    our friends;
For my heart speaks they are welcome.

First Murderer appears at the door.

Macb. See, they encounter thee with their
    hearts' thanks.   9
Both sides are even: here I'll sit i' the midst:
Be large in mirth; anon we'll drink a measure
The table round. [*Approaching the door.*]
            There's blood upon thy face.
Mur. 'Tis Banquo's then.
Macb. 'Tis better thee without than he
    within.
Is he dispatch'd?
Mur. My lord, his throat is cut; that I did
    for him.
Macb. Thou art the best o' the cut-
    throats: yet he's good
That did the like for Fleance: if thou didst it,
Thou art the nonpareil.
Mur.   Most royal sir,
Fleance is 'scaped.   20
Macb. Then comes my fit again: I had
    else been perfect,
Whole as the marble, founded as the rock,
As broad and general as the casing air:
But now I am cabin'd, cribb'd, confined,
    bound in
To saucy doubts and fears. But Banquo's
    safe?
Mur. Ay, my good lord: safe in a ditch he
    bides,
With twenty trenched gashes on his head;
The least a death to nature.
Macb.   Thanks for that:
There the grown serpent lies; the worm that's
    fled
Hath nature that in time will venom breed, 30
No teeth for the present. Get thee gone: to-
    morrow

We'll hear, ourselves, again. [*Exit Murderer.*
Lady M.   My royal lord,
You do not give the cheer: the feast is sold
That is not often vouch'd, while 'tis a-making,
'Tis given with welcome: to feed were best at
    home;
From thence the sauce to meat is ceremony;
Meeting were bare without it.
Macb.   Sweet remembrancer!
Now, good digestion wait on appetite,
And health on both!
Len.   May't please your highness sit.
    [*The Ghost of Banquo enters, and sits in
            Macbeth's place.*
Macb. Here had we now our country's
    honor roof'd,   40
Were the graced person of our Banquo pres-
    ent;
Who may I rather challenge for unkindness
Than pity for mischance!
Ross.   His absence, sir,
Lays blame upon his promise. Please't your
    highness
To grace us with your royal company.
Macb. The table's full.
Len.   Here is a place reserved, sir.
Macb. Where?
Len. Here, my good lord. What is't that
    moves your highness?
Macb. Which of you have done this?
Lords.   What, my good lord?
Macb. Thou canst not say I did it: never
    shake   50
Thy gory locks at me.
Ross. Gentlemen, rise: his highness is not
    well.
Lady M. Sit, worthy friends: my lord is
    often thus,
And hath been from his youth: pray you, keep
    seat;
The fit is momentary; upon a thought
He will again be well: if much you note him,
You shall offend him and extend his passion:
Feed, and regard him not. Are you a man?
Macb. Ay, and a bold one, that dare look
    on that
Which might appal the devil.
Lady M.   O proper stuff! 60
This is the very painting of your fear:
This is the air-drawn dagger which, you said,
Led you to Duncan. O, these flaws and starts,
Impostors to true fear, would well become
A woman's story at a winter's fire,
Authorized by her grandam. Shame itself!
Why do you make such faces? When all's
    done,
You look but on a stool.
Macb. Prithee, see there! behold! look!
    lo! how say you?
Why, what care I? If thou canst nod, speak
    too.   70
If charnel-houses and our graves must send
Those that we bury back, our monuments
Shall be the maws of kites. [*Ghost vanishes.*
Lady M. What, quite unmann'd in folly?
Macb. If I stand here, I saw him.
Lady M.   Fie, for shame!
Macb. Blood hath been shed ere now, i'
    the olden time,
Ere human statute purged the gentle weal;
Ay, and since too, murders have been per-
    form'd
Too terrible for the ear: the times have been,

That, when the brains were out, the man would
    die,
And there an end; but now they rise again, 80
With twenty mortal murders on their crowns,
And push us from our stools: this is more
    strange
Than such a murder is.
    Lady M.   My worthy lord,
Your noble friends do lack you.
    Macb.   I do forget.
Do not muse at me, my most worthy friends;
I have a strange infirmity, which is nothing
To those that know me. Come, love and health
    to all;
Then I'll sit down. Give me some wine; fill
    full.
I drink to the general joy o' the whole table,
And to our dear friend Banquo, whom we
    miss;
Would he were here! to all, and him, we
    thirst,
And all to all.
    Lords.   Our duties, and the pledge.

Re-enter Ghost.

    Macb.   Avaunt! and quit my sight! let the
        earth hide thee!
Thy bones are marrowless, thy blood is cold;
Thou hast no speculation in those eyes
Which thou dost glare with!
    Lady M.   Think of this, good peers,
But as a thing of custom: 'tis no other;
Only it spoils the pleasure of the time.
    Macb.   What man dare, I dare: 99
Approach thou like the rugged Russian bear,
The arm'd rhinoceros, or the Hyrcan tiger;
Take any shape but that, and my firm nerves
Shall never tremble: or be alive again,
And dare me to the desert with thy sword;
If trembling I inhabit then, protest me
The baby of a girl. Hence, horrible shadow!
Unreal mockery, hence!   [*Ghost vanishes.*
                    Why, so: being gone,
I am a man again. Pray you, sit still.
    Lady M.   You have displaced the mirth,
        broke the good meeting,
With most admired disorder.
    Macb.   Can such things be, 110
And overcome us like a summer's cloud,
Without our special wonder? You make me
    strange
Even to the disposition that I owe,
When now I think you can behold such sights,
And keep the natural ruby of your cheeks,
When mine is blanch'd with fear.
    Ross.   What sights, my lord?
    Lady M.   I pray you, speak not; he grows
        worse and worse;
Question enrages him. At once, good night:
Stand not upon the order of your going,
But go at once.
    Len.   Good night; and better health 120
Attend his majesty!
    Lady M.   A kind good night to all!
    [*Exeunt all but Macbeth and Lady M.*
    Macb.   It will have blood; they say, blood
        will have blood:
Stones have been known to move and trees to
    speak;
Augurs and understood relations have
By magot-pies and choughs and rooks brought
    forth

The secret'st man of blood. What is the night?
    Lady M.   Almost at odds with morning,
        which is which.
    Macb.   How say'st thou, that Macduff de-
        nies his person
At our great bidding?
    Lady M.   Did you send to him, sir?
    Macb.   I hear it by the way; but I will
        send:
There's not a one of them but in his house 131
I keep a servant fee'd. I will to-morrow,
And betimes I will, to the weird sisters:
More shall they speak; for now I am bent to
    know,
By the worst means, the worst. For mine own
    good,
All causes shall give way: I am in blood
Stepp'd in so far that, should I wade no more,
Returning were as tedious as go o'er:
Strange things I have in head, that will to
    hand;
Which must be acted ere they may be scann'd.
    Lady M.   You lack the season of all na-
        tures, sleep.   141
    Macb.   Come, we'll to sleep. My strange
        and self-abuse
Is the initiate fear that wants hard use:
We are yet but young in deed.   [*Exeunt.*

Scene V.   *A Heath.*

Thunder.   Enter the three Witches
    meeting Hecate.

First Witch.   Why, how now, Hecate! you
        look angerly.
    Hec.   Have I not reason, beldams as you
        are,
Saucy and overbold? How did you dare
To trade and traffic with Macbeth
In riddles and affairs of death;
And I, the mistress of your charms,
The close contriver of all harms,
Was never call'd to bear my part,
Or show the glory of our art?
And, which is worse, all you have done   10
Hath been but for a wayward son,
Spiteful and wrathful, who, as others do,
Loves for his own ends, not for you.
But make amends now: get you gone,
And at the pit of Acheron
Meet me i' the morning: thither he
Will come to know his destiny:
Your vessels and your spells provide,
Your charms and every thing beside.
I am for the air; this night I'll spend   20
Unto a dismal and a fatal end:
Great business must be wrought ere noon:
Upon the corner of the moon
There hangs a vaporous drop profound;
I'll catch it ere it come to ground:
And that distill'd by magic sleights
Shall raise such artificial sprites
As by the strength of their illusion
Shall draw him on to his confusion:
He shall spurn fate, scorn death, and bear 30
He hopes 'bove wisdom, grace and fear:
And you all know, security
Is mortals' chiefest enemy.
    [*Music and a song within:* 'Come away,
            come away,' &c.
Hark! I am call'd; my little spirit, see,
Sits in a foggy cloud, and stays for me. [*Exit.*

First Witch. Come, let's make haste ; she'll
    soon be back again.   [*Exeunt.*

SCENE VI. *Forres. The palace.*
    Enter LENNOX *and another* Lord.

Len. My former speeches have but hit your
    thoughts,
Which can interpret further : only, I say,
Things have been strangely borne. The gra-
    cious Duncan
Was pitied of Macbeth : marry, he was dead :
And the right-valiant Banquo walk'd too late ;
Whom, you may say, if't please you, Fleance
    kill'd,
For Fleance fled : men must not walk too late.
Who cannot want the thought how monstrous
It was for Malcolm and for Donalbain   9
To kill their gracious father ? damned fact !
How it did grieve Macbeth ! did he not straight
In pious rage the two delinquents tear,
That were the slaves of drink and thralls of
    sleep ?
Was not that nobly done ? Ay, and wisely too ;
For 'twould have anger'd any heart alive
To hear the men deny't. So that, I say,
He has borne all things well : and I do think
That had he Duncan's sons under his key—
As, an't please heaven, he shall not—they
    should find
What 'twere to kill a father ; so should Fle-
    ance.   20
But, peace ! for from broad words and 'cause
    he fail'd
His presence at the tyrant's feast, I hear
Macduff lives in disgrace : sir, can you tell
Where he bestows himself ?
    Lord.   The son of Duncan,
From whom this tyrant holds the due of birth
Lives in the English court, and is received
Of the most pious Edward with such grace
That the malevolence of fortune nothing
Takes from his high respect : thither Macduff
Is gone to pray the holy king, upon his aid 30
To wake Northumberland and warlike Si-
    ward :
That, by the help of these—with Him above
To ratify the work—we may again
Give to our tables meat, sleep to our nights,
Free from our feasts and banquets bloody
    knives,
Do faithful homage and receive free honors :
All which we pine for now : and this report
Hath so exasperate the king that he
Prepares for some attempt of war.
    Len.   Sent he to Macduff ?
    Lord. He did : and with an absolute ' Sir,
    not I,'   40
The cloudy messenger turns me his back,
And hums, as who should say ' You'll rue the
    time
That clogs me with this answer.'
    Len.   And that well might
Advise him to a caution, to hold what distance
His wisdom can provide. Some holy angel
Fly to the court of England and unfold
His message ere he come, that a swift blessing
May soon return to this our suffering country
Under a hand accursed !
    Lord.   I'll send my prayers with him.
                            [*Exeunt.*

ACT IV.

SCENE I. *A cavern. In the middle, a boiling
                    cauldron.*

Thunder. Enter the three Witches.

First Witch. Thrice the brinded cat hath
    mew'd.
Sec. Witch. Thrice and once the hedge-pig
    whined.
Third Witch. Harpier cries 'Tis time, 'tis
    time.
First Witch. Round about the cauldron
    go ;
In the poison'd entrails throw.
Toad, that under cold stone
Days and nights has thirty-one
Swelter'd venom sleeping got,
Boil thou first i' the charmed pot.
    All. Double, double toil and trouble ; 10
Fire burn, and cauldron bubble.
    Sec. Witch. Fillet of a fenny snake,
In the cauldron boil and bake ;
Eye of newt and toe of frog,
Wool of bat and tongue of dog,
Adder's fork and blind-worm's sting,
Lizard's leg and owlet's wing,
For a charm of powerful trouble,
Like a hell-broth boil and bubble.
    All. Double, double toil and trouble ; 20
Fire burn and cauldron bubble.
    Third Witch. Scale of dragon, tooth of
    wolf,
Witches' mummy, maw and gulf
Of the ravin'd salt-sea shark,
Root of hemlock digg'd i' the dark,
Liver of blaspheming Jew,
Gall of goat, and slips of yew
Silver'd in the moon's eclipse,
Nose of Turk and Tartar's lips,
Finger of birth-strangled babe   30
Ditch-deliver'd by a drab,
Make the gruel thick and slab :
Add thereto a tiger's chaudron,
For the ingredients of our cauldron.
    All. Double, double toil and trouble ;
Fire burn and cauldron bubble.
    Sec. Witch. Cool it with a baboon's
    blood,
Then the charm is firm and good.

Enter HECATE *to the other three* Witches.

Hec. O well done ! I commend your pains ;
And every one shall share i' the gains ;   40
And now about the cauldron sing,
Live elves and fairies in a ring,
Enchanting all that you put in.
    [*Music and a song :* ' Black spirits,' &c.
                            [*Hecate retires.*
Sec. Witch. By the pricking of my thumbs,
Something wicked this way comes.
            Open, locks,
            Whoever knocks !

Enter MACBETH.

Macb. How now, you secret, black, and
    midnight hags !
What is't you do ?
    All.   A deed without a name.
Macb. I conjure you, by that which you
    profess,   50
Howe'er you come to know it, answer me :

Though you untie the winds and let them fight
Against the churches ; though the yesty waves
Confound and swallow navigation up ;
Though bladed corn be lodged and trees blown
    down ;
Though castles topple on their warders' heads ;
Though palaces and pyramids do slope
Their heads to their foundations ; though the
    treasure
Of nature's germens tumble all together,
Even till destruction sicken ; answer me   60
To what I ask you.
    First Witch.   Speak.
    Sec. Witch.   Demand.
    Third Witch.   We'll answer.
    First Witch. Say, if thou'dst rather hear it
        from our mouths,
Or from our masters ?
    Macb.   Call 'em ; let me see 'em.
    First Witch. Pour in sow's blood, that
        hath eaten
Her nine farrow ; grease that's sweaten
From the murderer's gibbet throw
Into the flame.
    All.   Come, high or low ;
Thyself and office deftly show !

    Thunder. First Apparition : *an armed*
        Head.

    Macb. Tell me, thou unknown power,—
    First Witch.   He knows thy thought :
Hear his speech, but say thou nought.   70
    First App. Macbeth ! Macbeth ! Macbeth !
    beware Macduff ;
Beware the thane of Fife. Dismiss me. Enough.
                  [*Descends.*
    Macb. Whate'er thou art, for thy good
    caution, thanks ;
Thou hast harp'd my fear aright : but one
    word more,—
    First Witch. He will not be commanded :
    here's another,
More potent than the first.

    Thunder. Second Apparition : *A bloody*
        Child.

    Sec. App. Macbeth ! Macbeth ! Macbeth !
    Macb. Had I three ears, I'ld hear thee.
    Sec. App. Be bloody, bold, and resolute ;
    laugh to scorn
The power of man, for none of woman born
Shall harm Macbeth.   [*Descends.* 81
    Macb. Then live, Macduff : what need I
    fear of thee ?
But yet I'll make assurance double sure,
And take a bond of fate : thou shalt not live ;
That I may tell pale-hearted fear it lies,
And sleep in spite of thunder.

    Thunder. Third Apparition : *a Child*
    crowned, with a tree in his hand.

                  What is this
That rises like the issue of a king,
And wears upon his baby-brow the round
And top of sovereignty ?
    All.   Listen, but speak not to't.
    Third App. Be lion-mettled, proud ; and
    take no care   90
Who chafes, who frets, or where conspirers
    are :
Macbeth shall never vanquish'd be until
Great Birnam wood to high Dunsinane hill
Shall come against him.   [*Descends.*

    Macb.   That will never be
Who can impress the forest, bid the tree
Unfix his earth-bound root ? Sweet bode-
    ments ! good !
Rebellion's head, rise never till the wood
Of Birnam rise, and our high-placed Macbeth
Shall live the lease of nature, pay his breath
To time and mortal custom. Yet my heart
Throbs to know one thing : tell me, if your art
Can tell so much : shall Banquo's issue ever
Reign in this kingdom ?
    All.   Seek to know no more.
    Macb. I will be satisfied : deny me this,
And an eternal curse fall on you ! Let me
    know.
Why sinks that cauldron ? and what noise is
    this ?   [*Hautboys.*
    First Witch. Show !
    Sec. Witch. Show !
    Third Witch. Show !
    All. Show his eyes, and grieve his heart ;
Come like shadows, so depart !   111

    A show of Eight Kings, *the last with a glass in*
    his hand ; Banquo's *Ghost following.*

    Macb. Thou art too like the spirit of Ban-
    quo : down !
Thy crown does sear mine eye-balls. And thy
    hair,
Thou other gold-bound brow, is like the first.
A third is like the former. Filthy hags !
Why do you show me this ? A fourth ! Start,
    eyes !
What, will the line stretch out to the crack of
    doom ?
Another yet ! A seventh ! I'll see no more :
And yet the eighth appears, who bears a glass
Which shows me many more ; and some I see
That two-fold balls and treble scepters carry :
Horrible sight ! Now, I see, 'tis true ;
For the blood-bolter'd Banquo smiles upon me,
And points at them for his. [*Apparitions van-
    ish.*] What, is this so ?
    First Witch. Ay, sir, all this is so : but why
Stands Macbeth thus amazedly ?
Come, sisters, cheer we up his sprites,
And show the best of our delights :
I'll charm the air to give a sound,
While you perform your antic round :   130
That this great king may kindly say,
Our duties did his welcome pay.
        [*Music. The witches dance and then*
              vanish, with Hecate.
    Macb. Where are they ? Gone ? Let this
    pernicious hour
Stand aye accursed in the calendar !
Come in, without there !

               Enter Lennox.

    Len.   What's your grace's will ?
    Macb. Saw you the weird sisters ?
    Len.   No, my lord.
    Macb. Came they not by you ?
    Len.   No, indeed, my lord.
    Macb. Infected be the air whereon they
    ride ;
And damn'd all those that trust them ! I did
    hear
The galloping of horse : who was't came by ?
    Len. 'Tis two or three, my lord, that bring
    you word   141
Macduff is fled to England.
    Macb.   Fled to England !

Len. Ay, my good lord.

Macb. Time, thou anticipatest my dread
    exploits :
The flighty purpose never is o'ertook
Unless the deed go with it ; from this moment
The very firstlings of my heart shall be
The firstlings of my hand. And even now,
To crown my thoughts with acts, be it thought
    and done :
The castle of Macduff I will surprise ;   150
Seize upon Fife ; give to the edge o' the sword
His wife, his babes, and all unfortunate souls
That trace him in his line. No boasting like a
    fool ;
This deed I'll do before this purpose cool.
But no more sights !—Where are these gen-
    tlemen ?
Come, bring me where they are.   [*Exeunt.*

    SCENE II. *Fife. Macduff's castle.*

    Enter LADY MACDUFF, *her* Son, *and* ROSS.

L. Macd. What had he done, to make him
    fly the land ?

Ross. You must have patience, madam.

L. Macd.   He had none :
His flight was madness : when our actions do
    not,
Our fears do make us traitors.

Ross.   You know not
Whether it was his wisdom or his fear.

L. Macd. Wisdom ! to leave his wife, to
    leave his babes,
His mansion and his titles in a place
From whence himself does fly ? He loves us
    not ;
He wants the natural touch : for the poor
    wren,
The most diminutive of birds, will fight,   10
Her young ones in her nest, against the owl.
All is the fear and nothing is the love ;
As little is the wisdom, where the flight
So runs against all reason.

Ross.   My dearest coz,
I pray you, school yourself : but for your hus-
    band,
He is noble, wise, judicious, and best knows
The fits o' the season. I dare not speak much
    further ;
But cruel are the times, when we are traitors
And do not know ourselves, when we hold
    rumor
From what we fear, yet know not what we
    fear,   20
But float upon a wild and violent sea
Each way and move. I take my leave of you :
Shall not be long but I'll be here again :
Things at the worst will cease, or else climb
    upward
To what they were before. My pretty cousin,
Blessing upon you !

L. Macd. Father'd he is, and yet he's fa-
    therless.

Ross. I am so much a fool, should I stay
    longer,
It would be my disgrace and your discomfort :
I take my leave at once.   [*Exit.*

L. Macd. Sirrah, your father's dead ;   30
And what will you do now ? How will you
    live ?

Son. As birds do, mother.

L. Macd.   What, with worms and flies ?

Son. With what I get, I mean ; and so do
    they.

L. Macd. Poor bird ! thou'ldst never fear
    the net nor lime,
The pitfall nor the gin.

Son. Why should I, mother ? Poor birds
    they are not set for.
My father is not dead, for all your saying.

L. Macd. Yes, he is dead ; how wilt thou
    do for a father ?

Son. Nay, how will you do for a husband ?

L. Macd. Why, I can buy me twenty at
    any market.   40

Son. Then you'll buy 'em to sell again.

L. Macd. Thou speak'st with all thy wit :
    and yet, i' faith,
With wit enough for thee.

Son. Was my father a traitor, mother ?

L. Macd. Ay, that he was.

Son. What is a traitor ?

L. Macd. Why, one that swears and lies.

Son. And be all traitors that do so ?

L. Macd. Every one that does so is a traitor, and must be hanged.   50

Son. And must they all be hanged that
swear and lie ?

L. Macd. Every one.

Son. Who must hang them ?

L. Macd. Why, the honest men.

Son. Then the liars and swearers are fools,
for there are liars and swearers enow to beat
the honest men and hang up them.

L. Macd. Now, God help thee, poor mon-
    key !
But how wilt thou do for a father ?   60

Son. If he were dead, you'ld weep for
him : if you would not, it were a good sign
that I should quickly have a new father.

L. Macd. Poor prattler, how thou talk'st !

    Enter a Messenger.

Mess. Bless you, fair dame ! I am not to
    you known,
Though in your state of honor I am perfect.
I doubt some danger does approach you
    nearly :
If you will take a homely man's advice,
Be not found here ; hence, with your little
    ones.
To fright you thus, methinks, I am too sav-
    age ;   70
To do worse to you were fell cruelty,
Which is too nigh your person. Heaven pre-
    serve you !
I dare abide no longer.   [*Exit.*

L. Macd.   Whither should I fly ?
I have done no harm. But I remember now
I am in this earthly world ; where to do harm
Is often laudable, to do good sometime
Accounted dangerous folly : why then, alas,
Do I put up that womanly defence,
To say I have done no harm ?

    Enter Murderers.

          What are these faces ?

First Mur. Where is your husband ?   80

L. Macd. I hope, in no place so unsancti-
    fied
Where such as thou mayst find him.

First Mur.   He's a traitor.

Son. Thou liest, thou shag-hair'd villain !

First Mur.   What, you egg !
            [*Stabbing him.*
Young fry of treachery !

Son.   He has kill'd me, mother :
Run away, I pray you !   [*Dies.*
    [*Exit Lady Macduff, crying* 'Murder !'
        Exeunt Murderers, following her.

Scene III. *England. Before the King's
        palace.*

        Enter Malcolm *and* Macduff.

Mal. Let us seek out some desolate shade,
        and there
Weep our sad bosoms empty.
    Macd.   Let us rather
Hold fast the mortal sword, and like good
        men
Bestride our down-fall'n birthdom : each new
        morn
New widows howl, new orphans cry, new sor-
        rows
Strike heaven on the face, that it resounds
As if it felt with Scotland and yell'd out
Like syllable of dolour.
    Mal.   What I believe I'll wail,
What know believe, and what I can redress,
As I shall find the time to friend, I will.   10
What you have spoke, it may be so perchance.
This tyrant, whose sole name blisters our
        tongues,
Was once thought honest : you have loved him
        well.
He hath not touch'd you yet. I am young ; but
        something
You may deserve of him through me, and wis-
        dom
To offer up a weak poor innocent lamb
To appease an angry god.
    Macd. I am not treacherous.
    Mal.   But Macbeth is.
A good and virtuous nature may recoil
In an imperial charge. But I shall crave your
        pardon ;   20
That which you are my thoughts cannot trans-
        pose :
Angels are bright still, though the brightest
        fell ;
Though all things foul would wear the brows
        of grace,
Yet grace must still look so.
    Macd.   I have lost my hopes.
    Mal. Perchance even there where I did find
        my doubts.
Why in that rawness left you wife and child,
Those precious motives, those strong knots of
        love,
Without leave-taking ? I pray you,
Let not my jealousies be your dishonors,
But mine own safeties. You may be rightly
        just,   30
Whatever I shall think.
    Macd.   Bleed, bleed, poor country !
Great tyranny ! lay thou thy basis sure,
For goodness dare not check thee : wear thou
        thy wrongs ;
The title is affeer'd ! Fare thee well, lord :
I would not be the villain that thou think'st
For the whole space that's in the tyrant's
        grasp,
And the rich East to boot.
    Mal.   Be not offended :
I speak not as in absolute fear of you.
I think our country sinks beneath the yoke ;
It weeps, it bleeds ; and each new day a gash
Is added to her wounds : I think withal   41

There would be hands uplifted in my right ;
And here from gracious England have I offer
Of goodly thousands : but, for all this,
When I shall tread upon the tyrant's head,
Or wear it on my sword, yet my poor country
Shall have more vices than it had before,
More suffer and more sundry ways than ever,
By him that shall succeed.
    Macd.   What should he be ?
    Mal. It is myself I mean : in whom I
        know
All the particulars of vice so grafted   51
That, when they shall be open'd, black Mac-
        beth
Will seem as pure as snow, and the poor state
Esteem him as a lamb, being compared
With my confineless harms.
    Macd.   Not in the legions
Of horrid hell can come a devil more damn'd
In evils to top Macbeth.
    Mal.   I grant him bloody,
Luxurious, avaricious, false, deceitful,
Sudden, malicious, smacking of every sin
That has a name : but there's no bottom,
        none,   60
In my voluptuousness : your wives, your
        daughters,
Your matrons and your maids, could not fill
        up
The cistern of my lust, and my desire
All continent impediments would o'erbear
That did oppose my will : better Macbeth
Than such an one to reign.
    Macd.   Boundless intemperance
In nature is a tyranny ; it hath been
The untimely emptying of the happy throne
And fall of many kings. But fear not yet
To take upon you what is yours : you may   70
Convey your pleasures in a spacious plenty,
And yet seem cold, the time you may so
        hoodwink.
We have willing dames enough : there cannot
        be
That vulture in you, to devour so many
As will to greatness dedicate themselves,
Finding it so inclined.
    Mal.   With this there grows
In my most ill-composed affection such
A stanchless avarice that, were I king,
I should cut off the nobles for their lands,
Desire his jewels and this other's house :   80
And my more-having would be as a sauce
To make me hunger more ; that I should
        forge
Quarrels unjust against the good and loyal,
Destroying them for wealth.
    Macd.   This avarice
Sticks deeper, grows with more pernicious
        root
Than summer-seeming lust, and it hath been
The sword of our slain kings : yet do not fear ;
Scotland hath foisons to fill up your will.
Of your mere own : all these are portable,
With other graces weigh'd.   90
    Mal. But I have none : the king-becoming
        graces,
As justice, verity, temperance, stableness,
Bounty, perseverance, mercy, lowliness,
Devotion, patience, courage, fortitude,
I have no relish of them, but abound
In the division of each several crime,
Acting it many ways. Nay, had I power, I
        should

Pour the sweet milk of concord into hell,
Uproar the universal peace, confound
All unity on earth.
 Macd.   O Scotland, Scotland ! 100
 Mal. If such a one be fit to govern, speak :
I am as I have spoken.
 Macd.   Fit to govern !
No, not to live. O nation miserable,
With an untitled tyrant bloody-scepter'd,
When shalt thou see thy wholesome days
 again,
Since that the truest issue of thy throne
By his own interdiction stands accursed,
And does blaspheme his breed ? Thy royal
 father
Was a most sainted king : the queen that bore
 thee,
Oftener upon her knees than on her feet, 110
Died every day she lived. Fare thee well !
These evils thou repeat'st upon thyself
Have banish'd me from Scotland. O my
 breast,
Thy hope ends here !
 Mal.   Macduff, this noble passion,
Child of integrity, hath from my soul
Wiped the black scruples, reconciled my
 thoughts
To thy good truth and honor. Devilish Mac-
 beth
By many of these trains hath sought to win
 me
Into his power, and modest wisdom plucks me
From over-credulous haste : but God above
Deal between thee and me ! for even now 121
I put myself to thy direction, and
Unspeak mine own detraction, here abjure
The taints and blames I laid upon myself,
For strangers to my nature. I am yet
Unknown to woman, never was forsworn,
Scarcely have coveted what was mine own,
At no time broke my faith, would not betray
The devil to his fellow and delight
No less in truth than life : my first false
 speaking
Was this upon myself : what I am truly, 131
Is thine and my poor country's to command :
Whither indeed, before thy here-approach,
Old Siward, with ten thousand warlike men,
Already at a point, was setting forth.
Now we'll together ; and the chance of good-
 ness
Be like our warranted quarrel ! Why are you
 silent ?
 Macd. Such welcome and unwelcome
 things at once
'Tis hard to reconcile.

    Enter a Doctor.

 Mal. Well ; more anon.—Comes the king
 forth, I pray you ?   140
 Doct. Ay, sir ; there are a crew of
 wretched souls
That stay his cure : their malady convinces
The great assay of art ; but at his touch—
Such sanctity hath heaven given his hand—
They presently amend.
 Mal. I thank you, doctor. [*Exit Doctor.*
 Macd. What's the disease he means ?
 Mal.   'Tis call'd the evil :
A most miraculous work in this good king ;
Which often, since my here-remain in Eng-
 land,
I have seen him do. How he solicits heaven,

Himself best knows : but strangely-visited
 people,   150
All swoln and ulcerous, pitiful to the eye,
The mere despair of surgery, he cures,
Hanging a golden stamp about their necks,
Put on with holy prayers : and 'tis spoken,
To the succeeding royalty he leaves
The healing benediction. With this strange vir-
 tue,
He hath a heavenly gift of prophecy,
And sundry blessings hang about his throne,
That speak him full of grace.

    Enter Ross.

 Macd.   See, who comes here ?
 Mal. My countryman ; but yet I know him
 not.   160
 Macd. My ever-gentle cousin, welcome
 hither.
 Mal. I know him now. Good God, be-
 times remove
The means that makes us strangers !
 Ross.   Sir, amen.
 Macd. Stands Scotland where it did ?
 Ross.   Alas, poor country !
Almost afraid to know itself. It cannot
Be call'd our mother, but our grave ; where
 nothing,
But who knows nothing, is once seen to smile ;
Where sighs and groans and shrieks that rend
 the air
Are made, not mark'd ; where violent sorrow
 seems
A modern ecstasy ; the dead man's knell 170
Is there scarce ask'd for who ; and good men's
 lives
Expire before the flowers in their caps,
Dying or ere they sicken.
 Macd.   O, relation
Too nice, and yet too true !
 Mal.   What's the newest grief ?
 Ross. That of an hour's age doth hiss the
 speaker :
Each minute teems a new one.
 Macd.   How does my wife ?
 Ross. Why, well.
 Macd.   And all my children ?
 Ross.   Well too.
 Macd. The tyrant has not batter'd at their
 peace ?
 Ross. No ; they were well at peace when
 I did leave 'em.
 Macd. But not a niggard of your speech :
 how goes't ?   180
 Ross. When I came hither to transport the
 tidings,
Which I have heavily borne, there ran a ru-
 mor
Of many worthy fellows that were out ;
Which was to my belief witness'd the rather,
For that I saw the tyrant's power a-foot :
Now is the time of help ; your eye in Scot-
 land
Would create soldiers, make our women fight,
To doff their dire distresses.
 Mal.   Be't their comfort
We are coming thither : gracious England
 hath
Lent us good Siward and ten thousand men ;
An older and a better soldier none   191
That Christendom gives out.
 Ross.   Would I could answer
This comfort with the like ! But I have words

That would be howl'd out in the desert air,
Where hearing should not latch them.
    Macd.   What concern they ?
The general cause ? or is it a fee-grief
Due to some single breast ?
    Ross.   No mind that's honest
But in it shares some woe ; though the main
     part
Pertains to you alone.
    Macd.   If it be mine,
Keep it not from me, quickly let me have it.
    Ross. Let not your ears despise my tongue
     for ever,   201
Which shall possess them with the heaviest
     sound
That ever yet they heard.
    Macd.   Hum ! I guess at it.
    Ross. Your castle is surprised ; your wife
     and babes
Savagely slaughter'd : to relate the manner,
Were, on the quarry of these murder'd deer,
To add the death of you.
    Mal.   Merciful heaven !
What, man ! ne'er pull your hat upon your
     brows ;
Give sorrow words : the grief that does not
     speak
Whispers the o'er-fraught heart and bids it
     break.
    Macd. My children too ?   210
    Ross.   Wife, children, servants, all
That could be found.
    Macd.   And I must be from thence !
My wife kill'd too ?
    Ross.   I have said.
    Mal.   Be comforted :
Let's make us medicines of our great revenge,
To cure this deadly grief.
    Macd. He has no children. All my pretty
     ones ?
Did you say all ? O hell-kite ! All ?
What, all my pretty chickens and their dam
At one fell swoop ?
    Mal. Dispute it like a man.
    Macd.   I shall do so ; 220
But I must also feel it as a man :
I cannot but remember such things were,
That were most precious to me. Did heaven
     look on,
And would not take their part ? Sinful Mac-
     duff,
They were all struck for thee ! naught that I
     am,
Not for their own demerits, but for mine,
Fell slaughter on their souls. Heaven rest them
     now !
    Mal. Be this the whetstone of your sword :
     let grief
Convert to anger ; blunt not the heart, enrage
     it.
    Macd. O, I could play the woman with
     mine eyes   230
And braggart with my tongue ! But, gentle
     heavens,
Cut short all intermission ; front to front
Bring thou this fiend of Scotland and myself ;
Within my sword's length set him ; if he
     'scape,
Heaven forgive him too !
    Mal.   This tune goes manly.
Come, go we to the king ; our power is ready ;
Our lack is nothing but our leave ; Macbeth
Is ripe for shaking, and the powers above

Put on their instruments. Receive what cheer
     you may :
The night is long that never finds the day. 240
                                   [*Exeunt.*

ACT V.

Scene I. *Dunsinane. Ante-room in the castle.*

Enter a Doctor of Physic *and a* Waiting-
            Gentlewoman.

    Doct. I have two nights watched with you,
but can perceive no truth in your report.
When was it she last walked ?
    Gent. Since his majesty went into the
field, I have seen her rise from her bed, throw
her night-gown upon her, unlock her closet,
take forth paper, fold it, write upon't, read it,
afterwards seal it, and again return to bed ;
yet all this while in a most fast sleep.   9
    Doct. A great perturbation in nature, to
receive at once the benefit of sleep, and do the
effects of watching ! In this slumbery agita-
tion, besides her walking and other actual performances, what, at any time, have you heard
her say ?
    Gent. That, sir, which I will not report
after her.
    Doct. You may to me : and 'tis most meet
you should.
    Gent. Neither to you nor any one ; having
no witness to confirm my speech.   21

    Enter Lady Macbeth, *with a taper.*

Lo you, here she comes ! This is her very
guise ; and, upon my life, fast asleep. Observe
her ; stand close.
    Doct. How came she by that light ?
    Gent. Why, it stood by her : she has light
by her continually ; 'tis her command.
    Doct. You see, her eyes are open.
    Gent. Ay, but their sense is shut.
    Doct. What is it she does now ? Look, how
she rubs her hands.   31
    Gent. It is an accustomed action with her,
to seem thus washing her hands : I have
known her continue in this a quarter of an
hour.
    Lady M. Yet here's a spot.
    Doct. Hark ! she speaks : I will set down
what comes from her, to satisfy my remembrance the more strongly.
    Lady M. Out, damned spot ! out, I say !—
One : two : why, then, 'tis time to do't.—Hell
is murky !—Fie, my lord, fie ! a soldier, and
afeard ? What need we fear who knows it,
when none can call our power to account ?—
Yet who would have thought the old man to
have had so much blood in him.
    Doct. Do you mark that ?
    Lady M. The thane of Fife had a wife :
where is she now ?—What, will these hands
ne'er be clean ?—No more o' that, my lord,
no more o' that : you mar all with this starting.   50
    Doct. Go to, go to ; you have known what
you should not.
    Gent. She has spoke what she should not,
I am sure of that : heaven knows what she
has known.
    Lady M. Here's the smell of the blood

still : all the perfumes of Arabia will not
sweeten this little hand. Oh, oh, oh!

Doct. What a sigh is there ! The heart is
sorely charged.   60

Gent. I would not have such a heart in my
bosom for the dignity of the whole body.

Doct. Well, well, well,—

Gent. Pray God it be, sir.

Doct. This disease is beyond my practice :
yet I have known those which have walked in
their sleep who have died holily in their beds.

Lady M. Wash your hands, put on your
nightgown ; look not so pale.—I tell you yet
again, Banquo's buried ; he cannot come out
on's grave.   71

Doct. Even so ?

Lady M. To bed, to bed ! there's knocking
at the gate : come, come, come, come, give
me your hand. What's done cannot be undone.—To bed, to bed, to bed !   [*Exit.*

Doct. Will she go now to bed ?

Gent. Directly.

Doct. Foul whisperings are abroad : un-
natural deeds
Do breed unnatural troubles : infected minds
To their deaf pillows will discharge their se-
crets :   81
More needs she the divine than the physician.
God, God forgive us all ! Look after her ;
Remove from her the means of all annoyance,
And still keep eyes upon her. So, good night :
My mind she has mated, and amazed my sight.
I think, but dare not speak.

Gent.   Good night, good doctor.
                                          [*Exeunt.*

SCENE II. *The country near Dunsinane.*

Drum and colors. Enter MENTEITH, CAITH-
    NESS, ANGUS, LENNOX, *and* Soldiers.

Ment. The English power is near, led on
by Malcolm,
His uncle Siward and the good Macduff :
Revenges burn in them ; for their dear causes
Would to the bleeding and the grim alarm
Excite the mortified man.

Ang.   Near Birnam wood
Shall we well meet them ; that way are they
coming.

Caith. Who knows if Donalbain be with
his brother ?

Len. For certain, sir, he is not : I have a
file
Of all the gentry : there is Siward's son,
And many unrough youths that even now   10
Protest their first of manhood.

Ment.   What does the tyrant ?

Caith. Great Dunsinane he strongly forti-
fies :
Some say he's mad ; others that lesser hate
him
Do call it valiant fury : but, for certain,
He cannot buckle his distemper'd cause
Within the belt of rule.

Ang.   Now does he feel
His secret murders sticking on his hands ;
Now minutely revolts upbraid his faith-
breach ;
Those he commands move only in command,
Nothing in love : now does he feel his title   20
Hang loose about him, like a giant's robe
Upon a dwarfish thief.

Ment.   Who then shall blame
His pester'd senses to recoil and start,

When all that is within him does condemn
Itself for being there ?

Caith.   Well, march we on,
To give obedience where 'tis truly owed :
Meet we the medicine of the sickly weal,
And with him pour we in our country's purge
Each drop of us.

Len.   Or so much as it needs,
To dew the sovereign flower and drown the
weeds.   30
Make we our march towards Birnam.
                                    [*Exeunt, marching.*

SCENE III. *Dunsinane. A room in the castle.*

Enter MACBETH, Doctor, *and* Attendants.

Macb. Bring me no more reports ; let
them fly all :
Till Birnam wood remove to Dunsinane,
I cannot taint with fear. What's the boy
Malcolm ?
Was he not born of woman ? The spirits that
know
All mortal consequences have pronounced me
thus :
' Fear not, Macbeth ; no man that's born of
woman
Shall e'er have power upon thee.' Then fly,
false thanes,
And mingle with the English epicures :
The mind I sway by and the heart I bear
Shall never sag with doubt nor shake with
fear.   10

Enter a Servant.

The devil damn thee black, thou cream-faced
loon !
Where got'st thou that goose look ?

Serv. There is ten thousand—

Macb.   Geese, villain !

Serv.   Soldiers, sir.

Macb. Go prick thy face, and over-red thy
fear,
Thou lily-liver'd boy. What soldiers, patch ?
Death of thy soul ! those linen cheeks of thine
Are counsellors to fear. What soldiers, whey-
face ?

Serv. The English force, so please you.

Macb. Take thy face hence. [*Exit Servant.*
                    Seyton !—I am sick at heart,
When I behold—Seyton, I say !—This push   20
Will cheer me ever, or disseat me now.
I have lived long enough : my way of life
Is fall'n into the sear, the yellow leaf ;
And that which should accompany old age,
As honor, love, obedience, troops of friends,
I must not look to have ; but, in their stead,
Curses, not loud but deep, mouth-honor,
breath,
Which the poor heart would fain deny, and
dare not.
Seyton !

Enter SEYTON.

Sey. What is your gracious pleasure ?

Macb.   What news more ?   30

Sey. All is confirm'd, my lord, which was
reported.

Macb. I'll fight till from my bones my
flesh be hack'd.
Give me my armor.

Sey.   'Tis not needed yet.

Macb. I'll put it on.

Send out more horses; skirr the country
round;
Hang those that talk of fear. Give me mine
armor.
How does your patient, doctor?
    Doct.   Not so sick, my lord,
As she is troubled with thick coming fancies,
That keep her from her rest.
    Macb.   Cure her of that.
Canst thou not minister to a mind diseased, 40
Pluck from the memory a rooted sorrow,
Raze out the written troubles of the brain
And with some sweet oblivious antidote
Cleanse the stuff'd bosom of that perilous stuff
Which weighs upon the heart?
    Doct.   Therein the patient
Must minister to himself.
    Macb.   Throw physic to the dogs; I'll none
of it.
Come, put mine armor on; give me my staff.
Seyton, send out. Doctor, the thanes fly from
me.
Come, sir, dispatch. If thou couldst, doctor,
cast   50
The water of my land, find her disease,
And purge it to a sound and pristine health,
I would applaud thee to the very echo,
That should applaud again.—Pull't off, I
say.—
What rhubarb, cyme, or what purgative drug,
Would scour these English hence? Hear'st
thou of them?
    Doct.   Ay, my good lord; your royal prep-
aration
Makes us hear something.
    Macb.   Bring it after me.
I will not be afraid of death and bane,
Till Birnam forest come to Dunsinane.   60
    Doct. [*Aside.*]   Were I from Dunsinane
away and clear,
Profit again should hardly draw me here.
                                            [*Exeunt.*

SCENE IV. *Country near Birnam wood.*

Drum and colors. Enter MALCOLM, *old* SI-
WARD *and his* Son, MACDUFF, MENTEITH,
CAITHNESS, ANGUS, LENNOX, ROSS, *and*
Soldiers, *marching.*

    Mal. Cousins, I hope the days are near at
hand
That chambers will be safe.
    Ment.   We doubt it nothing.
    Siw. What wood is this before us?
    Ment.   The wood of Birnam.
    Mal. Let every soldier hew him down a
bough
And bear't before him: thereby shall we
shadow
The numbers of our host and make discovery
Err in report of us.
    Soldiers.   It shall be done.
    Siw. We learn no other but the confident
tyrant
Keeps still in Dunsinane, and will endure
Our setting down before 't.
    Mal.   'Tis his main hope: 10
For where there is advantage to be given,
Both more and less have given him the revolt,
And none serve with him but constrained
things
Whose hearts are absent too.
    Macd.   Let our just censures

Attend the true event, and put we on
Industrious soldiership.
    Siw. ·   The time approaches
That will with due decision make us know
What we shall say we have and what we owe.
Thoughts speculative their unsure hopes relate,
But certain issue strokes must arbitrate :   20
Towards which advance the war.
                                    [*Exeunt, marching.*

SCENE V. *Dunsinane. Within the castle.*

Enter MACBETH, SEYTON, *and* Soldiers, *with
drum and colors.*

    Macb. Hang out our banners on the out-
ward walls;
The cry is still 'They come:' our castle's
strength
Will laugh a siege to scorn: here let them lie
Till famine and the ague eat them up:
Were they not forced with those that should
be ours,
We might have met them dareful, beard to
beard,
And beat them backward home.
                        [*A cry of women within.*
                        What is that noise?
    Sey. It is the cry of women, my good lord.
                                            [*Exit.*
    Macb. I have almost forgot the taste of
fears;
The time has been, my senses would have
cool'd   10
To hear a night-shriek; and my fell of hair
Would at a dismal treatise rouse and stir
As life were in't: I have supp'd full with
horrors;
Direness, familiar to my slaughterous thoughts
Cannot once start me.

    Re-enter SEYTON.

                        Wherefore was that cry?
    Sey. The queen, my lord, is dead.
    Macb. She should have died hereafter;
There would have been a time for such a
word.
To-morrow, and to-morrow, and to-morrow,
Creeps in this petty pace from day to day 20
To the last syllable of recorded time,
And all our yesterdays have lighted fools
The way to dusty death. Out, out, brief
candle!
Life's but a walking shadow, a poor player
That struts and frets his hour upon the stage
And then is heard no more: it is a tale
Told by an idiot, full of sound and fury,
Signifying nothing.

    Enter a Messenger.

Thou comest to use thy tongue; thy story
quickly.
    Mess. Gracious my lord,   30
I should report that which I say I saw,
But know not how to do it.
    Macb.   Well, say, sir.
    Mess. As I did stand my watch upon the
hill,
I look'd toward Birnam, and anon, methought,
The wood began to move.
    Macb.   Liar and slave!
    Mess. Let me endure your wrath, if't be
not so:
Within this three mile may you see it coming;
I say, a moving grove.

Macb.   If thou speak'st false,
Upon the next tree shalt thou hang alive,
Till famine cling thee : if thy speech be sooth,
I care not if thou dost for me as much.   41
I pull in resolution, and begin
To doubt the equivocation of the fiend
That lies like truth : 'Fear not, till Birnam
    wood
Do come to Dunsinane : ' and now a wood
Comes toward Dunsinane. Arm, arm, and
    out !
If this which he avouches does appear,
There is nor flying hence nor tarrying here.
I gin to be aweary of the sun,
And wish the estate o' the world were now
    undone.   50
Ring the alarum-bell ! Blow, wind ! come,
    wrack !
At least we'll die with harness on our back.
            [*Exeunt.*

SCENE VI. *Dunsinane. Before the castle.*

Drum and colors. Enter MALCOLM, *old* SI-
    WARD, MACDUFF, *and their* Army, *with
    boughs.*

Mal. Now near enough : your leafy screens
    throw down,
And show like those you are. You, worthy
    uncle,
Shall, with my cousin, your right-noble son,
Lead our first battle : worthy Macduff and we
Shall take upon 's what else remains to do,
According to our order.
Siw.   Fare you well.
Do we but find the tyrant's power to-night,
Let us be beaten, if we cannot fight.
Macd. Make all our trumpets speak ; give
    them all breath,
Those clamorous harbingers of blood and
    death.   [*Exeunt.* 10

SCENE VII. *Another part of the field.*

Alarums. Enter MACBETH.

Macb. They have tied me to a stake ; I
    cannot fly,
But, bear-like, I must fight the course. What's
    he
That was not born of woman ? Such a one
Am I to fear, or none.

Enter young SIWARD.

Yo. Siw. What is thy name ?
Macb.   Thou'lt be afraid to hear it.
Yo. Siw. No ; though thou call'st thyself
    a hotter name
Than any is in hell.
Macb.   My name's Macbeth.
Yo. Siw. The devil himself could not pro-
    nounce a title
More hateful to mine ear.
Macb.   No, nor more fearful.
Yo. Siw. Thou liest, abhorred tyrant ; with
    my sword   10
I'll prove the lie thou speak'st.
    [*They fight and young Siward is slain.*
Macb.   Thou wast born of woman
But swords I smile at, weapons laugh to scorn,
Brandish'd by man that's of a woman born.
            [*Exit.*

Alarums. Enter MACDUFF.

Macd. That way the noise is. Tyrant, show
    thy face !

If thou be'st slain and with no stroke of mine,
My wife and children's ghosts will haunt me
    still.
I cannot strike at wretched kerns, whose arms
Are hired to bear their staves : either thou,
    Macbeth,
Or else my sword with an unbatter'd edge
I sheathe again undeeded. There thou shouldst
    be ;   20
By this great clatter, one of greatest note
Seems bruited. Let me find him, fortune !
And more I beg not.   [*Exit. Alarums.*

Enter MALCOLM *and old* SIWARD.

Siw. This way, my lord ; the castle's gen-
    tly render'd :
The tyrant's people on both sides do fight ;
The noble thanes do bravely in the war ;
The day almost itself professes yours,
And little is to do.
Mal.   We have met with foes
That strike beside us.
Siw.   Enter, sir, the castle.
            [*Exeunt. Alarums.*

SCENE VIII. *Another part of the field.*

Enter MACBETH.

Macb. Why should I play the Roman fool,
    and die
On mine own sword ? whiles I see lives, the
    gashes
Do better upon them.

Enter MACDUFF.

Macd.   Turn, hell-hound, turn !
Macb. Of all men else I have avoided
    thee :
But get thee back ; my soul is too much
    charged
With blood of thine already.
Macd.   I have no words :
My voice is in my sword : thou bloodier vil-
    lain
Than terms can give thee out !   [*They fight.*
Macb.   Thou losest labor :
As easy mayst thou the intrenchant air
With thy keen sword impress as make me
    bleed :
Let fall thy blade on vulnerable crests ;   11
I bear a charmed life, which must not yield,
To one of woman born.
Macd.   Despair thy charm ;
And let the angel whom thou still hast served
Tell thee, Macduff was from his mother's
    womb
Untimely ripp'd.
Macb. Accursed be that tongue that tells
    me so,
For it hath cow'd my better part of man !
And be these juggling fiends no more believed,
That palter with us in a double sense ;   20
That keep the word of promise to our ear,
And break it to our hope. I'll not fight with
    thee.
Macd. Then yield thee, coward,
And live to be the show and gaze o' the time :
We'll have thee, as our rarer monsters are,
Painted upon a pole, and underwrit,
'Here may you see the tyrant.'
Macb.   I will not yield,
To kiss the ground before young Malcolm's
    feet,
And to be baited with the rabble's curse.   29

Though Birnam wood be come to Dunsinane,
And thou opposed, being of no woman born,
Yet I will try the last. Before my body
I throw my warlike shield. Lay on, Macduff,
And damn'd be him that first cries, ' Hold,
    enough ! '   *[Exeunt, fighting. Alarums.*

*Retreat. Flourish. Enter, with drum and
colors,* MALCOLM, *old* SIWARD, ROSS, *the
other* Thanes, *and* Soldiers.

Mal. I would the friends we miss were safe
    arrived.
Siw. Some must go off : and yet, by these
    I see,
So great a day as this is cheaply bought.
Mal. Macduff is missing, and your noble
    son.
Ross. Your son, my lord, has paid a sol-
    dier's debt :
He only lived but till he was a man ;   40
The which no sooner had his prowess con-
    firm'd
In the unshrinking station where he fought,
But like a man he died.
Siw.   Then he is dead ?
Ross. Ay, and brought off the field : your
    cause of sorrow
Must not be measured by his worth, for then
It hath no end.
Siw.   Had he his hurts before ?
Ross. Ay, on the front.
Siw.   Why then, God's soldier be he !
Had I as many sons as I have hairs,
I would not wish them to a fairer death :
And so, his knell is knoll'd.
Mal.   He's worth more sorrow,   50

And that I'll spend for him.
Siw.   He's worth no more
They say he parted well, and paid his score :
And so, God be with him ! Here comes newer
    comfort.

Re-enter MACDUFF, *with* MACBETH'S *head.*

Macd. Hail, king ! for so thou art : be-
    hold, where stands
The usurper's cursed head : the time is free :
I see thee compass'd with thy kingdom's pearl,
That speak my salutation in their minds ;
Whose voices I desire aloud with mine :
Hail, King of Scotland !
All. Hail, King of Scotland !   *[Flourish.*
Mal. We shall not spend a large expense
    of time   60
Before we reckon with your several loves,
And make us even with you. My thanes and
    kinsmen,
Henceforth be earls, the first that ever Scot-
    land
In such an honor named. What's more to do,
Which would be planted newly with the time,
As calling home our exiled friends abroad
That fled the snares of watchful tyranny ;
Producing forth the cruel ministers
Of this dead butcher and his fiend-like queen,
Who, as 'tis thought, by self and violent
    hands   70
Took off her life ; this, and what needful else
That calls upon us, by the grace of Grace,
We will perform in measure, time and place :
So, thanks to all at once and to each one,
Whom we invite to see us crown'd at Scone.
    [Flourish. Exeunt.

ANTONY AND CLEOPATRA.

(WRITTEN ABOUT 1607.)

INTRODUCTION.

This play, though by the person of Antony it connects itself with *Julius Cæsar*, is a striking contrast to it in subject and style, and is separated from it in the chronological order by a wide interval. In May of the year 1608, Blount (afterwards one of the publishers of the First Folio) entered in the Stationers' register *A Book called Antony and Cleopatra*. This was probably Shakespeare's tragedy. The source of the play is the life of Antonius in North's *Plutarch*. Shakespeare had found in *Plutarch* his Brutus almost ready made to his hand ; he deemed it necessary to transform and transfigure the Antony of history, stained as he is not only by crimes of voluptuousness but of cruelty. "Of all Shakespeare's historical plays," says Coleridge, "*Antony and Cleopatra* is by far the most wonderful," and he calls attention to what he terms its "happy valiancy" of style. Shakespeare, indeed, nowhere seems a greater master of a great dramatic theme. The moral ideals, the doctrines, the stoical habits and stoical philosophy of Brutus and Portia, are as remote as possible from the sensuous splendors of the life in Egypt, from Antony's careless magnificence of strength, and the beauty, the arts, and the endless variety of Cleopatra. Yet, though the tragedy has all the glow and color of oriental magnificence, it remains true at heart to the moral laws which govern human life. The worship of pleasure by the Egyptian queen and her paramour is, after all, a failure, even from the first. There is no true confidence, no steadfast strength of love possible between Antony and his "serpent of old Nile." Each inspires the other with a mastering spirit of fascination, but Antony knows not the moment when Cleopatra may be faithless to him, and Cleopatra weaves her endless snares to retain her power over Antony. The great Roman soldier gradually loses his energy, his judgment, and even his joy in life ; at last, the despair of spent forces settles down upon him, and it is only out of despair that he snatches strength enough to fight fiercely when driven to bay. He is the ruin of Cleopatra's magic. Upon Cleopatra herself the genius of Shakespeare has been lavished. She is the most wonderful of his creations of women, formed of the greatest number of elements— apparently conflicting elements, yet united by the mystery of life. While creating, with so much imaginative ardor, his Cleopatra, Shakespeare yet stands away from her, and, in a manner, criticises her. Enobarbus, who sees through every wile and guile of the Queen, is, as it were, a chorus to the play, a looker-on at the game ; he stands clear of the golden haze which makes up the atmosphere around Cleopatra ; and yet he is not a mere critic or commentator (Shakespeare never permitting the presence of a person in his drama who is not a true portion of it). Enobarbus himself is under the influence of the charm of Antony, and slays himself because he has wronged his master. The figures of Antony and the Queen are ennobled and elevated by the strong power of attraction, even of devotion, which they exert over those about them— Antony over Enobarbus, Cleopatra over her attendants, Charmian and Iras.

DRAMATIS PERSONÆ.

MARK ANTONY,
OCTAVIUS CÆSAR, } triumvirs.
M. ÆMILIUS LEPIDUS,
SEXTUS POMPEIUS.
DOMITIUS ENOBARBUS,
VENTIDIUS,
EROS,
SCARUS, } friends to Antony.
DERCETAS,
DEMETRIUS,
PHILO,
MECÆNAS,
AGRIPPA,
DOLABELLA,
PROCULEIUS, } friends to Cæsar.
THYREUS,
GALLUS,
MENAS,
MENECRATES, } friends to Pompey.
VARRIUS,

TAURUS, lieutenant-general to Cæsar.
CANIDIUS, lieutenant-general to Antony.
SILIUS, an officer in Ventidius's army.
EUPHRONIUS, an ambassador from Antony to Cæsar.

ALEXAS,
MARDIAN, a Eunuch. } attendants on Cleopatra.
SELEUCUS,
DIOMEDES,
A Soothsayer.
A Clown.

CLEOPATRA, queen of Egypt.
OCTAVIA, sister to Cæsar and wife to Antony.
CHARMIAN, } attendants on Cleopatra.
IRAS,

Officers, Soldiers, Messengers, and other Attendants.

SCENE : *In several parts of the Roman empire.*

ACT I.

SCENE I. *Alexandria. A room in Cleopatra's palace.*

Enter DEMETRIUS *and* PHILO.

Phi. Nay, but this dotage of our general's
O'erflows the measure : those his goodly eyes,
That o'er the files and musters of the war
Have glow'd like plated Mars, now bend, now turn,
The office and devotion of their view
Upon a tawny front : his captain's heart,
Which in the scuffles of great fights hath burst
The buckles on his breast, reneges all temper,
And is become the bellows and the fan
To cool a gipsy's lust.

Flourish. Enter ANTONY, CLEOPATRA, *her Ladies, the Train, with Eunuchs fanning her.*

                  Look, where they come :   10
Take but good note, and you shall see in him.
The triple pillar of the world transform'd
Into a strumpet's fool : behold and see.

Cleo. If it be love indeed, tell me how much.

Ant. There's beggary in the love that can be reckon'd.

Cleo. I'll set a bourn how far to be beloved.

Ant. Then must thou needs find out new heaven, new earth.

Enter an Attendant.

Att. News, my good lord, from Rome.

Ant. Grates me : the sum.

Cleo. Nay, hear them, Antony :
Fulvia perchance is angry ; or, who knows 20
If the scarce-bearded Cæsar have not sent
His powerful mandate to you, ' Do this, or this ;
Take in that kingdom, and enfranchise that ;
Perform 't, or else we damn thee.'

Ant.   How, my love !

Cleo. Perchance ! nay, and most like :
You must not stay here longer, your dismission
Is come from Cæsar ; therefore hear it, Antony.
Where's Fulvia's process ? Cæsar's I would say ? both ?
Call in the messengers. As I am Egypt's queen,
Thou blushest, Antony ; and that blood of thine   30
Is Cæsar's homager : else so thy cheek pays shame
When shrill-tongued Fulvia scolds. The messengers !

Ant. Let Rome in Tiber melt, and the wide arch
Of the ranged empire fall ! Here is my space.
Kingdoms are clay : our dungy earth alike
Feeds beast as man : the nobleness of life
Is to do thus ; when such a mutual pair
                              [*Embracing.*
And such a twain can do 't, in which I bind,
On pain of punishment, the world to weet
We stand up peerless.

Cleo.   Excellent falsehood !   40
Why did he marry Fulvia, and not love her ?
I'll seem the fool I am not ; Antony
Will be himself.

Ant.   But stirr'd by Cleopatra.
Now, for the love of Love and her soft hours,
Let's not confound the time with conference harsh :
There's not a minute of our lives should stretch
Without some pleasure now. What sport to-night ?

Cleo. Hear the ambassadors.

Ant.   Fie, wrangling queen !
Whom every thing becomes, to chide, to laugh,
To weep ; whose every passion fully strives 50
To make itself, in thee, fair and admired !
No messenger, but thine ; and all alone
To-night we'll wander through the streets and note
The qualities of people. Come, my queen ;
Last night you did desire it : speak not to us.
[*Exeunt Ant. and Cleo. with their train.*

Dem. Is Cæsar with Antonius prized so slight ?

Phi. Sir, sometimes, when he is not Antony,
He comes too short of that great property
Which still should go with Antony.

Dem.   I am full sorry
That he approves the common liar, who   60
Thus speaks of him at Rome : but I will hope
Of better deeds to-morrow. Rest you happy !
                                    [*Exeunt.*

SCENE II. *The same. Another room.*

Enter CHARMIAN, IRAS, ALEXAS, *and a* Soothsayer.

Char. Lord Alexas, sweet Alexas, most any thing Alexas, almost most absolute Alexas, where's the soothsayer that you praised so to the queen ? O, that I knew this husband, which, you say, must charge his horns with garlands !

Alex. Soothsayer !

Sooth. Your will ?

Char. Is this the man ? Is't you, sir, that know things ?

Sooth. In nature's infinite book of secrecy A little I can read.

Alex.   Show him your hand.   10

Enter ENOBARBUS.

Eno. Bring in the banquet quickly ; wine enough
Cleopatra's health to drink.

Char. Good sir, give me good fortune.

Sooth. I make not, but foresee.

Char. Pray, then, foresee me one.

Sooth. You shall be yet far fairer than you are.

Char. He means in flesh.

Iras. No, you shall paint when you are old.

Char. Wrinkles forbid !

Alex. Vex not his prescience ; be attentive.

Char. Hush !   21

Sooth. You shall be more beloving than beloved.

Char. I had rather heat my liver with drinking.

Alex. Nay, hear him.

Char. Good now, some excellent fortune ! Let me be married to three kings in a forenoon, and widow them all : let me have a child at fifty, to whom Herod of Jewry may do homage : find me to marry me with Octavius Cæsar, and companion me with my mistress.

Sooth. You shall outlive the lady whom
you serve.   31
Char. O excellent! I love long life better
than figs.
Sooth. You have seen and proved a fairer
former fortune
Than that which is to approach.
Char. Then belike my children shall have
no names: prithee, how many boys and
wenches must I have?
Sooth. If every of your wishes had a
womb,
And fertile every wish, a million.
Char. Out, fool! I forgive thee for a
witch.
Alex. You think none but your sheets are
privy to your wishes.   41
Char. Nay, come, tell Iras hers.
Alex. We'll know all our fortunes.
Eno. Mine, and most of our fortunes, to-
night, shall be—drunk to bed.
Iras. There's a palm presages chastity, if
nothing else.
Char. E'en as the o'erflowing Nilus pre-
sageth famine.   50
Iras. Go, you wild bedfellow, you cannot
soothsay.
Char. Nay, if an oily palm be not a fruit-
ful prognostication, I cannot scratch mine ear.
Prithee, tell her but a worky-day fortune.
Sooth. Your fortunes are alike.
Iras. But how, but how? give me par-
ticulars.
Sooth. I have said.
Iras. Am I not an inch of fortune better
than she?   60
Char. Well, if you were but an inch of fortune better than I, where would you choose
it?
Iras. Not in my husband's nose.
Char. Our worser thoughts heavens mend!
Alexas,—come, his fortune, his fortune! O,
let him marry a woman that cannot go, sweet
Isis, I beseech thee! and let her die too, and
give him a worse! and let worst follow worse,
till the worst of all follow him laughing to his
grave, fifty-fold a cuckold! Good Isis, hear
me this prayer, though thou deny me a matter
of more weight; good Isis, I beseech thee!
Iras. Amen. Dear goddess, hear that
prayer of the people! for, as it is a heart-
breaking to see a handsome man loose-wived,
so it is a deadly sorrow to behold a foul knave
uncuckolded: therefore, dear Isis, keep decorum, and fortune him accordingly!
Char. Amen.   79
Alex. Lo, now, if it lay in their hands to
make me a cuckold, they would make themselves whores, but they'ld do't!
Eno. Hush! here comes Antony.
Char.   Not he; the queen.

Enter CLEOPATRA.

Cleo. Saw you my lord?
Eno.   No, lady.
Cleo.   Was he not here?
Char. No, madam.
Cleo. He was disposed to mirth; but on
the sudden
A Roman thought hath struck him. Enobar-
bus!
Eno. Madam?

Cleo. Seek him, and bring him hither.
Where's Alexas?
Alex. Here, at your service. My lord ap-
proaches.   90
Cleo. We will not look upon him: go with
us.   [*Exeunt.*

Enter ANTONY with a Messenger and Attend-
ants.

Mess. Fulvia thy wife first came into the
field.
Ant. Against my brother Lucius?
Mess. Ay:
But soon that war had end, and the time's
state
Made friends of them, joining their force
'gainst Cæsar;
Whose better issue in the war, from Italy,
Upon the first encounter, drave them.
Ant.   Well, what worst?
Mess. The nature of bad news infects the
teller.
Ant. When it concerns the fool or coward.
On: 100
Things that are past are done with me. 'Tis
thus:
Who tells me true, though in his tale lie death,
I hear him as he flatter'd.
Mess.   Labienus—
This is stiff news—hath, with his Parthian
force,
Extended Asia from Euphrates;
His conquering banner shook from Syria
To Lydia and to Ionia;
Whilst—
Ant. Antony, thou wouldst say,—
Mess.   O, my lord!
Ant. Speak to me home, mince not the
general tongue:
Name Cleopatra as she is call'd in Rome; 110
Rail thou in Fulvia's phrase; and taunt my
faults
With such full license as both truth and mal-
ice
Have power to utter. O, then we bring forth
weeds,
When our quick minds lie still; and our ills
told us
Is as our earing. Fare thee well awhile.
Mess. At your noble pleasure.   [*Exit.*
Ant. From Sicyon, ho, the news! Speak
there!
First Att. The man from Sicyon,—is there
such an one?
Sec. Att. He stays upon your will.
Ant.   Let him appear.
These strong Egyptian fetters I must break,
Or lose myself in dotage.   121

Enter another Messenger.

What are you?
Sec. Mess. Fulvia thy wife is dead.
Ant.   Where died she?
Sec. Mess. In Sicyon:
Her length of sickness, with what else more
serious
Importeth thee to know, this bears.
                             [*Gives a letter.*
Ant.   Forbear me.
                        [*Exit Sec. Messenger.*
There's a great spirit gone! Thus did I de-
sire it:
What our contempt doth often hurl from us,

We wish it ours again ; the present pleasure,
By revolution lowering, does become
The opposite of itself : she's good, being gone ;
The hand could pluck her back that shoved
   her on.   131
I must from this enchanting queen break off :
Ten thousand harms, more than the ills I
   know,
My idleness doth hatch. How now ! Enobar-
   bus !

Re-enter Enobarbus.

Eno. What's your pleasure, sir ?
Ant. I must with haste from hence.
Eno. Why, then, we kill all our women :
we see how mortal an unkindness is to them ;
if they suffer our departure, death's the word.
Ant. I must be gone.   140
Eno. Under a compelling occasion, let
women die ; it were pity to cast them away
for nothing ; though, between them and a great
cause, they should be esteemed nothing. Cleopatra, catching but the least noise of this, dies
instantly ; I have seen her die twenty times
upon far poorer moment : I do think there
is mettle in death, which commits some loving
act upon her, she hath such a celerity in dying.
Ant. She is cunning past man's thought. 150
Eno. Alack, sir, no ; her passions are made
of nothing but the finest part of pure love : we
cannot call her winds and waters sighs and
tears ; they are greater storms and tempests
than almanacs can report : this cannot be cunning in her ; if it be, she makes a shower of
rain as well as Jove.
Ant. Would I had never seen her.
Eno. O, sir, you had then left unseen a
wonderful piece of work ; which not to have
been blest withal would have discredited your
travel.
Ant. Fulvia is dead.
Eno. Sir ?
Ant. Fulvia is dead.
Eno. Fulvia !
Ant. Dead.
Eno. Why, sir, give the gods a thankful
sacrifice. When it pleaseth their deities to take
the wife of a man from him, it shows to man
the tailors of the earth ; comforting therein,
that when old robes are worn out, there are
members to make new. If there were no more
women but Fulvia, then had you indeed a cut,
and the case to be lamented : this grief is
crowned with consolation ; your old smock
brings forth a new petticoat : and indeed the
tears live in an onion that should water this
sorrow.
Ant. The business she hath broached in the
   state
Cannot endure my absence.   179
Eno. And the business you have broached
here cannot be without you ; especially that
of Cleopatra's, which wholly depends on your
abode.
Ant. No more light answers. Let our offi-
   cers
Have notice what we purpose. I shall break
The cause of our expedience to the queen,
And get her leave to part. For not alone
The death of Fulvia, with more urgent touches,
Do strongly speak to us ; but the letters too
Of many our contriving friends in Rome
Petition us at home : Sextus Pompeius   190
Hath given the dare to Cæsar, and commands
The empire of the sea : our slippery people,
Whose love is never link'd to the deserver
Till his deserts are past, begin to throw
Pompey the Great and all his dignities
Upon his son ; who, high in name and power,
Higher than both in blood and life, stands up
For the main soldier : whose quality, going on,
The sides o' the world may danger : much is
   breeding,
Which, like the courser's hair, hath yet but
   life,   200
And not a serpent's poison. Say, our pleasure,
To such whose place is under us, requires
Our quick remove from hence.
Eno. I shall do't.   [*Exeunt.*

Scene III. *The same. Another room.*

Enter Cleopatra, Charmian, Iras, *and*
   Alexas.

Cleo. Where is he ?
Char.   I did not see him since.
Cleo. See where he is, who's with him,
   what he does :
I did not send you : if you find him sad,
Say I am dancing ; if in mirth, report
That I am sudden sick : quick, and return.
   [*Exit Alexas.*
Char. Madam, methinks, if you did love
   him dearly,
You do not hold the method to enforce
The like from him.
Cleo.   What should I do, I do not ?
Char. In each thing give him way, cross
   him in nothing.
Cleo. Thou teachest like a fool ; the way
   to lose him.   10
Char. Tempt him not so too far ; I wish,
   forbear :
In time we hate that which we often fear.
But here comes Antony.

Enter Antony.

Cleo.   I am sick and sullen.
Ant. I am sorry to give breathing to my
   purpose,—
Cleo. Help me away, dear Charmian ; I
   shall fall :
It cannot be thus long, the sides of nature
Will not sustain it.
Ant.   Now, my dearest queen,—
Cleo. Pray you, stand further from me.
Ant.   What's the matter ?
Cleo. I know, by that same eye, there's
   some good news.
What says the married woman ? You may go :
Would she had never given you leave to
   come !   21
Let her not say 'tis I that keep you here :
I have no power upon you ; hers you are.
Ant. The gods best know,—
Cleo.   O, never was there queen
So mightily betray'd ! yet at the first
I saw the treasons planted.
Ant.   Cleopatra,—
Cleo. Why should I think you can be mine
   and true,
Though you in swearing shake the throned
   gods,
Who have been false to Fulvia ? Riotous mad-
   ness,
To be entangled with those mouth-made vows,
Which break themselves in swearing !   31

Ant. 　　　　　　　Most sweet queen,—
Cleo. Nay, pray you, seek no color for
　　your going,
But bid farewell, and go : when you sued
　　staying,
Then was the time for words : no going then ;
Eternity was in our lips and eyes,
Bliss in our brows' bent ; none our parts so
　　poor,
But was a race of heaven : they are so still,
Or thou, the greatest soldier of the world,
Art turn'd the greatest liar.
　　Ant. 　　　　　　How now, lady !
　　Cleo. I would I had thy inches ; thou
　　　　shouldst know　　　　　　　　40
There were a heart in Egypt.
　　Ant. 　　　　　　Hear me, queen :
The strong necessity of time commands
Our services awhile ; but my full heart
Remains in use with you. Our Italy
Shines o'er with civil swords : Sextus Pom-
　　peius
Makes his approaches to the port of Rome :
Equality of two domestic powers
Breed scrupulous faction : the hated, grown to
　　strength,
Are newly grown to love : the condemn'd
　　Pompey,
Rich in his father's honor, creeps apace,　50
Into the hearts of such as have not thrived
Upon the present state, whose numbers
　　threaten ;
And quietness, grown sick of rest, would purge
By any desperate change : my more particular,
And that which most with you should safe my
　　going,
Is Fulvia's death.
　　Cleo. Though age from folly could not give
　　me freedom,
It does from childishness : can Fulvia die ?
　　Ant. She's dead, my queen :　　　59
Look here, and at thy sovereign leisure read
The garboils she awaked ; at the last, best :
See when and where she died.
　　Cleo. 　　　　　O most false love !
Where be the sacred vials thou shouldst fill
With sorrowful water ? Now I see, I see,
In Fulvia's death, how mine received shall be.
　　Ant. Quarrel no more, but be prepared to
　　know
The purposes I bear ; which are, or cease,
As you shall give the advice. By the fire
That quickens Nilus' slime, I go from hence
Thy soldier, servant ; making peace or war　70
As thou affect'st.
　　Cleo. 　　Cut my lace, Charmian, come ;
But let it be : I am quickly ill, and well,
So Antony loves.
　　Ant. 　　　My precious queen, forbear ;
And give true evidence to his love, which
　　stands
An honorable trial.
　　Cleo. 　　　　So Fulvia told me.
I prithee, turn aside and weep for her,
Then bid adieu to me, and say the tears
Belong to Egypt : good now, play one scene
Of excellent dissembling ; and let it look
Life perfect honor.
　　Ant. 　　You'll heat my blood : no more.　80
　　Cleo. You can do better yet ; but this is
　　meetly.
　　Ant. Now, by my sword,—
　　Cleo. 　　　　　And target. Still he mends ;

But this is not the best. Look, prithee, Char-
　　mian,
How this Herculean Roman does become
The carriage of his chafe.
　　Ant. I'll leave you, lady.
　　Cleo. 　　　　Courteous lord, one word.
Sir, you and I must part, but that's not it :
Sir, you and I have loved, but there's not it ;
That you know well : something it is I would,
O, my oblivion is a very Antony,　　　90
And I am all forgotten.
　　Ant. 　　　But that your royalty
Holds idleness your subject, I should take you
For idleness itself.
　　Cleo. 　　　'Tis sweating labor
To bear such idleness so near the heart
As Cleopatra this. But, sir, forgive me ;
Since my becomings kill me, when they do not
Eye well to you : your honor calls you hence ;
Therefore be deaf to my unpitied folly.
And all the gods go with you ! upon your
　　sword
Sit laurel victory ! and smooth success　100
Be strew'd before your feet !
　　Ant. 　　　　Let us go. Come ;
Our separation so abides, and flies,
That thou, residing here, go'st yet with me,
And I, hence fleeting, here remain with thee.
Away !　　　　　　　　　　　　　[*Exeunt.*

SCENE IV. *Rome. Cæsar's house.*

Enter OCTAVIUS CÆSAR, *reading a letter,*
LEPIDUS, *and their* Train.

　　Cæs. You may see, Lepidus, and hence-
　　forth know,
It is not Cæsar's natural vice to hate
Our great competitor : from Alexandria
This is the news : he fishes, drinks, and wastes
The lamps of night in revel ; is not more man-
　　like
Than Cleopatra ; nor the queen of Ptolemy
More womanly than he ; hardly gave audience,
　　or
Vouchsafed to think he had partners : you
　　shall find there
A man who is the abstract of all faults
That all men follow.
　　Lep. 　　I must not think there are　10
Evils enow to darken all his goodness :
His faults in him seem as the spots of heaven,
More fiery by night's blackness ; hereditary,
Rather than purchased ; what he cannot
　　change,
Than what he chooses.
　　Cæs. You are too indulgent. Let us grant,
　　it is not
Amiss to tumble on the bed of Ptolemy ;
To give a kingdom for a mirth ; to sit
And keep the turn of tippling with a slave ;
To reel the streets at noon, and stand the
　　buffet　　　　　　　　　　　　20
With knaves that smell of sweat : say this be-
　　comes him,—
As his composure must be rare indeed
Whom these things cannot blemish,—yet must
　　Antony
No way excuse his soils, when we do bear
So great weight in his lightness. If he fill'd
His vacancy with his voluptuousness,
Full surfeits, and the dryness of his bones,
Call on him for't : but to confound such time,
That drums him from his sport, and speaks as
　　loud

As his own state and ours,—'tis to be chid 30
As we rate boys, who, being mature in knowl-
 edge,
Pawn their experience to their present pleas-
 ure,
And so rebel to judgment.

    Enter a Messenger.

Lep.   Here's more news.
 Mess. Thy biddings have been done; and
  every hour,
Most noble Cæsar, shalt thou have report
How 'tis abroad. Pompey is strong at sea;
And it appears he is beloved of those
That only have fear'd Cæsar : to the ports
The discontents repair, and men's reports
Give him much wrong'd.
 Cæs.   I should have known no less. 40
It hath been taught us from the primal state,
That he which is was wish'd until he were;
And the ebb'd man, ne'er loved till ne'er worth
 love,
Comes dear'd by being lack'd. This common
 body,
Like to a vagabond flag upon the stream,
Goes to and back, lackeying the varying tide,
To rot itself with motion.
 Mess.   Cæsar, I bring thee word,
Menecrates and Menas, famous pirates,
Make the sea serve them, which they ear and
 wound   49
With keels of every kind : many hot inroads
They make in Italy; the borders maritime
Lack blood to think on 't, and flush youth re-
 volt :
No vessel can peep forth, but 'tis as soon
Taken as seen; for Pompey's name strikes
 more
Than could his war resisted.
 Cæs.   Antony,
Leave thy lascivious wassails. When thou once
Wast beaten from Modena, where thou slew'st
Hirtius and Pansa, consuls, at thy heel
Did famine follow; whom thou fought'st
 against,
Though daintily brought up, with patience
 more   60
Than savages could suffer : thou didst drink
The stale of horses, and the gilded puddle
Which beasts would cough at : thy palate then
 did deign
The roughest berry on the rudest hedge;
Yea, like the stag, when snow the pasture
 sheets,
The barks of trees thou browsed'st; on the
 Alps
It is reported thou didst eat strange flesh,
Which some did die to look on : and all this—
It wounds thine honor that I speak it now—
Was borne so like a soldier, that thy cheek 70
So much as lank'd not.
 Lep.   'Tis pity of him.
 Cæs. Let his shames quickly
Drive him to Rome : 'tis time we twain
Did show ourselves i' the field; and to that
 end
Assemble we immediate council : Pompey
Thrives in our idleness.
 Lep.   To-morrow, Cæsar,
I shall be furnish'd to inform you rightly
Both what by sea and land I can be able
To front this present time.

 Cæs.   Till which encounter,
It is my business too. Farewell.   80
 Lep. Farewell, my lord : what you shall
  know meantime
Of stirs abroad, I shall beseech you, sir,
To let me be partaker.
 Cæs.   Doubt not, sir;
I knew it for my bond.   [*Exeunt.*

SCENE V. *Alexandria. Cleopatra's palace.*

 Enter CLEOPATRA, CHARMIAN, IRAS, *and*
     MARDIAN.

 Cleo. Charmian!
 Char. Madam?
 Cleo. Ha, ha!
Give me to drink mandragora.
 Char.   Why, madam?
 Cleo. That I might sleep out this great gap
  of time
My Antony is away.
 Char.   You think of him too much.
 Cleo. O, 'tis treason!
 Char.   Madam, I trust, not so.
 Cleo. Thou, eunuch Mardian!
 Mar.   What's your highness' pleasure?
 Cleo. Not now to hear thee sing; I take no
  pleasure
In aught an eunuch has : 'tis well for thee, 10
That, being unseminar'd, thy freer thoughts
May not fly forth of Egypt. Hast thou affec-
 tions?
 Mar. Yes, gracious madam.
 Cleo. Indeed!
 Mar. Not in deed, madam; for I can do
  nothing
But what indeed is honest to be done :
Yet have I fierce affections, and think
What Venus did with Mars.
 Cleo.   O Charmian,
Where think'st thou he is now? Stands he, or
 sits he?
Or does he walk? or is he on his horse? 20
O happy horse, to bear the weight of Antony!
Do bravely, horse! for wot'st thou whom thou
 movest?
The demi-Atlas of this earth, the arm
And burgonet of men. He's speaking now,
Or murmuring 'Where's my serpent of old
 Nile?'
For so he calls me : now I feed myself
With most delicious poison. Think on me,
That am with Phœbus' amorous pinches black,
And wrinkled deep in time? Broad-fronted
 Cæsar,
When thou wast here above the ground, I
 was   30
A morsel for a monarch : and great Pompey
Would stand and make his eyes grow in my
 brow;
There would he anchor his aspect and die
With looking on his life.

   Enter ALEXAS, *from* CÆSAR.

 Alex.   Sovereign of Egypt, hail!
 Cleo. How much unlike art thou Mark
  Antony!
Yet, coming from him, that great medicine
 hath
With his tinct gilded thee.
How goes it with my brave Mark Antony?
 Alex. Last thing he did, dear queen,
He kiss'd,—the last of many doubled kisses,—

This orient pearl. His speech sticks in my
    heart.   41
  Cleo. Mine ear must pluck it thence.
  Alex.   ' Good friend,' quoth he,
' Say, the firm Roman to great Egypt sends
This treasure of an oyster ; at whose foot,
To mend the petty present, I will piece
Her opulent throne with kingdoms ; all the
    east,
Say thou, shall call her mistress.' So he
    nodded,
And soberly did mount an arm-gaunt steed,
Who neigh'd so high, that what I would have
    spoke
Was beastly dumb'd by him.
  Cleo.   What, was he sad or merry ? 50
  Alex. Like to the time o' the year between
    the extremes
Of hot and cold, he was nor sad nor merry.
  Cleo. O well-divided disposition ! Note
    him,
Note him, good Charmian, 'tis the man ; but
    note him :
He was not sad, for he would shine on those
That make their looks by his ; he was not
    merry,
Which seem'd to tell them his remembrance
    lay
In Egypt with his joy ; but between both :
O heavenly mingle ! Be'st thou sad or merry,
The violence of either thee becomes,   60
So does it no man else. Met'st thou my posts ?
  Alex. Ay, madam, twenty several messen-
    gers :
Why do you send so thick ?
  Cleo.   Who's born that day
When I forget to send to Antony,
Shall die a beggar. Ink and paper, Charmian.
Welcome, my good Alexas. Did I, Charmian,
Ever love Cæsar so ?
  Char.   O that brave Cæsar !
  Cleo. Be choked with such another em-
    phasis !
Say, the brave Antony.
  Char.   The valiant Cæsar !
  Cleo. By Isis, I will give thee bloody teeth,
If thou with Cæsar paragon again   71
My man of men.
  Char.   By your most gracious pardon,
I sing but after you.
  Cleo.   My salad days,
When I was green in judgment : cold in blood,
To say as I said then ! But, come, away ;
Get me ink and paper :
He shall have every day a several greeting,
Or I'll unpeople Egypt.   [*Exeunt.*

ACT II.

SCENE I. *Messina. Pompey's house.*

Enter POMPEY, MENECRATES, *and* MENAS,
    in warlike manner.

  Pom. If the great gods be just, they shall
    assist
The deeds of justest men.
  Mene.   Know, worthy Pompey,
That what they do delay, they not deny.
  Pom. Whiles we are suitors to their throne,
    decays
The thing we sue for.
  Mene.   We, ignorant of ourselves,

Beg often our own harms, which the wise
    powers
Deny us for our good ; so find we profit
By losing of our prayers.
  Pom.   I shall do well :
The people love me, and the sea is mine ;
My powers are crescent, and my auguring
    hope   10
Says it will come to the full. Mark Antony
In Egypt sits at dinner, and will make
No wars without doors : Cæsar gets money
    where
He loses hearts : Lepidus flatters both,
Of both is flatter'd ; but he neither loves,
Nor either cares for him.
  Men.   Cæsar and Lepidus
Are in the field : a mighty strength they carry.
  Pom. Where have you this ? 'tis false.
  Men.   From Silvius, sir.
  Pom. He dreams : I know they are in
    Rome together,
Looking for Antony. But all the charms of
    love,   20
Salt Cleopatra, soften thy waned lip !
Let witchcraft join with beauty, lust with both !
Tie up the libertine in a field of feasts,
Keep his brain fuming ; Epicurean cooks
Sharpen with cloyless sauce his appetite ;
That sleep and feeding may prorogue his
    honor
Even till a Lethe'd dulness !

          Enter VARRIUS.

              How now, Varrius !
  Var. This is most certain that I shall de-
    liver :
Mark Antony is every hour in Rome
Expected : since he went from Egypt 'tis 30
A space for further travel.
  Pom.   I could have given less matter
A better ear. Menas, I did not think
This amorous surfeiter would have donn'd his
    helm
For such a petty war : his soldiership
Is twice the other twain : but let us rear
The higher our opinion, that our stirring
Can from the lap of Egypt's widow pluck
The ne'er-lust-wearied Antony.
  Men.   I cannot hope
Cæsar and Antony shall well greet together :
His wife that's dead did trespasses to Cæsar ;
His brother warr'd upon him ; although, I
    think,   40
Not moved by Antony.
  Pom.   I know not, Menas,
How lesser enmities may give way to greater.
Were't not that we stand up against them all,
'Twere pregnant they should square between
    themselves ;
For they have entertained cause enough
To draw their swords : but how the fear of us
May cement their divisions and bind up
The petty difference, we yet not know.
Be't as our gods will have't ! It only stands 50
Our lives upon to use our strongest hands.
Come, Menas.   [*Exeunt.*

SCENE II. *Rome. The house of Lepidus.*

    Enter ENOBARBUS *and* LEPIDUS.

  Lep. Good Enobarbus, 'tis a worthy deed,
And shall become you well, to entreat your
    captain
To soft and gentle speech.

Eno.   I shall entreat him
To answer like himself : if Cæsar move him,
Let Antony look over Cæsar's head
And speak as loud as Mars. By Jupiter,
Were I the wearer of Antonius' beard,
I would not shave't to-day.
Lep.   'Tis not a time
For private stomaching.
Eno.   Every time
Serves for the matter that is then born in't. 10
  Lep. But small to greater matters must
    give way.
  Eno. Not if the small come first.
  Lep.   Your speech is passion :
But, pray you, stir no embers up. Here comes
The noble Antony.

    Enter ANTONY *and* VENTIDIUS.

Eno.   And yonder, Cæsar.

  Enter CÆSAR, MECÆNAS, *and* AGRIPPA.

  Ant. If we compose well here, to Parthia :
Hark, Ventidius.
  Cæs.   I do not know,
Mecænas ; ask Agrippa.
  Lep.   Noble friends,
That which combined us was most great, and
    let not
A leaner action rend us. What's amiss,
May it be gently heard : when we debate 20
Our trivial difference loud, we do commit
Murder in healing wounds : then, noble part-
    ners,
The rather, for I earnestly beseech,
Touch you the sourest points with sweetest
    terms,
Nor curstness grow to the matter.
  Ant.   'Tis spoken well.
Were we before our armies, and to fight.
I should do thus.   [*Flourish.*
  Cæs. Welcome to Rome.
  Ant.   Thank you.
  Cæs.   Sit.
  Ant.   Sit, sir.
  Cæs.   Nay, then.
  Ant. I learn, you take things ill which are
    not so,
Or being, concern you not.
  Cæs.   I must be laugh'd at, 30
If, or for nothing or a little, I
Should say myself offended, and with you
Chiefly i' the world ; more laugh'd at, that I
    should
Once name you derogately, when to sound
    your name
It not concern'd me.
  Ant.   My being in Egypt, Cæsar,
What was't to you ?
  Cæs. No more than my residing here at
    Rome
Might be to you in Egypt : yet, if you there
Did practise on my state, your being in Egypt
Might be my question.
  Ant.   How intend you, practised ? 40
  Cæs. You may be pleased to catch at mine
    intent
By what did here befal me. Your wife and
    brother
Made wars upon me ; and their contestation
Was theme for you, you were the word of war.
  Ant. You do mistake your business ; my
    brother never
Did urge me in his act : I did inquire it ;

And have my learning from some true reports,
That drew their swords with you. Did he not
    rather
Discredit my authority with yours ;   49
And make the wars alike against my stomach,
Having alike your cause ? Of this my letters
Before did satisfy you. If you'll patch a quar-
    rel,
As matter whole you have not to make it with,
It must not be with this.
  Cæs.   You praise yourself
By laying defects of judgment to me ; but
You patch'd up your excuses.
  Ant.   Not so, not so ;
I know you could not lack, I am certain on't,
Very necessity of this thought, that I,
Your partner in the cause 'gainst which he
    fought,
Could not with graceful eyes attend those
    wars   60
Which fronted mine own peace. As for my
    wife,
I would you had her spirit in such another :
The third o' the world is yours ; which with a
    snaffle
You may pace easy, but not such a wife.
  Eno. Would we had all such wives, that
the men might go to wars with the women !
  Ant. So much uncurbable, her garboils,
    Cæsar,
Made out of her impatience, which not wanted
Shrewdness of policy too, I grieving grant
Did you too much disquiet : for that you must
But say, I could not help it.   71
  Cæs.   I wrote to you
When rioting in Alexandria ; you
Did pocket up my letters, and with taunts
Did gibe my missive out of audience.
  Ant.   Sir,
He fell upon me ere admitted : then
Three kings I had newly feasted, and did want
Of what I was i' the morning : but next day
I told him of myself ; which was as much
As to have ask'd him pardon. Let this fellow
Be nothing of our strife ; if we contend,   80
Out of our question wipe him.
  Cæs.   You have broken
The article of your oath ; which you shall
    never
Have tongue to charge me with.
  Lep.   Soft, Cæsar !
  Ant.   No,
Lepidus, let him speak :
The honor is sacred which he talks on now,
Supposing that I lack'd it. But, on, Cæsar ;
The article of my oath.
  Cæs. To lend me arms and aid when I re-
    quired them ;
The which you both denied.
  Ant.   Neglected, rather ;
And then when poison'd hours had bound me
    up   90
From mine own knowledge. As nearly as I
    may,
I'll play the penitent to you : but mine honesty
Shall not make poor my greatness, nor my
    power
Work without it. Truth is, that Fulvia,
To have me out of Egypt, made wars here ;
For which myself, the ignorant motive, do
So far ask pardon as befits mine honor
To stoop in such a case.
  Lep.   'Tis noble spoken.

Mec. If it might please you, to enforce no
   further
The griefs between ye : to forget them quite
Were to remember that the present need   101
Speaks to atone you.
   Lep.   Worthily spoken, Mecænas.
   Eno. Or, if you borrow one another's love
for the instant, you may, when you hear no
more words of Pompey, return it again : you
shall have time to wrangle in when you have
nothing else to do.
   Ant. Thou art a soldier only : speak no
      more.
   Eno. That truth should be silent I had al-
most forgot.   110
   Ant. You wrong this presence ; therefore
      speak no more.
   Eno. Go to, then ; your considerate stone.
   Cæs. I do not much dislike the matter, but
The manner of his speech ; for't cannot be
We shall remain in friendship, our conditions
So differing in their acts. Yet, if I knew
What hoop should hold us stanch, from edge
      to edge
O' the world I would pursue it.
   Agr.   Give me leave, Cæsar,—
   Cæs. Speak, Agrippa.
   Agr. Thou hast a sister by the mother's
      side,   120
Admired Octavia : great Mark Antony
Is now a widower.
   Cæs.   Say not so, Agrippa :
If Cleopatra heard you, your reproof
Were well deserved of rashness.
   Ant. I am not married, Cæsar : let me
      hear
Agrippa further speak.
   Agr. To hold you in perpetual amity,
To make you brothers, and to knit your hearts
With an unslipping knot, take Antony
Octavia to his wife ; whose beauty claims 130
No worse a husband than the best of men ;
Whose virtue and whose general graces speak
That which none else can utter. By this mar-
      riage,
All little jealousies, which now seem great,
And all great fears, which now import their
      dangers,
Would then be nothing : truths would be tales,
Where now half tales be truths : her love to
      both
Would, each to other and all loves to both,
Draw after her. Pardon what I have spoke ;
For 'tis a studied, not a present thought, 140
By duty ruminated.
   Ant.   Will Cæsar speak ?
   Cæs. Not till he hears how Antony is
      touch'd
With what is spoke already.
   Ant.   What power is in Agrippa,
If I would say, ' Agrippa, be it so,'
To make this good ?
   Cæs.   The power of Cæsar, and
His power unto Octavia.
   Ant.   May I never
To this good purpose, that so fairly shows,
Dream of impediment ! Let me have thy
      hand :
Further this act of grace : and from this hour
The heart of brothers govern in our loves 150
And sway our great designs !
   Cæs.   There is my hand.
A sister I bequeath you, whom no brother

Did ever love so dearly : let her live
To join our kingdoms and our hearts ; and
      never
Fly off our loves again !
   Lep.   Happily, amen !
   Ant. I did not think to draw my sword
      'gainst Pompey ;
For he hath laid strange courtesies and great
Of late upon me : I must thank him only,
Lest my remembrance suffer ill report ;
At heel of that, defy him.
   Lep.   Time calls upon's : 160
Of us must Pompey presently be sought,
Or else he seeks out us.
   Ant.   Where lies he ?
   Cæs. About the mount Misenum.
   Ant. What is his strength by land ?
   Cæs. Great and increasing : but by sea
He is an absolute master.
   Ant.   So is the fame.
Would we had spoke together ! Haste we for
      it :
Yet, ere we put ourselves in arms, dispatch
      we
The business we have talk'd of.
   Cæs.   With most gladness :
And do invite you to my sister's view,   170
Whither straight I'll lead you.
   Ant.   Let us, Lepidus,
Not lack your company.
   Lep.   Noble Antony,
Not sickness should detain me.
      [*Flourish. Exeunt Cæsar, Antony,
            and Lepidus.*

   Mec. Welcome from Egypt, sir.
   Eno. Half the heart of Cæsar, worthy
Mecænas ! My honorable friend, Agrippa !
   Agr. Good Enobarbus !
   Mec. We have cause to be glad that matters are so well digested. You stayed well by 't
in Egypt.   180
   Eno. Ay, sir ; we did sleep day out of
countenance, and made the night light with
drinking.
   Mec. Eight wild-boars roasted whole at a
breakfast, and but twelve persons there ; is
this true ?
   Eno. This was but as a fly by an eagle :
we had much more monstrous matter of feast,
which worthily deserved noting.
   Mec. She's a most triumphant lady, if re-
port be square to her.   190
   Eno. When she first met Mark Antony, she
pursed up his heart, upon the river of Cydnus.
   Agr. There she appeared indeed ; or my
reporter devised well for her.
   Eno. I will tell you.
The barge she sat in, like a burnish'd throne,
Burn'd on the water : the poop was beaten
      gold ;
Purple the sails, and so perfumed that
The winds were love-sick with them ; the oars
      were silver,
Which to the tune of flutes kept stroke, and
      made   200
The water which they beat to follow faster,
As amorous of their strokes. For her own
      person,
It beggar'd all description : she did lie
In her pavilion—cloth-of-gold of tissue—
O'er-picturing that Venus where we see
The fancy outwork nature : on each side her
Stood pretty dimpled boys, like smiling Cupids,

With divers-color'd fans, whose wind did seem
To glow the delicate cheeks which they did
    cool,
And what they undid did.
    Agr.   O, rare for Antony ! 210
    Eno. Her gentlewomen, like the Nereides,
So many mermaids, tended her i' the eyes,
And made their bends adornings : at the helm
A seeming mermaid steers : the silken tackle
Swell with the touches of those flower-soft
    hands,
That yarely frame the office. From the barge
A strange invisible perfume hits the sense
Of the adjacent wharfs. The city cast
Her people out upon her ; and Antony, 219
Enthroned i' the market-place, did sit alone,
Whistling to the air ; which, but for vacancy,
Had gone to gaze on Cleopatra too,
And made a gap in nature.
    Agr.   Rare Egyptian !
    Eno. Upon her landing, Antony sent to
    her,
Invited her to supper : she replied,
It should be better he became her guest ;
Which she entreated : our courteous Antony,
Whom ne'er the word of ' No ' woman heard
    speak,
Being barber'd ten times o'er, goes to the feast,
And for his ordinary pays his heart 230
For what his eyes eat only.
    Agr.   Royal wench !
She made great Cæsar lay his sword to bed :
He plough'd her, and she cropp'd.
    Eno.   I saw her once
Hop forty paces through the public street ;
And having lost her breath, she spoke, and
    panted,
That she did make defect perfection,
And, breathless, power breathe forth.
    Mec. Now Antony must leave her utterly.
    Eno. Never ; he will not :
Age cannot wither her, nor custom stale 240
Her infinite variety : other women cloy
The appetites they feed : but she makes hun-
    gry
Where most she satisfies ; for vilest things
Become themselves in her : that the holy
    priests
Bless her when she is riggish.
    Mec. If beauty, wisdom, modesty, can set-
    tle
The heart of Antony, Octavia is
A blessed lottery to him.
    Agr.   Let us go.
Good Enobarbus, make yourself my guest
Whilst you abide here. 250
    Eno. Humbly, sir, I thank you. [*Exeunt.*

SCENE III. *The same. Cæsar's house.*

Enter ANTONY, CÆSAR, OCTAVIA *between
them, and* Attendants.

    Ant. The world and my great office will
    sometimes
Divide me from your bosom.
    Octa.   All which time
Before the gods my knee shall bow my prayers
To them for you.
    Ant.   Good night, sir. My Octavia,
Read not my blemishes in the world's report :
I have not kept my square ; but that to come
Shall all be done by the rule. Good night, dear
    lady.

Good night, sir.
    Cæs. Good night.
        [*Exeunt Cæsar and Octavia.*

Enter Soothsayer.

    Ant. Now, sirrah ; you do wish yourself in
    Egypt ? 10
    Sooth. Would I had never come from
    thence, nor you
Thither !
    Ant. If you can, your reason ?
    Sooth.   I see it in
My motion, have it not in my tongue : but yet
Hie you to Egypt again.
    Ant.   Say to me,
Whose fortunes shall rise higher, Cæsar's or
    mine ?
    Sooth. Cæsar's.
Therefore, O Antony, stay not by his side :
Thy demon, that's thy spirit which keeps thee,
    is
Noble, courageous, high, unmatchable, 20
Where Cæsar's is not ; but, near him, thy
    angel
Becomes a fear, as being o'erpower'd : there-
    fore
Make space enough between you.
    Ant.   Speak this no more.
    Sooth. To none but thee ; no more, but
    when to thee.
If thou dost play with him at any game,
Thou art sure to lose ; and, of that natural
    luck,
He beats thee 'gainst the odds : thy lustre
    thickens,
When he shines by : I say again, thy spirit
Is all afraid to govern thee near him ;
But, he away, 'tis noble.
    Ant.   Get thee gone : 30
Say to Ventidius I would speak with him :
        [*Exit Soothsayer.*
He shall to Parthia. Be it art or hap,
He hath spoken true : the very dice obey him ;
And in our sports my better cunning faints
Under his chance : if we draw lots, he speeds ;
His cocks do win the battle still of mine,
When it is all to nought ; and his quails ever
Beat mine, inhoop'd, at odds. I will to Egypt :
And though I make this marriage for my
    peace,
I' the east my pleasure lies.

Enter VENTIDIUS.

        O, come, Ventidius, 40
You must to Parthia : your commission's
    ready ;
Follow me, and receive't.   [*Exeunt.*

SCENE IV. *The same. A street.*

Enter LEPIDUS, MECÆNAS, *and* AGRIPPA.

    Lep. Trouble yourselves no further : pray
    you, hasten
Your generals after.
    Agr.   Sir, Mark Antony
Will e'en but kiss Octavia, and we'll follow.
    Lep. Till I shall see you in your soldier's
    dress,
Which will become you both, farewell.
    Mec.   We shall,
As I conceive the journey, be at the Mount
Before you, Lepidus.
    Lep.   Your way is shorter ;
My purposes do draw me much about :

You'll win two days upon me.
Mec. }
Agr. }　　　　　　Sir, good success !
Lep. Farewell.　　　　　[*Exeunt.* 10

SCENE V. *Alexandria. Cleopatra's palace.*

Enter CLEOPATRA, CHARMIAN, IRAS, *and*
ALEXAS.

Cleo. Give me some music ; music, moody
food
Of us that trade in love.
Attend.　　　　　The music, ho !

Enter MARDIAN *the Eunuch.*

Cleo. Let it alone ; let's to billiards : come,
Charmian.
Char. My arm is sore ; best play with
Mardian.
Cleo. As well a woman with an eunuch
play'd
As with a woman. Come, you'll play with me,
sir ?
Mar. As well as I can, madam.
Cleo. And when good will is show'd,
though't come too short,
The actor may plead pardon. I'll none now :
Give me mine angle ; we'll to the river : there,
My music playing far off, I will betray　11
Tawny-finn'd fishes ; my bended hook shall
pierce
Their slimy jaws ; and, as I draw them up,
I'll think them every one an Antony,
And say ' Ah, ha ! you're caught.'
Char.　　　　　'Twas merry when
You wager'd on your angling ; when your
diver
Did hang a salt-fish on his hook, which he
With fervency drew up.
Cleo.　　　　That time,—O times !—
I laugh'd him out of patience ; and that night
I laugh'd him into patience ; and next morn,
Ere the ninth hour, I drunk him to his bed ;
Then put my tires and mantles on him, whilst
I wore his sword Philippan.

Enter a Messenger.

　　　　　　　O, from Italy
Ram thou thy fruitful tidings in mine ears,
That long time have been barren.
Mess.　　　　Madam, madam,—
Cleo. Antonius dead !—If thou say so, vil-
lain,
Thou kill'st thy mistress : but well and free,
If thou so yield him, there is gold, and here
My bluest veins to kiss ; a hand that kings
Have lipp'd, and trembled kissing.　30
Mess. First, madam, he is well.
Cleo.　　　　Why, there's more gold.
But, sirrah, mark, we use
To say the dead are well : bring it to that,
The gold I give thee will I melt and pour
Down thy ill-uttering throat.
Mess. Good madam, hear me.
Cleo.　　　　Well, go to, I will ;
But there's no goodness in thy face : if Antony
Be free and healthful,—so tart a favor
To trumpet such good tidings ! If not well,
Thou shouldst come like a Fury crown'd with
snakes,　40
Not like a formal man.
Mess.　　　　Will't please you hear me ?
Cleo. I have a mind to strike thee ere thou
speak'st :

Yet, if thou say Antony lives, is well,
Or friends with Cæsar, or not captive to him,
I'll set thee in a shower of gold, and hail
Rich pearls upon thee.
Mess.　　　　Madam, he's well.
Cleo.　　　　　　Well said.
Mess. And friends with Cæsar.
Cleo.　　　　Thou'rt an honest man.
Mess. Cæsar and he are greater friends
than ever.
Cleo. Make thee a fortune from me.
Mess.　　　　But yet, madam,—
Cleo. I do not like ' But yet,' it does allay
The good precedence ; fie upon ' But yet ' !　51
' But yet ' is as a gaoler to bring forth
Some monstrous malefactor. Prithee, friend,
Pour out the pack of matter to mine ear,
The good and bad together : he's friends with
Cæsar :
In state of health thou say'st ; and thou say'st
free.
Mess. Free, madam ! no ; I made no such
report :
He's bound unto Octavia.
Cleo.　　　　For what good turn ?
Mess. For the best turn i' the bed.
Cleo.　　　　I am pale, Charmian.
Mess. Madam, he's married to Octavia.　60
Cleo. The most infectious pestilence upon
thee !　　　　　[*Strikes him down.*
Mess. Good madam, patience.
Cleo.　　　　What say you ? Hence,
　　　　　　　[*Strikes him again.*
Horrible villain ! or I'll spurn thine eyes
Like balls before me ; I'll unhair thy head :
　　　　　[*She hales him up and down.*
Thou shalt be whipp'd with wire, and stew'd
in brine,
Smarting in lingering pickle.
Mess.　　　　Gracious madam,
I that do bring the news made not the match.
Cleo. Say 'tis not so, a province I will give
thee,
And make thy fortunes proud : the blow thou
hadst
Shall make thy peace for moving me to rage ;
And I will boot thee with what gift beside　71
Thy modesty can beg.
Mess.　　　　He's married, madam.
Cleo. Rogue, thou hast lived too long.
　　　　　　　[*Draws a knife.*
Mess.　　　　Nay, then I'll run.
What mean you, madam ? I have made no
fault.　　　　　　　[*Exit.*
Char. Good madam, keep yourself within
yourself :
The man is innocent.
Cleo. Some innocents 'scape not the thun-
derbolt.
Melt Egypt into Nile ! and kindly creatures
Turn all to serpents ! Call the slave again :
Though I am mad, I will not bite him : call.
Char. He is afeard to come.
Cleo.　　　　I will not hurt him.
　　　　　　　[*Exit Charmian.*
These hands do lack nobility, that they strike
A meaner than myself ; since I myself
Have given myself the cause.

Re-enter CHARMIAN *and* Messenger.

　　　　　　　Come hither, sir.
Though it be honest, it is never good

To bring bad news : give to a gracious mes-
  sage.
An host of tongues ; but let ill tidings tell
Themselves when they be felt.
 Mess.   I have done my duty.
 Cleo. Is he married ?
I cannot hate thee worser than I do, 90
If thou again say ' Yes.'
 Mess.   He's married, madam.
 Cleo. The gods confound thee ! dost thou
  hold there still ?
 Mess. Should I lie, madam ?
 Cleo.   O, I would thou didst,
So half my Egypt were submerged and made
A cistern for scaled snakes ! Go, get thee
 hence :
Hadst thou Narcissus in thy face, to me
Thou wouldst appear most ugly. He is mar-
 ried ?
 Mess. I crave your highness' pardon.
 Cleo.   He is married ?
 Mess. Take no offence that I would not
 offend you :
To punish me for what you make me do. 100
Seems much unequal : he's married to Octavia.
 Cleo. O, that his fault should make a
  knave of thee,
That art not what thou'rt sure of ! Get thee
 hence :
The merchandise which thou hast brought
 from Rome
Are all too dear for me : lie they upon thy
 hand,
And be undone by 'em ! *[Exit Messenger.*
 Char. Good your highness, patience.
 Cleo. In praising Antony, I have dispraised
  Caesar.
 Char. Many times, madam.
 Cleo.   I am paid for't now.
Lead me from hence :
I faint : O Iras, Charmian ! 'tis no matter. 110
Go to the fellow, good Alexas ; bid him
Report the feature of Octavia, her years,
Her inclination, let him not leave out
The color of her hair : bring me word quickly.
       [Exit Alexas.
Let him for ever go :—let him not—Charmian,
Though he be painted one way like a Gorgon,
The other way's a Mars. Bid you Alexas
       [To Mardian.
Bring me word how tall she is. Pity me,
 Charmian,
But do not speak to me. Lead me to my
 chamber.   *[Exeunt.*

  Scene VI. *Near Misenum.*

Flourish. Enter Pompey *and* Menas *at one
 door, with drum and trumpet : at another,*
 Caesar, Antony, Lepidus, Enobarbus,
 Mecaenas, *with* Soldiers *marching.*

 Pom. Your hostages I have, so have you
  mine ;
And we shall talk before we fight.
 Caes.   Most meet
That first we come to words ; and therefore
 have we
Our written purposes before us sent ;
Which, if thou hast consider'd, let us know
If 'twill tie up thy discontented sword,
And carry back to Sicily much tall youth
That else must perish here.
 Pom.   To you all three,
The senators alone of this great world,

Chief factors for the gods, I do not know 10
Wherefore my father should revengers want,
Having a son and friends ; since Julius Caesar,
Who at Philippi the good Brutus ghosted,
There saw you laboring for him. What was't
That moved pale Cassius to conspire ; and
 what
Made the all-honor'd, honest Roman, Brutus,
With the arm'd rest, courtiers and beauteous
 freedom,
To drench the Capitol ; but that they would
Have one man but a man ? And that is it 19
Hath made me rig my navy ; at whose burthen
The anger'd ocean foams ; with which I meant
To scourge the ingratitude that despiteful
 Rome
Cast on my noble father.
 Caes.   Take your time.
 Ant. Thou canst not fear us, Pompey, with
 thy sails ;
We'll speak with thee at sea : at land, thou
 know'st
How much we do o'er-count thee.
 Pom.   At land, indeed,
Thou dost o'er-count me of my father's house :
But, since the cuckoo builds not for himself,
Remain in't as thou mayst.
 Lep.   Be pleased to tell us—
For this is from the present—how you take 30
The offers we have sent you.
 Caes.   There's the point.
 Ant. Which do not be entreated to, but
 weigh
What it is worth embraced.
 Caes.   And what may follow,
To try a larger fortune.
 Pom. You have made me offer
Of Sicily, Sardinia ; and I must
Rid all the sea of pirates ; then, to send
Measures of wheat to Rome ; this 'greed upon
To part with unhack'd edges, and bear back
Our targes undinted.
 Caes. Ant. Lep. That's our offer.
 Pom.   Know, then, 40
I came before you here a man prepared
To take this offer : but that Mark Antony
Put me to some impatience : though I lose
The praise of it by telling, you must know,
When Caesar and your brother were at blows,
Your mother came to Sicily and did find
Her welcome friendly.
 Ant.   I have heard it, Pompey ;
And am well studied for a liberal thanks
Which I do owe you.
 Pom.   Let me have your hand :
I did not think, sir, to have met you here. 50
 Ant. The beds i' the east are soft ; and
 thanks to you,
That call'd me timelier than my purpose
 hither ;
For I have gain'd by 't.
 Caes.   Since I saw you last,
There is a change upon you.
 Pom.   Well, I know not
What counts harsh fortune casts upon my
 face ;
But in my bosom shall she never come,
To make my heart her vassal.
 Lep.   Well met here.
 Pom. I hope so, Lepidus. Thus we are
 agreed :
I crave our composition may be written,
And seal'd between us.

Cæs.   That's the next to do. 60
Pom. We'll feast each other ere we part;
and let's
Draw lots who shall begin.
Ant.   That will I, Pompey.
Pom. No, Antony, take the lot : but, first
Or last, your fine Egyptian cookery
Shall have the fame. I have heard that Julius
   Cæsar
Grew fat with feasting there.
Ant.   You have heard much.
Pom. I have fair meanings, sir.
Ant.   And fair words to them.
Pom. Then so much have I heard :
And I have heard, Apollodorus carried—
Eno. No more of that : he did so.
Pom.   What, I pray you ?   70
Eno. A certain queen to Cæsar in a mat-
tress.
Pom. I know thee now : how farest thou,
soldier ?
Eno.   Well ;
And well am like to do ; for, I perceive,
Four feasts are toward.
Pom.   Let me shake thy hand ;
I never hated thee : I have seen thee fight,
When I have envied thy behavior.
Eno.   Sir,
I never loved you much ; but I ha' praised ye,
When you have well deserved ten times as
much
As I have said you did.
Pom.   Enjoy thy plainness, 80
It nothing ill becomes thee.
Aboard my galley I invite you all :
Will you lead, lords ?
Cæs. Ant. Lep. Show us the way, sir.
Pom.   Come.
   [*Exeunt all but Menas and Enobarbus.*
Men. [*Aside*] Thy father, Pompey, would
ne'er have made this treaty.—You and I have
known, sir.
Eno. At sea, I think.
Men. We have, sir.
Eno. You have done well by water.
Men. And you by land.   90
Eno. I will praise any man that will praise
me ; though it cannot be denied what I have
done by land.
Men. Nor what I have done by water.
Eno. Yes, something you can deny for
your own safety : you have been a great thief
by sea.
Men. And you by land.
Eno. There I deny my land service. But
give me your hand, Menas : if our eyes had
authority, here they might take two thieves
kissing.   101
Men. All men's faces are true, what-
some'er their hands are.
Eno. But there is never a fair woman has
a true face.
Men. No slander ; they steal hearts.
Eno. We came hither to fight with you.
Men. For my part, I am sorry it is turned
to a drinking. Pompey doth this day laugh
away his fortune.   110
Eno. If he do, sure, he cannot weep't back
again.
Men. You've said, sir. We looked not for
Mark Antony here : pray you, is he married
to Cleopatra ?
Eno. Cæsar's sister is called Octavia.

Men. True, sir ; she was the wife of Caius
Marcellus.
Eno. But she is now the wife of Marcus
Antonius.
Men. Pray ye, sir ?   120
Eno. 'Tis true.
Men. Then is Cæsar and he for ever knit
together.
Eno. If I were bound to divine of this
unity, I would not prophesy so.
Men. I think the policy of that purpose
made more in the marriage than the love of
the parties.
Eno. I think so too. But you shall find, the
band that seems to tie their friendship together will be the very strangler of their
amity : Octavia is of a holy, cold, and still
conversation.   131
Men. Who would not have his wife so ?
Eno. Not he that himself is not so ; which
is Mark Antony. He will to his Egyptian dish
again : then shall the sighs of Octavia blow
the fire up in Cæsar ; and, as I said before,
that which is the strength of their amity shall
prove the immediate author of their variance.
Antony will use his affection where it is : he
married but his occasion here.   140
Men. And thus it may be. Come, sir, will
you aboard ? I have a health for you.
Eno. I shall take it, sir : we have used our
throats in Egypt.
Men. Come, let's away.   [*Exeunt.*

SCENE VII. *On board Pompey's galley, off
   Misenum.*

Music plays. Enter two or three Servants
   with a banquet.

First Serv. Here they'll be, man. Some o'
their plants are ill-rooted already ; the least
wind i' the world will blow them down.
Sec. Serv. Lepidus is high-colored.
First Serv. They have made him drink
alms-drink.
Sec. Serv. As they pinch one another by
the disposition, he cries out ' No more ; ' reconciles them to his entreaty, and himself to
the drink.
First Serv. But it raises the greater war
between him and his discretion.   11
Sec. Serv. Why, this is to have a name in
great men's fellowship : I had as lief have a
reed that will do me no service as a partisan
I could not heave.
First Serv. To be called into a huge sphere,
and not to be seen to move in't, are the holes
where eyes should be, which pitifully disaster
the cheeks.

A sennet sounded. Enter CÆSAR, ANTONY,
LEPIDUS, POMPEY, AGRIPPA, MECÆNAS,
ENOBARBUS, MENAS, *with other captains.*

Ant. [*To Cæsar*] Thus do they, sir : they
      take the flow o' the Nile   20
By certain scales i' the pyramid ; they know,
By the height, the lowness, or the mean, if
dearth
Or foison follow : the higher Nilus swells,
The more it promises : as it ebbs, the seeds-
man
Upon the slime and ooze scatters his grain,
And shortly comes to harvest.
Lep. You've strange serpents there.
Ant. Ay, Lepidus.

Lep. Your serpent of Egypt is bred now
of your mud by the operation of your sun : so
is your crocodile.　　　　　　　　　　　　31

Ant. They are so.

Pom. Sit,—and some wine ! A health to
Lepidus !

Lep. I am not so well as I should be, but
I'll ne'er out.

Eno. Not till you have slept ; I fear me
you'll be in till then.

Lep. Nay, certainly, I have heard the Ptolemies' pyramises are very goodly things ; without contradiction, I have heard that.　　　41

Men. [*Aside to Pom.*] Pompey, a word.

Pom.　　　　[*Aside to Men.*] Say
in mine ear : what is't ?

Men. [*Aside to Pom.*] Forsake thy seat, I
do beseech thee, captain,
And hear me speak a word.

Pom. [*Aside to Men.*] Forbear me till
anon.
This wine for Lepidus !

Lep. What manner o' thing is your crocodile ?

Ant. It is shaped, sir, like itself ; and it is
as broad as it hath breadth : it is just so high
as it is, and moves with its own organs : it
lives by that which nourisheth it ; and the elements once out of it, it transmigrates.　　51

Lep. What color is it of ?

Ant. Of it own color too.

Lep. 'Tis a strange serpent.

Ant. 'Tis so. And the tears of it are wet.

Cæs. Will this description satisfy him ?

Ant. With the health that Pompey gives
him, else he is a very epicure.

Pom. [*Aside to Men.*] Go hang, sir, hang !
Tell me of that ? away !
Do as I bid you. Where's this cup I call'd for ?

Men. [*Aside to Pom.*] If for the sake of
merit thou wilt hear me,　　　　　　61
Rise from thy stool.

Pom. [*Aside to Men.*] I think thou'rt mad.
The matter ?　[*Rises, and walks aside.*]

Men. I have ever held my cap off to thy
fortunes.

Pom. Thou hast served me with much
faith. What's else to say ?
Be jolly, lords.

Ant.　　　　These quick-sands, Lepidus,
Keep off them, for you sink.

Men. Wilt thou be lord of all the world ?

Pom.　　　　　　What say'st thou ?

Men. Wilt thou be lord of the whole
world ? That's twice.

Pom. How should that be ?

Men.　　　But entertain it,
And, though thou think me poor, I am the man
Will give thee all the world.　　　　　71

Pom.　　　Hast thou drunk well ?

Men. Now, Pompey, I have kept me from
the cup.
Thou art, if thou darest be, the earthly Jove :
Whate'er the ocean pales, or sky inclips,
Is thine, if thou wilt ha't.

Pom.　　　Show me which way.

Men. These three world-sharers, these com-
petitors,
Are in thy vessel : let me cut the cable ;
And, when we are put off, fall to their throats :
All there is thine.

Pom.　Ah, this thou shouldst have done,
And not have spoke on't ! In me 'tis villany ;

In thee't had been good service. Thou must
know,　　　　　　　　　　　　　　81
'Tis not my profit that does lead mine honor ;
Mine honor, it. Repent that e'er thy tongue
Hath so betray'd thine act : being done un-
known,
I should have found it afterwards well done ;
But must condemn it now. Desist, and drink.

Men. [*Aside*] For this,
I'll never follow thy pall'd fortunes more.
Who seeks, and will not take when once 'tis
offer'd,
Shall never find it more.

Pom.　　　This health to Lepidus ! 90

Ant. Bear him ashore. I'll pledge it for
him, Pompey.

Eno. Here's to thee, Menas !

Men.　　　　　Enobarbus, welcome !

Pom. Fill till the cup be hid.

Eno. There's a strong fellow, Menas.
[*Pointing to the Attendant who carries
off Lepidus.*

Men. Why ?

Eno. A' bears the third part of the world,
man ; see'st not ?

Men. The third part, then, is drunk : would
it were all,
That it might go on wheels !

Eno. Drink thou ; increase the reels. 100

Men. Come.

Pom. This is not yet an Alexandrian feast.

Ant. It ripens towards it. Strike the vessels, ho ?
Here is to Cæsar !

Cæs.　　I could well forbear 't.
It's monstrous labor, when I wash my brain,
And it grows fouler.

Ant.　　　Be a child o' the time.

Cæs. Possess it, I'll make answer :
But I had rather fast from all four days
Than drink so much in one.

Eno. Ha, my brave emperor ! [*To Antony.*
Shall we dance now the Egyptian Bacchanals,
And celebrate our drink ?

Pom.　　Let's ha't, good soldier. 111

Ant. Come, let's all take hands,
Till that the conquering wine hath steep'd our
sense
In soft and delicate Lethe.

Eno.　　　All take hands.
Make battery to our ears with the loud music :
The while I'll place you : then the boy shall
sing ;
The holding every man shall bear as loud
As his strong sides can volley.
[*Music plays. Enobarbus places them
hand in hand.*

THE SONG.

Come, thou monarch of the vine,　　120
Plumpy Bacchus with pink eyne !
In thy fats our cares be drown'd,
With thy grapes our hairs be crown'd :
Cup us, till the world go round,
Cup us, till the world go round !

Cæs. What would you more ? Pompey,
good night. Good brother,
Let me request you off : our graver business
Frowns at this levity. Gentle lords, let's part ;
You see we have burnt our cheeks : strong
Enobarb
Is weaker than the wine ; and mine own
tongue　　　　　　　　　　　　130

Splits what it speaks : the wild disguise hath
　almost
Antick'd us all. What needs more words ?
　Good night.
Good Antony, your hand.
　Pom.　　　　　　I'll try you on the shore.
　Ant. And shall, sir ; give's your hand.
　Pom.　　　　　　O Antony,
You have my father's house,—But, what ? we
　are friends.
Come, down into the boat.
　Eno.　　　　Take heed you fall not.
　　[*Exeunt all but Enobarbus and Menas.*
Menas, I'll not on shore.
　Men.　　　　No, to my cabin.
These drums ! these trumpets, flutes ! what !
Let Neptune hear we bid a loud farewell
To these great fellows : sound and be hang'd,
　sound out !
　　　　[*Sound a flourish, with drums.*
　Eno. Ho ! says a'. There's my cap.　141
　Men. Ho ! Noble captain, come. [*Exeunt.*

ACT III.

Scene I. *A plain in Syria.*

Enter Ventidius *as it were in triumph, with*
Silius, *and other* Romans, Officers, *and*
Soldiers ; *the dead body of* Pacorus *borne
before him.*

　Ven. Now, darting Parthia, art thou
　　struck ; and now
Pleased fortune does of Marcus Crassus' death
Make me revenger. Bear the king's son's body
Before our army. Thy Pacorus, Orodes,
Pays this for Marcus Crassus.
　Sil.　　　　　Noble Ventidius,
Whilst yet with Parthian blood thy sword is
　warm,
The fugitive Parthians follow ; spur through
　Media,
Mesopotamia, and the shelters whither
The routed fly : so thy grand captain Antony
Shall set thee on triumphant chariots and　10
Put garlands on thy head.
　Ven.　　　　O Silius, Silius,
I have done enough ; a lower place, note well,
May make too great an act : for learn this,
　Silius ;
Better to leave undone, than by our deed
Acquire too high a fame when him we serve's
　away.
Cæsar and Antony have ever won
More in their officer than person : Sossius,
One of my place in Syria, his lieutenant,
For quick accumulation of renown,　　19
Which he achieved by the minute, lost his
　favor.
Who does i' the wars more than his captain
　can
Becomes his captain's captain : and ambition,
The soldier's virtue, rather makes choice of
　loss,
Than gain which darkens him.
I could do more to do Antonius good,
But 'twould offend him ; and in his offence
Should my performance perish.
　Sil.　　　　Thou hast, Ventidius, that
Without the which a soldier, and his sword,
Grants scarce distinction. Thou wilt write to
　Antony !　　29

　Ven. I'll humbly signify what in his name,
That magical word of war, we have effected ;
How, with his banners and his well-paid ranks,
The ne'er-yet-beaten horse of Parthia
We have jaded out o' the field.
　Sil.　　　　　Where is he now ?
　Ven. He purposeth to Athens : whither,
　with what haste
The weight we must convey with 's will per-
　mit,
We shall appear before him. On there ; pass
　along !　　　　　　　[*Exeunt.*

Scene II. *Rome. An ante-chamber in Cæsar's house.*

Enter Agrippa *at one door,* Enobarbus
at another.

　Agr. What, are the brothers parted ?
　Eno. They have dispatch'd with Pompey,
　he is gone ;
The other three are sealing. Octavia weeps
To part from Rome ; Cæsar is sad ; and Lep-
　idus,
Since Pompey's feast, as Menas says, is trou-
　bled
With the green sickness.
　Agr.　　　　'Tis a noble Lepidus.
　Eno. A very fine one : O, how he loves
　Cæsar !
　Agr. Nay, but how dearly he adores Mark
　Antony !
　Eno. Cæsar ? Why, he's the Jupiter of
　men.
　Agr. What's Antony ? The god of Jupiter.
　Eno. Spake you of Cæsar ? How ! the non-
　pareil !　　11
　Agr. O Antony ! O thou Arabian bird !
　Eno. Would you praise Cæsar, say ' Cæ-
　sar : ' go no further.
　Agr. Indeed, he plied them both with ex-
　cellent praises.
　Eno. But he loves Cæsar best ; yet he loves
　Antony :
Ho ! hearts, tongues, figures, scribes, bards,
　poets, cannot
Think, speak, cast, write, sing, number, ho !
His love to Antony. But as for Cæsar,
Kneel down, kneel down, and wonder.
　Agr.　　　　　Both he loves.
　Eno. They are his shards, and he their
　beetle. [*Trumpets within*] So ;　20
This is to horse. Adieu, noble Agrippa.
　Agr. Good fortune, worthy soldier ; and
　farewell.

Enter Cæsar, Antony, Lepidus, *and* Octavia.

　Ant. No further, sir.
　Cæs. You take from me a great part of
　myself ;
Use me well in 't. Sister, prove such a wife
As my thoughts make thee, and as my farthest
　band
Shall pass on thy approof. Most noble An-
　tony,
Let not the piece of virtue, which is set
Betwixt us as the cement of our love,
To keep it builded, be the ram to batter　30
The fortress of it ; for better might we
Have loved without this mean, if on both parts
This be not cherish'd.
　Ant.　　　　Make me not offended
In your distrust.

Cæs.   I have said.

Ant.   You shall not find,
Though you be therein curious, the least cause
For what you seem to fear : so, the gods keep
you,
And make the hearts of Romans serve your
ends !
We will here part.

Cæs.   Farewell, my dearest sister, fare thee
well :
The elements be kind to thee, and make   40
Thy spirits all of comfort ! fare thee well.

Oct.   My noble brother !

Ant.   The April 's in her eyes : it is love's
spring,
And these the showers to bring it on. Be
cheerful.

Oct.   Sir, look well to my husband's house ;
and—

Cæs.   What,
Octavia ?

Oct.   I'll tell you in your ear.

Ant.   Her tongue will not obey her heart,
nor can
Her heart inform her tongue,—the swan's
down-feather,
That stands upon the swell at full of tide,
And neither way inclines.   50

Eno.   [*Aside to Agr.*] Will Cæsar weep ?

Agr.   [*Aside to Eno.*] He has a cloud in 's
face.

Eno.   [*Aside to Agr.*] He were the worse for
that, were he a horse ;
So is he, being a man.

Agr.   [*Aside to Eno.*] Why, Enobarbus,
When Antony found Julius Cæsar dead,
He cried almost to roaring ; and he wept
When at Philippi he found Brutus slain.

Eno.   [*Aside to Agr.*] That year, indeed, he
was troubled with a rheum ;
What willingly he did confound he wail'd,
Believe 't, till I wept too.

Cæs.   No, sweet Octavia,
You shall hear from me still ; the time shall
not
Out-go my thinking on you.

Ant.   Come, sir, come ;   60
I'll wrestle with you in my strength of love :
Look, here I have you ; thus I let you go,
And give you to the gods.

Cæs.   Adieu ; be happy !

Lep.   Let all the number of the stars give
light
To thy fair way !

Cæs.   Farewell, farewell ! [*Kisses Octavia.*

Ant.   Farewell !
[*Trumpets sound. Exeunt.*

SCENE III.   *Alexandria. Cleopatra's
palace.*

Enter CLEOPATRA, CHARMIAN, IRAS, *and*
ALEXAS.

Cleo.   Where is the fellow ?

Alex.   Half afeard to come.

Cleo.   Go to, go to.

Enter the Messenger *as before.*

Come hither, sir.

Alex.   Good majesty,
Herod of Jewry dare not look upon you
But when you are well pleased.

Cleo.   That Herod's head
I'll have : but how, when Antony is gone

Through whom I might command it ? Come
thou near.

Mess.   Most gracious majesty,—

Cleo.   Didst thou behold Octavia ?

Mess.   Ay, dread queen.

Cleo.   Where ?   10

Mess.   Madam, in Rome ;
I look'd her in the face, and saw her led
Between her brother and Mark Antony.

Cleo.   Is she as tall as me ?

Mess.   She is not, madam.

Cleo.   Didst hear her speak ? is she shrill-
tongued or low ?

Mess.   Madam, I heard her speak ; she is
low-voiced.

Cleo.   That's not so good : he cannot like
her long.

Char.   Like her ! O Isis ! 'tis impossible.

Cleo.   I think so, Charmian : dull of
tongue, and dwarfish !
What majesty is in her gait ? Remember,   20
If e'er thou look'dst on majesty.

Mess.   She creeps :
Her motion and her station are as one ;
She shows a body rather than a life,
A statue than a breather.

Cleo.   Is this certain ?

Mess.   Or I have no observance.

Char.   Three in Egypt
Cannot make better note.

Cleo.   He's very knowing ;
I do perceive 't : there's nothing in her yet :
The fellow has good judgment.

Char.   Excellent.

Cleo.   Guess at her years, I prithee.

Mess.   Madam,
She was a widow,—

Cleo.   Widow ! Charmian, hark.   30

Mess.   And I do think she's thirty.

Cleo.   Bear'st thou her face in mind ? is't
long or round ?

Mess.   Round even to faultiness.

Cleo.   For the most part, too, they are foolish that are so.
Her hair, what color ?

Mess.   Brown, madam : and her forehead
As low as she would wish it.

Cleo.   There's gold for thee.
Thou must not take my former sharpness ill :
I will employ thee back again ; I find thee
Most fit for business : go make thee ready ;   40
Our letters are prepared.   [*Exit Messenger.*

Char.   A proper man.

Cleo.   Indeed, he is so : I repent me much
That so I harried him. Why, methinks, by him,
This creature's no such thing.

Char.   Nothing, madam.

Cleo.   The man hath seen some majesty,
and should know.

Char.   Hath he seen majesty ? Isis else defend,
And serving you so long !

Cleo.   I have one thing more to ask him
yet, good Charmian :
But 'tis no matter ; thou shalt bring him to me
Where I will write. All may be well enough.   50

Char.   I warrant you, madam.   [*Exeunt.*

SCENE IV.   *Athens. A room in Antony's
house.*

Enter ANTONY *and* OCTAVIA.

Ant.   Nay, nay, Octavia, not only that,—
That were excusable, that, and thousands more

Of semblable import,—but he hath waged
New wars 'gainst Pompey ; made his will, and
    read it
To public ear :
Spoke scantly of me : when perforce he could
    not
But pay me terms of honor, cold and sickly
He vented them ; most narrow measure lent
    me :
When the best hint was given him, he not
    took 't,
Or did it from his teeth.
    Oct.   O my good lord,   10
Believe not all ; or, if you must believe,
Stomach not all. A more unhappy lady,
If this division chance, ne'er stood between,
Praying for both parts :
The good gods will mock me presently,
When I shall pray, ' O, bless my lord and hus-
    band ! '
Undo that prayer, by crying out as loud,
' O, bless my brother ! ' Husband win, win
    brother,
Prays, and destroys the prayer ; no midway
'Twixt these extremes at all.
    Ant.   Gentle Octavia,   20
Let your best love draw to that point, which
    seeks
Best to preserve it : if I lose mine honor,
I lose myself : better I were not yours
Than yours so branchless. But, as you re-
    quested,
Yourself shall go between 's : the mean time,
    lady,
I'll raise the preparation of a war
Shall stain your brother : make your soonest
    haste ;
So your desires are yours.
    Oct.   Thanks to my lord.
The Jove of power make me most weak, most
    weak,
Your reconciler ! Wars 'twixt you twain would
    be   30
As if the world should cleave, and that slain
    men
Should solder up the rift.
    Ant.   When it appears to you where this be-
    gins,
Turn your displeasure that way ; for our faults
Can never be so equal, that your love
Can equally move with them. Provide your
    going ;
Choose your own company, and command
    what cost
Your heart has mind to.   [*Exeunt.*

  SCENE V. *The same. Another room.*
  Enter ENOBARBUS *and* EROS, *meeting.*

Eno. How now, friend Eros !
Eros. There's strange news come, sir.
Eno. What, man ?
Eros. Cæsar and Lepidus have made wars
upon Pompey.
Eno. This is old : what is the success ?
Eros. Cæsar, having made use of him in
the wars 'gainst Pompey, presently denied him
rivality ; would not let him partake in the
glory of the action : and not resting here, accuses him of letters he had formerly wrote to
Pompey ; upon his own appeal, seizes him : so
the poor third is up, till death enlarge his
confine.

Eno. Then, world, thou hast a pair of
    chaps, no more ;
And throw between them all the food thou
    hast,
They'll grind the one the other. Where's An-
    tony ?
Eros. He's walking in the garden—thus ;
    and spurns
The rush that lies before him ; cries, ' Fool
    Lepidus ! '
And threats the throat of that his officer
That murder'd Pompey.
Eno.   Our great navy's rigg'd. 20
Eros. For Italy and Cæsar. More, Domi-
    tius ;
My lord desires you presently : my news
I might have told hereafter.
Eno.   'Twill be naught :
But let it be. Bring me to Antony.
Eros. Come, sir.   [*Exeunt.*

  SCENE VI. *Rome. Cæsar's house.*
  Enter CÆSAR, AGRIPPA, *and* MECÆNAS.

Cæs. Contemning Rome, he has done all
    this, and more,
In Alexandria : here's the manner of 't :
I' the market-place, on a tribunal silver'd,
Cleopatra and himself in chairs of gold
Were publicly enthroned : at the feet sat
Cæsarion, whom they call my father's son,
And all the unlawful issue that their lust
Since then hath made between them. Unto her
He gave the stablishment of Egypt ; made her
Of lower Syria, Cyprus, Lydia,   10
Absolute queen.
Mec.   This in the public eye ?
Cæs. I' the common show-place, where
    they exercise.
His sons he there proclaim'd the kings of
    kings :
Great Media, Parthia, and Armenia,
He gave to Alexander ; to Ptolemy he assign'd
Syria, Cilicia, and Phœnicia : she
In the habiliments of the goddess Isis
That day appear'd ; and oft before gave audi-
    ence,
As 'tis reported, so.
Mec.   Let Rome be thus
Inform'd.
Agr.   Who, queasy with his insolence   20
Already, will their good thoughts call from
    him.
Cæs. The people know it ; and have now
    received
His accusations.
Agr.   Who does he accuse ?
Cæs. Cæsar : and that, having in Sicily
Sextus Pompeius spoil'd, we had not rated him
His part o' the isle : then does he say, he lent
    me
Some shipping unrestored : lastly, he frets
That Lepidus of the triumvirate
Should be deposed ; and, being, that we detain
All his revenue.
Agr.   Sir, this should be answer'd.   30
Cæs. 'Tis done already, and the messenger
    gone.
I have told him, Lepidus was grown too cruel ;
That he his high authority abused,
And did deserve his change : for what I have
    conquer'd,
I grant him part ; but then, in his Armenia,

And other of his conquer'd kingdoms, I
Demand the like.

Mec.　　　　　He'll never yield to that.

Cæs.　Nor must not then be yielded to in
this.

Enter OCTAVIA *with her train.*

Oct.　Hail, Cæsar, and my lord ! hail, most
dear Cæsar !

Cæs.　That ever I should call thee castaway !　　　　　　　　　　　　　40

Oct.　You have not call'd me so, nor have
you cause.

Cæs.　Why have you stol'n upon us thus !
You come not
Like Cæsar's sister : the wife of Antony
Should have an army for an usher, and
The neighs of horse to tell of her approach
Long ere she did appear ; the trees by the way
Should have borne men ; and expectation
fainted,
Longing for what it had not ; nay, the dust
Should have ascended to the roof of heaven,
Raised by your populous troops : but you are
come　　　　　　　　　　　　　50
A market-maid to Rome ; and have prevented
The ostentation of our love, which, left un-
shown,
Is often left unloved ; we should have met you
By sea and land ; supplying every stage
With an augmented greeting.

Oct.　　　　　　Good my lord,
To come thus was I not constrain'd, but did
On my free will. My lord, Mark Antony,
Hearing that you prepared for war, acquainted
My grieved ear withal ; whereon, I begg'd
His pardon for return.

Cæs.　　　Which soon he granted,　60
Being an obstruct 'tween his lust and him.

Oct.　Do not say so, my lord.

Cæs.　　　　I have eyes upon him,
And his affairs come to me on the wind.
Where is he now ?

Oct.　　　　My lord, in Athens.

Cæs.　No, my most wronged sister ; Cleo-
patra
Hath nodded him to her. He hath given his
empire
Up to a whore ; who now are levying
The kings o' the earth for war ; he hath as-
sembled
Bocchus, the king of Libya ; Archelaus,
Of Cappadocia ; Philadelphos, king　70
Of Paphlagonia ; the Thracian king, Adallas ;
King Malchus of Arabia ; King of Pont ;
Herod of Jewry ; Mithridates, king
Of Comagene ; Polemon and Amyntas,
The kings of Mede and Lycaonia,
With a more larger list of sceptres.

Oct.　　　　Ay me, most wretched,
That have my heart parted betwixt two friends
That do afflict each other !

Cæs.　　　　Welcome hither :
Your letters did withhold our breaking forth ;
Till we perceived, both how you were wrong
led,　　　　　　　　　　　　　80
And we in negligent danger. Cheer your heart ;
Be you not troubled with the time, which
drives
O'er your content these strong necessities ;
But let determined things to destiny
Hold unbewail'd their way. Welcome to
Rome ;

Nothing more dear to me. You are abused
Beyond the mark of thought : and the high
gods,
To do you justice, make them ministers
Of us and those that love you. Best of com-
fort ;
And ever welcome to us.　　　　　90

Agr.　　　　Welcome, lady.

Mec.　Welcome, dear madam.
Each heart in Rome does love and pity you :
Only the adulterous Antony, most large
In his abominations, turns you off ;
And gives his potent regiment to a trull,
That noises it against us.

Oct.　　　　Is it so, sir ?

Cæs.　Most certain. Sister, welcome : pray
you,
Be ever known to patience : my dear'st sister !
　　　　　　　　　　　　　[*Exeunt.*

SCENE VII.　*Near Actium. Antony's camp.*

Enter CLEOPATRA *and* ENOBARBUS.

Cleo.　I will be even with thee, doubt it not.

Eno.　But why, why, why ?

Cleo.　Thou hast forspoke my being in these
wars,
And say'st it is not fit.

Eno.　　　　Well, is it, is it ?

Cleo.　If not denounced against us, why
should not we
Be there in person ?

Eno.　[*Aside*] Well, I could reply :
If we should serve with horse and mares to-
gether,
The horse were merely lost ; the mares would
bear
A soldier and his horse.

Cleo.　　　What is 't you say ?　10

Eno.　Your presence needs must puzzle An-
tony ;
Take from his heart, take from his brain,
from's time,
What should not then be spared. He is already
Traduced for levity ; and 'tis said in Rome
That Photinus an eunuch and your maids
Manage this war.

Cleo.　　　Sink Rome, and their tongues rot
That speak against us ! A charge we bear i'
the war,
And, as the president of my kingdom, will
Appear there for a man. Speak not against it :
I will not stay behind.

Eno.　　　　Nay, I have done.　20
Here comes the emperor.

Enter ANTONY *and* CANIDIUS.

Ant.　　　Is it not strange, Canidius,
That from Tarentum and Brundusium
He could so quickly cut the Ionian sea,
And take in Toryne ? You have heard on't,
sweet ?

Cleo.　Celerity is never more admired
Than by the negligent.

Ant.　　　A good rebuke,
Which might have well becomed the best of
men,
To taunt at slackness. Canidius, we
Will fight with him by sea.

Cleo.　　　By sea ! what else ?

Can.　Why will my lord do so ?

Ant.　　　For that he dares us to't.　30

Eno.　So hath my lord dared him to single
fight.

Can. Ay, and to wage this battle at Pharsalia.
Where Cæsar fought with Pompey : but these offers,
Which serve not for his vantage, he shakes off ;
And so should you.
Eno. Your ships are not well mann'd ;
Your mariners are muleters, reapers, people
Ingross'd by swift impress ; in Cæsar's fleet
Are those that often have 'gainst Pompey fought :
Their ships are yare ; yours, heavy : no disgrace
Shall fall you for refusing him at sea,   40
Being prepared for land.
Ant.   By sea, by sea.
Eno. Most worthy sir, you therein throw away
The absolute soldiership you have by land ;
Distract your army, which doth most consist
Of war-mark'd footmen ; leave unexecuted
Your own renowned knowledge ; quite forego
The way which promises assurance ; and
Give up yourself merely to chance and hazard,
From firm security.
Ant.   I'll fight at sea.   49
Cleo. I have sixty sails, Cæsar none better.
Ant. Our overplus of shipping will we burn ;
And, with the rest full-mann'd, from the head of Actium
Beat the approaching Cæsar. But if we fail,
We then can do't at land.

Enter a Messenger.

                    Thy business ?
Mess. The news is true, my lord ; he is descried ;
Cæsar has taken Toryne.
Ant. Can he be there in person ? 'tis impossible ;
Strange that his power should be. Canidius,
Our nineteen legions thou shalt hold by land,
And our twelve thousand horse. We'll to our ship :
Away, my Thetis !

Enter a Soldier.

                    How now, worthy soldier !   61
Sold. O noble emperor, do not fight by sea ;
Trust not to rotten planks : do you misdoubt
This sword and these my wounds ? Let the Egyptians
And the Phœnicians go a-ducking ; we
Have used to conquer, standing on the earth,
And fighting foot to foot.
Ant.   Well, well : away !
[*Exeunt Antony, Cleopatra, and Enobarbus.*
Sold. By Hercules, I think I am i' the right.
Can. Soldier, thou art : but his whole action grows
Not in the power on't : so our leader's led,   70
And we are women's men.
Sold.   You keep by land
The legions and the horse whole, do you not ?
Can. Marcus Octavius, Marcus Justeius,
Publicola, and Cælius, are for sea :
But we keep whole by land. This speed of Cæsar's
Carries beyond belief.
Sold.   While he was yet in Rome,

His power went out in such distractions as
Beguiled all spies.
Can.   Who's his lieutenant, hear you ?
Sold. They say, one Taurus.
Can.   Well I know the man.

Enter a Messenger.

Mess. The emperor calls Canidius.   80
Can. With news the time's with labor, and throes forth,
Each minute, some.   [*Exeunt.*

SCENE VIII. *A plain near Actium.*

Enter CÆSAR, *and* TAURUS, *with his army, marching.*

Cæs. Taurus !
Taur. My lord ?
Cæs. Strike not by land ; keep whole : provoke not battle,
Till we have done at sea. Do not exceed
The prescript of this scroll : our fortune lies
Upon this jump.   [*Exeunt.*

SCENE IX. *Another part of the plain.*

Enter ANTONY *and* ENOBARBUS.

Ant. Set we our squadrons on yond side o' the hill,
In eye of Cæsar's battle ; from which place
We may the number of the ships behold,
And so proceed accordingly.   [*Exeunt.*

SCENE X. *Another part of the plain.*

CANIDIUS *marcheth with his land army one way over the stage ; and* TAURUS, *the lieutenant of* CÆSAR, *the other way. After their going in, is heard the noise of a sea-fight.*

Alarum. Enter ENOBARBUS.

Eno. Naught, naught all, naught ! I can behold no longer :
The Antoniad, the Egyptian admiral,
With all their sixty, fly and turn the rudder :
To see't mine eyes are blasted.

Enter SCARUS.

Scar.   Gods and goddesses,
All the whole synod of them !
Eno.   What's thy passion ?
Scar. The greater cantle of the world is lost
With very ignorance ; we have kiss'd away
Kingdoms and provinces.
Eno.   How appears the fight ?
Scar. On our side like the token'd pestilence,
Where death is sure. Yon ribaudred nag of Egypt,—   10
Whom leprosy o'ertake !—i' the midst o' the fight,
When vantage like a pair of twins appear'd,
Both as the same, or rather ours the elder,
The breese upon her, like a cow in June,
Hoists sails and flies.
Eno. That I beheld :
Mine eyes did sicken at the sight, and could not
Endure a further view.
Scar.   She once being loof'd,
The noble ruin of her magic, Antony,
Claps on his sea-wing, and, like a doting mallard,   20
Leaving the fight in height, flies after her :
I never saw an action of such shame ;

Experience, manhood, honor, ne'er before
Did violate so itself.

   Eno.   Alack, alack!

        Enter CANIDIUS.

   Can. Our fortune on the sea is out of
breath,
And sinks most lamentably. Had our general
Been what he knew himself, it had gone well :
O, he has given example for our flight,
Most grossly, by his own !

   Eno.   Ay, are you thereabouts ?
Why, then, good night indeed.   30

   Can. Toward Peloponnesus are they fled.

   Scar. 'Tis easy to't ; and there I will attend
What further comes.

   Can.   To Cæsar will I render
My legions and my horse : six kings already
Show me the way of yielding.

   Eno.   I'll yet follow
The wounded chance of Antony, though my
    reason
Sits in the wind against me.   [*Exeunt.*

  SCENE XI. *Alexandria. Cleopatra's palace.*

    Enter ANTONY *with* Attendants.

   Ant. Hark ! the land bids me tread no
    more upon't ;
It is ashamed to bear me ! Friends, come
    hither :
I am so lated in the world, that I
Have lost my way for ever : I have a ship
Laden with gold ; take that, divide it ; fly,
And make your peace with Cæsar.

   All.   Fly ! not we.

   Ant. I have fled myself ; and have in-
    structed cowards
To run and show their shoulders. Friends, be
    gone ;
I have myself resolved upon a course
Which has no need of you ; be gone :   10
My treasure's in the harbor, take it. O,
I follow'd that I blush to look upon :
My very hairs do mutiny ; for the white
Reprove the brown for rashness, and they
    them
For fear and doting. Friends, be gone : you
    shall
Have letters from me to some friends that will
Sweep your way for you. Pray you, look not
    sad,
Nor make replies of loathness : take the hint
Which my despair proclaims ; let that be left
Which leaves itself : to the sea-side straight-
    way :   20
I will possess you of that ship and treasure.
Leave me, I pray, a little : pray you now :
Nay, do so ; for, indeed, I have lost command,
Therefore I pray you : I'll see you by and by.
                    [*Sits down.*

Enter CLEOPATRA *led by* CHARMIAN *and* IRAS ;
      EROS *following.*

   Eros. Nay, gentle madam, to him, comfort
    him.

   Iras. Do, most dear queen.

   Char. Do ! why : what else ?

   Cleo. Let me sit down. O Juno !

   Ant. No, no, no, no, no.

   Eros. See you here, sir ?   30

   Ant. O fie, fie, fie !

   Char. Madam !

   Iras. Madam, O good empress !

   Eros. Sir, sir,—

   Ant. Yes, my lord, yes ; he at Philippi kept
His sword e'en like a dancer ; while I struck
The lean and wrinkled Cassius ; and 'twas I
That the mad Brutus ended : he alone
Dealt on lieutenantry, and no practice had
In the brave squares of war : yet now—No
    matter.   40

   Cleo. Ah, stand by.

   Eros. The queen, my lord, the queen.

   Iras. Go to him, madam, speak to him :
He is unqualitied with very shame.

   Cleo. Well then, sustain him : O !

   Eros. Most noble sir, arise ; the queen ap-
    proaches :
Her head's declined, and death will seize her,
    but
Your comfort makes the rescue.

   Ant. I have offended reputation,
A most unnoble swerving.

   Eros.   Sir, the queen.   50

   Ant. O, whither hast thou led me, Egypt ?
    See,
How I convey my shame out of thine eyes
By looking back what I have left behind
'Stroy'd in dishonor.

   Cleo.   O my lord, my lord,
Forgive my fearful sails ! I little thought
You would have follow'd.

   Ant.   Egypt, thou knew'st too well
My heart was to thy rudder tied by the strings,
And thou shouldst tow me after : o'er my spirit
Thy full supremacy thou knew'st, and that
Thy beck might from the bidding of the gods
Command me.   61

   Cleo.   O, my pardon !

   Ant.   Now I must
To the young man send humble treaties, dodge
And palter in the shifts of lowness ; who
With half the bulk o' the world play'd as I
    pleased,
Making and marring fortunes. You did know
How much you were my conqueror ; and that
My sword, made weak by my affection, would
Obey it on all cause.

   Cleo.   Pardon, pardon !

   Ant. Fall not a tear, I say ; one of them
    rates
All that is won and lost : give me a kiss ;   70
Even this repays me. We sent our schoolmas-
    ter ;
Is he come back ? Love, I am full of lead.
Some wine, within there, and our viands !
Fortune knows
We scorn her most when most she offers
    blows.   [*Exeunt.*

    SCENE XII. *Egypt. Cæsar's camp.*

Enter CÆSAR, DOLABELLA, THYREUS, *with*
      others.

   Cæs. Let him appear that's come from
    Antony.
Know you him ?

   Dol.   Cæsar, 'tis his schoolmaster :
An argument that he is pluck'd, when hither
He sends so poor a pinion off his wing,
Which had superfluous kings for messengers
Not many moons gone by.

Enter EUPHRONIUS, *ambassador from Antony.*

   Cæs.   Approach, and speak.

   Euph. Such as I am, I come from Antony :
I was of late as petty to his ends

As is the morn-dew on the myrtle-leaf
To his grand sea.
Cæs.   Be't so : declare thine office. 10
Euph. Lord of his fortunes he salutes thee,
and
Requires to live in Egypt : which not granted,
He lessens his requests ; and to thee sues
To let him breathe between the heavens and
earth,
A private man in Athens : this for him.
Next, Cleopatra does confess thy greatness ;
Submits her to thy might ; and of thee craves
The circle of the Ptolemies for her heirs,
Now hazarded to thy grace.
Cæs.   For Antony,
I have no ears to his request. The queen   20
Of audience nor desire shall fail, so she
From Egypt drive her all-disgraced friend,
Or take his life there : this if she perform,
She shall not sue unheard. So to them both.
Euph. Fortune pursue thee !
Cæs.   Bring him through the bands.
                    [*Exit Euphronius.*
[*To Thyreus*] To try thy eloquence, now 'tis
time : dispatch ;
From Antony win Cleopatra : promise,
And in our name, what she requires ; add
more,
From thine invention, offers : women are not
In their best fortunes strong ; but want will
perjure   30
The ne'er touch'd vestal : try thy cunning,
Thyreus ;
Make thine own edict for thy pains, which we
Will answer as a law.
Thyr.   Cæsar, I go.
Cæs. Observe how Antony becomes his
flaw,
And what thou think'st his very action speaks
In every power that moves.
Thyr.   Cæsar, I shall. [*Exeunt.*

SCENE XIII. *Alexandria. Cleopatra's
palace.*

Enter CLEOPATRA, ENOBARBUS, CHARMIAN,
and IRAS.

Cleo. What shall we do, Enobarbus ?
Eno.   Think, and die.
Cleo. Is Antony or we in fault for this ?
Eno. Antony only, that would make his will
Lord of his reason. What though you fled
From that great face of war, whose several
ranges
Frighted each other ? why should he follow ?
The itch of his affection should not then
Have nick'd his captainship ; at such a point,
When half to half the world opposed, he being
The meered question : 'twas a shame no less
Than was his loss, to course your flying flags,
And leave his navy gazing.
Cleo.   Prithee, peace.

Enter ANTONY *with* EUPHRONIUS, *the
Ambassador.*

Ant. Is that his answer ?
Euph. Ay, my lord.
Ant. The queen shall then have courtesy,
so she
Will yield us up.
Euph.   He says so.
Ant.   Let her know't.
To the boy Cæsar send this grizzled head,
And he will fill thy wishes to the brim

With principalities.
Cleo.   That head, my lord ?
Ant. To him again : tell him he wears the
rose   20
Of youth upon him ; from which the world
should note
Something particular : his coin, ships, legions,
May be a coward's ; whose ministers would
prevail
Under the service of a child as soon
As i' the command of Cæsar : I dare him
therefore
To lay his gay comparisons apart,
And answer me declined, sword against sword,
Ourselves alone. I'll write it : follow me.
          [*Exeunt Antony and Euphronius.*
Eno. [*Aside*] Yes, like enough, high-bat-
tled Cæsar will
Unstate his happiness, and be staged to the
show,   30
Against a sworder ! I see men's judgments are
A parcel of their fortunes ; and things outward
Do draw the inward quality after them,
To suffer all alike. That he should dream,
Knowing all measures, the full Cæsar will
Answer his emptiness ! Cæsar, thou hast sub-
dued
His judgment too.

Enter an Attendant.

Att.   A messenger from Cæsar.
Cleo. What, no more ceremony ? See, my
women !
Against the blown rose may they stop their
nose   39
That kneel'd unto the buds. Admit him, sir.
                    [*Exit attendant.*
Eno. [*Aside*] Mine honesty and I begin to
square.
The loyalty well held to fools does make
Our faith mere folly : yet he that can endure
To follow with allegiance a fall'n lord
Does conquer him that did his master conquer
And earns a place i' the story.

Enter THYREUS.

Cleo.   Cæsar's will ?
Thyr. Hear it apart.
Cleo.   None but friends : say boldly.
Thyr. So, haply, are they friends to An-
tony.
Eno. He needs as many, sir, as Cæsar
has ;   49
Or needs not us. If Cæsar please, our master
Will leap to be his friend : for us, you know,
Whose he is we are, and that is, Cæsar's.
Thyr.   So.
Thus then, thou most renown'd : Cæsar en-
treats,
Not to consider in what case thou stand'st,
Further than he is Cæsar.
Cleo.   Go on : right royal.
Thyr. He knows that you embrace not
Antony
As you did love, but as you fear'd him.
Cleo.   O !
Thyr. The scars upon your honor, there-
fore, he
Does pity, as constrained blemishes,
Not as deserved.
Cleo.   He is a god, and knows 60
What is most right : mine honor was not
yielded,

But conquer'd merely.
　Eno.　　　[*Aside*] To be sure of that,
I will ask Antony. Sir, sir, thou art so leaky,
That we must leave thee to thy sinking, for
Thy dearest quit thee.　　　　　[*Exit.*
　Thyr.　　　Shall I say to Cæsar
What you require of him ? for he partly begs
To be desired to give. It much would please
him,
That of his fortunes you should make a staff
To lean upon : but it would warm his spirits,
To hear from me you had left Antony,　70
And put yourself under his shroud,
The universal landlord.
　Cleo.　　　What's your name ?
　Thyr. My name is Thyreus.
　Cleo.　　　Most kind messenger,
Say to great Cæsar this : in deputation
I kiss his conquering hand : tell him, I am
prompt
To lay my crown at 's feet, and there to kneel :
Tell him, from his all-obeying breath I hear
The doom of Egypt.
　Thyr.　　　'Tis your noblest course.
Wisdom and fortune combating together,
If that the former dare but what it can,　80
No chance may shake it. Give me grace to
lay
My duty on your hand.
　Cleo.　　　Your Cæsar's father oft,
When he hath mused of taking kingdoms in,
Bestow'd his lips on that unworthy place,
As it rain'd kisses.

　Re-enter Antony *and* Enobarbus.

　Ant.　　　Favors, by Jove that thunders !
What art thou, fellow ?
　Thyr.　　　One that but performs
The bidding of the fullest man, and worthiest
To have command obey'd.
　Eno.　　[*Aside*] You will be whipp'd.
　Ant. Approach, there ! Ah, you kite ! Now,
gods and devils !
Authority melts from me : of late, when I
cried ' Ho ! '　90
Like boys unto a muss, kings would start forth,
And cry ' Your will ? ' Have you no ears ? I
am
Antony yet.

　　　　Enter Attendants.

　　　Take hence this Jack, and whip him.
　Eno. [*Aside*] 'Tis better playing with a
lion's whelp
Than with an old one dying.
　Ant.　　　Moon and stars !
Whip him. Were't twenty of the greatest tribu-
taries
That do acknowledge Cæsar, should I find
them
So saucy with the hand of she here,—what's
her name,
Since she was Cleopatra ? Whip him, fellows,
Till, like a boy, you see him cringe his face,
And whine aloud for mercy : take him hence.
　Thyr. Mark Antony !
　Ant.　　　Tug him away : being whipp'd,
Bring him again : this Jack of Cæsar's shall
Bear us an errand to him.
　　　[*Exeunt Attendants with Thyreus.*
You were half blasted ere I knew you : ha !
Have I my pillow left unpress'd in Rome,
Forborne the getting of a lawful race,

And by a gem of women, to be abused
By one that looks on feeders ?
　Cleo.　　　Good my lord,—
　Ant. You have been a boggler ever :　110
But when we in our viciousness grow hard—
O misery on't !—the wise gods seel our eyes ;
In our own filth drop our clear judgments ;
make us
Adore our errors ; laugh at's, while we strut
To our confusion.
　Cleo.　　　O, is't come to this ?
　Ant. I found you as a morsel cold upon
Dead Cæsar's trencher ; nay, you were a
fragment
Of Cneius Pompey's ; besides what hotter
hours,
Unregister'd in vulgar fame, you have
Luxuriously pick'd out : for, I am sure,　120
Though you can guess what temperance should
be,
You know not what it is.
　Cleo.　　　Wherefore is this ?
　Ant. To let a fellow that will take rewards
And say ' God quit you ! ' be familiar with
My playfellow, your hand ; this kingly seal
And plighter of high hearts ! O, that I were
Upon the hill of Basan, to outroar
The horned herd ! for I have savage cause ;
And to proclaim it civilly, were like
A halter'd neck which does the hangman
thank
For being yare about him.

　　　Re-enter Attendants *with* Thyreus.

　　　　　　　Is he whipp'd ?　131
　First Att. Soundly, my lord.
　Ant.　　　Cried he ? and begg'd a' pardon ?
　First Att. He did ask favor.
　Ant. If that thy father live, let him repent
Thou wast not made his daughter ; and be
thou sorry
To follow Cæsar in his triumph, since
Thou hast been whipp'd for following him :
henceforth
The white hand of a lady fever thee,
Shake thou to look on 't. Get thee back to
Cæsar,　139
Tell him thy entertainment : look, thou say
He makes me angry with him ; for he seems
Proud and disdainful, harping on what I am,
Not what he knew I was : he makes me angry ;
And at this time most easy 'tis to do't,
When my good stars, that were my former
guides,
Have empty left their orbs, and shot their
fires
Into the abysm of hell. If he mislike
My speech and what is done, tell him he has
Hipparchus, my enfranched bondman, whom
He may at pleasure whip, or hang, or torture,
As he shall like, to quit me : urge it thou :
Hence with thy stripes, begone !
　　　　　　　　　[*Exit Thyreus.*
　Cleo. Have you done yet ?
　Ant.　　　Alack, our terrene moon
Is now eclipsed ; and it portends alone
The fall of Antony !
　Cleo.　　　I must stay his time.
　Ant. To flatter Cæsar, would you mingle
eyes
With one that ties his points ?
　Cleo.　　　Not know me yet ?
　Ant. Cold-hearted toward me ?

Cleo.   Ah, dear, if I be so,
From my cold heart let heaven engender hail,
And poison it in the source; and the first
    stone   160
Drop in my neck: as it determines, so
Dissolve my life! The next Cæsarion smite!
Till by degrees the memory of my womb,
Together with my brave Egyptians all,
By the discandying of this pelleted storm,
Lie graveless, till the flies and gnats of Nile
Have buried them for prey!
Ant.   I am satisfied.
Cæsar sits down in Alexandria; where
I will oppose his fate. Our force by land
Hath nobly held; our sever'd navy too   170
Have knit again, and fleet, threatening most
    sea-like.
Where hast thou been, my heart? Dost thou
    hear, lady?
If from the field I shall return once more
To kiss these lips, I will appear in blood;
I and my sword will earn our chronicle:
There's hope in't yet.
Cleo.   That's my brave lord!
Ant. I will be treble-sinew'd, hearted,
    breathed,
And fight maliciously: for when mine hours
Were nice and lucky, men did ransom lives
Of me for jests; but now I'll set my teeth,
And send to darkness all that stop me. Come,
Let's have one other gaudy night: call to me
All my sad captains; fill our bowls once more;
Let's mock the midnight bell.
Cleo.   It is my birth-day:
I had thought to have held it poor: but, since
    my lord
Is Antony again, I will be Cleopatra.
Ant. We will yet do well.
Cleo. Call all his noble captains to my lord.
Ant. Do so, we'll speak to them; and to-
    night I'll force   190
The wine peep through their scars. Come on,
    my queen;
There's sap in't yet. The next time I do fight,
I'll make death love me; for I will contend
Even with his pestilent scythe.
                    [*Exeunt all but Enobarbus.*
Eno. Now he'll outstare the lightning. To
    be furious,
Is to be frighted out of fear; and in that
    mood
The dove will peck the estridge; and I see
    still,
A diminution in our captain's brain
Restores his heart: when valor preys on rea-
    son,
It eats the sword it fights with. I will seek 200
Some way to leave him.   [*Exit.*

ACT IV.

SCENE I. *Before Alexandria. Cæsar's camp.*

Enter CÆSAR, AGRIPPA, *and* MECÆNAS, *with
    his Army;* CÆSAR *reading a letter.*

Cæs. He calls me boy; and chides, as he
    had power
To beat me out of Egypt; my messenger
He hath whipp'd with rods; dares me to per-
    sonal combat,
Cæsar to Antony: let the old ruffian know
I have many other ways to die; meantime

Laugh at his challenge.
Mec.   Cæsar must think,
When one so great begins to rage, he's hunted
Even to falling. Give him no breath, but now
Make boot of his distraction: never anger
Made good guard for itself.
Cæs.   Let our best heads 10
Know, that to-morrow the last of many bat-
    tles
We mean to fight: within our files there are,
Of those that served Mark Antony but late,
Enough to fetch him in. See it done:
And feast the army; we have store to do't,
And they have earn'd the waste. Poor Antony!
                                    [*Exeunt.*

SCENE II. *Alexandria. Cleopatra's palace.*

Enter ANTONY, CLEOPATRA, ENOBARBUS,
    CHARMIAN, IRAS, ALEXAS, *with others.*

Ant. He will not fight with me, Domitius.
Eno.   No.
Ant. Why should he not?
Eno. He thinks, being twenty times of bet-
    ter fortune,
He is twenty men to one.
Ant.   To-morrow, soldier,
By sea and land I'll fight: or I will live,
Or bathe my dying honor in the blood
Shall make it live again. Woo't thou fight
    well?
Eno. I'll strike, and cry 'Take all.'
Ant.   Well said; come on.
Call forth my household servants: let's to-
    night
Be bounteous at our meal.

Enter three or four Servitors.

                    Give me thy hand, 10
Thou hast been rightly honest;—so hast
    thou;—
Thou,—and thou,—and thou:—you have
    served me well,
And kings have been your fellows.
Cleo. [*Aside to Eno.*] What means this?
Eno. [*Aside to Cleo.*] 'Tis one of those
    odd tricks which sorrow shoots
Out of the mind.
Ant.   And thou art honest too.
I wish I could be made so many men,
And all of you clapp'd up together in
An Antony, that I might do you service
So good as you have done.
All.   The gods forbid!
Ant. Well, my good fellows, wait on me
    to-night: 20
Scant not my cups; and make as much of me
As when mine empire was your fellow too,
And suffer'd my command.
Cleo. [*Aside to Eno.*] What does he mean?
Eno. [*Aside to Cleo.*] To make his follow-
    ers weep.
Ant. Tend me to-night;
May be it is the period of your duty:
Haply you shall not see me more; or if,
A mangled shadow: perchance to-morrow
You'll serve another master. I look on you
As one that takes his leave. Mine honest
    friends,
I turn you not away; but, like a master 30
Married to your good service, stay till death:
Tend me to-night two hours, I ask no more,
And the gods yield you for't!
Eno.   What mean you, sir,

To give them this discomfort? Look, they
  weep;
And I, an ass, am onion-eyed: for shame,
Transform us not to women.
   Ant.   Ho, ho, ho!
Now the witch take me, if I meant it thus!
Grace grow where those drops fall! My hearty
  friends,
You take me in too dolorous a sense;
For I spake to you for your comfort; did
  desire you   40
To burn this night with torches: know, my
  hearts,
I hope well of to-morrow; and will lead you
Where rather I'll expect victorious life
Than death and honor. Let's to supper, come,
And drown consideration.   *[Exeunt.*

SCENE III. *The same. Before the palace.*

Enter two Soldiers *to their guard.*

First Sold. Brother, good night: to-mor-
  row is the day.
Sec. Sold. It will determine one way: fare
  you well.
Heard you of nothing strange about the
  streets?
First Sold. Nothing. What news?
Sec. Sold. Belike 'tis but a rumor. Good
  night to you.
First Sold. Well, sir, good night.

Enter two other Soldiers.

Sec. Sold. Soldiers, have careful watch.
Third Sold. And you. Good night, good
  night.
  [They place themselves in every corner of
                the stage.
Fourth Sold. Here we: and if to-morrow
Our navy thrive, I have an absolute hope   10
Our landmen will stand up.
Third Sold.   'Tis a brave army,
And full of purpose.
  [Music of the hautboys as under the stage.
Fourth Sold. Peace! what noise?
First Sold.   List, list!
Sec. Sold. Hark!
First Sold.   Music i' the air.
Third Sold.   Under the earth.
Fourth Sold. It signs well, does it not?
Third Sold.   No.
First Sold.   Peace, I say!
What should this mean?
Sec. Sold. 'Tis the god Hercules, whom
  Antony loved,
Now leaves him.
First Sold. Walk; let's see if other watch-
  men
Do hear what we do?
         [They advance to another post.
Sec. Sold.   How now, masters!
All.   *[Speaking together]* How now!
How now! do you hear this?
First Sold.   Ay; is't not strange? 20
Third Sold. Do you hear, masters? do you
  hear?
First Sold. Follow the noise so far as we
  have quarter;
Let's see how it will give off.
All.   Content. 'Tis strange. *[Exeunt.*

SCENE IV. *The same. A room in the palace.*

Enter ANTONY *and* CLEOPATRA, CHARMIAN,
    and others attending.

Ant. Eros! mine armor, Eros!
Cleo.   Sleep a little.
Ant. No, my chuck. Eros, come; mine
  armor, Eros!

Enter EROS *with armor.*

Come, good fellow, put mine iron on:
If fortune be not ours to-day, it is
Because we brave her: come.
Cleo.   Nay, I'll help too.
What's this for?
Ant.   Ah, let be, let be! thou art
The armorer of my heart: false, false; this,
  this.
Cleo. Sooth, la, I'll help: thus it must be.
Ant.   Well, well;
We shall thrive now. Seest thou, my good
  fellow?
Go put on thy defences.
Eros.   Briefly, sir.   10
Cleo. Is not this buckled well?
Ant.   Rarely, rarely:
He that unbuckles this, till we do please
To daff't for our repose, shall hear a storm.
Thou fumblest, Eros; and my queen's a squire
More tight at this than thou: dispatch. O love,
That thou couldst see my wars to-day, and
  knew'st
The royal occupation! thou shouldst see
A workman in't.

Enter an armed Soldier.

        Good morrow to thee; welcome:
Thou look'st like him that knows a warlike
  charge:
To business that we love we rise betime,   20
And go to't with delight.
Sold.   A thousand, sir,
Early though't be, have on their riveted trim,
And at the port expect you.
         [Shout. Trumpets flourish.

Enter Captains *and* Soldiers.

Capt. The morn is fair. Good morrow,
  general.
All. Good morrow, general.
Ant.   'Tis well blown, lads:
This morning, like the spirit of a youth
That means to be of note, begins betimes.
So, so; come, give me that: this way; well
  said.
Fare thee well, dame, whate'er becomes of me:
This is a soldier's kiss: rebukeable   30
                  [Kisses her.
And worthy shameful check it were, to stand
On more mechanic compliment; I'll leave thee
Now, like a man of steel. You that will fight,
Follow me close; I'll bring you to't. Adieu.
  [Exeunt Antony, Eros, Captains, and
                  Soldiers.
Char. Please you, retire to your chamber.
Cleo.   Lead me.
He goes forth gallantly. That he and Cæsar
  might
Determine this great war in single fight!
Then Antony,—but now—Well, on. *[Exeunt.*

SCENE V. *Alexandria. Antony's camp.*

Trumpets sound. Enter ANTONY *and* EROS;
    a Soldier *meeting them.*

Sold. The gods make this a happy day to
  Antony!

Ant. Would thou and those thy scars had
    once prevail'd
To make me fight at land !
    Sold.   Hadst thou done so,
The kings that have revolted, and the soldier
That has this morning left thee, would have
    still
Follow'd thy heels.
    Ant.   Who's gone this morning ?
    Sold.   Who !
One ever near thee : call for Enobarbus,
He shall not hear thee ; or from Cæsar's camp
Say 'I am none of thine.'
    Ant.   What say'st thou ?
    Sold.   Sir,
He is with Cæsar.
    Eros.   Sir, his chests and treasure 10
He has not with him.
    Ant.   Is he gone ?
    Sold.   Most certain.
    Ant. Go, Eros, send his treasure after ; do
    it ;
Detain no jot, I charge thee : write to him—
I will subscribe—gentle adieus and greetings ;
Say that I wish he never find more cause
To change a master. O, my fortunes have
Corrupted honest men ! Dispatch.—Enobar-
    bus !   [*Exeunt.*

    SCENE VI. *Alexandria. Cæsar's camp.*

Flourish. Enter CÆSAR, AGRIPPA, *with* ENO-
    BARBUS, *and others.*

    Cæs. Go forth, Agrippa, and begin the
    fight :
Our will is Antony be took alive ;
Make it so known.
    Agr. Cæsar, I shall.   [*Exit.*
    Cæs. The time of universal peace is near :
Prove this a prosperous day, the three-nook'd
    world
Shall bear the olive freely.

    Enter a Messenger.

    Mess.   Antony
Is come into the field.
    Cæs.   Go charge Agrippa
Plant those that have revolted in the van,
That Antony may seem to spend his fury 10
Upon himself.   [*Exeunt all but Enobarbus.*
    Eno. Alexas did revolt ; and went to Jewry
    on
Affairs of Antony ; there did persuade
Great Herod to incline himself to Cæsar,
And leave his master Antony : for this pains
Cæsar hath hang'd him. Canidius and the
    rest
That fell away have entertainment, but
No honorable trust. I have done ill ;
Of which I do accuse myself so sorely,
That I will joy no more.

    Enter a Soldier *of* CÆSAR'S.

    Sold.   Enobarbus, Antony 20
Hath after thee sent all thy treasure, with
His bounty overplus : the messenger
Came on my guard ; and at thy tent is now
Unloading of his mules.
    Eno.   I give it you.
    Sold. Mock not, Enobarbus.
I tell you true : best you safed the bringer
Out of the host ; I must attend mine office,
Or would have done 't myself. Your emperor
Continues still a Jove.   [*Exit.*

    Eno. I am alone the villain of the earth, 30
And feel I am so most. O Antony,
Thou mine of bounty, how wouldst thou have
    paid
My better service, when my turpitude
Thou dost so crown with gold ! This blows
    my heart :
If swift thought break it not, a swifter mean
Shall outstrike thought : but thought will do 't,
    I feel.
I fight against thee ! No : I will go seek
Some ditch wherein to die ; the foul'st best fits
My latter part of life.   [*Exit.*

    SCENE VII. *Field of battle between the camps.*
    Alarum. Drums and trumpets. Enter
    AGRIPPA *and others.*

    Agr. Retire, we have engaged ourselves too
    far :
Cæsar himself has work, and our oppression
Exceeds what we expected.   [*Exeunt.*

    Alarums. Enter ANTONY *and* SCARUS
        wounded.

    Scar. O my brave emperor, this is fought
    indeed !
Had we done so at first, we had droven them
    home
With clouts about their heads.
    Ant.   Thou bleed'st apace.
    Scar. I had a wound here that was like a T,
But now 'tis made an H.
    Ant.   They do retire.
    Scar. We'll beat 'em into bench-holes : I
    have yet
Room for six scotches more.   10

    Enter EROS.

    Eros. They are beaten, sir, and our ad-
    vantage serves
For a fair victory.
    Scar.   Let us score their backs,
And snatch 'em up, as we take hares, behind :
'Tis sport to maul a runner.
    Ant.   I will reward thee
Once for thy spritely comfort, and ten-fold
For thy good valor. Come thee on.
    Scar.   I'll halt after. [*Exeunt.*

    SCENE VIII. *Under the walls of Alexandria.*
    Alarum. Enter ANTONY, *in a march ;* SCARUS,
        with others.

    Ant. We have beat him to his camp : run
    one before,
And let the queen know of our gests. To-
    morrow,
Before the sun shall see 's, we'll spill the blood
That has to-day escaped. I thank you all ;
For doughty-handed are you, and have fought
Not as you served the cause, but as 't had been
Each man's like mine ; you have shown all
    Hectors.
Enter the city, clip your wives, your friends,
Tell them your feats ; whilst they with joy-
    ful tears
Wash the congealment from your wounds, and
    kiss   10
The honor'd gashes whole. [*To Scarus*] Give
    me thy hand ;

    Enter CLEOPATRA, *attended.*

To this great fairy I'll commend thy acts,

Make her thanks bless thee. [*To Cleo.*] O thou
　　day o' the world,
Chain mine arm'd neck ; leap thou, attire and
　　all,
Through proof of harness to my heart, and
　　there
Ride on the pants triumphing !
　　Cleo. 　　　　　　　Lord of lords !
O infinite virtue, comest thou smiling from
The world's great snare uncaught ?
　　Ant. 　　　　　　My nightingale,
We have beat them to their beds. What, girl !
　　though grey
Do something mingle with our younger brown,
　　yet ha' we 　　　　　　　　　20
A brain that nourishes our nerves, and can
Get goal for goal of youth. Behold this man ;
Commend unto his lips thy favoring hand ;
Kiss it, my warrior : he hath fought to-day
As if a god, in hate of mankind, had
Destroy'd in such a shape.
　　Cleo. 　　　　　I'll give thee, friend,
An armor all of gold ; it was a king's.
　　Ant. He has deserved it, were it carbuncled
Like holy Phœbus' car. Give me thy hand :
Through Alexandria make a jolly march ; 　30
Bear our hack'd targets like the men that owe
　　them :
Had our great palace the capacity
To camp this host, we all would sup together,
And drink carouses to the next day's fate,
Which promises royal peril. Trumpeters,
With brazen din blast you the city's ear ;
Make mingle with our rattling tabourines ;
That heaven and earth may strike their sounds
　　together,
Applauding our approach. 　[*Exeunt.* 39

　　SCENE IX. *Cæsar's camp.*
　　Sentinels *at their post.*

　First Sold. If we be not relieved within this
　　hour,
We must return to the court of guard : the
　　night
Is shiny ; and they say we shall embattle
By the second hour i' the morn.
　Sec. Sold. 　　　　This last day was
A shrewd one to's.

　　Enter ENOBARBUS.

　Eno. 　　O, bear me witness, night,—
　Third Sold. What man is this ?
　Sec. Sold. 　Stand close, and list him.
　Eno. Be witness to me, O thou blessed
　　moon,
When men revolted shall upon record
Bear hateful memory, poor Enobarbus did
Before thy face repent !
　First Sold. 　　　　Enobarbus !
　Third Sold. 　　　　　　Peace ! 10
Hark further.
　Eno. O sovereign mistress of true melan-
　　choly,
The poisonous damp of night disponge upon
　　me,
That life, a very rebel to my will,
May hang no longer on me : throw my heart
Against the flint and hardness of my fault ;
Which, being dried with grief, will break to
　　powder,
And finish all foul thoughts. O Antony,
Nobler than my revolt is infamous,
Forgive me in thine own particular ; 　　20

But let the world rank me in register
A master-leaver and a fugitive :
O Antony ! O Antony ! 　　　　[*Dies.*
　Sec. Sold. 　Let's speak
To him.
　First Sold. Let's hear him, for the things
　　he speaks
May concern Cæsar.
　Third Sold. 　Let's do so. But he sleeps.
　First Sold. Swoons rather ; for so bad a
　　prayer as his
Was never yet for sleep.
　Sec. Sold. 　　　　Go we to him.
　Third Sold. Awake, sir, awake ; speak to
　　us.
　Sec. Sold. 　　　Hear you, sir ?
　First Sold. The hand of death hath raught
　　him. [*Drums afar off.*] Hark ! the drums
Demurely wake the sleepers. Let us bear
　　him 　　　　　　　　　31
To the court of guard ; he is of note : our
　　hour
Is fully out.
　Third Sold. Come on, then ;
He may recover yet. [*Exeunt with the body.*

　　SCENE X. *Between the two camps.*
Enter ANTONY *and* SCARUS, *with their Army.*

　Ant. Their preparation is to-day by sea ;
We please them not by land.
　Scar. 　　　　For both, my lord.
　Ant. I would they 'ld fight i' the fire or i'
　　the air ;
We'ld fight there too. But this it is ; our foot
Upon the hills adjoining to the city
Shall stay with us : order for sea is given ;
They have put forth the haven . . . .
Where their appointment we may best dis-
　　cover,
And look on their endeavor. 　[*Exeunt.* 9

　　SCENE XI. *Another part of the same.*
　　Enter CÆSAR, *and his Army.*

　Cæs. But being charged, we will be still by
　　land,
Which, as I take't, we shall ; for his best force
Is forth to man his galleys. To the vales,
And hold our best advantage. 　[*Exeunt.*

　　SCENE XII. *Another part of the same.*
　　Enter ANTONY *and* SCARUS.

　Ant. Yet they are not join'd : where yond
　　pine does stand,
I shall discover all : I'll bring thee word
Straight, how 'tis like to go. 　　[*Exit.*
　Scar. 　　　　Swallows have built
In Cleopatra's sails their nests : the augurers
Say they know not, they cannot tell ; look
　　grimly,
And dare not speak their knowledge. Antony
Is valiant, and dejected ; and, by starts,
His fretted fortunes give him hope, and fear,
Of what he has, and has not.
　　[*Alarum afar off, as at a sea-fight.*

　　Re-enter ANTONY.

　Ant. 　　　　　All is lost ;
This foul Egyptian hath betrayed me : 　10
My fleet hath yielded to the foe ; and yonder
They cast their caps up and carouse together
Like friends long lost. Triple-turn'd whore !
　　'tis thou

Hast sold me to this novice ; and my heart
Makes only wars on thee. Bid them all fly ;
For when I am revenged upon my charm,
I have done all. Bid them all fly ; begone.
                  [*Exit* Scarus.
O sun, thy uprise shall I see no more :
Fortune and Antony part here ; even here
Do we shake hands. All come to this ? The
    hearts   20
That spaniel'd me at heels, to whom I gave
Their wishes, do discandy, melt their sweets
On blossoming Cæsar ; and this pine is bark'd,
That overtopp'd them all. Betray'd I am :
O this false soul of Egypt ! this grave charm,—
Whose eye beck'd forth my wars, and call'd
    them home ;
Whose bosom was my crownet, my chief end,—
Like a right gipsy, hath, at fast and loose,
Beguiled me to the very heart of loss.
What, Eros, Eros !

        Enter CLEOPATRA.

          Ah, thou spell ! Avaunt ! 30
  Cleo. Why is my lord enraged against his
    love ?
  Ant. Vanish, or I shall give thee thy de-
    serving,
And blemish Cæsar's triumph. Let him take
    thee,
And hoist thee up to the shouting plebeians :
Follow his chariot, like the greatest spot
Of all thy sex ; most monster-like, be shown
For poor'st diminutives, for doits ; and let
Patient Octavia plough thy visage up
With her prepared nails.   [*Exit* Cleopatra.
            'Tis well thou'rt gone,
If it be well to live ; but better 'twere   40
Thou fell'st into my fury, for one death
Might have prevented many. Eros, ho !
The shirt of Nessus is upon me : teach me,
Alcides, thou mine ancestor, thy rage :
Let me lodge Lichas on the horns o' the moon ;
And with those hands, that grasp'd the heavi-
    est club,
Subdue my worthiest self. The witch shall die :
To the young Roman boy she hath sold me,
    and I fall
Under this plot ; she dies for't. Eros, ho !
                    [*Exit.*

    SCENE XIII. *Alexandria. Cleopatra's*
              palace.

  Enter CLEOPATRA, CHARMIAN, IRAS, *and*
            MARDIAN.

  Cleo. Help me, my women ! O, he is more
    mad
Than Telamon for his shield ; the boar of
    Thessaly
Was never so emboss'd.
  Char.   To the monument !
There lock yourself, and send him word you
    are dead.
The soul and body rive not more in parting
Than greatness going off.
  Cleo.   To the monument !
Mardian, go tell him I have slain myself ;
Say, that the last I spoke was ' Antony,'
And word it, prithee, piteously : hence, Mar-
    dian,
And bring me how he takes my death. To the
    monument !   [*Exeunt.* 10

    SCENE XIV. *The same. Another room.*
        Enter ANTONY *and* EROS.

  Ant. Eros, thou yet behold'st me ?
  Eros.   Ay, noble lord.
  Ant. Sometimes we see a cloud that's drag-
    onish ;
A vapor sometime like a bear or lion,
A tower'd citadel, a pendent rock,
A forked mountain, or blue promontory
With trees upon't, that nod unto the world,
And mock our eyes with air : thou hast seen
    these signs ;
They are black vesper's pageants.
  Eros.   Ay, my lord,
  Ant. That which is now a horse, even with
    a thought
The rack dislimns, and makes it indistinct, 10
As water is in water.
  Eros.   It does, my lord.
  Ant. My good knave Eros, now thy captain
    is
Even such a body : here I am Antony :
Yet cannot hold this visible shape, my knave.
I made these wars for Egypt : and the queen,—
Whose heart I thought I had, for she had
    mine ;
Which whilst it was mine had annex'd unto't
A million more, now lost,—she, Eros, has
Pack'd cards with Cæsar, and false-play'd my
    glory
Unto an enemy's triumph.   20
Nay, weep not, gentle Eros ; there is left us
Ourselves to end ourselves.

        Enter MARDIAN.

                O, thy vile lady !
She has robb'd me of my sword.
  Mar.   No, Antony ;
My mistress loved thee, and her fortunes
    mingled
With thine entirely.
  Ant.   Hence, saucy eunuch ; peace !
She hath betray'd me and shall die the death.
  Mar. Death of one person can be paid but
    once,
And that she has discharged : what thou
    wouldst do
Is done unto thy hand : the last she spake
Was ' Antony ! most noble Antony ! '   30
Then in the midst a tearing groan did break
The name of Antony ; it was divided
Between her heart and lips : she render'd
    life,
Thy name so buried in her.
  Ant.   Dead, then ?
  Mar.   Dead.
  Ant. Unarm, Eros ; the long day's task is
    done,
And we must sleep. [*To Mar.*] That thou
    depart'st hence safe,
Does pay thy labor richly ; go. [*Exit Mardian.*
                      Off, pluck off.
The seven-fold shield of Ajax cannot keep
The battery from my heart. O, cleave, my
    sides !
Heart, once be stronger than thy continent, 40
Crack thy frail case ! Apace, Eros, apace.
No more a soldier : bruised pieces, go ;
You have been nobly borne. From me awhile.
                    [*Exit Eros.*
I will o'ertake thee, Cleopatra, and
Weep for my pardon. So it must be, for now

All length is torture : since the torch is out,
Lie down, and stray no farther : now all labor
Mars what it does ; yea, very force entangles
Itself with strength : seal then, and all is done.
Eros !—I come, my queen :—Eros !—Stay for
  me :   50
Where souls do couch on flowers, we'll hand
  in hand,
And with our sprightly port make the ghosts
  gaze :
Dido and her Æneas shall want troops,
And all the haunt be ours. Come, Eros, Eros !

Re-enter Eros.

Eros. What would my lord ?
Ant.   Since Cleopatra died,
I have lived in such dishonor, that the gods
Detest my baseness. I, that with my sword
Quarter'd the world, and o'er green Neptune's
  back
With ships made cities, condemn myself to
  lack
The courage of a woman ; less noble mind 60
Than she which by her death our Cæsar tells
' I am conqueror of myself.' Thou art sworn,
  Eros,
That, when the exigent should come, which
  now
Is come indeed, when I should see behind me
The inevitable prosecution of
Disgrace and horror, that, on my command,
Thou then wouldst kill me : do 't ; the time is
  come :
Thou strikest not me, 'tis Cæsar thou de-
  feat'st.
Put color in thy cheek.
Eros.   The gods withhold me !
Shall I do that which all the Parthian darts,
Though enemy, lost aim, and could not ?
Ant.   Eros,
Wouldst thou be window'd in great Rome and
  see
Thy master thus with pleach'd arms, bending
  down
His corrigible neck, his face subdued
To penetrative shame, whilst the wheel'd seat
Of fortunate Cæsar, drawn before him,
  branded
His baseness that ensued ?
Eros.   I would not see't.
Ant. Come, then ; for with a wound I must
  be cured.
Draw that thy honest sword, which thou hast
  worn
Most useful for thy country.
Eros.   O, sir, pardon me ! 80
Ant. When I did make thee free, sworest
  thou not then
To do this when I bade thee ? Do it at once ;
Or thy precedent services are all
But accidents unpurposed. Draw, and come.
Eros. Turn from me, then, that noble
  countenance,
Wherein the worship of the whole world lies.
Ant. Lo thee !   [*Turning from him.*
Eros. My sword is drawn.
Ant.   Then let it do at once
The thing why thou hast drawn it.
Eros.   My dear master,
My captain, and my emperor, let me say, 90
Before I strike this bloody stroke, farewell.
Ant. 'Tis said, man ; and farewell.

Eros. Farewell, great chief. Shall I strike
  now ?
Ant.   Now, Eros.
Eros. Why, there then : thus I do escape
  the sorrow
Of Antony's death.   [*Kills himself.*
Ant.   Thrice-nobler than myself !
Thou teachest me, O valiant Eros, what
I should, and thou couldst not. My queen and
  Eros
Have by their brave instruction got upon me
A nobleness in record : but I will be
A bridegroom in my death, and run into't 100
As to a lover's bed. Come, then ; and, Eros,
Thy master dies thy scholar : to do thus
              [*Falling on his sword.*
I learn'd of thee. How ! not dead ? not dead ?
The guard, ho ! O, dispatch me !

Enter Dercetas *and* Guard.

First Guard.   What's the noise ?
Ant. I have done my work ill, friends : O,
  make an end
Of what I have begun.
Sec. Guard.   The star is fall'n.
First Guard. And time is at his period.
All.   Alas, and woe !
Ant. Let him that loves me strike me dead.
First Guard.   Not I.
Sec. Guard. Nor I.   109
Third Guard. Nor any one.
                        [*Exeunt Guard.*
Der. Thy death and fortunes bid thy fol-
  lowers fly.
This sword but shown to Cæsar, with this
  tidings,
Shall enter me with him.

Enter Diomedes.

Dio. Where's Antony ?
Der.   There, Diomed there.
Dio.   Lives he ?
Wilt thou not answer, man ? [*Exit Dercetas.*
Ant. Art thou there, Diomed ? Draw thy
  sword, and give me
Sufficing strokes for death.
Dio.   Most absolute lord,
My mistress Cleopatra sent me to thee.
Ant. When did she send thee ?
Dio.   Now, my lord.
Ant.   Where is she ?
Dio. Lock'd in her monument. She had a
  prophesying fear   120
Of what hath come to pass : for when she
  saw—
Which never shall be found—you did suspect
She had disposed with Cæsar, and that your
  rage
Would not be purged, she sent you word she
  was dead ;
But, fearing since how it might work, hath
  sent
Me to proclaim the truth ; and I am come,
I dread, too late.
Ant. Too late, good Diomed : call my
  guard, I prithee.
Dio. What, ho, the emperor's guard ! The
  guard, what, ho !
Come, your lord calls !   130

Enter four or five of the Guard *of* Antony.

Ant. Bear me, good friends, where Cleopatra bides ;

'Tis the last service that I shall command you.
First Guard. Woe, woe are we, sir, you
    may not live to wear
All your true followers out.
    All.   Most heavy day!
    Ant. Nay, good my fellows, do not please
    sharp fate
To grace it with your sorrows : bid that wel-
    come
Which comes to punish us, and we punish it
Seeming to bear it lightly. Take me up :
I have led you oft : carry me now, good
    friends,
And have my thanks for all.   140
                [*Exeunt, bearing Antony.*

  SCENE XV. *The same. A monument.*

Enter CLEOPATRA *and her maids aloft, with*
    CHARMIAN *and* IRAS.

    Cleo. O Charmian, I will never go from
    hence.
    Char. Be comforted, dear madam.
    Cleo.   No, I will not :
All strange and terrible events are welcome,
But comforts we despise ; our size of sorrow,
Proportion'd to our cause, must be as great
As that which makes it.

    Enter, below, DIOMEDES.

              How now ! is he dead ?
    Dio. His death's upon him, but not dead.
Look out o' the other side your monument ;
His guard have brought him thither.

Enter, below, ANTONY, *borne by the* Guard.
    Cleo.   O sun,
Burn the great sphere thou movest in ! dark-
    ling stand   10
The varying shore o' the world. O Antony,
Antony, Antony ! Help, Charmian, help, Iras,
    help ;
Help, friends below ; let's draw him hither.
    Ant.   Peace !
Not Cæsar's valor hath o'erthrown Antony,
But Antony's hath triumph'd on itself.
    Cleo. So it should be, that none but An-
    tony
Should conquer Antony ; but woe 'tis so !
    Ant. I am dying, Egypt, dying ; only
I here importune death awhile, until
Of many thousand kisses the poor last   20
I lay upon thy lips.
    Cleo.   I dare not, dear,—
Dear my lord, pardon,—I dare not,
Lest I be taken : not the imperious show
Of the full-fortuned Cæsar ever shall
Be brooch'd with me ; if knife, drugs, serpents,
    have
Edge, sting, or operation, I am safe :
Your wife Octavia, with her modest eyes
And still conclusion, shall acquire no honor
Demuring upon me. But come, come, An-
    tony,—
Help me, my women,—we must draw thee up :
Assist, good friends.   31
    Ant.   O, quick, or I am gone.
    Cleo. Here's sport indeed ! How heavy
    weighs my lord !
Our strength is all gone into heaviness,
That makes the weight : had I great Juno's
    power,
The strong-wing'd Mercury should fetch thee
    up,

And set thee by Jove's side. Yet come a
    little,—
Wishes were ever fools,—O, come, come,
    come ;
        [*They heave Antony aloft to Cleopatra.*
And welcome, welcome ! die where thou hast
    lived ;
Quicken with kissing : had my lips that power,
Thus would I wear them out.
    All.   A heavy sight !   40
    Ant. I am dying, Egypt, dying :
Give me some wine, and let me speak a little.
    Cleo. No, let me speak ; and let me rail so
    high,
That the false housewife Fortune break her
    wheel,
Provoked by my offence.
    Ant.   One word, sweet queen :
Of Cæsar seek your honor, with your safety.
    O !
    Cleo. They do not go together.
    Ant.   Gentle, hear me :
None about Cæsar trust but Proculeius.
    Cleo. My resolution and my hands I'll
    trust ;
None about Cæsar.   50
    Ant. The miserable change now at my end
Lament nor sorrow at ; but please your
    thoughts
In feeding them with those my former fortunes
Wherein I lived, the greatest prince o' the
    world,
The noblest ; and do now not basely die,
Not cowardly put off my helmet to
My countryman,—a Roman by a Roman
Valiantly vanquish'd. Now my spirit is going ;
I can no more.
    Cleo.   Noblest of men, woo't die ?
Hast thou no care of me ? shall I abide   60
In this dull world, which in thy absence is
No better than a sty ? O, see, my women,
                  [*Antony dies.*
The crown o' the earth doth melt. My lord !
O, wither'd is the garland of the war,
The soldier's pole is fall'n : young boys and
    girls
Are level now with men ; the odds is gone,
And there is nothing left remarkable
Beneath the visiting moon.   [*Faints.*
    Char.   O, quietness, lady !
    Iras. She is dead too, our sovereign.
    Char.   Lady !
    Iras.   Madam !
    Char. O madam, madam, madam !
    Iras.   Royal Egypt,   70
Empress !
    Char. Peace, peace, Iras !
    Cleo. No more, but e'en a woman, and
    commanded
By such poor passion as the maid that milks
And does the meanest chares. It were for me
To throw my sceptre at the injurious gods ;
To tell them that this world did equal theirs
Till they had stol'n our jewel. All's but naught ;
Patience is scottish, and impatience does
Become a dog that's mad : then is it sin   80
To rush into the secret house of death,
Ere death dare come to us ? How do you,
    women ?
What, what ! good cheer ! Why, how now,
    Charmian !
My noble girls ! Ah, women, women, look,

Our lamp is spent, it's out! Good sirs, take
　　heart:
We'll bury him; and then, what's brave, what's
　　noble,
Let's do it after the high Roman fashion,
And make death proud to take us. Come,
　　away!
This case of that huge spirit now is cold:
Ah, women, women! come; we have no friend
But resolution, and the briefest end.　　91
　　|Exeunt; those above bearing off
　　　　　　　Antony's body.

ACT V.

SCENE I. *Alexandria. Cæsar's camp.*

Enter CÆSAR, AGRIPPA, DOLABELLA, MECÆ-
NAS, GALLUS, PROCULEIUS, *and others, his
council of war.*

　Cæs. Go to him, Dolabella, bid him yield;
Being so frustrate, tell him he mocks
The pauses that he makes.
　Dol.　　　　　Cæsar, I shall. [*Exit.*

Enter DERCETAS, *with the sword of* ANTONY.

　Cæs. Wherefore is that? and what art
　　thou that darest
Appear thus to us?
　Der.　　　　I am call'd Dercetas;
Mark Antony I served, who best was worthy
Best to be served: whilst he stood up and
　　spoke,
He was my master; and I wore my life
To spend upon his haters. If thou please
To take me to thee, as I was to him　　10
I'll be to Cæsar; if thou pleasest not,
I yield thee up my life.
　Cæs.　　　　What is't thou say'st?
　Der. I say, O Cæsar, Antony is dead.
　Cæs. The breaking of so great a thing
　　should make
A greater crack: the round world
Should have shook lions into civil streets,
And citizens to their dens: the death of An-
　　tony
Is not a single doom; in the name lay
A moiety of the world.
　Der.　　　　He is dead, Cæsar;
Not by a public minister of justice,　　20
Nor by a hired knife; but that self hand,
Which writ his honor in the acts it did,
Hath, with the courage which the heart did
　　lend it,
Splitted the heart. This is his sword;
I robb'd his wound of it; behold it stain'd
With his most noble blood.
　Cæs.　　　　Look you sad, friends?
The gods rebuke me, but it is tidings
To wash the eyes of kings.
　Agr.　　　　And strange it is,
That nature must compel us to lament
Our most persisted deeds.
　Mec.　　　　His taints and honors　30
Waged equal with him.
　Agr.　　　　A rarer spirit never
Did steer humanity: but you, gods, will give
　　us
Some faults to make us men. Cæsar is touch'd.
　Mec. When such a spacious mirror's set
　　before him,

He needs must see himself.
　Cæs.　　　　O Antony!
I have follow'd thee to this; but we do lance
Diseases in our bodies: I must perforce
Have shown to thee such a declining day,
Or look on thine; we could not stall together
In the whole world: but yet let me lament,　40
With tears as sovereign as the blood of hearts,
That thou, my brother, my competitor
In top of all design, my mate in empire,
Friend and companion in the front of war,
The arm of mine own body, and the heart
Where mine his thoughts did kindle,—that our
　　stars,
Unreconciliable, should divide
Our equalness to this. Hear me, good
　　friends,—
But I will tell you at some meeter season:

　　Enter an Egyptian.

The business of this man looks out of him;　50
We'll hear him what he says. Whence are
　　you?
　Egyp. A poor Egyptian yet. The queen my
　　mistress,
Confined in all she has, her monument,
Of thy intents desires instruction,
That she preparedly may frame herself
To the way she's forced to.
　Cæs.　　　　Bid her have good heart:
She soon shall know of us, by some of ours,
How honorable and how kindly we
Determine for her; for Cæsar cannot live
To be ungentle.
　Egyp. So the gods preserve thee! [*Exit.*　60
　Cæs. Come hither, Proculeius. Go and
　　say,
We purpose her no shame: give her what
　　comforts
The quality of her passion shall require,
Lest, in her greatness, by some mortal stroke
She do defeat us; for her life in Rome
Would be eternal in our triumph: go,
And with your speediest bring us what she
　　says,
And how you find of her.
　Pro.　　　　Cæsar, I shall. [*Exit.*
　Cæs. Gallus, go you along. [*Exit Gallus.*]
　　　Where's Dolabella,
To second Proculeius?
　All.　　　　Dolabella!　　70
　Cæs. Let him alone, for I remember now
How he's employ'd: he shall in time be ready.
Go with me to my tent; where you shall see
How hardly I was drawn into this war;
How calm and gentle I proceeded still
In all my writings: go with me, and see
What I can show in this.　　　[*Exeunt.*

SCENE II. *Alexandria. A room in the monument.*

Enter CLEOPATRA, CHARMIAN, *and* IRAS.

　Cleo. My desolation does begin to make
A better life. 'Tis paltry to be Cæsar;
Not being Fortune, he's but Fortune's knave,
A minister of her will: and it is great
To do that thing that ends all other deeds;
Which shackles accidents and bolts up
　　change;
Which sleeps, and never palates more the dug,
The beggar's nurse and Cæsar's.

*Enter, to the gates of the monument, PROCU-
        LEIUS, GALLUS and Soldiers.*

Pro. Cæsar sends greeting to the Queen of
        Egypt ;
And bids thee study on what fair demands   10
Thou mean'st to have him grant thee.
  Cleo.   What's thy name ?
  Pro. My name is Proculeius.
  Cleo.   Antony
Did tell me of you, bade me trust you ; but
I do not greatly care to be deceived,
That have no use for trusting. If your master
Would have a queen his beggar, you must tell
        him,
That majesty, to keep decorum, must
No less beg than a kingdom : if he please
To give me conquer'd Egypt for my son,
He gives me so much of mine own, as I   20
Will kneel to him with thanks.
  Pro.   Be of good cheer ;
You're fall'n into a princely hand, fear noth-
        ing :
Make your full reference freely to my lord,
Who is so full of grace, that it flows over
On all that need : let me report to him
Your sweet dependency ; and you shall find
A conqueror that will pray in aid for kindness,
Where he for grace is kneel'd to.
  Cleo.   Pray you, tell him
I am his fortune's vassal, and I send him
The greatness he has got. I hourly learn   30
A doctrine of obedience ; and would gladly
Look him i' the face.
  Pro.   This I'll report, dear lady.
Have comfort, for I know your plight is pitied
Of him that caused it.
  Gal. You see how easily she may be sur-
        prised :
  [*Here Proculeius and two of the Guard
        ascend the monument by a ladder
        placed against a window, and, having
        descended, come behind Cleopatra.
        Some of the Guard unbar and open
        the gates.*
  [*To Proculeius and the Guard*] Guard her
        till Cæsar come.   [*Exit.*
  Iras. Royal queen !
  Char. O Cleopatra ! thou art taken,
        queen.
  Cleo. Quick, quick, good hands.
                          [*Drawing a dagger.*
  Pro.   Hold, worthy lady, hold :
                    [*Seizes and disarms her.*
Do not yourself such wrong, who are in this
Relieved, but not betray'd.   41
  Cleo.   What, of death too,
That rids our dogs of languish ?
  Pro.   Cleopatra,
Do not abuse my master's bounty by
The undoing of yourself : let the world see
His nobleness well acted, which your death
Will never let come forth.
  Cleo.   Where art thou, death ?
Come hither, come ! come, come, and take a
        queen
Worthy many babes and beggars !
  Pro.   O, temperance, lady !
  Cleo. Sir, I will eat no meat, I'll not drink,
        sir ;
If idle talk will once be necessary,   50
I'll not sleep neither : this mortal house I'll
        ruin,

Do Cæsar what he can. Know, sir, that I
Will not wait pinion'd at your master's court ;
Nor once be chastised with the sober eye
Of dull Octavia. Shall they hoist me up
And show me to the shouting varletry
Of censuring Rome ? Rather a ditch in Egypt
Be gentle grave unto me ! rather on Nilus' mud
Lay me stark naked, and let the water-flies
Blow me into abhorring ! rather make   60
My country's high pyramides my gibbet,
And hang me up in chains !
  Pro.   You do extend
These thoughts of horror further than you
        shall
Find cause in Cæsar.

            Enter DOLABELLA.

  Dol.   Proculeius,
What thou hast done thy master Cæsar knows,
And he hath sent for thee : for the queen,
I'll take her to my guard.
  Pro.   So, Dolabella,
It shall content me best : be gentle to her.
  [*To Cleo.*] To Cæsar I will speak what you
        shall please,
If you'll employ me to him.
  Cleo.   Say, I would die.   70
            [*Exeunt Proculeius and Soldiers.*
  Dol. Most noble empress, you have heard
        of me ?
  Cleo. I cannot tell.
  Dol.   Assuredly you know me.
  Cleo. No matter, sir, what I have heard or
        known.
You laugh when boys or women tell their
        dreams ;
Is't not your trick ?
  Dol.   I understand not, madam.
  Cleo. I dream'd there was an Emperor An-
        tony :
O, such another sleep, that I might see
But such another man !
  Dol.   If it might please ye,—
  Cleo. His face was as the heavens ; and
        therein stuck
A sun and moon, which kept their course, and
        lighted   80
The little O, the earth.
  Dol.   Most sovereign creature,—
  Cleo. His legs bestrid the ocean : his
        rear'd arm
Crested the world : his voice was propertied
As all the tuned spheres, and that to friends ;
But when he meant to quail and shake the orb,
He was as rattling thunder. For his bounty,
There was no winter in't ; an autumn 'twas
That grew the more by reaping : his delights
Were dolphin-like ; they show'd his back
        above
The element they lived in : in his livery   90
Walk'd crowns and crownets ; realms and is-
        lands were
As plates dropp'd from his pocket.
  Dol.   Cleopatra !
  Cleo. Think you there was, or might be,
        such a man
As this I dream'd of ?
  Dol.   Gentle madam, no.
  Cleo. You lie, up to the hearing of the
        gods.
But, if there be, or ever were, one such,
It's past the size of dreaming : nature wants
        stuff

To vie strange forms with fancy; yet, to im-
agine
An Antony, were nature's piece 'gainst fancy,
Condemning shadows quite.
  Dol.   Hear me, good madam. 100
Your loss is as yourself, great; and you bear it
As answering to the weight: would I might
never
O'ertake pursued success, but I do feel,
By the rebound of yours, a grief that smites
My very heart at root.
  Cleo.   I thank you, sir,
Know you what Cæsar means to do with me?
  Dol. I am loath to tell you what I would
you knew.
  Cleo. Nay, pray you, sir,—
  Dol.   Though he be honorable,—
  Cleo. He'll lead me, then, in triumph?
  Dol. Madam, he will; I know't. 110
[*Flourish, and shout within,* ' Make way there :
Cæsar !'

Enter CÆSAR, GALLUS, PROCULEIUS, MECÆ-
NAS, SELEUCUS, *and others of his Train.*

  Cæs. Which is the Queen of Egypt?
  Dol. It is the emperor, madam.
               [*Cleopatra kneels.*
  Cæs. Arise, you shall not kneel:
I pray you, rise; rise, Egypt.
  Cleo.   Sir, the gods
Will have it thus; my master and my lord
I must obey.
  Cæs.   Take to you no hard thoughts:
The record of what injuries you did us,
Though written in our flesh, we shall remem-
ber
As things but done by chance.
  Cleo.   Sole sir o' the world, 120
I cannot project mine own cause so well
To make it clear; but do confess I have
Been laden with like frailties which before
Have often shamed our sex.
  Cæs.   Cleopatra, know,
We will extenuate rather than enforce:
If you apply yourself to our intents,
Which towards you are most gentle, you shall
find
A benefit in this change; but if you seek
To lay on me a cruelty, by taking   129
Antony's course, you shall bereave yourself
Of my good purposes, and put your children
To that destruction which I'll guard them
from,
If thereon you rely. I'll take my leave.
  Cleo. And may, through all the world: 'tis
yours; and we,
Your scutcheons and your signs of conquest,
shall
Hang in what place you please. Here, my good
lord.
  Cæs. You shall advise me in all for Cleo-
patra.
  Cleo. This is the brief of money, plate, and
jewels,
I am possess'd of: 'tis exactly valued;
Not petty things admitted. Where's Seleucus?
  Sel. Here, madam.   141
  Cleo. This is my treasurer: let him speak,
my lord,
Upon his peril, that I have reserved
To myself nothing. Speak the truth, Seleucus.
  Sel. Madam,
I had rather seal my lips, than, to my peril,

Speak that which is not.
  Cleo.   What have I kept back?
  Sel. Enough to purchase what you have
made known.
  Cæs. Nay, blush not, Cleopatra; I ap-
prove
Your wisdom in the deed.
  Cleo.   See, Cæsar! O, behold, 150
How pomp is follow'd! mine will now be
yours;
And, should we shift estates, yours would be
mine.
The ingratitude of this Seleucus does
Even make me wild: O slave, of no more trust
Than love that's hired! What, goest thou
back? thou shalt
Go back, I warrant thee; but I'll catch thine
eyes,
Though they had wings: slave, soulless vil-
lain, dog!
O rarely base!
  Cæs.   Good queen, let us entreat you.
  Cleo. O Cæsar, what a wounding shame
is this,
That thou, vouchsafing here to visit me, 160
Doing the honor of thy lordliness
To one so meek, that mine own servant should
Parcel the sum of my disgraces by
Addition of his envy! Say, good Cæsar,
That I some lady trifles have reserved,
Immoment toys, things of such dignity
As we greet modern friends withal; and say,
Some nobler token I have kept apart
For Livia and Octavia, to induce
Their mediation; must I be unfolded 170
With one that I have bred? The gods! it
smites me
Beneath the fall I have. [*To Seleucus*] Prithee,
go hence;
Or I shall show the cinders of my spirits
Through the ashes of my chance: wert thou
a man,
Thou wouldst have mercy on me.
  Cæs.   Forbear, Seleucus.
               [*Exit Seleucus.*
  Cleo. Be it known, that we, the greatest,
are misthought
For things that others do; and, when we fall,
We answer others' merits in our name,
Are therefore to be pitied.
  Cæs.   Cleopatra,
Not what you have reserved, nor what ac-
knowledged, 180
Put we i' the roll of conquest: still be 't yours,
Bestow it at your pleasure; and believe,
Cæsar's no merchant, to make prize with you
Of things that merchants sold. Therefore be
cheer'd;
Make not your thoughts your prisons: no,
dear queen;
For we intend so to dispose you as
Yourself shall give us counsel. Feed, and
sleep:
Our care and pity is so much upon you,
That we remain your friend; and so, adieu.
  Cleo. My master, and my lord!
  Cæs.   Not so. Adieu. 190
    [*Flourish. Exeunt Cæsar and his train.*
  Cleo. He words me, girls, he words me,
that I should not
Be noble to myself: but, hark thee, Charmian.
               [*Whispers Charmian.*

Iras. Finish, good lady ; the bright day is
done,
And we are for the dark.
   Cleo.   Hie thee again :
I have spoke already, and it is provided ;
Go put it to the haste.
   Char.   Madam, I will.

Re-enter DOLABELLA.

Dol. Where is the queen ?
   Char.   Behold, sir. [*Exit.*
   Cleo.   Dolabella !
Dol. Madam, as thereto sworn by your
command,
Which my love makes religion to obey,
I tell you this : Cæsar through Syria   200
Intends his journey ; and within three days
You with your children will he send before :
Make your best use of this : I have perform'd
Your pleasure and my promise.
   Cleo.   Dolabella,
I shall remain your debtor.
   Dol.   I your servant,
Adieu, good queen ; I must attend on Cæsar.
   Cleo. Farewell, and thanks.
                   [*Exit Dolabella.*
Now, Iras, what think'st thou ?
Thou, an Egyptian puppet, shalt be shown
In Rome, as well as I : mechanic slaves
With greasy aprons, rules, and hammers, shall
Uplift us to the view ; in their thick breaths,
Rank of gross diet, shall we be enclouded,
And forced to drink their vapor.
   Iras.   The gods forbid !
   Cleo. Nay, 'tis most certain, Iras : saucy
lictors
Will catch at us, like strumpets ; and scald
rhymers
Ballad us out o' tune : the quick comedians
Extemporally will stage us, and present
Our Alexandrian revels ; Antony
Shall be brought drunken forth, and I shall see
Some squeaking Cleopatra boy my greatness
I' the posture of a whore.   220
   Iras.   O the good gods !
   Cleo. Nay, that's certain.
   Iras. I'll never see 't ; for, I am sure, my
nails
Are stronger than mine eyes.
   Cleo.   Why, that's the way
To fool their preparation, and to conquer
Their most absurd intents.

Re-enter CHARMIAN.

              Now, Charmian !
Show me, my women, like a queen : go fetch
My best attires : I am again for Cydnus,
To meet Mark Antony : sirrah Iras, go.
Now, noble Charmian, we'll dispatch indeed ;
And, when thou hast done this chare, I'll give
thee leave   231
To play till doomsday. Bring our crown and
all.
Wherefore's this noise ?
           [*Exit Iras. A noise within.*

Enter a Guardsman.

   Guard.   Here is a rural fellow
That will not be denied your highness' pres-
ence :
He brings you figs.
   Cleo. Let him come in. [*Exit Guardsman.*
         What poor an instrument

May do a noble deed ! he brings me liberty.
My resolution's placed, and I have nothing
Of woman in me : now from head to foot
I am marble-constant ; now the fleeting moon
No planet is of mine.   241

Re-enter Guardsman, *with* Clown *bringing in
a basket.*

   Guard.   This is the man.
   Cleo. Avoid, and leave him.
                   [*Exit Guardsman.*
Hast thou the pretty worm of Nilus there,
That kills and pains not ?
   Clown. Truly, I have him : but I would not
be the party that should desire you to touch
him, for his biting is immortal ; those that do
die of it do seldom or never recover.
   Cleo. Rememberest thou any that have
died on 't ?   249
   Clown. Very many, men and women too.
I heard of one of them no longer than yesterday : a very honest woman, but something
given to lie ; as a woman should not do, but
in the way of honesty : how she died of the
biting of it, what pain she felt : truly, she
makes a very good report o' the worm ; but
he that will believe all that they say, shall
never be saved by half that they do : but this
is most fallible, the worm's an odd worm.
   Cleo. Get thee hence ; farewell.   260
   Clown. I wish you all joy of the worm.
            [*Setting down his basket.*
   Cleo. Farewell.
   Clown. You must think this, look you, that
the worm will do his kind.
   Cleo. Ay, ay ; farewell.
   Clown. Look you, the worm is not to be
trusted but in the keeping of wise people ; for,
indeed, there is no goodness in the worm.
   Cleo. Take thou no care ; it shall be
heeded.
   Clown. Very good. Give it nothing, I pray
you, for it is not worth the feeding.   271
   Cleo. Will it eat me ?
   Clown. You must not think I am so simple
but I know the devil himself will not eat a
woman : I know that a woman is a dish for
the gods, if the devil dress her not. But, truly,
these same whoreson devils do the gods great
harm in their women ; for in every ten that
they make, the devils mar five.
   Cleo. Well, get thee gone ; farewell.   280
   Clown. Yes, forsooth : I wish you joy o'
the worm.   [*Exit.*

Re-enter IRAS *with a robe, crown, &c.*

   Cleo. Give me my robe, put on my crown ;
I have
Immortal longings in me : now no more
The juice of Egypt's grape shall moist this lip :
Yare, yare, good Iras ; quick. Methinks I hear
Antony call ; I see him rouse himself
To praise my noble act ; I hear him mock
The luck of Cæsar, which the gods give men
To excuse their after wrath : husband, I
come :
Now to that name my courage prove my title !
I am fire and air ; my other elements
I give to baser life. So ; have you done ?
Come then, and take the last warmth of my
lips.
Farewell, kind Charmian ; Iras, long farewell.
         [*Kisses them. Iras falls and dies.*

Have I the aspic in my lips ? Dost fall ?
If thou and nature can so gently part,
The stroke of death is as a lover's pinch,
Which hurts, and is desired. Dost thou lie
    still ?
If thus thou vanishest, thou tell'st the world
It is not worth leave-taking.   301
 Char. Dissolve, thick cloud, and rain ; that
    I may say,
The gods themselves do weep !
 Cleo.   This proves me base :
If she first meet the curled Antony,
He'll make demand of her, and spend that kiss
Which is my heaven to have. Come, thou mor-
    tal wretch,
[*To an asp, which she applies to her breast.*
With thy sharp teeth this knot intrinsicate
Of life at once untie : poor venomous fool,
Be angry, and dispatch. O, couldst thou speak,
That I might hear thee call great Cæsar ass
Unpolicied !
 Char. O eastern star !
 Cleo.   Peace, peace !
Dost thou not see my baby at my breast,
That sucks the nurse asleep ?
 Char.   O, break ! O, break !
 Cleo. As sweet as balm, as soft as air, as
    gentle,—
O Antony !—Nay, I will take thee too.
    [*Applying another asp to her arm.*
What should I stay—   [*Dies.*
 Char. In this vile world ? So, fare thee
    well.
Now boast thee, death, in thy possession lies
A lass unparallel'd. Downy windows, close ;
And golden Phœbus never be beheld   320
Of eyes again so royal ! Your crown's awry ;
I'll mend it, and then play.

   Enter the Guard, *rushing in.*

 First Guard. Where is the queen ?
 Char.   Speak softly, wake her not.
 First Guard. Cæsar hath sent—
 Char.   Too slow a messenger.
        [*Applies an asp.*
O, come apace, dispatch ! I partly feel thee.
 First Guard. Approach, ho ! All's not
    well : Cæsar's beguiled.
 Sec. Guard. There's Dolabella sent from
    Cæsar ; call him.
 First Guard. What work is here ! Char-
    mian, is this well done ?
 Char. It is well done, and fitting for a
    princess
Descended of so many royal kings.   330
Ah, soldier !   [*Dies.*

Re-enter DOLABELLA.

 Dol. How goes it here ?
 Sec. Guard.   All dead.
 Dol.   Cæsar, thy thoughts
Touch their effects in this : thyself art coming
To see perform'd the dreaded act which thou
So sought'st to hinder.
 [*Within* ' A way there, a way for Cæsar ! '

Re-enter CÆSAR *and all his train marching.*

 Dol. O sir, you are too sure an augurer ;
That you did fear is done.
 Cæs.   Bravest at the last,
She levell'd at our purposes, and, being royal,
Took her own way. The manner of their
    deaths ?   340
I do not see them bleed.
 Dol.   Who was last with them ?
 First Guard. A simple countryman, that
    brought her figs :
This was his basket.
 Cæs.   Poison'd, then.
 First Guard.   O Cæsar,
This Charmian lived but now ; she stood and
    spake :
I found her trimming up the diadem
On her dead mistress ; tremblingly she stood
And on the sudden dropp'd.
 Cæs.   O noble weakness !
If they had swallow'd poison, 'twould appear
By external swelling : but she looks like sleep,
As she would catch another Antony   350
In her strong toil of grace.
 Dol.   Here, on her breast,
There is a vent of blood and something blown :
The like is on her arm.
 First Guard. This is an aspic's trail : and
    these fig-leaves
Have slime upon them, such as the aspic
    leaves
Upon the caves of Nile.
 Cæs.   Most probable
That so she died ; for her physician tells me
She hath pursued conclusions infinite
Of easy ways to die. Take up her bed ;
And bear her women from the monument :
She shall be buried by her Antony :   361
No grave upon the earth shall clip in it
A pair so famous. High events as these
Strike those that make them ; and their story
    is
No less in pity than his glory which
Brought them to be lamented. Our army shall
In solemn show attend this funeral ;
And then to Rome. Come, Dolabella, see
High order in this great solemnity.   [*Exeunt.*

CORIOLANUS.

(WRITTEN ABOUT 1608.)

INTRODUCTION.

The metrical test places *Coriolanus* next after *Antony and Cleopatra,* and it is probable that such is its actual place in the chronological order. Having rendered into art the history of the ruin of a noble nature through voluptuous self-indulgence, Shakespeare went on to represent the ruin of a noble nature through haughtiness and pride. From Egypt, with its splendors, its glow, its revels, its moral license, we pass back to austere republican Rome. But, although free from voluptuousness, the condition of Rome is not strong and sound ; there is political division between the patricians and plebeians. Shakespeare regards the people as an overgrown child with good and kindly instincts ; owning a basis of untutored common-sense, but capable of being led astray by its leaders ; possessed of little judgment and no reasoning powers, and without capacity for self-restraint. It is not for the people, however, that he reserves his scorn, but for their tribunes, the demagogues, who mislead and pervert them. Although nobler types of individual character are to be found among the patricians than the plebeians, the dramatist is not blind to the patrician vices, and indeed the whole tragedy turns upon the existence and the influence of these. Coriolanus is by nature of a kindly and generous disposition, but he inherits the aristocratical tradition, and his kindliness strictly limits itself to the circle which includes those of his own rank and class. For his mother, he has a veneration approaching to worship ; he is content to be subordinate under Cominius ; for the old Menenius he has an almost filial regard ; but the people are "slaves," "curs," "minnows." His haughtiness becomes towering, because his personal pride, which in itself is great, is built up over a solid and high-reared pride of class. When he is banished, his bitterness arises not only from his sense of the contemptible nature of the adversaries to whom he is forced to yield, but from the additional sense that he has been deserted by his own class, "the dastard nobles." And it is in this spirit of revolt against the bonds of society and of nature, that he advances against his native city. But his haughtiness cannot really place him above nature. In the presence of his wife, his boy, and his mother, the strong man gives way and is restored once more to human love. And so his fate comes upon him. To the last something of his pride remains, and the immediate occasion of his death, is an outbreak of that sudden passion, springing from his self-esteem, which had already often and grievously wronged him. The majestic figure of Volumnia is Shakespeare's ideal of the Roman matron. The gentle Virgilia is the most beautiful and tenderly loyal of wives, and her friend Valeria

> The moon of Rome, chaste as the icicle
> That's curdled by the frost from purest snow
> And hangs on Dian's temple.

DRAMATIS PERSONÆ.

CAIUS MARCIUS, afterwards CAIUS MARCIUS CORIOLANUS.
TITUS LARTIUS, } generals against the Volscians.
COMINIUS, }
MENENIUS AGRIPPA, friend to Coriolanus.
SICINIUS VELUTUS, } tribunes of the people.
JUNIUS BRUTUS, }
Young MARCIUS, son to Coriolanus.
A Roman Herald.
TULLUS AUFIDIUS, general of the Volscians.
Lieutenant to Aufidius.
Conspirators with Aufidius.

A Citizen of Antium.
Two Volscian Guards.
VOLUMNIA, mother to Coriolanus.
VIRGILIA, wife to Coriolanus.
VALERIA, friend to Virgilia.
Gentlewoman, attending on Virgilia.
Roman and Volscian Senators, Patricians, Ædiles, Lictors, Soldiers, Citizens, Messengers, Servants to Aufidius, and other Attendants.

SCENE : *Rome and the neighborhood ; Corioli and the neighborhood ; Antium.*

ACT I.

SCENE I. *Rome. A street.*

Enter a company of mutinous Citizens, *with staves, clubs, and other weapons.*

First Cit. Before we proceed any further, hear me speak.

All. Speak, speak.

First Cit. You are all resolved rather to die than to famish ?

All. Resolved, resolved.

First Cit. First, you know Caius Marcius is chief enemy to the people.

All. We know't, we know't.

First Cit. Let us kill him, and we'll have corn at our own price. Is't a verdict ?   11

All. No more talking on't ; let it be done : away, away !

Sec. Cit. One word, good citizens.

First Cit. We are accounted poor citizens, the patricians good. What authority surfeits on would relieve us : if they would yield us but the superfluity, while it were wholesome, we might guess they relieved us humanely ; but they think we are too dear : the leanness that afflicts us, the object of our misery, is as an inventory to particularize their abundance ; our sufferance is a gain to them. Let us revenge this with our pikes, ere we become rakes : for the gods know I speak this in hunger for bread, not in thirst for revenge.

Sec. Cit. Would you proceed especially against Caius Marcius ?

All. Against him first : he's a very dog to the commonalty.   29

Sec. Cit. Consider you what services he has done for his country ?

First Cit. Very well ; and could be content to give him good report for't, but that he pays himself with being proud.

Sec. Cit. Nay, but speak not maliciously.

First Cit. I say unto you, what he hath done famously, he did it to that end : though soft-conscienced men can be content to say it was for his country, he did it to please his mother, and to be partly proud ; which he is, even to the altitude of his virtue.   41

Sec. Cit. What he cannot help in his nature, you account a vice in him. You must in no way say he is covetous.

First Cit. If I must not, I need not be barren of accusations ; he hath faults, with surplus, to tire in repetition. [*Shouts within.*] What shouts are these ? The other side o' the city is risen : why stay we prating here ? to the Capitol !

All. Come, come.   50

First Cit. Soft ! who comes here ?

Enter MENENIUS AGRIPPA.

Sec. Cit. Worthy Menenius Agrippa ; one that hath always loved the people.

First Cit. He's one honest enough : would all the rest were so !

Men. What work's, my countrymen, in hand ? where go you
With bats and clubs ? The matter ? speak, I pray you.

First Cit. Our business is not unknown to the senate ; they have had inkling this fortnight what we intend to do, which now we'll show 'em in deeds. They say poor suitors have strong breaths : they shall know we have strong arms too.

Men. Why, masters, my good friends, mine honest neighbors,
Will you undo yourselves ?

First Cit. We cannot, sir, we are undone already.

Men. I tell you, friends, most charitable care
Have the patricians of you. For your wants,
Your suffering in this dearth, you may as well
Strike at the heaven with your staves as lift them   70
Against the Roman state, whose course will on
The way it takes, cracking ten thousand curbs
Of more strong link asunder than can ever
Appear in your impediment. For the dearth,
The gods, not the patricians, make it, and
Your knees to them, not arms, must help. Alack,
You are transported by calamity
Thither where more attends you, and you slander
The helms o' the state, who care for you like fathers,
When you curse them as enemies.   80

First Cit. Care for us ! True, indeed ! They ne'er cared for us yet : suffer us to famish, and their store-houses crammed with grain ; make edicts for usury, to support usurers ; repeal daily any wholesome act established against the rich, and provide more piercing statutes daily, to chain up and restrain the poor. If the wars eat us not up, they will ; and there's all the love they bear us.

Men. Either you must   90
Confess yourselves wondrous malicious,
Or be accused of folly. I shall tell you
A pretty tale : it may be you have heard it ;
But, since it serves my purpose, I will venture
To stale 't a little more.

First Cit. Well, I'll hear it, sir : yet you must not think to fob off our disgrace with a tale : but, an 't please you, deliver.

Men. There was a time when all the body's members
Rebell'd against the belly, thus accused it :   100
That only like a gulf it did remain
I' the midst o' the body, idle and unactive,
Still cupboarding the viand, never bearing
Like labor with the rest, where the other instruments
Did see and hear, devise, instruct, walk, feel,
And, mutually participate, did minister
Unto the appetite and affection common
Of the whole body. The belly answer'd—

First Cit. Well, sir, what answer made the belly ?   110

Men. Sir, I shall tell you. With a kind of smile,
Which ne'er came from the lungs, but even thus—
For, look you, I may make the belly smile
As well as speak—it tauntingly replied
To the discontented members, the mutinous parts
That envied his receipt ; even so most fitly
As you malign our senators for that
They are not such as you.

First Cit. Your belly's answer ? What !
The kingly-crowned head, the vigilant eye,
The counsellor heart, the arm our soldier,   120

Our steed the leg, the tongue our trumpeter,
With other muniments and petty helps
In this our fabric, if that they—
Men.   What then ?
'Fore me, this fellow speaks ! What then ?
    what then ?
    First Cit. Should by the cormorant belly
        be restrain'd,
Who is the sink o' the body,—
Men.   Well, what then ?
    First Cit. The former agents, if they did
        complain,
What could the belly answer ?
Men.   I will tell you ;
If you'll bestow a small—of what you have
    little—
Patience awhile, you'll hear the belly's an-
    swer.   130
    First Cit. Ye're long about it.
Men.   Note me this, good friend ;
Your most grave belly was deliberate,
Not rash like his accusers, and thus answer'd :
' True is it, my incorporate friends,' quoth he,
' That I receive the general food at first,
Which you do live upon ; and fit it is,
Because I am the store-house and the shop
Of the whole body : but, if you do remember,
I send it through the rivers of your blood,
Even to the court, the heart, to the seat o' the
    brain ;   140
And, through the cranks and offices of man,
The strongest nerves and small inferior veins
From me receive that natural competency
Whereby they live : and though that all at
    once,
You, my good friends,'—this says the belly,
    mark me,—
    First Cit. Ay, sir ; well, well.
Men.   ' Though all at once cannot
See what I do deliver out to each,
Yet I can make my audit up, that all
From me do back receive the flour of all,
And leave me but the bran.' What say you
    to't ?   150
    First Cit. It was an answer : how apply
        you this ?
Men. The senators of Rome are this good
    belly,
And you the mutinous members ; for examine
Their counsels and their cares, digest things
    rightly
Touching the weal o' the common, you shall
    find
No public benefit which you receive
But it proceeds or comes from them to you
And no way from yourselves. What do you
    think,
You, the great toe of this assembly ?
    First Cit. I the great toe ! why the great
        toe ?   160
Men. For that, being one o' the lowest,
    basest, poorest,
Of this most wise rebellion, thou go'st fore-
    most :
Thou rascal, that art worst in blood to run,
Lead'st first to win some vantage.
But make you ready your stiff bats and clubs :
Rome and her rats are at the point of battle ;
The one side must have bale.

    Enter CAIUS MARCIUS.

                    Hail, noble Marcius !

    Mar. Thanks. What's the matter, you dis-
        sentious rogues,
That, rubbing the poor itch of your opinion,
Make yourselves scabs ?
    First Cit. We have ever your good word.
    Mar. He that will give good words to thee
        will flatter   171
Beneath abhorring. What would you have, you
    curs,
That like nor peace nor war ? the one affrights
    you,
The other makes you proud. He that trusts to
    you,
Where he should find you lions, finds you
    hares ;
Where foxes, geese : you are no surer, no,
Than is the coal of fire upon the ice,
Or hailstone in the sun. Your virtue is
To make him worthy whose offence subdues
    him
And curse that justice did it. Who deserves
    greatness   180
Deserves your hate ; and your affections are
A sick man's appetite, who desires most that
Which would increase his evil. He that de-
    pends
Upon your favors swims with fins of lead
And hews down oaks with rushes. Hang ye !
    Trust ye ?
With every minute you do change a mind,
And call him noble that was now your hate,
Him vile that was your garland. What's the
    matter,
That in these several places of the city
You cry against the noble senate, who,   190
Under the gods, keep you in awe, which else
Would feed on one another ? What's their
    seeking ?
    Men. For corn at their own rates ;
        whereof, they say,
The city is well stored.
    Mar.   Hang 'em ! They say !
They'll sit by the fire, and presume to know
What's done i' the Capitol ; who's like to rise,
Who thrives and who declines ; side factions
    and give out
Conjectural marriages ; making parties strong
And feebling such as stand not in their liking
Below their cobbled shoes. They say there's
    grain enough !   200
Would the nobility lay aside their ruth,
And let me use my sword, I'll make a quarry
With thousands of these quarter'd slaves, as
    high
As I could pick my lance.
    Men. Nay, these are almost thoroughly
        persuaded ;
For though abundantly they lack discretion,
Yet are they passing cowardly. But, I beseech
    you,
What says the other troop ?
    Mar.   They are dissolved : hang 'em !
They said they were an-hungry ; sigh'd forth
    proverbs,
That hunger broke stone walls, that dogs must
    eat,   210
That meat was made for mouths, that the gods
    sent not
Corn for the rich men only : with these shreds
They vented their complainings ; which being
    answer'd,
And a petition granted them, a strange one—
To break the heart of generosity,

And make bold power look pale—they threw
    their caps
As they would hang them on the horns o' the
    moon,
Shouting their emulation.
  Men.   What is granted them?
  Mar. Five tribunes to defend their vulgar
    wisdoms,   219
Of their own choice : one's Junius Brutus,
Sicinius Velutus, and I know not—'Sdeath !
The rabble should have first unroof'd the city,
Ere so prevail'd with me : it will in time
Win upon power and throw forth greater
    themes
For insurrection's arguing.
  Men.   This is strange.
  Mar. Go, get you home, you fragments !

        Enter a Messenger, hastily.

  Mess. Where's Caius Marcius ?
  Mar.   Here : what's the matter ?
  Mess. The news is, sir, the Volsces are in
    arms.
  Mar. I am glad on 't : then we shall ha'
    means to vent
Our musty superfluity. See, our best elders.

Enter COMINIUS, TITUS LARTIUS, *and other*
    Senators ; JUNIUS BRUTUS *and* SICINIUS
    VELUTUS.

  First Sen. Marcius, 'tis true that you have
    lately told us ;   231
The Volsces are in arms.
  Mar.   They have a leader,
Tullus Aufidius, that will put you to 't.
I sin in envying his nobility,
And were I any thing but what I am,
I would wish me only he.
  Com.   You have fought together.
  Mar. Were half to half the world by the
    ears and he
Upon my party, I'ld revolt, to make
Only my wars with him : he is a lion
That I am proud to hunt.
  First Sen.   Then, worthy Marcius, 240
Attend upon Cominius to these wars.
  Com. It is your former promise.
  Mar.   Sir, it is ;
And I am constant. Titus Lartius, thou
Shalt see me once more strike at Tullus' face.
What, art thou stiff ? stand'st out ?
  Tit.   No, Caius Marcius ;
I'll lean upon one crutch and fight with t'other,
Ere stay behind this business.
  Men.   O, true-bred !
  First Sen. Your company to the Capitol ;
    where, I know,
Our greatest friends attend us.
  Tit.   [*To Com.*] Lead you on.
[*To Mar.*] Follow Cominius ; we must fol-
    low you ;   250
Right worthy you priority.
  Com.   Noble Marcius !
  First Sen. [*To the Citizens*] Hence to your
    homes ; be gone !
  Mar.   Nay, let them follow :
The Volsces have much corn ; take these rats
    thither
To gnaw their garners. Worshipful mutiners,
Your valor puts well forth : pray, follow.
        [*Citizens steal away. Exeunt all but
               Sicinius and Brutus.*

  Sic. Was ever man so proud as is this
    Marcius ?
  Bru. He has no equal.
  Sic. When we were chosen tribunes for the
    people,—
  Bru. Mark'd you his lip and eyes ?
  Sic.   Nay, but his taunts.
  Bru. Being moved, he will not spare to gird
    the gods.   260
  Sic. Be-mock the modest moon.
  Bru. The present wars devour him : he is
    grown
Too proud to be so valiant.
  Sic.   Such a nature,
Tickled with good success, disdains the shadow
Which he treads on at noon : but I do wonder
His insolence can brook to be commanded
Under Cominius.
  Bru. Fame, at the which he aims,
In whom already he's well graced, can not
Better be held nor more attain'd than by
A place below the first : for what miscarries
Shall be the general's fault, though he per-
    form   271
To the utmost of a man, and giddy censure
Will then cry out of Marcius 'O if he
Had borne the business ! '
  Sic.   Besides, if things go well,
Opinion that so sticks on Marcius shall
Of his demerits rob Cominius.
  Bru.   Come :
Half all Cominius' honors are to Marcius,
Though Marcius earned them not, and all his
    faults
To Marcius shall be honors, though indeed
In aught he merit not.   279
  Sic.   Let's hence, and hear
How the dispatch is made, and in what fash-
    ion,
More than his singularity, he goes
Upon this present action.
  Bru.   Let's along. [*Exeunt.*

   SCENE II. *Corioli. The Senate-house.*

Enter TULLUS AUFIDIUS *and certain* Senators.

  First Sen. So, your opinion is, Aufidius,
That they of Rome are entered in our counsels
And know how we proceed.
  Auf.   Is it not yours ?
What ever have been thought on in this state,
That could be brought to bodily act ere Rome
Had circumvention ? 'Tis not four days gone
Since I heard thence ; these are the words : I
    think
I have the letter here ; yes, here it is.
[*Reads*] ' They have press'd a power, but it
    is not known
Whether for east or west : the dearth is great ;
The people mutinous ; and it is rumor'd,   11
Cominius, Marcius your old enemy,
Who is of Rome worse hated than of you,
And Titus Lartius, a most valiant Roman,
These three lead on this preparation
Whither 'tis bent : most likely 'tis for you :
Consider of it.'
  First Sen. Our army's in the field :
We never yet made doubt but Rome was ready
To answer us.
  Auf.   Nor did you think it folly
To keep your great pretences veil'd till when
They needs must show themselves ; which in
    the hatching,   21
It seem'd, appear'd to Rome. By the discovery

We shall be shorten'd in our aim, which was
To take in many towns ere almost Rome
Should know we were afoot.

Sec. Sen.   Noble Aufidius,
Take your commission; hie you to your
    bands:
Let us alone to guard Corioli:
If they set down before 's, for the remove
Bring up your army; but, I think, you'll find
They've not prepared for us.

Auf.   O, doubt not that; 30
I speak from certainties. Nay, more,
Some parcels of their power are forth already,
And only hitherward. I leave your honors.
If we and Caius Marcius chance to meet,
'Tis sworn between us we shall ever strike
Till one can do no more.

All.   The gods assist you!
Auf. And keep your honors safe!
First Sen.   Farewell.
Sec. Sen.   Farewell.
All. Farewell.   [*Exeunt.*

SCENE III. *Rome. A room in Marcius'
    house.*

Enter VOLUMNIA *and* VIRGILIA: *they set them
    down on two low stools, and sew.*

Vol. I pray you, daughter, sing; or express yourself in a more comfortable sort: if
my son were my husband, I should freelier rejoice in that absence wherein he won honor
than in the embracements of his bed where he
would show most love. When yet he was but
tender-bodied and the only son of my womb,
when youth with comeliness plucked all gaze
his way, when for a day of kings' entreaties a
mother should not sell him an hour from her
beholding, I, considering how honor would become such a person, that it was no better
than picture-like to hang by the wall, if renown made it not stir, was pleased to let him
seek danger where he was like to find fame.
To a cruel war I sent him; from whence he
returned, his brows bound with oak. I tell thee,
daughter, I sprang not more in joy at first
hearing he was a man-child than now in first
seeing he had proved himself a man.   19

Vir. But had he died in the business,
madam; how then?

Vol. Then his good report should have
been my son; I therein would have found issue. Hear me profess sincerely: had I a dozen
sons, each in my love alike and none less dear
than thine and my good Marcius, I had rather
had eleven die nobly for their country than
one voluptuously surfeit out of action.

Enter a Gentlewoman.

Gent. Madam, the Lady Valeria is come to
visit you.

Vir. Beseech you, give me leave to retire
myself.   30

Vol. Indeed, you shall not.
Methinks I hear hither your husband's drum,
See him pluck Aufidius down by the hair,
As children from a bear, the Volsces shunning
    him:
Methinks I see him stamp thus, and call thus:
'Come on, you cowards! you were got in fear,
Though you were born in Rome:' his bloody
    brow
With his mail'd hand then wiping, forth he
    goes,

Like to a harvest-man that's task'd to mow
Or all or lose his hire.   40

Vir. His bloody brow! O Jupiter, no
    blood!

Vol. Away, you fool! it more becomes a
    man
Than gilt his trophy: the breasts of Hecuba,
When she did suckle Hector, look'd not love-
    lier
Than Hector's forehead when it spit forth
    blood
At Grecian sword, contemning. Tell Valeria,
We are fit to bid her welcome.   [*Exit Gent.*

Vir. Heavens bless my lord from fell Au-
    fidius!

Vol. He'll beat Aufidius 'head below his
    knee
And tread upon his neck.   50

Enter VALERIA, *with an* Usher *and* Gentle-
    woman.

Val. My ladies both, good day to you.
Vol. Sweet madam.
Vir. I am glad to see your ladyship.
Val. How do you both? you are manifest
house-keepers. What are you sewing here? A
fine spot, in good faith. How does your little
son?

Vir. I thank your ladyship; well, good
madam.

Vol. He had rather see the swords, and
hear a drum, than look upon his schoolmaster.   61

Val. O' my word, the father's son: I'll
swear, 'tis a very pretty boy. O' my troth, I
looked upon him o' Wednesday half an hour
together: has such a confirmed countenance.
I saw him run after a gilded butterfly; and
when he caught it, he let it go again; and after
it again; and over and over he comes, and up
again; catched it again; or whether his fall
enraged him, or how 'twas, he did so set his
teeth and tear it; O, I warrant it, how he
mammocked it!   71

Vol. One on 's father's moods.
Val. Indeed, la, 'tis a noble child.
Vir. A crack, madam.
Val. Come, lay aside your stitchery; I
must have you play the idle huswife with me
this afternoon.

Vir. No, good madam; I will not out of
doors.

Val. Not out of doors!
Vol. She shall, she shall.   80
Vir. Indeed, no, by your patience; I'll not
over the threshold till my lord return from the
wars.

Val. Fie, you confine yourself most un-
reasonably: come, you must go visit the good
lady that lies in.

Vir. I will wish her speedy strength, and
visit her with my prayers; but I cannot go
thither.

Vol. Why, I pray you?
Vir. 'Tis not to save labor, nor that I want
love.   91

Val. You would be another Penelope: yet,
they say, all the yarn she spun in Ulysses' absence did but fill Ithaca full of moths. Come;
I would your cambric were sensible as your
finger, that you might leave pricking it for
pity. Come, you shall go with us.

Vir. No, good madam, pardon me ; indeed,
I will not forth.

Val. In truth, la, go with me ; and I'll tell
you excellent news of your husband.   101

Vir. O, good madam, there can be none
yet.

Val. Verily, I do not jest with you ; there
came news from him last night.

Vir. Indeed, madam ?

Val. In earnest, it's true ; I heard a senator
speak it. Thus it is : the Volsces have an army
forth ; against whom Cominius the general is
gone, with one part of our Roman power :
your lord and Titus Lartius are set down before their city Corioli ; they nothing doubt pre-
vailing and to make it brief wars. This is true,
on mine honor ; and so, I pray, go with us.

Vir. Give me excuse, good madam ; I will
obey you in every thing hereafter.

Vol. Let her alone, lady : as she is now,
she will but disease our better mirth.

Val. In troth, I think she would. Fare you
well, then. Come, good sweet lady. Prithee,
Virgilia, turn thy solemness out o' door, and
go along with us.   121

Vir. No, at a word, madam ; indeed, I
must not. I wish you much mirth.

Val. Well, then, farewell.   [*Exeunt.*

Scene IV. *Before Corioli.*

Enter, with drum and colors, Marcius, Titus
Lartius, *Captains and* Soldiers. *To them
a* Messenger.

Mar. Yonder comes news. A wager they
have met.

Lart. My horse to yours, no.

Mar.   'Tis done.

Lart.   Agreed.

Mar. Say, has our general met the enemy ?

Mess. They lie in view ; but have not spoke
as yet.

Lart. So, the good horse is mine.

Mar.   I'll buy him of you.

Lart. No, I'll nor sell nor give him : lend
you him I will
For half a hundred years. Summon the town.

Mar. How far off lie these armies ?

Mess.   Within this mile and half.

Mar. Then shall we hear their 'larum, and
they ours.
Now, Mars, I prithee, make us quick in work,
That we with smoking swords may march
from hence,   11
To help our fielded friends ! Come, blow thy
blast.

They sound a parley. Enter two Senators *with
others on the walls.*

Tullus Aufidius, is he within your walls ?

First Sen. No, nor a man that fears you
less than he,
That's lesser than a little. [*Drums afar off.*]
Hark ! our drums
Are bringing forth our youth. We'll break our
walls,
Rather than they shall pound us up : our gates,
Which yet seem shut, we have but pinn'd with
rushes ;
They'll open of themselves. [*Alarum afar off.*]
Hark you, far off !
There is Aufidius ; list, what work he makes
Amongst your cloven army.   21

Mar.   O, they are at it !

Lart. Their noise be our instruction. Lad-
ders, ho !

Enter the army of the Volsces.

Mar. They fear us not, but issue forth their
city.
Now put your shields before your hearts, and
fight
With hearts more proof than shields. Advance,
brave Titus :
They do disdain us much beyond our thoughts,
Which makes me sweat with wrath. Come on,
my fellows :
He that retires I'll take him for a Volsce,
And he shall feel mine edge.

Alarum. The Romans *are beat back to their
trenches. Re-enter* Marcius, *cursing.*

Mar. All the contagion of the south light
on you,   30
You shames of Rome ! you herd of—Boils
and plagues
Plaster you o'er, that you may be abhorr'd
Further than seen and one infect another
Against the wind a mile ! You souls of geese,
That bear the shapes of men, how have you
run
From slaves that apes would beat ! Pluto and
hell !
All hurt behind ; backs red, and faces pale
With flight and agued fear ! Mend and charge
home,
Or, by the fires of heaven, I'll leave the foe
And make my wars on you : look to't : come
on ;   40
If you'll stand fast, we'll beat them to their
wives,
As they us to our trenches followed.

Another alarum. The Volsces *fly, and* Marcius *follows them to the gates.*

So, now the gates are ope : now prove good
seconds :
'Tis for the followers fortune widens them,
Not for the fliers : mark me, and do the like.
     [*Enters the gates.*

First Sol. Fool-hardiness ; not I.

Sec. Sol.   Nor I.
     [*Marcius is shut in.*

First Sol. See, they have shut him in.

All.   To the pot, I warrant him.
     [*Alarum continues.*

Re-enter Titus Lartius.

Lart. What is become of Marcius ?

All.   Slain, sir, doubtless.

First Sol. Following the fliers at the very
heels,   49
With them he enters ; who, upon the sudden,
Clapp'd to their gates : he is himself alone,
To answer all the city.

Lart.   O noble fellow !
Who sensibly outdares his senseless sword,
And, when it bows, stands up. Thou art left,
Marcius :
A carbuncle entire, as big as thou art,
Were not so rich a jewel. Thou wast a soldier
Even to Cato's wish, not fierce and terrible
Only in strokes ; but, with thy grim looks and
The thunder-like percussion of thy sounds,
Thou madst thine enemies shake, as if the
world   60
Were feverous and did tremble.

Re-enter MARCIUS, *bleeding, assaulted by the enemy.*

First Sol. Look, sir.
Lart. O, 'tis Marcius!
Let's fetch him off, or make remain alike.
  [*They fight, and all enter the city.*

SCENE V. *Corioli. A street.*

Enter certain Romans, *with spoils.*

First Rom. This will I carry to Rome.
Sec. Rom. And I this.
Third Rom. A murrain on't! I took this
for silver. [*Alarum continues still afar off.*

Enter MARCIUS *and* TITUS LARTIUS *with a trumpet.*

Mar. See here these movers that do prize
    their hours
At a crack'd drachm! Cushions, leaden
    spoons,
Irons of a doit, doublets that hangmen would
Bury with those that wore them, these base
    slaves,
Ere yet the fight be done, pack up: down with
    them!
And hark, what noise the general makes! To
    him!   10
There is the man of my soul's hate, Aufidius,
Piercing our Romans: then, valiant Titus, take
Convenient numbers to make good the city;
Whilst I, with those that have the spirit, will
    haste
To help Cominius.
Lart.   Worthy sir, thou bleed'st;
Thy exercise hath been too violent for
A second course of fight.
Mar.   Sir, praise me not;
My work hath yet not warm'd me: fare you
    well:
The blood I drop is rather physical
Than dangerous to me: to Aufidius thus   20
I will appear, and fight.
Lart.   Now the fair goddess, Fortune,
Fall deep in love with thee; and her great
    charms
Misguide thy opposers' swords! Bold gentle-
    man,
Prosperity be thy page!
Mar.   Thy friend no less
Than those she placeth highest! So, farewell.
Lart. Thou worthiest Marcius!
              [*Exit Marcius.*
Go, sound thy trumpet in the market-place;
Call thither all the officers o' the town,
Where they shall know our mind: away!
              [*Exeunt.*

SCENE VI. *Near the camp of Cominius.*

Enter COMINIUS, *as it were in retire, with sol-
    diers.*

Com. Breathe you, my friends: well
    fought; we are come off
Like Romans, neither foolish in our stands,
Nor cowardly in retire: believe me, sirs,
We shall be charged again. Whiles we have
    struck,
By interims and conveying gusts we have heard
The charges of our friends. Ye Roman gods!
Lead their successes as we wish our own,
That both our powers, with smiling fronts en-
    countering,
May give you thankful sacrifice.

Enter a Messenger.
              Thy news?   9
Mess. The citizens of Corioli have issued,
And given to Lartius and to Marcius battle:
I saw our party to their trenches driven,
And then I came away.
Com.   Though thou speak'st truth,
Methinks thou speak'st not well. How long is't
    since?
Mess. Above an hour, my lord.
Com.   'Tis not a mile; briefly we heard
    their drums:
How couldst thou in a mile confound an hour,
And bring thy news so late?
Mess.   Spies of the Volsces
Held me in chase, that I was forced to wheel
Three or four miles about, else had I, sir,   20
Half an hour since brought my report.
Com.   Who's yonder,
That does appear as he were flay'd? O gods!
He has the stamp of Marcius; and I have
Before-time seen him thus.
Mar.   [*Within*] Come I too late?
Com. The shepherd knows not thunder
    from a tabor
More than I know the sound of Marcius'
    tongue
From every meaner man.

Enter MARCIUS.

Mar.   Come I too late?
Com. Ay, if you come not in the blood of
    others,
But mantled in your own.
Mar.   O, let me clip ye
In arms as sound as when I woo'd, in heart 30
As merry as when our nuptial day was done,
And tapers burn'd to bedward!
Com.   Flower of warriors,
How is it with Titus Lartius?
Mar. As with a man busied about decrees:
Condemning some to death, and some to
    exile;
Ransoming him, or pitying, threatening the
    other;
Holding Corioli in the name of Rome,
Even like a fawning greyhound in the leash,
To let him slip at will.
Com.   Where is that slave
Which told me they had beat you to your
    trenches?   40
Where is he? call him hither.
Mar.   Let him alone;
He did inform the truth: but for our gentle-
    men,
The common file—a plague! tribunes for
    them!—
The mouse ne'er shunn'd the cat as they did
    budge
From rascals worse than they.
Com.   But how prevail'd you?
Mar. Will the time serve to tell? I do not
    think.
Where is the enemy? are you lords o' the
    field?
If not, why cease you till you are so?
Com.   Marcius,
We have at disadvantage fought and did
Retire to win our purpose.   50
Mar. How lies their battle? know you on
    which side
They have placed their men of trust?

Com.   As I guess, Marcius,
Their bands i' the vaward are the Antiates,
Of their best trust ; o'er them Aufidius,
Their very heart of hope.
Mar.   I do beseech you,
By all the battles wherein we have fought,
By the blood we have shed together, by the
    vows
We have made to endure friends, that you
    directly
Set me against Aufidius and his Antiates ;
And that you not delay the present, but,   60
Filling the air with swords advanced and darts,
We prove this very hour.
Com.   Though I could wish
You were conducted to a gentle bath
And balms applied to you, yet dare I never
Deny your asking : take your choice of those
That best can aid your action.
Mar.   Those are they
That most are willing. If any such be here—
As it were sin to doubt—that love this painting
Wherein you see me smear'd ; if any fear
Lesser his person than an ill report ;   70
If any think brave death outweighs bad life
And that his country's dearer than himself ;
Let him alone, or so many so minded,
Wave thus, to express his disposition,
And follow Marcius.
    [*They all shout and wave their swords, take
    him up in their arms, and cast up their
    caps.*
O, me alone ! make you a sword of me ?
If these shows be not outward, which of you
But is four Volsces ? none of you but is
Able to bear against the great Aufidius
A shield as hard as his. A certain number,   80
Though thanks to all, must I select from all :
    the rest
Shall bear the business in some other fight,
As cause will be obey'd. Please you to march ;
And four shall quickly draw out my com-
    mand,
Which men are best inclined.
Com.   March on, my fellows :
Make good this ostentation, and you shall
Divide in all with us.   [*Exeunt.*

SCENE VII.   *The gates of Corioli.*

TITUS LARTIUS, *having set a guard upon Corioli, going with drum and trumpet toward
COMINIUS and CAIUS MARCIUS, enters with
a Lieutenant, other Soldiers, and a Scout.*

Lart. So, let the ports be guarded : keep
    your duties,
As I have set them down. If I do send, dis-
    patch
Those centuries to our aid : the rest will serve
For a short holding : if we lose the field,
We cannot keep the town.
Lieu.   Fear not our care, sir.
Lart. Hence, and shut your gates upon's.
Our guider, come ; to the Roman camp con-
    duct us.   [*Exeunt.*

SCENE VIII.   *A field of battle.*

*Alarum as in battle. Enter, from opposite
sides, MARCIUS and AUFIDIUS.*

Mar. I'll fight with none but thee ; for I
    do hate thee
Worse than a promise-breaker.
Auf.   We hate alike :
Not Afric owns a serpent I abhor
More than thy fame and envy. Fix thy foot.
Mar. Let the first budger die the other's
    slave,
And the gods doom him after !
Auf.   If I fly, Marcius,
Holloa me like a hare.
Mar.   Within these three hours, Tullus,
Alone I fought in your Corioli walls,
And made what work I pleased : 'tis not my
    blood
Wherein thou seest me mask'd ; for thy re-
    venge
Wrench up thy power to the highest.
Auf.   Wert thou the Hector 11
That was the whip of your bragg'd progeny,
Thou shouldst not scape me here.
    [*They fight, and certain Volsces come to
    the aid of Aufidius. Marcius fights till
    they be driven in breathless.*
Officious, and not valiant, you have shamed
    me
In your condemned seconds.   [*Exeunt.*

SCENE IX.   *The Roman camp.*

*Flourish. Alarum. A retreat is sounded.
Flourish. Enter, from one side, COMINIUS
with the Romans ; from the other side,
MARCIUS, with his arm in a scarf.*

Com. If I should tell thee o'er this thy
    day's work,
Thou'ldst not believe thy deeds : but I'll re-
    port it
Where senators shall mingle tears with smiles,
Where great patricians shall attend and shrug,
I' the end admire, where ladies shall be
    frighted,
And, gladly quaked, hear more ; where the
    dull tribunes,
That, with the fusty plebeians, hate thine
    honors,
Shall say against their hearts ' We thank the
    gods
Our Rome hath such a soldier.'
Yet camest thou to a morsel of this feast,   10
Having fully dined before.

*Enter TITUS LARTIUS, with his power, from
the pursuit.*

Lart.   O general,
Here is the steed, we the caparison :
Hadst thou beheld—
Mar.   Pray now, no more : my mother,
Who has a charter to extol her blood,
When she does praise me grieves me. I have
    done
As you have done ; that's what I can ; induced
As you have been ; that's for my country :
He that has but effected his good will
Hath overta'en mine act.
Com.   You shall not be
The grave of your deserving ; Rome must
    know   20
The value of her own : 'twere a concealment
Worse than a theft, no less than a traduce-
    ment,
To hide your doings ; and to silence that,
Which, to the spire and top of praises vouch'd,
Would seem but modest : therefore, I beseech
    you
In sign of what you are, not to reward
What you have done—before our army hear
    me.

Mar. I have some wounds upon me, and
   they smart
To hear themselves remember'd.
   Com.   Should they not,
Well might they fester 'gainst ingratitude,   30
And tent themselves with death. Of all the
   horses,
Whereof we have ta'en good and good store,
   of all
The treasure in this field achieved and city,
We render you the tenth, to be ta'en forth,
Before the common distribution, at
Your only choice.
   Mar.   I thank you, general;
But cannot make my heart consent to take
A bribe to pay my sword: I do refuse it;
And stand upon my common part with those
That have beheld the doing.   40
   [*A long flourish. They all cry* 'Marcius!
      Marcius!' *cast up their caps and lances:*
      Cominius and Lartius stand bare.
   Mar. May these same instruments, which
      you profane,
Never sound more! when drums and trum-
   pets shall
I' the field prove flatterers, let courts and
   cities be
Made all of false-faced soothing!
When steel grows soft as the parasite's silk,
Let him be made a coverture for the wars!
No more, I say! For that I have not wash'd
My nose that bled, or foil'd some debile
   wretch,—
Which, without note, here's many else have
   done,—
You shout me forth   50
In acclamations hyperbolical;
As if I loved my little should be dieted
In praises sauced with lies.
   Com.   Too modest are you;
More cruel to your good report than grateful
To us that give you truly: by your patience,
If 'gainst yourself you be incensed, we'll put
   you,
Like one that means his proper harm, in man-
   acles,
Then reason safely with you. Therefore, be it
   known,
As to us, to all the world, that Caius Marcius
Wears this war's garland: in token of the
   which,   60
My noble steed, known to the camp, I give
   him,
With all his trim belonging; and from this
   time,
For what he did before Corioli, call him,
With all the applause and clamor of the host,
Caius Marcius Coriolanus! Bear
The addition nobly ever!
   [*Flourish. Trumpets sound, and drums.*
   All. Caius Marcius Coriolanus!
   Cor. I will go wash;
And when my face is fair, you shall perceive
Whether I blush or no: howbeit, I thank you.
I mean to stride your steed, and at all times
To undercrest your good addition
To the fairness of my power.
   Com.   So, to our tent;
Where, ere we do repose us, we will write
To Rome of our success. You, Titus Lartius,
Must to Corioli back: send us to Rome
The best, with whom we may articulate,
For their own good and ours.

   Lart.   I shall, my lord.
   Cor. The gods begin to mock me. I, that
      now
Refused most princely gifts, am bound to beg
Of my lord general.   81
   Com. Take't; 'tis yours. What is't?
   Cor. I sometime lay here in Corioli
At a poor man's house; he used me kindly:
He cried to me; I saw him prisoner;
But then Aufidius was within my view,
And wrath o'erwhelm'd my pity: I request
   you
To give my poor host freedom.
   Com.   O, well begg'd!
Were he the butcher of my son, he should
Be free as is the wind. Deliver him, Titus.
   Lart. Marcius, his name?
   Cor.   By Jupiter! forgot.
I am weary; yea, my memory is tired.   91
Have we no wine here?
   Com.   Go we to our tent:
The blood upon your visage dries; 'tis time
It should be look'd to: come.   [*Exeunt.*

   SCENE X. *The camp of the Volsces.*

A flourish. Cornets. Enter TULLUS AUFID-
   IUS, *bloody, with two or three Soldiers.*

   Auf. The town is ta'en!
   First Sol. 'Twill be deliver'd back on good
      condition.
   Auf. Condition!
I would I were a Roman; for I cannot,
Being a Volsce, be that I am. Condition!
What good condition can a treaty find
I' the part that is at mercy? Five times, Mar-
   cius,
I have fought with thee: so often hast thou
   beat me,
And wouldst do so, I think, should we en-
   counter
As often as we eat. By the elements,   10
If e'er again I meet him beard to beard,
He's mine, or I am his: mine emulation
Hath not that honor in't it had; for where
I thought to crush him in an equal force,
True sword to sword, I'll potch at him some
   way
Or wrath or craft may get him.
   First Sol.   He's the devil.
   Auf. Bolder, though not so subtle. My
      valor's poison'd
With only suffering stain by him; for him
Shall fly out of itself: nor sleep nor sanctuary,
Being naked, sick, nor fane nor Capitol,   20
The prayers of priests nor times of sacrifice,
Embarquements all of fury, shall lift up
Their rotten privilege and custom 'gainst
My hate to Marcius: where I find him, were it
At home, upon my brother's guard, even there,
Against the hospitable canon, would I
Wash my fierce hand in's heart. Go you to
   the city;
Learn how 'tis held; and what they are that
   must
Be hostages for Rome.
   First Sol.   Will not you go?
   Auf. I am attended at the cypress grove:
      I pray you—   30
'Tis south the city mills—bring me word
   thither
How the world goes, that to the pace of it
I may spur on my journey.

First Sol.   I shall, sir.
                                              [*Exeunt.*

ACT II.

SCENE I. *Rome. A public place.*

Enter MENENIUS *with the two Tribunes of the people,* SICINIUS *and* BRUTUS.

Men. The augurer tells me we shall have news to-night.

Bru. Good or bad?

Men. Not according to the prayer of the people, for they love not Marcius.

Sic. Nature teaches beasts to know their friends.

Men. Pray you, who does the wolf love?

Sic. The lamb.

Men. Ay, to devour him; as the hungry plebeians would the noble Marcius.   11

Bru. He's a lamb indeed, that baes like a bear.

Men. He's a bear indeed, that lives like a lamb. You two are old men: tell me one thing that I shall ask you.

Both. Well, sir.

Men. In what enormity is Marcius poor in, that you two have not in abundance?

Bru. He's poor in no one fault, but stored with all.   21

Sic. Especially in pride.

Bru. And topping all others in boasting.

Men. This is strange now: do you two know how you are censured here in the city, I mean of us o' the right-hand file? do you?

Both. Why, how are we censured?

Men. Because you talk of pride now,—will you not be angry?

Both. Well, well, sir, well.   30

Men. Why, 'tis no great matter; for a very little thief of occasion will rob you of a great deal of patience: give your dispositions the reins, and be angry at your pleasures; at the least, if you take it as a pleasure to you in being so. You blame Marcius for being proud?

Bru. We do it not alone, sir.

Men. I know you can do very little alone; for your helps are many, or else your actions would grow wondrous single: your abilities are too infant-like for doing much alone. You talk of pride: O that you could turn your eyes toward the napes of your necks, and make but an interior survey of your good selves! O that you could!

Bru. What then, sir?

Men. Why, then you should discover a brace of unmeriting, proud, violent, testy magistrates, alias fools, as any in Rome.

Sic. Menenius, you are known well enough too.   50

Men. I am known to be a humorous patrician, and one that loves a cup of hot wine with not a drop of allaying Tiber in't; said to be something imperfect in favoring the first complaint; hasty and tinder-like upon too trivial motion; one that converses more with the buttock of the night than with the forehead of the morning: what I think I utter, and spend my malice in my breath. Meeting two such wealsmen as you are—I cannot call you Lycurguses—if the drink you give me touch my palate adversely, I make a crooked face at it. I can't say your worships have delivered the matter well, when I find the ass in compound with the major part of your syllables: and though I must be content to bear with those that say you are reverend grave men, yet they lie deadly that tell you you have good faces. If you see this in the map of my microcosm, follows it that I am known well enough too? what harm can your bisson conspectuities glean out of this character, if I be known well enough too?

Bru. Come, sir, come, we know you well enough.

Men. You know neither me, yourselves nor any thing. You are ambitious for poor knaves' caps and legs: you wear out a good wholesome forenoon in hearing a cause between an orange wife and a fosset-seller; and then rejourn the controversy of three pence to a second day of audience. When you are hearing a matter between party and party, if you chance to be pinched with the colic, you make faces like mummers; set up the bloody flag against all patience; and, in roaring for a chamber-pot, dismiss the controversy bleeding, the more entangled by your hearing: all the peace you make in their cause is, calling both the parties knaves. You are a pair of strange ones.   89

Bru. Come, come, you are well understood to be a perfecter giber for the table than a necessary bencher in the Capitol.

Men. Our very priests must become mockers, if they shall encounter such ridiculous subjects as you are. When you speak best unto the purpose, it is not worth the wagging of your beards; and your beards deserve not so honorable a grave as to stuff a botcher's cushion, or to be entombed in an ass's packsaddle. Yet you must be saying, Marcius is proud; who, in a cheap estimation, is worth all your predecessors since Deucalion, though peradventure some of the best of 'em were hereditary hangmen. God-den to your worships: more of your conversation would infect my brain, being the herdsmen of the beastly plebeians: I will be bold to take my leave of you.

[*Brutus and Sicinius go aside.*

Enter VOLUMNIA, VIRGILIA, *and* VALERIA.

How now, my as fair as noble ladies,—and the moon, were she earthly, no nobler,—whither do you follow your eyes so fast?   109

Vol. Honorable Menenius, my boy Marcius approaches; for the love of Juno, let's go.

Men. Ha! Marcius coming home!

Vol. Ay, worthy Menenius; and with most prosperous approbation.

Men. Take my cap, Jupiter, and I thank thee. Hoo! Marcius coming home!

Vol. Vir. Nay, 'tis true.

Vol. Look, here's a letter from him: the state hath another, his wife another; and, I think, there's one at home for you.   120

Men. I will make my very house reel to-night: a letter for me!

Vir. Yes, certain, there's a letter for you; I saw't.

Men. A letter for me! it gives me an estate of seven years' health; in which time I will make a lip at the physician: the most sovereign prescription in Galen is but em-

piricutic, and, to this preservative, of no better report than a horse-drench. Is he not
wounded ? he was wont to come home
wounded. 131

Vir. O, no, no, no.

Vol. O, he is wounded; I thank the gods
for't.

Men. So do I too, if it be not too much :
brings a' victory in his pocket ? the wounds
become him.

Vol. On's brows : Menenius, he comes the
third time home with the oaken garland.

Men. Has he disciplined Aufidius soundly ?

Vol. Titus Lartius writes, they fought together, but Aufidius got off. 141

Men. And 'twas time for him too, I'll warrant him that : an he had stayed by him, I
would not have been so fidiused for all the
chests in Corioli, and the gold that's in them.
Is the senate possessed of this ?

Vol. Good ladies, let's go. Yes, yes, yes ;
the senate has letters from the general, wherein he gives my son the whole name of the war :
he hath in this action outdone his former deeds
doubly. 151

Val. In troth, there's wondrous things
spoke of him.

Men. Wondrous ! ay, I warrant you, and
not without his true purchasing.

Vir. The gods grant them true !

Vol. True ! pow, wow.

Men. True ! I'll be sworn they are true.
Where is he wounded ? [*To the Tribunes*]
God save your good worships ! Marcius is
coming home : he has more cause to be proud.
Where is he wounded ?

Vol. I' the shoulder and i' the left arm :
there will be large cicatrices to show the people, when he shall stand for his place. He received in the repulse of Tarquin seven hurts
i' the body.

Men. One i' the neck, and two i' the thigh,
—there's nine that I know.

Vol. He had, before this last expedition,
twenty-five wounds upon him. 170

Men. Now it's twenty-seven : every gash
was an enemy's grave. [*A shout and flourish.*]
Hark ! the trumpets.

Vol. These are the ushers of Marcius : before him he carries noise, and behind him he
leaves tears :
Death, that dark spirit, in 's nervy arm doth
lie ;
Which, being advanced, declines, and then
men die.

A sennet. Trumpets sound. Enter COMINIUS
the general, and TITUS LARTIUS ; *between
them,* CORIOLANUS, *crowned with an oaken
garland ; with* Captains *and* Soldiers, *and a*
Herald.

Her. Know, Rome, that all alone Marcius
did fight
Within Corioli gates : where he hath won, 180
With fame, a name to Caius Marcius ; these
In honor follows Coriolanus.
Welcome to Rome, renowned Coriolanus !
[*Flourish.*

All. Welcome to Rome, renowned Coriolanus !

Cor. No more of this ; it does offend my
heart :
Pray now, no more.

Com. Look, sir, your mother !

Cor. O,
You have, I know, petition'd all the gods
For my prosperity ! [*Kneels.*

Vol. Nay, my good soldier, up ;
My gentle Marcius, worthy Caius, and
By deed-achieving honor newly named,— 190
What is it ?—Coriolanus must I call thee ?—
But, O, thy wife !

Cor. My gracious silence, hail !
Wouldst thou have laugh'd had I come coffin'd
home,
That weep'st to see me triumph ? Ay, my
dear,
Such eyes the widows in Corioli wear,
And mothers that lack sons.

Men. Now, the gods crown thee !

Cor. And live you yet ? [*To Valeria*] O my
sweet lady, pardon.

Vol. I know not where to turn : O, welcome home :
And welcome, general : and ye're welcome all.

Men. A hundred thousand welcomes. I
could weep 200
And I could laugh, I am light and heavy.
Welcome.
A curse begin at very root on's heart,
That is not glad to see thee ! You are three
That Rome should dote on : yet, by the faith
of men,
We have some old crab-trees here at home
that will not
Be grafted to your relish. Yet welcome, war-
riors :
We call a nettle but a nettle and
The faults of fools but folly.

Com. Ever right.

Cor. Menenius ever, ever.

Her. Give way there, and go on !

Cor. [*To Volumnia and Virgilia*] Your
hand, and yours : 210
Ere in our own house I do shade my head,
The good patricians must be visited ;
From whom I have received not only greet-
ings,
But with them change of honors.

Vol. I have lived
To see inherited my very wishes
And the buildings of my fancy : only
There's one thing wanting, which I doubt not
but
Our Rome will cast upon thee.

Cor. Know, good mother,
I had rather be their servant in my way,
Than sway with them in theirs.

Com. On, to the Capitol ! 220
[*Flourish. Cornets. Exeunt in state, as
before. Brutus and Sicinius come forward.*

Bru. All tongues speak of him, and the
bleared sights
Are spectacled to see him : your prattling
nurse
Into a rapture lets her baby cry
While she chats him : the kitchen malkin pins
Her richest lockram 'bout her reechy neck,
Clambering the walls to eye him : stalls, bulks,
windows,
Are smother'd up, leads fill'd, and ridges
horsed
With variable complexions, all agreeing
In earnestness to see him : seld-shown fla-
mens

Do press among the popular throngs and puff
To win a vulgar station : or veil'd dames 231
Commit the war of white and damask in
Their nicely-gawded cheeks to the wanton
   spoil
Of Phœbus' burning kisses : such a pother
As if that whatsoever god who leads him
Were slily crept into his human powers
And gave him graceful posture.

  Sic.   On the sudden,
I warrant him consul.

  Bru.   Then our office may,
During his power, go sleep.

  Sic. He cannot temperately transport his
   honors   240
From where he should begin and end, but will
Lose those he hath won.

  Bru.   In that there's comfort.

  Sic.   Doubt not
The commoners, for whom we stand, but they
Upon their ancient malice will forget
With the least cause these his new honors,
   which
That he will give them make I as little ques-
   tion
As he is proud to do't.

  Bru.   I heard him swear,
Were he to stand for consul, never would he
Appear i' the market-place nor on him put
The napless vesture of humility ;   250
Nor, showing, as the manner is, his wounds
To the people, beg their stinking breaths.

  Sic.   'Tis right.

  Bru. It was his word : O, he would miss it
   rather
Than carry it but by the suit of the gentry to
   him,
And the desire of the nobles.

  Sic.   I wish no better
Than have him hold that purpose and to put
   it
In execution.

  Bru. 'Tis most like he will.

  Sic. It shall be to him then as our good
   wills,
A sure destruction.

  Bru.   So it must fall out
To him or our authorities. For an end,   260
We must suggest the people in what hatred
He still hath held them ; that to's power he
   would
Have made them mules, silenced their plead-
   ers and
Dispropertied their freedoms, holding them,
In human action and capacity,
Of no more soul nor fitness for the world
Than camels in the war, who have their
   provand
Only for bearing burdens, and sore blows
For sinking under them.

  Sic. This, as you say, suggested
At some time when his soaring insolence 270
Shall touch the people—which time shall not
   want,
If he be put upon 't ; and that's as easy
As to set dogs on sheep—will be his fire
To kindle their dry stubble ; and their blaze
Shall darken him for ever.

   Enter a Messenger.

  Bru.   What's the matter ?

  Mess. You are sent for to the Capitol. 'Tis
   thought

That Marcius shall be consul :
I have seen the dumb men throng to see him
   and
The blind to hear him speak : matrons flung
   gloves,
Ladies and maids their scarfs and handker-
   chers,   280
Upon him as he pass'd : the nobles bended,
As to Jove's statue, and the commons made
A shower and thunder with their caps and
   shouts :
I never saw the like.

  Bru.   Let's to the Capitol ;
And carry with us ears and eyes for the time,
But hearts for the event.

  Sic.   Have with you. [*Exeunt.*

   Scene II. *The same. The Capitol.*

   Enter two Officers, *to lay cushions.*

  First Off. Come, come, they are almost
here. How many stand for consulships ?

  Sec. Off. Three, they say : but 'tis thought
of every one Coriolanus will carry it.

  First Off. That's a brave fellow ; but he's
vengeance proud, and loves not the common
people.

  Sec. Off. Faith, there had been many great
men that have flattered the people, who ne'er
loved them ; and there be many that they have
loved, they know not wherefore : so that, if
they love they know not why, they hate upon
no better a ground : therefore, for Coriolanus
neither to care whether they love or hate him
manifests the true knowledge he has in their
disposition ; and out of his noble carelessness
lets them plainly see't.

  First Off. If he did not care whether he
had their love or no, he waved indifferently
'twixt doing them neither good nor harm : but
he seeks their hate with greater devotion than
they can render it him ; and leaves nothing
undone that may fully discover him their opposite. Now, to seem to affect the malice and
displeasure of the people is as bad as that
which he dislikes, to flatter them for their
love.

  Sec. Off. He hath deserved worthily of his
country : and his ascent is not by such easy
degrees as those who, having been supple and
courteous to the people, bonneted, without any
further deed to have them at all into their estimation and report : but he hath so planted
his honors in their eyes, and his actions in
their hearts, that for their tongues to be silent,
and not confess so much, were a kind of ingrateful injury ; to report otherwise, were a
malice, that, giving itself the lie, would pluck
reproof and rebuke from every ear that heard
it.

  First Off. No more of him ; he is a worthy
man : make way, they are coming.   40

   A sennet. *Enter, with* Lictors *before them,*
COMINIUS *the consul,* MENENIUS, CORIOLA-
NUS, Senators, SICINIUS *and* BRUTUS. *The*
Senators *take their places ; the* Tribunes
take their places by themselves. CORIO-
LANUS *stands.*

  Men. Having determined of the Volsces
   and
To send for Titus Lartius, it remains,
As the main point of this our after-meeting,
To gratify his noble service that

Hath thus stood for his country : therefore,
please you,
Most reverend and grave elders, to desire
The present consul, and last general
In our well-found successes, to report
A little of that worthy work perform'd
By Caius Marcius Coriolanus, whom   50
We met here both to thank and to remember
With honors like himself.
   First Sen.   Speak, good Cominius :
Leave nothing out for length, and make us
think
Rather our state's defective for requital
Than we to stretch it out. [*To the Tribunes.*]
   Masters o' the people,
We do request your kindest ears, and after,
Your loving motion toward the common body,
To yield what passes here.
   Sic.   We are convented
Upon a pleasing treaty, and have hearts
Inclinable to honor and advance   60
The theme of our assembly.
   Bru.   Which the rather
We shall be blest to do, if he remember
A kinder value of the people than
He hath hereto prized them at.
   Men.   That's off, that's off ;
I would you rather had been silent. Please you
To hear Cominius speak ?
   Bru.   Most willingly ;
But yet my caution was more pertinent
Than the rebuke you give it.
   Men.   He loves your people
But tie him not to be their bedfellow.
Worthy Cominius, speak. [*Coriolanus offers
   to go away.*] Nay, keep your place.   70
   First Sen.   Sit, Coriolanus ; never shame to
   hear
What you have nobly done.
   Cor.   Your honor's pardon :
I had rather have my wounds to heal again
Than hear say how I got them.
   Bru.   Sir, I hope
My words disbench'd you not.
   Cor.   No, sir : yet oft,
When blows have made me stay, I fled from
words.
You soothed not, therefore hurt not : but your
people,
I love them as they weigh.
   Men.   Pray now, sit down.
   Cor. I had rather have one scratch my
head i' the sun
When the alarum were struck than idly sit   80
To hear my nothings monster'd.   [*Exit.*
   Men.   Masters of the people,
Your multiplying spawn how can he flatter—
That's thousand to one good one—when you
now see
He had rather venture all his limbs for honor
Than one on's ears to hear it ? Proceed,
Cominius.
   Com. I shall lack voice : the deeds of
Coriolanus
Should not be utter'd feebly. It is held
That valor is the chiefest virtue, and
Most dignifies the haver : if it be,
The man I speak of cannot in the world   90
Be singly counterpoised. At sixteen years,
When Tarquin made a head for Rome, he
fought
Beyond the mark of others : our then dictator,

Whom with all praise I point at, saw him
fight,
When with his Amazonian chin he drove
The bristled lips before him : he bestrid
An o'er-press'd Roman and i' the consul's
view
Slew three opposers : Tarquin's self he met,
And struck him on his knee : in that day's
feats,
When he might act the woman in the scene,
He proved best man i' the field, and for his
meed   101
Was brow-bound with the oak. His pupil age
Man-enter'd thus, he waxed like a sea,
And in the brunt of seventeen battles since
He lurch'd all swords of the garland. For this
last,
Before and in Corioli, let me say,
I cannot speak him home : he stopp'd the
fliers ;
And by his rare example made the coward
Turn terror into sport : as weeds before
A vessel under sail, so men obey'd   110
And fell below his stem : his sword, death's
stamp,
Where it did mark, it took ; from face to foot
He was a thing of blood, whose every motion
Was timed with dying cries : alone he enter'd
The mortal gate of the city, which he painted
With shunless destiny ; aidless came off,
And with a sudden re-inforcement struck
Corioli like a planet : now all's his :
When, by and by, the din of war gan pierce
His ready sense ; then straight his doubled
spirit   120
Re-quicken'd what in flesh was fatigate,
And to the battle came he ; where he did
Run reeking o'er the lives of men, as if
'Twere a perpetual spoil : and till we call'd
Both field and city ours, he never stood
To ease his breast with panting.
   Men.   Worthy man !
   First Sen. He cannot but with measure fit
   the honors
Which we devise him.
   Com.   Our spoils he kick'd at,
And look'd upon things precious as they were
The common muck of the world : he covets
less   130
Than misery itself would give ; rewards
His deeds with doing them, and is content
To spend the time to end it.
   Men.   He's right noble :
Let him be call'd for.
   First Sen.   Call Coriolanus.
   Off. He doth appear.

          Re-enter CORIOLANUS.

   Men. The senate, Coriolanus, are well
pleased
To make thee consul.
   Cor.   I do owe them still
My life and services.
   Men.   It then remains
That you do speak to the people.
   Cor.   I do beseech you,
Let me o'erleap that custom, for I cannot   140
Put on the gown, stand naked and entreat
them,
For my wounds' sake, to give their suffrage :
please you
That I may pass this doing.
   Sic.   Sir, the people

Must have their voices ; neither will they bate
One jot of ceremony.
  Men.   Put them not to't :
Pray you, go fit you to the custom and
Take to you, as your predecessors have,
Your honor with your form.
  Cor.   It is apart
That I shall blush in acting, and might well
Be taken from the people.
  Bru.   Mark you that ? 150
  Cor. To brag unto them, thus I did, and
    thus ;
Show them the unaching scars which I should
    hide,
As if I had received them for the hire
Of their breath only !
  Men.   Do not stand upon't.
We recommend to you, tribunes of the people,
Our purpose to them : and to our noble con-
    sul
Wish we all joy and honor.
  Senators. To Coriolanus come all joy and
    honor ! [*Flourish of cornets. Exeunt
    all but Sicinius and Brutus.*
  Bru. You see how he intends to use the
    people.
  Sic. May they perceive's intent ! He will
    require them,   160
As if he did contemn what he requested
Should be in them to give.
  Bru.   Come, we'll inform them
Of our proceedings here : on the market-
    place,
I know, they do attend us.   [*Exeunt.*

    Scene III. *The same. The Forum.*
    Enter seven or eight Citizens.

  First Cit. Once, if he do require our
voices, we ought not to deny him.
  Sec. Cit. We may, sir, if we will.
  Third Cit. We have power in ourselves to
do it, but it is a power that we have no power
to do ; for if he show us his wounds and tell
us his deeds, we are to put our tongues into
those wounds and speak for them ; so, if he
tell us his noble deeds, we must also tell him
our noble acceptance of them. Ingratitude is
monstrous, and for the multitude to be ingrateful, were to make a monster of the multitude : of the which we being members,
should bring ourselves to be monstrous members.
  First Cit. And to make us no better
thought of, a little help will serve ; for once
we stood up about the corn, he himself stuck
not to call us the many-headed multitude.
  Third Cit. We have been called so of
many ; not that our heads are some brown,
some black, some auburn, some bald, but that
our wits are so diversely colored : and truly I
think if all our wits were to issue out of one
skull, they would fly east, west, north, south,
and their consent of one direct way should be
at once to all the points o' the compass.
  Sec. Cit. Think you so ? Which way do
you judge my wit would fly ?
  Third Cit. Nay, your wit will not so soon
out as another man's will ; 'tis strongly wedged
up in a block-head, but if it were at liberty,
'twould, sure, southward.
  Sec. Cit. Why that way ?
  Third Cit. To lose itself in a fog, where

being three parts melted away with rotten
dews, the fourth would return for conscience
sake, to help to get thee a wife.
  Sec. Cit. You are never without your
tricks : you may, you may.   39
  Third Cit. Are you all resolved to give
your voices ? But that's no matter, the greater
part carries it. I say, if he would incline to the
people, there was never a worthier man.

    Enter Coriolanus *in a gown of humility,
    with* Menenius.

Here he comes, and in the gown of humility :
mark his behavior. We are not to stay all together, but to come by him where he stands,
by ones, by twos, and by threes. He's to make
his requests by particulars ; wherein every one
of us has a single honor, in giving him our
own voices with our own tongues : therefore
follow me, and I'll direct you how you shall
go by him.
  All. Content, content.   [*Exeunt Citizens.*
  Men. O sir, you are not right : have you
    not known
The worthiest men have done't ?
  Cor.   What must I say ?
' I pray, sir '—Plague upon't ! I cannot bring
My tongue to such a pace :—' Look, sir, my
    wounds !
I got them in my country's service, when
Some certain of your brethren roar'd and ran
From the noise of our own drums.'   60
  Men.   O me, the gods !
You must not speak of that : you must desire
    them
To think upon you.
  Cor.   Think upon me ! hang 'em !
I would they would forget me, like the virtues
Which our divines lose by 'em.
  Men.   You'll mar all :
I'll leave you : pray you, speak to 'em, I pray
    you,
In wholesome manner.   [*Exit.*
  Cor.   Bid them wash their faces
And keep their teeth clean. [*Re-enter two of
    the Citizens.*] So, here comes a brace.
    [*Re-enter a third Citizen.*]
You know the cause, sir, of my standing here.
  Third Cit. We do, sir ; tell us what hath
brought you to't.   70
  Cor. Mine own desert.
  Sec. Cit. Your own desert !
  Cor. Ay, but not mine own desire.
  Third Cit. How not your own desire ?
  Cor. No, sir, 'twas never my desire yet to
trouble the poor with begging.
  Third Cit. You must think, if we give you
any thing, we hope to gain by you.
  Cor. Well then, I pray, your price o' the
consulship ?   80
  First Cit. The price is to ask it kindly.
  Cor. Kindly ! Sir, I pray, let me ha't : I
have wounds to show you, which shall be
yours in private. Your good voice, sir ; what
say you ?
  Sec. Cit. You shall ha' it, worthy sir.
  Cor. A match, sir. There's in all two
worthy voices begged. I have your alms :
adieu.
  Third Cit. But this is something odd.
  Sec. Cit. An 'twere to give again,—but 'tis
no matter.   [*Exeunt the three Citizens.* 90

Re-enter two other Citizens.

Cor. Pray you now, if it may stand with the tune of your voices that I may be consul, I have here the customary gown.

Fourth Cit. You have deserved nobly of your country, and you have not deserved nobly.

Cor. Your enigma ?

Fourth Cit. You have been a scourge to her enemies, you have been a rod to her friends ; you have not indeed loved the common people. 99

Cor. You should account me the more virtuous that I have not been common in my love. I will, sir, flatter my sworn brother, the people, to earn a dearer estimation of them ; 'tis a condition they account gentle : and since the wisdom of their choice is rather to have my hat than my heart, I will practise the insinuating nod and be off to them most counterfeitly ; that is, sir, I will counterfeit the bewitchment of some popular man and give it bountiful to the desirers. Therefore, beseech you, I may be consul.

Fifth Cit. We hope to find you our friend ; and therefore give you our voices heartily.

Fourth Cit. You have received many wounds for your country.

Cor. I will not seal your knowledge with showing them. I will make much of your voices, and so trouble you no further.

Both Cit. The gods give you joy, sir, heartily !   [*Exeunt.*

Cor. Most sweet voices !
Better it is to die, better to starve, 120
Than crave the hire which first we do deserve.
Why in this woolvish toge should I stand here,
To beg of Hob and Dick, that do appear,
Their needless vouches ? Custom calls me to't :
What custom wills, in all things should we do 't,
The dust on antique time would lie unswept,
And mountainous error be too highly heapt
For truth to o'er-peer. Rather than fool it so,
Let the high office and the honor go
To one that would do thus. I am half through ;
The one part suffer'd, the other will I do. 131

Re-enter three Citizens *more.*

Here come moe voices.
Your voices : for your voices I have fought ;
Watch'd for your voices ; for your voices bear
Of wounds two dozen odd ; battles thrice six
I have seen and heard of ; for your voices have
Done many things, some less, some more :
your voices :
Indeed, I would be consul.

Sixth Cit. He has done nobly, and cannot go without any honest man's voice. 140

Seventh Cit. Therefore let him be consul : the gods give him joy, and make him good friend to the people !

All Cit. Amen, amen. God save thee, noble consul !   [*Exeunt.*

Cor. Worthy voices !

Re-enter MENENIUS, *with* BRUTUS *and* SICINIUS.

Men. You have stood your limitation ; and the tribunes
Endue you with the people's voice : remains
That, in the official marks invested, you
Anon do meet the senate.

Cor.   Is this done ?

Sic. The custom of request you have discharged :   150
The people do admit you, and are summon'd
To meet anon, upon your approbation.

Cor. Where ? at the senate-house ?

Sic.   There, Coriolanus.

Cor. May I change these garments ?

Sic.   You may, sir.

Cor. That I'll straight do ; and, knowing myself again,
Repair to the senate-house.

Men. I'll keep you company. Will you along ?

Bru. We stay here for the people.

Sic.   Fare you well.
                [*Exeunt Coriolanus and Menenius.*
He has it now, and by his looks methink
'Tis warm at 's heart.   160

Bru. With a proud heart he wore his humble weeds.
Will you dismiss the people ?

Re-enter Citizens.

Sic. How now, my masters ! have you chose this man ?

First Cit. He has our voices, sir.

Bru. We pray the gods he may deserve your loves.

Sec. Cit. Amen, sir : to my poor unworthy notice,
He mock'd us when he begg'd our voices.

Third Cit.   Certainly
He flouted us downright.

First Cit. No, 'tis his kind of speech : he did not mock us.

Sec. Cit. Not one amongst us, save yourself, but says   170
He used us scornfully : he should have show'd us
His marks of merit, wounds received for's country.

Sic. Why, so he did, I am sure.

Citizens.   No, no ; no man saw 'em.

Third Cit. He said he had wounds, which he could show in private ;
And with his hat, thus waving it in scorn,
' I would be consul,' says he : ' aged custom,
But by your voices, will not so permit me ;
Your voices therefore.' When we granted that,
Here was ' I thank you for your voices : thank you :
Your most sweet voices : now you have left your voices,   180
I have no further with you.' Was not this mockery ?

Sic. Why either were you ignorant to see't,
Or, seeing it, of such childish friendliness
To yield your voices ?

Bru.   Could you not have told him
As you were lesson'd, when he had no power,
But was a petty servant to the state,
He was your enemy, ever spake against
Your liberties and the charters that you bear
I' the body of the weal ; and now, arriving
A place of potency and sway o' the state, 190
If he should still malignantly remain
Fast foe to the plebeii, your voices might
Be curses to yourselves ? You should have said
That as his worthy deeds did claim no less
Than what he stood for, so his gracious nature

Would think upon you for your voices and
Translate his malice towards you into love,
Standing your friendly lord.
 Sic.   Thus to have said,
As you were fore-advised, had touch'd his
  spirit   199
And tried his inclination; from him pluck'd
Either his gracious promise, which you might;
As cause had call'd you up, have held him to;
Or else it would have gall'd his surly nature,
Which easily endures not article
Tying him to aught; so putting him to rage,
You should have ta'en the advantage of his
  choler
And pass'd him unelected.
 Bru.   Did you perceive
He did solicit you in free contempt
When he did need your loves, and do you
  think
That his contempt shall not be bruising to
  you,   210
When he hath power to crush? Why, had
  your bodies
No heart among you? or had you tongues to
  cry
Against the rectorship of judgment?
 Sic.   Have you
Ere now denied the asker? and now again
Of him that did not ask, but mock, bestow
Your sued-for tongues?
  Third Cit. He's not confirm'd; we may
   deny him yet.
  Sec. Cit. And will deny him:
I'll have five hundred voices of that sound.
  First Cit. I twice five hundred and their
   friends to piece 'em.   220
 Bru. Get you hence instantly, and tell those
  friends,
They have chose a consul that will from them
  take
Their liberties; make them of no more voice
Than dogs that are as often beat for barking
As therefore kept to do so.
 Sic.   Let them assemble,
And on a safer judgment all revoke
Your ignorant election; enforce his pride,
And his old hate unto you; besides, forget not
With what contempt he wore the humble weed,
How in his suit he scorn'd you; but your
  loves,   230
Thinking upon his services, took from you
The apprehension of his present portance,
Which most gibingly, ungravely, he did
  fashion
After the inveterate hate he bears you.
 Bru.   Lay
A fault on us, your tribunes; that we labor'd,
No impediment between, but that you must
Cast your election on him.
 Sic.   Say, you chose him
More after our commandment than as guided
By your own true affections, and that your
  minds,
Pre-occupied with what you rather must do
Than what you should, made you against the
  grain   241
To voice him consul: lay the fault on us.
 Bru. Ay, spare us not. Say we read lec-
  tures to you.
How youngly he began to serve his country,
How long continued, and what stock he
  springs of,

The noble house o' the Marcians, from whence
  came
That Ancus Marcius, Numa's daughter's son,
Who, after great Hostilius, here was king;
Of the same house Publius and Quintus were,
That our best water brought by conduits
  hither;   250
And [Censorinus,] nobly named so,
Twice being [by the people chosen] censor,
Was his great ancestor.
 Sic.   One thus descended,
That hath beside well in his person wrought
To be set high in place, we did commend
To your remembrances: but you have found,
Scaling his present bearing with his past,
That he's your fixed enemy, and revoke
Your sudden approbation.
 Bru.   Say, you ne'er had done't—
Harp on that still—but by our putting on; 260
And presently, when you have drawn your
  number,
Repair to the Capitol.
 All.   We will so: almost all
Repent in their election. *[Exeunt Citizens.*
 Bru.   Let them go on;
This mutiny were better put in hazard,
Than stay, past doubt, for greater:
If, as his nature is, he fall in rage
With their refusal, both observe and answer
The vantage of his anger.
 Sic.   To the Capitol, come;
We will be there before the stream o' the
  people;   269
And this shall seem, as partly 'tis, their own,
Which we have goaded onward. *[Exeunt.*

ACT III.

SCENE I. *Rome. A street.*

Cornets. Enter CORIOLANUS, MENENIUS, *all
 the Gentry,* COMINIUS, TITUS LARTIUS, *and
 other* Senators.

 Cor. Tullus Aufidius then had made new
  head?
 Lart. He had, my lord; and that it was
  which caused
Our swifter composition.
 Cor. So then the Volsces stand but as at
  first,
Ready, when time shall prompt them, to make
  road
Upon's again.
 Com.   They are worn, lord consul, so,
That we shall hardly in our ages see
Their banners wave again.
 Cor.   Saw you Aufidius?
 Lart. On safe-guard he came to me; and
  did curse
Against the Volsces, for they had so vilely 10
Yielded the town: he is retired to Antium.
 Cor. Spoke he of me?
 Lart.   He did, my lord.
 Cor.   How? what?
 Lart. How often he had met you, sword to
  sword;
That of all things upon the earth he hated
Your person most, that he would pawn his
  fortunes
To hopeless restitution, so he might
Be call'd your vanquisher.
 Cor.   At Antium lives he?

Lart. At Antium.

Cor. I wish I had a cause to seek him
there, 19
To oppose his hatred fully. Welcome home.

Enter SICINIUS *and* BRUTUS.

Behold, these are the tribunes of the people,
The tongues o' the common mouth : I do de-
spise them ;
For they do prank them in authority,
Against all noble sufferance.

Sic. Pass no further.

Cor. Ha ! what is that ?

Bru. It will be dangerous to go on : no
further.

Cor. What makes this change ?

Men. The matter ?

Com. Hath he not pass'd the noble and the
common ?

Bru. Cominius, no.

Cor. Have I had children's voices ? 30

First Sen. Tribunes, give way ; he shall to
the market-place.

Bru. The people are incensed against him.

Sic. Stop,
Or all will fall in broil.

Cor. Are these your herd ?
Must these have voices, that can yield them
now
And straight disclaim their tongues ? What are
your offices ?
You being their mouths, why rule you not their
teeth ?
Have you not set them on ?

Men. Be calm, be calm.

Cor. It is a purposed thing, and grows by
plot,
To curb the will of the nobility :
Suffer't, and live with such as cannot rule 40
Nor ever will be ruled.

Bru. Call't not a plot :
The people cry you mock'd them, and of late,
When corn was given them gratis, you re-
pined ;
Scandal'd the suppliants for the people, call'd
them
Time-pleasers, flatterers, foes to nobleness.

Cor. Why, this was known before.

Bru. Not to them all.

Cor. Have you inform'd them sithence ?

Bru. How ! I inform them !

Cor. You are like to do such business.

Bru. Not unlike,
Each way, to better yours.

Cor. Why then should I be consul ? By
yond clouds, 50
Let me deserve so ill as you, and make me
Your fellow tribune.

Sic. You show too much of that
For which the people stir : if you will pass
To where you are bound, you must inquire
your way,
Which you are out of, with a gentler spirit,
Or never be so noble as a consul,
Nor yoke with him for tribune.

Men. Let's be calm.

Com. The people are abused ; set on. This
paltering
Becomes not Rome, nor has Coriolanus
Deserved this so dishonor'd rub, laid falsely
I' the plain way of his merit. 61

Cor. Tell me of corn !
This was my speech, and I will speak't again—

Men. Not now, not now.

First Sen. Not in this heat, sir, now.

Cor. Now, as I live, I will. My nobler
friends,
I crave their pardons :
For the mutable, rank-scented many, let them
Regard me as I do not flatter, and
Therein behold themselves : I say again,
In soothing them, we nourish 'gainst our senate
The cockle of rebellion, insolence, sedition, 70
Which we ourselves have plough'd for, sow'd,
and scatter'd,
By mingling them with us, the honor'd num-
ber,
Who lack not virtue, no, nor power, but that
Which they have given to beggars.

Men. Well, no more.

First Sen. No more words, we beseech you.

Cor. How ! no more !
As for my country I have shed my blood,
Not fearing outward force, so shall my lungs
Coin words till their decay against those mea-
sles,
Which we disdain should tetter us, yet sought
The very way to catch them.

Bru. You speak o' the people, 80
As if you were a god to punish, not
A man of their infirmity.

Sic. 'Twere well
We let the people know't.

Men. What, what ? his choler ?

Cor. Choler !
Were I as patient as the midnight sleep,
By Jove, 'twould be my mind !

Sic. It is a mind
That shall remain a poison where it is,
Not poison any further.

Cor. Shall remain !
Hear you this Triton of the minnows ? mark
you
His absolute ' shall ' ?

Com. 'Twas from the canon.

Cor. ' Shall ' ! 90
O good but most unwise patricians ! why,
You grave but reckless senators, have you thus
Given Hydra here to choose an officer,
That with his peremptory ' shall,' being but
The horn and noise o' the monster's, wants
not spirit
To say he'll turn your current in a ditch,
And make your channel his ? If he have power
Then vail your ignorance ; if none, awake
Your dangerous lenity. If you are learn'd,
Be not as common fools ; if you are not, 100
Let them have cushions by you. You are ple-
beians,
If they be senators : and they are no less,
When, both your voices blended, the great'st
taste
Most palates theirs. They choose their mag-
istrate,
And such a one as he, who puts his ' shall,'
His popular ' shall,' against a graver bench
Than ever frown'd in Greece. By Jove him-
self !
It makes the consuls base : and my soul aches
To know, when two authorities are up,
Neither supreme, how soon confusion 110
May enter 'twixt the gap of both and take
The one by the other.

Com. Well, on to the market-place.

Cor. Whoever gave that counsel, to give
forth

The corn o' the storehouse gratis, as 'twas used
Sometime in Greece,—
  Men.   Well, well, no more of that.
  Cor. Though there the people had more
      absolute power,
I say, they nourish'd disobedience, fed
The ruin of the state.
  Bru.   Why, shall the people give
One that speaks thus their voice ?
  Cor.   I'll give my reasons,
More worthier than their voices. They know
      the corn   120
Was not our recompense, resting well assured
That ne'er did service for't : being press'd to
      the war,
Even when the navel of the state was touch'd,
They would not thread the gates. This kind of
      service
Did not deserve corn gratis. Being i' the war
Their mutinies and revolts, wherein they
      show'd
Most valor, spoke not for them : the accusa-
      tion
Which they have often made against the sen-
      ate,
All cause unborn, could never be the motive
Of our so frank donation. Well, what then ?
How shall this bisson multitude digest
The senate's courtesy ? Let deeds express
What's like to be their words : ' We did re-
      quest it ;
We are the greater poll, and in true fear
They gave us our demands.' Thus we debase
The nature of our seats and make the rabble
Call our cares fears ; which will in time
Break ope the locks o' the senate and bring in
The crows to peck the eagles.
  Men.   Come, enough.
  Bru. Enough, with over-measure.
  Cor.   No, take more :   140
What may be sworn by, both divine and hu-
      man,
Seal what I end withal ! This double worship,
Where one part does disdain with cause, the
      other
Insult without all reason, where gentry, title,
      wisdom,
Cannot conclude but by the yea and no
Of general ignorance,—it must omit
Real necessities, and give way the while
To unstable slightness : purpose so barr'd, it
      follows,
Nothing is done to purpose. Therefore, be-
      seech you,—
You that will be less fearful than discreet,   150
That love the fundamental part of state
More than you doubt the change on't, that
      prefer
A noble life before a long, and wish
To jump a body with a dangerous physic
That's sure of death without it, at once pluck
      out
The multitudinous tongue ; let them not lick
The sweet which is their poison : your dis-
      honor
Mangles true judgment and bereaves the state
Of that integrity which should become't,
Not having the power to do the good it would,
For the ill which doth control't.
  Bru.   Has said enough.   161
  Sic. Has spoken like a traitor, and shall
      answer
As traitors do.

  Cor. Thou wretch, despite o'erwhelm thee !
What should the people do with these bald
      tribunes ?
On whom depending, their obedience fails
To the greater bench : in a rebellion,
When what's not meet, but what must be, was
      law,
Then were they chosen : in a better hour,
Let what is meet be said it must be meet,   170
And throw their power i' the dust.
  Bru. Manifest treason !
  Sic.   This a consul ? no.
  Bru. The ædiles, ho !

              Enter an Ædile.

                    Let him be apprehended.
  Sic. Go, call the people : [*Exit Ædile*] in
      whose name myself
Attach thee as a traitorous innovator,
A foe to the public weal : obey, I charge thee,
And follow to thine answer.
  Cor.   Hence, old goat !
  Senators, &c. We'll surety him.
  Com.   Aged sir, hands off.
  Cor. Hence, rotten thing ! or I shall shake
      thy bones
Out of thy garments.
  Sic.   Help, ye citizens !   180

Enter a rabble of Citizens (*Plebeians*), *with
      the* Ædiles.

  Men. On both sides more respect.
  Sic. Here's he that would take from you
      all your power.
  Bru. Seize him, ædiles !
  Citizens. Down with him ! down with him !
  Senators, &c. Weapons, weapons, weap-
      ons !
      [*They all bustle about Coriolanus, crying*
' Tribunes ! ' ' Patricians ! ' ' Citizens ! ' ' What,
      ho ! '
' Sicinius ! ' ' Brutus ! ' ' Coriolanus ! ' ' Citi-
      zens ! '
' Peace, peace, peace ! ' ' Stay, hold, peace ! '
  Men. What is about to be ? I am out of
      breath ;
Confusion's near ; I cannot speak. You, trib-
      unes   190
To the people ! Coriolanus, patience !
Speak, good Sicinius.
  Sic.   Hear me, people ; peace !
  Citizens. Let's hear our tribune : peace !
      Speak, speak, speak.
  Sic. You are at point to lose your liber-
      ties :
Marcius would have all from you ; Marcius,
Whom late you have named for consul.
  Men.   Fie, fie, fie !
This is the way to kindle, not to quench.
  First Sen. To unbuild the city and to lay
      all flat.
  Sic. What is the city but the people ?
  Citizens.   True,
The people are the city.   200
  Bru. By the consent of all, we were estab-
      lish'd
The people's magistrates.
  Citizens.   You so remain.
  Men. And so are like to do.
  Com. That is the way to lay the city flat ;
To bring the roof to the foundation,
And bury all, which yet distinctly ranges,
In heaps and piles of ruin.

Sic.   This deserves death.
Bru. Or let us stand to our authority,
Or let us lose it. We do here pronounce,   209
Upon the part o' the people, in whose power
We were elected theirs, Marcius is worthy
Of present death.
Sic.   Therefore lay hold of him ;
Bear him to the rock Tarpeian, and from
    thence
Into destruction cast him.
Bru.   Ædiles, seize him !
Citizens. Yield, Marcius, yield !
Men.   Hear me one word ;
Beseech you, tribunes, hear me but a word.
Æd. Peace, peace !
Men. [*To Brutus*] Be that you seem, truly
    your country's friend,
And temperately proceed to what you would
Thus violently redress.
Bru.   Sir, those cold ways, 220
That seem like prudent helps, are very poison-
    ous
Where the disease is violent. Lay hands upon
    him,
And bear him to the rock.
Cor.   No, I'll die here.
                    [*Drawing his sword.*
There's some among you have beheld me fight-
    ing :
Come, try upon yourselves what you have seen
    me.
Men. Down with that sword ! Tribunes,
    withdraw awhile.
Bru. Lay hands upon him.
Com.   Help Marcius, help,
You that be noble ; help him, young and old !
Citizens. Down with him, down with him !
    [*In this mutiny, the Tribunes, the Ædiles,
        and the People, are beat in.*
Men. Go, get you to your house ; be gone,
    away !   230
All will be naught else.
Sec. Sen.   Get you gone.
Com.   Stand fast ;
We have as many friends as enemies.
Men. Shall it be put to that ?
First Sen.   The gods forbid !
I prithee, noble friend, home to thy house ;
Leave us to cure this cause.
Men.   For 'tis a sore upon us,
You cannot tent yourself : be gone, beseech
    you.
Com. Come, sir, along with us.
Cor. I would they were barbarians—as
    they are,
Though in Rome litter'd—not Romans—as
    they are not,
Though calved i' the porch o' the Capitol—
Men.   Be gone ; 240
Put not your worthy rage into your tongue ;
One time will owe another.
Cor.   On fair ground
I could beat forty of them.
Com.   I could myself
Take up a brace o' the best of them ; yea, the
    two tribunes :
But now 'tis odds beyond arithmetic ;
And manhood is call'd foolery, when it stands
Against a falling fabric. Will you hence,
Before the tag return ? whose rage doth rend
Like interrupted waters and o'erbear
What they are used to bear.
Men.   Pray you, be gone : 250

I'll try whether my old wit be in request
With those that have but little : this must be
    patch'd
With cloth of any color.
Com.   Nay, come away.
    [*Exeunt Coriolanus, Cominius, and others.*
A Patrician. This man has marr'd his for-
    tune.
Men. His nature is too noble for the
    world :
He would not flatter Neptune for his trident,
Or Jove for's power to thunder. His heart's
    his mouth :
What his breast forges, that his tongue must
    vent ;
And, being angry, does forget that ever   259
He heard the name of death. [*A noise within.*
Here's goodly work !
Sec. Pat.   I would they were a-bed !
Men. I would they were in Tiber ! What
    the vengeance !
Could he not speak 'em fair ?

    Re-enter BRUTUS *and* SICINIUS, *with the
        rabble.*

Sic.   Where is this viper
That would depopulate the city and
Be every man himself ?
Men.   You worthy tribunes,—
Sic. He shall be thrown down the Tarpeian
    rock
With rigorous hands : he hath resisted law,
And therefore law shall scorn him further trial
Than the severity of the public power
Which he so sets at nought.
First Cit.   He shall well know 270
The noble tribunes are the people's mouths,
And we their hands.
Citizens. He shall, sure on't.
Men.   Sir, sir,—
Sic. Peace !
Men. Do not cry havoc, where you should
    but hunt
With modest warrant.
Sic.   Sir, how comes't that you
Have holp to make this rescue ?
Men.   Hear me speak :
As I do know the consul's worthiness,
So can I name his faults,—
Sic.   Consul ! what consul ?
Men. The consul Coriolanus.
Bru.   He consul ! 280
Citizens. No, no, no, no, no.
Men. If, by the tribunes' leave, and yours,
    good people,
I may be heard, I would crave a word or two ;
The which shall turn you to no further harm
Than so much loss of time.
Sic.   Speak briefly then ;
For we are peremptory to dispatch
This viperous traitor : to eject him hence
Were but one danger, and to keep him here
Our certain death : therefore it is decreed
He dies to-night.
Men.   Now the good gods forbid 290
That our renowned Rome, whose gratitude
Towards her deserved children is enroll'd
In Jove's own book, like an unnatural dam
Should now eat up her own !
Sic. He's a disease that must be cut away.
Men. O, he's a limb that has but a dis-
    ease ;
Mortal, to cut it off ; to cure it, easy.

What has he done to Rome that's worthy
death ?
Killing our enemies, the blood he hath lost—
Which, I dare vouch, is more than that he
hath,   300
By many an ounce—he dropp'd it for his
country ;
And what is left, to lose it by his country,
Were to us all, that do't and suffer it,
A brand to the end o' the world.
  Sic.   This is clean kam.
  Bru. Merely awry : when he did love his
country,
It honor'd him.
  Men.   The service of the foot
Being once gangrened, is not then respected
For what before it was.
  Bru.   We'll hear no more.
Pursue him to his house, and pluck him
thence ;
Lest his infection, being of catching nature,
Spread further.   311
  Men.   One word more, one word.
This tiger-footed rage, when it shall find
The harm of unscann'd swiftness, will too late
Tie leaden pounds to's heels. Proceed by
process ;
Lest parties, as he is beloved, break out,
And sack great Rome with Romans.
  Bru.   If it were so,—
  Sic. What do ye talk ?
Have we not had a taste of his obedience ?
Our ædiles smote ? ourselves resisted ? Come.
  Men. Consider this : he has been bred i'
the wars   320
Since he could draw a sword, and is ill
school'd
In bolted language ; meal and bran together
He throws without distinction. Give me leave,
I'll go to him, and undertake to bring him
Where he shall answer, by a lawful form,
In peace, to his utmost peril.
  First Sen.   Noble tribunes,
It is the humane way : the other course
Will prove too bloody, and the end of it
Unknown to the beginning.
  Sic.   Noble Menenius,
Be you then as the people's officer.   330
Masters, lay down your weapons.
  Bru.   Go not home.
  Sic. Meet on the market-place. We'll at-
tend you there :
Where, if you bring not Marcius, we'll proceed
In our first way.
  Men.   I'll bring him to you.
[*To the Senators*] Let me desire your com-
pany : he must come,
Or what is worst will follow.
  First Sen.   Pray you, let's to him.
                                        [*Exeunt.*

SCENE II. *A room in Coriolanus's house.*

Enter CORIOLANUS *with* Patricians.

  Cor. Let them pull all about mine ears,
present me
Death on the wheel or at wild horses' heels,
Or pile ten hills on the Tarpeian rock,
That the precipitation might down stretch
Below the beam of sight, yet will I still
Be thus to them.
  A Patrician. You do the nobler.
  Cor. I muse my mother
Does not approve me further, who was wont

To call them woollen vassals, things created
To buy and sell with groats, to show bare
heads   10
In congregations, to yawn, be still and wonder,
When one but of my ordinance stood up
To speak of peace or war.

Enter VOLUMNIA.

                   I talk of you :
Why did you wish me milder ? would you have
me
False to my nature ? Rather say I play
The man I am.
  Vol.   O, sir, sir, sir,
I would have had you put your power well on,
Before you had worn it out.
  Cor.   Let go.
  Vol. You might have been enough the man
you are,
With striving less to be so ; lesser had been
The thwartings of your dispositions, if   21
You had not show'd them how ye were dis-
posed
Ere they lack'd power to cross you.
  Cor.   Let them hang.
  A Patrician. Ay, and burn too.

Enter MENENIUS *and* Senators.

  Men. Come, come, you have been too
rough, something too rough ;
You must return and mend it.
  First Sen.   There's no remedy ;
Unless, by not so doing, our good city
Cleave in the midst, and perish.
  Vol.   Pray, be counsell'd :
I have a heart as little apt as yours,
But yet a brain that leads my use of anger 30
To better vantage.
  Men.   Well said, noble woman ?
Before he should thus stoop to the herd, but
that
The violent fit o' the time craves it as physic
For the whole state, I would put mine armor
on,
Which I can scarcely bear.
  Cor.   What must I do ?
  Men. Return to the tribunes.
  Cor.   Well, what then ? what then ?
  Men. Repent what you have spoke.
  Cor. For them ! I cannot do it to the gods ;
Must I then do't to them ?
  Vol.   You are too absolute ;
Though therein you can never be too noble,
But when extremities speak. I have heard you
say,
Honor and policy, like unsever'd friends,
I' the war do grow together : grant that, and
tell me,
In peace what each of them by the other lose,
That they combine not there.
  Cor.   Tush, tush !
  Men.   A good demand.
  Vol. If it be honor in your wars to seem
The same you are not, which, for your best
ends,
You adopt your policy, how is it less or worse,
That it shall hold companionship in peace
With honor, as in war, since that to both 50
It stands in like request ?
  Cor.   Why force you this ?
  Vol. Because that now it lies you on to
speak
To the people ; not by your own instruction,

Nor by the matter which your heart prompts you,
But with such words that are but rooted in
Your tongue, though but bastards and syllables
Of no allowance to your bosom's truth.
Now, this no more dishonors you at all
Than to take in a town with gentle words,
Which else would put you to your fortune and
The hazard of much blood.   61
I would dissemble with my nature where
My fortunes and my friends at stake required
I should do so in honor : I am in this,
Your wife, your son, these senators, the nobles ;
And you will rather show our general louts
How you can frown than spend a fawn upon 'em,
For the inheritance of their loves and safe-guard
Of what that want might ruin.
  Men.   Noble lady !
Come, go with us ; speak fair : you may salve so,
Not what is dangerous present, but the loss 71
Of what is past.
  Vol.   I prithee now, my son,
Go to them, with this bonnet in thy hand ;
And thus far having stretch'd it—here be with them—
Thy knee bussing the stones—for in such business
Action is eloquence, and the eyes of the ignorant
More learned than the ears—waving thy head,
Which often, thus, correcting thy stout heart,
Now humble as the ripest mulberry
That will not hold the handling : or say to them,   80
Thou art their soldier, and being bred in broils
Hast not the soft way which, thou dost confess,
Were fit for thee to use as they to claim,
In asking their good loves, but thou wilt frame
Thyself, forsooth, hereafter theirs, so far
As thou hast power and person.
  Men.   This but done,
Even as she speaks, why, their hearts were yours ;
For they have pardons, being ask'd, as free
As words to little purpose.
  Vol.   Prithee now,
Go, and be ruled : although I know thou hadst rather   90
Follow thine enemy in a fiery gulf
Than flatter him in a bower. Here is Cominius.

Enter COMINIUS.

  Com. I have been i' the market-place ; and, sir, 'tis fit
You make strong party, or defend yourself
By calmness or by absence : all's in anger.
  Men. Only fair speech.
  Com.   I think 'twill serve, if he
Can thereto frame his spirit.
  Vol.   He must, and will
Prithee now, say you will, and go about it.
  Cor. Must I go show them my unbarbed sconce ?   99
Must I with base tongue give my noble heart
A lie that it must bear ? Well, I will do't :

Yet, were there but this single plot to lose,
This mould of Marcius, they to dust should grind it
And throw't against the wind. To the market-place !
You have put me now to such a part which never
I shall discharge to the life.
  Com.   Come, come, we'll prompt you.
  Vol. I prithee now, sweet son, as thou hast said
My praises made thee first a soldier, so,
To have my praise for this, perform a part
Thou hast not done before.
  Cor.   Well, I must do't :
Away, my disposition, and possess me   111
Some harlot's spirit ! my throat of war be turn'd,
Which quired with my drum, into a pipe
Small as an eunuch, or the virgin voice
That babies lulls asleep ! the smiles of knaves
Tent in my cheeks, and schoolboys' tears take up
The glasses of my sight ! a beggar's tongue
Make motion through my lips, and my arm'd knees,
Who bow'd but in my stirrup, bend like his
That hath received an alms ! I will not do't,
Lest I surcease to honor mine own truth 121
And by my body's action teach my mind
A most inherent baseness.
  Vol.   At thy choice, then :
To beg of thee, it is my more dishonor
Than thou of them. Come all to ruin ; let
Thy mother rather feel thy pride than fear
Thy dangerous stoutness, for I mock at death
With as big heart as thou. Do as thou list.
Thy valiantness was mine, thou suck'dst it from me,
But owe thy pride thyself.
  Cor.   Pray, be content : 130
Mother, I am going to the market-place ;
Chide me no more. I'll mountebank their loves,
Cog their hearts from them, and come home beloved
Of all the trades in Rome. Look, I am going :
Commend me to my wife. I'll return consul ;
Or never trust to what my tongue can do
I' the way of flattery further.
  Vol.   Do your will. [*Exit.*
  Com. Away ! the tribunes do attend you : arm yourself
To answer mildly ; for they are prepared
With accusations, as I hear, more strong 140
Than are upon you yet.
  Cor.   The word is ' mildly.' Pray you, let us go :
Let them accuse me by invention, I
Will answer in mine honor.
  Men.   Ay, but mildly.
  Cor. Well, mildly be it then. Mildly !
                              [*Exeunt.*

SCENE III. *The same. The Forum.*
Enter SICINIUS and BRUTUS.

  Bru. In this point charge him home, that he affects
Tyrannical power : if he evade us there,
Enforce him with his envy to the people,
And that the spoil got on the Antiates
Was ne'er distributed.

Enter an Ædile.

What, will he come ?
Æd.   He's coming.
Bru.   How accompanied ?
Æd. With old Menenius, and those sena-
    tors
That always favor'd him.
Sic.   Have you a catalogue
Of all the voices that we have procured
Set down by the poll ?
Æd.   I have ; 'tis ready. 10
Sic. Have you collected them by tribes ?
Æd.   I have.
Sic. Assemble presently the people hither ;
And when they hear me say ' It shall be so
I' the right and strength o' the commons,' be
    it either
For death, for fine, or banishment, then let
    them
If I say fine, cry ' Fine ; ' if death, cry ' Death.'
Insisting on the old prerogative
And power i' the truth o' the cause.
Æd.   I shall inform them.
Bru. And when such time they have begun
    to cry,
Let them not cease, but with a din confused 20
Enforce the present execution
Of what we chance to sentence.
Æd.   Very well.
Sic. Make them be strong and ready for
    this hint,
When we shall hap to give 't them.
Bru.   Go about it. [*Exit Ædile.*
Put him to choler straight : he hath been used
Ever to conquer, and to have his worth
Of contradiction : being once chafed, he can-
    not
Be rein'd again to temperance ; then he speaks
What's in his heart ; and that is there which
    looks
With us to break his neck.
Sic.   Well, here he comes. 30

Enter Coriolanus, Menenius, *and* Cominius, *with* Senators *and* Patricians.

Men. Calmly, I do beseech you.
Cor. Ay, as an ostler, that for the poorest
    piece
Will bear the knave by the volume. The
    honor'd gods
Keep Rome in safety, and the chairs of justice
Supplied with worthy men ! plant love
    among 's !
Throng our large temples with the shows of
    peace,
And not our streets with war !
First Sen.   Amen, amen.
Men. A noble wish.

Re-enter Ædile, *with* Citizens.

Sic. Draw near, ye people.
Æd. List to your tribunes. Audience :
    peace, I say !   40
Cor. First, hear me speak.
Both Tri.   Well, say. Peace, ho !
Cor. Shall I be charged no further than
    this present ?
Must all determine here ?
Sic.   I do demand,
If you submit you to the people's voices,
Allow their officers and are content
To suffer lawful censure for such faults

As shall be proved upon you ?
Cor.   I am content.
Men. Lo, citizens, he says he is content :
The warlike service he has done, consider ;
    think
Upon the wounds his body bears, which show
Like graves i' the holy churchyard.   51
Cor.   Scratches with briers,
Scars to move laughter only.
Men.   Consider further,
That when he speaks not like a citizen,
You find him like a soldier : do not take
His rougher accents for malicious sounds,
But, as I say, such as become a soldier,
Rather than envy you.
Com.   Well, well, no more.
Cor. What is the matter
That being pass'd for consul with full voice,
I am so dishonor'd that the very hour   60
You take it off again ?
Sic.   Answer to us.
Cor. Say, then : 'tis true, I ought so.
Sic. We charge you, that you have con-
    trived to take
From Rome all season'd office and to wind
Yourself into a power tyrannical ;
For which you are a traitor to the people.
Cor. How ! traitor !
Men.   Nay, temperately ; your promise.
Cor. The fires i' the lowest hell fold-in the
    people !
Call me their traitor ! Thou injurious tribune !
Within thine eyes sat twenty thousand deaths,
In thy hand clutch'd as many millions, in 71
Thy lying tongue both numbers, I would say
' Thou liest ' unto thee with a voice as free
As I do pray the gods.
Sic.   Mark you this, people ?
Citizens. To the rock, to the rock with
    him !
Sic.   Peace !
We need not put new matter to his charge :
What you have seen him do and heard him
    speak,
Beating your officers, cursing yourselves,
Opposing laws with strokes and here defying
Those whose great power must try him ; even
    this,   80
So criminal and in such capital kind,
Deserves the extremest death.
Bru.   But since he hath
Served well for Rome,—
Cor.   What do you prate of service ?
Bru. I talk of that, that know it.
Cor.   You ?
Men. Is this the promise that you made
    your mother ?
Com. Know, I pray you,—
Cor.   I know no further :
Let them pronounce the steep Tarpeian death,
Vagabond exile, flaying, pent to linger
But with a grain a day, I would not buy   90
Their mercy at the price of one fair word ;
Nor check my courage for what they can give,
To have't with saying ' Good morrow.'
Sic.   For that he has,
As much as in him lies, from time to time
Envied against the people, seeking means
To pluck away their power, as now at last
Given hostile strokes, and that not in the
    presence
Of dreaded justice, but on the ministers

That do distribute it; in the name o' the
people
And in the power of us the tribunes, we, 100
Even from this instant, banish him our city,
In peril of precipitation
From off the rock Tarpeian never more
To enter our Rome gates: i' the people's
name,
I say it shall be so.

Citizens. It shall be so, it shall be so; let
him away:
He's banish'd, and it shall be so.

Com. Hear me, my masters, and my common friends,—

Sic. He's sentenced; no more hearing.

Com.　　　　　　　　　Let me speak:
I have been consul, and can show for Rome
Her enemies' marks upon me. I do love 111
My country's good with a respect more ten-
der,
More holy and profound, than mine own life,
My dear wife's estimate, her womb's increase,
And treasure of my loins; then if I would
Speak that,—

Sic. We know your drift: speak what?

Bru. There's no more to be said, but he is
banish'd,
As enemy to the people and his country:
It shall be so.

Citizens. It shall be so, it shall be so.

Cor. You common cry of curs! whose
breath I hate　　　　　　　　　　120
As reek o' the rotten fens, whose loves I prize
As the dead carcasses of unburied men
That do corrupt my air, I banish you;
And here remain with your uncertainty!
Let every feeble rumor shake your hearts!
Your enemies, with nodding of their plumes,
Fan you into despair! Have the power still
To banish your defenders; till at length
Your ignorance, which finds not till it feels,
Making not reservation of yourselves,　130
Still your own foes, deliver you as most
Abated captives to some nation
That won you without blows! Despising,
For you, the city, thus I turn my back:
There is a world elsewhere.

　　　[*Exeunt Coriolanus, Cominius, Mene-
　　　　nius, Senators, and Patricians.*

Æd. The people's enemy is gone, is gone!

Citizens. Our enemy is banish'd! he is
gone! Hoo! hoo!

　　　[*Shouting, and throwing up their caps.*

Sic. Go, see him out at gates, and follow
him,
As he hath followed you, with all despite;
Give him deserved vexation. Let a guard　140
Attend us through the city.

Citizens. Come, come; let's see him out at
gates; come.
The gods preserve our noble tribunes! Come.
　　　　　　　　　　　　　　　[*Exeunt.*

———————

ACT IV.

SCENE I. *Rome. Before a gate of the city.*

Enter CORIOLANUS, VOLUMNIA, VIRGILIA, ME-
NENIUS, COMINIUS, *with the young Nobility
of Rome.*

Cor. Come, leave your tears: a brief farewell: the beast

With many heads butts me away. Nay, mother,
Where is your ancient courage? you were
used
To say extremity was the trier of spirits;
That common chances common men could
bear;
That when the sea was calm all boats alike
Show'd mastership in floating; fortune's blows,
When most struck home, being gentle
wounded, craves
A noble cunning: you were used to load me
With precepts that would make invincible 10
The heart that conn'd them.

Vir. O heavens! O heavens!

Cor.　　　　　　Nay, I prithee, woman,—

Vol. Now the red pestilence strike all
trades in Rome,
And occupations perish!

Cor.　　　　　　What, what, what!
I shall be loved when I am lack'd. Nay,
mother,
Resume that spirit, when you were wont to
say,
If you had been the wife of Hercules,
Six of his labors you'ld have done, and saved
Your husband so much sweat. Cominius,
Droop not; adieu. Farewell, my wife, my
mother:　　　　　　　　　　　　20
I'll do well yet. Thou old and true Menenius,
Thy tears are salter than a younger man's,
And venomous to thine eyes. My sometime
general,
I have seen thee stern, and thou hast oft be-
held
Heart-hardening spectacles; tell these sad
women
'Tis fond to wail inevitable strokes,
As 'tis to laugh at 'em. My mother, you wot
well
My hazards still have been your solace: and
Believe't not lightly—though I go alone,
Like to a lonely dragon, that his fen　30
Makes fear'd and talk'd of more than seen—
your son
Will or exceed the common or be caught
With cautelous baits and practice.

Vol.　　　　　　My first son.
Whither wilt thou go? Take good Cominius
With thee awhile: determine on some course,
More than a wild exposture to each chance
That starts i' the way before thee.

Cor.　　　　　　O the gods!

Com. I'll follow thee a month, devise with
thee
Where thou shalt rest, that thou mayst hear
of us
And we of thee: so if the time thrust forth 40
A cause for thy repeal, we shall not send
O'er the vast world to seek a single man,
And lose advantage, which doth ever cool
I' the absence of the needer.

Cor.　　　　　　Fare ye well:
Thou hast years upon thee; and thou art too
full
Of the wars' surfeits, to go rove with one
That's yet unbruised: bring me but out at
gate.
Come, my sweet wife, my dearest mother, and
My friends of noble touch, when I am forth,
Bid me farewell, and smile. I pray you, come.
While I remain above the ground, you shall
Hear from me still, and never of me aught
But what is like me formerly.

Men.　　　　　　　　　　That's worthily
As any ear can hear. Come, let's not weep.
If I could shake off but one seven years
From these old arms and legs, by the good
　　　gods,
I'ld with thee every foot.
Cor.　　　　　　　Give me thy hand :
Come.　　　　　　　　　　　　[*Exeunt.*

SCENE II. *The same. A street near the gate.*

Enter SICINIUS, BRUTUS, *and an* Ædile.

Sic. Bid them all home ; he's gone, and
　　we'll no further.
The nobility are vex'd, whom we see have
　　sided
In his behalf.
Bru.　　　　Now we have shown our power,
Let us seem humbler after it is done
Than when it was a-doing.
Sic.　　　　　　　Bid them home :
Say their great enemy is gone, and they
Stand in their ancient strength.
Bru.　　　　Dismiss them home. [*Exit Ædile.*
Here comes his mother.
Sic.　　　　　　Let's not meet her.
Bru.　　　　　　　　　　　　Why ?
Sic. They say she's mad.
Bru. They have ta'en note of us : keep on
　　your way.　　　　　　　　　　　　10

Enter VOLUMNIA, VIRGILIA, *and* MENENIUS.

Vol. O, ye're well met : the hoarded plague
　　o' the gods
Requite your love !
Men.　　Peace, peace ; be not so loud.
Vol. If that I could for weeping, you
　　should hear,—
Nay, and you shall hear some. [*To Brutus*]
　　Will you be gone ?
Vir. [*To Sicinius*] You shall stay too : I
　　would I had the power
To say so to my husband.
Sic.　　　　　　Are you mankind ?
Vol. Ay, fool ; is that a shame ? Note but
　　this fool.
Was not a man my father ? Hadst thou fox-
　　ship
To banish him that struck more blows for
　　Rome
Than thou hast spoken words ?
Sic.　　　　　　O blessed heavens !
Vol. More noble blows than ever thou
　　wise words ;　　　　　　　　　　　21
And for Rome's good. I'll tell thee what ; yet
　　go :
Nay, but thou shalt stay too : I would my son
Were in Arabia, and thy tribe before him,
His good sword in his hand.
Sic.　　　　　　What then ?
Vir.　　　　　　　　What then !
He'ld make an end of thy posterity.
Vol. Bastards and all.
Good man, the wounds that he does bear for
　　Rome !
Men. Come, come, peace.
Sic. I would he had continued to his coun-
　　try　　　　　　　　　　　　　　30
As he began, and not unknit himself
The noble knot he made.
Bru.　　　　　　I would he had.
Vol. 'I would he had' ! 'Twas you in-
　　censed the rabble :
Cats, that can judge as fitly of his worth

As I can of those mysteries which heaven
Will not have earth to know.
Bru.　　　　　　Pray, let us go.
Vol. Now, pray, sir, get you gone :
You have done a brave deed. Ere you go, hear
　　this :—　　　　　　　　　　　　39
As far as doth the Capitol exceed
The meanest house in Rome, so far my son—
This lady's husband here, this, do you see—
Whom you have banish'd, does exceed you all.
Bru. Well, well, we'll leave you.
Sic.　　　　Why stay we to be baited
With one that wants her wits ?
Vol.　　　　　Take my prayers with you.
　　　　　　　　　　　　[*Exeunt Tribunes.*
I would the gods had nothing else to do
But to confirm my curses ! Could I meet 'em
But once a-day, it would unclog my heart
Of what lies heavy to 't.
Men.　　　　You have told them home ;
And, by my troth, you have cause. You'll sup
　　with me ?
Vol. Anger's my meat ; I sup upon my-
　　self,　　　　　　　　　　　　　50
And so shall starve with feeding. Come, let's
　　go :
Leave this faint puling and lament as I do,
In anger, Juno-like. Come, come, come.
Men. Fie, fie, fie !　　　　　　[*Exeunt.*

SCENE III. *A highway between Rome and
　　　　　　　　Antium.*

Enter a Roman *and a* Volsce, *meeting.*

Rom. I know you well, sir, and you know
me : your name, I think, is Adrian.
Vols. It is so, sir : truly, I have forgot you.
Rom. I am a Roman ; and my services are,
as you are, against 'em : know you me yet ?
Vols. Nicanor ? no.
Rom. The same, sir.
Vols. You had more beard when I last saw
you ; but your favor is well approved by your
tongue. What's the news in Rome ? I have a
note from the Volscian state, to find you out
there : you have well saved me a day's journey.
Rom. There hath been in Rome strange in-
surrections ; the people against the senators,
patricians, and nobles !
Vols. Hath been ! is it ended, then ? Our
state thinks not so : they are in a most warlike preparation, and hope to come upon them
in the heat of their division.　　　　　19
Rom. The main blaze of it is past, but a
small thing would make it flame again : for
the nobles receive so to heart the banishment
of that worthy Coriolanus, that they are in a
ripe aptness to take all power from the people
and to pluck from them their tribunes for
ever. This lies glowing, I can tell you, and is
almost mature for the violent breaking out.
Vols. Coriolanus banished !
Rom. Banished, sir.　　　　　　　29
Vols. You will be welcome with this intelligence, Nicanor.
Rom. The day serves well for them now.
I have heard it said, the fittest time to corrupt
a man's wife is when she's fallen out with her
husband. Your noble Tullus Aufidius will appear well in these wars, his great opposer,
Coriolanus, being now in no request of his
country.
Vols. He cannot choose. I am most fortu-

nate, thus accidentally to encounter you : you
have ended my business, and I will merrily
accompany you home.

Rom. I shall, between this and supper, tell
you most strange things from Rome ; all tending to the good of their adversaries. Have you
an army ready, say you ?

Vols. A most royal one ; the centurions
and their charges, distinctly billeted, already
in the entertainment, and to be on foot at an
hour's warning. 50

Rom. I am joyful to hear of their readiness, and am the man, I think, that shall set
them in present action. So, sir, heartily well
met, and most glad of your company.

Vols. You take my part from me, sir ; I
have the most cause to be glad of yours.

Rom. Well, let us go together. [*Exeunt.*

SCENE IV. *Antium. Before Aufidius's house.*

Enter CORIOLANUS *in mean apparel, disguised
and muffled.*

Cor. A goodly city is this Antium. City,
'Tis I that made thy widows : many an heir
Of these fair edifices 'fore my wars
Have I heard groan and drop : then know me
　　not,
Lest that thy wives with spits and boys with
　　stones
In puny battle slay me.

Enter a Citizen.
　　　　　　　　Save you, sir.

Cit. And you.
Cor. 　　　　　Direct me, if it be your will,
Where great Aufidius lies : is he in Antium ?
Cit. He is, and feasts the nobles of the
　　state
At his house this night.
Cor. 　　Which is his house, beseech you ? 10
Cit. This, here before you.
Cor. 　　　　　　Thank you, sir : farewell.
　　　　　　　　　　　　　[*Exit Citizen.*
O world, thy slippery turns ! Friends now
　　fast sworn,
Whose double bosoms seem to wear one heart,
Whose house, whose bed, whose meal, and ex-
　　ercise,
Are still together, who twin, as 'twere, in love
Unseparable, shall within this hour,
On a dissension of a doit, break out
To bitterest enmity : so, fellest foes,
Whose passions and whose plots have broke
　　their sleep,
To take the one the other, by some chance, 20
Some trick not worth an egg, shall grow dear
　　friends
And interjoin their issues. So with me :
My birth-place hate I, and my love's upon
This enemy town. I'll enter : if he slay me,
He does fair justice ; if he give me way,
I'll do his country service. 　　　[*Exit.*

SCENE V. *The same. A hall in Aufidius's
house.*

Music within. Enter a Servingman.

First Serv. Wine, wine, wine ! What service is here ! I think our fellows are asleep.
　　　　　　　　　　　　　　　　[*Exit.*

Enter a second Servingman.

Sec. Serv. Where's Cotus ? my master calls
for him. Cotus ! 　　　　　　　[*Exit.*

Enter CORIOLANUS.

Cor. A goodly house : the feast smells
　　well ; but I
Appear not like a guest.

Re-enter the first Servingman.

First Serv. What would you have, friend ?
whence are you ? Here's no place for you :
pray, go to the door. 　　　　　　[*Exit.*
Cor. I have deserved no better entertainment,
In being Coriolanus. 　　　　　　　11

Re-enter second Servingman.

Sec. Serv. Whence are you, sir ? Has the
porter his eyes in his head, that he gives en-
trance to such companions ? Pray, get you out.
Cor. Away !
Sec. Serv. Away ! get you away.
Cor. Now thou'rt troublesome.
Sec. Serv. Are you so brave ? I'll have you
talked with anon.

Enter a third Servingman. *The first meets
him.*

Third Serv. What fellow's this ? 　　20
First Serv. A strange one as ever I looked
on : I cannot get him out of the house :
prithee, call my master to him. 　　[*Retires.*
Third Serv. What have you to do here,
fellow ? Pray you, avoid the house.
Cor. Let me but stand ; I will not hurt
your hearth.
Third Serv. What are you ?
Cor. A gentleman.
Third Serv. A marvellous poor one. 　30
Cor. True, so I am.
Third Serv. Pray you, poor gentleman,
take up some other station ; here's no place
for you ; pray you, avoid : come.
Cor. Follow your function, go, and batten
on cold bits. 　　　　　　[*Pushes him away.*
Third Serv. What, you will not ? Prithee,
tell my master what a strange guest he has
here.
Sec. Serv. And I shall. 　　　　[*Exit.*
Third Serv. Where dwellest thou ? 　　40
Cor. Under the canopy.
Third Serv. Under the canopy !
Cor. Ay.
Third Serv. Where's that ?
Cor. I' the city of kites and crows.
Third Serv. I' the city of kites and crows !
What an ass it is ! Then thou dwellest with
daws too ?
Cor. No, I serve not thy master.
Third Serv. How, sir ! do you meddle with
my master ? 　　　　　　　　　　51
Cor. Ay ; 'tis an honester service than to
meddle with thy mistress.
Thou pratest, and pratest ; serve with thy
　　trencher, hence !
　　[*Beats him away. Exit third Servingman.*

Enter AUFIDIUS *with the second* Servingman.

Auf. Where is this fellow ?
Sec. Serv. Here, sir : I'ld have beaten him
like a dog, but for disturbing the lords within.
　　　　　　　　　　　　　　　　[*Retires.*
Auf. Whence comest thou ? what wouldst
　　thou ? thy name ?

Why speak'st not ? speak, man : what's thy
    name ?
  Cor. If, Tullus,   [*Unmuffling.* 60
Not yet thou knowest me, and, seeing me,
    dost not
Think me for the man I am, necessity
Commands me name myself.
  Auf.   What is thy name ?
  Cor. A name unmusical to the Volscians'
    ears,
And harsh in sound to thine.
  Auf.   Say, what's thy name ?
Thou hast a grim appearance, and thy face
Bears a command in't ; though thy tackle's
    torn.
Thou show'st a noble vessel : what's thy
    name ?
  Cor. Prepare thy brow to frown : know'st
    thou me yet ?
  Auf. I know thee not : thy name ?   70
  Cor. My name is Caius Marcius, who hath
    done
To thee particularly and to all the Volsces
Great hurt and mischief ; thereto witness may
My surname, Coriolanus : the painful service,
The extreme dangers and the drops of blood
Shed for my thankless country are requited
But with that surname ; a good memory,
And witness of the malice and displeasure
Which thou shouldst bear me : only that name
    remains ;
The cruelty and envy of the people,   80
Permitted by our dastard nobles, who
Have all forsook me, hath devour'd the rest ;
And suffer'd me by the voice of slaves to be
Whoop'd out of Rome. Now this extremity
Hath brought me to thy hearth ; not out of
    hope—
Mistake me not—to save my life, for if
I had fear'd death, of all the men i' the world
I would have 'voided thee, but in mere spite,
To be full quit of those my banishers,
Stand I before thee here. Then if thou hast 90
A heart of wreak in thee, that wilt revenge
Thine own particular wrongs and stop those
    maims
Of shame seen through thy country, speed thee
    straight,
And make my misery serve thy turn : so use it
That my revengeful services may prove
As benefits to thee, for I will fight
Against my canker'd country with the spleen
Of all the under fiends. But if so be
Thou darest not this and that to prove more
    fortunes
Thou'rt tired, then, in a word, I also am 100
Longer to live most weary, and present
My throat to thee and to thy ancient malice ;
Which not to cut would show thee but a fool,
Since I have ever follow'd thee with hate,
Drawn tuns of blood out of thy country's
    breast,
And cannot live but to thy shame, unless
It be to do thee service.
  Auf.   O Marcius, Marcius !
Each word thou hast spoke hath weeded from
    my heart
A root of ancient envy. If Jupiter
Should from yond cloud speak divine things,
And say ''Tis true,' I'ld not believe them
    more   111
Than thee, all noble Marcius. Let me twine
Mine arms about that body, where against

My grained ash an hundred times hath broke
And scarr'd the moon with splinters : here I
    clip
The anvil of my sword, and do contest
As hotly and as nobly with thy love
As ever in ambitious strength I did
Contend against thy valor. Know thou first,
I loved the maid I married ; never man   120
Sigh'd truer breath ; but that I see thee here,
Thou noble thing ! more dances my rapt heart
Than when I first my wedded mistress saw
Bestride my threshold. Why, thou Mars ! I
    tell thee,
We have a power on foot ; and I had purpose
Once more to hew thy target from thy brawn,
Or lose mine arm for't : thou hast beat me out
Twelve several times, and I have nightly since
Dreamt of encounters 'twixt thyself and me ;
We have been down together in my sleep, 130
Unbuckling helms, fisting each other's throat,
And waked half dead with nothing. Worthy
    Marcius,
Had we no quarrel else to Rome, but that
Thou art thence banish'd, we would muster all
From twelve to seventy, and pouring war
Into the bowels of ungrateful Rome,
Like a bold flood o'er-bear. O, come, go in,
And take our friendly senators by the hands ;
Who now are here, taking their leaves of me,
Who am prepared against your territories,
Though not for Rome itself.   141
  Cor.   You bless me, gods !
  Auf. Therefore, most absolute sir, if thou
    wilt have
The leading of thine own revenges, take
The one half of my commission ; and set
    down—
As best thou art experienced, since thou
    know'st
Thy country's strength and weakness,—thine
    own ways ;
Whether to knock against the gates of Rome,
Or rudely visit them in parts remote,
To fright them, ere destroy. But come in :
Let me commend thee first to those that shall
Say yea to thy desires. A thousand wel-
    comes !   151
And more a friend than e'er an enemy ;
Yet, Marcius, that was much. Your hand :
    most welcome !
    [*Exeunt Coriolanus and Aufidius. The*
        two Servingmen come forward.
  First Serv. Here's a strange alteration !
  Sec. Serv. By my hand, I had thought to
have strucken him with a cudgel ; and yet my
mind gave me his clothes made a false report
of him.
  First Serv. What an arm he has ! he turned
me about with his finger and his thumb, as
one would set up a top.   161
  Sec. Serv. Nay, I knew by his face that
there was something in him : he had, sir, a
kind of face, methought,—I cannot tell how to
term it.
  First Serv. He had so ; looking as it were
—would I were hanged, but I thought there
was more in him than I could think.
  Sec. Serv. So did I, I'll be sworn : he is
simply the rarest man i' the world.
  First Serv. I think he is : but a greater soldier than he you wot on.   171
  Sec. Serv. Who, my master ?
  First Serv. Nay, it's no matter for that.

Sec. Serv. Worth six on him.

First Serv. Nay, not so neither : but I take him to be the greater soldier.

Sec. Serv. Faith, look you, one cannot tell how to say that : for the defence of a town, our general is excellent.

First Serv. Ay, and for an assault too. 180

Re-enter third Servingman.

Third Serv. O slaves, I can tell you news,— news, you rascals !

First and Sec. Serv. What, what, what ? let's partake.

Third Serv. I would not be a Roman, of all nations ; I had as lieve be a condemned man.

First and Sec. Serv. Wherefore ? wherefore ?

Third Serv. Why, here's he that was wont to thwack our general, Caius Marcius.

First Serv. Why do you say 'thwack our general ' ? 191

Third Serv. I do not say 'thwack our general ;' but he was always good enough for him.

Sec. Serv. Come, we are fellows and friends : he was ever too hard for him ; I have heard him say so himself.

First Serv. He was too hard for him directly, to say the troth on't : before Corioli he scotched him and notched him like a carbonado.

Sec. Serv. An he had been cannibally given, he might have broiled and eaten him too. 201

First Serv. But, more of thy news ?

Third Serv. Why, he is so made on here within, as if he were son and heir to Mars ; set at upper end o' the table ; no question asked him by any of the senators, but they stand bald before him : our general himself makes a mistress of him ; sanctifies himself with's hand and turns up the white o' the eye to his discourse. But the bottom of the news is, our general is cut i' the middle and but one half of what he was yesterday ; for the other has half, by the entreaty and grant of the whole table. He'll go, he says, and sowl the porter of Rome gates by the ears : he will mow all down before him, and leave his passage polled.

Sec. Serv. And he's as like to do't as any man I can imagine.

Third Serv. Do't ! he will do't ; for, look you, sir, he has as many friends as enemies ; which friends, sir, as it were, durst not, look you, sir, show themselves, as we term it, his friends whilst he's in directitude.

First Serv. Directitude ! what's that ?

Third Serv. But when they shall see, sir, his crest up again, and the man in blood, they will out of their burrows, like conies after rain, and revel all with him.

First Serv. But when goes this forward ?

Third Serv. To-morrow ; to-day ; presently ; you shall have the drum struck up this afternoon : 'tis, as it were, a parcel of their feast, and to be executed ere they wipe their lips.

Sec. Serv. Why, then we shall have a stirring world again. This peace is nothing, but to rust iron, increase tailors, and breed ballad-makers.

First Serv. Let me have war, say I ; it exceeds peace as far as day does night ; it's

spritely, waking, audible, and full of vent. Peace is a very apoplexy, lethargy ; mulled, deaf, sleepy, insensible ; a getter of more bastard children than war's a destroyer of men. 241

Sec. Serv. 'Tis so : and as war, in some sort, may be said to be a ravisher, so it cannot be denied but peace is a great maker of cuckolds.

First Serv. Ay, and it makes men hate one another.

Third Serv. Reason ; because they then less need one another. The wars for my money. I hope to see Romans as cheap as Volscians. They are rising, they are rising. 250

All. In, in, in, in ! [*Exeunt.*

SCENE VI. *Rome. A public place.*

Enter SICINIUS *and* BRUTUS.

Sic. We hear not of him, neither need we
fear him ;
His remedies are tame i' the present peace
And quietness of the people, which before
Were in wild hurry. Here do we make his
friends
Blush that the world goes well, who rather
had,
Though they themselves did suffer by't, behold
Dissentious numbers pestering streets than see
Our tradesmen singing in their shops and
going
About their functions friendly.

Bru.   We stood to't in good time. [*Enter*
Menenius.] Is this Menenius ? 10

Sic. 'Tis he, 'tis he : O, he is grown most
kind of late.

Both Tri. Hail, sir !

Men.   Hail to you both !

Sic.   Your Coriolanus
Is not much miss'd, but with his friends :
The commonwealth doth stand, and so would
do,
Were he more angry at it.

Men.   All's well ; and might have been
much better, if
He could have temporized.

Sic.   Where is he, hear you ?

Men.   Nay, I hear nothing : his mother and
his wife
Hear nothing from him.

Enter three or four Citizens.

Citizens. The gods preserve you both !

Sic.   God-den, our neighbors. 20

Bru. God-den to you all, god-den to you
all.

First Cit. Ourselves, our wives, and children, on our knees,
Are bound to pray for you both.

Sic.   Live, and thrive !

Bru. Farewell, kind neighbors : we wish'd
Coriolanus
Had loved you as we did.

Citizens.   Now the gods keep you !

Both Tri. Farewell, farewell.

                    [*Exeunt Citizens.*

Sic. This is a happier and more comely
time
Than when these fellows ran about the streets,
Crying confusion.

Bru. Caius Marcius was
A worthy officer i' the war ; but insolent, 30
O'ercome with pride, ambitious past all think-
          ing,
Self-loving,—
  Sic.   And affecting one sole throne,
Without assistance.
  Men.   I think not so.
  Sic. We should by this, to all our lamen-
          tation,
If he had gone forth consul, found it so.
  Bru. The gods have well prevented it, and
          Rome
Sits safe and still without him.

Enter an ÆDILE.

  Æd.   Worthy tribunes,
There is a slave, whom we have put in prison,
Reports, the Volsces with two several powers
Are enter'd in the Roman territories,   40
And with the deepest malice of the war
Destroy what lies before 'em.
  Men.   'Tis Aufidius,
Who, hearing of our Marcius' banishment,
Thrusts forth his horns again into the world ;
Which were inshell'd when Marcius stood for
          Rome,
And durst not once peep out.
  Sic.   Come, what talk you
Of Marcius ?
  Bru.   Go see this rumorer whipp'd. It
          cannot be
The Volsces dare break with us.
  Men.   Cannot be !
We have record that very well it can,
And three examples of the like have been   50
Within my age. But reason with the fellow,
Before you punish him, where he heard this,
Lest you shall chance to whip your infor-
          mation
And beat the messenger who bids beware
Of what is to be dreaded.
  Sic.   Tell not me :
I know this cannot be.
  Bru.   Not possible.

Enter a MESSENGER.

  Mess. The nobles in great earnestness are
          going
All to the senate-house : some news is come
That turns their countenances.
  Sic.   'Tis this slave ;—
Go whip him, 'fore the people's eyes :—his
          raising ;   60
Nothing but his report.
  Mess.   Yes, worthy sir,
The slave's report is seconded ; and more,
More fearful, is deliver'd.
  Sic.   What more fearful ?
  Mess. It is spoke freely out of many
          mouths—
How probable I do not know—that Marcius,
Join'd with Aufidius, leads a power 'gainst
          Rome,
And vows revenge as spacious as between
The young'st and oldest thing.
  Sic.   This is most likely !
  Bru. Raised only, that the weaker sort may
          wish
Good Marcius home again.
  Sic.   The very trick on't.   70

  Men. This is unlikely :
He and Aufidius can no more atone
Than violentest contrariety.

Enter a second MESSENGER.

  Sec. Mess. You are sent for to the senate :
A fearful army, led by Caius Marcius
Associated with Aufidius, rages
Upon our territories ; and have already
O'erborne their way, consumed with fire, and
          took
What lay before them.

Enter COMINIUS.

  Com. O, you have made good work !
  Men.   What news ? what news ?   80
  Com. You have holp to ravish your own
          daughters and
To melt the city leads upon your pates,
To see your wives dishonor'd to your noses,—
  Men. What's the news ? what's the news ?
  Com. Your temples burned in their cement,
          and
Your franchises, whereon you stood, confined
Into an auger's bore.
  Men.   Pray now, your news ?
You have made fair work, I fear me.—Pray,
          your news ?—
If Marcius should be join'd with Volscians,—
  Com.   If !
He is their god : he leads them like a thing   91
Made by some other deity than nature,
That shapes man better ; and they follow him,
Against us brats, with no less confidence
Than boys pursuing summer butterflies,
Or butchers killing flies.
  Men.   You have made good work,
You and your apron-men ; you that stood so
          much
Upon the voice of occupation and
The breath of garlic-eaters !
  Com.   He will shake
Your Rome about your ears.
  Men.   As Hercules
Did shake down mellow fruit. You have made
          fair work !   100
  Bru. But is this true, sir ?
  Com.   Ay ; and you'll look pale
Before you find it other. All the regions
Do smilingly revolt ; and who resist
Are mock'd for valiant ignorance,
And perish constant fools. Who is't can blame
          him ?
Your enemies and his find something in him.
  Men. We are all undone, unless
The noble man have mercy.
  Com.   Who shall ask it ?
The tribunes cannot do't for shame ; the peo-
          ple
Deserve such pity of him as the wolf   110
Does of the shepherds : for his best friends, if
          they
Should say 'Be good to Rome,' they charged
          him even
As those should do that had deserved his hate,
And therein show'd like enemies.
  Men.   'Tis true :
If he were putting to my house the brand
That should consume it, I have not the face
To say 'Beseech you, cease.' You have made
          fair hands,

You and your crafts! you have crafted fair!
 Com.   You have brought
A trembling upon Rome, such as was never
So incapable of help.
 Both Tri. Say not we brought it. 120
 Men. How! Was it we? we loved him;
  but, like beasts
And cowardly nobles, gave way unto your
  clusters,
Who did hoot him out o' the city.
 Com.   But I fear
They'll roar him in again. Tullus Aufidius,
The second name of men, obeys his points
As if he were his officer: desperation
Is all the policy, strength and defence,
That Rome can make against them.

   Enter a troop of Citizens.

 Men.   Here come the clusters.
And is Aufidius with him? You are they
That made the air unwholesome, when you
  cast   130
Your stinking greasy caps in hooting at
Coriolanus' exile. Now he's coming;
And not a hair upon a soldier's head
Which will not prove a whip: as many cox-
  combs
As you threw caps up will he tumble down,
And pay you for your voices. 'Tis no matter;
If he could burn us all into one coal,
We have deserved it.
 Citizens. Faith, we hear fearful news.
 First Cit. For mine own part,
When I said, banish him, I said 'twas pity.
 Sec. Cit. And so did I.   141
 Third Cit. And so did I; and, to say the
truth, so did very many of us: that we did,
we did for the best; and though we willingly
consented to his banishment, yet it was against
our will.
 Com. Ye're goodly things, you voices!
 Men.   You have made
Good work, you and your cry! Shall's to the
  Capitol?
 Com. O, ay, what else?
   [*Exeunt Cominius and Menenius.*
 Sic. Go, masters, get you home; be not
  dismay'd: 150
These are a side that would be glad to have
This true which they so seem to fear. Go
  home,
And show no sign of fear.
 First Cit. The gods be good to us! Come,
masters, let's home. I ever said we were i' the
wrong when we banished him.
 Sec. Cit. So did we all. But, come, let's
home.   [*Exeunt Citizens.*
 Bru. I do not like this news.
 Sic. Nor I.
 Bru. Let's to the Capitol. Would half my
  wealth   160
Would buy this for a lie!
 Sic.   Pray, let us go.
          [*Exeunt.*

 Scene VII. *A camp, at a small distance
    from Rome.*

  Enter AUFIDIUS *and his* Lieutenant.

 Auf. Do they still fly to the Roman?
 Lieu. I do not know what witchcraft's in
  him, but
Your soldiers use him as the grace 'fore meat,

Their talk at table, and their thanks at end;
And you are darken'd in this action, sir,
Even by your own.
 Auf.   I cannot help it now,
Unless, by using means, I lame the foot
Of our design. He bears himself more proud-
  lier,
Even to my person, than I thought he would
When first I did embrace him: yet his nature
In that's no changeling; and I must excuse
What cannot be amended.
 Lieu.   Yet I wish, sir,—
I mean for your particular,—you had not
Join'd in commission with him; but either
Had borne the action of yourself, or else
To him had left it solely.
 Auf. I understand thee well; and be thou
  sure,
When he shall come to his account, he knows
  not
What I can urge against him. Although it
  seems,
And so he thinks, and is no less apparent 20
To the vulgar eye, that he bears all things
  fairly.
And shows good husbandry for the Volscian
  state,
Fights dragon-like, and does achieve as soon
As draw his sword; yet he hath left undone
That which shall break his neck or hazard
  mine,
Whene'er we come to our account.
 Lieu. Sir, I beseech you, think you he'll
  carry Rome?
 Auf. All places yield to him ere he sits
  down;
And the nobility of Rome are his:
The senators and patricians love him too: 30
The tribunes are no soldiers; and their people
Will be as rash in the repeal, as hasty
To expel him thence. I think he'll be to Rome
As is the osprey to the fish, who takes it
By sovereignty of nature. First he was
A noble servant to them; but he could not
Carry his honors even: whether 'twas pride,
Which out of daily fortune ever taints
The happy man; whether defect of judgment,
To fail in the disposing of those chances 40
Which he was lord of; or whether nature,
Not to be other than one thing, not moving
From the casque to the cushion, but command-
  ing peace
Even with the same austerity and garb
As he controll'd the war; but one of these—
As he hath spices of them all, not all,
For I dare so far free him—made him fear'd,
So hated, and so banish'd: but he has a merit,
To choke it in the utterance. So our virtues
Lie in the interpretation of the time: 50
And power, unto itself most commendable,
Hath not a tomb so evident as a chair
To extol what it hath done.
One fire drives out one fire; one nail, one
  nail;
Rights by rights falter, strengths by strengths
  do fail.
Come, let's away. When, Caius, Rome is
  thine,
Thou art poor'st of all; then shortly art thou
  mine.   [*Exeunt.*

ACT V.

Scene I. *Rome. A public place.*

Enter Menenius, Cominius, Sicinius, Brutus, *and others.*

Men.　No, I'll not go : you hear what he
　　hath said
Which was sometime his general ; who loved
　　him
In a most dear particular. He call'd me father :
But what o' that ? Go, you that banish'd him ;
A mile before his tent fall down, and knee
The way into his mercy : nay, if he coy'd
To hear Cominius speak, I'll keep at home.
Com.　He would not seem to know me.
Men.　　　　　　　　　Do you hear ?
Com.　Yet one time he did call me by my
　　name :
I urged our old acquaintance, and the drops　10
That we have bled together. Coriolanus
He would not answer to : forbad all names ;
He was a kind of nothing, titleless,
Till he had forged himself a name o' the fire
Of burning Rome.
Men.　Why, so : you have made good
　　work !
A pair of tribunes that have rack'd for Rome,
To make coals cheap,—a noble memory !
Com.　I minded him how royal 'twas to par-
　　don
When it was less expected : he replied,
It was a bare petition of a state　　　　　20
To one whom they had punish'd.
Men.　　　　　　　　Very well :
Could he say less ?
Com.　I offer'd to awaken his regard
For's private friends : his answer to me was,
He could not stay to pick them in a pile
Of noisome musty chaff : he said 'twas folly,
For one poor grain or two, to leave unburnt,
And still to nose the offence.
Men.　　　　For one poor grain or two !
I am one of those ; his mother, wife, his
　　child,　　　　　　　　　　　　　29
And this brave fellow too, we are the grains :
You are the musty chaff ; and you are smelt
Above the moon : we must be burnt for you.
Sic.　Nay, pray, be patient : if you refuse
　　your aid
In this so never-needed help, yet do not
Upbraid's with our distress. But, sure, if you
Would be your country's pleader, your good
　　tongue,
More than the instant army we can make,
Might stop our countryman.
Men.　　　　No, I'll not meddle.
Sic.　Pray you, go to him.
Men.　　　　What should I do ?
Bru.　Only make trial what your love can
　　do　　　　　　　　　　　　　　40
For Rome, towards Marcius.
Men.　　　　Well, and say that Marcius
Return me, as Cominius is return'd,
Unheard ; what then ?
But as a discontented friend, grief-shot
With his unkindness ? say't be so ?
Sic.　　　　　　　Yet your good will
Must have that thanks from Rome, after the
　　measure
As you intended well.
Men.　　　　　I'll undertake 't :

I think he'll hear me. Yet, to bite his lip
And hum at good Cominius, much unhearts
　　me.
He was not taken well ; he had not dined :　50
The veins unfill'd, our blood is cold, and then
We pout upon the morning, are unapt
To give or to forgive ; but when we have stuff'd
These pipes and these conveyances of our
　　blood
With wine and feeding, we have suppler souls
Than in our priest-like fasts : therefore I'll
　　watch him
Till he be dieted to my request,
And then I'll set upon him.
Bru.　You know the very road into his
　　kindness,
And cannot lose your way.
Men.　　　Good faith, I'll prove him,　60
Speed how it will. I shall ere long have knowl-
　　edge
Of my success.　　　　　　　　　[*Exit.*
Com.　　　He'll never hear him.
Sic.　　　　　　　　　Not ?
Com.　I tell you, he does sit in gold, his eye
Red as 'twould burn Rome ; and his injury
The gaoler to his pity. I kneel'd before him ;
'Twas very faintly he said ' Rise ; ' dismiss'd
　　me
Thus, with his speechless hand : what he would
　　do,
He sent in writing after me ; what he would
　　not,
Bound with an oath to yield to his conditions :
So that all hope is vain,　　　　　　　70
Unless his noble mother, and his wife ;
Who, as I hear, mean to solicit him
For mercy to his country. Therefore, let's
　　hence,
And with our fair entreaties haste them on.
　　　　　　　　　　　　　[*Exeunt.*

Scene II. *Entrance of the Volscian camp
before Rome. Two Sentinels on guard.*

Enter to them, Menenius.

First Sen.　Stay : whence are you ?
Sec. Sen.　　　　Stand, and go back.
Men.　You guard like men ; 'tis well : but,
　　by your leave,
I am an officer of state, and come
To speak with Coriolanus.
First Sen.　　　　From whence ?
Men.　　　　　　　From Rome.
First Sen.　You may not pass, you must re-
　　turn : our general
Will no more hear from thence.
Sec. Sen.　You'll see your Rome embraced
　　with fire before
You'll speak with Coriolanus.
Men.　　　　　Good my friends,
If you have heard your general talk of Rome,
And of his friends there, it is lots to blanks,
My name hath touch'd your ears : it is Me-
　　nenius.　　　　　　　　　　　11
First Sen.　Be it so ; go back : the virtue
　　of your name
Is not here passable.
Men.　　　　I tell thee, fellow,
The general is my lover : I have been
The book of his good acts, whence men have
　　read
His name unparallel'd, haply amplified ;
For I have ever verified my friends,

Of whom he's chief, with all the size that
verity
Would without lapsing suffer : nay, some-
times,
Like to a bowl upon a subtle ground, 20
I have tumbled past the throw ; and in his
praise
Have almost stamp'd the leasing : therefore,
fellow,
I must have leave to pass.

First Sen. Faith, sir, if you had told as
many lies in his behalf as you have uttered
words in your own, you should not pass here ;
no, though it were as virtuous to lie as to live
chastely. Therefore, go back.

Men. Prithee, fellow, remember my name
is Menenius, always factionary on the party of
your general. 31

Sec. Sen. Howsoever you have been his liar,
as you say you have, I am one that, telling
true under him, must say, you cannot pass.
Therefore, go back.

Men. Has he dined, canst thou tell ? for I
would not speak with him till after dinner.

First Sen. You are a Roman, are you ?

Men. I am, as thy general is. 39

First Sen. Then you should hate Rome, as
he does. Can you, when you have pushed out
your gates the very defender of them, and,
in a violent popular ignorance, given your
enemy your shield, think to front his revenges
with the easy groans of old women, the virginal palms of your daughters, or with the
palsied intercession of such a decayed dotant
as you seem to be ? Can you think to blow
out the intended fire your city is ready to
flame in, with such weak breath as this ? No,
you are deceived ; therefore, back to Rome,
and prepare for your execution : you are condemned, our general has sworn you out of reprieve and pardon.

Men. Sirrah, if thy captain knew I were
here, he would use me with estimation.

Sec. Sen. Come, my captain knows you not.

Men. I mean, thy general.

First Sen. My general cares not for you.
Back, I say, go ; lest I let forth your half-pint
of blood ; back,—that's the utmost of your
having : back.

Men. Nay, but, fellow, fellow,—

Enter CORIOLANUS *and* AUFIDIUS.

Cor. What's the matter ?

Men. Now, you companion, I'll say an
errand for you : you shall know now that I am
in estimation ; you shall perceive that a Jack
guardant cannot office me from my son Coriolanus : guess, but by my entertainment with
him, if thou standest not i' the state of hanging,
or of some death more long in spectatorship,
and crueller in suffering ; behold now presently, and swoon for what's to come upon
thee. [*To Cor.*] The glorious gods sit in
hourly synod about thy particular prosperity,
and love thee no worse than thy old father
Menenius does ! O my son, my son ! thou art
preparing fire for us ; look thee, here's water
to quench it. I was hardly moved to come to
thee ; but being assured none but myself could
move thee, I have been blown out of your
gates with sighs ; and conjure thee to pardon
Rome, and thy petitionary countrymen. The
good gods assuage thy wrath, and turn the

dregs of it upon this varlet here,—this, who,
like a block, hath denied my access to thee.

Cor. Away !

Men. How ! away !

Cor. Wife, mother, child, I know not. My
affairs
Are servanted to others : though I owe
My revenge properly, my remission lies 90
In Volscian breasts. That we have been famil-
iar,
Ingrate forgetfulness shall poison, rather
Than pity note how much. Therefore, be gone.
Mine ears against your suits are stronger than
Your gates against my force. Yet, for I loved
thee,
Take this along ; I writ it for thy sake,
[*Gives a letter.*
And would have sent it. Another word, Me-
nenius,
I will not hear thee speak. This man, Aufidius,
Was my beloved in Rome : yet thou behold'st !

Auf. You keep a constant temper. 100
[*Exeunt Coriolanus and Aufidius.*

First Sen. Now, sir, is your name Menenius ?

Sec. Sen. 'Tis a spell, you see, of much
power : you know the way home again.

First Sen. Do you hear how we are shent
for keeping your greatness back ?

Sec. Sen. What cause, do you think, I have
to swoon ?

Men. I neither care for the world nor your
general : for such things as you, I can scarce
think there's any, ye're so slight. He that hath
a will to die by himself fears it not from another : let your general do his worst. For you,
be that you are, long ; and your misery increase with your age ! I say to you, as I was
said to, Away ! [*Exit.*

First Sen. A noble fellow, I warrant him.

Sec. Sen. The worthy fellow is our general :
he's the rock, the oak not to be wind-shaken.
[*Exeunt.*

SCENE III. *The tent of Coriolanus.*

Enter CORIOLANUS, AUFIDIUS, *and others.*

Cor. We will before the walls of Rome to-
morrow
Set down our host. My partner in this action,
You must report to the Volscian lords, how
plainly
I have borne this business.

Auf.   Only their ends
You have respected ; stopp'd your ears against
The general suit of Rome ; never admitted
A private whisper, no, not with such friends
That thought them sure of you.

Cor.   This last old man,
Whom with a crack'd heart I have sent to
Rome,
Loved me above the measure of a father ; 10
Nay, godded me, indeed. Their latest refuge
Was to send him ; for whose old love I have,
Though I show'd sourly to him, once more
offer'd
Th first conditions, which they did refuse
And cannot now accept ; to grace him only
That thought he could do more, a very little
I have yielded to : fresh embassies and suits,
Nor from the state nor private friends, here-
after
Will I lend ear to. Ha ! what shout is this ?
[*Shout within.*

Shall I be tempted to infringe my vow   20
In the same time 'tis made ? I will not.

Enter in mourning habits, VIRGILIA, VO-
LUMNIA, *leading young* MARCIUS, VALERIA,
and Attendants.

My wife comes foremost ; then the honor'd
   mould
Wherein this trunk was framed, and in her
   hand
The grandchild to her blood. But, out, affec-
   tion !
All bond and privilege of nature, break !
Let it be virtuous to be obstinate.
What is that curt'sy worth ? or those doves'
   eyes,
Which can make gods forsworn ? I melt, and
   am not
Of stronger earth than others. My mother
   bows ;
As if Olympus to a molehill should   30
In supplication nod : and my young boy
Hath an aspect of intercession, which
Great nature cries ' Deny not.' Let the Volsces
Plough Rome, and harrow Italy : I'll never
Be such a gosling to obey instinct, but stand,
As if a man were author of himself
And knew no other kin.
  Vir.   My lord and husband !
  Cor. These eyes are not the same I wore
in Rome.
  Vir. The sorrow that delivers us thus
   changed
Makes you think so.
  Cor.   Like a dull actor now,   40
I have forgot my part, and I am out,
Even to a full disgrace. Best of my flesh,
Forgive my tyranny ; but do not say
For that 'Forgive our Romans.' O, a kiss
Long as my exile, sweet as my revenge !
Now, by the jealous queen of heaven, that
   kiss
I carried from thee, dear ; and my true lip
Hath virgin'd it e'er since. You gods ! I prate,
And the most noble mother of the world
Leave unsaluted : sink, my knee, i' the earth ;
                    [*Kneels.*
Of thy deep duty more impression show   51
Than that of common sons.
  Vol.   O, stand up blest !
Whilst, with no softer cushion than the flint,
I kneel before thee ; and unproperly
Show duty, as mistaken all this while
Between the child and parent.   [*Kneels.*
  Cor.   What is this ?
Your knees to me ? to your corrected son ?
Then let the pebbles on the hungry beach
Fillip the stars ; then let the mutinous winds
Strike the proud cedars 'gainst the fiery sun ;
Murdering impossibility, to make   61
What cannot be, slight work.
  Vol.   Thou art my warrior ;
I holp to frame thee. Do you know this lady ?
  Cor. The noble sister of Publicola,
The moon of Rome, chaste as the icicle
That's curdied by the frost from purest snow
And hangs on Dian's temple : dear Valeria !
  Vol. This is a poor epitome of yours,
Which by the interpretation of full time
May show like all yourself.
  Cor.   The god of soldiers,   70
With the consent of supreme Jove, inform

Thy thoughts with nobleness ; that thou mayst
   prove
To shame unvulnerable, and stick i' the wars
Like a great sea-mark, standing every flaw,
And saving those that eye thee !
  Vol.   Your knee, sirrah.
  Cor. That's my brave boy !
  Vol. Even he, your wife, this lady, and
   myself,
Are suitors to you.
  Cor.   I beseech you, peace :
Or, if you'ld ask, remember this before :
The thing I have forsworn to grant may never
Be held by you denials. Do not bid me   81
Dismiss my soldiers, or capitulate
Again with Rome's mechanics : tell me not
Wherein I seem unnatural : desire not
To ally my rages and revenges with
Your colder reasons.
  Vol.   O, no more, no more !
You have said you will not grant us any thing ;
For we have nothing else to ask, but that
Which you deny already : yet we will ask ;
That, if you fail in our request, the blame   90
May hang upon your hardness : therefore hear
   us.
  Cor. Aufidius, and you Volsces, mark ; for
   we'll
Hear nought from Rome in private. Your re-
   quest ?
  Vol. Should we be silent and not speak, our
   raiment
And state of bodies would bewray what life
We have led since thy exile. Think with thy-
   self
How more unfortunate than all living women
Are we come hither : since that thy sight,
   which should
Make our eyes flow with joy, hearts dance
   with comforts,
Constrains them weep and shake with fear and
   sorrow ;   100
Making the mother, wife and child to see
The son, the husband and the father tearing
His country's bowels out. And to poor we
Thine enmity's most capital : thou barr'st us
Our prayers to the gods, which is a comfort
That all but we enjoy ; for how can we,
Alas, how can we for our country pray,
Whereto we are bound, together with thy
   victory,
Whereto we are bound ? alack, or we must lose
The country, our dear nurse, or else thy per-
   son,   110
Our comfort in the country. We must find
An evident calamity, though we had
Our wish, which side should win : for either
   thou
Must, as a foreign recreant, be led
With manacles thorough our streets, or else
Triumphantly tread on thy country's ruin,
And bear the palm for having bravely shed
Thy wife and children's blood. For myself,
   son,
I purpose not to wait on fortune till
These wars determine : if I cannot persuade
   thee   120
Rather to show a noble grace to both parts
Than seek the end of one, thou shalt no sooner
March to assault thy country than to tread—
Trust to't, thou shalt not—on thy mother's
   womb,
That brought thee to this world.

Vir.   Ay, and mine,
That brought you forth this boy, to keep your
      name
Living to time.
Young Mar. A' shall not tread on me;
I'll run away till I am bigger, but then I'll fight.
Cor. Not of a woman's tenderness to be,
Requires nor child nor woman's face to see.
I have sat too long.   [*Rising.* 131
Vol.   Nay, go not from us thus.
If it were so that our request did tend
To save the Romans, thereby to destroy
The Volsces whom you serve, you might con-
      demn us,
As poisonous of your honor : no ; our suit
Is, that you reconcile them : while the Volsces
May say ' This mercy we have show'd ; ' the
      Romans,
' This we received ; ' and each in either side
Give the all-hail to thee, and cry ' Be blest
For making up this peace ! ' Thou know'st,
      great son,   140
The end of war's uncertain, but this certain,
That, if thou conquer Rome, the benefit
Which thou shalt thereby reap is such a name,
Whose repetition will be dogg'd with curses ;
Whose chronicle thus writ : ' The man was
      noble,
But with his last attempt he wiped it out ;
Destroy'd his country, and his name remains
To the ensuing age abhorr'd.' Speak to me,
      son :
Thou hast affected the fine strains of honor,
To imitate the graces of the gods ;   150
To tear with thunder the wide cheeks o' the
      air,
And yet to charge thy sulphur with a bolt
That should but rive an oak. Why dost not
      speak ?
Think'st thou it honorable for a noble man
Still to remember wrongs ? Daughter, speak
      you :
He cares not for your weeping. Speak thou,
      boy :
Perhaps thy childishness will move him more
Than can our reasons. There's no man in the
      world
More bound to 's mother ; yet here he lets me
      prate
Like one i' the stocks. Thou hast never in thy
      life   160
Show'd thy dear mother any courtesy,
When she, poor hen, fond of no second brood,
Has cluck'd thee to the wars and safely home,
Loaden with honor. Say my request's unjust,
And spurn me back : but if it be not so,
Thou art not honest ; and the gods will plague
      thee,
That thou restrain'st from me the duty which
To a mother's part belongs. He turns away :
Down, ladies ; let us shame him with our
      knees.   169
To his surname Coriolanus 'longs more pride
Than pity to our prayers. Down : an end ;
This is the last : so we will home to Rome,
And die among our neighbors. Nay, be-
      hold 's :
This boy, that cannot tell what he would have,
But kneels and holds up hands for fellowship,
Does reason our petition with more strength
Than thou hast to deny 't. Come, let us go :
This fellow had a Volscian to his mother ;
His wife is in Corioli and his child

Like him by chance. Yet give us our dis-
      patch :   180
I am hush'd until our city be a-fire,
And then I'll speak a little.
            [*He holds her by the hand, silent.*
Cor.   O mother, mother !
What have you done ? Behold, the heavens
      do ope,
The gods look down, and this unnatural scene
They laugh at. O my mother, mother ! O !
You have won a happy victory to Rome ;
But, for your son,—believe it, O, believe it,
Most dangerously you have with him pre-
      vail'd,
If not most mortal to him. But, let it come.
Aufidius, though I cannot make true wars, 190
I'll frame convenient peace. Now, good Au-
      fidius,
Were you in my stead, would you have heard
A mother less ? or granted less, Aufidius ?
Auf. I was moved withal.
Cor.   I dare be sworn you were :
And, sir, it is no little thing to make
Mine eyes to sweat compassion. But, good
      sir,
What peace you'll make, advise me : for my
      part,
I'll not to Rome, I'll back with you ; and pray
      you,
Stand to me in this cause. O mother ! wife !
Auf. [*Aside.*] I am glad thou hast set thy
      mercy and thy honor   200
At difference in thee : out of that I'll work
Myself a former fortune.
            [*The Ladies make signs to Coriolanus.*
Cor.   Ay, by and by ;
            [*To Volumnia, Virgilia, &c.*
But we will drink together ; and you shall
      bear
A better witness back than words, which we,
On like conditions, will have counter-seal'd.
Come, enter with us. Ladies, you deserve
To have a temple built you : all the swords
In Italy, and her confederate arms,
Could not have made this peace. [*Exeunt.* 209

SCENE IV.   *Rome.   A public place.*

Enter MENENIUS *and* SICINIUS.

Men. See you yond coign o' the Capitol,
yond corner-stone ?
Sic. Why, what of that ?
Men. If it be possible for you to displace it
with your little finger, there is some hope the
ladies of Rome, especially his mother, may
prevail with him. But I say there is no hope
in't : our throats are sentenced and stay upon
execution.
Sic. Is't possible that so short a time can
alter the condition of a man !   10
Men. There is difference between a grub
and a butterfly ; yet your butterfly was a grub.
This Marcius is grown from man to dragon :
he has wings ; he's more than a creeping thing.
Sic. He loved his mother dearly.
Men. So did he me : and he no more remembers his mother now than an eight-year-
old horse. The tartness of his face sours ripe
grapes : when he walks, he moves like an engine, and the ground shrinks before his tread-
ing : he is able to pierce a corslet with his
eye ; talks like a knell, and his hum is a battery. He sits in his state, as a thing made for
Alexander. What he bids be done is finished

with his bidding. He wants nothing of a god
but eternity and a heaven to throne in.

Sic. Yes, mercy, if you report him truly.

Men. I paint him in the character. Mark
what mercy his mother shall bring from him :
there is no more mercy in him than there is
milk in a male tiger ; that shall our poor city
find : and all this is long of you.

Sic. The gods be good unto us !

Men. No, in such a case the gods will not
be good unto us. When we banished him, we
respected not them ; and, he returning to break
our necks, they respect not us.

Enter a Messenger.

Mess. Sir, if you'ld save your life, fly to
    your house :
The plebeians have got your fellow-tribune
And hale him up and down, all swearing, if 40
The Roman ladies bring not comfort home,
They'll give him death by inches.

Enter a second Messenger.

Sic.   What's the news ?

Sec. Mess. Good news, good news ; the la-
    dies have prevail'd,
The Volscians are dislodged, and Marcius
    gone :
A merrier day did never yet greet Rome,
No, not the expulsion of the Tarquins.

Sic.   Friend,
Art thou certain this is true ? is it most cer-
    tain ?

Sec. Mess. As certain as I know the sun is
    fire :
Where have you lurk'd, that you make doubt
    of it ?
Ne'er through an arch so hurried the blown
    tide,   50
As the recomforted through the gates. Why,
    hark   you !   *[Trumpets;   hautboys;*
            drums beat ; all together.
The trumpets, sackbuts, psalteries and fifes,
Tabors and cymbals and the shouting Romans,
Make the sun dance. Hark you !
                      [A shout within.

Men.   This is good news :
I will go meet the ladies. This Volumnia
Is worth of consuls, senators, patricians,
A city full ; of tribunes, such as you,
A sea and land full. You have pray'd well
    to-day :
This morning for ten thousand of your throats
I'd not have given a doit. Hark, how they
    joy !   *[Music still, with shouts.* 60

Sic. First, the gods bless you for your tid-
    ings ; next,
Accept my thankfulness.

Sec. Mess.   Sir, we have all
Great cause to give great thanks.

Sic.   They are near the city ?

Sec. Mess. Almost at point to enter.

Sic.   We will meet them,
And help the joy.   *[Exeunt.*

SCENE V. *The same. A street near the gate.*

Enter two Senators *with* VOLUMNIA, VIRGILIA,
VALERIA, *&c. passing over the stage, followed by Patricians and others.*

First Sen. Behold our patroness, the life of
    Rome !
Call all your tribes together, praise the gods,

And make triumphant fires ; strew flowers be-
    fore them :
Unshout the noise that banish'd Marcius,
Repeal him with the welcome of his mother ;
Cry ' Welcome, ladies, welcome ! '

All.   Welcome, ladies,
Welcome !   *[A flourish with drums and trum-
                     pets. Exeunt.*

SCENE VI. *Antium. A public place.*

Enter TULLUS AUFIDIUS, *with* Attendants.

Auf. Go tell the lords o' the city I am
    here :
Deliver them this paper : having read it,
Bid them repair to the market place ; where I,
Even in theirs and in the commons' ears,
Will vouch the truth of it. Him I accuse
The city ports by this hath enter'd and
Intends to appear before the people, hoping
To purge himself with words : dispatch.
              [Exeunt Attendants.

Enter three or four Conspirators *of* AUFIDIUS'
    faction.

Most welcome !

First Con. How is it with our general ?

Auf.   Even so   10
As with a man by his own alms empoison'd,
And with his charity slain.

Sec. Con.   Most noble sir,
If you do hold the same intent wherein
You wish'd us parties, we'll deliver you
Of your great danger.

Auf.   Sir, I cannot tell :
We must proceed as we do find the people.

Third Con. The people will remain uncer-
    tain whilst
'Twixt you there's difference ; but the fall of
    either
Makes the survivor heir of all.

Auf.   I know it ;
And my pretext to strike at him admits   20
A good construction. I raised him, and I
    pawn'd
Mine honor for his truth : who being so
    heighten'd,
He water'd his new plants with dews of flat-
    tery,
Seducing so my friends ; and, to this end,
He bow'd his nature, never known before
But to be rough, unswayable and free.

Third Con. Sir, his stoutness
When he did stand for consul, which he lost
By lack of stooping,—

Auf.   That I would have spoke of : 29
Being banish'd for't, he came unto my hearth ;
Presented to my knife his throat : I took him ;
Made him joint-servant with me ; gave him
    way
In all his own desires ; nay, let him choose
Out of my files, his projects to accomplish,
My best and freshest men ; served his design-
    ments
In mine own person ; holp to reap the fame
Which he did end all his ; and took some pride
To do myself this wrong : till, at the last,
I seem'd his follower, not partner, and
He waged me with his countenance, as if   40
I had been mercenary.

First Con.   So he did, my lord :
The army marvell'd at it, and, in the last,
When he had carried Rome and that we look'd
For no less spoil than glory,—

Auf.   There was it :
For which my sinews shall be stretch'd upon
    him.
At a few drops of women's rheum, which are
As cheap as lies, he sold the blood and labor
Of our great action : therefore shall he die,
And I'll renew me in his fall. But, hark !
    [*Drums and trumpets sound, with great
                shouts of the People.*
First Con.   Your native town you enter'd
    like a post,   50
And had no welcomes home : but he returns,
Splitting the air with noise.
Sec. Con.   And patient fools,
Whose children he hath slain, their base
    throats tear
With giving him glory.
Third Con.   Therefore, at your vantage,
Ere he express himself, or move the people
With what he would say, let him feel your
    sword,
Which we will second. When he lies along,
After your way his tale pronounced shall bury
His reasons with his body.
Auf.   Say no more :
Here come the lords.   60

        Enter the Lords *of the city.*

All the Lords. You are most welcome
    home.
Auf.   I have not deserved it.
But, worthy lords, have you with heed perused
What I have written to you ?
Lords.   We have.
First Lord.   And grieve to hear't.
What faults he made before the last, I think
Might have found easy fines : but there to end
Where he was to begin and give away
The benefit of our levies, answering us
With our own charge, making a treaty where
There was a yielding,—this admits no excuse.
Auf. He approaches : you shall hear him.

Enter CORIOLANUS, *marching with drum and
    colors ; commoners being with him.*

Cor. Hail, lords ! I am return'd your sol-
    dier,
No more infected with my country's love
Than when I parted hence, but still subsisting
Under your great command. You are to know
That prosperously I have attempted and
With bloody passage led your wars even to
The gates of Rome. Our spoils we have
    brought home
Do more than counterpoise a full third part
The charges of the action. We have made
    peace
With no less honor to the Antiates   80
Than shame to the Romans : and we here de-
    liver,
Subscribed by the consuls and patricians,
Together with the seal o' the senate, what
We have compounded on.
Auf.   Read it not, noble lords ;
But tell the traitor, in the high'st degree
He hath abused your powers.
Cor. Traitor ! how now !
Auf.   Ay, traitor, Marcius !
Cor.   Marcius !
Auf. Ay, Marcius, Caius Marcius : dost
    thou think
I'll grace thee with that robbery, thy stol'n
    name

Coriolanus in Corioli ?   90
You lords and heads o' the state, perfidiously
He has betray'd your business, and given up,
For certain drops of salt, your city Rome,
I say ' your city,' to his wife and mother ;
Breaking his oath and resolution like
A twist of rotten silk, never admitting
Counsel o' the war, but at his nurse's tears
He whined and roar'd away your victory,
That pages blush'd at him and men of heart
Look'd wondering each at other.
Cor.   Hear'st thou, Mars ? 100
Auf. Name not the god, thou boy of tears !
Cor.   Ha !
Auf. No more.
Cor. Measureless liar, thou hast made my
    heart
Too great for what contains it. Boy ! O slave !
Pardon me, lords, 'tis the first time that ever
I was forced to scold. Your judgments, my
    grave lords,
Must give this cur the lie : and his own no-
    tion—
Who wears my stripes impress'd upon him ;
    that
Must bear my beating to his grave—shall join
To thrust the lie unto him.   110
First Lord. Peace, both, and hear me
    speak.
Cor. Cut me to pieces, Volsces ; men and
    lads,
Stain all your edges on me. Boy ! false hound !
If you have writ your annals true, 'tis there,
That, like an eagle in a dove-cote, I
Flutter'd your Volscians in Corioli :
Alone I did it. Boy !
Auf.   Why, noble lords,
Will you be put in mind of his blind fortune,
Which was your shame, by this unholy brag-
    gart,
'Fore your own eyes and ears ?
All Consp.   Let him die for't. 120
All the people. ' Tear him to pieces.' ' Do
it presently.' ' He killed my son.' ' My daugh-
ter.' ' He killed my cousin Marcus.' ' He killed
my father.'
Sec. Lord. Peace, ho ! no outrage : peace !
The man is noble and his fame folds-in
This orb o' the earth. His last offences to us
Shall have judicious hearing. Stand, Aufidius,
And trouble not the peace.
Cor.   O that I had him,
With six Aufidiuses, or more, his tribe,   130
To use my lawful sword !
Auf.   Insolent villain !
All Consp. Kill, kill, kill, kill, kill him !
    [*The Conspirators draw, and kill Corio-
        lanus : Aufidius stands on his body.*
Lords.   Hold, hold, hold, hold !
Auf. My noble masters, hear me speak.
First Lord.   O Tullus,—
Sec. Lord. Thou hast done a deed whereat
    valor will weep.
Third Lord. Tread not upon him. Masters
    all, be quiet ;
Put up your swords.
Auf. My lords, when you shall know—as
    in this rage,
Provoked by him, you cannot—the great dan-
    ger
Which this man's life did owe you, you'll re-
    joice
That he is thus cut off. Please it your honors

To call me to your senate, I'll deliver   141
Myself your loyal servant, or endure
Your heaviest censure.
    First Lord.   Bear from hence his body;
And mourn you for him : let him be regarded
As the most noble corse that ever herald
Did follow to his urn.
    Sec. Lord.   His own impatience
Takes from Aufidius a great part of blame.
Let's make the best of it.

    Auf.   My rage is gone ;
And I am struck with sorrow. Take him up.
Help, three o' the chiefest soldiers ; I'll be one.
Beat thou the drum, that it speak mournfully :
Trail your steel pikes. Though in this city he
Hath widow'd and unchilded many a one,
Which to this hour bewail the injury,
Yet he shall have a noble memory.
Assist.   [*Exeunt, bearing the body of Corio-
          lanus. A dead march sounded.*

TIMON OF ATHENS.

(WRITTEN ABOUT 1607–1608.)

INTRODUCTION.

This play is, beyond reasonable doubt, only in part the work of Shakespeare. Whether Shakespeare worked upon materials furnished by an older play, or whether he left his play a fragment to be completed by another hand, is uncertain : the former supposition is perhaps the correct one, and the older writer may possibly have been George Wilkins. There is a substantial agreement among the best critics as to what portions of the play are Shakespeare's and what are not. The following may be distinguished, with some confidence, as the non-Shakespearian parts : Act I., Sc. I., L. 189–240, 258–273 (or ? from entrance of Apemantus to end of scene), II. (certainly) ; Act II., Sc. II., L. 45–124 ; all Act III., except Sc. VI., L. 98–115 ; Act IV., Sc. II., L. 30–50, (?) III., L. 292–362, 399–413, 454–543 ; Act V. (?) Sc. I., L. i.–59, II., III. There is no external evidence which helps to determine the date at which Shakespeare wrote his part of the play, but it was probably later than *Macbeth* and earlier than *Pericles.* The year 1607 is a date which cannot be very far astray. The sources of the play were Paynter's *Palace of Pleasure,* a passage in Plutarch's Life of Mark Antony, and in particular, a dialogue of Lucian. But if Shakespeare worked upon an older play, it may have been through it that he obtained the materials which appear to come through Lucian. Although only a fragment, Shakespeare's part of *Timon* is written with the highest dramatic energy. Nothing is more intense than the conception and rendering of Timon's feelings when he turns in hatred from the evil world. The rich Lord Timon has lived in a rose-colored mist of pleasant delusions. The conferring of favors has been with him a mode of kindly self-indulgence, and he has assumed that every one is as liberal-hearted and of as easy generosity as himself. Out of his pleasant dream he wakes to find the baseness, the selfishness, the ingratitude of the world ; and he passes violently over from his former lax philanthropy to a fierce hatred of mankind. The practical Alcibiades sets at once about righting the wrongs which he has suffered ; but Timon can only rage and then die. His rage implies the elements of a possible nobleness in him ; he cannot acclimatize himself, as Alcibiades can, to the harsh and polluted air of the world ; yet the rage also proceeds from a weakness of nature. The dog-like Apemantus accepts, well-contented, the evil which Alcibiades would punish, and from which Timon flies : he barks and snarls, but does not really suffer. The play is a painful one, unrelieved by the presence of beauty or human worth.

DRAMATIS PERSONÆ.

TIMON, of Athens.
LUCIUS,
LUCULLUS,   } flattering lords.
SEMPRONIUS,
VENTIDIUS, one of Timon's false friends.
ALCIBIADES, an Athenian captain.
APEMANTUS, a churlish philosopher.
FLAVIUS, steward to Timon.
Poet, Painter, Jeweller, and Merchant.
An old Athenian.
FLAMINIUS,
LUCILIUS,   } servants to Timon.
SERVILIUS,

CAPHIS,
PHILOTUS,
TITUS,   } servants to Timon's creditors.
LUCIUS,
HORTENSIUS,
And others,
A Page. A Fool. Three Strangers.

PHRYNIA,   } mistresses to Alcibiades.
TIMANDRA,

Cupid and Amazons in the mask.
Other Lords, Senators, Officers, Soldiers, Banditti, and Attendants.

SCENE : *Athens, and the neighboring woods.*

ACT I.

Scene I. *Athens. A hall in Timon's house.*

Enter Poet, Painter, Jeweller, Merchant, *and others, at several doors.*

Poet. Good day, sir.
Pain.   I am glad you're well.
Poet. I have not seen you long : how goes
   the world ?
Pain. It wears, sir, as it grows.
Poet.   Ay, that's well known :
But what particular rarity ? what strange,
Which manifold record not matches ? See,
Magic of bounty ! all these spirits thy power
Hath conjured to attend. I know the merchant.
Pain. I know them both ; th' other's a
   jeweller.
Mer. O, 'tis a worthy lord.
Jew.   Nay, that's most fix'd.
Mer. A most incomparable man, breathed,
   as it were,   10
To an untirable and continuate goodness :
He passes.
Jew. I have a jewel here—
Mer. O, pray, let's see't : for the Lord
   Timon, sir ?
Jew. If he will touch the estimate : but, for
   that—
Poet. [*Reciting to himself*] ' When we for
   recompense have praised the vile,
It stains the glory in that happy verse
Which aptly sings the good.'
Mer.   'Tis a good form.
            [*Looking at the jewel.*
Jew. And rich : here is a water, look ye.
Pain. You are rapt, sir, in some work,
   some dedication
To the great lord.
Poet.   A thing slipp'd idly from me. 20
Our poesy is as a gum, which oozes
From whence 'tis nourish'd : the fire i' the flint
Shows not till it be struck ; our gentle flame
Provokes itself and like the current flies
Each bound it chafes. What have you there ?
Pain. A picture, sir. When comes your
   book forth ?
Poet. Upon the heels of my presentment,
   sir.
Let's see your piece.
Pain.   'Tis a good piece.
Poet. So 'tis : this comes off well and ex-
   cellent.
Pain. Indifferent.
Poet.   Admirable : how this grace 30
Speaks his own standing ! what a mental power
This eye shoots forth ! how big imagination
Moves in this lip ! to the dumbness of the ges-
   ture
One might interpret.
Pain. It is a pretty mocking of the life.
Here is a touch ; is't good ?
Poet.   I will say of it,
It tutors nature : artificial strife
Lives in these touches, livelier than life.

Enter certain Senators, *and pass over.*

Pain. How this lord is follow'd !
Poet. The senators of Athens : happy man !
Pain. Look, more !   41
Poet. You see this confluence, this great
   flood of visitors.

I have, in this rough work, shaped out a man,
Whom this beneath world doth embrace and
   hug
With amplest entertainment : my free drift
Halts not particularly, but moves itself
In a wide sea of wax : no levell'd malice
Infects one comma in the course I hold ;
But flies an eagle flight, bold and forth on,
Leaving no tract behind.   50
Pain. How shall I understand you ?
Poet.   I will unbolt to you.
You see how all conditions, how all minds,
As well of glib and slippery creatures as
Of grave and austere quality, tender down
Their services to Lord Timon : his large for-
   tune
Upon his good and gracious nature hanging
Subdues and properties to his love and tend-
   ance
All sorts of hearts ; yea, from the glass-faced
   flatterer
To Apemantus, that few things loves better
Than to abhor himself : even he drops down
The knee before him and returns in peace   61
Most rich in Timon's nod.
Pain.   I saw them speak together.
Poet. Sir, I have upon a high and pleasant
   hill
Feign'd Fortune to be throned : the base o'
   the mount
Is rank'd with all deserts, all kind of natures,
That labor on the bosom of this sphere
To propagate their states : amongst them all,
Whose eyes are on this sovereign lady fix'd,
One do I personate of Lord Timon's frame,
Whom Fortune with her ivory hand wafts to
   her ;   70
Whose present grace to present slaves and
   servants
Translates his rivals.
Pain.   'Tis conceived to scope.
This throne, this Fortune, and this hill, me-
   thinks,
With one man beckon'd from the rest below,
Bowing his head against the steepy mount
To climb his happiness, would be well ex-
   press'd
In our condition.
Poet.   Nay, sir, but hear me on.
All those which were his fellows but of late,
Some better than his value, on the moment
Follow his strides, his lobbies fill with tend-
   ance,   80
Rain sacrificial whisperings in his ear,
Make sacred even his stirrup, and through him
Drink the free air.
Pain.   Ay, marry, what of these ?
Poet. When Fortune in her shift and
   change of mood
Spurns down her late beloved, all his depend-
   ants
Which labor'd after him to the mountain's top
Even on their knees and hands, let him slip
   down,
Not one accompanying his declining foot.
Pain. 'Tis common :
A thousand moral paintings I can show   90
That shall demonstrate these quick blows of
   Fortune's
More pregnantly than words. Yet you do well
To show Lord Timon that mean eyes have seen
The foot above the head.

Trumpets sound. Enter LORD TIMON, *addressing himself courteously to every suitor; a Messenger from* VENTIDIUS *talking with him;* LUCILIUS *and other servants following.*

Tim.　　　　　Imprison'd is he, say you?
Mess. Ay, my good lord : five talents is his debt,
His means most short, his creditors most strait :
Your honorable letter he desires
To those have shut him up ; which failing,
Periods his comfort.
Tim.　　　　　Noble Ventidius ! Well ;
I am not of that feather to shake off　　100
My friend when he must need me. I do know him
A gentleman that well deserves a help :
Which he shall have : I'll pay the debt, and free him.
Mess. Your lordship ever binds him.
Tim. Commend me to him : I will send his ransom ;
And being enfranchised, bid him come to me.
'Tis not enough to help the feeble up,
But to support him after. Fare you well.
Mess. All happiness to your honor ! [*Exit.*

　　Enter an old Athenian.

Old Ath. Lord Timon, hear me speak.
Tim.　　Freely, good father.　110
Old Ath. Thou hast a servant named Lucilius.
Tim. I have so : what of him ?
Old Ath. Most noble Timon, call the man before thee.
Tim. Attends he here, or no ? Lucilius !
Luc. Here, at your lordship's service.
Old Ath. This fellow here, Lord Timon, this thy creature,
By night frequents my house. I am a man
That from my first have been inclined to thrift ;
And my estate deserves an heir more raised
Than one which holds a trencher.
Tim.　　Well ; what further ? 120
Old Ath. One only daughter have I, no kin else,
On whom I may confer what I have got :
The maid is fair, o' the youngest for a bride,
And I have bred her at my dearest cost
In qualities of the best. This man of thine
Attempts her love : I prithee, noble lord,
Join with me to forbid him her resort ;
Myself have spoke in vain.
Tim.　　　　The man is honest.
Old Ath. Therefore he will be, Timon :
His honesty rewards him in itself ;　　130
It must not bear my daughter.
Tim.　　　　Does she love him ?
Old Ath. She is young and apt :
Our own precedent passions do instruct us
What levity's in youth.
Tim. [*To Lucilius*] Love you the maid ?
Luc. Ay, my good lord, and she accepts of it.
Old Ath. If in her marriage my consent be missing,
I call the gods to witness, I will choose
Mine heir from forth the beggars of the world,
And dispossess her all.
Tim.　　　　How shall she be endow'd,
If she be mated with an equal husband ? 140

Old Ath. Three talents on the present ; in future, all.
Tim. This gentleman of mine hath served me long :
To build his fortune I will strain a little,
For 'tis a bond in men. Give him thy daughter :
What you bestow, in him I'll counterpoise,
And make him weigh with her.
Old Ath.　　Most noble lord,
Pawn me to this your honor, she is his.
Tim. My hand to thee ; mine honor on my promise.
Luc. Humbly I thank your lordship : never may
The state or fortune fall into my keeping, 150
Which is not owed to you !
　　　　[*Exeunt Lucilius and Old Athenian.*
Poet. Vouchsafe my labor, and long live your lordship !
Tim. I thank you ; you shall hear from me anon :
Go not away. What have you there, my friend ?
Pain. A piece of painting, which I do beseech
Your lordship to accept.
Tim.　　　Painting is welcome.
The painting is almost the natural man ;
For since dishonor traffics with man's nature,
He is but outside : these pencill'd figures are
Even such as they give out. I like your work ;
And you shall find I like it : wait attendance
Till you hear further from me.
Pain.　　The gods preserve ye !
Tim. Well fare you, gentleman : give me your hand ;
We must needs dine together. Sir, your jewel
Hath suffer'd under praise.
Jew.　　What, my lord ! dispraise ?
Tim. A mere satiety of commendations.
If I should pay you for't as 'tis extoll'd,
It would unclew me quite.
Jew.　　My lord, 'tis rated
As those which sell would give : but you well know,
Things of like value differing in the owners
Are prized by their masters : believe't, dear lord,　　171
You mend the jewel by the wearing it.
Tim. Well mock'd.
Mer. No, my good lord ; he speaks the common tongue,
Which all men speak with him.
Tim. Look, who comes here : will you be chid ?

　　Enter APEMANTUS.

Jew. We'll bear, with your lordship.
Mer.　　　He'll spare none.
Tim. Good morrow to thee, gentle Apemantus !
Apem. Till I be gentle, stay thou for thy good morrow ;
When thou art Timon's dog, and these knaves honest.　　180
Tim. Why dost thou call them knaves ? thou know'st them not.
Apem. Are they not Athenians ?
Tim. Yes.
Apem. Then I repent not.
Jew. You know me, Apemantus ?

Apem. Thou know'st I do : I call'd thee by thy name.

Tim. Thou art proud, Apemantus.

Apem. Of nothing so much as that I am not like Timon.   190

Tim. Whither art going ?

Apem. To knock out an honest Athenian's brains.

Tim. That's a deed thou'lt die for.

Apem. Right, if doing nothing be death by the law.

Tim. How likest thou this picture, Apemantus ?   199

Apem. The best, for the innocence.

Tim. Wrought he not well that painted it ?

Apem. He wrought better that made the painter ; and yet he's but a filthy piece of work.

Pain. You're a dog.

Apem. Thy mother's of my generation : what's she, if I be a dog ?

Tim. Wilt dine with me, Apemantus ?

Apem. No ; I eat not lords.

Tim. An thou shouldst, thou 'ldst anger ladies.

Apem. O, they eat lords ; so they come by great bellies.   210

Tim. That's a lascivious apprehension.

Apem. So thou apprehendest it : take it for thy labor.

Tim. How dost thou like this jewel, Apemantus ?

Apem. Not so well as plain-dealing, which will not cost a man a doit.

Tim. What dost thou think 'tis worth ?

Apem. Not worth my thinking. How now, poet !   220

Poet. How now, philosopher !

Apem. Thou liest.

Poet. Art not one ?

Apem. Yes.

Poet. Then I lie not.

Apem. Art not a poet ?

Poet. Yes.

Apem. Then thou liest : look in thy last work, where thou hast feigned him a worthy fellow.

Poet. That's not feigned ; he is so.   230

Apem. Yes, he is worthy of thee, and to pay thee for thy labor : he that loves to be flattered is worthy o' the flatterer. Heavens, that I were a lord !

Tim. What wouldst do then, Apemantus ?

Apem. E'en as Apemantus does now ; hate a lord with my heart.

Tim. What, thyself ?

Apem. Ay.

Tim. Wherefore ?   240

Apem. That I had no angry wit to be a lord.
Art not thou a merchant ?

Mer. Ay, Apemantus.

Apem. Traffic confound thee, if the gods will not !

Mer. If traffic do it, the gods do it.

Apem. Traffic's thy god ; and thy god confound thee !

Trumpet sounds. Enter a Messenger.

Tim. What trumpet's that ?

Mess. 'Tis Alcibiades, and some twenty horse,   250
All of companionship.

Tim. Pray, entertain them ; give them guide to us.   [*Exeunt some Attendants.*
You must needs dine with me : go not you hence
Till I have thank'd you : when dinner's done,
Show me this piece. I am joyful of your sights.

Enter ALCIBIADES, *with the rest.*

Most welcome, sir !

Apem.   So, so, there !
Aches contract and starve your supple joints !
That there should be small love 'mongst these sweet knaves,
And all this courtesy ! The strain of man's bred out
Into baboon and monkey.   260

Alcib. Sir, you have saved my longing, and I feed
Most hungerly on your sight.

Tim.   Right welcome, sir !
Ere we depart, we'll share a bounteous time
In different pleasures. Pray you, let us in.
               [*Exeunt all except Apemantus.*

Enter two Lords.

First Lord. What time o' day is't, Apemantus ?

Apem. Time to be honest.

First Lord. That time serves still.

Apem. The more accursed thou, that still omitt'st it.

Sec. Lord. Thou art going to Lord Timon's feast ?   270

Apem. Ay, to see meat fill knaves and wine heat fools.

Sec. Lord. Fare thee well, fare thee well.

Apem. Thou art a fool to bid me farewell twice.

Sec. Lord. Why, Apemantus ?

Apem. Shouldst have kept one to thyself, for I mean to give thee none.

First Lord. Hang thyself !

Apem. No, I will do nothing at thy bidding : make thy requests to thy friend.

Sec. Lord. Away, unpeaceable dog, or I'll spurn thee hence !   281

Apem. I will fly, like a dog, the heels o' the ass.   [*Exit.*

First Lord. He's opposite to humanity. Come, shall we in,
And taste Lord Timon's bounty ? he outgoes
The very heart of kindness.

Sec. Lord. He pours it out ; Plutus, the god of gold,
Is but his steward : no meed, but he repays
Sevenfold above itself ; no gift to him,
But breeds the giver a return exceeding   290
All use of quittance.

First Lord.   The noblest mind he carries
That ever govern'd man.

Sec. Lord. Long may he live in fortunes ! Shall we in ?

First Lord. I'll keep you company.
                                        [*Exeunt.*

SCENE II. *A banqueting-room in Timon's house.*

Hautboys playing loud music. A great banquet served in ; FLAVIUS *and others attending ; then enter* LORD TIMON, ALCIBIADES, *Lords, Senators, and* VENTIDIUS. *Then*

comes, dropping, after all, APEMANTUS, *dis-
contentedly, like himself.*

Ven. Most honor'd Timon,
It hath pleased the gods to remember my fa-
ther's age,
And call him to long peace.
He is gone happy, and has left me rich :
Then, as in grateful virtue I am bound
To your free heart, I do return those talents,
Doubled with thanks and service, from whose
help
I derived liberty.
    Tim.   O, by no means,
Honest Ventidius ; you mistake my love :
I gave it freely ever ; and there's none   10
Can truly say he gives, if he receives :
If our betters play at that game, we must not
dare
To imitate them ; faults that are rich are fair.
    Ven. A noble spirit !
    Tim.   Nay, my lords,
    [*They all stand ceremoniously looking
                                    on Timon.*
Ceremony was but devised at first
To set a gloss on faint deeds, hollow welcomes,
Recanting goodness, sorry ere 'tis shown ;
But where there is true friendship, there needs
none.
Pray, sit ; more welcome are ye to my fortunes
Than my fortunes to me   [*They sit.*   20
    First Lord. My lord, we always have con-
fess'd it.
    Apem. Ho, ho, confess'd it ! hang'd it,
have you not ?
    Tim. O, Apemantus, you are welcome.
    Apem.   No ;
You shall not make me welcome :
I come to have thee thrust me out of doors.
    Tim. Fie, thou'rt a churl ; ye've got a hu-
mor there
Does not become a man ; 'tis much to blame.
They say, my lords, ' ira furor brevis est ; ' but
yond man is ever angry. Go, let him have a
table by himself, for he does neither affect
company, nor is he fit for't, indeed.   31
    Apem. Let me stay at thine apperil,
Timon : I come to observe ; I give thee warning on't.
    Tim. I take no heed of thee ; thou'rt an
Athenian, therefore welcome : I myself would
have no power ; prithee, let my meat make
thee silent.
    Apem. I scorn thy meat ; 'twould choke
me, for I should ne'er flatter thee. O you gods,
what a number of men eat Timon, and he sees
'em not ! It grieves me to see so many dip their
meat in one man's blood ; and all the madness
is, he cheers them up too.
I wonder men dare trust themselves with men :
Methinks they should invite them without
knives ;
Good for their meat, and safer for their lives.
There's much example for't ; the fellow that
sits next him now, parts bread with him,
pledges the breath of him in a divided draught,
is the readiest man to kill him : 't has been
proved. If I were a huge man, I should fear
to drink at meals ;   51
Lest they should spy my windpipe's dangerous
notes :
Great men should drink with harness on their
throats.

    Tim. My lord, in heart ; and let the health
go round.
    Sec. Lord. Let it flow this way, my good
lord.
    Apem. Flow this way ! A brave fellow ! he
keeps his tides well. Those healths will make
thee and thy state look ill, Timon. Here's that
which is too weak to be a sinner, honest water,
which ne'er left man i' the mire :   60
This and my food are equals ; there's no odds :
Feasts are too proud to give thanks to the
gods.

Apemantus' grace.

Immortal gods, I crave no pelf ;
I pray for no man but myself :
Grant I may never prove so fond,
To trust man on his oath or bond ;
Or a harlot, for her weeping ;
Or a dog, that seems a-sleeping :
Or a keeper with my freedom ;
Or my friends, if I should need 'em.   70
Amen. So fall to't :
Rich men sin, and I eat root.
    [*Eats and drinks.*
Much good dich thy good heart, Apemantus !
    Tim. Captain Alcibiades, your heart's in
the field now.
    Alcib. My heart is ever at your service, my
lord.
    Tim. You had rather be at a breakfast of
enemies than a dinner of friends.   79
    Alcib. So they were bleeding-new, my lord,
there's no meat like 'em : I could wish my best
friend at such a feast.
    Apem. Would all those flatterers were
thine enemies then, that then thou mightst kill
'em and bid me to 'em !
    First Lord. Might we but have that happi-
ness, my lord, that you would once use our
hearts, whereby we might express some part of
our zeals, we should think ourselves for ever
perfect.   90
    Tim. O, no doubt, my good friends, but
the gods themselves have provided that I shall
have much help from you : how had you been
my friends else ? why have you that charitable
title from thousands, did not you chiefly belong to my heart ? I have told more of you
to myself than you can with modesty speak in
your own behalf ; and thus far I confirm you.
O you gods, think I, what need we have any
friends, if we should ne'er have need of 'em ?
they were the most needless creatures living,
should we ne'er have use for 'em, and would
most resemble sweet instruments hung up in
cases that keep their sounds to themselves.
Why, I have often wished myself poorer, that
I might come nearer to you. We are born to
do benefits : and what better or properer can
we call our own than the riches of our
friends ? O, what a precious comfort 'tis, to
have so many, like brothers, commanding one
another's fortunes ! O joy, e'en made away
ere 't can be born ! Mine eyes cannot hold out
water, methinks : to forget their faults, I drink
to you.
    Apem. Thou weepest to make them drink,
Timon.
    Sec. Lord. Joy had the like conception in
our eyes
And at that instant like a babe sprung up.

Apem. Ho, ho ! I laugh to think that babe
a bastard.
Third Lord. I promise you, my lord, you
moved me much.
Apem. Much !   [*Tucket, within.*
Tim. What means that trump ?

Enter a Servant.

How now ? 120
Serv. Please you, my lord, there are certain
ladies most desirous of admittance.
Tim. Ladies ! what are their wills ?
Serv. There comes with them a forerunner,
my lord, which bears that office, to signify
their pleasures.
Tim. I pray, let them be admitted.

Enter CUPID.

Cup. Hail to thee, worthy Timon, and to
all
That of his bounties taste ! The five best senses
Acknowledge thee their patron ; and come
freely   130
To gratulate thy plenteous bosom : th' ear,
Taste, touch and smell, pleased from thy table
rise ;
They only now come but to feast thine eyes.
Tim. They're welcome all ; let 'em have
kind admittance :
Music, make their welcome !   [*Exit Cupid.*
First Lord. You see, my lord, how ample
you're beloved.

Music. Re-enter CUPID *with a mask of* Ladies
as Amazons, *with lutes in their hands, dancing and playing.*

Apem. Hoy-day, what a sweep of vanity
comes this way !
They dance ! they are mad women.
Like madness is the glory of this life,
As this pomp shows to a little oil and root. 140
We make ourselves fools, to disport ourselves ;
And spend our flatteries, to drink those men
Upon whose age we void it up again,
With poisonous spite and envy.
Who lives that's not depraved or depraves ?
Who dies, that bears not one spurn to their
graves
Of their friends' gift ?
I should fear those that dance before me now
Would one day stamp upon me : 't has been
done ;
Men shut their doors against a setting sun. 150

The Lords *rise from table, with much adoring
of* TIMON ; *and to show their loves, each
singles out an* Amazon, *and all dance, men
with women, a lofty strain or two to the
hautboys, and cease.*

Tim. You have done our pleasures much
grace, fair ladies,
Set a fair fashion on our entertainment,
Which was not half so beautiful and kind ;
You have added worth unto 't and lustre,
And entertain'd me with mine own device ;
I am to thank you for 't.
First Lady. My lord, you take us even at
the best.
Apem. 'Faith, for the worst is filthy ; and
would not hold taking, I doubt me.
Tim. Ladies, there is an idle banquet at-
tends you :   160
Please you to dispose yourselves.

All Ladies. Most thankfully, my lord.
[*Exeunt Cupid and Ladies.*
Tim. Flavius.
Flav. My lord ?
Tim.   The little casket bring me hither.
Flav. Yes, my lord. More jewels yet !
There is no crossing him in 's humor ;
[*Aside*
Else I should tell him,—well, i' faith, I should,
When all's spent, he 'ld be cross'd then, an he
could.
'Tis pity bounty had not eyes behind,
That man might ne'er be wretched for his
mind.   [*Exit.*
First Lord. Where be our men ?   171
Serv. Here, my lord, in readiness.
Sec. Lord. Our horses !

Re-enter FLAVIUS, *with the casket.*

Tim.   O my friends,
I have one word to say to you : look you, my
good lord,
I must entreat you, honor me so much
As to advance this jewel ; accept it and wear
it,
Kind my lord.
First Lord. I am so far already in your
gifts,—
All. So are we all.

Enter a Servant.

Serv. My lord, there are certain nobles of
the senate   180
Newly alighted, and come to visit you.
Tim. They are fairly welcome.
Flav.   I beseech your honor,
Vouchsafe me a word ; it does concern you
near.
Tim. Near ! why then, another time I'll
hear thee :
I prithee, let's be provided to show them enter-
tainment.
Flav. [*Aside*] I scarce know how.

Enter a second Servant.

Sec. Serv. May it please your honor, Lord
Lucius,
Out of his free love, hath presented to you
Four milk-white horses, trapp'd in silver.
Tim. I shall accept them fairly ; let the
presents
Be worthily entertain'd.

Enter a third Servant.

How now ! what news ? 191
Third Serv. Please you, my lord, that hon-
orable gentleman, Lord Lucullus, entreats your
company to-morrow to hunt with him, and has
sent your honor two brace of greyhounds.
Tim. I'll hunt with him ; and let them be
received,
Not without fair reward.
Flav.   [*Aside*] What will this come to ?
He commands us to provide, and give great
gifts,
And all out of an empty coffer :
Nor will he know his purse, or yield me this,
To show him what a beggar his heart is, 201
Being of no power to make his wishes good :
His promises fly so beyond his state
That what he speaks is all in debt ; he owes
For every word : he is so kind that he now
Pays interest for 't ; his land's put to their
books.

Well, would I were gently put out of office
Before I were forced out!
Happier is he that has no friend to feed
Than such that do e'en enemies exceed. 210
I bleed inwardly for my lord. [*Exit.*
 Tim.   You do yourselves
Much wrong, you bate too much of your own
 merits:
Here, my lord, a trifle of our love.
 Sec. Lord. With more than common
 thanks I will receive it.
 Third Lord. O, he's the very soul of
 bounty!
 Tim. And now I remember, my lord, you
 gave
Good words the other day of a bay courser
I rode on: it is yours, because you liked it.
 Sec. Lord. O, I beseech you, pardon me,
 my lord, in that.
 Tim. You may take my word, my lord; I
 know, no man   220
Can justly praise but what he does affect:
I weigh my friend's affection with mine own;
I'll tell you true. I'll call to you.
 All Lords.   O, none so welcome.
 Tim. I take all and your several visitations
So kind to heart, 'tis not enough to give;
Methinks, I could deal kingdoms to my
 friends,
And ne'er be weary. Alcibiades,
Thou art a soldier, therefore seldom rich;
It comes in charity to thee: for all thy living
Is 'mongst the dead, and all the lands thou
 hast
Lie in a pitch'd field.
 Alcib. Ay, defiled land, my lord. 231
 First Lord. We are so virtuously bound—
 Tim.   And so
Am I to you.
 Sec. Lord. So infinitely endear'd—
 Tim. All to you. Lights, more lights!
 First Lord. The best of happiness,
Honor and fortunes, keep with you, Lord
 Timon!
 Tim. Ready for his friends.
  [*Exeunt all but Apemantus and Timon.*
 Apem.   What a coil's here!
Serving of becks and jutting-out of bums!
I doubt whether their legs be worth the sums
That are given for 'em. Friendship's full of
 dregs:
Methinks, false hearts should never have sound
 legs,
Thus honest fools lay out their wealth on
 court'sies.
 Tim. Now, Apemantus, if thou wert not
sullen, I would be good to thee.
 Apem. No, I'll nothing: for if I should be
bribed too, there would be none left to rail
upon thee, and then thou wouldst sin the faster.
Thou givest so long, Timon, I fear me thou
wilt give away thyself in paper shortly: what
need these feasts, pomps and vain-glories? 249
 Tim. Nay, an you begin to rail on society
once, I am sworn not to give regard to you.
Farewell; and come with better music. [*Exit.*
 Apem. So:
Thou wilt not hear me now; thou shalt not
 then:
I'll lock thy heaven from thee.
O, that men's ears should be
To counsel deaf, but not to flattery! [*Exit.*

ACT II.

Scene I. *A Senator's house.*

Enter Senator, *with papers in his hand.*

 Sen. And late, five thousand: to Varro and
 to Isidore
He owes nine thousand; besides my former
 sum,
Which makes it five and twenty. Still in mo-
 tion
Of raging waste? It cannot hold; it will not.
If I want gold, steal but a beggar's dog,
And give it Timon, why, the dog coins gold.
If I would sell my horse, and buy twenty more
Better than he, why, give my horse to Timon,
Ask nothing, give it him, it foals me, straight,
And able horses. No porter at his gate, 10
But rather one that smiles and still invites
All that pass by. It cannot hold: no reason
Can found his state in safety. Caphis, ho!
Caphis, I say!

Enter Caphis.

 Caph. Here, sir; what is your pleasure?
 Sen. Get on your cloak, and haste you to
 Lord Timon;
Importune him for my moneys; be not ceased
With slight denial, nor then silenced when—
' Commend me to your master'—and the cap
Plays in the right hand, thus: but tell him,
My uses cry to me, I must serve my turn 20
Out of mine own; his days and times are past
And my reliances on his fracted dates
Have smit my credit: I love and honor him,
But must not break my back to heal his finger;
Immediate are my needs, and my relief
Must not be toss'd and turn'd to me in words,
But find supply immediate. Get you gone:
Put on a most importunate aspect,
A visage of demand; for, I do fear,
When every feather sticks in his own wing,
Lord Timon will be left a naked gull, 31
Which flashes now a phœnix. Get you gone.
 Caph. I go, sir.
 Sen. ' I go, sir!'—Take the bonds along
 with you,
And have the dates in compt.
 Caph.   I will, sir.
 Sen.   Go. [*Exeunt.*

Scene II. *The same. A hall in Timon's house.*

Enter Flavius, *with many bills in his hand.*

 Flav. No care, no stop! so senseless of
 expense,
That he will neither know how to maintain it,
Nor cease his flow of riot: takes no account
How things go from him, nor resumes no care
Of what is to continue: never mind
Was to be so unwise, to be so kind.
What shall be done? he will not hear, till
 feel:
I must be round with him, now he comes from
 hunting.
Fie, fie, fie, fie!

Enter Caphis, *and the Servants of* Isidore
and Varro.

 Caph. Good even, Varro: what,
You come for money?
 Var. Serv. Is't not your business too? 10

Caph. It is : and yours too, Isidore ?
Isid. Serv.   It is so.
Caph. Would we were all discharged !
Var. Serv.   I fear it.
Caph. Here comes the lord.

Enter TIMON, ALCIBIADES, *and* Lords, &c.

Tim. So soon as dinner's done, we'll forth
  again,
My Alcibiades. With me ? what is your will ?
Caph. My lord, here is a note of certain
  dues.
Tim. Dues ! Whence are you ?
Caph.   Of Athens here, my lord.
Tim. Go to my steward.
Caph. Please it your lordship, he hath put
  me off
To the succession of new days this month : 20
My master is awaked by great occasion
To call upon his own, and humbly prays you
That with your other noble parts you'll suit
In giving him his right.
Tim.   Mine honest friend,
I prithee, but repair to me next morning.
Caph. Nay, good my lord,—
Tim.   Contain thyself, good friend.
Var. Serv. One Varro's servant, my good
  lord,—
Isid. Serv.   From Isidore ;
He humbly prays your speedy payment.
Caph. If you did know, my lord, my mas-
  ter's wants—
Var. Serv. 'Twas due on forfeiture, my
  lord, six weeks   30
And past.
Isid. Serv. Your steward puts me off, my
  lord ;
And I am sent expressly to your lordship.
Tim. Give me breath.
I do beseech you, good my lords, keep on ;
I'll wait upon you instantly.
            [*Exeunt Alcibiades and Lords.*
        [*To Flav.*] Come hither : pray you,
How goes the world, that I am thus encoun-
  ter'd
With clamorous demands of date-broke bonds,
And the detention of long-since-due debts,
Against my honor ?
Flav.   Please you, gentlemen, 40
The time is unagreeable to this business :
Your importunacy cease till after dinner,
That I may make his lordship understand
Wherefore you are not paid.
Tim. Do so, my friends. See them well en-
  tertain'd.   [*Exit.*
Flav. Pray, draw near.   [*Exit.*

Enter APEMANTUS *and* Fool.

Caph. Stay, stay, here comes the fool with
Apemantus : let's ha' some sport with 'em.
Var. Serv. Hang him, he'll abuse us.
Isid. Serv. A plague upon him, dog !   50
Var. Serv. How dost, fool ?
Apem. Dost dialogue with thy shadow ?
Var. Serv. I speak not to thee.
Apem. No, 'tis to thyself. [*To the Fool*]
Come away.
Isid. Serv. There's the fool hangs on your
back already.
Apem. No, thou stand'st single, thou'rt not
  on him yet.
Caph. Where's the fool now ?
Apem. He last asked the question. Poor

rogues, and usurers' men ! bawds between gold
and want !
All Serv. What are we, Apemantus ?
Apem. Asses.
All Serv. Why ?
Apem. That you ask me what you are, and
do not know yourselves. Speak to 'em, fool.
Fool. How do you, gentlemen ?
All Serv. Gramercies, good fool : how does
your mistress ?   70
Fool. She's e'en setting on water to scald
such chickens as you are. Would we could see
you at Corinth !
Apem. Good ! gramercy.

Enter Page.

Fool. Look you, here comes my mistress'
page.
Page. [*To the Fool*] Why, how now, captain ! what do you in this wise company ? How
dost thou, Apemantus ?
Apem. Would I had a rod in my mouth,
that I might answer thee profitably.   80
Page. Prithee, Apemantus, read me the
superscription of these letters : I know not
which is which.
Apem. Canst not read ?
Page. No.
Apem. There will little learning die then,
that day thou art hanged. This is to Lord
Timon ; this to Alcibiades. Go ; thou wast
born a bastard, and thou't die a bawd.   89
Page. Thou wast whelped a dog, and thou
shalt famish a dog's death. Answer not; I am
gone.   [*Exit.*
Apem. E'en so thou outrunnest grace.
Fool, I will go with you to Lord Timon's.
Fool. Will you leave me there ?
Apem. If Timon stay at home. You three
serve three usurers ?
All Serv. Ay ; would they served us !
Apem. So would I,—as good a trick as
ever hangman served thief.   100
Fool. Are you three usurers' men ?
All Serv. Ay, fool.
Fool. I think no usurer but has a fool to
his servant : my mistress is one, and I am her
fool. When men come to borrow of your mas-
ters, they approach sadly, and go away merry ;
but they enter my mistress' house merrily, and
go away sadly : the reason of this ?
Var. Serv. I could render one.   109
Apem. Do it then, that we may account
thee a whoremaster and a knave ; which notwithstanding, thou shalt be no less esteemed.
Var. Serv. What is a whoremaster, fool ?
Fool. A fool in good clothes, and something like thee. 'Tis a spirit : sometime't appears like a lord ; sometime like a lawyer ;
sometime like a philosopher, with two stones
moe than's artificial one : he is very often like
a knight ; and, generally, in all shapes that
man goes up and down in from fourscore to
thirteen, this spirit walks in.   121
Var. Serv. Thou art not altogether a fool.
Fool. Nor thou altogether a wise man : as
much foolery as I have, so much wit thou
lackest.
Apem. That answer might have become
Apemantus.
All Serv. Aside, aside ; here comes Lord
Timon.

Re-enter TIMON *and* FLAVIUS.

Apem. Come with me, fool, come.

Fool. I do not always follow lover, elder brother and woman ; sometime the philosopher. [*Exeunt Apemantus and Fool.* 131

Flav. Pray you, walk near : I'll speak with you anon.   [*Exeunt Servants.*

Tim. You make me marvel : wherefore ere this time
Had you not fully laid my state before me,
That I might so have rated my expense,
As I had leave of means ?

Flav.   You would not hear me,
At many leisures I proposed.

Tim.   Go to :
Perchance some single vantages you took.
When my indisposition put you back :
And that unaptness made your minister,   140
Thus to excuse yourself.

Flav.   O my good lord,
At many times I brought in my accounts,
Laid them before you ; you would throw them off,
And say, you found them in mine honesty.
When, for some trifling present, you have bid me
Return so much, I have shook my head and wept ;
Yea, 'gainst the authority of manners, pray'd you
To hold your hand more close : I did endure
Not seldom, nor no slight checks, when I have
Prompted you in the ebb of your estate   150
And your great flow of debts. My loved lord,
Though you hear now, too late—yet now's a time—
The greatest of your having lacks a half
To pay your present debts.

Tim.   Let all my land be sold.

Flav. 'Tis all engaged, some forfeited and gone ;
And what remains will hardly stop the mouth
Of present dues : the future comes apace :
What shall defend the interim ? and at length
How goes our reckoning ?

Tim. To Lacedæmon did my land extend.

Flav. O my good lord, the world is but a word :   161
Were it all yours to give it in a breath,
How quickly were it gone !

Tim.   You tell me true.

Flav. If you suspect my husbandry or falsehood,
Call me before the exactest auditors
And set me on the proof. So the gods bless me,
When all our offices have been oppress'd
With riotous feeders, when our vaults have wept
With drunken spilth of wine, when every room
Hath blazed with lights and bray'd with minstrelsy,   170
I have retired me to a wasteful cock,
And set mine eyes at flow.

Tim.   Prithee, no more.

Flav. Heavens, have I said, the bounty of this lord !
How many prodigal bits have slaves and peasants
This night englutted ! Who is not Timon's ?
What heart, head, sword, force, means, but is Lord Timon's ?
Great Timon, noble, worthy, royal Timon !

Ah, when the means are gone that buy this praise,
The breath is gone whereof this praise is made :
Feast-won, fast-lost ; one cloud of winter showers,
These flies are couch'd.

Tim.   Come, sermon me no further :
No villanous bounty yet hath pass'd my heart ;
Unwisely, not ignobly, have I given.
Why dost thou weep ? Canst thou the conscience lack,
To think I shall lack friends ? Secure thy heart ;
If I would broach the vessels of my love,
And try the argument of hearts by borrowing,
Men and men's fortunes could I frankly use
As I can bid thee speak.

Flav.   Assurance bless your thoughts !

Tim. And, in some sort, these wants of mine are crown'd,   190
That I account them blessings ; for by these
Shall I try friends : you shall perceive how you
Mistake my fortunes ; I am wealthy in my friends.
Within there ! Flaminius ! Servilius !

Enter FLAMINIUS, SERVILIUS, *and other* Servants.

Servants. My lord ? my lord ?

Tim. I will dispatch you severally ; you to Lord Lucius ; to Lord Lucullus you : I hunted with his honor to-day : you, to Sempronius : commend me to their loves, and, I am proud, say, that my occasions have found time to use 'em toward a supply of money : let the request be fifty talents.

Flam. As you have said, my lord.

Flav. [*Aside*] Lord Lucius and Lucullus ? hum !

Tim. Go you, sir, to the senators—
Of whom, even to the state's best health, I have
Deserved this hearing—bid 'em send o' the instant
A thousand talents to me.

Flav.   I have been bold—
For that I knew it the most general way—
To them to use your signet and your name ;
But they do shake their heads, and I am here
No richer in return.

Tim.   Is't true ? can't be ?

Flav. They answer, in a joint and corporate voice,
That now they are at fall, want treasure, cannot
Do what they would ; are sorry—you are honorable,—
But yet they could have wish'd—they know not—
Something hath been amiss—a noble nature
May catch a wrench—would all were well—
'tis pity ;—
And so, intending other serious matters,   220
After distasteful looks and these hard fractions,
With certain half-caps and cold-moving nods
They froze me into silence.

Tim.   You gods, reward them !
Prithee, man, look cheerly. These old fellows
Have their ingratitude in them hereditary :
Their blood is caked, 'tis cold, it seldom flows ;
'Tis lack of kindly warmth they are not kind ;

And nature, as it grows again toward earth,
Is fashion'd for the journey, dull and heavy.
[*To a Serv.*] Go to Ventidius. [*To Flav.*]
   Prithee, be not sad,   229
Thou art true and honest; ingeniously I speak,
No blame belongs to thee. [*To Serv.*] Ventid-
   ius lately
Buried his father; by whose death he's stepp'd
Into a great estate: when he was poor,
Imprison'd and in scarcity of friends,
I clear'd him with five talents: greet him from
   me;
Bid him suppose some good necessity
Touches his friend, which craves to be remem-
   ber'd
With those five talents [*Exit Serv.*] [*To Flav.*]
   That had, give't these fellows
To whom 'tis instant due. Ne'er speak, or
   think,
That Timon's fortunes 'mong his friends can
   sink.   240
  Flav. I would I could not think it : that
   thought is bounty's foe;
Being free itself, it thinks all others so.
                          [*Exeunt.*

ACT III.

Scene I. *A room in Lucullus' house.*

Flaminius *waiting. Enter a* Servant *to him.*

  Serv. I have told my lord of you; he is
   coming down to you.
  Flam. I thank you, sir.

Enter Lucullus.

  Serv. Here's my lord.
  Lucul. [*Aside*] One of Lord Timon's
men ? a gift, I warrant. Why, this hits right; I
dreamt of a silver basin and ewer to-night.
Flaminius, honest Flaminius; you are very respectively welcome, sir. Fill me some wine.
[*Exit Serv.*] And how does that honorable,
complete, free-hearted gentleman of Athens,
thy very bountiful good lord and master ?   11
  Flam. His health is well sir.
  Lucul. I am right glad that his health is
well, sir : and what hast thou there under thy
cloak, pretty Flaminius ?
  Flam. 'Faith, nothing but an empty box,
sir; which, in my lord's behalf, I come to entreat your honor to supply; who, having great
and instant occasion to use fifty talents, hath
sent to your lordship to furnish him, nothing
doubting your present assistance therein.   21
  Lucul. La, la, la, la! 'nothing doubting,'
says he ? Alas, good lord! a noble gentleman
'tis, if he would not keep so good a house.
Many a time and often I ha' dined with him,
and told him on't, and come again to supper to
him, of purpose to have him spend less, and
yet he would embrace no counsel, take no
warning by my coming. Every man has his
fault, and honesty is his : I ha' told him on't,
but I could ne'er get him from't.   31

Re-enter Servant, *with wine.*

  Serv. Please your lordship, here is the wine.
  Lucul. Flaminius, I have noted thee always
wise. Here's to thee.
  Flam. Your lordship speaks your pleasure.
  Lucul. I have observed thee always for a

towardly prompt spirit—give thee thy due—
and one that knows what belongs to reason;
and canst use the time well, if the time use
thee well : good parts in thee. [*To Serv.*] Get
you gone, sirrah [*Exit Serv.*]. Draw nearer,
honest Flaminius. Thy lord's a bountiful gentleman : but thou art wise; and thou knowest
well enough, although thou comest to me, that
this is no time to lend money, especially upon
bare friendship, without security. Here's three
solidares for thee : good boy, wink at me, and
say thou sawest me not. Fare thee well.
  Flam. Is't possible the world should so
   much differ,
And we alive that lived ? Fly, damned baseness,
To him that worships thee!   51
         [*Throwing the money back.*
  Lucul. Ha! now I see thou art a fool, and
fit for thy master.   [*Exit.*
  Flam. May these add to the number that
   may scald thee!
Let molten coin be thy damnation,
Thou disease of a friend, and not himself!
Has friendship such a faint and milky heart,
It turns in less than two nights ? O you gods,
I feel my master's passion! this slave,   59
Unto his honor, has my lord's meat in him :
Why should it thrive and turn to nutriment,
When he is turn'd to poison ?
O, may diseases only work upon't!
And, when he's sick to death, let not that part
   of nature
Which my lord paid for, be of any power
To expel sickness, but prolong his hour! [*Exit.*

Scene II. *A public place.*

Enter Lucius, *with three Strangers.*

  Luc. Who, the Lord Timon ? he is my very
good friend, and an honorable gentleman.
  First Stran. We know him for no less,
though we are but strangers to him. But I can
tell you one thing, my lord, and which I hear
from common rumors : now Lord Timon's
happy hours are done and past, and his estate
shrinks from him.
  Luc. Fie, no, do not believe it; he cannot
want for money.   10
  Sec. Stran. But believe you this, my lord,
that, not long ago, one of his men was with
the Lord Lucullus to borrow so many talents,
nay, urged extremely for't and showed what
necessity belonged to't, and yet was denied.
  Luc. How!
  Sec. Stran. I tell you, denied, my lord.
  Luc. What a strange case was that! now,
before the gods, I am ashamed on't. Denied
that honorable man! there was very little
honor showed in't. For my own part, I must
needs confess, I have received some small
kindnesses from him, as money, plate, jewels
and such-like trifles, nothing comparing to
his; yet, had he mistook him and sent to me, I
should ne'er have denied his occasion so many
talents.

Enter Servilius.

  Ser. See, by good hap, yonder's my lord;
I have sweat to see his honor. My honored
lord,—   [*To Lucius.*
  Luc. Servilius! you are kindly met, sir.
Fare thee well : commend me to thy honor-
able virtuous lord, my very exquisite friend.

Ser. May it please your honor, my lord
hath sent—

Luc. Ha! what has he sent? I am so much
endeared to that lord; he's ever sending: how
shall I thank him, thinkest thou? And what
has he sent now?

Ser. Has only sent his present occasion
now, my lord; requesting your lordship to supply his instant use with so many talents.   41

Luc. I know his lordship is but merry with
me;
He cannot want fifty five hundred talents.

Ser. But in the mean time he wants less,
my lord.
If his occasion were not virtuous,
I should not urge it half so faithfully.

Luc. Dost thou speak seriously, Servilius?

Ser. Upon my soul, 'tis true, sir.

Luc. What a wicked beast was I to disfurnish myself against such a good time, when
I might ha' shown myself honorable! how unluckily it happened, that I should purchase
the day before for a little part, and undo a
great deal of honor! Servilius, now, before
the gods, I am not able to do,—the more beast,
I say:—I was sending to use Lord Timon myself, these gentlemen can witness! but I would
not, for the wealth of Athens, I had done't
now. Commend me bountifully to his good
lordship; and I hope his honor will conceive
the fairest of me, because I have no power to
be kind: and tell him this from me, I count
it one of my greatest afflictions, say, that I
cannot pleasure such an honorable gentleman.
Good Servilius, will you befriend me so far,
as to use mine own words to him?

Ser. Yes, sir, I shall.

Luc. I'll look you out a good turn, Servil-
ius.   [*Exit Servilius.*
True, as you said, Timon is shrunk indeed;
And he that's once denied will hardly speed.
                             [*Exit.*

First Stran. Do you observe this, Hostilius?

Sec. Stran.   Ay, too well.   70

First Stran. Why, this is the world's soul;
     and just of the same piece
Is every flatterer's spirit. Who can call him
His friend that dips in the same dish? for, in
My knowing, Timon has been this lord's fa-
     ther,
And kept his credit with his purse,
Supported his estate; nay, Timon's money
Has paid his men their wages: he ne'er drinks,
But Timon's silver treads upon his lip;
And yet—O, see the monstrousness of man
When he looks out in an ungrateful shape!—
He does deny him, in respect of his,   81
What charitable men afford to beggars.

Third Stran. Religion groans at it.

First Stran.   For mine own part,
I never tasted Timon in my life,
Nor came any of his bounties over me,
To mark me for his friend; yet, I protest,
For his right noble mind, illustrious virtue
And honorable carriage,
Had his necessity made use of me,
I would have put my wealth into donation,   90
And the best half should have return'd to him,
So much I love his heart: but, I perceive,
Men must learn now with pity to dispense;
For policy sits above conscience.   [*Exeunt.*

SCENE III.   *A room in Sempronius' house.*

Enter SEMPRONIUS, *and a* Servant *of* TIMON'S.

Sem. Must he needs trouble me in 't,—
     hum!—'bove all others?
He might have tried Lord Lucius or Lucullus;
And now Ventidius is wealthy too,
Whom he redeem'd from prison: all these
Owe their estates unto him.

Serv.   My lord,
They have all been touch'd and found base
     metal, for
They have all denied him.

Sem.   How! have they denied him?
Has Ventidius and Lucullus denied him?
And does he send to me? Three? hum!   9
It shows but little love or judgment in him:
Must I be his last refuge! His friends, like
     physicians,
Thrive, give him over: must I take the cure
     upon me?
Has much disgraced me in't; I'm angry at
     him,
That might have known my place: I see no
     sense for't,
But his occasion might have woo'd me first;
For, in my conscience, I was the first man
That e'er received gift from him:
And does he think so backwardly of me now,
That I'll requite his last? No:
So it may prove an argument of laughter   20
To the rest, and 'mongst lords I be thought a
     fool.
I'ld rather than the worth of thrice the sum,
Had sent to me first, but for my mind's sake;
I'd such a courage to do him good. But now
     return,
And with their faint reply this answer join;
Who bates mine honor shall not know my
     coin.   [*Exit.*

Serv. Excellent! Your lordship's a goodly
villain. The devil knew not what he did when
he made man politic; he crossed himself by
't: and I cannot think but, in the end, the
villainies of man will set him clear. How
fairly this lord strives to appear foul! takes
virtuous copies to be wicked, like those that
under hot ardent zeal would set whole realms
on fire:
Of such a nature is his politic love.
This was my lord's best hope; now all are fled,
Save only the gods: now his friends are dead,
Doors, that were ne'er acquainted with their
     wards
Many a bounteous year must be employ'd
Now to guard sure their master.   40
And this is all a liberal course allows;
Who cannot keep his wealth must keep his
     house.   [*Exit.*

SCENE IV.   *The same. A hall in Timon's
house.*

Enter two Servants *of* VARRO, *and the* Servant
of LUCIUS, *meeting* TITUS, HORTENSIUS, *and
other* Servants *of* TIMON'S *creditors, waiting
his coming out.*

First Var. Serv. Well met; good morrow,
Titus and Hortensius.

Tit. The like to you kind Varro.

Hor.   Lucius!
What, do we meet together?

Luc. Serv.   Ay, and I think

One business does command us all ; for mine
Is money.
Tit. So is theirs and ours.

Enter Philotus.

Luc. Serv.   And Sir Philotus too !
Phi. Good day at once.
Luc. Serv.   Welcome, good brother.
What do you think the hour ?
Phi.   Laboring for nine.
Luc. Serv. So much ?
Phi.   Is not my lord seen yet ?
Luc. Serv.   Not yet.
Phi. I wonder on't ; he was wont to shine
at seven.   10
Luc. Serv. Ay, but the days are wax'd
shorter with him :
You must consider that a prodigal course
Is like the sun's ; but not, like his, recover-
able.
I fear 'tis deepest winter in Lord Timon's
purse ;
That is, one may reach deep enough, and yet
Find little.
Phi. I am of your fear for that.
Tit. I'll show you how to observe a strange
event.
Your lord sends now for money.
Hor.   Most true, he does.
Tit. And he wears jewels now of Timon's
gift,
For which I wait for money.   20
Hor. It is against my heart.
Luc. Serv.   Mark, how strange it shows,
Timon in this should pay more than he owes :
And e'en as if your lord should wear rich
jewels,
And send for money for 'em.
Hor. I'm weary of this charge, the gods
can witness :
I know my lord hath spent of Timon's wealth,
And now ingratitude makes it worse than
stealth.
First Var. Serv. Yes, mine's three thou-
sand crowns : what's yours ?
Luc. Serv. Five thousand mine.
First Var. Serv. 'Tis much deep : and it
should seem by the sun,   30
Your master's confidence was above mine ;
Else, surely, his had equall'd.

Enter Flaminius.

Tit. One of Lord Timon's men.
Luc. Serv. Flaminius ! Sir, a word : pray,
is my lord ready to come forth ?
Flam. No, indeed, he is not.
Tit. We attend his lordship ; pray, signify
so much.
Flam. I need not tell him that ; he knows
you are too diligent.   [*Exit.* 40

Enter Flavius *in a cloak, muffled.*

Luc. Serv. Ha ! is not that his steward
muffled so ?
He goes away in a cloud : call him, call him.
Tit. Do you hear, sir ?
Sec. Var. Serv. By your leave, sir,—
Flav. What do ye ask of me, my friend ?
Tit. We wait for certain money here, sir.
Flav.   Ay,
If money were as certain as your waiting,
'Twere sure enough.

Why then preferr'd you not your sums and
bills,
When your false masters eat of my lord's
meat ?   50
Then they could smile and fawn upon his
debts
And take down the interest into their glutton-
ous maws.
You do yourselves but wrong to stir me up ;
Let me pass quietly :
Believe 't, my lord and I have made an end ;
I have no more to reckon, he to spend.
Luc. Serv. Ay, but this answer will not
serve.
Flav. If 'twill not serve, 'tis not so base as
you ;
For you serve knaves.   [*Exit.*
First Var. Serv. How ! what does his cash-
iered worship mutter ?   61
Sec. Var. Serv. No matter what ; he's poor,
and that's revenge enough. Who can speak
broader than he that has no house to put his
head in ? such may rail against great buildings.

Enter Servilius.

Tit. O, here's Servilius ; now we shall know
some answer.
Ser. If I might beseech you, gentlemen, to
repair some other hour, I should derive much
from't ; for, take't of my soul, my lord leans
wondrously to discontent : his comfortable
temper has forsook him ; he's much out of
health, and keeps his chamber.
Luc. Serv. Many do keep their chambers
are not sick :
And, if it be so far beyond his health,
Methinks he should the sooner pay his debts,
And make a clear way to the gods.
Ser.   Good gods !
Tit. We cannot take this for answer, sir.
Flam. [*Within*] Servilius, help ! My lord !
my lord !

Enter Timon, *in a rage,* Flaminius *following.*

Tim. What, are my doors opposed against
my passage ?   80
Have I been ever free, and must my house
Be my retentive enemy, my gaol ?
The place which I have feasted, does it now,
Like all mankind, show me an iron heart ?
Luc. Serv. Put in now, Titus.
Tit. My lord, here is my bill.
Luc. Serv. Here's mine.
Hor. And mine, my lord.
Both Var. Serv. And ours, my lord.
Phi. All our bills.   90
Tim. Knock me down with 'em : cleave
me to the girdle.
Luc. Serv. Alas, my lord,—
Tim. Cut my heart in sums.
Tit. Mine, fifty talents.
Tim. Tell out my blood.
Luc. Serv. Five thousand crowns, my lord.
Tim. Five thousand drops pays that. What
yours ?—and yours ?
First Var. Serv. My lord,—
Sec. Var. Serv. My lord,—
Tim. Tear me, take me, and the gods fall
upon you !   [*Exit.* 100
Hor. 'Faith, I perceive our masters may
throw their caps at their money : these debts
may well be called desperate ones, for a mad-
man owes 'em.   [*Exeunt.*

Re-enter TIMON *and* FLAVIUS.

Tim. They have e'en put my breath from
　me, the slaves.
Creditors ? devils !
Flav. My dear lord,—
Tim. What if it should be so ?
Flav. My lord,—
Tim. I'll have it so. My steward !
Flav. Here, my lord.　　　　　　110
Tim. So fitly ? Go, bid all my friends
　again,
Lucius, Lucullus, and Sempronius :
All, sirrah, all :
I'll once more feast the rascals.
Flav.　　　　　　O my lord,
You only speak from your distracted soul ;
There is not so much left, to furnish out
A moderate table.
Tim.　　　Be't not in thy care ; go,
I charge thee, invite them all : let in the tide
Of knaves once more ; my cook and I'll pro-
　vide.　　　　　　　　　[*Exeunt.*

SCENE V. *The same.　The senate-house.*

The Senate sitting.

First Sen. My lord, you have my voice to
　it ; the fault's
Bloody ; 'tis necessary he should die :
Nothing emboldens sin so much as mercy.
Sec. Sen. Most true ; the law shall bruise
　him.

Enter ALCIBIADES, *with* Attendants.

Alcib. Honor, health, and compassion to
　the senate !
First Sen. Now, captain ?
Alcib. I am an humble suitor to your
　virtues ;
For pity is the virtue of the law,
And none but tyrants use it cruelly.
It pleases time and fortune to lie heavy　10
Upon a friend of mine, who, in hot blood,
Hath stepp'd into the law, which is past depth
To those that, without heed, do plunge into 't.
He is a man, setting his fate aside,
Of comely virtues :
Nor did he soil the fact with cowardice—
An honor in him which buys out his fault—
But with a noble fury and fair spirit,
Seeing his reputation touch'd to death,
He did oppose his foe :　　　　　20
And with such sober and unnoted passion
He did behave his anger, ere 'twas spent,
As if he had but proved an argument.
First Sen. You undergo too strict a para-
　dox,
Striving to make an ugly deed look fair :
Your words have took such pains as if they
　labor'd
To bring manslaughter into form and set
　quarrelling
Upon the head of valor ; which indeed
Is valor misbegot and came into the world
When sects and factions were newly born : 30
He's truly valiant that can wisely suffer
The worst that man can breathe, and make
　his wrongs
His outsides, to wear them like his raiment,
　carelessly,
And ne'er prefer his injuries to his heart,
To bring it into danger.

If wrongs be evils and enforce us kill,
What folly 'tis to hazard life for ill !
Alcib. My lord,—
First Sen.　　　You cannot make gross sins
　look clear :
To revenge is no valor, but to bear.
Alcib. My lords, then, under favor, pardon
　me,　　　　　　　　　　40
If I speak like a captain.
Why do fond men expose themselves to battle,
And not endure all threats ? sleep upon 't,
And let the foes quietly cut their throats,
Without repugnancy ? If there be
Such valor in the bearing, what make we
Abroad ? why then, women are more valiant
That stay at home, if bearing carry it,
And the ass more captain than the lion, the
　felon
Loaden with irons wiser than the judge,　50
If wisdom be in suffering. O my lords,
As you are great, be pitifully good :
Who cannot condemn rashness in cold blood ?
To kill, I grant, is sin's extremest gust ;
But, in defence, by mercy, 'tis most just.
To be in anger is impiety ;
But who is man that is not angry ?
Weigh but the crime with this.
Sec. Sen.　　　You breathe in vain.
Alcib.　　　　　In vain ! his service done
At Lacedæmon and Byzantium　　　60
Were a sufficient briber for his life.
First Sen. What's that ?
Alcib. I say, my lords, he has done fair
　service,
And slain in fight many of your enemies :
How full of valor did he bear himself
In the last conflict, and made plenteous
　wounds !
Sec. Sen. He has made too much plenty
　with 'em ;
He's a sworn rioter : he has a sin that often
Drowns him, and takes his valor prisoner :
If there were no foes, that were enough　70
To overcome him : in that beastly fury
He has been known to commit outrages,
And cherish factions : 'tis inferr'd to us,
His days are foul and his drink dangerous.
First Sen. He dies.
Alcib. Hard fate ! he might have died in
　war.
My lords, if not for any parts in him—
Though his right arm might purchase his own
　time
And be in debt to none—yet, more to move
　you,
Take my deserts to his, and join 'em both :
And, for I know your reverend ages love　80
Security, I'll pawn my victories, all
My honors to you, upon his good returns.
If by this crime he owes the law his life,
Why, let the war receive 't in valiant gore ;
For law is strict, and war is nothing more.
First Sen. We are for law : he dies ; urge
　it no more,
On height of our displeasure : friend or
　brother,
He forfeits his own blood that spills another.
Alcib. Must it be so ? it must not be. My
　lords,
I do beseech you, know me.　　　　90
Sec. Sen. How !
Alcib. Call me to your remembrances.

Third Sen.   What !
Alcib. I cannot think but your age has for-
    got me ;
It could not else be, I should prove so base,
To sue, and be denied such common grace :
My wounds ache at you.
First Sen.   Do you dare our anger ?
'Tis in few words, but spacious in effect ;
We banish thee for ever.
Alcib.   Banish me !
Banish your dotage ; banish usury,
That makes the senate ugly.   100
First Sen. If, after two days' shine, Athens
    contain thee,
Attend our weightier judgment. And, not to
    swell our spirit,
He shall be executed presently.
                          [*Exeunt Senators.*
Alcib. Now the gods keep you old enough ;
    that you may live
Only in bone, that none may look on you !
I'm worse than mad : I have kept back their
    foes,
While they have told their money and let out
Their coin upon large interest, I myself
Rich only in large hurts. All those for this ?
Is this the balsam that the usuring senate 110
Pours into captains' wounds ? Banishment !
It comes not ill ; I hate not to be banish'd ;
It is a cause worthy my spleen and fury,
That I may strike at Athens. I'll cheer up
My discontented troops, and lay for hearts.
'Tis honor with most lands to be at odds ;
Soldiers should brook as little wrongs as gods.
                                    [*Exit.*

SCENE VI. *The same. A banqueting-room
            in Timon's house.*

Music. Tables set out : Servants *attending.
    Enter divers* Lords, Senators *and others, at
    several doors.*

First Lord. The good time of day to you,
    sir.
Sec. Lord. I also wish it to you. I think
this honorable lord did but try us this other
day.
First Lord. Upon that were my thoughts
tiring, when we encountered : I hope it is not
so low with him as he made it seem in the
trial of his several friends.
Sec. Lord. It should not be, by the persuasion of his new feasting.   9
First Lord. I should think so : he hath sent
me an earnest inviting, which many my near
occasions did urge me to put off ; but he hath
conjured me beyond them, and I must needs
appear.
Sec. Lord. In like manner was I in debt to
my importunate business, but he would not
hear my excuse. I am sorry, when he sent to
borrow of me, that my provision was out.
First Lord. I am sick of that grief too, as
I understand how all things go.   20
Sec. Lord. Every man here 's so. What
would he have borrowed of you ?
First Lord. A thousand pieces.
Sec. Lord. A thousand pieces !
First Lord. What of you ?
Sec. Lord. He sent to me, sir,—Here he
comes.

Enter TIMON *and* Attendants.

Tim. With all my heart, gentlemen both ;
and how fare you ?
First Lord. Ever at the best, hearing well
of your lordship.   30
Sec. Lord. The swallow follows not summer more willing than we your lordship.
Tim. [*Aside*] Nor more willingly leaves
winter ; such summer-birds are men. Gentlemen, our dinner will not recompense this long
stay : feast your ears with the music awhile,
if they will fare so harshly o' the trumpet's
sound ; we shall to 't presently.
First Lord. I hope it remains not unkindly
with your lordship that I returned you an
empty messenger.   41
Tim. O, sir, let it not trouble you.
Sec. Lord. My noble lord,—
Tim. Ah, my good friend, what cheer ?
Sec. Lord. My most honorable lord, I am
e'en sick of shame, that, when your lordship
this other day sent to me, I was so unfortunate
a beggar.
Tim. Think not on 't, sir.
Sec. Lord. If you had sent but two hours
before,—   51
Tim. Let it not cumber your better remem-
brance. [*The banquet brought in.*] Come,
bring in all together.
Sec. Lord. All covered dishes !
First Lord Royal cheer, I warrant you.
Third Lord. Doubt not that, if money and
the season can yield it.
First Lord. How do you ? What's the
news ?
Third Lord. Alcibiades is banished : hear
you of it ?   61
First and Sec. Lord. Alcibiades banished !
Third Lord. 'Tis so, be sure of it.
First Lord. How ! how !
Sec. Lord. I pray you, upon what ?
Tim. My worthy friends, will you draw
    near ?
Third Lord. I'll tell you more anon. Here's
a noble feast toward.
Sec. Lord. This is the old man still.
Third Lord. Will 't hold ? will 't hold ? 70
Sec. Lord. It does : but time will—and
so—
Third Lord. I do conceive.
Tim. Each man to his stool, with that spur
as he would to the lip of his mistress : your
diet shall be in all places alike. Make not a
city feast of it, to let the meat cool ere we can
agree upon the first place : sit, sit. The gods
require our thanks.

You great benefactors, sprinkle our society
with thankfulness. For your own gifts, make
yourselves praised : but reserve still to give,
lest your deities be despised. Lend to each
man enough, that one need not lend to another ; for, were your godheads to borrow of
men, men would forsake the gods. Make the
meat be beloved more than the man that gives
it. Let no assembly of twenty be without a
score of villains : if there sit twelve women
at the table, let a dozen of them be—as they
are. The rest of your fees, O gods—the senators of Athens, together with the common lag
of people—what is amiss in them, you gods,
make suitable for destruction. For these my
present friends, as they are to me nothing, so

in nothing bless them, and to nothing are they welcome.

Uncover, dogs, and lap.

[*The dishes are uncovered and seen to be full of warm water.*

Some speak. What does his lordship mean ?
Some other. I know not.
Tim. May you a better feast never behold,
You knot of mouth-friends ! smoke and luke-
    warm water
Is your perfection. This is Timon's last ;   100
Who, stuck and spangled with your flatteries,
Washes it off, and sprinkles in your faces
Your reeking villany.

[*Throwing the water in their faces.*
           Live loathed and long,
Most smiling, smooth, detested parasites,
Courteous destroyers, affable wolves, meek
    bears,
You fools of fortune, trencher-friends, time's
    flies,
Cap and knee slaves, vapors, and minute-
    jacks !
Of man and beast the infinite malady
Crust you quite o'er ! What, dost thou go ?
Soft ! take thy physic first—thou too—and
    thou ;—   110
Stay, I will lend thee money, borrow none.

[*Throws the dishes at them, and drives them out.*

What, all in motion ? Henceforth be no feast,
Whereat a villain 's not a welcome guest.
Burn, house ! sink, Athens ! henceforth hated
    be
Of Timon man and all humanity !   [*Exit.*

Re-enter the Lords, Senators, &c.

First Lord. How now, my lords !
Sec. Lord. Know you the quality of Lord
Timon's fury ?
Third Lord. Push ! did you see my cap ?
Fourth Lord. I have lost my gown.   120
First Lord. He's but a mad lord, and
nought but humor sways him. He gave me a
jewel th' other day, and now he has beat it
out of my hat : did you see my jewel ?
Third Lord. Did you see my cap ?
Sec. Lord. Here 'tis.
Fourth Lord. Here lies my gown.
First Lord. Let's make no stay.
Sec. Lord. Lord Timon 's mad.
Third Lord. I feel 't upon my bones. 130
Fourth Lord. One day he gives us dia-
    monds, next day stones.   [*Exeunt.*

ACT IV.

SCENE I. *Without the walls of Athens.*

Enter TIMON.

Tim. Let me look back upon thee. O thou
    wall,
That girdlest in those wolves, dive in the earth,
And fence not Athens ! Matrons, turn incon-
    tinent !
Obedience fail in children ! slaves and fools,
Pluck the grave wrinkled senate from the
    bench,
And minister in their steads ! to general filths
Convert o' the instant, green virginity,

Do 't in your parents' eyes ! bankrupts, hold
    fast ;
Rather than render back, out with your knives,
And cut your trusters' throats ! bound serv-
    ants, steal !   10
Large-handed robbers your grave masters are,
And pill by law. Maid, to thy master's bed ;
Thy mistress is o' the brothel ! Son of six-
    teen,
Pluck the lined crutch from thy old limping
    sire,
With it beat out his brains ! Piety, and fear,
Religion to the gods, peace, justice, truth,
Domestic awe, night-rest, and neighborhood,
Instruction, manners, mysteries, and trades,
Degrees, observances, customs, and laws,
Decline to your confounding contraries,   20
And let confusion live ! Plagues, incident to
    men,
Your potent and infectious fevers heap
On Athens, ripe for stroke ! Thou cold
    sciatica,
Cripple our senators, that their limbs may halt
As lamely as their manners. Lust and liberty
Creep in the minds and marrows of our youth,
That 'gainst the stream of virtue they may
    strive,
And drown themselves in riot ! Itches, blains,
Sow all the Athenian bosoms ; and their crop
Be general leprosy ! Breath infect breath, 30
That their society, as their friendship, may
Be merely poison ! Nothing I'll bear from
    thee,
But nakedness, thou detestable town !
Take thou that too, with multiplying bans !
Timon will to the woods ; where he shall find
The unkindest beast more kinder than man-
    kind.
The gods confound—hear me, you good gods
    all—
The Athenians both within and out that wall !
And grant, as Timon grows, his hate may
    grow
To the whole race of mankind, high and low !
Amen.   [*Exit.* 41

SCENE II. *Athens. A room in Timon's house.*

Enter FLAVIUS, *with two or three* Servants.

First Serv.   Hear you, master steward,
where's our master ?
Are we undone ? cast off ? nothing remaining ?
Flav. Alack, my fellows, what should I say
    to you ?
Let me be recorded by the righteous gods,
I am as poor as you.
First Serv.   Such a house broke !
So noble a master fall'n ! All gone ! and not
One friend to take his fortune by the arm,
And go along with him !
Sec. Serv.   As we do turn our backs
From our companion thrown into his grave,
So his familiars to his buried fortunes   10
Slink all away, leave their false vows with him,
Like empty purses pick'd ; and his poor self,
A dedicated beggar to the air,
With his disease of all-shunn'd poverty,
Walks, like contempt, alone. More of our
    fellows.

Enter other Servants.

Flav. All broken implements of a ruin'd
house.

Third Serv. Yet do our hearts wear
      Timon's livery;
That see I by our faces; we are fellows still,
Serving alike in sorrow: leak'd is our bark,
And we, poor mates, stand on the dying deck,
Hearing the surges threat: we must all part
Into this sea of air.
   Flav.   Good fellows all,
The latest of my wealth I'll share amongst
      you.
Wherever we shall meet, for Timon's sake,
Let's yet be fellows; let's shake our heads,
      and say,
As 'twere a knell unto our master's fortunes,
'We have seen better days.' Let each take
      some;
Nay, put out all your hands. Not one word
      more:
Thus part we rich in sorrow, parting poor.
   [*Servants embrace, and part several ways.*
O, the fierce wretchedness that glory brings
      us!   30
Who would not wish to be from wealth
      exempt,
Since riches point to misery and contempt?
Who would be so mock'd with glory? or to
      live
But in a dream of friendship?
To have his pomp and all what state com-
      pounds
But only painted, like his varnish'd friends?
Poor honest lord, brought low by his own
      heart,
Undone by goodness! Strange, unusual blood,
When man's worst sin is, he does too much
      good!
Who, then, dares to be half so kind again? 40
For bounty, that makes gods, does still mar
      men.
My dearest lord, bless'd, to be most accursed,
Rich, only to be wretched, thy great fortunes
Are made thy chief afflictions. Alas, kind
      lord!
He's flung in rage from this ingrateful seat
Of monstrous friends, nor has he with him to
Supply his life, or that which can command it.
I'll follow and inquire him out:
I'll ever serve his mind with my best will;
Whilst I have gold, I'll be his steward still. 50
                                        [*Exit.*

Scene III. *Woods and cave, near the sea-
      shore.*

   Enter Timon, *from the cave.*

   Tim. O blessed breeding sun, draw from
      the earth
Rotten humidity; below thy sister's orb
Infect the air! Twinn'd brothers of one womb,
Whose procreation, residence, and birth,
Scarce is dividant, touch them with several
      fortunes;
The greater scorns the lesser: not nature,
To whom all sores lay siege, can bear great
      fortune,
But by contempt of nature.
Raise me this beggar, and deny 't that lord; 10
The senator shall bear contempt hereditary,
The beggar native honor.
It is the pasture lards the rother's sides,
The want that makes him lean. Who dares,
      who dares,
In purity of manhood stand upright,

And say 'This man's a flatterer?' if one be,
So are they all; for every grise of fortune
Is smooth'd by that below: the learned pate
Ducks to the golden fool: all is oblique;
There's nothing level in our cursed natures,
But direct villany. Therefore, be abhorr'd 20
All feasts, societies, and throngs of men!
His semblable, yea, himself, Timon disdains:
Destruction fang mankind! Earth, yield me
      roots!   [*Digging.*
Who seeks for better of thee, sauce his palate
With thy most operant poison! What is here?
Gold? yellow, glittering, precious gold? No,
      gods,
I am no idle votarist: roots, you clear heav-
      ens!
Thus much of this will make black white, foul
      fair,
Wrong right, base noble, old young, coward
      valiant.
Ha, you gods! why this? what this, you
      gods? Why, this   30
Will lug your priests and servants from your
      sides,
Pluck stout men's pillows from below their
      heads:
This yellow slave
Will knit and break religions, bless the ac-
      cursed,
Make the hoar leprosy adored, place thieves
And give them title, knee and approbation
With senators on the bench: this is it
That makes the wappen'd widow wed again;
She, whom the spital-house and ulcerous sores
Would cast the gorge at, this embalms and
      spices   40
To the April day again. Come, damned earth,
Thou common whore of mankind, that put'st
      odds
Among the route of nations, I will make thee
Do thy right nature. [*March afar off.*] Ha! a
      drum? Thou'rt quick,
But yet I'll bury thee: thou'lt go, strong thief,
When gouty keepers of the cannot stand.
Nay, stay thou out for earnest.
                        [*Keeping some gold.*

Enter Alcibiades, *with drum and fife, in
      warlike manner;* Phrynia *and* Timandra.

   Alcib. What art thou there? speak.
   Tim. A beast, as thou art. The canker
      gnaw thy heart,
For showing me again the eyes of man!   50
   Alcib. What is thy name? Is man so hate-
      ful to thee,
That art thyself a man?
   Tim. I am Misanthropos, and hate man-
      kind.
For thy part, I do wish thou wert a dog,
That I might love thee something.
   Alcib.   I know thee well;
But in thy fortunes am unlearn'd and strange.
   Tim. I know thee too; and more than that
      I know thee,
I not desire to know. Follow thy drum;
With man's blood paint the ground, gules,
      gules:
Religious canons, civil laws are cruel;   60
Then what should war be? This fell whore of
      thine
Hath in her more destruction than thy sword,
For all her cherubin look.
   Phry.   Thy lips rot off!

Tim. I will not kiss thee; then the rot returns
To thine own lips again.

Alcib. How came the noble Timon to this change?

Tim. As the moon does, by wanting light to give:
But then renew I could not, like the moon;
There were no suns to borrow of.

Alcib. Noble Timon,
What friendship may I do thee?

Tim. None, but to 70
Maintain my opinion.

Alcib. What is it, Timon?

Tim. Promise me friendship, but perform none: if thou wilt not promise, the gods plague thee, for thou art a man! if thou dost perform, confound thee, for thou art a man!

Alcib. I have heard in some sort of thy miseries.

Tim. Thou saw'st them, when I had prosperity.

Alcib. I see them now; then was a blessed time.

Tim. As thine is now, held with a brace of harlots.

Timan. Is this the Athenian minion, whom the world 80
Voiced so regardfully?

Tim. Art thou Timandra?

Timan. Yes.

Tim. Be a whore still: they love thee not that use thee;
Give them diseases, leaving with thee their lust.
Make use of thy salt hours: season the slaves
For tubs and baths; bring down rose-cheeked youth
To the tub-fast and the diet.

Timan. Hang thee, monster!

Alcib. Pardon him, sweet Timandra; for his wits
Are drown'd and lost in his calamities.
I have but little gold of late, brave Timon, 90
The want whereof doth daily make revolt
In my penurious band: I have heard, and grieved,
How cursed Athens, mindless of thy worth,
Forgetting thy great deeds, when neighbor states,
But for thy sword and fortune, trod upon them,—

Tim. I prithee, beat thy drum, and get thee gone.

Alcib. I am thy friend, and pity thee, dear Timon.

Tim. How dost thou pity him whom thou dost trouble?
I had rather be alone.

Alcib. Why, fare thee well:
Here is some gold for thee.

Tim. Keep it, I cannot eat it. 100

Alcib. When I have laid proud Athens on a heap,—

Tim. Warr'st thou 'gainst Athens?

Alcib. Ay, Timon, and have cause.

Tim. The gods confound them all in thy conquest;
And thee after, when thou hast conquer'd!

Alcib. Why me, Timon?

Tim. That, by killing of villains,
Thou wast born to conquer my country.
Put up thy gold: go on,—here's gold,—go on;

Be as a planetary plague, when Jove
Will o'er some high-viced city hang his poison
In the sick air: let not thy sword skip one:
Pity not honor'd age for his white beard; 111
He is an usurer: strike me the counterfeit matron;
It is her habit only that is honest,
Herself's a bawd: let not the virgin's cheek
Make soft thy trenchant sword; for those milk-paps,
That through the window-bars bore at men's eyes,
Are not within the leaf of pity writ,
But set them down horrible traitors: spare not the babe,
Whose dimpled smiles from fools exhaust their mercy;
Think it a bastard, whom the oracle 120
Hath doubtfully pronounced thy throat shall cut,
And mince it sans remorse: swear against objects;
Put armor on thine ears and on thine eyes;
Whose proof, nor yells of mothers, maids, nor babes,
Nor sight of priests in holy vestments bleeding,
Shall pierce a jot. There's gold to pay thy soldiers:
Make large confusion; and, thy fury spent,
Confounded be thyself! Speak not, be gone.

Alcib. Hast thou gold yet? I'll take the gold thou givest me,
Not all thy counsel. 130

Tim. Dost thou, or dost thou not, heaven's curse upon thee!

Phr. and Timan. Give us some gold, good Timon: hast thou more?

Tim. Enough to make a whore forswear her trade,
And to make whores, a bawd. Hold up, you sluts,
Your aprons mountant: you are not oathable,
Although, I know, you 'll swear, terribly swear
Into strong shudders and to heavenly agues
The immortal gods that hear you,—spare your oaths,
I'll trust to your conditions: be whores still;
And he whose pious breath seeks to convert you, 149
Be strong in whore, allure him, burn him up;
Let your close fire predominate his smoke,
And be no turncoats: yet may your pains, six months,
Be quite contrary: and thatch your poor thin roofs
With burthens of the dead;—some that were hang'd,
No matter:—wear them, betray with them: whore still;
Paint till a horse may mire upon your face,
A pox of wrinkles!

Phr. and Timan. Well, more gold: what then?
Believe 't, that we'll do any thing for gold. 150

Tim. Consumptions sow
In hollow bones of man; strike their sharp shins,
And mar men's spurring. Crack the lawyer's voice,
That he may never more false title plead,
Nor sound his quillets shrilly: hoar the flamen,

That scolds against the quality of flesh,
And not believes himself : down with the nose,
Down with it flat ; take the bridge quite away
Of him that, his particular to foresee,
Smells from the general weal : make curl'd- 160
    pate ruffians bald ;
And let the unscarr'd braggarts of the war
Derive some pain from you : plague all ;
That your activity may defeat and quell
The source of all erection. There's more gold :
Do you damn others, and let this damn you,
And ditches grave you all !
  Phr. and Timan. More counsel with more
    money, bounteous Timon.
  Tim. More whore, more mischief first ; I
    have given you earnest.
  Alcib. Strike up the drum towards Athens !
    Farewell, Timon :
If I thrive well, I'll visit thee again.   170
  Tim. If I hope well, I'll never see thee
    more.
  Alcib. I never did thee harm.
  Tim. Yes, thou spokest well of me.
  Alcib.   Call'st thou that harm ?
  Tim. Men daily find it. Get thee away, and
    take
Thy beagles with thee.
  Alcib.   We but offend him. Strike !
    [*Drum beats. Exeunt Alcibiades,*
        Phrynia, and Timandra.
  Tim. That nature, being sick of man's un-
    kindness,
Should yet be hungry ! Common mother,
    thou,   [*Digging.*
Whose womb unmeasurable, and infinite
    breast,
Teems, and feeds all ; whose self-same mettle,
Whereof thy proud child, arrogant man, is 180
    puff'd,
Engenders the black toad and adder blue,
The gilded newt and eyeless venom'd worm,
With all the abhorred births below crisp
    heaven
Whereon Hyperion's quickening fire doth
    shine ;
Yield him, who all thy human sons doth hate,
From forth thy plenteous bosom, one poor
    root !
Ensear thy fertile and conceptious womb,
Let it no more bring out ingrateful man !
Go great with tigers, dragons, wolves, and
    bears ;
Teem with new monsters, whom thy upward
    face
Hath to the marbled mansion all above   191
Never presented !—O, a root,—dear thanks !—
Dry up thy marrows, vines, and plough-torn
    leas ;
Whereof ingrateful man, with liquorish
    draughts
And morsels unctuous, greases his pure mind,
That from it all consideration slips !

    Enter Apemantus.

More man ? plague, plague !
  Apem. I was directed hither : men report
Thou dost affect my manners, and dost use
    them.
  Tim. 'Tis, then, because thou dost not keep
    a dog,   200
Whom I would imitate : consumption catch
    thee !

  Apem. This is in thee a nature but in-
    fected ;
A poor unmanly melancholy sprung
From change of fortune. Why this spade ? this
    place ?
This slave-like habit ? and these looks of care ?
Thy flatterers yet wear silk, drink wine, lie
    soft ;
Hug their diseased perfumes, and have forgot
That ever Timon was. Shame not these woods,
By putting on the cunning of a carper.
Be thou a flatterer now, and seek to thrive 210
By that which has undone thee : hinge thy
    knee,
And let his very breath, whom thou'lt observe,
Blow off thy cap ; praise his most vicious
    strain,
And call it excellent : thou wast told thus ;
Thou gavest thine ears like tapsters that bid
    welcome
To knaves and all approachers : 'tis most just
That thou turn rascal ; hadst thou wealth
    again,
Rascals should have 't. Do not assume my
    likeness.
  Tim. Were I like thee, I'd throw away
    myself.
  Apem. Thou hast cast away thyself, being
    like thyself ;   220
A madman so long, now a fool. What, think'st
That the bleak air, thy boisterous chamber-
    lain,
Will put thy shirt on warm ? will these moss'd
    trees,
That have outlived the eagle, page thy heels,
And skip where thou point'st out ? will the
    cold brook,
Candied with ice, caudle thy morning taste,
To cure thy o'er-night's surfeit ? Call the crea-
    tures
Whose naked natures live in all the spite
Of wreakful heaven, whose bare unhoused
    trunks,
To the conflicting elements exposed,   230
Answer mere nature ; bid them flatter thee ;
O, thou shalt find—
  Tim.   A fool of thee : depart.
  Apem. I love thee better now than e'er I
    did.
  Tim. I hate thee worse.
  Apem.   Why ?
  Tim.   Thou flatter'st misery.
  Apem. I flatter not ; but say thou art a
    caitiff.
  Tim. Why dost thou seek me out ?
  Apem.   To vex thee.
  Tim. Always a villain's office or a fool's.
Dost please thyself in't ?
  Apem.   Ay.
  Tim.   What ! a knave too ?
  Apem. If thou didst put this sour-cold
    habit on   239
To castigate thy pride, 'twere well : but thou
Dost it enforcedly ; thou'ldst courtier be again,
Wert thou not beggar. Willing misery
Outlives incertain pomp, is crown'd before :
The one is filling still, never complete ;
The other, at high wish : best state, content-
    less,   249
Hath a distracted and most wretched being,
Worse than the worst, content.
Thou shouldst desire to die, being miserable.

Tim. Not by his breath that is more miserable.
Thou art a slave, whom Fortune's tender arm
With favor never clasp'd ; but bred a dog.
Hadst thou, like us from our first swath, proceeded
The sweet degrees that this brief world affords
To such as may the passive drugs of it
Freely command, thou wouldst have plunged thyself
In general riot ; melted down thy youth
In different beds of lust ; and never learn'd
The icy precepts of respect, but follow'd
The sugar'd game before thee. But myself,
Who had the world as my confectionary, 260
The mouths, the tongues, the eyes and hearts of men
At duty, more than I could frame employment,
That numberless upon me stuck as leaves
Do on the oak, have with one winter's brush
Fell from their boughs and left me open, bare
For every storm that blows : I, to bear this,
That never knew but better, is some burden :
Thy nature did commence in sufferance, time
Hath made thee hard in't. Why shouldst thou hate men ?
They never flatter'd thee : what hast thou given ? 270
If thou wilt curse, thy father, that poor rag,
Must be thy subject, who in spite put stuff
To some she beggar and compounded thee
Poor rogue hereditary. Hence, be gone !
If thou hadst not been born the worst of men,
Thou hadst been a knave and flatterer.

Apem. 　　　　　　Art thou proud yet ?
Tim. Ay, that I am not thee.
Apem. 　　　　　　　I, that I was
No prodigal.
Tim. 　　　　I, that I am one now :
Were all the wealth I have shut up in thee,
I'ld give thee leave to hang it. Get thee gone.
That the whole life of Athens were in this ! 281
Thus would I eat it. 　　　　[*Eating a root.*
Apem. 　　　　Here ; I will mend thy feast.
　　　　　　　　　　[*Offering him a root.*
Tim. First mend my company, take away thyself.
Apem. So I shall mend mine own, by the lack of thine.
Tim. 'Tis not well mended so, it is but botch'd ;
If not, I would it were.
Apem. What wouldst thou have to Athens ?
Tim. Thee thither in a whirlwind. If thou wilt,
Tell them there I have gold ; look, so I have.
Apem. Here is no use for gold.
Tim. 　　　　　　The best and truest ; 290
For here it sleeps, and does no hired harm.
Apem. Where liest o' nights, Timon ?
Tim. 　　　　　　Under that's above me.
Where feed'st thou o' days, Apemantus ?
Apem. Where my stomach finds meat ; or, rather, where I eat it.
Tim. Would poison were obedient and knew my mind !
Apem. Where wouldst thou send it ?
Tim. To sauce thy dishes. 　　　　299
Apem. The middle of humanity thou never knewest, but the extremity of both ends : when thou wast in thy gilt and thy perfume, they mocked thee for too much curiosity ; in thy rags thou knowest none, but art despised for

the contrary. There's a medlar for thee, eat it.
Tim. On what I hate I feed not.
Apem. Dost hate a medlar ?
Tim. Ay, though it look like thee.
Apem. An thou hadst hated meddlers sooner, thou shouldst have loved thyself better now. What man didst thou ever know unthrift that was beloved after his means ?
Tim. Who, without those means thou talk'st of, didst thou ever know beloved ?
Apem. Myself.
Tim. I understand thee ; thou hadst some means to keep a dog.
Apem. What things in the world canst thou nearest compare to thy flatterers ? 319
Tim. Women nearest ; but men, men are the things themselves. What wouldst thou do with the world, Apemantus, if it lay in thy power ?
Apem. Give it the beasts, to be rid of the men.
Tim. Wouldst thou have thyself fall in the confusion of men, and remain a beast with the beasts ?
Apem. Ay, Timon.
Tim. A beastly ambition, which the gods grant thee t' attain to ! If thou wert the lion, the fox would beguile thee ; if thou wert the lamb, the fox would eat thee : if thou wert the fox, the lion would suspect thee, when peradventure thou wert accused by the ass : if thou wert the ass, thy dulness would torment thee, and still thou livedst but as a breakfast to the wolf : if thou wert the wolf, thy greediness would afflict thee, and oft thou shouldst hazard thy life for thy dinner : wert thou the unicorn, pride and wrath would confound thee and make thine own self the conquest of thy fury : wert thou a bear, thou wouldst be killed by the horse : wert thou a horse, thou wouldst be seized by the leopard : wert thou a leopard, thou wert german to the lion and the spots of thy kindred were jurors on thy life : all thy safety were remotion and thy defence absence. What beast couldst thou be, that were not subject to a beast ? and what a beast art thou already, that seest not thy loss in transformation ! 349
Apem. If thou couldst please me with speaking to me, thou mightst have hit upon it here : the commonwealth of Athens is become a forest of beasts.
Tim. How has the ass broke the wall, that thou art out of the city ?
Apem. Yonder comes a poet and a painter : the plague of company light upon thee ! I will fear to catch it and give way : when I know not what else to do, I'll see thee again. 359
Tim. When there is nothing living but thee, thou shalt be welcome. I had rather be a beggar's dog than Apemantus.
Apem. Thou art the cap of all the fools alive.
Tim. Would thou wert clean enough to spit upon !
Apem. A plague on thee ! thou art too bad to curse.
Tim. All villains that do stand by thee are pure.
Apem. There is no leprosy but what thou speak'st.

Tim. If I name thee.
I'll beat thee, but I should infect my hands.
Apem. I would my tongue could rot them
    off !   370
Tim. Away, thou issue of a mangy dog !
Choler does kill me that thou art alive ;
I swound to see thee.
Apem.   Would thou wouldst burst !
Tim.   Away,
Thou tedious rogue ! I am sorry I shall lose
A stone by thee. [*Throws a stone at him.*
Apem.   Beast !
Tim.   Slave !
Apem.   Toad !
Tim.   Rogue, rogue, rogue !
I am sick of this false world, and will love
    nought
But even the mere necessities upon 't.
Then, Timon, presently prepare thy grave ;
Lie where the light foam of the sea may beat
Thy grave-stone daily : make thine epitaph,
That death in me at others' lives may laugh.
[*To the gold*] O thou sweet king-killer, and
    dear divorce
'Twixt natural son and sire ! thou bright de-
    filer
Of Hymen's purest bed ! thou valiant Mars !
Thou ever young, fresh, loved and delicate
    wooer,
Whose blush doth thaw the consecrated snow
That lies on Dian's lap ! thou visible god,
That solder'st close impossibilities,
And makest them kiss ! that speak'st with ev-
    ery tongue,
To every purpose ! O thou touch of hearts !
Think, thy slave man rebels, and by thy vir-
    tue   391
Set them into confounding odds, that beasts
May have the world in empire !
Apem.   Would 'twere so !
But not till I am dead. I'll say thou'st gold :
Thou wilt be throng'd to shortly.
Tim.   Throng'd to !
Apem.   Ay.
Tim. Thy back, I prithee.
Apem.   Live, and love thy misery.
Tim. Long live so, and so die. [*Exit Ape-
    mantus.*] I am quit.
Moe things like men ! Eat, Timon, and abhor
    them.

Enter Banditti.

First Ban. Where should he have this
gold ? It is some poor fragment, some slender
ort of his remainder : the mere want of gold,
and the falling-from of his friends, drove him
into this melancholy.
Sec. Ban. It is noised he hath a mass of
treasure.
Third Ban. Let us make the assay upon
him : if he care not for't, he will supply us
easily ; if he covetously reserve it, how shall's
get it ?
Sec. Ban. True ; for he bears it not about
him, 'tis hid.
First Ban. Is not this he ?   410
Banditti. Where ?
Sec. Ban. 'Tis his description.
Third Ban. He ; I know him.
Banditti. Save thee, Timon.
Tim. Now, thieves ?
Banditti. Soldiers, not thieves.
Tim. Both too ; and women's sons.

Banditti. We are not thieves, but men that
much do want.
Tim. Your greatest want is, you want much
of meat.
Why should you want ? Behold, the earth hath
    roots ;   420
Within this mile break forth a hundred
    springs ;
The oaks bear mast, the briers scarlet hips ;
The bounteous housewife, nature, on each bush
Lays her full mess before you. Want ! why
    want ?
First Ban. We cannot live on grass, on ber-
    ries, water,
As beasts and birds and fishes.
Tim. Nor on the beasts themselves, the
    birds, and fishes ;
You must eat men. Yet thanks I must you con
That you are thieves profess'd, that you work
    not   429
In holier shapes : for there is boundless theft
In limited professions. Rascal thieves,
Here's gold. Go, suck the subtle blood o' the
    grape,
Till the high fever seethe your blood to froth,
And so 'scape hanging : trust not the physi-
    cian ;
His antidotes are poison, and he slays
Moe than you rob : take wealth and lives to-
    gether ;
Do villany, do, since you protest to do't,
Like workmen. I'll example you with thievery.
The sun's a thief, and with his great attrac-
    tion   439
Robs the vast sea : the moon's an arrant thief,
And her pale fire she snatches from the sun :
The sea's a thief, whose liquid surge resolves
The moon into salt tears : the earth's a thief,
That feeds and breeds by a composture stolen
From general excrement : each thing's a thief :
The laws, your curb and whip, in their rough
    power
Have uncheck'd theft. Love not yourselves :
    away,
Rob one another. There's more gold. Cut
    throats :
All that you meet are thieves : to Athens go,
Break open shops ; nothing can you steal, 450
But thieves do lose it : steal no less for this
I give you ; and gold confound you howsoe'er !
Amen.
Third Ban. Has almost charmed me from
my profession, by persuading me to it.
First Ban. 'Tis in the malice of mankind
that he thus advises us ; not to have us thrive
in our mystery.
Sec. Ban. I'll believe him as an enemy, and
give over my trade.   460
First Ban. Let us first see peace in Athens :
there is no time so miserable but a man may
be true.   [*Exeunt Banditti.*

Enter FLAVIUS.

Flav. O you gods !
Is yond despised and ruinous man my lord ?
Full of decay and failing ? O monument
And wonder of good deeds evilly bestow'd !
What an alteration of honor
Has desperate want made !   469
What viler thing upon the earth than friends
Who can bring noblest minds to basest ends !
How rarely does it meet with this time's guise,
When man was wish'd to love his enemies !

Grant I may ever love, and rather woo
Those that would mischief me than those that
　do!
Has caught me in his eye: I will present
My honest grief unto him; and, as my lord,
Still serve him with my life. My dearest mas-
　ter!
　Tim. Away! what art thou?
　Flav. Have you forgot me, sir?
　Tim. Why dost ask that? I have forgot all
　men; 480
Then, if thou grant'st thou'rt a man, I have
　forgot thee.
　Flav. An honest poor servant of yours.
　Tim. Then I know thee not:
I never had honest man about me, I; all
I kept were knaves, to serve in meat to vil-
　lains.
　Flav. The gods are witness,
Ne'er did poor steward wear a truer grief
For his undone lord than mine eyes for you.
　Tim. What, dost thou weep? Come nearer.
　Then I love thee,
Because thou art a woman, and disclaim'st 490
Flinty mankind; whose eyes do never give
But thorough lust and laughter. Pity's sleep-
　ing:
Strange times, that weep with laughing, not
　with weeping!
　Flav. I beg of you to know me, good my
　lord,
To accept my grief and whilst this poor wealth
　lasts
To entertain me as your steward still.
　Tim. Had I a steward
So true, so just, and now so comfortable?
It almost turns my dangerous nature mild.
Let me behold thy face. Surely, this man 500
Was born of woman.
Forgive my general and exceptless rashness,
You perpetual-sober gods! I do proclaim
One honest man—mistake me not—but one;
No more, I pray,—and he's a steward.
How fain would I have hated all mankind!
And thou redeem'st thyself: but all, save thee,
I fell with curses.
Methinks thou art more honest now than wise;
For, by oppressing and betraying me, 510
Thou mightst have sooner got another service:
For many so arrive at second masters,
Upon their first lord's neck. But tell me true—
For I must ever doubt, though ne'er so sure—
Is not thy kindness subtle, covetous,
If not a usuring kindness, and, as rich men
　deal gifts,
Expecting in return twenty for one?
　Flav. No, my most worthy master; in
　whose breast
Doubt and suspect, alas, are placed too late:
You should have fear'd false times when you
　did feast: 520
Suspect still comes where an estate is least.
That which I show, heaven knows, is merely
　love,
Duty and zeal to your unmatched mind,
Care of your food and living; and, believe it,
My most honor'd lord,
For any benefit that points to me,
Either in hope or present, I'ld exchange
For this one wish, that you had power and
　wealth
To requite me, by making rich yourself.

　Tim. Look thee, 'tis so! Thou singly hon-
　est man, 530
Here, take: the gods out of my misery
Have sent thee treasure. Go, live rich and
　happy;
But thus condition'd: thou shalt build from
　men;
Hate all, curse all, show charity to none,
But let the famish'd flesh slide from the bone,
Ere thou relieve the beggar; give to dogs
What thou deny'st to men; let prisons swal-
　low 'em,
Debts wither 'em to nothing; be men like
　blasted woods,
And may diseases lick up their false bloods!
And so farewell and thrive.
　Flav. O, let me stay, 540
And comfort you, my master.
　Tim. If thou hatest curses,
Stay not; fly, whilst thou art blest and free:
Ne'er see thou man, and let me ne'er see thee.
　　　[Exit Flavius. Timon retires to his cave.

ACT V.

SCENE I. *The woods. Before Timon's cave.*

　Enter Poet *and* Painter; TIMON *watching
　　　them from his cave.*

　Pain. As I took note of the place, it cannot
be far where he abides.
　Poet. What's to be thought of him? does
the rumor hold for true, that he's so full of
gold?
　Pain. Certain: Alcibiades reports it; Phrynia and Timandra had gold of him: he likewise enriched poor straggling soldiers with
great quantity: 'tis said he gave unto his steward a mighty sum.
　Poet. Then this breaking of his has been
but a try for his friends. 11
　Pain. Nothing else: you shall see him a
palm in Athens again, and flourish with the
highest. Therefore 'tis not amiss we tender our
loves to him, in this supposed distress of his:
it will show honestly in us; and is very likely
to load our purposes with what they travail
for, if it be a just and true report that goes
of his having.
　Poet. What have you now to present unto
him?
　Pain. Nothing at this time but my visitation: only I will promise him an excellent
piece. 21
　Poet. I must serve him so too, tell him of
an intent that's coming toward him.
　Pain. Good as the best. Promising is the
very air o' the time: it opens the eyes of expectation: performance is ever the duller for
his act; and, but in the plainer and simpler
kind of people, the deed of saying is quite out
of use. To promise is most courtly and fashionable: performance is a kind of will or testament which argues a great sickness in his
judgment that makes it.
　　　[Timon comes from his cave, behind.
　Tim. [*Aside*] Excellent workman! thou
canst not paint a man so bad as is thyself.
　Poet. I am thinking what I shall say I have
provided for him: it must be a personating of
himself; a satire against the softness of pros-

perity, with a discovery of the infinite flatteries that follow youth and opulency.

Tim. [*Aside*] Must thou needs stand for
a villain in thine own work? wilt thou whip
thine own faults in other men? Do so, I have
gold for thee.

Poet. Nay, let's seek him:
Then do we sin against our own estate,
When we may profit meet, and come too late.

Pain. True;
When the day serves, before black-corner'd
night,
Find what thou want'st by free and offer'd
light.
Come.

Tim. [*Aside*] I'll meet you at the turn.
What a god's gold,   50
That he is worship'd in a baser temple
Than where swine feed!
'Tis thou that rigg'st the bark and plough'st
the foam,
Settlest admired reverence in a slave:
To thee be worship! and thy saints for aye
Be crown'd with plagues that thee alone obey!
Fit I meet them.   [*Coming forward.*

Poet. Hail, worthy Timon!

Pain.   Our late noble master!

Tim. Have I once lived to see two honest
men?

Poet. Sir,   60
Having often of your open bounty tasted,
Hearing you were retired, your friends fall'n
off,
Whose thankless natures—O abhorred spir-
its!—
Not all the whips of heaven are large enough:
What! to you,
Whose star-like nobleness gave life and influ-
ence
To their whole being! I am rapt and cannot
cover
The monstrous bulk of this ingratitude
With any size of words.

Tim. Let it go naked, men may see't the
better: 70
You that are honest, by being what you are,
Make them best seen and known.

Pain.   He and myself
Have travail'd in the great shower of your
gifts,
And sweetly felt it.

Tim.   Ay, you are honest men.

Pain. We are hither come to offer you our
service.

Tim. Most honest men! Why, how shall I
requite you?
Can you eat roots, and drink cold water? no.

Both. What we can do, we'll do, to do you
service.

Tim. Ye're honest men: ye've heard that I
have gold;
I am sure you have: speak truth; ye're honest men.   80

Pain. So it is said, my noble lord; but
therefore
Came not my friend nor I.

Tim. Good honest men! Thou draw'st a
counterfeit
Best in all Athens: thou'rt, indeed, the best;
Thou counterfeit'st most lively.

Pain.   So, so, my lord.

Tim. E'en so, sir, as I say. And, for thy
fiction,

Why, thy verse swells with stuff so fine and
smooth
That thou art even natural in thine art.
But, for all this, my honest-natured friends,
I must needs say you have a little fault: 90
Marry, 'tis not monstrous in you, neither wish
I
You take much pains to mend.

Both.   Beseech your honor
To make it known to us.

Tim.   You'll take it ill.

Both. Most thankfully, my lord.

Tim.   Will you, indeed?

Both. Doubt it not, worthy lord.

Tim. There's never a one of you but trusts
a knave,
That mightily deceives you.

Both.   Do we, my lord?

Tim. Ay, and you hear him cog, see him
dissemble,
Know his gross patchery, love him, feed him,
Keep in your bosom: yet remain assured   100
That he's a made-up villain.

Pain. I know none such, my lord.

Poet.   Nor I.

Tim. Look you, I love you well; I'll give
you gold,
Rid me these villains from your companies:
Hang them or stab them, drown them in a
draught,
Confound them by some course, and come to
me,
I'll give you gold enough.

Both. Name them, my lord, let's know
them.

Tim. You that way and you this, but two
in company;
Each man apart, all single and alone,   110
Yet an arch-villain keeps him company.
If where thou art two villains shall not be,
Come not near him. If thou wouldst not reside
But where one villain is, then him abandon.
Hence, pack! there's gold; you came for gold,
ye slaves:
[*To Painter*] You have work'd for me; there's
payment for you: hence!
[*To Poet*] You are an alchemist; make gold
of that.
Out, rascal dogs! [*Beats them out, and then
retires to his cave.*

Enter Flavius *and two* Senators.

Flav. It is in vain that you would speak
with Timon;
For he is set so only to himself   120
That nothing but himself which looks like man
Is friendly with him.

First Sen.   Bring us to his cave:
It is our part and promise to the Athenians
To speak with Timon.

Sec. Sen.   At all times alike
Men are not still the same: 'twas time and
griefs
That framed him thus: time, with his fairer
hand,
Offering the fortunes of his former days,
The former man may make him. Bring us to
him,
And chance it as it may.

Flav.   Here is his cave.
Peace and content be here! Lord Timon!
Timon!   130

Look out, and speak to friends : the Athe-
    nians,
By two of their most reverend senate, greet
    thee :
Speak to them, noble Timon.

    Timon comes from his cave.

Tim. Thou sun, that comfort'st, burn !
    Speak, and be hang'd :
For each true word, a blister ! and each false
Be as cauterizing to the root o' the tongue,
Consuming it with speaking !
    First Sen.   Worthy Timon,—
Tim. Of none but such as you, and you of
    Timon.
First Sen. The senators of Athens greet
    thee, Timon.
Tim. I thank them ; and would send them
    back the plague,   140
Could I but catch it for them.
    First Sen.   O, forget
What we are sorry for ourselves in thee.
The senators with one consent of love
Entreat thee back to Athens ; who have
    thought
On special dignities, which vacant lie
For thy best use and wearing.
    Sec. Sen.   They confess
Toward thee forgetfulness too general, gross :
Which now the public body, which doth sel-
    dom
Play the recanter, feeling in itself
A lack of Timon's aid, hath sense withal 150
Of its own fail, restraining aid to Timon ;
And send forth us, to make their sorrow'd
    render,
Together with a recompense more fruitful
Than their offence can weigh down by the
    dram ;
Ay, even such heaps and sums of love and
    wealth
As shall to thee blot out what wrongs were
    theirs
And write in thee the figures of their love,
Ever to read them thine.
    Tim.   You witch me in it ;
Surprise me to the very brink of tears :
Lend me a fool's heart and a woman's eyes,
And I'll beweep these comforts, worthy sena-
    tors.   161
    First Sen. Therefore, so please thee to re-
    turn with us
And of our Athens, thine and ours, to take
The captainship, thou shalt be met with thanks,
Allow'd with absolute power and thy good
    name
Live with authority : so soon we shall drive
    back
Of Alcibiades the approaches wild,
Who, like a boar too savage, doth root up
His country's peace.
    Sec. Sen. And shakes his threatening sword
Against the walls of Athens.
    First Sen.   Therefore, Timon,— 170
    Tim. Well, sir, I will ; therefore, I will, sir ;
    thus :
If Alcibiades kill my countrymen,
Let Alcibiades know this of Timon,
That Timon cares not. But if he sack fair
    Athens,
And take our goodly aged men by the beards,
Giving our holy virgins to the stain
Of contumelious, beastly, mad-brain'd war,

Then let him know, and tell him Timon speaks
    it,
In pity of our aged and our youth,
I cannot choose but tell him, that I care not,
And let him take't at worst ; for their knives
    care not,   181
While you have throats to answer : for myself,
There's not a whittle in the unruly camp
But I do prize it at my love before
The reverend'st throat in Athens. So I leave
    you
To the protection of the prosperous gods,
As thieves to keepers.
    Flav.   Stay not, all's in vain.
    Tim. Why, I was writing of my epitaph ;
It will be seen to-morrow : my long sickness
Of health and living now begins to mend, 190
And nothing brings me all things. Go, live
    still ;
Be Alcibiades your plague, you his,
And last so long enough !
    First Sen.   We speak in vain.
    Tim. But yet I love my country, and am
    not
One that rejoices in the common wreck,
As common bruit doth put it.
    First Sen.   That's well spoke.
    Tim. Commend me to my loving country-
    men,—
    First Sen. These words become your lips
    as they pass thorough them.
    Sec. Sen. And enter in our ears like great
    triumphers
In their applauding gates.
    Tim.   Commend me to them, 200
And tell them that, to ease them of their griefs,
Their fears of hostile strokes, their aches,
    losses,
Their pangs of love, with other incident throes
That nature's fragile vessel doth sustain
In life's uncertain voyage, I will some kindness
    do them :
I'll teach them to prevent wild Alcibiades'
    wrath.
    First Sen. I like this well ; he will return
    again.
    Tim. I have a tree, which grows here in
    my close,
That mine own use invites me to cut down,
And shortly must I fell it : tell my friends, 210
Tell Athens, in the sequence of degree
From high to low throughout, that whoso
    please
To stop affliction, let him take his haste,
Come hither, ere my tree hath felt the axe,
And hang himself. I pray you, do my greeting.
    Flav. Trouble him no further ; thus you
    still shall find him.
    Tim. Come not to me again : but say to
    Athens,
Timon hath made his everlasting mansion
Upon the beached verge of the salt flood ;
Who once a day with his embossed froth 220
The turbulent surge shall cover : thither come,
And let my grave-stone be your oracle.
Lips, let sour words go by and language end :
What is amiss plague and infection mend !
Graves only be men's works and death their
    gain !
Sun, hide thy beams ! Timon hath done his
    reign.   [*Retires to his cave.*
    First Sen. His discontents are unremove-
    ably

Coupled to nature.

Sec. Sen. Our hope in him is dead : let us
return,
And strain what other means is left unto us
In our dear peril.   231
First Sen. It requires swift foot. [*Exeunt.*

Scene II. *Before the walls of Athens.*

Enter two Senators *and a* Messenger.

First Sen. Thou hast painfully discover'd :
are his files
As full as thy report ?
Mess.   I have spoke the least :
Besides, his expedition promises
Present approach.
Sec. Sen. We stand much hazard, if they
bring not Timon.
Mess. I met a courier, one mine ancient
friend ;
Whom, though in general part we were op-
posed,
Yet our old love made a particular force,
And made us speak like friends : this man was
riding
From Alcibiades to Timon's cave,   10
With letters of entreaty, which imported
His fellowship i' the cause against your city,
In part for his sake moved.
First Sen.   Here come our brothers.

Enter the Senators *from* Timon.

Third Sen. No talk of Timon, nothing of
him expect.
The enemies' drum is heard, and fearful scour-
ing
Doth choke the air with dust : in, and prepare :
Ours is the fall, I fear ; our foes the snare.
                                            [*Exeunt.*

Scene III. *The woods. Timon's cave, and a
rude tomb seen.*

Enter a Soldier, *seeking* Timon.

Sold. By all description this should be the
place.
Who's here ? speak, ho ! No answer ! What is
this ?
Timon is dead, who hath outstretch'd his
span :
Some beast rear'd this ; there does not live a
man.
Dead, sure ; and this his grave. What's on this
tomb
I cannot read ; the character I'll take with
wax :
Our captain hath in every figure skill,
An aged interpreter, though young in days :
Before proud Athens he's set down by this,
Whose fall the mark of his ambition is. [*Exit.*

Scene IV. *Before the walls of Athens.*

Trumpets sound. Enter Alcibiades *with his
powers.*

Alcib. Sound to this coward and lascivious
town
Our terrible approach.   [*A parley sounded.*

Enter Senators *on the walls.*

Till now you have gone on and fill'd the time
With all licentious measure, making your wills
The scope of justice ; till now myself and such

As slept within the shadow of your power
Have wander'd with our traversed arms and
breathed
Our sufferance vainly : now the time is flush,
When crouching marrow in the bearer strong
Cries of itself ' No more : ' now breathless
wrong   10
Shall sit and pant in your great chairs of ease,
And pursy insolence shall break his wind
With fear and horrid flight.
First Sen.   Noble and young,
When thy first griefs were but a mere conceit,
Ere thou hadst power or we had cause of fear,
We sent to thee, to give thy rages balm,
To wipe out our ingratitude with loves
Above their quantity.
Sec. Sen.   So did we woo
Transformed Timon to our city's love
By humble message and by promised means :
We were not all unkind, nor all deserve   21
The common stroke of war.
First Sen.   These walls of ours
Were not erected by their hands from whom
You have received your griefs ; nor are they
such
That these great towers, trophies and schools
should fall
For private faults in them.
Sec. Sen.   Nor are they living
Who were the motives that you first went out ;
Shame that they wanted cunning, in excess
Hath broke their hearts. March, noble lord,
Into our city with thy banners spread :   30
By decimation, and a tithed death—
If thy revenges hunger for that food
Which nature loathes—take thou the destined
tenth,
And by the hazard of the spotted die
Let die the spotted.
First Sen.   All have not offended ;
For those that were, it is not square to take
On those that are : revenges : crimes, like lands,
Are not inherited. Then, dear countryman,
Bring in thy ranks, but leave without thy rage :
Spare thy Athenian cradle and those kin   40
Which in the bluster of thy wrath must fall
With those that have offended : like a shep-
herd,
Approach the fold and cull the infected forth,
But kill not all together.
Sec. Sen.   What thou wilt,
Thou rather shalt enforce it with thy smile
Than hew to't with thy sword.
First Sen.   Set but thy foot
Against our rampired gates, and they shall
ope ;
So thou wilt send thy gentle heart before,
To say thou'lt enter friendly.
Sec. Sen.   Throw thy glove,
Or any token of thine honor else,   50
That thou wilt use the wars as thy redress
And not as our confusion, all thy powers
Shall make their harbor in our town, till we
Have seal'd thy full desire.
Alcib.   Then there's my glove ;
Descend, and open your uncharged ports :
Those enemies of Timon's and mine own
Whom you yourselves shall set out for reproof
Fall and no more : and, to atone your fears
With my more noble meaning, not a man
Shall pass his quarter, or offend the stream

Of regular justice in your city's bounds,   61
But shall be render'd to your public laws
At heaviest answer.
  Both.   'Tis most nobly spoken.
  Alcib. Descend, and keep your words.
[*The Senators descend, and open the gates.*

           Enter Soldier.

  Sold. My noble general, Timon is dead ;
Entomb'd upon the very hem o' the sea ;
And on his grave-stone this insculpture, which
With wax I brought away, whose soft impression
Interprets for my poor ignorance.   69
  Alcib. [*Reads the epitaph*] ' Here lies a
    wretched corse, of wretched soul bereft :
Seek not my name : a plague consume you
    wicked caitiffs left !

Here lie I, Timon ; who, alive, all living men
    did hate :
Pass by and curse thy fill, but pass and stay
    not here thy gait.'
These well express in thee thy latter spirits :
Though thou abhorr'dst in us our human
    griefs,
Scorn'dst our brain's flow and those our droplets which
From niggard nature fall, yet rich conceit
Taught thee to make vast Neptune weep for
    aye
On thy low grave, on faults forgiven. Dead
Is noble Timon : of whose memory   80
Hereafter more. Bring me into your city,
And I will use the olive with my sword,
Make war breed peace, make peace stint war,
    make each
Prescribe to other as each other's leech.
Let our drums strike.   [*Exeunt.*

PERICLES, PRINCE OF TYRE.

(WRITTEN ABOUT 1608.)

INTRODUCTION.

Shakespeare's portion of this play has something of the slightness of a preliminary sketch. The first two Acts are evidently by another writer than Shakespeare, and probably the scenes in Act IV. (Sc. II., V., and VI.), so revolting to our moral sense, are also to be assigned away from him. What remains (Acts III., IV., V., omitting the scenes just mentioned) is the pure and charming romance of Marina, the sea-born child of Pericles, her loss, and the recovery of both child and mother by the afflicted Prince. Whether Shakespeare worked upon the foundation of an earlier play, or whether the non-Shakespearean parts of *Pericles* were additions made to what he had written, cannot be determined with certainty. It is supposed by some critics that three hands can be distinguished : that of a general reviser who wrote the first two acts and Gower's choruses—possibly the dramatist, George Wilkins ; that of a second writer who contributed the offensive scenes of Act IV. ; and thirdly the hand of Shakespeare. *Pericles* was entered in the Stationers' register in 1608 by the book-seller Blount, and was published with a very ill arranged text the next year (1609) by another book-seller who had, it is believed, surreptitiously obtained his copy. It was not included among the plays given in the first or second folios, but appeared, with six added plays, in the third folio (1663). The story upon which *Pericles* was founded is that given in Lawrence Twine's *Patterne of Painfull Adventures* (1607), itself a reprint of an early printed version from the French ; given also in Gower's *Confessio Amantis*, and originally written about the fifth or sixth century of our era, in Greek. Both Twine and Gower appear to have been made use of by the writers of *Pericles*, and the debt to Gower is acknowledged by his introduction as the "presenter" of the play. The drama as a whole is singularly undramatic. It entirely lacks unity of action, and the prominent figures of the opening scenes quickly drop out of the play. Most of the story is briefly told in rhymed verse by the presenter, Gower, or is set forth in dumb show. But Shakespeare's portion is one and indivisible. It opens on ship board with a tempest, and in Shakespeare's later play of storm and wreck he has not attempted to rival the earlier treatment of the subject. "No poetry of shipwreck and the sea," a living poet writes, "has ever equalled the great scene of *Pericles* ; no such note of music was ever struck out of the clash and contention of tempestuous elements." Cerimon, who is master of the secrets of nature, and who is liberal in his "learned charity," is like a first study of Prospero. In the fifth act Marina, so named from her birth at sea, has grown to the age of fourteen years, and is, as it were, a sister of Miranda and Perdita (note in each case the significant name). She, like Perdita, is a child lost by her parents, and, like Perdita, we see her flower-like with her flowers—only these flowers of Marina are not for a merrymaking, but a grave. The melancholy of Pericles is a clear-obscure of sadness, not a gloom of cloudy remorse like that of Leontes. His meeting with his lost Marina is like an anticipation of the scene in which Cymbeline recovers his sons and daughter ; but the scene in *Pericles* is filled with a rarer, keener version of joy.

DRAMATIS PERSONÆ.

ANTIOCHUS, king of Antioch.
PERICLES, prince of Tyre.
HELICANUS, } two lords of Tyre.
ESCANES, }
SIMONIDES, king of Pentapolis.
CLEON, governor of Tarsus.
LYSIMACHUS, governor of Mytilene.
CERIMON, a lord of Ephesus.
THALIARD, a lord of Antioch.
PHILEMON, servant to Cerimon.
LEONINE, servant to Dionyza.
Marshal.
A Pandar.

BOULT, his servant.
The Daughter of Antiochus.
DIONYZA, wife to Cleon.
THAISA, daughter to Simonides.
MARINA, daughter to Pericles and Thaisa.
LYCHORIDA, nurse to Marina.
A Bawd.
Lords, Knights, Gentlemen, Sailors, Pirates, Fishermen, and Messengers.

DIANA.

GOWER, as Chorus.

SCENE : *Dispersedly in various countries.*

ACT I.

Enter GOWER.

Before the palace of Antioch.

To sing a song that old was sung,
From ashes ancient Gower is come ;
Assuming man's infirmities,
To glad your ear, and please your eyes.
It hath been sung at festivals,
On ember-eves and holy-ales ;
And lords and ladies in their lives
Have read it for restoratives :
The purchase is to make men glorious ;
Et bonum quo antiquius, eo melius. 10
If you, born in these latter times,
When wit's more ripe, accept my rhymes.
And that to hear an old man sing
May to your wishes pleasure bring,
I life would wish, and that I might
Waste it for you, like taper-light.
This Antioch, then, Antiochus the Great
Built up, this city, for his chiefest seat :
The fairest in all Syria,
I tell you what mine authors say : 20
This king unto him took a fere,
Who died and left a female heir,
So buxom, blithe, and full of face,
As heaven had lent her all his grace ;
With whom the father liking took,
And her to incest did provoke :
Bad child ; worse father ! to entice his own
To evil should be done by none :
But custom what they did begin
Was with long use account no sin. 30
The beauty of this sinful dame
Made many princes thither frame,
To seek her as a bed-fellow,
In marriage-pleasures play-fellow :
Which to prevent he made a law,
To keep her still, and men in awe,
That whoso ask'd her for his wife,
His riddle told not, lost his life :
So for her many a wight did die,
As yon grim looks do testify. 40
What now ensues, to the judgment of your
eye
I give, my cause who best can justify. [*Exit.*

SCENE I. *Antioch. A room in the palace.*

Enter ANTIOCHUS, PRINCE PERICLES, *and
followers.*

Ant. Young prince of Tyre, you have at
large received
The danger of the task you undertake.
Per. I have, Antiochus, and, with a soul
Embolden'd with the glory of her praise,
Think death no hazard in this enterprise.
Ant. Bring in our daughter, clothed like a
bride,
For the embracements even of Jove himself ;
At whose conception, till Lucina reign'd,
Nature this dowry gave, to glad her presence,
The senate-house of planets all did sit, 10
To knit in her their best perfections.

Music. Enter the Daughter of Antiochus.

Per. See where she comes, apparell'd like
the spring,
Graces her subjects, and her thoughts the king
Of every virtue gives renown to men !
Her face the book of praises, where is read

Nothing but curious pleasures, as from thence
Sorrow were ever razed, and testy wrath
Could never be her mild companion.
You gods that made me man, and sway in
love,
That have inflamed desire in my breast 20
To taste the fruit of yon celestial tree,
Or die in the adventure, be my helps,
As I am son and servant to your will,
To compass such a boundless happiness !
Ant. Prince Pericles,—
Per. That would be son to great Antiochus.
Ant. Before thee stands this fair Hesper-
ides,
With golden fruit, but dangerous to be
touch'd ;
For death-like dragons here affright thee
hard :
Her face, like heaven, enticeth thee to view 30
Her countless glory, which desert must gain ;
And which, without desert, because thine eye
Presumes to reach, all thy whole heap must
die.
Yon sometimes famous princes, like thyself,
Drawn by report, adventurous by desire,
Tell thee, with speechless tongues and sem-
blance pale,
That without covering, save yon field of stars,
Here they stand martyrs, slain in Cupid's
wars ;
And with dead cheeks advise thee to desist
For going on death's net, whom none resist.
Per. Antiochus, I thank thee, who hath
taught 41
My frail mortality to know itself,
And by those fearful objects to prepare
This body, like to them, to what I must ;
For death remember'd should be like a mirror,
Who tells us life's but breath, to trust it error.
I'll make my will then, and, as sick men do
Who know the world, see heaven, but, feeling
woe,
Gripe not at earthly joys as erst they did ;
So I bequeath a happy peace to you 50
And all good men, as every prince should do ;
My riches to the earth from whence they
came ;
But my unspotted fire of love to you.
          [*To the daughter of Antiochus.*
Thus ready for the way of life or death,
I wait the sharpest blow, Antiochus.
Ant. Scorning advice, read the conclusion
then :
Which read and not expounded, 'tis decreed,
As these before thee thou thyself shalt bleed.
Daugh. Of all say'd yet, mayst thou prove
prosperous !
Of all say'd yet, I wish thee happiness ! 60
Per. Like a bold champion, I assume the
lists,
Nor ask advice of any other thought
But faithfulness and courage.

He reads the riddle.

I am no viper, yet I feed
On mother's flesh which did me breed.
I sought a husband, in which labor
I found that kindness in a father :
He's father, son, and husband mild ;
I mother, wife, and yet his child.
How they may be, and yet in two, 70
As you will live, resolve it you.
Sharp physic is the last : but, O you powers

That give heaven countless eyes to view men's
　　acts,
Why cloud they not their sights perpetually,
If this be true, which makes me pale to read
　　it ?
Fair glass of light, I loved you, and could
　　still,
　　　[*Takes hold of the hand of the Princess.*
Were not this glorious casket stored with ill :
But I must tell you, now my thoughts revolt ;
For he's no man on whom perfections wait　79
That, knowing sin within, will touch the gate.
You are a fair viol, and your sense the strings ;
Who, finger'd to make man his lawful music,
Would draw heaven down, and all the gods,
　　to hearken :
But being play'd upon before your time,
Hell only danceth at so harsh a chime.
Good sooth, I care not for you.
　　Ant. Prince Pericles, touch not, upon thy
　　life,
For that's an article within our law,
As dangerous as the rest. Your time's ex-
　　pired :
Either expound now, or receive your sen-
　　tence.　　　　　　　　　　　　　　　　　90
　　Per. Great king,
Few love to hear the sins they love to act ;
'Twould braid yourself too near for me to tell
　　it.
Who has a book of all that monarchs do,
He's more secure to keep it shut than shown :
For vice repeated is like the wandering wind,
Blows dust in others' eyes, to spread itself ;
And yet the end of all is bought thus dear,
The breath is gone, and the sore eyes see
　　clear :
To stop the air would hurt them. The blind
　　mole casts　　　　　　　　　　　　　　100
Copp'd hills towards heaven, to tell the earth
　　is throng'd
By man's oppression ; and the poor worm doth
　　die for't.
Kings are earth's gods ; in vice their law's
　　their will ;
And if Jove stray, who dares say Jove doth
　　ill ?
It is enough you know ; and it is fit,
What being more known grows worse, to
　　smother it.
All love the womb that their first being bred,
Then give my tongue like leave to love my
　　head.
　　Ant. [*Aside*] Heaven, that I had thy head !
　　he has found the meaning :
But I will gloze with him.—Young prince of
　　Tyre,　　　　　　　　　　　　　　　　110
Though by the tenor of our strict edict,
Your exposition misinterpreting,
We might proceed to cancel of your days ;
Yet hope, succeeding from so fair a tree
As your fair self, doth tune us otherwise :
Forty days longer we do respite you ;
If by which time our secret be undone,
This mercy shows we'll joy in such a son :
And until then your entertain shall be
As doth befit our honor and your worth.　120
　　　　　　　　　[*Exeunt all but Pericles.*
　　Per. How courtesy would seem to cover
　　sin,
When what is done is like an hypocrite,

The which is good in nothing but in sight !
If it be true that I interpret false,
Then were it certain you were not so bad
As with foul incest to abuse your soul ;
Where now you're both a father and a son,
By your untimely claspings with your child,
Which pleasure fits an husband, not a father ;
And she an eater of her mother's flesh,　　130
By the defiling of her parent's bed ;
And both like serpents are, who though they
　　feed
On sweetest flowers, yet they poison breed.
Antioch, farewell ! for wisdom sees, those men
Blush not in actions blacker than the night,
Will shun no course to keep them from the
　　light.
One sin, I know, another doth provoke ;
Murder's as near to lust as flame to smoke :
Poison and treason are the hands of sin,
Ay, and the targets, to put off the shame : 140
Then, lest my life be cropp'd to keep you
　　clear,
By flight I'll shun the danger which I fear.
　　　　　　　　　　　　　　　　　　[*Exit.*

　　　　　　Re-enter Antiochus.

　　Ant. He hath found the meaning, for which
　　we mean
To have his head.
He must not live to trumpet forth my infamy,
Nor tell the world Antiochus doth sin
In such a loathed manner ;
And therefore instantly this prince must die :
For by his fall my honor must keep high.
Who attends us there ?

　　　　　　Enter Thaliard.

　　Thal.　　　Doth your highness call ?　150
　　Ant. Thaliard,
You are of our chamber, and our mind par-
　　takes
Her private actions to your secrecy ;
And for your faithfulness we will advance you.
Thaliard, behold, here's poison, and here's
　　gold ;
We hate the prince of Tyre, and thou must
　　kill him :
It fits thee not to ask the reason why,
Because we bid it. Say, is it done ?
　　Thal.　　　　　　　　　　　My lord,
'Tis done.
　　Ant. Enough.　　　　　　　　　　160

　　　　　　Enter a Messenger.

Let your breath cool yourself, telling your
　　haste.
　　Mess. My lord, prince Pericles is fled.
　　　　　　　　　　　　　　　　　　[*Exit.*
　　Ant.　　　　　　　　　　As thou
Wilt live, fly after : and like an arrow shot
From a well-experienced archer hits the mark
His eye doth level at, so thou ne'er return
Unless thou say 'Prince Pericles is dead.'
　　Thal. My lord,
If I can get him within my pistol's length,
I'll make him sure enough : so, farewell to
　　your highness.
　　Ant. Thaliard, adieu ! [*Exit Thal.*] Till
Pericles be dead,　　　　　　　　　　　170
My heart can lend no succor to my head.
　　　　　　　　　　　　　　　　　　[*Exit.*

SCENE II. *Tyre. A room in the palace.*
Enter PERICLES.

Per. [*To Lords without*] Let none dis-
   turb us.—Why should this change of
   thoughts,
The sad companion, dull-eyed melancholy,
Be my so used a guest as not an hour,
In the day's glorious walk, or peaceful night,
The tomb where grief should sleep, can breed
   me quiet ?
Here pleasures court mine eyes, and mine eyes
   shun them,
And danger, which I fear'd, is at Antioch,
Whose aim seems far too short to hit me
   here :
Yet neither pleasure's art can joy my spirits,
Nor yet the other's distance comfort me.   10
Then it is thus : the passions of the mind,
That have their first conception by mis-dread,
Have after-nourishment and life by care ;
And what was first but fear what might be
   done,
Grows elder now and cares it be not done.
And so with me : the great Antiochus,
'Gainst whom I am too little to contend,
Since he's so great can make his will his act,
Will think me speaking, though I swear to
   silence ;
Nor boots it me to say I honor him.   20
If he suspect I may dishonor him :
And what may make him blush in being
   known,
He'll stop the course by which it might be
   known :
With hostile forces he'll o'erspread the land,
And with the ostent of war will look so huge,
Amazement shall drive courage from the state ;
Our men be vanquish'd ere they do resist,
And subjects punish'd that ne'er thought
   offence :
Which care of them, not pity of myself,
Who am no more but as the tops of trees,
Which fence the roots they grow by and de-
   fend them,   30
Makes both my body pine and soul to lan-
   guish,
And punish that before that he would punish.

Enter HELICANUS, *with other* Lords.

First Lord. Joy and all comfort in your
   sacred breast !
Sec. Lord. And keep your mind, till you
   return to us,
Peaceful and comfortable !
Hel. Peace, peace, and give experience
   tongue.
They do abuse the king that flatter him :
For flattery is the bellows blows up sin ;
The thing the which is flatter'd, but a spark,
To which that blast gives heat and stronger
   glowing ;   41
Whereas reproof, obedient and in order,
Fits kings, as they are men, for they may err.
When Signior Sooth here does proclaim a
   peace,
He flatters you, makes war upon your life.
Prince, pardon me, or strike me, if you please ;
I cannot be much lower than my knees.
Per. All leave us else ; but let your cares
   o'erlook
What shipping and what lading's in our
   haven,

And then return to us. [*Exeunt Lords.*] Helica-
   nus, thou   50
Hast moved us : what seest thou in our looks ?
Hel. An angry brow, dread lord.
Per. If there be such a dart in princes'
   frowns,
How durst thy tongue move anger to our face ?
Hel. How dare the plants look up to
   heaven, from whence
They have their nourishment ?
Per.   Thou know'st I have power
To take thy life from thee.
Hel. [*Kneeling.*] I have ground the axe
   myself ;
Do you but strike the blow.
Per.   Rise, prithee, rise.
Sit down : thou art no flatterer :   60
I thank thee for it ; and heaven forbid
That kings should let their ears hear their
   faults hid !
Fit counsellor and servant for a prince,
Who by thy wisdom makest a prince thy serv-
   ant,
What wouldst thou have me do ?
Hel.   To bear with patience
Such griefs as you yourself do lay upon your-
   self.
Per. Thou speak'st like a physician, Heli-
   canus,
That minister'st a potion unto me
That thou wouldst tremble to receive thyself.
Attend me, then : I went to Antioch,   70
Where as thou know'st, against the face of
   death,
I sought the purchase of a glorious beauty,
From whence an issue I might propagate,
Are arms to princes, and bring joys to sub-
   jects.
Her face was to mine eye beyond all wonder ;
The rest—hark in thine ear—as black as in-
   cest :
Which by my knowledge found, the sinful
   father
Seem'd not to strike, but smooth : but thou
   know'st this,
'Tis time to fear when tyrants seem to kiss.
Which fear so grew in me, I hither fled,   80
Under the covering of a careful night,
Who seem'd my good protector ; and, being
   here,
Bethought me what was past, what might
   succeed.
I knew him tyrannous ; and tyrants' fears
Decrease not, but grow faster than the years :
And should he doubt it, as no doubt he doth,
That I should open to the listening air
How many worthy princes' bloods were shed,
To keep his bed of blackness unlaid ope,
To lop that doubt, he'll fill this land with
   arms,   90
And make pretence of wrong that I have done
   him :
When all, for mine, if I may call offence,
Must feel war's blow, who spares not in-
   nocence :
Which love to all, of which thyself art one,
Who now reprovest me for it,—
Hel.   Alas, sir !
Per. Drew sleep out of mine eyes, blood
   from my cheeks,
Musings into my mind, with thousand doubts
How I might stop this tempest ere it came ;

And finding little comfort to relieve them,
I thought it princely charity to grieve them. 100
Hel. Well, my lord, since you have given
me leave to speak,
Freely will I speak. Antiochus you fear,
And justly too, I think, you fear the tyrant,
Who either by public war or private treason
Will take away your life.
Therefore, my lord, go travel for a while,
Till that his rage and anger be forgot,
Or till the Destinies do cut his thread of life.
Your rule direct to any ; if to me. 109
Day serves not light more faithful than I'll be.
Per. I do not doubt thy faith ;
But should he wrong my liberties in my ab-
sence ?
Hel. We'll mingle our bloods together in
the earth,
From whence we had our being and our birth.
Per. Tyre, I now look from thee then, and
to Tarsus
Intend my travel, where I'll hear from thee ;
And by whose letters I'll dispose myself.
The care I had and have of subjects' good
On thee I lay, whose wisdom's strength can
bear it.
I'll take thy word for faith, not ask thine
oath : 120
Who shuns not to break one will sure crack
both :
But in our orbs we'll live so round and safe,
That time of both this truth shall ne'er con-
vince,
Thou show'dst a subject's shine, I a true
prince. [*Exeunt.*

SCENE III. *Tyre. An ante-chamber in the
palace.*

Enter THALIARD.

Thal. So, this is Tyre, and this the court.
Here must I kill King Pericles ; and if I do it
not, I am sure to be hanged at home : 'tis dangerous. Well, I perceive he was a wise fellow,
and had good discretion, that, being bid to
ask what he would of the king, desired he
might know none of his secrets : now do I see
he had some reason for 't ; for if a king bid a
man be a villain, he's bound by the indenture
of his oath to be one ! Hush ! here come the
lords of Tyre.

Enter HELICANUS *and* ESCANES, *with other*
Lords *of Tyre.*

Hel. You shall not need, my fellow peers
of Tyre, 10
Further to question me of your king's depar-
ture :
His seal'd commission, left in trust with me,
Doth speak sufficiently he's gone to travel.
Thal. [*Aside*] How ! the king gone !
Hel. If further yet you will be satisfied,
Why, as it were unlicensed of your loves,
He would depart, I'll give some light unto
you.
Being at Antioch——
Thal. [*Aside*] What from Antioch ?
Hel. Royal Antiochus—on what cause I
know not— 20
Took some displeasure at him ; at least he
judged so :
And doubting lest that he had err'd or sinn'd,
To show his sorrow, he'ld correct himself ;

So puts himself unto the shipman's toil,
With whom each minute threatens life or
death.
Thal. [*Aside*] Well, I perceive
I shall not be hang'd now, although I would ;
But since he's gone, the king's seas must
please :
He 'scaped the land, to perish at the sea.
I'll present myself. Peace to the lords of
Tyre ! 30
Hel. Lord Thaliard from Antiochus is wel-
come.
Thal. From him I come
With message unto princely Pericles ;
But since my landing I have understood
Your lord has betook himself to unknown
travels,
My message must return from whence it came.
Hel. We have no reason to desire it,
Commended to our master, not to us :
Yet, ere you shall depart, this we desire,
As friends to Antioch, we may feast in Tyre.
[*Exeunt.* 40

SCENE IV. *Tarsus. A room in the Governor's house.*

Enter CLEON, *the governor of Tarsus, with*
DIONYZA, *and others.*

Cle. My Dionyza, shall we rest us here,
And by relating tales of others' griefs,
See if 'twill teach us to forget our own ?
Dio. That were to blow at fire in hope to
quench it ;
For who digs hills because they do aspire
Throws down one mountain to cast up a
higher.
O my distressed lord, even such our griefs
are ;
Here they're but felt, and seen with mischief's
eyes,
But like to groves, being topp'd, they higher
rise.
Cle. O Dionyza, 10
Who wanteth food, and will not say he wants
it,
Or can conceal his hunger till he famish ?
Our tongues and sorrows do sound deep
Our woes into the air ; our eyes do weep,
Till tongues fetch breath that may proclaim
them louder ;
That, if heaven slumber while their creatures
want,
They may awake their helps to comfort them.
I'll then discourse our woes, felt several years,
And wanting breath to speak help me with
tears.
Dio. I'll do my best, sir. 20
Cle. This Tarsus, o'er which I have the
government,
A city on whom plenty held full hand,
For riches strew'd herself even in the streets ;
Whose towers bore heads so high they kiss'd
the clouds,
And strangers ne'er beheld but wonder'd at ;
Whose men and dames so jetted and adorn'd,
Like one another's glass to trim them by :
Their tables were stored full, to glad the sight,
And not so much to feed on as delight ;
All poverty was scorn'd, and pride so great,
The name of help grew odious to repeat. 31
Dio. O, 'tis too true.

Cle. But see what heaven can do ! By this
 our change,
These mouths, who but of late, earth, sea,
 and air,
Were all too little to content and please,
Although they gave their creatures in abun-
 dance,
As houses are defiled for want of use,
They are now starved for want of exercise :
Those palates who, not yet two summers
 younger,
Must have inventions to delight the taste,   40
Would now be glad of bread, and beg for it :
Those mothers who, to nousle up their babes,
Thought nought too curious, are ready now
To eat those little darlings whom they loved.
So sharp are hunger's teeth, that man and
 wife
Draw lots who first shall die to lengthen life :
Here stands a lord, and there a lady weeping ;
Here many sink, yet those which see them fall
Have scarce strength left to give them burial.
Is not this true ?   50
Dio. Our cheeks and hollow eyes do wit-
 ness it.
Cle. O, let those cities that of plenty's cup
And her prosperities so largely taste,
With their superfluous riots, hear these tears !
The misery of Tarsus may be theirs.

Enter a Lord.

Lord. Where's the lord governor ?
Cle.   Here.
Speak out thy sorrows which thou bring'st in
 haste,
For comfort is too far for us to expect.
Lord. We have descried, upon our neigh-
 boring shore,   60
A portly sail of ships make hitherward.
Cle. I thought as much.
One sorrow never comes but brings an heir,
That may succeed as his inheritor ;
And so in ours : some neighboring nation,
Taking advantage of our misery,
Hath stuff'd these hollow vessels with their
 power,
To beat us down, the which are down al-
 ready ;
And make a conquest of unhappy me,
Whereas no glory's got to overcome.   70
Lord. That's the least fear ; for, by the
 semblance
Of their white flags display'd, they bring us
 peace,
And come to us as favorers, not as foes.
Cle. Thou speak'st like him's untutor'd to
 repeat :
Who makes the fairest show means most de-
 ceit.
But bring they what they will and what they
 can,
What need we fear ?
The ground's the lowest, and we are half way
 there.
Go tell their general we attend him here,
To know for what he comes, and whence he
 comes,   80
And what he craves.
Lord. I go, my lord.   [*Exit.*
Cle. Welcome is peace, if he on peace con-
 sist ;
If wars, we are unable to resist.

Enter PERICLES with Attendants.

Per. Lord governor, for so we hear you
 are,
Let not our ships and number of our men
Be like a beacon fired to amaze your eyes.
We have heard your miseries as far as Tyre,
And seen the desolation of your streets :
Nor come we to add sorrow to your tears,   90
But to relieve them of their heavy load ;
And these our ships, you happily may think
Are like the Trojan horse was stuff'd within
With bloody veins, expecting overthrow,
Are stored with corn to make your needy
 bread,
And give them life whom hunger starved half
 dead.
All. The gods of Greece protect you !
And we'll pray for you.
Per.   Arise, I pray you, rise :
We do not look for reverence, but for love,
And harborage for ourself, our ships, and
 men.   100
Cle. The which when any shall not gratify,
Or pay you with unthankfulness in thought,
Be it our wives, our children, or ourselves,
The curse of heaven and men succeed their
 evils !
Till when,—the which I hope shall ne'er be
 seen,—
Your grace is welcome to our town and us.
Per. Which welcome we'll accept ; feast
 here awhile,
Until our stars that frown lend us a smile.
                                    [*Exeunt.*

ACT II.

Enter GOWER.

Gow. Here have you seen a mighty king
His child, I wis, to incest bring ;
A better prince and benign lord,
That will prove awful both in deed and
 word.
Be quiet then as men should be,
Till he hath pass'd necessity.
I'll show you those in troubles reign,
Losing a mite, a mountain gain.
The good in conversation,
To whom I give my benison,   10
Is still at Tarsus, where each man
Thinks all is writ he spoken can ;
And, to remember what he does,
Build his statue to make him glorious :
But tidings to the contrary
Are brought your eyes ; what need speak I ?

DUMB SHOW.

Enter at one door PERICLES *talking with*
CLEON ; *all the train with them. Enter at
another door a Gentleman, with a letter to*
PERICLES ; PERICLES *shows the letter to*
CLEON ; *gives the* Messenger *a reward, and
knights him. Exit* PERICLES *at one door,
and* CLEON *at another.*

Good Helicane, that stay'd at home,
Not to eat honey like a drone
From others' labors ; for though he strive
To killen bad, keep good alive ;   20
And to fulfil his prince' desire,
Sends word of all that haps in Tyre :

How Thaliard came full bent with sin
And had intent to murder him ;
And that in Tarsus was not best
Longer for him to make his rest.
He, doing so, put forth to seas,
Where when men been, there's seldom ease ;
For now the wind begins to blow ;
Thunder above and deeps below   30
Make such unquiet, that the ship
Should house him safe is wreck'd and split ;
And he, good prince, having all lost,
By waves from coast to coast is tost :
All perishen of man, of pelf,
Ne aught escapen but himself ;
Till fortune, tired with doing bad,
Threw him ashore, to give him glad :
And here he comes. What shall be next,
Pardon old Gower,—this longs the text.   40
                                   [*Exit.*

SCENE I. *Pentapolis. An open place by the
                    sea-side.*

            Enter PERICLES, *wet.*

Per.   Yet cease your ire, you angry stars of
              heaven !
Wind, rain, and thunder, remember, earthly
              man
Is but a substance that must yield to you ;
And I, as fits my nature, do obey you :
Alas, the sea hath cast me on the rocks,
Wash'd me from shore to shore, and left me
              breath
Nothing to think on but ensuing death :
Let it suffice the greatness of your powers
To have bereft a prince of all his fortunes ;
And having thrown him from your watery
              grave,   10
Here to have death in peace is all he'll crave.

            Enter three Fishermen.

First Fish.   What, ho, Pilch !
Sec. Fish.   Ha, come and bring away the
              nets !
First Fish.   What, Patch-breech, I say !
Third Fish.   What say you, master ?
First Fish.   Look how thou stirrest now !
come away, or I'll fetch thee with a wanion.
Third Fish.   'Faith, master, I am thinking
of the poor men that were cast away before
us even now.   20
First Fish.   Alas, poor souls, it grieved my
heart to hear what pitiful cries they made to
us to help them, when, well-a-day, we could
scarce help ourselves.
Third Fish.   Nay, master, said not I as
much when I saw the porpus how he bounced
and tumbled ? they say they're half fish, half
flesh : a plague on them, they ne'er come but
I look to be washed. Master, I marvel how
the fishes live in the sea.   30
First Fish.   Why, as men do a-land ; the
great ones eat up the little ones : I can compare our rich misers to nothing so fitly as to a
whale ; a' plays and tumbles, driving the poor
fry before him, and at last devours them all
at a mouthful : such whales have I heard on
o' the land, who never leave gaping till they've
swallowed the whole parish, church, steeple,
bells, and all.
Per.   [*Aside*] A pretty moral.   39
Third Fish.   But, master, if I had been the
sexton, I would have been that day in the
belfry.

Sec. Fish.   Why, man ?
Third Fish.   Because he should have swallowed me too : and when I had been in his
belly, I would have kept such a jangling of
the bells, that he should never have left, till
he cast bells, steeple, church, and parish up
again. But if the good King Simonides were
of my mind,—
Per.   [*Aside*] Simonides !   49
Third Fish.   We would purge the land of
these drones, that rob the bee of her honey.
Per.   [*Aside*] How from the finny subject of
              the sea
These fishers tell the infirmities of men ;
And from their watery empire recollect
All that may men approve or men detect !
Peace be at your labor, honest fishermen.
Sec. Fish.   Honest ! good fellow, what's
that ? If it be a day fits you, search out of
the calendar, and nobody look after it.
Per.   May see the sea hath cast upon your
              coast.   60
Sec. Fish.   What a drunken knave was the
sea to cast thee in our way !
Per.   A man whom both the waters and the
              wind,
In that vast tennis-court, have made the ball
For them to play upon, entreats you pity him ;
He asks of you, that never used to beg.
First Fish.   No, friend, cannot you beg ?
Here's them in our country of Greece gets
more with begging than we can do with work-
ing.
Sec. Fish.   Canst thou catch any fishes,
then ?   70
Per.   I never practiced it.
Sec. Fish.   Nay, then thou wilt starve, sure ;
for here's nothing to be got now-a-days, un-
less thou canst fish for't.
Per.   What I have been I have forgot to
              know ;
But what I am, want teaches me to think on :
A man throng'd up with cold : my veins are
              chill,
And have no more of life than may suffice
To give my tongue that heat to ask your help ;
Which if you shall refuse, when I am dead, 80
For that I am a man, pray see me buried.
First Fish.   Die quoth-a ? Now gods for-
bid ! I have a gown here ; come, put it on ;
keep thee warm. Now, afore me, a handsome
fellow ! Come, thou shalt go home, and we'll
have flesh for holidays, fish for fasting-days,
and moreo'er puddings and flap-jacks, and
thou shalt be welcome.
Per.   I thank you, sir.
Sec. Fish.   Hark you, my friend ; you said
you could not beg.   90
Per.   I did but crave.
Sec. Fish.   But crave ! Then I'll turn craver
too, and so I shall 'scape whipping.
Per.   Why, are all your beggars whipped,
              then ?
Sec. Fish.   O, not all, my friend, not all ;
for if all your beggars were whipped, I would
wish no better office than to be beadle. But,
master, I'll go draw up the net.
                    [*Exit with Third Fisherman.*
Per.   [*Aside*] How well this honest mirth
              becomes their labor !
First Fish.   Hark you, sir, do you know
where ye are ?   101

Per. Not well.

First Fish. Why, I'll tell you : this is called Pentapolis, and our king the good Simonides.

Per. The good King Simonides, do you call him.

First Fish. Ay, sir ; and he deserves so to be called for his peaceable reign and good government.

Per. He is a happy king, since he gains from his subjects the name of good by his government. How far is his court distant from this shore ?   111

First Fish. Marry, sir, half a day's journey : and I'll tell you, he hath a fair daughter, and to-morrow is her birth-day ; and there are princes and knights come from all parts of the world to just and tourney for her love.

Per. Were my fortunes equal to my desires, I could wish to make one there.

First Fish. O, sir, things must be as they may ; and what a man cannot get, he may lawfully deal for—his wife's soul.   121

Re-enter Second *and* Third Fishermen, *drawing up a net.*

Sec. Fish. Help, master, help ! here's a fish hangs in the net, like a poor man's right in the law ; 'twill hardly come out. Ha ! bots on't, 'tis come at last, and 'tis turned to a rusty armor.

Per. An armor, friends ! I pray you, let me see it.

Thanks, fortune, yet, that, after all my crosses, Thou givest me somewhat to repair myself ;
And though it was mine own, part of my heritage,   129
Which my dead father did bequeath to me,
With this strict charge, even as he left his life,
'Keep it, my Pericles ; it hath been a shield
'Twixt me and death ; '—and pointed to this
     brace ;—
'For that it saved me, keep it ; in like necessity—
The which the gods protect thee from !—may defend thee.'
It kept where I kept, I so dearly loved it ;
Till the rough seas, that spare not any man,
Took it in rage, though calm'd have given't again :
I thank thee for't : my shipwreck now's no ill,
Since I have here my father's gift in's will.

First Fish. What mean you, sir ?   141

Per. To beg of you, kind friends, this coat of worth,
For it was sometime target to a king ;
I know it by this mark. He loved me dearly,
And for his sake I wish the having of it ;
And that you'ld guide me to your sovereign's
     court,
Where with it I may appear a gentleman ;
And if that ever my low fortune's better,
I'll pay your bounties ; till then rest your debtor.

First Fish. Why, wilt thou tourney for the lady ?   150

Per. I'll show the virtue I have borne in arms.

First Fish. Why, do 'e take it, and the gods give thee good on't !

Sec. Fish. Ay, but hark you, my friend ; 'twas we that made up this garment through the rough seams of the waters : there are certain condolements, certain vails. I hope, sir, if you thrive, you'll remember from whence you had it.

Per. Believe 't, I will.

By your furtherance I am clothed in steel ; 160
And, spite of all the rapture of the sea,
This jewel holds his building on my arm :
Unto thy value I will mount myself
Upon a courser, whose delightful steps
Shall make the gazer joy to see him tread.
Only, my friend, I yet am unprovided
Of a pair of bases.

Sec. Fish. We'll sure provide : thou shalt
have my best gown to make thee a pair ; and
I'll bring thee to the court myself.   170

Per. Then honor be but a goal to my will,
This day I'll rise, or else add ill to ill. [*Exeunt.*

SCENE II. *The same. A public way or platform leading to the lists. A pavilion by the side of it for the reception of the King, Princess, Lords, &c.*

Enter SIMONIDES, THAISA, Lords, *and* Attendants.

Sim. Are the knights ready to begin the triumph ?

First Lord. They are, my liege ;
And stay your coming to present themselves.

Sim. Return them, we are ready ; and our daughter,
In honor of whose birth these triumphs are,
Sits here, like beauty's child, whom nature gat
For men to see, and seeing wonder at.
            [*Exit a Lord.*

Thai. It pleaseth you, my royal father, to express
My commendations great, whose merit's less.

Sim. It's fit it should be so ; for princes are
A model, which heaven makes like to itself :
As jewels lose their glory if neglected,
So princes their renowns if not respected.
'Tis now your honor, daughter, to explain
The labor of each knight in his device.

Thai. Which, to preserve mine honor, I'll perform.

Enter a Knight ; *he passes over, and his* Squire *presents his shield to the* Princess.

Sim. Who is the first that doth prefer himself ?

Thai. A knight of Sparta, my renowned father ;
And the device he bears upon his shield
Is a black Ethiope reaching at the sun ;   20
The word, ' Lux tua vita mihi.'

Sim. He loves you well that holds his life of you.
            [*The Second Knight passes over.*
Who is the second that presents himself ?

Thai. A prince of Macedon, my royal father ;
And the device he bears upon his shield
Is an arm'd knight that's conquer'd by a lady ;
The motto thus, in Spanish, ' Piu por dulzura
que por fuerza.'
            [*The Third Knight passes over.*

Sim. And what's the third ?

Thai.   The third of Antioch ;
And his device, a wreath of chivalry ;
The word, ' Me pompæ provexit apex.'   30
            [*The Fourth Knight passes over.*

Sim. What is the fourth ?

Thai. A burning torch that's turned upside
down ;
The word, ' Quod me alit, me extinguit.'
Sim. Which shows that beauty hath his
power and will,
Which can as well inflame as it can kill.
[*The Fifth Knight passes over.*
Thai. The fifth, an hand environed with
clouds,
Holding out gold that's by the touchstone
tried ;
The motto thus, ' Sic spectanda fides.'
[*The Sixth Knight, Pericles, passes over.*
Sim. And what's
The sixth and last, the which the knight him-
self   40
With such a graceful courtesy deliver'd ?
Thai. He seems to be a stranger ; but his
present is
A wither'd branch, that's only green at top ;
The motto, ' In hac spe vivo.'
Sim. A pretty moral ;
From the dejected state wherein he is,
He hopes by you his fortunes yet may flour-
ish.
First Lord. He had need mean better than
his outward show
Can any way speak in his just commend ;
For by his rusty outside he appears   50
To have practiced more the whipstock than
the lance.
Sec. Lord. He well may be a stranger, for
he comes
To an honor'd triumph strangely furnished.
Third Lord. And on set purpose let his
armor rust
Until this day, to scour it in the dust.
Sim. Opinion's but a fool, that makes us
scan
The outward habit by the inward man.
But stay, the knights are coming : we will
withdraw
Into the gallery.   [*Exeunt.*
[*Great shouts within and all cry* ' The mean
knight ! '

SCENE III. *The same. A hall of state : a
banquet prepared.*

Enter SIMONIDES, THAISA, *Lords, Attendants,
and* Knights, *from tilting.*

Sim. Knights,
To say you're welcome were superfluous.
To place upon the volume of your deeds,
As in a title-page, your worth in arms,
Were more than you expect, or more than's
fit,
Since every worth in show commends itself.
Prepare for mirth, for mirth becomes a feast :
You are princes and my guests.
Thai. But you, my knight and guest ;
To whom this wreath of victory I give,   10
And crown you king of this day's happiness.
Per. 'Tis more by fortune, lady, than by
merit.
Sim. Call it by what you will, the day is
yours ;
And here, I hope, is none that envies it.
In framing an artist, art hath thus decreed,
To make some good, but others to exceed ;
And you are her labor'd scholar. Come, queen
o' the feast,—

For, daughter, so you are,—here take your
place ;
Marshal the rest, as they deserve their grace.
Knights. We are honor'd much by good
Simonides.   20
Sim. Your presence glads our days : honor
we love ;
For who hates honor hates the gods above.
Marshal. Sir, yonder is your place.
Per.   Some other is more fit.
First Knight. Contend not, sir ; for we are
gentlemen
That neither in our hearts nor outward eyes
Envy the great nor do the low despise.
Per. You are right courteous knights.
Sim.   Sit, sir, sit.
Per. By Jove, I wonder, that is king of
thoughts,
These cates resist me, she but thought upon.
Thai. By Juno, that is queen of marriage,
All viands that I eat do seem unsavory,   31
Wishing him my meat. Sure, he's a gallant
gentleman.
Sim. He's but a country gentleman ;
Has done no more than other knights have
done ;
Has broken a staff or so ; so let it pass.
Thai. To me he seems like diamond to
glass.
Per. Yon king's to me like to my father's
picture,
Which tells me in that glory once he was ;
Had princes sit, like stars, about his throne,
And he the sun, for them to reverence ;   40
None that beheld him, but, like lesser lights,
Did vail their crowns to his supremacy :
Where now his son's like a glow-worm in the
night,
The which hath fire in darkness, none in light :
Whereby I see that Time's the king of men,
He's both their parent, and he is their grave,
And gives them what he will, not what they
crave.
Sim. What, are you merry, knights ?
Knights. Who can be other in this royal
presence ?
Sim. Here, with a cup that's stored unto
the brim,—   50
As you do love, fill to your mistress' lips,—
We drink this health to you.
Knights.   We thank your grace.
Sim. Yet pause awhile :
Yon knight doth sit too melancholy,
As if the entertainment in our court
Had not a show might countervail his worth.
Note it not you, Thaisa ?
Thai.   What is it
To me, my father ?
Sim.   O, attend, my daughter :
Princes in this should live like gods above,
Who freely give to every one that comes   60
To honor them :
And princes not doing so are like to gnats,
Which make a sound, but kill'd are wonder'd
at.
Therefore to make his entrance more sweet,
Here, say we drink this standing-bowl of wine
to him.
Thai. Alas, my father, it befits not me
Unto a stranger knight to be so bold :
He may my proffer take for an offence,
Since men take women's gifts for impudence.

Sim. How !   70
Do as I bid you, or you'll move me else.
   Thai. [*Aside*] Now, by the gods, he could
      not please me better.
   Sim. And furthermore tell him, we desire
      to know of him,
Of whence he is, his name and parentage.
   Thai. The king my father, sir, has drunk
      to you.
   Per. I thank him.
   Thai. Wishing it so much blood unto your
      life.
   Per. I thank both him and you, and pledge
      him freely.
   Thai. And further he desires to know of
      you,   79
Of whence you are, your name and parentage.
   Per. A gentleman of Tyre ; my name,
      Pericles ;
My education been in arts and arms ;
Who, looking for adventures in the world,
Was by the rough seas reft of ships and men,
And after shipwreck driven upon this shore.
   Thai. He thanks your grace ; names him-
      self Pericles,
A gentleman of Tyre,
Who only by misfortune of the seas
Bereft of ships and men, cast on this shore.
   Sim. Now, by the gods, I pity his misfor-
      tune,   90
And will awake him from his melancholy.
Come, gentlemen, we sit too long on trifles,
And waste the time, which looks for other
      revels.
Even in your armors, as you are address'd,
Will very well become a soldier's dance.
I will not have excuse, with saying this
Loud music is too harsh for ladies' heads,
Since they love men in arms as well as beds.
                              [*The Knights dance.*
So, this was well ask'd, 'twas so well per-
      form'd.
Come, sir ;   100
Here is a lady that wants breathing too ;
And I have heard, you knights of Tyre
Are excellent in making ladies trip ;
And that their measures are as excellent.
   Per. In those that practice them they are,
      my lord.
   Sim. O, that's as much as you would be
      denied
Of your fair courtesy.
              [*The Knights and Ladies dance.*
              Unclasp, unclasp :
Thanks, gentlemen, to all ; all have done well,
[*To Per.*] But you the best. Pages and lights,
      to conduct
These knights unto their several lodgings ! [*To
   Per.*] Yours, sir,   110
We have given order to be next our own.
   Per. I am at your grace's pleasure.
   Sim. Princes, it is too late to talk of love ;
And that's the mark I know you level at :
Therefore each one betake him to his rest ;
To-morrow all for speeding do their best.
                                       [*Exeunt.*

SCENE IV. *Tyre. A room in the Governor's
      house.*

      Enter HELICANUS *and* ESCANES.

   Hel. No, Escanes, know this of me,
Antiochus from incest lived not free :

For which, the most high gods not minding
      longer
To withhold the vengeance that they had in
      store,
Due to this heinous capital offence,
Even in the height and pride of all his glory,
When he was seated in a chariot
Of an inestimable value, and his daughter with
      him,
A fire from heaven came and shrivell'd up
Their bodies, even to loathing ; for they so
      stunk,   10
That all those eyes adored them ere their fall
Scorn now their hand should give them burial.
   Esca. 'Twas very strange.
   Hel.   And yet but justice ; for though
This king were great, his greatness was no
      guard
To bar heaven's shaft, but sin had his reward.
   Esca. 'Tis very true.

      Enter two or three Lords.

   First Lord. See, not a man in private con-
      ference
Or council has respect with him but he.
   Sec. Lord. It shall no longer grieve without
      reproof.
   Third Lord. And cursed be he that will not
      second it.   20
   First Lord. Follow me, then. Lord Heli-
      cane, a word.
   Hel. With me ? and welcome : happy day,
      my lords.
   First Lord. Know that our griefs are risen
      to the top,
And now at length they overflow their banks.
   Hel. Your griefs ! for what ? wrong not
      your prince you love.
   First Lord. Wrong not yourself, then, no-
      ble Helicane ;
But if the prince do live, let us salute him,
Or know what ground's made happy by his
      breath.
If in the world he live, we'll seek him out ;
If in his grave he rest, we'll find him there ;
And be resolved he lives to govern us,   31
Or dead, give's cause to mourn his funeral,
And leave us to our free election.
   Sec. Lord. Whose death indeed's the
      strongest in our censure :
And knowing this kingdom is without a
      head,—
Like goodly buildings left without a roof
Soon fall to ruin,—your noble self,
That best know how to rule and how to reign,
We thus submit unto,—our sovereign.
   All. Live, noble Helicane !   40
   Hel. For honor's cause, forbear your suf-
      frages :
If that you love Prince Pericles, forbear.
Take I your wish, I leap into the seas,
Where's hourly trouble for a minute's ease.
A twelvemonth longer, let me entreat you to
Forbear the absence of your king :
If in which time expired, he not return,
I shall with aged patience bear your yoke.
But if I cannot win you to this love,
Go search like nobles, like noble subjects,   50
And in your search spend your adventurous
      worth ;
Whom if you find, and win unto return,
You shall like diamonds sit about his crown.

First Lord. To wisdom he's a fool that will
  not yield;
And since Lord Helicane enjoineth us,
We with our travels will endeavor us.
  Hel. Then you love us, we you, and we'll
    clasp hands:
When peers thus knit, a kingdom ever stands.
                                        [*Exeunt.*

SCENE V. *Pentapolis. A room in the palace.*

Enter SIMONIDES, *reading a letter, at one
  door: the* Knights *meet him.*

  First Knight. Good morrow to the good Si-
    monides.
  Sim. Knights, from my daughter this I let
    you know,
That for this twelvemonth she'll not undertake
A married life.
Her reason to herself is only known,
Which yet from her by no means can I get.
  Sec. Knight. May we not get access to her,
    my lord?
  Sim. 'Faith, by no means; she has so
    strictly tied
Her to her chamber, that 'tis impossible.
One twelve moons more she'll wear Diana's
  livery;   10
This by the eye of Cynthia hath she vow'd,
And on her virgin honor will not break it.
  Third Knight. Loath to bid farewell, we
    take our leaves.   [*Exeunt Knights.*
  Sim. So,
They are well dispatch'd; now to my daugh-
  ter's letter:
She tells me here, she'll wed the stranger
  knight,
Or never more to view nor day nor light.
'Tis well, mistress; your choice agrees with
  mine;
I like that well: nay, how absolute she's in't,
Not minding whether I dislike or no!   20
Well, I do commend her choice;
And will no longer have it be delay'd.
Soft! here he comes: I must dissemble it.

Enter PERICLES.

  Per. All fortune to the good Simonides!
  Sim. To you as much, sir! I am beholding
    to you
For your sweet music this last night: I do
Protest my ears were never better fed
With such delightful pleasing harmony.
  Per. It is your grace's pleasure to com-
    mend;
Not my desert.
  Sim. Sir, you are music's master.   30
  Per. The worst of all her scholars, my good
    lord.
  Sim. Let me ask you one thing:
What do you think of my daughter, sir?
  Per. A most virtuous princess.
  Sim. And she is fair too, is she not?
  Per. As a fair day in summer, wondrous
    fair.
  Sim. Sir, my daughter thinks very well of
    you;
Ay, so well, that you must be her master,
And she will be your scholar: therefore look
  to it.   39
  Per. I am unworthy for her schoolmaster.
  Sim. She thinks not so; peruse this writing
    else.

  Per. [*Aside*] What's here?
A letter, that she loves the knight of Tyre!
'Tis the king's subtilty to have my life.
O, seek not to entrap me, gracious lord,
A stranger and distressed gentleman,
That never aim'd so high to love your daugh-
  ter,
But bent all offices to honor her.
  Sim. Thou hast bewitch'd my daughter,
    and thou art
A villain.   50
  Per. By the gods, I have not:
Never did thought of mine levy offence;
Nor never did my actions yet commence
A deed might gain her love or your displeas-
  ure.
  Sim. Traitor, thou liest.
  Per.   Traitor!
  Sim.   Ay, traitor.
  Per. Even in his throat—unless it be the
    king—
That calls me traitor, I return the lie.
  Sim. [*Aside*] Now, by the gods, I do ap-
    plaud his courage.
  Per. My actions are as noble as my
    thoughts,
That never relish'd of a base descent.   60
I came unto your court for honor's cause,
And not to be a rebel to her state;
And he that otherwise accounts of me,
This sword shall prove he's honor's enemy.
  Sim. No?
Here comes my daughter, she can witness it.

Enter THAISA.

  Per. Then, as you are as virtuous as fair,
Resolve your angry father, if my tongue
Did ere solicit, or my hand subscribe
To any syllable that made love to you.   70
  Thai. Why, sir, say if you had,
Who takes offence at that would make me
  glad?
  Sim. Yea, mistress, are you so peremp-
    tory?
[*Aside*] I am glad on't with all my heart.—
I'll tame you; I'll bring you in subjection.
Will you, not having my consent,
Bestow your love and your affections
Upon a stranger? [*Aside*] who, for aught I
  know,
May be, nor can I think the contrary,
As great in blood as I myself.—   80
Therefore hear you, mistress; either frame
Your will to mine,—and you, sir, hear you,
Either be ruled by me, or I will make you—
Man and wife:
Nay, come, your hands and lips must seal it
  too:
And being join'd, I'll thus your hopes destroy;
And for a further grief,—God give you joy!—
What, are you both pleased?
  Thai.   Yes, if you love me, sir.
  Per. Even as my life, or blood that fosters
    it.
  Sim. What, are you both agreed?   90
  Both. Yes, if it please your majesty.
  Sim. It pleaseth me so well, that I will see
    you wed;
And then with what haste you can get you to
  bed.   [*Exeunt.*

ACT III.

Enter GOWER.

Gow. Now sleep yslaked hath the rout;
No din but snores the house about,
Made louder by the o'er-fed breast
Of this most pompous marriage-feast.
The cat, with eyne of burning coal,
Now crouches fore the mouse's hole;
And crickets sing at the oven's mouth,
E'er the blither for their drouth.
Hymen hath brought the bride to bed,
Where, by the loss of maidenhead,   10
A babe is moulded. Be attent,
And time that is so briefly spent
With your fine fancies quaintly eche:
What's dumb in show I'll plain with speech.

DUMB SHOW.

Enter, PERICLES *and* SIMONIDES *at one door,
with* Attendants; *a* Messenger *meets them,
kneels, and gives* PERICLES *a letter:* PERI-
CLES *shows it* SIMONIDES; *the* Lords *kneel
to him. Then enter* THAISA *with child, with*
LYCHORIDA *a nurse. The* KING *shows her
the letter; she rejoices: she and* PERICLES
takes leave of her father, and depart with
LYCHORIDA *and their* Attendants. *Then exeunt* SIMONIDES *and the rest.*

By many a dern and painful perch
Of Pericles the careful search,
By the four opposing coigns
Which the world together joins,
Is made with all due diligence
That horse and sail and high expense   20
Can stead the quest. At last from Tyre,
Fame answering the most strange inquire,
To the court of King Simonides
Are letters brought, the tenor these:
Antiochus and his daughter dead;
The men of Tyrus on the head
Of Helicanus would set on
The crown of Tyre, but he will none:
The mutiny he there hastes t' oppress;
Says to 'em, if King Pericles   30
Come not home in twice six moons,
He, obedient to their dooms,
Will take the crown. The sum of this,
Brought hither to Pentapolis,
Y-ravished the regions round,
And every one with claps can sound,
' Our heir-apparent is a king!
Who dream'd, who thought of such a
        thing?'
Brief, he must hence depart to Tyre:
His queen with child makes her desire—   40
Which who shall cross?—along to go:
Omit we all their dole and woe:
Lychorida, her nurse, she takes,
And so to sea. Their vessel shakes
On Neptune's billow; half the flood
Hath their keel cut: but fortune's mood
Varies again; the grisly north
Disgorges such a tempest forth,
That, as a duck for life that dives,
So up and down the poor ship drives: 50
The lady shrieks, and well-a-near
Does fall in travail with her fear:
And what ensues in this fell storm
Shall for itself itself perform.

I nill relate, action may
Conveniently the rest convey;
Which might not what by me is told.
In your imagination hold
This stage the ship, upon whose deck   59
The sea-tost Pericles appears to speak. [*Exit.*

SCENE I.

Enter PERICLES, *on shipboard.*

Per. Thou god of this great vast, rebuke
        these surges,
Which wash both heaven and hell; and thou,
        that hast
Upon the winds command, bind them in brass,
Having call'd them from the deep! O, still
Thy deafening, dreadful thunders; gently
        quench
Thy nimble, sulphurous flashes! O, how, Ly-
        chorida,
How does my queen? Thou stormest venom-
        ously;
Wilt thou spit all thyself? The seaman's
        whistle
Is as a whisper in the ears of death,
Unheard. Lychorida!—Lucina, O   10
Divinest patroness, and midwife gentle
To those that cry by night, convey thy deity
Aboard our dancing boat; make swift the
        pangs
Of my queen's travails!

Enter LYCHORIDA, *with an Infant.*

                Now, Lychorida!
Lyc. Here is a thing too young for such a
        place,
Who, if it had conceit, would die, as I
Am like to do: take in your arms this piece
Of your dead queen.
Per.   How, how, Lychorida!
Lyc. Patience, good sir; do not assist the
        storm.
Here's all that is left living of your queen,   20
A little daughter: for the sake of it,
Be manly, and take comfort.
Per.   O you gods!
Why do you make us love your goodly gifts,
And snatch them straight away? We here be-
        low
Recall not what we give, and therein may
Use honor with you.
Lyc.   Patience, good sir,
Even for this charge.
Per.   Now, mild may be thy life!
For a more blustrous birth had never babe:
Quiet and gentle thy conditions! for   29
Thou art the rudeliest welcome to this world
That ever was prince's child. Happy what fol-
        lows!
Thou hast as chiding a nativity
As fire, air, water, earth, and heaven can make,
To herald thee from the womb: even at the
        first
Thy loss is more than can thy portage quit,
With all thou canst find here. Now, the good
        gods
Throw their best eyes upon't!

Enter two Sailors.

First Sail. What courage, sir? God save
        you!
Per. Courage enough: I do not fear the
        flaw;
It hath done to me the worst. Yet, for the love

Of this poor infant, this fresh-new sea-farer,
I would it would be quiet.
   First Sail. Slack the bolins there ! Thou
wilt not, wilt thou ? Blow, and split thyself.
   Sec. Sail. But sea-room, an the brine and
cloudy billow kiss the moon, I care not.
   First Sail. Sir, your queen must over-
board : the sea works high, the wind is loud,
and will not lie till the ship be cleared of the
dead.
   Per. That's your superstition.   50
   First Sail. Pardon us, sir ; with us at sea
it hath been still observed : and we are strong
in custom. Therefore briefly yield her ; for she
must overboard straight.
   Per. As you think meet. Most wretched
      queen !
   Lyc. Here she lies, sir.
   Per. A terrible childbed hast thou had, my
      dear ;
No light, no fire : the unfriendly elements
Forgot thee utterly : nor have I time   59
To give thee hallow'd to thy grave, but straight
Must cast thee, scarcely coffin'd, in the ooze ;
Where, for a monument upon thy bones,
And e'er-remaining lamps, the belching whale
And humming water must o'erwhelm thy
     corpse,
Lying with simple shells. O Lychorida,
Bid Nestor bring me spices, ink and paper,
My casket and my jewels ; and bid Nicander
Bring me the satin coffer : lay the babe
Upon the pillow : hie thee, whiles I say   69
A priestly farewell to her : suddenly, woman.
                [*Exit Lychorida.*
   Sec. Sail. Sir, we have a chest beneath the
hatches, caulked and bitumed ready.
   Per. I thank thee. Mariner, say what coast
     is this ?
   Sec. Sail. We are near Tarsus.
   Per. Thither, gentle mariner.
Alter thy course for Tyre. When canst thou
     reach it ?
   Sec. Sail. By break of day, if the wind
     cease.
   Per. O, make for Tarsus !
There will I visit Cleon, for the babe   79
Cannot hold out to Tyrus : there I'll leave it
At careful nursing. Go thy ways, good mar-
     iner :
I'll bring the body presently.   [*Exeunt.*

SCENE II. *Ephesus. A room in Cerimon's
house.*

Enter CERIMON, *with a Servant, and some
Persons who have been shipwrecked.*

   Cer. Philemon, ho !

       Enter PHILEMON.

   Phil. Doth my lord call ?
   Cer. Get fire and meat for these poor
     men :
'T has been a turbulent and stormy night.
   Serv. I have been in many ; but such a
     night as this,
Till now, I ne'er endured.
   Cer. Your master will be dead ere you re-
     turn ;
There's nothing can be minister'd to nature
That can recover him. [*To Philemon*] Give
     this to the 'pothecary,
And tell me how it works.
          [*Exeunt all but Cerimon.*

      Enter two Gentlemen.

   First Gent.   Good morrow.   10
   Sec. Gent. Good morrow to your lordship.
   Cer.   Gentlemen,
Why do you stir so early ?
   First Gent.   Sir,
Our lodgings, standing bleak upon the sea,
Shook as the earth did quake ;
The very principals did seem to rend,
And all-to topple : pure surprise and fear
Made me to quit the house.
   Sec. Gent. That is the cause we trouble you
     so early ;
'Tis not our husbandry.
   Cer.   O, you say well.   20
   First Gent. But I much marvel that your
     lordship, having
Rich tire about you, should at these early
     hours
Shake off the golden slumber of repose.
'Tis most strange,
Nature should be so conversant with pain,
Being thereto not compell'd.
   Cer.   I hold it ever,
Virtue and cunning were endowments greater
Than nobleness and riches : careless heirs
May the two latter darken and expend ;
But immortality attends the former,   30
Making a man a god. 'Tis known, I ever
Have studied physic, through which secret art,
By turning o'er authorities, I have,
Together with my practice, made familiar
To me and to my aid the blest infusions
That dwell in vegetives, in metals, stones ;
And I can speak of the disturbances
That nature works, and of her cures ; which
     doth give me
A more content in course of true delight
Than to be thirsty after tottering honor,   40
Or tie my treasure up in silken bags,
To please the fool and death.
   Sec. Gent. Your honor has through Ephe-
     sus pour'd forth
Your charity, and hundreds call themselves
Your creatures, who by you have been re-
     stored :
And not your knowledge, your personal pain,
     but even
Your purse, still open, hath built Lord Ceri-
     mon
Such strong renown as time shall ne'er decay.

   Enter two or three Servants *with a chest.*

   First Serv. So ; lift there.
   Cer.   What is that ?
   First Serv.   Sir, even now
Did the sea toss upon our shore this chest : 50
'Tis of some wreck.
   Cer.   Set 't down, let's look upon't.
   Sec. Gent. 'Tis like a coffin, sir.
   Cer.   Whate'er it be,
'Tis wondrous heavy. Wrench it open straight :
If the sea's stomach be o'ercharged with gold,
'Tis a good constraint of fortune it belches
     upon us.
   Sec. Gent. 'Tis so, my lord.
   Cer. How close 'tis caulk'd and bitumed !
Did the sea cast it up ?
   First Serv. I never saw so huge a billow,
     sir,
As toss'd it upon shore.

Cer.   Wrench it open ;
Soft ! it smells most sweetly in my sense.   60
Sec. Gent. A delicate odor.
Cer. As ever hit my nostril. So, up with it.
O you most potent gods ! what's here ? a
    corse !
First Gent. Most strange !
Cer. Shrouded in cloth of state ; balm'd
    and entreasured
With full bags of spices ! A passport too !
Apollo, perfect me in the characters !
                [*Reads from a scroll.*
' Here I give to understand,
    If e'er this coffin drive a-land,
    I, King Pericles, have lost   70
    This queen, worth all our mundane cost.
    Who finds her, give her burying ;
    She was the daughter of a king :
    Besides this treasure for a fee,
    The gods requite his charity ! '
If thou livest, Pericles, thou hast a heart
That even cracks for woe ! This chanced to-
    night.
Sec. Gent. Most likely, sir.
Cer.   Nay, certainly to-night ;
For look how fresh she looks ! They were too
    rough
That threw her in the sea. Make a fire within :
Fetch hither all my boxes in my closet.   81
                [*Exit a Servant.*
Death may usurp on nature many hours,
And yet the fire of life kindle again
The o'erpress'd spirits. I heard of an Egyp-
    tian
That had nine hours lien dead,
Who was by good appliance recovered.

Re-enter a Servant, *with boxes, napkins, and
    fire.*

Well said, well said ; the fire and cloths.
The rough and woeful music that we have,
Cause it to sound, beseech you.
The viol once more : how thou stirr'st, thou
    block !   90
The music there !—I pray you, give her air.
Gentlemen.
This queen will live : nature awakes ; a
    warmth
Breathes out of her : she hath not been en-
    tranced
Above five hours : see how she gins to blow
Into life's flower again !
First Gent.   The heavens,
Through you, increase our wonder and set up
Your fame forever.
Cer.   She is alive ; behold,
Her eyelids, cases to those heavenly jewels
Which Pericles hath lost,   100
Begin to part their fringes of bright gold ;
The diamonds of a most praised water
Do appear, to make the world twice rich.
Live,
And make us weep to hear your fate, fair crea-
    ture,
Rare as you seem to be.   [*She moves.*
Thai.   O dear Diana,
Where am I ? Where's my lord ? What world
    is this ?
Sec. Gent. Is not this strange ?
First Gent.   Most rare.
Cer.   Hush, my gentle neighbors !

Lend me your hands ; to the next chamber
    bear her.
Get linen : now this matter must be look'd to,
For her relapse is mortal. Come, come ;   110
And Æsculapius guide us !
                [*Exeunt, carrying her away.*

SCENE III. *Tarsus.   A room in Cleon's
                house.*

Enter PERICLES, CLEON, DIONYZA, *and* LY-
    CHORIDA *with* MARINA *in her arms.*

Per. Most honor'd Cleon, I must needs be
    gone ;
My twelve months are expired, and Tyrus
    stands
In a litigious peace. You, and your lady,
Take from my heart all thankfulness ! The
    gods
Make up the rest upon you !
Cle. Your shafts of fortune, though they
    hurt you mortally,
Yet glance full wanderingly on us.
Dion.   O your sweet queen !
That the strict fates had pleased you had
    brought her hither,
To have bless'd mine eyes with her !
Per.   We cannot but obey
The powers above us. Could I rage and roar
As doth the sea she lies in, yet the end   11
Must be as 'tis. My gentle babe Marina, whom,
For she was born at sea, I have named so, here
I charge your charity withal, leaving her
The infant of your care ; beseeching you
To give her princely training, that she may be
Manner'd as she is born.
Cle.   Fear not, my lord, but think
Your grace, that fed my country with your
    corn,
For which the people's prayers still fall upon
    you,
Must in your child be thought on. If neglec-
    tion   20
Should therein make me vile, the common
    body,
By you relieved, would force me to my duty :
But if to that my nature need a spur,
The gods revenge it upon me and mine,
To the end of generation !
Per.   I believe you ;
Your honor and your goodness teach me to't,
Without your vows. Till she be married,
    madam,
By bright Diana, whom we honor, all
Unscissar'd shall this hair of mine remain,
Though I show ill in't. So I take my leave.   30
Good madam, make me blessed in your care
In bringing up my child.
Dion.   I have one myself,
Who shall not be more dear to my respect
Than yours, my lord.
Per.   Madam, my thanks and prayers.
Cle. We'll bring your grace e'en to the
    edge o' the shore,
Then give you up to the mask'd Neptune and
The gentlest winds of heaven.
Per.   I will embrace
Your offer. Come, dearest madam. O, no tears,
Lychorida, no tears :
Look to your little mistress, on whose grace   40
You may depend hereafter. Come, my lord.
                [*Exeunt.*

SCENE IV. *Ephesus. A room in Cerimon's*
house.

Enter CERIMON *and* THAISA.

Cer. Madam, this letter, and some certain
jewels,
Lay with you in your coffer : which are now
At your command. Know you the character ?
Thai. It is my lord's.
That I was shipp'd at sea, I well remember,
Even on my eaning time ; but whether there
Deliver'd, by the holy gods,
I cannot rightly say. But since King Pericles,
My wedded lord, I ne'er shall see again,
A vestal livery will I take me to,   10
And never more have joy.
Cer. Madam, if this you purpose as ye
speak,
Diana's temple is not distant far,
Where you may abide till your date expire.
Moreover, if you please, a niece of mine
Shall there attend you.
Thai. My recompense is thanks, that's all ;
Yet my good will is great, though the gift
small.   [*Exeunt.*

ACT IV.

Enter GOWER.

Gow. Imagine Pericles arrived at Tyre,
Welcomed and settled to his own desire.
His woeful queen we leave at Ephesus,
Unto Diana there a votaress.
Now to Marina bend your mind,
Whom our fast-growing scene must find
At Tarsus, and by Cleon train'd
In music, letters ; who hath gain'd
Of education all the grace,
Which makes her both the heart and place
Of general wonder. But, alack,   11
That monster envy, oft the wrack
Of earned praise, Marina's life
Seeks to take off by treason's knife.
And in this kind hath our Cleon
One daughter, and a wench full grown,
Even ripe for marriage-rite ; this maid
Hight Philoten : and it is said
For certain in our story, she
Would ever with Marina be :   20
Be't when she weaved the sleided silk
With fingers long, small, white as milk ;
Or when she would with sharp needle
wound
The cambric, which she made more sound
By hurting it ; or when to the lute
She sung, and made the night-bird mute,
That still records with moan ; or when
She would with rich and constant pen
Vail to her mistress Dian ; still
This Philoten contends in skill   30
With absolute Marina : so
With the dove of Paphos might the crow
Vie feathers white. Marina gets
All praises, which are paid as debts,
And not as given. This so darks
In Philoten all graceful marks,
That Cleon's wife, with envy rare,
A present murderer does prepare
For good Marina, that her daughter
Might stand peerless by this slaughter.   40

The sooner her vile thoughts to stead,
Lychorida, our nurse, is dead :
And cursed Dionyza hath
The pregnant instrument of wrath
Prest for this blow. The unborn event
I do commend to your content :
Only I carry winged time
Post on the lame feet of my rhyme ;
Which never could I so convey,
Unless your thoughts went on my way.   50
Dionyza does appear,
With Leonine, a murderer.   [*Exit.*

SCENE I. *Tarsus. An open place near the*
sea-shore.

Enter DIONYZA *and* LEONINE.

Dion. Thy oath remember ; thou hast
sworn to do't :
'Tis but a blow, which never shall be known.
Thou canst not do a thing in the world so
soon,
To yield thee so much profit. Let not con-
science,
Which is but cold, inflaming love i' thy bosom,
Inflame too nicely ; nor let pity, which
Even women have cast off, melt thee, but be
A soldier to thy purpose.
Leon. I will do't ; but yet she is a goodly
creature.   9
Dion. The fitter, then, the gods should have
her. Here she comes weeping for her only
mistress' death. Thou art resolved ?
Leon. I am resolved.

Enter MARINA, *with a basket of flowers.*

Mar. No, I will rob Tellus of her weed,
To strew thy green with flowers : the yellows,
blues,
The purple violets, and marigolds,
Shall as a carpet hang upon thy grave,
While summer-days do last. Ay me ! poor
maid,
Born in a tempest, when my mother died,
This world to me is like a lasting storm,   20
Whirring me from my friends.
Dion. How now, Marina ! why do you
keep alone ?
How chance my daughter is not with you ?
Do not
Consume your blood with sorrowing : you
have
A nurse of me. Lord, how your favor's
changed
With this unprofitable woe !
Come, give me your flowers, ere the sea mar
it.
Walk with Leonine ; the air is quick there,
And it pierces and sharpens the stomach.
Come,
Leonine, take her by the arm, walk with her.
Mar. No, I pray you ;   31
I'll not bereave you of your servant.
Dion.   Come, come ;
I love the king your father, and yourself,
With more than foreign heart. We every day
Expect him here : when he shall come and find
Our paragon to all reports thus blasted,
He will repent the breadth of his great voy-
age ;
Blame both my lord and me, that we have
taken
No care to your best courses. Go, I pray you,

Walk, and be cheerful once again ; reserve 40
That excellent complexion, which did steal
The eyes of young and old. Care not for me ;
I can go home alone.
Mar. 　　　　Well, I will go ;
But yet I have no desire to it.
Dion. Come, come, I know 'tis good for
　　you.
Walk half an hour, Leonine, at the least :
Remember what I have said.
Leon. 　　　　I warrant you, madam.
Dion. I'll leave you, my sweet lady, for a
　　while :
Pray, walk softly, do not heat your blood :
What ! I must have a care of you.
Mar. 　　　　My thanks, sweet madam. 50
　　　　　　　　[*Exit Dionyza.*
Is this wind westerly that blows ?
Leon. 　　　　South-west.
Mar. When I was born, the wind was
　　north.
Leon. 　　　　Was't so ?
Mar. My father, as nurse said, did never
　　fear,
But cried ' Good seaman ! ' to the sailors,
　　galling
His kingly hands, haling ropes ;
And, clasping to the mast, endured a sea
That almost burst the deck.
Leon. When was this ?
Mar. When I was born :
Never was waves nor wind more violent ; 60
And from the ladder-tackle washes off
A canvas-climber. ' Ha ! ' says one, ' wilt
　　out ? '
And with a dropping industry they skip
From stem to stern : the boatswain whistles,
　　and
The master calls, and trebles their confusion.
Leon. Come, say your prayers.
Mar. What mean you ?
Leon. If you require a little space for
　　prayer,
I grant it : pray ; but be not tedious,
For the gods are quick of ear, and I am sworn
To do my work with haste. 71
Mar. 　　　　Why will you kill me ?
Leon. To satisfy my lady.
Mar. Why would she have me kill'd ?
Now, as I can remember, by my troth,
I never did her hurt in all my life :
I never spake bad word, nor did ill turn
To any living creature : believe me, la,
I never kill'd a mouse, nor hurt a fly ;
I trod upon a worm against my will,
But I wept for it. How have I offended, 80
Wherein my death might yield her any profit,
Or my life imply her any danger ?
Leon. My commission
Is not to reason of the deed, but do it.
Mar. You will not do't for all the world,
　　I hope.
You are well favor'd, and your looks foreshow
You have a gentle heart. I saw you lately,
When you caught hurt in parting two that
　　fought :
Good sooth, it show'd well in you : do so
　　now :
Your lady seeks my life ; come you between,
And save poor me, the weaker. 91
Leon. 　　　　I am sworn,
And will dispatch. 　　[*He seizes her.*

Enter Pirates.

First Pirate. Hold, villain !
　　　　　　　　[*Leonine runs away.*
Sec. Pirate. A prize ! a prize !
Third Pirate. Half-part, mates, half-part.
Come, let 's have her aboard suddenly.
　　　　　　　[*Exeunt Pirates with Marina.*

Re-enter LEONINE.

Leon. These roguing thieves serve the great
　　pirate Valdes ;
And they have seized Marina. Let her go :
There's no hope she will return. I'll swear
　　she's dead,
And thrown into the sea. But I'll see further :
Perhaps they will but please themselves upon
　　her, 101
Not carry her aboard. If she remain,
Whom they have ravish'd must by me be slain.
　　　　　　　　[*Exit.*

SCENE II. *Mytilene. A room in a brothel.*

Enter PANDAR, Bawd, *and* BOULT.

Pand. Boult !
Boult. Sir ?
Pand. Search the market narrowly ; Mytilene is full of gallants. We lost too much
money this mart by being too wenchless.
Bawd. We were never so much out of
creatures. We have but poor three, and they
can do no more than they can do ; and they
with continual action are even as good as
rotten. 9
Pand. Therefore let's have fresh ones,
whate'er we pay for them. If there be not a
conscience to be used in every trade, we shall
never prosper.
Bawd. Thou sayest true : 'tis not our bringing up of poor bastards,—as, I think, I have
brought up some eleven—
Boult. Ay, to eleven ; and brought them
down again. But shall I search the market ?
Bawd. What else, man ? The stuff we
have, a strong wind will blow it to pieces, they
are so pitifully sodden. 21
Pand. Thou sayest true ; they're too unwholesome, o' conscience. The poor Tran-
sylvanian is dead, that lay with the little baggage.
Boult. Ay, she quickly pooped him ; she
made him roast-meat for worms. But I'll go
search the market. 　　　　[*Exit.*
Pand. Three or four thousand chequins
were as pretty a proportion to live quietly,
and so give over. 30
Bawd. Why to give over, I pray you ? is it
a shame to get when we are old ?
Pand. O, our credit comes not in like the
commodity, nor the commodity wages not
with the danger : therefore, if in our youths
we could pick up some pretty estate, 'twere
not amiss to keep our door hatched. Besides,
the sore terms we stand upon with the gods
will be strong with us for giving over. 39
Bawd. Come, other sorts offend as well as
we.
Pand. As well as we ! ay, and better too ;
we offend worse. Neither is our profession
any trade ; it's no calling. But here comes
Boult.

Re-enter Boult, *with the* Pirates *and* Marina.

Boult. [*To Marina*] Come your ways. My masters, you say she's a virgin ?

First Pirate. O, sir, we doubt it not.

Boult. Master, I have gone through for this piece, you see : if you like her, so ; if not, I have lost my earnest.

Bawd. Boult, has she any qualities ?	50

Boult. She has a good face, speaks well, and has excellent good clothes : there's no further necessity of qualities can make her be refused.

Bawd. What's her price, Boult ?

Boult. I cannot be bated one doit of a thousand pieces.

Pand. Well, follow me, my masters, you shall have your money presently. Wife, take her in ; instruct her what she has to do, that she may not be raw in her entertainment. 60

[*Exeunt Pandar and Pirates.*

Bawd. Boult, take you the marks of her, the color of her hair, complexion, height, age, with warrant of her virginity ; and cry ' He that will give most shall have her first.' Such a maidenhead were no cheap thing, if men were as they have been. Get this done as I command you.

Boult. Performance shall follow.	[*Exit.*

Mar. Alack that Leonine was so slack, so slow !
He should have struck, not spoke ; or that these pirates,
Not enough barbarous, had not o'erboard thrown me	70
For to seek my mother !

Bawd. Why lament you, pretty one ?

Mar. That I am pretty.

Bawd. Come, the gods have done their part in you.

Mar. I accuse them not.

Bawd. You are light into my hands, where you are like to live.

Mar. The more my fault
To scape his hands where I was like to die. 80

Bawd. Ay, and you shall live in pleasure.

Mar. No.

Bawd. Yes, indeed shall you, and taste gentlemen of all fashions : you shall fare well ; you shall have the difference of all complexions. What ! do you stop your ears ?

Mar. Are you a woman ?

Bawd. What would you have me be, an I be not a woman ?	89

Mar. An honest woman, or not a woman.

Bawd. Marry, whip thee, gosling : I think I shall have something to do with you. Come, you're a young foolish sapling, and must be bowed as I would have you.

Mar. The gods defend me !

Bawd. If it please the gods to defend you by men, then men must comfort you, men must feed you, men must stir you up. Boult's returned.

Re-enter Boult.

Now, sir, hast thou cried her through the market ?

Boult. I have cried her almost to the number of her hairs ; I have drawn her picture with my voice.

Bawd. And I prithee tell me, how dost thou find the inclination of the people, especially of the younger sort ?

Boult. 'Faith, they listened to me as they would have hearkened to their father's testament. There was a Spaniard's mouth so watered, that he went to bed to her very description.	109

Bawd. We shall have him here to-morrow with his best ruff on.

Boult. To-night, to-night. But, mistress, do you know the French knight that cowers i' the hams ?

Bawd. Who, Monsieur Veroles ?

Boult. Ay, he : he offered to cut a caper at the proclamation ; but he made a groan at it, and swore he would see her to-morrow.

Bawd. Well, well ; as for him, he brought his disease hither : here he does but repair it. I know he will come in our shadow, to scatter his crowns in the sun.

Boult. Well, if we had of every nation a traveller, we should lodge them with this sign.

Bawd. [*To Mar.*] Pray you, come hither awhile. You have fortunes coming upon you. Mark me : you must seem to do that fearfully which you commit willingly, despise profit where you have most gain. To weep that you live as ye do makes pity in your lovers : seldom but that pity begets you a good opinion, and that opinion a mere profit.

Mar. I understand you not.

Boult. O, take her home, mistress, take her home : these blushes of hers must be quenched with some present practice.

Bawd. Thou sayest true, i' faith, so they must ; for your bride goes to that with shame which is her way to go with warrant.	139

Boult. 'Faith, some do, and some do not. But, mistress, if I have bargained for the joint,—

Bawd. Thou mayst cut a morsel off the spit.

Boult. I may so.

Bawd. Who should deny it ? Come, young one, I like the manner of your garments well.

Boult. Ay, by my faith, they shall not be changed yet.

Bawd. Boult, spend thou that in the town : report what a sojourner we have ; you'll lose nothing by custom. When nature framed this piece, she meant thee a good turn ; therefore say what a paragon she is, and thou hast the harvest out of thine own report.

Boult. I warrant you, mistress, thunder shall not so awake the beds of eels as my giving out her beauty stir up the lewdly-inclined. I'll bring home some to-night.

Bawd. Come your ways ; follow me.

Mar. If fires be hot, knives sharp, or waters deep,
Untied I still my virgin knot will keep.	160
Diana, aid my purpose !

Bawd. What have we to do with Diana ? Pray you, will you go with us ?	[*Exeunt.*

Scene III. *Tarsus. A room in Cleon's house.*

Enter Cleon *and* Dionyza.

Dion. Why, are you foolish ? Can it be undone ?

Cle. O Dionyza, such a piece of slaughter The sun and moon ne'er look'd upon !

Dion.　　　　　　　　　　　　I think
You'll turn a child again.
　　Cle.　Were I chief lord of all this spacious
　　　　world,
I'ld give it to undo the deed. O lady,
Much less in blood than virtue, yet a princess
To equal any single crown o' the earth
I' the justice of compare! O villain Leonine!
Whom thou hast poison'd too :　　　　　　10
If thou hadst drunk to him, 't had been a
　　kindness
Becoming well thy fact : what canst thou say
When noble Pericles shall demand his child ?
　　Dion.　That she is dead. Nurses are not the
　　　　fates,
To foster it, nor ever to preserve.
She died at night ; I'll say so. Who can
　　cross it ?
Unless you play the pious innocent,
And for an honest attribute cry out
' She died by foul play.'
　　Cle.　　　　　　O, go to. Well, well,
Of all the faults beneath the heavens, the gods
Do like this worst.
　　Dion.　　　　Be one of those that think
The petty wrens of Tarsus will fly hence,
And open this to Pericles. I do shame
To think of what a noble strain you are,
And of how coward a spirit.
　　Cle.　　　　　　To such proceeding
Who ever but his approbation added,
Though not his prime consent, he did not flow
From honorable sources.
　　Dion.　　　　　Be it so, then :
Yet none does know, but you, how she came
　　dead,
Nor none can know, Leonine being gone.　　30
She did distain my child, and stood between
Her and her fortunes : none would look on
　　her,
But cast their gazes on Marina's face ;
Whilst ours was blurted at and held a malkin
Not worth the time of day. It pierced me
　　thorough ;
And though you call my course unnatural,
You not your child well loving, yet I find
It greets me as an enterprise of kindness
Perform'd to your sole daughter.
　　Cle.　　　　　　Heavens forgive it !
　　Dion.　And as for Pericles,　　　　　40
What should he say ? We wept after her
　　hearse,
And yet we mourn : her monument
Is almost finish'd, and her epitaphs
In glittering golden characters express
A general praise to her, and care in us
At whose expense 'tis done.
　　Cle.　　　　　Thou art like the harpy,
Which, to betray, dost, with thine angel's face,
Seize with thine eagle's talons.
　　Dion.　You are like one that superstitiously
Doth swear to the gods that winter kills the
　　flies :　　　　　　　　　　　　　50
But yet I know you'll do as I advise. [*Exeunt.*

SCENE IV.

*Enter GOWER, before the monument of
MARINA at Tarsus.*

　　Gow.　Thus time we waste, and longest
　　　　leagues make short ;
Sail seas in cockles, have an wish but for't ;
Making, to take your imagination,
From bourn to bourn, region to region.

By you being pardon'd, we commit no crime
To use one language in each several clime
Where our scenes seem to live. I do beseech
　　you
To learn of me, who stand i' the gaps to
　　teach you,
The stages of our story. Pericles
Is now again thwarting the wayward seas,
Attended on by many a lord and knight,
To see his daughter, all his life's delight.
Old Escanes, whom Helicanus late
Advanced in time to great and high estate,
Is left to govern. Bear you it in mind,
Old Helicanus goes along behind.
Well-sailing ships and bounteous winds have
　　brought
This king to Tarsus,—think his pilot
　　thought ;
So with his steerage shall your thoughts
　　grow on,—　　　　　　　　　　　19
To fetch his daughter home, who first is
　　gone.
Like motes and shadows see them move
　　awhile ;
Your ears unto your eyes I'll reconcile.

DUMB SHOW.

*Enter PERICLES, at one door, with all his train ;
CLEON and DIONYZA, at the other. CLEON
shows PERICLES the tomb ; whereat PERICLES
makes lamentation, puts on sackcloth, and
in a mighty passion departs. Then exeunt
CLEON and DIONYZA.*

See how belief may suffer by foul show !
This borrow'd passion stands for true old
　　woe ;
And Pericles, in sorrow all devour'd,
With sighs shot through, and biggest tears
　　o'ershower'd,
Leaves Tarsus and again embarks. He swears
Never to wash his face, nor cut his hairs :
He puts on sackcloth, and to sea. He bears
A tempest, which his mortal vessel tears,　　30
And yet he rides it out. Now please you wit.
The epitaph is for Marina writ
By wicked Dionyza.
　　　　　　　　[*Reads the inscription on Marina's
　　　　　　　　　　　　　　　　　　monument.*
' The fairest, sweet'st, and best lies here,
Who wither'd in her spring of year.
She was of Tyrus the king's daughter,
On whom foul death hath made this slaugh-
　　ter ;
Marina was she call'd ; and at her birth,
Thetis, being proud, swallow'd some part o'
　　the earth :
Therefore the earth, fearing to be o'erflow'd,
Hath Thetis' birth-child on the heavens be-
　　stow'd :
Wherefore she does, and swears she'll never
　　stint,
Make raging battery upon shores of flint.'
No visor does become black villany
So well as soft and tender flattery.
Let Pericles believe his daughter's dead,
And bear his courses to be ordered
By Lady Fortune ; while our scene must
　　play
His daughter's woe and heavy well-a-day
In her unholy service. Patience, then,　　50
And think you now are all in Mytilene.
　　　　　　　　　　　　　　　　　[*Exit.*

Scene V. *Mytilene. A street before
the brothel.*

Enter, from the brothel, two Gentlemen.

First Gent. Did you ever hear the like ?
Sec. Gent. No, nor never shall do in such
a place as this, she being once gone.
First Gent. But to have divinity preached
there ! did you ever dream of such a thing ?
Sec. Gent. No, no. Come, I am for no
more bawdy-houses : shall's go hear the vestals sing ?
First Gent. I'll do any thing now that is
virtuous ; but I am out of the road of rutting
for ever.   [*Exeunt.* 10

Scene VI. *The same. A room in the brothel.*

Enter Pandar, Bawd, *and* Boult.

Pand. Well, I had rather than twice the
worth of her she had ne'er come here.
Bawd. Fie, fie upon her ! she's able to
freeze the god Priapus, and undo a whole generation. We must either get her ravished, or
be rid of her. When she should do for clients
her fitment, and do me the kindness of our
profession, she has me her quirks, her reasons, her master reasons, her prayers, her
knees ; that she would make a puritan of the
devil, if he should cheapen a kiss of her.
Boult. 'Faith, I must ravish her, or she'll
disfurnish us of all our cavaliers, and make
our swearers priests.
Pand. Now, the pox upon her green-sickness for me !
Bawd. 'Faith, there's no way to be rid on't
but by the way to the pox. Here comes the
Lord Lysimachus disguised.
Boult. We should have both lord and
lown, if the peevish baggage would but give
way to customers.   21

Enter Lysimachus.

Lys. How now ! How a dozen of virginities ?
Bawd. Now, the gods to-bless your honor !
Boult. I am glad to see your honor in good
health.
Lys. You may so ; 'tis the better for you
that your resorters stand upon sound legs.
How now ! wholesome iniquity have you that
a man may deal withal, and defy the surgeon ?
Bawd. We have here one, sir, if she would
—but there never came her like in Mytilene.
Lys. If she'ld do the deed of darkness,
thou wouldst say.
Bawd. Your honor knows what 'tis to say
well enough.
Lys. Well, call forth, call forth.
Boult. For flesh and blood, sir, white and
red, you shall see a rose ; and she were a rose
indeed, if she had but—
Lys. What, prithee ?   40
Boult. O, sir, I can be modest.
Lys. That dignifies the renown of a bawd,
no less than it gives a good report to a number
to be chaste.   [*Exit Boult.*
Bawd. Here comes that which grows to the
stalk ; never plucked yet, I can assure you.

Re-enter Boult *with* Marina.

Is she not a fair creature ?
Lys. 'Faith, she would serve after a long

voyage at sea. Well, there's for you : leave us.
Bawd. I beseech your honor, give me
leave : a word, and I'll have done presently. 51
Lys. I beseech you, do.
Bawd. [*To* Marina] First, I would have
you note, this is an honorable man.
Mar. I desire to find him so, that I may
worthily note him.
Bawd. Next, he's the governor of this country, and a man whom I am bound to.
Mar. If he govern the country, you are
bound to him indeed ; but how honorable he
is in that, I know not.   61
Bawd. Pray you, without any more virginal fencing, will you use him kindly ? He
will line your apron with gold.
Mar. What he will do graciously, I will
thankfully receive.
Lys. Ha' you done ?
Bawd. My lord, she's not paced yet : you
must take some pains to work her to your
manage. Come, we will leave his honor and
her together. Go thy ways.
          [*Exeunt Bawd, Pandar, and Boult.*
Lys. Now, pretty one, how long have you
been at this trade ?
Mar. What trade, sir ?
Lys. Why, I cannot name't but I shall
offend.
Mar. I cannot be offended with my trade.
Please you to name it.
Lys. How long have you been of this profession ?
Mar. E'er since I can remember.
Lys. Did you go to 't so young ? Were
you a gamester at five or at seven ?   81
Mar. Earlier too, sir, if now I be one.
Lys. Why, the house you dwell in proclaims you to be a creature of sale.
Mar. Do you know this house to be a
place of such resort, and will come into 't ? I
hear say you are of honorable parts, and are
the governor of this place.
Lys. Why, hath your principal made
known unto you who I am ?   90
Mar. Who is my principal ?
Lys. Why, your herb-woman ; she that
sets seeds and roots of shame and iniquity. O,
you have heard something of my power, and
so stand aloof for more serious wooing. But I
protest to thee, pretty one, my authority shall
not see thee, or else look friendly upon thee.
Come, bring me to some private place : come,
come.
Mar. If you were born to honor, show it
now ;
If put upon you, make the judgment good
That thought you worthy of it.   101
Lys. How's this ? how's this ? Some more ;
be sage.
Mar.   For me,
That am a maid, though most ungentle fortune
Have placed me in this sty, where, since I
came,
Diseases have been sold dearer than physic,
O, that the gods
Would set me free from this unhallow'd place,
Though they did change me to the meanest
bird
That flies i' the purer air !
Lys.   I did not think

Thou couldst have spoke so well; ne'er
 dream'd thou couldst. 110
Had I brought hither a corrupted mind,
Thy speech had alter'd it. Hold, here's gold
 for thee :
Persever in that clear way thou goest,
And the gods strengthen thee !
 Mar.   The good gods preserve you !
 Lys. For me, be you thoughten
That I came with no ill intent ; for to me
The very doors and windows savor vilely.
Fare thee well. Thou art a piece of virtue, and
I doubt not but thy training hath been noble.
Hold, here's more gold for thee. 120
A curse upon him, die he like a thief,
That robs thee of thy goodness ! If thou dost
Hear from me, it shall be for thy good.

Re-enter BOULT.

 Boult. I beseech your honor, one piece for
me.
 Lys. Avaunt, thou damned door-keeper !
Your house, but for this virgin that doth prop
it,
Would sink and overwhelm you. Away ! [*Exit.*
 Boult. How's this ? We must take another
course with you. If your peevish chastity,
which is not worth a breakfast in the cheapest
country under the cope, shall undo a whole
household, let me be gelded like a spaniel.
Come your ways.
 Mar. Whither would you have me ?
 Boult. I must have your maidenhead taken
off, or the common hangman shall execute it.
Come your ways. We'll have no more gentlemen driven away. Come your ways, I say.

Re-enter Bawd.

 Bawd. How now ! what's the matter ? 140
 Boult. Worse and worse, mistress ; she has
here spoken holy words to the Lord Lysimachus.
 Bawd. O abominable !
 Boult. She makes our profession as it were
to stink afore the face of the gods.
 Bawd. Marry, hang her up for ever !
 Boult. The nobleman would have dealt
with her like a nobleman, and she sent him
away as cold as a snowball ; saying his
prayers too. 149
 Bawd. Boult, take her away ; use her at
thy pleasure : crack the glass of her virginity,
and make the rest malleable.
 Boult. An if she were a thornier piece of
ground than she is, she shall be ploughed.
 Mar. Hark, hark, you gods !
 Bawd. She conjures : away with her !
Would she had never come within my doors !
Marry, hang you ! She's born to undo us.
Will you not go the way of women-kind ?
Marry, come up, my dish of chastity with rose-
mary and bays ! [*Exit.*
 Boult. Come, mistress ; come your ways
with me.
 Mar. Whither wilt thou have me ?
 Boult. To take from you the jewel you
hold so dear.
 Mar. Prithee, tell me one thing first.
 Boult. Come now, your one thing.
 Mar. What canst thou wish thine enemy
to be ?
 Boult. Why, I could wish him to be my
master, or rather, my mistress. 170

 Mar. Neither of these are so bad as thou
art,
Since they do better thee in their command.
Thou hold'st a place, for which the pained'st
 fiend
Of hell would not in reputation change :
Thou art the damned doorkeeper to every
Coistrel that comes inquiring for his Tib ;
To the choleric fisting of every rogue
Thy ear is liable ; thy food is such 178
As hath been belch'd on by infected lungs.
 Boult. What would you have me do ? go
to the wars, would you ? where a man may
serve seven years for the loss of a leg, and
have not money enough in the end to buy him
a wooden one ?
 Mar. Do any thing but this thou doest.
Empty
Old receptacles, or common shores, of filth ;
Serve by indenture to the common hangman :
Any of these ways are yet better than this ;
For what thou professest, a baboon, could he
 speak,
Would own a name too dear. O, that the
 gods
Would safely deliver me from this place ! 191
Here, here's gold for thee.
If that thy master would gain by me,
Proclaim that I can sing, weave, sew, and
 dance,
With other virtues, which I'll keep from
 boast ;
And I will undertake all these to teach.
I doubt not but this populous city will
Yield many scholars.
 Boult. But can you teach all this you speak
of ?
 Mar. Prove that I cannot, take me home
 again,
And prostitute me to the basest groom 201
That doth frequent your house.
 Boult. Well, I will see what I can do for
thee : if I can place thee, I will.
 Mar. But amongst honest women.
 Boult. 'Faith, my acquaintance lies little
amongst them. But since my master and mis-
tress have bought you, there's no going but by
their consent : therefore I will make them ac-
quainted with your purpose, and I doubt not
but I shall find them tractable enough. Come,
I'll do for thee what I can ; come your ways.
 [*Exeunt.*

***

ACT V.

Enter GOWER.

 Gow. Marina thus the brothel 'scapes, and
 chances
Into an honest house, our story says.
She sings like one immortal, and she dances
As goddess-like to her admired lays ;
Deep clerks she dumbs ; and with her needle
 composes
Nature's own shape, of bud, bird, branch, or
 berry,
That even her art sisters the natural roses ;
Her inkle, silk, twin with the rubied cherry :
That pupils lacks she none of noble race, 9
Who pour their bounty on her ; and her gain
She gives the cursed bawd. Here we her place ;
And to her father turn our thoughts again,

Where we left him, on the sea. We there him
    lost ;
Whence, driven before the winds, he is arrived
Here where his daughter dwells ; and on this
    coast
Suppose him now at anchor. The city strived
God Neptune's annual feast to keep : from
    whence
Lysimachus our Tyrian ship espies,
His banners sable, trimm'd with rich expense ;
And to him in his barge with fervor hies.   20
In your supposing once more put your sight
Of heavy Pericles ; think this his bark :
Where what is done in action, more, if might,
Shall be discover'd ; please you, sit and hark.
                        [*Exit.*

Scene I. *On board Pericles' ship, off Myti-*
   lene. A close pavilion on deck, with a cur-
   tain before it ; Pericles within it, reclined on
   a couch. A barge lying beside the Tyrian
   vessel.

Enter two Sailors, *one belonging to the Tyrian*
   vessel, the other to the barge ; to them Helicanus.

Tyr. Sail. [*To the Sailor of Mytilene*]
   Where is lord Helicanus ? he can re-
   solve you.
O, here is he.
Sir, there's a barge put off from Mytilene,
And in it is Lysimachus the governor,
Who craves to come aboard. What is your
   will ?
   Hel.   That he have his. Call up some gen-
   tlemen.
   Tyr. Sail. Ho, gentlemen ! my lord calls.

Enter two or three Gentlemen.

First Gent. Doth your lordship call ?
   Hel.   Gentlemen, there's some of worth
   would come aboard ;
I pray ye, greet them fairly.   10
[*The Gentlemen and the two Sailors descend,*
        and go on board the barge.

Enter, *from thence,* Lysimachus *and* Lords ;
   with the Gentlemen *and the two* Sailors.

Tyr. Sail. Sir,
This is the man that can, in aught you would,
Resolve you.
   Lys.   Hail, reverend sir ! the gods preserve
   you !
   Hel.   And you, sir, to outlive the age I am,
And die as I would do.
   Lys.   You wish me well.
Being on shore, honoring of Neptune's tri-
   umphs,
Seeing this goodly vessel ride before us,
I made to it, to know of whence you are.
   Hel.   First, what is your place ?   20
   Lys.   I am the governor of this place you
   lie before.
   Hel.   Sir,
Our vessel is of Tyre, in it the king ;
A man who for this three months hath not
   spoken
To any one, nor taken sustenance
But to prorogue his grief.
   Lys.   Upon what ground is his distem-
   perature ?
   Hel.   'Twould be too tedious to repeat ;
But the main grief springs from the loss
Of a beloved daughter and a wife.   30

   Lys.   May we not see him ?
   Hel.   You may ;
But bootless is your sight : he will not speak
To any.
   Lys.   Yet let me obtain my wish.
   Hel.   Behold him. [*Pericles discovered.*]
      This was a goodly person,
Till the disaster that, one mortal night,
Drove him to this.
   Lys.   Sir king, all hail ! the gods preserve
   you !
Hail, royal sir !   40
   Hel.   It is in vain ; he will not speak to you.
   First Lord. Sir,
We have a maid in Mytilene, I durst wager,
Would win some words of him.
   Lys.   'Tis well bethought.
She questionless with her sweet harmony
And other chosen attractions, would allure,
And make a battery through his deafen'd
   parts,
Which now are midway stopp'd :
She is all happy as the fairest of all,
And, with her fellow maids, is now upon 50
The leafy shelter that abuts against
The island's side.
      [*Whispers a Lord, who goes off in the*
               barge of Lysimachus.
   Hel.   Sure, all's effectless ; yet nothing we'll
   omit
That bears recovery's name. But, since your
   kindness
We have stretch'd thus far, let us beseech you
That for our gold we may provision have,
Wherein we are not destitute for want,
But weary for the staleness.
   Lys.   O, sir, a courtesy
Which if we should deny, the most just gods
For every graff would send a caterpillar,   60
And so afflict our province. Yet once more
Let me entreat to know at large the cause
Of your king's sorrow.
   Hel.   Sit, sir, I will recount it to you :
But, see, I am prevented.

Re-enter, *from the barge,* Lord, *with* Marina,
   and a young Lady.

   Lys.   O, here is
The lady that I sent for. Welcome, fair one !
Is't not a goodly presence ?
   Hel.   She's a gallant lady.
   Lys.   She's such a one, that, were I well
   assured
Came of a gentle kind and noble stock,
I'ld wish no better choice, and think me rarely
   wed.   69
Fair one, all goodness that consists in bounty
Expect even here, where is a kingly patient :
If that thy prosperous and artificial feat
Can draw him but to answer thee in aught,
Thy sacred physic shall receive such pay
As thy desires can wish.
   Mar.   Sir, I will use
My utmost skill in his recovery,
   Provided
That none but I and my companion maid
Be suffer'd to come near him.
   Lys.   Come, let us leave her ;
And the gods make her prosperous !   80
                       [*Marina sings.*
   Lys.   Mark'd he your music ?
   Mar.   No, nor look'd on us.
   Lys.   See, she will speak to him.

Mar. Hail, sir! my lord, lend ear.
Per. Hum, ha!
Mar. I am a maid,
My lord, that ne'er before invited eyes,
But have been gazed on like a comet : she
      speaks,
My lord, that, may be, hath endured a grief
Might equal yours, if both were justly weigh'd.
Though wayward fortune did malign my state,
My derivation was from ancestors   91
Who stood equivalent with mighty kings :
But time hath rooted out my parentage,
And to the world and awkward casualties
Bound me in servitude. [*Aside*] I will desist;
But there is something glows upon my cheek,
And whispers in mine ear 'Go not till he
      speak.'
Per. My fortunes—parentage—good par-
      entage—
To equal mine !—was it not thus ? what say
      you ?
Mar. I said, my lord, if you did know my
      parentage,   100
You would not do me violence.
Per. I do think so. Pray you, turn your
      eyes upon me.
You are like something that—What country-
      woman ?
Here of these shores ?
Mar.   No, nor of any shores :
Yet I was mortally brought forth, and am
No other than I appear.
Per. I am great with woe, and shall deliver
      weeping.
My dearest wife was like this maid, and such
      a one
My daughter might have been : my queen's
      square brows ;
Her stature to an inch ; as wand-like straight ;
As silver-voiced ; her eyes as jewel-like   111
And cased as richly ; in pace another Juno ;
Who starves the ears she feeds, and makes
      them hungry,
The more she gives them speech. Where do
      you live ?
Mar. Where I am but a stranger : from
      the deck
You may discern the place.
Per.   Where were you bred ?
And how achieved you these endowments,
      which
You make more rich to owe ?
Mar. If I should tell my history, it would
      seem
Like lies disdain'd in the reporting.
Per.   Prithee, speak :   120
Falseness cannot come from thee ; for thou
      look'st
Modest as Justice, and thou seem'st a palace
For the crown'd Truth to dwell in : I will be-
      lieve thee,
And make my senses credit thy relation
To points that seem impossible ; for thou
      look'st
Like one I loved indeed. What were thy
      friends ?
Didst thou not say, when I did push thee
      back—
Which was when I perceived thee—that thou
      camest
From good descending ?
Mar.   So indeed I did.

Per. Report thy parentage. I think thou
      said'st   130
Thou hadst been toss'd from wrong to injury,
And that thou thought'st thy griefs might
      equal mine,
If both were open'd.
Mar.   Some such thing
I said, and said no more but what my thoughts
Did warrant me was likely.
Per.   Tell thy story ;
If thine consider'd prove the thousandth part
Of my endurance, thou art a man, and I
Have suffer'd like a girl : yet thou dost look
Like Patience gazing on kings' graves, and
      smiling
Extremity out of act. What were thy friends ?
How lost thou them ? Thy name, my most
      kind virgin ?   141
Recount, I do beseech thee : come, sit by me.
Mar. My name is Marina.
Per.   O, I am mock'd,
And thou by some incensed god sent hither
To make the world to laugh at me.
Mar.   Patience, good sir,
Or here I'll cease.
Per.   Nay, I'll be patient.
Thou little know'st how thou dost startle me,
To call thyself Marina.
Mar.   The name
Was given me by one that had some power,
My father, and a king.   151
Per.   How ! a king's daughter ?
And call'd Marina ?
Mar.   You said you would believe me ;
But, not to be a troubler of your peace,
I will end here.
Per.   But are you flesh and blood ?
Have you a working pulse ? and are no fairy ?
Motion ! Well ; speak on. Where were you
      born?
And wherefore call'd Marina ?
Mar.   Call'd Marina
For I was born at sea.
Per.   At sea ! what mother ?
Mar. My mother was the daughter of a
      king ;
Who ᶜdied the minute I was born,   160
As my good nurse Lychorida hath oft
Deliver'd weeping.
Per.   O, stop there a little !
[*Aside*] This is the rarest dream that e'er dull
      sleep
Did mock sad fools withal : this cannot be :
My daughter's buried. Well : where were you
      bred ?
I'll hear you more, to the bottom of your story,
And never interrupt you.
Mar. You scorn : believe me, 'twere best I
      did give o'er.   169
Per. I will believe you by the syllable
Of what you shall deliver. Yet, give me leave :
How came you in these parts ? where were
      you bred ?
Mar. The king my father did in Tarsus
      leave me ;
Till cruel Cleon, with his wicked wife,
Did seek to murder me : and having woo'd
A villain to attempt it, who having drawn to
      do't,
A crew of pirates came and rescued me ;
Brought me to Mytilene. But, good sir,

Whither will you have me ? Why do you
    weep ? It may be,
You think me an impostor : no, good faith ;
I am the daughter to King Pericles,   180
If good King Pericles be.
    Per. Ho, Helicanus !
    Hel. Calls my lord ?
    Per. Thou art a grave and noble counsel-
    lor,
Most wise in general : tell me, if thou canst,
What this maid is, or what is like to be,
That thus hath made me weep ?
    Hel.   I know not ; but
Here is the regent, sir, of Mytilene
Speaks nobly of her.
    Lys.   She would never tell
Her parentage ; being demanded that,   190
She would sit still and weep.
    Per. O Helicanus, strike me, honor'd sir ;
Give me a gash, put me to present pain ;
Lest this great sea of joys rushing upon me
O'erbear the shores of my mortality,
And drown me with their sweetness. O, come
    hither,
Thou that beget'st him that did thee beget ;
Thou that wast born at sea, buried at Tarsus,
And found at sea again ! O Helicanus,
Down on thy knees, thank the holy gods as
    loud   200
As thunder threatens us : this is Marina.
What was thy mother's name ? tell me but
    that,
For truth can never be confirm'd enough,
Though doubts did ever sleep.
    Mar.   First, sir, I pray,
What is your title ?
    Per. I am Pericles of Tyre : but tell me
    now
My drown'd queen's name, as in the rest you
    said
Thou hast been godlike perfect,
The heir of kingdoms and another like
To Pericles thy father.   210
    Mar. Is it no more to be your daughter
    than
To say my mother's name was Thaisa ?
Thaisa was my mother, who did end
The minute I began.
    Per. Now, blessing on thee ! rise ; thou art
    my child.
Give me fresh garments. Mine own, Heli-
    canus ;
She is not dead at Tarsus, as she should have
    been,
By savage Cleon : she shall tell thee all ;
When thou shalt kneel, and justify in knowl-
    edge
She is thy very princess. Who is this ?   220
    Hel. Sir, 'tis the governor of Mytilene,
Who, hearing of your melancholy state,
Did come to see you.
    Per.   I embrace you.
Give me my robes. I am wild in my beholding.
O heavens bless my girl ! But, hark, what
    music ;
Tell Helicanus, my Marina, tell him
O'er, point by point, for yet he seems to doubt,
How sure you are my daughter. But, what
    music ?
    Hel. My lord, I hear none.
    Per. None !   230
The music of the spheres ! List, my Marina.

    Lys. It is not good to cross him ; give him
    way.
    Per. Rarest sounds ! Do ye not hear ?
    Lys.   My lord, I hear. [*Music.*
    Per. Most heavenly music !
It nips me unto listening, and thick slumber
Hangs upon mine eyes : let me rest. [*Sleeps.*
    Lys. A pillow for his head :
So, leave him all. Well, my companion friends,
If this but answer to my just belief,
I'll well remember you.   240
                    [*Exeunt all but Pericles.*

DIANA *appears to* PERICLES *as in a vision.*

    Dia. My temple stands in Ephesus : hie
    thee thither,
And do upon mine altar sacrifice.
There, when my maiden priests are met to-
    gether,
Before the people all,
Reveal how thou at sea didst lose thy wife :
To mourn thy crosses, with thy daughter's, call
And give them repetition to the life.
Or perform my bidding, or thou livest in woe ;
Do it, and happy ; by my silver bow !
Awake, and tell thy dream. [*Disappears.*   250
    Per. Celestial Dian, goddess argentine,
I will obey thee. Helicanus !

    Re-enter HELICANUS, LYSIMACHUS, *and*
        MARINA.

    Hel.   Sir ?
    Per. My purpose was for Tarsus, there to
    strike
The inhospitable Cleon ; but I am
For other service first : toward Ephesus
Turn our blown sails ; eftsoons I'll tell thee
    why.
[*To Lysimachus*] Shall we refresh us, sir,
    upon your shore,
And give you gold for such provision
As our intents will need ?
    Lys. Sir,   260
With all my heart ; and, when you come
    ashore,
I have another suit.
    Per.   You shall prevail,
Were it to woo my daughter ; for it seems
You have been noble towards her.
    Lys.   Sir, lend me your arm.
    Per. Come, my Marina.   [*Exeunt.*

SCENE II. *Enter* GOWER, *before the temple of*
        DIANA *at Ephesus.*

    Gow. Now our sands are almost run ;
More a little, and then dumb.
This, my last boon, give me,
For such kindness must relieve me,
That you aptly will suppose   270
What pageantry, what feats, what shows,
What minstrelsy, and pretty din,
The regent made in Mytilene
To greet the king. So he thrived,
That he is promised to be wived
To fair Marina ; but in no wise
Till he had done his sacrifice,
As Dian bade : whereto being bound,
The interim, pray you, all confound.
In feather'd briefness sails are fill'd,   280
And wishes fall out as they're will'd.
At Ephesus, the temple see,
Our king and all his company.

That he can hither come so soon,
Is by your fancy's thankful doom.   [*Exit.*

SCENE III.   *The temple of Diana at Ephesus;*
THAISA *standing near the altar, as high
priestess; a number of Virgins on each side;*
CERIMON *and other Inhabitants of Ephesus
attending.*

Enter PERICLES, *with his train;* LYSIMACHUS,
HELICANUS, MARINA, *and a* Lady.

Per. Hail, Dian! to perform thy just com-
        mand,
I here confess myself the king of Tyre;
Who, frighted from my country, did wed
At Pentapolis the fair Thaisa.
At sea in childbed died she, but brought forth
A maid-child call'd Marina; who, O goddess,
Wears yet thy silver livery. She at Tarsus
Was nursed with Cleon; who at fourteen years
He sought to murder : but her better stars
Brought her to Mytilene; 'gainst whose shore
Riding, her fortunes brought the maid aboard
        us,
Where, by her own most clear remembrance,
        she
Made known herself my daughter.
Thai.   Voice and favor!
You are, you are—O royal Pericles! [*Faints.*
Per. What means the nun? she dies! help,
        gentlemen!
Cer. Noble sir,
If you have told Diana's altar true,
This is your wife.
Per.   Reverend appearer, no;
I threw her overboard with these very arms.
Cer. Upon this coast, I warrant you.
Per.   'Tis most certain. 20
Cer. Look to the lady; O, she's but o'er-
        joy'd.
Early in blustering morn this lady was
Thrown upon this shore. I oped the coffin,
Found there rich jewels; recover'd her, and
        placed her
Here in Diana's temple.
Per.   May we see them?
Cer. Great sir, they shall be brought you
        to my house,
Whither I invite you. Look, Thaisa is
Recovered.
Thai. O, let me look!
If he be none of mine, my sanctity
Will to my sense bend no licentious ear,   30
But curb it, spite of seeing. O, my lord,
Are you not Pericles? Like him you spake,
Like him you are : did you not name a tem-
        pest,
A birth, and death?
Per.   The voice of dead Thaisa!
Thai. That Thaisa am I, supposed dead
And drown'd.
Per. Immortal Dian!
Thai.   Now I know you better.
When we with tears parted Pentapolis,
The king my father gave you such a ring.
                            [*Shows a ring.*
Per. This, this : no more, you gods! your
        present kindness   40
Makes my past miseries sports : you shall do
        well,
That on the touching of her lips I may
Melt and no more be seen. O, come, be buried
A second time within these arms.

Mar.   My heart
Leaps to be gone into my mother's bosom.
                        [*Kneels to Thaisa.*
Per. Look, who kneels here! Flesh of thy
        flesh, Thaisa;
Thy burden at the sea, and call'd Marina
For she was yielded there.
Thai.   Blest, and mine own!
Hel. Hail, madam, and my queen!
Thai.   I know you not.
Per. You have heard me say, when I did
        fly from Tyre,   50
I left behind an ancient substitute :
Can you remember what I call'd the man?
I have named him oft.
Thai.   'Twas Helicanus then.
Per. Still confirmation :
Embrace him, dear Thaisa; this is he.
Now do I long to hear how you were found;
How possibly preserved; and who to thank,
Besides the gods, for this great miracle.
Thai. Lord Cerimon, my lord; this man,
Through whom the gods have shown their
        power; that can   60
From first to last resolve you.
Per.   Reverend sir,
The gods can have no mortal officer
More like a god than you. Will you deliver
How this dead queen re-lives?
Cer.   I will, my lord.
Beseech you, first go with me to my house,
Where shall be shown you all was found with
        her;
How she came placed here in the temple;
No needful thing omitted.
Per. Pure Dian, bless thee for thy vision! I
Will offer night-oblations to thee. Thaisa,   70
This prince, the fair-betrothed of your daugh-
        ter,
Shall marry her at Pentapolis. And now,
This ornament
Makes me look dismal will I clip to form;
And what this fourteen years no razor touch'd,
To grace thy marriage-day, I'll beautify.
Thai. Lord Cerimon hath letters of good
        credit, sir,
My father's dead.
Per. Heavens make a star of him! Yet
        there, my queen,
We'll celebrate their nuptials, and ourselves
Will in that kingdom spend our following
        days :   81
Our son and daughter shall in Tyrus reign.
Lord Cerimon, we do our longing stay
To hear the rest untold : sir, lead's the way.
                            [*Exeunt.*

Enter GOWER.

Gow. In Antiochus and his daughter you
        have heard
Of monstrous lust the due and just reward :
In Pericles, his queen and daughter, seen,
Although assail'd with fortune fierce and
        keen,
Virtue preserved from fell destruction's
        blast,
Led on by heaven, and crown'd with joy at
        last :   90
In Helicanus may you well descry
A figure of truth, of faith, of loyalty :
In reverend Cerimon there well appears
The worth that learned charity aye wears :
For wicked Cleon and his wife, when fame

Had spread their cursed deed, and honor'd
    name
Of Pericles, to rage the city turn,
That him and his they in his palace burn;
The gods for murder seemed so content

To punish them; although not done, but
    meant.
So, on your patience evermore attending, 100
New joy wait on you! Here our play has
    ending.   [*Exit.*

CYMBELINE.

(WRITTEN ABOUT 1609.)

INTRODUCTION.

Cymbeline interweaves with a fragment of British history taken from Holinshed, a story from Boccacio's *Decameron* (9th Novel of 2nd Day), the Geneura of the Italian novel corresponding to Shakespeare's Imogen. The story is told in a tract called *Westward for Smelts*, 1620 (stated by Steevens and Malone to have been published as early as 1603) ; but Shakespeare appears in some way, directly or indirectly, to have made acquaintance with it as given by Boccacio. The names of the two princes Shakespeare found, as well as the king's name, in Holinshed ; but the incidents of their having been stolen, and their life, among the mountains of Wales, appear to have been invented by the dramatist. Dr. Forman records in his MS *Booke of Plaies and Notes thereof* that he saw Cymbeline acted ; but he gives no date. His book, however, belongs to the years 1610–1611, and the metrical and other internal evidence point to that time as about the period when the drama must have been written. It is loosely constructed, and some passages possess little dramatic intensity. Several critics have questioned whether the vision of Posthumus (Act V. Sc. IV.) is of Shakespeare's authorship, and it is certainly poorly conceived and written. Nevertheless, the play is one of singular charm, and contains in Imogen one of the loveliest of Shakespeare's creations of female character. Except grandeur and majesty, which were reserved for Hermione and Queen Katherine, every thing that can make a woman lovely is given by the poet to Imogen : quick and exquisite feelings, brightness of intellect, delicate imagination, energy to hate evil and to right what was wrong, scorn for what is mean or rude, culture, dainty womanly accomplishments, the gift of song, a capacity for exquisite happiness and no less sensitiveness to the sharpness of sorrow, a power of quick recovery from disaster when the warmth of love breathes upon her once more, beauty of a type which is noble and refined. And her lost brothers are gallant youths, bred happily far from the court, in wilds where their generous instincts and love of freedom and activity find innocent if insufficient modes of gratification. As in all the works of this period, an open-air feeling pervades a great part of the drama ; nature, itself joyous and free, ministers to what is beautiful, simple, or heroic in man, while yet by Shakespeare nature alone is never anywhere conceived as sufficient to satisfy the heart or the imagination of a human being. With reconciliation and reunion this, like the other Romances, closes. The faith of Posthumus in Imogen is of a half-romantic kind, unconfirmed by calm and deep acquaintance with her heart : that faith is not subtly poisoned, like the love of Othello, but suddenly, in one brief and desperate encounter, overthrown. His jealousy is not heroic, like Othello's ; it shows something of grossness, unworthy of his true self. In due time penitential sorrow does its work, his nobler nature reasserts itself, and in the final reunion of parent and lost children, the erring husband is also restored to the quick-beating, joyous heart of his wife.

DRAMATIS PERSONÆ.

CYMBELINE, king of Britain.
CLOTEN, son to the Queen by a former husband.
POSTHUMUS LEONATUS, a gentleman, husband to Imogen.
BELARIUS, a banished lord, disguised under the name of Morgan.
GUIDERIUS, } sons to Cymbeline, disguised
ARVIRAGUS, } under the names of Polydore and Cadwal, supposed sons to Morgan.
PHILARIO, friend to Posthumus, } Italians.
IACHIMO, friend to Philario, }
CAIUS LUCIUS, general of the Roman forces.
PISANIO, servant to Posthumus.
CORNELIUS, a physician.

A Roman Captain.
Two British Captains.
A Frenchman, friend to Philario.
Two Lords of Cymbeline's court.
Two Gentlemen of the same.
Two Gaolers.

Queen, wife to Cymbeline.
IMOGEN, daughter to Cymbeline by a former queen.
HELEN, a lady attending on Imogen.

Lords, Ladies, Roman Senators, Tribunes, a Soothsayer, a Dutchman, a Spaniard, Musicians, Officers, Captains, Soldiers, Messengers, and other Attendants.

Apparitions.

SCENE : *Britain ; Rome.*

ACT I.

Scene I. *Britain. The garden of Cymbeline's palace.*

Enter two Gentlemen.

First Gent. You do not meet a man but
  frowns : our bloods
No more obey the heavens than our courtiers
Still seem as does the king.
  Sec. Gent.   But what's the matter ?
  First Gent. His daughter, and the heir of's
  kingdom, whom
He purposed to his wife's sole son—a widow
That late he married—hath referr'd herself
Unto a poor but worthy gentleman : she's
  wedded ;
Her husband banish'd ; she imprison'd : all
Is outward sorrow ; though I think the king
Be touch'd at very heart.
  Sec. Gent.   None but the king ?   10
  First Gent. He that hath lost her too ; so is
  the queen,
That most desired the match ; but not a cour-
  tier,
Although they wear their faces to the bent
Of the king's look's, hath a heart that is not
Glad at the thing they scowl at.
  Sec. Gent.   And why so ?
  First Gent. He that hath miss'd the prin-
  cess is a thing
Too bad for bad report : and he that hath
  her—
I mean, that married her, alack, good man !
And therefore banish'd—is a creature such   19
As, to seek through the regions of the earth
For one his like, there would be something
  failing
In him that should compare. I do not think
So fair an outward and such stuff within
Endows a man but he.
  Sec. Gent.   You speak him far.
  First Gent. I do extend him, sir, within
  himself,
Crush him together rather than unfold
His measure duly.
  Sec. Gent.   What's his name and birth ?
  First Gent. I cannot delve him to the root :
  his father
Was call'd Sicilius, who did join his honor
Against the Romans with Cassibelan,   30
But had his titles by Tenantius whom
He served with glory and admired success,
So gain'd the sur-addition Leonatus ;
And had, besides this gentleman in question,
Two other sons, who in the wars o' the time
Died with their swords in hand ; for which
  their father,
Then old and fond of issue, took such sorrow
That he quit being, and his gentle lady,
Big of this gentleman our theme, deceased
As he was born. The king he takes the babe
To his protection, calls him Posthumus Leon-
  atus,   41
Breeds him and makes him of his bed-cham-
  ber,
Puts to him all the learnings that his time
Could make him the receiver of ; which he
  took,
As we do air, fast as 'twas minister'd,
And in's spring became a harvest, lived in
  court—

Which rare it is to do—most praised, most
  loved,
A sample to the youngest, to the more mature
A glass that feated them, and to the graver
A child that guided dotards ; to his mistress,
For whom he now is banish'd, her own price
Proclaims how she esteem'd him and his vir-
  tue ;
By her election may be truly read
What kind of man he is.
  Sec. Gent.   I honor him
Even out of your report. But, pray you, tell
  me,
Is she sole child to the king ?
  First Gent.   His only child.
He had two sons : if this be worth your hear-
  ing,
Mark it : the eldest of them at three years old,
I' the swathing-clothes the other, from their
  nursery
Were stol'n, and to this hour no guess in
  knowledge   60
Which way they went.
  Sec. Gent.   How long is this ago ?
  First Gent. Some twenty years.
  Sec. Gent. That a king's children should be
  so convey'd,
So slackly guarded, and the search so slow,
That could not trace them !
  First Gent. Howsoe'er 'tis strange,
Or that the negligence may well be laugh'd at,
Yet is it true, sir.
  Sec. Gent.   I do well believe you.
  First Gent. We must forbear : here comes
  the gentleman,
The queen, and princess.   [*Exeunt.*

Enter the Queen, Posthumus, *and* Imogen.

  Queen. No, be assured you shall not find
  me, daughter,   70
After the slander of most stepmothers,
Evil-eyed unto you : you're my prisoner, but
Your gaoler shall deliver you the keys
That lock up your restraint. For you, Posthu-
  mus,
So soon as I can win the offended king,
I will be known your advocate : marry, yet
The fire of rage is in him, and 'twere good
You lean'd unto his sentence with what pa-
  tience
Your wisdom may inform you.
  Post.   Please your highness,
I will from hence to-day.
  Queen.   You know the peril.   80
I'll fetch a turn about the garden, pitying
The pangs of barr'd affections, though the king
Hath charged you should not speak together.
  [*Exit.*
  Imo.   O
Dissembling courtesy ! How fine this tyrant
Can tickle where she wounds ! My dearest
  husband,
I something fear my father's wrath ; but noth-
  ing—
Always reserved my holy duty—what
His rage can do on me : you must be gone ;
And I shall here abide the hourly shot
Of angry eyes, not comforted to live,   90
But that there is this jewel in the world
That I may see again.
  Post.   My queen ! my mistress !
O lady, weep no more, lest I give cause
To be suspected of more tenderness

Than doth become a man. I will remain
The loyal'st husband that did e'er plight troth :
My residence in Rome at one Philario's,
Who to my father was a friend, to me
Known but by letter : thither write, my queen,
And with mine eyes I'll drink the words you
    send,
Though ink be made of gall.

Re-enter QUEEN.

Queen. Be brief, I pray you : 101
If the king come, I shall incur I know not
How much of his displeasure. [*Aside*] Yet
    I'll move him
To walk this way : I never do him wrong,
But he does buy my injuries, to be friends ;
Pays dear for my offences. [*Exit.*
Post. Should we be taking leave
As long a term as yet we have to live,
The loathness to depart would grow. Adieu !
Imo. Nay, stay a little :
Were you but riding forth to air yourself, 110
Such parting were too petty. Look here, love ;
This diamond was my mother's : take it, heart ;
But keep it till you woo another wife,
When Imogen is dead.
Post. How, how ! another ?
You gentle gods, give me but this I have,
And sear up my embracements from a next
With bonds of death ! [*Putting on the ring.*]
    Remain, remain thou here
While sense can keep it on. And, sweetest,
    fairest,
As I my poor self did exchange for you,
To your so infinite loss, so in our trifles 120
I still win of you : for my sake wear this ;
It is a manacle of love ; I'll place it
Upon this fairest prisoner.
    [*Putting a bracelet upon her arm.*
Imo. O the gods !
When shall we see again ?

Enter CYMBELINE *and* Lords.

Post. Alack, the king !
Cym. Thou basest thing, avoid ! hence,
    from my sight !
If after this command thou fraught the court
With thy unworthiness, thou diest : away !
Thou'rt poison to my blood.
Post. The gods protect you !
And bless the good remainders of the court !
I am gone. [*Exit.*
Imo. There cannot be a pinch in death 130
More sharp than this is.
Cym. O disloyal thing,
That shouldst repair my youth, thou heap'st
A year's age on me.
Imo. I beseech you, sir,
Harm not yourself with your vexation :
I am senseless of your wrath ; a touch more
    rare
Subdues all pangs, all fears.
Cym. Past grace ? obedience ?
Imo. Past hope, and in despair ; that way,
    past grace.
Cym. That mightst have had the sole son
    of my queen !
Imo. O blest, that I might not ! I chose an
    eagle,
And did avoid a puttock. 140
Cym. Thou took'st a beggar ; wouldst have
    made my throne
A seat for baseness.

Imo. No ; I rather added
A lustre to it.
Cym. O thou vile one !
Imo. Sir,
It is your fault that I have loved Posthumus :
You bred him as my playfellow, and he is
A man worth any woman, overbuys me
Almost the sum he pays.
Cym. What, art thou mad ?
Imo. Almost, sir : heaven restore me !
    Would I were
A neat-herd's daughter, and my Leonatus
Our neighbor shepherd's son !
Cym. Thou foolish thing ! 150

Re-enter QUEEN.

They were again together : you have done
Not after our command. Away with her,
And pen her up.
Queen. Beseech your patience. Peace,
Dear lady daughter, peace ! Sweet sovereign,
Leave us to ourselves ; and make yourself
    some comfort
Out of your best advice.
Cym. Nay, let her languish
A drop of blood a day ; and, being aged,
Die of this folly !
    [*Exeunt Cymbeline and Lords.*
Queen. Fie ! you must give way.

Enter PISANIO.

Here is your servant. How now, sir ! What
    news ?
Pis. My lord your son drew on my master.
Queen. Ha ! 160
No harm, I trust, is done ?
Pis. There might have been,
But that my master rather play'd than fought
And had no help of anger : they were parted
By gentlemen at hand.
Queen. I am very glad on't.
Imo. Your son's my father's friend ; he
    takes his part.
To draw upon an exile ! O brave sir !
I would they were in Afric both together ;
Myself by with a needle, that I might prick
The goer-back. Why came you from your
    master ?
Pis. On his command : he would not suffer
    me 170
To bring him to the haven ; left these notes
Of what commands I should be subject to,
When 't pleased you to employ me.
Queen. This hath been
Your faithful servant : I dare lay mine honor
He will remain so.
Pis. I humbly thank your highness.
Queen. Pray, walk awhile.
Imo. About some half-hour hence,
I pray you, speak with me : you shall at least
Go see my lord aboard : for this time leave
    me. [*Exeunt.*

SCENE II. *The same. A public place.*

Enter CLOTEN *and two* Lords.

First Lord. Sir, I would advise you to shift
a shirt ; the violence of action hath made you
reek as a sacrifice : where air comes out, air
comes in : there's none abroad so wholesome
as that you vent.
Clo. If my shirt were bloody, then to shift
it. Have I hurt him ?

Sec. Lord. [*Aside*] No, 'faith; not so
much as his patience.   9
First Lord. Hurt him! his body's a passable carcass, if he be not hurt : it is a thor-
oughfare for steel, if it be not hurt.
Sec. Lord. [*Aside*] His steel was in debt;
it went o' the backside the town.
Clo. The villain would not stand me.
Sec. Lord. [*Aside*] No; but he fled forward still, toward your face.
First Lord. Stand you! You have land
enough of your own : but he added to your
having ; gave you some ground.   20
Sec. Lord. [*Aside*] As many inches as you
have oceans. Puppies!
Clo. I would they had not come between
us.
Sec. Lord. [*Aside*] So would I, till you
had measured how long a fool you were upon
the ground.
Clo. And that she should love this fellow
and refuse me!
Sec. Lord. [*Aside*] If it be a sin to make a
true election, she is damned.   30
First Lord. Sir, as I told you always, her
beauty and her brain go not together : she's a
good sign, but I have seen small reflection of
her wit.
Sec. Lord. [*Aside*] She shines not upon
fools, lest the reflection should hurt her.
Clo. Come, I'll to my chamber. Would
there had been some hurt done!
Sec. Lord. [*Aside*] I wish not so; unless it
had been the fall of an ass, which is no great
hurt.   40
Clo. You'll go with us?
First Lord. I'll attend your lordship.
Clo. Nay, come, let's go together.
Sec. Lord. Well, my lord.   [*Exeunt.*

Scene III.   *A room in Cymbeline's palace.*

Enter IMOGEN *and* PISANIO.

Imo. I would thou grew'st unto the shores
          o' the haven,
And question'dst every sail : if he should write
And I not have it, 'twere a paper lost,
As offer'd mercy is. What was the last
That he spake to thee?
Pis.   It was his queen, his queen!
Imo. Then waved his handkerchief?
Pis.   And kiss'd it, madam.
Imo. Senseless linen! happier therein than
          I!
And that was all?
Pis.   No, madam ; for so long
As he could make me with this eye or ear
Distinguish him from others, he did keep   10
The deck, with glove, or hat, or handkerchief,
Still waving, as the fits and stirs of 's mind
Could best express how slow his soul sail'd on,
How swift his ship.
Imo.   Thou shouldst have made him
As little as a crow, or less, ere left
To after-eye him.
Pis.   Madam, so I did.
Imo. I would have broke mine eye-strings ;
          crack'd them, but
To look upon him, till the diminution
Of space had pointed him sharp as my needle,
Nay, follow'd him, till he had melted from 20
The smallness of a gnat to air, and then
Have turn'd mine eye and wept. But, good
Pisanio,

When shall we hear from him?
Pis.   Be assured, madam,
With his next vantage.
Imo.   I did not take my leave of him, but
          had
Most pretty things to say : ere I could tell him
How I would think on him at certain hours
Such thoughts and such, or I could make him
          swear
The shes of Italy should not betray
Mine interest and his honor, or have charged
          him,   30
At the sixth hour of morn, at noon, at mid-
          night,
To encounter me with orisons, for then
I am in heaven for him ; or ere I could
Give him that parting kiss which I had set
Betwixt two charming words, comes in my
          father
And like the tyrannous breathing of the north
Shakes all our buds from growing.

Enter a Lady.

Lady.   The queen, madam,
Desires your highness' company.
Imo. Those things I bid you do, get them
          dispatch'd.
I will attend the queen.
Pis.   Madam, I shall. [*Exeunt.* 40

Scene IV.   *Rome.   Philario's house.*

Enter PHILARIO, IACHIMO, *a* Frenchman, *a*
Dutchman, *and a* Spaniard.

Iach. Believe it, sir, I have seen him in
Britain : he was then of a crescent note, expected to prove so worthy as since he hath
been allowed the name of; but I could then
have looked on him without the help of admiration, though the catalogue of his endowments had been tabled by his side and I to
peruse him by items.
Phi. You speak of him when he was less
furnished than now he is with that which
makes him both without and within.   10
French. I have seen him in France : we
had very many there could behold the sun
with as firm eyes as he.
Iach. This matter of marrying his king's
daughter, wherein he must be weighed rather
by her value than his own, words him, I doubt
not, a great deal from the matter.
French. And then his banishment.
Iach. Ay, and the approbation of those
that weep this lamentable divorce under her
colors are wonderfully to extend him ; be it
but to fortify her judgment, which else an easy
battery might lay flat, for taking a beggar without less quality. But how comes it he is to
sojourn with you? How creeps acquaintance?
Phi. His father and I were soldiers together ; to whom I have been often bound for
no less than my life. Here comes the Briton :
let him be so entertained amongst you as suits,
with gentlemen of your knowing, to a stranger
of his quality.   30

Enter POSTHUMUS.

I beseech you all, be better known to this gentleman ; whom I commend to you as a noble
friend of mine : how worthy he is I will leave
to appear hereafter, rather than story him in
his own hearing.

French. Sir, we have known together in Orleans.

Post. Since when I have been debtor to you for courtesies, which I will be ever to pay and yet pay still.　　　　　　　　　　　　40

French. Sir, you o'er-rate my poor kindness : I was glad I did atone my countryman and you ; it had been pity you should have been put together with so mortal a purpose as then each bore, upon importance of so slight and trivial a nature.

Post. By your pardon, sir, I was then a young traveller ; rather shunned to go even with what I heard than in my every action to be guided by others' experiences : but upon my mended judgment—if I offend not to say it is mended—my quarrel was not altogether slight.　　　　　　　　　　　　51

French. 'Faith, yes, to be put to the arbitrement of swords, and by such two that would by all likelihood have confounded one the other, or have fallen both.

Iach. Can we, with manners, ask what was the difference ?

French. Safely, I think : 'twas a contention in public, which may, without contradiction, suffer the report. It was much like an argument that fell out last night, where each of us fell in praise of our country mistresses ; this gentleman at that time vouching—and upon warrant of bloody affirmation—his to be more fair, virtuous, wise, chaste, constant-qualified and less attemptable than any the rarest of our ladies in France.

Iach. That lady is not now living, or this gentleman's opinion by this worn out.

Post. She holds her virtue still and I my mind.

Iach. You must not so far prefer her 'fore ours of Italy.　　　　　　　　　　　71

Post. Being so far provoked as I was in France, I would abate her nothing, though I profess myself her adorer, not her friend.

Iach. As fair and as good—a kind of hand-in-hand comparison—had been something too fair and too good for any lady in Britain. If she went before others I have seen, as that diamond of yours outlustres many I have beheld, I could not but believe she excelled many : but I have not seen the most precious diamond that is, nor you the lady.

Post. I praised her as I rated her : so do I my stone.

Iach. What do you esteem it at ?

Post. More than the world enjoys.

Iach. Either your unparagoned mistress is dead, or she's outprized by a trifle.

Post. You are mistaken : the one may be sold, or given, if there were wealth enough for the purchase, or merit for the gift : the other is not a thing for sale, and only the gift of the gods.

Iach. Which the gods have given you ?

Post. Which, by their graces, I will keep.

Iach. You may wear her in title yours : but, you know, strange fowl light upon neighboring ponds. Your ring may be stolen too : so your brace of unprizable estimations ; the one is but frail and the other casual ; a cunning thief, or a that way accomplished courtier, would hazard the winning both of first and last.

Post. Your Italy contains none so accomplished a courtier to convince the honor of my mistress, if, in the holding or loss of that, you term her frail. I do nothing doubt you have store of thieves ; notwithstanding, I fear not my ring.

Phi. Let us leave here, gentlemen.　　　　109

Post. Sir, with all my heart. This worthy signior, I thank him, makes no stranger of me ; we are familiar at first.

Iach. With five times so much conversation, I should get ground of your fair mistress, make her go back, even to the yielding, had I admittance and opportunity to friend.

Post. No, no.

Iach. I dare thereupon pawn the moiety of my estate to your ring ; which, in my opinion, o'ervalues it something : but I make my wager rather against your confidence than her reputation : and, to bar your offence herein too, I durst attempt it against any lady in the world.

Post. You are a great deal abused in too bold a persuasion ; and I doubt not you sustain what you're worthy of by your attempt.

Iach. What's that ?

Post. A repulse : though your attempt, as you call it, deserve more ; a punishment too.

Phi. Gentlemen, enough of this : it came in too suddenly ; let it die as it was born, and, I pray you, be better acquainted.

Iach. Would I had put my estate and my neighbor's on the approbation of what I have spoke !

Post. What lady would you choose to assail ?

Iach. Yours ; whom in constancy you think stands so safe. I will lay you ten thousand ducats to your ring, that, commend me to the court where your lady is, with no more advantage than the opportunity of a second conference, and I will bring from thence that honor of hers which you imagine so reserved.

Post. I will wage against your gold, gold to it : my ring I hold dear as my finger ; 'tis part of it.

Iach. You are afraid, and therein the wiser. If you buy ladies' flesh at a million a dram, you cannot preserve it from tainting : but I see you have some religion in you, that you fear.　　　　　　　　　　　149

Post. This is but a custom in your tongue ; you bear a graver purpose, I hope.

Iach. I am the master of my speeches, and would undergo what's spoken, I swear.

Post. Will you ? I shall but lend my diamond till your return : let there be covenants drawn between's : my mistress exceeds in goodness the hugeness of your unworthy thinking : I dare you to this match : here's my ring.

Phi. I will have it no lay.　　　　　　　159

Iach. By the gods, it is one. If I bring you no sufficient testimony that I have enjoyed the dearest bodily part of your mistress, my ten thousand ducats are yours ; so is your diamond too : if I come off, and leave her in such honor as you have trust in, she your jewel, this your jewel, and my gold are yours : provided I have your commendation for my more free entertainment.

Post. I embrace these conditions ; let us have articles betwixt us. Only, thus far you shall answer : if you make your voyage upon her and give me directly to understand you have prevailed, I am no further your enemy ;

she is not worth our debate : if she remain un-
seduced, you not making it appear otherwise,
for your ill opinion and the assault you have
made to her chastity you shall answer me with
your sword.

Iach. Your hand ; a covenant : we will
have these things set down by lawful counsel,
and straight away for Britain, lest the bargain
should catch cold and starve : I will fetch my
gold and have our two wagers recorded.   181

Post. Agreed.
     [*Exeunt Posthumus and Iachimo.*
French. Will this hold, think you ?

Phi. Signior Iachimo will not from it.
Pray, let us follow 'em.   [*Exeunt.*

SCENE V. *Britain. A room in Cymbeline's
palace.*

Enter QUEEN, *Ladies, and* CORNELIUS.

Queen. Whiles yet the dew's on ground,
    gather those flowers ;
Make haste : who has the note of them ?

First Lady.   I, madam.

Queen. Dispatch.   [*Exeunt Ladies.*
Now, master doctor, have you brought those
    drugs ?

Cor. Pleaseth your highness, ay : here they
    are, madam : [*Presenting a small box.*
But I beseech your grace, without offence,—
My conscience bids me ask—wherefore you
    have
Commanded of me those most poisonous com-
    pounds,
Which are the movers of a languishing death ;
But though slow, deadly ?

Queen.   I wonder, doctor,   10
Thou ask'st me such a question. Have I not
    been
Thy pupil long ? Hast thou not learn'd me how
To make perfumes ? distil ? preserve ? yea, so
That our great king himself doth woo me oft
For my confections ? Having thus far pro-
    ceeded,—
Unless thou think'st me devilish—is't not meet
That I did amplify my judgment in
Other conclusions ? I will try the forces
Of these thy compounds on such creatures as
We count not worth the hanging, but none
    human,   20
To try the vigor of them and apply
Allayments to their act, and by them gather
Their several virtues and effects.

Cor.   Your highness
Shall from this practice but make hard your
    heart :
Besides, the seeing these effects will be
Both noisome and infectious.

Queen.   O, content thee.

Enter PISANIO.

[*Aside*] Here comes a flattering rascal ; upon
    him
Will I first work : he's for his master,
An enemy to my son. How now, Pisanio !
Doctor, your service for this time is ended ; 30
Take your own way.

Cor. [*Aside*] I do suspect you, madam ;
But you shall do no harm.

Queen. [*To Pisanio*] Hark thee, a word.

Cor. [*Aside*] I do not like her. She doth
    think she
Strange lingering poisons : I do know her
    spirit,

And will not trust one of her malice with
A drug of such damn'd nature. Those she has
Will stupefy and dull the sense awhile ;
Which first, perchance, she'll prove on cats
    and dogs,
Then afterward up higher : but there is   39
No danger in what show of death it makes,
More than the locking-up the spirits a time,
To be more fresh, reviving. She is fool'd
With a most false effect ; and I the truer,
So to be false with her.

Queen.   No further service, doctor,
Until I send for thee.

Cor.   I humbly take my leave. [*Exit.*

Queen. Weeps she still, say'st thou ? Dost
    thou think in time
She will not quench and let instructions enter
Where folly now possesses ? Do thou work :
When thou shalt bring me word she loves my
    son,
I'll tell thee on the instant thou art then   50
As great as is thy master, greater, for
His fortunes all lie speechless and his name
Is at last gasp : return he cannot, nor
Continue where he is : to shift his being
Is to exchange one misery with another,
And every day that comes to comes to decay
A day's work in him. What shalt thou expect,
To be depender on a thing that leans,
Who cannot be new built, nor has no friends,
So much as but to prop him ? [*The Queen
    drops the box : Pisanio takes it up.*]
    Thou takest up
Thou know'st not what ; but take it for thy
    labor :
It is a thing I made, which hath the king
Five times redeem'd from death : I do not
    know
What is more cordial. Nay, I prithee, take it ;
It is an earnest of a further good
That I mean to thee. Tell thy mistress how
The case stands with her ; do't as from thy-
    self.
Think what a chance thou changest on, but
    think
Thou hast thy mistress still, to boot, my son,
Who shall take notice of thee : I'll move the
    king   70
To any shape of thy preferment such
As thou'lt desire ; and then myself, I chiefly,
That set thee on to this desert, am bound
To load thy merit richly. Call my women :
Think on my words.   [*Exit Pisanio.*
     A sly and constant knave,
Not to be shaked ; the agent for his master
And the remembrancer of her to hold
The hand-fast to her lord. I have given him
    that
Which, if he take, shall quite unpeople her 79
Of liegers for her sweet, and which she after,
Except she bend her humor, shall be assured
To taste of too.

Re-enter PISANIO *and* Ladies.

     So, so : well done, well done :
The violets, cowslips, and the primroses,
Bear to my closet. Fare thee well, Pisanio ;
Think on my words.
     [*Exeunt Queen and Ladies.*

Pis.   And shall do :
But when to my good lord I prove untrue,
I'll choke myself : there's all I'll do for you.
     [*Exit.*

Scene VI. *The same. Another room in the
palace.*

Enter IMOGEN.

Imo. A father cruel, and a step-dame
false ;
A foolish suitor to a wedded lady,
That hath her husband banish'd ;—O, that
husband !
My supreme crown of grief ! and those re-
peated
Vexations of it ! Had I been thief-stol'n,
As my two brothers, happy ! but most miser-
able
Is the desire that's glorious : blest be those,
How mean soe'er, that have their honest wills,
Which seasons comfort. Who may this be ?
Fie !

Enter PISANIO *and* IACHIMO.

Pis. Madam, a noble gentleman of Rome,
Comes from my lord with letters.   11
Iach. Change you, madam ?
The worthy Leonatus is in safety
And greets your highness dearly.
                        [*Presents a letter.*
Imo.   Thanks, good sir :
You're kindly welcome.
Iach. [*Aside*] All of her that is out of door
most rich !
If she be furnish'd with a mind so rare,
She is alone the Arabian bird, and I
Have lost the wager. Boldness be my friend !
Arm me, audacity, from head to foot !
Or, like the Parthian, I shall flying fight ;   20
Rather, directly fly.
Imo. [*Reads*] 'He is one of the noblest
note, to whose kindnesses I am most infinitely
tied. Reflect upon him accordingly, as you
value your trust—   LEONATUS.'
So far I read aloud :
But even the very middle of my heart
Is warm'd by the rest, and takes it thankfully.
You are as welcome, worthy sir, as I
Have words to bid you, and shall find it so 30
In all that I can do.
Iach.   Thanks, fairest lady.
What, are men mad ? Hath nature given them
eyes
To see this vaulted arch, and the rich crop
Of sea and land, which can distinguish 'twixt
The fiery orbs above and the twinn'd stones
Upon the number'd beach ? and can we not
Partition make with spectacles so precious
'Twixt fair and foul ?
Imo.   What makes your admiration ?
Iach. It cannot be i' the eye, for apes and
monkeys
'Twixt two such shes would chatter this way
and   40
Contemn with mows the other ; nor i' the
judgment,
For idiots in this case of favor would
Be wisely definite ; nor i' the appetite ;
Sluttery to such neat excellence opposed
Should make desire vomit emptiness,
Not so allured to feed.
Imo. What is the matter, trow ?
Iach.   The cloyed will,
That satiate yet unsatisfied desire, that tub
Both fill'd and running, ravening first the lamb
Longs after for the garbage.

Imo.   What, dear sir, 50
Thus raps you ? Are you well ?
Iach. Thanks, madam ; well. [*To Pisanio*]
Beseech you, sir, desire
My man's abode where I did leave him : he
Is strange and peevish.
Pis.   I was going, sir,
To give him welcome.   [*Exit.*
Imo. Continues well my lord ? His health,
beseech you ?
Iach. Well, madam.
Imo. Is he disposed to mirth ? I hope he is.
Iach. Exceeding pleasant ; none a stranger
there
So merry and so gamesome : he is call'd   60
The Briton reveller.
Imo.   When he was here,
He did incline to sadness, and oft-times
Not knowing why.
Iach.   I never saw him sad.
There is a Frenchman his companion, one
An eminent monsieur, that, it seems, much
loves
A Gallian girl at home ; he furnaces
The thick sighs from him, whiles the jolly
Briton—
Your lord, I mean—laughs from's free lungs,
cries ' O,
Can my sides hold, to think that man, who
knows
By history, report, or his own proof,   70
What woman is, yea, what she cannot choose
But must be, will his free hours languish for
Assured bondage ? '
Imo.   Will my lord say so ?
Iach. Ay, madam, with his eyes in flood
with laughter :
It is a recreation to be by
And hear him mock the Frenchman. But,
heavens know,
Some men are much to blame.
Imo.   Not he, I hope.
Iach. Not he : but yet heaven's bounty to-
wards him might
Be used more thankfully. In himself, 'tis
much ;
In you, which I account his beyond all talents,
Whilst I am bound to wonder, I am bound 81
To pity too.
Imo. What do you pity, sir ?
Iach. Two creatures heartily.
Imo.   Am I one, sir ?
You look on me : what wreck discern you in
me
Deserves your pity ?
Iach.   Lamentable ! What,
To hide me from the radiant sun and solace
I' the dungeon by a snuff ?
Imo.   I pray you, sir,
Deliver with more openness your answers
To my demands. Why do you pity me ?
Iach. That others do—   90
I was about to say—enjoy your——But
It is an office of the gods to venge it,
Not mine to speak on 't.
Imo.   You do seem to know
Something of me, or what concerns me : pray
you,—
Since doubting things go ill often hurts more
Than to be sure they do ; for certainties
Either are past remedies, or, timely knowing,
The remedy then born—discover to me
What both you spur and stop.

Iach.   Had I this cheek
To bathe my lips upon; this hand, whose
    touch,   100
Whose every touch, would force the feeler's
    soul
To the oath of loyalty; this object, which
Takes prisoner the wild motion of mine eye,
Fixing it only here; should I, damn'd then,
Slaver with lips as common as the stairs
That mount the Capitol; join gripes with
    hands
Made hard with hourly falsehood—falsehood,
    as
With labor; then by-peeping in an eye
Base and unlustrous as the smoky light
That's fed with stinking tallow; it were fit 110
That all the plagues of hell should at one time
Encounter such revolt.
    Imo.   My lord, I fear,
Has forgot Britain.
    Iach.   And himself. Not I,
Inclined to this intelligence, pronounce
The beggary of his change; but 'tis your
    graces
That from my mutest conscience to my tongue
Charms this report out.
    Imo.   Let me hear no more.
    Iach. O dearest soul! your cause doth
    strike my heart
With pity, that doth make me sick. A lady
So fair, and fasten'd to an empery,   120
Would make the great'st king double,—to be
    partner'd
With tomboys hired with that self-exhibition
Which your own coffers yield! with diseased
    ventures
That play with all infirmities for gold
Which rottenness can lend nature! such boil'd
    stuff
As well might poison poison! Be revenged;
Or she that bore you was no queen, and you
Recoil from your great stock.
    Imo.   Revenged!
How should I be revenged? If this be true,—
As I have such a heart that both mine ears 130
Must not in haste abuse—if it be true,
How should I be revenged?
    Iach.   Should he make me
Live, like Diana's priest, betwixt cold sheets,
Whiles he is vaulting variable ramps,
In your despite, upon your purse? Revenge it.
I dedicate myself to your sweet pleasure,
More noble than that runagate to your bed,
And will continue fast to your affection,
Still close as sure.
    Imo.   What, ho, Pisanio!
    Iach. Let me my service tender on your
    lips.
    Imo. Away! I do condemn mine ears that
    have   141
So long attended thee. If thou wert honorable,
Thou wouldst have told this tale for virtue, not
For such an end thou seek'st,—as base as
    strange.
Thou wrong'st a gentleman, who is as far
From thy report as thou from honor, and
Solicit'st here a lady that disdains
Thee and the devil alike. What ho, Pisanio!
The king my father shall be made acquainted
Of thy assault: if he shall think it fit,   150
A saucy stranger in his court to mart
As in a Romish stew and to expound
His beastly mind to us, he hath a court

He little cares for and a daughter who
He not respects at all. What, ho, Pisanio!
    Iach. O happy Leonatus! I may say:
The credit that thy lady hath of thee
Deserves thy trust, and thy most perfect good-
    ness
Her assured credit. Blessed live you long!
A lady to the worthiest sir that ever   160
Country call'd his! and you his mistress, only
For the most worthiest fit! Give me your par-
    don.
I have spoke this, to know if your affiance
Were deeply rooted; and shall make your
    lord,
That which he is, new o'er: and he is one
The truest manner'd; such a holy witch
That he enchants societies into him;
Half all men's hearts are his.
    Imo.   You make amends.
    Iach. He sits 'mongst men like a descended
    god:
He hath a kind of honor sets him off,   170
More than a mortal seeming. Be not angry,
Most mighty princess, that I have adventured
To try your taking of a false report; which
    hath
Honor'd with confirmation your great judg-
    ment
In the election of a sir so rare,
Which you know cannot err: the love I bear
    him
Made me to fan you thus, but the gods made
    you,
Unlike all others, chaffless. Pray, your par-
    don.
    Imo. All's well, sir: take my power i' the
    court for yours.
    Iach. My humble thanks. I had almost
    forgot   180
To entreat your grace but in a small request,
And yet of moment too, for it concerns
Your lord; myself and other noble friends,
Are partners in the business.
    Imo.   Pray, what is't?
    Iach. Some dozen Romans of us and your
    lord—
The best feather of our wing—have mingled
    sums
To buy a present for the emperor
Which I, the factor for the rest, have done
In France: 'tis plate of rare device, and
    jewels   189
Of rich and exquisite form; their values
    great;
And I am something curious, being strange,
To have them in safe stowage: may it please
    you
To take them in protection?
    Imo.   Willingly;
And pawn mine honor for their safety: since
My lord hath interest in them, I will keep
    them
In my bedchamber.
    Iach.   They are in a trunk,
Attended by my men: I will make bold
To send them to you, only for this night;
I must aboard to-morrow.
    Imo.   O, no, no.
    Iach. Yes, I beseech; or I shall short my
    word   200
By lengthening my return. From Gallia
I cross'd the seas on purpose and on promise
To see your grace.

Imo.   I thank you for your pains :
But not away to-morrow !
Iach.   O, I must, madam :
Therefore I shall beseech you, if you please
To greet your lord with writing, do't to-night :
I have outstood my time ; which is material
To the tender of our present.
Imo.   I will write.
Send your trunk to me ; it shall safe be kept,
And truly yielded you. You're very welcome.
[*Exeunt.* 210

ACT II.

Scene I. *Britain. Before Cymbeline's palace.*

Enter Cloten *and two* Lords.

Clo. Was there ever man had such luck !
when I kissed the jack, upon an up-cast to be
hit away ! I had a hundred pound on't : and
then a whoreson jackanapes must take me up
for swearing ; as if I borrowed mine oaths of
him and might not spend them at my pleasure.
First Lord. What got he by that ? You
have broke his pate with your bowl.
Sec. Lord. [*Aside*] If his wit had been like
him that broke it, it would have run all out.
Clo. When a gentleman is disposed to
swear, it is not for any standers-by to curtail
his oaths, ha ?
Sec. Lord. No, my lord ; [*Aside*] nor crop
the ears of them.
Clo. Whoreson dog ! I give him satisfaction ? Would he had been one of my rank !
Sec. Lord. [*Aside*] To have smelt like a
fool.
Clo. I am not vexed more at any thing in
the earth : a pox on't ! I had rather not be so
noble as I am ; they dare not fight with me,
because of the queen my mother : every Jack-
slave hath his bellyful of fighting, and I must
go up and down like a cock that nobody can
match.
Sec. Lord. [*Aside*] You are cock and ca-
pon too ; and you crow, cock, with your comb
on.
Clo. Sayest thou ?
Sec. Lord. It is not fit your lordship should
undertake every companion that you give offence to.   30
Clo. No, I know that : but it is fit I should
commit offence to my inferiors.
Sec. Lord. Ay, it is fit for your lordship
only.
Clo. Why, so I say.
First Lord. Did you hear of a stranger
that's come to court to-night ?
Clo. A stranger, and I not know on't !
Sec. Lord. [*Aside*] He's a strange fellow
himself, and knows it not.
First Lord. There's an Italian come ; and,
'tis thought, one of Leonatus' friends.   41
Clo. Leonatus ! a banished rascal ; and
he's another, whatsoever he be. Who told you
of this stranger ?
First Lord. One of your lordship's pages.
Clo. Is it fit I went to look upon him ? is
there no derogation in't ?
Sec. Lord. You cannot derogate, my lord.
Clo. Not easily, I think.   49
Sec. Lord. [*Aside*] You are a fool granted ;

therefore your issues, being foolish, do not
derogate.
Clo. Come, I'll go see this Italian : what I
have lost to-day at bowls I'll win to-night of
him. Come, go.
Sec. Lord. I'll attend your lordship.
[*Exeunt Cloten and First Lord.*
That such a crafty devil as is his mother
Should yield the world this ass ! a woman that
Bears all down with her brain ; and this her
son
Cannot take two from twenty, for his heart,
And leave eighteen. Alas, poor princess,   61
Thou divine Imogen, what thou endurest,
Betwixt a father by thy step-dame govern'd,
A mother hourly coining plots, a wooer
More hateful than the foul expulsion is
Of thy dear husband, than that horrid act
Of the divorce he'ld make ! The heavens hold
firm
The walls of thy dear honor, keep unshaked
That temple, thy fair mind, that thou mayst
stand,
To enjoy thy banish'd lord and this great
land !   [*Exit.* 70

Scene II. *Imogen's bedchamber in Cymbe-line's palace : a trunk in one corner of it.*

Imogen *in bed, reading ; a* Lady *attending.*

Imo. Who's there ? my woman Helen ?
Lady.   Please you, madam.
Imo. What hour is it ?
Lady.   Almost midnight, madam.
Imo. I have read three hours then : mine
eyes are weak :
Fold down the leaf where I have left : to bed :
Take not away the taper, leave it burning ;
And if thou canst awake by four o' the clock,
I prithee, call me. Sleep hath seized me
wholly.   [*Exit Lady.*
To your protection I commend me, gods.
From fairies and the tempters of the night
Guard me, beseech ye.   10
[*Sleeps. Iachimo comes from the trunk.*
Iach. The crickets sing, and man's o'er-
labor'd sense
Repairs itself by rest. Our Tarquin thus
Did softly press the rushes, ere he waken'd
The chastity he wounded. Cytherea,
How bravely thou becomest thy bed, fresh lily,
And whiter than the sheets ! That I might
touch !
But kiss ; one kiss ! Rubies unparagon'd,
How dearly they do't ! 'Tis her breathing that
Perfumes the chamber thus : the flame o' the
taper
Bows toward her, and would under-peep her
lids,   20
To see the enclosed lights, now canopied
Under these windows, white and azure laced
With blue of heaven's own tinct. But my de-
sign,
To note the chamber : I will write all down :
Such and such pictures ; there the window ;
such
The adornment of her bed ; the arras ; figures,
Why, such and such ; and the contents o' the
story.
Ah, but some natural notes about her body,
Above ten thousand meaner moveables
Would testify, to enrich mine inventory.   30

O sleep, thou ape of death, lie dull upon her !
And be her sense but as a monument,
Thus in a chapel lying ! Come off, come off :
     [*Taking off her bracelet.*
As slippery as the Gordian knot was hard !
'Tis mine ; and this will witness outwardly,
As strongly as the conscience does within,
To the madding of her lord. On her left
  breast
A mole cinque-spotted, like the crimson drops
I' the bottom of a cowslip : here's a voucher,
Stronger than ever law could make : this
  secret   40
Will force him think I have pick'd the lock
  and ta'en
The treasure of her honor. No more. To
  what end ?
Why should I write this down, that's riveted,
Screw'd to my memory ? She hath been read-
  ing late
The tale of Tereus ; here the leaf's turn'd down
Where Philomel gave up. I have enough :
To the trunk again, and shut the spring of it.
Swift, swift, you dragons of the night, that
  dawning
May bare the raven's eye ! I lodge in fear ;
Though this a heavenly angel, hell is here. 50
      [*Clock strikes.*
One, two, three : time, time !
 [*Goes into the trunk. The scene closes.*

SCENE III. *An ante-chamber adjoining Imogen's apartments.*

Enter CLOTEN *and* Lords.

First Lord. Your lordship is the most patient man in loss, the most coldest that ever
turned up ace.
 Clo. It would make any man cold to lose.
 First Lord. But not every man patient
after the noble temper of your lordship. You
are most hot and furious when you win.
 Clo. Winning will put any man into courage. If I could get this foolish Imogen, I
should have gold enough. It's almost morning,
is't not ?   10
 First Lord. Day, my lord.
 Clo. I would this music would come : I
am advised to give her music o' mornings ;
they say it will penetrate.

Enter Musicians.

Come on ; tune : if you can penetrate her
with your fingering, so ; we'll try with tongue
too : if none will do, let her remain ; but I'll
never give o'er. First, a very excellent good-
conceited thing ; after, a wonderful sweet air,
with admirable rich words to it : and then let
her consider.   20

SONG.

Hark, hark ! the lark at heaven's gate sings,
 And Phœbus 'gins arise,
His steeds to water at those springs
 On chaliced flowers that lies ;
And winking Mary-buds begin
 To ope their golden eyes :
With every thing that pretty is,
 My lady sweet, arise :
  Arise, arise.   30

 Clo. So, get you gone. If this penetrate, I
will consider your music the better : if it do
not, it is a vice in her ears, which horse-hairs

and calves'-guts, nor the voice of unpaved
eunuch to boot, can never amend.
      [*Exeunt Musicians.*
 Sec. Lord. Here comes the king.
 Clo. I am glad I was up so late ; for that's
the reason I was up so early : he cannot
choose but take this service I have done fa-
therly.

Enter CYMBELINE *and* QUEEN.

Good morrow to your majesty and to my
gracious mother.   41
 Cym. Attend you here the door of our
  stern daughter ?
Will she not forth ?
 Clo. I have assailed her with music, but
she vouchsafes no notice.
 Cym. The exile of her minion is too new ;
She hath not yet forgot him : some more time
Must wear the print of his remembrance out,
And then she's yours.
 Queen.   You are most bound to the king,
Who lets go by no vantages that may 50
Prefer you to his daughter. Frame yourself
To orderly soliciting, and be friended
With aptness of the season ; make denials
Increase your services ; so seem as if
You were inspired to do those duties which
You tender to her ; that you in all obey her,
Save when command to your dismission tends,
And therein you are senseless.
 Clo.   Senseless ! not so.

Enter a Messenger.

 Mess. So like you, sir, ambassadors from
  Rome ;
The one is Caius Lucius.
 Cym.   A worthy fellow, 60
Albeit he comes on angry purpose now ;
But that's no fault of his : we must receive
  him
According to the honor of his sender ;
And towards himself, his goodness forespent
  on us,
We must extend our notice. Our dear son,
When you have given good morning to your
  mistress,
Attend the queen and us ; we shall have need
To employ you towards this Roman. Come,
  our queen. [*Exeunt all but Cloten.*
 Clo. If she be up, I'll speak with her ; if
  not,
Let her lie still and dream. [*Knocks*] By your
  leave, ho !   70
I know her women are about her : what
If I do line one of their hands ? 'Tis gold
Which buys admittance ; oft it doth ; yea, and
  makes
Diana's rangers false themselves, yield up
Their deer to the stand o' the stealer ; and 'tis
  gold
Which makes the true man kill'd and saves
  the thief ;
Nay, sometime hangs both thief and true
  man : what
Can it not do and undo ? I will make
One of her women lawyer to me, for
I yet not understand the case myself. 80
[*Knocks*] By your leave.

Enter a Lady.

 Lady. Who's there that knocks ?
 Clo.   A gentleman.

Lady.   No more ?
Clo. Yes, and a gentlewoman's son.
Lady.   That's more
Than some, whose tailors are as dear as yours,
Can justly boast of. What's your lordship's
    pleasure ?
Clo. Your lady's person : is she ready ?
Lady.   Ay,
To keep her chamber.
Clo.   There is gold for you ;
Sell me your good report.
Lady. How ! my good name ? or to report
    of you
What I shall think is good ?—The princess ! 90

Enter IMOGEN.

Clo. Good morrow, fairest : sister, your
    sweet hand.   [*Exit Lady.*
Imo. Good morrow, sir. You lay out too
    much pains
For purchasing but trouble : the thanks I give
Is telling you that I am poor of thanks
And scarce can spare them.
Clo.   Still, I swear I love you.
Imo. If you but said so, 'twere as deep
    with me :
If you swear still, your recompense is still
That I regard it not.
Clo.   This is no answer.
Imo. But that you shall not say I yield
    being silent,
I would not speak. I pray you, spare me :
    'faith,   100
I shall unfold equal discourtesy
To your best kindness : one of your great
    knowing
Should learn, being taught, forbearance.
Clo. To leave you in your madness, 'twere
    my sin :
I will not.
Imo. Fools are not mad folks.
Clo.   Do you call me fool ?
Imo. As I am mad, I do :
If you'll be patient, I'll no more be mad ;
That cures us both. I am much sorry, sir,
You put me to forget a lady's manners, 110
By being so verbal : and learn now, for all,
That I, which know my heart, do here pro-
    nounce,
By the very truth of it, I care not for you,
And am so near the lack of charity—
To accuse myself—I hate you ; which I had
    rather
You felt than make't my boast.
Clo.   You sin against
Obedience, which you owe your father. For
The contract you pretend with that base
    wretch,
One bred of alms and foster'd with cold dishes,
With scraps o' the court, it is no contract,
    none :   120
And though it be allow'd in meaner parties—
Yet who than he more mean ?—to knit their
    souls,
On whom there is no more dependency
But brats and beggary, in self-figured knot ;
Yet you are curb'd from that enlargement by
The consequence o' the crown, and must not
    soil
The precious note of it with a base slave.
A hilding for a livery, a squire's cloth,
A pantler, not so eminent.
Imo.   Profane fellow

Wert thou the son of Jupiter and no more 130
But what thou art besides, thou wert too base
To be his groom : thou wert dignified enough,
Even to the point of envy, if 'twere made
Comparative for your virtues, to be styled
The under-hangman of his kingdom, and hated
For being preferr'd so well.
Clo.   The south-fog rot him !
Imo. He never can meet more mischance
    than come
To be but named of thee. His meanest gar-
    ment,
That ever hath but clipp'd his body, is dearer
In my respect than all the hairs above thee,
Were they all made such men. How now,
    Pisanio !   141

Enter PISANIO.

Clo. 'His garment !' Now the devil—
Imo. To Dorothy my woman hie thee pres-
    ently—
Clo. 'His garment !'
Imo.   I am sprited with a fool,
Frighted, and anger'd worse : go bid my
    woman
Search for a jewel that too casually
Hath left mine arm : it was thy master's :
    'shrew me,
If I would lose it for a revenue
Of any king's in Europe. I do think
I saw't this morning : confident I am   150
Last night 'twas on mine arm ; I kiss'd it :
I hope it be not gone to tell my lord
That I kiss aught but he.
Pis.   'Twill not be lost.
Imo. I hope so : go and search.
             [*Exit Pisanio.*
Clo.   You have abused me :
' His meanest garment ! '
Imo.   Ay, I said so, sir :
If you will make't an action, call witness to't.
Clo. I will inform your father.
Imo.   Your mother too :
She's my good lady, and will conceive, I hope,
But the worst of me. So, I leave you, sir,
To the worst of discontent.   [*Exit.*
Clo.   I'll be revenged :   160
' His meanest garment ! ' Well.   [*Exit.*

SCENE IV. *Rome. Philario's house.*

Enter POSTHUMUS *and* PHILARIO.

Post. Fear it not, sir : I would I were so
    sure
To win the king as I am bold her honor
Will remain hers.
Phi.   What means do you make to him ?
Post. Not any, but abide the change of
    time,
Quake in the present winter's state and wish
That warmer days would come : in these
    sear'd hopes,
I barely gratify your love ; they failing,
I must die much your debtor.
Phi.   Your very goodness and your com-
    pany
O'erpays all I can do. By this, your king   10
Hath heard of great Augustus : Caius Lucius
Will do's commission throughly : and I think
He'll grant the tribute, send the arrearages,
Or look upon our Romans, whose remem-
    brance
Is yet fresh in their grief.
Post.   I do believe,

Statist though I am none, nor like to be,
That this will prove a war; and you shall
hear
The legions now in Gallia sooner landed
In our not-fearing Britain than have tidings
Of any penny tribute paid. Our countrymen
Are men more order'd than when Julius Cæsar
Smiled at their lack of skill, but found their
courage
Worthy his frowning at : their discipline,
Now mingled with their courages, will make
known
To their approvers they are people such
That mend upon the world.

Enter IACHIMO.

Phi.   See ! Iachimo !
Post. The swiftest harts have posted you
by land ;
And winds of all the corners kiss'd your sails,
To make your vessel nimble.
Phi.   Welcome, sir.
Post. I hope the briefness of your answer
made
The speediness of your return.
Iach.   Your lady 31
Is one of the fairest that I have look'd upon.
Post. And therewithal the best ; or let her
beauty
Look through a casement to allure false hearts
And be false with them.
Iach.   Here are letters for you.
Post. Their tenor good, I trust.
Iach.   'Tis very like.
Phi. Was Caius Lucius in the Britain court
When you were there ?
Iach.   He was expected then,
But not approach'd.
Post.   All is well yet.
Sparkles this stone as it was wont? or is't
not   40
Too dull for your good wearing ?
Iach.   If I had lost it,
I should have lost the worth of it in gold.
I'll make a journey twice as far, to enjoy
A second night of such sweet shortness which
Was mine in Britain, for the ring is won.
Post. The stone's too hard to come by.
Iach.   Not a whit,
Your lady being so easy.
Post.   Make not, sir,
Your loss your sport : I hope you know that
we
Must not continue friends.
Iach.   Good sir, we must,
If you keep covenant. Had I not brought 50
The knowledge of your mistress home, I grant
We were to question further : but I now
Profess myself the winner of her honor,
Together with your ring ; and not the wronger
Of her or you, having proceeded but
By both your wills.
Post.   If you can make't apparent
That you have tasted her in bed, my hand
And ring is yours ; if not, the foul opinion
You had of her pure honor gains or loses
Your sword or mine, or masterless leaves both
To who shall find them.
Iach.   Sir, my circumstances,
Being so near the truth as I will make them,
Must first induce you to believe : whose
strength
I will confirm with oath ; which, I doubt not,

You'll give me leave to spare, when you shall
find
You need it not.
Post.   Proceed.
Iach.   First, her bedchamber,—
Where, I confess, I slept not, but profess
Had that was well worth watching—it was
hang'd
With tapestry of silk and silver ; the story
Proud Cleopatra, when she met her Roman, 70
And Cydnus swell'd above the banks, or for
The press of boats or pride : a piece of work
So bravely done, so rich, that it did strive
In workmanship and value ; which I wonder'd
Could be so rarely and exactly wrought,
Since the true life on't was—
Post.   This is true ;
And this you might have heard of here, by me,
Or by some other.
Iach.   More particulars
Must justify my knowledge.
Post.   So they must,
Or do your honor injury.
Iach.   The chimney 80
Is south the chamber, and the chimney-piece
Chaste Dian bathing : never saw I figures
So likely to report themselves : the cutter
Was as another nature, dumb ; outwent her,
Motion and breath left out.
Post.   This is a thing
Which you might from relation likewise reap,
Being, as it is, much spoke of.
Iach.   The roof o' the chamber
With golden cherubins is fretted : her and-
irons—
I had forgot them—were two winking Cupids
Of silver, each on one foot standing, nicely 90
Depending on their brands.
Post.   This is her honor !
Let it be granted you have seen all this—and
praise
Be given to your remembrance—the descrip-
tion
Of what is in her chamber nothing saves
The wager you have laid.
Iach.   Then, if you can,
                              [*Showing the bracelet.*
Be pale : I beg but leave to air this jewel ;
see !
And now 'tis up again : it must be married
To that your diamond ; I'll keep them.
Post.   Jove !
Once more let me behold it : is it that
Which I left with her ?
Iach.   Sir—I thank her—that : 100
She stripp'd it from her arm ; I see her yet ;
Her pretty action did outsell her gift,
And yet enrich'd it too : she gave it me, and
said
She prized it once.
Post.   May be she pluck'd it off
To send it me.
Iach.   She writes so to you, doth she ?
Post. O, no, no, no ! 'tis true. Here, take
this too ;   [*Gives the ring.*
It is a basilisk unto mine eye,
Kills me to look on't. Let there be no honor
Where there is beauty ; truth, where sem-
blance ; love,
Where there's another man : the vows of
women   110
Of no more bondage be, to where they are
made,

Than they are to their virtues ; which is noth-
　　ing.
O, above measure false !
　　Phi.　　　　　　　　Have patience, sir,
And take your ring again ; 'tis not yet won :
It may be probable she lost it ; or
Who knows if one of her women, being cor-
　　rupted,
Hath stol'n it from her ?
　　Post.　　　　　　　　Very true ;
And so, I hope, he came by't. Back my ring :
Render to me some corporal sign about her,
More evident than this ; for this was stolen.
　　Iach. By Jupiter, I had it from her arm.
　　Post. Hark you, he swears ; by Jupiter he
　　swears.
'Tis true :—nay, keep the ring—'tis true : I
　　am sure
She would not lose it : her attendants are
All sworn and honorable :—they induced to
　　steal it !
And by a stranger !—No, he hath enjoyed
　　her :
The cognizance of her incontinency
Is this : she hath bought the name of whore
　　thus dearly.
There, take thy hire ; and all the fiends of
　　hell
Divide themselves between you !
　　Phi.　　　　　　Sir, be patient :　130
This is not strong enough to be believed
Of one persuaded well of—
　　Post.　　　　　　Never talk on't ;
She hath been colted by him.
　　Iach.　　　　　　If you seek
For further satisfying, under her breast—
Worthy the pressing—lies a mole, right proud
Of that most delicate lodging : by my life,
I kiss'd it ; and it gave me present hunger
To feed again, though full. You do remem-
　　ber
This stain upon her ?
　　Post.　　　　　Ay, and it doth confirm
Another stain, as big as hell can hold,　140
Were there no more but it.
　　Iach.　　　　　Will you hear more ?
　　Post.　　　Spare your arithmetic : never count
　　the turns ;
Once, and a million !
　　Iach.　　　　　I'll be sworn—
　　Post.　　　　　　No swearing.
If you will swear you have not done't, you
　　lie ;
And I will kill thee, if thou dost deny
Thou'st made me cuckold.
　　Iach.　　　　　I'll deny nothing.
　　Post. O, that I had her here, to tear her
　　limb-meal !
I will go there and do't, i' the court, before
Her father. I'll do something—　　[*Exit.*
　　Phi.　　　　　　Quite besides
The government of patience ! You have won :
Let's follow him, and pervert the present
　　wrath　　　　　　　　　151
He hath against himself.
　　Iach.　　　With all my heart. [*Exeunt.*

SCENE V. *Another room in Philario's house.*
　　　　Enter POSTHUMUS.

　　Post. Is there no way for men to be but
　　women
Must be half-workers ? We are all bastards ;
And that most venerable man which I

Did call my father, was I know not where
When I was stamp'd ; some coiner with his
　　tools
Made me a counterfeit : yet my mother seem'd
The Dian of that time : so doth my wife
The nonpareil of this. O, vengeance, venge-
　　ance !
Me of my lawful pleasure she restrain'd
And pray'd me oft forbearance ; did it with
A pudency so rosy the sweet view on't　　11
Might well have warm'd old Saturn ; that I
　　thought her
As chaste as unsunn'd snow. O, all the devils !
This yellow Iachimo, in an hour,—was't
　　not ?—
Or less,—at first ?—perchance he spoke not,
　　but,
Like a full-acorn'd boar, a German one,
Cried ' O ! ' and mounted ; found no opposi-
　　tion
But what he look'd for should oppose and she
Should from encounter guard. Could I find
　　out
The woman's part in me ! For there's no mo-
　　tion　　　　　　　　　　　　　20
That tends to vice in man, but I affirm
It is the woman's part : be it lying, note it,
The woman's ; flattering, hers ; deceiving,
　　hers ;
Lust and rank thoughts, hers, hers ; revenges,
　　hers ;
Ambitions, covetings, change of prides, dis-
　　dain,
Nice longing, slanders, mutability,
All faults that may be named, nay, that hell
　　knows,
Why, hers, in part or all ; but rather, all ;
For even to vice
They are not constant, but are changing still
One vice, but of a minute old, for one　　31
Not half so old as that. I'll write against them,
Detest them, curse them : yet 'tis greater skill
In a true hate, to pray they have their will :
The very devils cannot plague them better.
　　　　　　　　　　　　　　[*Exit.*

ACT III.

SCENE I. *Britain. A hall in Cymbeline's
　　palace.*

Enter in state, CYMBELINE, QUEEN, CLOTEN,
and Lords *at one door, and at another,*
CAIUS LUCIUS *and* Attendants.

　　Cym. Now say, what would Augustus Cæ-
　　sar with us ?
　　Luc. When Julius Cæsar, whose remem-
　　brance yet
Lives in men's eyes and will to ears and
　　tongues
Be theme and hearing ever, was in this Britain
And conquer'd it, Cassibelan, thine uncle,—
Famous in Cæsar's praises, no whit less
Than in his feats deserving it—for him
And his succession granted Rome a tribute,
Yearly three thousand pounds, which by thee
　　lately
Is left untender'd.
　　Queen.　　　And, to kill the marvel,　10
Shall be so ever.
　　Clo.　　　There be many Cæsars,
Ere such another Julius. Britain is

A world by itself; and we will nothing pay
For wearing our own noses.

Queen.   That opportunity
Which then they had to take from 's, to re-
    sume
We have again. Remember, sir, my liege,
The kings your ancestors, together with
The natural bravery of your isle, which stands
As Neptune's park, ribbed and paled in
With rocks unscalable and roaring waters, 20
With sands that will not bear your enemies'
    boats,
But suck them up to the topmast. A kind of
    conquest
Cæsar made here; but made not here his brag
Of ' Came ' and ' saw ' and ' overcame : ' with
    shame—
That first that ever touch'd him—he was car-
    ried
From off our coast, twice beaten; and his
    shipping—
Poor ignorant baubles !—on our terrible seas,
Like egg-shells moved upon their surges,
    crack'd
As easily 'gainst our rocks : for joy whereof
The famed Cassibelan, who was once at
    point—   30
O giglot fortune !—to master Cæsar's sword,
Made Lud's town with rejoicing fires bright
And Britons strut with courage.

Clo.   Come, there's no more tribute to be
paid : our kingdom is stronger than it was at
that time; and, as I said, there is no moe
such Cæsars : other of them may have crook'd
noses, but to owe such straight arms, none.

Cym.   Son, let your mother end.   39

Clo.   We have yet many among us can
gripe as hard as Cassibelan : I do not say I
am one; but I have a hand. Why tribute ?
why should we pay tribute ? If Cæsar can hide
the sun from us with a blanket, or put the
moon in his pocket, we will pay him tribute
for light; else, sir, no more tribute, pray you
now.

Cym.   You must know,
Till the injurious Romans did extort
This tribute from us, we were free : Cæsar's
    ambition,
Which swell'd so much that it did almost
    stretch   50
The sides o' the world, against all color here
Did put the yoke upon 's; which to shake off
Becomes a warlike people, whom we reckon
Ourselves to be.

Clo. and Lords.   We do.

Cym.   Say, then, to Cæsar,
Our ancestor was that Mulmutius which
Ordain'd our laws, whose use the sword of
    Cæsar
Hath too much mangled; whose repair and
    franchise
Shall, by the power we hold, be our good deed,
Though Rome be therefore angry : Mulmutius
    made our laws,
Who was the first of Britain which did put 60
His brows within a golden crown and call'd
Himself a king.

Luc.   I am sorry, Cymbeline,
That I am to pronounce Augustus Cæsar—
Cæsar, that hath more kings his servants than
Thyself domestic officers—thine enemy :
Receive it from me, then : war and confusion

In Cæsar's name pronounce I 'gainst thee :
    look
For fury not to be resisted. Thus defied,
I thank thee for myself.

Cym.   Thou art welcome, Caius.
Thy Cæsar knighted me; my youth I spent
Much under him; of him I gather'd honor;
Which he to seek of me again, perforce,
Behoves me keep at utterance. I am perfect
That the Pannonians and Dalmatians for
Their liberties are now in arms; a precedent
Which not to read would show the Britons
    cold :
So Cæsar shall not find them.

Luc.   Let proof speak.

Clo.   His majesty bids you welcome. Make
pastime with us a day or two, or longer : if
you seek us afterwards in other terms, you
shall find us in our salt-water girdle : if you
beat us out of it, it is yours; if you fall in
the adventure, our crows shall fare the better
for you; and there's an end.

Luc.   So, sir.

Cym.   I know your master's pleasure and
    he mine :
All the remain is ' Welcome ! '   [*Exeunt.*

SCENE II.   *Another room in the palace.*

Enter PISANIO, *with a letter.*

Pis.   How ! of adultery ? Wherefore write
    you not
What monster's her accuser ? Leonatus !
O master ! what a strange infection
Is fall'n into thy ear ! What false Italian,
As poisonous-tongued as handed, hath pre-
    vail'd
On thy too ready hearing ? Disloyal ! No :
She's punish'd for her truth, and undergoes,
More goddess-like than wife-like, such assaults
As would take in some virtue. O my master !
Thy mind to her is now as low as were   10
Thy fortunes. How ! that I should murder her ?
Upon the love and truth and vows which I
Have made to thy command ? I, her ? her
    blood ?
If it be so to do good service, never
Let me be counted serviceable. How look I,
That I should seem to lack humanity
So much as this fact comes to ?   [*Reading*]
' Do't : the letter
That I have sent her, by her own command
Shall give thee opportunity.' O damn'd paper !
Black as the ink that's on thee ! Senseless
    bauble,   20
Art thou a feodary for this act, and look'st
So virgin-like without ? Lo, here she comes.
I am ignorant in what I am commanded.

Enter IMOGEN.

Imo.   How now, Pisanio !

Pis.   Madam, here is a letter from my lord.

Imo.   Who ? thy lord ? that is my lord,
    Leonatus !
O, learn'd indeed were that astronomer
That knew the stars as I his characters;
He'ld lay the future open. You good gods,
Let what is here contain'd relish of love,   30
Of my lord's health, of his content, yet not
That we two are asunder; let that grieve him :
Some griefs are med'cinable; that is one of
    them,
For it doth physic love : of his content,

All but in that ! Good wax, thy leave. Blest be
You bees that make these locks of counsel !
    Lovers
And men in dangerous bonds pray not alike :
Though forfeiters you cast in prison, yet
You clasp young Cupid's tables. Good news,
    gods !   39
  [*Reads*] ' Justice, and your father's wrath,
should he take me in his dominion, could not
be so cruel to me, as you, O the dearest of
creatures, would even renew me with your
eyes. Take notice that I am in Cambria, at
Milford-Haven : what your own love will out
of this advise you, follow. So he wishes you
all happiness, that remains loyal to his vow,
and your, increasing in love,
                LEONATUS . POSTHUMUS.'
O, for a horse with wings ! Hear'st thou, Pi-
    sanio ?   50
He is at Milford-Haven : read, and tell me
How far 'tis thither. If one of mean affairs
May plod it in a week, why may not I
Glide thither in a day ? Then, true Pisanio,—
Who long'st, like me, to see thy lord ; who
    long'st,—
O, let me bate,—but not like me—yet long'st,
But in a fainter kind :—O, not like me ;
For mine's beyond beyond—say, and speak
    thick ;
Love's counsellor should fill the bores of hear-
    ing,   59
To the smothering of the sense—how far it is
To this same blessed Milford : and by the way
Tell me how Wales was made so happy as
To inherit such a haven : but first of all,
How we may steal from hence, and for the gap
That we shall make in time, from our hence-
    going
And our return, to excuse : but first, how get
    hence :
Why should excuse be born or e'er begot ?
We'll talk of that hereafter. Prithee, speak,
How many score of miles may we well ride
'Twixt hour and hour ?
  Pis.   One score 'twixt sun and sun,
Madam, 's enough for you : [*Aside*] and too
    much too.   71
  Imo. Why, one that rode to's execution,
    man,
Could never go so slow : I have heard of rid-
    ing wagers,
Where horses have been nimbler than the
    sands
That run i' the clock's behalf. But this is
    foolery :
Go bid my woman feign a sickness ; say
She'll home to her father : and provide me
    presently
A riding-suit, no costlier than would fit
A franklin's housewife.
  Pis.   Madam, you're best consider.
  Imo. I see before me, man : nor here, nor
    here,   80
Nor what ensues, but have a fog in them,
That I cannot look through. Away, I prithee ;
Do as I bid thee : there's no more to say ;
Accessible is none but Milford way. [*Exeunt.*

SCENE III. *Wales: a mountainous country
    with a cave.*

Enter, from the cave, BELARIUS ; GUIDERIUS,
    and ARVIRAGUS *following.*

  Bel. A goodly day not to keep house, with
    such
Whose roof's as low as ours ! Stoop, boys ;
    this gate
Instructs you how to adore the heavens and
    bows you
To a morning's holy office : the gates of mon-
    archs
Are arch'd so high that giants may jet through
And keep their impious turbans on, without
Good morrow to the sun. Hail, thou fair
    heaven !
We house i' the rock, yet use thee not so
    hardly
As prouder livers do.
  Gui.   Hail, heaven !
  Arv.   Hail, heaven !
  Bel. Now for our mountain sport : up to
    yond hill ;   10
Your legs are young ; I'll tread these flats.
    Consider,
When you above perceive me like a crow,
That it is place which lessens and sets off ;
And you may then revolve what tales I have
    told you
Of courts, of princes, of the tricks in war :
This service is not service, so being done,
But being so allow'd : to apprehend thus,
Draws us a profit from all things we see ;
And often, to our comfort, shall we find
The sharded beetle in a safer hold   20
Than is the full-wing'd eagle. O, this life
Is nobler than attending for a check,
Richer than doing nothing for a bauble,
Prouder than rustling in unpaid-for silk :
Such gain the cap of him that makes 'em fine,
Yet keeps his book uncross'd : no life to ours.
  Gui. Out of your proof you speak : we,
    poor unfledged,
Have never wing'd from view o' the nest, nor
    know not
What air's from home. Haply this life is best,
If quiet life be best ; sweeter to you   30
That have a sharper known ; well correspond-
    ing
With your stiff age : but unto us it is
A cell of ignorance ; travelling a-bed ;
A prison for a debtor, that not dares
To stride a limit.
  Arv.   What should we speak of
When we are old as you ? when we shall hear
The rain and wind beat dark December, how,
In this our pinching cave, shall we discourse
The freezing hours away ? We have seen noth-
    ing ;
We are beastly, subtle as the fox for prey, 40
Like warlike as the wolf for what we eat ;
Our valor is to chase what flies ; our cage
We make a quire, as doth the prison'd bird,
And sing our bondage freely.
  Bel.   How you speak !
Did you but know the city's usuries
And felt them knowingly ; the art o' the court
As hard to leave as keep ; whose top to climb
Is certain falling, or so slippery that
The fear's as bad as falling ; the toil o' the
    war,
A pain that only seems to seek out danger 50
I' the name of fame and honor ; which dies i'
    the search,
And hath as oft a slanderous epitaph
As record of fair act ; nay, many times,

Doth ill deserve by doing well; what's worse,
Must court'sy at the censure :—O boys, this
    story
The world may read in me : my body's mark'd
With Roman swords, and my report was once
First with the best of note : Cymbeline loved
    me,
And when a soldier was the theme, my name
Was not far off : then was I as a tree   60
Whose boughs did bend with fruit : but in one
    night,
A storm or robbery, call it what you will,
Shook down my mellow hangings, nay, my
    leaves,
And left me bare to weather.

Gui.   Uncertain favor !

Bel. My fault being nothing—as I have
    told you oft—
But that two villains, whose false oaths pre-
    vail'd
Before my perfect honor, swore to Cymbeline
I was confederate with the Romans : so
Follow'd my banishment, and this twenty years
This rock and these demesnes have been my
    world ;   70
Where I have lived at honest freedom, paid
More pious debts to heaven than in all
The fore-end of my time. But up to the moun-
    tains !
This is not hunters' language : he that strikes
The venison first shall be the lord o' the feast ;
To him the other two shall minister ;
And we will fear no poison, which attends
In place of greater state. I'll meet you in the
    valleys.
        [*Exeunt Guiderius and Arviragus.*
How hard it is to hide the sparks of nature !
These boys know little they are sons to the
    king ;   80
Nor Cymbeline dreams that they are alive.
They think they are mine ; and though train'd
    up thus meanly
I' the cave wherein they bow, their thoughts
    do hit
The roofs of palaces, and nature prompts them
In simple and low things to prince it much
Beyond the trick of others. This Polydore,
The heir of Cymbeline and Britain, who
The king his father call'd Guiderius,—Jove !
When on my three-foot stool I sit and tell
The warlike feats I have done, his spirits fly
    out   90
Into my story : say 'Thus, mine enemy fell,
And thus I set my foot on 's neck ; ' even then
The princely blood flows in his cheek, he
    sweats,
Strains his young nerves and puts himself in
    posture
That acts my words. The younger brother,
    Cadwal,
Once Arviragus, in as like a figure,
Strikes life into my speech and shows much
    more
His own conceiving.—Hark, the game is
    roused !
O Cymbeline ! heaven and my conscience
    knows
Thou didst unjustly banish me : whereon,   100
At three and two years old, I stole these
    babes ;
Thinking to bar thee of succession, as
Thou reft'st me of my lands. Euriphile,

Thou wast their nurse ; they took thee for
    their mother,
And every day do honor to her grave :
Myself, Belarius, that am Morgan call'd,
They take for natural father. The game is up.
                                        [*Exit.*

SCENE IV. *Country near Milford-Haven.*

Enter PISANIO *and* IMOGEN.

Imo. Thou told'st me, when we came from
    horse, the place
Was near at hand : ne'er long'd my mother so
To see me first, as I have now. Pisanio ! man !
Where is Posthumus ? What is in thy mind,
That makes thee stare thus ? Wherefore breaks
    that sigh
From the inward of thee ? One, but painted
    thus,
Would be interpreted a thing perplex'd
Beyond self-explication : put thyself
Into a havior of less fear, ere wildness
Vanquish my staider senses. What's the mat-
    ter ?   10
Why tender'st thou that paper to me, with
A look untender ? If 't be summer news,
Smile to 't before ; if winterly, thou need'st
But keep that countenance still. My husband's
    hand !
That drug-damn'd Italy hath out-crafted him,
And he's at some hard point. Speak, man : thy
    tongue
May take off some extremity, which to read
Would be even mortal to me.

Pis.   Please you, read ;
And you shall find me, wretched man, a thing
The most disdain'd of fortune.   20

Imo. [*Reads*] 'Thy mistress, Pisanio, hath
played the strumpet in my bed ; the testimonies whereof lie bleeding in me. I speak not
out of weak surmises, but from proof as strong
as my grief and as certain as I expect my revenge. That part thou, Pisanio, must act for
me, if thy faith be not tainted with the breach
of hers. Let thine own hands take away her
life : I shall give thee opportunity at Milford-
Haven. She hath my letter for the purpose :
where, if thou fear to strike and to make me
certain it is done, thou art the pandar to her
dishonor and equally to me disloyal.'

Pis. What shall I need to draw my sword ?
    the paper
Hath cut her throat already. No, 'tis slander,
Whose edge is sharper than the sword, whose
    tongue
Outvenoms all the worms of Nile, whose
    breath
Rides on the posting winds and doth belie
All corners of the world : kings, queens and
    states,
Maids, matrons, nay, the secrets of the grave
This viperous slander enters. What cheer,
    madam ?   41

Imo. False to his bed ! What is it to be
    false ?
To lie in watch there and to think on him ?
To weep 'twixt clock and clock ? if sleep
    charge nature,
To break it with a fearful dream of him
And cry myself awake ? that's false to 's bed,
    is it ?

Pis. Alas, good lady !

Imo. I false! Thy conscience witness: Iachimo,
Thou didst accuse him of incontinency;
Thou then look'dst like a villain; now me-
thinks   50
Thy favor's good enough. Some jay of Italy
Whose mother was her painting, hath betray'd
him:
Poor I am stale, a garment out of fashion;
And, for I am richer than to hang by the walls,
I must be ripp'd:—to pieces with me!—O,
Men's vows are women's traitors! All good
seeming,
By thy revolt, O husband, shall be thought
Put on for villany; not born where't grows,
But worn a bait for ladies.
    Pis.   Good madam, hear me.
    Imo. True honest men being heard, like
false Æneas,   60
Were in his time thought false, and Sinon's
weeping
Did scandal many a holy tear, took pity
From most true wretchedness: so thou, Post-
humus,
Wilt lay the leaven on all proper men;
Goodly and gallant shall be false and perjured
From thy great fail. Come, fellow, be thou
honest:
Do thou thy master's bidding: when thou
see'st him,
A little witness my obedience: look!
I draw the sword myself: take it, and hit   69
The innocent mansion of my love, my heart:
Fear not; 'tis empty of all things but grief;
Thy master is not there, who was indeed
The riches of it: do his bidding; strike
Thou mayst be valiant in a better cause;
But now thou seem'st a coward.
    Pis.   Hence, vile instrument!
Thou shalt not damn my hand.
    Imo.   Why, I must die;
And if I do not by thy hand, thou art
No servant of thy master's. Against self-
slaughter
There is a prohibition so divine
That cravens my weak hand. Come, here's my
heart.   80
Something's afore't. Soft, soft! we'll no de-
fence;
Obedient as the scabbard. What is here?
The scriptures of the loyal Leonatus,
All turn'd to heresy? Away, away,
Corrupters of my faith! you shall no more
Be stomachers to my heart. Thus may poor
fools
Believe false teachers: though those that are
betray'd
Do feel the treason sharply, yet the traitor
Stands in worse case of woe.   89
And thou, Posthumus, thou that didst set up
My disobedience 'gainst the king my father
And make me put into contempt the suits
Of princely fellows, shalt hereafter find
It is no act of common passage, but
A strain of rareness: and I grieve myself
To think, when thou shalt be disedged by her
That now thou tirest on, how thy memory
Will then be pang'd by me. Prithee, dispatch:
The lamb entreats the butcher: where's thy
knife?
Thou art too slow to do thy master's bidding,
When I desire it too.   101
    Pis.   O gracious lady,

Since I received command to do this business
I have not slept one wink.
    Imo.   Do't, and to bed then.
    Pis. I'll wake mine eye-balls blind first.
    Imo.   Wherefore then
Didst undertake it? Why hast thou abused
So many miles with a pretence? this place?
Mine action and thine own? our horses'
labor?
The time inviting thee? the perturb'd court,
For my being absent? whereunto I never
Purpose return. Why hast thou gone so far,
To be unbent when thou hast ta'en thy stand,
The elected deer before thee?
    Pis.   But to win time
To lose so bad employment; in the which
I have consider'd of a course. Good lady,
Hear me with patience.
    Imo.   Talk thy tongue weary; speak:
I have heard I am a strumpet; and mine ear,
Therein false struck, can take no greater
wound,
Nor tent to bottom that. But speak.
    Pis.   Then, madam,
I thought you would not back again.
    Imo.   Most like;
Bringing me here to kill me.
    Pis.   Not so, neither: 120
But if I were as wise as honest, then
My purpose would prove well. It cannot be
But that my master is abused:
Some villain, ay, and singular in his art,
Hath done you both this cursed injury.
    Imo. Some Roman courtezan.
    Pis.   No, on my life.
I'll give but notice you are dead and send him
Some bloody sign of it; for 'tis commanded
I should do so: you shall be miss'd at court,
And that will well confirm it.
    Imo.   Why, good fellow, 130
What shall I do the while? where bide? how
live?
Or in my life what comfort, when I am
Dead to my husband?
    Pis.   If you'll back to the court—
    Imo. No court, no father; nor no more
ado
With that harsh, noble, simple nothing,
That Cloten, whose love-suit hath been to me
As fearful as a siege.
    Pis.   If not at court,
Then not in Britain must you bide.
    Imo.   Where then?
Hath Britain all the sun that shines? Day,
night,
Are they not but in Britain? I' the world's
volume   140
Our Britain seems as of it, but not in 't;
In a great pool a swan's nest: prithee, think
There's livers out of Britain.
    Pis.   I am most glad
You think of other place. The ambassador,
Lucius the Roman, comes to Milford-Haven
To-morrow: now, if you could wear a mind
Dark as your fortune is, and but disguise
That which, to appear itself, must not yet be
But by self-danger, you should tread a course
Pretty and full of view; yea, haply, near   150
The residence of Posthumus; so nigh at least
That though his actions were not visible, yet
Report should render him hourly to your ear
As truly as he moves.

Imo.   O, for such means !
Though peril to my modesty, not death on't,
I would adventure.
Pis.   Well, then, here's the point :
You must forget to be a woman ; change
Command into obedience ; fear and niceness—
The handmaids of all women, or, more truly,
Woman its pretty self—into a waggish cour-
        age :   160
Ready in gibes, quick-answer'd, saucy and
As quarrelous as the weasel ; nay, you must
Forget that rarest treasure of your cheek,
Exposing it—but, O, the harder heart !
Alack, no remedy !—to the greedy touch
Of common-kissing Titan, and forget
Your laborsome and dainty trims, wherein
You made great Juno angry.
Imo.   Nay, be brief :
I see into thy end, and am almost
A man already.
Pis.   First, make yourself but like one.   170
Fore-thinking this, I have already fit—
'Tis in my cloak-bag—doublet, hat, hose, all
That answer to them : would you in their serv-
        ing,
And with what imitation you can borrow
From youth of such a season, 'fore noble
        Lucius
Present yourself, desire his service, tell him
Wherein you're happy,—which you'll make
        him know,
If that his head have ear in music,—doubtless
With joy he will embrace you, for he's honor-
        able
And doubling that, most holy. Your means
        abroad,   180
You have me, rich ; and I will never fail
Beginning nor supplyment.
Imo.   Thou art all the comfort
The gods will diet me with. Prithee, away :
There's more to be consider'd ; but we'll even
All that good time will give us : this attempt
I am soldier to, and will abide it with
A prince's courage. Away, I prithee.
Pis.   Well, madam, we must take a short
        farewell,
Lest, being miss'd, I be suspected of
Your carriage from the court. My noble mis-
        tress,   190
Here is a box ; I had it from the queen :
What's in't is precious ; if you are sick at sea,
Or stomach-qualm'd at land, a dram of this
Will drive away distemper. To some shade,
And fit you to your manhood. May the gods
Direct you to the best !
Imo.   Amen : I thank thee.
                        [*Exeunt, severally.*

Scene V.   *A room in Cymbeline's palace.*

Enter Cymbeline, Queen, Cloten, Lucius,
        Lords, *and* Attendants.

Cym.   Thus far ; and so farewell.
Luc.   Thanks, royal sir.
My emperor hath wrote, I must from hence ;
And am right sorry that I must report ye
My master's enemy.
Cym.   Our subjects, sir,
Will not endure his yoke ; and for ourself
To show less sovereignty than they, must needs
Appear unkinglike.
Luc.   So, sir : I desire of you
A conduct over-land to Milford-Haven.
Madam, all joy befal your grace !

Queen.   And you !
Cym.   My lords, you are appointed for that
        office ;   10
The due of honor in no point omit.
So farewell, noble Lucius.
Luc.   Your hand, my lord.
Clo.   Receive it friendly ; but from this
        time forth
I wear it as your enemy.
Luc.   Sir, the event
Is yet to name the winner : fare you well.
Cym.   Leave not the worthy Lucius, good
        my lords,
Till he have cross'd the Severn. Happiness !
                    [*Exeunt Lucius and Lords.*
Queen.   He goes hence frowning : but it
        honors us
That we have given him cause.
Clo.   'Tis all the better ;
Your valiant Britons have their wishes in it.
Cym.   Lucius hath wrote already to the em-
        peror   21
How it goes here. It fits us therefore ripely
Our chariots and our horsemen be in readiness :
The powers that he already hath in Gallia
Will soon be drawn to head, from whence he
        moves
His war for Britain.
Queen.   'Tis not sleepy business ;
But must be look'd to speedily and strongly.
Cym.   Our expectation that it would be
        thus
Hath made us forward. But, my gentle queen,
Where is our daughter ? She hath not appear'd
Before the Roman, nor to us hath tender'd   31
The duty of the day : she looks us like
A thing more made of malice than of duty :
We have noted it. Call her before us ; for
We have been too slight in sufferance.
                        [*Exit an Attendant.*
Queen.   Royal sir,
Since the exile of Posthumus, most retired
Hath her life been ; the cure whereof, my lord,
'Tis time must do. Beseech your majesty,
Forbear sharp speeches to her : she's a lady
So tender of rebukes that words are strokes 40
And strokes death to her.

Re-enter Attendant.

Cym.   Where is she, sir ? How
Can her contempt be answer'd ?
Atten.   Please you, sir,
Her chambers are all lock'd ; and there's no
        answer
That will be given to the loudest noise we
        make.
Queen.   My lord, when last I went to visit
        her,
She pray'd me to excuse her keeping close,
Whereto constrain'd by her infirmity,
She should that duty leave unpaid to you,
Which daily she was bound to proffer : this
She wish'd me to make known ; but our great
        court   50
Made me to blame in memory.
Cym.   Her doors lock'd ?
Not seen of late ? Grant, heavens, that which
        I fear
Prove false !   [*Exit.*
Queen.   Son, I say, follow the king.
Clo.   That man of hers, Pisanio, her old
        servant,
I have not seen these two days.

Queen. Go, look after. [*Exit Cloten.*
Pisanio, thou that stand'st so for Posthumus !
He hath a drug of mine ; I pray his absence
Proceed by swallowing that, for he believes
It is a thing most precious. But for her,
Where is she gone ? Haply, despair hath seized
  her, 60
Or, wing'd with fervor of her love, she's flown
To her desired Posthumus : gone she is
To death or to dishonor ; and my end
Can make good use of either : she being down,
I have the placing of the British crown.

Re-enter CLOTEN.

How now, my son !
Clo. 'Tis certain she is fled.
Go in and cheer the king : he rages ; none
Dare come about him.
Queen. [*Aside*] All the better : may
This night forestall him of the coming day !
                     [*Exit.*
Clo. I love and hate her : for she's fair and
  royal, 70
And that she hath all courtly parts more ex-
  quisite
Than lady, ladies, woman ; from every one
The best she hath, and she, of all compounded,
Outsells them all ; I love her therefore : but
Disdaining me and throwing favors on
The low Posthumus slanders so her judgment
That what's else rare is choked ; and in that
  point
I will conclude to hate her, nay, indeed,
To be revenged upon her. For when fools 79
Shall—

Enter PISANIO.

Who is here ? What, are you packing,
  sirrah ?
Come hither : ah, you precious pander ! Vil-
  lain,
Where is thy lady ? In a word ; or else
Thou art straightway with the fiends.
Pis. O, good my lord !
Clo. Where is thy lady ? or, by Jupiter,—
I will not ask again. Close villain,
I'll have this secret from thy heart, or rip
Thy heart to find it. Is she with Posthumus ?
From whose so many weights of baseness can-
  not
A dram of worth be drawn.
Pis. Alas, my lord,
How can she be with him ? When was she
  miss'd ? 90
He is in Rome.
Clo. Where is she, sir ? Come nearer ;
No further halting : satisfy me home
What is become of her.
Pis. O, my all-worthy lord !
Clo. All-worthy villain !
Discover where thy mistress is at once,
At the next word : no more of ' worthy lord ! '
Speak, or thy silence on the instant is
Thy condemnation and thy death.
Pis. Then, sir,
This paper is the history of my knowledge 99
Touching her flight. [*Presenting a letter.*
Clo. Let's see't. I will pursue her
Even to Augustus' throne.
Pis. [*Aside*] Or this, or perish.
She's far enough ; and what he learns by this
May prove his travel, not her danger.
Clo. Hum !

Pis. [*Aside*] I'll write to my lord she's dead.
  O Imogen,
Safe mayst thou wander, safe return again !
Clo. Sirrah, is this letter true ?
Pis. Sir, as I think.
Clo. It is Posthumus' hand ; I know't.
Sirrah, if thou wouldst not be a villain, but
do me true service, undergo those employ-
ments wherein I should have cause to use thee
with a serious industry, that is, what villany
soe'er I bid thee do, to perform it directly and
truly, I would think thee an honest man : thou
shouldst neither want my means for thy relief
nor my voice for thy preferment.
Pis. Well, my good lord.
Clo. Wilt thou serve me ? for since patiently and constantly thou hast stuck to the
bare fortune of that beggar Posthumus, thou
canst not, in the course of gratitude, but be a
diligent follower of mine : wilt thou serve me ?
Pis. Sir, I will.
Clo. Give me thy hand ; here's my purse.
Hast any of thy late master's garments in thy
possession ?
Pis. I have, my lord, at my lodging, the
same suit he wore when he took leave of my
lady and mistress. 129
Clo. The first service thou dost me, fetch
that suit hither : let it be thy first service ; go.
Pis. I shall, my lord. [*Exit.*
Clo. Meet thee at Milford-Haven !—I forgot to ask him one thing ; I'll remember't
anon :—even there, thou villain Posthumus,
will I kill thee. I would these garments were
come. She said upon a time—the bitterness of
it I now belch from my heart—that she held
the very garment of Posthumus in more respect
than my noble and natural person, together
with the adornment of my qualities. With that
suit upon my back, will I ravish her : first kill
him, and in her eyes ; there shall she see my
valor, which will then be a torment to her contempt. He on the ground, my speech of insult-
ment ended on his dead body, and when my
lust hath dined,—which, as I say, to vex her I
will execute in the clothes that she so praised,
—to the court I'll knock her back, foot her
home again. She hath despised me rejoicingly,
and I'll be merry in my revenge. 150

Re-enter PISANIO, *with the clothes.*

Be those the garments ?
Pis. Ay, my noble lord.
Clo. How long is't since she went to Mil-
ford-Haven ?
Pis. She can scarce be there yet.
Clo. Bring this apparel to my chamber ;
that is the second thing that I have com-
manded thee : the third is, that thou wilt be a
voluntary mute to my design. Be but duteous,
and true preferment shall tender itself to thee.
My revenge is now at Milford : would I had
wings to follow it ! Come, and be true. [*Exit.*
Pis. Thou bid'st me to my loss : for true
  to thee
Were I to prove false, which I will never be,
To him that is most true. To Milford go,
And find not her whom thou pursuest. Flow,
  flow,
You heavenly blessings, on her ! This fool's
  speed
Be cross'd with slowness ; labor be his meed !
                    [*Exit.*

Scene VI. *Wales. Before the cave of
Belarius.*

Enter Imogen, *in boy's clothes.*

Imo.   I see a man's life is a tedious one :
I have tired myself, and for two nights to-
    gether
Have made the ground my bed. I should be
    sick,
But that my resolution helps me. Milford,
When from the mountain-top Pisanio show'd
    thee,
Thou wast within a ken : O Jove ! I think
Foundations fly the wretched ; such, I mean,
Where they should be relieved. Two beggars
    told me
I could not miss my way : will poor folks lie,
That have afflictions on them, knowing 'tis 10
A punishment or trial ? Yes ; no wonder,
When rich ones scarce tell true. To lapse in
    fulness
Is sorer than to lie for need, and falsehood
Is worse in kings than beggars. My dear lord !
Thou art one o' the false ones. Now I think
    on thee,
My hunger's gone ; but even before, I was
At point to sink for food. But what is this ?
Here is a path to't : 'tis some savage hold :
I were best not call ; I dare not call : yet
    famine,   19
Ere clean it o'erthrow nature, makes it valiant,
Plenty and peace breeds cowards : hardness
    ever
Of hardiness is mother. Ho ! who's here ?
If any thing that's civil, speak ; if savage,
Take or lend. Ho ! No answer ? Then I'll
    enter.
Best draw my sword ; and if mine enemy
But fear the sword like me, he'll scarcely look
    on't.
Such a foe, good heavens ! [*Exit, to the cave.*

Enter Belarius, Guiderius, *and* Arviragus.

Bel.   You, Polydore, have proved best
    woodman and
Are master of the feast : Cadwal and I
Will play the cook and servant ; 'tis our
    match :   30
The sweat of industry would dry and die,
But for the end it works to. Come ; our stom-
    achs
Will make what's homely savory : weariness
Can snore upon the flint, when resty sloth
Finds the down pillow hard. Now peace be
    here,
Poor house, that keep'st thyself !
Gui.   I am thoroughly weary.
Arv.   I am weak with toil, yet strong in ap-
    petite.
Gui.   There is cold meat i' the cave ; we'll
    browse on that,
Whilst what we have kill'd be cook'd.
Bel. [*Looking into the cave*] Stay ; come
    not in.   40
But that it eats our victuals, I should think
Here were a fairy.
Gui.   What's the matter, sir ?
Bel.   By Jupiter, an angel ! or, if not,
An earthly paragon ! Behold divineness
No elder than a boy !

Re-enter Imogen.

Imo.   Good masters, harm me not :

Before I enter'd here, I call'd ; and thought
To have begg'd or bought what I have took :
    good troth,
I have stol'n nought, nor would not, though I
    had found
Gold strew'd i' the floor. Here's money for my
    meat :   50
I would have left it on the board so soon
As I had made my meal, and parted
With prayers for the provider.
Gui.   Money, youth ?
Arv.   All gold and silver rather turn to
    dirt !
As 'tis no better reckon'd, but of those
Who worship dirty gods.
Imo.   I see you're angry :
Know, if you kill me for my fault, I should
Have died had I not made it.
Bel.   Whither bound ?
Imo.   To Milford-Haven.
Bel.   What's your name ?   60
Imo.   Fidele, sir. I have a kinsman who
Is bound for Italy ; he embark'd at Milford ;
To whom being going, almost spent with hun-
    ger,
I am fall'n in this offence.
Bel.   Prithee, fair youth,
Think us no churls, nor measure our good
    minds
By this rude place we live in. Well encoun-
    ter'd !
'Tis almost night : you shall have better cheer
Ere you depart ; and thanks to stay and eat it.
Boys, bid him welcome.
Gui.   Were you a woman, youth,
I should woo hard but be your groom. In
    honesty,   70
I bid for you as I'ld buy.
Arv.   I'll make't my comfort
He is a man ; I'll love him as my brother :
And such a welcome as I'ld give to him
After long absence, such is yours : most wel-
    come !
Be sprightly, for you fall 'mongst friends.
Imo.   'Mongst friends,
If brothers. [*Aside*] Would it had been so,
    that they
Had been my father's sons ! then had my prize
Been less, and so more equal ballasting
To thee, Posthumus.
Bel.   He wrings at some distress.
Gui.   Would I could free't !
Arv.   Or I, whate'er it be, 80
What pain it cost, what danger. God's !
Bel.   Hark, boys.
                                   [*Whispering.*
Imo.   Great men,
That had a court no bigger than this cave,
That did attend themselves and had the virtue
Which their own conscience seal'd them—lay-
    ing by
That nothing-gift of differing multitudes—
Could not out-peer these twain. Pardon me,
    gods !
I'ld change my sex to be companion with
    them,
Since Leonatus's false.
Bel.   It shall be so.
Boys, we'll go dress our hunt. Fair youth,
    come in :   90
Discourse is heavy, fasting ; when we have
    supp'd,

We'll mannerly demand thee of thy story,
So far as thou wilt speak it.

Gui.　　　　　　　　Pray, draw near.

Arv. The night to the owl and morn to the
lark less welcome.

Imo. Thanks, sir.

Arv. I pray, draw near.　　　　[*Exeunt.*

SCENE VII. *Rome. A public place.*

Enter two Senators and Tribunes.

First Sen. This is the tenor of the emper-
or's writ:
That since the common men are now in action
'Gainst the Pannonians and Dalmatians,
And that the legions now in Gallia are
Full weak to undertake our wars against
The fall'n-off Britons, that we do incite
The gentry to this business. He creates
Lucius proconsul : and to you the tribunes,
For this immediate levy, he commends 9
His absolute commission. Long live Cæsar !

First Tri. Is Lucius general of the forces ?

Sec. Sen.　　　　　　　　Ay.

First Tri. Remaining now in Gallia ?

First Sen.　　　　　　　With those legions
Which I have spoke of, whereunto your levy
Must be supplyant : the words of your com-
mission
Will tie you to the numbers and the time
Of their dispatch.

First Tri. We will discharge our duty.
　　　　　　　　　　　　　　　[*Exeunt.*

ACT IV.

SCENE I. *Wales : near the cave of Belarius.*

Enter CLOTEN.

Clo. I am near to the place where they
should meet, if Pisanio have mapped it truly.
How fit his garments serve me ! Why should
his mistress, who was made by him that made
the tailor, not be fit too ? the rather—saving
reverence of the word—for 'tis said a woman's
fitness comes by fits. Therein I must play the
workman. I dare speak it to myself—for it is
not vain-glory for a man and his glass to confer in his own chamber—I mean, the lines of
my body are as well drawn as his ; no less
young, more strong, not beneath him in fortunes, beyond him in the advantage of the
time, above him in birth, alike conversant in
general services, and more remarkable in single oppositions : yet this imperceiverant thing
loves him in my despite. What mortality is !
Posthumus, thy head, which now is growing
upon thy shoulders, shall within this hour be
off ; thy mistress enforced ; thy garments cut
to pieces before thy face : and all this done,
spurn her home to her father ; who may haply
be a little angry for my so rough usage ; but
my mother, having power of his testiness, shall
turn all into my commendations. My horse is
tied up safe : out, sword, and to a sore purpose ! Fortune, put them into my hand ! This
is the very description of their meeting-place ;
and the fellow dares not deceive me. [*Exit.*

SCENE II. *Before the cave of Belarius.*

Enter, from the cave, BELARIUS, GUIDERIUS,
ARVIRAGUS, *and* IMOGEN.

Bel. [*To Imogen*] You are not well : remain here in the cave ;
We'll come to you after hunting.

Arv.　　　　[*To Imogen*] Brother, stay here :
Are we not brothers ?

Imo.　　　　So man and man should be ;
But clay and clay differs in dignity,
Whose dust is both alike. I am very sick.

Gui. Go you to hunting ; I'll abide with
him.

Imo. So sick I am not, yet I am not well ;
But not so citizen a wanton as
To seem to die ere sick : so please you, leave
me ;
Stick to your journal course : the breach of
custom　　　　　　　　　　　　　　10
Is breach of all. I am ill, but your being by me
Cannot amend me ; society is no comfort
To one not sociable : I am not very sick,
Since I can reason of it. Pray you, trust me
here :
I'll rob none but myself ; and let me die,
Stealing so poorly.

Gui.　　　　I love thee ; I have spoke it :
How much the quantity, the weight as much,
As I do love my father.

Bel.　　　　　　　What ! how ! how !

Arv. If it be sin to say so, sir, I yoke me
In my good brother's fault : I know not why
I love this youth ; and I have heard you say,
Love's reason's without reason : the bier at
door,
And a demand who is't shall die, I'ld say
' My father, not this youth.'

Bel.　　　　　[*Aside*] O noble strain !
O worthiness of nature ! breed of greatness !
Cowards father cowards and base things sire
base :
Nature hath meal and bran, contempt and
grace.
I'm not their father ; yet who this should be,
Doth miracle itself, loved before me.
'Tis the ninth hour o' the morn.

Arv.　　　　　　　Brother, farewell. 30

Imo. I wish ye sport.

Arv.　　　　You health. So please you, sir.

Imo. [*Aside*] These are kind creatures.
Gods, what lies I have heard !
Our courtiers say all's savage but at court :
Experience, O, thou disprovest report !
The imperious seas breed monsters, for the
dish
Poor tributary rivers as sweet fish.
I am sick still ; heart-sick. Pisanio,
I'll now taste of thy drug. [*Swallows some.*

Gui.　　　　　I could not stir him :
He said he was gentle, but unfortunate ;
Dishonestly afflicted, but yet honest.　　40

Arv. Thus did he answer me : yet said,
hereafter
I might know more.

Bel.　　　　To the field, to the field !
We'll leave you for this time : go in and rest.

Arv. We'll not be long away.

Bel.　　　　　　Pray, be not sick,
For you must be our housewife.

Imo.　　　　　Well or ill,
I am bound to you.

Bel.　　　　And shalt be ever.
　　　　　　[*Exit Imogen, to the cave.*
This youth, how'er distress'd, appears he hath
had
Good ancestors.

Arv.   How angel-like he sings !
Gui. But his neat cookery ! he cut our
        roots
In characters,
And sauced our broths, as Juno had been sick
And he her dieter.   51
Arv.   Nobly he yokes
A smiling with a sigh, as if the sigh
Was that it was, for not being such a smile ;
The smile mocking the sigh, that it would fly
From so divine a temple, to commix
With winds that sailors rail at.
Gui.   I do note
That grief and patience, rooted in him both,
Mingle their spurs together.
Arv.   Grow, patience !
And let the stinking elder, grief, untwine
His perishing root with the increasing vine !
Bel. It is great morning. Come, away !—
Who's there ?   61

Enter Cloten.

Clo. I cannot find those runagates ; that
        villain
Hath mock'd me. I am faint.
Bel.   'Those runagates ! '
Means he not us ? I partly know him : 'tis
Cloten, the son o' the queen. I fear some am-
        bush.
I saw him not these many years, and yet
I know 'tis he. We are held as outlaws : hence !
Gui. He is but one : you and my brother
        search
What companies are near : pray you, away !
Let me alone with him.
        [*Exeunt Belarius and Arviragus.*
Clo.   Soft ! What are you   70
That fly me thus ? some villain mountaineers ?
I have heard of such. What slave art thou ?
Gui.   A thing
More slavish did I ne'er than answering
A slave without a knock.
Clo.   Thou art a robber,
A law-breaker, a villain : yield thee, thief.
Gui. To who ? to thee ? What art thou ?
        Have not I
An arm as big as thine ? a heart as big ?
Thy words, I grant, are bigger, for I wear not
My dagger in my mouth. Say what thou art,
Why I should yield to thee ?
Clo.   Thou villain base,   80
Know'st me not by my clothes ?
Gui.   No, nor thy tailor, rascal,
Who is thy grandfather : he made those
        clothes,
Which, as it seems, make thee.
Clo.   Thou precious varlet,
My tailor made them not.
Gui.   Hence, then, and thank
The man that gave them thee. Thou art some
        fool ;
I am loath to beat thee.
Clo.   Thou injurious thief,
Hear but my name, and tremble.
Gui.   What's thy name ?
Clo. Cloten, thou villain.
Gui. Cloten, thou double villain, be thy
        name,
I cannot tremble at it : were it Toad, or Ad-
        der, Spider,   90
'Twould move me sooner.
Clo.   To thy further fear,

Nay, to thy mere confusion, thou shalt know
I am son to the queen.
Gui.   I am sorry for 't ; not seeming
So worthy as thy birth.
Clo.   Art not afeard ?
Gui. Those that I reverence those I fear,
        the wise :
At fools I laugh, not fear them.
Clo.   Die the death :
When I have slain thee with my proper hand,
I'll follow those that even now fled hence,
And on the gates of Lud's-town set your
        heads :
Yield, rustic mountaineer.   [*Exeunt, fighting.*

Re-enter Belarius *and* Arviragus.

Bel. No companies abroad ?   101
Arv. None in the world : you did mistake
        him, sure.
Bel. I cannot tell : long is it since I saw
        him,
But time hath nothing blurr'd those lines of
        favor
Which then he wore ; the snatches in his voice,
And burst of speaking, were as his : I am ab-
        solute
'Twas very Cloten.
Arv.   In this place we left them :
I wish my brother make good time with him,
You say he is so fell.
Bel.   Being scarce made up,
I mean, to man, he had not apprehension   110
Of roaring terrors ; for the effect of judgment
Is oft the cause of fear. But, see, thy brother.

Re-enter Guiderius, *with* Cloten's *head.*

Gui. This Cloten was a fool, an empty
        purse ;
There was no money in't : not Hercules
Could have knock'd out his brains, for he had
        none :
Yet I not doing this, the fool had borne
My head as I do his.
Bel.   What hast thou done ?
Gui. I am perfect what : cut off one Clo-
        ten's head,
Son to the queen, after his own report ;
Who call'd me traitor, mountaineer, and swore
With his own single hand he'ld take us in   121
Displace our heads where—thank the gods !—
        they grow,
And set them on Lud's-town.
Bel.   We are all undone.
Gui. Why, worthy father, what have we to
        lose,
But that he swore to take, our lives ? The law
Protects not us : then why should we be tender
To let an arrogant piece of flesh threat us,
Play judge and executioner all himself,
For we do fear the law ? What company
Discover you abroad ?
Bel.   No single soul   130
Can we set eye on ; but in all safe reason
He must have some attendants. Though his
        humor
Was nothing but mutation, ay, and that
From one bad thing to worse ; not frenzy, not
Absolute madness could so far have raved
To bring him here alone ; although perhaps
It may be heard at court that such as we
Cave here, hunt here, are outlaws, and in time
May make some stronger head ; the which he
        hearing—

As it is like him—might break out, and swear
He'ld fetch us in ; yet is't not probable   141
To come alone, either he so undertaking,
Or they so suffering : then on good ground we
    fear,
If we do fear this body hath a tail
More perilous than the head.

Arv.   Let ordinance
Come as the gods foresay it : howsoe'er,
My brother hath done well.

Bel.   I had no mind
To hunt this day : the boy Fidele's sickness
Did make my way long forth.

Gui.   With his own sword,
Which he did wave against my throat, I have
    ta'en   150
His head from him : I'll throw't into the creek
Behind our rock ; and let it to the sea,
And tell the fishes he's the queen's son, Clo-
    ten :
That's all I reck.   [*Exit.*

Bel.   I fear 'twill be revenged :
Would, Polydore, thou hadst not done't !
    though valor
Becomes thee well enough.

Arv.   Would I had done't,
So the revenge alone pursued me ! Polydore,
I love thee brotherly, but envy much
Thou hast robb'd me of this deed : I would
    revenges,
That possible strength might meet, would seek
    us through   160
And put us to our answer.

Bel.   Well, 'tis done :
We'll hunt no more to-day, nor seek for dan-
    ger
Where there's no profit. I prithee, to our rock ;
You and Fidele play the cooks : I'll stay
Till hasty Polydore return, and bring him
To dinner presently.

Arv.   Poor sick Fidele !
I'll willingly to him : to gain his color
I'ld let a parish of such Clotens' blood,
And praise myself for charity.   [*Exit.*

Bel.   O thou goddess,
Thou divine Nature, how thyself thou blazon'st
In these two princely boys ! They are as gentle
As zephyrs blowing below the violet,   172
Not wagging his sweet head ; and yet as rough,
Their royal blood enchafed, as the rudest
    wind,
That by the top doth take the mountain pine,
And make him stoop to the vale. 'Tis wonder
That an invisible instinct should frame them
To royalty unlearn'd, honor untaught,
Civility not seen from other, valor   179
That wildly grows in them, but yields a crop
As if it had been sow'd. Yet still it's strange
What Cloten's being here to us portends,
Or what his death will bring us.

Re-enter GUIDERIUS.

Gui.   Where's my brother ?
I have sent Cloten's clotpoll down the stream,
In embassy to his mother : his body's hostage
For his return.   [*Solemn music.*

Bel.   My ingenious instrument !
Hark, Polydore, it sounds ! But what occasion
Hath Cadwal now to give it motion ? Hark !

Gui. Is he at home ?

Bel.   He went hence even now.

Gui. What does he mean ? since death of
my dear'st mother   190

It did not speak before. All solemn things
Should answer solemn accidents. The matter ?
Triumphs for nothing and lamenting toys
Is jollity for apes and grief for boys.
Is Cadwal mad ?

Bel.   Look, here he comes,
And brings the dire occasion in his arms
Of what we blame him for.

Re-enter ARVIRAGUS, *with* IMOGEN, *as dead,
    bearing her in his arms.*

Arv.   The bird is dead
That we have made so much on. I had rather
Have skipp'd from sixteen years of age to
    sixty,
To have turn'd my leaping-time into a crutch,
Than have seen this.   201

Gui.   O sweetest, fairest lily !
My brother wears thee not the one half so well
As when thou grew'st thyself.

Bel.   O melancholy !
Who ever yet could sound thy bottom ? find
The ooze, to show what coast thy sluggish
    crare
Might easiliest harbor in ? Thou blessed
    thing !
Jove knows what man thou mightst have
    made ; but I,
Thou diedst, a most rare boy, of melancholy.
How found you him ?

Arv.   Stark, as you see :
Thus smiling, as some fly had tickled slumber,
Not as death's dart, being laugh'd at ; his right
    cheek   211
Reposing on a cushion.

Gui.   Where ?

Arv.   O' the floor ;
His arms thus leagued : I thought he slept, and
    put
My clouted brogues from off my feet, whose
    rudeness
Answer'd my steps too loud.

Gui.   Why, he but sleeps :
If he be gone, he'll make his grave a bed ;
With female fairies will his tomb be haunted,
And worms will not come to thee.

Arv.   With fairest flowers
Whilst summer lasts and I live here, Fidele,
I'll sweeten thy sad grave : thou shalt not lack
The flower that's like thy face, pale primrose,
    nor   221
The azured harebell, like thy veins, no, nor
The leaf of eglantine, whom not to slander,
Out-sweeten'd not thy breath : the ruddock
    would,
With charitable bill,—O bill, sore-shaming
Those rich-left heirs that let their fathers lie
Without a monument !—bring thee all this ;
Yea, and furr'd moss besides, when flowers are
    none,
To winter-ground thy corse.

Gui.   Prithee, have done ;
And do not play in wench-like words with that
Which is so serious. Let us bury him,   231
And not protract with admiration what
Is now due debt. To the grave !

Arv.   Say, where shall's lay him ?

Gui. By good Euriphile, our mother.

Arv.   Be't so :
And let us, Polydore, though now our voices
Have got the mannish crack, sing him to the
    ground,
As once our mother ; use like note and words,

Save that Euriphile must be Fidele.
  Gui. Cadwal,
I cannot sing : I'll weep, and word it with
  thee ;   240
For notes of sorrow out of tune are worse
Than priests and fanes that lie.
  Arv.   We'll speak it, then.
  Bel. Great griefs, I see, medicine the less ;
Is quite forgot. He was a queen's son, boys ;
And though he came our enemy, remember
He was paid for that : though mean and
  mighty, rotting
Together, have one dust, yet reverence,
That angel of the world, doth make distinction
Of place 'tween high and low. Our foe was
  princely ;
And though you took his life, as being our foe,
Yet bury him as a prince.
  Gui.   Pray you, fetch him hither. 251
Thersites' body is as good as Ajax',
When neither are alive.
  Arv.   If you'll go fetch him,
We'll say our song the whilst. Brother, begin.
                   [*Exit Belarius.*
  Gui. Nay, Cadwal, we must lay his head
  to the east ;
My father hath a reason for't.
  Arv.   'Tis true.
  Gui. Come on then, and remove him.
  Arv.   So. Begin.

SONG.

  Gui. Fear no more the heat o' the sun,
      Nor the furious winter's rages ;
    Thou thy worldly task hast done, 260
      Home art gone, and ta'en thy
      wages :
    Golden lads and girls all must,
    As chimney-sweepers, come to dust.
  Arv. Fear no more the frown o' the great ;
    Thou art past the tyrant's stroke ;
    Care no more to clothe and eat ;
      To thee the reed is as the oak :
    The sceptre, learning, physic, must
    All follow this, and come to dust.
  Gui. Fear no more the lightning flash, 270
  Arv.   Nor the all-dreaded thunder-stone ;
  Gui. Fear not slander, censure rash ;
  Arv.   Thou hast finish'd joy and moan :
  Both. All lovers young, all lovers must
    Consign to thee, and come to dust.
  Gui. No exorciser harm thee !
  Arv. Nor no witchcraft charm thee !
  Gui. Ghost unlaid forbear thee !
  Arv. Nothing ill come near thee !
  Both. Quiet consummation have ;   280
    And renowned be thy grave !

Re-enter BELARIUS, *with the body of* CLOTEN.

  Gui. We have done our obsequies : come,
  lay him down.
  Bel. Here's a few flowers ; but 'bout mid-
  night, more :
The herbs that have on them cold dew o' the
  night
Are strewings fitt'st for graves. Upon their
  faces.
You were as flowers, now wither'd : even so
These herblets shall, which we upon you strew.
Come on, away : apart upon our knees.

The ground that gave them first has them
  again :   289
Their pleasures here are past, so is their pain.
      [*Exeunt Belarius, Guiderius, and Arviragus.*
  Imo. [*Awaking*] Yes, sir, to Milford-
  Haven ; which is the way ?—
I thank you.—By yond bush ?—Pray, how far
  thither ?
'Ods pittikins ! can it be six mile yet ?—
I have gone all night. 'Faith, I'll lie down and
  sleep.
But, soft ! no bedfellow !—O gods and god-
  desses !   [*Seeing the body of Cloten.*
These flowers are like the pleasures of the
  world ;
This bloody man, the care on't. I hope I
  dream ;
For so I thought I was a cave-keeper,
And cook to honest creatures : but 'tis not so ;
'Twas but a bolt of nothing, shot at nothing,
Which the brain makes of fumes : our very
  eyes   301
Are sometimes like our judgments, blind. Good
  faith,
I tremble still with fear : but if there be
Yet left in heaven as small a drop of pity
As a wren's eye, fear'd gods, a part of it !
The dream's here still : even when I wake, it is
Without me, as within me ; not imagined, felt.
A headless man ! The garments of Posthu-
  mus !
I know the shape of's leg : this is his hand ;
His foot Mercurial ; his Martial thigh ;   310
The brawns of Hercules : but his Jovial face
Murder in heaven ?—How !—'Tis gone. Pi-
  sanio,
All curses madded Hecuba gave the Greeks,
And mine to boot, be darted on thee ! Thou,
Conspired with that irregulous devil, Cloten,
Hast here cut off my lord. To write and read
Be henceforth treacherous ! Damn'd Pisanio
Hath with his forged letters,—damn'd Pi-
  sanio—
From this most bravest vessel of the world
Struck the main-top ! O Posthumus ! alas,
Where is thy head ? where's that ? Ay me !
  where's that ?   321
Pisanio might have kill'd thee at the heart,
And left this head on. How should this be ?
  Pisanio ?
'Tis he and Cloten : malice and lucre in them
Have laid this woe here. O, 'tis pregnant, preg-
  nant !
The drug he gave me, which he said was pre-
  cious
And cordial to me, have I not found it
Murderous to the senses ? That confirms it
  home :
This is Pisanio's deed, and Cloten's : O !
Give color to my pale cheek with thy blood,
That we the horrider may seem to those   331
Which chance to find us : O, my lord, my
  lord !   [*Falls on the body.*

Enter LUCIUS, *a* Captain *and other* Officers,
      and a Soothsayer.

  Cap. To them the legions garrison'd in
  Gallia,
After your will, have cross'd the sea, attending
You here at Milford-Haven with your ships :
They are in readiness.
  Luc.   But what from Rome ?

Cap. The senate hath stirr'd up the con-
    finers
And gentlemen of Italy, most willing spirits,
That promise noble service : and they come
Under the conduct of bold Iachimo,   340
Syenna's brother.
    Luc.   When expect you them ?
    Cap. With the next benefit o' the wind.
    Luc.   This forwardness
Makes our hopes fair. Command our present
    numbers
Be muster'd ; bid the captains look to't. Now,
    sir,
What have you dream'd of late of this war's
    purpose ?
    Sooth. Last night the very gods show'd me
        a vision—
I fast and pray'd for their intelligence—thus :
I saw Jove's bird, the Roman eagle, wing'd
From the spongy south to this part of the
    west,
There vanish'd in the sunbeams : which por-
    tends—   350
Unless my sins abuse my divination—
Success to the Roman host.
    Luc.   Dream often so,
And never false. Soft, ho ! what trunk is here
Without his top ? The ruin speaks that some-
    time
It was a worthy building. How ! a page !
Or dead, or sleeping on him ? But dead rather ;
For nature doth abhor to make his bed
With the defunct, or sleep upon the dead.
Let's see the boy's face.
    Cap.   He's alive, my lord.
    Luc. He'll then instruct us of this body.
        Young one,   360
Inform us of thy fortunes, for it seems
They crave to be demanded. Who is this
Thou makest thy bloody pillow ? Or who was
    he
That, otherwise than noble nature did,
Hath alter'd that good picture ? What's thy
    interest
In this sad wreck ? How came it ? Who is it ?
What art thou ?
    Imo.   I am nothing : or if not,
Nothing to be were better. This was my master,
A very valiant Briton and a good,
That here by mountaineers lies slain. Alas !
There is no more such masters : I may wander
From east to occident, cry out for service, 372
Try many, all good, serve truly, never
Find such another master.
    Luc.   'Lack, good youth !
Thou movest no less with thy complaining than
Thy master in bleeding : say his name, good
    friend.
    Imo. Richard du Champ. [*Aside*] If I do
        lie and do
No harm by it, though the gods hear, I hope
They'll pardon it.—Say you, sir ?
    Luc.   Thy name ?
    Imo.   Fidele, sir.
    Luc. Thou dost approve thyself the very
        same :   380
Thy name well fits thy faith, thy faith thy
    name.
Wilt take thy chance with me ? I will not say
Thou shalt be so well master'd, but, be sure,
No less beloved. The Roman emperor's letters,
Sent by a consul to me, should not sooner

Than thine own worth prefer thee : go with
    me.
    Imo. I'll follow, sir. But first, an't please
        the gods,
I'll hide my master from the flies, as deep
As these poor pickaxes can dig ; and when
With wild wood-leaves and weeds I ha' strew'd
        his grave,   390
And on it said a century of prayers,
Such as I can, twice o'er, I'll weep and sigh ;
And leaving so his service, follow you,
So please you entertain me.
    Luc.   Ay, good youth !
And rather father thee than master thee.
My friends,
The boy hath taught us manly duties : let us
Find out the prettiest daisied plot we can,
And make him with our pikes and partisans
A grave : come, arm him. Boy, he is preferr'd
By thee to us, and he shall be interr'd   401
As soldiers can. Be cheerful ; wipe thine eyes :
Some falls are means the happier to arise.
        [*Exeunt.*

SCENE III. *A room in Cymbeline's palace.*

    Enter CYMBELINE, *Lords,* PISANIO, *and*
        Attendants.

Cym. Again ; and bring me word how 'tis
        with her.   [*Exit an Attendant.*
A fever with the absence of her son,
A madness, of which her life's in danger.
        Heavens,
How deeply you at once do touch me ! Imo-
    gen,
The great part of my comfort, gone ; my queen
Upon a desperate bed, and in a time
When fearful wars point at me ; her son gone,
So needful for this present : it strikes me, past
The hope of comfort. But for thee, fellow,
Who needs must know of her departure and
Dost seem so ignorant, we'll enforce it from
    thee   11
By a sharp torture.
    Pis.   Sir, my life is yours ;
I humbly set it at your will ; but, for my mis-
    tress,
I nothing know where she remains, why gone,
Nor when she purposes return. Beseech your
    highness,
Hold me your loyal servant.
    First Lord.   Good my liege,
The day that she was missing he was here :
I dare be bound he's true and shall perform
All parts of his subjection loyally. For Cloten,
There wants no diligence in seeking him,   20
And will, no doubt, be found.
    Cym.   The time is troublesome.
[*To Pisanio*] We'll slip you for a season ; but
        our jealousy
Does yet depend.
    First Lord.   So please your majesty,
The Roman legions, all from Gallia drawn,
Are landed on your coast, with a supply
Of Roman gentlemen, by the senate sent.
    Cym. Now for the counsel of my son and
        queen !
I am amazed with matter.
    First Lord.   Good my liege,
Your preparation can affront no less
Than what you hear of : come more, for more
        you're ready :   30
The want is but to put those powers in motion
That long to move.

Cym.   I thank you. Let's withdraw ;
And meet the time as it seeks us. We fear not
What can from Italy annoy us ; but
We grieve at chances here. Away !
                    [*Exeunt all but Pisanio.*
  Pis.   I heard no letter from my master since
I wrote him Imogen was slain : 'tis strange :
Nor hear I from my mistress, who did promise
To yield me often tidings : neither know I
What is betid to Cloten ; but remain   40
Perplex'd in all. The heavens still must work.
Wherein I am false I am honest ; not true, to
        be true.
These present wars shall find I love my coun-
        try,
Even to the note o' the king, or I'll fall in
        them.
All other doubts, by time let them be clear'd :
Fortune brings in some boats that are not
        steer'd.   [*Exit.*

SCENE IV. *Wales : before the cave of*
Belarius.

Enter BELARIUS, GUIDERIUS, *and* ARVIRAGUS.
  Gui.   The noise is round about us.
  Bel.   Let us from it.
  Arv.   What pleasure, sir, find we in life, to
        lock it
From action and adventure ?
  Gui.   Nay, what hope
Have we in hiding us ? This way, the Romans
Must or for Britons slay us, or receive us
For barbarous and unnatural revolts
During their use, and slay us after.
  Bel.   Sons,
We'll higher to the mountains ; there secure
        us.
To the king's party there's no going : newness
Of Cloten's death—we being not known, not
        muster'd   10
Among the bands—may drive us to a render
Where we have lived, and so extort from's that
Which we have done, whose answer would be
        death
Drawn on with torture.
  Gui.   This is, sir, a doubt
In such a time nothing becoming you,
Nor satisfying us.
  Arv.   It is not likely
That when they hear the Roman horses neigh,
Behold their quarter'd fires, have both their
        eyes
And ears so cloy'd importantly as now,
That they will waste their time upon our note,
To know from whence we are.   21
  Bel.   O, I am known
Of many in the army : many years,
Though Cloten then but young, you see, not
        wore him
From my remembrance. And, besides, the
        king
Hath not deserved my service nor your loves ;
Who find in my exile the want of breeding,
The certainty of this hard life ; aye hopeless
To have the courtesy your cradle promised,
But to be still hot summer's tanlings and
The shrinking slaves of winter.
  Gui.   Than be so   30
Better to cease to be. Pray, sir, to the army :
I and my brother are not known ; yourself
So out of thought, and thereto so o'ergrown,
Cannot be question'd.
  Arv.   By this sun that shines,

I'll thither : what thing is it that I never
Did see man die ! scarce ever look'd on blood,
But that of coward hares, hot goats, and ven-
        ison !
Never bestrid a horse, save one that had
A rider like myself, who ne'er wore rowel
Nor iron on his heel ! I am ashamed   40
To look upon the holy sun, to have
The benefit of his blest beams, remaining
So long a poor unknown.
  Gui.   By heavens, I'll go :
If you will bless me, sir, and give me leave,
I'll take the better care, but if you will not,
The hazard therefore due fall on me by
The hands of Romans !
  Arv.   So say I : amen.
  Bel.   No reason I, since of your lives you
        set
So slight a valuation, should reserve
My crack'd one to more care. Have with you,
        boys !   50
If in your country wars you chance to die,
That is my bed too, lads, and there I'll lie :
Lead, lead. [*Aside*] The time seems long ;
        their blood thinks scorn,
Till it fly out and show them princes born.
                              [*Exeunt.*

ACT V.

SCENE I. *Britain. The Roman camp.*

Enter POSTHUMUS, *with a bloody handkerchief.*
  Post.   Yea, bloody cloth, I'll keep thee, for
        I wish'd
Thou shouldst be color'd thus. You married
        ones,
If each of you should take this course, how
        many
Must murder wives much better than them-
        selves
For wrying but a little ! O Pisanio !
Every good servant does not all commands :
No bond but to do just ones. Gods ! if you
Should have ta'en vengeance on my faults, I
        never
Had lived to put on this : so had you saved
The noble Imogen to repent, and struck   10
Me, wretch more worth your vengeance. But,
        alack,
You snatch some hence for little faults ; that's
        love,
To have them fall no more : you some permit
To second ills with ills, each elder worse,
And make them dread it, to the doers' thrift.
But Imogen is your own : do your best wills,
And make me blest to obey ! I am brought
        hither
Among the Italian gentry, and to fight
Against my lady's kingdom : 'tis enough
That, Britain, I have kill'd thy mistress ;
        peace !   20
I'll give no wound to thee. Therefore, good
        heavens,
Hear patiently my purpose : I'll disrobe me
Of these Italian weeds and suit myself
As does a Briton peasant : so I'll fight
Against the part I come with ; so I'll die
For thee, O Imogen, even for whom my life
Is every breath a death ; and thus, unknown,
Pitied nor hated, to the face of peril
Myself I'll dedicate. Let me make men know

More valor in me than my habits show. 30
Gods, put the strength o' the Leonati in me!
To shame the guise o' the world, I will begin
The fashion, less without and more within.
[*Exit.*

SCENE II. *Field of battle between the British
and Roman camps.*

Enter, from one side, LUCIUS, IACHIMO, *and
the* Roman Army: *from the other side, the
British Army;* LEONATUS POSTHUMUS *following, like a poor soldier. They march
over and go out. Then enter again, in skir-
mish,* IACHIMO *and* POSTHUMUS: *he van-
quisheth and disarmeth* IACHIMO, *and then
leaves him.*

Iach. The heaviness and guilt within my
bosom
Takes off my manhood: I have belied a lady,
The princess of this country, and the air on't
Revengingly enfeebles me; or could this carl,
A very drudge of nature's, have subdued me
In my profession? Knighthoods and honors,
borne
As I wear mine, are titles but of scorn.
If that thy gentry, Britain, go before
This lout as he exceeds our lords, the odds
Is that we scarce are men and you are gods. 10
[*Exit.*

The battle continues; the Britons *fly;* CYM-
BELINE *is taken: then enter, to his rescue,*
BELARIUS, GUIDERIUS, *and* ARVIRAGUS.

Bel. Stand, stand! We have the advan-
tage of the ground;
The lane is guarded: nothing routs us but
The villany of our fears.

Gui. }
Arv. }   Stand, stand, and fight!

Re-enter POSTHUMUS, *and seconds the* Brit-
ons: *they rescue* CYMBELINE, *and exeunt.
Then re-enter* LUCIUS, *and* IACHIMO, *with*
IMOGEN.

Luc. Away, boy, from the troops, and save
thyself;
For friends kill friends, and the disorder's
such
As war were hoodwink'd.

Iach.   'Tis their fresh supplies.

Luc. It is a day turn'd strangely: or betimes
Let's re-inforce, or fly.   [*Exeunt.*

SCENE III. *Another part of the field.*

Enter POSTHUMUS *and a* British Lord.

Lord. Camest thou from where they made
the stand?

Post.   I did:
Though you, it seems, come from the fliers.

Lord.   I did.

Post. No blame be to you, sir; for all was
lost,
But that the heavens fought: the king him-
self
Of his wings destitute, the army broken,
And but the backs of Britons seen, all flying
Through a straight lane; the enemy full-
hearted,
Lolling the tongue with slaughtering, having
work
More plentiful than tools to do't, struck down

Some mortally, some slightly touch'd, some
falling   10
Merely through fear; that the straight pass
was damm'd
With dead men hurt behind, and cowards living
To die with lengthen'd shame.

Lord.   Where was this lane?

Post. Close by the battle, ditch'd, and
wall'd with turf;
Which gave advantage to an ancient soldier,
An honest one, I warrant; who deserved
So long a breeding as his white beard came to,
In doing this for's country: athwart the lane,
He, with two striplings—lads more like to run
The country base than to commit such slaugh-
ter;   20
With faces fit for masks, or rather fairer
Than those for preservation cased, or shame,—
Made good the passage; cried to those that
fled,
'Our Britain's harts die flying, not our men:
To darkness fleet souls that fly backwards.
Stand;
Or we are Romans and will give you that
Like beasts which you shun beastly, and may
save,
But to look back in frown: stand, stand.'
These three,
Three thousand confident, in act as many—
For three performers are the file when all 30
The rest do nothing—with this word 'Stand,
stand,'
Accommodated by the place, more charming
With their own nobleness, which could have
turn'd
A distaff to a lance, gilded pale looks,
Part shame, part spirit renew'd; that some,
turn'd coward
But by example—O, a sin in war,
Damn'd in the first beginners!—gan to look
The way that they did, and to grin like lions
Upon the pikes o' the hunters. Then began
A stop i' the chaser, a retire, anon 40
A rout, confusion thick; forthwith they fly
Chickens, the way which they stoop'd eagles;
slaves,
The strides they victors made: and now our
cowards,
Like fragments in hard voyages, became
The life o' the need: having found the back-
door open
Of the unguarded hearts, heavens, how they
wound!
Some slain before; some dying; some their
friends
O'er borne i' the former wave: ten, chased by
one,
Are now each one the slaughter-man of
twenty:
Those that would die or ere resist are grown
The mortal bugs o' the field. 51

Lord.   This was strange chance:
A narrow lane, an old man, and two boys.

Post. Nay, do not wonder at it: you are
made
Rather to wonder at the things you hear
Than to work any. Will you rhyme upon't,
And vent it for a mockery? Here is one:
'Two boys, an old man twice a boy, a lane,
Preserved the Britons, was the Romans' bane.'

Lord. Nay, be not angry, sir.

Post.   'Lack, to what end ?
Who dares not stand his foe, I'll be his friend ;
For if he'll do as he is made to do,   61
I know he'll quickly fly my friendship too.
You have put me into rhyme.
     Lord.   Farewell ; you're angry.
     Post. Still going ? [*Exit Lord.*] This is a
          lord ! O noble misery,
To be i' the field, and ask ' what news ?' of
          me !
To-day how many would have given their
          honors
To have saved their carcases ! took heel to
          do't,
And yet died too ! I, in mine own woe
          charm'd,
Could not find death where I did hear him
          groan,
Nor feel him where he struck : being an ugly
          monster,   70
'Tis strange he hides him in fresh cups, soft
          beds,
Sweet words ; or hath more ministers than we
That draw his knives i' the war. Well, I will
          find him :
For being now a favorer to the Briton,
No more a Briton, I have resumed again
The part I came in : fight I will no more,
But yield me to the veriest hind that shall
Once touch my shoulder. Great the slaughter
          is
Here made by the Roman ; great the answer
          be
Britons must take. For me, my ransom's
          death ;   80
On either side I come to spend my breath ;
Which neither here I'll keep nor bear again,
But end it by some means for Imogen.

     Enter two British Captains *and* Soldiers.

     First Cap. Great Jupiter be praised ! Lu-
          cius is taken.
'Tis thought the old man and his sons were
          angels.
     Sec. Cap. There was a fourth man, in a
          silly habit,
That gave the affront with them.
     First Cap.   So 'tis reported :
But none of 'em can be found. Stand ! who's
          there ?
     Post. A Roman,
Who had not now been drooping here, if sec-
          onds
Had answer'd him.   90
     Sec. Cap.   Lay hands on him ; a dog !
A leg of Rome shall not return to tell
What crows have peck'd them here. He brags
          his service
As if he were of note : bring him to the king.

Enter Cymbeline, Belarius, Guiderius,
Arviragus, Pisanio, Soldiers, Attendants,
and Roman Captives. *The* Captains *present* Posthumus *to* Cymbeline, *who delivers him over to a* Gaoler : *then exeunt
omnes.*

          Scene IV. *A British prison.*
     Enter Posthumus *and two* Gaolers.

     First Gaol. You shall not now be stol'n,
          you have locks upon you ;
So graze as you find pasture.

     Sec. Gaol.   Ay, or a stomach.
                              [*Exeunt Gaolers.*
     Post. Most welcome, bondage ! for thou art
          a way,
I think, to liberty : yet am I better
Than one that's sick o' the gout ; since he had
          rather
Groan so in perpetuity than be cured
By the sure physician, death, who is the key
To unbar these locks. My conscience, thou
          art fetter'd
More than my shanks and wrists : you good
          gods, give me
The penitent instrument to pick that bolt,   10
Then, free for ever ! Is't enough I am sorry ?
So children temporal fathers do appease ;
Gods are more full of mercy. Must I repent ?
I cannot do it better than in gyves,
Desired more than constrain'd : to satisfy,
If of my freedom 'tis the main part, take
No stricter render of me than my all.
I know you are more clement than vile men,
Who of their broken debtors take a third,
A sixth, a tenth, letting them thrive again   20
On their abatement : that's not my desire :
For Imogen's dear life take mine ; and though
'Tis not so dear, yet 'tis a life ; you coin'd it :
'Tween man and man they weigh not every
          stamp ;
Though light, take pieces for the figure's sake :
You rather mine, being yours : and so, great
          powers,
If you will take this audit, take this life,
And cancel these cold bonds. O Imogen !
I'll speak to thee in silence.   [*Sleeps.*

Solemn music. Enter, as in an apparition,
Sicilius Leonatus, *father to Posthumus, an
old man, attired like a warrior ; leading in
his hand an ancient matron, his wife, and
mother to Posthumus, with music before
them : then, after other music, follow the
two young* Leonati, *brothers to Posthumus,
with wounds as they died in the wars. They
circle* Posthumus *round, as he lies sleeping.*

     Sici. No more, thou thunder-master, show
          Thy spite on mortal flies :   31
     With Mars fall out, with Juno chide,
          That thy adulteries
               Rates and revenges.
     Hath my poor boy done aught but well,
          Whose face I never saw ?
     I died whilst in the womb he stay'd
          Attending nature's law :
     Whose father then, as men report
          Thou orphans' father art,   40
     Thou shouldst have been, and shielded
          him
          From this earth-vexing smart.
     Moth. Lucina lent not me her aid,
          But took me in my throes ;
     That from me was Posthumus ript,
          Came crying 'mongst his foes,
          A thing of pity !
     Sici. Great nature, like his ancestry,
          Moulded the stuff so fair,
     That he deserved the praise o' the world,
          As great Sicilius' heir.   51
     First Bro. When once he was mature for
          man,
          In Britain where was he
          That could stand up his parallel ;

Or fruitful object be
In eye of Imogen, that best
Could deem his dignity ?

Moth. With marriage wherefore was he
　　mock'd,
To be exiled, and thrown
From Leonati seat, and cast　　　　60
From her his dearest one,
　　Sweet Imogen ?

Sici. Why did you suffer Iachimo,
Slight thing of Italy,
To taint his nobler heart and brain
With needless jealousy ;
And to become the geck and scorn
O' th' other's villany ?

Sec. Bro. For this from stiller seats we came,
　Our parents and us twain,　　　　70
That striking in our country's cause
Fell bravely and were slain,
Our fealty and Tenantius' right
With honor to maintain.

First Bro. Like hardiment Posthumus hath
To Cymbeline perform'd :
Then, Jupiter, thou king of gods,
Why hast thou thus adjourn'd
The graces for his merits due,
Being all to dolours turn'd ?　　　80

Sici. Thy crystal window ope ; look out ;
No longer exercise
Upon a valiant race thy harsh
And potent injuries.

Moth. Since, Jupiter, our son is good,
Take off his miseries.

Sici. Peep through thy marble mansion ;
　　help ;
Or we poor ghosts will cry
To the shining synod of the rest
Against thy deity.　　　　　90

Both Bro. Help, Jupiter ; or we appeal,
And from thy justice fly.

JUPITER *descends in thunder and lightning,
sitting upon an eagle : he throws a thunderbolt. The Ghosts fall on their knees.*

Jup. No more, you petty spirits of region
low,
Offend our hearing ; hush ! How dare you
　ghosts
Accuse the thunderer, whose bolt, you know,
Sky-planted batters all rebelling coasts ?
Poor shadows of Elysium, hence, and rest
Upon your never-withering banks of flow-
　ers :
Be not with mortal accidents opprest ;　　99
No care of yours it is ; you know 'tis ours.
Whom best I love I cross ; to make my gift,
The more delay'd, delighted. Be content ;
Your low-laid son our godhead will uplift :
His comforts thrive, his trials well are spent.
Our Jovial star reign'd at his birth, and in
Our temple was he married. Rise, and fade.
He shall be lord of lady Imogen,
And happier much by his affliction made.
This tablet lay upon his breast, wherein
Our pleasure his full fortune doth confine :
And so, away : no further with your din　111
Express impatience, lest you stir up mine.
Mount, eagle, to my palace crystalline.
　　　　　　　　　　　　　[*Ascends.*

Sici. He came in thunder ; his celestial
　breath
Was sulphurous to smell : the holy eagle
Stoop'd as to foot us : his ascension is
More sweet than our blest fields : his royal
　bird
Prunes the immortal wing and cloys his beak,
As when his god is pleased.

All.　　　　　　　　Thanks, Jupiter !

Sici. The marble pavement closes, he is
　enter'd　　　　　　　　　120
His radiant roof. Away ! and, to be blest,
Let us with care perform his great behest.
　　　　　　　　　　[*The Ghosts vanish.*

Post. [*Waking*] Sleep, thou hast been a
　grandsire, and begot
A father to me ; and thou hast created
A mother and two brothers : but, O scorn !
Gone ! they went hence so soon as they were
　born :
And so I am awake. Poor wretches that de-
　pend
On greatness' favor dream as I have done,
Wake and find nothing. But, alas, I swerve :
Many dream not to find, neither deserve,　130
And yet are steep'd in favors ; so am I,
That have this golden chance and know not
　why.
What fairies haunt this ground ? A book ? O
　rare one !
Be not, as is our fangled world, a garment
Nobler than that it covers : let thy effects
So follow, to be most unlike our courtiers,
As good as promise.

[*Reads*] ' When as a lion's whelp shall, to
himself unknown, without seeking find, and
be embraced by a piece of tender air ; and
when from a stately cedar shall be lopped
branches, which, being dead many years, shall
after revive, be jointed to the old stock and
freshly grow ; then shall Posthumus end his
miseries, Britain be fortunate and flourish in
peace and plenty.'
'Tis still a dream, or else such stuff as madmen
Tongue and brain not ; either both or nothing ;
Or senseless speaking or a speaking such
As sense cannot untie. Be what it is,
The action of my life is like it, which　　150
I'll keep, if but for sympathy.

Re-enter First Gaoler.

First Gaol. Come, sir, are you ready for
death ?

Post. Over-roasted rather ; ready long ago.

First Gaol. Hanging is the word, sir : if
you be ready for that, you are well cooked.

Post. So, if I prove a good repast to the
spectators, the dish pays the shot.

First Gaol. A heavy reckoning for you,
sir. But the comfort is, you shall be called to
no more payments, fear no more tavern-bills ;
which are often the sadness of parting, as the
procuring of mirth : you come in faint for
want of meat, depart reeling with too much
drink ; sorry that you have paid too much,
and sorry that you are paid too much ; purse
and brain both empty ; the brain the heavier
for being too light, the purse too light, being
drawn of heaviness : of this contradiction you
shall now be quit. O, the charity of a penny
cord ! it sums up thousands in a trice : you
have no true debitor and creditor but it ; of
what's past, is, and to come, the discharge :

your neck, sir, is pen, book and counters ; so
the acquittance follows.

Post. I am merrier to die than thou art to
live.

First Gaol. Indeed, sir, he that sleeps feels
not the tooth-ache : but a man that were to
sleep your sleep, and a hangman to help him
to bed, I think he would change places with
his officer ; for, look you, sir, you know not
which way you shall go.

Post. Yes, indeed do I, fellow.

First Gaol. Your death has eyes in 's head
then ; I have not seen him so pictured : you
must either be directed by some that take upon
them to know, or do take upon yourself that
which I am sure you do not know, or jump
the after inquiry on your own peril : and how
you shall speed in your journey's end, I think
you'll never return to tell one.   191

Post. I tell thee, fellow, there are none
want eyes to direct them the way I am going,
but such as wink and will not use them.

First Gaol. What an infinite mock is this,
that a man should have the best use of eyes to
see the way of blindness ! I am sure hanging's
the way of winking.

Enter a Messenger.

Mess. Knock off his manacles ; bring your
prisoner to the king.   200

Post. Thou bring'st good news ; I am called
to be made free.

First Gaol. I'll be hang'd then.

Post. Thou shalt be then freer than a
gaoler ; no bolts for the dead.

[*Exeunt Posthumus and Messenger.*

First Gaol. Unless a man would marry a
gallows and beget young gibbets, I never saw
one so prone. Yet, on my conscience, there
are verier knaves desire to live, for all he be a
Roman : and there be some of them too that
die against their wills ; so should I, if I were
one. I would we were all of one mind, and one
mind good ; O, there were desolation of
gaolers and gallowses ! I speak against my
present profit, but my wish hath a preferment
in 't.   [*Exeunt.*

SCENE V. *Cymbeline's tent.*

Enter CYMBELINE, BELARIUS, GUIDERIUS,
ARVIRAGUS, PISANIO, Lords, Officers, *and*
Attendants.

Cym.   Stand by my side, you whom the
        gods have made
Preservers of my throne. Woe is my heart
That the poor soldier that so richly fought,
Whose rags shamed gilded arms, whose naked
        breast
Stepp'd before targes of proof, cannot be
        found !
He shall be happy that can find him, if
Our grace can make him so.

Bel.   I never saw
Such noble fury in so poor a thing ;
Such precious deeds in one that promised
        nought
But beggary and poor looks.

Cym.   No tidings of him ?   10

Pis. He hath been search'd among the
        dead and living,
But no trace of him.

Cym.   To my grief, I am

The heir of his reward ; [*To Belarius, Guide-
      rius, and Arviragus*] which I will add
To you, the liver, heart and brain of Britain,
By whom I grant she lives. 'Tis now the time
To ask of whence you are. Report it.

Bel.   Sir,
In Cambria are we born, and gentlemen :
Further to boast were neither true nor modest,
Unless I add, we are honest.

Cym.   Bow your knees.
Arise my knights o' the battle : I create you
Companions to our person and will fit you 21
With dignities becoming your estates.

Enter CORNELIUS *and* Ladies.

There's business in these faces. Why so sadly
Greet you our victory ? you look like Romans,
And not o' the court of Britain.

Cor.   Hail, great king !
To sour your happiness, I must report
The queen is dead.

Cym.   Who worse than a physician
Would this report become ? But I consider,
By medicine life may be prolong'd, yet death
Will seize the doctor too. How ended she ? 30

Cor. With horror, madly dying, like her
        life,
Which, being cruel to the world, concluded
Most cruel to herself. What she confess'd
I will report, so please you : these her women
Can trip me, if I err ; who with wet cheeks
Were present when she finish'd.

Cym.   Prithee, say.

Cor. First, she confess'd she never loved
        you, only
Affected greatness got by you, not you :
Married your royalty, was wife to your place ;
Abhorr'd your person.

Cym.   She alone knew this ; 40
And, but she spoke it dying, I would not
Believe her lips in opening it. Proceed.

Cor. Your daughter, whom she bore in
        hand to love
With such integrity, she did confess
Was as a scorpion to her sight ; whose life,
But that her flight prevented it, she had
Ta'en off by poison.

Cym.   O most delicate fiend !
Who is 't can read a woman ? Is there more ?

Cor. More, sir, and worse. She did con-
        fess she had
For you a mortal mineral ; which, being took,
Should by the minute feed on life and linger-
        ing   51
By inches waste you : in which time she pur-
        posed,
By watching, weeping, tendance, kissing, to
O'ercome you with her show, and in time,
When she had fitted you with her craft, to
        work
Her son into the adoption of the crown :
But, failing of her end by his strange absence,
Grew shameless-desperate ; open'd, in despite
Of heaven and men, her purposes ; repented
The evils she hatch'd were not effected ; so 60
Despairing died.

Cym.   Heard you all this, her women ?

First Lady. We did, so please your high-
        ness.

Cym.   Mine eyes
Were not in fault, for she was beautiful ;
Mine ears, that heard her flattery ; nor my
        heart,

That thought her like her seeming; it had
　　been vicious
To have mistrusted her : yet, O my daughter !
That it was folly in me, thou mayst say,
And prove it in thy feeling. Heaven mend all !

Enter LUCIUS, IACHIMO, *the* Soothsayer, *and
other* Roman Prisoners, *guarded ;* POSTHU-
MUS *behind, and* IMOGEN.

Thou comest not, Caius, now for tribute ;
　　that
The Britons have razed out, though with the
　　loss　　　　　　　　　　　　　　　　70
Of many a bold one ; whose kinsmen have
　　made suit
That their good souls may be appeased with
　　slaughter
Of you their captives, which ourself have
　　granted :
So think of your estate.
　　Luc.　Consider, sir, the chance of war : the
　　　　day
Was yours by accident ; had it gone with us,
We should not, when the blood was cool, have
　　threaten'd
Our prisoners with the sword. But since the
　　gods
Will have it thus, that nothing but our lives
May be call'd ransom, let it come : sufficeth 80
A Roman with a Roman's heart can suffer :
Augustus lives to think on't : and so much
For my peculiar care. This one thing only
I will entreat ; my boy, a Briton born,
Let him be ransom'd : never master had
A page so kind, so duteous, diligent,
So tender over his occasions, true,
So feat, so nurse-like : let his virtue join
With my request, which I'll make bold your
　　highness
Cannot deny ; he hath done no Briton harm, 90
Though he have served a Roman : save him,
　　sir,
And spare no blood beside.
　　Cym.　　　　　　I have surely seen him :
His favor is familiar to me. Boy,
Thou hast look'd thyself into my grace,
And art mine own. I know not why, where-
　　fore,
To say ' live, boy : ' ne'er thank thy master ;
　　live :
And ask of Cymbeline what boon thou wilt,
Fitting my bounty and thy state, I'll give it ;
Yea, though thou do demand a prisoner,
The noblest ta'en.
　　Imo.　I humbly thank your highness. 100
　　Luc.　I do not bid thee beg my life, good
　　　　lad ;
And yet I know thou wilt.
　　Imo.　　　　　　No, no : alack,
There's other work in hand : I see a thing
Bitter to me as death : your life, good master,
Must shuffle for itself.
　　Luc.　　　　The boy disdains me,
He leaves me, scorns me : briefly die their
　　joys
That place them on the truth of girls and boys.
Why stands he so perplex'd ?
　　Cym.　　　　　What wouldst thou, boy ?
I love thee more and more : think more and
　　more
What's best to ask. Know'st him thou look'st
　　on ? speak,　　　　　　　　　　　110

Wilt have him live ? Is he thy kin ? thy
　　friend ?
　　Imo.　He is a Roman ; no more kin to me
Than I to your highness ; who, being born
　　your vassal,
Am something nearer.
　　Cym.　　　　　Wherefore eyest him so ?
　　Imo.　I'll tell you, sir, in private, if you
　　　　please
To give me hearing.
　　Cym.　　　　Ay, with all my heart,
And lend my best attention. What's thy name ?
　　Imo.　Fidele, sir.
　　Cym.　　　Thou'rt my good youth, my page ;
I'll be thy master : walk with me ; speak freely.
　　　　[*Cymbeline and Imogen converse apart.*
　　Bel.　Is not this boy revived from death ?
　　Arv.　　　　　　One sand another 120
Not more resembles that sweet rosy lad
Who died, and was Fidele. What think you ?
　　Gui.　The same dead thing alive.
　　Bel.　　Peace, peace ! see further ; he eyes us
　　　　not ; forbear ;
Creatures may be alike : were 't he, I am sure
He would have spoke to us.
　　Gui.　　　　　But we saw him dead.
　　Bel.　Be silent ; let's see further.
　　Pis.　　　　[*Aside*] It is my mistress :
Since she is living, let the time run on
To good or bad.
　　　　[*Cymbeline and Imogen come forward.*
　　Cym.　　　Come, stand thou by our side ;
Make thy demand aloud. [*To Iachimo*] Sir,
　　step you forth ;　　　　　　　　　　130
Give answer to this boy, and do it freely ;
Or, by our greatness and the grace of it,
Which is our honor, bitter torture shall
Winnow the truth from falsehood. On, speak
　　to him.
　　Imo.　My boon is, that this gentleman may
　　render
Of whom he had this ring.
　　Post.　　　[*Aside*] What's that to him ?
　　Cym.　That diamond upon your finger, say
How came it yours ?
　　Iach.　Thou'lt torture me to leave unspoken
　　that
Which, to be spoke, would torture thee.
　　Cym.　　　　　　How ! me ? 140
　　Iach.　I am glad to be constrain'd to utter
　　that
Which torments me to conceal. By villany
I got this ring : 'twas Leonatus' jewel ;
Whom thou didst banish ; and—which more
　　may grieve thee,
As it doth me—a nobler sir ne'er lived
'Twixt sky and ground. Wilt thou hear more,
　　my lord ?
　　Cym.　All that belongs to this.
　　Iach.　　　　That paragon, thy daughter,—
For whom my heart drops blood, and my false
　　spirits
Quail to remember— Give me leave ; I faint.
　　Cym.　My daughter ! what of her ? Renew
　　thy strength :　　　　　　　　　　150
I had rather thou shouldst live while nature
　　will
Than die ere I hear more : strive, man, and
　　speak.
　　Iach.　Upon a time,—unhappy was the
　　clock

That struck the hour!—it was in Rome,—ac-
    cursed
The mansion where!—'twas at a feast,—O,
    would
Our viands had been poison'd, or at least
Those which I heaved to head!—the good
    Posthumus—
What should I say? he was too good to be
Where ill men were; and was the best of all
Amongst the rarest of good ones,—sitting
    sadly,   160
Hearing us praise our loves of Italy
For beauty that made barren the swell'd boast
Of him that best could speak, for feature, lam-
    ing
The shrine of Venus, or straight-pight Mi-
    nerva.
Postures beyond brief nature, for condition,
A shop of all the qualities that man
Loves woman for, besides that hook of wiving,
Fairness which strikes the eye—
    Cym.   I stand on fire:
Come to the matter.
    Iach.   All too soon I shall,
Unless thou wouldst grieve quickly. This
    Posthumus,   170
Most like a noble lord in love and one
That had a royal lover, took his hint;
And, not dispraising whom we praised,—
    therein
He was as calm as virtue—he began
His mistress' picture; which by his tongue be-
    ing made,
And then a mind put in't, either our brags
Were crack'd of kitchen-trulls, or his de-
    scription
Proved us unspeaking sots.
    Cym.   Nay, nay, to the purpose.
    Iach. Your daughter's chastity—there it
    begins.
He spake of her, as Dian had hot dreams, 180
And she alone were cold: whereat I, wretch,
Made scruple of his praise; and wager'd with
    him
Pieces of gold 'gainst this which then he wore
Upon his honor'd finger, to attain
In suit the place of's bed and win this ring
By hers and mine adultery. He, true knight,
No lesser of her honor confident
Than I did truly find her, stakes this ring;
And would so, had it been a carbuncle
Of Phœbus' wheel, and might so safely, had
    it   190
Been all the worth of's car. Away to Britain
Post I in this design: well may you, sir,
Remember me at court; where I was taught
Of your chaste daughter the wide difference
'Twixt amorous and villanous. Being thus
    quench'd
Of hope, not longing, mine Italian brain
'Gan in your duller Britain operate
Most vilely; for my vantage, excellent:
And, to be brief, my practice so prevail'd,
That I return'd with simular proof enough
To make the noble Leonatus mad,   201
By wounding his belief in her renown
With tokens thus, and thus; averring notes
Of chamber-hanging, pictures, this her brace-
    let,—
O cunning, how I got it!—nay, some marks
Of secret on her person, that he could not
But think her bond of chastity quite crack'd,
I having ta'en the forfeit. Whereupon—

Methinks, I see him now—
    Post.   [*Advancing*] Ay, so thou dost,
Italian fiend! Ay me, most credulous fool,
Egregious murderer, thief, any thing   211
That's due to all the villains past, in being,
To come! O, give me cord, or knife, or
    poison,
Some upright justicer! Thou, king, send out
For torturers ingenious: it is I
That all the abhorred things o' the earth
    amend
By being worse than they. I am Posthumus,
That kill'd thy daughter:—villain-like, I lie—
That caused a lesser villain than myself,
A sacrilegious thief, to do't: the temple   220
Of virtue was she; yea, and she herself.
Spit, and throw stones, cast mire upon me, set
The dogs o' the street to bay me: every villain
Be call'd Posthumus Leonatus; and
Be villany less than 'twas! O Imogen!
My queen, my life, my wife! O Imogen,
Imogen, Imogen!
    Imo.   Peace, my lord; hear, hear—
    Post. Shall's have a play of this? Thou
    scornful page,
There lie thy part.   [*Striking her: she falls.*
    Pis.   O, gentlemen, help!
Mine and your mistress! O, my lord Post-
    humus!   230
You ne'er kill'd Imogen till now. Help, help!
Mine honor'd lady!
    Cym.   Does the world go round?
    Post. How come these staggers on me?
    Pis.   Wake, my mistress!
    Cym. If this be so, the gods do mean to
    strike me
To death with mortal joy.
    Pis.   How fares my mistress?
    Imo. O, get thee from my sight;
Thou gavest me poison: dangerous fellow,
    hence!
Breathe not where princes are.
    Cym.   The tune of Imogen!
    Pis. Lady,   239
The gods throw stones of sulphur on me, if
That box I gave you was not thought by me
A precious thing: I had it from the queen.
    Cym. New matter still?
    Imo.   It poison'd me.
    Cor.   O gods!
I left out one thing which the queen confess'd,
Which must approve thee honest: 'If Pisanio
Have,' said she, 'given his mistress that con-
    fection
Which I gave him for cordial, she is served
As I would serve a rat.'
    Cym.   What's this, Cornelius?
    Cor. The queen, sir, very oft importuned
    me
To temper poisons for her, still pretending 250
The satisfaction of her knowledge only
In killing creatures vile, as cats and dogs,
Of no esteem: I, dreading that her purpose
Was of more danger, did compound for her
A certain stuff, which, being ta'en, would cease
The present power of life, but in short time
All offices of nature should again
Do their due functions. Have you ta'en of it?
    Imo. Most like I did, for I was dead.
    Bel.   My boys,
There was our error.
    Gui.   This is, sure, Fidele. 260

Imo. Why did you throw your wedded
　　lady from you ?
Think that you are upon a rock ; and now
Throw me again.　　　　　　[*Embracing him.*
Post.　　　Hang there like fruit, my soul,
Till the tree die !
Cym.　　　How now, my flesh, my child !
What, makest thou me a dullard in this act ?
Wilt thou not speak to me ?
Imo.　　　[*Kneeling*] Your blessing, sir.
Bel. [*To Guiderius and Arviragus*] Though
　　you did love this youth, I blame ye not :
You had a motive for't.
Cym.　　　　　My tears that fall
Prove holy water on thee ! Imogen,
Thy mother's dead.
Imo.　　　I am sorry for't, my lord. 270
Cym. O, she was naught ; and long of her
　　it was
That we meet here so strangely : but her son
Is gone, we know not how nor where.
Pis.　　　　　　　　My lord,
Now fear is from me, I'll speak troth. Lord
　　Cloten,
Upon my lady's missing, came to me
With his sword drawn ; foam'd at the mouth,
　　and swore,
If I discover'd not which way she was gone,
It was my instant death. By accident,
I had a feigned letter of my master's
Then in my pocket ; which directed him 280
To seek her on the mountains near to Mil-
　　ford ;
Where, in a frenzy, in my master's garments,
Which he enforced from me, away he posts
With unchaste purpose and with oath to vio-
　　late
My lady's honor : what became of him
I further know not.
Gui.　　　　Let me end the story :
I slew him there.
Cym.　　　Marry, the gods forfend !
I would not thy good deeds should from my
　　lips
Pluck a hard sentence : prithee, valiant youth,
Deny't again.
Gui.　　　I have spoke it, and I did it. 290
Cym. He was a prince.
Gui.　　A most incivil one : the wrongs he
　　did me
Were nothing prince-like ; for he did provoke
　　me
With language that would make me spurn the
　　sea,
If it could so roar to me : I cut off's head ;
And am right glad he is not standing here
To tell this tale of mine.
Cym.　　　　I am sorry for thee :
By thine own tongue thou art condemn'd, and
　　must
Endure our law : thou'rt dead.
Imo.　　　　That headless man
I thought had been my lord.
Cym.　　　　Bind the offender, 300
And take him from our presence.
Bel.　　　　　Stay, sir king :
This man is better than the man he slew,
As well descended as thyself ; and hath
More of thee merited than a band of Clotens
Had ever scar for. [*To the Guard*] Let his
　　arms alone :
They were not born for bondage.
Cym.　　　　　Why, old soldier,

Wilt thou undo the worth thou art unpaid for,
By tasting of our wrath ? How of descent
As good as we ?
Arv.　　　In that he spake too far.
Cym. And thou shalt die for't.
Bel.　　　We will die all three : 310
But I will prove that two on's are as good
As I have given out him. My sons, I must,
For mine own part, unfold a dangerous speech,
Though, haply, well for you.
Arv.　　　　Your danger's ours.
Gui. And our good his.
Bel.　　　　Have at it then, by leave.
Thou hadst, great king, a subject who
Was call'd Belarius.
Cym.　　　　What of him ? he is
A banish'd traitor.
Bel.　　　He it is that hath
Assumed this age ; indeed a banish'd man ;
I know not how a traitor.
Cym.　　　Take him hence : 320
The whole world shall not save him.
Bel.　　　　Not too hot :
First pay me for the nursing of thy sons ;
And let it be confiscate all, so soon
As I have received it.
Cym.　　　Nursing of my sons !
Bel. I am too blunt and saucy : here's my
　　knee :
Ere I arise, I will prefer my sons ;
Then spare not the old father. Mighty sir,
These two young gentlemen, that call me father
And think they are my sons, are none of mine ;
They are the issue of your loins, my liege,
And blood of your begetting.　　　　331
Cym.　　　How ! my issue !
Bel. So sure as you your father's. I, old
　　Morgan,
Am that Belarius whom you sometime ban-
　　ish'd :
Your pleasure was my mere offence, my pun-
　　ishment
Itself, and all my treason ; that I suffer'd
Was all the harm I did. These gentle princes—
For such and so they are—these twenty years
Have I train'd up : those arts they have as I
Could put into them ; my breeding was, sir, as
Your highness knows. Their nurse, Euriphile,
Whom for the theft I wedded, stole these chil-
　　dren　　　　　　　　　　　341
Upon my banishment : I moved her to't,
Having received the punishment before,
For that which I did then : beaten for loyalty
Excited me to treason : their dear loss,
The more of you 'twas felt, the more it shaped
Unto my end of stealing them. But, gracious
　　sir,
Here are your sons again ; and I must lose
Two of the sweet'st companions in the world.
The benediction of these covering heavens 350
Fall on their heads like dew ! for they are
　　worthy
To inlay heaven with stars.
Cym.　　　Thou weep'st, and speak'st.
The service that you three have done is more
Unlike than this thou tell'st. I lost my chil-
　　dren :
If these be they, I know not how to wish
A pair of worthier sons.
Bel.　　　Be pleased awhile.
This gentleman, whom I call Polydore,
Most worthy prince, as yours, is true Guide-
　　rius :

This gentleman, my Cadwal, Arviragus,   359
Your younger princely son ; he, sir, was lapp'd
In a most curious mantle, wrought by the hand
Of his queen mother, which for more proba-
    tion
I can with ease produce.
  Cym.   Guiderius had
Upon his neck a mole, a sanguine star ;
It was a mark of wonder.
  Bel.   This is he ;
Who hath upon him still that natural stamp :
It was wise nature's end in the donation,
To be his evidence now.
  Cym.   O, what, am I
A mother to the birth of three ? Ne'er mother
Rejoiced deliverance more. Blest pray you be,
That, after this strange starting from your
    orbs,   371
You may reign in them now ! O Imogen,
Thou hast lost by this a kingdom.
  Imo.   No, my lord ;
I have got two worlds by 't. O my gentle
    brothers,
Have we thus met ? O, never say hereafter
But I am truest speaker : you call'd me
    brother,
When I was but your sister ; I you brothers,
When ye were so indeed.
  Cym.   Did you e'er meet ?
  Arv.   Ay, my good lord.
  Gui.   And at first meeting loved ;
Continued so, until we thought he died.   380
  Cor.   By the queen's dram she swallow'd.
  Cym.   O rare instinct !
When shall I hear all through ? This fierce
    abridgement
Hath to it circumstantial branches, which
Distinction should be rich in. Where ? how
    lived you ?
And when came you to serve our Roman cap-
    tive ?
How parted with your brothers ? how first met
    them ?
Why fled you from the court ? and whither ?
    These,
And your three motives to the battle, with
I know not how much more, should be de-
    manded ;
And all the other by-dependencies,   390
From chance to chance : but nor the time nor
    place
Will serve our long inter'gatories. See,
Posthumus anchors upon Imogen,
And she, like harmless lightning, throws her
    eye
On him, her brothers, me, her master, hitting
Each object with a joy : the counterchange
Is severally in all. Let's quit this ground,
And smoke the temple with our sacrifices.
  [*To Belarius*] Thou art my brother ; so we'll
    hold thee ever.
  Imo.   You are my father too, and did re-
    lieve me,   400
To see this gracious season.
  Cym.   All o'erjoy'd,
Save these in bonds : let them be joyful too,
For they shall taste our comfort.
  Imo.   My good master,
I will yet do you service.
  Luc.   Happy be you !
  Cym.   The forlorn soldier, that so nobly
    fought,

He would have well becomed this place, and
    graced
The thankings of a king.
  Post.   I am, sir,
The soldier that did company these three
In poor beseeming ; 'twas a fitment for   409
The purpose I then follow'd. That I was he,
Speak, Iachimo : I had you down and might
Have made you finish.
  Iach.   [*Kneeling*] I am down again :
But now my heavy conscience sinks my knee,
As then your force did. Take that life, beseech
    you,
Which I so often owe : but your ring first ;
And here the bracelet of the truest princess
That ever swore her faith.
  Post.   Kneel not to me :
The power that I have on you is to spare you ;
The malice towards you to forgive you : live,
And deal with others better.
  Cym.   Nobly doom'd ! 420
We'll learn our freeness of a son-in-law ;
Pardon's the word to all.
  Arv.   You holp us, sir,
As you did mean indeed to be our brother ;
Joy'd are we that you are.
  Post.   Your servant, princes. Good my lord
    of Rome,
Call forth your soothsayer : as I slept, me-
    thought
Great Jupiter, upon his eagle back'd,
Appear'd to me, with other spritely shows
Of mine own kindred : when I waked, I found
This label on my bosom ; whose containing
Is so from sense in hardness, that I can   431
Make no collection of it : let him show
His skill in the construction.
  Luc.   Philarmonus !
  Sooth.   Here, my good lord.
  Luc.   Read, and declare the meaning.
  Sooth.   [*Reads*] 'When as a lion's whelp
shall, to himself unknown, without seeking
find, and be embraced by a piece of tender
air ; and when from a stately cedar shall be
lopped branches, which, being dead many
years, shall after revive, be jointed to the old
stock, and freshly grow ; then shall Posthu-
mus end his miseries, Britain be fortunate and
flourish in peace and plenty.'
Thou, Leonatus, art the lion's whelp ;
The fit and apt construction of thy name,
Being Leo-natus, doth import so much.
[*To Cymbeline*] The piece of tender air, thy
    virtuous daughter,
Which we call ' mollis aer ; ' and ' mollis aer '
We term it ' mulier : ' which ' mulier ' I divine
Is this most constant wife ; who, even now,
Answering the letter of the oracle,   450
Unknown to you, unsought, were clipp'd about
With this most tender air.
  Cym.   This hath some seeming.
  Sooth.   The lofty cedar, royal Cymbeline,
Personates thee : and thy lopp'd branches point
Thy two sons forth ; who, by Belarius stol'n,
For many years thought dead, are now revived,
To the majestic cedar join'd, whose issue
Promises Britain peace and plenty.
  Cym.   Well ;
My peace we will begin. And, Caius Lucius,
Although the victor, we submit to Cæsar,   460
And to the Roman empire ; promising
To pay our wonted tribute, from the which

We were dissuaded by our wicked queen ;
Whom heavens, in justice, both on her and
    hers,
Have laid most heavy hand.
    Sooth.   The fingers of the powers above do
    tune
The harmony of this peace. The vision
Which I made known to Lucius, ere the stroke
Of this yet scarce-cold battle, at this instant
Is full accomplish'd ; for the Roman eagle, 470
From south to west on wing soaring aloft,
Lessen'd herself, and in the beams o' the sun
So vanish'd : which foreshow'd our princely
    eagle,
The imperial Cæsar, should again unite

His favor with the radiant Cymbeline,
Which shines here in the west.
    Cym.   Laud we the gods ;
And let our crooked smokes climb to their
    nostrils
From our blest altars. Publish we this peace
To all our subjects. Set we forward : let
A Roman and a British ensign wave   480
Friendly together : so through Lud's-town
    march :
And in the temple of great Jupiter
Our peace we'll ratify ; seal it with feasts.
Set on there ! Never was a war did cease,
Ere bloody hands were wash'd, with such a
    peace.   *[Exeunt.*

THE TEMPEST.

(WRITTEN ABOUT 1610.)

INTRODUCTION.

The Tempest was probably written late in the year 1610. A few months previously had appeared an account of the wreck of Sir George Somers' ship in a tempest off the Bermudas, entitled *A Discovery of the Bermudas, otherwise called the Ile of Divels, etc.*, written by Silvester Jourdan. Shakespeare (Act I., Sc. II., L. 229) makes mention of "the still-vexed Bermoothes;" and several points of resemblance render it probable that in writing the play he had Jourdan's tract before him. Beyond the suggestions obtained from this tract no source of the story of the play can be pointed out. Mention was made by the poet Collins of a tale called *Aurelis and Isabella* containing the same incidents, but in this point he was mistaken, though he may have seen some other Italian story which resembled *The Tempest.* The name Setebos (Sycorax's god) and perhaps other names of persons Shakespeare found in Eden's *History of Travaile,* published in 1577. *The Tempest,* although far from lacking dramatic or human interest, has something in its spirit of the nature of a clear and solemn vision. It expresses Shakespeare's highest and serenest view of life. Prospero, the great enchanter, is altogether the opposite of the vulgar magician. With command over the elemental powers, which study has brought to him, he possesses moral grandeur, and a command over himself, in spite of occasional fits of involuntary abstraction and of intellectual impatience ; he looks down on life, and sees through it, yet will not refuse to take his part in it. In Shakespeare's early play of supernatural agencies—*A Midsummer Night's Dream*—the "human mortals" were made the sport of the frolic-loving elves ; here the supernatural powers attend on and obey their ruler, man. It has been suggested that Prospero, the great enchanter, is Shakespeare himself, and that when he breaks his staff, drowns his book, and dismisses his airy spirits, going back to the duties of his dukedom, Shakespeare was thinking of his own resigning of his powers of imaginative enchantment, his parting from the theatre, where his attendant spirits had played their parts, and his return to Stratford. The persons in this play, while remaining real and living, are conceived in a more abstract way, more as types than those in any other work of Shakespeare. Prospero is the highest wisdom and moral attainment ; Gonzalo is humorous common-sense incarnated ; all that is meanest and most despicable appears in the wretched conspirators ; Miranda, whose name seems to suggest wonder, is almost an elemental being, framed in the purest and simplest type of womanhood, yet made substantial by contrast with Ariel, who is an unbodied joy, too much a creature of light and air to know human affection or human sorrow ; Caliban (the name formed from cannibal) stands at the other extreme, with all the elements in him—appetites, intellect, even imagination—out of which man emerges into early civilization, but with a moral nature that is still gross and malignant. Over all presides Prospero like a providence ; and the spirit of reconciliation, of forgiveness, harmonizing the contentions of men, appears in *The Tempest* in the same noble manner as in *The Winter's Tale, Cymbeline,* and *Henry VIII.* The action of the play is comprised within three hours.

DRAMATIS PERSONÆ.

ALONSO, King of Naples.
SEBASTIAN, his brother.
PROSPERO, the right Duke of Milan.
ANTONIO, his brother, the usurping Duke of Milan.
FERDINAND, son to the King of Naples.
GONZALO, an honest old Counsellor.
ADRIAN, } Lords.
FRANCISCO, }
CALIBAN, a savage and deformed Slave.
TRINCULO, a Jester.
STEPHANO, a drunken Butler.

Master of a Ship.
Boatswain.
Mariners.
MIRANDA, daughter to Prospero.
ARIEL, an airy Spirit.
IRIS,
CERES,
JUNO, } presented by Spirits.
NYMPHS,
REAPERS,
Other Spirits attending on Prospero.

SCENE—*A ship at Sea : an island.*

ACT I.

SCENE I. *On a ship at sea: a tempestuous noise of thunder and lightning heard.*

Enter a Ship-Master *and* a Boatswain.

Mast. Boatswain!

Boats. Here, master: what cheer?

Mast. Good, speak to the mariners: fall to't, yarely, or we run ourselves aground: bestir, bestir.   [*Exit.*

Enter Mariners.

Boats. Heigh, my hearts! cheerly, cheerly, my hearts! yare, yare! Take in the topsail. Tend to the master's whistle. Blow, till thou burst thy wind, if room enough!

Enter ALONSO, SEBASTIAN, ANTONIO, FERDI-
NAND, GONZALO, *and others.*

Alon. Good boatswain, have care. Where's the master? Play the men.   11

Boats. I pray now, keep below.

Ant. Where is the master, boatswain?

Boats. Do you not hear him? You mar our labor: keep your cabins: you do assist the storm.

Gon. Nay, good, be patient.

Boats. When the sea is. Hence! What cares these roarers for the name of king? To cabin: silence! trouble us not.

Gon. Good, yet remember whom thou hast aboard.   21

Boats. None that I more love than myself. You are a counsellor; if you can command these elements to silence, and work the peace of the present, we will not hand a rope more; use your authority: if you cannot, give thanks you have lived so long, and make yourself ready in your cabin for the mischance of the hour, if it so hap. Cheerly, good hearts! Out of our way, I say.   [*Exit.*

Gon. I have great comfort from this fellow: methinks he hath no drowning mark upon him; his complexion is perfect gallows. Stand fast, good Fate, to his hanging: make the rope of his destiny our cable, for our own doth little advantage. If he be not born to be hanged, our case is miserable.   [*Exeunt.*

Re-enter Boatswain.

Boats. Down with the topmast! yare! lower, lower! Bring her to try with maincourse. [*A cry within.*] A plague upon this howling! they are louder than the weather or our office.   40

Re-enter SEBASTIAN, ANTONIO, *and* GONZALO.

Yet again! what do you here? Shall we give o'er and drown? Have you a mind to sink?

Seb. A pox o' your throat, you bawling, blasphemous, incharitable dog!

Boats. Work you then.

Ant. Hang, cur! hang, you whoreson, insolent noisemaker! We are less afraid to be drowned than thou art.

Gon. I'll warrant him for drowning; though the ship were no stronger than a nutshell and as leaky as an unstanched wench.

Boats. Lay her a-hold, a-hold! set her two courses off to sea again; lay her off.

Enter Mariners *wet.*

Mariners. All lost! to prayers, to prayers! all lost!

Boats. What, must our mouths be cold?

Gon. The king and prince at prayers! let's assist them,
For our case is as theirs.

Seb.   I'm out of patience.

Ant. We are merely cheated of our lives by drunkards:
This wide-chapp'd rascal—would thou mightst lie drowning   60
The washing of ten tides!

Gon.   He'll be hang'd yet,
Though every drop of water swear against it
And gape at widest to glut him.

[*A confused noise within:* 'Mercy on us!'—
'We split, we split!'—'Farewell, my wife and children!'—
'Farewell, brother!'—'We split, we split, we split!']

Ant. Let's all sink with the king.

Seb. Let's take leave of him.

[*Exeunt Ant. and Seb.*

Gon. Now would I give a thousand furlongs of sea for an acre of barren ground, long heath, brown furze, any thing. The wills above be done! but I would fain die a dry death.   [*Exeunt.*

SCENE II. *The island. Before* PROSPERO'S *cell.*

Enter PROSPERO *and* MIRANDA.

Mir. If by your art, my dearest father, you have
Put the wild waters in this roar, allay them.
The sky, it seems, would pour down stinking pitch,
But that the sea, mounting to the welkin's cheek,
Dashes the fire out. O, I have suffered
With those that I saw suffer: a brave vessel,
Who had, no doubt, some noble creature in her,
Dash'd all to pieces. O, the cry did knock
Against my very heart. Poor souls, they perish'd.
Had I been any god of power, I would   10
Have sunk the sea within the earth or ere
It should the good ship so have swallow'd and
The fraughting souls within her.

Pros.   Be collected:
No more amazement: tell your piteous heart
There's no harm done.

Mir.   O, woe the day!

Pros.   No harm.
I have done nothing but in care of thee,
Of thee, my dear one, thee, my daughter, who
Art ignorant of what thou art, nought knowing
Of whence I am, nor that I am more better
Than Prospero, master of a full poor cell,   20
And thy no greater father.

Mir.   More to know
Did never meddle with my thoughts.

Pros.   'Tis time
I should inform thee farther. Lend thy hand,
And pluck my magic garment from me. So:
[*Lays down his mantle.*
Lie there, my art. Wipe thou thine eyes; have comfort.

The direful spectacle of the wreck, which
   touch'd
The very virtue of compassion in thee,
I have with such provision in mine art
So safely ordered that there is no soul—
No, not so much perdition as an hair   30
Betid to any creature in the vessel
Which thou heard'st cry, which thou saw'st
   sink. Sit down ;
For thou must now know farther.
   Mir.   You have often
Begun to tell me what I am, but stopp'd
And left me to a bootless inquisition,
Concluding ' Stay : not yet.'
   Pros.   The hour's now come ;
The very minute bids thee ope thine ear ;
Obey and be attentive. Canst thou remember
A time before we came unto this cell ?
I do not think thou canst, for then thou wast
   not   40
Out three years old.
   Mir.   Certainly, sir, I can.
   Pros. By what ? by any other house or
   person ?
Of any thing the image tell me that
Hath kept with thy remembrance.
   Mir.   'Tis far off
And rather like a dream than an assurance
That my remembrance warrants. Had I not
Four or five women once that tended me ?
   Pros. Thou hadst, and more, Miranda. But
   how is it
That this lives in thy mind ? What seest thou
   else
In the dark backward and abysm of time ? 50
If thou remember'st aught ere thou camest
   here,
How thou camest here thou mayst.
   Mir.   But that I do not.
   Pros. Twelve year since, Miranda, twelve
   year since,
Thy father was the Duke of Milan and
A prince of power.
   Mir.   Sir, are not you my father ?
   Pros. Thy mother was a piece of virtue,
   and
She said thou wast my daughter ; and thy
   father
Was Duke of Milan ; and thou his only heir
And princess no worse issued.
   Mir.   O the heavens !
What foul play had we, that we came from
   thence ?
Or blessed was't we did ?
   Pros.   Both, both, my girl : 61
By foul play, as thou say'st, were we heaved
   thence,
But blessedly holp hither.
   Mir.   O, my heart bleeds
To think o' the teen that I have turn'd you to,
Which is from my remembrance ! Please you,
   farther.
   Pros. My brother and thy uncle, call'd An-
   tonio—
I pray thee, mark me—that a brother should
Be so perfidious !—he whom next thyself
Of all the world I loved and to him put
The manage of my state ; as at that time 70
Through all the signories it was the first
And Prospero the prime duke, being so re-
   puted
In dignity, and for the liberal arts
Without a parallel ; those being all my study,

The government I cast upon my brother
And to my state grew stranger, being trans-
   ported
And rapt in secret studies. Thy false uncle—
Dost thou attend me ?
   Mir.   Sir, most heedfully.
   Pros. Being once perfected how to grant
   suits,
How to deny them, who to advance and who
To trash for over-topping, new created 81
The creatures that were mine, I say, or
   changed 'em,
Or else new form'd 'em ; having both the key
Of officer and office, set all hearts i' the state
To what tune pleased his ear ; that now he was
The ivy which had hid my princely trunk,
And suck'd my verdure out on't. Thou at-
   tend'st not.
   Mir.   O, good sir, I do.
   Pros.   I pray thee, mark me.
I, thus neglecting worldly ends, all dedicated
To closeness and the bettering of my mind 90
With that which, but by being so retired,
O'er-prized all popular rate, in my false
   brother
Awaked an evil nature ; and my trust,
Like a good parent, did beget of him
A falsehood in its contrary as great
As my trust was ; which had indeed no limit,
A confidence sans bound. He being thus
   lorded,
Not only with what my revenue yielded,
But what my power might else exact, like one
Who having into truth, by telling of it, 100
Made such a sinner of his memory,
To credit his own lie, he did believe
He was indeed the duke ; out o' the substitu-
   tion,
And executing the outward face of royalty,
With all prerogative : hence his ambition
   growing—
Dost thou hear ?
   Mir.   Your tale, sir, would cure deafness.
   Pros. To have no screen between this part
   he play'd
And him he play'd it for, he needs will be
Absolute Milan. Me, poor man, my library
Was dukedom large enough : of temporal roy-
   alties 110
He thinks me now incapable ; confederates—
So dry he was for sway—wi' the King of
   Naples
To give him annual tribute, do him homage,
Subject his coronet to his crown and bend
The dukedom yet unbow'd—alas, poor Mi-
   lan !—
To most ignoble stooping.
   Mir.   O the heavens !
   Pros. Mark his condition and the event ;
   then tell me
If this might be a brother.
   Mir.   I should sin
To think but nobly of my grandmother :
Good wombs have borne bad sons.
   Pros.   Now the condition. 120
The King of Naples, being an enemy
To me inveterate, hearkens my brother's suit ;
Which was, that he, in lieu o' the premises
Of homage and I know not how much tribute,
Should presently extirpate me and mine
Out of the dukedom and confer fair Milan
With all the honors on my brother : whereon,
A treacherous army levied, one midnight

Fated to the purpose did Antonio open
The gates of Milan, and, i' the dead of dark-
　　ness,　　　　　　　　　　　　　130
The ministers for the purpose hurried thence
Me and thy crying self.
　　Mir.　　　　　　　Alack, for pity!
I, not remembering how I cried out then,
Will cry it o'er again : it is a hint
That wrings mine eyes to't.
　　Pros.　　　　　Hear a little further
And then I'll bring thee to the present business
Which now's upon's ; without the which this
　　story
Were most impertinent.
　　Mir.　　　　Wherefore did they not
That hour destroy us?
　　Pros.　　　　Well demanded, wench :
My tale provokes that question. Dear, they
　　durst not,　　　　　　　　　　140
So dear the love my people bore me, nor set
A mark so bloody on the business, but
With colors fairer painted their foul ends.
In few, they hurried us aboard a bark,
Bore us some leagues to sea ; where they pre-
　　pared
A rotten carcass of a boat, not rigg'd,
Nor tackle, sail, nor mast ; the very rats
Instinctively had quit it : there they hoist us,
To cry to the sea that roar'd to us, to sigh
To the winds whose pity, sighing back again,
Did us but loving wrong.　　　　　　151
　　Mir.　　　　Alack, what trouble
Was I then to you!
　　Pros.　　　　O, a cherubin
Thou wast that did preserve me. Thou didst
　　smile,
Infused with a fortitude from heaven,
When I have deck'd the sea with drops full
　　salt,
Under my burthen groan'd ; which raised in
　　me
An undergoing stomach, to bear up
Against what should ensue.
　　Mir.　　　　How came we ashore?
　　Pros. By Providence divine.
Some food we had and some fresh water that
A noble Neapolitan, Gonzalo,　　　161
Out of his charity, being then appointed
Master of this design, did give us, with
Rich garments, linens, stuffs and necessaries,
Which since have steaded much ; so, of his
　　gentleness,
Knowing I loved my books, he furnish'd me
From mine own library with volumes that
I prize above my dukedom.
　　Mir.　　　　Would I might
But ever see that man!
　　Pros. Now I arise : [*Resumes his mantle.*
Sit still, and hear the last of our sea-sorrow.
Here in this island we arrived ; and here　171
Have I, thy schoolmaster, made thee more
　　profit
Than other princesses can that have more time
For vainer hours and tutors not so careful.
　　Mir. Heavens thank you for't! And now,
　　I pray you, sir,
For still 'tis beating in my mind, your reason
For raising this sea-storm?
　　Pros.　　　　Know thus far forth.
By accident most strange, bountiful Fortune,
Now my dear lady, hath mine enemies
Brought to this shore ; and by my prescience

I find my zenith doth depend upon　　181
A most auspicious star, whose influence
If now I court not but omit, my fortunes
Will ever after droop. Here cease more ques-
　　tions :
Thou art inclined to sleep ; 'tis a good dulness,
And give it way : I know thou canst not
　　choose.　　　　　[*Miranda sleeps.*
Come away, servant, come. I am ready now.
Approach, my Ariel, come.

Enter ARIEL.

　　Ari. All hail, great master! grave sir, hail!
　　I come
To answer thy best pleasure ; be't to fly,　190
To swim, to dive into the fire, to ride
On the curl'd clouds, to thy strong bidding
　　task
Ariel and all his quality.
　　Pros.　　　　Hast thou, spirit,
Perform'd to point the tempest that I bade
　　thee?
　　Ari. To every article.
I boarded the king's ship ; now on the beak,
Now in the waist, the deck, in every cabin,
I flamed amazement : sometime I'd divide,
And burn in many places ; on the topmast,
The yards and bowsprit, would I flame dis-
　　tinctly,　　　　　　　　　　200
Then meet and join. Jove's lightnings, the pre-
　　cursors
O' the dreadful thunder-claps, more momen-
　　tary
And sight-outrunning were not ; the fire and
　　cracks
Of sulphurous roaring the most mighty Nep-
　　tune
Seem to besiege and make his bold waves
　　tremble,
Yea, his dread trident shake.
　　Pros.　　　　My brave spirit!
Who was so firm, so constant, that this coil
Would not infect his reason?
　　Ari.　　　　Not a sou
But felt a fever of the mad and play'd
Some tricks of desperation. All but mariners
Plunged in the foaming brine and quit the
　　vessel,　　　　　　　　　　211
Then all afire with me : the king's son, Ferdi-
　　nand,
With hair up-staring,—then like reeds, not
　　hair,—
Was the first man that leap'd ; cried, ' Hell is
　　empty,
And all the devils are here.'
　　Pros.　　　　Why, that's my spirit!
But was not this nigh shore?
　　Ari.　　　　Close by, my master.
　　Pros. But are they, Ariel, safe?
　　Ari.　　　　Not a hair perish'd ;
On their sustaining garments not a blemish,
But fresher than before : and, as thou badest
　　me,
In troops I have dispersed them 'bout the isle.
The king's son have I landed by himself ;　221
Whom I left cooling of the air with sighs
In an odd angle of the isle and sitting,
His arms in this sad knot.
　　Pros.　　　　Of the king's ship
The mariners say how thou hast disposed
And all the rest o' the fleet.
　　Ari.　　　　Safely in harbor

Is the king's ship ; in the deep nook, where
    once
Thou call'dst me up at midnight to fetch dew
From the still-vex'd Bermoothes, there she's
    hid :
The mariners all under hatches stow'd ;   230
Who, with a charm join'd to their suffer'd
    labor,
I have left asleep ; and for the rest o' the fleet
Which I dispersed, they all have met again
And are upon the Mediterranean flote,
Bound sadly home for Naples,
Supposing that they saw the king's ship
    wreck'd
And his great person perish.

    Pros.   Ariel, thy charge
Exactly is perform'd : but there's more work.
What is the time o' the day ?
    Ari.   Past the mid season.
    Pros. At least two glasses. The time 'twixt
    six and now   240
Must by us both be spent most preciously.
    Ari. Is there more toil ? Since thou dost
    give me pains,
Let me remember thee what thou hast prom-
    ised,
Which is not yet perform'd me.
    Pros.   How now ? moody ?
What is't thou canst demand ?
    Ari.   My liberty.
    Pros. Before the time be out ? no more !
    Ari.   I prithee,
Remember I have done thee worthy service ;
Told thee no lies, made thee no mistakings,
    served
Without or grudge or grumblings : thou didst
    promise
To bate me a full year.
    Pros.   Dost thou forget   250
From what a torment I did free thee ?
    Ari.   No.
    Pros. Thou dost, and think'st it much to
    tread the ooze
Of the salt deep,
To run upon the sharp wind of the north,
To do me business in the veins o' the earth
When it is baked with frost.
    Ari.   I do not, sir.
    Pros. Thou liest, malignant thing ! Hast
    thou forgot
The foul witch Sycorax, who with age and
    envy
Was grown into a hoop ? hast thou forgot
    her ?
    Ari. No, sir.
    Pros.   Thou hast. Where was she born ?
    speak ; tell me.   260
    Ari. Sir, in Argier.
    Pros.   O, was she so ? I must
Once in a month recount what thou hast been,
Which thou forget'st. This damn'd witch
    Sycorax,
For mischiefs manifold and sorceries terrible
To enter human hearing, from Argier,
Thou know'st, was banish'd : for one thing she
    did
They would not take her life. Is not this true ?
    Ari. Ay, sir.
    Pros. This blue-eyed hag was hither
    brought with child
And here was left by the sailors. Thou, my
    slave,

As thou report'st thyself, wast then her serv-
    ant ;
And, for thou wast a spirit too delicate
To act her earthy and abhorr'd commands,
Refusing her grand hests, she did confine thee,
By help of her more potent ministers
And in her most unmitigable rage,
Into a cloven pine ; within which rift
Imprison'd thou didst painfully remain
A dozen years ; within which space she died
And left thee there ; where thou didst vent thy
    groans   280
As fast as mill-wheels strike. Then was this
    island—
Save for the son that she did litter here,
A freckled whelp hag-born—not honor'd with
A human shape.
    Ari.   Yes, Caliban her son.
    Pros. Dull thing, I say so ; he, that Caliban
Whom now I keep in service. Thou best
    know'st
What torment I did find thee in ; thy groans
Did make wolves howl and penetrate the
    breasts
Of ever angry bears : it was a torment
To lay upon the damn'd, which Sycorax   290
Could not again undo : it was mine art,
When I arrived and heard thee, that made
    gape
The pine and let thee out.
    Ari.   I thank thee, master.
    Pros. If thou more murmur'st, I will rend
    an oak
And peg thee in his knotty entrails till
Thou hast howl'd away twelve winters.
    Ari.   Pardon, master ;
I will be correspondent to command
And do my spiriting gently.
    Pros.   Do so, and after two days
I will discharge thee.
    Ari.   That's my noble master !
What shall I do ? say what ; what shall I do ?
    Pros. Go make thyself like a nymph o' the
    sea : be subject   301
To no sight but thine and mine, invisible
To every eyeball else. Go take this shape
And hither come in't : go, hence with dili-
    gence !   [*Exit Ariel.*
Awake, dear heart, awake ! thou hast slept
    well ;
Awake !
    Mir. The strangeness of your story put
Heaviness in me.
    Pros.   Shake it off. Come on ;
We'll visit Caliban my slave, who never
Yields us kind answer.
    Mir.   'Tis a villain, sir,
I do not love to look on.
    Pros.   But, as 'tis,   310
We cannot miss him : he does make our fire,
Fetch in our wood and serves in offices
That profit us. What, ho ! slave ! Caliban !
Thou earth, thou ! speak.
    Cal. [*Within*] There's wood enough within.
    Pros. Come forth, I say ! there's other
    business for thee :
Come, thou tortoise ! when ?

    Re-enter Ariel *like a water-nymph.*

Fine apparition ! My quaint Ariel,
Hark in thine ear.

Ari.   My lord, it shall be done. [*Exit.*
Pros. Thou poisonous slave, got by the
devil himself
Upon thy wicked dam, come forth!   320

Enter CALIBAN.

Cal. As wicked dew as e'er my mother
brush'd
With raven's feather from unwholesome fen
Drop on you both! a south-west blow on ye
And blister you all o'er!
Pros. For this, be sure, to-night thou shalt
have cramps,
Side-stitches that shall pen thy breath up;
urchins
Shall, for that vast of night that they may
work,
All exercise on thee; thou shalt be pinch'd
As thick as honeycomb, each pinch more
stinging
Than bees that made 'em.
Cal.   I must eat my dinner.   330
This island's mine, by Sycorax my mother,
Which thou takest from me. When thou
camest first,
Thou strokedst me and madest much of me,
wouldst give me
Water with berries in't, and teach me how
To name the bigger light, and how the less,
That burn by day and night: and then I loved
thee
And show'd thee all the qualities o' the isle,
The fresh springs, brine-pits, barren place and
fertile:
Cursed be I that did so! All the charms
Of Sycorax, toads, beetles, bats, light on you!
For I am all the subjects that you have,   341
Which first was mine own king: and here you
sty me
In this hard rock, whiles you do keep from me
The rest o' the island.
Pros.   Thou most lying slave,
Whom stripes may move, not kindness! I have
used thee,
Filth as thou art, with human care, and lodged
thee
In mine own cell, till thou didst seek to vio-
late
The honor of my child.
Cal. O ho, O ho! would't had been done!
Thou didst prevent me; I had peopled else
This isle with Calibans.   351
Pros.   Abhorred slave,
Which any print of goodness wilt not take,
Being capable of all ill! I pitied thee,
Took pains to make thee speak, taught thee
each hour
One thing or other: when thou didst not,
savage,
Know thine own meaning, but wouldst gabble
like
A thing most brutish, I endow'd thy purposes
With words that made them known. But thy
vile race,
Though thou didst learn, had that in't which
good natures
Could not abide to be with; therefore wast
thou   360
Deservedly confined into this rock,
Who hadst deserved more than a prison.
Cal. You taught me language; and my
profit on't

Is, I know how to curse. The red plague rid
you
For learning me your language!
Pros.   Hag-seed, hence!
Fetch us in fuel; and be quick, thou'rt best,
To answer other business. Shrug'st thou,
malice?
If thou neglect'st or dost unwillingly
What I command, I'll rack thee with old
cramps,
Fill all thy bones with aches, make thee roar
That beasts shall tremble at thy din.   371
Cal.   No, pray thee.
[*Aside*] I must obey: his art is of such power,
It would control my dam's god, Setebos,
And make a vassal of him.
Pros.   So, slave; hence! [*Exit Caliban.*

Re-enter ARIEL, *invisible, playing and singing;*
FERDINAND *following.*

ARIEL'S *song.*

Come unto these yellow sands,
        And then take hands:
Courtsied when you have and kiss'd
        The wild waves whist,
Foot it featly here and there;   380
And, sweet sprites, the burthen bear.
Burthen [*dispersedly*]. Hark, hark!
        Bow-wow.
        The watch-dogs bark:
        Bow-wow
Ari. Hark, hark! I hear
        The strain of strutting chanticleer
        Cry, Cock-a-diddle-dow.

Fer. Where should this music be? i' the air
        or the earth?
It sounds no more: and, sure, it waits upon
Some god o' the island. Sitting on a bank,
Weeping again the king my father's wreck,
This music crept by me upon the waters,   391
Allaying both their fury and my passion
With its sweet air: thence I have follow'd it,
Or it hath drawn me rather. But 'tis gone.
No, it begins again.

ARIEL *sings.*

Full fathom five thy father lies;
        Of his bones are coral made;
Those are pearls that were his eyes:
        Nothing of him that doth fade
But doth suffer a sea-change   400
Into something rich and strange.
Sea-nymphs hourly ring his knell:
        Burthen. Ding-dong.
Ari. Hark! now I hear them,—Ding-dong,
bell.
Fer. The ditty does remember my drown'd
father.
This is no mortal business, nor no sound
That the earth owes. I hear it now above me.
Pros. The fringed curtains of thine eye ad-
vance
And say what thou seest yond.
Mir.   What is't? a spirit?
Lord, how it looks about! Believe me, sir,
It carries a brave form. But 'tis a spirit.   411
Pros. No, wench; it eats and sleeps and
hath such senses
As we have, such. This gallant which thou
seest
Was in the wreck; and, but he's something
stain'd

With grief that's beauty's canker, thou mightst
  call him
A goodly person : he hath lost his fellows
And strays about to find 'em.
 Mir.   I might call him
A thing divine, for nothing natural
I ever saw so noble.
 Pros. [*Aside*] It goes on, I see,
As my soul prompts it. Spirit, fine spirit ! I'll
  free thee   420
Within two days for this.
 Fer.   Most sure, the goddess
On whom these airs attend ! Vouchsafe my
  prayer
May know if you remain upon this island ;
And that you will some good instruction give
How I may bear me here : my prime request,
Which I do last pronounce, is, O you wonder !
If you be maid or no ?
 Mir.   No wonder, sir ;
But certainly a maid.
 Fer.   My language ! heavens !
I am the best of them that speak this speech,
Were I but where 'tis spoken.
 Pros.   How ? the best ? 430
What wert thou, if the King of Naples heard
  thee ?
 Fer. A single thing, as I am now, that won-
  ders
To hear thee speak of Naples. He does hear
  me ;
And that he does I weep : myself am Naples,
Who with mine eyes, never since at ebb, be-
  held
The king my father wreck'd.
 Mir.   Alack, for mercy !
 Fer. Yes, faith, and all his lords ; the Duke
  of Milan
And his brave son being twain.
 Pros.   [*Aside*] The Duke of Milan
And his more braver daughter could control
  thee,
If now 'twere fit to do't. At the first sight 440
They have changed eyes. Delicate Ariel,
I'll set thee free for this. [*To Fer.*] A word,
  good sir ;
I fear you have done yourself some wrong : a
  word.
 Mir. Why speaks my father so ungently ?
  This
Is the third man that e'er I saw, the first,
That e'er I sigh'd for : pity move my father
To be inclined my way !
 Fer.   O, if a virgin,
And your affection not gone forth, I'll make
  you
The queen of Naples.
 Pros.   Soft, sir ! one word more.
[*Aside*] They are both in either's powers ; but
  this swift business   450
I must uneasy make, lest too light winning
Make the prize light. [*To Fer.*] One word
  more ; I charge thee
That thou attend me : thou dost here usurp
The name thou owest not ; and hast put thy-
  self
Upon this island as a spy, to win it
From me, the lord on't.
 Fer.   No, as I am a man.
 Mir. There's nothing ill can dwell in such
  a temple :

If the ill spirit have so fair a house,
Good things will strive to dwell with't.
 Pros.   Follow me.
Speak not you for him ; he's a traitor. Come ;
I'll manacle thy neck and feet together : 461
Sea-water shalt thou drink ; thy food shall be
The fresh-brook muscles, wither'd roots and
  husks
Wherein the acorn cradled. Follow.
 Fer.   No ;
I will resist such entertainment till
Mine enemy has more power.
   [*Draws, and is charmed from moving.*
 Mir.   O dear father,
Make not too rash a trial of him, for
He's gentle and not fearful.
 Pros.   What ? I say,
My foot my tutor ? Put thy sword up, traitor ;
Who makest a show but darest not strike, thy
  conscience   470
Is so possess'd with guilt : come from thy
  ward,
For I can here disarm thee with this stick
And make thy weapon drop.
 Mir.   Beseech you, father.
 Pros. Hence ! hang not on my garments.
 Mir.   Sir, have pity ;
I'll be his surety.
 Pros.   Silence ! one word more
Shall make me chide thee, if not hate thee.
  What !
An advocate for an impostor ! hush !
Thou think'st there is no more such shapes as
  he,
Having seen but him and Caliban : foolish
  wench !
To the most of men this is a Caliban 480
And they to him are angels.
 Mir.   My affections
Are then most humble ; I have no ambition
To see a goodlier man.
 Pros.   Come on ; obey :
Thy nerves are in their infancy again
And have no vigor in them.
 Fer.   So they are ;
My spirits, as in a dream, are all bound up.
My father's loss, the weakness which I feel,
The wreck of all my friends, nor this man's
  threats,
To whom I am subdued, are but light to me,
Might I but through my prison once a day 490
Behold this maid : all corners else o' the earth
Let liberty make use of ; space enough
Have I in such a prison.
 Pros. [*Aside*] It works. [*To Fer.*] Come
  on.
Thou hast done well, fine Ariel ! [*To Fer.*]
  Follow me.
[*To Ari.*] Hark what thou else shalt do me.
 Mir.   Be of comfort ;
My father's of a better nature, sir,
Than he appears by speech : this is unwonted
Which now came from him.
 Pros.   Thou shalt be free
As mountain winds : but then exactly do
All points of my command.
 Ari.   To the syllable. 500
 Pros. Come, follow. Speak not for him.
         [*Exeunt.*

ACT II.

SCENE I. *Another part of the island.*

Enter ALONSO, SEBASTIAN, ANTONIO, GON-
ZALO, ADRIAN, FRANCISCO, *and others.*

Gon. Beseech you, sir, be merry ; you have
cause,
So have we all, of joy ; for our escape
Is much beyond our loss. Our hint of woe
Is common ; every day some sailor's wife,
The masters of some merchant and the mer-
chant
Have just our theme of woe ; but for the mir-
acle,
I mean our preservation, few in millions
Can speak like us : then wisely, good sir, weigh
Our sorrow with our comfort.
Alon. Prithee, peace.
Seb. He receives comfort like cold por-
ridge.
Ant. The visitor will not give him o'er so.
Seb. Look, he's winding up the watch of
his wit ; by and by it will strike.
Gon. Sir,—
Seb. One : tell.
Gon. When every grief is entertain'd that's
offer'd,
Comes to the entertainer—
Seb. A dollar.
Gon. Dolour comes to him, indeed : you
have spoken truer than you purposed. 20
Seb. You have taken it wiselier than I
meant you should.
Gon. Therefore, my lord,—
Ant. Fie, what a spendthrift is he of his
tongue !
Alon. I prithee, spare.
Gon. Well, I have done : but yet,—
Seb. He will be talking.
Ant. Which, of he or Adrian, for a good
wager, first begins to crow ?
Seb. The old cock. 30
Ant. The cockerel.
Seb. Done. The wager ?
Ant. A laughter.
Seb. A match !
Adr. Though this island seem to be des-
ert,—
Seb. Ha, ha, ha ! So, you're paid.
Adr. Uninhabitable and almost inacces-
sible,—
Seb. Yet,—
Adr. Yet,—
Ant. He could not miss't. 40
Adr. It must needs be of subtle, tender and
delicate temperance.
Ant. Temperance was a delicate wench.
Seb. Ay, and a subtle ; as he most learn-
edly delivered.
Adr. The air breathes upon us here most
sweetly.
Seb. As if it had lungs and rotten ones.
Ant. Or as 'twere perfumed by a fen.
Gon. Here is everything advantageous to
life.
Ant. True ; save means to live. 50
Seb. Of that there's none, or little.
Gon. How lush and lusty the grass looks !
how green !
Ant. The ground indeed is tawny.
Seb. With an eye of green in't.

Ant. He misses not much.
Seb. No ; he doth but mistake the truth
totally.
Gon. But the rarity of it is,—which is indeed almost beyond credit,—
Seb. As many vouched rarities are.
Gon. That our garments, being, as they
were, drenched in the sea, hold notwithstanding their freshness and glosses, being rather
new-dyed than stained with salt water.
Ant. If but one of his pockets could speak,
would it not say he lies ?
Seb. Ay, or very falsely pocket up his re-
port.
Gon. Methinks our garments are now as
fresh as when we put them on first in Afric,
at the marriage of the king's fair daughter
Claribel to the King of Tunis. 71
Seb. 'Twas a sweet marriage, and we pros-
per well in our return.
Adr. Tunis was never graced before with
such a paragon to their queen.
Gon. Not since widow Dido's time.
Ant. Widow ! a pox o' that ! How came
that widow in ? widow Dido !
Seb. What if he had said 'widower
Æneas' too ? Good Lord, how you take it !
Adr. 'Widow Dido' said you ? you make
me study of that : she was of Carthage, not of
Tunis.
Gon. This Tunis, sir, was Carthage.
Adr. Carthage ?
Gon. I assure you, Carthage.
Seb. His word is more than the miraculous
harp ; he hath raised the wall and houses too.
Ant. What impossible matter will he make
easy next ?
Seb. I think he will carry this island home
in his pocket and give it his son for an apple.
Ant. And, sowing the kernels of it in the
sea, bring forth more islands.
Gon. Ay.
Ant. Why, in good time.
Gon. Sir, we were talking that our gar-
ments seem now as fresh as when we were at
Tunis at the marriage of your daughter, who
is now queen.
Ant. And the rarest that e'er came there.
Seb. Bate, I beseech you, widow Dido. 100
Ant. O, widow Dido ! ay, widow Dido.
Gon. Is not, sir, my doublet as fresh as the
first day I wore it ? I mean, in a sort.
Ant. That sort was well fished for.
Gon. When I wore it at your daughter's
marriage ?
Alon. You cram these words into mine
ears against
The stomach of my sense. Would I had never
Married my daughter there ! for, coming
thence,
My son is lost and, in my rate, she too,
Who is so far from Italy removed 110
I ne'er again shall see her. O thou mine heir
Of Naples and of Milan, what strange fish
Hath made his meal on thee ?
Fran. Sir, he may live :
I saw him beat the surges under him,
And ride upon their backs ; he trod the water,
Whose enmity he flung aside, and breasted
The surge most swoln that met him ; his bold
head
'Bove the contentious waves he kept, and oar'd

Himself with his good arms in lusty stroke
To the shore, that o'er his wave-worn basis
    bow'd,   120
As stooping to relieve him : I not doubt
He came alive to land.
    Alon.   No, no, he's gone.
    Seb. Sir, you may thank yourself for this
        great loss,
That would not bless our Europe with your
    daughter,
But rather lose her to an African ;
Where she at least is banish'd from your eye,
Who hath cause to wet the grief on't.
    Alon.   Prithee, peace.
    Seb. You were kneel'd to and importuned
        otherwise
By all of us, and the fair soul herself   129
Weigh'd between loathness and obedience, at
Which end o' the beam should bow. We have
    lost your son,
I fear, for ever : Milan and Naples have
More widows in them of this business' making
Than we bring men to comfort them :
The fault's your own.
    Alon.   So is the dear'st o' the loss.
    Gon. My lord Sebastian,
The truth you speak doth lack some gentle-
    ness
And time to speak it in : you rub the sore,
When you should bring the plaster.
    Seb.   Very well.
    Ant. And most chirurgeonly.   140
    Gon. It is foul weather in us all, good sir,
When you are cloudy.
    Seb.   Foul weather ?
    Ant.   Very foul.
    Gon. Had I plantation of this isle, my
    lord,—
    Ant. He'ld sow't with nettle-seed.
    Seb.   Or docks, or mallows.
    Gon. And were the king on't, what would
    I do ?
    Seb. 'Scape being drunk for want of wine.
    Gon. I' the commonwealth I would by con-
    traries
Execute all things ; for no kind of traffic
Would I admit ; no name of magistrate ;
Letters should not be known ; riches, poverty,
And use of service, none ; contract, succession,
Bourn, bound of land, tilth, vineyard, none ;
No use of metal, corn, or wine, or oil ;
No occupation ; all men idle, all ;
And women too, but innocent and pure ;
No sovereignty ;—
    Seb.   Yet he would be king on't.
    Ant. The latter end of his commonwealth
forgets the beginning.
    Gon. All things in common nature should
    produce
Without sweat or endeavor : treason, felony,
Sword, pike, knife, gun, or need of any en-
    gine,   161
Would I not have ; but nature should bring
    forth,
Of its own kind, all foison, all abundance,
To feed my innocent people.
    Seb. No marrying 'mong his subjects ?
    Ant. None, man ; all idle : whores and
    knaves.
    Gon. I would with such perfection govern,
    sir,
To excel the golden age.
    Seb.   God save his majesty !

    Ant. Long live Gonzalo !
    Gon.   And,—do you mark me, sir ?
    Alon. Prithee, no more : thou dost talk
nothing to me.   171
    Gon. I do well believe your highness ; and
did it to minister occasion to these gentlemen,
who are of such sensible and nimble lungs that
they always use to laugh at nothing.
    Ant. 'Twas you we laughed at.
    Gon. Who in this kind of merry fooling
am nothing to you : so you may continue and
laugh at nothing still.
    Ant. What a blow was there given !   180
    Seb. An it had not fallen flat-long.
    Gon. You are gentlemen of brave metal ;
you would lift the moon out of her sphere, if
she would continue in it five weeks without
changing.

Enter Ariel, *invisible, playing solemn music.*

    Seb. We would so, and then go a bat-
fowling.
    Ant. Nay, good my lord, be not angry.
    Gon. No, I warrant you ; I will not adven-
ture my discretion so weakly. Will you laugh
me asleep, for I am very heavy ?
    Ant. Go sleep, and hear us.   190
        [*All sleep except Alon., Seb., and Ant.*
    Alon. What, all so soon asleep ! I wish
    mine eyes
Would, with themselves, shut up my thoughts :
    I find
They are inclined to do so.
    Seb.   Please you, sir,
Do not omit the heavy offer of it :
It seldom visits sorrow ; when it doth,
It is a comforter.
    Ant.   We two, my lord,
Will guard your person while you take your
    rest,
And watch your safety.
    Alon.   Thank you. Wondrous heavy.
        [*Alonso sleeps. Exit Ariel.*
    Seb. What a strange drowsiness possesses
    them !
    Ant. It is the quality o' the climate.
    Seb.   Why   200
Doth it not then our eyelids sink ? I find not
Myself disposed to sleep.
    Ant.   Nor I ; my spirits are nimble.
They fell together all, as by consent ;
They dropp'd, as by a thunder-stroke. What
    might,
Worthy Sebastian ? O, what might ?—No
    more :—
And yet me thinks I see it in thy face,
What thou shouldst be : the occasion speaks
    thee, and
My strong imagination sees a crown
Dropping upon thy head.
    Seb.   What, art thou waking ?
    Ant. Do you not hear me speak ?
    Seb.   I do ; and surely
It is a sleepy language and thou speak'st   211
Out of thy sleep. What is it thou didst say ?
This is a strange repose, to be asleep
With eyes wide open ; standing, speaking,
    moving,
And yet so fast asleep.
    Ant.   Noble Sebastian,
Thou let'st thy fortune sleep—die, rather ;
    wink'st
Whiles thou art waking.

Seb.   Thou dost snore distinctly;
There's meaning in thy snores.
Ant. I am more serious than my custom:
            you
Must be so too, if heed me; which to do   220
Trebles thee o'er.
Seb.   Well, I am standing water.
Ant. I'll teach you how to flow.
Seb.   Do so: to ebb
Hereditary sloth instructs me.
Ant.   O,
If you but knew how you the purpose cherish
Whiles thus you mock it! how, in stripping it,
You more invest it! Ebbing men, indeed,
Most often do so near the bottom run
By their own fear or sloth.
Seb.   Prithee, say on:
The setting of thine eye and cheek proclaim
A matter from thee, and a birth indeed   230
Which throes thee much to yield.
Ant.   Thus, sir:
Although this lord of weak remembrance, this,
Who shall be of as little memory
When he is earth'd, hath here almost per-
            suaded,—
For he's a spirit of persuasion, only
Professes to persuade,—the king his son's
            alive,
'Tis as impossible that he's undrown'd
As he that sleeps here swims.
Seb.   I have no hope
That he's undrown'd.
Ant.   O, out of that ' no hope '
What great hope have you! no hope that way
            is   240
Another way so high a hope that even
Ambition cannot pierce a wink beyond,
But doubt discovery there. Will you grant with
            me
That Ferdinand is drown'd?
Seb.   He's gone.
Ant.   Then, tell me,
Who's the next heir of Naples?
Seb.   Claribel.
Ant. She that is queen of Tunis; she that
            dwells
Ten leagues beyond man's life; she that from
            Naples
Can have no note, unless the sun were post—
The man i' the moon's too slow—till new-born
            chins
Be rough and razorable; she that—from
            whom?   250
We all were sea-swallow'd, though some cast
            again,
And by that destiny to perform an act
Whereof what's past is prologue, what to come
In yours and my discharge.
Seb. What stuff is this! how say you?
'Tis true, my brother's daughter's queen of
            Tunis;
So is she heir of Naples; 'twixt which regions
There is some space.
Ant.   A space whose every cubit
Seems to cry out, ' How shall that Claribel
Measure us back to Naples? Keep in Tunis,
And let Sebastian wake.' Say, this were death
That now hath seized them; why, they were
            no worse   261
Than now they are. There be that can rule
            Naples
As well as he that sleeps; lords that can prate
As amply and unnecessarily

As this Gonzalo; I myself could make
A chough of as deep chat. O, that you bore
The mind that I do! what a sleep were this
For your advancement! Do you understand
            me?
Seb. Methinks I do.
Ant.   And how does your content
Tender your own good fortune?
Seb.   I remember   270
You did supplant your brother Prospero.
Ant.   True:
And look how well my garments sit upon me;
Much feater than before: my brother's serv-
            ants
Were then my fellows; now they are my men.
Seb. But, for your conscience?
Ant. Ay, sir; where lies that? if 'twere a
            kibe,
'Twould put me to my slipper: but I feel not
This deity in my bosom: twenty consciences,
That stand 'twixt me and Milan, candied be
            they
And melt ere they molest! Here lies your
            brother,   280
No better than the earth he lies upon,
If he were that which now he's like, that's
            dead;
Whom I, with this obedient steel, three inches
            of it,
Can lay to bed for ever; whiles you, doing
            thus,
To the perpetual wink for aye might put
This ancient morsel, this Sir Prudence, who
Should not upbraid our course. For all the
            rest,
They'll take suggestion as a cat laps milk;
They'll tell the clock to any business that
We say befits the hour.
Seb.   Thy case, dear friend, 290
Shall be my precedent; as thou got'st Milan,
I'll come by Naples. Draw thy sword: one
            stroke
Shall free thee from the tribute which thou
            payest;
And I the king shall love thee.
Ant.   Draw together;
And when I rear my hand, do you the like,
To fall it on Gonzalo.
Seb. O, but one word. [*They talk apart.*

            Re-enter ARIEL, *invisible.*

Ari. My master through his art foresees
            the danger
That you, his friend, are in; and sends me
            forth—
For else his project dies—to keep them living.
            [*Sings in Gonzalo's ear.*
While you here do snoring lie,   300
Open-eyed conspiracy
            His time doth take.
If of life you keep a care,
Shake off slumber, and beware:
            Awake, awake!
Ant. Then let us both be sudden.
Gon.   Now, good angels
Preserve the king.   [*They wake.*
Alon. Why, how now? ho, awake! Why
            are you drawn?
Wherefore this ghastly looking?
Gon.   What's the matter?
Seb. Whiles we stood here securing your
            repose,   310

Even now, we heard a hollow burst of bellow-
　ing
Like bulls, or rather lions : did't not wake
　you ?
It struck mine ear most terribly.
　Alon.　　　　　　　　　I heard nothing.
　Ant.　O, 'twas a din to fright a monster's
　ear,
To make an earthquake ! sure, it was the roar
Of a whole herd of lions.
　Alon.　　　　　Heard you this, Gonzalo ?
　Gon.　Upon mine honor, sir, I heard a
　humming,
And that a strange one too, which did awake
　me :
I shaked you, sir, and cried : as mine eyes
　open'd,
I saw their weapons drawn : there was a noise,
That's verily. 'Tis best we stand upon our
　guard,　　　　　　　　　　　　　321
Or that we quit this place ; let's draw our
　weapons.
　Alon.　Lead off this ground ; and let's make
　further search
For my poor son.
　Gon.　Heavens keep him from these beasts !
For he is, sure, i' the island.
　Alon.　　　　　　　　Lead away.
　Ari.　Prospero my lord shall know what I
　have done :
So, king, go safely on to seek thy son. [*Exeunt.*

　SCENE II.　*Another part of the island.*

Enter CALIBAN *with a burden of wood. A
　noise of thunder heard.*

　Cal.　All the infections that the sun sucks
　up
From bogs, fens, flats, on Prosper fall and
　make him
By inch-meal a disease ! His spirits hear me
And yet I needs must curse. But they'll nor
　pinch,
Fright me with urchin-shows, pitch me i' the
　mire,
Nor lead me, like a firebrand, in the dark
Out of my way, unless he bid 'em ; but
For every trifle are they set upon me ;
Sometime like apes that mow and chatter at
　me　　　　　　　　　　　　　　9
And after bite me, then like hedgehogs which
Lie tumbling in my barefoot way and mount
Their pricks at my footfall ; sometime am I
All wound with adders who with cloven
　tongues
Do hiss me into madness.

　　　　　Enter TRINCULO.

　　　　　　　　　　Lo, now, lo !
Here comes a spirit of his, and to torment me
For bringing wood in slowly. I'll fall flat ;
Perchance he will not mind me.
　Trin.　Here's neither bush nor shrub, to
bear off any weather at all, and another storm
brewing ; I hear it sing i' the wind : yond same
black cloud, yond huge one, looks like a foul
bombard that would shed his liquor. If it
should thunder as it did before, I know not
where to hide my head : yond same cloud cannot choose but fall by pailfuls. What have we
here ? a man or a fish ? dead or alive ? A fish :
he smells like a fish ; a very ancient and fish-
like smell ; a kind of not of the newest Poor-
John. A strange fish ! Were I in England now,

as once I was, and had but this fish painted,
not a holiday fool there but would give a piece
of silver : there would this monster make a
man ; any strange beast there makes a man :
when they will not give a doit to relieve a lame
beggar, they will lay out ten to see a dead Indian. Legged like a man ! and his fins like
arms ! Warm o' my troth ! I do now let loose
my opinion ; hold it no longer : this is no fish,
but an islander, that hath lately suffered by a
thunderbolt. [*Thunder.*] Alas, the storm is
come again ! my best way is to creep under
his gaberdine ; there is no other shelter here-
abouts : misery acquaints a man with strange
bed-fellows. I will here shroud till the dregs of
the storm be past.

Enter STEPHANO, *singing : a bottle in his
　hand.*

　Ste.　I shall no more to sea, to sea,
　　　　　Here shall I die ashore—
This is a very scurvy tune to sing at a man's
funeral : well, here's my comfort.　[*Drinks.*
[*Sings.*
The master, the swabber, the boatswain and I,
　　The gunner and his mate
Loved Mall, Meg and Marian and Margery, 50
　　But none of us cared for Kate ;
　　For she had a tongue with a tang,
　　Would cry to a sailor, Go hang !
She loved not the savor of tar nor of pitch,
Yet a tailor might scratch her where'er she did
　itch :
　　Then to sea, boys, and let her go hang !
This is a scurvy tune too : but here's my com-
　fort.　　　　　　　　　　　　　[*Drinks.*
　Cal.　Do not torment me : Oh !
　Ste.　What's the matter ? Have we devils
here ? Do you put tricks upon 's with savages
and men of Ind, ha ? I have not scaped drown-
ing to be afeard now of your four legs ; for
it hath been said, As proper a man as ever
went on four legs cannot make him give
ground ; and it shall be said so again while
Stephano breathes at's nostrils.
　Cal.　The spirit torments me ; Oh !
　Ste.　This is some monster of the isle with
four legs, who hath got, as I take it, an ague.
Where the devil should he learn our language ?
I will give him some relief, if it be but for
that. If I can recover him and keep him tame
and get to Naples with him, he's a present for
any emperor that ever trod on neat's leather.
　Cal.　Do not torment me, prithee ; I'll bring
my wood home faster.
　Ste.　He's in his fit now and does not talk
after the wisest. He shall taste of my bottle :
if he have never drunk wine afore, it will go
near to remove his fit. If I can recover him
and keep him tame, I will not take too much
for him ; he shall pay for him that hath him,
and that soundly.
　Cal.　Thou dost me yet but little hurt ; thou
wilt anon, I know it by thy trembling : now
Prosper works upon thee.
　Ste.　Come on your ways ; open your
mouth ; here is that which will give language
to you, cat : open your mouth ; this will shake
your shaking, I can tell you, and that soundly :
you cannot tell who's your friend : open your
chaps again.
　Trin.　I should know that voice : it should

be—but he is drowned; and these are devils:
O defend me!

Ste. Four legs and two voices: a most delicate monster! His forward voice now is to speak well of his friend; his backward voice is to utter foul speeches and to detract. If all the wine in my bottle will recover him, I will help his ague. Come. Amen! I will pour some in thy other mouth.

Trin. Stephano! 100

Ste. Doth thy other mouth call me? Mercy, mercy! This is a devil, and no monster: I will leave him; I have no long spoon.

Trin. Stephano! If thou beest Stephano, touch me and speak to me: for I am Trinculo—be not afeard—thy good friend Trinculo.

Ste. If thou beest Trinculo, come forth: I'll pull thee by the lesser legs: if any be Trinculo's legs, these are they. Thou art very Trinculo indeed! How camest thou to be the siege of this moon-calf? can he vent Trinculos?

Trin. I took him to be killed with a thunder-stroke. But art thou not drowned, Stephano? I hope now thou art not drowned. Is the storm overblown? I hid me under the dead moon-calf's gaberdine for fear of the storm. And art thou living, Stephano? O Stephano, two Neapolitans 'scaped!

Ste. Prithee, do not turn me about; my stomach is not constant.

Cal. [*Aside*] These be fine things, an if they be not sprites. 121

That's a brave god and bears celestial liquor. I will kneel to him.

Ste. How didst thou 'scape? How camest thou hither? swear by this bottle how thou camest hither. I escaped upon a butt of sack which the sailors heaved o'erboard, by this bottle; which I made of the bark of a tree with mine own hands since I was cast ashore.

Cal. I'll swear upon that bottle to be thy true subject; for the liquor is not earthly.

Ste. Here; swear then how thou escapedst.

Trin. Swum ashore, man, like a duck: I can swim like a duck, I'll be sworn.

Ste. Here, kiss the book. Though thou canst swim like a duck, thou art made like a goose.

Trin. O Stephano, hast any more of this?

Ste. The whole butt, man: my cellar is in a rock by the sea-side where my wine is hid. How now, moon-calf! how does thine ague?

Cal. Hast thou not dropp'd from heaven?

Ste. Out o' the moon, I do assure thee: I was the man i' the moon when time was.

Cal. I have seen thee in her and I do adore thee:
My mistress show'd me thee and thy dog and thy bush.

Ste. Come, swear to that; kiss the book: I will furnish it anon with new contents: swear.

Trin. By this good light, this is a very shallow monster! I afeard of him! A very weak monster! The man i' the moon! A most poor credulous monster! Well drawn, monster, in good sooth!

Cal. I'll show thee every fertile inch o' th' island;
And I will kiss thy foot: I prithee, be my god.

Trin. By this light, a most perfidious and

drunken monster! when 's god's asleep, he'll rob his bottle.

Cal. I'll kiss thy foot; I'll swear myself thy subject.

Ste. Come on then; down, and swear.

Trin. I shall laugh myself to death at this puppy-headed monster. A most scurvy monster! I could find in my heart to beat him,—

Ste. Come, kiss. 161

Trin. But that the poor monster's in drink: an abominable monster!

Cal. I'll show thee the best springs; I'll pluck thee berries;
I'll fish for thee and get thee wood enough.
A plague upon the tyrant that I serve!
I'll bear him no more sticks, but follow thee,
Thou wondrous man.

Trin. A most ridiculous monster, to make a wonder of a poor drunkard! 170

Cal. I prithee, let me bring thee where crabs grow;
And I with my long nails will dig thee pignuts;
Show thee a jay's nest and instruct thee how
To snare the nimble marmoset; I'll bring thee
To clustering filberts and sometimes I'll get thee
Young scamels from the rock. Wilt thou go with me?

Ste. I prithee now, lead the way without any more talking. Trinculo, the king and all our company else being drowned, we will inherit here: here; bear my bottle: fellow Trinculo, we'll fill him by and by again.

Cal. [*Sings drunkenly*]
Farewell, master; farewell, farewell!

Trin. A howling monster: a drunken monster!

Cal. No more dams I'll make for fish;
    Nor fetch in firing
        At requiring;
    Nor scrape trencher, nor wash dish:
    'Ban, 'Ban, Cacaliban
        Has a new master: get a new man.

Freedom, hey-day! hey-day, freedom! freedom, hey-day, freedom! 191

Ste. O brave monster! Lead the way.
[*Exeunt.*

ACT III.

SCENE I. *Before* PROSPERO'S *cell.*

Enter FERDINAND, *bearing a log.*

Fer. There be some sports are painful, and their labor
Delight in them sets off: some kinds of baseness
Are nobly undergone and most poor matters
Point to rich ends. This my mean task
Would be as heavy to me as odious, but
The mistress which I serve quickens what's dead
And makes my labors pleasures: O, she is
Ten times more gentle than her father's crabbed,
And he's composed of harshness. I must remove
Some thousands of these logs and pile them up,
Upon a sore injunction: my sweet mistress

Weeps when she sees me work, and says, such
  baseness
Had never like executor. I forget :
But these sweet thoughts do even refresh my
  labors,
Most busy lest, when I do it.

Enter MIRANDA ; *and* PROSPERO *at a distance,
  unseen.*

Mir.   Alas, now, pray you,
Work not so hard : I would the lightning had
Burnt up those logs that you are enjoin'd to
  pile !
Pray, set it down and rest you : when this
  burns,
'Twill weep for having wearied you. My fa-
  ther
Is hard at study ; pray now, rest yourself ; 20
He's safe for these three hours.
Fer.   O most dear mistress,
The sun will set before I shall discharge
What I must strive to do.
Mir.   If you'll sit down,
I'll bear your logs the while : pray, give me
  that ;
I'll carry it to the pile.
Fer.   No, precious creature ;
I had rather crack my sinews, break my back,
Than you should such dishonor undergo,
While I sit lazy by.
Mir.   It would become me
As well as it does you : and I should do it
With much more ease ; for my good will is to
  it,
And yours it is against.
Pros.   Poor worm, thou art infected !
This visitation shows it.
Mir.   You look wearily.
Fer. No, noble mistress ; 'tis fresh morn-
  ing with me
When you are by at night. I do beseech you—
Chiefly that I might set it in my prayers—
What is your name ?
Mir.   Miranda.—O my father,
I have broke your hest to say so !
Fer.   Admired Miranda !
Indeed the top of admiration ! worth
What's dearest to the world ! Full many a
  lady
I have eyed with best regard and many a time
The harmony of their tongues hath into bond-
  age   41
Brought my too diligent ear : for several vir-
  tues
Have I liked several women ; never any
With so full soul, but some defect in her
Did quarrel with the noblest grace she owed
And put it to the foil : but you, O you,
So perfect and so peerless, are created
Of every creature's best !
Mir.   I do not know
One of my sex ; no woman's face remember,
Save, from my glass, mine own ; nor have I
  seen
More that I may call men than you, good
  friend,
And my dear father : how features are abroad,
I am skilless of ; but, by my modesty,
The jewel in my dower, I would not wish
Any companion in the world but you,
Nor can imagination form a shape,
Besides yourself, to like of. But I prattle

Something too wildly and my father's precepts
I therein do forget.
Fer.   I am in my condition
A prince, Miranda ; I do think, a king ;   60
I would, not so !—and would no more endure
This wooden slavery than to suffer
The flesh-fly blow my mouth. Hear my soul
  speak :
The very instant that I saw you, did
My heart fly to your service ; there resides,
To make me slave to it ; and for your sake
Am I this patient log-man.
Mir.   Do you love me ?
Fer. O heaven, O earth, bear witness to this
  sound
And crown what I profess with kind event
If I speak true ! if hollowly, invert   70
What best is boded me to mischief ! I
Beyond all limit of what else i' the world
Do love, prize, honor you.
Mir.   I am a fool
To weep at what I am glad of.
Pros.   Fair encounter
Of two most rare affections ! Heavens rain
  grace
On that which breeds between 'em !
Fer.   Wherefore weep you ?
Mir. At mine unworthiness that dare not
  offer
What I desire to give, and much less take
What I shall die to want. But this is trifling ;
And all the more it seeks to hide itself,   80
The bigger bulk it shows. Hence, bashful cun-
  ning !
And prompt me, plain and holy innocence !
I am your wife, if you will marry me ;
If not, I'll die your maid : to be your fellow
You may deny me ; but I'll be your servant,
Whether you will or no.
Fer.   My mistress, dearest ;
And I thus humble ever.
Mir.   My husband, then ?
Fer. Ay, with a heart as willing
As bondage e'er of freedom : here's my hand.
Mir. And mine, with my heart in't ; and
  now farewell   90
Till half an hour hence.
Fer.   A thousand thousand !
    [*Exeunt Fer. and Mir. severally.*
Pros. So glad of this as they I cannot be,
Who are surprised withal ; but my rejoicing
At nothing can be more. I'll to my book,
For yet ere supper-time must I perform
Much business appertaining.   [*Exit.*

  SCENE II. *Another part of the island.*

Enter CALIBAN, STEPHANO, *and* TRINCULO.

Ste. Tell not me ; when the butt is out, we
will drink water ; not a drop before : therefore
bear up, and board 'em. Servant-monster,
drink to me.
Trin. Servant-monster ! the folly of this
island ! They say there's but five upon this
isle : we are three of them ; if th' other two
be brained like us, the state totters.
Ste. Drink, servant-monster, when I bid
thee : thy eyes are almost set in thy head. 10
Trin. Where should they be set else ? he
were a brave monster indeed, if they were set
in his tail.
Ste. My man-monster hath drown'd his
tongue in sack : for my part, the sea cannot

drown me; I swam, ere I could recover the shore, five and thirty leagues off and on. By this light, thou shalt be my lieutenant, monster, or my standard.

Trin. Your lieutenant, if you list; he's no standard.   20

Ste. We'll not run, Monsieur Monster.

Trin. Nor go neither; but you'll lie like dogs and yet say nothing neither.

Ste. Moon-calf, speak once in thy life, if thou beest a good moon-calf.

Cal. How does thy honor? Let me lick thy shoe. I'll not serve him; he's not valiant.

Trin. Thou liest, most ignorant monster: I am in case to justle a constable. Why, thou deboshed fish, thou, was there ever man a coward that hath drunk so much sack as I to-day? Wilt thou tell a monstrous lie, being but half a fish and half a monster?

Cal. Lo, how he mocks me! wilt thou let him, my lord?

Trin. 'Lord' quoth he! That a monster should be such a natural!

Cal. Lo, lo, again! bite him to death, I prithee.

Ste. Trinculo, keep a good tongue in your head: if you prove a mutineer,—the next tree! The poor monster's my subject and he shall not suffer indignity.

Cal. I thank my noble lord. Wilt thou be pleased to hearken once again to the suit I made to thee?

Ste. Marry, will I: kneel and repeat it; I will stand, and so shall Trinculo.

Enter ARIEL, *invisible.*

Cal. As I told thee before, I am subject to a tyrant, a sorcerer, that by his cunning hath cheated me of the island.   50

Ari. Thou liest.

Cal. Thou liest, thou jesting monkey, thou: I would my valiant master would destroy thee! I do not lie.

Ste. Trinculo, if you trouble him any more in's tale, by this hand, I will supplant some of your teeth.

Trin. Why, I said nothing.

Ste. Mum, then, and no more. Proceed.

Cal. I say, by sorcery he got this isle;   60 From me he got it. If thy greatness will Revenge it on him,—for I know thou darest, But this thing dare not,—

Ste. That's most certain.

Cal. Thou shalt be lord of it and I'll serve thee.

Ste. How now shall this be compassed? Canst thou bring me to the party?

Cal. Yea, yea, my lord: I'll yield him thee asleep, Where thou mayst knock a nail into his head.

Ari. Thou liest; thou canst not.   70

Cal. What a pied ninny's this! Thou scurvy patch! I do beseech thy greatness, give him blows And take his bottle from him: when that's gone He shall drink nought but brine; for I'll not show him Where the quick freshes are.

Ste. Trinculo, run into no further danger: interrupt the monster one word further, and,

by this hand, I'll turn my mercy out o' doors and make a stock-fish of thee.

Trin. Why, what did I? I did nothing. I'll go farther off.   81

Ste. Didst thou not say he lied?

Ari. Thou liest.

Ste. Do I so? take thou that. [*Beats Trin.*] As you like this, give me the lie another time.

Trin. I did not give the lie. Out o' your wits and hearing too? A pox o' your bottle! this can sack and drinking do. A murrain on your monster, and the devil take your fingers!

Cal. Ha, ha, ha!   90

Ste. Now, forward with your tale. Prithee, stand farther off.

Cal. Beat him enough: after a little time I'll beat him too.

Ste.   Stand farther. Come, proceed.

Cal. Why, as I told thee, 'tis a custom with him, I' th' afternoon to sleep: there thou mayst brain him, Having first seized his books, or with a log Batter his skull, or paunch him with a stake, Or cut his wezand with thy knife. Remember First to possess his books; for without them He's but a sot, as I am, nor hath not   101 One spirit to command: they all do hate him As rootedly as I. Burn but his books. He has brave utensils,—for so he calls them,— Which, when he has a house, he'll deck withal And that most deeply to consider is The beauty of his daughter; he himself Calls her a nonpareil: I never saw a woman, But only Sycorax my dam and she; But she as far surpasseth Sycorax   110 As great'st does least.

Ste.   Is it so brave a lass?

Cal. Ay, lord; she will become thy bed, I warrant. And bring thee forth brave brood.

Ste. Monster, I will kill this man: his daughter and I will be king and queen,—save our graces!—and Trinculo and thyself shall be viceroys. Dost thou like the plot, Trinculo?

Trin. Excellent.

Ste. Give me thy hand: I am sorry I beat thee; but, while thou livest, keep a good tongue in thy head.   121

Cal. Within this half hour will he be asleep: Wilt thou destroy him then?

Ste.   Ay, on mine honor.

Ari. This will I tell my master.

Cal. Thou makest me merry; I am full of pleasure: Let us be jocund: will you troll the catch You taught me but while-ere?

Ste. At thy request, monster, I will do reason, any reason. Come on, Trinculo, let us sing.   [*Sings.*

Flout 'em and scout 'em And scout 'em and flout 'em; Thought is free.

Cal. That's not the tune.

[*Ariel plays the tune on a tabor and pipe.*

Ste. What is this same?

Trin. This is the tune of our catch, played by the picture of Nobody.

Ste. If thou beest a man, show thyself in thy likeness: if thou beest a devil, take't as thou list.

Trin. O, forgive me my sins !
Ste. He that dies pays all debts : I defy
thee. Mercy upon us !   141
Cal. Art thou afeard ?
Ste. No, monster, not I.
Cal. Be not afeard ; the isle is full of
noises,
Sounds and sweet airs, that give delight and
hurt not.
Sometimes a thousand twangling instruments
Will hum about mine ears, and sometime
voices
That, if I then had waked after long sleep,
Will make me sleep again : and then, in
dreaming,
The clouds methought would open and show
riches   150
Ready to drop upon me, that, when I waked,
I cried to dream again.
Ste. This will prove a brave kingdom to
me, where I shall have my music for nothing.
Cal. When Prospero is destroyed.
Ste. That shall be by and by : I remember
the story.
Trin. The sound is going away ; let's fol-
low it, and after do our work.
Ste. Lead, monster ; we'll follow. I would
I could see this taborer ; he lays it on.   160
Trin. Wilt come ? I'll follow, Stephano.
                                    [*Exeunt.*

SCENE III. *Another part of the island.*

Enter ALONSO, SEBASTIAN, ANTONIO, GON-
ZALO, ADRIAN, FRANCISCO, *and others.*

Gon. By'r lakin, I can go no further, sir ;
My old bones ache : here's a maze trod indeed
Through forth-rights and meanders ! By your
patience,
I needs must rest me.
Alon. Old lord, I cannot blame thee,
Who am myself attach'd with weariness,
To the dulling of my spirits : sit down, and
rest.
Even here I will put off my hope and keep it
No longer for my flatterer : he is drown'd
Whom thus we stray to find, and the sea
mocks
Our frustrate search on land. Well, let him
go.   10
Ant. [*Aside to Seb.*] I am right glad that
he's so out of hope.
Do not, for one repulse, forego the purpose
That you resolved to effect.
Seb. [*Aside to Ant.*] The next advantage
Will we take throughly.
Ant. [*Aside to Seb.*] Let it be to-night ;
For, now they are oppress'd with travel, they
Will not, nor cannot, use such vigilance
As when they are fresh.
Seb. [*Aside to Ant.*] I say, to-night : no
more.   [*Solemn and strange music.*
Alon. What harmony is this ? My good
friends, hark !
Gon. Marvellous sweet music !

Enter PROSPERO *above, invisible. Enter several strange Shapes, bringing in a banquet ;
they dance about it with gentle actions of
salutation ; and, inviting the King, &c. to
eat, they depart.*

Alon. Give us kind keepers, heavens !
What were these ?   20
Seb. A living drollery. Now I will believe

That there are unicorns, that in Arabia
There is one tree, the phœnix' throne, one
phœnix
At this hour reigning there.
Ant.   I'll believe both ;
And what does else want credit, come to me,
And I'll be sworn 'tis true : travellers ne'er
did lie,
Though fools at home condemn 'em.
Gon.   If in Naples
I should report this now, would they believe
me ?
If I should say, I saw such islanders—
For, certes, these are people of the island— 30
Who, though they are of monstrous shape, yet,
note,
Their manners are more gentle-kind than of
Our human generation you shall find
Many, nay, almost any.
Pros.   [*Aside*] Honest lord,
Thou hast said well ; for some of you there
present
Are worse than devils.
Alon.   I cannot too much muse
Such shapes, such gesture and such sound,
expressing,
Although they want the use of tongue, a kind
Of excellent dumb discourse.
Pros.   [*Aside*] Praise in departing.
Fran. They vanish'd strangely.
Seb.   No matter, since   40
They have left their viands behind ; for we
have stomachs.
Will't please you taste of what is here ?
Alon.   Not I.
Gon. Faith, sir, you need not fear. When
we were boys,
Who would believe that there were moun-
taineers
Dew-lapp'd like bulls, whose throats had hang-
ing at 'em
Wallets of flesh ? or that there were such men
Whose heads stood in their breasts ? which
now we find
Each putter-out of five for one will bring us
Good warrant of.
Alon.   I will stand to and feed,
Although my last : no matter, since I feel   50
The best is past. Brother, my lord the duke,
Stand to and do as we.

Thunder and lightning. Enter ARIEL, *like a
harpy ; claps his wings upon the table ; and,
with a quaint device, the banquet vanishes.*

Ari. You are three men of sin, whom
Destiny,
That hath to instrument this lower world
And what is in't, the never-surfeited sea
Hath caused to belch up you ; and on this
island
Where man doth not inhabit ; you 'mongst
men
Being most unfit to live. I have made you
mad ;
And even with such-like valor men hang and
drown
Their proper selves.
          [*Alon., Seb. &c. draw their swords.*
                You fools ! I and my fellows   60
Are ministers of Fate : the elements,
Of whom your swords are temper'd, may as
well

Wound the loud winds, or with bemock'd-at
    stabs
Kill the still-closing waters, as diminish
One dowle that's in my plume : my fellow-
    ministers
Are like invulnerable. If you could hurt,
Your swords are now too massy for your
    strengths
And will not be uplifted. But remember—
For that's my business to you—that you three
From Milan did supplant good Prospero ;   70
Exposed unto the sea, which hath requit it,
Him and his innocent child : for which foul
    deed
The powers, delaying, not forgetting, have
Incensed the seas and shores, yea, all the
    creatures,
Against your peace. Thee of thy son, Alonso,
They have bereft ; and do pronounce by me :
Lingering perdition, worse than any death
Can be at once, shall step by step attend
You and your ways ; whose wraths to guard
    you from—
Which here, in this most desolate isle, else
    falls   80
Upon your heads—is nothing but heart-sorrow
And a clear life ensuing.

He vanishes in thunder ; then, to soft music,
*   enter the Shapes again, and dance, with*
*   mocks and mows, and carrying out the table.*

  Pros.   Bravely the figure of this harpy hast
    thou
Perform'd, my Ariel ; a grace it had, devour-
    ing :
Of my instruction hast thou nothing bated
In what thou hadst to say : so, with good life
And observation strange, my meaner minis-
    ters
Their several kinds have done. My high
    charms work
And these mine enemies are all knit up
In their distractions ; they now are in my
    power ;   90
And in these fits I leave them, while I visit
Young Ferdinand, whom they suppose is
    drown'd,
And his and mine loved darling. [*Exit above.*
  Gon. I' the name of something holy, sir,
    why stand you
In this strange stare ?
  Alon.   O, it is monstrous, monstrous :
Methought the billows spoke and told me of
    it ;
The winds did sing it to me, and the thunder,
That deep and dreadful organ-pipe, pro-
    nounced
The name of Prosper : it did bass my tres-
    pass.
Therefore my son i' the ooze is bedded, and
I'll seek him deeper than e'er plummet
    sounded   101
And with him there lie mudded.   [*Exit.*
  Seb.   But one fiend at a time,
I'll fight their legions o'er.
  Ant.   I'll be thy second.
              [*Exeunt Seb. and Ant.*
  Gon. All three of them are desperate :
    their great guilt,
Like poison given to work a great time after,
Now 'gins to bite the spirits. I do beseech
    you

That are of suppler joints, follow them swiftly
And hinder them from what this ecstasy
May now provoke them to.
  Adr.   Follow, I pray you.   [*Exeunt.*

ACT IV.

SCENE I. *Before* PROSPERO'S *cell.*

Enter PROSPERO, FERDINAND, *and* MIRANDA.

  Pros. If I have too austerely punish'd you,
Your compensation makes amends, for I
Have given you here a third of mine own life,
Or that for which I live ; who once again
I tender to thy hand : all thy vexations
Were but my trials of thy love, and thou
Hast strangely stood the test : here, afore
    Heaven,
I ratify this my rich gift. O Ferdinand,
Do not smile at me that I boast her off,
For thou shalt find she will outstrip all praise
And make it halt behind her.   11
  Fer.   I do believe it
Against an oracle.
  Pros.   Then, as my gift and thine own ac-
    quisition
Worthily purchased, take my daughter : but
If thou dost break her virgin-knot before
All sanctimonious ceremonies may
With full and holy rite be minister'd,
No sweet aspersion shall the heavens let fall
To make this contract grow : but barren hate,
Sour-eyed disdain and discord shall bestrew   20
The union of your bed with weeds so loathly
That you shall hate it both : therefore take
    heed,
As Hymen's lamps shall light you.
  Fer.   As I hope
For quiet days, fair issue and long life,
With such love as 'tis now, the murkiest den,
The most opportune place, the strong'st sug-
    gestion
Our worser genius can, shall never melt
Mine honor into lust, to take away
The edge of that day's celebration
When I shall think, or Phœbus' steeds are
    founder'd,   30
Or Night kept chain'd below.
  Pros.   Fairly spoke.
Sit then and talk with her ; she is thine own.
What, Ariel ! my industrious servant, Ariel !

Enter ARIEL.

  Ari. What would my potent master ? here
    I am.
  Pros. Thou and thy meaner fellows your
    last service
Did worthily perform ; and I must use you
In such another trick. Go bring the rabble,
O'er whom I give thee power, here to this
    place :
Incite them to quick motion ; for I must
Bestow upon the eyes of this young couple   40
Some vanity of mine art : it is my promise,
And they expect it from me.
  Ari.   Presently ?
  Pros.   Ay, with a twink.
  Ari.   Before you can say ' come ' and ' go,'
    And breathe twice and cry ' so, so,'
    Each one, tripping on his toe,
    Will be here with mop and mow.
    Do you love me, master ? no ?

Pros. Dearly, my delicate Ariel. Do not approach
Till thou dost hear me call.
   Ari.   Well, I conceive. [*Exit.* 50
   Pros. Look thou be true ; do not give dalliance
Too much the rein : the strongest oaths are straw
To the fire i' the blood : be more abstemious,
Or else, good night your vow !
   Fer.   I warrant you, sir ;
The white cold virgin snow upon my heart
Abates the ardor of my liver.
   Pros.   Well.
Now come, my Ariel ! bring a corollary,
Rather than want a spirit : appear and pertly !
No tongue ! all eyes ! be silent. [*Soft music.*

Enter IRIS.

   Iris. Ceres, most bounteous lady, thy rich leas
Of wheat, rye, barley, vetches, oats and pease ;
Thy turfy mountains, where live nibbling sheep,
And flat meads thatch'd with stover, them to keep ;
Thy banks with pioned and twilled brims,
Which spongy April at thy hest betrims,
To make cold nymphs chaste crowns ; and thy broom-groves,
Whose shadow the dismissed bachelor loves,
Being lass-lorn ; thy pole-clipt vineyard ;
And thy sea-marge, sterile and rocky-hard,
Where thou thyself dost air ;—the queen o' the sky,   70
Whose watery arch and messenger am I,
Bids thee leave these, and with her sovereign grace,
Here on this grass-plot, in this very place,
To come and sport : her peacocks fly amain :
Approach, rich Ceres, her to entertain.

Enter CERES.

   Cer. Hail, many-color'd messenger, that ne'er
Dost disobey the wife of Jupiter ;
Who with thy saffron wings upon my flowers
Diffusest honey-drops, refreshing showers,
And with each end of thy blue bow dost crown   80
My bosky acres and my unshrubb'd down,
Rich scarf to my proud earth ; why hath thy queen
Summon'd me hither, to this short-grass'd green ?
   Iris. A contract of true love to celebrate ;
And some donation freely to estate
On the blest lovers.
   Cer.   Tell me, heavenly bow,
If Venus or her son, as thou dost know,
Do now attend the queen ? Since they did plot
The means that dusky Dis my daughter got,
Her and her blind boy's scandal'd company 90
I have forsworn.
   Iris.   Of her society
Be not afraid : I met her deity
Cutting the clouds towards Paphos and her son
Dove-drawn with her. Here thought they to have done
Some wanton charm upon this man and maid,
Whose vows are, that no bed-right shall be paid

Till Hymen's torch be lighted : but in vain ;
Mars's hot minion is returned again ;
Her waspish-headed son has broke his arrows,
Swears he will shoot no more but play with sparrows   100
And be a boy right out.
   Cer.   High'st queen of state,
Great Juno, comes ; I know her by her gait.

Enter JUNO.

   Juno. How does my bounteous sister ? Go with me
To bless this twain, that they may prosperous be
And honor'd in their issue.   [*They sing:*
   Juno. Honor, riches, marriage-blessing,
         Long continuance, and increasing,
         Hourly joys be still upon you !
         Juno sings her blessings on you.
   Cer.   Earth's increase, foison plenty,   110
         Barns and garners never empty,
         Vines and clustering bunches growing,
         Plants with goodly burthen bowing ;
         Spring come to you at the farthest
         In the very end of harvest !
         Scarcity and want shall shun you ;
         Ceres' blessing so is on you.
   Fer. This is a most majestic vision, and
Harmonious charmingly. May I be bold
To think these spirits ?
   Pros.   Spirits, which by mine art   120
I have from their confines call'd to enact
My present fancies.
   Fer.   Let me live here ever ;
So rare a wonder'd father and a wife
Makes this place Paradise.
         [*Juno and Ceres whisper, and send*
                 Iris on employment.
   Pros.   Sweet, now, silence !
Juno and Ceres whisper seriously ;
There's something else to do : hush, and be mute,
Or else our spell is marr'd.
   Iris. You nymphs, call'd Naiads, of the windring brooks,
With your sedged crowns and ever-harmless looks,
Leave your crisp channels and on this green land
Answer your summons ; Juno does command :
Come, temperate nymphs, and help to celebrate
A contract of true love ; be not too late.

Enter certain Nymphs.

You sunburnt sicklemen, of August weary,
Come hither from the furrow and be merry :
Make holiday ; your rye-straw hats put on
And these fresh nymphs encounter every one
In country footing.

Enter certain Reapers, properly habited : they join with the Nymphs in a graceful dance ; towards the end whereof PROSPERO *starts suddenly, and speaks ; after which, to a strange, hollow, and confused noise, they heavily vanish.*

   Pros. [*Aside*] I had forgot that foul conspiracy
Of the beast Caliban and his confederates 140
Against my life : the minute of their plot

Is almost come. [*To the Spirits.*] Well done!
    avoid; no more!
  Fer. This is strange: your father's in some
        passion
That works him strongly.
  Mir.   Never till this day
Saw I him touch'd with anger so distemper'd.
  Pros. You do look, my son, in a moved
        sort,
As if you were dismay'd: be cheerful, sir.
Our revels now are ended. These our actors,
As I foretold you, were all spirits and
Are melted into air, into thin air: 150
And, like the baseless fabric of this vision,
The cloud-capp'd towers, the gorgeous palaces,
The solemn temples, the great globe itself,
Yea, all which it inherit, shall dissolve
And, like this insubstantial pageant faded,
Leave not a rack behind. We are such stuff
As dreams are made on, and our little life
Is rounded with a sleep. Sir, I am vex'd;
Bear with my weakness; my old brain is
        troubled:
Be not disturb'd with my infirmity: 160
If you be pleased, retire into my cell
And there repose: a turn or two I'll walk,
To still my beating mind.
  Fer. Mir. We wish your peace. [*Exeunt.*
  Pros. Come with a thought. I thank thee,
Ariel: come.

              Enter ARIEL.
  Ari. Thy thoughts I cleave to. What's thy
        pleasure?
  Pros.   Spirit,
We must prepare to meet with Caliban.
  Ari. Ay, my commander: when I pre-
        sented Ceres,
I thought to have told thee of it, but I fear'd
Lest I might anger thee.
  Pros. Say again, where didst thou leave
        these varlets?   170
  Ari. I told you, sir, they were red-hot with
        drinking;
So full of valor that they smote the air
For breathing in their faces; beat the ground
For kissing of their feet; yet always bending
Towards their project. Then I beat my tabor;
At which, like unback'd colts, they prick'd
        their ears,
Advanced their eyelids, lifted up their noses
As they smelt music: so I charm'd their ears
That calf-like they my lowing follow'd through
Tooth'd briers, sharp furzes, pricking goss and
        thorns,   180
Which entered their frail shins: at last I left
        them
I' the filthy-mantled pool beyond your cell,
There dancing up to the chins, that the foul
        lake
O'erstunk their feet.
  Pros.   This was well done, my bird.
Thy shape invisible retain thou still:
The trumpery in my house, go bring it hither,
For stale to catch these thieves.
  Ari.   I go, I go. [*Exit.*
  Pros. A devil, a born devil, on whose na-
        ture
Nurture can never stick; on whom my pains,
Humanely taken, all, all lost, quite lost; 190
And as with age his body uglier grows,
So his mind cankers. I will plague them all,
Even to roaring.

Re-enter ARIEL, *loaden with glistering ap-*
        parel, &c.
Come, hang them on this line.

PROSPERO *and* ARIEL *remain invisible. Enter*
CALIBAN, STEPHANO, *and* TRINCULO, *all*
wet.
  Cal. Pray you, tread softly, that the blind
        mole may not
Hear a foot fall: we now are near his cell.
  Ste. Monster, your fairy, which you say is
a harmless fairy, has done little better than
played the Jack with us.
  Trin. Monster, I do smell all horse-piss; at
which my nose is in great indignation.   200
  Ste. So is mine. Do you hear, monster?
If I should take a displeasure against you,
look you,—
  Trin. Thou wert but a lost monster.
  Cal. Good my lord, give me thy favor still.
Be patient, for the prize I'll bring thee to
Shall hoodwink this mischance: therefore
        speak softly.
All's hush'd as midnight yet.
  Trin. Ay, but to lose our bottles in the
        pool,—
  Ste. There is not only disgrace and dis-
honor in that, monster, but an infinite loss. 210
  Trin. That's more to me than my wetting:
yet this is your harmless fairy, monster.
  Ste. I will fetch off my bottle, though I be
o'er ears for my labor.
  Cal. Prithee, my king, be quiet. See'st thou
        here,
This is the mouth o' the cell: no noise, and
        enter.
Do that good mischief which may make this
        island
Thine own for ever, and I, thy Caliban,
For aye thy foot-licker.
  Ste. Give me thy hand. I do begin to have
bloody thoughts.   220
  Trin. O king Stephano! O peer! O worthy
Stephano! look what a wardrobe here is for
thee!
  Cal. Let it alone, thou fool; it is but trash.
  Trin. O, ho, monster! we know what be-
longs to a frippery. O king Stephano!
  Ste. Put off that gown, Trinculo; by this
hand, I'll have that gown.
  Trin. Thy grace shall have it.
  Cal. The dropsy drown this fool! what do
        you mean   230
To dote thus on such luggage? Let's alone
And do the murder first: if he awake,
From toe to crown he'll fill our skins with
        pinches,
Make us strange stuff.
  Ste. Be you quiet, monster. Mistress line,
is not this my jerkin? Now is the jerkin under
the line: now, jerkin, you are like to lose your
hair and prove a bald jerkin.
  Trin. Do, do: we steal by line and level,
an't like your grace.   240
  Ste. I thank thee for that jest; here's a
garment for't: wit shall not go unrewarded
while I am king of this country. 'Steal by line
and level' is an excellent pass of pate; there's
another garment for't.
  Trin. Monster, come, put some lime upon
your fingers, and away with the rest.

Cal. I will have none on't : we shall lose
   our time,
And all be turn'd to barnacles, or to apes
With foreheads villanous low.   250
   Ste. Monster, lay-to your fingers : help to
bear this away where my hogshead of wine
is, or I'll turn you out of my kingdom : go
to, carry this.
   Trin. And this.
   Ste. Ay, and this.

A noise of hunters heard. Enter divers Spir-
   its, in shape of dogs and hounds, and hunt
   them about, PROSPERO *and* ARIEL *setting*
   them on.

   Pros. Hey, Mountain, hey !
   Ari. Silver ! there it goes, Silver !
   Pros. Fury, Fury ! there, Tyrant, there !
       hark ! hark ! [*Cal., Ste., and Trin. are*
                          driven out.
Go charge my goblins that they grind their
   joints
With dry convulsions, shorten up their sinews
With aged cramps, and more pinch-spotted
   make them
Than pard or cat o' mountain.
   Ari.   Hark, they roar !
   Pros. Let them be hunted soundly. At this
   hour
Lie at my mercy all mine enemies :
Shortly shall all my labors end, and thou
Shalt have the air at freedom : for a little
Follow, and do me service.   [*Exeunt.*

ACT V.

Scene I. *Before* Prospero's *cell.*

Enter PROSPERO *in his magic robes, and*
   ARIEL.

   Pros. Now does my project gather to a
   head :
My charms crack not ; my spirits obey ; and
   time
Goes upright with his carriage. How's the
   day ?
   Ari. On the sixth hour ; at which time, my
   lord,
You said our work should cease.
   Pros.   I did say so,
When first I raised the tempest. Say, my spirit,
How fares the king and's followers ?
   Ari.   Confined together
In the same fashion as you gave in charge,
Just as you left them ; all prisoners, sir,
In the line-grove which weather-fends your
   cell ;
They cannot budge till your release. The
   king,
His brother and yours, abide all three dis-
   tracted
And the remainder mourning over them,
Brimful of sorrow and dismay ; but chiefly
Him that you term'd, sir, ' The good old lord,
   Gonzalo ; '
His tears run down his beard, like winter's
   drops
From eaves of reeds. Your charm so strongly
   works 'em
That if you now beheld them, your affections
Would become tender.
   Pros.   Dost thou think so, spirit ?

   Ari. Mine would, sir, were I human.
   Pros.   And mine shall.   20
Hast thou, which art but air, a touch, a feel-
   ing
Of their afflictions, and shall not myself,
One of their kind, that relish all as sharply,
Passion as they, be kindlier moved than thou
   art ?
Though with their high wrongs I am struck
   to the quick,
Yet with my nobler reason 'gainst my fury
Do I take part : the rarer action is
In virtue than in vengeance : they being pen-
   itent,
The sole drift of my purpose doth extend   29
Not a frown further. Go release them, Ariel :
My charms I'll break, their senses I'll restore,
And they shall be themselves.
   Ari.   I'll fetch them, sir. [*Exit.*
   Pros. Ye elves of hills, brooks, standing
       lakes and groves,
And ye that on the sands with printless foot
Do chase the ebbing Neptune and do fly him
When he comes back ; you demi-puppets that
By moonshine do the green sour ringlets
   make,
Whereof the ewe not bites, and you whose
   pastime
Is to make midnight mushrooms, that rejoice
To hear the solemn curfew ; by whose aid   40
Weak masters though ye be, I have bedimm'd
The noontide sun, call'd forth the mutinous
   winds,
And 'twixt the green sea and the azured vault
Set roaring war : to the dread rattling thun-
   der
Have I given fire and rifted Jove's stout oak
With his own bolt ; the strong-based prom-
   ontory
Have I made shake and by the spurs pluck'd
   up
The pine and cedar : graves at my command
Have waked their sleepers, oped, and let 'em
   forth
By my so potent art. But this rough magic   50
I here abjure, and, when I have required
Some heavenly music, which even now I do,
To work mine end upon their senses that
This airy charm is for, I'll break my staff,
Bury it certain fathoms in the earth,
And deeper than did ever plummet sound
I'll drown my book.   [*Solemn music.*

Re-enter ARIEL *before : then* ALONSO, *with a*
   frantic gesture, attended by GONZALO ; SE-
   BASTIAN *and* ANTONIO *in like manner, at-*
   tended by ADRIAN *and* FRANCISCO : *they all*
   enter the circle which PROSPERO *had made,*
   and there stand charmed ; which PROSPERO
   observing, speaks :

A solemn air and the best comforter
To an unsettled fancy cure thy brains,
Now useless, boil'd within thy skull ! There
   stand,
For you are spell-stopp'd.
Holy Gonzalo, honorable man,
Mine eyes, even sociable to the show of thine,
Fall fellowly drops. The charm dissolves
   apace,
And as the morning steals upon the night,
Melting the darkness, so their rising senses
Begin to chase the ignorant fumes that man-
   tle

Their clearer reason. O good Gonzalo,
My true preserver, and a loyal sir   69
To him thou follow'st ! I will pay thy graces
Home both in word and deed. Most cruelly
Didst thou, Alonso, use me and my daughter :
Thy brother was a furtherer in the act.
Thou art pinch'd for't now, Sebastian. Flesh
  and blood,
You, brother mine, that entertain'd ambition,
Expell'd remorse and nature ; who, with Se-
  bastian,
Whose inward pinches therefore are most
  strong,
Would here have kill'd your king ; I do for-
  give him,
Unnatural though thou art. Their understand-
  ing
Begins to swell, and the approaching tide   80
Will shortly fill the reasonable shore
That now lies foul and muddy. Not one of
  them
That yet looks on me, or would know me :
  Ariel,
Fetch me the hat and rapier in my cell :
I will discase me, and myself present
As I was sometime Milan : quickly, spirit ;
Thou shalt ere long be free.

      ARIEL *sings and helps to attire him.*
      Where the bee sucks, there suck I :
      In a cowslip's bell I lie ;
      There I couch when owls do cry.   90
      On the bat's back I do fly
      After summer merrily.
    Merrily, merrily shall I live now
    Under the blossom that hangs on the bough.
  Pros. Why, that's my dainty Ariel ! I shall
    miss thee :
But yet thou shalt have freedom : so, so, so.
To the king's ship, invisible as thou art :
There shalt thou find the mariners asleep
Under the hatches ; the master and the boat-
  swain
Being awake, enforce them to this place,   100
And presently, I prithee.
  Ari. I drink the air before me, and return
Or ere your pulse twice beat.   [*Exit.*
  Gon. All torment, trouble, wonder and
  amazement
Inhabits here : some heavenly power guide us
Out of this fearful country !
  Pros.   Behold, sir king,
The wronged Duke of Milan, Prospero :
For more assurance that a living prince
Does now speak to thee, I embrace thy body ;
And to thee and thy company I bid   110
A hearty welcome.
  Alon.   Whether thou be'st he or no,
Or some enchanted trifle to abuse me,
As late I have been, I not know : thy pulse
Beats as of flesh and blood ; and, since I saw
  thee,
The affliction of my mind amends, with which,
I fear, a madness held me : this must crave,
An if this be at all, a most strange story.
Thy dukedom I resign and do entreat
Thou pardon me my wrongs. But how should
  Prospero
Be living and be here ?
  Pros.   First, noble friend, 120
Let me embrace thine age, whose honor can-
  not

Be measured or confined.
  Gon.   Whether this be
Or be not, I'll not swear.
  Pros.   You do yet taste
Some subtilties o' the isle, that will not let
  you
Believe things certain. Welcome, my friends
  all !
[*Aside to Seb. and Ant.*] But you, my brace
  of lords, were I so minded,
I here could pluck his highness' frown upon
  you
And justify you traitors : at this time
I will tell no tales.
  Seb. [*Aside*] The devil speaks in him.
  Pros.   No.
For you, most wicked sir, whom to call brother
Would even infect my mouth, I do forgive
Thy rankest fault ; all of them ; and require
My dukedom of thee, which perforce, I know,
Thou must restore.
  Alon.   If thou be'st Prospero,
Give us particulars of thy preservation ;
How thou hast met us here, who three hours
  since
Were wreck'd upon this shore ; where I have
  lost—
How sharp the point of this remembrance
  is !—
My dear son Ferdinand.
  Pros.   I am woe for't, sir.
  Alon. Irreparable is the loss, and patience
Says it is past her cure.   141
  Pros.   I rather think
You have not sought her help, of whose soft
  grace
For the like loss I have her sovereign aid
And rest myself content.
  Alon.   You the like loss !
  Pros. As great to me as late ; and, sup-
  portable
To make the dear loss, have I means much
  weaker
Than you may call to comfort you, for I
Have lost my daughter.
  Alon.   A daughter ?
O heavens, that they were living both in
  Naples,
The king and queen there ! that they were, I
  wish
Myself were mudded in that oozy bed
Where my son lies. When did you lose your
  daughter ?
  Pros. In this last tempest. I perceive these
  lords
At this encounter do so much admire
That they devour their reason and scarce think
Their eyes do offices of truth, their words
Are natural breath : but, howsoe'er you have
Been justled from your senses, know for cer-
  tain
That I am Prospero and that very duke
Which was thrust forth of Milan, who most
  strangely   160
Upon this shore, where you were wreck'd,
  was landed,
To be the lord on't. No more yet of this ;
For 'tis a chronicle of day by day,
Not a relation for a breakfast nor
Befitting this first meeting. Welcome, sir ;
This cell's my court : here have I few attend-
  ants
And subjects none abroad : pray you, look in.

My dukedom since you have given me again,
I will requite you with as good a thing;
At least bring forth a wonder, to content ye
As much as me my dukedom.   171

Here Prospero *discovers* Ferdinand *and* Mi-
    randa *playing at chess.*

Mir. Sweet lord, you play me false.
Fer.   No, my dear'st love,
I would not for the world.
Mir. Yes, for a score of kingdoms you
    should wrangle,
And I would call it fair play.
Alon.   If this prove
A vision of the Island, one dear son
Shall I twice lose.
Seb.   A most high miracle!
Fer. Though the seas threaten, they are
    merciful;
I have cursed them without cause. [*Kneels.*
Alon.   Now all the blessings
Of a glad father compass thee about!   180
Arise, and say how thou camest here.
Mir.   O, wonder!
How many goodly creatures are there here!
How beauteous mankind is! O brave new
    world,
That has such people in't!
Pros.   'Tis new to thee.
Alon. What is this maid with whom thou
    wast at play?
Your eld'st acquaintance cannot be three
    hours:
Is she the goddess that hath sever'd us,
And brought us thus together?
Fer.   Sir, she is mortal;
But by immortal Providence she's mine : 189
I chose her when I could not ask my father
For his advice, nor thought I had one. She
Is daughter to this famous Duke of Milan,
Of whom so often I have heard renown,
But never saw before; of whom I have
Received a second life; and second father
This lady makes him to me.
Alon.   I am hers:
But, O, how oddly will it sound that I
Must ask my child forgiveness!
Pros.   There, sir, stop:
Let us not burthen our remembrance with
A heaviness that's gone.
Gon.   I have inly wept, 200
Or should have spoke ere this. Look down,
    you gods,
And on this couple drop a blessed crown!
For it is you that have chalk'd forth the way
Which brought us hither.
Alon.   I say, Amen, Gonzalo!
Gon. Was Milan thrust from Milan, that
    his issue
Should become kings of Naples? O, rejoice
Beyond a common joy, and set it down
With gold on lasting pillars : In one voyage
Did Claribel her husband find at Tunis,
And Ferdinand, her brother, found a wife 210
Where he himself was lost, Prospero his duke-
    dom
In a poor isle and all of us ourselves
When no man was his own.
Alon. [*To Fer. and Mir.*] Give me your
    hands:
Let grief and sorrow still embrace his heart
That doth not wish you joy!
Gon.   Be it so! Amen!

Re-enter Ariel, *with the* Master *and* Boat-
    swain *amazedly following.*

O, look, sir, look, sir! here is more of us:
I prophesied, if a gallows were on land,
This fellow could not drown. Now, blas-
    phemy,
That swear'st grace o'erboard, not an oath on
    shore?
Hast thou no mouth by land? What is the
    news?   220
Boats. The best news is, that we have safely
    found
Our king and company; the next, our ship—
Which, but three glasses since, we gave out
    split—
Is tight and yare and bravely rigg'd as when
We first put out to sea.
Ari. [*Aside to Pros.*] Sir, all this service
Have I done since I went.
Pros. [*Aside to Ari.*] My tricksy spirit!
Alon. These are not natural events; they
    strengthen
From strange to stranger. Say, how came you
    hither?
Boats. If I did think, sir, I were well
    awake,
I'ld strive to tell you. We were dead of sleep,
And—how we know not—all clapp'd under
    hatches;
Where but even now with strange and several
    noises
Of roaring, shrieking, howling, jingling chains,
And more diversity of sounds, all horrible,
We were awaked; straightway, at liberty;
Where we, in all her trim, freshly beheld
Our royal, good and gallant ship, our master
Capering to eye her : on a trice, so please
    you,
Even in a dream, were we divided from them
And were brought moping hither.
Ari. [*Aside to Pros.*] Was't well done? 240
Pros. [*Aside to Ari.*] Bravely, my diligence.
Thou shalt be free.
Alon. This is as strange a maze as e'er men
    trod;
And there is in this business more than nature
Was ever conduct of : some oracle
Must rectify our knowledge.
Pros.   Sir, my liege,
Do not infest your mind with beating on
The strangeness of this business; at pick'd
    leisure
Which shall be shortly, single I'll resolve you,
Which to you shall seem probable, of every
These happen'd accidents; till when, be cheer-
    ful   250
And think of each thing well. [*Aside to Ari.*]
    Come hither, spirit :
Set Caliban and his companions free;
Untie the spell. [*Exit Ariel.*] How fares my
    gracious sir?
There are yet missing of your company
Some few odd lads that you remember not.

Re-enter Ariel, *driving in* Caliban, Stephano
    and Trinculo, *in their stolen apparel.*

Ste. Every man shift for all the rest, and
let no man take care for himself; for all is
but fortune. Coragio, bully-monster, coragio!
Trin. If these be true spies which I wear
in my head, here's a goodly sight.   260

Cal. O Setebos, these be brave spirits in-
    deed !
How fine my master is ! I am afraid
He will chastise me.
    Seb.   Ha, ha !
What things are these, my lord Antonio ?
Will money buy 'em ?
    Ant.   Very like ; one of them
Is a plain fish, and, no doubt, marketable.
    Pros. Mark but the badges of these men,
    my lords,
Then say if they be true. This mis-shapen
    knave,
His mother was a witch, and one so strong
That could control the moon, make flows and
    ebbs,   270
And deal in her command without her power.
These three have robb'd me ; and this demi-
    devil—
For he's a bastard one—had plotted with them
To take my life. Two of these fellows you
Must know and own ; this thing of darkness I
Acknowledge mine.
    Cal.   I shall be pinch'd to death.
    Alon. Is not this Stephano, my drunken
    butler ?
    Seb. He is drunk now : where had he
    wine ?
    Alon. And Trinculo is reeling ripe : where
    should they
Find this grand liquor that hath gilded 'em ?
How camest thou in this pickle ?   281
    Trin. I have been in such a pickle since I
saw you last that, I fear me, will never out of
my bones : I shall not fear fly-blowing.
    Seb. Why, how now, Stephano !
    Ste. O, touch me not ; I am not Stephano,
but a cramp.
    Pros. You'ld be king o' the isle, sirrah ?
    Ste. I should have been a sore one then.
    Alon. This is a strange thing as e'er I
    look'd on.   [*Pointing to Caliban.*
    Pros. He is as disproportion'd in his man-
    ners   290
As in his shape. Go, sirrah, to my cell ;
Take with you your companions ; as you look
To have my pardon, trim it handsomely.
    Cal. Ay, that I will ; and I'll be wise here-
    after
And seek for grace. What a thrice-double ass
Was I, to take this drunkard for a god
And worship this dull fool !
    Pros.   Go to ; away !
    Alon. Hence, and bestow your luggage
    where you found it.

    Seb. Or stole it, rather.
                    [*Exeunt Cal., Ste., and Trin.*
    Pros. Sir, I invite your highness and your
    train   300
To my poor cell, where you shall take your
    rest
For this one night ; which, part of it, I'll
    waste
With such discourse as, I not doubt, shall
    make it
Go quick away ; the story of my life
And the particular accidents gone by
Since I came to this isle : and in the morn
I'll bring you to your ship and so to Naples,
Where I have hope to see the nuptial
Of these our dear-beloved solemnized ;
And thence retire me to my Milan, where 310
Every third thought shall be my grave.
    Alon.   I long
To hear the story of your life, which must
Take the ear strangely.
    Pros.   I'll deliver all ;
And promise you calm seas, auspicious gales
And sail so expeditious that shall catch
Your royal fleet far off. [*Aside to Ari.*] My
    Ariel, chick,
That is thy charge : then to the elements
Be free, and fare thou well ! Please you, draw
    near.   [*Exeunt.*

EPILOGUE.

SPOKEN BY PROSPERO.

Now my charms are all o'erthrown,
And what strength I have's mine own,
Which is most faint : now, 'tis true,
I must be here confined by you,
Or sent to Naples. Let me not,
Since I have my dukedom got
And pardon'd the deceiver, dwell
In this bare island by your spell ;
But release me from my bands
With the help of your good hands :   10
Gentle breath of yours my sails
Must fill, or else my project fails,
Which was to please. Now I want
Spirits to enforce, art to enchant,
And my ending is despair,
Unless I be relieved by prayer,
Which pierces so that it assaults
Mercy itself and frees all faults.
As you from crimes would pardon'd be,
Let your indulgence set me free.   20

THE WINTER'S TALE.

(WRITTEN ABOUT 1610–11.)

INTRODUCTION.

The Winter's Tale was seen at the Globe on May 15, 1611, by Dr. Forman, and is described in his MS. *Booke of Plaies and Notes thereof.* The versification is that of Shakespeare's latest group of plays : no five-measure lines are rhymed ; run-on lines and double endings are numerous. Its tone and feeling place it in the same period with *The Tempest* and *Cymbeline ;* its breezy air is surely that which blew over Warwickshire fields upon Shakespeare now returned to Stratford ; its country lads and lasses, and their junketings, are those with which the poet had in a happy spirit renewed his acquaintance. *The Winter's Tale* is perhaps the last complete play that Shakespeare wrote. It is founded upon Greene's *Pandosto* (or, as it was afterward named, *Dorastus and Fawnia*) first published in 1588. The idea of introducing Time as a chorus comes from Greene, and all the principal characters, except Paulina and the incomparable rogue Autolycus. After his manner, Shakespeare drives forward to what chiefly interests him in the subject. The jealousy of Leontes is not a detailed dramatic study like the love and jealousy of Othello. It is a gross madness which mounts to the brain, and turns Leontes' whole nature into unreasoning passion. The character of the noble sufferer Hermione is that with which the dramatist is above all concerned—this first ; and, secondly, the grace, beauty, and girlish happiness of Perdita ; while of the subordinate persons of the drama, Shakespeare delights chiefly in his own creation, Autolycus, the most charming of rogues and rovers. Hermione may be placed side by side with the Queen Katharine of *Henry VIII.*, which play belongs to this period. Both are noble sufferers, who by the dignity and purity of their natures transcend all feeling of vulgar resentment. Deep and even quick feeling never renders Hermione incapable of an admirable justice, nor deprives her of a true sense of pity for him who so gravely wrongs both her and himself. The meeting of kindred, with forgiveness and reconciliation, if these are called for by past offences, forms the common ending of the last plays of Shakespeare. Perdita belongs to the group of exquisite youthful figures set over against those of their graver and sadder elders in the plays of this period. She is one of the same company with Miranda and Marina, and the youthful sons of Cymbeline. The shepherdess-princess, " queen of curds and cream," is less a vision than Miranda, the child of wonder, but more perhaps a creature of this earth. There is nothing lovelier or more innocently joyous in poetry than Perdita at the rustic merry-making, sharing her flowers with old and young. And in Florizel she has found a lover, full of the innocence and chivalry of unstained early manhood. Autolycus stands by himself among the creations of the dramatist. The art of thieving as practised by him is no crime, but the gift of some knavish god. He does not trample on the laws of morality, but dances or leaps over them with so nimble a foot that we forbear to stay him. In the sad world which contains a Leontes and can lose a Mamillius, so light-hearted a wanderer must be pardoned even if he be light-fingered, and sometimes mistakes for his own the sheet bleaching on the hedge, which happens to be ours.

DRAMATIS PERSONÆ.

LEONTES, king of Sicilia.
MAMILLIUS, young prince of Sicilia.
CAMILLO,
ANTIGONUS,   } Four Lords of Sicilia.
CLEOMENES,
DION,
POLIXENES, king of Bohemia.
FLORIZEL, prince of Bohemia.
ARCHIDAMUS, a Lord of Bohemia.
Old Shepherd, reputed father of Perdita.
Clown, his son.
AUTOLYCUS, a rogue.

A Mariner.
A Gaoler.
HERMIONE, queen to Leontes.
PERDITA, daughter to Leontes and Hermione.
PAULINA, wife to Antigonus.
EMILIA, a lady attending on Hermione.
MOPSA,
DORCAS,   } Shepherdesses.

Other Lords and Gentlemen, Ladies, Officers, and Servants, Shepherds, and Shepherdesses.

Time, as Chorus.

SCENE : *Sicilia, and Bohemia.*

ACT I.

SCENE I. *Antechamber in* LEONTES' *palace.*

Enter CAMILLO *and* ARCHIDAMUS.

Arch. If you shall chance, Camillo, to visit Bohemia, on the like occasion whereon my services are now on foot, you shall see, as I have said, great difference betwixt our Bohemia and your Sicilia.

Cam. I think, this coming summer, the King of Sicilia means to pay Bohemia the visitation which he justly owes him.

Arch. Wherein our entertainment shall shame us we will be justified in our loves; for indeed—　　　　　　　　　　　　　　　10

Cam. Beseech you,—

Arch. Verily, I speak it in the freedom of my knowledge: we cannot with such magnificence—in so rare—I know not what to say. We will give you sleepy drinks, that your senses, unintelligent of our insufficience, may, though they cannot praise us, as little accuse us.

Cam. You pay a great deal too dear for what's given freely.　　　　　　　　　19

Arch. Believe me, I speak as my understanding instructs me and as mine honesty puts it to utterance.

Cam. Sicilia cannot show himself over-kind to Bohemia. They were trained together in their childhoods; and there rooted betwixt them then such an affection, which cannot choose but branch now. Since their more mature dignities and royal necessities made separation of their society, their encounters, though not personal, have been royally attorneyed with interchange of gifts, letters, loving embassies; that they have seemed to be together, though absent, shook hands, as over a vast, and embraced, as it were, from the ends of opposed winds. The heavens continue their loves!

Arch. I think there is not in the world either malice or matter to alter it. You have an unspeakable comfort of your young prince Mamillius: it is a gentleman of the greatest promise that ever came into my note.　40

Cam. I very well agree with you in the hopes of him: it is a gallant child; one that indeed physics the subject, makes old hearts fresh: they that went on crutches ere he was born desire yet their life to see him a man.

Arch. Would they else be content to die?

Cam. Yes; if there were no other excuse why they should desire to live.

Arch. If the king had no son, they would desire to live on crutches till he had one.　50

[*Exeunt.*

SCENE II. *A room of state in the same.*

Enter LEONTES, HERMIONE, MAMILLIUS, POLIXENES, CAMILLO, *and* Attendants.

Pol. Nine changes of the watery star hath been
The shepherd's note since we have left our throne
Without a burthen: time as long again
Would be fill'd up, my brother, with our thanks;
And yet we should, for perpetuity,
Go hence in debt: and therefore, like a cipher,
Yet standing in rich place, I multiply
With one 'We thank you' many thousands moe
That go before it.

Leon.　　　　Stay your thanks a while;
And pay them when you part.

Pol.　　　　Sir, that's to-morrow.　10
I am question'd by my fears, of what may chance
Or breed upon our absence; that may blow
No sneaping winds at home, to make us say
'This is put forth too truly:' besides, I have stay'd
To tire your royalty.

Leon.　　　　We are tougher, brother,
Than you can put us to't.

Pol.　　　　No longer stay.

Leon. One seven-night longer.

Pol.　　　　Very sooth, to-morrow.

Leon. We'll part the time between's then; and in that
I'll no gainsaying.

Pol.　　　　Press me not, beseech you, so.
There is no tongue that moves, none, none i' the world,　20
So soon as yours could win me: so it should now,
Were there necessity in your request, although
'Twere needful I denied it. My affairs
Do even drag me homeward: which to hinder
Were in your love a whip to me; my stay
To you a charge and trouble: to save both,
Farewell, our brother.

Leon. Tongue-tied, our queen? speak you.

Her. I had thought, sir, to have held my peace until
You have drawn oaths from him not to stay. You, sir,
Charge him too coldly. Tell him, you are sure
All in Bohemia's well; this satisfaction　31
The by-gone day proclaim'd: say this to him,
He's beat from his best ward.

Leon.　　　　Well said, Hermione.

Her. To tell, he longs to see his son, were strong:
But let him say so then, and let him go;
But let him swear so, and he shall not stay,
We'll thwack him hence with distaffs.
Yet of your royal presence I'll adventure
The borrow of a week. When at Bohemia
You take my lord, I'll give him my commission　40
To let him there a month behind the gest
Prefix'd for's parting: yet, good deed, Leontes,
I love thee not a jar o' the clock behind
What lady-she her lord. You'll stay?

Pol.　　　　No, madam.

Her. Nay, but you will?

Pol.　　　　I may not, verily.

Her. Verily!
You put me off with limber vows; but I,
Though you would seek to unsphere the stars with oaths,
Should yet say 'Sir, no going.' Verily,
You shall not go: a lady's 'Verily''s　50
As potent as a lord's. Will you go yet?
Force me to keep you as a prisoner,
Not like a guest; so you shall pay your fees
When you depart, and save your thanks. How say you?
My prisoner? or my guest? by your dread 'Verily,'

One of them you shall be.

Pol.   Your guest, then, madam :
To be your prisoner should import offending ;
Which is for me less easy to commit
Than you to punish.

Her.   Not your gaoler, then,
But your kind hostess. Come, I'll question
    you   60
Of my lord's tricks and yours when you were
    boys :
You were pretty lordings then ?

Pol.   We were, fair queen,
Two lads that thought there was no more be-
    hind
But such a day to-morrow as to-day,
And to be boy eternal.

Her.   Was not my lord
The verier wag o' the two ?

Pol.   We were as twinn'd lambs that did
    frisk i' the sun,
And bleat the one at the other : what we
    changed
Was innocence for innocence ; we knew not
The doctrine of ill-doing, nor dream'd   70
That any did. Had we pursued that life,
And our weak spirits ne'er been higher rear'd
With stronger blood, we should have answer'd
    heaven
Boldly ' not guilty ; ' the imposition clear'd
Hereditary ours.

Her.   By this we gather
You have tripp'd since.

Pol.   O my most sacred lady !
Temptations have since then been born to's ;
    for
In those unfledged days was my wife a girl ;
Your precious self had then not cross'd the
    eyes
Of my young play-fellow.

Her.   Grace to boot !   80
Of this make no conclusion, lest you say
Your queen and I are devils : yet go on ;
The offences we have made you do we'll an-
    swer,
If you first sinn'd with us and that with us
You did continue fault and that you slipp'd
    not
With any but with us.

Leon.   Is he won yet ?

Her. He'll stay, my lord.

Leon.   At my request he would not.
Hermione, my dearest, thou never spokest
To better purpose.

Her.   Never ?

Leon.   Never, but once.

Her. What ! have I twice said well ? when
    was't before ?   90
I prithee tell me ; cram's with praise, and
    make's
As fat as tame things : one good deed dying
    tongueless
Slaughters a thousand waiting upon that.
Our praises are our wages : you may ride's
With one soft kiss a thousand furlongs ere
With spur we beat an acre. But to the goal :
My last good deed was to entreat his stay :
What was my first ? it has an elder sister,
Or I mistake you : O, would her name were
    Grace !
But once before I spoke to the purpose :
    when ?
Nay, let me have't ; I long.

Leon.   Why, that was when 101

Three crabbed months had sour'd themselves
    to death,
Ere I could make thee open thy white hand
And clap thyself my love : then didst thou
    utter
' I am yours for ever.'

Her.   'Tis grace indeed.
Why, lo you now, I have spoke to the purpose
    twice :
The one for ever earn'd a royal husband ;
The other for some while a friend.

Leon.   [*Aside*] Too hot, too hot !
To mingle friendship far is mingling bloods.
I have tremor cordis on me : my heart
    dances ;
But not for joy ; not joy. This entertainment
May a free face put on, derive a liberty
From heartiness, from bounty, fertile bosom,
And well become the agent ; 't may, I grant ;
But to be paddling palms and pinching fingers,
As now they are, and making practised smiles,
As in a looking-glass, and then to sigh, as
    'twere
The mort o' the deer ; O, that is entertain-
    ment
My bosom likes not, nor my brows ! Mamil-
    lius,
Art thou my boy ?

Mam.   Ay, my good lord.

Leon.   I' fecks !   120
Why, that's my bawcock. What, hast smutch'd
    thy nose ?
They say it is a copy out of mine. Come, cap-
    tain,
We must be neat ; not neat, but cleanly, cap-
    tain :
And yet the steer, the heifer and the calf
Are all call'd neat.—Still virginalling
Upon his palm !—How now, you wanton calf !
Art thou my calf ?

Mam.   Yes, if you will, my lord.

Leon. Thou want'st a rough pash and the
    shoots that I have,
To be full like me : but they say we are
Almost as like as eggs ; women say so,   130
That will say anything : but were they false
As o'er-dyed blacks, as wind, as waters, false
As dice are to be wish'd by one that fixes
No bourn 'twixt his and mine, yet were it true
To say this boy were like me. Come, sir page,
Look on me with your welkin eye : sweet vil-
    lain !
Most dear'st ! my collop ! Can thy dam ?—
    may't be ?—
Affection ! thy intention stabs the centre :
Thou dost make possible things not so held,
Communicatest with dreams ;—how can this
    be ?—   140
With what's unreal thou coactive art,
And fellow'st nothing : then 'tis very credent
Thou mayst co-join with something ; and thou
    dost,
And that beyond commission, and I find it,
And that to the infection of my brains
And hardening of my brows.

Pol.   What means Sicilia ?

Her. He something seems unsettled.

Pol.   How, my lord !
What cheer ? how is't with you, best brother ?

Her.   You look
As if you held a brow of much distraction :
Are you moved, my lord ?

Leon.   No, in good earnest. 150

How sometimes nature will betray its folly,
Its tenderness, and make itself a pastime
To harder bosoms! Looking on the lines
Of my boy's face, methoughts I did recoil
Twenty-three years, and saw myself un-
    breech'd,
In my green velvet coat, my dagger muzzled,
Lest it should bite its master, and so prove,
As ornaments oft do, too dangerous :
How like, methought, I then was to this
    kernel,
This squash, this gentleman. Mine honest
    friend,   160
Will you take eggs for money ?
    Mam.   No, my lord, I'll fight.
    Leon. You will! why, happy man be's
    dole! My brother,
Are you so fond of your young prince as we
Do seem to be of ours ?
    Pol.   If at home, sir,
He's all my exercise, my mirth, my matter,
Now my sworn friend and then mine enemy,
My parasite, my soldier, statesman, all :
He makes a July's day short as December,
And with his varying childness cures in me
Thoughts that would thick my blood.   171
    Leon.   So stands this squire
Officed with me : we two will walk, my lord,
And leave you to your graver steps. Hermi-
    one,
How thou lovest us, show in our brother's
    welcome ;
Let what is dear in Sicily be cheap :
Next to thyself and my young rover, he's
Apparent to my heart.
    Her.   If you would seek us,
We are yours i' the garden : shall's attend you
    there ?
    Leon. To your own bents dispose you :
    you'll be found,
Be you beneath the sky. [*Aside*] I am angling
    now,   180
Though you perceive me not how I give line.
Go to, go to!
How she holds up the neb, the bill to him!
And arms her with the boldness of a wife
To her allowing husband!
        [*Exeunt Polixenes, Hermione, and
                Attendants.*
                        Gone already!
Inch-thick, knee-deep, o'er head and ears a
    fork'd one!
Go, play, boy : thy mother plays, and I
Play too, but so disgraced a part, whose issue
Will hiss me to my grave : contempt and
    clamor
Will be my knell. Go, play, boy, play. There
    have been,   190
Or I am much deceived, cuckolds ere now ;
And many a man there is, even at this present,
Now while I speak this, holds his wife by the
    arm,
That little thinks she has been sluiced in's
    absence
And his pond fish'd by his next neighbor, by
Sir Smile, his neighbor : nay, there's comfort
    in't
Whiles other men have gates and those gates
    open'd,
As mine, against their will. Should all de-
    spair
That have revolted wives, the tenth of man-
    kind

Would hang themselves. Physic for't there is
    none ;   200
It is a bawdy planet, that will strike
Where 'tis predominant ; and 'tis powerful,
    think it,
From east, west, north and south : be it con-
    cluded,
No barricado for a belly ; know't ;
It will let in and out the enemy
With bag and baggage : many thousand on's
Have the disease, and feel't not. How now,
    boy!
    Mam. I am like you, they say.
    Leon.   Why that's some comfort.
What, Camillo there ?
    Cam. Ay, my good lord.   210
    Leon. Go play, Mamillius ; thou'rt an hon-
    est man.   [*Exit Mamillius.*
Camillo, this great sir will yet stay longer.
    Cam. You had much ado to make his an-
    chor hold :
When you cast out, it still came home.
    Leon.   Didst note it ?
    Cam. He would not stay at your petitions :
    made
His business more material.
    Leon.   Didst perceive it ?
[*Aside*] They're here with me already, whis-
    pering, rounding
' Sicilia is a so-forth : ' 'tis far gone,
When I shall gust it last. How came't, Ca-
    millo,
That he did stay ?
    Cam. At the good queen's entreaty.   220
    Leon. At the queen's be't : ' good ' should
    be pertinent ;
But, so it is, it is not. Was this taken
By any understanding pate but thine ?
For thy conceit is soaking, will draw in
More than the common blocks : not noted, is't,
But of the finer natures ? by some severals
Of head-piece extraordinary ? lower messes
Perchance are to this business purblind ? say.
    Cam. Business, my lord! I think most un-
    derstand
Bohemia stays here longer.
    Leon.   Ha!
    Cam.   Stays here longer. 230
    Leon. Ay, but why ?
    Cam. To satisfy your highness and the en-
    treaties
Of our most gracious mistress.
    Leon.   Satisfy!
The entreaties of your mistress! satisfy!
Let that suffice. I have trusted thee, Camillo,
With all the nearest things to my heart, as
    well
My chamber-councils, wherein, priest-like,
    thou
Hast cleansed my bosom, I from thee departed
Thy penitent reform'd : but we have been
Deceived in thy integrity, deceived   240
In that which seems so.
    Cam.   Be it forbid, my lord!
    Leon. To bide upon't, thou art not honest,
    or,
If thou inclinest that way, thou art a coward,
Which hoxes honesty behind, restraining
From course required ; or else thou must be
    counted
A servant grafted in my serious trust
And therein negligent ; or else a fool

That seest a game play'd home, the rich stake
    drawn,
And takest it all for jest.
    Cam.   My gracious lord,
I may be negligent, foolish and fearful ;   250
In every one of these no man is free,
But that his negligence, his folly, fear,
Among the infinite doings of the world,
Sometime puts forth. In your affairs, my lord,
If ever I were wilful-negligent,
It was my folly ; if industriously
I play'd the fool, it was my negligence,
Not weighing well the end ; if ever fearful
To do a thing, where I the issue doubted,
Where of the execution did cry out   260
Against the non-performance, 'twas a fear
Which oft infects the wisest : these, my lord,
Are such allow'd infirmities that honesty
Is never free of. But, beseech your grace,
Be plainer with me ; let me know my trespass
By its own visage : if I then deny it,
'Tis none of mine.
    Leon.   Ha' not you seen, Camillo,—
But that's past doubt, you have, or your eye-
    glass
Is thicker than a cuckold's horn,—or heard,—
For to a vision so apparent rumor   270
Cannot be mute,—or thought,—for cogitation
Resides not in that man that does not think,—
My wife is slippery ? If thou wilt confess,
Or else be impudently negative,
To have no eyes nor ears nor thought, then
    say
My wife's a hobby-horse, deserves a name
As rank as any flax-wench that puts to
Before her troth-plight : say't and justify't.
    Cam.   I would not be a stander-by to hear
My sovereign mistress clouded so, without 280
My present vengeance taken : 'shrew my heart,
You never spoke what did become you less
Than this ; which to reiterate were sin
As deep as that, though true.
    Leon.   Is whispering nothing ?
Is leaning cheek to cheek ? is meeting noses ?
Kissing with inside lip ? stopping the career
Of laughing with a sigh ?—a note infallible
Of breaking honesty—horsing foot on foot ?
Skulking in corners ? wishing clocks more
    swift ?
Hours, minutes ? noon, midnight ? and all eyes
Blind with the pin and web but theirs, theirs
    only,
That would unseen be wicked ? is this noth-
    ing ?
Why, then the world and all that's in't is
    nothing ;
The covering sky is nothing ; Bohemia noth-
    ing ;
My wife is nothing ; nor nothing have these
    nothings,
If this be nothing.
    Cam.   Good my lord, be cured
Of this diseased opinion, and betimes ;
For 'tis most dangerous.
    Leon.   Say it be, 'tis true.
    Cam.   No, no, my lord.
    Leon.   It is ; you lie, you lie :
I say thou liest, Camillo, and I hate thee, 300
Pronounce thee a gross lout, a mindless slave,
Or else a hovering temporizer, that
Canst with thine eyes at once see good and
    evil,
Inclining to them both : were my wife's liver

Infected as her life, she would not live
The running of one glass.
    Cam.   Who does infect her ?
    Leon.   Why, he that wears her like a medal,
    hanging
About his neck, Bohemia : who, if I
Had servants true about me, that bare eyes
To see alike mine honor as their profits,   310
Their own particular thrifts, they would do
    that
Which should undo more doing : ay, and thou,
His cupbearer,—whom I from meaner form
Have bench'd and rear'd to worship, who
    mayst see
Plainly as heaven sees earth and earth sees
    heaven,
How I am galled,—mightst bespice a cup,
To give mine enemy a lasting wink ;
Which draught to me were cordial.
    Cam.   Sir, my lord,
I could do this, and that with no rash potion,
But with a lingering dram that should not
    work   320
Maliciously like poison : but I cannot
Believe this crack to be in my dread mistress,
So sovereignly being honorable.
I have loved thee,—
    Leon.   Make that thy question, and go
    rot !
Dost think I am so muddy, so unsettled,
To appoint myself in this vexation, sully
The purity and whiteness of my sheets,
Which to preserve is sleep, which being spot-
    ted
Is goads, thorns, nettles, tails of wasps,
Give scandal to the blood o' the prince my
    son,   330
Who I do think is mine and love as mine,
Without ripe moving to't ? Would I do this ?
Could man so blench ?
    Cam.   I must believe you, sir :
I do ; and will fetch off Bohemia for't ;
Provided that, when he's removed, your high-
    ness
Will take again your queen as yours at first,
Even for your son's sake ; and thereby for
    sealing
The injury of tongues in courts and kingdoms
Known and allied to yours.
    Leon.   Thou dost advise me
Even so as I mine own course have set down :
I'll give no blemish to her honor, none.   341
    Cam.   My lord,
Go then ; and with a countenance as clear
As friendship wears at feasts, keep with Bo-
    hemia
And with your queen. I am his cupbearer :
If from me he have wholesome beverage,
Account me not your servant.
    Leon.   This is all :
Do't and thou hast the one half of my heart ;
Do't not, thou split'st thine own.
    Cam.   I'll do't, my lord.
    Leon.   I will seem friendly, as thou hast
    advised me.   [*Exit.* 350
    Cam.   O miserable lady ! But, for me,
What case stand I in ? I must be the poisoner
Of good Polixenes ; and my ground to do't
Is the obedience to a master, one
Who in rebellion with himself will have
All that are his so too. To do this deed,
Promotion follows. If I could find example
Of thousands that had struck anointed kings

And flourish'd after, I'ld not do't; but since
Nor brass nor stone nor parchment bears not
 one,   360
Let villany itself forswear't. I must
Forsake the court : to do't, or no, is certain
To me a break-neck. Happy star, reign now !
Here comes Bohemia.

    Re-enter POLIXENES.

Pol.   This is strange : methinks
My favor here begins to warp. Not speak ?
Good day, Camillo.
 Cam.   Hail, most royal sir !
 Pol. What is the news i' the court ?
 Cam.   None rare, my lord.
 Pol. The king hath on him such a counte-
  nance
As he had lost some province and a region
Loved as he loves himself : even now I met
 him   370
With customary compliment ; when he,
Wafting his eyes to the contrary and falling
A lip of much contempt, speeds from me and
So leaves me to consider what is breeding
That changeth thus his manners.
 Cam. I dare not know, my lord.
 Pol. How ! dare not ! do not. Do you
  know, and dare not ?
Be intelligent to me : 'tis thereabouts :
For, to yourself, what you do know, you must,
And cannot say, you dare not. Good Camillo,
Your changed complexions are to me a mirror
Which shows me mine changed too ; for I
  must be
A party in this alteration, finding
Myself thus alter'd with 't.
 Cam.   There is a sickness
Which puts some of us in distemper, but
I cannot name the disease ; and it is caught
Of you that yet are well.
 Pol.   How ! caught of me !
Make me not sighted like the basilisk :
I have look'd on thousands, who have sped the
  better
By my regard, but kill'd none so. Camillo,—
As you are certainly a gentleman, thereto 391
Clerk-like experienced, which no less adorns
Our gentry than our parents' noble names,
In whose success we are gentle,—I beseech
  you,
If you know aught which does behove my
  knowledge
Thereof to be inform'd, imprison't not
In ignorant concealment.
 Cam.   I may not answer.
 Pol. A sickness caught of me, and yet I
  well !
I must be answer'd. Dost thou hear, Camillo,
I conjure thee, by all the parts of man 400
Which honor does acknowledge, whereof the
  least
Is not this suit of mine, that thou declare
What incidency thou dost guess of harm
Is creeping toward me ; how far off, how near ;
Which way to be prevented, if to be ;
If not, how best to bear it.
 Cam.   Sir, I will tell you ;
Since I am charged in honor and by him
That I think honorable : therefore mark my
  counsel,
Which must be even as swiftly follow'd as
I mean to utter it, or both yourself and me
Cry lost, and so good night !

 Pol.   On, good Camillo.
 Cam. I am appointed him to murder you.
 Pol. By whom, Camillo ?
 Cam.   By the king.
 Pol.   For what ?
 Cam. He thinks, nay, with all confidence
  he swears,
As he had seen't or been an instrument
To vice you to't, that you have touch'd his
  queen
Forbiddenly.
 Pol. O, then my best blood turn
To an infected jelly and my name
Be yoked with his that did betray the Best !
Turn then my freshest reputation to 420
A savor that may strike the dullest nostril
Where I arrive, and my approach be shunn'd,
Nay, hated too, worse than the great'st infec-
  tion
That e'er was heard or read !
 Cam.   Swear his thought over
By each particular star in heaven and
By all their influences, you may as well
Forbid the sea for to obey the moon
As or by oath remove or counsel shake
The fabric of his folly, whose foundation
Is piled upon his faith and will continue 430
The standing of his body.
 Pol.   How should this grow ?
 Cam. I know not : but I am sure 'tis safer
  to
Avoid what's grown than question how 'tis
  born.
If therefore you dare trust my honesty,
That lies enclosed in this trunk which you
Shall bear along impawn'd, away to-night !
Your followers I will whisper to the business,
And will by twos and threes at several pos-
  terns
Clear them o' the city. For myself, I'll put
My fortunes to your service, which are here
By this discovery lost. Be not uncertain ; 441
For, by the honor of my parents, I
Have utter'd truth : which if you seek to prove,
I dare not stand by ; nor shall you be safer
Than one condemn'd by the king's own mouth,
  thereon
His execution sworn.
 Pol.   I do believe thee :
I saw his heart in 's face. Give me thy hand :
Be pilot to me and thy places shall
Still neighbor mine. My ships are ready and
My people did expect my hence departure 450
Two days ago. This jealousy
Is for a precious creature : as she's rare,
Must it be great, and as his person's mighty,
Must it be violent, and as he does conceive
He is dishonor'd by a man which ever
Profess'd to him, why, his revenges must
In that be made more bitter. Fear o'ershades
  me :
Good expedition be my friend, and comfort
The gracious queen, part of his theme, but
  nothing   459
Of his ill-ta'en suspicion ! Come, Camillo ;
I will respect thee as a father if
Thou bear'st my life off hence : let us avoid.
 Cam. It is in mine authority to command
The keys of all the posterns : please your high-
  ness
To take the urgent hour. Come, sir, away.
            [*Exeunt.*

ACT II.

Scene I. *A room in* Leontes' *palace.*

Enter Hermione, Mamillius, *and* Ladies.

Her. Take the boy to you : he so troubles
me,
'Tis past enduring.
First Lady. Come, my gracious lord,
Shall I be your playfellow ?
Mam. No, I'll none of you.
First Lady. Why, my sweet lord ?
Mam. You'll kiss me hard and speak to
me as if
I were a baby still. I love you better.
Sec. Lady. And why so, my lord ?
Mam. Not for because
Your brows are blacker ; yet black brows,
they say,
Become some women best, so that there be
not
Too much hair there, but in a semicircle   10
Or a half-moon made with a pen.
Sec. Lady. Who taught you this ?
Mam. I learnt it out of women's faces.
Pray now
What color are your eyebrows ?
First Lady. Blue, my lord.
Mam. Nay, that's a mock : I have seen a
lady's nose
That has been blue, but not her eyebrows.
First Lady. Hark ye ;
The queen your mother rounds apace : we
shall
Present our services to a fine new prince
One of these days ; and then you'ld wanton
with us,
If we would have you.
Sec. Lady. She is spread of late
Into a goodly bulk : good time encounter her !
Her. What wisdom stirs amongst you ?
Come, sir, now   21
I am for you again : pray you, sit by us,
And tell 's a tale.
Mam. Merry or sad shall't be ?
Her. As merry as you will.
Mam. A sad tale's best for winter : I have
one
Of sprites and goblins.
Her. Let's have that, good sir.
Come on, sit down : come on, and do your
best
To fright me with your sprites ; you're power-
ful at it.
Mam. There was a man—
Her. Nay, come, sit down ; then on.
Mam. Dwelt by a churchyard : I will tell
it softly ;   30
Yond crickets shall not hear it.
Her. Come on, then,
And give't me in mine ear.

Enter Leontes, *with* Antigonus, Lords
and others.

Leon. Was he met there ? his train ? Ca-
millo with him ?
First Lord. Behind the tuft of pines I met
them ; never
Saw I men scour so on their way : I eyed them
Even to their ships.
Leon. How blest am I
In my just censure, in my true opinion !
Alack, for lesser knowledge ! how accursed
In being so blest ! There may be in the cup
A spider steep'd, and one may drink, depart,
And yet partake no venom, for his knowledge
Is not infected : but if one present
The abhorr'd ingredient to his eye, make
known
How he hath drunk, he cracks his gorge, his
sides,
With violent hefts. I have drunk, and seen
the spider.
Camillo was his help in this, his pander :
There is a plot against my life, my crown ;
All's true that is mistrusted : that false villain
Whom I employ'd was pre-employ'd by him :
He has discover'd my design, and I   50
Remain a pinch'd thing ; yea, a very trick
For them to play at will. How came the pos-
terns
So easily open ?
First Lord. By his great authority ;
Which often hath no less prevail'd than so
On your command.
Leon. I know't too well.
Give me the boy : I am glad you did not nurse
him :
Though he does bear some signs of me, yet
you
Have too much blood in him.
Her. What is this ? sport ?
Leon. Bear the boy hence ; he shall not
come about her ;
Away with him ! and let her sport herself   60
With that she's big with ; for 'tis Polixenes
Has made thee swell thus.
Her. But I'd say he had not,
And I'll be sworn you would believe my say-
ing,
Howe'er you lean to the nayward.
Leon. You, my lords,
Look on her, mark her well ; be but about
To say 'she is a goodly lady,' and
The justice of your hearts will thereto add
' 'Tis pity she's not honest, honorable : '
Praise her but for this her without-door form,
Which on my faith deserves high speech, and
straight   70
The shrug, the hum or ha, these petty brands
That calumny doth use—O, I am out—
That mercy does, for calumny will sear
Virtue itself : these shrugs, these hums and
ha's,
When you have said 'she's goodly,' come be-
tween
Ere you can say 'she's honest : ' but be 't
known,
From him that has most cause to grieve it
should be,
She's an adulteress.
Her. Should a villain say so,
The most replenish'd villain in the world,
He were as much more villain : you, my lord,
Do but mistake.   81
Leon. You have mistook, my lady,
Polixenes for Leontes : O thou thing !
Which I'll not call a creature of thy place,
Lest barbarism, making me the precedent,
Should a like language use to all degrees
And mannerly distinguishment leave out
Betwixt the prince and beggar : I have said
She's an adulteress ; I have said with whom :
More, she's a traitor and Camillo is
A federary with her, and one that knows   90

What she should shame to know herself
But with her most vile principal, that she's
A bed-swerver, even as bad as those
That vulgars give bold'st titles, ay, and privy
To this their late escape.
 Her.   No, by my life,
Privy to none of this. How will this grieve
 you,
When you shall come to clearer knowledge,
 that
You thus have publish'd me ! Gentle my lord,
You scarce can right me throughly then to
 say
You did mistake.
 Leon. No ; if I mistake 100
In those foundations which I build upon,
The centre is not big enough to bear
A school-boy's top. Away with her ! to prison !
He who shall speak for her is afar off guilty
But that he speaks.
 Her.   There's some ill planet reigns :
I must be patient till the heavens look
With an aspect more favorable. Good my
 lords,
I am not prone to weeping, as our sex
Commonly are ; the want of which vain dew
Perchance shall dry your pities : but I have
That honorable grief lodged here which burns
Worse than tears drown : beseech you all, my
 lords,
With thoughts so qualified as your charities
Shall best instruct you, measure me ; and so
The king's will be perform'd !
 Leon.   Shall I be heard ?
 Her. Who is't that goes with me ? Beseech
 your highness,
My women may be with me ; for you see
My plight requires it. Do not weep, good
 fools ;
There is no cause : when you shall know your
 mistress
Has deserved prison, then abound in tears 120
As I come out : this action I now go on
Is for my better grace. Adieu, my lord :
I never wish'd to see you sorry ; now
I trust I shall. My women, come ; you have
 leave.
 Leon. Go, do our bidding ; hence !
    [*Exit Queen, guarded ; with Ladies.*
 First Lord. Beseech your highness, call the
 queen again.
 Ant. Be certain what you do, sir, lest your
 justice
Prove violence ; in the which three great ones
 suffer,
Yourself, your queen, your son.
 First Lord.   For her, my lord,
I dare my life lay down and will do't, sir, 130
Please you to accept it, that the queen is spot-
 less
I' the eyes of heaven and to you ; I mean,
In this which you accuse her.
 Ant.   If it prove
She's otherwise, I'll keep my stables where
I lodge my wife ; I'll go in couples with her ;
Than when I feel and see her no farther trust
 her ;
For every inch of woman in the world,
Ay, every dram of woman's flesh is false,
If she be.
 Leon. Hold your peaces.
 First Lord.   Good my lord,—

 Ant. It is for you we speak, not for our-
 selves : 140
You are abused and by some putter-on
That will be damn'd for't ; would I knew the
 villain,
I would land-damn him. Be she honor-
 flaw'd,
I have three daughters ; the eldest is eleven ;
The second and the third, nine, and some
 five ;
If this prove true, they'll pay for't : by mine
 honor,
I'll geld 'em all ; fourteen they shall not see,
To bring false generations : they are co-
 heirs ;
And I had rather glib myself than they
Should not produce fair issue. 149
 Leon.   Cease ; no more.
You smell this business with a sense as cold
As is a dead man's nose : but I do see't and
 feel't,
As you feel doing thus ; and see withal
The instruments that feel.
 Ant.   If it be so,
We need no grave to bury honesty :
There's not a grain of it the face to sweeten
Of the whole dungy earth.
 Leon.   What ! lack I credit ?
 First Lord. I had rather you did lack than
 I, my lord,
Upon this ground ; and more it would content
 me
To have her honor true than your suspicion,
Be blamed for't how you might.
 Leon.   Why, what need we
Commune with you of this, but rather follow
Our forceful instigation ? Our prerogative
Calls not your counsels, but our natural good-
 ness
Imparts this ; which if you, or stupefied
Or seeming so in skill, cannot or will not
Relish a truth like us, inform yourselves
We need no more of your advice : the matter,
The loss, the gain, the ordering on't, is all
Properly ours.
 Ant. And I wish, my liege, 170
You had only in your silent judgment tried it,
Without more overture.
 Leon.   How could that be ?
Either thou art most ignorant by age,
Or thou wert born a fool. Camillo's flight,
Added to their familiarity,
Which was as gross as ever touch'd conjecture,
That lack'd sight only, nought for approba-
 tion
But only seeing, all other circumstances
Made up to the deed, doth push on this pro-
 ceeding :
Yet, for a greater confirmation, 180
For in an act of this importance 'twere
Most piteous to be wild, I have dispatch'd in
 post
To sacred Delphos, to Apollo's temple,
Cleomenes and Dion, whom you know
Of stuff'd sufficiency : now from the oracle
They will bring all ; whose spiritual counsel
 had,
Shall stop or spur me. Have I done well ?
 First Lord. Well done, my lord.
 Leon. Though I am satisfied and need no
 more
Than what I know, yet shall the oracle 190
Give rest to the minds of others, such as he

Whose ignorant credulity will not
Come up to the truth. So have we thought it
    good
From our free person she should be confined,
Lest that the treachery of the two fled hence
Be left her to perform. Come, follow us ;
We are to speak in public ; for this business
Will raise us all.
   Ant. [*Aside*] To laughter, as I take it,
If the good truth were known.   [*Exeunt.*

        Scene II. *A prison.*

Enter Paulina, *a* Gentleman, *and* Attendants.

   Paul. The keeper of the prison, call to
    him ;
Let him have knowledge who I am.
                    [*Exit Gent.*
                  Good lady,
No court in Europe is too good for thee ;
What dost thou then in prison ?

    Re-enter Gentleman, *with the* Gaoler.

                   Now, good sir,
You know me, do you not ?
   Gaol.   For a worthy lady
And one whom much I honor.
   Paul.   Pray you then,
Conduct me to the queen.
   Gaol.   I may not, madam :
To the contrary I have express commandment.
   Paul. Here's ado,
To lock up honesty and honor from   10
The access of gentle visitors ! Is't lawful, pray
    you,
To see her women ? any of them ? Emilia ?
   Gaol. So please you, madam,
To put apart these your attendants, I
Shall bring Emilia forth.
   Paul.   I pray now, call her.
Withdraw yourselves.
       [*Exeunt Gentleman and Attendants.*
   Gaol.   And, madam,
I must be present at your conference.
   Paul. Well, be't so, prithee. [*Exit Gaoler.*
Here's such ado to make no stain a stain
As passes coloring.

    Re-enter Gaoler, *with* Emilia.

            Dear gentlewoman,   20
How fares our gracious lady ?
   Emil. As well as one so great and so for-
    lorn
May hold together : on her frights and griefs,
Which never tender lady hath born greater,
She is something before her time deliver'd.
   Paul. A boy ?
   Emil.   A daughter, and a goodly babe,
Lusty and like to live : the queen receives
Much comfort in't ; says ' My poor prisoner,
I am innocent as you.'
   Paul.   I dare be sworn :
These dangerous unsafe lunes i' the king, be-
    shrew them !   30
He must be told on't, and he shall : the office
Becomes a woman best ; I'll take't upon me :
If I prove honey-mouth'd, let my tongue blister
And never to my red-look'd anger be
The trumpet any more. Pray you, Emilia,
Commend my best obedience to the queen :
If she dares trust me with her little babe,
I'll show't the king and undertake to be
Her advocate to the loud'st. We do not know
How he may soften at the sight o' the child :

The silence often of pure innocence   41
Persuades when speaking fails.
   Emil.   Most worthy madam,
Your honor and your goodness is so evident
That your free undertaking cannot miss
A thriving issue : there is no lady living
So meet for this great errand. Please your
    ladyship
To visit the next room, I'll presently
Acquaint the queen of your most noble offer ;
Who but to-day hammer'd of this design,
But durst not tempt a minister of honor,   50
Lest she should be denied.
   Paul.   Tell her, Emilia,
I'll use that tongue I have : if wit flow from't
As boldness from my bosom, let 't not be
    doubted
I shall do good.
   Emil.   Now be you blest for it !
I'll to the queen : please you, come something
    nearer.
   Gaol. Madam, if't please the queen to send
    the babe,
I know not what I shall incur to pass it,
Having no warrant.
   Paul.   You need not fear it, sir :
This child was prisoner to the womb and is
By law and process of great nature thence   60
Freed and enfranchised, not a party to
The anger of the king nor guilty of,
If any be, the trespass of the queen.
   Gaol. I do believe it.
   Paul. Do not you fear : upon mine honor, I
Will stand betwixt you and danger. [*Exeunt.*

   Scene III. *A room in* Leontes' *palace.*

   Enter Leontes, Antigonus, Lords, *and*
              Servants.

   Leon. Nor night nor day no rest : it is but
    weakness
To bear the matter thus ; mere weakness. If
The cause were not in being,—part o' the
    cause,
She the adulteress ; for the harlot king
Is quite beyond mine arm, out of the blank
And level of my brain, plot-proof ; but she
I can hook to me : say that she were gone,
Given to the fire, a moiety of my rest
Might come to me again. Who's there ?
   First Serv.   My lord ?
   Leon. How does the boy ?
   First Serv. He took good rest to-night ;   10
'Tis hoped his sickness is discharged.
   Leon.   To see his nobleness !
Conceiving the dishonor of his mother,
He straight declined, droop'd, took it deeply,
Fasten'd and fix'd the shame on't in himself,
Threw off his spirit, his appetite, his sleep,
And downright languish'd. Leave me solely :
    go,
See how he fares. [*Exit Serv.*] Fie, fie ! no
    thought of him :
The very thought of my revenges that way
Recoil upon me : in himself too mighty,   20
And in his parties, his alliance ; let him be
Until a time may serve : for present venge-
    ance,
Take it on her. Camillo and Polixenes
Laugh at me, make their pastime at my sor-
    row :
They should not laugh if I could reach them,
    nor

Shall she within my power.

Enter PAULINA, *with a child.*

First Lord.   You must not enter.
Paul. Nay, rather, good my lords, be sec-
    ond to me :
Fear you his tyrannous passion more, alas,
Than the queen's life ? a gracious innocent
    soul,
More free than he is jealous.
Ant.   That's enough. 30
Sec. Serv. Madam, he hath not slept to-
    night ; commanded
None should come at him.
Paul.   Not so hot, good sir :
I come to bring him sleep. 'Tis such as you,
That creep like shadows by him and do sigh
At each his needless heavings, such as you
Nourish the cause of his awaking : I
Do come with words as medicinal as true,
Honest as either, to purge him of that humor
That presses him from sleep.
Leon.   What noise there, ho ?
Paul. No noise, my lord ; but needful con-
    ference   40
About some gossips for your highness.
Leon.   How !
Away with that audacious lady ! Antigonus,
I charged thee that she should not come about
    me :
I knew she would.
Ant.   I told her so, my lord,
On your displeasure's peril and on mine,
She should not visit you.
Leon.   What, canst not rule her ?
Paul. From all dishonesty he can : in this,
Unless he take the course that you have done,
Commit me for committing honor, trust it,
He shall not rule me.
Ant.   La you now, you hear : 50
When she will take the rein I let her run ;
But she'll not stumble.
Paul.   Good my liege, I come ;
And, I beseech you, hear me, who profess
Myself your loyal servant, your physician,
Your most obedient counsellor, yet that dare
Less appear so in comforting your evils,
Than such as most seem yours : I say, I come
From your good queen.
Leon.   Good queen !
Paul.   Good queen, my lord,
Good queen ; I say good queen ;
And would by combat make her good, so
    were I
A man, the worst about you.
Leon.   61
                Force her hence.
Paul. Let him that makes but trifles of his
    eyes
First hand me : on mine own accord I'll off ;
But first I'll do my errand. The good queen,
For she is good, hath brought you forth a
    daughter ;
Here 'tis ; commends it to your blessing.
                [*Laying down the child.*
Leon.   Out !
A mankind witch ! Hence with her, out o'
    door :
A most intelligencing bawd !
Paul.   Not so :
I am as ignorant in that as you
In so entitling me, and no less honest   70
Than you are mad ; which is enough, I'll war-
    rant,

As this world goes, to pass for honest.
Leon.   Traitors !
Will you not push her out ? Give her the bas-
    tard.
Thou dotard ! thou art woman-tired, unroosted
By thy dame Partlet here. Take up the bas-
    tard ;
Take't up, I say ; give't to thy crone.
Paul.   For ever
Unvenerable be thy hands, if thou
Takest up the princess by that forced baseness
Which he has put upon't !
Leon.   He dreads his wife.
Paul. So I would you did ; then 'twere
    past all doubt   80
You'ld call your children yours.
Leon.   A nest of traitors !
Ant. I am none, by this good light.
Paul.   Nor I, nor any
But one that's here, and that's himself, for he
The sacred honor of himself, his queen's,
His hopeful son's, his babe's, betrays to slan-
    der,
Whose sting is sharper than the sword's ; and
    will not—
For, as the case now stands, it is a curse
He cannot be compell'd to't—once remove
The root of his opinion, which is rotten
As ever oak or stone was sound.
Leon.   A callat 90
Of boundless tongue, who late hath beat her
    husband
And now baits me ! This brat is none of mine ;
It is the issue of Polixenes :
Hence with it, and together with the dam
Commit them to the fire !
Paul.   It is yours ;
And, might we lay the old proverb to your
    charge,
So like you, 'tis the worse. Behold, my lords,
Although the print be little, the whole matter
And copy of the father, eye, nose, lip,
The trick of's frown, his forehead, nay, the
    valley,   100
The pretty dimples of his chin and cheek,
His smiles,
The very mould and frame of hand, nail,
    finger :
And thou, good goddess Nature, which hast
    made it
So like to him that got it, if thou hast
The ordering of the mind too, 'mongst all
    colors
No yellow in't, lest she suspect, as he does,
Her children not her husband's !
Leon.   A gross hag
And, lozel, thou art worthy to be hang'd,
That wilt not stay her tongue.
Ant.   Hang all the husbands 110
That cannot do that feat, you'll leave yourself
Hardly one subject.
Leon.   Once more, take her hence.
Paul. A most unworthy and unnatural lord
Can do no more.
Leon.   I'll ha' thee burnt.
Paul.   I care not :
It is an heretic that makes the fire,
Not she which burns in't. I'll not call you
    tyrant ;
But this most cruel usage of your queen,
Not able to produce more accusation
Than your own weak-hinged fancy, something
    savors

Of tyranny and will ignoble make you,   120
Yea, scandalous to the world.
 Leon.   On your allegiance,
Out of the chamber with her ! Were I a tyrant,
Where were her life ? she durst not call me so,
If she did know me one. Away with her !
 Paul. I pray you, do not push me ; I'll be gone.
Look to your babe, my lord ; 'tis yours : Jove send her
A better guiding spirit ! What needs these hands ?
You, that are thus so tender o'er his follies,
Will never do him good, not one of you.
So, so : farewell ; we are gone. [*Exit.* 130
 Leon. Thou, traitor, hast set on thy wife to this.
My child ? away with't ! Even thou, that hast
A heart so tender o'er it, take it hence
And see it instantly consumed with fire ;
Even thou and none but thou. Take it up straight :
Within this hour bring me word 'tis done,
And by good testimony, or I'll seize thy life,
With what thou else call'st thine. If thou refuse
And wilt encounter with my wrath, say so ;
The bastard brains with these my proper hands
Shall I dash out. Go, take it to the fire ;   140
For thou set'st on thy wife.
 Ant.   I did not, sir :
These lords, my noble fellows, if they please,
Can clear me in't.
 Lords. We can : my royal liege,
He is not guilty of her coming hither.
 Leon. You're liars all.
 First Lord. Beseech your highness, give us better credit.
We have always truly served you, and beseech you
So to esteem of us, and on our knees we beg,
As recompense of our dear services   150
Past and to come, that you do change this purpose,
Which being so horrible, so bloody, must
Lead on to some foul issue : we all kneel.
 Leon. I am a feather for each wind that blows :
Shall I live on to see this bastard kneel
And call me father ? better burn it now
Than curse it then. But be it ; let it live.
It shall not neither. You, sir, come you hither ;
You that have been so tenderly officious
With Lady Margery, your midwife there,   160
To save this bastard's life,—for 'tis a bastard,
So sure as this beard's grey,—what will you adventure
To save this brat's life ?
 Ant.   Any thing, my lord,
That my ability may undergo
And nobleness impose : at least thus much :
I'll pawn the little blood which I have left
To save the innocent : any thing possible.
 Leon. It shall be possible. Swear by this sword
Thou wilt perform my bidding.
 Ant.   I will, my lord.
 Leon. Mark and perform it, see'st thou ! for the fail   170

Of any point in't shall not only be
Death to thyself but to thy lewd-tongued wife,
Whom for this time we pardon. We enjoin thee,
As thou art liege-man to us, that thou carry
This female bastard hence and that thou bear it
To some remote and desert place quite out
Of our dominions, and that there thou leave it,
Without more mercy, to its own protection
And favor of the climate. As by strange fortune
It came to us, I do in justice charge thee,   180
On thy soul's peril and thy body's torture,
That thou commend it strangely to some place
Where chance may nurse or end it. Take it up.
 Ant. I swear to do this, though a present death
Had been more merciful. Come on, poor babe :
Some powerful spirit instruct the kites and ravens
To be thy nurses ! Wolves and bears, they say
Casting their savageness aside have done
Like offices of pity. Sir, be prosperous
In more than this deed does require ! And blessing   190
Against this cruelty fight on thy side,
Poor thing, condemn'd to loss !
    [*Exit with the child.*
 Leon.   No, I'll not rear
Another's issue.

    Enter a Servant.

 Serv. Please your highness, posts
From those you sent to the oracle are come
An hour since : Cleomenes and Dion,
Being well arrived from Delphos, are both landed,
Hasting to the court.
 First Lord. So please you, sir, their speed
Hath been beyond account.
 Leon.   Twenty-three days
They have been absent : 'tis good speed ; foretells
The great Apollo suddenly will have   200
The truth of this appear. Prepare you, lords ;
Summon a session, that we may arraign
Our most disloyal lady, for, as she hath
Been publicly accused, so shall she have
A just and open trial. While she lives
My heart will be a burthen to me. Leave me,
And think upon my bidding. [*Exeunt.*

ACT III.

Scene I. *A sea-port in Sicilia.*

   Enter Cleomenes *and* Dion.

 Cleo. The climate's delicate, the air most sweet,
Fertile the isle, the temple much surpassing
The common praise it bears.
 Dion.   I shall report,
For most it caught me, the celestial habits,
Methinks I so should term them, and the reverence
Of the grave wearers. O, the sacrifice !
How ceremonious, solemn and unearthly
It was i' the offering !
 Cleo.   But of all, the burst

And the ear-deafening voice o' the oracle,
Kin to Jove's thunder, so surprised my sense,
That I was nothing.   11
    Dion.   If the event o' the journey
Prove as successful to the queen,—O be 't
so !—
As it hath been to us rare, pleasant, speedy,
The time is worth the use on 't.
    Cleo.   Great Apollo
Turn all to the best ! These proclamations,
So forcing faults upon Hermione,
I little like.
    Dion. The violent carriage of it
Will clear or end the business : when the
    oracle,
Thus by Apollo's great divine seal'd up,
Shall the contents discover, something rare 20
Even then will rush to knowledge. Go : fresh
    horses !
And gracious be the issue !   [*Exeunt.*

SCENE II. *A court of Justice.*

Enter LEONTES, *Lords, and* Officers.

    Leon. This sessions, to our great grief we
    pronounce,
Even pushes 'gainst our heart : the party tried
The daughter of a king, our wife, and one
Of us too much beloved. Let us be clear'd
Of being tyrannous, since we so openly
Proceed in justice, which shall have due
    course,
Even to the guilt or the purgation.
Produce the prisoner.
    Off. It is his highness' pleasure that the
    queen
Appear in person here in court. Silence ! 10

Enter HERMIONE *guarded ;* PAULINA *and*
Ladies *attending.*

    Leon. Read the indictment.
    Off. [*Reads*] Hermione, queen to the
worthy Leontes, king of Sicilia, thou art here
accused and arraigned of high treason, in
committing adultery with Polixenes, king of
Bohemia, and conspiring with Camillo to take
away the life of our sovereign lord the king,
thy royal husband : the pretence whereof being by circumstances partly laid open, thou,
Hermione, contrary to the faith and alle-
giance of a true subject, didst counsel and aid
them, for their better safety, to fly away by
night.
    Her. Since what I am to say must be but
    that
Which contradicts my accusation and
The testimony on my part no other
But what comes from myself, it shall scarce
    boot me
To say ' not guilty : ' mine integrity
Being counted falsehood, shall, as I express it,
Be so received. But thus : if powers divine
Behold our human actions, as they do,   30
I doubt not then but innocence shall make
False accusation blush and tyranny
Tremble at patience. You, my lord, best
    know,
Who least will seem to do so, my past life
Hath been as continent, as chaste, as true,
As I am now unhappy ; which is more
Than history can pattern, though devised
And play'd to take spectators. For behold me
A fellow of the royal bed, which owe

A moiety of the throne a great king's daugh-
    ter,   40
The mother to a hopeful prince, here standing
To prate and talk for life and honor 'fore
Who please to come and hear. For life, I
    prize it
As I weigh grief, which I would spare : for
    honor,
'Tis a derivative from me to mine,
And only that I stand for. I appeal
To your own conscience, sir, before Polixenes
Came to your court, how I was in your grace,
How merited to be so ; since he came,
With what encounter so uncurrent I   50
Have strain'd to appear thus : if one jot be-
    yond
The bound of honor, or in act or will
That way inclining, harden'd be the hearts
Of all that hear me, and my near'st of kin
Cry fie upon my grave !
    Leon.   I ne'er heard yet
That any of these bolder vices wanted
Less impudence to gainsay what they did
Than to perform it first.
    Her.   That's true enough ;
Though 'tis a saying, sir, not due to me.
    Leon. You will not own it.
    Her.   More than mistress of 60
Which comes to me in name of fault, I must
    not
At all acknowledge. For Polixenes,
With whom I am accused, I do confess
I loved him as in honor he required,
With such a kind of love as might become
A lady like me, with a love even such,
So and no other, as yourself commanded :
Which not to have done I think had been in
    me
Both disobedience and ingratitude
To you and toward your friend, whose love
    had spoke,   70
Even since it could speak, from an infant,
    freely
That it was yours. Now, for conspiracy,
I know not how it tastes ; though it be dish'd
For me to try how : all I know of it
Is that Camillo was an honest man ;
And why he left your court, the gods them-
    selves,
Wotting no more than I, are ignorant.
    Leon. You knew of his departure, as you
    know
What you have underta'en to do in 's absence.
    Her. Sir,   80
You speak a language that I understand not :
My life stands in the level of your dreams,
Which I'll lay down.
    Leon.   Your actions are my dreams ;
You had a bastard by Polixenes,
And I but dream'd it. As you were past all
    shame,—
Those of your fact are so—so past all truth :
Which to deny concerns more than avails ;
    for as
Thy brat hath been cast out, like to itself,
No father owning it,—which is, indeed,
More criminal in thee than it,—so thou   90
Shalt feel our justice, in whose easiest passage
Look for no less than death.
    Her.   Sir, spare your threats :
The bug which you would fright me with I
    seek.
To me can life be no commodity :

The crown and comfort of my life, your favor,
I do give lost ; for I do feel it gone,
But know not how it went. My second joy
And first-fruits of my body, from his presence
I am barr'd, like one infectious. My third
   comfort
Starr'd most unluckily, is from my breast, 100
The innocent milk in its most innocent mouth,
Haled out to murder : myself on every post
Proclaimed a strumpet : with immodest hatred
The child-bed privilege denied, which 'longs
To women of all fashion ; lastly, hurried
Here to this place, i' the open air, before
I have got strength of limit. Now, my liege,
Tell me what blessings I have here alive,
That I should fear to die ? Therefore proceed.
But yet hear this : mistake me not ; no life,
I prize it not a straw, but for mine honor, 111
Which I would free, if I shall be condemn'd
Upon surmises, all proofs sleeping else
But what your jealousies awake, I tell you
'Tis rigor and not law. Your honors all,
I do refer me to the oracle :
Apollo be my judge !
   First Lord.   This your request
Is altogether just : therefore bring forth,
And in Apollo's name, his oracle.
          [*Exeunt certain Officers.*
   Her. The Emperor of Russia was my fa-
   ther :   120
O that he were alive, and here beholding
His daughter's trial ! that he did but see
The flatness of my misery, yet with eyes
Of pity, not revenge !

Re-enter Officers, *with* Cleomenes *and* Dion.

   Off. You here shall swear upon this sword
     of justice,
That you, Cleomenes and Dion, have
Been both at Delphos, and from thence have
   brought
The seal'd-up oracle, by the hand deliver'd
Of great Apollo's priest ; and that, since then,
You have not dared to break the holy seal 130
Nor read the secrets in't.
   Cleo. Dion.   All this we swear.
   Leon. Break up the seals and read.
   Off. [*Reads*] Hermione is chaste ; Polix-
enes blameless ; Camillo a true subject ; Le-
ontes a jealous tyrant ; his innocent babe
truly begotten ; and the king shall live with-
out an heir, if that which is lost be not found.
   Lords. Now blessed be the great Apollo !
   Her.   Praised !
   Leon. Hast thou read truth ?
   Off.   Ay, my lord ; even so
As it is here set down.   140
   Leon. There is no truth at all i' the oracle :
The sessions shall proceed : this is mere false-
hood.

Enter Servant.

   Serv. My lord the king, the king !
   Leon.   What is the business ?
   Serv. O sir, I shall be hated to report it !
The prince your son, with mere conceit and
   fear
Of the queen's speed, is gone.
   Leon.   How ! gone !
   Serv.   Is dead.
   Leon. Apollo's angry ; and the heavens
   themselves

Do strike at my injustice. [*Hermione swoons*]
   How now there !
   Paul. This news is mortal to the queen :
   look down
And see what death is doing.
   Leon.   Take her hence : 150
Her heart is but o'ercharged ; she will re-
   cover :
I have too much believed mine own suspi-
   cion :
Beseech you, tenderly apply to her
Some remedies for life.
    [*Exeunt Paulina and Ladies, with Hermione.*
             Apollo, pardon
My great profaneness 'gainst thine oracle !
I'll reconcile me to Polixenes,
New woo my queen, recall the good Camillo,
Whom I proclaim a man of truth, of mercy ;
For, being transported by my jealousies
To bloody thoughts and to revenge, I chose
Camillo for the minister to poison   161
My friend Polixenes : which had been done,
But that the good mind of Camillo tardied
My swift command, though I with death and
   with
Reward did threaten and encourage him,
Not doing 't and being done : he, most hu-
   mane
And fill'd with honor, to my kingly guest
Unclasp'd my practice, quit his fortunes here,
Which you knew great, and to the hazard
Of all incertainties himself commended, 170
No richer than his honor : how he glisters
Thorough my rust ! and how his piety
Does my deeds make the blacker !

Re-enter Paulina.

   Paul.   Woe the while !
O, cut my lace, lest my heart, cracking it,
Break too.
   First Lord. What fit is this, good lady ?
   Paul. What studied torments, tyrant, hast
     for me ?
What wheels ? racks ? fires ? what flaying ?
     boiling ?
In leads or oils ? what old or newer torture
Must I receive, whose every word deserves
To taste of thy most worst ? Thy tyranny 180
Together working with thy jealousies,
Fancies too weak for boys, too green and idle
For girls of nine, O, think what they have
   done
And then run mad indeed, stark mad ! for all
Thy by-gone fooleries were but spices of it.
That thou betray'dst Polixenes, 'twas nothing ;
That did but show thee, of a fool, inconstant
And damnable ingrateful : nor was't much,
Thou wouldst have poison'd good Camillo's
   honor,
To have him kill a king : poor trespasses, 190
More monstrous standing by : whereof I
   reckon
The casting forth to crows thy baby-daughter
To be or none or little ; though a devil
Would have shed water out of fire ere done't :
Nor is't directly laid to thee, the death
Of the young prince, whose honorable
   thoughts,
Thoughts high for one so tender, cleft the heart
That could conceive a gross and foolish sire
Blemish'd his gracious dam : this is not, no,
Laid to thy answer : but the last,—O lords,

When I have said, cry 'woe!' the queen, the
queen,								201
The sweet'st, dear'st creature's dead, and
vengeance for't
Not dropp'd down yet.
 First Lord.   The higher powers forbid!
 Paul. I say she's dead; I'll swear't. If word
nor oath
Prevail not, go and see : if you can bring
Tincture or lustre in her lip, her eye,
Heat outwardly or breath within, I'll serve you
As I would do the gods. But, O thou tyrant!
Do not repent these things, for they are heavier
Than all thy woes can stir; therefore betake
thee
To nothing but despair. A thousand knees		211
Ten thousand years together, naked, fasting,
Upon a barren mountain, and still winter
In storm perpetual, could not move the gods
To look that way thou wert.
 Leon.   Go on, go on :
Thou canst not speak too much; I have de-
served
All tongues to talk their bitterest.
 First Lord.   Say no more :
Howe'er the business goes, you have made
fault
I' the boldness of your speech.
 Paul.   I am sorry for't :
All faults I make, when I shall come to know
them,								220
I do repent. Alas! I have show'd too much
The rashness of a woman : he is touch'd
To the noble heart. What's gone and what's
past help
Should be past grief : do not receive affliction
At my petition; I beseech you, rather
Let me be punish'd, that have minded you
Of what you should forget. Now, good my
liege,
Sir, royal sir, forgive a foolish woman :
The love I bore your queen—lo, fool again!—
I'll speak of her no more, nor of your chil-
dren;								230
I'll not remember you of my own lord,
Who is lost too : take your patience to you,
And I'll say nothing.
 Leon.   Thou didst speak but well
When most the truth; which I receive much
better
Than to be pitied of thee. Prithee, bring me
To the dead bodies of my queen and son :
One grave shall be for both : upon them shall
The causes of their death appear, unto
Our shame perpetual. Once a day I'll visit
The chapel where they lie, and tears shed
there								240
Shall be my recreation : so long as nature
Will bear up with this exercise, so long
I daily vow to use it. Come and lead me
Unto these sorrows.						[*Exeunt.*

SCENE III. *Bohemia. A desert country near
the sea.*

Enter ANTIGONUS *with a Child, and a* Mariner.

 Ant. Thou art perfect then, our ship hath
touch'd upon
The deserts of Bohemia ?
 Mar.   Ay, my lord : and fear
We have landed in ill time : the skies look
grimly
And threaten present blusters. In my con-
science,
The heavens with that we have in hand are
angry
And frown upon 's.
 Ant. Their sacred wills be done! Go, get
aboard;
Look to thy bark : I'll not be long before
I call upon thee.
 Mar. Make your best haste, and go not		10
Too far i' the land : 'tis like to be loud
weather;
Besides, this place is famous for the creatures
Of prey that keep upon't.
 Ant.   Go thou away :
I'll follow instantly.
 Mar.   I am glad at heart
To be so rid o' the business.				[*Exit.*
 Ant.   Come, poor babe :
I have heard, but not believed, the spirits o'
the dead
May walk again : if such thing be, thy mother
Appear'd to me last night, for ne'er was dream
So like a waking. To me comes a creature,
Sometimes her head on one side, some an-
other;								20
I never saw a vessel of like sorrow,
So fill'd and so becoming : in pure white robes,
Like very sanctity, she did approach
My cabin where I lay; thrice bow'd before
me,
And gasping to begin some speech, her eyes
Became two spouts : the fury spent, anon
Did this break from her : ' Good Antigonus,
Since fate, against thy better disposition,
Hath made thy person for the thrower-out
Of my poor babe, according to thine oath,		30
Places remote enough are in Bohemia,
There weep and leave it crying; and, for the
babe
Is counted lost for ever, Perdita,
I prithee, call't. For this ungentle business
Put on thee by my lord, thou ne'er shalt see
Thy wife Paulina more.' And so, with shrieks
She melted into air. Affrighted much,
I did in time collect myself and thought
This was so and no slumber. Dreams are toys :
Yet for this once, yea, superstitiously,		40
I will be squared by this. I do believe
Hermione hath suffer'd death, and that
Apollo would, this being indeed the issue
Of King Polixenes, it should here be laid,
Either for life or death, upon the earth
Of its right father. Blossom, speed thee well!
There lie, and there thy character : there
these;
Which may, if fortune please, both breed thee,
pretty,
And still rest thine. The storm begins; poor
wretch,
That for thy mother's fault art thus exposed
To loss and what may follow! Weep I can-
not,								51
But my heart bleeds; and most accursed am I
To be by oath enjoin'd to this. Farewell!
The day frowns more and more : thou'rt like
to have
A lullaby too rough : I never saw
The heavens so dim by day. A savage clamor!
Well may I get aboard! This is the chase :
I am gone for ever.		[*Exit, pursued by a bear.*

Enter a Shepherd.

 Shep. I would there were no age between
sixteen and three-and-twenty, or that youth

would sleep out the rest; for there is nothing in the between but getting wenches with child, wronging the ancientry, stealing, fighting— Hark you now! Would any but these boiled brains of nineteen and two-and-twenty hunt this weather? They have scared away two of my best sheep, which I fear the wolf will sooner find than the master: if any where I have them, 'tis by the seaside, browsing of ivy. Good luck, an't be thy will! what have we here! Mercy on 's, a barne; a very pretty barne! A boy or a child, I wonder? A pretty one; a very pretty one: sure, some 'scape: though I am not bookish, yet I can read waiting-gentlewoman in the 'scape. This has been some stair-work, some trunk-work, some behind-door-work: they were warmer that got this than the poor thing is here. I'll take it up for pity: yet I'll tarry till my son come; he hallooed but even now. Whoa, ho, hoa!

Enter Clown.

Clo. Hilloa, loa!   80
Shep. What, art so near? If thou'lt see a thing to talk on when thou art dead and rotten, come hither. What ailest thou, man?
Clo. I have seen two such sights, by sea and by land! but I am not to say it is a sea, for it is now the sky: betwixt the firmament and it you cannot thrust a bodkin's point.
Shep. Why, boy, how is it?
Clo. I would you did but see how it chafes, how it rages, how it takes up the shore! but that's not to the point. O, the most piteous cry of the poor souls! sometimes to see 'em, and not to see 'em; now the ship boring the moon with her main-mast, and anon swallowed with yest and froth, as you'ld thrust a cork into a hogshead. And then for the land-service, to see how the bear tore out his shoulder-bone; how he cried to me for help and said his name was Antigonus, a nobleman. But to make an end of the ship, to see how the sea flap-dragoned it: but, first, how the poor souls roared, and the sea mocked them; and how the poor gentleman roared and the bear mocked him, both roaring louder than the sea or weather.
Shep. Name of mercy, when was this, boy?
Clo. Now, now: I have not winked since I saw these sights: the men are not yet cold under water, nor the bear half dined on the gentleman: he's at it now.
Shep. Would I had been by, to have helped the old man!   111
Clo. I would you had been by the ship side, to have helped her: there your charity would have lacked footing.
Shep. Heavy matters! heavy matters! but look thee here, boy. Now bless thyself: thou mettest with things dying, I with things new-born. Here's a sight for thee; look thee, a bearing-cloth for a squire's child! look thee here; take up, take up, boy; open't. So, let's see: it was told me I should be rich by the fairies. This is some changeling: open't. What's within, boy?
Clo. You're a made old man: if the sins of your youth are forgiven you, you're well to live. Gold! all gold!
Shep. This is fairy gold, boy, and 'twill prove so: up with't, keep it close: home, home, the next way. We are lucky, boy; and

to be so still requires nothing but secrecy. Let my sheep go: come, good boy, the next way home.
Clo. Go you the next way with your findings. I'll go see if the bear be gone from the gentleman and how much he hath eaten: they are never curst but when they are hungry: if there be any of him left, I'll bury it.
Shep. That's a good deed. If thou mayest discern by that which is left of him what he is, fetch me to the sight of him.
Clo. Marry, will I; and you shall help to put him i' the ground.   141
Shep. 'Tis a lucky day, boy, and we'll do good deeds on't.   [*Exeunt.*

ACT IV. Scene I.

Enter Time, *the* Chorus.

Time. I, that please some, try all, both joy
    and terror
Of good and bad, that makes and unfolds
    error,
Now take upon me, in the name of Time,
To use my wings. Impute it not a crime
To me or my swift passage, that I slide
O'er sixteen years and leave the growth un-
    tried
Of that wide gap, since it is in my power
To o'erthrow law and in one self-born hour
To plant and o'erwhelm custom. Let me pass
The same I am, ere ancient'st order was   10
Or what is now received; I witness to
The times that brought them in; so shall I do
To the freshest things now reigning and make
    stale
The glistering of this present, as my tale
Now seems to it. Your patience this allowing,
I turn my glass and give my scene such grow-
    ing
As you had slept between: Leontes leaving,
The effects of his fond jealousies so grieving
That he shuts up himself, imagine me,
Gentle spectators, that I now may be   20
In fair Bohemia; and remember well,
I mentioned a son o' the king's, which Florizel
I now name to you; and with speed so pace
To speak of Perdita, now grown in grace
Equal with wondering: what of her ensues
I list not prophesy; but let Time's news
Be known when 'tis brought forth. A shep-
    herd's daughter,
And what to her adheres, which follows after,
Is the argument of Time. Of this allow,
If ever you have spent time worse ere now; 30
If never, yet that Time himself doth say
He wishes earnestly you never may.   [*Exit.*

Scene II. *Bohemia. The palace of*
Polixenes.

Enter Polixenes *and* Camillo.

Pol. I pray thee, good Camillo, be no more importunate: 'tis a sickness denying thee any thing; a death to grant this.
Cam. It is fifteen years since I saw my country: though I have for the most part been aired abroad, I desire to lay my bones there. Besides, the penitent king, my master, hath sent for me; to whose feeling sorrows I might be some allay, or I o'erween to think so, which is another spur to my departure.   10
Pol. As thou lovest me, Camillo, wipe not

out the rest of thy services by leaving me now : the need I have of thee thine own goodness hath made ; better not to have had thee than thus to want thee : thou, having made me businesses which none without thee can sufficiently manage, must either stay to execute them thyself or take away with thee the very services thou hast done ; which if I have not enough considered, as too much I cannot, to be more thankful to thee shall be my study, and my profit therein the heaping friendships. Of that fatal country, Sicilia, prithee speak no more ; whose very naming punishes me with the remembrance of that penitent, as thou callest him, and reconciled king, my brother ; whose loss of his most precious queen and children are even now to be afresh lamented. Say to me, when sawest thou the Prince Florizel, my son ? Kings are no less unhappy, their issue not being gracious, than they are in losing them when they have approved their virtues.

Cam. Sir, it is three days since I saw the prince. What his happier affairs may be, are to me unknown : but I have missingly noted, he is of late much retired from court and is less frequent to his princely exercises than formerly he hath appeared.

Pol. I have considered so much, Camillo, and with some care ; so far that I have eyes under my service which look upon his removedness ; from whom I have this intelligence, that he is seldom from the house of a most homely shepherd ; a man, they say, that from very nothing, and beyond the imagination of his neighbors, is grown into an unspeakable estate.

Cam. I have heard, sir, of such a man, who hath a daughter of most rare note : the report of her is extended more than can be thought to begin from such a cottage.   50

Pol. That's likewise part of my intelligence ; but, I fear, the angle that plucks our son thither. Thou shalt accompany us to the place ; where we will, not appearing what we are, have some question with the shepherd ; from whose simplicity I think it not uneasy to get the cause of my son's resort thither. Prithee, be my present partner in this business, and lay aside the thoughts of Sicilia.

Cam. I willingly obey your command.

Pol. My best Camillo ! We must disguise ourselves.   [*Exeunt.*

SCENE III. *A road near the* Shepherd's *cottage.*

Enter AUTOLYCUS, *singing.*

When daffodils begin to peer,
     With heigh ! the doxy over the dale,
Why, then comes in the sweet o' the year ;
     For the red blood reigns in the winter's pale.

The white sheet bleaching on the hedge,
     With heigh ! the sweet birds, O, how they
          sing !
Doth set my pugging tooth on edge ;
     For a quart of ale is a dish for a king.

The lark, that tirra-lyra chants,
     With heigh ! with heigh ! the thrush and the
          jay,   10
Are summer songs for me and my aunts,
     While we lie tumbling in the hay.

I have served Prince Florizel and in my time

wore three-pile ; but now I am out of service :

But shall I go mourn for that, my dear ?
     The pale moon shines by night :
And when I wander here and there,
     I then do most go right.

If tinkers may have leave to live,
     And bear the sow-skin budget,   20
Then my account I well may give,
     And in the stocks avouch it.

My traffic is sheets ; when the kite builds, look to lesser linen. My father named me Autolycus ; who being, as I am, littered under Mercury, was likewise a snapper-up of unconsidered trifles. With die and drab I purchased this caparison, and my revenue is the silly cheat. Gallows and knock are too powerful on the highway : beating and hanging are terrors to me : for the life to come, I sleep out the thought of it. A prize ! a prize !

Enter Clown.

Clo. Let me see : every 'leven wether tods ; every tod yields pound and odd shilling ; fifteen hundred shorn, what comes the wool to ?

Aut. [*Aside*] If the springe hold, the cock's mine.

Clo. I cannot do't without counters. Let me see ; what am I to buy for our sheepshearing feast ? Three pound of sugar, five pound of currants, rice,—what will this sister of mine do with rice ? But my father hath made her mistress of the feast, and she lays it on. She hath made me four and twenty nosegays for the shearers, three-man-song-men all, and very good ones ; but they are most of them means and bases ; but one puritan amongst them, and he sings psalms to horn-pipes. I must have saffron to color the warden pies ; mace ; dates ?—none, that's out of my note ; nutmegs, seven ; a race or two of ginger, but that I may beg ; four pound of prunes, and as many of raisins o' the sun.

Aut. O that ever I was born !
          [*Grovelling on the ground.*

Clo. I' the name of me—

Aut. O, help me, help me ! pluck but off these rags ; and then, death, death !

Clo. Alack, poor soul ! thou hast need of more rags to lay on thee, rather than have these off.

Aut. O sir, the loathsomeness of them offends me more than the stripes I have received, which are mighty ones and millions.

Clo. Alas, poor man ! a million of beating may come to a great matter.

Aut. I am robbed, sir, and beaten ; my money and apparel ta'en from me, and these detestable things put upon me.

Clo. What, by a horseman, or a footman ?

Aut. A footman, sweet sir, a footman.

Clo. Indeed, he should be a footman by the garments he has left with thee : if this be a horseman's coat, it hath seen very hot service. Lend me thy hand, I'll help thee : come, lend me thy hand.

Aut. O, good sir, tenderly, O !

Clo. Alas, poor soul !

Aut. O, good sir, softly, good sir ! I fear, sir, my shoulder-blade is out.

Clo. How now ! canst stand ?

Aut. [*Picking his pocket*] Softly, dear sir ;

good sir, softly. You ha' done me a charitable
office.   81

Clo.   Dost lack any money ? I have a little
money for thee.

Aut.   No, good sweet sir ; no, I beseech
you, sir : I have a kinsman not past three
quarters of a mile hence, unto whom I was
going ; I shall there have money, or any thing
I want : offer me no money, I pray you ; that
kills my heart.

Clo.   What manner of fellow was he that
robbed you ?   90

Aut.   A fellow, sir, that I have known to
go about with troll-my-dames ; I knew him
once a servant of the prince : I cannot tell,
good sir, for which of his virtues it was, but
he was certainly whipped out of the court.

Clo.   His vices, you would say ; there's no
virtue whipped out of the court : they cherish
it to make it stay there ; and yet it will no
more but abide.   99

Aut.   Vices, I would say, sir. I know this
man well : he hath been since an ape-bearer ;
then a process-server, a bailiff ; then he compassed a motion of the Prodigal Son, and married a tinker's wife within a mile where my
land and living lies ; and, having flown over
many knavish professions, he settled only in
rogue : some call him Autolycus.

Clo.   Out upon him ! prig, for my life,
prig : he haunts wakes, fairs and bear-bait-
ings.

Aut.   Very true, sir ; he, sir, he ; that's the
rogue that put me into this apparel.   111

Clo.   Not a more cowardly rogue in all Bohemia : if you had but looked big and spit at
him, he'd have run.

Aut.   I must confess to you, sir, I am no
fighter : I am false of heart that way ; and
that he knew, I warrant him.

Clo.   How do you now ?

Aut.   Sweet sir, much better than I was ; I
can stand and walk : I will even take my leave
of you, and pace softly towards my kinsman's.

Clo.   Shall I bring thee on the way ?

Aut.   No, good-faced sir ; no, sweet sir.

Clo.   Then fare thee well : I must go buy
spices for our sheep-shearing.

Aut.   Prosper you, sweet sir ! [*Exit Clown.*]
Your purse is not hot enough to purchase your
spice. I'll be with you at your sheep-shearing
too : if I make not this cheat bring out another and the shearers prove sheep, let me be
unrolled and my name put in the book of
virtue !

[*Sings*] Jog on, jog on, the foot-path way,
       And merrily hent the stile-a :
    A merry heart goes all the day,
       Your sad tires in a mile-a. [*Exit.*

SCENE IV.   *The* Shepherd's *cottage.*

Enter FLORIZEL *and* PERDITA.

Flo.   These your unusual weeds to each
       part of you
Do give a life : no shepherdess, but Flora
Peering in April's front. This your sheep-
       shearing
Is as a meeting of the petty gods,
And you the queen on't.

Per.   Sir, my gracious lord,
To chide at your extremes it not becomes me :
O, pardon, that I name them ! Your high self,

The gracious mark o' the land, you have ob-
       scured
With a swain's wearing, and me, poor lowly
       maid,
Most goddess-like prank'd up : but that our
       feasts   10
In every mess have folly and the feeders
Digest it with a custom, I should blush
To see you so attired, sworn, I think,
To show myself a glass.

Flo.   I bless the time
When my good falcon made her flight across
Thy father's ground.

Per.   Now Jove afford you cause !
To me the difference forges dread ; your great-
       ness
Hath not been used to fear. Even now I trem-
       ble
To think your father, by some accident,
Should pass this way as you did : O, the
       Fates !   20
How would he look, to see his work so noble
Vilely bound up ? What would he say ? Or
       how
Should I, in these my borrow'd flaunts, behold
The sternness of his presence ?

Flo.   Apprehend
Nothing but jollity. The gods themselves,
Humbling their deities to love, have taken
The shapes of beasts upon them : Jupiter
Became a bull, and bellow'd ; the green Nep-
       tune
A ram, and bleated ; and the fire-robed god,
Golden Apollo, a poor humble swain,   30
As I seem now. Their transformations
Were never for a piece of beauty rarer,
Nor in a way so chaste, since my desires
Run not before mine honor, nor my lusts
Burn hotter than my faith.

Per.   O, but, sir,
Your resolution cannot hold, when 'tis
Opposed, as it must be, by the power of the
       king :
One of these two must be necessities,
Which then will speak, that you must change
       this purpose,
Or I my life.

Flo.   Thou dearest Perdita,   40
With these forced thoughts, I prithee, darken
       not
The mirth o' the feast. Or I'll be thine, my
       fair,
Or not my father's. For I cannot be
Mine own, nor any thing to any, if
I be not thine. To this I am most constant,
Though destiny say no. Be merry, gentle ;
Strangle such thoughts as these with any thing
That you behold the while. Your guests are
       coming :
Lift up your countenance, as it were the day
Of celebration of that nuptial which   50
We two have sworn shall come.

Per.   O lady Fortune,
Stand you auspicious !

Flo.   See, your guests approach :
Address yourself to entertain them sprightly,
And let's be red with mirth.

Enter Shepherd, Clown, MOPSA, DORCAS, *and
    others, with* POLIXENES *and* CAMILLO *dis-
    guised.*

Shep.   Fie, daughter ! when my old wife
       lived, upon

This day she was both pantler, butler, cook,
Both dame and servant; welcomed all, served
    all;
Would sing her song and dance her turn; now
    here,
At upper end o' the table, now i' the middle;
On his shoulder, and his; her face o' fire   60
With labor and the thing she took to quench it,
She would to each one sip. You are retired,
As if you were a feasted one and not
The hostess of the meeting: pray you, bid
These unknown friends to's welcome; for it is
A way to make us better friends, more known.
Come, quench your blushes and present your-
    self
That which you are, mistress o' the feast:
    come on,
And bid us welcome to your sheep-shearing,
As your good flock shall prosper.
    Per.   [To Pol.] Sir, welcome: 70
It is my father's will I should take on me
The hostess-ship o' the day. [To Cam.]
    You're welcome, sir.
Give me those flowers there, Dorcas. Reverend
    sirs,
For you there's rosemary and rue; these keep
Seeming and savor all the winter long:
Grace and remembrance be to you both,
And welcome to our shearing!
    Pol.   Shepherdess,
A fair one are you—well you fit our ages
With flowers of winter.
    Per.   Sir, the year growing ancient,
Not yet on summer's death, nor on the birth
Of trembling winter, the fairest flowers o' the
    season   81
Are our carnations and streak'd gillyvors,
Which some call nature's bastards: of that
    kind
Our rustic garden's barren; and I care not
To get slips of them.
    Pol.   Wherefore, gentle maiden,
Do you neglect them?
    Per.   For I have heard it said
There is an art which in their piedness shares
With great creating nature.
    Pol.   Say there be;
Yet nature is made better by no mean
But nature makes that mean: so, over that
    art   90
Which you say adds to nature, is an art
That nature makes. You see, sweet maid, we
    marry
A gentler scion to the wildest stock,
And make conceive a bark of baser kind
By bud of nobler race: this is an art
Which does mend nature, change it rather, but
The art itself is nature.
    Per.   So it is.
    Pol. Then make your garden rich in gilly-
    vors,
And do not call them bastards.
    Per.   I'll not put
The dibble in earth to set one slip of them;
No more than were I painted I would wish 101
This youth should say 'twere well and only
    therefore
Desire to breed by me. Here's flowers for you;
Hot lavender, mints, savory, marjoram;
The marigold, that goes to bed wi' the sun
And with him rises weeping: these are flow-
    ers
Of middle summer, and I think they are given

To men of middle age. You're very welcome.
    Cam. I should leave grazing, were I of
    your flock,
And only live by gazing.
    Per.   Out, alas!   110
You'd be so lean, that blasts of January
Would blow you through and through. Now,
    my fair'st friend,
I would I had some flowers o' the spring that
    might
Become your time of day; and yours, and
    yours,
That wear upon your virgin branches yet
Your maidenheads growing: O Proserpina,
For the flowers now, that frighted thou let'st
    fall
From Dis's waggon! daffodils,
That come before the swallow dares, and take
The winds of March with beauty; violets dim,
But sweeter than the lids of Juno's eyes   121
Or Cytherea's breath; pale primroses,
That die unmarried, ere they can behold
Bight Phœbus in his strength—a malady
Most incident to maids; bold oxlips and
The crown imperial; lilies of all kinds,
The flower-de-luce being one! O, these I lack,
To make you garlands of, and my sweet
    friend,
To strew him o'er and o'er!
    Flo.   What, like a corse?
    Per. No, like a bank for love to lie and
    play on;   130
Not like a corse; or if, not to be buried,
But quick and in mine arms. Come, take your
    flowers:
Methinks I play as I have seen them do
In Whitsun pastorals: sure this robe of mine
Does change my disposition.
    Flo.   What you do
Still betters what is done. When you speak,
    sweet,
I'ld have you do it ever: when you sing,
I'ld have you buy and sell so, so give alms,
Pray so; and, for the ordering your affairs,
To sing them too: when you do dance, I wish
    you   140
A wave o' the sea, that you might ever do
Nothing but that; move still, still so,
And own no other function: each your doing,
So singular in each particular,
Crowns what you are doing in the present
    deed,
That all your acts are queens.
    Per.   O Doricles,
Your praises are too large: but that your
    youth,
And the true blood which peepeth fairly
    through't,
Do plainly give you out an unstain'd shepherd,
With wisdom I might fear, my Doricles,   150
You woo'd me the false way.
    Flo.   I think you have
As little skill to fear as I have purpose
To put you to't. But come; our dance, I
    pray:
Your hand, my Perdita: so turtles pair,
That never mean to part.
    Per.   I'll swear for 'em.
    Pol. This is the prettiest low-born lass that
    ever
Ran on the green-sward: nothing she does or
    seems

But smacks of something greater than herself,
Too noble for this place.
  Cam.   He tells her something
That makes her blood look out : good sooth,
    she is   160
The queen of curds and cream.
  Clo.   Come on, strike up !
  Dor. Mopsa must be your mistress :
    marry, garlic,
To mend her kissing with !
  Mop.   Now, in good time !
  Clo. Not a word, a word ; we stand upon
    our manners.
Come, strike up !
  [*Music. Here a dance of Shepherds and*
                    Shepherdesses.
  Pol. Pray, good shepherd, what fair swain
    is this
Which dances with your daughter ?
  Shep. They call him Doricles ; and boasts
    himself
To have a worthy feeding : but I have it
Upon his own report and I believe it ;   170
He looks like sooth. He says he loves my
    daughter :
I think so too ; for never gazed the moon
Upon the water as he'll stand and read
As 'twere my daughter's eyes : and, to be plain,
I think there is not half a kiss to choose
Who loves another best.
  Pol.   She dances featly.
  Shep. So she does any thing ; though I re-
    port it,
That should be silent : if young Doricles
Do light upon her, she shall bring him that
Which he not dreams of.   180

Enter Servant.

  Serv. O master, if you did but hear the
pedlar at the door, you would never dance
again after a tabor and pipe ; no, the bagpipe
could not move you : he sings several tunes
faster than you'll tell money ; he utters them
as he had eaten ballads and all men's ears
grew to his tunes.
  Clo. He could never come better ; he shall
come in. I love a ballad but even too well, if
it be doleful matter merrily set down, or a
very pleasant thing indeed and sung lamentably.
  Serv. He hath songs for man or woman,
of all sizes ; no milliner can so fit his customers with gloves : he has the prettiest love-
songs for maids ; so without bawdry, which is
strange ; with such delicate burthens of dil-
dos and fadings, ' jump her and thump her ; '
and where some stretch-mouthed rascal
would, as it were, mean mischief and break a
foul gap into the matter, he makes the maid
to answer ' Whoop, do me no harm, good
man ; ' puts him off, slights him, with ' Whoop,
do me no harm, good man.'   201
  Pol. This is a brave fellow.
  Clo. Believe me, thou talkest of an admirable conceited fellow. Has he any un-
braided wares ?
  Serv. He hath ribbons of all the colors i'
the rainbow ; points more than all the lawyers
in Bohemia can learnedly handle, though they
come to him by the gross : inkles, caddisses,
cambrics, lawns : why, he sings 'em over as
they were gods or goddesses ; you would think
a smock were a she-angel, he so chants to the

sleeve-hand and the work about the square
on't.
  Clo. Prithee bring him in ; and let him approach singing.
  Per. Forewarn him that he use no scurrilous words in 's tunes.   [*Exit Servant.*
  Clo. You have of these pedlars, that have
more in them than you'ld think, sister.
  Per. Ay, good brother, or go about to
think.

Enter AUTOLYCUS, *singing.*

Lawn as white as driven snow ;   220
Cyprus black as e'er was crow ;
Gloves as sweet as damask roses ;
Masks for faces and for noses ;
Bugle bracelet, necklace amber,
Perfume for a lady's chamber ;
Golden quoifs and stomachers,
For my lads to give their dears :
Pins and poking-sticks of steel,
What maids lack from head to heel :
Come buy of me, come ; come buy, come
    buy ;
Buy, lads, or else your lasses cry :   231
Come buy.
  Clo. If I were not in love with Mopsa, thou
shouldst take no money of me ; but being en-
thralled as I am, it will also be the bondage of
certain ribbons and gloves.
  Mop. I was promised them against the
feast ; but they come not too late now.
  Dor. He hath promised you more than that,
or there be liars.   240
  Mop. He hath paid you all he promised
you ; may be, he has paid you more, which
will shame you to give him again.
  Clo. Is there no manners left among
maids ? will they wear their plackets where
they should bear their faces ? Is there not
milking-time, when you are going to bed, or
kiln-hole, to whistle off these secrets, but you
must be tittle-tattling before all our guests ?
'tis well they are whispering : clamor your
tongues, and not a word more.   251
  Mop. I have done. Come, you promised
me a tawdry-lace and a pair of sweet gloves.
  Clo. Have I not told thee how I was coz-
ened by the way and lost all my money ?
  Aut. And indeed, sir, there are cozeners
abroad ; therefore it behoves men to be wary.
  Clo. Fear not thou, man, thou shalt lose
nothing here.
  Aut. I hope so, sir ; for I have about me
many parcels of charge.   261
  Clo. What hast here ? ballads ?
  Mop. Pray now, buy some : I love a ballad
in print o' life, for then we are sure they are
true.
  Aut. Here's one to a very doleful tune, how
a usurer's wife was brought to bed of twenty
money-bags at a burthen and how she longed
to eat adders' heads and toads carbonadoed.
  Mop. Is it true, think you ?
  Aut. Very true, and but a month old. 270
  Dor. Bless me from marrying a usurer !
  Aut. Here's the midwife's name to't, one
Mistress Tale-porter, and five or six honest
wives that were present. Why should I carry
lies abroad ?
  Mop. Pray you now, buy it.
  Clo. Come on, lay it by : and let's first see
moe ballads ; we'll buy the other things anon.

Aut. Here's another ballad of a fish, that appeared upon the coast on Wednesday the four-score of April, forty thousand fathom above water, and sung this ballad against the hard hearts of maids : it was thought she was a woman and was turned into a cold fish for she would not exchange flesh with one that loved her : the ballad is very pitiful and as true.

Dor. Is it true too, think you ?

Aut. Five justices' hands at it, and witnesses more than my pack will hold.

Clo. Lay it by too : another. 290

Aut. This is a merry ballad, but a very pretty one.

Mop. Let's have some merry ones.

Aut. Why, this is a passing merry one and goes to the tune of ' Two maids wooing a man : ' there's scarce a maid westward but she sings it ; 'tis in request, I can tell you.

Mop. We can both sing it : if thou'lt bear a part, thou shalt hear ; 'tis in three parts. 299

Dor. We had the tune on't a month ago.

Aut. I can bear my part ; you must know 'tis my occupation ; have at it with you.

SONG.

A. Get you hence, for I must go
    Where it fits not you to know.
      D. Whither ? *M.* O, whither ? *D.*
        Whither ?
  M. It becomes thy oath full well,
    Thou to me thy secrets tell.
      D. Me too, let me go thither.
  M. Or thou goest to the grange or mill.
  D. If to either, thou dost ill. 310
A. Neither. *D.* What, neither ? *A.* Neither.
  D. Thou hast sworn my love to be.
  M. Thou hast sworn it more to me :
    Then whither goest ? say, whither ?

Clo. We'll have this song out anon by ourselves : my father and the gentlemen are in sad talk, and we'll not trouble them. Come, bring away thy pack after me. Wenches, I'll buy for you both. Pedlar, let's have the first choice. Follow me, girls. [*Exit with Dorcas and Mopsa.*

Aut. And you shall pay well for 'em.
               [*Follows singing.*
    Will you buy any tape,
    Or lace for your cape,
My dainty duck, my dear-a ?
    Any silk, any thread,
    Any toys for your head,
Of the new'st and finest, finest wear-a ?
    Come to the pedlar ;
    Money's a medler.
That doth utter all men's ware-a. [*Exit.* 330

Re-enter Servant.

Serv. Master, there is three carters, three shepherds, three neat-herds, three swine-herds, that have made themselves all men of hair, they call themselves Saltiers, and they have a dance which the wenches say is a gallimaufry of gambols, because they are not in't ; but they themselves are o' the mind, if it be not too rough for some that know little but bowling, it will please plentifully. 339

Shep. Away ! we'll none on 't : here has been too much homely foolery already. I know, sir, we weary you.

Pol. You weary those that refresh us : pray, let's see these four threes of herdsmen.

Serv. One three of them, by their own report, sir, hath danced before the king ; and not the worst of the three but jumps twelve foot and a half by the squier.

Shep. Leave your prating : since these good men are pleased, let them come in ; but quickly now. 351

Serv. Why, they stay at door, sir. [*Exit.*

Here a dance of twelve Satyrs.

Pol. O, father, you'll know more of that hereafter.
[*To Cam.*] Is it not too far gone ? 'Tis time to part them.
He's simple and tells much. [*To Flor.*] How now, fair shepherd !
Your heart is full of something that does take
Your mind from feasting. Sooth, when I was young
And handed love as you do, I was wont
To load my she with knacks : I would have ransack'd 360
The pedlar's silken treasury and have pour'd it
To her acceptance ; you have let him go
And nothing marted with him. If your lass
Interpretation should abuse and call this
Your lack of love or bounty, you were straited
For a reply, at least if you make a care
Of happy holding her.
Flo.   Old sir, I know
She prizes not such trifles as these are :
The gifts she looks from me are pack'd and lock'd 369
Up in my heart ; which I have given already,
But not deliver'd. O, hear me breathe my life
Before this ancient sir, who, it should seem,
Hath sometime loved ! I take thy hand, this hand,
As soft as dove's down and as white as it,
Or Ethiopian's tooth, or the fann'd snow that's bolted
By the northern blasts twice o'er.
Pol.   What follows this ?
How prettily the young swain seems to wash
The hand was fair before ! I have put you out :
But to your protestation ; let me hear
What you profess.
Flo.   Do, and be witness to 't. 380
Pol. And this my neighbor too ?
Flo.   And he, and more
Than he, and men, the earth, the heavens, and all :
That, were I crown'd the most imperial monarch,
Thereof most worthy, were I the fairest youth
That ever made eye swerve, had force and knowledge
More than was ever man's, I would not prize them
Without her love ; for her employ them all,
Commend them and condemn them to her service
Or to their own perdition.
Pol.   Fairly offer'd.
Cam. This shows a sound affection.
Shep.   But, my daughter, 390
Say you the like to him ?
Per.   I cannot speak
So well, nothing so well ; no, nor mean better :
By the pattern of mine own thoughts I cut out
The purity of his.

Shep.   Take hands, a bargain!
And, friends unknown, you shall bear witness
            to 't:
I give my daughter to him, and will make
Her portion equal his.
    Flo.   O, that must be
I' the virtue of your daughter: one being dead,
I shall have more than you can dream of yet;
Enough then for your wonder. But, come on,
Contract us 'fore these witnesses.   401
    Shep.   Come, your hand;
And, daughter, yours.
    Pol.   Soft, swain, awhile, beseech you;
Have you a father?
    Flo.   I have: but what of him?
    Pol. Knows he of this?
    Flo.   He neither does nor shall.
    Pol. Methinks a father
Is at the nuptial of his son a guest
That best becomes the table. Pray you once
            more,
Is not your father grown incapable
Of reasonable affairs? is he not stupid
With age and altering rheums? can he speak?
            hear?   410
Know man from man? dispute his own estate?
Lies he not bed-rid? and again does nothing
But what he did being childish?
    Flo.   No, good sir;
He has his health and ampler strength indeed
Than most have of his age.
    Pol.   By my white beard,
You offer him, if this be so, a wrong
Something unfilial: reason my son
Should choose himself a wife, but as good
            reason
The father, all whose joy is nothing else
But fair posterity, should hold some counsel
In such a business.   421
    Flo.   I yield all this;
But for some other reasons, my grave sir,
Which 'tis not fit you know, I not acquaint
My father of this business.
    Pol.   Let him know't.
    Flo. He shall not.
    Pol.   Prithee, let him.
    Flo.   No, he must not.
    Shep. Let him, my son: he shall not need
            to grieve
At knowing of thy choice.
    Flo.   Come, come, he must not.
Mark our contract.
    Pol.   Mark your divorce, young sir,
                        [*Discovering himself.*
Whom son I dare not call; thou art too base
To be acknowledged: thou a sceptre's heir,
That thus affect'st a sheep-hook! Thou old
            traitor,   431
I am sorry that by hanging thee I can
But shorten thy life one week. And thou,
            fresh piece
Of excellent witchcraft, who of force must
            know
The royal fool thou copest with,—
    Shep. O, my heart!
    Pol. I'll have thy beauty scratch'd with
            briers, and made
More homely than thy state. For thee, fond
            boy,
If I may ever know thou dost but sigh
That thou no more shalt see this knack, as
            never

I mean thou shalt, we'll bar thee from suc-
            cession;
Not hold thee of our blood, no, not our
            kin,   441
Far than Deucalion off: mark thou my words:
Follow us to the court. Thou churl, for this
            time,
Though full of our displeasure, yet we free
            thee
From the dead blow of it. And you, enchant-
            ment.—
Worthy enough a herdsman; yea, him too,
That makes himself, but for our honor therein,
Unworthy thee,—if ever henceforth thou
These rural latches to his entrance open,
Or hoop his body more with thy embraces,
I will devise a death as cruel for thee   451
As thou art tender to't.   [*Exit.*
    Per.   Even here undone!
I was not much afeard; for once or twice
I was about to speak and tell him plainly,
The selfsame sun that shines upon his court
Hides not his visage from our cottage but
Looks on alike. Will't please you, sir, be
            gone?
I told you what would come of this: beseech
            you,
Of your own state take care: this dream of
            mine,—
Being now awake, I'll queen it no inch far-
            ther,
But milk my ewes and weep.   461
    Cam.   Why, how now, father!
Speak ere thou diest.
    Shep.   I cannot speak, nor think,
Nor dare to know that which I know. O sir!
You have undone a man of fourscore three,
That thought to fill his grave in quiet, yea,
To die upon the bed my father died,
To lie close by his honest bones: but now
Some hangman must put on my shroud and
            lay me
Where no priest shovels in dust. O cursed
            wretch,
That knew'st this was the prince, and wouldst
            adventure   470
To mingle faith with him! Undone! undone!
If I might die within this hour, I have lived
To die when I desire.   [*Exit.*
    Flo.   Why look you so upon me?
I am but sorry, not afeard; delay'd,
But nothing alter'd: what I was, I am;
More straining on for plucking back, not fol-
            lowing
My leash unwillingly.
    Cam.   Gracious my lord,
You know your father's temper: at this time
He will allow no speech, which I do guess
You do not purpose to him; and as hardly
Will he endure your sight as yet, I fear: 481
Then, till the fury of his highness settle,
Come not before him.
    Flo.   I not purpose it.
I think, Camillo?
    Cam.   Even he, my lord.
    Per. How often have I told you 'twould be
            thus!
How often said, my dignity would last
But till 'twere known!
    Flo.   It cannot fail but by
The violation of my faith; and then
Let nature crush the sides o' the earth together
And mar the seeds within! Lift up thy looks:

From my succession wipe me, father ; I   491
Am heir to my affection.
  Cam.   Be advised.
  Flo.   I am, and by my fancy : if my rea-
      son
Will thereto be obedient, I have reason ;
If not, my senses, better pleased with mad-
      ness,
Do bid it welcome.
  Cam.   This is desperate, sir.
  Flo.   So call it : but it does fulfil my vow ;
I needs must think it honesty. Camillo,
Not for Bohemia, nor the pomp that may
Be thereat glean'd, for all the sun sees or 500
The close earth wombs or the profound sea
      hides
In unknown fathoms, will I break my oath
To this my fair beloved : therefore, I pray
      you,
As you have ever been my father's honor'd
      friend,
When he shall miss me,—as, in faith, I mean
      not
To see him any more,—cast your good coun-
      sels
Upon his passion ; let myself and fortune
Tug for the time to come. This you may know
And so deliver, I am put to sea
With her whom here I cannot hold on shore ;
And most opportune to our need I have   511
A vessel rides fast by, but not prepared
For this design. What course I mean to hold
Shall nothing benefit your knowledge, nor
Concern me the reporting.
  Cam.   O my lord !
I would your spirit were easier for advice,
Or stronger for your need.
  Flo.   Hark, Perdita [*Drawing her aside.*
I'll hear you by and by.
  Cam.   He's irremoveable,
Resolved for flight. Now were I happy, if
His going I could frame to serve my turn, 520
Save him from danger, do him love and
      honor,
Purchase the sight again of dear Sicilia
And that unhappy king, my master, whom
I so much thirst to see.
  Flo.   Now, good Camillo ;
I am so fraught with curious business that
I leave out ceremony.
  Cam.   Sir, I think
You have heard of my poor services, i' the
      love
That I have borne your father ?
  Flo.   Very nobly
Have you deserved : it is my father's music
To speak your deeds, not little of his care 530
To have them recompensed as thought on.
  Cam.   Well, my lord,
If you may please to think I love the king
And through him what is nearest to him, which
      is
Your gracious self, embrace but my direction :
If your more ponderous and settled project
May suffer alteration, on mine honor,
I'll point you where you shall have such re-
      ceiving
As shall become your highness ; where you
      may
Enjoy your mistress, from the whom, I see,
There's no disjunction to be made, but by—
As heavens forefend !—your ruin ; marry her,
And, with my best endeavors in your absence,

Your discontenting father strive to qualify
And bring him up to liking.
  Flo.   How, Camillo,
May this, almost a miracle, be done ?
That I may call thee something more than
      man
And after that trust to thee.
  Cam.   Have you thought on
A place whereto you'll go ?
  Flo.   Not any yet :
But as the unthought-on accident is guilty
To what we wildly do, so we profess   550
Ourselves to be the slaves of chance and flies
Of every wind that blows.
  Cam.   Then list to me :
This follows, if you will not change your pur-
      pose
But undergo this flight, make for Sicilia,
And there present yourself and your fair prin-
      cess,
For so I see she must be, 'fore Leontes :
She shall be habited as it becomes
The partner of your bed. Methinks I see
Leontes opening his free arms and weeping
His welcomes forth ; asks thee the son for-
      giveness,   560
As 'twere i' the father's person ; kisses the
      hands
Of your fresh princess ; o'er and o'er divides
      him
'Twixt his unkindness and his kindness ; the
      one
He chides to hell and bids the other grow
Faster than thought or time.
  Flo.   Worthy Camillo,
What color for my visitation shall I
Hold up before him ?
  Cam.   Sent by the king your father
To greet him and to give him comforts. Sir,
The manner of your bearing towards him,
      with   569
What you as from your father shall deliver,
Things known betwixt us three, I'll write you
      down :
The which shall point you forth at every sit-
      ting
What you must say ; that he shall not per-
      ceive
But that you have your father's bosom there
And speak his very heart.
  Flo.   I am bound to you :
There is some sap in this.
  Cam.   A cause more promising
Than a wild dedication of yourselves
To unpath'd waters, undream'd shores, most
      certain
To miseries enough ; no hope to help you,
But as you shake off one to take another ; 580
Nothing so certain as your anchors, who
Do their best office, if they can but stay you
Where you'll be loath to be : besides you
      know
Prosperity's the very bond of love,
Whose fresh complexion and whose heart to-
      gether
Affliction alters.
  Per.   One of these is true :
I think affliction may subdue the cheek,
But not take in the mind.
  Cam.   Yea, say you so ?
There shall not at your father's house these
      seven years
Be born another such.

Flo.   My good Camillo, 590
She is as forward of her breeding as
She is i' the rear our birth.
Cam.   I cannot say 'tis pity
She lacks instructions, for she seems a mis-
    tress
To most that teach.
Per.   Your pardon, sir; for this
I'll blush you thanks.
Flo.   My prettiest Perdita!
But O, the thorns we stand upon! Camillo,
Preserver of my father, now of me,
The medicine of our house, how shall we do?
We are not furnish'd like Bohemia's son,
Nor shall appear in Sicilia.
Cam.   My lord,   600
Fear none of this: I think you know my for-
    tunes
Do all lie there: it shall be so my care
To have you royally appointed as if
The scene you play were mine. For instance,
    sir,
That you may know you shall not want, one
    word.   [*They talk aside.*

Re-enter AUTOLYCUS.

Aut. Ha, ha! what a fool Honesty is! and
Trust, his sworn brother, a very simple gentleman! I have sold all my trumpery; not
a counterfeit stone, not a ribbon, glass, pomander, brooch, table-book, ballad, knife, tape,
glove, shoe-tie, bracelet, horn-ring, to keep my
pack from fasting: they throng who should
buy first, as if my trinkets had been hallowed
and brought a benediction to the buyer: by
which means I saw whose purse was best in
picture; and what I saw, to my good use I remembered. My clown, who wants but something to be a reasonable man, grew so in
love with the wenches' song, that he would
not stir his pettitoes till he had both tune and
words; which so drew the rest of the herd to
me that all their other senses stuck in ears:
you might have pinched a placket, it was
senseless; 'twas nothing to geld a codpiece of
a purse; I could have filed keys off that hung
in chains: no hearing, no feeling, but my sir's
song, and admiring the nothing of it. So that
in this time of lethargy I picked and cut most
of their festival purses; and had not the old
man come in with a whoo-bub against his
daughter and the king's son and scared my
choughs from the chaff, I had not left a purse
alive in the whole army.   631
[*Camillo, Florizel, and Perdita come forward.*
Cam. Nay, but my letters, by this means
    being there
So soon as you arrive, shall clear that doubt.
Flo. And those that you'll procure from
    King Leontes—
Cam.   Shall satisfy your father.
Per.   Happy be you!
All that you speak shows fair.
Cam.   Who have we here?
                   [*Seeing Autolycus.*
We'll make an instrument of this, omit
Nothing may give us aid.
Aut. If they have overheard me now, why,
hanging.   640
Cam. How now, good fellow! why shakest
thou so? Fear not, man; here's no harm in-
tended to thee.
Aut. I am a poor fellow, sir.

Cam. Why, be so still; here's nobody will
steal that from thee: yet for the outside of thy
poverty we must make an exchange; therefore discase thee instantly,—thou must think
there's a necessity in't,—and change garments
with this gentleman: though the pennyworth
on his side be the worst, yet hold thee, there's
some boot.
Aut. I am a poor fellow, sir. [*Aside*] I
know ye well enough.
Cam. Nay, prithee, dispatch: the gentle-
man is half flayed already.
Aut. Are you in earnest, sir? [*Aside*] I
smell the trick on't.
Flo. Dispatch, I prithee.
Aut. Indeed, I have had earnest: but I
cannot with conscience take it.   660
Cam. Unbuckle, unbuckle.
[*Florizel and Autolycus exchange garments.*
Fortunate mistress,—let my prophecy
Come home to ye!—you must retire yourself
Into some covert: take your sweetheart's hat
And pluck it o'er your brows, muffle your
    face,
Dismantle you, and, as you can, disliken
The truth of your own seeming; that you
    may—
For I do fear eyes over—to shipboard
Get undescried.
Per.   I see the play so lies
That I must bear a part.
Cam.   No remedy.   670
Have you done there?
Flo.   Should I now meet my father,
He would not call me son.
Cam.   Nay, you shall have no hat.
                   [*Giving it to Perdita.*
Come, lady, come. Farewell, my friend.
Aut.   Adieu, sir.
Flo. O Perdita, what have we twain for-
    got!
Pray you, a word.
Cam. [*Aside*] What I do next, shall be to
    tell the king
Of this escape and whither they are bound;
Wherein my hope is I shall so prevail
To force him after: in whose company
I shall review Sicilia, for whose sight   680
I have a woman's longing.
Flo.   Fortune speed us!
Thus we set on, Camillo, to the sea-side.
Cam. The swifter speed the better.
       [*Exeunt Florizel, Perdita, and Camillo.*
Aut. I understand the business, I hear it:
to have an open ear, a quick eye, and a nimble hand, is necessary for a cut-purse; a good
nose is requisite also, to smell out work for
the other senses. I see this is the time that
the unjust man doth thrive. What an exchange had this been without boot! What a
boot is here with this exchange! Sure the
gods do this year connive at us, and we may
do any thing extempore. The prince himself
is about a piece of iniquity, stealing away
from his father with his clog at his heels: if
I thought it were a piece of honesty to acquaint the king withal, I would not do't: I
hold it the more knavery to conceal it; and
therein am I constant to my profession.

Re-enter Clown and Shepherd.

Aside, aside; here is more matter for a hot
brain: every lane's end, every shop, church,

session, hanging, yields a careful man work.

Clo. See, see; what a man you are now! There is no other way but to tell the king she's a changeling and none of your flesh and blood.

Shep. Nay, but hear me.

Clo. Nay, but hear me.

Shep. Go to, then. 709

Clo. She being none of your flesh and blood, your flesh and blood has not offended the king; and so your flesh and blood is not to be punished by him. Show those things you found about her, those secret things, all but what she has with her: this being done, let the law go whistle: I warrant you.

Shep. I will tell the king all, every word, yea, and his son's pranks too; who, I may say, is no honest man, neither to his father nor to me, to go about to make me the king's brother-in-law. 721

Clo. Indeed, brother-in-law was the farthest off you could have been to him and then your blood had been the dearer by I know how much an ounce.

Aut. [*Aside*] Very wisely, puppies!

Shep. Well, let us to the king: there is that in this fardel will make him scratch his beard.

Aut. [*Aside*] I know not what impediment this complaint may be to the flight of my master.

Clo. Pray heartily he be at palace. 731

Aut. [*Aside*] Though I am not naturally honest, I am so sometimes by chance: let me pocket up my pedlar's excrement. [*Takes off his false beard.*] How now, rustics! whither are you bound?

Shep. To the palace, an it like your worship.

Aut. Your affairs there, what, with whom, the condition of that fardel, the place of your dwelling, your names, your ages, of what having, breeding, and any thing that is fitting to be known, discover.

Clo. We are but plain fellows, sir.

Aut. A lie; you are rough and hairy. Let me have no lying: it becomes none but tradesmen, and they often give us soldiers the lie: but we pay them for it with stamped coin, not stabbing steel; therefore they do not give us the lie.

Clo. Your worship had like to have given us one, if you had not taken yourself with the manner.

Shep. Are you a courtier, an't like you, sir?

Aut. Whether it like me or no, I am a courtier. Seest thou not the air of the court in these enfoldings? hath not my gait in it the measure of the court? receives not thy nose court-odor from me? reflect I not on thy baseness court-contempt? Thinkest thou, for that I insinuate, or toaze from thee thy business, I am therefore no courtier? I am courtier cap-a-pe; and one that will either push on or pluck back thy business there: whereupon I command thee to open thy affair.

Shep. My business, sir, is to the king.

Aut. What advocate hast thou to him?

Shep. I know not, an't like you.

Clo. Advocate's the court-word for a pheasant: say you have none.

Shep. None, sir; I have no pheasant, cock nor hen. 771

Aut. How blessed are we that are not simple men! Yet nature might have made me as these are, Therefore I will not disdain.

Clo. This cannot be but a great courtier.

Shep. His garments are rich, but he wears them not handsomely.

Clo. He seems to be the more noble in being fantastical: a great man, I'll warrant; I know by the picking on's teeth. 780

Aut. The fardel there? what's i' the fardel? Wherefore that box?

Shep. Sir, there lies such secrets in this fardel and box, which none must know but the king; and which he shall know within this hour, if I may come to the speech of him.

Aut. Age, thou hast lost thy labor.

Shep. Why, sir?

Aut. The king is not at the palace; he is gone aboard a new ship to purge melancholy and air himself: for, if thou beest capable of things serious, thou must know the king is full of grief.

Shep. So 'tis said, sir; about his son, that should have married a shepherd's daughter.

Aut. If that shepherd be not in hand-fast, let him fly: the curses he shall have, the tortures he shall feel, will break the back of man, the heart of monster.

Clo. Think you so, sir? 799

Aut. Not he alone shall suffer what wit can make heavy and vengeance bitter; but those that are germane to him, though removed fifty times, shall all come under the hangman: which though it be great pity, yet it is necessary. An old sheep-whistling rogue, a ram-tender, to offer to have his daughter come into grace! Some say he shall be stoned; but that death is too soft for him, say I: draw our throne into a sheep-cote! all deaths are too few, the sharpest too easy.

Clo. Has the old man e'er a son, sir, do you hear, an't like you, sir? 811

Aut. He has a son, who shall be flayed alive; then 'nointed over with honey, set on the head of a wasp's nest; then stand till he be three quarters and a dram dead; then recovered again with aqua-vitæ or some other hot infusion; then, raw as he is, and in the hottest day prognostication proclaims, shall he be set against a brick-wall, the sun looking with a southward eye upon him, where he is to behold him with flies blown to death. But what talk we of these traitorly rascals, whose miseries are to be smiled at, their offences being so capital? Tell me, for you seem to be honest plain men, what you have to the king: being something gently considered, I'll bring you where he is aboard, tender your persons to his presence, whisper him in your behalfs; and if it be in man besides the king to effect your suits, here is man shall do it. 829

Clo. He seems to be of great authority: close with him, give him gold; and though authority be a stubborn bear, yet he is oft led by the nose with gold: show the inside of your purse to the outside of his hand, and no more ado. Remember 'stoned,' and 'flayed alive.'

Shep. An't please you, sir, to undertake

the business for us, here is that gold I have :
I'll make it as much more and leave this
young man in pawn till I bring it you.

Aut. After I have done what I promised ?
Shep. Ay, sir.   841
Aut. Well, give me the moiety. Are you
a party in this business ?
Clo. In some sort, sir : but though my case
be a pitiful one, I hope I shall not be flayed
out of it.
Aut. O, that's the case of the shepherd's
son : hang him, he'll be made an example.
Clo. Comfort, good comfort ! We must to
the king and show our strange sights : he must
know 'tis none of your daughter nor my sister ; we are gone else. Sir, I will give you
as much as this old man does when the business is performed, and remain, as he says,
your pawn till it be brought you.
Aut. I will trust you. Walk before toward
the sea-side ; go on the right hand : I will but
look upon the hedge and follow you.
Clo. We are blest in this man, as I may
say, even blest.
Shep. Let's before as he bids us : he was
provided to do us good.   861
                    [*Exeunt Shepherd and Clown.*
Aut. If I had a mind to be honest, I see
Fortune would not suffer me : she drops
booties in my mouth. I am courted now with
a double occasion, gold and a means to do
the prince my master good ; which who knows
how that may turn back to my advancement ?
I will bring these two moles, these blind ones,
aboard him : if he think it fit to shore them
again and that the complaint they have to the
king concerns him nothing, let him call me
rogue for being so far officious ; for I am
proof against that title and what shame else
belongs to't. To him will I present them :
there may be matter in it.   [*Exit.*

ACT V.

SCENE I. *A room in* LEONTES' *palace.*

Enter LEONTES, CLEOMENES, DION, PAULINA,
and Servants.

Cleo. Sir, you have done enough, and have
        perform'd
A saint-like sorrow : no fault could you make,
Which you have not redeem'd ; indeed, paid
        down
More penitence than done trespass : at the
        last,
Do as the heavens have done, forget your
        evil ;
With them forgive yourself.
Leon.   Whilst I remember
Her and her virtues, I cannot forget
My blemishes in them, and so still think of
The wrong I did myself ; which was so much,
That heirless it hath made my kingdom and
Destroy'd the sweet'st companion that e'er
        man   11
Bred his hopes out of.
Paul.   True, too true, my lord :
If, one by one, you wedded all the world,
Or from the all that are took something good,
To make a perfect woman, she you kill'd
Would be unparallel'd.
Leon.   I think so. Kill'd !

She I kill'd ! I did so : but thou strikest me
Sorely, to say I did ; it is as bitter
Upon thy tongue as in my thought : now,
        good now,
Say so but seldom.
Cleo.   Not at all, good lady :   20
You might have spoken a thousand things that
        would
Have done the time more benefit and graced
Your kindness better.
Paul.   You are one of those
Would have him wed again.
Dion.   If you would not so,
You pity not the state, nor the remembrance
Of his most sovereign name ; consider little
What dangers, by his highness' fail of issue,
May drop upon his kingdom and devour
Incertain lookers on. What were more holy
Than to rejoice the former queen is well ?   30
What holier than, for royalty's repair,
For present comfort and for future good,
To bless the bed of majesty again
With a sweet fellow to't ?
Paul.   There is none worthy,
Respecting her that's gone. Besides, the gods
Will have fulfill'd their secret purposes ;
For has not the divine Apollo said,
Is't not the tenor of his oracle,
That King Leontes shall not have an heir
Till his lost child be found ? which that it
        shall,   40
Is all as monstrous to our human reason
As my Antigonus to break his grave
And come again to me ; who, on my life,
Did perish with the infant. 'Tis your counsel
My lord should to the heavens be contrary,
Oppose against their wills. [*To Leontes.*]
        Care not for issue ;
The crown will find an heir : great Alexander
Left his to the worthiest ; so his successor
Was like to be the best.
Leon.   Good Paulina,
Who hast the memory of Hermione,   50
I know, in honor, O, that ever I
Had squared me to thy counsel ! then, even
        now,
I might have look'd upon my queen's full eyes,
Have taken treasure from her lips—
Paul.   And left them
More rich for what they yielded.
Leon.   Thou speak'st truth.
No more such wives ; therefore, no wife : one
        worse,
And better used, would make her sainted
        spirit
Again possess her corpse, and on this stage,
Where we're offenders now, appear soul-vex'd,
And begin, ' Why to me ? '
Paul.   Had she such power,   60
She had just cause.
Leon.   She had ; and would incense me
To murder her I married.
Paul.   I should so.
Were I the ghost that walk'd, I'ld bid you
        mark
Her eye, and tell me for what dull part in't
You chose her ; then I'ld shriek, that even
        your ears
Should rift to hear me ; and the words that
        follow'd
Should be ' Remember mine.'
Leon.   Stars, stars,

And all eyes else dead coals ! Fear thou no
  wife ;
I'll have no wife, Paulina.

Paul.   Will you swear
Never to marry but by my free leave ?   70
  Leon. Never, Paulina ; so be blest my
    spirit !
  Paul. Then, good my lords, bear witness
    to his oath.
  Cleo. You tempt him over-much.
  Paul.   Unless another,
As like Hermione as is her picture,
Affront his eye.

  Cleo.   Good madam,—
  Paul.   I have done.
Yet, if my lord will marry,—if you will, sir,
No remedy, but you will,—give me the office
To choose you a queen : she shall not be so
    young
As was your former ; but she shall be such
As, walk'd your first queen's ghost, it should
    take joy   80
To see her in your arms.

  Leon.   My true Paulina,
We shall not marry till thou bid'st us.

  Paul.   That
Shall be when your first queen's again in
    breath ;
Never till then.

Enter a Gentleman.

  Gent. One that gives out himself Prince
    Florizel,
Son of Polixenes, with his princess, she
The fairest I have yet beheld, desires access
To your high presence.

  Leon.   What with him ? he comes not
Like to his father's greatness : his approach,
So out of circumstance and sudden, tells us 90
'Tis not a visitation framed, but forced
By need and accident. What train ?

  Gent.   But few,
And those but mean.

  Leon. His princess, say you, with him ?
  Gent. Ay, the most peerless piece of earth,
    I think,
That e'er the sun shone bright on.

  Paul.   O Hermione,
As every present time doth boast itself
Above a better gone, so must thy grave
Give way to what's seen now ! Sir, you your-
    self
Have said and writ so, but your writing now
Is colder than that theme, ' She had not been,
Nor was not to be equall'd ; '—thus your verse
Flow'd with her beauty once : 'tis shrewdly
    ebb'd,
To say you have seen a better.

  Gent.   Pardon, madam :
The one I have almost forgot,—your pardon,—
The other, when she has obtain'd your eye,
Will have your tongue too. This is a creature,
Would she begin a sect, might quench the zeal
Of all professors else, make proselytes
Of who she but bid follow.

  Paul.   How ! not women ?
  Gent. Women will love her, that she is a
    woman   110
More worth than any man ; men, that she is
The rarest of all women.

  Leon.   Go, Cleomenes ;
Yourself, assisted with your honor'd friends,
Bring them to our embracement. Still, 'tis

strange   [*Exeunt Cleomenes and others.*
He thus should steal upon us.

  Paul.   Had our prince,
Jewel of children, seen this hour, he had pair'd
Well with this lord : there was not full a
    month
Between their births.

  Leon. Prithee, no more ; cease ; thou
    know'st
He dies to me again when talk'd of : sure, 120
When I shall see this gentleman, thy speeches
Will bring me to consider that which may
Unfurnish me of reason. They are come.

Re-enter CLEOMENES and others, with
FLORIZEL and PERDITA.

Your mother was most true to wedlock,
    prince ;
For she did print your royal father off,
Conceiving you : were I but twenty-one,
Your father's image is so hit in you,
His very air, that I should call you brother,
As I did him, and speak of something wildly
By us perform'd before. Most dearly wel-
    come !   130
And your fair princess,—goddess !—O, alas !
I lost a couple, that 'twixt heaven and earth
Might thus have stood begetting wonder as
You, gracious couple, do : and then I lost—
All mine own folly—the society,
Amity too, of your brave father, whom,
Though bearing misery, I desire my life
Once more to look on him.

  Flo.   By his command
Have I here touch'd Sicilia and from him
Give you all greetings that a king, at friend,
Can send his brother : and, but infirmity 141
Which waits upon worn times hath something
    seized
His wish'd ability, he had himself
The lands and waters 'twixt your throne and
    his
Measured to look upon you ; whom he loves—
He bade me say so—more than all the sceptres
And those that bear them living.

  Leon.   O my brother,
Good gentleman ! the wrongs I have done thee
    stir
Afresh within me, and these thy offices,
So rarely kind, are as interpreters   150
Of my behind-hand slackness. Welcome hither,
As is the spring to the earth. And hath he too
Exposed this paragon to the fearful usage,
At least ungentle, of the dreadful Neptune,
To greet a man not worth her pains, much less
The adventure of her person ?

  Flo.   Good my lord,
She came from Libya.

  Leon.   Where the warlike Smalus,
That noble honor'd lord, is fear'd and loved ?

  Flo. Most royal sir, from thence ; from
    him, whose daughter
His tears proclaim'd his, parting with her :
    thence,   160
A prosperous south-wind friendly, we have
    cross'd,
To execute the charge my father gave me
For visiting your highness : my best train
I have from your Sicilian shores dismiss'd ;
Who for Bohemia bend, to signify
Not only my success in Libya, sir,
But my arrival and my wife's in safety
Here where we are.

Leon.   The blessed gods
Purge all infection from our air whilst you
Do climate here ! You have a holy father,
A graceful gentleman ; against whose person,
So sacred as it is, I have done sin :
For which the heavens, taking angry note,
Have left me issueless ; and your father's blest,
As he from heaven merits it, with you
Worthy his goodness. What might I have been,
Might I a son and daughter now have look'd
    on,
Such goodly things as you !

Enter a Lord.

Lord.   Most noble sir,
That which I shall report will bear no credit,
Were not the proof so nigh. Please you, great
    sir,   180
Bohemia greets you from himself by me ;
Desires you to attach his son, who has—
His dignity and duty both cast off—
Fled from his father, from his hopes, and with
A shepherd's daughter.
Leon.   Where's Bohemia ? speak.
Lord. Here in your city ; I now came from
    him :
I speak amazedly ; and it becomes
My marvel and my message. To your court
Whiles he was hastening, in the chase, it seems,
Of this fair couple, meets he on the way   190
The father of this seeming lady and
Her brother, having both their country quitted
With this young prince.
Flo.   Camillo has betray'd me ;
Whose honor and whose honesty till now
Endured all weathers.
Lord.   Lay't so to his charge :
He's with the king your father.
Leon.   Who ? Camillo ?
Lord. Camillo, sir ; I spake with him ; who
    now
Has these poor men in question. Never saw I
Wretches so quake : they kneel, they kiss the
    earth ;   199
Forswear themselves as often as they speak :
Bohemia stops his ears, and threatens them
With divers deaths in death.
Per.   O my poor father !
The heaven sets spies upon us, will not have
Our contract celebrated.
Leon.   You are married ?
Flo. We are not, sir, nor are we like to be ;
The stars, I see, will kiss the valleys first :
The odds for high and low's alike.
Leon.   My lord,
Is this the daughter of a king ?
Flo.   She is,
When once she is my wife.
Leon. That ' once,' I see by your good fa-
    ther's speed,   210
Will come on very slowly. I am sorry,
Most sorry, you have broken from his liking
Where you were tied in duty, and as sorry
Your choice is not so rich in worth as beauty,
That you might well enjoy her.
Flo.   Dear, look up :
Though Fortune, visible an enemy,
Should chase us with my father, power no jot
Hath she to change our loves. Beseech you, sir,
Remember since you owed no more to time
Than I do now : with thought of such affec-
    tions,   220
Step forth mine advocate ; at your request

My father will grant precious things as trifles.
Leon. Would he do so, I'ld beg your pre-
    cious mistress,
Which he counts but a trifle.
Paul.   Sir, my liege,
Your eye hath too much youth in't : not a
    month
'Fore your queen died, she was more worth
    such gazes
Than what you look on now.
Leon.   I thought of her,
Even in these looks I made. [*To Florizel.*]
    But your petition
Is yet unanswer'd. I will to your father :
Your honor not o'erthrown by your desires,
I am friend to them and you : upon which
    errand   231
I now go toward him ; therefore follow me
And mark what way I make : come, good my
    lord.   [*Exeunt.*

SCENE II. *Before* LEONTES' *palace.*

Enter AUTOLYCUS *and a* Gentleman.

Aut. Beseech you, sir, were you present at
this relation ?
First Gent. I was by at the opening of the
fardel, heard the old shepherd deliver the manner how he found it : whereupon, after a little
amazedness, we were all commanded out of
the chamber ; only this methought I heard the
shepherd say, he found the child.
Aut. I would most gladly know the issue
of it.
First Gent. I make a broken delivery of
the business ; but the changes I perceived in
the king and Camillo were very notes of admiration : they seemed almost, with staring on
one another, to tear the cases of their eyes ;
there was speech in their dumbness, language
in their very gesture ; they looked as they had
heard of a world ransomed, or one destroyed :
a notable passion of wonder appeared in them ;
but the wisest beholder, that knew no more but
seeing, could not say if the importance were
joy or sorrow ; but in the extremity of the one,
it must needs be.

Enter another Gentleman.

Here comes a gentleman that haply knows
    more.
The news, Rogero ?
Sec. Gent. Nothing but bonfires : the oracle is fulfilled ; the king's daughter is found :
such a deal of wonder is broken out within
this hour that ballad-makers cannot be able to
express it.

Enter a third Gentleman.

Here comes the Lady Paulina's steward : he
can deliver you more. How goes it now, sir ?
this news which is called true is so like an old
tale, that the verity of it is in strong suspicion :
has the king found his heir ?
Third Gent. Most true, if ever truth were
pregnant by circumstance : that which you
hear you'll swear you see, there is such unity
in the proofs. The mantle of Queen Hermione's, her jewel about the neck of it, the
letters of Antigonus found with it which they
know to be his character, the majesty of the
creature in resemblance of the mother, the affection of nobleness which nature shows above
her breeding, and many other evidences pro-

claim her with all certainty to be the king's daughter. Did you see the meeting of the two kings ?

Sec. Gent. No.

Third Gent. Then have you lost a sight, which was to be seen, cannot be spoken of. There might you have beheld one joy crown another, so and in such manner that it seemed sorrow wept to take leave of them, for their joy waded in tears. There was casting up of eyes, holding up of hands, with countenances of such distraction that they were to be known by garment, not by favor. Our king, being ready to leap out of himself for joy of his found daughter, as if that joy were now become a loss, cries 'O, thy mother, thy mother !' then asks Bohemia forgiveness ; then embraces his son-in-law ; then again worries he his daughter with clipping her ; now he thanks the old shepherd, which stands by like a weather-bitten conduit of many kings' reigns. I never heard of such another encounter, which lames report to follow it and undoes description to do it.

Sec. Gent. What, pray you, became of Antigonus, that carried hence the child ?

Third Gent. Like an old tale still, which will have matter to rehearse, though credit be asleep and not an ear open. He was torn to pieces with a bear : this avouches the shepherd's son ; who has not only his innocence, which seems much, to justify him, but a handkerchief and rings of his that Paulina knows.

First Gent. What became of his bark and his followers ?

Third Gent. Wrecked the same instant of their master's death and in the view of the shepherd : so that all the instruments which aided to expose the child were even then lost when it was found. But O, the noble combat that 'twixt joy and sorrow was fought in Paulina ! She had one eye declined for the loss of her husband, another elevated that the oracle was fulfilled : she lifted the princess from the earth, and so locks her in embracing, as if she would pin her to her heart that she might no more be in danger of losing.

First Gent. The dignity of this act was worth the audience of kings and princes ; for by such was it acted.

Third Gent. One of the prettiest touches of all and that which angled for mine eyes, caught the water though not the fish, was when, at the relation of the queen's death, with the manner how she came to't bravely confessed and lamented by the king, how attentiveness wounded his daughter ; till, from one sign of dolour to another, she did, with an 'Alas,' I would fain say, bleed tears ; for I am sure my heart wept blood. Who was most marble there changed color ; some swooned, all sorrowed : if all the world could have seen 't, the woe had been universal.   100

First Gent. Are they returned to the court ?

Third Gent. No : the princess hearing of her mother's statue, which is in the keeping of Paulina,—a piece many years in doing and now newly performed by that rare Italian master, Julio Romano, who, had he himself eternity and could put breath into his work, would beguile Nature of her custom, so perfectly he is her ape : he so near to Hermione hath done Hermione that they say one would speak to her and stand in hope of answer : thither with all greediness of affection are they gone, and there they intend to sup.

Sec. Gent. I thought she had some great matter there in hand ; for she hath privately twice or thrice a day, ever since the death of Hermione, visited that removed house. Shall we thither and with our company piece the rejoicing ?

First Gent. Who would be thence that has the benefit of access ? every wink of an eye some new grace will be born : our absence makes us unthrifty to our knowledge. Let's along.   [*Exeunt Gentlemen.* 121

Aut. Now, had I not the dash of my former life in me, would preferment drop on my head. I brought the old man and his son aboard the prince ; told him I heard them talk of a fardel and I know not what : but he at that time, overfond of the shepherd's daughter, so he then took her to be, who began to be much sea-sick, and himself little better, extremity of weather continuing, this mystery remained undiscovered. But 'tis all one to me ; for had I been the finder out of this secret, it would not have relished among my other discredits.

Enter Shepherd *and* Clown.

Here come those I have done good to against my will, and already appearing in the blossoms of their fortune.

Shep. Come, boy ; I am past moe children, but thy sons and daughters will be all gentlemen born.

Clo. You are well met, sir. You denied to fight with me this other day, because I was no gentleman born. See you these clothes ? say you see them not and think me still no gentleman born : you were best say these robes are not gentlemen born : give me the lie, do, and try whether I am not now a gentleman born.

Aut. I know you are now, sir, a gentleman born.

Clo. Ay, and have been so any time these four hours.

Shep. And so have I, boy.   149

Clo. So you have : but I was a gentleman born before my father ; for the king's son took me by the hand, and called me brother ; and then the two kings called my father brother ; and then the prince my brother and the princess my sister called my father father ; and so we wept, and there was the first gentleman-like tears that ever we shed.

Shep. We may live, son, to shed many more.

Clo. Ay ; or else 'twere hard luck, being in so preposterous estate as we are.   159

Aut. I humbly beseech you, sir, to pardon me all the faults I have committed to your worship and to give me your good report to the prince my master.

Shep. Prithee, son, do ; for we must be gentle, now we are gentlemen.

Clo. Thou wilt amend thy life ?

Aut. Ay, an it like your good worship.

Clo. Give me thy hand : I will swear to the prince thou art as honest a true fellow as any is in Bohemia.   170

Shep. You may say it, but not swear it.

Clo. Not swear it, now I am a gentleman ? Let boors and franklins say it, I'll swear it.

Shep. How if it be false, son ?

Clo. If it be ne'er so false, a true gentleman may swear it in the behalf of his friend :
and I'll swear it to the prince thou art a tall
fellow of thy hands and that thou wilt not be
drunk ; but I know thou art no tall fellow of
thy hands and that thou wilt be drunk : but
I'll swear it, and I would thou wouldst be a
tall fellow of thy hands.

Aut. I will prove so, sir, to my power.

Clo. Ay, by any means prove a tall fellow :
if I do not wonder how thou darest venture to
be drunk, not being a tall fellow, trust me not.
Hark ! the kings and the princes, our kindred,
are going to see the queen's picture. Come, follow us : we'll be thy good masters.   [*Exeunt.*

SCENE III.   *A chapel in* PAULINA'S *house.*

Enter LEONTES, POLIXENES, FLORIZEL, PER-
DITA, CAMILLO, PAULINA, Lords, *and* Attendants.

Leon. O grave and good Paulina, the great
         comfort
That I have had of thee !

Paul.   What, sovereign sir,
I did not well I meant well. All my services
You have paid home : but that you have
         vouchsafed,
With your crown'd brother and these your
         contracted
Heirs of your kingdoms, my poor house to
         visit,
It is a surplus of your grace, which never
My life may last to answer.

Leon.   O Paulina,
We honor you with trouble : but we came
To see the statue of our queen : your gallery
Have we pass'd through, not without much
         content   11
In many singularities ; but we saw not
That which my daughter came to look upon,
The statue of her mother.

Paul.   As she lived peerless,
So her dead likeness, I do well believe,
Excels whatever yet you look'd upon
Or hand of man hath done ; therefore I keep it
Lonely, apart. But here it is : prepare
To see the life as lively mock'd as ever
Still sleep mock'd death : behold, and say 'tis
         well.   20
[*Paulina draws a curtain, and discovers
         Hermione standing like a statue.*
I like your silence, it the more shows off
Your wonder : but yet speak ; first, you, my
         liege,
Comes it not something near ?

Leon.   Her natural posture !
Chide me, dear stone, that I may say indeed
Thou art Hermione ; or rather, thou art she
In thy not chiding, for she was as tender
As infancy and grace. But yet, Paulina,
Hermione was not so much wrinkled, nothing
So aged as this seems.

Pol.   O, not by much.

Paul. So much the more our carver's ex-
         cellence ;   30
Which lets go by some sixteen years and makes
         her
As she lived now.

Leon.   As now she might have done,
So much to my good comfort, as it is
Now piercing to my soul. O, thus she stood,
Even with such life of majesty, warm life,

As now it coldly stands, when first I woo'd
         her !
I am ashamed : does not the stone rebuke me
For being more stone than it ? O royal piece,
There's magic in thy majesty, which has
My evils conjured to remembrance and   40
From thy admiring daughter took the spirits,
Standing like stone with thee.

Per.   And give me leave,
And do not say 'tis superstition, that
I kneel and then implore her blessing. Lady,
Dear queen, that ended when I but began,
Give me that hand of yours to kiss.

Paul.   O, patience !
The statue is but newly fix'd, the color's
Not dry.

Cam. My lord, your sorrow was too sore
         laid on,
Which sixteen winters cannot blow away,   50
So many summers dry ; scarce any joy
Did ever so long live ; no sorrow
But kill'd itself much sooner.

Pol.   Dear my brother,
Let him that was the cause of this have power
To take off so much grief from you as he
Will piece up in himself.

Paul.   Indeed, my lord,
If I had thought the sight of my poor image
Would thus have wrought you,—for the stone
         is mine—
I'ld not have show'd it.

Leon.   Do not draw the curtain.

Paul. No longer shall you gaze on't, lest
         your fancy   60
May think anon it moves.

Leon.   Let be, let be.
Would I were dead, but that, methinks, al-
         ready—
What was he that did make it ? See, my lord,
Would you not deem it breathed ? and that
         those veins
Did verily bear blood ?

Pol.   Masterly done :
The very life seems warm upon her lip.

Leon. The fixture of her eye has motion
         in't,
As we are mock'd with art.

Paul.   I'll draw the curtain :
My lord's almost so far transported that
He'll think anon it lives.

Leon.   O sweet Paulina,   70
Make me to think so twenty years together !
No settled senses of the world can match
The pleasure of that madness. Let 't alone.

Paul. I am sorry, sir, I have thus far stirr'd
         you : but
I could afflict you farther.

Leon.   Do, Paulina ;
For this affliction has a taste as sweet
As any cordial comfort. Still, methinks,
There is an air comes from her : what fine
         chisel
Could ever yet cut breath ? Let no man mock
         me,
For I will kiss her.

Paul.   Good my lord, forbear : 80
The ruddiness upon her lip is wet ;
You'll mar it if you kiss it, stain your own
With oily painting. Shall I draw the curtain ?

Leon. No, not these twenty years.

Per.   So long could I
Stand by, a looker on.

Paul.   Either forbear,

Quit presently the chapel, or resolve you
For more amazement. If you can behold it,
I'll make the statue move indeed, descend
And take you by the hand; but then you'll
    think—
Which I protest against—I am assisted   90
By wicked powers.

Leon.   What you can make her do,
I am content to look on: what to speak,
I am content to hear; for 'tis as easy
To make her speak as move.

Paul.   It is required
You do awake your faith. Then all stand still;
On: those that think it is unlawful business
I am about, let them depart.

Leon.   Proceed:
No foot shall stir.

Paul. Music, awake her; strike!   [*Music.*
'Tis time; descend; be stone no more; ap-
    proach;   99
Strike all that look upon with marvel. Come,
I'll fill your grave up: stir, nay, come away,
Bequeath to death your numbness, for from
    him
Dear life redeems you. You perceive she stirs:
                [*Hermione comes down.*
Start not; her actions shall be holy as
You hear my spell is lawful: do not shun her
Until you see her die again; for then
You kill her double. Nay, present your hand:
When she was young you woo'd her; now in
    age
Is she become the suitor?

Leon.   O, she's warm!
If this be magic, let it be an art   110
Lawful as eating.

Pol.   She embraces him.

Cam. She hangs about his neck:
If she pertain to life let her speak too.

Pol. Ay, and make't manifest where she has
    lived,
Or how stolen from the dead.

Paul.   That she is living,
Were it but told you, should be hooted at
Like an old tale: but it appears she lives,
Though yet she speak not. Mark a little while.
Please you to interpose, fair madam: kneel

And pray your mother's blessing. Turn, good
    lady;   120
Our Perdita is found.

Her.   You gods, look down
And from your sacred vials pour your graces
Upon my daughter's head! Tell me, mine own,
Where hast thou been preserved? where lived?
    how found
Thy father's court? for thou shalt hear that I,
Knowing by Paulina that the oracle
Gave hope thou wast in being, have preserved
Myself to see the issue.

Paul.   There's time enough for that;
Lest they desire upon this push to trouble
Your joys with like relation. Go together,   130
You precious winners all; your exultation
Partake to every one. I, an old turtle,
Will wing me to some wither'd bough and there
My mate, that's never to be found again,
Lament till I am lost.

Leon.   O, peace, Paulina!
Thou shouldst a husband take by my consent,
As I by thine a wife: this is a match,
And made between's by vows. Thou hast found
    mine;
But how, is to be question'd; for I saw her,
As I thought, dead, and have in vain said
    many   140
A prayer upon her grave. I'll not seek far—
For him, I partly know his mind—to find thee
An honorable husband. Come, Camillo,
And take her by the hand, whose worth and
    honesty
Is richly noted and here justified
By us, a pair of kings. Let's from this place.
What! look upon my brother: both your par-
    dons,
That e'er I put between your holy looks
My ill suspicion. This is your son-in-law,   149
And son unto the king, who, heavens directing,
Is troth-plight to your daughter. Good Paulina,
Lead us from hence, where we may leisurely
Each one demand and answer to his part
Perform'd in this wide gap of time since first
We were dissever'd: hastily lead away.

                           [*Exeunt.*

KING HENRY VIII.

(WRITTEN ABOUT 1612–13.)

INTRODUCTION.

This play, as we learn from Sir Henry Wotton and from T. Lorking, was being enacted as a new play at the Globe Theatre, under the name of *All is True*, in June, 1613, when some burning paper shot off from a cannon set fire to the thatch and occasioned the destruction of the building. It has been shown conclusively by Mr. Spedding that the play is in part from Shakespeare's hand, in part from Fletcher's. The latter's verse had certain strongly-marked characteristics, one of which is the very frequent occurrence of double endings. Going over the play, scene by scene, and applying the various tests, Mr. Spedding arrived at the following result : Shakespeare's part : Act I., Sc. I. II. ; Act II., Sc. III. IV. ; Act III., Sc. II. (to exit of the king) ; Act V, Sc. I. The rest of the play is by Fletcher. A German critic (Hertzberg) has described *Henry VIII.* as " a chronicle-history with three and a half catastrophes, varied by a marriage and a coronation pageant, ending abruptly with the baptism of a child." It is indeed incoherent in structure. After all our sympathies have been engaged upon the side of the wronged Queen Katharine, we are called upon to rejoice in the marriage triumph of her rival, Anne Boleyn. " The greater part of the fifth act, in which the interest ought to be gathering to a head, is occupied with matters in which we have not been prepared to take any interest by what went before, and on which no interest is reflected by what comes after." But viewed from another side, that of its metrical workmanship, the play is equally deficient in unity, and indeed betrays unmistakably the presence of two writers. Nevertheless, there are three great figures in the play clearly and strongly conceived by Shakespeare : The King, Queen Katharine, and Cardinal Wolsey. The Queen is one of the noble, long-enduring sufferers, just-minded, disinterested, truly charitable, who give their moral gravity and grandeur to Shakespeare's last plays. She has clear-sighted penetration to see through the Cardinal's cunning practice, and a lofty indignation against what is base, but no unworthy personal resentment. Henry, if we judge him sternly, is cruel and self-indulgent ; but Shakespeare will hardly allow us to judge Henry sternly. He is a lordly figure, with a full, abounding strength of nature, a self-confidence, an ease and mastery of life, a power of effortless sway, and seems born to pass on in triumph over those who have fallen and are afflicted. Wolsey is drawn with superb power : ambition, fraud, vindictiveness, have made him their own, yet cannot quite ruin a nature possessed of noble qualities. It is hard at first to refuse to Shakespeare the authorship of Wolsey's famous soliloquy in which he bids his greatness farewell, but it is certainly Fletcher's, and when one has perceived this one perceives also that it was an error ever to suppose it written in Shakespeare's manner. The scene in which the vision appears to the dying Queen is also Fletcher's, and in his highest style. We can see from this play that if Shakespeare had returned at the age of fifty to the historical drama, the works written then would have been greater in moral grandeur than those written from his thirtieth to his thirty-fifth years.

DRAMATIS PERSONÆ.

KING HENRY the Eighth.
CARDINAL WOLSEY.
CARDINAL CAMPEIUS.
CAPUCIUS, Ambassador from the Emperor Charles V.
CRANMER, Archbishop of Canterbury.
DUKE OF NORFOLK.
DUKE OF BUCKINGHAM.
DUKE OF SUFFOLK.
EARL OF SURREY.
Lord Chamberlain.
Lord Chancellor.
GARDINER, Bishop of Winchester.
Bishop of Lincoln.
LORD ABERGAVENNY.
LORD SANDS.

SIR HENRY GUILDFORD.
SIR THOMAS LOVELL.
SIR ANTHONY DENNY.
SIR NICHOLAS VAUX.
Secretaries to Wolsey.
CROMWELL, Servant to Wolsey.
GRIFFITH, Gentleman-usher to Queen Katharine.
Three Gentlemen.
DOCTOR BUTTS, Physician to the King.
Garter King-at-Arms.
Surveyor to the Duke of Buckingham.
BRANDON, and a Sergeant-at-Arms.
Door-keeper of the Council-chamber. Porter, and his Man.
Page to Gardiner. A Crier.

QUEEN KATHARINE, wife to King Henry, afterwards divorced.
ANNE BULLEN, her Maid of Honor, afterwards Queen.
An old Lady, friend to Anne Bullen.
PATIENCE, woman to Queen Katharine.

Several Lords and Ladies in the Dumb Shows ; Women attending upon the Queen ; Scribes, Officers, Guards, and other Attendants.
Spirits.

SCENE : *London ; Westminster ; Kimbolton.*

THE PROLOGUE.

I COME no more to make you laugh : things
 now,
That bear a weighty and a serious brow,
Sad, high, and working, full of state and woe,
Such noble scenes as draw the eye to flow,
We now present. Those that can pity, here
May, if they think it well, let fall a tear ;
The subject will deserve it. Such as give
Their money out of hope they may believe,
May here find truth too. Those that come to
 see
Only a show or two, and so agree   10
The play may pass, if they be still and willing,
I'll undertake may see away their shilling
Richly in two short hours. Only they
That come to hear a merry bawdy play,
A noise of targets, or to see a fellow
In a long motley coat guarded with yellow,
Will be deceived ; for, gentle hearers, know,
To rank our chosen truth with such a show
As fool and fight is, beside forfeiting
Our own brains, and the opinion that we bring,
To make that only true we now intend,   21
Will leave us never an understanding friend.
Therefore, for goodness' sake, and as you are
 known
The first and happiest hearers of the town,
Be sad, as we would make ye : think ye see
The very persons of our noble story
As they were living ; think you see them great,
And follow'd with the general throng and
 sweat
Of thousand friends ; then in a moment, see
How soon this mightiness meets misery :   30
And, if you can be merry then, I'll say
A man may weep upon his wedding-day.

ACT I.

SCENE I. *London. An ante-chamber in the palace.*

Enter the DUKE OF NORFOLK *at one door ; at the other, the* DUKE OF BUCKINGHAM *and the* LORD ABERGAVENNY.

Buck. Good morrow, and well met. How
 have ye done
Since last we saw in France ?
 Nor.   I thank your grace,
Healthful ; and ever since a fresh admirer
Of what I saw there.
 Buck.   An untimely ague
Stay'd me a prisoner in my chamber when
Those suns of glory, those two lights of men,
Met in the vale of Andren.
 Nor.   'Twixt Guynes and Arde :
I was then present, saw them salute on horse-
 back ;
Beheld them, when they lighted, how they
 clung

In their embracement, as they grew together ;
Which had they, what four throned ones could
 have weigh'd   11
Such a compounded one ?
 Buck.   All the whole time
I was my chamber's prisoner.
 Nor.   Then you lost
The view of earthly glory : men might say,
Till this time pomp was single, but now mar-
 ried
To one above itself. Each following day
Became the next day's master, till the last
Made former wonders its. To-day the French,
All clinquant, all in gold, like heathen gods,
Shone down the English ; and, to-morrow, they
Made Britain India : every man that stood   21
Show'd like a mine. Their dwarfish pages were
As cherubins, all gilt : the madams too,
Not used to toil, did almost sweat to bear
The pride upon them, that their very labor
Was to them as a painting : now this masque
Was cried incomparable ; and the ensuing
 night
Made it a fool and beggar. The two kings,
Equal in lustre, were now best, now worst,
As presence did present them ; him in eye,   30
Still him in praise : and, being present both,
'Twas said they saw but one ; and no discerner
Durst wag his tongue in censure. When these
 suns—
For so they phrase 'em—by their heralds chal-
 lenged
The noble spirits to arms, they did perform
Beyond thought's compass ; that former fabu-
 lous story,
Being now seen possible enough, got credit,
That Bevis was believed.
 Buck.   O, you go far.
 Nor. As I belong to worship and affect
In honor honesty, the tract of every thing   40
Would by a good discourser lose some life,
Which action's self was tongue to. All was
 royal ;
To the disposing of it nought rebell'd,
Order gave each thing view ; the office did
Distinctly his full function.
 Buck.   Who did guide,
I mean, who set the body and the limbs
Of this great sport together, as you guess ?
 Nor. One, certes, that promises no element
In such a business.
 Buck.   I pray you, who, my lord ?
 Nor. All this was order'd by the good dis-
 cretion   50
Of the right reverend Cardinal of York.
 Buck. The devil speed him ! no man's pie
 is freed
From his ambitious finger. What had he
To do in these fierce vanities ? I wonder
That such a keech can with his very bulk
Take up the rays o' the beneficial sun
And keep it from the earth.
 Nor.   Surely, sir,

There's in him stuff that puts him to these
    ends ;
For, being not propp'd by ancestry, whose
    grace
Chalks successors their way, nor call'd upon
For high feats done to the crown ; neither
    allied   61
To eminent assistants ; but, spider-like,
Out of his self-drawing web, he gives us note,
The force of his own merit makes his way ;
A gift that heaven gives for him, which buys
A place next to the king.
  Aber.   I cannot tell
What heaven hath given him,—let some graver
    eye
Pierce into that ; but I can see his pride
Peep through each part of him : whence has
    he that,
If not from hell ? the devil is a niggard,   70
Or has given all before, and he begins
A new hell in himself.
  Buck.   Why the devil,
Upon this French going out, took he upon him,
Without the privity o' the king, to appoint
Who should attend on him ? He makes up the
    file
Of all the gentry ; for the most part such
To whom as great a charge as little honor
He meant to lay upon : and his own letter,
The honorable board of council out,
Must fetch him in the papers.
  Aber.   I do know 80
Kinsmen of mine, three at the least, that have
By this so sicken'd their estates, that never
They shall abound as formerly.
  Buck.   O, many
Have broke their backs with laying manors on
    'em
For this great journey. What did this vanity
But minister communication of
A most poor issue ?
  Nor.   Grievingly I think,
The peace between the French and us not
    values
The cost that did conclude it.
  Buck.   Every man,
After the hideous storm that follow'd, was 90
A thing inspired ; and, not consulting, broke
Into a general prophecy ; That this tempest,
Dashing the garment of this peace, aboded
The sudden breach on't.
  Nor.   Which is budded out ;
For France hath flaw'd the league, and hath
    attach'd
Our merchants' goods at Bourdeaux.
  Aber.   Is it therefore
The ambassador is silenced ?
  Nor.   Marry, is't.
  Aber. A proper title of a peace ; and pur-
    chased
At a superfluous rate !
  Buck.   Why, all this business
Our reverend cardinal carried.
  Nor.   Like it your grace, 100
The state takes notice of the private difference
Betwixt you and the cardinal. I advise you—
And take it from a heart that wishes towards
    you
Honor and plenteous safety—that you read
The cardinal's malice and his potency
Together ; to consider further that
What his high hatred would effect wants not
A minister in his power. You know his nature,

That he's revengeful, and I know his sword
Hath a sharp edge : it's long and, 't may be
    said,   110
It reaches far, and where 'twill not extend,
Thither he darts it. Bosom up my counsel,
You'll find it wholesome. Lo, where comes that
    rock
That I advise your shunning.

Enter CARDINAL WOLSEY, *the purse borne before him, certain of the* Guard, *and two Secretaries* with papers. *The* CARDINAL *in his
passage fixeth his eye on* BUCKINGHAM, *and*
BUCKINGHAM *on him, both full of disdain.*

  Wol. The Duke of Buckingham's surveyor,
    ha ?
Where's his examination ?
  First Secr.   Here, so please you.
  Wol. Is he in person ready ?
  First Secr.   Ay, please your grace.
  Wol. Well, we shall then know more ; and
    Buckingham
Shall lessen this big look.
             [*Exeunt Wolsey and his Train.*
  Buck. This butcher's cur is venom-mouth'd,
    and I   120
Have not the power to muzzle him ; therefore
    best
Not wake him in his slumber. A beggar's book
Outworths a noble's blood.
  Nor.   What, are you chafed ?
Ask God for temperance ; that's the appliance
    only
Which your disease requires.
  Buck.   I read in's looks
Matter against me ; and his eye reviled
Me, as his abject object : at this instant
He bores me with some trick : he's gone to the
    king ;
I'll follow and outstare him.
  Nor.   Stay, my lord, 129
And let your reason with your choler question
What 'tis you go about : to climb steep hills
Requires slow pace at first : anger is like
A full-hot horse, who being allow'd his way,
Self-mettle tires him. Not a man in England
Can advise me like you : be to yourself
As you would to your friend.
  Buck.   I'll to the king ;
And from a mouth of honor quite cry down
This Ipswich fellow's insolence ; or proclaim
There's difference in no persons.
  Nor.   Be advised ;
Heat not a furnace for your foe so hot   140
That it do singe yourself : we may outrun,
By violent swiftness, that which we run at,
And lose by over-running. Know you not,
The fire that mounts the liquor till't run o'er,
In seeming to augment it wastes it ? Be ad-
    vised :
I say again, there is no English soul
More stronger to direct you than yourself,
If with the sap of reason you would quench,
Or but allay, the fire of passion.
  Buck.   Sir,
I am thankful to you ; and I'll go along 150
By your prescription : but this top-proud fel-
    low,
Whom from the flow of gall I name not but
From sincere motions, by intelligence,
And proofs as clear as founts in July when
We see each grain of gravel, I do know
To be corrupt and treasonous.

Nor. Say not ' treasonous.'
Buck. To the king I'll say't ; and make my
 vouch as strong
As shore of rock. Attend. This holy fox,
Or wolf, or both,—for he is equal ravenous
As he is subtle, and as prone to mischief 160
As able to perform't ; his mind and place
Infecting one another, yea, reciprocally—
Only to show his pomp as well in France
As here at home, suggests the king our master
To this last costly treaty, the interview,
That swallow'd so much treasure, and like a
 glass
Did break i' the rinsing.
Nor. Faith, and so it did.
Buck. Pray, give me favor, sir. This cun-
 ning cardinal
The articles o' the combination drew 169
As himself pleased ; and they were ratified
As he cried ' Thus let be ' : to as much end
As give a crutch to the dead : but our count-
 cardinal
Has done this, and 'tis well ; for worthy Wol-
 sey,
Who cannot err, he did it. Now this follows,—
Which, as I take it, is a kind of puppy
To the old dam, treason,—Charles the em-
 peror,
Under pretence to see the queen his aunt—
For 'twas indeed his color, but he came
To whisper Wolsey,—here makes visitation :
His fears were, that the interview betwixt 180
England and France might, through their
 amity,
Breed him some prejudice ; for from this
 league
Peep'd harms that menaced him : he privily
Deals with our cardinal ; and, as I trow,—
Which I do well ; for I am sure the emperor
Paid ere he promised ; whereby his suit was
 granted
Ere it was ask'd ; but when the way was made,
And paved with gold, the emperor thus desired,
That he would please to alter the king's course,
And break the foresaid peace. Let the king
 know, 190
As soon he shall by me, that thus the cardinal
Does buy and sell his honor as he pleases,
And for his own advantage.
Nor. I am sorry
To hear this of him ; and could wish he were
Something mistaken in't.
Buck. No, not a syllable :
I do pronounce him in that very shape
He shall appear in proof.

Enter BRANDON, *a* Sergeant-at-arms *before
 him, and two or three of the* Guard.

Bran. Your office, sergeant ; execute it.
Serg. Sir,
My lord the Duke of Buckingham, and Earl
Of Hereford, Stafford, and Northampton, I
Arrest thee of high treason, in the name 201
Of our most sovereign king.
Buck. Lo, you, my lord,
The net has fall'n upon me ! I shall perish
Under device and practice.
Bran. I am sorry
To see you ta'en from liberty, to look on
The business present : 'tis his highness' pleas-
 ure
You shall to the Tower.
Buck. It will help me nothing

To plead mine innocence ; for that dye is on
 me
Which makes my whitest part black. The will
 of heaven
Be done in this and all things ! I obey. 210
O my Lord Abergavenny, fare you well !
Bran. Nay, he must bear you company.
 The king [*To Abergavenny.*
Is pleased you shall to the Tower, till you
 know
How he determines further.
Aber. As the duke said,
The will of heaven be done, and the king's
 pleasure
By me obey'd !
Bran. Here is a warrant from
The king to attach Lord Montacute ; and the
 bodies
Of the duke's confessor, John de la Car,
One Gilbert Peck, his chancellor,—
Buck. So, so ;
These are the limbs o' the plot : no more, I
 hope. 220
Bran. A monk o' the Chartreux.
Buck. O, Nicholas Hopkins ?
Bran. He.
Buck. My surveyor is false ; the o'er-great
 cardinal
Hath show'd him gold ; my life is spann'd al-
 ready :
I am the shadow of poor Buckingham,
Whose figure even this instant cloud puts on,
By darkening my clear sun. My lord, farewell.
 [*Exeunt.*

SCENE II. *The same. The council-chamber.*

Cornets. Enter the KING, *leaning on the* CAR-
DINAL'S *shoulder, the* Nobles, *and* SIR
THOMAS LOVELL ; *the* CARDINAL *places him-
self under the* KING'S *feet on his right side.*

King. My life itself, and the best heart of
 it,
Thanks you for this great care : I stood i' the
 level
Of a full-charged confederacy, and give thanks
To you that choked it. Let be call'd before us
That gentleman of Buckingham's ; in person
I'll hear him his confessions justify ;
And point by point the treasons of his master
He shall again relate.

A noise within, crying ' Room for the Queen ! '
Enter QUEEN KATHARINE, *ushered by the*
DUKE OF NORFOLK, *and the* DUKE OF SUF-
FOLK : *she kneels. The* KING *riseth from
his state, takes her up, kisses and placeth her
by him.*

Q. Kath. Nay, we must longer kneel : I am
 a suitor.
King. Arise, and take place by us : half
 your suit 10
Never name to us ; you have half our power :
The other moiety, ere you ask, is given ;
Repeat your will and take it.
Q. Kath. Thank your majesty.
That you would love yourself, and in that love
Not unconsider'd leave your honor, nor
The dignity of your office, is the point
Of my petition.
King. Lady mine, proceed.
Q. Kath. I am solicited, not by a few,
And those of true condition, that your subjects

Are in great grievance : there have been com-
   missions   20
Sent down among 'em, which hath flaw'd the
   heart
Of all their loyalties : wherein, although,
My good lord cardinal, they vent reproaches
Most bitterly on you, as putter on
Of these exactions, yet the king our master—
Whose honor heaven shield from soil !—even
   he escapes not
Language unmannerly, yea, such which breaks
The sides of loyalty, and almost appears
In loud rebellion.

Nor.   Not almost appears,
It doth appear ; for, upon these taxations, 30
The clothiers all, not able to maintain
The many to them longing, have put off
The spinsters, carders, fullers, weavers, who,
Unfit for other life, compell'd by hunger
And lack of other means, in desperate manner
Daring the event to the teeth, are all in uproar,
And danger serves among them.

King.   Taxation !
Wherein ? and what taxation ? My lord car-
   dinal,
You that are blamed for it alike with us,
Know you of this taxation ?

Wol.   Please you, sir, 40
I know but of a single part, in aught
Pertains to the state ; and front but in that file
Where others tell steps with me.

Q. Kath.   No, my lord,
You know no more than others ; but you
   frame
Things that are known alike ; which are not
   wholesome
To those which would not know them, and yet
   must
Perforce be their acquaintance. These exac-
   tions,
Whereof my sovereign would have note, they
   are
Most pestilent to the hearing ; and, to bear
   'em,
The back is sacrifice to the load. They say 50
They are devised by you ; or else you suffer
Too hard an exclamation.

King.   Still exaction !
The nature of it ? in what kind, let's know,
Is this exaction ?

Q. Kath.   I am much too venturous
In tempting of your patience ; but am bolden'd
Under your promised pardon. The subjects'
   grief
Comes through commissions, which compel
   from each
The sixth part of his substance, to be levied
Without delay ; and the pretence for this
Is named, your wars in France : this makes
   bold mouths : 60
Tongues spit their duties out, and cold hearts
   freeze
Allegiance in them ; their curses now
Live where their prayers did : and it's come to
   pass,
This tractable obedience is a slave
To each incensed will. I would your highness
Would give it quick consideration, for
There is no primer business.

King.   By my life,
This is against our pleasure.

Wol.   And for me,
I have no further gone in this than by

A single voice ; and that not pass'd me but 70
By learned approbation of the judges. If I am
Traduced by ignorant tongues, which neither
   know
My faculties nor person, yet will be
The chronicles of my doing, let me say
'Tis but the fate of place, and the rough brake
That virtue must go through. We must not
   stint
Our necessary actions, in the fear
To cope malicious censurers ; which ever,
As ravenous fishes, do a vessel follow
That is new-trimm'd, but benefit no further 80
Than vainly longing. What we oft do best,
By sick interpreters, once weak ones, is
Not ours, or not allow'd ; what worst, as oft,
Hitting a grosser quality, is cried up
For our best act. If we shall stand still,
In fear our motion will be mock'd or carp'd at,
We should take root here where we sit, or sit
State-statues only.

King.   Things done well,
And with a care, exempt themselves from fear ;
Things done without example, in their issue
Are to be fear'd. Have you a precedent 91
Of this commission ? I believe, not any.
We must not rend our subjects from our laws,
And stick them in our will. Sixth part of each ?
A trembling contribution ! Why, we take
From every tree lop, bark, and part o' the
   timber ;
And, though we leave it with a root, thus
   hack'd,
The air will drink the sap. To every county
Where this is question'd send our letters, with
Free pardon to each man that has denied 100
The force of this commission : pray, look to't ;
I put it to your care.

Wol.   A word with you.
                   [To the Secretary.
Let there be letters writ to every shire,
Of the king's grace and pardon. The grieved
   commons
Hardly conceive of me ; let it be noised
That through our intercession this revokement
And pardon comes : I shall anon advise you
Further in the proceeding.   *[Exit Secretary.*

        Enter Surveyor.

Q. Kath. I am sorry that the Duke of
   Buckingham
Is run in your displeasure.

King.   It grieves many : 110
The gentleman is learn'd, and a most rare
   speaker ;
To nature none more bound ; his training such,
That he may furnish and instruct great teach-
   ers,
And never seek for aid out of himself. Yet see,
When these so noble benefits shall prove
Not well disposed, the mind growing once cor-
   rupt,
They turn to vicious forms, ten times more
   ugly
Than ever they were fair. This man so com-
   plete,
Who was enroll'd 'mongst wonders, and when
   we, 119
Almost with ravish'd listening, could not find
His hour of speech a minute ; he, my lady,
Hath into monstrous habits put the graces
That once were his, and is become as black

As if besmear'd in hell. Sit by us ; you shall
    hear—
This was his gentleman in trust—of him
Things to strike honor sad. Bid him recount
The fore-recited practices ; whereof
We cannot feel too little, hear too much.
  Wol. Stand forth, and with bold spirit re-
    late what you,
Most like a careful subject, have collected 130
Out of the Duke of Buckingham.
  King.   Speak freely.
  Surv. First, it was usual with him, every
    day
It would infect his speech, that if the king
Should without issue die, he'll carry it so
To make the sceptre his : these very words
I've heard him utter to his son-in-law,
Lord Abergavenny ; to whom by oath he men-
    aced
Revenge upon the cardinal.
  Wol.   Please your highness, note
This dangerous conception in this point. 139
Not friended by his wish, to your high person
His will is most malignant ; and it stretches
Beyond you, to your friends.
  Q. Kath.   My learn'd lord cardinal,
Deliver all with charity.
  King.   Speak on :
How grounded he his title to the crown,
Upon our fail ? to this point hast thou heard
    him
At any time speak aught ?
  Surv.   He was brought to this
By a vain prophecy of Nicholas Hopkins.
  King. What was that Hopkins ?
  Surv.   Sir, a Chartreux friar,
His confessor, who fed him every minute
With words of sovereignty.
  King.   How know'st thou this ? 150
  Surv. Not long before your highness sped
    to France,
The duke being at the Rose, within the parish
Saint Lawrence Poultney, did of me demand
What was the speech among the Londoners
Concerning the French journey : I replied,
Men fear'd the French would prove perfidious,
To the king's danger. Presently the duke
Said, 'twas the fear, indeed ; and that he
    doubted
'Twould prove the verity of certain words 159
Spoke by a holy monk ; ' that oft,' says he,
' Hath sent to me, wishing me to permit
John de la Car, my chaplain, a choice hour
To hear from him a matter of some moment :
Whom after under the confession's seal
He solemnly had sworn, that what he spoke
My chaplain to no creature living, but
To me, should utter, with demure confidence
This pausingly ensued : neither the king nor's
    heirs,
Tell you the duke, shall prosper : bid him
    strive
To gain the love o' the commonalty : the duke
Shall govern England.'   171
  Q. Kath.   If I know you well,
You were the duke's surveyor, and lost your
    office
On the complaint o' the tenants : take good
    heed
You charge not in your spleen a noble person
And spoil your nobler soul : I say, take heed ;
Yes, heartily beseech you.

  King.   Let him on.
Go forward.
  Surv.   On my soul, I'll speak but truth.
I told my lord the duke, by the devil's illusions
The monk might be deceived ; and that 'twas
    dangerous for him
To ruminate on this so far, until   180
It forged him some design, which, being be-
    lieved,
It was much like to do : he answer'd, ' Tush,
It can do me no damage ; ' adding further,
That, had the king in his last sickness fail'd,
The cardinal's and Sir Thomas Lovell's heads
Should have gone off.
  King.   Ha ! what, so rank ? Ah ha !
There's mischief in this man : canst thou say
    further ?
  Surv. I can, my liege.
  King.   Proceed.
  Surv.   Being at Greenwich,
After your highness had reproved the duke
About Sir William Blomer,—
  King.   I remember 190
Of such a time : being my sworn servant,
The duke retain'd him his. But on ; what
    hence ?
  Surv. ' If,' quoth he, ' I for this had been
    committed,
As, to the Tower, I thought, I would have
    play'd
The part my father meant to act upon
The usurper Richard ; who, being at Salisbury,
Made suit to come in's presence ; which if
    granted,
As he made semblance of his duty, would
Have put his knife into him.'
  King.   A giant traitor !
  Wol. Now, madam, may his highness live
    in freedom,   200
And this man out of prison ?
  Q. Kath.   God mend all !
  King. There's something more would out
    of thee ; what say'st ?
  Surv. After ' the duke his father,' with
    ' the knife,'
He stretch'd him, and, with one hand on his
    dagger,
Another spread on 's breast, mounting his eyes
He did discharge a horrible oath ; whose tenor
Was,—were he evil used, he would outgo
His father by as much as a performance
Does an irresolute purpose.
  King.   There's his period,
To sheathe his knife in us. He is attach'd ;
Call him to present trial : if he may   211
Find mercy in the law, 'tis his ; if none,
Let him not seek 't of us : by day and night,
He's traitor to the height.   [*Exeunt.*

SCENE III.   *An ante-chamber in the palace.*

  Enter the LORD CHAMBERLAIN *and* LORD
    SANDS.

  Cham. Is't possible the spells of France
    should juggle
Men into such strange mysteries ?
  Sands.   New customs,
Though they be never so ridiculous,
Nay, let 'em be unmanly, yet are follow'd.
  Cham. As far as I see, all the good our
    English
Have got by the late voyage is but merely
A fit or two o' the face ; but they are shrewd
    ones ;

For when they hold 'em, you would swear
directly
Their very noses had been counsellors
To Pepin or Clotharius, they keep state so. 10
  Sands. They have all new legs, and lame
    ones : one would take it,
That never saw 'em pace before, the spavin
Or springhalt reign'd among 'em.
  Cham.   Death ! my lord,
Their clothes are after such a pagan cut too,
That, sure, they've worn out Christendom.

Enter Sir Thomas Lovell.

                      How now !
What news, Sir Thomas Lovell ?
  Lov.   Faith, my lord,
I hear of none, but the new proclamation
That's clapp'd upon the court-gate.
  Cham.   What is't for ?
  Lov. The reformation of our travell'd gal-
    lants,
That fill the court with quarrels, talk, and
    tailors.   20
  Cham. I'm glad 'tis there : now I would
    pray our monsieurs
To think an English courtier may be wise,
And never see the Louvre.
  Lov.   They must either,
For so run the conditions, leave those rem-
    nants
Of fool and feather that they got in France,
With all their honorable points of ignorance
Pertaining thereunto, as fights and fireworks,
Abusing better men than they can be,
Out of a foreign wisdom, renouncing clean
The faith they have in tennis, and tall stock-
    ings,   30
Short blister'd breeches, and those types of
    travel,
And understand again like honest men ;
Or pack to their old playfellows : there, I take
    it,
They may, ' cum privilegio,' wear away
The lag end of their lewdness and be laugh'd
    at.
  Sands. 'Tis time to give 'em physic, their
    diseases
Are grown so catching.
  Cham.   What a loss our ladies
Will have of these trim vanities !
  Lov.   Ay, marry,
There will be woe indeed, lords : the sly
    whoresons   39
Have got a speeding trick to lay down ladies ;
A French song and a fiddle has no fellow.
  Sands. The devil fiddle 'em ! I am glad
    they are going,
For, sure, there's no converting of 'em : now
An honest country lord, as I am, beaten
A long time out of play, may bring his plain-
    song
And have an hour of hearing ; and, by'r lady,
Held current music too.
  Cham.   Well said, Lord Sands ;
Your colt's tooth is not cast yet.
  Sands.   No, my lord ;
Nor shall not, while I have a stump.
  Cham.   Sir Thomas,
Whither were you a-going ?
  Lov.   To the cardinal's : 50
Your lordship is a guest too.
  Cham.   O, 'tis true :
This night he makes a supper, and a great one,
To many lords and ladies ; there will be
The beauty of this kingdom, I'll assure you.
  Lov. That churchman bears a bounteous
    mind indeed,
A hand as fruitful as the land that feeds us ;
His dews fall every where.
  Cham.   No doubt he's noble ;
He had a black mouth that said other of him.
  Sands. He may, my lord ; has where-
    withal : in him
Sparing would show a worse sin than ill doc-
    trine :   60
Men of his way should be most liberal ;
They are set here for examples.
  Cham.   True, they are so :
But few now give so great ones. My barge
    stays ;
Your lordship shall along. Come, good Sir
    Thomas,
We shall be late else ; which I would not be,
For I was spoke to, with Sir Henry Guildford
This night to be comptrollers.
  Sands. I am your lordship's. [*Exeunt.*

Scene IV. *A Hall in York Place.*

Hautboys. A small table under a state for the
  Cardinal, *a longer table for the guests.*
  Then enter Anne Bullen *and divers other*
  Ladies *and* Gentlemen *as guests, at one*
  door ; at another door, enter Sir Henry
  Guildford.

  Guild. Ladies, a general welcome from his
    grace
Salutes ye all ; this night he dedicates
To fair content and you : none here, he hopes,
In all this noble bevy, has brought with her
One care abroad ; he would have all as merry
As, first, good company, good wine, good wel-
    come,
Can make good people. O, my lord, you're
    tardy :

Enter Lord Chamberlain, Lord Sands, *and*
  Sir Thomas Lovell.

The very thought of this fair company
Clapp'd wings to me.
  Cham. You are young, Sir Harry Guild-
    ford.
  Sands. Sir Thomas Lovell, had the cardinal
But half my lay thoughts in him, some of these
Should find a running banquet ere they rested,
I think would better please 'em : by my life,
They are a sweet society of fair ones.
  Lov. O, that your lordship were but now
    confessor
To one or two of these !
  Sands.   I would I were ;
They should find easy penance.
  Lov.   Faith, how easy ?
  Sands. As easy as a down-bed would afford
    it.
  Cham. Sweet ladies, will it please you sit ?
    Sir Harry,
Place you that side ; I'll take the charge of
    this :   20
His grace is entering. Nay, you must not
    freeze ;
Two women placed together makes cold
    weather :
My Lord Sands, you are one will keep 'em
    waking ;
Pray, sit between these ladies.
  Sands.   By my faith,

And thank your lordship. By your leave, sweet
  ladies :
If I chance to talk a little wild, forgive me ;
I had it from my father.
Anne.   Was he mad, sir ?
Sands.   O, very mad, exceeding mad, in love
  too :
But he would bite none ; just as I do now,
He would kiss you twenty with a breath.
                      [Kisses her.
Cham.   Well said, my lord. 30
So, now you're fairly seated. Gentlemen,
The penance lies on you, if these fair ladies
Pass away frowning.
Sands.   For my little cure,
Let me alone.

    Hautboys. Enter CARDINAL WOLSEY, *and*
        takes his state.

Wol. You're welcome, my fair guests : that
  noble lady,
Or gentleman, that is not freely merry,
Is not my friend : this, to confirm my wel-
  come ;
And to you all, good health.   *[Drinks.*
Sands.   Your grace is noble :
Let me have such a bowl may hold my thanks,
And save me so much talking.
Wol.   My Lord Sands, 40
I am beholding to you : cheer your neighbors.
Ladies, you are not merry : gentlemen,
Whose fault is this ?
Sands.   The red wine first must rise
In their fair cheeks, my lord ; then we shall
  have 'em
Talk us to silence.
Anne.   You are a merry gamester,
My Lord Sands.
Sands.   Yes, if I make my play.
Here's to your ladyship : and pledge it,
  madam,
For 'tis to such a thing,—
Anne.   You cannot show me.
Sands. I told your grace they would talk
  anon.
  [Drum and trumpet, chambers discharged.
Wol.   What's that ?
Cham. Look out there, some of ye.
                     [Exit Servant.
Wol.   What warlike voice, 50
And to what end is this ? Nay, ladies, fear not ;
By all the laws of war you're privileged.

    Re-enter Servant.

Cham. How now ! what is't ?
Serv.   A noble troop of strangers ;
For so they seem : they've left their barge and
  landed ;
And hither make, as great ambassadors
From foreign princes.
Wol.   Good lord chamberlain,
Go, give 'em welcome ; you can speak the
  French tongue ;
And, pray, receive 'em nobly, and conduct 'em
Into our presence, where this heaven of beauty
Shall shine at full upon them. Some attend
  him.
  [Exit Chamberlain, attended. All rise,
          and tables removed.
You have now a broken banquet ; but we'll
  mend it.   61
A good digestion to you all : and once more
I shower a welcome on ye ; welcome all.

    Hautboys. Enter the KING *and others, as*
    masquers, habited like shepherds, ushered by
    the LORD CHAMBERLAIN. *They pass directly*
    before the CARDINAL, *and gracefully salute*
    him.

A noble company ! what are their pleasures ?
Cham. Because they speak no English, thus
  they pray'd
To tell your grace, that, having heard by fame
Of this so noble and so fair assembly
This night to meet here, they could do no less
Out of the great respect they bear to beauty,
But leave their flocks ; and, under your fair
  conduct,   70
Crave leave to view these ladies and entreat
An hour of revels with 'em.
Wol.   Say, lord chamberlain,
They have done my poor house grace ; for
  which I pay 'em
A thousand thanks, and pray 'em take their
  pleasures.
  [They choose Ladies for the dance. The
      King chooses Anne Bullen.
King. The fairest hand I ever touch'd ! O
  beauty,
Till now I never knew thee ! [*Music. Dance.*
Wol. My lord !
Cham. Your grace ?
Wol. Pray, tell 'em thus much from me :
There should be one amongst 'em, by his per-
  son,
More worthy this place than myself ; to whom,
If I but knew him, with my love and duty 80
I would surrender it.
Cham.   I will, my lord.
              [Whispers the Masquers.
Wol. What say they ?
Cham.   Such a one, they all confess,
There is indeed ; which they would have your
  grace
Find out, and he will take it.
Wol.   Let me see, then.
By all your good leaves, gentlemen ; here I'll
  make
My royal choice.
King.   Ye have found him, cardinal :
                    [Unmasking.
You hold a fair assembly ; you do well, lord :
You are a churchman, or, I'll tell you, cardi-
  nal,
I should judge now unhappily.
Wol.   I am glad
Your grace is grown so pleasant.
King.   My lord chamberlain, 90
Prithee, come hither : what fair lady's that ?
Cham. An't please your grace, Sir Thomas
  Bullen's daughter,—
The Viscount Rochford,—one of her highness'
  women.
King. By heaven, she is a dainty one.
  Sweetheart,
I were unmannerly, to take you out,
And not to kiss you. A health, gentlemen !
Let it go round.
Wol. Sir Thomas Lovell, is the banquet
  ready
I' the privy chamber ?
Lov.   Yes, my lord.
Wol.   Your grace,
I fear, with dancing is a little heated.   100
King. I fear, too much.

Wol.   There's fresher air, my lord,
In the next chamber.
King.   Lead in your ladies, every one :
      sweet partner,
I must not yet forsake you : let's be merry :
Good my lord cardinal, I have half a dozen
      healths
To drink to these fair ladies, and a measure
To lead 'em once again ; and then let's dream
Who's best in favor. Let the music knock it.
                    [*Exeunt with trumpets.*

ACT II.

SCENE I. *Westminster. A street.*

Enter two Gentlemen, *meeting.*

First Gent.   Whither away so fast ?
Sec. Gent.   O, God save ye !
Even to the hall, to hear what shall become
Of the great Duke of Buckingham.
First Gent.   I'll save you
That labor, sir. All's now done, but the cere-
      mony
Of bringing back the prisoner.
Sec. Gent.   Were you there ?
First Gent.   Yes, indeed, was I.
Sec. Gent.   Pray, speak what has happen'd.
First Gent.   You may guess quickly what.
Sec. Gent.   Is he found guilty ?
First Gent.   Yes, truly is he, and condemn'd
      upon't.
Sec. Gent.   I am sorry for't.
First Gent.   So are a number more.
Sec. Gent.   But, pray, how pass'd it ?   10
First Gent.   I'll tell you in a little. The great
      duke
Came to the bar ; where to his accusations
He pleaded still not guilty and alleged
Many sharp reasons to defeat the law.
The king's attorney on the contrary
Urged on the examinations, proofs, confessions
Of divers witnesses ; which the duke desired
To have brought vivâ voce to his face :
At which appear'd against him his surveyor ;
Sir Gilbert Peck his chancellor ; and John Car,
Confessor to him ; with that devil-monk,   21
Hopkins, that made this mischief.
Sec. Gent.   That was he
That fed him with his prophecies ?
First Gent.   The same.
All these accused him strongly ; which he fain
Would have flung from him, but, indeed, he
      could not :
And so his peers, upon this evidence,
Have found him guilty of high treason. Much
He spoke, and learnedly, for life ; but all
Was either pitied in him or forgotten.
Sec. Gent.   After all this, how did he bear
      himself ?   30
First Gent.   When he was brought again to
      the bar, to hear
His knell rung out, his judgment, he was stirr'd
With such an agony, he sweat extremely,
And something spoke in choler, ill, and hasty :
But he fell to himself again, and sweetly
In all the rest show'd a most noble patience.
Sec. Gent.   I do not think he fears death.
First Gent.   Sure, he does not :
He never was so womanish ; the cause
He may a little grieve at.
Sec. Gent.   Certainly

The cardinal is the end of this.
First Gent.   'Tis likely, 40
By all conjectures : first, Kildare's attainder,
Then deputy of Ireland ; who removed,
Earl Surrey was sent thither, and in haste too,
Lest he should help his father.
Sec. Gent.   That trick of state
Was a deep envious one.
First Gent.   At his return
No doubt he will requite it. This is noted,
And generally, whoever the king favors,
The cardinal instantly will find employment,
And far enough from court too.
Sec. Gent.   All the commons
Hate him perniciously, and, o' my conscience,
Wish him ten fathom deep : this duke as much
They love and dote on ; call him bounteous
      Buckingham,   52
The mirror of all courtesy ;—
First Gent.   Stay there, sir,
And see the noble ruin'd man you speak of.

Enter BUCKINGHAM *from his arraignment ; tip-
staves before him ; the axe with the edge
towards him ; halberds on each side : accompanied with* SIR THOMAS LOVELL, SIR
NICHOLAS VAUX, SIR WILLIAM SANDS, *and
common people.*

Sec. Gent.   Let's stand close, and behold
      him.
Buck.   All good people,
You that thus far have come to pity me,
Hear what I say, and then go home and lose
      me.
I have this day received a traitor's judgment,
And by that name must die : yet, heaven bear
      witness,
And if I have a conscience, let it sink me,   60
Even as the axe falls, if I be not faithful !
The law I bear no malice for my death ;
'T has done, upon the premises, but justice :
But those that sought it I could wish more
      Christians :
Be what they will, I heartily forgive 'em :
Yet let 'em look they glory not in mischief,
Nor build their evils on the graves of great
      men ;
For then my guiltless blood must cry against
      'em.
For further life in this world I ne'er hope,
Nor will I sue, although the king have mer-
      cies   70
More than I dare make faults. You few that
      loved me,
And dare be bold to weep for Buckingham,
His noble friends and fellows, whom to leave
Is only bitter to him, only dying,
Go with me, like good angels, to my end ;
And, as the long divorce of steel falls on me,
Make of your prayers one sweet sacrifice,
And lift my soul to heaven. Lead on, o' God's
      name.
Lov.   I do beseech your grace, for charity,
If ever any malice in your heart   80
Were hid against me, now to forgive me
      frankly.
Buck.   Sir Thomas Lovell, I as free forgive
      you
As I would be forgiven : I forgive all ;
There cannot be those numberless offences
'Gainst me, that I cannot take peace with : no
      black envy

Shall mark my grave. Commend me to his
     grace ;
And, if he speak of Buckingham, pray, tell him
You met him half in heaven : my vows and
     prayers
Yet are the king's ; and, till my soul forsake,
Shall cry for blessings on him : may he live   90
Longer than I have time to tell his years !
Ever beloved and loving may his rule be !
And when old time shall lead him to his end,
Goodness and he fill up one monument !
    Lov. To the water side I must conduct
     your grace ;
Then give my charge up to Sir Nicholas Vaux,
Who undertakes you to your end.
    Vaux.   Prepare there,
The duke is coming : see the barge be ready ;
And fit it with such furniture as suits
The greatness of his person.
    Buck.   Nay, Sir Nicholas,   100
Let it alone ; my state now will but mock me.
When I came hither, I was lord high constable
And Duke of Buckingham ; now, poor Edward
     Bohun :
Yet I am richer than my base accusers,
That never knew what truth meant : I now
     seal it ;
And with that blood will make 'em one day
     groan for't.
My noble father, Henry of Buckingham,
Who first raised head against usurping Rich-
     ard,
Flying for succor to his servant Banister,
Being distress'd, was by that wretch betray'd,
And without trial fell ; God's peace be with
     him !   111
Henry the Seventh succeeding, truly pitying
My father's loss, like a most royal prince,
Restored me to my honors, and, out of ruins,
Made my name once more noble. Now his
     son,
Henry the Eighth, life, honor, name and all
That made me happy at one stroke has taken
For ever from the world. I had my trial,
And, must needs say, a noble one ; which
     makes me
A little happier than my wretched father :   120
Yet thus far we are one in fortunes : both
Fell by our servants, by those men we loved
     most ;
A most unnatural and faithless service !
Heaven has an end in all : yet, you that hear
     me,
This from a dying man receive as certain :
Where you are liberal of your loves and coun-
     sels
Be sure you be not loose ; for those you make
     friends
And give your hearts to, when they once per-
     ceive
The least rub in your fortunes, fall away
Like water from ye, never found again   130
But where they mean to sink ye. All good
     people,
Pray for me ! I must now forsake ye : the last
     hour
Of my long weary life is come upon me.
Farewell :
And when you would say something that is
     sad,
Speak how I fell. I have done ; and God for-
     give me !   [*Exeunt Duke and Train.*

    First Gent. O, this is full of pity ! Sir, it
     calls,
I fear, too many curses on their heads
That were the authors.
    Sec. Gent.   If the duke be guiltless,
'Tis full of woe : yet I can give you inkling
Of an ensuing evil, if it fall,   141
Greater than this.
    First Gent.   Good angels keep it from us !
What may it be ? You do not doubt my faith,
     sir ?
    Sec. Gent. This secret is so weighty, 'twill
     require
A strong faith to conceal it.
    First Gent.   Let me have it ;
I do not talk much.
    Sec. Gent.   I am confident,
You shall, sir : did you not of late days hear
A buzzing of a separation
Between the king and Katharine ?
    First Gent.   Yes, but it held not :
For when the king once heard it, out of anger
He sent command to the lord mayor straight
To stop the rumor, and allay those tongues
That durst disperse it.
    Sec. Gent.   But that slander, sir,
Is found a truth now : for it grows again
Fresher than e'er it was ; and held for certain
The king will venture at it. Either the cardinal,
Or some about him near, have, out of malice
To the good queen, possess'd him with a scru-
     ple
That will undo her : to confirm this too,
Cardinal Campeius is arrived, and lately ;   160
As all think, for this business.
    First Gent.   'Tis the cardinal ;
And merely to revenge him on the emperor
For not bestowing on him, at his asking,
The archbishopric of Toledo, this is purposed.
    Sec. Gent. I think you have hit the mark :
     but is't not cruel
That she should feel the smart of this ? The
     cardinal
Will have his will, and she must fall.
    First Gent.   'Tis woful.
We are too open here to argue this ;
Let's think in private more.   [*Exeunt.*

SCENE II. *An ante-chamber in the palace.*
Enter the LORD CHAMBERLAIN, *reading a
letter.*

    Cham. 'My lord, the horses your lordship
sent for, with all the care I had, I saw well
chosen, ridden, and furnished. They were
young and handsome, and of the best breed in
the north. When they were ready to set out
for London, a man of my lord cardinal's, by
commission and main power, took 'em from
me ; with this reason : His master would be
served before a subject, if not before the king ;
which stopped our mouths, sir.'   10
I fear he will indeed : well, let him have them :
He will have all, I think.

Enter, to the LORD CHAMBERLAIN, *the* DUKES
OF NORFOLK *and* SUFFOLK.

    Nor. Well met, my lord chamberlain.
    Cham. Good day to both your graces.
    Suf. How is the king employ'd ?
    Cham.   I left him private,
Full of sad thoughts and troubles.

Nor. What's the cause?
Cham. It seems the marriage with his
brother's wife
Has crept too near his conscience.
Suf. No, his conscience
Has crept too near another lady.
Nor. 'Tis so:
This is the cardinal's doing, the king-cardinal:
That blind priest, like the eldest son of for-
tune, 21
Turns what he list. The king will know him
one day.
Suf. Pray God he do! he'll never know
himself else.
Nor. How holily he works in all his busi-
ness!
And with what zeal! for, now he has crack'd
the league
Between us and the emperor, the queen's great
nephew,
He dives into the king's soul, and there scat-
ters
Dangers, doubts, wringing of the conscience,
Fears, and despairs; and all these for his mar-
riage:
And out of all these to restore the king, 30
He counsels a divorce; a loss of her
That, like a jewel, has hung twenty years
About his neck, yet never lost her lustre;
Of her that loves him with that excellence
That angels love good men with; even of her
That, when the greatest stroke of fortune falls,
Will bless the king: and is not this course
pious?
Cham. Heaven keep me from such coun-
sel! 'Tis most true
These news are every where; every tongue
speaks 'em,
And every true heart weeps for't: all that
dare 40
Look into these affairs see this main end,
The French king's sister. Heaven will one day
open
The king's eyes, that so long have slept upon
This bold bad man.
Suf. And free us from his slavery.
Nor. We had need pray,
And heartily, for our deliverance;
Or this imperious man will work us all
From princes into pages: all men's honors
Lie like one lump before him, to be fashion'd
Into what pitch he please.
Suf. For me, my lords, 50
I love him not, nor fear him; there's my
creed:
As I am made without him, so I'll stand,
If the king please; his curses and his bless-
ings
Touch me alike, they're breath I not believe
in.
I knew him, and I know him; so I leave him
To him that made him proud, the pope.
Nor. Let's in;
And with some other business put the king
From these sad thoughts, that work too much
upon him:
My lord, you'll bear us company?
Cham. Excuse me;
The king has sent me otherwhere: besides, 60
You'll find a most unfit time to disturb him:
Health to your lordships.

Nor. Thanks, my good lord chamberlain.
[*Exit Lord Chamberlain; and the
King draws the curtain, and sits
reading pensively.*
Suf. How sad he looks! sure, he is much
afflicted.
King. Who's there, ha?
Nor. Pray God he be not angry.
King. Who's there, I say? How dare you
thrust yourselves
Into my private meditations?
Who am I? ha?
Nor. A gracious king that pardons all of-
fences
Malice ne'er meant: our breach of duty this
way
Is business of estate; in which we come 70
To know your royal pleasure.
King. Ye are too bold:
Go to; I'll make ye know your times of busi-
ness:
Is this an hour for temporal affairs, ha?

Enter WOLSEY *and* CAMPEIUS, *with a commission.*

Who's there? my good lord cardinal? O my
Wolsey,
The quiet of my wounded conscience;
Thou art a cure fit for a king. [*To Camp.*]
You're welcome,
Most learned reverend sir, into our kingdom:
Use us and it. [*To Wol.*] My good lord, have
great care
I be not found a talker.
Wol. Sir, you cannot.
I would your grace would give us but an hour
Of private conference. 81
King. [*To Nor. and Suf.*] We are busy;
go.
Nor. [*Aside to Suf.*] This priest has no
pride in him?
Suf. [*Aside to Nor.*] Not to speak of:
I would not be so sick though for his place:
But this cannot continue.
Nor. [*Aside to Suf.*] If it do,
I'll venture one have-at-him.
Suf. [*Aside to Nor.*] I another.
[*Exeunt Nor. and Suf.*
Wol. Your grace has given a precedent of
wisdom
Above all princes, in committing freely
Your scruple to the voice of Christendom:
Who can be angry now? what envy reach
you? 89
The Spaniard, tied by blood and favor to her,
Must now confess, if they have any goodness,
The trial just and noble. All the clerks,
I mean the learned ones, in Christian king-
doms
Have their free voices: Rome, the nurse of
judgment,
Invited by your noble self, hath sent
One general tongue unto us, this good man,
This just and learned priest, Cardinal Cam-
peius;
Whom once more I present unto your high-
ness.
King. And once more in mine arms I bid
him welcome,
And thank the holy conclave for their loves:
They have sent me such a man I would have
wish'd for. 101

Cam. Your grace must needs deserve all strangers' loves,
You are so noble. To your highness' hand
I tender my commission; by whose virtue,
The court of Rome commanding, you, my lord
Cardinal of York, are join'd with me their servant
In the unpartial judging of this business.
  King. Two equal men. The queen shall be acquainted
Forthwith for what you come. Where's Gardiner?
  Wol. I know your majesty has always loved her   110
So dear in heart, not to deny her that
A woman of less place might ask by law:
Scholars allow'd freely to argue for her.
  King. Ay, and the best she shall have; and my favor
To him that does best: God forbid else. Cardinal,
Prithee, call Gardiner to me, my new secretary:
I find him a fit fellow.   [*Exit Wolsey.*

  Re-enter WOLSEY, *with* GARDINER.

  Wol. [*Aside to Gard.*] Give me your hand: much joy and favor to you;
You are the king's now.
  Gard. [*Aside to Wol.*] But to be commanded
For ever by your grace, whose hand has raised me.   120
  King. Come hither, Gardiner.
        [*Walks and whispers.*
  Cam. My Lord of York, was not one Doctor Pace
In this man's place before him?
  Wol.   Yes, he was.
  Cam. Was he not held a learned man?
  Wol.   Yes, surely.
  Cam. Believe me, there's an ill opinion spread then
Even of yourself, lord cardinal.
  Wol.   How! of me?
  Cam. They will not stick to say you envied him,
And fearing he would rise, he was so virtuous,
Kept him a foreign man still; which so grieved him,
That he ran mad and died.
  Wol.   Heaven's peace be with him!
That's Christian care enough: for living murmurers   131
There's places of rebuke. He was a fool;
For he would needs be virtuous: that good fellow,
If I command him, follows my appointment:
I will have none so near else. Learn this, brother,
We live not to be grip'd by meaner persons.
  King. Deliver this with modesty to the queen.   [*Exit Gardiner.*
The most convenient place that I can think of
For such receipt of learning is Black-Friars;
There ye shall meet about this weighty business.   140
My Wolsey, see it furnish'd. O, my lord,
Would it not grieve an able man to leave
So sweet a bedfellow? But, conscience, conscience!

O, 'tis a tender place; and I must leave her.
        [*Exeunt.*

SCENE III. *An ante-chamber of the* QUEEN'S *apartments.*

  Enter ANNE BULLEN *and an* Old Lady.

  Anne. Not for that neither: here's the pang that pinches:
His highness having lived so long with her, and she
So good a lady that no tongue could ever
Pronounce dishonor of her; by my life,
She never knew harm-doing: O, now, after
So many courses of the sun enthroned,
Still growing in a majesty and pomp, the which
To leave a thousand-fold more bitter than
'Tis sweet at first to acquire,—after this process,
To give her the avaunt! it is a pity   10
Would move a monster.
  Old L.   Hearts of most hard temper
Melt and lament for her.
  Anne.   O, God's will! much better
She ne'er had known pomp: though't be temporal,
Yet, if that quarrel, fortune, do divorce
It from the bearer, 'tis a sufferance panging
As soul and body's severing.
  Old L.   Alas, poor lady!
She's a stranger now again.
  Anne.   So much the more
Must pity drop upon her. Verily,
I swear, 'tis better to be lowly born,
And range with humble livers in content,   20
Than to be perk'd up in a glistering grief,
And wear a golden sorrow.
  Old L.   Our content
Is our best having.
  Anne.   By my troth and maidenhead,
I would not be a queen.
  Old L.   Beshrew me, I would,
And venture maidenhead for't; and so would you,
For all this spice of your hypocrisy:
You, that have so fair parts of woman on you,
Have too a woman's heart; which ever yet
Affected eminence, wealth, sovereignty;
Which, to say sooth, are blessings; and which gifts,   30
Saving your mincing, the capacity
Of your soft cheveril conscience would receive,
If you might please to stretch it.
  Anne.   Nay, good troth.
  Old L. Yes, troth, and troth; you would not be a queen?
  Anne. No, not for all the riches under heaven.
  Old L. 'Tis strange: a three-pence bow'd would hire me,
Old as I am, to queen it: but, I pray you,
What think you of a duchess? have you limbs
To bear that load of title?
  Anne.   No, in truth.
  Old L. Then you are weakly made: pluck off a little;   40
I would not be a young count in your way,
For more than blushing comes to: if your back
Cannot vouchsafe this burthen, 'tis too weak
Ever to get a boy.

Anne.　　　　　How you do talk!
I swear again, I would not be a queen
For all the world.
　　Old L.　　　In faith, for little England
You'ld venture an emballing: I myself
Would for Carnarvonshire, although there
　　long'd
No more to the crown but that. Lo, who
　　comes here?

Enter the LORD CHAMBERLAIN.

　　Cham.　Good morrow, ladies. What were't
worth to know　　　　　　　　　　50
The secret of your conference?
　　Anne.　　　　　　My good lord,
Not your demand; it values not your asking:
Our mistress' sorrows we were pitying.
　　Cham.　It was a gentle business, and be-
coming
The action of good women: there is hope
All will be well.
　　Anne.　　Now, I pray God, amen!
　　Cham.　You bear a gentle mind, and heav-
enly blessings
Follow such creatures. That you may, fair
　　lady,
Perceive I speak sincerely, and high note's
Ta'en of your many virtues, the king's maj-
esty　　　　　　　　　　　　　　60
Commends his good opinion of you, and
Does purpose honor to you no less flowing
Than Marchioness of Pembroke: to which
　　title
A thousand pound a year, annual support,
Out of his grace he adds.
　　Anne.　　　　　I do not know
What kind of my obedience I should tender;
More than my all is nothing: nor my prayers
Are not words duly hallow'd, nor my wishes
More worth than empty vanities; yet prayers
　　and wishes
Are all I can return. Beseech your lordship,
Vouchsafe to speak my thanks and my obe-
dience,　　　　　　　　　　　　71
As from a blushing handmaid, to his high-
ness;
Whose health and royalty I pray for.
　　Cham.　　　　　　　　Lady,
I shall not fail to approve the fair conceit
The king hath of you. [*Aside*] I have pe-
rused her well;
Beauty and honor in her are so mingled
That they have caught the king: and who
　　knows yet
But from this lady may proceed a gem
To lighten all this isle? I'll to the king,
And say I spoke with you.
　　　　　　[*Exit Lord Chamberlain.*
　　Anne.　　　　My honor'd lord.　　80
　　Old L.　Why, this it is; see, see!
I have been begging sixteen years in court,
Am yet a courtier beggarly, nor could
Come pat betwixt too early and too late
For any suit of pounds; and you, O fate!
A very fresh-fish here—fie, fie upon
This compell'd fortune!—have your mouth
　　fill'd up
Before you open it.
　　Anne.　　　　This is strange to me.
　　Old L.　How tastes it? is it bitter? forty
pence, no.
There was a lady once, 'tis an old story,　90

That would not be a queen, that would she
　　not,
For all the mud in Egypt: have you heard
　　it?
　　Anne.　Come, you are pleasant.
　　Old L.　　　　With your theme, I could
O'ermount the lark. The Marchioness of
　　Pembroke!
A thousand pounds a year for pure respect!
No other obligation! By my life,
That promises moe thousands: honor's train
Is longer than his foreskirt. By this time
I know your back will bear a duchess: say,
Are you not stronger than you were?
　　Anne.　　　　　Good lady,　100
Make yourself mirth with your particular
　　fancy,
And leave me out on't. Would I had no be-
ing,
If this salute my blood a jot: it faints me,
To think what follows.
The queen is comfortless, and we forgetful
In our long absence: pray, do not deliver
What here you've heard to her.
　　Old L.　　　　What do you think me?
　　　　　　　　　　　　[*Exeunt.*

SCENE IV. *A hall in Black-Friars.*

Trumpets, sennet, and cornets. Enter two
　　Vergers, with short silver wands; next them,
　　two Scribes, in the habit of doctors; after
　　them, the ARCHBISHOP OF CANTERBURY
　　alone; after him, the BISHOPS OF LINCOLN,
　　ELY, ROCHESTER, *and* SAINT ASAPH; *next*
　　them, with some small distance, follows a
　　Gentleman bearing the purse, with the great
　　seal, and a cardinal's hat; then two Priests,
　　bearing each a silver cross; then a Gentle-
　　man-usher *bare-headed, accompanied with*
　　a Sergeant-at-arms *bearing a silver mace;*
　　then two Gentlemen *bearing two great silver*
　　pillars; after them, side by side, the two
　　CARDINALS; *two* Noblemen *with the sword*
　　and mace. The KING *takes place under the*
　　cloth of state; the two CARDINALS *sit under*
　　him as judges. The QUEEN *takes place*
　　some distance from the KING. *The* Bishops
　　place themselves on each side the court, in
　　manner of a consistory; below them, the
　　Scribes. *The* Lords *sit next the* Bishops.
　　The rest of the Attendants *stand in con-*
　　venient order about the stage.

　　Wol.　Whilst our commission from Rome
　　　　is read,
Let silence be commanded.
　　King.　　　　　What's the need?
It hath already publicly been read,
And on all sides the authority allow'd;
You may, then, spare that time.
　　Wol.　　　　　Be't so. Proceed.
　　Scribe.　Say, Henry King of England, come
into the court.
　　Crier.　Henry King of England, &c.
　　King.　Here.
　　Scribe.　Say, Katharine Queen of England,
come into the court.　　　　　　　11
　　Crier.　Katharine Queen of England, &c.
　　　　　[*The Queen makes no answer, rises out*
　　　　　　of her chair, goes about the court,
　　　　　　comes to the King, and kneels at his
　　　　　　feet; then speaks.

Q. Kath. Sir, I desire you do me right and
    justice ;
And to bestow your pity on me : for
I am a most poor woman, and a stranger,
Born out of your dominions ; having here
No judge indifferent, nor no more assurance
Of equal friendship and proceeding. Alas, sir,
In what have I offended you ? what cause 19
Hath my behavior given to your displeasure,
That thus you should proceed to put me off,
And take your good grace from me ? Heaven
    witness,
I have been to you a true and humble wife,
At all times to your will conformable ;
Ever in fear to kindle your dislike,
Yea, subject to your countenance, glad or
    sorry
As I saw it inclined : when was the hour
I ever contradicted your desire,
Or made it not mine too ? Or which of your
    friends
Have I not strove to love, although I knew 30
He were mine enemy ? what friend of mine
That had to him derived your anger, did I
Continue in my liking ? nay, gave notice
He was from thence discharged. Sir, call to
    mind
That I have been your wife, in this obe-
    dience,
Upward of twenty years, and have been blest
With many children by you : if, in the course
And process of this time, you can report,
And prove it too, against mine honor aught,
My bond to wedlock, or my love and duty, 40
Against your sacred person, in God's name,
Turn me away ; and let the foul'st contempt
Shut door upon me, and so give me up
To the sharp'st kind of justice. Please you sir,
The king, your father, was reputed for
A prince most prudent, of an excellent
And unmatch'd wit and judgment : Ferdi-
    nand,
My father, king of Spain, was reckon'd one
The wisest prince that there had reign'd by
    many
A year before : it is not to be question'd 50
That they had gather'd a wise council to them
Of every realm, that did debate this business,
Who deem'd our marriage lawful : wherefore
    I humbly
Beseech you, sir, to spare me, till I may
Be by my friends in Spain advised ; whose
    counsel
I will implore : if not, i' the name of God,
Your pleasure be fulfill'd !
  Wol.   You have here, lady,
And of your choice, these reverend fathers ;
    men
Of singular integrity and learning,
Yea, the elect o' the land, who are assembled
To plead your cause : it shall be therefore
    bootless 61
That longer you desire the court ; as well
For your own quiet, as to rectify
What is unsettled in the king.
  Cam.   His grace
Hath spoken well and justly : therefore,
    madam,
It's fit this royal session do proceed ;
And that, without delay, their arguments
Be now produced and heard.
  Q. Kath.   Lord cardinal,
To you I speak.

Wol.   Your pleasure, madam ?
  Q. Kath.   Sir,
I am about to weep ; but, thinking that 70
We are a queen, or long have dream'd so,
    certain
The daughter of a king, my drops of tears
I'll turn to sparks of fire.
  Wol.   Be patient yet.
  Q. Kath. I will, when you are humble ;
    nay, before,
Or God will punish me. I do believe,
Induced by potent circumstances, that
You are mine enemy, and make my challenge
You shall not be my judge : for it is you
Have blown this coal betwixt my lord and
    me ;
Which God's dew quench ! Therefore I say
    again, 80
I utterly abhor, yea, from my soul
Refuse you for my judge ; whom, yet once
    more,
I hold my most malicious foe, and think not
At all a friend to truth.
  Wol.   I do profess
You speak not like yourself ; who ever yet
Have stood to charity, and display'd the ef-
    fects
Of disposition gentle, and of wisdom
O'ertopping woman's power. Madam, you do
    me wrong :
I have no spleen against you ; nor injustice
For you or any : how far I have proceeded, 90
Or how far further shall, is warranted
By a commission from the consistory,
Yea, the whole consistory of Rome. You
    charge me
That I have blown this coal : I do deny it :
The king is present : if it be known to him
That I gainsay my deed, how may he wound,
And worthily, my falsehood ! yea, as much
As you have done my truth. If he know
That I am free of your report, he knows
I am not of your wrong. Therefore in him 100
It lies to cure me : and the cure is, to
Remove these thoughts from you : the which
    before
His highness shall speak in, I do beseech
You, gracious madam, to unthink your speak-
    ing
And to say so no more.
  Q. Kath.   My lord, my lord,
I am a simple woman, much too weak
To oppose your cunning. You're meek and
    humble-mouth'd ;
You sign your place and calling, in full seem-
    ing,
With meekness and humility ; but your heart
Is cramm'd with arrogancy, spleen, and pride.
You have, by fortune and his highness' fa-
    vors, 111
Gone slightly o'er low steps and now are
    mounted
Where powers are your retainers, and your
    words,
Domestics to you, serve your will as't please
Yourself pronounce their office. I must tell
    you,
You tender more your person's honor than
Your high profession spiritual : that again
I do refuse you for my judge ; and here,
Before you all, appeal unto the pope,
To bring my whole cause 'fore his holiness,

And to be judged by him.   121
[*She curtsies to the King, and offers to depart.*
  Cam.   The queen is obstinate,
Stubborn to justice, apt to accuse it, and
Disdainful to be tried by't : 'tis not well.
She's going away.
  King. Call her again.
  Crier. Katharine Queen of England, come
    into the court.
  Grif. Madam, you are call'd back.
  Q. Kath. What need you note it ? pray
    you, keep your way :
When you are call'd, return. Now, the Lord
    help,
They vex me past my patience ! Pray you,
    pass on :   130
I will not tarry ; no, nor ever more
Upon this business my appearance make
In any of their courts.
    [*Exeunt Queen and her Attendants.*
  King.   Go thy ways, Kate :
That man i' the world who shall report he has
A better wife, let him in nought be trusted,
For speaking false in that : thou art, alone,
If thy rare qualities, sweet gentleness,
Thy meekness saint-like, wife-like government,
Obeying in commanding, and thy parts
Sovereign and pious else, could speak thee out,
The queen of earthly queens : she's noble
    born ;   141
And, like her true nobility, she has
Carried herself towards me.
  Wol.   Most gracious sir,
In humblest manner I require your highness,
That it shall please you to declare, in hearing
Of all these ears,—for where I am robb'd and
    bound,
There must I be unloosed, although not there
At once and fully satisfied,—whether ever I
Did broach this business to your highness ; or
Laid any scruple in your way, which might
Induce you to the question on't ? or ever 151
Have to you, but with thanks to God for such
A royal lady, spake one the least word that
    might
Be to the prejudice of her present state,
Or touch of her good person ?
  King.   My lord cardinal,
I do excuse you ; yea, upon mine honor,
I free you from't. You are not to be taught
That you have many enemies, that know not
Why they are so, but, like to village-curs,
Bark when their fellows do : by some of these
The queen is put in anger. You're excused :
But will you be more justified ? You ever 162
Have wish'd the sleeping of this business ;
    never desired
It to be stirr'd ; but oft have hinder'd, oft,
The passages made toward it : on my honor,
I speak my good lord cardinal to this point,
And thus far clear him. Now, what moved
    me to't,
I will be bold with time and your attention :
Then mark the inducement. Thus it came ;
    give heed to't :
My conscience first received a tenderness, 170
Scruple, and prick, on certain speeches utter'd
By the Bishop of Bayonne, then French am-
    bassador ;
Who had been hither sent on the debating
A marriage 'twixt the Duke of Orleans and
Our daughter Mary : i' the progress of this
    business,

Ere a determinate resolution, he,
I mean the bishop, did require a respite ;
Wherein he might the king his lord advertise
Whether our daughter were legitimate,
Respecting this our marriage with the dowa-
    ger,   180
Sometimes our brother's wife. This respite
    shook
The bosom of my conscience, enter'd me,
Yea, with a splitting power, and made to
    tremble
The region of my breast ; which forced such
    way,
That many mazed considerings did throng
And press'd in with this caution. First,
    methought
I stood not in the smile of heaven ; who had
Commanded nature, that my lady's womb,
If it conceived a male child by me, should
Do no more offices of life to't than   190
The grave does to the dead ; for her male
    issue
Or died where they were made, or shortly
    after
This world had air'd them : hence I took a
    thought,
This was a judgment on me ; that my king-
    dom,
Well worthy the best heir o' the world, should
    not
Be gladded in't by me : then follows, that
I weigh'd the danger which my realms stood in
By this my issue's fail ; and that gave to me
Many a groaning throe. Thus hulling in
The wild sea of my conscience, I did steer 200
Toward this remedy, whereupon we are
Now present here together ; that's to say,
I meant to rectify my conscience,—which
I then did feel full sick, and yet not well,—
By all the reverend fathers of the land
And doctors learn'd : first I began in private
With you, my Lord of Lincoln ; you remember
How under my oppression I did reek,
When I first moved you.
  Lin.   Very well, my liege.
  King. I have spoke long : be pleased your-
    self to say   210
How far you satisfied me.
  Lin.   So please your highness,
The question did at first so stagger me,
Bearing a state of mighty moment in't
And consequence of dread, that I committed
The daring'st counsel which I had to doubt ;
And did entreat your highness to this course
Which you are running here.
  King.   I then moved you,
My Lord of Canterbury ; and got your leave
To make this present summons : unsolicited
I left no reverend person in this court ;   220
But by particular consent proceeded
Under your hands and seals : therefore, go on ;
For no dislike i' the world against the person
Of the good queen, but the sharp thorny points
Of my alleged reasons, drive this forward :
Prove but our marriage lawful, by my life
And kingly dignity, we are contented
To wear our mortal state to come with her,
Katharine our queen, before the primest crea-
    ture
That's paragon'd o' the world.
  Cam.   So please your highness, 230
The queen being absent, 'tis a needful fitness
That we adjourn this court till further day :

Meanwhile must be an earnest motion
Made to the queen, to call back her appeal
She intends unto his holiness.
 King. [*Aside*] I may perceive
These cardinals trifle with me : I abhor
This dilatory sloth and tricks of Rome.
My learn'd and well-beloved servant, Cran-
 mer,
Prithee, return : with thy approach, I know,
My comfort comes along. Break up the court :
I say, set on. 241
  [*Exeunt in manner as they entered.*

ACT III.

SCENE I. *London. The* QUEEN'S *apartments.*

Enter the QUEEN *and her Women, as at work.*

 Q. Kath. Take thy lute, wench : my soul
  grows sad with troubles ;
Sing, and disperse 'em, if thou canst : leave
 working.

     SONG.

 Orpheus with his lute made trees,
 And the mountain tops that freeze,
  Bow themselves when he did sing :
 To his music plants and flowers
 Ever sprung ; as sun and showers
  There had made a lasting spring.

 Every thing that heard him play,
 Even the billows of the sea, 10
  Hung their heads, and then lay by.
 In sweet music is such art,
 Killing care and grief of heart
  Fall asleep, or hearing, die.

   Enter a Gentleman.

 Q. Kath. How now !
 Gent. An't please your grace, the two
  great cardinals
Wait in the presence.
 Q. Kath. Would they speak with me ?
 Gent. They will'd me say so, madam.
 Q. Kath. Pray their graces
To come near. [*Exit Gent.*] What can be
 their business
With me, a poor weak woman, fall'n from
 favor ? 20
I do not like their coming. Now I think on't,
They should be good men ; their affairs as
 righteous :
But all hoods make not monks.

Enter the two Cardinals, WOLSEY *and* CAM-
    PEIUS.

 Wol. Peace to your highness !
 Q. Kath. Your graces find me here part of
 a housewife,
I would be all, against the worst may happen.
What are your pleasures with me, reverend
 lords ?
 Wol. May it please you noble madam, to
 withdraw
Into your private chamber, we shall give you
The full cause of our coming.
 Q. Kath. Speak it here :
There's nothing I have done yet, o' my con-
 science, 30
Deserves a corner : would all other women
Could speak this with as free a soul as I do !
My lords, I care not, so much I am happy

Above a number, if my actions
Were tried by every tongue, every eye saw
 'em,
Envy and base opinion set against 'em,
I know my life so even. If your business
Seek me out, and that way I am wife in,
Out with it boldly : truth loves open dealing.
 Wol. Tanta est erga te mentis integritas,
regina serenissima,— 41
 Q. Kath. O, good my lord, no Latin ;
I am not such a truant since my coming,
As not to know the language I have lived in :
A strange tongue makes my cause more
 strange, suspicious ;
Pray, speak in English : here are some will
 thank you,
If you speak truth, for their poor mistress'
 sake ;
Believe me, she has had much wrong : lord
 cardinal,
The willing'st sin I ever yet committed
May be absolved in English.
 Wol. Noble lady, 50
I am sorry my integrity should breed,
And service to his majesty and you,
So deep suspicion, where all faith was meant.
We come not by the way of accusation,
To taint that honor every good tongue blesses,
Nor to betray you any way to sorrow,
You have too much, good lady ; but to know
How you stand minded in the weighty dif-
 ference
Between the king and you ; and to deliver,
Like free and honest men, our just opinions
And comforts to your cause. 61
 Cam. Most honor'd madam,
My Lord of York, out of his noble nature,
Zeal and obedience he still bore your grace,
Forgetting, like a good man your late censure
Both of his truth and him, which was too far,
Offers, as I do, in a sign of peace,
His service and his counsel.
 Q. Kath. [*Aside*] To betray me.—
My lords, I thank you both for your good
 wills ;
Ye speak like honest men ; pray God, ye
 prove so !
But how to make ye suddenly an answer, 70
In such a point of weight, so near mine
 honor,—
More near my life, I fear,—with my weak
 wit,
And to such men of gravity and learning,
In truth, I know not. I was set at work
Among my maids : full little, God knows,
 looking
Either for such men or such business.
For her sake that I have been,—for I feel
The last fit of my greatness,—good your
 graces,
Let me have time and counsel for my cause :
Alas, I am a woman, friendless, hopeless ! 80
 Wol. Madam, you wrong the king's love
 with these fears :
Your hopes and friends are infinite.
 Q. Kath. In England
But little for my profit : can you think, lords,
That any Englishman dare give me counsel ?
Or be a known friend, 'gainst his highness'
 pleasure,
Though he be grown so desperate to be honest,
And live a subject ? Nay, forsooth, my friends,

They that must weigh out my afflictions,
They that my trust must grow to, live not
    here :
They are, as all my other comforts, far hence
In mine own country, lords.   91
  Cam.   I would your grace
Would leave your griefs, and take my counsel.
  Q. Kath.   How, sir ?
  Cam.   Put your main cause into the king's
    protection ;
He's loving and most gracious : 'twill be much
Both for your honor better and your cause ;
For if the trial of the law o'ertake ye,
You'll part away disgraced.
  Wol.   He tells you rightly.
  Q. Kath. Ye tell me what ye wish for both,
    —my ruin :
Is this your Christian counsel ? out upon ye !
Heaven is above all yet ; there sits a judge
That no king can corrupt.   101
  Cam.   Your rage mistakes us.
  Q. Kath. The more shame for ye : holy
    men I thought ye,
Upon my soul, two reverend cardinal virtues ;
But cardinal sins and hollow hearts I fear ye :
Mend 'em, for shame, my lords. Is this your
    comfort ?
The cordial that ye bring a wretched lady,
A woman lost among ye, laugh'd at, scorn'd ?
I will not wish ye half my miseries ;
I have more charity : but say, I warn'd ye ;
Take heed, for heaven's sake, take heed, lest
    at once   110
The burthen of my sorrows fall upon ye.
  Wol. Madam, this is a mere distraction ;
You turn the good we offer into envy.
  Q. Kath. Ye turn me into nothing : woe
    upon ye
And all such false professors ! would you have
    me—
If you have any justice, any pity ;
If ye be any thing but churchmen's habits—
Put my sick cause into his hands that hates
    me ?
Alas, has banish'd me his bed already,
His love, too long ago ! I am old, my lords, 120
And all the fellowship I hold now with him
Is only my obedience. What can happen
To me above this wretchedness ? all your
    studies
Make me a curse like this.
  Cam.   Your fears are worse.
  Q. Kath. Have I lived thus long—let me
    speak myself,
Since virtue finds no friends—a wife, a true
    one ?
A woman, I dare say without vain-glory,
Never yet branded with suspicion ?
Have I with all my full affections
Still met the king ? loved him next heaven ?
    obey'd him ?   130
Been, out of fondness, superstitious to him ?
Almost forgot my prayers to content him ?
And am I thus rewarded ? 'tis not well, lords.
Bring me a constant woman to her husband,
One that ne'er dream'd a joy beyond his
    pleasure ;
And to that woman, when she has done most,
Yet will I add an honor, a great patience.
  Wol. Madam, you wander from the good
    we aim at.
  Q. Kath. My lord, I dare not make myself
    so guilty,

To give up willingly that noble title   140
Your master wed me to : nothing but death
Shall e'er divorce my dignities.
  Wol.   Pray, hear me.
  Q. Kath. Would I had never trod this
    English earth,
Or felt the flatteries that grow upon it !
Ye have angels' faces, but heaven knows your
    hearts.
What will become of me now, wretched lady !
I am the most unhappy woman living.
Alas, poor wenches, where are now your for-
    tunes !
Shipwreck'd upon a kingdom, where no pity,
No friend, no hope ; no kindred weep for me ;
Almost no grave allow'd me : like the lily,
That once was mistress of the field and flour-
    ish'd,
I'll hang my head and perish.
  Wol.   If your grace
Could but be brought to know our ends are
    honest,
You'ld feel more comfort : why should we,
    good lady,
Upon what cause, wrong you ? alas, our
    places,
The way of our profession is against it :
We are to cure such sorrows, not to sow 'em.
For goodness' sake, consider what you do ;
How you may hurt yourself, ay, utterly   160
Grow from the king's acquaintance, by this
    carriage.
The hearts of princes kiss obedience,
So much they love it ; but to stubborn spirits
They swell, and grow as terrible as storms.
I know you have a gentle, noble temper,
A soul as even as a calm : pray, think us
Those we profess, peace-makers, friends, and
    servants.
  Cam. Madam, you'll find it so. You wrong
    your virtues
With these weak women's fears : a noble
    spirit,
As yours was put into you, ever casts   170
Such doubts, as false coin, from it. The king
loves you ;
Beware you lose it not : for us, if you please
To trust us in your business, we are ready
To use our utmost studies in your service.
  Q. Kath. Do what ye will, my lords : and,
    pray, forgive me,
If I have used myself unmannerly ;
You know I am a woman, lacking wit
To make a seemly answer to such persons.
Pray, do my service to his majesty :
He has my heart yet ; and shall have my
    prayers   180
While I shall have my life. Come, reverend
    fathers,
Bestow your counsels on me : she now begs,
That little thought, when she set footing here,
She should have bought her dignities so dear.
    [*Exeunt.*

Scene II.   *Ante-chamber to the* King's
    apartment.

Enter the Duke of Norfolk, *the* Duke of
  Suffolk, *the* Earl of Surrey, *and the*
  Lord Chamberlain.

  Nor. If you will now unite in your com-
    plaints,
And force them with a constancy, the cardinal

Cannot stand under them : if you omit
The offer of this time, I cannot promise
But that you shall sustain moe new disgraces,
With these you bear already.
 Sur.   I am joyful
To meet the least occasion that may give me
Remembrance of my father-in-law, the duke,
To be revenged on him.
 Suf.   Which of the peers
Have uncontemn'd gone by him, or at least 10
Strangely neglected ? when did he regard
The stamp of nobleness in any person
Out of himself ?
 Cham. My lords, you speak your pleasures :
What he deserves of you and me I know ;
What we can do to him, though now the time
Gives way to us, I much fear. If you cannot
Bar his access to the king, never attempt
Any thing on him ; for he hath a witchcraft
Over the king in's tongue.
 Nor.   O, fear him not ;
His spell in that is out : the king hath found
Matter against him that for ever mars 21
The honey of his language. No, he's settled,
Not to come off, in his displeasure.
 Sur.   Sir,
I should be glad to hear such news as this
Once every hour.
 Nor. Believe it, this is true :
In the divorce his contrary proceedings
Are all unfolded ; wherein he appears
As I would wish mine enemy.
 Sur.   How came
His practices to light ?
 Suf.   Most strangely.
 Sur.   O, how, how ?
 Suf. The cardinal's letters to the pope miscarried, 30
And came to the eye o' the king : wherein
  was read,
How that the cardinal did entreat his holiness
To stay the judgment o' the divorce ; for if
It did take place, ' I do,' quoth he, ' perceive
My king is tangled in affection to
A creature of the queen's, Lady Anne Bullen.'
 Sur. Has the king this ?
 Suf.   Believe it.
 Sur.   Will this work ?
 Cham. The king in this perceives him, how
  he coasts
And hedges his own way. But in this point
All his tricks founder, and he brings his physic
After his patient's death : the king already 41
Hath married the fair lady.
 Sur.   Would he had !
 Suf. May you be happy in your wish, my
  lord !
For, I profess, you have it.
 Sur.   Now, all my joy
Trace the conjunction !
 Suf. My amen to't !
 Nor.   All men's !
 Suf. There's order given for her coronation :
Marry, this is yet but young, and may be left
To some ears unrecounted. But, my lords,
She is a gallant creature, and complete
In mind and feature : I persuade me, from her
Will fall some blessing to this land, which
  shall 51
In it be memorized.

 Sur.   But, will the king
Digest this letter of the cardinal's ?
The Lord forbid !
 Nor.   Marry, amen !
 Suf.   No, no ;
There be moe wasps that buzz about his nose
Will make this sting the sooner. Cardinal
  Campeius
Is stol'n away to Rome ; hath ta'en no leave ;
Has left the cause o' the king unhandled ; and
Is posted, as the agent of our cardinal,
To second all his plot. I do assure you 60
The king cried Ha ! at this.
 Cham. Now, God incense him,
And let him cry Ha ! louder !
 Nor.   But, my lord,
When returns Cranmer ?
 Suf. He is return'd in his opinions ; which
Have satisfied the king for his divorce,
Together with all famous colleges
Almost in Christendom : shortly, I believe,
His second marriage shall be publish'd, and
Her coronation. Katharine no more
Shall be call'd queen, but princess dowager
And widow to Prince Arthur. 71
 Nor. This same Cranmer's
A worthy fellow, and hath ta'en much pain
In the king's business.
 Suf. He has ; and we shall see him
For it an archbishop.
 Nor.   So I hear.
 Suf.   'Tis so.
The cardinal !

   Enter WOLSEY *and* CROMWELL.

 Nor. Observe, observe, he's moody.
 Wol. The packet, Cromwell.
Gave't you the king ?
 Crom. To his own hand, in's bedchamber.
 Wol. Look'd he o' the inside of the paper ?
 Crom.   Presently
He did unseal them : and the first he view'd,
He did it with a serious mind ; a heed 80
Was in his countenance. You he bade
Attend him here this morning.
 Wol.   Is he ready
To come abroad ?
 Crom. I think, by this he is.
 Wol. Leave me awhile. [*Exit Cromwell.*
[*Aside*] It shall be to the Duchess of Alençon,
The French king's sister : he shall marry her.
Anne Bullen ! No ; I'll no Anne Bullens for
  him :
There's more in't than fair visage. Bullen !
No, we'll no Bullens. Speedily I wish
To hear from Rome. The Marchioness of Pembroke ! 90
 Nor. He's discontented.
 Suf. May be, he hears the king
Does whet his anger to him.
 Sur.   Sharp enough,
Lord, for thy justice !
 Wol. [*Aside*] The late queen's gentlewoman, a knight's daughter,
To be her mistress' mistress ! the queen's
  queen !
This candle burns not clear : 'tis I must snuff
  it ;
Then out it goes. What though I know her
  virtuous
And well deserving ? yet I know her for
A spleeny Lutheran ; and not wholesome to

Our cause, that she should lie i' the bosom of
Our hard-ruled king. Again, there is sprung
   up   101
An heretic, an arch one, Cranmer ; one
Hath crawl'd into the favor of the king,
And is his oracle.
   Nor.   He is vex'd at something.
   Sur. I would 'twere something that would
      fret the string,
The master-cord on's heart !

Enter the King, *reading of a schedule, and*
      Lovell.

   Suf.   The king, the king !
   King. What piles of wealth hath he accu-
      mulated
To his own portion ! and what expense by the
      hour
Seems to flow from him ! How, i' the name
      of thrift,
Does he rake this together ! Now, my lords,
Saw you the cardinal ?   111
   Nor.   My lord, we have
Stood here observing him : some strange com-
      motion
Is in his brain : he bites his lip, and starts ;
Stops on a sudden, looks upon the ground,
Then lays his finger on his temple, straight
Springs out into fast gait ; then stops again,
Strikes his breast hard, and anon he casts
His eye against the moon : in most strange
      postures
We have seen him set himself.
   King.   It may well be ;
There is a mutiny in's mind. This morning
Papers of state he sent me to peruse,   121
As I required : and wot you what I found
There,—on my conscience, put unwittingly ?
Forsooth, an inventory, thus importing ;
The several parcels of his plate, his treasure,
Rich stuffs, and ornaments of household ;
      which
I find at such proud rate, that it out-speaks
Possession of a subject.
   Nor.   It's heaven's will :
Some spirit put this paper in the packet,
To bless your eye withal.
   King.   If we did think 130
His contemplation were above the earth,
And fix'd on spiritual object, he should still
Dwell in his musings : but I am afraid
His thinkings are below the moon, not worth
His serious considering.
   [*King takes his seat ; whispers Lovell, who
      goes to the Cardinal.*
   Wol.   Heaven forgive me !
Ever God bless your highness !
   King.   Good my lord,
You are full of heavenly stuff, and bear the
      inventory
Of your best graces in your mind ; the which
You were now running o'er : you have scarce
      time
To steal from spiritual leisure a brief span 140
To keep your earthly audit : sure, in that
I deem you an ill husband, and am glad
To have you therein my companion.
   Wol.   Sir,
For holy offices I have a time ; a time
To think upon the part of business which
I bear i' the state ; and nature does require
Her times of preservation, which perforce
I, her frail son, amongst my brethren mortal,

Must give my tendence to.
   King.   You have said well.
   Wol. And ever may your highness yoke
      together,   150
As I will lend you cause, my doing well
With my well saying !
   King.   'Tis well said again ;
And 'tis a kind of good deed to say well :
And yet words are no deeds. My father loved
      you :
He said he did ; and with his deed did crown
His word upon you. Since I had my office,
I have kept you next my heart ; have not alone
Employ'd you where high profits might come
      home,
But pared my present havings, to bestow
My bounties upon you.
   Wol. [*Aside*] What should this mean ? 160
   Sur. [*Aside*] The Lord increase this busi-
      ness !
   King.   Have I not made you,
The prime man of the state ? I pray you, tell
      me,
If what I now pronounce you have found true :
And, if you may confess it, say withal,
If you are bound to us or no. What say you ?
   Wol. My sovereign, I confess your royal
      graces,
Shower'd on me daily, have been more than
      could
My studied purposes requite ; which went
Beyond all man's endeavors : my endeavors
Have ever come too short of my desires, 170
Yet filed with my abilities : mine own ends
Have been mine so that evermore they pointed
To the good of your most sacred person and
The profit of the state. For your great graces
Heap'd upon me, poor undeserver, I
Can nothing render but allegiant thanks,
My prayers to heaven for you, my loyalty,
Which ever has and ever shall be growing,
Till death, that winter, kill it.
   King.   Fairly answer'd ;
A loyal and obedient subject is   180
Therein illustrated : the honor of it
Does pay the act of it ; as, i' the contrary,
The foulness is the punishment. I presume
That, as my hand has open'd bounty to you,
My heart dropp'd love, my power rain'd
      honor, more
On you than any ; so your hand and heart,
Your brain, and every function of your power,
Should, notwithstanding that your bond of
      duty,
As 'twere in love's particular, be more
To me, your friend, than any.
   Wol.   I do profess 190
That for your highness' good I ever labor'd
More than mine own ; that am, have, and
      will be—
Though all the world should crack their duty
      to you,
And throw it from their soul ; though perils
      did
Abound, as thick as thought could make 'em,
      and
Appear in forms more horrid,—yet my duty,
As doth a rock against the chiding flood,
Should the approach of this wild river break,
And stand unshaken yours.
   King.   'Tis nobly spoken :
Take notice, lords, he has a loyal breast, 200

For you have seen him open't. Read o'er
this ;   [*Giving him papers.*
And after, this : and then to breakfast with
What appetite you have.

     [*Exit King, frowning upon Cardinal
     Wolsey : the Nobles throng
     after him, smiling and whisper-
     ing.*

Wol.   What should this mean ?
What sudden anger's this ? how have I reap'd
it ?
He parted frowning from me, as if ruin
Leap'd from his eyes : so looks the chafed lion
Upon the daring huntsman that has gall'd
him ;
Then makes him nothing. I must read this
paper ;
I fear, the story of his anger. 'Tis so ;
This paper has undone me : 'tis the account
Of all that world of wealth I have drawn to-
gether   211
For mine own ends ; indeed, to gain the pope-
dom,
And fee my friends in Rome. O negligence !
Fit for a fool to fall by : what cross devil
Made me put this main secret in the packet
I sent the king ? Is there no way to cure this ?
No new device to beat this from his brains ?
I know 'twill stir him strongly ; yet I know
A way, if it take right, in spite of fortune
Will bring me off again. What's this ? ' To
the Pope ! '   220
The letter, as I live, with all the business
I writ to's holiness. Nay then, farewell !
I have touch'd the highest point of all my
greatness ;
And, from that full meridian of my glory,
I haste now to my setting : I shall fall
Like a bright exhalation in the evening,
And no man see me more.

Re-enter to WOLSEY, *the* DUKES OF NORFOLK
and SUFFOLK, *the* EARL OF SURREY, *and the*
LORD CHAMBERLAIN.

Nor.   Hear the king's pleasure, cardinal :
who commands you
To render up the great seal presently
Into our hands ; and to confine yourself   230
To Asher House, my Lord of Winchester's,
Till you hear further from his highness.

Wol.   Stay :
Where's your commission, lords ? words can-
not carry
Authority so weighty.

Suf.   Who dare cross 'em,
Bearing the king's will from his mouth expressly ?

Wol.   Till I find more than will or words to
do it,
I mean your malice, know, officious lords,
I dare and must deny it. Now I feel
Of what coarse metal ye are moulded, envy :
How eagerly ye follow my disgraces,   240
As if it fed ye ! and how sleek and wanton
Ye appear in every thing may bring my ruin !
Follow your envious courses, men of malice ;
You have Christian warrant for 'em, and, no
doubt,
In time will find their fit rewards. That seal,
You ask with such a violence, the king,
Mine and your master, with his own hand
gave me ;
Bade me enjoy it, with the place and honors,

During my life ; and, to confirm his goodness,
Tied it by letters-patents : now, who'll take it ?

Sur.   The king, that gave it.

Wol.   It must be himself, then. 251

Sur.   Thou art a proud traitor, priest.

Wol.   Proud lord, thou liest :
Within these forty hours Surrey durst better
Have burnt that tongue than said so.

Sur.   Thy ambition,
Thou scarlet sin, robb'd this bewailing land
Of noble Buckingham, my father-in-law :
The heads of all thy brother cardinals,
With thee and all thy best parts bound to-
gether,
Weigh'd not a hair of his. Plague of your
policy !
You sent me deputy for Ireland ;   260
Far from his succor, from the king, from all
That might have mercy on the fault thou
gavest him ;
Whilst your great goodness, out of holy pity,
Absolved him with an axe.

Wol.   This, and all else
This talking lord can lay upon my credit,
I answer is most false. The duke by law
Found his deserts : how innocent I was
From any private malice in his end,
His noble jury and foul cause can witness.
If I loved many words, lord, I should tell you
You have as little honesty as honor,   271
That in the way of loyalty and truth
Toward the king, my ever royal master,
Dare mate a sounder man than Surrey can be,
And all that love his follies.

Sur.   By my soul,
Your long coat, priest, protects you ; thou
shouldst feel
My sword i' the life-blood of thee else. My
lords,
Can ye endure to hear this arrogance ?
And from this fellow ? If we live thus tamely,
To be thus jaded by a piece of scarlet,   280
Farewell nobility ; let his grace go forward,
And dare us with his cap like larks.

Wol.   All goodness
Is poison to thy stomach.

Sur.   Yes, that goodness
Of gleaning all the land's wealth into one,
Into your own hands, cardinal, by extortion ;
The goodness of your intercepted packets
You writ to the pope against the king : your
goodness,
Since you provoke me, shall be most notorious.
My Lord of Norfolk, as you are truly noble,
As you respect the common good, the state
Of our despised nobility, our issues,   291
Who, if he live, will scarce be gentlemen,
Produce the grand sum of his sins, the articles
Collected from his life. I'll startle you
Worse than the scaring bell, when the brown
wench
Lay kissing in your arms, lord cardinal.

Wol.   How much, methinks, I could despise
this man,
But that I am bound in charity against it !

Nor.   Those articles, my lord, are in the
king's hand :
But, thus much, they are foul ones.

Wol.   So much fairer 300
And spotless shall mine innocence arise,
When the king knows my truth.

Sur.   This cannot save you :
I thank my memory, I yet remember

Some of these articles ; and out they shall.
Now, if you can blush and cry ' guilty,' cardi-
  nal,
You'll show a little honesty.
Wol.   Speak on, sir ;
I dare your worst objections : if I blush,
It is to see a nobleman want manners.
  Sur. I had rather want those than my
  head. Have at you !
First, that, without the king's assent or knowl-
  edge,   310
You wrought to be a legate ; by which power
You maim'd the jurisdiction of all bishops.
  Nor. Then, that in all you writ to Rome,
  or else
To foreign princes, ' Ego et Rex meus '
Was still inscribed ; in which you brought the
  king
To be your servant.
  Suf.   Then that, without the knowledge
Either of king or council, when you went
Ambassador to the emperor, you made bold
To carry into Flanders the great seal.
  Sur. Item, you sent a large commission
To Gregory de Cassado, to conclude,   321
Without the king's will or the state's allowance,
A league between his highness and Ferrara.
  Suf. That, out of mere ambition, you have
  caused
Your holy hat to be stamp'd on the king's coin.
  Sur. Then that you have sent innumerable
  substance—
By what means got, I leave to your own con-
  science—
To furnish Rome, and to prepare the ways
You have for dignities ; to the mere undoing
Of all the kingdom. Many more there are ;
Which, since they are of you, and odious, 331
I will not taint my mouth with.
  Cham.   O my lord,
Press not a falling man too far ! 'tis virtue :
His faults lie open to the laws ; let them,
Not you, correct him. My heart weeps to see
  him
So little of his great self.
  Sur.   I forgive him.
  Suf. Lord cardinal, the king's further
  pleasure is,
Because all those things you have done of late,
By your power legatine, within this kingdom,
Fall into the compass of a præmunire,   340
That therefore such a writ be sued against
  you ;
To forfeit all your goods, lands, tenements,
Chattels, and whatsoever, and to be
Out of the king's protection. This is my
  charge.
  Nor. And so we'll leave you to your medi-
  tations
How to live better. For your stubborn answer
About the giving back the great seal to us,
The king shall know it, and, no doubt, shall
  thank you.
So fare you well, my little good lord cardinal.
               [*Exeunt all but Wolsey.*
  Wol. So farewell to the little good you
  bear me.   350
Farewell ! a long farewell, to all my greatness !
This is the state of man : to-day he puts forth
The tender leaves of hopes ; to-morrow blos-
  soms,
And bears his blushing honors thick upon
  him ;

The third day comes a frost, a killing frost,
And, when he thinks, good easy man, full
  surely
His greatness is a-ripening, nips his root,
And then he falls, as I do. I have ventured,
Like little wanton boys that swim on bladders,
This many summers in a sea of glory,   360
But far beyond my depth : my high-blown
  pride
At length broke under me and now has left me,
Weary and old with service, to the mercy
Of a rude stream, that must for ever hide me.
Vain pomp and glory of this world, I hate ye :
I feel my heart new open'd. O, how wretched
Is that poor man that hangs on princes'
  favors !
There is, betwixt that smile we would aspire to,
That sweet aspect of princes, and their ruin,
More pangs and fears than wars or women
  have :   370
And when he falls, he falls like Lucifer,
Never to hope again.

      Enter CROMWELL, *and stands amazed.*
            Why, how now, Cromwell !
  Crom. I have no power to speak, sir.
  Wol.   What, amazed
At my misfortunes ? can thy spirit wonder
A great man should decline ? Nay, an you
  weep,
I am fall'n indeed.
  Crom.   How does your grace ?
  Wol.   Why, well ;
Never so truly happy, my good Cromwell.
I know myself now ; and I feel within me
A peace above all earthly dignities,
A still and quiet conscience. The king has
  cured me,   380
I humbly thank his grace ; and from these
  shoulders,
These ruin'd pillars, out of pity, taken
A load would sink a navy, too much honor :
O, 'tis a burthen, Cromwell, 'tis a burthen
Too heavy for a man that hopes for heaven !
  Crom. I am glad your grace has made that
  right use of it.
  Wol. I hope I have : I am able now, me-
  thinks,
Out of a fortitude of soul I feel,
To endure more miseries and greater far
Than my weak-hearted enemies dare offer. 390
What news abroad ?
  Crom.   The heaviest and the worst
Is your displeasure with the king.
  Wol.   God bless him !
  Crom. The next is, that Sir Thomas More
  is chosen
Lord chancellor in your place.
  Wol.   That's somewhat sudden :
But he's a learned man. May he continue
Long in his highness' favor, and do justice
For truth's sake and his conscience ; that his
  bones,
When he has run his course and sleeps in
  blessings,
May have a tomb of orphans' tears wept on
  'em !
What more ?   400
  Crom. That Cranmer is return'd with wel-
  come,
Install'd lord archbishop of Canterbury.
  Wol. That's news indeed.

Crom.   Last, that the Lady Anne,
Whom the king hath in secrecy long married,
This day was view'd in open as his queen,
Going to chapel ; and the voice is now
Only about her coronation.
  Wol.   There was the weight that pull'd me
      down. O Cromwell,
The king has gone beyond me : all my glories
In that one woman I have lost for ever :   410
No sun shall ever usher forth mine honors,
Or gild again the noble troops that waited
Upon my smiles. Go, get thee from me, Crom-
      well ;
I am a poor fall'n man, unworthy now
To be thy lord and master : seek the king ;
That sun, I pray, may never set ! I have told
      him
What and how true thou art : he will advance
      thee ;
Some little memory of me will stir him—
I know his noble nature—not to let
Thy hopeful service perish too : good Crom-
      well,   420
Neglect him not ; make use now, and provide
For thine own future safety.
  Crom.   O my lord,
Must I, then, leave you ? must I needs forego
So good, so noble and so true a master ?
Bear witness, all that have not hearts of iron,
With what a sorrow Cromwell leaves his lord.
The king shall have my service : but my
      prayers
For ever and for ever shall be yours.
  Wol.   Cromwell, I did not think to shed a
      tear   429
In all my miseries ; but thou hast forced me,
Out of thy honest truth, to play the woman.
Let's dry our eyes : and thus far hear me,
      Cromwell ;
And, when I am forgotten, as I shall be,
And sleep in dull cold marble, where no men-
      tion
Of me more must be heard of, say, I taught
      thee,
Say, Wolsey, that once trod the ways of glory,
And sounded all the depths and shoals of
      honor,
Found thee a way, out of his wreck, to rise in ;
A sure and safe one, though thy master miss'd
      it.   439
Mark but my fall, and that that ruin'd me.
Cromwell, I charge thee, fling away ambition :
By that sin fell the angels ; how can man,
      then,
The image of his Maker, hope to win by it ?
Love thyself last : cherish those hearts that
      hate thee ;
Corruption wins not more than honesty.
Still in thy right hand carry gentle peace,
To silence envious tongues. Be just, and fear
      not :
Let all the ends thou aim'st at be thy country's,
Thy God's, and truth's ; then if thou fall'st, O
      Cromwell,
Thou fall'st a blessed martyr ! Serve the king ;
And,—prithee, lead me in :   451
There take an inventory of all I have,
To the last penny ; 'tis the king's : my robe,
And my integrity to heaven, is all
I dare now call mine own. O Cromwell, Crom-
      well !
Had I but served my God with half the zeal
I served my king, he would not in mine age

Have left me naked to mine enemies.
  Crom.   Good sir, have patience.
  Wol.   So I have. Farewell
The hopes of court ! my hopes in heaven do
      dwell.   [*Exeunt.* 460

ACT IV.

SCENE I.   *A street in Westminster.*

Enter two Gentlemen, *meeting one another.*

  First Gent.   You're well met once again.
  Sec. Gent.   So are you.
  First Gent.   You come to take your stand
      here, and behold
The Lady Anne pass from her coronation ?
  Sec. Gent.   'Tis all my business. At our
      last encounter,
The Duke of Buckingham came from his trial.
  First Gent.   'Tis very true : but that time
      offer'd sorrow ;
This, general joy.
  Sec. Gent.   'Tis well : the citizens,
I am sure, have shown at full their royal
      minds—
As, let 'em have their rights, they are ever for-
      ward—
In celebration of this day with shows,   10
Pageants and sights of honor.
  First Gent.   Never greater,
Nor, I'll assure you, better taken, sir.
  Sec. Gent.   May I be bold to ask what that
      contains,
That paper in your hand ?
  First Gent.   Yes ; 'tis the list
Of those that claim their offices this day
By custom of the coronation.
The Duke of Suffolk is the first, and claims
To be high-steward ; next, the Duke of Nor-
      folk,
He to be earl marshal : you may read the rest.
  Sec. Gent.   I thank you, sir : had I not
      known those customs,   20
I should have been beholding to your paper.
But, I beseech you, what's become of Katha-
      rine,
The princess dowager ? how goes her busi-
      ness ?
  First Gent.   That I can tell you too. The
      Archbishop
Of Canterbury, accompanied with other
Learned and reverend fathers of his order,
Held a late court at Dunstable, six miles off
From Ampthill where the princess lay ; to
      which
She was often cited by them, but appear'd
      not :
And, to be short, for not appearance and 30
The king's late scruple, by the main assent
Of all these learned men she was divorced,
And the late marriage made of none effect :
Since which she was removed to Kimbolton,
Where she remains now sick.
  Sec. Gent.   Alas, good lady !
                                    [*Trumpets.*
The trumpets sound : stand close, the queen
      is coming.   [*Hautboys.*

THE ORDER OF THE CORONATION.

1. *A lively flourish of Trumpets.*
2. *Then, two Judges.*

3. Lord Chancellor, *with the purse and mace before him.*
4. Choristers, *singing.* [*Music.*
5. Mayor of London, *bearing the mace. Then Garter, in his coat of arms, and on his head a gilt copper crown.*
6. Marquess DORSET, *bearing a sceptre of gold, on his head a demi-coronal of gold. With him, the* EARL of SURREY, *bearing the rod of silver with the dove, crowned with an earl's coronet. Collars of SS.*
7. Duke of SUFFOLK, *in his robe of estate, his coronet on his head, bearing a long white wand, as high-steward. With him, the* Duke of NORFOLK, *with the rod of marshalship, a coronet on his head. Collars of SS.*
8. *A canopy borne by four of the* Cinque-ports ; *under it, the* Queen *in her robe ; in her hair richly adorned with pearl, crowned. On each side her, the* Bishops of London *and* Winchester.
9. *The old* Duchess of NORFOLK, *in a coronal of gold, wrought with flowers, bearing the* Queen's *train.*
10. *Certain* Ladies *or* Countesses, *with plain circlets of gold without flowers.*
They pass over the stage in order and state.

Sec. Gent. A royal train, believe me.
These I know :
Who's that that bears the sceptre ?
First Gent. Marquess Dorset :
And that the Earl of Surrey, with the rod.
Sec. Gent. A bold brave gentleman. That should be 40
The Duke of Suffolk ?
First Gent. 'Tis the same : high-steward.
Sec. Gent. And that my Lord of Norfolk ?
First Gent. Yes.
Sec. Gent. Heaven bless thee !
[*Looking on the Queen.*
Thou hast the sweetest face I ever look'd on.
Sir, as I have a soul, she is an angel ;
Our king has all the Indies in his arms,
And more and richer, when he strains that lady :
I cannot blame his conscience.
First Gent. They that bear
The cloth of honor over her, are four barons
Of the Cinque-ports.
Sec. Gent. Those men are happy ; and so are all are near her. 50
I take it, she that carries up the train
Is that old noble lady, Duchess of Norfolk.
First Gent. It is ; and all the rest are count-esses.
Sec. Gent. Their coronets say so. These are stars indeed ;
And sometimes falling ones.
First Gent. No more of that.
[*Exit procession, and then a great flourish of trumpets.*

Enter a third Gentleman.

First Gent. God save you, sir ! where have you been broiling ?
Third Gent. Among the crowd i' the Ab-bey ; where a finger
Could not be wedged in more : I am stifled
With the mere rankness of their joy.

Sec. Gent. You saw
The ceremony ?
Third Gent. That I did.
First Gent. How was it ? 60
Third Gent. Well worth the seeing.
Sec. Gent. Good sir, speak it to us.
Third Gent. As well as I am able. The rich stream
Of lords and ladies, having brought the queen
To a prepared place in the choir, fell off
A distance from her ; while her grace sat down
To rest awhile, some half an hour or so,
In a rich chair of state, opposing freely
The beauty of her person to the people.
Believe me, sir, she is the goodliest woman
That ever lay by man : which when the peo-ple 70
Had the full view of, such a noise arose
As the shrouds make at sea in a stiff tempest,
As loud, and to as many tunes : hats, cloaks,—
Doublets, I think,—flew up ; and had their faces
Been loose, this day they had been lost. Such joy
I never saw before. Great-bellied women,
That had not half a week to go, like rams
In the old time of war, would shake the press,
And make 'em reel before 'em. No man living
Could say 'This is my wife' there ; all were woven
So strangely in one piece.
Sec. Gent. But, what follow'd ? 81
Third Gent. At length her grace rose, and with modest paces
Came to the altar ; where she kneel'd, and saint-like
Cast her fair eyes to heaven and pray'd de-voutly.
Then rose again and bow'd her to the people :
When by the Archbishop of Canterbury
She had all the royal makings of a queen ;
As holy oil, Edward Confessor's crown,
The rod, and bird of peace, and all such em-blems
Laid nobly on her : which perform'd, the choir, 90
With all the choicest music of the kingdom,
Together sung 'Te Deum.' So she parted,
And with the same full state paced back again
To York-place, where the feast is held.
First Gent. Sir,
You must no more call it York-place, that's past ;
For, since the cardinal fell, that title's lost :
'Tis now the king's, and call'd Whitehall.
Third Gent. I know it ;
But 'tis so lately alter'd, that the old name
Is fresh about me.
Sec. Gent. What two reverend bishops
Were those that went on each side of the queen ?
Third Gent. Stokesly and Gardiner ; the one of Winchester, 101
Newly preferr'd from the king's secretary,
The other, London.
Sec. Gent. He of Winchester
Is held no great good lover of the arch-bishop's,
The virtuous Cranmer.
Third Gent. All the land knows that :
However, yet there is no great breach ; when it comes,

Cranmer will find a friend will not shrink from
him.
Sec. Gent.   Who may that be, I pray you ?
Third Gent.   Thomas Cromwell ;
A man in much esteem with the king, and
truly
A worthy friend. The king has made him mas-
ter   110
O' the jewel house,
And one, already, of the privy council.
Sec. Gent. He will deserve more.
Third Gent.   Yes, without all doubt.
Come, gentlemen, ye shall go my way, which
Is to the court, and there ye shall be my
guests :
Something I can command. As I walk thither,
I'll tell ye more.
Both. You may command us, sir. [*Exeunt.*

SCENE II. *Kimbolton.*

Enter KATHARINE, *Dowager, sick ; led between*
GRIFFITH, *her gentleman usher, and* PA-
TIENCE, *her woman.*

Grif. How does your grace ?
Kath.   O Griffith, sick to death !
My legs, like loaden branches, bow to the
earth,
Willing to leave their burthen. Reach a chair :
So ; now, methinks, I feel a little ease.
Didst thou not tell me, Griffith, as thou led'st
me,
That the great child of honor, Cardinal Wol-
sey,
Was dead ?
Grif. Yes, madam ; but I think your grace,
Out of the pain you suffer'd, gave no ear to't.
Kath. Prithee, good Griffith, tell me how
he died :
If well, he stepp'd before me, happily   10
For my example.
Grif.   Well, the voice goes, madam :
For after the stout Earl Northumberland
Arrested him at York, and brought him for-
ward,
As a man sorely tainted, to his answer,
He fell sick suddenly, and grew so ill
He could not sit his mule.
Kath.   Alas, poor man !
Grif. At last, with easy roads, he came to
Leicester,
Lodged in the abbey ; where the reverend
abbot,
With all his covent, honorably received him ;
To whom he gave these words, ' O, father
abbot,   20
An old man, broken with the storms of state,
Is come to lay his weary bones among ye ;
Give him a little earth for charity ! '
So went to bed ; where eagerly his sickness
Pursued him still : and, three nights after this,
About the hour of eight, which he himself
Foretold should be his last, full of repentance,
Continual meditations, tears, and sorrows,
He gave his honors to the world again,
His blessed part to heaven, and slept in peace.
Kath. So may he rest ; his faults lie gently
on him !   31
Yet thus far, Griffith, give me leave to speak
him,
And yet with charity. He was a man
Of an unbounded stomach, ever ranking
Himself with princes ; one that, by suggestion,

Tied all the kingdom : simony was fair-play ;
His own opinion was his law : i' the presence
He would say untruths ; and be ever double
Both in his words and meaning : he was never,
But where he meant to ruin, pitiful :   40
His promises were, as he then was, mighty ;
But his performance, as he is now, nothing :
Of his own body he was ill, and gave
The clergy ill example.
Grif.   Noble madam,
Men's evil manners live in brass ; their virtues
We write in water. May it please your high-
ness
To hear me speak his good now ?
Kath.   Yes, good Griffith ;
I were malicious else.
Grif.   This cardinal,
Though from an humble stock, undoubtedly
Was fashion'd to much honor from his cradle.
He was a scholar, and a ripe and good one ;
Exceeding wise, fair-spoken, and persuading :
Lofty and sour to them that loved him not ;
But to those men that sought him sweet as
summer.
And though he were unsatisfied in getting,
Which was a sin, yet in bestowing, madam,
He was most princely : ever witness for him
Those twins of learning that he raised in you,
Ipswich and Oxford ! one of which fell with
him,
Unwilling to outlive the good that did it ;   60
The other, though unfinish'd, yet so famous,
So excellent in art, and still so rising,
That Christendom shall ever speak his virtue.
His overthrow heap'd happiness upon him ;
For then, and not till then, he felt himself,
And found the blessedness of being little :
And, to add greater honors to his age
Than man could give him, he died fearing
God.
Kath. After my death I wish no other
herald,
No other speaker of my living actions,   70
To keep mine honor from corruption,
But such an honest chronicler as Griffith.
Whom I most hated living, thou hast made
me,
With thy religious truth and modesty,
Now in his ashes honor : peace be with him !
Patience, be near me still ; and set me lower :
I have not long to trouble thee. Good Grif-
fith,
Cause the musicians play me that sad note
I named my knell, whilst I sit meditating
On that celestial harmony I go to.   80
                  [*Sad and solemn music.*
Grif. She is asleep : good wench, let's sit
down quiet,
For fear we wake her : softly, gentle Patience.

*The vision. Enter, solemnly tripping one after
another, six personages, clad in white robes,
wearing on their heads garlands of bays, and
golden vizards on their faces ; branches of
bays or palm in their hands. They first con-
gee unto her, then dance ; and, at certain
changes, the first two hold a spare garland
over her head ; at which the other four
make reverent curtsies ; then the two that
held the garland deliver the same to the
other next two, who observe the same order
in their changes, and holding the garland
over her head : which done, they deliver the*

*same garland to the last two, who likewise
observe the same order : at which, as it were
by inspiration, she makes in her sleep signs
of rejoicing, and holdeth up her hands to
heaven : and so in their dancing vanish, carrying the garland with them. The music
continues.*

Kath. Spirits of peace, where are ye ? are
ye all gone,
And leave me here in wretchedness behind ye ?
Grif. Madam, we are here.
Kath.   It is not you I call for :
Saw ye none enter since I slept ?
Grif.   None, madam.
Kath. No ? Saw you not, even now, a
blessed troop
Invite me to a banquet ; whose bright faces
Cast thousand beams upon me, like the sun ?
They promised me eternal happiness ;   90
And brought me garlands, Griffith, which I
feel
I am not worthy yet to wear : I shall, as-
suredly.
Grif. I am most joyful, madam, such good
dreams
Possess your fancy.
Kath.   Bid the music leave,
They are harsh and heavy to me.
                        [*Music ceases.*
Pat.   Do you note
How much her grace is alter'd on the sudden ?
How long her face is drawn ? how pale she
looks,
And of an earthy cold ? Mark her eyes !
Grif. She is going, wench : pray, pray.
Pat.   Heaven comfort her !

        Enter a Messenger.

Mess. An't like your grace,—
Kath.   You are a saucy fellow : 100
Deserve we no more reverence ?
Grif.   You are to blame,
Knowing she will not lose her wonted great-
ness,
To use so rude behavior ; go to, kneel.
Mess. I humbly do entreat your highness'
pardon ;
My haste made me unmannerly. There is stay-
ing
A gentleman, sent from the king, to see you.
Kath. Admit him entrance, Griffith : but
this fellow
Let me ne'er see again.
                [*Exeunt Griffith and Messenger.*

Re-enter Griffith, *with* Capucius.

                If my sight fail not,
You should be lord ambassador from the em-
peror,   109
My royal nephew, and your name Capucius.
Cap. Madam, the same ; your servant.
Kath.   O, my lord,
The times and titles now are alter'd strangely
With me since first you knew me. But, I pray
you,
What is your pleasure with me ?
Cap.   Noble lady,
First mine own service to your grace ; the next,
The king's request that I would visit you ;
Who grieves much for your weakness, and by
me
Sends you his princely commendations,
And heartily entreats you take good comfort.

Kath. O my good lord, that comfort comes
too late ;   120
'Tis like a pardon after execution :
That gentle physic, given in time, had cured
me ;
But now I am past all comforts here, but
prayers.
How does his highness ?
Cap.   Madam, in good health.
Kath. So may he ever do ! and ever flour-
ish,
When I shall dwell with worms, and my poor
name
Banish'd the kingdom ! Patience, is that letter,
I caused you write, yet sent away ?
Pat.   No, madam.
                [*Giving it to Katharine.*
Kath. Sir, I most humbly pray you to de-
liver
This to my lord the king.
Cap.   Most willing, madam. 130
Kath. In which I have commended to his
goodness
The model of our chaste loves, his young
daughter ;
The dews of heaven fall thick in blessings on
her !
Beseeching him to give her virtuous breed-
ing,—
She is young, and of a noble modest nature,
I hope she will deserve well,—and a little
To love her for her mother's sake, that loved
him,
Heaven knows how dearly. My next poor
petition
Is, that his noble grace would have some pity 140
Upon my wretched women, that so long
Have follow'd both my fortunes faithfully :
Of which there is not one, I dare avow,
And now I should not lie, but will deserve
For virtue and true beauty of the soul,
For honesty and decent carriage,
A right good husband, let him be a noble
And, sure, those men are happy that shall have
'em.
The last is, for my men ; they are the poorest,
But poverty could never draw 'em from me ;
That they may have their wages duly paid 'em,
And something over to remember me by : 151
If heaven had pleased to have given me longer
life
And able means, we had not parted thus.
These are the whole contents : and, good my
lord,
By that you love the dearest in this world,
As you wish Christian peace to souls departed,
Stand these poor people's friend, and urge the
king
To do me this last right.
Cap.   By heaven, I will,
Or let me lose the fashion of a man !
Kath. I thank you, honest lord. Remember
me   160
In all humility unto his highness :
Say his long trouble now is passing
Out of this world ; tell him, in death I bless'd
him,
For so I will. Mine eyes grow dim. Farewell,
My lord. Griffith, farewell. Nay, Patience,
You must not leave me yet : I must to bed ;
Call in more women. When I am dead, good
wench,
Let me be used with honor : strew me over

With maiden flowers, that all the world may
　　know
I was a chaste wife to my grave : embalm me,
Then lay me forth : although unqueen'd, yet
　　like　　　　　　　　　　　　　　　　171
A queen, and daughter to a king, inter me.
I can no more. [*Exeunt, leading Katharine.*

ACT V.

SCENE I. *London. A gallery in the palace.*

Enter GARDINER, *Bishop of Winchester, a
Page with a torch before him, met by* SIR
THOMAS LOVELL.

Gar. It's one o'clock, boy, is't not ?
Boy. 　　　　　　　　　　　It hath struck.
Gar. These should be hours for necessities,
Not for delights ; times to repair our nature
With comforting repose, and not for us
To waste these times. Good hour of night, Sir
　　Thomas !
Whither so late ?
Lov. Came you from the king, my lord ?
Gar. I did, Sir Thomas : and left him at
　　primero
With the Duke of Suffolk.
Lov. 　　　　　　　I must to him too,
Before he go to bed. I'll take my leave.
Gar. Not yet, Sir Thomas Lovell. What's
　　the matter ?　　　　　　　　　　　10
It seems you are in haste : an if there be
No great offence belongs to't, give your friend
Some touch of your late business : affairs, that
　　walk,
As they say spirits do, at midnight, have
In them a wilder nature than the business
That seeks dispatch by day.
Lov. 　　　　　　My lord, I love you ;
And durst commend a secret to your ear
Much weightier than this work. The queen's
　　in labor,
They say, in great extremity ; and fear'd
She'll with the labor end.
Gar. 　　　　　The fruit she goes with 20
I pray for heartily, that it may find
Good time, and live : but for the stock, Sir
　　Thomas,
I wish it grubb'd up now.
Lov. 　　　　　　Methinks I could
Cry the amen ; and yet my conscience says
She's a good creature, and, sweet lady, does
Deserve our better wishes.
Gar. 　　　　　But, sir, sir,
Hear me, Sir Thomas : you're a gentleman
Of mine own way ; I know you wise, religious ;
And, let me tell you, it will ne'er be well,
'Twill not, Sir Thomas Lovell, take't of me,
Till Cranmer, Cromwell, her two hands, and
　　she,　　　　　　　　　　　　　31
Sleep in their graves.
Lov. 　　　　Now, sir, you speak of two
The most remark'd i' the kingdom. As for
　　Cromwell,
Beside that of the jewel house, is made master
O' the rolls, and the king's secretary ; further,
　　sir,
Stands in the gap and trade of moe prefer-
　　ments,
With which the time will load him. The arch-
　　bishop

Is the king's hand and tongue ; and who dare
　　speak
One syllable against him ?
Gar. 　　　　　Yes, yes, Sir Thomas,
There are that dare ; and I myself have ven-
　　tured　　　　　　　　　　　　40
To speak my mind of him : and indeed this
　　day,
Sir, I may tell it you, I think I have
Incensed the lords o' the council, that he is,
For so I know he is, they know he is,
A most arch heretic, a pestilence
That does infect the land : with which they
　　moved
Have broken with the king ; who hath so far
Given ear to our complaint, of his great grace
And princely care foreseeing those fell mis-
　　chiefs
Our reasons laid before him, hath commanded
To-morrow morning to the council-board　51
He be convented. He's a rank weed, Sir
　　Thomas,
And we must root him out. From your affairs
I hinder you too long : good night, Sir Thomas.
Lov. Many good nights, my lord : I rest
　　your servant.
　　　　　　　[*Exeunt Gardiner and Page.*

Enter the KING *and* SUFFOLK.

King. Charles, I will play no more to-
　　night ;
My mind's not on't ; you are too hard for me.
Suf. Sir, I did never win of you before.
King. But little, Charles ;
Nor shall not, when my fancy's on my play.
Now, Lovell, from the queen what is the
　　news ?　　　　　　　　　　　61
Lov. I could not personally deliver to her
What you commanded me, but by her woman
I sent your message ; who return'd her thanks
In the great'st humbleness, and desired your
　　highness
Most heartily to pray for her.
King. 　　　　　What say'st thou, ha ?
To pray for her ? what, is she crying out ?
Lov. So said her woman ; and that her
　　sufferance made
Almost each pang a death.
King. 　　　　　Alas, good lady !
Suf. God safely quit her of her burthen,
　　and　　　　　　　　　　　　　70
With gentle travail, to the gladding of
Your highness with an heir !
King. 　　　　　'Tis midnight, Charles ;
Prithee, to bed ; and in thy prayers remember
The estate of my poor queen. Leave me alone ;
For I must think of that which company
Would not be friendly to.
Suf. 　　　　　I wish your highness
A quiet night ; and my good mistress will
Remember in my prayers.
King. Charles, good night. [*Exit Suffolk.*

Enter SIR ANTHONY DENNY.

Well, sir, what follows ?
Den. Sir, I have brought my lord the arch-
　　bishop,　　　　　　　　　　　80
As you commanded me.
King. 　　　　　Ha ! Canterbury ?
Den. Ay, my good lord.
King. 　　　　　'Tis true : where is he, Denny ?
Den. He attends your highness' pleasure.

King.   Bring him to us.
                              [*Exit Denny.*
Lov. [*Aside*] This is about that which the
    bishop spake :
I am happily come hither.

Re-enter DENNY, *with* CRANMER.

King. Avoid the gallery. [*Lovell seems to
    stay.*] Ha ! I have said. Be gone.
What !   [*Exeunt Lovell and Denny.*
Cran. [*Aside*] I am fearful : wherefore
    frowns he thus ?
'Tis his aspect of terror. All's not well.
King. How now, my lord ! you desire to
    know   90
Wherefore I sent for you.
Cran. [*Kneeling*] It is my duty
To attend your highness' pleasure.
King.   Pray you, arise,
My good and gracious Lord of Canterbury.
Come, you and I must walk a turn together ;
I have news to tell you : come, come, give me
    your hand.
Ah, my good lord, I grieve at what I speak,
And am right sorry to repeat what follows :
I have, and most unwillingly, of late
Heard many grievous, I do say, my lord,
Grievous complaints of you ; which, being
    consider'd,   100
Have moved us and our council, that you shall
This morning come before us ; where, I know,
You cannot with such freedom purge yourself,
But that, till further trial in those charges
Which will require your answer, you must
    take
Your patience to you, and be well contented
To make your house our Tower : you a
    brother of us,
It fits we thus proceed, or else no witness
Would come against you.
Cran. [*Kneeling*] I humbly thank your
    highness ;
And am right glad to catch this good occasion
Most throughly to be winnow'd, where my
    chaff   111
And corn shall fly asunder : for, I know,
There's none stands under more calumnious
    tongues
Than I myself, poor man.
King.   Stand up, good Canterbury :
Thy truth and thy integrity is rooted
In us, thy friend : give me thy hand, stand up :
Prithee, let's walk. Now, by my holidame.
What manner of man are you ? My lord, I
    look'd
You would have given me your petition, that
I should have ta'en some pains to bring to-
    gether   120
Yourself and your accusers ; and to have
    heard you,
Without indurance, further.
Cran.   Most dread liege,
The good I stand on is my truth and honesty :
If they shall fail, I, with mine enemies,
Will triumph o'er my person ; which I weigh
    not,
Being of those virtues vacant. I fear nothing
What can be said against me.
King.   Know you not
How your state stands i' the world, with the
    whole world ?
Your enemies are many, and not small ; their
    practices

Must bear the same proportion ; and not ever
The justice and the truth o' the question car-
    ries   131
The due o' the verdict with it : at what ease
Might corrupt minds procure knaves as cor-
    rupt
To swear against you ? such things have been
    done.
You are potently opposed ; and with a malice
Of as great size. Ween you of better luck,
I mean, in perjured witness, than your master,
Whose minister you are, whiles here he lived
Upon this naughty earth ? Go to, go to ;   139
You take a precipice for no leap of danger,
And woo your own destruction.
Cran.   God and your majesty
Protect mine innocence, or I fall into
The trap is laid for me !
King.   Be of good cheer ;
They shall no more prevail than we give way
    to.
Keep comfort to you ; and this morning see
You do appear before them : if they shall
    chance,
In charging you with matters, to commit you,
The best persuasions to the contrary
Fail not to use, and with what vehemency
The occasion shall instruct you : if entreaties
Will render you no remedy, this ring   151
Deliver them, and your appeal to us
There make before them. Look, the good man
    weeps !
He's honest, on mine honor. God's blest
    mother !
I swear he is true-hearted ; and a soul
None better in my kingdom. Get you gone,
And do as I have bid you. [*Exit Cranmer.*]
                      He has strangled
His language in his tears.

Enter Old Lady, LOVELL *following.*

Gent. [*Within*] Come back : what mean
    you ?
Old L. I'll not come back ; the tidings that
    I bring   160
Will make my boldness manners. Now, good
    angels
Fly o'er thy royal head, and shade thy person
Under their blessed wings !
King.   Now, by thy looks
I guess thy message. Is the queen deliver'd ?
Say, ay ; and of a boy.
Old L.   Ay, ay, my liege ;
And of a lovely boy : the God of heaven
Both now and ever bless her ! 'tis a girl,
Promises boys hereafter. Sir, your queen
Desires your visitation, and to be   169
Acquainted with this stranger : 'tis as like you
As cherry is to cherry.
King.   Lovell !
Lov.   Sir ?
King. Give her an hundred marks. I'll to
    the queen.   [*Exit.*
Old L. An hundred marks ! By this light,
    I'll ha' more.
An ordinary groom is for such payment.
I will have more, or scold it out of him.
Said I for this, the girl was like to him ?
I will have more, or else unsay't ; and now,
While it is hot, I'll put it to the issue.
                                      [*Exeunt.*

SCENE II. *Before the council-chamber.*
Pursuivants, Pages, &c. attending.

Enter CRANMER, *Archbishop of Canterbury.*

Cran. I hope I am not too late ; and yet
    the gentleman,
That was sent to me from the council, pray'd
    me
To make great haste. All fast ? what means
    this ? Ho !
Who waits there ? Sure, you know me ?

    Enter Keeper.

Keep.   Yes, my lord ;
But yet I cannot help you.
Cran. Why ?

    Enter DOCTOR BUTTS.

Keep. Your grace must wait till you be
    call'd for.
Cran. So.
Butts. [*Aside*] This is a piece of malice. I
    am glad
I came this way so happily : the king
Shall understand it presently.   [*Exit.*
Cran.   [*Aside*] 'Tis Butts,   10
The king's physician : as he pass'd along,
How earnestly he cast his eyes upon me !
Pray heaven, he sound not my disgrace ! For
    certain,
This is of purpose laid by some that hate me—
God turn their hearts ! I never sought their
    malice—
To quench mine honor : they would shame to
    make me
Wait else at door, a fellow-counsellor,
'Mong boys, grooms, and lackeys. But their
    pleasures
Must be fulfill'd, and I attend with patience.

Enter the KING *and* BUTTS *at a window above.*

Butts. I'll show your grace the strangest
    sight—
King.   What's that, Butts ?   20
Butts. I think your highness saw this many
    a day.
King. Body o' me, where is it ?
Butts.   There, my lord :
The high promotion of his grace of Canter-
    bury ;
Who holds his state at door, 'mongst pursui-
    vants,
Pages, and footboys.
King.   Ha ! 'tis he, indeed :
Is this the honor they do one another ?
'Tis well there's one above 'em yet. I had
    thought
They had parted so much honesty among 'em
At least, good manners, as not thus to suffer
A man of his place, and so near our favor,   30
To dance attendance on their lordships' pleas-
    ures,
And at the door too, like a post with packets.
By holy Mary, Butts, there's knavery :
Let 'em alone, and draw the curtain close :
We shall hear more anon.   [*Exeunt.*

SCENE III. *The Council-Chamber.*

Enter LORD CHANCELLOR ; *places himself at
the upper end of the table on the left hand ;
a seat being left void above him, as for* CAN-
TERBURY'S *seat.* DUKE OF SUFFOLK, DUKE
OF NORFOLK, SURREY, LORD CHAMBERLAIN,
GARDINER, *seat themselves in order on each
side.* CROMWELL *at lower end, as secretary.*
Keeper *at the door.*

Chan. Speak to the business, master-secre-
    tary :
Why are we met in council ?
Crom.   Please your honors,
The chief cause concerns his grace of Canter-
    bury.
Gar. Has he had knowledge of it ?
Crom.   Yes.
Nor.   Who waits there ?
Keep. Without, my noble lords ?
Gar.   Yes.
Keep.   My lord archbishop ;
And has done half an hour, to know your
    pleasures.
Chan. Let him come in.
Keep.   Your grace may enter now.
            [*Cranmer enters and approaches
                the council-table.*
Chan. My good lord archbishop, I'm very
    sorry
To sit here at this present, and behold
That chair stand empty : but we all are men,
In our own natures frail, and capable   11
Of our flesh ; few are angels : out of which
    frailty
And want of wisdom, you, that best should
    teach us,
Have misdemean'd yourself, and not a little,
Toward the king first, then his laws, in filling
The whole realm, by your teaching and your
    chaplains,
For so we are inform'd, with new opinions,
Divers and dangerous ; which are heresies,
And, not reform'd, may prove pernicious.
Gar. Which reformation must be sudden
    too,   20
My noble lords ; for those that tame wild
    horses
Pace 'em not in their hands to make 'em gen-
    tle,
But stop their mouths with stubborn bits, and
    spur 'em,
Till they obey the manage. If we suffer,
Out of our easiness and childish pity
To one man's honor, this contagious sickness,
Farewell all physic : and what follows then ?
Commotions, uproars, with a general taint
Of the whole state : as, of late days, our
    neighbors,
The upper Germany, can dearly witness,   30
Yet freshly pitied in our memories.
Cran. My good lords, hitherto, in all the
    progress
Both of my life and office, I have labor'd,
And with no little study, that my teaching
And the strong course of my authority
Might go one way, and safely ; and the end
Was ever, to do well : nor is there living,
I speak it with a single heart, my lords,
A man that more detests, more stirs against,
Both in his private conscience and his place,
Defacers of a public peace, than I do.   41
Pray heaven, the king may never find a heart
With less allegiance in it ! Men that make
Envy and crooked malice nourishment
Dare bite the best. I do beseech your lord-
    ships,
That, in this case of justice, my accusers,

Be what they will, may stand forth face to
    face,
And freely urge against me.
    Suf.   Nay, my lord,
That cannot be : you are a counsellor,   49
And, by that virtue, no man dare accuse you.
    Gar. My lord, because we have business of
        more moment,
We will be short with you. 'Tis his highness'
    pleasure,
And our consent, for better trial of you,
From hence you be committed to the Tower ;
Where, being but a private man again,
You shall know many dare accuse you boldly,
More than, I fear, you are provided for.
    Cran. Ah, my good Lord of Winchester, I
        thank you ;
You are always my good friend ; if your will
    pass,
I shall both find your lordship judge and juror,
You are so merciful : I see your end ;   61
'Tis my undoing : love and meekness, lord,
Become a churchman better than ambition :
Win straying souls with modesty again,
Cast none away. That I shall clear myself,
Lay all the weight ye can upon my patience,
I make as little doubt, as you do conscience
In doing daily wrongs. I could say more,
But reverence to your calling makes me
    modest.
    Gar. My lord, my lord, you are a sectary,
That's the plain truth : your painted gloss dis-
        covers,   71
To men that understand you, words and weak-
    ness.
    Crom. My Lord of Winchester, you are a
    little,
By your good favor, too sharp ; men so noble,
However faulty, yet should find respect
For what they have been : 'tis a cruelty
To load a falling man.
    Gar.   Good master secretary,
I cry your honor mercy ; you may, worst
Of all this table, say so.
    Crom.   Why, my lord ?
    Gar. Do not I know you for a favorer   80
Of this new sect ? ye are not sound.
    Crom.   Not sound ?
    Gar. Not sound, I say.
    Crom. Would you were half so honest !
Men's prayers then would seek you, not their
    fears.
    Gar. I shall remember this bold language.
    Crom.   Do.
Remember your bold life too.
    Chan.   This is too much ;
Forbear, for shame, my lords.
    Gar.   I have done.
    Crom.   And I.
    Chan. Then thus for you, my lord : it
        stands agreed,
I take it, by all voices, that forthwith
You be convey'd to the Tower a prisoner ; 89
There to remain till the king's further pleasure
Be known unto us : are you all agreed, lords ?
    All. We are.
    Cran.   Is there no other way of mercy,
But I must needs to the Tower, my lords ?
    Gar.   What other
Would you expect ? you are strangely trouble-
    some.
Let some o' the guard be ready there.

              Enter Guard.

    Cran.   For me ?
Must I go like a traitor thither ?
    Gar.   Receive him,
And see him safe i' the Tower.
    Cran.   Stay, good my lords,
I have a little yet to say. Look there, my
    lords ;
By virtue of that ring, I take my cause   99
Out of the gripes of cruel men, and give it
To a most noble judge, the king my master.
    Cham. This is the king's ring.
    Sur.   'Tis no counterfeit.
    Suf. 'Tis the right ring, by heaven : I told
    ye all,
When we first put this dangerous stone a-roll-
    ing,
'Twould fall upon ourselves.
    Nor.   Do you think, my lords,
The king will suffer but the little finger
Of this man to be vex'd ?
    Chan.   'Tis now too certain :
How much more is his life in value with him ?
Would I were fairly out on't !
    Crom.   My mind gave me,
In seeking tales and informations   110
Against this man, whose honesty the devil
And his disciples only envy at,
Ye blew the fire that burns ye : now have at
    ye !

    Enter KING, *frowning on them ; takes his seat.*

    Gar. Dread sovereign, how much are we
        bound to heaven
In daily thanks, that gave us such a prince ;
Not only good and wise, but most religious :
One that, in all obedience, makes the church
The chief aim of his honor ; and, to strengthen
That holy duty, out of dear respect,
His royal self in judgment comes to hear 120
The cause betwixt her and this great offender.
    King. You were ever good at sudden com-
        mendations,
Bishop of Winchester. But know, I come not
To hear such flattery now, and in my pres-
    ence ;
They are too thin and bare to hide offences.
To me you cannot reach, you play the span-
    iel,
And think with wagging of your tongue to win
    me ;
But, whatsoe'er thou takest me for, I'm sure
Thou hast a cruel nature and a bloody.
[*To Cranmer*] Good man, sit down. Now let
    me see the proudest   130
He, that dares most, but wag his finger at
    thee :
By all that's holy, he had better starve
Than but once think this place becomes thee
    not.
    Sur. May it please your grace,—
    King.   No, sir, it does not please me.
I had thought I had had men of some under-
    standing
And wisdom of my council ; but I find none.
Was it discretion, lords, to let this man,
This good man,—few of you deserve that
    title,—
This honest man, wait like a lousy footboy
At chamber-door ? and one as great as you
    are ?   140

Why, what a shame was this! Did my com-
mission
Bid ye so far forget yourselves? I gave ye
Power as he was a counsellor to try him,
Not as a groom: there's some of ye, I see,
More out of malice than integrity,
Would try him to the utmost, had ye mean;
Which ye shall never have while I live.
　　Chan.　　　　　　　　Thus far,
My most dread sovereign, may it like your
grace
To let my tongue excuse all. What was pur-
posed
Concerning his imprisonment, was rather, 150
If there be faith in men, meant for his trial,
And fair purgation to the world, than malice,
I'm sure, in me.
　　King. Well, well, my lords, respect him;
Take him, and use him well, he's worthy of it.
I will say thus much for him, if a prince
May be beholding to a subject, I
Am, for his love and service, so to him.
Make me no more ado, but all embrace him:
Be friends, for shame, my lords! My Lord of
Canterbury,　　　　　　　　　160
I have a suit which you must not deny me;
That is, a fair young maid that yet wants
baptism,
You must be godfather, and answer for her.
　　Cran. The greatest monarch now alive may
glory
In such an honor: how may I deserve it
That am a poor and humble subject to you?
　　King. Come, come, my lord, you'ld spare
your spoons: you shall have two noble part-
ners with you; the old Duchess of Norfolk,
and Lady Marquess Dorset: will these please
you?　　　　　　　　　　　170
Once more, my Lord of Winchester, I charge
you,
Embrace and love this man.
　　Gar.　　　　　　　With a true heart
And brother-love I do it.
　　Cran.　　　　　　And let heaven
Witness, how dear I hold this confirmation.
　　King. Good man, those joyful tears show
thy true heart:
The common voice, I see, is verified
Of thee, which says thus, 'Do my Lord of
Canterbury
A shrewd turn, and he is your friend for ever.'
Come, lords, we trifle time away; I long
To have this young one made a Christian. 180
As I have made ye one, lords, one remain;
So I grow stronger, you more honor gain.
　　　　　　　　　　　　[Exeunt.

　　SCENE IV. *The palace yard.*

Noise and tumult within. Enter Porter *and
his* Man.

　　Port. You'll leave your noise anon, ye
rascals: do you take the court for Paris-gar-
den? ye rude slaves, leave your gaping.
　　[*Within*] Good master porter, I belong to
the larder.
　　Port. Belong to the gallows, and be hanged,
ye rogue! is this a place to roar in? Fetch
me a dozen crab-tree staves, and strong ones:
these are but switches to 'em. I'll scratch your
heads: you must be seeing christenings? do

you look for ale and cakes here, you rude
rascals?　　　　　　　　　　11
　　Man. Pray, sir, be patient: 'tis as much
impossible—
Unless we sweep 'em from the door with can-
nons—
To scatter 'em, as 'tis to make 'em sleep
On May-day morning; which will never be:
We may as well push against Powle's, as stir
'em.
　　Port. How got they in, and be hang'd?
　　Man. Alas, I know not; how gets the tide
in?
As much as one sound cudgel of four foot—
You see the poor remainder—could distribute,
I made no spare, sir.
　　Port.　　　　　　You did nothing, sir.
　　Man. I am not Samson, nor Sir Guy, nor
Colbrand,
To mow 'em down before me: but if I spared
any
That had a head to hit, either young or old,
He or she, cuckold or cuckold-maker,
Let me ne'er hope to see a chine again;
And that I would not for a cow, God save
her!
　　[*Within*] Do you hear, master porter?
　　Port. I shall be with you presently, good
master puppy. Keep the door close, sirrah. 30
　　Man. What would you have me do?
　　Port. What should you do, but knock 'em
down by the dozens? Is this Moorfields to
muster in? or have we some strange Indian
with the great tool come to court, the women
so besiege us? Bless me, what a fry of fornication is at door! On my Christian conscience, this one christening will beget a
thousand; here will be father, godfather, and
all together.　　　　　　　　　39
　　Man. The spoons will be the bigger, sir.
There is a fellow somewhat near the door, he
should be a brazier by his face, for, o' my
conscience, twenty of the dog-days now reign
in's nose; all that stand about him are under
the line, they need no other penance: that
fire-drake did I hit three times on the head,
and three times was his nose discharged
against me; he stands there, like a mortar-
piece, to blow us. There was a haberdasher's
wife of small wit near him, that railed upon
me till her pinked porringer fell off her head,
for kindling such a combustion in the state.
I missed the meteor once, and hit that
woman; who cried out 'Clubs!' when I
might see from far some forty truncheoners
draw to her succor, which were the hope o'
the Strand, where she was quartered. They fell
on; I made good my place: at length they
came to the broom-staff to me; I defied 'em
still: when suddenly a file of boys behind 'em,
loose shot, delivered such a shower of pebbles, that I was fain to draw mine honor in,
and let 'em win the work: the devil was
amongst 'em, I think, surely.
　　Port. These are the youths that thunder at
a playhouse, and fight for bitten apples; that
no audience, but the tribulation of Tower-
hill, or the limbs of Limehouse, their dear
brothers, are able to endure. I have some of
'em in Limbo Patrum, and there they are like
to dance these three days; besides the running banquet of two beadles that is to come.

Enter LORD CHAMBERLAIN.

Cham. Mercy o' me, what a multitude are
here !
They grow still too ; from all parts they are
coming,
As if we kept a fair here ! Where are these
porters,
These lazy knaves ? Ye have made a fine
hand, fellows :
There's a trim rabble let in : are all these
Your faithful friends o' the suburbs ? We shall
have
Great store of room, no doubt, left for the
ladies,
When they pass back from the christening.
Port. An't please your honor,
We are but men ; and what so many may do,
Not being torn a-pieces, we have done :   80
An army cannot rule 'em.
Cham. As I live,
If the king blame me for't, I'll lay ye all
By the heels, and suddenly ; and on your
heads
Clap round fines for neglect : ye are lazy
knaves ;
And here ye lie baiting of bombards, when
Ye should do service. Hark ! the trumpets
sound ;
They're come already from the christening :
Go, break among the press, and find a way
out
To let the troop pass fairly ; or I'll find
A Marshalsea shall hold ye play these two
months.   90
Port. Make way there for the princess.
Man. You great fellow,
Stand close up, or I'll make your head ache.
Port. You i' the camlet, get up o' the rail ;
I'll peck you o'er the pales else.   [*Exeunt.*

SCENE V. *The palace.*

Enter trumpets, sounding ; then two Alder-
men, LORD MAYOR, GARTER, CRANMER,
DUKE OF NORFOLK *with his marshal's staff,*
DUKE OF SUFFOLK, *two* Noblemen *bearing
great standing-bowls for the christening-
gifts ; then four* Noblemen *bearing a canopy, under which the* DUCHESS OF NOR-
FOLK, *godmother, bearing the child richly
habited in a mantle, &c., train borne by a*
Lady ; *then follows the* MARCHIONESS DOR-
SET, *the other godmother, and Ladies. The
troop pass once about the stage, and* GAR-
TER *speaks.*

Gart. Heaven, from thy endless goodness,
send prosperous life, long, and ever happy, to
the high and mighty princess of England,
Elizabeth !

Flourish. Enter KING *and Guard.*

Cran. [*Kneeling*] And to your royal grace,
and the good queen,
My noble partners, and myself, thus pray :
All comfort, joy, in this most gracious lady,
Heaven ever laid up to make parents happy,
May hourly fall upon ye !
King. Thank you, good lord archbishop :
What is her name ?
Cran. Elizabeth.
King. Stand up, lord.   10
[*The King kisses the child.*

With this kiss take my blessing : God protect
thee !
Into whose hand I give thy life.
Cran. Amen.
King. My noble gossips, ye have been too
prodigal :
I thank ye heartily ; so shall this lady,
When she has so much English.
Cran. Let me speak, sir,
For heaven now bids me ; and the words I
utter
Let none think flattery, for they'll find 'em
truth.
This royal infant—heaven still move about
her !—
Though in her cradle, yet now promises
Upon this land a thousand thousand blessings,
Which time shall bring to ripeness : she shall
be—   21
But few now living can behold that goodness—
A pattern to all princes living with her,
And all that shall succeed : Saba was never
More covetous of wisdom and fair virtue
Than this pure soul shall be : all princely
graces,
That mould up such a mighty piece as this is,
With all the virtues that attend the good,
Shall still be doubled on her : truth shall
nurse her,
Holy and heavenly thoughts still counsel her :
She shall be loved and fear'd : her own shall
bless her ;   31
Her foes shake like a field of beaten corn,
And hang their heads with sorrow : good
grows with her :
In her days every man shall eat in safety,
Under his own vine, what he plants ; and sing
The merry songs of peace to all his neighbors :
God shall be truly known ; and those about
her
From her shall read the perfect ways of honor,
And by those claim their greatness, not by
blood.
Nor shall this peace sleep with her : but as
when   40
The bird of wonder dies, the maiden phœnix,
Her ashes new create another heir,
As great in admiration as herself ;
So shall she leave her blessedness to one,
When heaven shall call her from this cloud of
darkness,
Who from the sacred ashes of her honor
Shall star-like rise, as great in fame as she
was,
And so stand fix'd : peace, plenty, love, truth,
terror,
That were the servants to this chosen infant,
Shall then be his, and like a vine grow to
him :   50
Wherever the bright sun of heaven shall shine,
His honor and the greatness of his name
Shall be, and make new nations : he shall
flourish,
And, like a mountain cedar, reach his
branches
To all the plains about him : our children's
children
Shall see this, and bless heaven.
King. Thou speakest wonders.
Cran. She shall be, to the happiness of
England,
An aged princess ; many days shall see her,

And yet no day without a deed to crown it.
Would I had known no more! but she must
    die,   60
She must, the saints must have her; yet a
    virgin,
A most unspotted lily shall she pass
To the ground, and all the world shall mourn
    her.
  King.   O lord archbishop,
Thou hast made me now a man! never, be-
    fore
This happy child, did I get any thing:
This oracle of comfort has so pleased me,
That when I am in heaven I shall desire
To see what this child does, and praise my
    Maker.
I thank ye all. To you, my good lord mayor,
And your good brethren, I am much behold-
    ing;   71
I have received much honor by your presence,
And ye shall find me thankful. Lead the way,
    lords:
Ye must all see the queen, and she must thank
    ye,

She will be sick else. This day, no man think
Has business at his house; for all shall stay:
This little one shall make it holiday. [*Exeunt.*

EPILOGUE.

'Tis ten to one this play can never please
All that are here: some come to take their
    ease,
And sleep an act or two; but those, we fear,
We have frighted with our trumpets; so, 'tis
    clear,
They'll say 'tis naught: others, to hear the city
Abused extremely, and to cry 'That's witty!'
Which we have not done neither: that, I fear,
All the expected good we're like to hear
For this play at this time, is only in
The merciful construction of good women; 10
For such a one we show'd 'em: if they smile,
And say 'twill do, I know, within a while
All the best men are ours; for 'tis ill hap,
If they hold when their ladies bid 'em clap.

VENUS AND ADONIS.

(WRITTEN ABOUT 1592.)

INTRODUCTION.

Venus and Adonis was entered in the Stationers' register on April 18, 1593, and was published the same year. The poem became popular at once, and before the close of 1602 it had been reprinted no fewer than six times. "As the soul of Euphorbus," wrote Meres in his *Wit's Treasury* (1598), "was thought to live in Pythagoras, so the sweete wittie soule of Ovid lives in mellifluous and hony-tongued Shakespeare; witness his *Venus and Adonis*, his *Lucrece*, his sugred Sonnets among his private friends, &c." Ovid has told the story of the love of Venus for Adonis and the death of the beautiful hunter by a wild boar's tusk; the coldness of Adonis, his boyish disdain of love, was an invention of later times. It is in this later form that Shakespeare imagines the subject; and in his treatment of it he has less in common with Ovid than with a short poem by a contemporary writer of sonnets and lyrical poems, Henry Constable, which appeared in a collection of verse published in 1600, under the name of *England's Helicon*. It is uncertain which of the two poems, Constable's or Shakespeare's, was the earlier written. When *Venus and Adonis* appeared Shakespeare was twenty-nine years of age; the Earl of Southampton, to whom it was dedicated, was not yet twenty. In the dedication the poet speaks of these "unpolish'd lines" as "the first heire of my invention." Did he mean by this that *Venus and Adonis* was written before any of his plays, or before any plays that were strictly original—his own "invention?" or does he, setting plays altogether apart, which were not looked upon as literature, in a high sense of the word, call it his first poem because he had written no earlier narrative or lyrical verse? We cannot be sure. It is possible, but not likely, that he may have written this poem before he left Stratford, and have brought it up with him to London. More probably it was written in London, and perhaps not long before its publication. The year 1593, in which the poem appeared, was a year of plague; the London theatres were closed: it may be that Shakespeare, idle in London, or having returned for a while to Stratford, then wrote the poem. Whenever written, it was elaborated with peculiar care. The subject of the poem is sensual, but with Shakespeare it becomes rather a study or analysis of passion and the objects of passion, than in itself passionate. Without being dramatic, the poem contains the materials for dramatic poetry, set forth at large. The descriptions of English landscape and country life are numerous, and give a spirit of breezy life and health to portions of the poem which could ill afford to lose anything that is fresh and healthful.

'Vilia miretur vulgus; mihi flavus Apollo
Pocula Castalia plena ministret aqua.'

TO THE
RIGHT HONORABLE HENRY WRIOTHESLY,
EARL OF SOUTHAMPTON, AND BARON OF TICHFIELD.

RIGHT HONORABLE,

I KNOW not how I shall offend in dedicating my unpolished lines to your lordship, nor how the world will censure me for choosing so strong a prop to support so weak a burden : only, if your honor seem but pleased, I account myself highly praised, and vow to take advantage of all idle hours, till I have honored you with some graver labor. But if the first heir of my invention prove deformed, I shall be sorry it had so noble a god-father, and never after ear so barren a land, for fear it yield me still so bad a harvest. I leave it to your honorable survey, and your honor to your heart's content; which I wish may always answer your own wish and the world's hopeful expectation.

Your honor's in all duty,
WILLIAM SHAKESPEARE.

EVEN as the sun with purple-color'd face
Had ta'en his last leave of the weeping morn,
Rose-cheek'd Adonis hied him to the chase ;
Hunting he loved, but love he laugh'd to
    scorn ;
  Sick-thoughted Venus makes amain unto
    him,
  And like a bold-faced suitor 'gins to woo
    him.

' Thrice-fairer than myself,' thus she began,
' The field's chief flower, sweet above compare,
Stain to all nymphs, more lovely than a man,
More white and red than doves or roses are ;
  Nature that made thee, with herself at strife,
  Saith that the world hath ending with thy
    life.

' Vouchsafe, thou wonder, to alight thy steed,
And rein his proud head to the saddle-bow ;
If thou wilt deign this favor, for thy meed
A thousand honey secrets shalt thou know :
  Here come and sit, where never serpent
    hisses,
  And being set, I'll smother thee with kisses ;

' And yet not cloy thy lips with loathed sa-
    tiety,
But rather famish them amid their plenty, 20
Making them red and pale with fresh variety,
Ten kisses short as one, one long as twenty :
  A summer's day will seem an hour but
    short,
  Being wasted in such time-beguiling sport.'

With this she seizeth on his sweating palm,
The precedent of pith and livelihood,
And trembling in her passion, calls it balm,
Earth's sovereign salve to do a goddess good :
  Being so enraged, desire doth lend her force
  Courageously to pluck him from his horse.

Over one arm the lusty courser's rein,   31
Under her other was the tender boy,
Who blush'd and pouted in a dull disdain,
With leaden appetite, unapt to toy ;
  She red and hot as coals of glowing fire,
  He red for shame, but frosty in desire.

The studded bridle on a ragged bough
Nimbly she fastens :—O, how quick is love !—
The steed is stalled up, and even now
To tie the rider she begins to prove :   40
  Backward she push'd him, as she would be
    thrust,
  And govern'd him in strength, though not
    in lust.

So soon was she along as he was down,
Each leaning on their elbows and their hips :
Now doth she stroke his cheek, now doth he
    frown,
And 'gins to chide, but soon she stops his lips ;
  And kissing speaks, with lustful language
    broken,
  ' If thou wilt chide, thy lips shall never
    open.'

He burns with bashful shame : she with her
    tears
Doth quench the maiden burning of his
    cheeks ;   50
Then with her windy sighs and golden hairs
To fan and blow them dry again she seeks :
  He saith she is immodest, blames her 'miss ;
  What follows more she murders with a kiss.

Even as an empty eagle, sharp by fast,
Tires with her beak on feathers, flesh and
    bone,
Shaking her wings, devouring all in haste,
Till either gorge be stuff'd or prey be gone ;
  Even so she kissed his brow, his cheek, his
    chin,
  And where she ends she doth anew begin.

Forced to content, but never to obey,   61
Panting he lies and breatheth in her face ;
She feedeth on the steam as on a prey,
And calls it heavenly moisture, air of grace ;
  Wishing her cheeks were gardens full of
    flowers,
  So they were dew'd with such distilling
    showers.

Look, how a bird lies tangled in a net,
So fasten'd in her arms Adonis lies ;
Pure shame and awed resistance made him
    fret,
Which bred more beauty in his angry eyes : 70
  Rain added to a river that is rank
  Perforce will force it overflow the bank.

Still she entreats, and prettily entreats,
For to a pretty ear she tunes her tale ;
Still is he sullen, still he lours and frets,
'Twixt crimson shame and anger ashy-pale :
  Being red, she loves him best ; and being
    white,
  Her best is better'd with a more delight.

Look how he can, she cannot choose but love ;
And by her fair immortal hand she swears, 80
From his soft bosom never to remove,
Till he take truce with her contending tears,
  Which long have rain'd, making her cheeks
    all wet ;
  And one sweet kiss shall pay this countless
    debt.

Upon this promise did he raise his chin,
Like a dive-dapper peering through a wave,
Who, being look'd on, ducks as quickly in ;
So offers he to give what she did crave ;
  But when her lips were ready for his pay,
  He winks, and turns his lips another way. 90

Never did passenger in summer's heat
More thirst for drink than she for this good
    turn.
Her help she sees, but help she cannot get ;
She bathes in water, yet her fire must burn :
  ' O, pity,' 'gan she cry, ' flint-hearted boy !
  'Tis but a kiss I beg ; why art thou coy ?

' I have been woo'd, as I entreat thee now,
Even by the stern and direful god of war,
Whose sinewy neck in battle ne'er did bow,
Who conquers where he comes in every jar ;
  Yet hath he been my captive and my slave,
  And begg'd for that which thou unask'd shalt
    have.

' Over my altars hath he hung his lance,
His batter'd shield, his uncontrolled crest,
And for my sake hath learn'd to sport and
    dance,
To toy, to wanton, dally, smile and jest,
  Scorning his churlish drum and ensign red,
  Making my arms his field, his tent my bed.

'Thus he that overruled I oversway'd,
Leading him prisoner in a red-rose chain : 110
Strong-tempered steel his stronger strength
obey'd,
Yet was he servile to my coy disdain.
  O, be not proud, nor brag not of thy might,
  For mastering her that foil'd the god of
    fight !

'Touch but my lips with those fair lips of
    thine,—
Though mine be not so fair, yet are they
    red—
The kiss shall be thine own as well as mine.
What seest thou in the ground ? hold up thy
    head :
  Look in mine eye-balls, there thy beauty
    lies ;
  Then why not lips on lips, since eyes in
    eyes ?   120

'Art thou ashamed to kiss ? then wink again,
And I will wink ; so shall the day seem night ;
Love keeps his revels where they are but
    twain ;
Be bold to play, our sport is not in sight :
  These blue-vein'd violets whereon we lean
  Never can blab, nor know not what we
    mean.

'The tender spring upon thy tempting lip
Shows thee unripe ; yet mayst thou well be
    tasted :
Make use of time, let not advantage slip ;
Beauty within itself should not be wasted : 130
  Fair flowers that are not gather'd in their
    prime
  Rot and consume themselves in little time.

'Were I hard-favor'd, foul, or wrinkled-old,
Ill-nurtured, crooked, churlish, harsh in voice,
O'erworn, despised, rheumatic and cold,
Thick-sighted, barren, lean and lacking juice,
  Then mightst thou pause, for then I were
    not for thee ;
  But having no defects, why dost abhor me ?

'Thou canst not see one wrinkle in my brow ;
Mine eyes are gray and bright and quick in
    turning :   140
My beauty as the spring doth yearly grow,
My flesh is soft and plump, my marrow burn-
    ing ;
  My smooth moist hand, were it with thy
    hand felt,
  Would in thy palm dissolve, or seem to melt.

'Bid me discourse, I will enchant thine ear,
Or, like a fairy, trip upon the green,
Or, like a nymph, with long dishevell'd hair,
Dance on the sands, and yet no footing seen :
  Love is a spirit all compact of fire,
  Not gross to sink, but light, and will aspire.

'Witness this primrose bank whereon I lie ; 151
These forceless flowers like sturdy trees sup-
    port me ;
Two strengthless doves will draw me through
    the sky,
From morn till night, even where I list to sport
    me :
  Is love so light, sweet boy, and may it be
  That thou shouldst think it heavy unto thee ?

'Is thine own heart to thine own face affected ?
Can thy right hand seize love upon thy left ?
Then woo thyself, be of thyself rejected,

Steal thine own freedom and complain on
    theft.   160
Narcissus so himself himself forsook,
And died to kiss his shadow in the brook.

'Torches are made to light, jewels to wear,
Dainties to taste, fresh beauty for the use,
Herbs for their smell, and sappy plants to
    bear :
Things growing to themselves are growth's
    abuse :
  Seeds spring from seeds and beauty breedeth
    beauty ;
  Thou wast begot ; to get it is thy duty.

'Upon the earth's increase why shouldst thou
    feed,
Unless the earth with thy increase be fed ? 170
By law of nature thou art bound to breed,
That thine may live when thou thyself art
    dead ;
  And so, in spite of death, thou dost survive,
  In that thy likeness still is left alive.'

By this the love-sick queen began to sweat,
For where they lay the shadow had forsook
    them,
And Titan, tired in the mid-day heat,
With burning eye did hotly overlook them ;
  Wishing Adonis had his team to guide,
  So he were like him and by Venus' side. 180

And now Adonis, with a lazy spright,
And with a heavy, dark, disliking eye,
His louring brows o'erwhelming his fair sight,
Like misty vapors when they blot the sky,
  Souring his cheeks cries 'Fie, no more of
    love !
  The sun doth burn my face : I must re-
    move.'

'Ay me,' quoth Venus, 'young, and so un-
    kind ?
What bare excuses makest thou to be gone !
I'll sigh celestial breath, whose gentle wind
Shall cool the heat of this descending sun : 190
  I'll make a shadow for thee of my hairs ;
  If they burn too, I'll quench them with my
    tears.

'The sun that shines from heaven shines but
    warm,
And, lo, I lie between that sun and thee :
The heat I have from thence doth little harm,
Thine eye darts forth the fire that burneth me ;
  And were I not immortal, life were done
  Between this heavenly and earthly sun.

'Art thou obdurate, flinty, hard as steel,
Nay, more than flint, for stone at rain relent-
    eth ?
Art thou a woman's son, and canst not feel 200
What 'tis to love ? how want of love torment-
    eth ?
  O, had thy mother borne so hard a mind,
  She had not brought forth thee, but died un-
    kind.

'What am I, that thou shouldst contemn me
    this ?
Or what great danger dwells upon my suit ?
What were thy lips the worse for one poor
    kiss ?
Speak, fair ; but speak fair words, or else be
    mute :
  Give me one kiss, I'll give it thee again, 209
  And one for interest, if thou wilt have twain.

'Fie, lifeless picture, cold and senseless stone,
Well-painted idol, image dull and dead,
Statue contenting but the eye alone,
Thing like a man, but of no woman bred !
    Thou art no man, though of a man's complexion,
    For men will kiss even by their own direction.'

This said, impatience chokes her pleading
    tongue,
And swelling passion doth provoke a pause ;
Red cheeks and fiery eyes blaze forth her
    wrong ;
Being judge in love, she cannot right her
    cause :   220
    And now she weeps, and now she fain would
    speak,
    And now her sobs do her intendments break.

Sometimes she shakes her head and then his
    hand,
Now gazeth she on him, now on the ground ;
Sometimes her arms infold him like a band :
She would, he will not in her arms be bound ;
    And when from thence he struggles to be
    gone,
    She locks her lily fingers one in one.

'Fondling,' she saith, 'since I have hemm'd
    thee here
Within the circuit of this ivory pale,   230
I'll be a park, and thou shalt be my deer ;
Feed where thou wilt, on mountain or in dale :
    Graze on my lips ; and if those hills be dry,
    Stray lower, where the pleasant fountains
    lie.

'Within this limit is relief enough,
Sweet bottom-grass and high delightful plain,
Round rising hillocks, brakes obscure and
    rough,
To shelter thee from tempest and from rain
    Then be my deer, since I am such a park ;
    No dog shall rouse thee, though a thousand
    bark.'   240

At this Adonis smiles as in disdain,
That in each cheek appears a pretty dimple :
Love made those hollows, if himself were
    slain,
He might be buried in a tomb so simple ;
    Foreknowing well, if there he came to lie,
    Why, there Love lived and there he could
    not die.

These lovely caves, these round enchanting
    pits,
Open'd their mouths to swallow Venus' liking.
Being mad before, how doth she now for wits ?
Struck dead at first, what needs a second
    striking ?   250
    Poor queen of love, in thine own law forlorn,
    To love a cheek that smiles at thee in scorn !

Now which way shall she turn ? what shall she
    say ?
Her words are done, her woes are more increasing ;
The time is spent, her object will away,
And from her twining arms doth urge releasing.

'Pity,' she cries, 'some favor, some remorse ! '
Away he springs and hasteth to his horse.

But, lo, from forth a copse that neighbors by,
A breeding jennet, lusty, young and proud,
Adonis' trampling courser doth espy,   261
And forth she rushes, snorts and neighs aloud :
    The strong-neck'd steed, being tied unto a
    tree,
    Breaketh his rein, and to her straight goes
    he.

Imperiously he leaps, he neighs, he bounds,
And now his woven girths he breaks asunder ;
The bearing earth with his hard hoof he
    wounds,
Whose hollow womb resounds like heaven's
    thunder ;
    The iron bit he crusheth 'tween his teeth,
    Controlling what he was controlled with. 270

His ears up-prick'd ; his braided hanging mane
Upon his compass'd crest now stand on end ;
His nostrils drink the air, and forth again,
As from a furnace, vapors doth he send :
    His eye, which scornfully glisters like fire,
    Shows his hot courage and his high desire.

Sometime he trots, as if he told the steps,
With gentle majesty and modest pride ;
Anon he rears upright, curvets and leaps,
As who should say 'Lo, thus my strength is
    tried,   280
    And this I do to captivate the eye
    Of the fair breeder that is standing by.'

What recketh he his rider's angry stir,
His flattering 'Holla,' or his 'Stand, I say ' ?
What cares he now for curb or pricking spur ?
For rich caparisons or trapping gay ?
    He sees his love, and nothing else he sees,
    For nothing else with his proud sight agrees.

Look, when a painter would surpass the life,
In limning out a well-proportion'd steed,   290
His art with nature's workmanship at strife,
As if the dead the living should exceed ;
    So did this horse excel a common one
    In shape, in courage, color, pace and bone.

Round-hoof'd, short-jointed, fetlocks shag and
    long,
Broad breast, full eye, small head and nostril
    wide,
High crest, short ears, straight legs and passing strong,
Thin mane, thick tail, broad buttock, tender
    hide :
    Look, what a horse should have he did not
    lack,
    Save a proud rider on so proud a back. 300

Sometime he scuds far off and there he stares ;
Anon he starts at stirring of a feather ;
To bid the wind a base he now prepares,
And whether he run or fly they know not
    whether ;
    For through his mane and tail the high wind
    sings,
    Fanning the hairs, who wave like feather'd
    wings.

He looks upon his love and neighs unto her ;
She answers him as if she knew his mind :
Being proud, as females are, to see him woo
   her,
She puts on outward strangeness, seems un-
   kind,
   Spurns at his love and scorns the heat he
    feels,
   Beating his kind embracements with her
    heels.

Then, like a melancholy malcontent,
He veils his tail that, like a falling plume,
Cool shadow to his melting buttock lent :
He stamps and bites the poor flies in his fume.
   His love, perceiving how he is enraged,
   Grew kinder, and his fury was assuaged.

His testy master goeth about to take him ; 319
When, lo, the unback'd breeder, full of fear,
Jealous of catching, swiftly doth forsake him,
With her the horse, and left Adonis there :
   As they were mad, unto the wood they hie
    them,
   Out-stripping crows that strive to over-fly
    them.

All swoln with chafing, down Adonis sits,
Banning his boisterous and unruly beast :
And now the happy season once more fits,
That love-sick Love by pleading may be blest ;
   For lovers say, the heart hath treble wrong
   When it is barr'd the aidance of the tongue.

An oven that is stopp'd, or river stay'd,   331
Burneth more hotly, swelleth with more rage :
So of concealed sorrow may be said ;
Free vent of words love's fire doth assuage :
   But when the heart's attorney once is mute,
   The client breaks, as desperate in his suit.

He sees her coming, and begins to glow,
Even as a dying coal revives with wind,
And with his bonnet hides his angry brow ;
Looks on the dull earth with disturbed mind,
   Taking no notice that she is so nigh,   341
   For all askance he holds her in his eye.

O, what a sight it was, wistly to view
How she came stealing to the wayward boy !
To note the fighting conflict of her hue,
How white and red each other did destroy !
   But now her cheek was pale, and by and by
   It flash'd forth fire, as lightning from the
    sky.

Now was she just before him as he sat,
And like a lowly lover down she kneels ; 350
With one fair hand she heaveth up his hat,
Her other tender hand his fair cheek feels :
   His tenderer cheek receives her soft hand's
    print,
   As apt as new-fall'n snow takes any dint.

O, what a war of looks was then between
   them !
Her eyes petitioners to his eyes suing ;
His eyes saw her eyes as they had not seen
   them ;
Her eyes woo'd still, his eyes disdain'd the
   wooing :
   And all this dumb play had his acts made
   plain

With tears, which, chorus-like, her eyes did
   rain.   360

Full gently now she takes him by the hand,
A lily prison'd in a gaol of snow,
Or ivory in an alabaster band ;
So white a friend engirts so white a foe :
   This beauteous combat, wilful and unwill-
    ing,
   Show'd like two silver doves that sit a-bill-
    ing.

Once more the engine of her thoughts began :
' O fairest mover on this mortal round,
Would thou wert as I am, and I a man,
My heart all whole as thine, thy heart my
   wound ;   370
   For one sweet look thy help I would assure
    thee,
   Though nothing but my body's bane would
    cure thee ! '

' Give me my hand,' saith he, ' why dost thou
   feel it ? '
' Give me my heart,' saith she, ' and thou shalt
   have it :
O, give it me, lest thy hard heart do steel it,
And being steel'd, soft sighs can never grave
   it :
   Then love's deep groans I never shall re-
    gard,
   Because Adonis' heart hath made mine
    hard.'

' For shame,' he cries, ' let go, and let me go ;
My day's delight is past, my horse is gone, 380
And 'tis your fault I am bereft him so :
I pray you hence, and leave me here alone ;
   For all my mind, my thought, my busy care,
   Is how to get my palfrey from the mare.'

Thus she replies : ' Thy palfrey, as he should,
Welcomes the warm approach of sweet desire :
Affection is a coal that must be cool'd ;
Else, suffer'd, it will set the heart on fire :
   The sea hath bounds, but deep desire hath
    none ;
   Therefore no marvel though thy horse be
    gone.   390

' How like a jade he stood, tied to the tree,
Servilely master'd with a leathern rein !
But when he saw his love, his youth's fair fee,
He held such petty bondage in disdain ;
   Throwing the base thong from his bending
    crest,
   Enfranchising his mouth, his back, his
    breast.

' Who sees his true-love in her naked bed,
Teaching the sheets a whiter hue than white,
But, when his glutton eye so full hath fed,
His other agents aim at like delight ?   400
   Who is so faint, that dare not be so bold
   To touch the fire, the weather being cold ?

' Let me excuse thy courser, gentle boy ;
And learn of him, I heartily beseech thee,
To take advantage on presented joy ;
Though I were dumb, yet his proceedings
   teach thee ;
   O, learn to love ; the lesson is but plain,
   And once made perfect, never lost again.'

'I know not love,' quoth he, 'nor will not
    know it,
Unless it be a boar, and then I chase it ;   410
'Tis much to borrow, and I will not owe it ;
My love to love is love but to disgrace it ;
    For I have heard it is a life in death,
    That laughs and weeps, and all but with a
      breath.

' Who wears a garment shapeless and unfin-
    ish'd ?
Who plucks the bud before one leaf put forth ?
If springing things be any jot diminish'd,
They wither in their prime, prove nothing
    worth :
    The colt that's back'd and burden'd being
      young
    Loseth his pride and never waxeth strong.

' You hurt my hand with wringing ; let us
    part,   421
And leave this idle theme, this bootless chat :
Remove your siege from my unyielding heart ;
To love's alarms it will not ope the gate :
    Dismiss your vows, your feigned tears, your
      flattery ;
    For where a heart is hard they make no
      battery.'

' What ! canst thou talk ? ' quoth she, ' hast
    thou a tongue ?
O, would thou hadst not, or I had no hearing !
Thy mermaid's voice hath done me double
    wrong ;
I had my load before, now press'd with bear-
    ing :   430
    Melodious discord, heavenly tune harsh-
      sounding,
    Ear's deep-sweet music, and heart's deep-
      sore wounding.

' Had I no eyes but ears, my ears would love
That inward beauty and invisible ;
Or were I deaf, thy outward parts would move
Each part in me that were but sensible :
    Though neither eyes nor ears, to hear nor
      see,
    Yet should I be in love by touching thee.

' Say, that the sense of feeling were bereft me,
And that I could not see, nor hear, nor touch,
And nothing but the very smell were left me,
Yet would my love to thee be still as much ;
    For from the stillitory of thy face excelling
    Comes breath perfumed that breedeth love
      by smelling.

' But, O, what banquet wert thou to the taste,
Being nurse and feeder of the other four !
Would they not wish the feast might ever last,
And bid Suspicion double-lock the door,
    Lest Jealousy, that sour unwelcome guest,
    Should, by his stealing in, disturb the feast ? '

Once more the ruby-color'd portal open'd, 451
Which to his speech did honey passage yield ;
Like a red morn, that ever yet betoken'd
Wreck to the seaman, tempest to the field,
    Sorrow to shepherds, woe unto the birds,
    Gusts and foul flaws to herdmen and to
      herds.

This ill presage advisedly she marketh :
Even as the wind is hush'd before it raineth,
Or as the wolf doth grin before he barketh,
Or as the berry breaks before it staineth, 460
    Or like the deadly bullet of a gun,
    His meaning struck her ere his words begun.

And at his look she flatly falleth down,
For looks kill love and love by looks reviveth ;
A smile recures the wounding of a frown ;
But blessed bankrupt, that by love so thriveth !
    The silly boy, believing she is dead,
    Claps her pale cheek, till clapping makes it
      red ;

And all amazed brake off his late intent,
For sharply he did think to reprehend her, 470
Which cunning love did wittily prevent :
Fair fall the wit that can so well defend her !
    For on the grass she lies as she were slain,
    Till his breath breatheth life in her again.

He wrings her nose, he strikes her on the
    cheeks,
He bends her fingers, holds her pulses hard,
He chafes her lips ; a thousand ways he seeks
To mend the hurt that his unkindness marr'd :
    He kisses her ; and she, by her good will,
    Will never rise, so he will kiss her still. 480

The night of sorrow now is turn'd to day :
Her two blue windows faintly she up-heaveth,
Like the fair sun, when in his fresh array
He cheers the morn and all the earth relieveth ;
    And as the bright sun glorifies the sky,
    So is her face illumined with her eye ;

Whose beams upon his hairless face are fix'd,
As if from thence they borrow'd all their
    shine.
Were never four such lamps together mix'd,
Had not his clouded with his brow's repine ;
    But hers, which through the crystal tears
      gave light,   491
    Shone like the moon in water seen by night.

' O, where am I ? ' quoth she, ' in earth or
    heaven,
Or in the ocean drench'd, or in the fire ?
What hour is this ? or morn or weary even ?
Do I delight to die, or life desire ?
    But now I lived, and life was death's annoy ;
    But now I died, and death was lively joy.

' O, thou didst kill me : kill me once again :
Thy eyes' shrewd tutor, that hard heart of
    thine,   500
Hath taught them scornful tricks and such dis-
    dain
That they have murder'd this poor heart of
    mine ;
    And these mine eyes, true leaders to their
      queen,
    But for thy piteous lips no more had seen.

' Long may they kiss each other, for this cure !
O, never let their crimson liveries wear !
And as they last, their verdure still endure,
To drive infection from the dangerous year !
    That the star-gazers, having writ on death,
    May say, the plague is banish'd by thy
      breath.   510

' Pure lips, sweet seals in my soft lips im-
    printed,
What bargains may I make, still to be seal-
    ing ?
To sell myself I can be well contented,
So thou wilt buy and pay and use good deal-
    ing ;
    Which purchase if thou make, for fear of
      slips
    Set thy seal-manual on my wax-red lips.

'A thousand kisses buys my heart from me;
And pay them at thy leisure, one by one.
What is ten hundred touches unto thee? 519
Are they not quickly told and quickly gone?
  Say, for non-payment that the debt should double,
  Is twenty hundred kisses such a trouble?'

'Fair queen,' quoth he, 'if any love you owe me,
Measure my strangeness with my unripe years:
Before I know myself, seek not to know me;
No fisher but the ungrown fry forbears:
  The mellow plum doth fall, the green sticks fast,
  Or being early pluck'd is sour to taste.

'Look, the world's comforter, with weary gait,
His day's hot task hath ended in the west;
The owl, night's herald, shrieks, "'Tis very late;" 531
The sheep are gone to fold, birds to their nest,
  And coal-black clouds that shadow heaven's light
  Do summon us to part and bid good night.

'Now let me say "Good night," and so say you;
If you will say so, you shall have a kiss.'
'Good night,' quoth she, and, ere he says 'Adieu,'
The honey fee of parting tender'd is:
  Her arms do lend his neck a sweet embrace;
  Incorporate then they seem; face grows to face.   540

Till, breathless, he disjoin'd, and backward drew
The heavenly moisture, that sweet coral mouth,
Whose precious taste her thirsty lips well knew,
Whereon they surfeit, yet complain on drouth:
  He with her plenty press'd, she faint with dearth
  Their lips together glued, fall to the earth.

Now quick desire hath caught the yielding prey,
And glutton-like she feeds, yet never filleth;
Her lips are conquerors, his lips obey,
Paying what ransom the insulter willeth;   550
  Whose vulture thought doth pitch the price so high,
  That she will draw his lips' rich treasure dry:

And having felt the sweetness of the spoil,
With blindfold fury she begins to forage;
Her face doth reek and smoke, her blood doth boil,
And careless lust stirs up a desperate courage,
  Planting oblivion, beating reason back,
  Forgetting shame's pure blush and honor's wrack.

Hot, faint, and weary, with her hard embracing,
Like a wild bird being tamed with too much handling,   560
Or as the fleet-foot roe that's tired with chasing,
Or like the froward infant still'd with dandling,

He now obeys, and now no more resisteth,
While she takes all she can, not all she listeth.

What wax so frozen but dissolves with tempering,
And yields at last to every light impression?
Things out of hope are compass'd oft with venturing,
Chiefly in love, whose leave exceeds commission:
  Affection faints not like a pale-faced coward,
  But then woos best when most his choice is froward.   570

When he did frown, O, had she then gave over,
Such nectar from his lips she had not suck'd.
Foul words and frowns must not repel a lover;
What though the rose have prickles, yet 'tis pluck'd:
  Were beauty under twenty locks kept fast,
  Yet love breaks through and picks them all at last.

For pity now she can no more detain him;
The poor fool prays her that he may depart:
She is resolved no longer to restrain him;
Bids him farewell, and look well to her heart,
  The which, by Cupid's bow she doth protest,
  He carries thence incaged in his breast.

'Sweet boy,' she says, 'this night I'll waste in sorrow,
For my sick heart commands mine eyes to watch.
Tell me, Love's master, shall we meet to-morrow?
Say, shall we? shall we? wilt thou make the match?'
  He tells her, no; to-morrow he intends
  To hunt the boar with certain of his friends.

'The boar!' quoth she; whereat a sudden pale,
Like lawn being spread upon the blushing rose,
Usurps her cheek; she trembles at his tale,
And on his neck her yoking arms she throws:
  She sinketh down, still hanging by his neck,
  He on his belly falls, she on her back.

Now is she in the very lists of love,
Her champion mounted for the hot encounter:
All is imaginary she doth prove,
He will not manage her, although he mount her;
  That worse than Tantalus' is her annoy,
  To clip Elysium and to lack her joy.   600

Even as poor birds, deceived with painted grapes,
Do surfeit by the eye and pine the maw,
Even so she languisheth in her mishaps,
As those poor birds that helpless berries saw.
  The warm effects which she in him finds missing
  She seeks to kindle with continual kissing.

But all in vain; good queen, it will not be:
She hath assay'd as much as may be proved;
Her pleading hath deserved a greater fee;   609
She's Love, she loves, and yet she is not loved.
  'Fie, fie,' he says, 'you crush me; let me go;
  You have no reason to withhold me so.'

' Thou hadst been gone,' quoth she, ' sweet boy,
ere this,
But that thou told'st me thou wouldst hunt the
boar.
O, be advised ! thou know'st not what it is
With javelin's point a churlish swine to gore,
Whose tushes never sheathed he whetteth
still,
Like to a mortal butcher bent to kill.

' On his bow-back he hath a battle set
Of bristly pikes, that ever threat his foes ;   620
His eyes, like glow-worms, shine when he doth
fret ;
His snout digs sepulchres where'er he goes ;
Being moved, he strikes whate'er is in his
way,
And whom he strikes his cruel tushes slay.

' His brawny sides, with hairy bristles arm'd,
Are better proof than thy spear's point can
enter ;
His short thick neck cannot be easily harm'd ;
Being ireful, on the lion he will venture :
The thorny brambles and embracing bushes,
As fearful of him, part, through whom he
rushes.   630

' Alas, he nought esteems that face of thine,
To which Love's eyes pay tributary gazes ;
Nor thy soft hands, sweet lips and crystal eyne,
Whose full perfection all the world amazes ;
But having thee at vantage,—wondrous
dread !—
Would root these beauties as he roots the
mead.

' O, let him keep his loathsome cabin still ;
Beauty hath nought to do with such foul
fiends :
Come not within his danger by thy will ;   639
They that thrive well take counsel of their
friends.
When thou didst name the boar, not to dis-
semble,
I fear'd thy fortune, and my joints did trem-
ble.

' Didst thou not mark my face ? was it not
white ?
Saw'st thou not signs of fear lurk in mine eye ?
Grew I not faint ? and fell I not downright ?
Within my bosom, whereon thou dost lie,
My boding heart pants, beats, and takes no
rest,
But, like an earthquake, shakes thee on my
breast.

' For where Love reigns, disturbing Jealousy
Doth call himself Affection's sentinel ;   650
Gives false alarms, suggesteth mutiny,
And in a peaceful hour doth cry " Kill, kill ! "
Distempering gentle Love in his desire,
As air and water do abate the fire.

' This sour informer, this bate-breeding spy,
This canker that eats up Love's tender spring,
This carry-tale, dissentious Jealousy,
That sometime true news, sometime false doth
bring,
Knocks at my heart and whispers in mine
ear   659
That if I love thee, I thy death should fear :

' And more than so, presenteth to mine eye
The picture of an angry-chafing boar,

Under whose sharp fangs on his back doth lie
An image like thyself, all stain'd with gore ;
Whose blood upon the fresh flowers being
shed
Doth make them droop with grief and hang
the head.

' What should I do, seeing thee so indeed,
That tremble at the imagination ?
The thought of it doth make my faint heart
bleed,
And fear doth teach it divination :   670
I prophesy thy death, my living sorrow,
If thou encounter with the boar to-morrow.

' But if thou needs wilt hunt, be ruled by me ;
Uncouple at the timorous flying hare,
Or at the fox which lives by subtlety,
Or at the roe which no encounter dare :
Pursue these fearful creatures o'er the
downs,
And on thy well-breath'd horse keep with
thy hounds.

' And when thou hast on foot the purblind
hare,
Mark the poor wretch, to overshoot his trou-
bles   680
How he outruns the wind and with what care
He cranks and crosses with a thousand dou-
bles :
The many musets through the which he goes
Are like a labyrinth to amaze his foes.

' Sometime he runs among a flock of sheep,
To make the cunning hounds mistake their
smell,
And sometime where earth-delving conies
keep,
To stop the loud pursuers in their yell,
And sometime sorteth with a herd of deer :
Danger deviseth shifts ; wit waits on fear :

' For there his smell with others being mingled,
The hot scent-snuffing hounds are driven to
doubt,   692
Ceasing their clamorous cry till they have sin-
gled
With much ado the cold fault cleanly out ;
Then do they spend their mouths : Echo re-
plies,
As if another chase were in the skies.

' By this, poor Wat, far off upon a hill,
Stands on his hinder legs with listening ear,
To harken if his foes pursue him still :
Anon their loud alarums he doth hear ;   700
And now his grief may be compared well
To one sore sick that hears the passing-bell.

' Then shalt thou see the dew-bedabbled wretch
Turn, and return, indenting with the way ;
Each envious brier his weary legs doth scratch,
Each shadow makes him stop, each murmur
stay :
For misery is trodden on by many,
And being low never relieved by any.

' Lie quietly, and hear a little more ;   709
Nay, do not struggle, for thou shalt not rise :
To make thee hate the hunting of the boar,
Unlike myself thou hear'st me moralize,
Applying this to that, and so to so ;
For love can comment upon every woe.

'Where did I leave?' 'No matter where,'
    quoth he,
'Leave me, and then the story aptly ends:
The night is spent.' 'Why, what of that?'
    quoth she.
'I am,' quoth he, 'expected of my friends;
    And now 'tis dark, and going I shall fall.'
'In night,' quoth she, 'desire sees best of all.

'But if thou fall, O, then imagine this, 721
The earth, in love with thee, thy footing trips,
And all is but to rob thee of a kiss.
Rich preys make true men thieves; so do thy
    lips
  Make modest Dian cloudy and forlorn,
  Lest she should steal a kiss and die for-
    sworn.

'Now of this dark night I perceive the reason:
Cynthia for shame obscures her silver shine,
Till forging Nature be condemn'd of treason,
For stealing moulds from heaven that were di-
    vine; 730
  Wherein she framed thee in high heaven's
    despite,
  To shame the sun by day and her by night.

'And therefore hath she bribed the Destinies
To cross the curious workmanship of nature,
To mingle beauty with infirmities,
And pure perfection with impure defeature,
  Making it subject to the tyranny
  Of mad mischances and much misery;

'As burning fevers, agues pale and faint, 739
Life-poisoning pestilence and frenzies wood,
The marrow-eating sickness, whose attaint
Disorder breeds by heating of the blood:
  Surfeits, imposthumes, grief, and damn'd de-
    spair,
  Swear nature's death for framing thee so
    fair.

'And not the least of all these maladies
But in one minute's fight brings beauty under:
Both favor, savor, hue and qualities,
Whereat the impartial gazer late did wonder,
  Are on the sudden wasted, thaw'd and done,
  As mountain-snow melts with the midday
    sun.

'Therefore, despite of fruitless chastity, 751
Love-lacking vestals and self-loving nuns,
That on the earth would breed a scarcity
And barren dearth of daughters and of sons,
  Be prodigal: the lamp that burns by night
  Dries up his oil to lend the world his light.

'What is thy body but a swallowing grave,
Seeming to bury that posterity
Which by the rights of time thou needs must
    have, 759
If thou destroy them not in dark obscurity?
  If so, the world will hold thee in disdain,
  Sith in thy pride so fair a hope is slain.

'So in thyself thyself art made away;
A mischief worse than civil home-bred strife,
Or theirs whose desperate hands themselves do
    slay,
Or butcher-sire that reaves his son of life.
  Foul-cankering rust the hidden treasure
    frets,
  But gold that's put to use more gold begets.'

'Nay, then,' quoth Adon, 'you will fall again
Into your idle over-handled theme: 770
The kiss I gave you is bestow'd in vain,
And all in vain you strive against the stream;

For, by this black-faced night, desire's foul
    nurse,
Your treatise makes me like you worse and
    worse.

'If love have lent you twenty thousand tongues,
And every tongue more moving than your own,
Bewitching like the wanton mermaid's songs,
Yet from mine ear the tempting tune is blown:
  For know, my heart stands armed in mine
    ear,
  And will not let a false sound enter there;

'Lest the deceiving harmony should run 781
Into the quiet closure of my breast;
And then my little heart were quite undone,
In his bedchamber to be barr'd of rest.
  No, lady, no; my heart longs not to groan,
  But soundly sleeps, while now it sleeps alone.

'What have you urged that I cannot reprove?
The path is smooth that leadeth on to danger:
I hate not love, but your device in love, 789
That lends embracements unto every stranger.
  You do it for increase: O strange excuse,
  When reason is the bawd to lust's abuse!

'Call it not love, for Love to heaven is fled,
Since sweating Lust on earth usurp'd his
    name;
Under whose simple semblance he hath fed
Upon fresh beauty, blotting it with blame;
  Which the hot tyrant stains and soon be-
    reaves,
  As caterpillars do the tender leaves.

'Love comforteth like sunshine after rain,
But Lust's effect is tempest after sun; 800
Love's gentle spring doth always fresh remain,
Lust's winter comes ere summer half be done;
  Love surfeits not, Lust like a glutton dies;
  Love is all truth, Lust full of forged lies.

'More I could tell, but more I dare not say;
The text is old, the orator too green.
Therefore, in sadness, now I will away;
My face is full of shame, my heart of teen:
  Mine ears, that to your wanton talk at-
    tended,
  Do burn themselves for having so offended.'

With this, he breaketh from the sweet em-
    brace, 811
Of those fair arms which bound him to her
    breast,
And homeward through the dark laund runs
    apace;
  Leaves Love upon her back deeply distress'd.
  Look, how a bright star shooteth from the
    sky,
  So glides he in the night from Venus' eye.

Which after him she darts, as one on shore
Gazing upon a late-embarked friend,
Till the wild waves will have him seen no more,
Whose ridges with the meeting clouds con-
    tend:
  So did the merciless and pitchy night 821
  Fold in the object that did feed her sight.

Whereat amazed, as one that unaware
Hath dropp'd a precious jewel in the flood,
Or stonish'd as night-wanderers often are,
Their light blown out in some mistrustful
    wood,
  Even so confounded in the dark she lay,
  Having lost the fair discovery of her way.

And now she beats her heart, whereat it
  groans,
That all the neighbor caves, as seeming trou-
  bled,   830
Make verbal repetition of her moans ;
Passion on passion deeply is redoubled :
  ' Ay me ! ' she cries, and twenty times ' Woe,
    woe ! '
  And twenty echoes twenty times cry so.

She marking them begins a wailing note
And sings extemporally a woeful ditty ;
How love makes young men thrall and old
  men dote ;
How love is wise in folly, foolish-witty :
  Her heavy anthem still concludes in woe,
  And still the choir of echoes answer so. 840

Her song was tedious and outwore the night,
For lovers' hours are long, though seeming
  short :
If pleased themselves, others, they think, de-
  light
In such-like circumstance, with such-like
  sport :
  Their copious stories oftentimes begun
  End without audience and are never done.

For who hath she to spend the night withal
But idle sounds resembling parasites,
Like shrill-tongued tapsters answering every
  call,
Soothing the humor of fantastic wits ?   850
  She says ' 'Tis so : ' they answer all ' 'Tis
    so ; '
  And would say after her, if she said ' No.'

Lo, here the gentle lark, weary of rest,
From his moist cabinet mounts up on high,
And wakes the morning, from whose silver
  breast
The sun ariseth in his majesty ;
  Who doth the world so gloriously behold
  That cedar-tops and hills seem burnish'd
    gold.

Venus salutes him with this fair good-morrow :
' O thou clear god, and patron of all light, 860
From whom each lamp and shining star doth
  borrow
The beauteous influence that makes him bright,
  There lives a son that suck'd an earthly
    mother,
  May lend thee light, as thou dost lend to
    other.'

This said, she hasteth to a myrtle grove,
Musing the morning is so much o'erworn,
And yet she hears no tidings of her love :
She hearkens for his hounds and for his horn :
  Anon she hears them chant it lustily,
  And all in haste she coasteth to the cry. 870

And as she runs, the bushes in the way
Some catch her by the neck, some kiss her
  face,
Some twine about her thigh to make her stay :
She wildly breaketh from their strict embrace,
  Like a milch doe, whose swelling dugs do
    ache,
  Hasting to feed her fawn hid in some brake.

By this, she hears the hounds are at a bay ;
Whereat she starts, like one that spies an adder
Wreathed up in fatal folds just in his way,
The fear whereof doth make him shake and
  shudder ;   880

Even so the timorous yelping of the hounds
Appals her senses and her spirit confounds.

For now she knows it is no gentle chase,
But the blunt boar, rough bear, or lion proud,
Because the cry remaineth in one place,
Where fearfully the dogs exclaim aloud :
  Finding their enemy to be so curst,
  They all strain courtesy who shall cope him
    first.

This dismal cry rings sadly in her ear,   889
Through which it enters to surprise her heart ;
Who, overcome by doubt and bloodless fear,
With cold-pale weakness numbs each feeling
  part :
  Like soldiers, when their captain once doth
    yield,
  They basely fly and dare not stay the field.

Thus stands she in a trembling ecstasy ;
Till, cheering up her senses all dismay'd,
She tells them 'tis a causeless fantasy,
And childish error, that they are afraid ;
  Bids them leave quaking, bids them fear no
    more :—
  And with that word she spied the hunted
    boar,   900

Whose frothy mouth, bepainted all with red,
Like milk and blood being mingled both to-
  gether,
A second fear through all her sinews spread,
Which madly hurries her she knows not
  whither :
  This way she runs, and now she will no fur-
    ther,
  But back retires to rate the boar for mur-
    ther.

A thousand spleens bear her a thousand ways ;
She treads the path that she untreads again ;
Her more than haste is mated with delays,
Like the proceedings of a drunken brain, 910
  Full of respects, yet nought at all respect-
    ing ;
  In hand with all things, nought at all effect-
    ing.

Here kennell'd in a brake she finds a hound,
And asks the weary caitiff for his master,
And there another licking of his wound,
'Gainst venom'd sores the only sovereign plas-
  ter ;
  And here she meets another sadly scowling,
  To whom she speaks, and he replies with
    howling.

When he hath ceased his ill-resounding noise,
Another flap-mouth'd mourner, black and
  grim,   920
Against the welkin volleys out his voice ;
Another and another answer him,
  Clapping their proud tails to the ground be-
    low,
  Shaking their scratch'd ears, bleeding as they
    go.

Look, how the world's poor people are amazed
At apparitions, signs and prodigies,
Whereon with fearful eyes they long have
  gazed,
Infusing them with dreadful prophecies ;
  So she at these sad signs draws up her
    breath
  And sighing it again, exclaims on Death. 930

' Hard-favor'd tyrant, ugly, meagre, lean,
Hateful divorce of love,'—thus chides she
　　Death,—
' Grim-grinning ghost, earth's worm, what dost
　　thou mean
To stifle beauty and to steal his breath,
　Who when he lived, his breath and beauty
　　set
　　Gloss on the rose, smell to the violet ?

' If he be dead,—O no, it cannot be,
Seeing his beauty, thou shouldst strike at it :—
O yes, it may ; thou hast no eyes to see,
But hatefully at random dost thou hit.　940
　Thy mark is feeble age, but thy false dart
　Mistakes that aim and cleaves an infant's
　　heart.

' Hadst thou but bid beware, then he had
　　spoke,
And, hearing him, thy power had lost his
　　power.
The Destinies will curse thee for this stroke ;
They bid thee crop a weed, thou pluck'st a
　　flower :
　Love's golden arrow at him should have fled,
　And not Death's ebon dart, to strike him
　　dead.

' Dost thou drink tears, that thou provokest
　　such weeping ?
What may a heavy groan advantage thee ?
Why hast thou cast into eternal sleeping　951
Those eyes that taught all other eyes to see ?
　Now Nature cares not for thy mortal vigor,
　Since her best work is ruin'd with thy rigor.'

Here overcome, as one full of despair,
She vail'd her eyelids, who, like sluices, stopt
The crystal tide that from her two cheeks fair
In the sweet channel of her bosom dropt ;
　But through the flood-gates breaks the silver
　　rain,
　And with his strong course opens them
　　again.　　960

O, how her eyes and tears did lend and bor-
　　row !
Her eyes seen in the tears, tears in her eye ;
Both crystals, where they view'd each other's
　　sorrow,
Sorrow that friendly sighs sought still to dry ;
　But like a stormy day, now wind, now rain,
　Sighs dry her cheeks, tears make them wet
　　again.

Variable passions throng her constant woe,
As striving who should best become her grief ;
All entertain'd, each passion labors so,
That every present sorrow seemeth chief,　970
　But none is best : then join they all together,
　Like many clouds consulting for foul
　　weather.

By this, far off she hears some huntsman
　　hollo ;
A nurse's song ne'er pleased her babe so well :
The dire imagination she did follow
This sound of hope doth labor to expel ;
　For now reviving joy bids her rejoice,
　And flatters her it is Adonis' voice.

Whereat her tears began to turn their tide,
Being prison'd in her eye like pearls in glass ;
Yet sometimes falls an orient drop beside,　981

Which her cheek melts, as scorning it should
　　pass,
　To wash the foul face of the sluttish ground,
　Who is but drunken when she seemeth
　　drown'd.

O hard-believing love, how strange it seems
Not to believe, and yet too credulous !
Thy weal and woe are both of them extremes ;
Despair and hope makes thee ridiculous :
　The one doth flatter thee in thoughts un-
　　likely,
　In likely thoughts the other kills thee
　　quickly.

Now she unweaves the web that she hath
　　wrought ;　　991
Adonis lives, and Death is not to blame ;
It was not she that call'd him, all-to naught :
Now she adds honors to his hateful name ;
　She clepes him king of graves and grave for
　　kings,
　Imperious supreme of all mortal things.

' No, no,' quoth she, ' sweet Death, I did but
　　jest ;
Yet pardon me I felt a kind of fear
When as I met the boar, that bloody beast,
Which knows no pity, but is still severe ; 1000
　Then, gentle shadow,—truth I must con-
　　fess,—
　I rail'd on thee, fearing my love's decease.

' 'Tis not my fault : the boar provoked my
　　tongue ;
Be wreak'd on him, invisible commander ;
'Tis he, foul creature, that hath done thee
　　wrong ;
I did but act, he's author of thy slander :
　Grief hath two tongues, and never woman
　　yet
　Could rule them both without ten women's
　　wit.'

Thus hoping that Adonis is alive,
Her rash suspect she doth extenuate ;　1010
And that his beauty may the better thrive,
With Death she humbly doth insinuate ;
　Tells him of trophies, statues, tombs, and
　　stories
　His victories, his triumphs and his glories.

' O Jove,' quoth she, ' how much a fool was I
To be of such a weak and silly mind
To wail his death who lives and must not die
Till mutual overthrow of mortal kind !　1018
　For he being dead, with him is beauty slain,
　And, beauty dead, black chaos comes again.

' Fie, fie, fond love, thou art so full of fear
As one with treasure laden, hemm'd thieves ;
Trifles, unwitnessed with eye or ear,
Thy coward heart with false bethinking
　　grieves.'
　Even at this word she hears a merry horn,
　Whereat she leaps that was but late forlorn.

As falcon to the lure, away she flies ;
The grass stoops not, she treads on it so light ;
And in her haste unfortunately spies　1029
The foul boar's conquest on her fair delight ;
　Which seen, her eyes, as murder'd with the
　　view,
　Like stars ashamed of day, themselves with-
　　drew ;

Or, as the snail, whose tender horns being hit,
Shrinks backward in his shelly cave with pain,
And there, all smother'd up, in shade doth sit,
Long after fearing to creep forth again ;
　　So, at his bloody view, her eyes are fled
　　Into the deep dark cabins of her head :

Where they resign their office and their light
To the disposing of her troubled brain ;　1040
Who bids them still consort with ugly night,
And never wound the heart with looks again ;
　　Who, like a king perplexed in his throne,
　　By their suggestion gives a deadly groan,

Whereat each tributary subject quakes ;
As when the wind, imprison'd in the ground,
Struggling for passage, earth's foundation
　　shakes,
Which with cold terror doth men's minds con-
　　found.
　　This mutiny each part doth so surprise
　　That from their dark beds once more leap
　　　her eyes ;　　　　　　　　　　　　1050

And, being open'd, threw unwilling light
Upon the wide wound that the boar had
　　trench'd
In his soft flank ; whose wonted lily white
With purple tears, that his wound wept, was
　　drench'd :
　　No flower was nigh, no grass, herb, leaf, or
　　　weed,
　　But stole his blood and seem'd with him to
　　　bleed.

This solemn sympathy poor Venus noteth ;
Over one shoulder doth she hang her head ;
Dumbly she passions, franticly she doteth ;
She thinks he could not die, he is not dead :
　　Her voice is stopt, her joints forget to bow ;
　　Her eyes are mad that they have wept til
　　　now.

Upon his hurt she looks so steadfastly,
That her sight dazzling makes the wound seem
　　three ;
And then she reprehends her mangling eye,
That makes more gashes where no breach
　　should be :
　　His face seems twain, each several limb is
　　　doubled ;
　　For oft the eye mistakes, the brain being
　　　troubled.

' My tongue cannot express my grief for one,
And yet,' quoth she, ' behold two Adons dead !
My sighs are blown away, my salt tears gone,
Mine eyes are turn'd to fire, my heart to lead :
　　Heavy heart's lead, melt at mine eyes' red
　　　fire !
　　So shall I die by drops of hot desire.

' Alas, poor world, what treasure hast thou
　　lost !
What face remains alive that's worth the view-
　　ing ?
Whose tongue is music now ? what canst thou
　　boast
Of things long since, or any thing ensuing ?
　　The flowers are sweet, their colors fresh and
　　　trim ;
　　But true-sweet beauty lived and died with
　　　him.　　　　　　　　　　　　　1080

' Bonnet nor veil henceforth no creature wear !
Nor sun nor wind will ever strive to kiss you :
Having no fair to lose, you need not fear ;
The sun doth scorn you and the wind doth hiss
　　you :
　　But when Adonis lived, sun and sharp air
　　Lurk'd like two thieves, to rob him of his
　　　fair :

' And therefore would he put his bonnet on,
Under whose brim the gaudy sun would peep ;
The wind would blow it off and, being gone,
Play with his locks : then would Adonis weep ;
　　And straight, in pity of his tender years,
　　They both would strive who first should dry
　　　his tears.

' To see his face the lion walk'd along
Behind some hedge, because he would not fear
　　him ;
To recreate himself when he hath sung,
The tiger would be tame and gently hear him ;
　　If he had spoke, the wolf would leave his
　　　prey
　　And never fright the silly lamb that day.

' When he beheld his shadow in the brook,
The fishes spread on it their golden gills ;　1100
When he was by, the birds such pleasure took,
That some would sing, some other in their bills
　　Would bring him mulberries and ripe-red
　　　cherries ;
　　He fed them with his sight, they him with
　　　berries.

' But this foul, grim, and urchin-snouted boar,
Whose downward eye still looketh for a grave,
Ne'er saw the beauteous livery that he wore ;
Witness the entertainment that he gave :
　　If he did see his face, why then I know
　　He thought to kiss him, and hath kill'd him
　　　so.　　　　　　　　　　　　　1110

' 'Tis true, 'tis true ; thus was Adonis slain :
He ran upon the boar with his sharp spear,
Who did not whet his teeth at him again,
But by a kiss thought to persuade him there ;
　　And nuzzling in his flank, the loving swine
　　Sheathed unaware the tusk in his soft groin.

' Had I been tooth'd like him, I must confess,
With kissing him I should have kill'd him first ;
But he is dead, and never did he bless　1119
My youth with his ; the more am I accurst.'
　　With this, she falleth in the place she stood,
　　And stains her face with his congealed
　　　blood.

She looks upon his lips, and they are pale ;
She takes him by the hand, and that is cold ;
She whispers in his ears a heavy tale,
As if they heard the woeful words she told ;
　　She lifts the coffer-lids that close his eyes,
　　Where, lo, two lamps, burnt out, in darkness
　　　lies ;

Two glasses, where herself herself beheld
A thousand times, and now no more reflect ;
Their virtue lost, wherein they late excell'd,
And every beauty robb'd of his effect :
　　' Wonder of time,' quoth she, ' this is my
　　　spite,
　　That, thou being dead, the day should yet be
　　　light.

' Since thou art dead, lo, here I prophesy :
Sorrow on love hereafter shall attend :
It shall be waited on with jealousy,
Find sweet beginning, but unsavory end,
   Ne'er settled equally, but high or low,
   That all love's pleasure shall not match his
     woe. 1140

' It shall be fickle, false and full of fraud,
Bud and be blasted in a breathing-while ;
The bottom poison, and the top o'erstraw'd
With sweets that shall the truest sight beguile :
   The strongest body shall it make most weak,
   Strike the wise dumb and teach the fool to
     speak.

' It shall be sparing and too full of riot,
Teaching decrepit age to tread the measures ;
The staring ruffian shall it keep in quiet,
Pluck down the rich, enrich the poor with
     treasures ; 1150
   It shall be raging-mad and silly-mild,
   Make the young old, the old become a child.

' It shall suspect where is no cause of fear ;
It shall not fear where it should most mistrust ;
It shall be merciful and too severe,
And most deceiving when it seems most just ;
   Perverse it shall be where it shows most to-
     ward,
   Put fear to valor, courage to the coward.

' It shall be cause of war and dire events,
And set dissension 'twixt the son and sire ;
Subject and servile to all discontents, 1161
As dry combustious matter is to fire :
   Sith in his prime Death doth my love de-
     stroy,
   They that love best their loves shall not en-
     joy.'

By this, the boy that by her side lay kill'd
Was melted like a vapor from her sight,
And in his blood that on the ground lay spill'd,

A purple flower sprung up, chequer'd with
     white,
   Resembling well his pale cheeks and the
     blood
   Which in round drops upon their whiteness
     stood.

She bows her head, the new-sprung flower to
     smell, 1171
Comparing it to her Adonis' breath,
And says, within her bosom it shall dwell,
Since he himself is reft from her by death :
   She crops the stalk, and in the breach ap-
     pears
   Green dropping sap, which she compares to
     tears.

' Poor flower,' quoth she, ' this was thy father's
     guise—
Sweet issue of a more sweet-smelling sire—
For every little grief to wet his eyes :
To grow unto himself was his desire, 1180
   And so 'tis thine ; but know, it is as good
   To wither in my breast as in his blood.

' Here was thy father's bed, here in my breast ;
Thou art the next of blood, and 'tis thy right :
Lo, in this hollow cradle take thy rest,
My throbbing heart shall rock thee day and
     night :
   There shall not be one minute in an hour
   Wherein I will not kiss my sweet love's
     flower.'

Thus weary of the world, away she hies, 1189
And yokes her silver doves ; by whose swift aid
Their mistress mounted through the empty
     skies
In her light chariot quickly is convey'd ;
   Holding their course to Paphos, where their
     queen
   Means to immure herself and not be seen.

LUCRECE.

(WRITTEN ABOUT 1593-4.)

INTRODUCTION.

Lucrece was entered in the Stationers' register May 9, 1594, and was published the same year. Like the *Venus and Adonis*, it is dedicated to the Earl of Southampton, having been perhaps the "graver labor" promised in the dedication of that poem. The two poems resemble each other in several respects, especially in the detailed description style, which draws out at length the particulars of a scene, an incident, or an emotion. The poem of later date, however, exhibits far less immaturity than does the "first heire" of Shakespeare's invention. Part of this may be due to the fact that the subject is deeper and more passionate : instead of the enamored Venus we have here the pure and noble Lucretia ; instead of the boy Adonis, the powerful figure of the evil Tarquin. *Lucrece* was highly admired by Shakespeare's contemporaries, and was several times republished, though less often than the *Venus*. The story of Lucretia is told by Livy and Ovid, and was versified by Gower, and again related in Paynter's *Palace of Pleasure*, 1567.

TO THE
RIGHT HONORABLE HENRY WRIOTHESLY,
EARL OF SOUTHAMPTON, AND BARON OF TICHFIELD.

THE love I dedicate to your lordship is without end ; whereof this pamphlet, without beginning, is but a superfluous moiety. The warrant I have of your honorable disposition, not the worth of my untutored lines, makes it assured of acceptance. What I have done is yours ; what I have to do is yours ; being part in all I have, devoted yours. Were my worth greater, my duty would show greater ; meantime, as it is, it is bound to your lordship, to whom I wish long life, still lengthened with all happiness.

Your lordship's in all duty,

WILLIAM SHAKESPEARE.

THE ARGUMENT.

LUCIUS TARQUINIUS, for his excessive pride surnamed Superbus, after he had caused his own father-in-law Servius Tullius to be cruelly murdered, and, contrary to the Roman laws and customs, not requiring or staying for the people's suffrages, had possessed himself of the kingdom, went, accompanied with his sons and other noblemen of Rome, to besiege Ardea. During which siege the principal men of the army meeting one evening at the tent of Sextus Tarquinius, the king's son, in their discourses after supper every one commended the virtues of his own wife : among whom Collatinus extolled the incomparable chastity of his wife Lucretia. In that pleasant humor they all posted to Rome ; and intending, by their secret and sudden arrival, to make trial of that which every one had before avouched, only Collatinus finds his wife, though it were late in the night, spinning amongst her maids : the other ladies were all found dancing and revelling, or in several disports. Whereupon the noblemen yielded Collatinus the victory, and his wife the fame. At that time Sextus Tarquinius being inflamed with Lucrece' beauty, yet smothering his passions for the present, departed with the rest back to the camp ; from whence he shortly after privily withdrew himself, and was, according to his estate, royally entertained and lodged by Lucrece at Collatium. The same night he treacherously stealeth into her chamber, violently ravished her, and early in the morning speedeth away. Lucrece, in this lamentable plight, hastily dispatcheth messengers, one to Rome for her father, another to the camp for Collatine. They came, the one accompanied with Junius Brutus, the other with Publius Valerius ; and finding Lucrece attired in mourning habit, demanded the cause of her sorrow. She, first taking an oath of them for her revenge, revealed the actor, and whole manner of his dealing, and withal suddenly stabbed herself. Which done, with one consent they all vowed to root out the whole hated family of the Tarquins ; and bearing the dead body to Rome, Brutus acquainted the people with the doer and manner of the vile deed, with a bitter invective against the tyranny of the king : wherewith the people were so moved, that with one consent and a general acclamation the Tarquins were all exiled, and the state government changed from kings to consuls.

From the besieged Ardea all in post,
Borne by the trustless wings of false desire,
Lust-breathed Tarquin leaves the Roman host,
And to Collatium bears the lightless fire
Which, in pale embers hid, lurks to aspire
    And girdle with embracing flames the waist
    Of Collatine's fair love, Lucrece the chaste.

Haply that name of ' chaste ' unhappily set
This bateless edge on his keen appetite ;
When Collatine unwisely did not let   10
To praise the clear unmatched red and white
Which triumph'd in that sky of his delight,
    Where mortal stars, as bright as heaven's
        beauties,
    With pure aspects did him peculiar duties.

For he the night before, in Tarquin's tent,
Unlock'd the treasure of his happy state ;
What priceless wealth the heavens had him
        lent
In the possession of his beauteous mate ;
Reckoning his fortune at such high-proud rate,
    That kings might be espoused to more fame,
    But king nor peer to such a peerless dame.

O happiness enjoy'd but of a few !
And, if possess'd, as soon decay'd and done
As is the morning's silver-melting dew
Against the golden splendor of the sun !
An expired date, cancell'd ere well begun :
    Honor and beauty, in the owner's arms,
    Are weakly fortress'd from a world of
        harms.

Beauty itself doth of itself persuade
The eyes of men without an orator ;   30
What needeth then apologies be made,
To set forth that which is so singular ?
Or why is Collatine the publisher
    Of that rich jewel he should keep unknown
    From thievish ears, because it is his own ?

Perchance his boast of Lucrece' sovereignty
Suggested this proud issue of a king ;
For by our ears our hearts oft tainted be :
Perchance that envy of so rich a thing,
Braving compare, disdainfully did sting   40
    His high-pitch'd thoughts, that meaner men
        should vaunt
    That golden hap which their superiors
        want.

But some untimely thought did instigate
His all-too-timeless speed, if none of those :
His honor, his affairs, his friends, his state,
Neglected all, with swift intent he goes
To quench the coal which in his liver glows.
    O rash false heat, wrapp'd in repentant cold,
    Thy hasty spring still blasts, and ne'er grows
        old !

When at Collatium this false lord arrived, 50
Well was he welcomed by the Roman dame,
Within whose face beauty and virtue strived
Which of them both should underprop her
        fame :
    When virtue bragg'd, beauty would blush for
        shame ;
    When beauty boasted blushes, in despite
    Virtue would stain that o'er with silver
        white.

But beauty, in that white intituled,
From Venus' doves doth challenge that fair
        field :
Then virtue claims from beauty beauty's red,
Which virtue gave the golden age to gild   60

Their silver cheeks, and call'd it then their
        shield ;
    Teaching them thus to use it in the fight,
    When shame assail'd, the red should fence
        the white.

This heraldry in Lucrece' face was seen,
Argued by beauty's red and virtue's white
Of either's color was the other queen,
Proving from world's minority their right :
Yet their ambition makes them still to fight ;
    The sovereignty of either being so great,
    That oft they interchange each other's seat.

Their silent war of lilies and of roses,   71
Which Tarquin view'd in her fair face's field,
In their pure ranks his traitor eye encloses ;
Where, lest between them both it should be
        kill'd,
    The coward captive vanquished doth yield
    To those two armies that would let him go,
    Rather than triumph in so false a foe.

Now thinks he that her husband's shallow
        tongue,—
The niggard prodigal that praised her so,—
In that high task hath done her beauty wrong,
Which far exceeds his barren skill to show :
Therefore that praise which Collatine doth owe
    Enchanted Tarquin answers with surmise,
    In silent wonder of still-gazing eyes.

This earthly saint, adored by this devil,
Little suspecteth the false worshipper ;
For unstain'd thoughts do seldom dream on
        evil ;
Birds never limed no secret bushes fear :
So guiltless she securely gives good cheer
    And reverend welcome to her princely guest,
    Whose inward ill no outward harm ex-
        press'd :   91

For that he color'd with his high estate,
Hiding base sin in plaits of majesty ;
That nothing in him seem'd inordinate,
Save something too much wonder of his eye,
Which, having all, all could not satisfy ;
    But, poorly rich, so wanteth in his store,
    That, cloy'd with much, he pineth still for
        more.

But she, that never coped with stranger eyes,
Could pick no meaning from their parling
        looks,   100
Nor read the subtle-shining secrecies
Writ in the glassy margents of such books :
She touch'd no unknown baits, nor fear'd no
        hooks ;
    Nor could she moralize his wanton sight,
    More than his eyes were open'd to the light.

He stories to her ears her husband's fame,
Won in the fields of fruitful Italy ;
And decks with praises Collatine's high name,
Made glorious by his manly chivalry
With bruised arms and wreaths of victory :
    Her joy with heaved-up hand she doth ex-
        press,   111
    And, wordless, so greets heaven for his suc-
        cess.

Far from the purpose of his coming hither,
He makes excuses for his being there :
No cloudy show of stormy blustering weather
Doth yet in his fair welkin once appear ;
Till sable Night, mother of Dread and Fear,
    Upon the world dim darkness doth display,
    And in her vaulty prison stows the Day.

For then is Tarquin brought unto his bed, 120
Intending weariness with heavy spright ;
For, after supper, long he questioned
With modest Lucrece, and wore out the night :
Now leaden slumber with life's strength doth fight ;
  And every one to rest themselves betake,
  Save thieves, and cares, and troubled minds, that wake.

As one of which doth Tarquin lie revolving
The sundry dangers of his will's obtaining ;
Yet ever to obtain his will resolving,
Though weak-built hopes persuade him to abstaining : 130
Despair to gain doth traffic oft for gaining ;
  And when great treasure is the meed proposed,
  Though death be adjunct, there's no death supposed.

Those that much covet are with gain so fond,
For what they have not, that which they possess
They scatter and unloose it from their bond,
And so, by hoping more, they have but less ;
Or, gaining more, the profit of excess
  Is but to surfeit, and such griefs sustain,
  That they prove bankrupt in this poor-rich gain. 140

The aim of all is but to nurse the life
With honor, wealth, and ease, in waning age ;
And in this aim there is such thwarting strife,
That one for all, or all for one we gage ;
As life for honor in fell battle's rage ;
  Honor for wealth ; and oft that wealth doth cost
  The death of all, and all together lost.

So that in venturing ill we leave to be
The things we are for that which we expect ;
And this ambitious foul infirmity, 150
In having much, torments us with defect
Of that we have : so then we do neglect
  The thing we have ; and, all for want of wit,
  Make something nothing by augmenting it.

Such hazard now must doting Tarquin make,
Pawning his honor to obtain his lust ;
And for himself himself he must forsake :
Then where is truth, if there be no self-trust ?
When shall he think to find a stranger just,
  When he himself himself confounds, betrays
  To slanderous tongues and wretched hateful days ? 161

Now stole upon the time the dead of night,
When heavy sleep had closed up mortal eyes :
No comfortable star did lend his light,
No noise but owls' and wolves' death-boding cries ;
Now serves the season that they may surprise
  The silly lambs : pure thoughts are dead and still,
  While lust and murder wake to stain and kill.

And now this lustful lord leap'd from his bed,
Throwing his mantle rudely o'er his arm ; 170
Is madly toss'd between desire and dread ;
Th' one sweetly flatters, th' other feareth harm ;
But honest fear, bewitch'd with lust's foul charm,

Doth too too oft betake him to retire,
Beaten away by brain-sick rude desire.

His falchion on a flint he softly smiteth,
That from the cold stone sparks of fire do fly ;
Whereat a waxen torch forthwith he lighteth,
Which must be lode-star to his lustful eye ;
And to the flame thus speaks advisedly, 180
  ' As from this cold flint I enforced this fire,
  So Lucrece must I force to my desire.'

Here pale with fear he doth premeditate
The dangers of his loathsome enterprise,
And in his inward mind he doth debate
What following sorrow may on this arise :
Then looking scornfully, he doth despise
  His naked armor of still-slaughter'd lust,
  And justly thus controls his thoughts unjust :

' Fair torch, burn out thy light, and lend it not
To darken her whose light excelleth thine : 191
And die, unhallow'd thoughts, before you blot
With your uncleanness that which is divine ;
Offer pure incense to so pure a shrine :
  Let fair humanity abhor the deed
  That spots and stains love's modest snow-white weed.

' O shame to knighthood and to shining arms !
O foul dishonor to my household's grave !
O impious act, including all foul harms !
A martial man to be soft fancy's slave ! 200
True valor still a true respect should have ;
  Then my digression is so vile, so base,
  That it will live engraven in my face.

' Yea, though I die, the scandal will survive,
And be an eye-sore in my golden coat ;
Some loathsome dash the herald will contrive,
To cipher me how fondly I did dote ;
That my posterity, shamed with the note
  Shall curse my bones, and hold it for no sin
  To wish that I their father had not bin. 210

' What win I, if I gain the thing I seek ?
A dream, a breath, a froth of fleeting joy.
Who buys a minute's mirth to wail a week ?
Or sells eternity to get a toy ?
For one sweet grape who will the vine destroy ?
  Or what fond beggar, but to touch the crown,
  Would with the sceptre straight be strucken down ?

' If Collatinus dream of my intent,
Will he not wake, and in a desperate rage
Post hither, this vile purpose to prevent ? 220
This siege that hath engirt his marriage,
This blur to youth, this sorrow to the sage,
  This dying virtue, this surviving shame,
  Whose crime will bear an ever-during blame ?

' O, what excuse can my invention make,
When thou shalt charge me with so black a deed ?
Will not my tongue be mute, my frail joints shake,
Mine eyes forego their light, my false heart bleed ?
The guilt being great, the fear doth still exceed ; 229
  And extreme fear can neither fight nor fly,
  But coward-like with trembling terror die.

' Had Collatinus kill'd my son or sire,
Or lain in ambush to betray my life,
Or were he not my dear friend, this desire
Might have excuse to work upon his wife,
As in revenge or quittal of such strife :
  But as he is my kinsman, my dear friend,
  The shame and fault finds no excuse nor
    end.

' Shameful it is ; ay, if the fact be known :
Hateful it is ; there is no hate in loving : 240
I'll beg her love ; but she is not her own :
The worst is but denial and reproving :
My will is strong, past reason's weak removing.
  Who fears a sentence or an old man's saw
  Shall by a painted cloth be kept in awe.'

Thus, graceless, holds he disputation
'Tween frozen conscience and hot-burning will,
And with good thoughts makes dispensation,
Urging the worser sense for vantage still ; 249
Which in a moment doth confound and kill
  All pure effects, and doth so far proceed,
  That what is vile shows like a virtuous deed.

Quoth he, ' She took me kindly by the hand,
And gazed for tidings in my eager eyes,
Fearing some hard news from the warlike
    band,
Where her beloved Collatinus lies.
O, how her fear did make her color rise !
  First red as roses that on lawn we lay,
  Then white as lawn, the roses took away.

' And how her hand, in my hand being lock'd,
Forced it to tremble with her loyal fear ! 261
Which struck her sad, and then it faster
    rock'd,
Until her husband's welfare she did hear ;
Whereat she smiled with so sweet a cheer,
  That had Narcissus seen her as she stood,
  Self-love had never drown'd him in the flood.

' Why hunt I then for color or excuses ?
All orators are dumb when beauty pleadeth ;
Poor wretches have remorse in poor abuses ;
Love thrives not in the heart that shadows
    dreadeth : 270
Affection is my captain, and he leadeth ;
  And when his gaudy banner is display'd,
  The coward fights and will not be dismay'd.

' Then, childish fear, avaunt ! debating, die !
Respect and reason, wait on wrinkled age !
My heart shall never countermand mine eye :
Sad pause and deep regard beseem the sage ;
My part is youth, and beats these from the
    stage :
  Desire my pilot is, beauty my prize ;
  Then who fears sinking where such treasure
    lies ? ' 280

As corn o'ergrown by weeds, so heedful fear
Is almost choked by unresisted lust.
Away he steals with open listening ear,
Full of foul hope and full of fond mistrust ;
Both which, as servitors to the unjust,
  So cross him with their opposite persuasion,
  That now he vows a league, and now inva-
    sion.

Within his thought her heavenly image sits,
And in the self-same seat sits Collatine :
That eye which looks on her confounds his
    wits ; 290
That eye which him beholds, as more divine,

Unto a view so false will not incline ;
  But with a pure appeal seeks to the heart,
  Which once corrupted takes the worser
    part ;

And therein heartens up his servile powers,
Who, flatter'd by their leader's jocund show,
Stuff up his lust, as minutes fill up hours ;
And as their captain, so their pride doth grow,
Paying more slavish tribute than they owe.
  By reprobate desire thus madly led, 300
  The Roman lord marcheth to Lucrece' bed.

The locks between her chamber and his will,
Each one by him enforced, retires his ward ;
But, as they open, they all rate his ill,
Which drives the creeping thief to some re-
    gard :
The threshold grates the door to have him
    heard ;
  Night-wandering weasels shriek to see him
    there ;
  They fright him, yet he still pursues his fear.

As each unwilling portal yields him way, 309
Through little vents and crannies of the place
The wind wars with his torch to make him
    stay,
And blows the smoke of it into his face,
Extinguishing his conduct in this case ;
  But his hot heart, which fond desire doth
    scorch,
  Puffs forth another wind that fires the
    torch :

And being lighted, by the light he spies
Lucretia's glove, wherein her needle sticks :
He takes it from the rushes where it lies,
And griping it, the needle his finger pricks ;
As who should say ' This glove to wanton
    tricks 320
  Is not inured ; return again in haste ;
  Thou see'st our mistress' ornaments are
    chaste.'

But all these poor forbiddings could not stay
    him ;
He in the worst sense construes their denial :
The doors, the wind, the glove, that did delay
    him,
He takes for accidental things of trial ;
Or as those bars which stop the hourly dial,
  Who with a lingering stay his course doth
    let,
  Till every minute pays the hour his debt.

' So, so,' quoth he, ' these lets attend the time,
Like little frosts that sometime threat the
    spring, 331
To add a more rejoicing to the prime,
And give the sneaped birds more cause to sing.
Pain pays the income of each precious thing ;
  Huge rocks, high winds, strong pirates,
    shelves and sands,
  The merchant fears, ere rich at home he
    lands.'

Now is he come unto the chamber-door,
That shuts him from the heaven of his thought,
Which with a yielding latch, and with no more,
Hath barr'd him from the blessed thing he
    sought. 340
So from himself impiety hath wrought,
  That for his prey to pray he doth begin,
  As if the heavens should countenance his sin.

But in the midst of his unfruitful prayer,
Having solicited th' eternal power
That his foul thoughts might compass his fair
fair,
And they would stand auspicious to the hour,
Even there he starts : quoth he, ' I must de-
flower :
　The powers to whom I pray abhor this fact,
　How can they then assist me in the act? 350

' Then Love and Fortune be my gods, my
guide !
My will is back'd with resolution :
Thoughts are but dreams till their effects be
tried ;
The blackest sin is clear'd with absolution ;
Against love's fire fear's frost hath dissolution.
　The eye of heaven is out, and misty night
　Covers the shame that follows sweet delight.'

This said, his guilty hand pluck'd up the latch,
And with his knee the door he opens wide.
The dove sleeps fast that this night-owl will
catch :　　　　　　　　　　　　　360
Thus treason works ere traitors be espied.
Who sees the lurking serpent steps aside ;
　But she, sound sleeping, fearing no such
thing,
　Lies at the mercy of his mortal sting.

Into the chamber wickedly he stalks,
And gazeth on her yet unstained bed.
The curtains being close, about he walks,
Rolling his greedy eyeballs in his head :
By their high treason is his heart misled ;
　Which gives the watch-word to his hand full
soon　　　　　　　　　　　　　370
　To draw the cloud that hides the silver
moon.

Look, as the fair and fiery-pointed sun,
Rushing from forth a cloud, bereaves our
sight ;
Even so, the curtain drawn, his eyes begun
To wink, being blinded with a greater light :
Whether it is that she reflects so bright,
　That dazzleth them, or else some shame sup-
posed ;
　But blind they are, and keep themselves en-
closed.

O, had they in that darksome prison died !
Then had they seen the period of their ill ;
Then Collatine again, by Lucrece' side,　381
In his clear bed might have reposed still :
But they must ope, this blessed league to kill ;
　And holy-thoughted Lucrece to their sight
　Must sell her joy, her life, her world's de-
light.

Her lily hand her rosy cheek lies under,
Cozening the pillow of a lawful kiss ;
Who, therefore angry, seems to part in sunder,
Swelling on either side to want his bliss ;
Between whose hills her head entombed is :
　Where, like a virtuous monument, she lies,
　To be admired of lewd unhallow'd eyes.

Without the bed her other fair hand was,
On the green coverlet ; whose perfect white
Show'd like an April daisy on the grass,
With pearly sweat, resembling dew of night.
Her eyes, like marigolds, had sheathed their
light,
　And canopied in darkness sweetly lay,
　Till they might open to adorn the day.

Her hair, like golden threads, play'd with her
breath ;　　　　　　　　　　　　400
O modest wantons ! wanton modesty !
Showing life's triumph in the map of death,
And death's dim look in life's mortality :
Each in her sleep themselves so beautify,
　As if between them twain there were no
strife,
　But that life lived in death, and death in life.

Her breasts, like ivory globes circled with blue,
A pair of maiden worlds unconquered,
Save of their lord no bearing yoke they knew,
And him by oath they truly honored.　410
These worlds in Tarquin new ambition bred ;
　Who, like a foul usurper, went about
　From this fair throne to heave the owner
out.

What could he see but mightily he noted ?
What did he note but strongly he desired ?
What he beheld, on that he firmly doted,
And in his will his wilful eye he tired.
With more than admiration he admired
　Her azure veins, her alabaster skin,
　Her coral lips, her snow-white dimpled chin.

As the grim lion fawneth o'er his prey,　421
Sharp hunger by the conquest satisfied,
So o'er this sleeping soul doth Tarquin stay,
His rage of lust by gazing qualified ;
Slack'd, not suppress'd ; for standing by her
side,
　His eye, which late this mutiny restrains,
　Unto a greater uproar tempts his veins :

And they, like straggling slaves for pillage
fighting,
Obdurate vassals fell exploits effecting,
In bloody death and ravishment delighting,
Nor children's tears nor mothers' groans re-
specting,　　　　　　　　　　　431
Swell in their pride, the onset still expecting :
　Anon his beating heart, alarum striking,
　Gives the hot charge and bids them do their
liking.

His drumming heart cheers up his burning eye,
His eye commends the leading to his hand ;
His hand, as proud of such a dignity,
Smoking with pride, march'd on to make his
stand
On her bare breast, the heart of all her land ;
　Whose ranks of blue veins, as his hand did
scale,　　　　　　　　　　　　440
　Left there round turrets destitute and pale.

They, mustering to the quiet cabinet
Where their dear governess and lady lies,
Do tell her she is dreadfully beset,
And fright her with confusion of their cries :
She, much amazed, breaks ope her lock'd-up
eyes,
　Who, peeping forth this tumult to behold,
　Are by his flaming torch dimm'd and con-
troll'd.

Imagine her as one in dead of night
From forth dull sleep by dreadful fancy wak-
ing,　　　　　　　　　　　　　450
That thinks she hath beheld some ghastly
sprite,
Whose grim aspect sets every joint a-shaking ;
What terror 'tis ! but she, in worser taking,
　From sleep disturbed, heedfully doth view
　The sight which makes supposed terror true.

Wrapp'd and confounded in a thousand fears,
Like to a new-kill'd bird she trembling lies;
She dares not look; yet, winking, there ap-
pears
Quick-shifting antics, ugly in her eyes:
Such shadows are the weak brain's forgeries;
    Who, angry that the eyes fly from their
        lights, 461
    In darkness daunts them with more dreadful
        sights.

His hand, that yet remains upon her breast,—
Rude ram, to batter such an ivory wall!—
May feel her heart—poor citizen!—distress'd,
Wounding itself to death, rise up and fall,
Beating her bulk, that his hand shakes withal.
    This moves in him more rage and lesser pity,
    To make the breach and enter this sweet
        city.

First, like a trumpet, doth his tongue begin
To sound a parley to his heartless foe; 471
Who o'er the white sheet peers her whiter chin,
The reason of this rash alarm to know,
Which he by dumb demeanor seeks to show;
    But she with vehement prayers urgeth still
    Under what color he commits this ill.

Thus he replies: 'The color in thy face,
That even for anger makes the lily pale,
And the red rose blush at her own disgrace,
Shall plead for me and tell my loving tale:
Under that color am I come to scale 481
    Thy never-conquer'd fort: the fault is thine,
    For those thine eyes betray thee unto mine.

'Thus I forestall thee, if thou mean to chide:
Thy beauty hath ensnared thee to this night,
Where thou with patience must my will abide;
My will that marks thee for my earth's delight,
Which I to conquer sought with all my might;
    But as reproof and reason beat it dead,
    By thy bright beauty was it newly bred. 490

'I see what crosses my attempt will bring;
I know what thorns the growing rose defends;
I think the honey guarded with a sting;
All this beforehand counsel comprehends:
But will is deaf and hears no heedful friends;
    Only he hath an eye to gaze on beauty,
    And dotes on what he looks, 'gainst law or
        duty.

'I have debated, even in my soul,
What wrong, what shame, what sorrow I shall
    breed;
But nothing can affection's course control, 500
Or stop the headlong fury of his speed.
I know repentant tears ensue the deed,
    Reproach, disdain, and deadly enmity,
    Yet strive I to embrace mine infamy.'

This said, he shakes aloft his Roman blade,
Which, like a falcon towering in the skies,
Coucheth the fowl below with his wings' shade,
Whose crooked beak threats if he mount he
    dies:
So under his insulting falchion lies
    Harmless Lucretia, marking what he tells
    With trembling fear, as fowl hear falcon's
        bells. 511

'Lucrece,' quoth he, 'this night I must enjoy
    thee:
If thou deny, then force must work my way,
For in thy bed I purpose to destroy thee:

That done, some worthless slave of thine I'll
    slay,
To kill thine honor with thy life's decay;
    And in thy dead arms do I mean to place
        him,
    Swearing I slew him, seeing thee embrace
        him.

'So thy surviving husband shall remain
The scornful mark of every open eye; 520
Thy kinsmen hang their heads at this disdain,
Thy issue blurr'd with nameless bastardy:
And thou, the author of their obloquy,
    Shalt have thy trespass cited up in rhymes,
    And sung by children in succeeding times.

'But if thou yield, I rest thy secret friend:
The fault unknown is as a thought unacted;
A little harm done to a great good end
For lawful policy remains enacted.
The poisonous simple sometimes is compacted
    In a pure compound; being so applied, 531
    His venom in effect is purified.

'Then, for thy husband and thy children's
    sake,
Tender my suit: bequeath not to their lot
The shame that from them no device can take,
The blemish that will never be forgot;
Worse than a slavish wipe or birth-hour's
    blot:
    For marks descried in men's nativity
    Are nature's faults, not their own infamy.'

Here with a cockatrice' dead-killing eye 540
He rouseth up himself and makes a pause;
While she, the picture of pure piety,
Like a white hind under the gripe's sharp
    claws,
Pleads, in a wilderness where are no laws,
    To the rough beast that knows no gentle
        right,
    Nor aught obeys but his foul appetite.

But when a black-faced cloud the world doth
    threat,
In his dim mist the aspiring mountains hiding,
From earth's dark womb some gentle gust doth
    get,
Which blows these pitchy vapors from their
    bidding, 550
Hindering their present fall by this dividing;
    So his unhallow'd haste her words delays,
    And moody Pluto winks while Orpheus
        plays.

Yet, foul night-waking cat, he doth but dally,
While in his hold-fast foot the weak mouse
    panteth:
Her sad behavior feeds his vulture folly,
A swallowing gulf that even in plenty wanteth:
His ear her prayers admits, but his heart
    granteth
    No penetrable entrance to her plaining:
    Tears harden lust, though marble wear with
        raining. 560

Her pity-pleading eyes are sadly fix'd
In the remorseless wrinkles of his face;
Her modest eloquence with sighs is mix'd,
Which to her oratory adds more grace.
She puts the period often from his place;
    And midst the sentence so her accent breaks,
    That twice she doth begin ere once she
        speaks.

She conjures him by high almighty Jove,
By knighthood, gentry, and sweet friendship's
        oath,
By her untimely tears, her husband's love, 570
By holy human law, and common troth,
By heaven and earth, and all the power of
        both,
    That to his borrow'd bed he make retire,
    And stoop to honor, not to foul desire.

Quoth she, 'Reward not hospitality
With such black payment as thou hast pre-
        tended ;
Mud not the fountain that gave drink to thee ;
Mar not the thing that cannot be amended ;
End thy ill aim before thy shoot be ended ;
    He is no woodman that doth bend his bow
    To strike a poor unseasonable doe.   581

' My husband is thy friend ; for his sake spare
        me :
Thyself art mighty ; for thine own sake leave
        me :
Myself a weakling ; do not then ensnare me :
Thou look'st not like deceit ; do not deceive
        me.
My sighs, like whirlwinds, labor hence to
        heave thee :
    If ever man were moved with woman's
        moans,
    Be moved with my tears, my sighs, my
        groans :

' All which together, like a troubled ocean,
Beat at thy rocky and wreck-threatening heart,
To soften it with their continual motion ; 591
For stones dissolved to water do convert.
O, if no harder than a stone thou art,
    Melt at my tears, and be compassionate !
    Soft pity enters at an iron gate.

' In Tarquin's likeness I did entertain thee :
Hast thou put on his shape to do him shame ?
To all the host of heaven I complain me,
Thou wrong'st his honor, wound'st his princely
        name.
Thou art not what thou seem'st ; and if the
        same,   600
    Thou seem'st not what thou art, a god, a
        king ;
    For kings like gods should govern every
        thing.

' How will thy shame be seeded in thine age,
When thus thy vices bud before thy spring !
If in thy hope thou darest do such outrage,
What darest thou not when once thou art a
        king ?
O, be remember'd, no outrageous thing
    From vassal actors can be wiped away ;
    Then kings' misdeeds cannot be hid in clay.

' This deed will make thee only loved for fear ;
But happy monarchs still are fear'd for love :
With foul offenders thou perforce must bear,
When they in thee the like offences prove :
If but for fear of this, thy will remove :
    For princes are the glass, the school, the
        book,
    Where subjects' eyes do learn, do read, do
        look.

' And wilt thou be the school where Lust shall
        learn ?
Must he in thee read lectures of such shame ?
Wilt thou be glass wherein it shall discern

Authority for sin, warrant for blame,   620
To privilege dishonor in thy name ?
    Thou back'st reproach against long-living
        laud,
    And makest fair reputation but a bawd.

' Hast thou command ? by him that gave it
        thee,
From a pure heart command thy rebel will :
Draw not thy sword to guard iniquity,
For it was lent thee all that brood to kill.
Thy princely office how canst thou fulfil,
    When, pattern'd by thy fault, foul sin may
        say,
    He learn'd to sin, and thou didst teach the
        way ?   630

' Think but how vile a spectacle it were,
To view thy present trespass in another.
Men's faults do seldom to themselves appear ;
Their own transgressions partially they
        smother :
This guilt would seem death-worthy in thy
        brother.
    O, how are they wrapp'd in with infamies
    That from their own misdeeds askance their
        eyes !

' To thee, to thee, my heaved-up hands appeal,
Not to seducing lust, thy rash relier :
I sue for exiled majesty's repeal ;   640
Let him return, and flattering thoughts retire :
His true respect will prison false desire,
    And wipe the dim mist from thy doting eyne,
    That thou shalt see thy state and pity mine.'

' Have done,' quoth he : ' my uncontrolled tide
Turns not, but swells the higher by this let.
Small lights are soon blown out, huge fires
        abide,
And with the wind in greater fury fret :
The petty streams that pay a daily debt
    To their salt sovereign, with their fresh falls'
        haste   650
    Add to his flow, but alter not his taste.'

' Thou art,' quoth she, ' a sea, a sovereign
        king ;
And, lo, there falls into thy boundless flood
Black lust, dishonor, shame, misgoverning,
Who seek to stain the ocean of thy blood.
If all these pretty ills shall change thy good,
    Thy sea within a puddle's womb is hearsed,
    And not the puddle in thy sea dispersed.

' So shall these slaves be king, and thou their
        slave ;
Thou nobly base, they basely dignified ;   660
Thou their fair life, and they thy fouler grave :
Thou loathed in their shame, they in thy
        pride :
The lesser thing should not the greater hide ;
    The cedar stoops not to the base shrub's
        foot,
    But low shrubs wither at the cedar's root.

' So let thy thoughts, low vassals to thy
        state'—
' No more,' quoth he ; ' by heaven, I will not
        hear thee :
Yield to my love ; if not, enforced hate,
Instead of love's coy touch, shall rudely tear
        thee ;   669
That done, despitefully I mean to bear thee
    Unto the base bed of some rascal groom,
    To be thy partner in this shameful doom.'

This said, he sets his foot upon the light,
For light and lust are deadly enemies :
Shame folded up in blind concealing night,
When most unseen, then most doth tyrannize.
The wolf hath seized his prey, the poor lamb
    cries ;
  Till with her own white fleece her voice con-
    troll'd
  Entombs her outcry in her lips' sweet fold :

For with the nightly linen that she wears 680
He pens her piteous clamors in her head ;
Cooling his hot face in the chastest tears
That ever modest eyes with sorrow shed.
O, that prone lust should stain so pure a bed !
  The spots whereof could weeping purify,
  Her tears should drop on them perpetually.

But she hath lost a dearer thing than life,
And he hath won what he would lose again :
This forced league doth force a further strife ;
This momentary joy breeds months of pain ;
This hot desire converts to cold disdain : 691
  Pure Chastity is rifled of her store,
  And Lust, the thief, far poorer than before.

Look, as the full-fed hound or gorged hawk,
Unapt for tender smell or speedy flight,
Make slow pursuit, or altogether balk
The prey wherein by nature they delight ;
So surfeit-taking Tarquin fares this night :
  His taste delicious, in digestion souring,
  Devours his will, that lived by foul devour-
    ing. 700

O, deeper sin than bottomless conceit
Can comprehend in still imagination !
Drunken Desire must vomit his receipt,
Ere he can see his own abomination.
While Lust is in his pride, no exclamation
  Can curb his heat or rein his rash desire,
  Till like a jade Self-will himself doth tire.

And then with lank and lean discolor'd cheek,
With heavy eye, knit brow, and strengthless
    pace,
Feeble Desire, all recreant, poor, and meek,
Like to a bankrupt beggar wails his case : 711
The flesh being proud, Desire doth fight with
    Grace,
  For there it revels ; and when that decays,
  The guilty rebel for remission prays.

So fares it with this faultful lord of Rome,
Who this accomplishment so hotly chased ;
For now against himself he sounds this doom,
That through the length of times he stands
    disgraced :
Besides, his soul's fair temple is defaced ;
  To whose weak ruins muster troops of
    cares, 720
  To ask the spotted princess how she fares.

She says, her subjects with foul insurrection
Have batter'd down her consecrated wall,
And by their mortal fault brought in subjec-
    tion
Her immortality, and made her thrall
To living death and pain perpetual :
  Which in her prescience she controlled still,
  But her foresight could not forestall their
    will.

Even in this thought through the dark night
    he stealeth,
A captive victor that hath lost in gain ; 730
Bearing away the wound that nothing healeth,
The scar that will, despite of cure, remain ;
Leaving his spoil perplex'd in greater pain.
  She bears the load of lust he left behind,
  And he the burden of a guilty mind.

He like a thievish dog creeps sadly thence ;
She like a wearied lamb lies panting there ;
He scowls and hates himself for his offence ;
She, desperate, with her nails her flesh doth
    tear ;
He faintly flies, sweating with guilty fear ; 740
  She stays, exclaiming on the direful night :
  He runs, and chides his vanish'd, loathed
    delight.

He thence departs a heavy convertite ;
She there remains a hopeless castaway ;
He in his speed looks for the morning light ;
She prays she never may behold the day,
' For day,' quoth she, ' night's scapes doth
    open lay,
  And my true eyes have never practiced how
  To cloak offences with a cunning brow.

' They think not but that every eye can see
The same disgrace which they themselves be-
    hold ; 751
And therefore would they still in darkness be,
To have their unseen sin remain untold ;
For they their guilt with weeping will unfold,
  And grave, like water that doth eat in steel,
  Upon my cheeks what helpless shame I feel.'

Here she exclaims against repose and rest,
And bids her eyes hereafter still be blind.
She wakes her heart by beating on her breast,
And bids it leap from thence, where it may
    find 760
Some purer chest to close so pure a mind.
  Frantic with grief thus breathes she forth
    her spite
  Against the unseen secrecy of night :

' O comfort-killing Night, image of hell !
Dim register and notary of shame !
Black stage for tragedies and murders fell !
Vast sin-concealing chaos ! nurse of blame !
Blind muffled bawd ! dark harbor for defame !
  Grim cave of death ! whispering conspirator
  With close-tongued treason and the rav-
    isher ! 770

' O hateful, vaporous, and foggy Night !
Since thou art guilty of my cureless crime,
Muster thy mists to meet the eastern light,
Make war against proportion'd course of time ;
Or if thou wilt permit the sun to climb
  His wonted height, yet ere he go to bed,
  Knit poisonous clouds about his golden
    head.

' With rotten damps ravish the morning air ;
Let their exhaled unwholesome breaths make
    sick
The life of purity, the supreme fair, 780
Ere he arrive his weary noon-tide prick ;
And let thy misty vapors march so thick,
  That in their smoky ranks his smother'd
    light
  May set at noon and make perpetual night.

'Were Tarquin Night, as he is but Night's
　　child,
The silver-shining queen he would distain ;
Her twinkling handmaids too, by him defiled,
Through Night's black bosom should not peep
　　again :
So should I have co-partners in my pain ;
　　And fellowship in woe doth woe assuage,
　　As palmers' chat makes short their pilgrim-
　　　age.　　　　　　　　　　　791

'Where now I have no one to blush with me,
To cross their arms and hang their heads with
　　mine,
To mask their brows and hide their infamy ;
But I alone alone must sit and pine,
Seasoning the earth with showers of silver
　　brine,
　　Mingling my talk with tears, my grief with
　　　groans,
　　Poor wasting monuments of lasting moans.

'O Night, thou furnace of foul-reeking smoke,
Let not the jealous Day behold that face　　800
Which underneath thy black all-hiding cloak
Immodestly lies martyr'd with disgrace !
Keep still possession of thy gloomy place,
　　That all the faults which in thy reign are
　　　made
　　May likewise be sepulchred in thy shade !

'Make me not object to the tell-tale Day !
The light will show, character'd in my brow,
The story of sweet chastity's decay,
The impious breach of holy wedlock vow :
Yea, the illiterate, that know not how　　810
　　To cipher what is writ in learned books,
　　Will quote my loathsome trespass in my
　　　looks.

'The nurse, to still her child, will tell my
　　story,
And fright her crying babe with Tarquin's
　　name ;
The orator, to deck his oratory,
Will couple my reproach to Tarquin's shame ;
Feast-finding minstrels, tuning my defame,
　　Will tie the hearers to attend each line,
　　How Tarquin wronged me, I Collatine.

'Let my good name, that senseless reputa-
　　tion,　　　　　　　　　　　820
For Collatine's dear love be kept unspotted :
If that be made a theme for disputation,
The branches of another root are rotted,
And undeserved reproach to him allotted
　　That is as clear from this attaint of mine
　　As I, ere this, was pure to Collatine.

'O unseen shame ! invisible disgrace !
O unfelt sore ! crest-wounding, private scar !
Reproach is stamp'd in Collatinus' face,
And Tarquin's eye may read the mot afar, 830
How he in peace is wounded, not in war.
　　Alas, how many bear such shameful blows,
　　Which not themselves, but he that gives
　　　them knows !

'If, Collatine, thine honor lay in me,
From me by strong assault it is bereft.
My honey lost, and I, a drone-like bee,
Have no perfection of my summer left,
But robb'd and ransack'd by injurious theft :
　　In thy weak hive a wandering wasp hath
　　　crept,
　　And suck'd the honey which thy chaste bee
　　　kept.　　　　　　　　　　　840

'Yet am I guilty of thy honor's wrack ;
Yet for thy honor did I entertain him ;
Coming from thee, I could not put him back,
For it had been dishonor to disdain him :
Besides, of weariness he did complain him,
　　And talk'd of virtue : O unlook'd-for evil,
　　When virtue is profaned in such a devil !

'Why should the worm intrude the maiden
　　bud ?
Or hateful cuckoos hatch in sparrows' nests ?
Or toads infect fair founts with venom mud ?
Or tyrant folly lurk in gentle breasts ?　　851
Or kings be breakers of their own behests ?
　　But no perfection is so absolute,
　　That some impurity doth not pollute.

'The aged man that coffers-up his gold
Is plagued with cramps and gouts and pain-
　　ful fits ;
And scarce hath eyes his treasure to behold,
But like still-pining Tantalus he sits,
And useless barns the harvest of his wits ;
　　Having no other pleaure of his gain　　860
　　But torment that it cannot cure his pain.

'So then he hath it when he cannot use it,
And leaves it to be master'd by his young ;
Who in their pride do presently abuse it :
Their father was too weak, and they too
　　strong,
To hold their cursed-blessed fortune long.
　　The sweets we wish for turn to loathed
　　　sours
　　Even in the moment that we call them ours.

'Unruly blasts wait on the tender spring ;
Unwholesome weeds take root with precious
　　flowers ;　　　　　　　　　870
The adder hisses where the sweet birds sing ;
What virtue breeds iniquity devours :
We have no good that we can say is ours,
　　But ill-annexed Opportunity
　　Or kills his life or else his quality.

'O Opportunity, thy guilt is great !
'Tis thou that executest the traitor's treason :
Thou set'st the wolf where he the lamb may
　　get ;
Whoever plots the sin, thou 'point'st the sea-
　　son ;
'Tis thou that spurn'st at right, at law, at rea-
　　son ;　　　　　　　　　880
　　And in thy shady cell, where none may spy
　　　him,
　　Sits Sin, to seize the souls that wander by
　　　him.

'Thou makest the vestal violate her oath ;
Thou blow'st the fire when temperance is
　　thaw'd ;
Thou smother'st honesty, thou murder'st
　　troth ;
Thou foul abettor ! thou notorious bawd !
Thou plantest scandal and displacest laud :
　　Thou ravisher, thou traitor, thou false thief,
　　Thy honey turns to gall, thy joy to grief !

'Thy secret pleasure turns to open shame, 890
Thy private feasting to a public fast,
Thy smoothing titles to a ragged name,
Thy sugar'd tongue to bitter wormwood taste :
　　Thy violent vanities can never last.
　　How comes it then, vile Opportunity,
　　Being so bad, such numbers seek for thee ?

'When wilt thou be the humble suppliant's
  friend,
And bring him where his suit may be obtain'd ?
When wilt thou sort an hour great strifes to
  end ?
Or free that soul which wretchedness hath
  chain'd ? 900
Give physic to the sick, ease to the pain'd ?
    The poor, lame, blind, halt, creep, cry out
      for thee ;
    But they ne'er meet with Opportunity.

'The patient dies while the physician sleeps ;
The orphan pines while the oppressor feeds ;
Justice is feasting while the widow weeps ;
Advice is sporting while infection breeds :
Thou grant'st no time for charitable deeds :
    Wrath, envy, treason, rape, and murder's
      rages,
    Thy heinous hours wait on them as their
      pages. 910

'When Truth and Virtue have to do with thee,
A thousand crosses keep them from thy aid :
They buy thy help ; but Sin ne'er gives a fee,
He gratis comes ; and thou art well appaid
As well to hear as grant what he hath said.
    My Collatine would else have come to me
    When Tarquin did, but he was stay'd by
      thee.

'Guilty thou art of murder and of theft,
Guilty of perjury and subornation,
Guilty of treason, forgery, and shift, 920
Guilty of incest, that abomination ;
An accessary by thine inclination
    To all sins past, and all that are to come,
    From the creation to the general doom.

'Mis-shapen Time, copesmate of ugly Night,
Swift subtle post, carrier of grisly care,
Eater of youth, false slave to false delight,
Base watch of woes, sin's pack-horse, vir-
  tue's snare ;
Thou nursest all and murder'st all that are :
    O, hear me then, injurious, shifting Time !
    Be guilty of my death, since of my crime.

'Why hath thy servant, Opportunity,
Betray'd the hours thou gavest me to repose,
Cancell'd my fortunes, and enchained me
To endless date of never-ending woes ?
Time's office is to fine the hate of foes ;
    To eat up errors by opinion bred,
    Not spend the dowry of a lawful bed.

'Time's glory is to calm contending kings,
To unmask falsehood and bring truth to light,
To stamp the seal of time in aged things, 941
To wake the morn and sentinel the night,
To wrong the wronger till he render right,
    To ruinate proud buildings with thy hours,
    And smear with dust their glittering golden
      towers ;

'To fill with worm-holes stately monuments,
To feed oblivion with decay of things,
To blot old books and alter their contents,
To pluck the quills from ancient ravens'
  wings,
To dry the old oak's sap and cherish springs,

To spoil antiquities of hammer'd steel, 951
    And turn the giddy round of Fortune's
      wheel ;

'To show the beldam daughters of her daugh-
  ter,
To make the child a man, the man a child,
To slay the tiger that doth live by slaughter,
To tame the unicorn and lion wild,
To mock the subtle in themselves beguiled,
    To cheer the ploughman with increaseful
      crops,
    And waste huge stones with little water
      drops.

'Why work'st thou mischief in thy pilgrim-
  age, 960
Unless thou couldst return to make amends ?
One poor retiring minute in an age
Would purchase thee a thousand thousand
  friends,
Lending him wit that to bad debtors lends :
    O, this dread night, wouldst thou one hour
      come back,
    I could prevent this storm and shun thy
      wrack !

'Thou ceaseless lackey to eternity,
With some mischance cross Tarquin in his
  flight :
Devise extremes beyond extremity,
To make him curse this cursed crimeful
  night : 970
    Let ghastly shadows his lewd eyes affright ;
    And the dire thought of his committed evil
    Shape every bush a hideous shapeless devil.

'Disturb his hours of rest with restless trances,
Afflict him in his bed with bedrid groans ;
Let there bechance him pitiful mischances,
To make him moan ; but pity not his moans :
Stone him with harden'd hearts, harder than
  stones ;
    And let mild women to him lose their mild-
      ness, 979
    Wilder to him than tigers in their wildness.

'Let him have time to tear his curled hair,
Let him have time against himself to rave,
Let him have time of Time's help to despair,
Let him have time to live a loathed slave,
Let him have time a beggar's orts to crave,
    And time to see one that by alms doth live
    Disdain to him disdained scraps to give.

'Let him have time to see his friends his foes,
And merry fools to mock at him resort ;
Let him have time to mark how slow time
  goes 990
In time of sorrow, and how swift and short
His time of folly and his time of sport ;
    And ever let his unrecalling crime
    Have time to wail th' abusing of his time.

'O Time, thou tutor both to good and bad,
Teach me to curse him that thou taught'st
  this ill !
At his own shadow let the thief run mad,
Himself himself seek every hour to kill !
Such wretched hands such wretched blood
  should spill ;
    For who so base would such an office have
    As slanderous death's-man to so base a
      slave ? 1001

' The baser is he, coming from a king,
To shame his hope with deeds degenerate :
The mightier man, the mightier is the thing
That makes him honor'd, or begets him hate ;
For greatest scandal waits on greatest state.
    The moon being clouded presently is miss'd,
    But little stars may hide them when they
      list.

' The crow may bathe his coal-black wings in
    mire,
And unperceived fly with the filth away ; 1010
But if the like the snow-white swan desire,
The stain upon his silver down will stay.
Poor grooms are sightless night, kings glori-
    ous day :
    Gnats are unnoted wheresoe'er they fly,
    But eagles gazed upon with every eye.

' Out, idle words, servants to shallow fools !
Unprofitable sounds, weak arbitrators !
Busy yourselves in skill-contending schools ;
Debate where leisure serves with dull debat-
    ers ;
To trembling clients be you mediators : 1020
    For me, I force not argument a straw,
    Since that my case is past the help of law.

' In vain I rail at Opportunity,
At Time, at Tarquin, and uncheerful Night ;
In vain I cavil with mine infamy,
In vain I spurn at my confirm'd despite :
This helpless smoke of words doth me no
    right.
    The remedy indeed to do me good
    Is to let forth my foul-defiled blood.

' Poor hand, why quiver'st thou at this de-
    cree ?   1030
Honor thyself to rid me of this shame :
For if I die, my honor lives in thee ;
But if I live, thou livest in my defame :
Since thou couldst not defend thy loyal dame,
    And wast afeard to scratch her wicked foe,
    Kill both thyself and her for yielding so.'

This said, from her be-tumbled couch she
    starteth,
To find some desperate instrument of death :
But this no slaughterhouse no tool imparteth
To make more vent for passage of her breath ;
Which, thronging through her lips, so van-
    isheth   1041
    As smoke from Ætna, that in air consumes,
    Or that which from discharged cannon
    fumes.

' In vain,' quoth she, ' I live, and seek in vain
Some happy mean to end a hapless life.
I fear'd by Tarquin's falchion to be slain,
Yet for the self-same purpose seek a knife :
But when I fear'd I was a loyal wife :
    So am I now : O no, that cannot be ;   1049
    Of that true type hath Tarquin rifled me.

' O, that is gone for which I sought to live,
And therefore now I need not fear to die.
To clear this spot by death, at least I give
A badge of fame to slander's livery ;
A dying life to living infamy :
    Poor helpless help, the treasure stol'n away,
    To burn the guiltless casket where it lay !

' Well, well, dear Collatine, thou shalt not
    know

The stained taste of violated troth ;
I will not wrong thy true affection so,   1060
To flatter thee with an infringed oath ;
This bastard graff shall never come to growth :
    He shall not boast who did thy stock pol-
      lute
    That thou art doting father of his fruit.

' Nor shall he smile at thee in secret thought,
Nor laugh with his companions at thy state :
But thou shalt know thy interest was not
    bought
Basely with gold, but stol'n from forth thy
    gate.
For me, I am the mistress of my fate,   1069
    And with my trespass never will dispense,
    Till life to death acquit my forced offence.

' I will not poison thee with my attaint,
Nor fold my fault in cleanly-coin'd excuses ;
My sable ground of sin I will not paint,
To hide the truth of this false night's abuses :
My tongue shall utter all ; mine eyes, like
    sluices,
    As from a mountain-spring that feeds a
      dale,
    Shall gush pure streams to purge my impure
      tale.'

By this, lamenting Philomel had ended
The well-tuned warble of her nightly sorrow,
And solemn night with slow sad gait de-
    scended   1081
To ugly hell ; when, lo, the blushing morrow
Lends light to all fair eyes that light will bor-
    row :
    But cloudy Lucrece shames herself to see,
    And therefore still in night would cloister'd
    be.

Revealing day through every cranny spies,
And seems to point her out where she sits
    weeping ;
To whom she sobbing speaks : ' O eye of eyes,
Why pry'st thou through my window ? leave
    thy peeping :
Mock with thy tickling beams eyes that are
    sleeping :   1090
    Brand not my forehead with thy piercing
    light,
    For day hath nought to do what's done by
    night.'

Thus cavils she with every thing she sees :
True grief is fond and testy as a child,
Who wayward once, his mood with nought
    agrees :
Old woes, not infant sorrows, bear them mild ;
Continuance tames the one ; the other wild,
    Like an unpractised swimmer plunging still,
    With too much labor drowns for want of
    skill.

So she, deep-drenched in a sea of care,   1100
Holds disputation with each thing she views,
And to herself all sorrow doth compare ;
No object but her passion's strength renews ;
And as one shifts, another straight ensues :
    Sometime her grief is dumb and hath no
      words ;
    Sometime 'tis mad and too much talk af-
      fords.

The little birds that tune their morning's joy
Make her moans mad with their sweet melody :
For mirth doth search the bottom of annoy ;
Sad souls are slain in merry company ;   1110
Grief best is pleased with grief's society :
  True sorrow then is feelingly sufficed
  When with like semblance it is sympathized.

'Tis double death to drown in ken of shore ;
He ten times pines that pines beholding food ;
To see the salve doth make the wound ache
    more ;
Great grief grieves most at that would do it
    good ;
Deep woes roll forward like a gentle flood,
  Who, being stopp'd, the bounding banks
    o'erflows ;
  Grief dallied with nor law nor limit knows.

'You mocking-birds,' quoth she, 'your tunes
    entomb   1121
Within your hollow-swelling feather'd breasts,
And in my hearing be you mute and dumb :
My restless discord loves no stops nor rests ;
A woeful hostess brooks not merry guests :
  Relish your nimble notes to pleasing ears ;
  Distress likes dumps when time is kept with
    tears.

'Come, Philomel, that sing'st of ravishment,
Make thy sad grove in my dishevell'd hair :
As the dank earth weeps at thy languishment,
So I at each sad strain will strain a tear, 1131
And with deep groans the diapason bear ;
  For burden-wise I'll hum on Tarquin still,
  While thou on Tereus descant'st better skill.

'And whiles against a thorn thou bear'st thy
    part,
To keep thy sharp woes waking, wretched I,
To imitate thee well, against my heart
Will fix a sharp knife to affright mine eye ;
Who, if it wink, shall thereon fall and die.
  These means, as frets upon an instrument,
  Shall tune our heart-strings to true languishment.   1141

'And for, poor bird, thou sing'st not in the
    day,
As shaming any eye should thee behold,
Some dark deep desert, seated from the way,
That knows not parching heat nor freezing
    cold,
Will we find out ; and there we will unfold
  To creatures stern sad tunes, to change their
    kinds :
  Since men prove beasts, let beasts bear gentle minds.'

As the poor frighted deer, that stands at gaze,
Wildly determining which way to fly,   1150
Or one encompass'd with a winding maze,
That cannot tread the way out readily ;
So with herself is she in mutiny,
  To live or die which of the twain were better,
  When life is shamed, and death reproach's
    debtor.

'To kill myself,' quoth she, 'alack, what were
    it,
But with my body my poor soul's pollution ?
They that lose half with greater patience bear
    it

Than they whose whole is swallow'd in confusion.
That mother tries a merciless conclusion 1160
  Who, having two sweet babes, when death
    takes one,
  Will slay the other and be nurse to none.

'My body or my soul, which was the dearer,
When the one pure, the other made divine ?
Whose love of either to myself was nearer,
When both were kept for heaven and Collatine ?
Ay me ! the bark peel'd from the lofty pine,
  His leaves will wither and his sap decay ;
  So must my soul, her bark being peel'd
    away.

'Her house is sack'd, her quiet interrupted,
Her mansion batter'd by the enemy ;   1171
Her sacred temple spotted, spoil'd, corrupted,
Grossly engirt with daring infamy :
Then let it not be call'd impiety,
  If in this blemish'd fort I make some hole
  Through which I may convey this troubled
    soul.

'Yet die I will not till my Collatine
Have heard the cause of my untimely death ;
That he may vow, in that sad hour of mine,
Revenge on him that made me stop my breath.
My stained blood to Tarquin I'll bequeath,
  Which by him tainted shall for him be spent,
  And as his due writ in my testament.

'My honor I'll bequeath unto the knife
That wounds my body so dishonored.
'Tis honor to deprive dishonor'd life ;
The one will live, the other being dead :
So of shame's ashes shall my fame be bred ;
  For in my death I murder shameful scorn :
  My shame so dead, mine honor is newborn.   1190

'Dear lord of that dear jewel I have lost,
What legacy shall I bequeath to thee ?
My resolution, love, shall be thy boast,
By whose example thou revenged mayst be.
How Tarquin must be used, read it in me :
  Myself, thy friend, will kill myself, thy foe,
  And for my sake serve thou false Tarquin
    so.

'This brief abridgement of my will I make :
My soul and body to the skies and ground ;
My resolution, husband, do thou take ;   1200
Mine honor be the knife's that makes my
    wound ;
My shame be his that did my fame confound ;
  And all my fame that lives disbursed be
  To those that live, and think no shame of
    me.

'Thou, Collatine, shalt oversee this will ;
How was I overseen that thou shalt see it !
My blood shall wash the slander of mine ill ;
My life's foul deed, my life's fair end shall free
    it.
Faint not, faint heart, but stoutly say "So be
    it : "
  Yield to my hand ; my hand shall conquer
    thee :   1210
  Thou dead, both die, and both shall victors
    be.'

This plot of death when sadly she had laid,
And wiped the brinish pearl from her bright
    eyes,
With untuned tongue she hoarsely calls her
    maid,
Whose swift obedience to her mistress hies;
For fleet-wing'd duty with thought's feathers
    flies.
    Poor Lucrece' cheeks unto her maid seem so
    As winter meads when sun doth melt their
    snow.

Her mistress she doth give demure good-mor-
    row,
With soft-slow tongue, true mark of modesty,
And sorts a sad look to her lady's sorrow, 1221
For why her face wore sorrow's livery;
But durst not ask of her audaciously
    Why her two suns were cloud-eclipsed so,
    Nor why her fair cheeks over-wash'd with
    woe.

But as the earth doth weep, the sun being set,
Each flower moisten'd like a melting eye;
Even so the maid with swelling drops gan wet
Her circled eyne, enforced by sympathy
Of those fair suns set in her mistress' sky,
    Who in a salt-waved ocean quench their
    light,   1231
    Which makes the maid weep like the dewy
    night.

A pretty while these pretty creatures stand,
Like ivory conduits coral cisterns filling:
One justly weeps; the other takes in hand
No cause, but company, of her drops spilling:
Their gentle sex to weep are often willing;
    Grieving themselves to guess at others'
    smarts,
    And then they drown their eyes or break
    their hearts.   1239

For men have marble, women waxen, minds,
And therefore are they form'd as marble will;
The weak oppress'd, the impression of strange
    kinds
Is form'd in them by force, by fraud, or skill:
Then call them not the authors of their ill,
    No more than wax shall be accounted evil
    Wherein is stamp'd the semblance of a devil.

Their smoothness, like a goodly champaign
    plain,
Lays open all the little worms that creep;
In men, as in a rough-grown grove, remain
Cave-keeping evils that obscurely sleep : 1250
Through crystal walls each little mote will
    peep :
    Though men can cover crimes with bold
    stern looks,
    Poor women's faces are their own fault's
    books.

No man inveigh against the wither'd flower,
But chide rough winter that the flower hath
    kill'd :
Not that devour'd, but that which doth de-
    vour,
Is worthy blame. O, let it not be hild
Poor women's faults, that they are so fulfill'd

With men's abuses : those proud lords, to
    blame,
Make weak-made women tenants to their
    shame.   1260

The precedent whereof in Lucrece view,
Assail'd by night with circumstances strong
Of present death, and shame that might ensue
By that her death, to do her husband wrong :
Such danger to resistance did belong,
    That dying fear through all her body spread;
    And who cannot abuse a body dead ?

By this, mild patience bid fair Lucrece speak
To the poor counterfeit of her complaining :
' My girl,' quoth she, ' on what occasion break
Those tears from thee, that down thy cheeks
    are raining ?   1271
If thou dost weep for grief of my sustaining,
    Know, gentle wench, it small avails my
    mood :
    If tears could help, mine own would do me
    good.

' But tell me, girl, when went '—and there she
    stay'd
Till after a deep groan—' Tarquin from
    hence ? '
' Madam, ere I was up,' replied the maid,
' The more to blame my sluggard negligence :
Yet with the fault I thus far can dispense ;
    Myself was stirring ere the break of day,
    And, ere I rose, was Tarquin gone away.

' But, lady, if your maid may be so bold,
She would request to know your heaviness.'
' O, peace ! ' quoth Lucrece : ' if it should be
    told,
The repetition cannot make it less ;
For more it is than I can well express :
    And that deep torture may be call'd a hell
    When more is felt than one hath power to
    tell.

' Go, get me hither paper, ink, and pen :
Yet save that labor, for I have them here.
What should I say ? One of my husband's
    men   1291
Bid thou be ready, by and by, to bear
A letter to my lord, my love, my dear ;
    Bid him with speed prepare to carry it ;
    The cause craves haste, and it will soon be
    writ.'

Her maid is gone, and she prepares to write,
First hovering o'er the paper with her quill :
Conceit and grief an eager combat fight ;
What wit sets down is blotted straight with
    will ;
This is too curious-good, this blunt and ill :
    Much like a press of people at a door, 1301
    Throng her inventions, which shall go be-
    fore.

At last she thus begins : ' Thou worthy lord
Of that unworthy wife that greeteth thee,
Health to thy person ! next vouchsafe t' af-
    ford—
If ever, love, thy Lucrece thou wilt see—
Some present speed to come and visit me.
    So, I commend me from our house in grief :
    My woes are tedious, though my words are
    brief.'

Here folds she up the tenor of her woe, 1310
Her certain sorrow writ uncertainly.
By this short schedule Collatine may know
Her grief, but not her grief's true quality :
She dares not thereof make discovery,
  Lest he should hold it her own gross abuse,
  Ere she with blood had stain'd her stain'd
    excuse.

Besides, the life and feeling of her passion
She hoards, to spend when he is by to hear
    her :
When sighs and groans and tears may grace
    the fashion
Of her disgrace, the better so to clear her 1320
From that suspicion which the world might
    bear her.
  To shun this blot, she would not blot the
    letter
  With words, till action might become them
    better.

To see sad sights moves more than hear them
    told ;
For then the eye interprets to the ear
The heavy motion that it doth behold,
When every part a part of woe doth bear.
'Tis but a part of sorrow that we hear :
  Deep sounds make lesser noise than shallow
    fords,
  And sorrow ebbs, being blown with wind of
    words. 1330

Her letter now is seal'd, and on it writ
' At Ardea to my lord with more than haste.'
The post attends, and she delivers it,
Charging the sour-faced groom to hie as fast
As lagging fowls before the northern blast :
  Speed more than speed but dull and slow
    she deems :
  Extremity still urgeth such extremes.

The homely villain court'sies to her low ;
And, blushing on her, with a steadfast eye
Receives the scroll without or yea or no, 1340
And forth with bashful innocence doth hie.
But they whose guilt within their bosoms lie
  Imagine every eye beholds their blame ;
  For Lucrece thought he blush'd to see her
    shame !

When, silly groom ! God wot, it was defect
Of spirit, life, and bold audacity.
Such harmless creatures have a true respect
To talk in deeds, while others saucily
Promise more speed, but do it leisurely :
  Even so this pattern of the worn-out age
  Pawn'd honest looks, but laid no words to
    gage. 1351

His kindled duty kindled her mistrust,
That two red fires in both their faces blazed ;
She thought he blush'd, as knowing Tarquin's
    lust,
And, blushing with him, wistly on him gazed ;
Her earnest eye did make him more amazed :
  The more she saw the blood his cheeks re-
    plenish,
  The more she thought he spied in her some
    blemish.

But long she thinks till he return again,
And yet the duteous vassal scarce is gone.
The weary time she cannot entertain, 1361
For now 'tis stale to sigh, to weep, and groan :
So woe hath wearied woe, moan tired moan,

That she her plaints a little while doth stay,
Pausing for means to mourn some newer
    way.

At last she calls to mind where hangs a piece
Of skilful painting, made for Priam's Troy :
Before the which is drawn the power of
    Greece,
For Helen's rape the city to destroy, 1369
Threatening cloud-kissing Ilion with annoy ;
  Which the conceited painter drew so proud,
  As heaven, it seem'd, to kiss the turrets
    bow'd.

A thousand lamentable objects there,
In scorn of nature, art gave lifeless life :
Many a dry drop seem'd a weeping tear,
Shed for the slaughter'd husband by the wife :
The red blood reek'd, to show the painter's
    strife ;
  And dying eyes gleam'd forth their ashy
    lights,
  Like dying coals burnt out in tedious nights.

There might you see the laboring pioner 1380
Begrimed with sweat, and smeared all with
    dust ;
And from the towers of Troy there would ap-
    pear
The very eyes of men through loop-holes
    thrust,
Gazing upon the Greeks with little lust :
  Such sweet observance in this work was had,
  That one might see those far-off eyes look
    sad.

In great commanders grace and majesty
You might behold, triumphing in their faces ;
In youth, quick bearing and dexterity ;
And here and there the painter interlaces 1390
Pale cowards, marching on with trembling
    paces ;
  Which heartless peasants did so well resem-
    ble,
  That one would swear he saw them quake
    and tremble.

In Ajax and Ulysses, O, what art
Of physiognomy might one behold !
The face of either cipher'd either's heart ;
Their face their manners most expressly told :
In Ajax' eyes blunt rage and rigor roll'd ;
  But the mild glance that sly Ulysses lent
  Show'd deep regard and smiling govern-
    ment. 1400

There pleading might you see grave Nestor
    stand,
As 'twere encouraging the Greeks to fight ;
Making such sober action with his hand,
That it beguiled attention, charm'd the sight :
In speech, it seem'd, his beard, all silver white,
  Wagg'd up and down, and from his lips did
    fly
  Thin winding breath, which purl'd up to the
    sky.

About him were a press of gaping faces,
Which seem'd to swallow up his sound advice ;
All jointly listening, but with several graces,
As if some mermaid did their ears entice, 1411
Some high, some low, the painter was so nice ;
  The scalps of many, almost hid behind,
  To jump up higher seem'd, to mock the
    mind.

Here one man's hand lean'd on another's head,
His nose being shadow'd by his neighbor's
    ear;
Here one being throng'd bears back, all boll'n
    and red;
Another smother'd seems to pelt and swear;
And in their rage such signs of rage they bear,
    As, but for loss of Nestor's golden words,
    It seem'd they would debate with angry
        swords.   1421

For much imaginary work was there;
Conceit deceitful, so compact, so kind,
That for Achilles' image stood his spear,
Griped in an armed hand; himself, behind,
Was left unseen, save to the eye of mind:
    A hand, a foot, a face, a leg, a head,
    Stood for the whole to be imagined.

And from the walls of strong-besieged Troy
When their brave hope, bold Hector, march'd
    to field,   1430
Stood many Trojan mothers, sharing joy
To see their youthful sons bright weapons
    wield;
And to their hope they such odd action yield,
    That through their light joy seemed to ap-
        pear,
    Like bright things stain'd, a kind of heavy
        fear.

And from the strand of Dardan, where they
    fought,
To Simois' reedy banks the red blood ran,
Whose waves to imitate the battle sought
With swelling ridges; and their ranks began
To break upon the galled shore, and than   1440
    Retire again, till, meeting greater ranks,
    They join and shoot their foam at Simois'
        banks.

To this well-painted piece is Lucrece come,
To find a face where all distress is stell'd.
Many she sees where cares have carved some,
But none where all distress and dolor dwell'd,
Till she despairing Hecuba beheld,
    Staring on Priam's wounds with her old
        eyes,
    Which bleeding under Pyrrhus' proud foot
        lies.

In her the painter had anatomized   1450
Time's ruin, beauty's wreck, and grim care's
    reign;
Her cheeks with chaps and wrinkles were dis-
    guised;
Of what she was no semblance did remain:
Her blue blood changed to black in every vein,
    Wanting the spring that those shrunk pipes
        had fed,
    Show'd life imprison'd in a body dead.

On this sad shadow Lucrece spends her eyes,
And shapes her sorrow to the beldam's woes,
Who nothing wants to answer her but cries,
And bitter words to ban her cruel foes;   1460
The painter was no god to lend her those;
    And therefore Lucrece swears he did her
        wrong,
    To give her so much grief and not a tongue.

'Poor instrument,' quoth she, 'without a
    sound,
I'll tune thy woes with my lamenting tongue;

And drop sweet balm in Priam's painted
    wound,
And rail on Pyrrhus that hath done him
    wrong;
And with my tears quench Troy that burns so
    long;
    And with my knife scratch out the angry
        eyes   1469
    Of all the Greeks that are thine enemies.

'Show me the strumpet that began this stir,
That with my nails her beauty I may tear.
Thy heat of lust, fond Paris, did incur
This load of wrath that burning Troy doth
    bear:
Thy eye kindled the fire that burneth here;
    And here in Troy, for trespass of thine eye,
    The sire, the son, the dame, and daughter
        die.

'Why should the private pleasure of some one
Become the public plague of many moe?
Let sin, alone committed, light alone   1480
Upon his head that hath transgressed so;
Let guiltless souls be freed from guilty woe:
    For one's offence why should so many fall,
    To plague a private sin in general?

'Lo, here weeps Hecuba, here Priam dies,
Here manly Hector faints, here Troilus
    swounds,
Here friend by friend in bloody channel lies,
And friend to friend gives unadvised wounds,
And one man's lust these many lives con-
    founds:
    Had doting Priam check'd his son's desire,
    Troy had been bright with fame and not
        with fire.'   1491

Here feelingly she weeps Troy's painted woes:
For sorrow, like a heavy-hanging bell,
Once set on ringing, with his own weight goes;
Then little strength rings out the doleful knell;
So Lucrece, set a-work, sad tales doth tell
    To pencill'd pensiveness and color'd sorrow;
    She lends them words, and she their looks
        doth borrow.

She throws her eyes about the painting round,
And whom she finds forlorn she doth lament.
At last she sees a wretched image bound, 1501
That piteous looks to Phrygian shepherds lent:
His face, though full of cares, yet show'd con-
    tent:
    Onward to Troy with the blunt swains he
        goes,
    So mild, that Patience seem'd to scorn his
        woes.

In him the painter labor'd with his skill
To hide deceit, and give the harmless show
An humble gait, calm looks, eyes wailing still,
A brow unbent, that seem'd to welcome woe;
Cheeks neither red nor pale, but mingled so
    That blushing red no guilty instance gave,
    Nor ashy pale the fear that false hearts have.

But, like a constant and confirmed devil,
He entertain'd a show so seeming just,
And therein so ensconced his secret evil,
That jealousy itself could not mistrust
False-creeping craft and perjury should thrust
    Into so bright a day such black-faced storms,
    Or blot with hell-born sin such saint-like
        forms.   1519

The well-skill'd workman this mild image drew
For perjured Sinon, whose enchanting story
The credulous old Priam after slew ;
Whose words like wildfire burnt the shining
  glory
Of rich-built Ilion, that the skies were sorry,
  And little stars shot from their fixed places,
  When their glass fell wherein they view'd
    their faces.

This picture she advisedly perused,
And chid the painter for his wondrous skill,
Saying, some shape in Sinon's was abused :
So fair a form lodged not a mind so ill : 1530
And still on him she gazed ; and gazing still,
  Such signs of truth in his plain face she
    spied,
  That she concludes the picture was belied.

' It cannot be,' quoth she, ' that so much
    guile '—
She would have said ' can lurk in such a
    look ; '
But Tarquin's shape came in her mind the
    while,
And from her tongue ' can lurk ' from ' can-
    not ' took :
' It cannot be ' she in that sense forsook,
  And turn'd it thus, ' It cannot be, I find,
  But such a face should bear a wicked mind.

' For even as subtle Sinon here is painted, 1541
So sober-sad, so weary, and so mild,
As if with grief or travail he had fainted,
To me came Tarquin armed ; so beguiled
With outward honesty, but yet defiled
  With inward vice : as Priam him did cher-
    ish,
  So did I Tarquin ; so my Troy did perish.

' Look, look, how listening Priam wets his
    eyes,
To see those borrow'd tears that Sinon sheds !
Priam, why art thou old and yet not wise ?
For every tear he falls a Trojan bleeds : 1551
His eye drops fire, no water thence proceeds ;
  Those round clear pearls of his, that move
    thy pity,
  Are balls of quenchless fire to burn thy city.

' Such devils steal effects from lightless hell !
For Sinon in his fire doth quake with cold,
And in that cold hot-burning fire doth dwell ;
These contraries such unity do hold,
Only to flatter fools and make them bold :
  So Priam's trust false Sinon's tears doth flat-
    ter, 1560
  That he finds means to burn his Troy with
    water.'

Here, all enraged, such passion her assails,
That patience is quite beaten from her breast.
She tears the senseless Sinon with her nails,
Comparing him to that unhappy guest
Whose deed hath made herself herself detest :
  At last she smilingly with this gives o'er ;
  ' Fool, fool ! ' quoth she, ' his wounds will
    not be sore.'

Thus ebbs and flows the current of her sorrow,
And time doth weary time with her complain-
    ing. 1570
She looks for night, and then she longs for
    morrow,
And both she thinks too long with her remain-
    ing :

Short time seems long in sorrow's sharp sus-
    taining :
Though woe be heavy, yet it seldom sleeps,
And they that watch see time how slow it
    creeps.

Which all this time hath overslipp'd her
    thought,
That she with painted images hath spent ;
Being from the feeling of her own grief
    brought
By deep surmise of others' detriment ;
Losing her woes in shows of discontent. 1580
  It easeth some, though none it ever cured,
  To think their dolor others have endured.

But now the mindful messenger, come back,
Brings home his lord and other company ;
Who finds his Lucrece clad in mourning
    black :
And round about her tear-distained eye
Blue circles stream'd ; like rainbows in the
    sky :
  These water-galls in her dim element
  Foretell new storms to those already spent.

Which when her sad-beholding husband saw,
Amazedly in her sad face he stares :   1591
Her eyes, though sod in tears, look'd red and
    raw,
Her lively color kill'd with deadly cares.
He hath no power to ask her how she fares :
  Both stood, like old acquaintance in a
    trance,
  Met far from home, wondering each other's
    chance.

At last he takes her by the bloodless hand,
And thus begins : ' What uncouth ill event
Hath thee befall'n, that thou dost trembling
    stand ?
Sweet love, what spite hath thy fair color
    spent ?   1600
Why art thou thus attired in discontent ?
  Unmask, dear dear, this moody heaviness,
  And tell thy grief, that we may give redress.'

Three times with sighs she gives her sorrow
    fire,
Ere once she can discharge one word of woe :
At length address'd to answer his desire,
She modestly prepares to let them know
Her honor is ta'en prisoner by the foe ;
  While Collatine and his consorted lords
  With sad attention long to hear her words.

And now this pale swan in her watery nest
Begins the sad dirge of her certain ending ;
' Few words,' quoth she, ' shall fit the trespass
    best,
Where no excuse can give the fault amending :
In me moe woes than words are now depend-
    ing ;
  And my laments would be drawn out too
    long,
  To tell them all with one poor tired tongue.

' Then be this all the task it hath to say
Dear husband, in the interest of thy bed
A stranger came, and on that pillow lay 1620
Where thou was wont to rest thy weary head ;
And what wrong else may be imagined
  By foul enforcement might be done to me,
  From that, alas, thy Lucrece is not free.

' For in the dreadful dead of dark midnight,
With shining falchion in my chamber came
A creeping creature, with a flaming light,
And softly cried " Awake, thou Roman dame,
And entertain my love ; else lasting shame
  On thee and thine this night I will inflict,
  If thou my love's desire do contradict. 1631

' " For some hard-favor'd groom of thine,"
    quoth he,
" Unless thou yoke thy liking to my will,
I'll murder straight, and then I'll slaughter thee
And swear I found you where you did fulfil
The loathsome act of lust, and so did kill
  The lechers in their deed : this act will be
  My fame and thy perpetual infamy."

' With this, I did begin to start and cry ;
And then against my heart he sets his sword,
Swearing, unless I took all patiently,   1641
I should not live to speak another word ;
So should my shame still rest upon record,
  And never be forgot in mighty Rome
  Th' adulterate death of Lucrece and her
    groom.

' Mine enemy was strong, my poor self weak,
And far the weaker with so strong a fear :
My bloody judge forbade my tongue to speak ;
No rightful plea might plead for justice there :
His scarlet lust came evidence to swear   1650
  That my poor beauty had purloin'd his eyes ;
  And when the judge is robb'd the prisoner
    dies.

' O, teach me how to make mine own excuse !
Or at the least this refuge let me find ;
Though my gross blood be stain'd with this
    abuse,
Immaculate and spotless is my mind ;
That was not forced ; that never was inclined
  To accessary yieldings, but still pure
  Doth in her poison'd closet yet endure.'

Lo, here, the hopeless merchant of this loss,
With head declined, and voice damm'd up
    with woe,   1661
With sad set eyes, and wretched arms across,
From lips new-waxen pale begins to blow
The grief away that stops his answer so :
  But, wretched as he is, he strives in vain ;
  What he breathes out his breath drinks up
    again.

As through an arch the violent roaring tide
Outruns the eye that doth behold his haste,
Yet in the eddy boundeth in his pride   1669
Back to the strait that forced him on so fast ;
In rage sent out, recall'd in rage, being past :
  Even so his sighs, his sorrows, make a saw,
  To push grief on, and back the same grief
    draw.

Which speechless woe of his poor she at-
    tendeth,
And his untimely frenzy thus awaketh :
' Dear lord, thy sorrow to my sorrow lendeth
Another power ; no flood by raining slaketh.
My woe too sensible thy passion maketh
  More feeling-painful : let it then suffice
  To drown one woe, one pair of weeping
    eyes.   1680

' And for my sake, when I might charm thee
    so,
For she that was thy Lucrece, now attend me :

Be suddenly revenged on my foe,
Thine, mine, his own : suppose thou dost de-
    fend me
From what is past : the help that thou shalt
    lend me
  Comes all too late, yet let the traitor die ;
  For sparing justice feeds iniquity.

' But ere I name him, you fair lords,' quoth
    she,
Speaking to those that came with Collatine,
' Shall plight your honorable faiths to me,
With swift pursuit to venge this wrong of
    mine ;   1691
For 'tis a meritorious fair design
  To chase injustice with revengeful arms :
  Knights, by their oaths, should right poor
    ladies' harms.'

At this request, with noble disposition
Each present lord began to promise aid,
As bound in knighthood to her imposition,
Longing to hear the hateful foe bewray'd.
But she, that yet her sad task hath not said,
  The protestation stops. ' O, speak,' quoth
    she,   1700
  ' How may this forced stain be wiped from
    me ?

' What is the quality of mine offence,
Being constrain'd with dreadful circumstance ?
May my pure mind with the foul act dispense,
My low-declined honor to advance ?
May any terms acquit me from this chance ?
  The poison's fountain clears itself again ;
  And why not I from this compelled stain ? '

With this, they all at once began to say,   1709
Her body's stain her mind untainted clears ;
While with a joyless smile she turns away
The face, that map which deep impression
    bears
Of hard misfortune, carved in it with tears.
  ' No, no,' quoth she, ' no dame, hereafter
    living,
  By my excuse shall claim excuse's giving.'

Here with a sigh, as if her heart would break,
She throws forth Tarquin's name ; ' He, he,'
    she says,
But more than ' he ' her poor tongue could not
    speak ;
Till after many accents and delays,   1719
Untimely breathings, sick and short assays,
  She utters this, ' He, he, fair lords, 'tis he,
  That guides this hand to give this wound to
    me.'

Even here she sheathed in her harmless breast
A harmful knife, that thence her soul un-
    sheathed :
That blow did bail it from the deep unrest
Of that polluted prison where it breathed :
  Her contrite sighs unto the clouds bequeath'd
  Her winged sprite, and through her wounds
    doth fly
  Life's lasting date from cancell'd destiny.

Stone-still, astonish'd with this deadly deed,
Stood Collatine and all his lordly crew ;   1731
Till Lucrece' father, that beholds her bleed,
Himself on her self-slaughter'd body threw ;
And from the purple fountain Brutus drew
  The murderous knife, and, as it left the
    place,
  Her blood, in poor revenge, held it in chase ;

And bubbling from her breast, it doth divide
In two slow rivers, that the crimson blood
Circles her body in on every side,
Who, like a late-sack'd island, vastly stood
Bare and unpeopled in this fearful flood. 1741
    Some of her blood still pure and red re-
        main'd,
    And some look'd black, and that false Tar-
        quin stain'd.

About the mourning and congealed face
Of that black blood a watery rigol goes,
Which seems to weep upon the tainted place :
And ever since, as pitying Lucrece' woes,
Corrupted blood some watery token shows ;
    And blood untainted still doth red abide,
    Blushing at that which is so putrified. 1750

'Daughter, dear daughter,' old Lucretius
    cries,
'That life was mine which thou hast here de-
    prived.
If in the child the father's image lies,
Where shall I live now Lucrece is unlived ?
Thou wast not to this end from me derived.
    If children pre-decease progenitors,
    We are their offspring, and they none of
      ours.

'Poor broken glass, I often did behold
In thy sweet semblance my old age new born ;
But now that fresh fair mirror, dim and old,
Shows me a bare-boned death by time out-
    worn : 1761
O, from thy cheeks my image thou hast torn,
    And shivered all the beauty of my glass,
    That I no more can see what once I was !

'O time, cease thou thy course and last no
    longer,
If they surcease to be that should survive.
Shall rotten death make conquest of the
    stronger
And leave the faltering feeble souls alive ?
The old bees die, the young possess their hive :
    Then live, sweet Lucrece, live again and see
    Thy father die, and not thy father thee ! '

By this, starts Collatine as from a dream,
And bids Lucretius give his sorrow place ;
And then in key-cold Lucrece' bleeding stream
He falls, and bathes the pale fear in his face,
And counterfeits to die with her a space ;
    Till manly shame bids him possess his
      breath
    And live to be revenged on her death.

The deep vexation of his inward soul 1779
Hath served a dumb arrest upon his tongue ;
Who, mad that sorrow should his use control,
Or keep him from heart-easing words so long,
Begins to talk ; but through his lips do throng
    Weak words, so thick come in his poor
      heart's aid,
    That no man could distinguish what he said.

Yet sometime 'Tarquin' was pronounced
    plain,
But through his teeth, as if the name he tore.
This windy tempest, till it blow up rain,
Held back his sorrow's tide, to make it more ;
At last it rains, and busy winds give o'er :

Then son and father weep with equal strife
Who should weep most, for daughter or for
    wife.

The one doth call her his, the other his,
Yet neither may possess the claim they lay.
The father says ' She's mine.' ' O, mine she is,'
Replies her husband : ' do not take away
My sorrow's interest ; let no mourner say
    He weeps for her, for she was only mine,
    And only must be wail'd by Collatine.'

' O,' quoth Lucretius, ' I did give that life 1800
Which she too early and too late hath spill'd.'
' Woe, woe,' quoth Collatine, ' she was my
    wife,
I owed her, and 'tis mine that she hath kill'd.'
' My daughter ' and ' my wife ' with clamors
    fill'd
    The dispersed air, who, holding Lucrece'
      life,
    Answer'd their cries, ' my daughter ' and
      ' my wife.'

Brutus, who pluck'd the knife from Lucrece'
    side,
Seeing such emulation in their woe,
Began to clothe his wit in state and pride,
Burying in Lucrece' wound his folly's show.
He with the Romans was esteemed so 1811
    As silly-jeering idiots are with kings,
    For sportive words and uttering foolish
      things :

But now he throws that shallow habit by,
Wherein deep policy did him disguise ;
And arm'd his long-hid wits advisedly,
To check the tears in Collatinus' eyes.
' Thou wronged lord of Rome,' quoth he,
    ' arise '
    Let my unsounded self, supposed a fool,
    Now set thy long-experienced wit to school.

' Why, Collatine, is woe the cure for woe ?
Do wounds help wounds, or grief help grievous
    deeds ?
Is it revenge to give thyself a blow
For his foul act by whom thy fair wife bleeds ?
Such childish humor from weak minds pro-
    ceeds :
    Thy wretched wife mistook the matter so,
    To slay herself, that should have slain her
      foe.

' Courageous Roman, do not steep thy heart
In such relenting dew of lamentations ; 1829
But kneel with me and help to bear thy part,
To rouse our Roman gods with invocations,
That they will suffer these abominations,
    Since Rome herself in them doth stand dis-
      graced,
    By our strong arms from forth her fair
      streets chased.

' Now, by the Capitol that we adore,
And by this chaste blood so unjustly stain'd,
By heaven's fair sun that breeds the fat earth's
    store,
By all our country rights in Rome maintain'd,
And by chaste Lucrece' soul that late com-
    plain'd 1839
    Her wrongs to us, and by this bloody knife,
    We will revenge the death of this true wife.'

This said, he struck his hand upon his breast,
And kiss'd the fatal knife, to end his vow ;
And to his protestation urged the rest,
Who, wondering at him, did his words allow :
Then jointly to the ground their knees they
    bow ;
  And that deep vow, which Brutus made be-
      fore,
  He doth again repeat, and that they swore.

When they had sworn to this advised doom,
They did conclude to bear dead Lucrece
    thence ;   1850
To show her bleeding body thorough Rome,
And so to publish Tarquin's foul offence :
Which being done with speedy diligence,
  The Romans plausibly did give consent
  To Tarquin's everlasting banishment.

THE PASSIONATE PILGRIM.

INTRODUCTION.

The Passionate Pilgrim was published by William Jaggard, in 1599. It was a piratical book-seller's venture, and although the popular name of Shakespeare was put upon the title-page the little volume really consisted of a collection from several authors. Shakespeare, as Heywood tells us, was much offended when Jaggard, in 1612, republished the volume, with added poems of Heywood, and with Shakespeare's name upon the title-page : a cancel of the title-page was thereupon made, and one printed without any author's name. Of the collection, Nos. I., II., III., V., XII., and XVII., are probably Shakespeare's ; Nos. IV., VI., VII., IX., and XIX. are possibly Shakespeare's ; and the rest are certainly *not* Shakespeare's. After the fifteenth poem in the original collection occurs a second title—*Sonnets to Sundry Notes of Music.*

I.

WHEN my love swears that she is made of
    truth,
I do believe her, though I know she lies,
That she might think me some untutor'd youth,
Unskilful in the world's false forgeries.
Thus vainly thinking that she thinks me young,
Although I know my years be past the best,
I smiling credit her false-speaking tongue,
Outfacing faults in love with love's ill rest.
But wherefore says my love that she is young ?
And wherefore say not I that I am old ?   10
O, love's best habit is a soothing tongue,
And age, in love, loves not to have years told.
    Therefore I'll lie with love, and love with
      me,
    Since that our faults in love thus smother'd
      be.

II.

Two loves I have, of comfort and despair,
That like two spirits do suggest me still ;
My better angel is a man right fair,
My worser spirit a woman color'd ill.
To win me soon to hell, my female evil
Tempteth my better angel from my side,   20
And would corrupt my saint to be a devil,
Wooing his purity with her fair pride.
And whether that my angel be turn'd fiend,
Suspect I may, yet not directly tell :
For being both to me, both to each friend,
I guess one angel in another's hell :
    The truth I shall not know, but live in doubt,
    Till my bad angel fire my good one out.

III.

Did not the heavenly rhetoric of thine eye,
'Gainst whom the world could not hold argu-
    ment,   30
Persuade my heart to this false perjury ?
Vows for thee broke deserve not punishment.
A woman I forswore ; but I will prove,
Thou being a goddess, I forswore not thee :
My vow was earthly, thou a heavenly love ;
Thy grace being gain'd cures all disgrace in
    me.

My vow was breath, and breath a vapor is ;
Then, thou fair sun, that on this earth doth
    shine,
Exhale this vapor vow ; in thee it is :
If broken, then it is no fault of mine.   40
    If by me broke, what fool is not so wise
    To break an oath, to win a paradise ?

IV.

Sweet Cytherea, sitting by a brook
With young Adonis, lovely, fresh, and green,
Did court the lad with many a lovely look,
Such looks as none could look but beauty's
    queen.
She told him stories to delight his ear ;
She showed him favors to allure his eye ;
To win his heart, she touch'd him here and
    there,—
Touches so soft still conquer chastity.   50
But whether unripe years did want conceit,
Or he refused to take her figured proffer,
The tender nibbler would not touch the bait,
But smile and jest at every gentle offer :
    Then fell she on her back, fair queen, and
      toward :
    He rose and ran away ; ah, fool too fro-
      ward !

V.

If love make me forsworn, how shall I swear
    to love ?
O never faith could hold, if not to beauty
    vow'd :
Though to myself forsworn, to thee I'll con-
    stant prove ;
Those thoughts, to me like oaks, to thee like
    osiers bow'd.   60
Study his bias leaves, and makes his book thine
    eyes,
Where all those pleasures live that art can
    comprehend.
If knowledge be the mark, to know thee shall
    suffice ;
Well learned is that tongue that well can thee
    commend ;

All ignorant that soul that sees thee without
  wonder ;
Which is to me some praise, that I thy parts
  admire :
Thine eye Jove's lightning seems, thy voice his
  dreadful thunder,
Which, not to anger bent, is music and sweet
  fire.
  Celestial as thou art, O do not love that
    wrong,
  To sing heaven's praise with such an earthly
    tongue.   70

VI.

Scarce had the sun dried up the dewy morn,
And scarce the herd gone to the hedge for
  shade,
When Cytherea, all in love forlorn,
A longing tarriance for Adonis made
Under an osier growing by a brook,
A brook where Adon used to cool his spleen :
Hot was the day ; she hotter that did look
For his approach, that often there had been.
Anon he comes, and throws his mantle by,
And stood stark naked on the brook's green
  brim :   80
The sun look'd on the world with glorious eye,
Yet not so wistly as this queen on him.
  He, spying her, bounced in, whereas he
    stood :
  'O Jove,' quoth she, 'why was not I a
    flood ! '

VII.

Fair is my love, but not so fair as fickle ;
Mild as a dove, but neither true nor trusty ;
Brighter than glass, and yet, as glass is, brittle ;
Softer than wax, and yet, as iron, rusty :
  A lily pale, with damask dye to grace her,
  None fairer, nor none falser to deface her.
Her lips to mine how often hath she joined,
Between each kiss her oaths of true love swear-
  ing !
How many tales to please me hath she coined,
Dreading my love, the loss thereof still fear-
  ing !
  Yet in the midst of all her pure protestings,
  Her faith, her oaths, her tears, and all were
    jestings.
She burn'd with love, as straw with fire
  flameth ;
She burn'd out love, as soon as straw out-
  burneth ;
She framed the love, and yet she foil'd the
  framing ;
She bade love last, and yet she fell a-turning.
  Was this a lover, or a lecher whether ? 101
  Bad in the best, though excellent in neither.

VIII.

If music and sweet poetry agree,
As they must needs, the sister and the brother,
Then must the love be great 'twixt thee and
  me,
Because thou lovest the one, and I the other.
Dowland to thee is dear, whose heavenly touch
Upon the lute doth ravish human sense ;
Spenser to me, whose deep conceit is such
As, passing all conceit, needs no defence.   110
Thou lovest to hear the sweet melodious sound
That Phœbus' lute, the queen of music,
  makes ;

And I in deep delight am chiefly drown'd
When as himself to singing he betakes.
  One god is god of both, as poets feign ;
  One knight loves both, and both in thee re-
    main.

IX.

Fair was the morn when the fair queen of
  love,
* * * * * * *
Paler for sorrow than her milk-white dove,
For Adon's sake, a youngster proud and wild ;
Her stand she takes upon a steep-up hill : 121
Anon Adonis comes with horn and hounds ;
She, silly queen, with more than love's good
  will,
Forbade the boy he should not pass those
  grounds :
'Once,' quoth she, 'did I see a fair sweet
  youth
Here in these brakes deep-wounded with a
  boar,
Deep in the thigh, a spectacle of ruth !
See, in my thigh,' quoth she, 'here was the
  sore.'
  She showed hers : he saw more wounds than
    one,
  And blushing fled, and left her all alone. 130

X.

Sweet rose, fair flower, untimely pluck'd, soon
  vaded,
Pluck'd in the bud, and vaded in the spring !
Bright orient pearl, alack, too timely shaded !
Fair creature, kill'd too soon by death's sharp
  sting !
  Like a green plum that hangs upon a tree,
  And falls, through wind, before the fall
    should be.
I weep for thee, and yet no cause I have ;
For why thou left'st me nothing in thy will :
And yet thou left'st me more than I did crave ;
For why I craved nothing of thee still :   140
  O yes, dear friend, I pardon crave of thee,
  Thy discontent thou didst bequeath to me.

XI.

Venus, with young Adonis sitting by her
Under a myrtle shade, began to woo him :
She told the youngling how god Mars did try
  her,
And as he fell to her, so fell she to him.
'Even thus,' quoth she, 'the warlike god em-
  braced me,'
And then she clipp'd Adonis in her arms ;
'Even thus,' quoth she, 'the warlike god un-
  laced me,'   149
As if the boy should use like loving charms ;
'Even thus,' quoth she, 'he seized on my lips,'
And with her lips on his did act the seizure :
And as she fetched breath, away he skips,
And would not take her meaning nor her
  pleasure.
  Ah, that I had my lady at this bay,
  To kiss and clip me till I run away !

XII.

Crabbed age and youth cannot live together :
Youth is full of pleasance, age is full of care ;
Youth like summer morn, age like winter
  weather ;
Youth like summer brave, age like winter
  bare.   160

Youth is full of sport, age's breath is short ;
  Youth is nimble, age is lame ;
Youth is hot and bold, age is weak and cold ;
  Youth is wild, and age is tame.
Age, I do abhor thee ; youth, I do adore thee ;
  O, my love, my love is young !
Age, I do defy thee : O, sweet shepherd, hie
    thee,
  For methinks thou stay'st too long,

XIII.

Beauty is but a vain and doubtful good ;
A shining gloss that vadeth suddenly ;   170
A flower that dies when first it gins to bud ;
A brittle glass that's broken presently :
  A doubtful good, a gloss, a glass, a flower,
  Lost, vaded, broken, dead within an hour.

And as goods lost are seld or never found,
As vaded gloss no rubbing will refresh,
As flowers dead lie wither'd on the ground,
As broken glass no cement can redress,
  So beauty blemish'd once's for ever lost,
  In spite of physic, painting, pain and cost.

XIV.

Good night, good rest. Ah, neither be my
    share :   181
She bade good night that kept my rest away ;
And daff'd me to a cabin hang'd with care,
To descant on the doubts of my decay.
  'Farewell,' quoth she, 'and come again to-
    morrow : '
  Fare well I could not, for I supp'd with sor-
    row.

Yet at my parting sweetly did she smile,
In scorn or friendship, nill I construe
    whether :
'T may be, she joy'd to jest at my exile,
'T may be, again to make me wander thither :
  'Wander,' a word for shadows like myself,
  As take the pain, but cannot pluck the pelf.

XV.

Lord, how mine eyes throw gazes to the east !
My heart doth charge the watch ; the morn-
    ing rise
Doth cite each moving sense from idle rest.
Not daring trust the office of mine eyes,
  While Philomela sits and sings, I sit and
    mark,
  And wish her lays were tuned like the lark ;

For she doth welcome daylight with her ditty,
And drives away dark dismal-dreaming night :
The night so pack'd, I post unto my pretty ;
Heart hath his hope, and eyes their wished
    sight ;
  Sorrow changed to solace, solace mix'd with
    sorrow ;
  For why, she sigh'd and bade me come to-
    morrow.

Were I with her, the night would post too
    soon ;
But now are minutes added to the hours ;
To spite me now, each minute seems a moon ;
Yet not for me, shine sun to succor flowers !
  Pack night, peep day ; good day, of night
    now borrow :
  Short, night, to-night, and length thyself to-
    morrow.   210

SONNETS TO SUNDRY NOTES OF MUSIC

[XVI.]

IT was a lording's daughter, the fairest one of
    three,
That liked of her master as well as well might
    be,
Till looking on an Englishman, the fair'st that
    eye could see,
  Her fancy fell a-turning.
Long was the combat doubtful that love with
    love did fight,
To leave the master loveless, or kill the gal-
    lant knight :
To put in practice either, alas, it was a spite
  Unto the silly damsel !
But one must be refused ; more mickle was
    the pain
That nothing could be used to turn them both
    to gain,   220
For of the two the trusty knight was wounded
    with disdain :
  Alas, she could not help it !
Thus art with arms contending was victor of
    the day,
Which by a gift of learning did bear the maid
    away :
Then, lullaby, the learned man hath got the
    lady gay ;
  For now my song is ended.

XVII.

On a day, alack the day !
Love, whose month was ever May,

Spied a blossom passing fair,
Playing in the wanton air :   230
Through the velvet leaves the wind
All unseen, gan passage find ;
That the lover, sick to death,
Wish'd himself the heaven's breath,
'Air,' quoth he, 'thy cheeks may blow ;
Air, would I triumph so !
But, alas ! my hand hath sworn
Ne'er to pluck thee from thy thorn :
Vow, alack ! for youth unmeet :
Youth, so apt to pluck a sweet.   240
Thou for whom Jove would swear
Juno but an Ethiope were ;
And deny himself for Jove,
Turning mortal for thy love.'

[XVIII.]

My flocks feed not,
My ewes breed not,
My rams speed not,
  All is amiss :
Love's denying,
Faith's defying,   250
Heart's renying,
  Causer of this.
All my merry jigs are quite forgot,
All my lady's love is lost, God wot :
Where her faith was firmly fix'd in love,
There a nay is placed without remove.
One silly cross
Wrought all my loss ;

O frowning Fortune, cursed, fickle
     dame !
For now I see   260
Inconstancy
     More in women than in men remain.

In black mourn I,
All fears scorn I,
Love hath forlorn me,
     Living in thrall :
Heart is bleeding,
All help needing,
O cruel speeding,
     Fraughted with gall.   270
My shepherd's pipe can sound no deal ;
My wether's bell rings doleful knell ;
My curtail dog, that wont to have play'd,
Plays not at all, but seems afraid ;
My sighs so deep
Procure to weep,
     In howling wise, to see my doleful
          plight.
How sighs resound
Through heartless ground,
     Like a thousand vanquish'd men in
          bloody fight !   280

Clear wells spring not,
Sweet birds sing not,
Green plants bring not
     Forth their dye ;
Herds stand weeping,
Flocks all sleeping,
Nymphs back peeping
     Fearfully :
All our pleasure known to us poor swains,
All our merry meetings on the plains,   290
All our evening sport from us is fled,
All our love is lost, for Love is dead
Farewell, sweet lass,
Thy like ne'er was
     For a sweet content, the cause of all
          my moan :
Poor Corydon
Must live alone ;
     Other help for him I see that there is
          none.

XIX.

When as thine eye hath chose the dame,
And stall'd the deer that thou shouldst strike,
Let reason rule things worthy blame,   301
As well as fancy partial might :
     Take counsel of some wiser head,
     Neither too young nor yet unwed.

And when thou comest thy tale to tell,
Smooth not thy tongue with filed talk,
Lest she some subtile practice smell,—
A cripple soon can find a halt ;—
     But plainly say thou lovest her well,
     And set thy person forth to sell.   310

What though her frowning brows be bent,
Her cloudy looks will calm ere night :
And then too late she will repent
That thus dissembled her delight ;
     And twice desire, ere it be day,
     That which with scorn she put away.

What though she strive to try her strength,
And ban and brawl, and say thee nay,
Her feeble force will yield at length,
When craft hath taught her thus to say,   320
     ' Had women been so strong as men,
     In faith, you had not had it then.'

And to her will frame all thy ways ;
Spare not to spend, and chiefly there
Where thy desert may merit praise,
By ringing in thy lady's ear :
     The strongest castle, tower, and town,
     The golden bullet beats it down.

Serve always with assured trust,
And in thy suit be humble true ;   330
Unless thy lady prove unjust,
Press never thou to choose anew :
     When time shall serve, be thou not slack
     To proffer, though she put thee back.

The wiles and guiles that women work,
Dissembled with an outward show,
The tricks and toys that in them lurk,
The cock that treads them shall not know.
     Have you not heard it said full oft,
     A woman's nay doth stand for nought ? 340

Think women still to strive with men,
To sin and never for to saint :
There is no heaven, by holy then,
When time with age doth them attaint.
     Were kisses all the joys in bed,
     One woman would another wed.

But, soft ! enough, too much, I fear
Lest that my mistress hear my song,
She will not stick to round me i' the ear,
To teach my tongue to be so long :   350
     Yet will she blush, here be it said,
     To hear her secrets so bewray'd.

[XX.]

Live with me, and be my love,
And we will all the pleasures prove
That hills and valleys, dales and fields,
And all the craggy mountains yields.

There will we sit upon the rocks,
And see the shepherds feed their flocks,
By shallow rivers, by whose falls
Melodious birds sing madrigals.   360

There will I make thee a bed of roses,
With a thousand fragrant posies,
A cap of flowers, and a kirtle
Embroider'd all with leaves of myrtle.

A belt of straw and ivy buds,
With coral clasps and amber studs ;
And if these pleasures may thee move,
Then live with me and be my love.

LOVE'S ANSWER.

If that the world and love were young,
And truth in every shepherd's tongue,   370
These pretty pleasures might me move
To live with thee and be thy love.

[XXI.]

As it fell upon a day
In the merry month of May,
Sitting in a pleasant shade
Which a grove of myrtles made,
Beasts did leap, and birds did sing,
Trees did grow, and plants did spring ;
Every thing did banish moan,
Save the nightingale alone :   380
She, poor bird, as all forlorn,
Lean'd her breast up-till a thorn
And there sung the dolefull'st ditty,
That to hear it was great pity :
' Fie, fie, fie,' now would she cry ;
' Tereu, tereu ! ' by and by ;

That to hear her so complain,
Scarce I could from tears refrain ;
For her griefs, so lively shown,
Made me think upon mine own.   390
Ah, thought I, thou mourn'st in vain !
None takes pity on thy pain :
Senseless trees they cannot hear thee ;
Ruthless beasts they will not cheer thee :
King Pandion he is dead ;
All thy friends are lapp'd in lead ;
All thy fellow birds do sing,
Careless of thy sorrowing.
Even so, poor bird, like thee,
None alive will pity me.   400
Whilst as fickle Fortune smiled,
Thou and I were both beguiled.
  Every one that flatters thee
Is no friend in misery.
Words are easy, like the wind ;
Faithful friends are hard to find :
Every man will be thy friend
Whilst thou hast wherewith to spend ;

But if store of crowns be scant,
No man will supply thy want.   410
If that one be prodigal,
Bountiful they will him call,
And with such-like flattering,
' Pity but he were a king ; '
If he be addict to vice,
Quickly him they will entice ;
If to women he be bent,
They have at commandement :
But if Fortune once do frown,
Then farewell his great renown   420
They that fawn'd on him before
Use his company no more.
He that is thy friend indeed,
He will help thee in thy need :
If thou sorrow, he will weep ;
If thou wake, he cannot sleep ;
Thus of every grief in heart
He with thee doth bear a part.
These are certain signs to know
Faithful friend from flattering foe.   430

SONNETS.

(WRITTEN BETWEEN 1595–1605.)

INTRODUCTION.

The Sonnets of Shakespeare suggest, perhaps, the most difficult questions in Shakespearean criticism. In 1609 appeared these poems in a quarto (published almost certainly without the author's sanction), which also contained *A Lover's Complaint*. The publisher, Thomas Thorpe, dedicated them " To the onlie begetter of these ensuing sonnets, Mr. W. H." Does " begetter " mean the person who inspired them and so brought them into existence, or only the obtainer of the *Sonnets* for Thorpe ? Probably the former. And who is Mr. W. H. ? It is clear from sonnet 135 that the Christian-name of Shakespeare's friend to whom the first 126 sonnets were addressed was William. But what William ? There is not even an approach to certainty in any answer offered to this question. Some have supposed that W. H. is a blind to conceal and yet express the initials H. W. *i.e.* Henry Wriothesley, Earl of Southampton, Shakespeare's patron. Others hold that William Herbert, Earl of Pembroke (to whom, together with his brother, the first folio was dedicated), is here addressed. When were the *Sonnets* written ? We know that Meres in 1598 spoke of Shakespeare's " sugred sonnets among his private friends," and that in 1599 two (138 and 144) were printed in *The Passionate Pilgrim*. Some, to judge by their style, seem to belong to the time when *Romeo and Juliet* was written. Others—as for example 66–74 —echo the sadder tone which is heard in *Hamlet* and *Measure for Measure*. The writing of the *Sonnets* certainly extended over a considerable period of time, at least three years (see 104), and perhaps a longer period. They all, probably, lie somewhere between 1595 and 1605. The *Sonnets* consist of two series, the first (from 1 to 126) addressed to a young man ; the other (from 127 to 154) addressed to or referring to a woman. But both series allude to events which connect the two persons with one another and with Shakespeare. The young friend, whom Shakespeare loved with a fond idolatry, was beautiful, clever, rich in the gifts of fortune, and of high rank. The woman was of stained character, false to her husband, the reverse of beautiful, dark-eyed, pale-faced, a musician, possessed of a strange power of attraction. To her fascination Shakespeare yielded himself, and in his absence she laid her snares for Shakespeare's friend and won him. Hence a coldness, estrangement, and for some time a complete severance between Shakespeare and his friend, after a time followed by acknowledgment of fault on both sides and a complete reconciliation. So the *Sonnets* must be interpreted if we accept the natural sense they seem to bear. But several critics have held that they are either altogether of an ideal nature or allegorical, or were written in part by Shakespeare not for himself but for the use of others. The natural sense, however, is probably the true one.

TO THE ONLIE BEGETTER OF
THESE INSUING SONNETS
MR. W. H. ALL HAPPINESSE
AND THAT ETERNITIE
PROMISED BY
OUR EVER-LIVING POET
WISHETH
THE WELL-WISHING
ADVENTURER IN
SETTING
FORTH
T. T.

FROM fairest creatures we desire increase,
That thereby beauty's rose might never die,
But as the riper should by time decease,
His tender heir might bear his memory :
But thou, contracted to thine own bright eyes,
Feed'st thy light'st flame with self-substantial
fuel,
Making a famine where abundance lies,
Thyself thy foe, to thy sweet self too cruel.
Thou that art now the world's fresh orna-
ment
And only herald to the gaudy spring,
Within thine own bud buriest thy content
And, tender churl, makest waste in niggard-
ing.
    Pity the world, or else this glutton be,
    To eat the world's due, by the grave and
    thee.

II.

When forty winters shall besiege thy brow,
And dig deep trenches in thy beauty's field,
Thy youth's proud livery, so gazed on now,
Will be a tatter'd weed, of small worth held :
Then being ask'd where all thy beauty lies,
Where all the treasure of thy lusty days,
To say, within thine own deep-sunken eyes,
Were an all-eating shame and thriftless praise.
How much more praise deserved thy beauty's
use,
If thou couldst answer 'This fair child of
mine
Shall sum my count and make my old excuse,'
Proving his beauty by succession thine !
    This were to be new made when thou art
    old,
    And see thy blood warm when thou feel'st
    it cold.

III.

Look in thy glass, and tell the face thou view-
est
Now is the time that face should form an-
other ;
Whose fresh repair if now thou not renewest,
Thou dost beguile the world, unbless some
mother.
For where is she so fair whose unear'd womb
Disdains the tillage of thy husbandry ?
Or who is he so fond will be the tomb
Of his self-love, to stop posterity ?
Thou art thy mother's glass, and she in thee
Calls back the lovely April of her prime :
So thou through windows of thine age shall
see
Despite of wrinkles this thy golden time.
    But if thou live, remember'd not to be,
    Die single, and thine image dies with thee.

IV.

Unthrifty loveliness, why dost thou spend
Upon thyself thy beauty's legacy ?
Nature's bequest gives nothing but doth lend,
And being frank she lends to those are free.
Then, beauteous niggard, why dost thou abuse
The bounteous largess given thee to give ?
Profitless usurer, why dost thou use
So great a sum of sums, yet canst not live ?
For having traffic with thyself alone,
Thou of thyself thy sweet self dost deceive.

Then how, when nature calls thee to be gone,
What acceptable audit canst thou leave ?
    Thy unused beauty must be tomb'd with
    thee,
    Which, used, lives th' executor to be.

V.

Those hours, that with gentle work did frame
The lovely gaze where every eye doth dwell,
Will play the tyrants to the very same
And that unfair which fairly doth excel :
For never-resting time leads summer on
To hideous winter and confounds him there ;
Sap check'd with frost and lusty leaves quite
gone,
Beauty o'ersnow'd and bareness every where :
Then, were not summer's distillation left,
A liquid prisoner pent in walls of glass,
Beauty's effect with beauty were bereft,
Nor it nor no remembrance what it was :
    But flowers distill'd, though they with win-
    ter meet,
    Leese but their show ; their substance still
    lives sweet.

VI.

Then let not winter's ragged hand deface
In thee thy summer, ere thou be distill'd :
Make sweet some vial ; treasure thou some
place
With beauty's treasure, ere it be self-kill'd.
That use is not forbidden usury,
Which happies those that pay the willing
loan ;
That's for thyself to breed another thee,
Or ten times happier, be it ten for one ;
Ten times thyself were happier than thou art,
If ten of thine ten times refigured thee :
Then what could death do, if thou shouldst
depart,
Leaving thee living in posterity ?
    Be not self-will'd, for thou art much too
    fair
    To be death's conquest and make worms
    thine heir.

VII.

Lo ! in the orient when the gracious light
Lifts up his burning head, each under eye
Doth homage to his new-appearing sight,
Serving with looks his sacred majesty ;
And having climb'd the steep-up heavenly hill,
Resembling strong youth in his middle age,
Yet mortal looks adore his beauty still,
Attending on his golden pilgrimage ;
But when from highmost pitch, with weary
car,
Like feeble age, he reeleth from the day,
The eyes, 'fore duteous, now converted are
From his low tract and look another way :
    So thou, thyself out-going in thy noon,
    Unlook'd on diest, unless thou get a son.

VIII.

Music to hear, why hear'st thou music sadly ?
Sweets with sweets war not, joy delights in
joy.
Why lovest thou that which thou receivest not
gladly,
Or else receivest with pleasure thine annoy ?

If the true concord of well-tuned sounds,
By unions married, do offend thine ear,
They do but sweetly chide thee, who confounds
In singleness the parts that thou shouldst bear.
Mark how one string, sweet husband to another,
Strikes each in each by mutual ordering,
Resembling sire and child and happy mother
Who all in one, one pleasing note do sing :
   Whose speechless song, being many, seeming one,
   Sings this to thee : ' thou single wilt prove none.'

IX.

Is it for fear to wet a widow's eye
That thou consumest thyself in single life ?
Ah ! if thou issueless shalt hap to die,
The world will wail thee, like a makeless wife ;
The world will be thy widow and still weep
That thou no form of thee hast left behind,
When every private widow well may keep
By children's eyes her husband's shape in mind.
Look, what an unthrift in the world doth spend
Shifts but his place, for still the world enjoys it ;
But beauty's waste hath in the world an end,
And kept unused, the user so destroys it.
   No love toward others in that bosom sits
   That on himself such murderous shame commits.

X.

For shame ! deny that thou bear'st love to any,
Who for thyself art so unprovident.
Grant, if thou wilt, thou art beloved of many,
But that thou none lovest is most evident ;
For thou art so possess'd with murderous hate
That 'gainst thyself thou stick'st not to conspire,
Seeking that beauteous roof to ruinate
Which to repair should be thy chief desire.
O, change thy thought, that I may change my mind!
Shall hate be fairer lodged than gentle love ?
Be, as thy presence is, gracious and kind,
Or to thyself at least kind-hearted prove :
   Make thee another self, for love of me,
   That beauty still may live in thine or thee.

XI.

As fast as thou shalt wane, so fast thou growest
In one of thine, from that which thou departest ;
And that fresh blood which youngly thou bestowest
Thou mayst call thine when thou from youth convertest.
Herein lives wisdom, beauty and increase :
Without this, folly, age and cold decay :
If all were minded so, the times should cease
And threescore year would make the world away.

Let those whom Nature hath not made for store,
Harsh featureless and rude, barrenly perish :
Look, whom she best endow'd she gave the more ;
Which bounteous gift thou shouldst in bounty cherish :
   She carved thee for her seal, and meant thereby
   Thou shouldst print more, not let that copy die.

XII.

When I do count the clock that tells the time,
And see the brave day sunk in hideous night ;
When I behold the violet past prime,
And sable curls all silver'd o'er with white ;
When lofty trees I see barren of leaves
Which erst from heat did canopy the herd,
And summer's green all girded up in sheaves
Borne on the bier with white and bristly beard,
Then of thy beauty do I question make,
That thou among the wastes of time must go,
Since sweets and beauties do themselves forsake
And die as fast as they see others grow ;
   And nothing 'gainst Time's scythe can make defence
   Save breed, to brave him when he takes thee hence.

XIII.

O, that you were yourself ! but, love, you are
No longer yours than you yourself here live :
Against this coming end you should prepare,
And your sweet semblance to some other give.
So should that beauty which you hold in lease
Find no determination : then you were
Yourself again after yourself's decease,
When your sweet issue your sweet form should bear.
Who lets so fair a house fall to decay,
Which husbandry in honor might uphold
Against the stormy gusts of winter's day
And barren rage of death's eternal cold ?
   O, none but unthrifts ! Dear my love, you know
   You had a father : let your son say so.

XIV.

Not from the stars do I my judgment pluck ;
And yet methinks I have astronomy,
But not to tell of good or evil luck,
Of plagues, of dearths, or seasons' quality ;
Nor can I fortune to brief minutes tell,
Pointing to each his thunder, rain and wind,
Or say with princes if it shall go well,
By oft predict that I in heaven find :
But from thine eyes my knowledge I derive,
And, constant stars, in them I read such art
As truth and beauty shall together thrive,
If from thyself to store thou wouldst convert ;
   Or else of thee this I prognosticate :
   Thy end is truth's and beauty's doom and date.

XV.

When I consider every thing that grows
Holds in perfection but a little moment,
That this huge stage presenteth nought but shows
Whereon the stars in secret influence comment ;

When I perceive that men as plants increase,
Cheered and check'd even by the self-same
    sky,
Vaunt in their youthful sap, at height de-
    crease,
And wear their brave state out of memory ;
Then the conceit of this inconstant stay
Sets you most rich in youth before my sight,
Where wasteful Time debateth with Decay,
To change your day of youth to sullied night ;
    And all in war with Time for love of you,
    As he takes from you, I engraft you new.

XVI.

But wherefore do not you a mightier way
Make war upon this bloody tyrant, Time ?
And fortify yourself in your decay
With means more blessed than my barren
    rhyme ?
Now stand you on the top of happy hours,
And many maiden gardens yet unset
With virtuous wish would bear your living
    flowers,
Much liker than your painted counterfeit :
So should the lines of life that life repair,
Which this, Time's pencil, or my pupil pen,
Neither in inward worth nor outward fair,
Can make you live yourself in eyes of men.
    To give away yourself keeps yourself still,
    And you must live, drawn by your own
        sweet skill.

XVII.

Who will believe my verse in time to come,
If it were fill'd with your most high deserts ?
Though yet, heaven knows, it is but as a tomb
Which hides your life and shows not half your
    parts.
If I could write the beauty of your eyes
And in fresh numbers number all your graces,
The age to come would say ' This poet lies ;
Such heavenly touches ne'er touch'd earthly
    faces.'
So should my papers yellow'd with their age
Be scorn'd like old men of less truth than
    tongue,
And your true rights be term'd a poet's rage
And stretched metre of an antique song :
    But were some child of yours alive that
        time,
    You should live twice ; in it and in my
        rhyme.

XVIII.

Shall I compare thee to a summer's day ?
Thou art more lovely and more temperate :
Rough winds do shake the darling buds of
    May,
And summer's lease hath all too short a date :
Sometime too hot the eye of heaven shines,
And often is his gold complexion dimm'd ;
And every fair from fair sometime declines,
By chance or nature's changing course un-
    trimm'd ;
But thy eternal summer shall not fade
Nor lose possession of that fair thou owest ;
Nor shall Death brag thou wander'st in his
    shade,
When in eternal lines to time thou growest :
    So long as men can breathe or eyes can see,
    So long lives this and this gives life to thee.

XIX.

Devouring Time, blunt thou the lion's paws,
And make the earth devour her own sweet
    brood ;
Pluck the keen teeth from the fierce tiger's
    jaws,
And burn the long-lived phœnix in her blood ;
Make glad and sorry seasons as thou fleets,
And do whate'er thou wilt, swift-footed Time,
To the wide world and all her fading sweets ;
But I forbid thee one most heinous crime :
O, carve not with thy hours my love's fair
    brow,
Nor draw no lines there with thine antique
    pen ;
Him in thy course untainted do allow
For beauty's pattern to succeeding men.
    Yet, do thy worst, old Time : despite thy
        wrong,
    My love shall in my verse ever live young.

XX.

A woman's face with Nature's own hand
    painted
Hast thou, the master-mistress of my passion ;
A woman's gentle heart, but not acquainted
With shifting change, as is false women's
    fashion ;
An eye more bright than theirs, less false in
    rolling,
Gilding the object whereupon it gazeth ;
A man in hue, all ' hues ' in his controlling,
Which steals men's eyes and women's souls
    amazeth.
And for a woman wert thou first created ;
Till Nature, as she wrought thee, fell a-dot-
    ing,
And by addition me of thee defeated,
By adding one thing to my purpose nothing.
    But since she prick'd thee out for women's
        pleasure,
    Mine be thy love and thy love's use their
        treasure.

XXI.

So is it not with me as with that Muse
Stirr'd by a painted beauty to his verse,
Who heaven itself for ornament doth use
And every fair with his fair doth rehearse
Making a couplement of proud compare,
With sun and moon, with earth and sea's rich
    gems,
With April's first-born flowers, and all things
    rare
That heaven's air in this huge rondure hems.
O, let me, true in love, but truly write,
And then believe me, my love is as fair
As any mother's child, though not so bright
As those gold candles fix'd in heaven's air :
    Let them say more that like of hearsay
        well ;
    I will not praise that purpose not to sell.

XXII.

My glass shall not persuade me I am old,
So long as youth and thou are of one date ;
But when in thee time's furrows I behold,
Then look I death my days should expiate.
For all that beauty that doth cover thee
Is but the seemly raiment of my heart,
Which in thy breast doth live, as thine in me :
How can I then be elder than thou art ?

O, therefore, love, be of thyself so wary
As I, not for myself, but for thee will ;
Bearing thy heart, which I will keep so chary
As tender nurse her babe from faring ill.
　　Presume not on thy heart when mine is
　　　　slain ;
　　Thou gavest me thine, not to give back
　　　　again.

XXIII.

As an unperfect actor on the stage
Who with his fear is put besides his part,
Or some fierce thing replete with too much
　　rage,
Whose strength's abundance weakens his own
　　heart,
So I, for fear of trust, forget to say
The perfect ceremony of love's rite,
And in mine own love's strength seem to de-
　　cay,
O'ercharged with burden of mine own love's
　　might.
O, let my books be then the eloquence
And dumb presagers of my speaking breast,
Who plead for love and look for recompense
More than that tongue that more hath more
　　express'd.
　　O, learn to read what silent love hath writ :
　　To hear with eyes belongs to love's fine wit.

XXIV.

Mine eye hath play'd the painter and hath
　　stell'd
Thy beauty's form in table of my heart ;
My body is the frame wherein 'tis held,
And perspective it is best painter's art.
For through the painter must you see his skill,
To find where your true image pictured lies ;
Which in my bosom's shop is hanging still,
That hath his windows glazed with thine eyes.
Now see what good turns eyes for eyes have
　　done :
Mine eyes have drawn thy shape, and thine
　　for me
Are windows to my breast, where-through the
　　sun
Delights to peep, to gaze therein on thee ;
　　Yet eyes this cunning want to grace their
　　　　art ;
　　They draw but what they see, know not the
　　　　heart.

XXV.

Let those who are in favor with their stars
Of public honor and proud titles boast,
Whilst I, whom fortune of such triumph bars,
Unlook'd for joy in that I honor most.
Great princes' favorites their fair leaves spread
But as the marigold at the sun's eye,
And in themselves their pride lies buried,
For at a frown they in their glory die.
The painful warrior famoused for fight,
After a thousand victories once foil'd,
Is from the book of honor razed quite,
And all the rest forgot for which he toil'd :
　　Then happy I, that love and am beloved
　　Where I may not remove nor be removed.

XXVI.

Lord of my love, to whom in vassalage
Thy merit hath my duty strongly knit,
To thee I send this written embassage,
To witness duty, not to show my wit :

Duty so great, which wit so poor as mine
May make seem bare, in wanting words to
　　show it,
But that I hope some good conceit of thine
In thy soul's thought, all naked, will bestow
　　it ;
Till whatsoever star that guides my moving
Points on me graciously with fair aspect
And puts apparel on my tatter'd loving,
To show me worthy of thy sweet respect :
　　Then may I dare to boast how I do love
　　　　thee ;
　　Till then not show my head where thou
　　　　mayst prove me.

XXVII.

Weary with toil, I haste me to my bed,
The dear repose for limbs with travel tired ;
But then begins a journey in my head,
To work my mind, when body's work's ex-
　　pired :
For then my thoughts, from far where I abide,
Intend a zealous pilgrimage to thee,
And keep my drooping eyelids open wide,
Looking on darkness which the blind do see
Save that my soul's imaginary sight
Presents thy shadow to my sightless view,
Which, like a jewel hung in ghastly night,
Makes black night beauteous and her old face
　　new.
　　Lo ! thus, by day my limbs, by night my
　　　　mind,
　　For thee and for myself no quiet find.

XXVIII.

How can I then return in happy plight,
That am debarr'd the benefit of rest ?
When day's oppression is not eased by night,
But day by night, and night by day, oppress'd ?
And each, though enemies to either's reign,
Do in consent shake hands to torture me ;
The one by toil, the other to complain
How far I toil, still farther off from thee.
I tell the day, to please him thou art bright
And dost him grace when clouds do blot the
　　heaven :
So flatter I the swart-complexion'd night,
When sparkling stars twire not thou gild'st the
　　even.
　　But day doth daily draw my sorrows longer
　　And night doth nightly make grief's strength
　　　　seem stronger.

XXIX.

When, in disgrace with fortune and men's eyes,
I all alone beweep my outcast state
And trouble deaf heaven with my bootless
　　cries
And look upon myself and curse my fate,
Wishing me like to one more rich in hope,
Featured like him, like him with friends pos-
　　sess'd,
Desiring this man's art and that man's scope,
With what I most enjoy contented least ;
Yet in these thoughts myself almost despising,
Haply I think on thee, and then my state,
Like to the lark at break of day arising
From sullen earth, sings hymns at heaven's
　　gate ;
　　For thy sweet love remember'd such wealth
　　　　brings
　　That then I scorn to change my state with
　　　　kings.

XXX.

When to the sessions of sweet silent thought
I summon up remembrance of things past,
I sigh the lack of many a thing I sought,
And with old woes new wail my dear time's
    waste :
Then can I drown an eye, unused to flow,
For precious friends hid in death's dateless
    night,
And weep afresh love's long since cancell'd
    woe,
And moan the expense of many a vanish'd
    sight :
Then can I grieve at grievances foregone,
And heavily from woe to woe tell o'er
The sad account of fore-bemoaned moan,
Which I new pay as if not paid before.
    But if the while I think on thee, dear friend,
    All losses are restored and sorrows end.

XXXI.

Thy bosom is endeared with all hearts,
Which I by lacking have supposed dead,
And there reigns love and all love's loving
    parts,
And all those friends which I thought buried.
How many a holy and obsequious tear
Hath dear religious love stol'n from mine eye
As interest of the dead, which now appear
But things removed that hidden in thee lie !
Thou art the grave where buried love doth live,
Hung with the trophies of my lovers gone,
Who all their parts of me to thee did give ;
That due of many now is thine alone :
    Their images I loved I view in thee,
    And thou, all they, hast all the all of me.

XXXII.

If thou survive my well-contented day,
When that churl Death my bones with dust
    shall cover,
And shalt by fortune once more re-survey
These poor rude lines of thy deceased lover,
Compare them with the bettering of the time,
And though they be outstripp'd by every pen,
Reserve them for my love, not for their rhyme,
Exceeded by the height of happier men.
O, then vouchsafe me but this loving thought :
' Had my friend's Muse grown with this grow-
    ing age,
A dearer birth than this his love had brought,
To march in ranks of better equipage :
    But since he died and poets better prove,
    Theirs for their style I'll read, his for his
    love.'

XXXIII.

Full many a glorious morning have I seen
Flatter the mountain-tops with sovereign eye,
Kissing with golden face the meadows green,
Gilding pale streams with heavenly alchemy ;
Anon permit the basest clouds to ride
With ugly rack on his celestial face,
And from the forlorn world his visage hide,
Stealing unseen to west with this disgrace :
Even so my sun one early morn did shine
With all triumphant splendor on my brow ;
But out, alack ! he was but one hour mine ;
The region cloud hath mask'd him from me
    now.
    Yet him for this my love no whit disdaineth ;
    Suns of the world may stain when heaven's
    sun staineth.

XXXIV.

Why didst thou promise such a beauteous day,
And make me travel forth without my cloak,
To let base clouds o'ertake me in my way,
Hiding thy bravery in their rotten smoke ?
'Tis not enough that through the cloud thou
    break,
To dry the rain on my storm-beaten face,
For no man well of such a salve can speak
That heals the wound and cures not the dis-
    grace :
Nor can thy shame give physic to my grief ;
Though thou repent, yet I have still the loss :
The offender's sorrow lends but weak relief
To him that bears the strong offence's cross.
    Ah ! but those tears are pearl which thy love
    sheds,
    And they are rich and ransom all ill deeds.

XXXV.

No more be grieved at that which thou hast
    done :
Roses have thorns, and silver fountains mud ;
Clouds and eclipses stain both moon and sun,
And loathsome canker lives in sweetest bud.
All men make faults, and even I in this,
Authorizing thy trespass with compare,
Myself corrupting, salving thy amiss,
Excusing thy sins more than thy sins are ;
For to thy sensual fault I bring in sense—
Thy adverse party is thy advocate—
And 'gainst myself a lawful plea commence :
Such civil war is in my love and hate
    That I an accessary needs must be
    To that sweet thief which sourly robs from
    me.

XXXVI.

Let me confess that we two must be twain,
Although our undivided loves are one :
So shall those blots that do with me remain
Without thy help by me be borne alone.
In our two loves there is but one respect,
Though in our lives a separable spite,
Which though it alter not love's sole effect,
Yet doth it steal sweet hours from love's de-
    light.
I may not evermore acknowledge thee,
Lest my bewailed guilt should do thee shame,
Nor thou with public kindness honor me,
Unless thou take that honor from thy name :
    But do not so ; I love thee in such sort
    As, thou being mine, mine is thy good re-
    port.

XXXVII.

As a decrepit father takes delight
To see his active child do deeds of youth,
So I, made lame by fortune's dearest spite,
Take all my comfort of thy worth and truth.
For whether beauty, birth, or wealth, or wit,
Or any of these all, or all, or more,
Entitled in thy parts do crowned sit,
I make my love engrafted to this store :
So then I am not lame, poor, nor despised,
Whilst that this shadow doth such substance
    give
That I in thy abundance am sufficed
And by a part of all thy glory live.
    Look, what is best, that best I wish in thee :
    This wish I have ; then ten times happy me !

XXXVIII.

How can my Muse want subject to invent,
While thou dost breathe, that pour'st into my
    verse
Thine own sweet argument, too excellent
For every vulgar paper to rehearse ?
O, give thyself the thanks, if aught in me
Worthy perusal stand against thy sight ;
For who's so dumb that cannot write to thee,
When thou thyself dost give invention light ?
Be thou the tenth Muse, ten times more in
    worth
Than those old nine which rhymers invocate ;
And he that calls on thee, let him bring forth
Eternal numbers to outlive long date.
    If my slight Muse do please these curious
        days,
    The pain be mine, but thine shall be the
        praise.

XXXIX.

O, how thy worth with manners may I sing,
When thou art all the better part of me ?
What can mine own praise to mine own self
    bring ?
And what is 't but mine own when I praise
    thee ?
Even for this let us divided live,
And our dear love lose name of single one,
That by this separation I may give
That due to thee which thou deservest alone.
O absence, what a torment wouldst thou
    prove,
Were it not thy sour leisure gave sweet leave
To entertain the time with thoughts of love,
Which time and thoughts so sweetly doth de-
    ceive,
    And that thou teachest how to make one
        twain,
    By praising him here who doth hence re-
        main !

XL.

Take all my loves, my love, yea, take them
    all ;
What hast thou then more than thou hadst
    before ?
No love, my love, that thou mayst true love
    call ;
All mine was thine before thou hadst this
    more.
Then if for my love thou my love receivest,
I cannot blame thee for my love thou usest ;
But yet be blamed, if thou thyself deceivest
By wilful taste of what thyself refusest.
I do forgive thy robbery, gentle thief,
Although thou steal thee all my poverty ;
And yet, love knows, it is a greater grief
To bear love's wrong than hate's known in-
    jury.
    Lascivious grace, in whom all ill well shows,
    Kill me with spites ; yet we must not be
        foes.

XLI.

Those petty wrongs that liberty commits,
When I am sometime absent from thy heart,
Thy beauty and thy years full well befits,
For still temptation follows where thou art.
Gentle thou art and therefore to be won,
Beauteous thou art, therefore to be assailed ;
And when a woman woos, what woman's son
Will sourly leave her till she have prevailed ?
Ay me ! but yet thou mightest my seat forbear,
And chide thy beauty and thy straying youth,
Who lead thee in their riot even there
Where thou art forced to break a twofold
    truth,
    Hers by thy beauty tempting her to thee,
    Thine, by thy beauty being false to me.

XLII.

That thou hast her, it is not all my grief,
And yet it may be said I loved her dearly ;
That she hath thee, is of my wailing chief,
A loss in love that touches me more nearly.
Loving offenders, thus I will excuse ye :
Thou dost love her, because thou knowst I love
    her ;
And for my sake even so doth she abuse me,
Suffering my friend for my sake to approve
    her.
If I lose thee, my loss is my love's gain,
And losing her, my friend hath found that
    loss ;
Both find each other, and I lose both twain,
And both for my sake lay on me this cross :
    But here's the joy ; my friend and I are
        one ;
    Sweet flattery ! then she loves but me alone.

XLIII.

When most I wink, then do mine eyes best see,
For all the day they view things unrespected ;
But when I sleep, in dreams they look on thee,
And darkly bright are bright in dark directed.
Then thou, whose shadow shadows doth make
    bright,
How would thy shadow's form form happy
    show
To the clear day with thy much clearer light,
When to unseeing eyes thy shade shines so !
How would, I say, mine eyes be blessed made
By looking on thee in the living day,
When in dead night thy fair imperfect shade
Through heavy sleep on sightless eyes doth
    stay !
    All days are nights to see till I see thee,
    And nights bright days when dreams do
        show thee me.

XLIV.

If the dull substance of my flesh were thought,
Injurious distance should not stop my way ;
For then despite of space I would be brought,
From limits far remote where thou dost stay.
No matter then although my foot did stand
Upon the farthest earth removed from thee ;
For nimble thought can jump both sea and
    land
As soon as think the place where he would be.
But ah ! thought kills me that I am not
    thought,
To leap large lengths of miles when thou art
    gone,
But that so much of earth and water wrought
I must attend time's leisure with my moan,
    Receiving nought by elements so slow
    But heavy tears, badges of either's woe.

XLV.

The other two, slight air and purging fire,
Are both with thee, wherever I abide ;
The first my thought, the other my desire,
These present-absent with swift motion slide.

For when these quicker elements are gone
In tender embassy of love to thee,
My life, being made of four, with two alone
Sinks down to death, oppress'd with melancholy ;
Until life's composition be recured
By those swift messengers return'd from thee,
Who even but now come back again, assured
Of thy fair health, recounting it to me :
    This told, I joy ; but then no longer glad,
    I send them back again and straight grow sad.

XLVI.

Mine eye and heart are at a mortal war
How to divide the conquest of thy sight ;
Mine eye my heart thy picture's sight would bar,
My heart mine eye the freedom of that right.
My heart doth plead that thou in him dost lie,—
A closet never pierced with crystal eyes—
But the defendant doth that plea deny
And says in him thy fair appearance lies.
To 'cide this title is impanneled
A quest of thoughts, all tenants to the heart,
And by their verdict is determined
The clear eye's moiety and the dear heart's part :
    As thus ; mine eye's due is thy outward part,
    And my heart's right thy inward love of heart.

XLVII.

Betwixt mine eye and heart a league is took,
And each doth good turns now unto the other :
When that mine eye is famish'd for a look,
Or heart in love with sighs himself doth smother,
With my love's picture then my eye doth feast
And to the painted banquet bids my heart ;
Another time mine eye is my heart's guest
And in his thoughts of love doth share a part :
So, either by thy picture or my love,
Thyself away art present still with me ;
For thou not farther than my thoughts canst move,
And I am still with them and they with thee ;
    Or, if they sleep, thy picture in my sight
    Awakes my heart to heart's and eye's delight.

XLVIII.

How careful was I, when I took my way,
Each trifle under truest bars to thrust,
That to my use it might unused stay
From hands of falsehood, in sure wards of trust !
But thou, to whom my jewels trifles are,
Most worthy of comfort, now my greatest grief,
Thou, best of dearest and mine only care,
Art left the prey of every vulgar thief.
Thee have I not lock'd up in any chest,
Save where thou art not, though I feel thou art,
Within the gentle closure of my breast,
From whence at pleasure thou mayst come and part ;
    And even thence thou wilt be stol'n, I fear,
    For truth proves thievish for a prize so dear.

XLIX.

Against that time, if ever that time come,
When I shall see thee frown on my defects,
When as thy love hath cast his utmost sum,
Call'd to that audit by advised respects ;
Against that time when thou shalt strangely pass
And scarcely greet me with that sun, thine eye,
When love, converted from the thing it was,
Shall reasons find of settled gravity,—
Against that time do I ensconce me here
Within the knowledge of mine own desert,
And this my hand against myself uprear,
To guard the lawful reasons on thy part :
    To leave poor me thou hast the strength of laws,
    Since why to love I can allege no cause.

L.

How heavy do I journey on the way,
When what I seek, my weary travel's end,
Doth teach that ease and that repose to say
' Thus far the miles are measured from thy friend ! '
The beast that bears me, tired with my woe,
Plods dully on, to bear that weight in me,
As if by some instinct the wretch did know
His rider loved not speed, being made from thee :
The bloody spur cannot provoke him on
That sometimes anger thrusts into his hide ;
Which heavily he answers with a groan,
More sharp to me than spurring to his side ;
    For that same groan doth put this in my mind ;
    My grief lies onward and my joy behind.

LI.

Thus can my love excuse the slow offence
Of my dull bearer when from thee I speed :
From where thou art why should I haste me thence ?
Till I return, of posting is no need.
O, what excuse will my poor beast then find,
When swift extremity can seem but slow ?
Then should I spur, though mounted on the wind ;
In winged speed no motion shall I know :
Then can no horse with my desire keep pace ;
Therefore desire of perfect'st love being made,
Shall neigh—no dull flesh—in his fiery race ;
But love, for love, thus shall excuse my jade ;
    Since from thee going he went wilful-slow,
    Towards thee I'll run, and give him leave to go.

LII.

So am I as the rich, whose blessed key
Can bring him to his sweet up-locked treasure,
The which he will not every hour survey,
For blunting the fine point of seldom pleasure.
Therefore are feasts so solemn and so rare,
Since, seldom coming, in the long year set,
Like stones of worth they thinly placed are,
Or captain jewels in the carcanet.
So is the time that keeps you as my chest,
Or as the wardrobe which the robe doth hide,
To make some special instant special blest,
By new unfolding his imprison'd pride.
    Blessed are you, whose worthiness gives scope,
    Being had, to triumph, being lack'd, to hope.

LIII.

What is your substance, whereof are you made,
That millions of strange shadows on you tend ?
Since every one hath, every one, one shade,
And you, but one, can every shadow lend.
Describe Adonis, and the counterfeit
Is poorly imitated after you ;
On Helen's cheek all art of beauty set,
And you in Grecian tires are painted new :
Speak of the spring and foison of the year ;
The one doth shadow of your beauty show,
The other as your bounty doth appear ;
And you in every blessed shape we know.
  In all external grace you have some part,
  But you like none, none you, for constant
    heart.

LIV.

O, how much more doth beauty beauteous
    seem
By that sweet ornament which truth doth give !
The rose looks fair, but fairer we it deem
For that sweet odor which doth in it live.
The canker-blooms have full as deep a dye
As the perfumed tincture of the roses,
Hang on such thorns and play as wantonly
When summer's breath their masked buds dis-
    closes :
But, for their virtue only is their show,
They live unwoo'd and unrespected fade,
Die to themselves. Sweet roses do not so ;
Of their sweet deaths are sweetest odors
    made :
  And so of you, beauteous and lovely youth,
  When that shall fade, my verse distills your
    truth.

LV.

Not marble, nor the gilded monuments
Of princes, shall outlive this powerful rhyme ;
But you shall shine more bright in these con-
    tents
Than unswept stone besmear'd with sluttish
    time.
When wasteful war shall statues overturn,
And broils root out the work of masonry,
Nor Mars his sword nor war's quick fire shall
    burn
The living record of your memory.
'Gainst death and all-oblivious enmity
Shall you pace forth ; your praise shall still
    find room
Even in the eyes of all posterity
That wear this world out to the ending doom.
  So, till the judgment that yourself arise,
  You live in this, and dwell in lovers' eyes.

LVI.

Sweet love, renew thy force ; be it not said
Thy edge should blunter be than appetite,
Which but to-day by feeding is allay'd,
To-morrow sharpen'd in his former might :
So, love, be thou ; although to-day thou fill
Thy hungry eyes even till they wink with full-
    ness,
To-morrow see again, and do not kill
The spirit of love with a perpetual dullness.
Let this sad interim like the ocean be
Which parts the shore, where two contracted
    new
Come daily to the banks, that, when they see
Return of love, more blest may be the view ;

Else call it winter, which being full of care
Makes summer's welcome thrice more
    wish'd, more rare.

LVII.

Being your slave, what should I do but tend
Upon the hours and times of your desire ?
I have no precious time at all to spend,
Nor services to do, till you require.
Nor dare I chide the world-without-end hour
Whilst I, my sovereign, watch the clock for
    you,
Nor think the bitterness of absence sour
When you have bid your servant once adieu ;
Nor dare I question with my jealous thought
Where you may be, or your affairs suppose,
But, like a sad slave, stay and think of nought
Save, where you are how happy you make
    those.
  So true a fool is love that in your will,
  Though you do any thing, he thinks no ill.

LVIII.

That god forbid that made me first your slave,
I should in thought control your times of
    pleasure,
Or at your hand the account of hours to crave,
Being your vassal, bound to stay your leisure !
O, let me suffer, being at your beck,
The imprison'd absence of your liberty ;
And patience, tame to sufferance, bide each
    check,
Without accusing you of injury.
Be where you list, your charter is so strong
That you yourself may privilege your time
To what you will ; to you it doth belong
Yourself to pardon of self-doing crime.
  I am to wait, though waiting so be hell ;
  Not blame your pleasure, be it ill or well.

LIX.

If there be nothing new, but that which is
Hath been before, how are our brains be-
    guiled,
Which, laboring for invention, bear amiss
The second burden of a former child !
O, that record could with a backward look,
Even of five hundred courses of the sun,
Show me your image in some antique book,
Since mind at first in character was done !
That I might see what the old world could say
To this composed wonder of your frame ;
Whether we are mended, or whether better
    they,
Or whether revolution be the same.
  O, sure I am, the wits of former days
  To subjects worse have given admiring
    praise.

LX.

Like as the waves make towards the pebbled
    shore,
So do our minutes hasten to their end ;
Each changing place with that which goes be-
    fore,
In sequent toil all forwards do contend.
Nativity, once in the main of light,
Crawls to maturity, wherewith being crown'd,
Crooked eclipses 'gainst his glory fight,
And Time that gave doth now his gift con-
    found.

Time doth transfix the flourish set on youth
And delves the parallels in beauty's brow,
Feeds on the rarities of nature's truth,
And nothing stands but for his scythe to mow :
  And yet to times in hope my verse shall
    stand,
  Praising thy worth, despite his cruel hand.

LXI.

Is it thy will thy image should keep open
My heavy eyelids to the weary night ?
Dost thou desire my slumbers should be
  broken,
While shadows like to thee do mock my sight ?
Is it thy spirit that thou send'st from thee
So far from home into my deeds to pry,
To find out shames and idle hours in me,
The scope and tenor of thy jealousy ?
O, no ! thy love, though much, is not so great :
It is my love that keeps mine eye awake ;
Mine own true love that doth my rest defeat,
To play the watchman ever for thy sake :
  For thee watch I whilst thou dost wake else-
    where,
  From me far off, with others all too near.

LXII.

Sin of self-love possesseth all mine eye
And all my soul and all my every part ;
And for this sin there is no remedy,
It is so grounded inward in my heart.
Methinks no face so gracious is as mine,
No shape so true, no truth of such account ;
And for myself mine own worth do define,
As I all other in all worths surmount.
But when my glass shows me myself indeed,
Beated and chopp'd with tann'd antiquity,
Mine own self-love quite contrary I read ;
Self so self-loving were iniquity.
  'Tis thee, myself, that for myself I praise,
  Painting my age with beauty of thy days.

LXIII.

Against my love shall be, as I am now,
With Time's injurious hand crush'd and o'er-
  worn ;
When hours have drain'd his blood and fill'd
  his brow
With lines and wrinkles ; when his youthful
  morn
Hath travell'd on to age's steepy night,
And all those beauties whereof now he's king
Are vanishing or vanish'd out of sight,
Stealing away the treasure of his spring ;
For such a time do I now fortify
Against confounding age's cruel knife,
That he shall never cut from memory
My sweet love's beauty, though my lover's life :
  His beauty shall in these black lines be seen,
  And they shall live, and he in them still
    green.

LXIV.

When I have seen by Time's fell hand defaced
The rich proud cost of outworn buried age ;
When sometime lofty towers I see down-razed
And brass eternal slave to mortal rage ;
When I have seen the hungry ocean gain
Advantage on the kingdom of the shore,
And the firm soil win of the watery main,
Increasing store with loss and loss with store ;
When I have seen such interchange of state,
Or state itself confounded to decay ;

Ruin hath taught me thus to ruminate,
That Time will come and take my love away.
  This thought is as a death, which cannot
    choose
  But weep to have that which it fears to lose.

LXV.

Since brass, nor stone, nor earth, nor bound-
  less sea,
But sad mortality o'er-sways their power,
How with this rage shall beauty hold a plea,
Whose action is no stronger than a flower ?
O, how shall summer's honey breath hold out
Against the wreckful siege of battering days,
When rocks impregnable are not so stout,
Nor gates of steel so strong, but Time decays ?
O fearful meditation ! where, alack,
Shall Time's best jewel from Time's chest lie
  hid ?
Or what strong hand can hold his swift foot
  back ?
Or who his spoil of beauty can forbid ?
  O, none, unless this miracle have might,
  That in black ink my love may still shine
    bright.

LXVI.

Tired with all these, for restful death I cry,
As, to behold desert a beggar born,
And needy nothing trimm'd in jollity,
And purest faith unhappily forsworn,
And guilded honor shamefully misplaced,
And maiden virtue rudely strumpeted,
And right perfection wrongfully disgraced,
And strength by limping sway disabled,
And art made tongue-tied by authority,
And folly doctor-like controlling skill,
And simple truth miscall'd simplicity,
And captive good attending captain ill :
  Tired with all these, from these would I be
    gone,
  Save that, to die, I leave my love alone.

LXVII.

Ah ! wherefore with infection should he live,
And with his presence grace impiety,
That sin by him advantage should achieve
And lace itself with his society ?
Why should false painting imitate his cheek
And steal dead seeing of his living hue ?
Why should poor beauty indirectly seek
Roses of shadow, since his rose is true ?
Why should he live, now Nature bankrupt is,
Beggar'd of blood to blush through lively
  veins ?
For she hath no exchequer now but his,
And, proud of many, lives upon his gains.
  O, him she stores, to show what wealth she
    had
  In days long since, before these last so bad.

LXVIII.

Thus is his cheek the map of days outworn,
When beauty lived and died as flowers do
  now,
Before these bastard signs of fair were born,
Or durst inhabit on a living brow ;
Before the golden tresses of the dead,
The right of sepulchres, were shorn away,
To live a second life on second head ;
Ere beauty's dead fleece made another gay :

In him those holy antique hours are seen,
Without all ornament, itself and true,
Making no summer of another's green,
Robbing no old to dress his beauty new ;
　　And him as for a map doth Nature store,
　　To show false Art what beauty was of yore.

LXIX.

Those parts of thee that the world's eye doth
　　view
Want nothing that the thought of hearts can
　　mend ;
All tongues, the voice of souls, give thee that
　　due,
Uttering bare truth, even so as foes commend.
Thy outward thus with outward praise is
　　crown'd ;
But those same tongues that give thee so thine
　　own
In other accents do this praise confound
By seeing farther than the eye hath shown.
They look into the beauty of thy mind,
And that, in guess, they measure by thy deeds ;
Then, churls, their thoughts, although their
　　eyes were kind,
To thy fair flower add the rank smell of
　　weeds :
　　But why thy odor matcheth not thy show,
　　The solve is this, that thou dost common
　　grow.

LXX.

That thou art blamed shall not be thy defect,
For slander's mark was ever yet the fair ;
The ornament of beauty is suspect,
A crow that flies in heaven's sweetest air.
So thou be good, slander doth but approve
Thy worth the greater, being woo'd of time ;
For canker vice the sweetest buds doth love,
And thou present'st a pure unstained prime.
Thou hast pass'd by the ambush of young
　　days,
Either not assail'd or victor being charged ;
Yet this thy praise cannot be so thy praise,
To tie up envy evermore enlarged :
　　If some suspect of ill mask'd not thy show,
　　Then thou alone kingdoms of hearts shouldst
　　owe.

LXXI.

No longer mourn for me when I am dead
Then you shall hear the surly sullen bell
Give warning to the world that I am fled
From this vile world, with vilest worms to
　　dwell :
Nay, if you read this line, remember not
The hand that writ it ; for I love you so
That I in your sweet thoughts would be forgot
If thinking on me then should make you woe.
O, if, I say, you look upon this verse
When I perhaps compounded am with clay,
Do not so much as my poor name rehearse,
But let your love even with my life decay,
　　Lest the wise world should look into your
　　moan
　　And mock you with me after I am gone.

LXXII.

O, lest the world should task you to recite
What merit lived in me, that you should love
After my death, dear love, forget me quite,
For you in me can nothing worthy prove ;
Unless you would devise some virtuous lie,
To do more for me than mine own desert,
And hang more praise upon deceased I
Than niggard truth would willingly impart :
O, lest your true love may seem false in this,
That you for love speak well of me untrue,
My name be buried where my body is,
And live no more to shame nor me nor you.
　　For I am shamed by that which I bring
　　forth,
　　And so should you, to love things nothing
　　worth.

LXXIII.

That time of year thou mayst in me behold
When yellow leaves, or none, or few, do hang
Upon those boughs which shake against the
　　cold,
Bare ruin'd choirs, where late the sweet birds
　　sang.
In me thou see'st the twilight of such day
As after sunset fadeth in the west,
Which by and by black night doth take away,
Death's second self, that seals up all in rest.
In me thou see'st the glowing of such fire
That on the ashes of his youth doth lie,
As the death-bed whereon it must expire
Consumed with that which it was nourish'd by.
　　This thou perceivest, which makes thy love
　　more strong,
　　To love that well which thou must leave ere
　　long.

LXXIV.

But be contented : when that fell arrest
Without all bail shall carry me away,
My life hath in this line some interest,
Which for memorial still with thee shall stay.
When thou reviewest this, thou dost review
The very part was consecrate to thee :
The earth can have but earth, which is his
　　due ;
My spirit is thine, the better part of me :
So then thou hast but lost the dregs of life,
The prey of worms, my body being dead,
The coward conquest of a wretch's knife,
Too base of thee to be remembered.
　　The worth of that is that which it contains,
　　And that is this, and this with thee remains.

LXXV.

So are you to my thoughts as food to life,
Or as sweet-season'd showers are to the
　　ground ;
And for the peace of you I hold such strife
As 'twixt a miser and his wealth is found ;
Now proud as an enjoyer and anon
Doubting the filching age will steal his treas-
　　ure,
Now counting best to be with you alone,
Then better'd that the world may see my
　　pleasure ;
Sometime all full with feasting on your sight
And by and by clean starved for a look ;
Possessing or pursuing no delight,
Save what is had or must from you be took.
　　Thus do I pine and surfeit day by day,
　　Or gluttoning on all, or all away.

LXXVI.

Why is my verse so barren of new pride,
So far from variation or quick change ?
Why with the time do I not glance aside
To new-found methods and to compounds
　　strange ?

Why write I still all one, ever the same,
And keep invention in a noted weed,
That every word doth almost tell my name,
Showing their birth and where they did pro-
　　ceed ?
O, know, sweet love, I always write of you,
And you and love are still my argument ;
So all my best is dressing old words new,
Spending again what is already spent :
　For as the sun is daily new and old,
　So is my love still telling what is told.

LXXVII.

Thy glass will show thee how thy beauties
　　wear,
Thy dial how thy precious minutes waste ;
The vacant leaves thy mind's imprint will bear,
And of this book this learning mayst thou
　　taste.
The wrinkles which thy glass will truly show
Of mouthed graves will give thee memory ;
Thou by thy dial's shady stealth mayst know
Time's thievish progress to eternity.
Look, what thy memory can not contain
Commit to these waste blanks, and thou shalt
　　find
Those children nursed, deliver'd from thy
　　brain,
To take a new acquaintance of thy mind.
　These offices, so oft as thou wilt look,
　Shall profit thee and much enrich thy book.

LXXVIII.

So oft have I invoked thee for my Muse
And found such fair assistance in my verse
As every alien pen hath got my use
And under thee their poesy disperse.
Thine eyes that taught the dumb on high to
　　sing
And heavy ignorance aloft to fly
Have added feathers to the learned's wing
And given grace a double majesty.
Yet be most proud of that which I compile,
Whose influence is thine and born of thee :
In others' works thou dost but mend the style,
And arts with thy sweet graces graced be ;
　But thou art all my art and dost advance
　As high as learning my rude ignorance.

LXXIX.

Whilst I alone did call upon thy aid,
My verse alone had all thy gentle grace,
But now my gracious numbers are decay'd
And my sick Muse doth give another place.
I grant, sweet love, thy lovely argument
Deserves the travail of a worthier pen,
Yet what of thee thy poet doth invent
He robs thee of and pays it thee again.
He lends thee virtue and he stole that word
From thy behavior ; beauty doth he give
And found it in thy cheek ; he can afford
No praise to thee but what in thee doth live.
　Then thank him not for that which he doth
　　say,
　Since what he owes thee thou thyself dost
　　pay.

LXXX.

O, how I faint when I of you do write,
Knowing a better spirit doth use your name,
And in the praise thereof spends all his might,
To make me tongue-tied, speaking of your
　　fame !

But since your worth, wide as the ocean is,
The humble as the proudest sail doth bear,
My saucy bark inferior far to his
On your broad main doth wilfully appear.
Your shallowest help will hold me up afloat,
Whilst he upon your soundless deep doth ride ;
Or, being wreck'd, I am a worthless boat,
He of tall building and of goodly pride :
　Then if he thrive and I be cast away,
　The worst was this ; my love was my decay.

LXXXI.

Or I shall live your epitaph to make,
Or you survive when I in earth am rotten ;
From hence your memory death cannot take,
Although in me each part will be forgotten.
Your name from hence immortal life shall
　　have,
Though I, once gone, to all the world must
　　die :
The earth can yield me but a common grave,
When you entombed in men's eyes shall lie.
Your monument shall be my gentle verse,
Which eyes not yet created shall o'er-read,
And tongues to be your being shall rehearse
When all the breathers of this world are dead ;
　You still shall live—such virtue hath my
　　pen—
　Where breath most breathes, even in the
　　mouths of men.

LXXXII.

I grant thou wert not married to my Muse
And therefore mayst without attaint o'erlook
The dedicated words which writers use
Of their fair subject, blessing every book
Thou art as fair in knowledge as in hue,
Finding thy worth a limit past my praise,
And therefore art enforced to seek anew
Some fresher stamp of the time-bettering days
And do so, love ; yet when they have devised
What strained touches rhetoric can lend,
Thou truly fair wert truly sympathized
In true plain words by thy true-telling friend ;
　And their gross painting might be better used
　Where cheeks need blood ; in thee it is
　　abused.

LXXXIII.

I never saw that you did painting need
And therefore to your fair no painting set ;
I found, or thought I found, you did exceed
The barren tender of a poet's debt ;
And therefore have I slept in your report,
That you yourself being extant well might
　　show
How far a modern quill doth come too short,
Speaking of worth, what worth in you doth
　　grow.
This silence for my sin you did impute,
Which shall be most my glory, being dumb ;
For I impair not beauty being mute,
When others would give life and bring a tomb.
　There lives more life in one of your fair eyes
　Than both your poets can in praise devise.

LXXXIV.

Who is it that says most ? which can say more
Than this rich praise, that you alone are you ?
In whose confine immured is the store
Which should example where your equal grew.

Lean penury within that pen doth dwell
That to his subject lends not some small glory ;
But he that writes of you, if he can tell
That you are you, so dignifies his story,
Let him but copy what in you is writ,
Not making worse what nature made so clear,
And such a counterpart shall fame his wit,
Making his style admired every where.
　　You to your beauteous blessings add a curse,
　　Being fond on praise, which makes your
　　　　praises worse.

LXXXV.

My tongue-tied Muse in manners holds her
　　still,
While comments of your praise, richly com-
　　piled,
Reserve their character with golden quill
And precious phrase by all the Muses filed.
I think good thoughts whilst other write good
　　words,
And like unletter'd clerk still cry ' Amen '
To every hymn that able spirit affords
In polish'd form of well-refined pen.
Hearing you praised, I say ' 'Tis so, 'tis true,'
And to the most of praise add something
　　more ;
But that is in my thought, whose love to you,
Though words come hindmost, holds his rank
　　before.
　　Then others for the breath of words respect,
　　Me for my dumb thoughts, speaking in ef-
　　　　fect.

LXXXVI.

Was it the proud full sail of his great verse,
Bound for the prize of all too precious you,
That did my ripe thoughts in my brain in-
　　hearse,
Making their tomb the womb wherein they
　　grew ?
Was it his spirit, by spirits taught to write
Above a mortal pitch, that struck me dead ?
No, neither he, nor his compeers by night
Giving him aid, my verse astonished.
He, nor that affable familiar ghost
Which nightly gulls him with intelligence
As victors of my silence cannot boast ;
I was not sick of any fear from thence :
　　But when your countenance fill'd up his line,
　　Then lack'd I matter ; that enfeebled mine.

LXXXVII.

Farewell ! thou art too dear for my possessing,
And like enough thou know'st thy estimate :
The charter of thy worth gives thee releasing ;
My bonds in thee are all determinate.
For how do I hold thee but by thy granting ?
And for that riches where is my deserving ?
The cause of this fair gift in me is wanting,
And so my patent back again is swerving.
Thyself thou gavest, thy own worth then not
　　knowing,
Or me, to whom thou gavest it, else mistaking ;
So thy great gift, upon misprision growing,
Comes home again, on better judgment mak-
　　ing.
　　Thus have I had thee, as a dream doth flat-
　　　　ter,
　　In sleep a king, but waking no such matter.

LXXXVIII.

When thou shalt be disposed to set me light,
And place my merit in the eye of scorn,

Upon thy side against myself I'll fight,
And prove thee virtuous, though thou art for-
　　sworn.
With mine own weakness being best ac-
　　quainted,
Upon thy part I can set down a story
Of faults conceal'd, wherein I am attainted,
That thou in losing me shalt win much glory :
And I by this will be a gainer too ;
For bending all my loving thoughts on thee,
The injuries that to myself I do,
Doing thee vantage, double-vantage me.
　　Such is my love, to thee I so belong,
　　That for thy right myself will bear all wrong.

LXXXIX.

Say that thou didst forsake me for some fault,
And I will comment upon that offence ;
Speak of my lameness, and I straight will halt,
Against thy reasons making no defence.
Thou canst not, love, disgrace me half so ill,
To set a form upon desired change,
As I'll myself disgrace : knowing thy will,
I will acquaintance strangle and look strange,
Be absent from thy walks, and in my tongue
Thy sweet beloved name no more shall dwell,
Lest I, too much profane, should do it wrong
And haply of our old acquaintance tell.
　　For thee against myself I'll vow debate,
　　For I must ne'er love him whom thou dost
　　　　hate.

XC.

Then hate me when thou wilt ; if ever, now ;
Now, while the world is bent my deeds to
　　cross,
Join with the spite of fortune, make me bow,
And do not drop in for an after-loss :
Ah, do not, when my heart hath 'scaped this
　　sorrow,
Come in the rearward of a conquer'd woe ;
Give not a windy night a rainy morrow,
To linger out a purposed overthrow.
If thou wilt leave me, do not leave me last,
When other petty griefs have done their spite
But in the onset come ; so shall I taste
At first the very worst of fortune's might,
　　And other strains of woe, which now seem
　　　　woe,
　　Compared with loss of thee will not seem so.

XCI.

Some glory in their birth, some in their skill,
Some in their wealth, some in their bodies'
　　force,
Some in their garments, though new-fangled
　　ill,
Some in their hawks and hounds, some in their
　　horse ;
And every humor hath his adjunct pleasure,
Wherein it finds a joy above the rest :
But these particulars are not my measure ;
All these I better in one general best.
Thy love is better than high birth to me,
Richer than wealth, prouder than garments'
　　cost,
Of more delight than hawks or horses be ;
And having thee, of all men's pride I boast :
　　Wretched in this alone, that thou mayst
　　　　take
　　All this away and me most wretched make.

SONNETS.

1105

XCII.

But do thy worst to steal thyself away,
For term of life thou art assured mine,
And life no longer than thy love will stay,
For it depends upon that love of thine.
Then need I not to fear the worst of wrongs,
When in the least of them my life hath end.
I see a better state to me belongs
Than that which on thy humor doth depend;
Thou canst not vex me with inconstant mind,
Since that my life on thy revolt doth lie.
O, what a happy title do I find,
Happy to have thy love, happy to die!
  But what's so blessed-fair that fears no blot?
  Thou mayst be false, and yet I know it not.

XCIII.

So shall I live, supposing thou art true,
Like a deceived husband; so love's face
May still seem love to me, though alter'd new;
Thy looks with me, thy heart in other place:
For there can live no hatred in thine eye,
Therefore in that I cannot know thy change.
In many's looks the false heart's history
Is writ in moods and frowns and wrinkles
    strange,
But heaven in thy creation did decree
That in thy face sweet love should ever dwell;
Whate'er thy thoughts or thy heart's workings
    be,
Thy looks should nothing thence but sweet-
    ness tell.
  How like Eve's apple doth thy beauty grow,
  If thy sweet virtue answer not thy show!

XCIV.

They that have power to hurt and will do
    none,
That do not do the thing they most do show,
Who, moving others, are themselves as stone,
Unmoved, cold, and to temptation slow,
They rightly do inherit heaven's graces
And husband nature's riches from expense;
They are the lords and owners of their faces,
Others but stewards of their excellence.
The summer's flower is to the summer sweet,
Though to itself it only live and die,
But if that flower with base infection meet,
The basest weed outbraves his dignity:
  For sweetest things turn sourest by their
    deeds;
  Lilies that fester smell far worse than weeds.

XCV.

How sweet and lovely dost thou make the
    shame
Which, like a canker in the fragrant rose,
Doth spot the beauty of thy budding name!
O, in what sweets dost thou thy sins enclose!
That tongue that tells the story of thy days,
Making lascivious comments on thy sport,
Cannot dispraise but in a kind of praise;
Naming thy name blesses an ill report.
O, what a mansion have those vices got
Which for their habitation chose out thee,
Where beauty's veil doth cover every blot,
And all things turn to fair that eyes can see!
  Take heed, dear heart, of this large privi-
    lege;
  The hardest knife ill-used doth lose his edge.

XCVI.

Some say thy fault is youth, some wantonness;
Some say thy grace is youth and gentle sport;
Both grace and faults are loved of more and
    less;
Thou makest faults graces that to thee resort.
As on the finger of a throned queen
The basest jewel will be well esteem'd,
So are those errors that in thee are seen
To truths translated and for true things
    deem'd.
How many lambs might the stern wolf betray,
If like a lamb he could his looks translate!
How many gazers mightst thou lead away,
If thou wouldst use the strength of all thy
    state!
  But do not so; I love thee in such sort
  As, thou being mine, mine is thy good re-
    port.

XCVII.

How like a winter hath my absence been
From thee, the pleasure of the fleeting year!
What freezings have I felt, what dark days
    seen!
What old December's bareness every where!
And yet this time removed was summer's time,
The teeming autumn, big with rich increase,
Bearing the wanton burden of the prime,
Like widow'd wombs after their lords' de-
    cease:
Yet this abundant issue seem'd to me
But hope of orphans and unfather'd fruit;
For summer and his pleasures wait on thee,
And, thou away, the very birds are mute;
  Or, if they sing, 'tis with so dull a cheer
  That leaves look pale, dreading the winter's
    near.

XCVIII.

From you have I been absent in the spring,
When proud-pied April dress'd in all his trim
Hath put a spirit of youth in every thing,
That heavy Saturn laugh'd and leap'd with
    him.
Yet nor the lays of birds nor the sweet smell
Of different flowers in odor and in hue
Could make me any summer's story tell,
Or from their proud lap pluck them where
    they grew;
Nor did I wonder at the lily's white,
Nor praise the deep vermilion in the rose;
They were but sweet, but figures of delight,
Drawn after you, you pattern of all those.
  Yet seem'd it winter still, and, you away,
  As with your shadow I with these did play:

XCIX.

The forward violet thus did I chide:
Sweet thief, whence didst thou steal thy sweet
    that smells,
If not from my love's breath? The purple
    pride
Which on thy soft cheek for complexion
    dwells
In my love's veins thou hast too grossly dyed.
The lily I condemned for thy hand,
And buds of marjoram had stol'n thy hair:
The roses fearfully on thorns did stand,
One blushing shame, another white despair;

A third, nor red nor white, had stol'n of both
And to his robbery had annex'd thy breath ;
But, for his theft, in pride of all his growth
A vengeful canker eat him up to death.
 More flowers I noted, yet I none could see
 But sweet or color it had stol'n from thee.

C.

Where art thou, Muse, that thou forget'st so
   long
To speak of that which gives thee all thy
   might ?
Spend'st thou thy fury on some worthless song,
Darkening thy power to lend base subjects
   light ?
Return, forgetful Muse, and straight redeem
In gentle numbers time so idly spent ;
Sing to the ear that doth thy lays esteem
And gives thy pen both skill and argument.
Rise, resty Muse, my love's sweet face survey,
If Time have any wrinkle graven there ;
If any, be a satire to decay,
And make Time's spoils despised every where.
 Give my love fame faster than Time wastes
 life ;
 So thou prevent'st his scythe and crooked
 knife.

CI.

O truant Muse, what shall be thy amends
For thy neglect of truth in beauty dyed ?
Both truth and beauty on my love depends ;
So dost thou too, and therein dignified.
Make answer, Muse : wilt thou not haply say
' Truth needs no color, with his color fix'd ;
Beauty no pencil, beauty's truth to lay ;
But best is best, if never intermix'd ? '
Because he needs no praise, wilt thou be
   dumb ?
Excuse not silence so ; for't lies in thee
To make him much outlive a gilded tomb,
And to be praised of ages yet to be.
 Then do thy office, Muse ; I teach thee how
 To make him seem long hence as he shows
 now.

CII.

My love is strengthen'd, though more weak in
   seeming ;
I love not less, though less the show appear :
That love is merchandized whose rich esteem-
   ing
The owner's tongue doth publish every where.
Our love was new and then but in the spring
When I was wont to greet it with my lays,
As Philomel in summer's front doth sing
And stops her pipe in growth of riper days :
Not that the summer is less pleasant now
Than when her mournful hymns did hush the
   night,
But that wild music burthens every bough
And sweets grown common lose their dear de-
   light.
 Therefore like her I sometime hold my
 tongue,
 Because I would not dull you with my song.

CIII.

Alack, what poverty my Muse brings forth,
That having such a scope to show her pride,
The argument all bare is of more worth
Than when it hath my added praise beside !
O, blame me not, if I no more can write !

Look in your glass, and there appears a face
That over-goes my blunt invention quite,
Dulling my lines and doing me disgrace.
Were it not sinful then, striving to mend,
To mar the subject that before was well ?
For to no other pass my verses tend
Than of your graces and your gifts to tell ;
 And more, much more, than in my verse can
 sit
 Your own glass shows you when you look
 in it.

CIV.

To me, fair friend, you never can be old,
For as you were when first your eye I eyed,
Such seems your beauty still. Three winters
   cold
Have from the forests shook three summers'
   pride,
Three beauteous springs to yellow autumn
   turn'd
In process of the seasons have I seen,
Three April perfumes in three hot Junes
   burn'd,
Since first I saw you fresh, which yet are
   green.
Ah! yet doth beauty, like a dial-hand,
Steal from his figure and no pace perceived ;
So your sweet hue, which methinks still doth
   stand,
Hath motion and mine eye may be deceived :
 For fear of which, hear this, thou age un-
 bred ;
 Ere you were born was beauty's summer
 dead.

CV.

Let not my love be call'd idolatry,
Nor my beloved as an idol show,
Since all alike my songs and praises be
To one, of one, still such, and ever so.
Kind is my love to-day, to-morrow kind,
Still constant in a wondrous excellence ;
Therefore my verse to constancy confined,
One thing expressing, leaves out difference.
' Fair, kind and true ' is all my argument,
' Fair, kind, and true ' varying to other words ;
And in this change is my invention spent,
Three themes in one, which wondrous scope
   affords.
 ' Fair, kind, and true,' have often lived
 alone,
 Which three till now never kept seat in one.

CVI.

When in the chronicle of wasted time
I see descriptions of the fairest wights,
And beauty making beautiful old rhyme
In praise of ladies dead and lovely knights,
Then, in the blazon of sweet beauty's best,
Of hand, of foot, of lip, of eye, of brow,
I see their antique pen would have express'd
Even such a beauty as you master now.
So all their praises are but prophecies
Of this our time, all you prefiguring ;
And, for they look'd but with divining eyes,
They had not skill enough your worth to sing :
 For we, which now behold these present
 days,
 Had eyes to wonder, but lack tongues to
 praise.

CVII.

Not mine own fears, nor the prophetic soul
Of the wide world dreaming on things to come,
Can yet the lease of my true love control,
Supposed as forfeit to a confined doom.
The mortal moon hath her eclipse endured
And the sad augurs mock their own presage ;
Incertainties now crown themselves assured
And peace proclaims olives of endless age.
Now with the drops of this most balmy time
My love looks fresh, and death to me sub-
    scribes,
Since, spite of him, I'll live in this poor rhyme,
While he insults o'er dull and speechless
    tribes :
    And thou in this shalt find thy monument,
    When tyrants' crests and tombs of brass are
        spent.

CVIII.

What's in the brain that ink may character
Which hath not figured to thee my true spirit ?
What's new to speak, what new to register,
That may express my love or thy dear merit ?
Nothing, sweet boy ; but yet, like prayers di-
    vine,
I must, each day say o'er the very same,
Counting no old thing old, thou mine, I thine,
Even as when first I hallow'd thy fair name.
So that eternal love in love's fresh case
Weighs not the dust and injury of age,
Nor gives to necessary wrinkles place,
But makes antiquity for aye his page,
    Finding the first conceit of love there bred
    Where time and outward form would show
        it dead.

CIX.

O, never say that I was false of heart,
Though absence seem'd my flame to qualify.
As easy might I from myself depart
As from my soul, which in thy breast doth lie :
That is my home of love : if I have ranged,
Like him that travels I return again,
Just to the time, not with the time exchanged,
So that myself bring water for my stain.
Never believe, though in my nature reign'd
All frailties that besiege all kinds of blood,
That it could so preposterously be stain'd,
To leave for nothing all thy sum of good ;
    For nothing this wide universe I call,
    Save thou, my rose ; in it thou art my all.

CX.

Alas, 'tis true I have gone here and there
And made myself a motley to the view,
Gored mine own thoughts, sold cheap what is
    most dear,
Made old offences of affections new ;
Most true it is that I have look'd on truth
Askance and strangely : but, by all above,
These blenches gave my heart another youth,
And worse essays proved thee my best of love.
Now all is done, have what shall have no end :
Mine appetite I never more will grind
On newer proof, to try an older friend,
A god in love, to whom I am confined.
    Then give me welcome, next my heaven the
        best,
    Even to thy pure and most most loving
        breast.

CXI.

O, for my sake do you with Fortune chide,
The guilty goddess of my harmful deeds,
That did not better for my life provide
Than public means which public manners
    breeds.
Thence comes it that my name receives a
    brand,
And almost thence my nature is subdued
To what it works in, like the dyer's hand :
Pity me then and wish I were renew'd ;
Whilst, like a willing patient, I will drink
Potions of eisel 'gainst my strong infection
No bitterness that I will bitter think,
Nor double penance, to correct correction.
    Pity me then, dear friend, and I assure ye
    Even that your pity is enough to cure me.

CXII.

Your love and pity doth the impression fill
Which vulgar scandal stamp'd upon my brow ;
For what care I who calls me well or ill,
So you o'er-green my bad, my good allow ?
You are my all the world, and I must strive
To know my shames and praises from your
    tongue :
None else to me, nor I to none alive,
That my steel'd sense or changes right or
    wrong.
In so profound abysm I throw all care
Of others' voices, that my adder's sense
To critic and to flatterer stopped are.
Mark how with my neglect I do dispense :
    You are so strongly in my purpose bred
    That all the world besides methinks are
        dead.

CXIII.

Since I left you, mine eye is in my mind ;
And that which governs me to go about
Doth part his function and is partly blind,
Seems seeing, but effectually is out ;
For it no form delivers to the heart
Of bird, of flower, or shape, which it doth
    latch :
Of his quick objects hath the mind no part,
Nor his own vision holds what it doth catch :
For if it see the rudest or gentlest sight,
The most sweet favor or deformed'st creature,
The mountain or the sea, the day or night,
The crow or dove, it shapes them to your
    feature :
    Incapable of more, replete with you,
    My most true mind thus makes mine eye
        untrue.

CXIV.

Or whether doth my mind, being crown'd
    with you,
Drink up the monarch's plague, this flattery ?
Or whether shall I say, mine eye saith true,
And that your love taught it this alchemy,
To make of monsters and things indigest
Such cherubins as your sweet self resemble,
Creating every bad a perfect best,
As fast as objects to his beams assemble ?
O, 'tis the first ; 'tis flattery in my seeing,
And my great mind most kingly drinks it up :
Mine eye well knows what with his gust is
    'greeing,
And to his palate doth prepare the cup :
    If it be poison'd, 'tis the lesser sin
    That mine eye loves it and doth first begin.

CXV.

Those lines that I before have writ do lie,
Even those that said I could not love you
    dearer;
Yet then my judgment knew no reason why
My most full flame should afterwards burn
    clearer.
But reckoning time, whose million'd accidents
Creep in 'twixt vows and change decrees of
    kings,
Tan sacred beauty, blunt the sharp'st intents,
Divert strong minds to the course of altering
    things;
Alas, why, fearing of time's tyranny,
Might I not then say 'Now I love you best,'
When I was certain o'er incertainty,
Crowning the present, doubting of the rest?
    Love is a babe; then might I not say so,
    To give full growth to that which still doth
        grow?

CXVI.

Let me not to the marriage of true minds
Admit impediments. Love is not love
Which alters when it alteration finds,
Or bends with the remover to remove:
O, no! it is an ever-fixed mark
That looks on tempests and is never shaken;
It is the star to every wandering bark,
Whose worth's unknown, although his height
    be taken.
Love's not Time's fool, though rosy lips and
    cheeks
Within his bending sickle's compass come:
Love alters not with his brief hours and
    weeks,
But bears it out even to the edge of doom.
    If this be error and upon me proved,
    I never writ, nor no man ever loved.

CXVII.

Accuse me thus: that I have scanted all
Wherein I should your great deserts repay,
Forgot upon your dearest love to call,
Whereto all bonds do tie me day by day;
That I have frequent been with unknown
    minds
And given to time your own dear-purchased
    right
That I have hoisted sail to all the winds
Which should transport me farthest from your
    sight.
Book both my wilfulness and errors down
And on just proof surmise accumulate;
Bring me within the level of your frown,
But shoot not at me in your waken'd hate;
    Since my appeal says I did strive to prove
    The constancy and virtue of your love.

CXVIII.

Like as, to make our appetites more keen,
With eager compounds we our palate urge,
As, to prevent our maladies unseen,
We sicken to shun sickness when we purge,
Even so, being full of your ne'er-cloying sweet-
    ness,
To bitter sauces did I frame my feeding
And, sick of welfare, found a kind of meet-
    ness
To be diseased ere that there was true need-
    ing.

Thus policy in love, to anticipate
The ills that were not, grew to faults assured
And brought to medicine a healthful state
Which, rank of goodness, would by ill be
    cured:
    But thence I learn, and find the lesson true,
    Drugs poison him that so fell sick of you.

CXIX.

What potions have I drunk of Siren tears,
Distill'd from limbecks foul as hell within,
Applying fears to hopes and hopes to fears,
Still losing when I saw myself to win!
What wretched errors hath my heart com-
    mitted,
Whilst it hath thought itself so blessed never!
How have mine eyes out of their spheres been
    fitted
In the distraction of this madding fever!
O benefit of ill! now I find true
That better is by evil still made better;
And ruin'd love, when it is built anew,
Grows fairer than at first, more strong, far
    greater.
    So I return rebuked to my content
    And gain by ill thrice more than I have
        spent.

CXX.

That you were once unkind befriends me now,
And for that sorrow which I then did feel
Needs must I under my transgression bow,
Unless my nerves were brass or hammer'd
    steel.
For if you were by my unkindness shaken
As I by yours, you've pass'd a hell of time,
And I, a tyrant, have no leisure taken
To weigh how once I suffered in your crime.
O, that our night of woe might have remem-
    ber'd
My deepest sense, how hard true sorrow hits,
And soon to you, as you to me, then tender'd
The humble salve which wounded bosoms fits!
    But that your trespass now becomes a fee;
    Mine ransoms yours, and yours must ran-
        som me.

CXXI.

'Tis better to be vile than vile esteem'd,
When not to be receives reproach of being,
And the just pleasure lost which is so deem'd
Not by our feeling but by others' seeing:
For why should others' false adulterate eyes
Give salutation to my sportive blood?
Or on my frailties why are frailer spies,
Which in their wills count bad what I think
    good?
No, I am that I am, and they that level
At my abuses reckon up their own:
I may be straight, though they themselves be
    bevel;
By their rank thoughts my deeds must not be
    shown;
    Unless this general evil they maintain,
    All men are bad, and in their badness reign.

CXXII.

Thy gift, thy tables, are within my brain
Full character'd with lasting memory,
Which shall above that idle rank remain
Beyond all date, even to eternity;

Or at the least, so long as brain and heart
Have faculty by nature to subsist ;
Till each to razed oblivion yield his part
Of thee, thy record never can be miss'd.
That poor retention could not so much hold,
Nor need I tallies thy dear love to score ;
Therefore to give them from me was I bold,
To trust those tables that receive thee more :
  To keep an adjunct to remember thee
  Were to import forgetfulness in me.

CXXIII.

No, Time, thou shalt not boast that I do
    change :
Thy pyramids built up with newer might
To me are nothing novel, nothing strange ;
They are but dressings of a former sight.
Our dates are brief, and therefore we admire
What thou dost foist upon us that is old,
And rather make them born to our desire
Than think that we before have heard them
    told.
Thy registers and thee I both defy,
Not wondering at the present nor the past,
For thy records and what we see doth lie,
Made more or less by thy continual haste.
  This I do vow and this shall ever be ;
  I will be true, despite thy scythe and thee.

CXXIV.

If my dear love were but the child of state,
It might for Fortune's bastard be unfather'd,
As subject to Time's love or to Time's hate,
Weeds among weeds, or flowers with flowers
    gather'd.
No, it was builded far from accident ;
It suffers not in smiling pomp, nor falls
Under the blow of thralled discontent,
Whereto the inviting time our fashion calls :
It fears not policy, that heretic,
Which works on leases of short-number'd
    hours,
But all alone stands hugely politic,
That it nor grows with heat nor drowns with
    showers.
  To this I witness call the fools of time,
  Which die for goodness, who have lived for
    crime.

CXXV.

Were 't aught to me I bore the canopy,
With my extern the outward honoring,
Or laid great bases for eternity,
Which prove more short than waste or ruin-
    ing ?
Have I not seen dwellers on form and favor
Lose all, and more, by paying too much rent,
For compound sweet forgoing simple savor,
Pitiful thrivers, in their gazing spent ?
No, let me be obsequious in thy heart,
And take thou my oblation, poor but free,
Which is not mix'd with seconds, knows no
    art,
But mutual render, only me for thee.
  Hence, thou suborn'd informer ! a true soul
  When most impeach'd stands least in thy
    control.

CXXVI.

O thou, my lovely boy, who in thy power
Dost hold Time's fickle glass, his sickle, hour ;
Who hast by waning grown, and therein
    show'st
Thy lovers withering as thy sweet self grow'st ;

If Nature, sovereign mistress over wrack,
As thou goest onwards, still will pluck thee
    back,
She keeps thee to this purpose, that her skill
May time disgrace and wretched minutes kill.
Yet fear her, O thou minion of her pleasure !
She may detain, but not still keep, her treas-
    ure :
  Her audit, though delay'd, answer'd must be,
  And her quietus is to render thee.

CXXVII.

In the old age black was not counted fair,
Or if it were, it bore not beauty's name ;
But now is black beauty's successive heir,
And beauty slander'd with a bastard shame :
For since each hand hath put on nature's
    power,
Fairing the foul with art's false borrow'd face,
Sweet beauty hath no name, no holy bower,
But is profaned, if not lives in disgrace.
Therefore my mistress' brows are raven black,
Her eyes so suited, and they mourners seem
At such who, not born fair, no beauty lack,
Slandering creation with a false esteem :
  Yet so they mourn, becoming of their woe,
  That every tongue says beauty should look
    so.

CXXVIII.

How oft, when thou, my music, music play'st,
Upon that blessed wood whose motion sounds
With thy sweet fingers, when thou gently
    sway'st
The wiry concord that mine ear confounds,
Do I envy those jacks that nimble leap
To kiss the tender inward of thy hand,
Whilst my poor lips, which should that harvest
    reap,
At the wood's boldness by thee blushing
    stand !
To be so tickled, they would change their state
And situation with those dancing chips,
O'er whom thy fingers walk with gentle gait,
Making dead wood more blest than living lips.
  Since saucy jacks so happy are in this,
  Give them thy fingers, me thy lips to kiss.

CXXIX.

The expense of spirit in a waste of shame
Is lust in action ; and till action, lust
Is perjured, murderous, bloody, full of blame,
Savage, extreme, rude, cruel, not to trust,
Enjoy'd no sooner but despised straight,
Past reason hunted, and no sooner had
Past reason hated, as a swallow'd bait
On purpose laid to make the taker mad ;
Mad in pursuit and in possession so ;
Had, having, and in quest to have, extreme ;
A bliss in proof, and proved, a very woe ;
Before, a joy proposed ; behind, a dream.
  All this the world well knows ; yet none
    knows well
  To shun the heaven that leads men to this
    hell.

CXXX.

My mistress' eyes are nothing like the sun ;
Coral is far more red than her lips' red ;
If snow be white, why then her breasts are
    dun ;
If hairs be wires, black wires grow on her
    head.

I have seen roses damask'd, red and white,
But no such roses see I in her cheeks;
And in some perfumes is there more delight
Than in the breath that from my mistress
    reeks.
I love to hear her speak, yet well I know
That music hath a far more pleasing sound;
I grant I never saw a goddess go;
My mistress, when she walks, treads on the
    ground:
    And yet, by heaven, I think my love as rare
    As any she belied with false compare.

CXXXI.

Thou art as tyrannous, so as thou art,
As those whose beauties proudly make them
    cruel;
For well thou know'st to my dear doting heart
Thou art the fairest and most precious jewel.
Yet, in good faith, some say that thee behold
Thy face hath not the power to make love
    groan:
To say they err I dare not be so bold,
Although I swear it to myself alone.
And, to be sure that is not false I swear,
A thousand groans, but thinking on thy face,
One on another's neck, do witness bear
Thy black is fairest in my judgment's place.
    In nothing art thou black save in thy deeds,
    And thence this slander, as I think, pro-
    ceeds.

CXXXII.

Thine eyes I love, and they, as pitying me,
Knowing thy heart torments me with disdain,
Have put on black and loving mourners be,
Looking with pretty ruth upon my pain.
And truly not the morning sun of heaven
Better becomes the grey cheeks of the east,
Nor that full star that ushers in the even
Doth half that glory to the sober west,
As those two mourning eyes become thy face:
O, let it then as well beseem thy heart
To mourn for me, since mourning doth thee
    grace,
And suit thy pity like in every part.
    Then will I swear beauty herself is black
    And all they foul that thy complexion lack.

CXXXIII.

Beshrew that heart that makes my heart to
    groan
For that deep wound it gives my friend and
    me!
Is't not enough to torture me alone,
But slave to slavery my sweet'st friend must
    be?
Me from myself thy cruel eye hath taken,
And my next self thou harder hast engross'd:
Of him, myself, and thee, I am forsaken;
A torment thrice threefold thus to be cross'd.
Prison my heart in thy steel bosom's ward,
But then my friend's heart let my poor heart
    bail;
Whoe'er keeps me, let my heart be his guard;
Thou canst not then use rigor in my gaol:
    And yet thou wilt; for I, being pent in thee,
    Perforce am thine, and all that is in me.

CXXXIV.

So, now I have confess'd that he is thine,
And I myself am mortgaged to thy will,
Myself I'll forfeit, so that other mine

Thou wilt restore, to be my comfort still:
But thou wilt not, nor he will not be free,
For thou art covetous and he is kind;
He learn'd but surety-like to write for me
Under that bond that him as fast doth bind.
The statute of thy beauty thou wilt take,
Thou usurer, that put'st forth all to use,
And sue a friend came debtor for my sake;
So him I lose through my unkind abuse.
    Him have I lost; thou hast both him and
    me:
    He pays the whole, and yet am I not free.

CXXXV.

Whoever hath her wish, thou hast thy 'Will,'
And 'Will' to boot, and 'Will' in overplus;
More than enough am I that vex thee still,
To thy sweet will making addition thus.
Wilt thou, whose will is large and spacious,
Not once vouchsafe to hide my will in thine?
Shall will in others seem right gracious,
And in my will no fair acceptance shine?
The sea, all water, yet receives rain still
And in abundance addeth to his store;
So thou, being rich in 'Will,' add to thy
    'Will'
One will of mine, to make thy large 'Will'
    more.
    Let no unkind, no fair beseechers kill;
    Think all but one, and me in that one
    'Will.'

CXXXVI.

If thy soul check thee that I come so near,
Swear to thy blind soul that I was thy 'Will,'
And will, thy soul knows, is admitted there;
Thus far for love my love-suit, sweet, fulfil.
'Will' will fulfil the treasure of thy love,
Ay, fill it full with wills, and my will one.
In things of great receipt with ease we prove
Among a number one is reckon'd none:
Then in the number let me pass untold,
Though in thy stores' account I one must be;
For nothing hold me, so it please thee hold
That nothing me, a something sweet to thee:
    Make but my name thy love, and love that
    still,
    And then thou lovest me, for my name is
    'Will.'

CXXXVII.

Thou blind fool, Love, what dost thou to mine
    eyes,
That they behold, and see not what they see?
They know what beauty is, see where it lies,
Yet what the best is take the worst to be.
If eyes corrupt by over-partial looks
Be anchor'd in the bay where all men ride,
Why of eyes' falsehood hast thou forged
    hooks,
Whereto the judgment of my heart is tied?
Why should my heart think that a several plot
Which my heart knows the wide world's com-
    mon place?
Or mine eyes seeing this, say this is not,
To put fair truth upon so foul a face?
    In things right true my heart and eyes have
    erred,
    And to this false plague are they now trans-
    ferr'd.

CXXXVIII.

When my love swears that she is made of
truth
I do believe her, though I know she lies,
That she might think me some untutor'd
youth,
Unlearned in the world's false subtleties.
Thus vainly thinking that she thinks me young,
Although she knows my days are past the best,
Simply I credit her false speaking tongue :
On both sides thus is simple truth suppress'd.
But wherefore says she not she is unjust ?
And wherefore say not I that I am old ?
O, love's best habit is in seeming trust,
And age in love loves not to have years told :
  Therefore I lie with her and she with me,
  And in our faults by lies we flatter'd be.

CXXXIX.

O, call not me to justify the wrong
That thy unkindness lays upon my heart ;
Wound me not with thine eye but with thy
tongue ;
Use power with power and slay me not by art.
Tell me thou lovest elsewhere, but in my sight,
Dear heart, forbear to glance thine eye aside :
What need'st thou wound with cunning when
thy might
Is more than my o'er-press'd defence can bide ?
Let me excuse thee : ah ! my love well knows
Her pretty looks have been mine enemies,
And therefore from my face she turns my
foes,
That they elsewhere might dart their injuries :
  Yet do not so ; but since I am near slain,
  Kill me outright with looks and rid my pain.

CXL.

Be wise as thou art cruel ; do not press
My tongue-tied patience with too much dis-
dain ;
Lest sorrow lend me words and words express
The manner of my pity-wanting pain.
If I might teach thee wit, better it were,
Though not to love, yet, love, to tell me so ;
As testy sick men, when their deaths be near,
No news but health from their physicians
know ;
For if I should despair, I should grow mad,
And in my madness might speak ill of thee :
Now this ill-wresting world is grown so bad,
Mad slanderers by mad ears believed be,
  That I may not be so, nor thou belied,
  Bear thine eyes straight, though thy proud
    heart go wide.

CXLI.

In faith, I do not love thee with mine eyes,
For they in thee a thousand errors note ;
But 'tis my heart that loves what they de-
spise,
Who in despite of view is pleased to dote ;
Nor are mine ears with thy tongue's tune de-
lighted,
Nor tender feeling, to base touches prone,
Nor taste, nor smell, desire to be invited
To any sensual feast with thee alone :
But my five wits nor my five senses can
Dissuade one foolish heart from serving thee,
Who leaves unsway'd the likeness of a man,
Thy proud hearts slave and vassal wretch to
be :

Only my plague thus far I count my gain,
That she that makes me sin awards me pain.

CXLII.

Love is my sin and thy dear virtue hate,
Hate of my sin, grounded on sinful loving :
O, but with mine compare thou thine own
state,
And thou shalt find it merits not reproving ;
Or, if it do, not from those lips of thine,
That have profaned their scarlet ornaments
And seal'd false bonds of love as oft as mine,
Robb'd others' beds' revenues of their rents.
Be it lawful I love thee, as thou lovest those
Whom thine eyes woo as mine importune
thee :
Root pity in thy heart, that when it grows
Thy pity may deserve to pitied be.
  If thou dost seek to have what thou dost
    hide,
  By self-example mayst thou be denied !

CXLIII.

Lo ! as a careful housewife runs to catch
One of her feather'd creatures broke away,
Sets down her babe and makes all swift dis-
patch
In pursuit of the thing she would have stay,
Whilst her neglected child holds her in chase,
Cries to catch her whose busy care is bent
To follow that which flies before her face,
Not prizing her poor infant's discontent ;
So runn'st thou after that which flies from
thee,
Whilst I thy babe chase thee afar behind ;
But if thou catch thy hope, turn back to me,
And play the mother's part, kiss me, be kind :
  So will I pray that thou mayst have thy
    ' Will,'
  If thou turn back, and my loud crying still.

CXLIV.

Two loves I have of comfort and despair,
Which like two spirits do suggest me still :
The better angel is a man right fair,
The worser spirit a woman color'd ill.
To win me soon to hell, my female evil
Tempteth my better angel from my side,
And would corrupt my saint to be a devil,
Wooing his purity with her foul pride.
And whether that my angel be turn'd fiend
Suspect I may, yet not directly tell ;
But being both from me, both to each friend,
I guess one angel in another's hell :
  Yet this shall I ne'er know, but live in doubt,
  Till my bad angel fire my good one out.

CXLV.

Those lips that Love's own hand did make
Breathed forth the sound that said ' I hate '
To me that languish'd for her sake ;
But when she saw my woeful state,
Straight in her heart did mercy come,
Chiding that tongue that ever sweet
Was used in giving gentle doom,
And taught it thus anew to greet :
' I hate ' she alter'd with an end,
That follow'd it as gentle day
Doth follow night, who like a fiend
From heaven to hell is flown away ;
  ' I hate ' from hate away she threw,
  And saved my life, saying ' not you.'

CXLVI.

Poor soul, the centre of my sinful earth,
......these rebel powers that thee array,
Why dost thou pine within and suffer dearth,
Painting thy outward walls so costly gay ?
Why so large cost, having so short a lease,
Dost thou upon thy fading mansion spend ?
Shall worms, inheritors of this excess,
Eat up thy charge ? is this thy body's end ?
Then, soul, live thou upon thy servant's loss,
And let that pine to aggravate thy store ;
Buy terms divine in selling hours of dross ;
Within be fed, without be rich no more :
     So shalt thou feed on Death, that feeds on
        men,
        And Death once dead, there's no more dying
        then.

CXLVII.

My love is as a fever, longing still
For that which longer nurseth the disease,
Feeding on that which doth preserve the ill,
The uncertain sickly appetite to please.
My reason, the physician to my love,
Angry that his prescriptions are not kept,
Hath left me, and I desperate now approve
Desire is death, which physic did except.
Past cure I am, now reason is past care,
And frantic-mad with evermore unrest ;
My thoughts and my discourse as madmen's
    are,
    At random from the truth vainly express'd ;
        For I have sworn thee fair and thought thee
        bright,
        Who art as black as hell, as dark as night.

CXLVIII.

O me, what eyes hath Love put in my head,
Which have no correspondence with true
    sight !
Or, if they have, where is my judgment fled,
That censures falsely what they see aright ?
If that be fair whereon my false eyes dote,
What means the world to say it is not so ?
If it be not, then love doth well denote
Love's eye is not so true as all men's ' No.'
How can it ? O, how can Love's eye be true,
That is so vex'd with watching and with tears ?
No marvel then, though I mistake my view ;
The sun itself sees not till heaven clears.
     O cunning Love ! with tears thou keep'st
        me blind,
        Lest eyes well-seeing thy foul faults should
        find.

CXLIX.

Canst thou, O cruel ! say I love thee not,
When I against myself with thee partake ?
Do I not think on thee, when I forgot
Am of myself, all tyrant, for thy sake ?
Who hateth thee that I do call my friend ?
On whom frown'st thou that I do fawn upon ?
Nay, if thou lour'st on me, do I not spend
Revenge upon myself with present moan ?
What merit do I in myself respect,
That is so proud thy service to despise,
When all my best doth worship thy defect,
Commanded by the motion of thine eyes ?
     But, love, hate on, for now I know thy
        mind ;
        Those that can see thou lovest, and I am
        blind.

CL.

O, from what power hast thou this powerful
    might
With insufficiency my heart to sway ?
To make me give the lie to my true sight,
And swear that brightness doth not grace the
    day ?
Whence hast thou this becoming of things ill,
That in the very refuse of thy deeds
There is such strength and warrantize of skill
That, in my mind, thy worst all best exceeds ?
Who taught thee how to make me love thee
    more
The more I hear and see just cause of hate ?
O, though I love what others do abhor,
With others thou shouldst not abhor my state :
     If thy unworthiness raised love in me,
        More worthy I to be beloved of thee.

CLI.

Love is too young to know what conscience is ;
Yet who knows not conscience is born of love ?
Then, gentle cheater, urge not my amiss,
Lest guilty of my faults thy sweet self prove :
For, thou betraying me, I do betray
My nobler part to my gross body's treason ;
My soul doth tell my body that he may
Triumph in love ; flesh stays no father reason ;
But, rising at thy name, doth point out thee
As his triumphant prize. Proud of this pride,
He is contented thy poor drudge to be,
To stand in thy affairs, fall by thy side.
     No want of conscience hold it that I call
        Her ' love ' for whose dear love I rise and
        fall.

CLII.

In loving thee thou know'st I am forsworn,
But thou art twice forsworn, to me love swear-
    ing,
In act thy bed-vow broke and new faith torn,
In vowing new hate after new love bearing.
But why of two oaths' breach do I accuse thee,
When I break twenty ? I am perjured most ;
For all my vows are oaths but to misuse thee
And all my honest faith in thee is lost,
For I have sworn deep oaths of thy deep kind-
    ness,
Oaths of thy love, thy truth, thy constancy,
And, to enlighten thee, gave eyes to blindness,
Or made them swear against the thing they
    see ;
        For I have sworn thee fair ; more perjured
        I,
        To swear against the truth so foul a lie !

CLIII.

Cupid laid by his brand, and fell asleep :
A maid of Dian's this advantage found,
And his love-kindling fire did quickly steep
In a cold valley-fountain of that ground ;
Which borrow'd from this holy fire of Love
A dateless lively heat, still to endure,
And grew a seething bath, which yet men
    prove
Against strange maladies a sovereign cure.

But at my mistress' eye Love's brand new-
    fired,
The boy for trial needs would touch my
    breast;
I, sick withal, the help of bath desired,
And thither hied, a sad distemper'd guest,
    But found no cure: the bath for my help
        lies
        Where Cupid got new fire—my mistress'
            eyes.

CLIV.

The little Love-god lying once asleep
Laid by his side his heart-inflaming brand,
Whilst many nymphs that vow'd chaste life to
    keep
Came tripping by; but in her maiden hand
The fairest votary took up that fire
Which many legions of true hearts had
    warm'd;
And so the general of hot desire
Was sleeping by a virgin hand disarm'd.
This brand she quenched in a cool well by,
Which from Love's fire took heat perpetual,
Growing a bath and healthful remedy
For men diseased; but I, my mistress' thrall,
    Came there for cure, and this by that I
        prove,
    Love's fire heats water, water cools not love.

A LOVER'S COMPLAINT.

INTRODUCTION.

As already mentioned in the Introduction to the *Sonnets* this poem first appeared in the quarto containing the Sonnets published in 1609. In a letter to the Editor of the " Leopold Shakespeare," Professor Delius says : " *A Lover's Complaint* may belong to the end of Shakespeare's second period, or to the third and latest period ; so you may place it with *Othello*," in the chronological order.

FROM off a hill whose concave womb re-
  worded
A plaintful story from a sistering vale,
My spirits to attend this double voice ac-
  corded,
And down I laid to list the sad-tuned tale ;
Ere long espied a fickle maid full pale,
Tearing of papers, breaking rings a-twain,
Storming her world with sorrow's wind and
  rain.

Upon her head a platted hive of straw,
Which fortified her visage from the sun,
Whereon the thought might think sometime it
  saw   10
The carcass of beauty spent and done :
Time had not scythed all that youth begun,
Nor youth all quit ; but, spite of heaven's fell
  rage,
Some beauty peep'd through lattice of sear'd
  age.

Oft did she heave her napkin to her eyne,
Which on it had conceited characters,
Laundering the silken figures in the brine
That season'd woe had pelleted in tears,
And often reading what contents it bears ;
As often shrieking undistinguish'd woe, 20
In clamors of all size, both high and low.

Sometimes her levell'd eyes their carriage ride,
As they did battery to the spheres intend ;
Sometime diverted their poor balls are tied
To the orbed earth ; sometimes they do extend
Their view right on ; anon their gazes lend
To every place at once, and, nowhere fix'd,
The mind and sight distractedly commix'd.

Her hair, nor loose nor tied in formal plat,
Proclaim'd in her a careless hand of pride 30
For some, untuck'd, descended her sheaved
  hat,
Hanging her pale and pined cheek beside ;
Some in her threaden fillet still did bide,
And true to bondage would not break from
  thence,
Though slackly braided in loose negligence.

A thousand favors from a maund she drew
Of amber, crystal, and of beaded jet,
Which one by one she in a river threw,
Upon whose weeping margent she was set ;
Like usury, applying wet to wet, 40

Or monarch's hands that let not bounty fall
Where want cries some, but where excess begs
  all.

Of folded schedules had she many a one,
Which she perused, sigh'd, tore, and gave the
  flood ;
Crack'd many a ring of posied gold and bone
Bidding them find their sepulchres in mud ;
Found yet moe letters sadly penn'd in blood,
With sleided silk feat and affectedly
Enswathed, and seal'd to curious secrecy.

These often bathed she in her fluxive eyes, 50
And often kiss'd, and often 'gan to tear :
Cried ' O false blood, thou register of lies,
What unapproved witness dost thou bear !
Ink would have seem'd more black and
  damned here ! '
This said, in top of rage the lines she rents,
Big discontent so breaking their contents.

A reverend man that grazed his cattle nigh—
Sometime a blusterer, that the ruffle knew
Of court, of city, and had let go by
The swiftest hours, observed as they flew— 60
Towards this afflicted fancy fastly drew,
And, privileged by age, desires to know
In brief the grounds and motives of her woe.

So slides he down upon his grained bat,
And comely-distant sits he by her side ;
When he again desires her, being sat,
Her grievance with his hearing to divide :
If that from him there may be aught applied
Which may her suffering ecstasy assuage,
'Tis promised in the charity of age. 70

' Father,' she says, ' though in me you behold
The injury of many a blasting hour,
Let it not tell your judgment I am old ;
Not age, but sorrow, over me hath power :
I might as yet have been a spreading flower,
Fresh to myself, if I had self-applied
Love to myself and to no love beside.

' But, woe is me ! too early I attended
A youthful suit—it was to gain my grace—
Of one by nature's outwards so commended,
That maidens' eyes stuck over all his face : 81
Love lack'd a dwelling, and made him her
  place ;
And when in his fair parts she did abide,
She was new lodged and newly deified.

'His browny locks did hang in crooked curls ;
And every light occasion of the wind
Upon his lips their silken parcels hurls.
What's sweet to do, to do will aptly find :
Each eye that saw him did enchant the mind,
For on his visage was in little drawn　90
What largeness thinks in Paradise was sawn.

'Small show of man was yet upon his chin ;
His phœnix down began but to appear
Like unshorn velvet on that termless skin
Whose bare out-bragg'd the web it seem'd to
　　wear :
Yet show'd his visage by that cost more dear ;
And nice affections wavering stood in doubt
If best were as it was, or best without.

'His qualities were beauteous as his form,　99
For maiden-tongued he was, and thereof free ;
Yet, if men moved him, was he such a storm
As oft 'twixt May and April is to see,
When winds breathe sweet, unruly though they
　　be.
His rudeness so with his authorized youth
Did livery falseness in a pride of truth.

'Well could he ride, and often men would say
"That horse his mettle from his rider takes :
Proud of subjection, noble by the sway,
What rounds, what bounds, what course, what
　　stop he makes !"
And controversy hence a question takes,　110
Whether the horse by him became his deed,
Or he his manage by the well-doing steed.

'But quickly on this side the verdict went :
His real habitude gave life and grace
To appertainings and to ornament,
Accomplish'd in himself, not in his case :
All aids, themselves made fairer by their place,
Came for additions ; yet their purposed trim
Pieced not his grace, but were all graced by
　　him.

'So on the tip of his subduing tongue　120
All kind of arguments and question deep,
All replication prompt, and reason strong,
For his advantage still did wake and sleep :
To make the weeper laugh, the laugher weep,
He had the dialect and different skill,
Catching all passions in his craft of will :

'That he did in the general bosom reign
Of young, of old ; and sexes both enchanted,
To dwell with him in thoughts, or to remain
In personal duty, following where he haunted :
Consents bewitch'd, ere he desire, have
　　granted ;　131
And dialogued for him what he would say,
Ask'd their own wills, and made their wills
　　obey.

'Many there were that did his picture get,
To serve their eyes, and in it put their mind ;
Like fools that in th' imagination set
The goodly objects which abroad they find
Of lands and mansions, theirs in thought as-
　　sign'd ;
And laboring in moe pleasures to bestow them
Than the true gouty landlord which doth owe
　　them :　140

'So many have, that never touch'd his hand,
Sweetly supposed them mistress of his heart.
My woeful self, that did in freedom stand,
And was my own fee-simple, not in part,
What with his art in youth, and youth in art,
Threw my affections in his charmed power,
Reserved the stalk and gave him all my flower.

'Yet did I not, as some my equals did,
Demand of him, nor being desired yielded ;
Finding myself in honor so forbid,　150
With safest distance I mine honor shielded :
Experience for me many bulwarks builded
Of proofs new-bleeding, which remain'd the
　　foil
Of this false jewel, and his amorous spoil.

'But, ah, who ever shunn'd by precedent
The destined ill she must herself assay ?
Or forced examples, 'gainst her own content,
To put the by-past perils in her way ?
Counsel may stop awhile what will not stay ;
For when we rage, advice is often seen　160
By blunting us to make our wits more keen.

'Nor gives it satisfaction to our blood,
That we must curb it upon others' proof ;
To be forbod the sweets that seem so good,
For fear of harms that preach in our behoof.
O appetite, from judgment stand aloof !
The one a palate hath that needs will taste,
Though Reason weep, and cry, "It is thy
　　last."

'For further I could say "This man's untrue,"
And knew the patterns of his foul beguiling ;
Heard where his plants in others' orchards
　　grew,　171
Saw how deceits were gilded in his smiling ;
Knew vows were ever brokers to defiling ;
Thought characters and words merely but art,
And bastards of his foul adulterate heart.

'And long upon these terms I held my city,
Till thus he gan besiege me : "Gentle maid,
Have of my suffering youth some feeling pity,
And be not of my holy vows afraid :
That's to ye sworn to none was ever said ;　180
For feasts of love I have been call'd unto,
Till now did ne'er invite, nor never woo.

'"All my offences that abroad you see
Are errors of the blood, none of the mind ;
Love made them not : with acture they may
　　be,
Where neither party is nor true nor kind :
They sought their shame that so their shame
　　did find ;
And so much less of shame in me remains,
By how much of me their reproach contains.

'"Among the many that mine eyes have seen,
Not one whose flame my heart so much as
　　warm'd,　191
Or my affection put to the smallest teen,
Or any of my leisures ever charm'd :
Harm have I done to them, but ne'er was
　　harm'd ;
Kept hearts in liveries, but mine own was free,
And reign'd, commanding in his monarchy.

'"Look here, what tributes wounded fancies
　　sent me,
Of paled pearls and rubies red as blood ;
Figuring that they their passions likewise lent
　　me
Of grief and blushes, aptly understood　200
In bloodless white and the encrimson'd mood ;
Effects of terror and dear modesty,
Encamp'd in hearts, but fighting outwardly.

' " And, lo, behold these talents of their hair,
With twisted metal amorously impleach'd,
I have received from many a several fair,
Their kind acceptance weepingly beseech'd,
With the annexions of fair gems enrich'd,
And deep-brain'd sonnets that did amplify 209
Each stone's dear nature, worth, and quality.

' " The diamond,—why, 'twas beautiful and
    hard,
Whereto his invised properties did tend ;
The deep-green emerald, in whose fresh re-
    gard
Weak sights their sickly radiance do amend ;
The heaven-hued sapphire and the opal blend
With objects manifold : each several stone,
With wit well blazon'd, smiled or made some
    moan.

' " Lo, all these trophies of affections hot,
Of pensived and subdued desires the tender,
Nature hath charged me that I hoard them
    not,   220
But yield them up where I myself must ren-
    der,
That is, to you, my origin and ender ;
For these, of force, must your oblations be,
Since I their altar, you enpatron me.

' " O, then, advance of yours that phraseless
    hand,
Whose white weighs down the airy scale of
    praise ;
Take all these similes to your own command,
Hallow'd with sighs that burning lungs did
    raise ;
What me your minister, for you obeys,
Works under you ; and to your audit comes
Their distract parcels in combined sums. 231

' " Lo, this device was sent me from a nun,
Or sister sanctified, of holiest note ;
Which late her noble suit in court did shun,
Whose rarest havings made the blossoms dote ;
For she was sought by spirits of richest coat,
But kept cold distance, and did thence re-
    move,
To spend her living in eternal love.

' " But, O my sweet, what labor is't to leave
The thing we have not, mastering what not
    strives,   240
Playing the place which did no form receive,
Playing patient sports in unconstrained gyves ?
She that her fame so to herself contrives,
The scars of battle 'scapeth by the flight,
And makes her absence valiant, not her might.

' " O, pardon me, in that my boast is true :
The accident which brought me to her eye
Upon the moment did her force subdue,
And now she would the caged cloister fly :
Religious love put out Religion's eye :   250
Not to be tempted, would she be immured,
And now, to tempt, all liberty procured.

' " How mighty then you are, O, hear me tell !
The broken bosoms that to me belong
Have emptied all their fountains in my well,
And mine I pour your ocean all among :
I strong o'er them, and you o'er me being
    strong,
Must for your victory us all congest,
As compound love to physic your cold breast.

' " My parts had power to charm a sacred
    nun,   260

Who, disciplined, ay, dieted in grace,
Believed her eyes when they to assail begun,
All vows and consecrations giving place :
O most potential love ! vow, bond, nor space,
In thee hath neither sting, knot, nor confine,
For thou art all, and all things else are thine.

' " When thou impressest, what are precepts
    worth
Of stale example ? When thou wilt inflame,
How coldly those impediments stand forth 269
Of wealth, of filial fear, law, kindred, fame !
Love's arms are peace, 'gainst rule, 'gainst
    sense, 'gainst shame,
And sweetens, in the suffering pangs it bears,
The aloes of all forces, shocks, and fears.

' " Now all these hearts that do on mine de-
    pend,
Feeling it break, with bleeding groans they
    pine ;
And supplicant their sighs to you extend,
To leave the battery that you make 'gainst
    mine,
Lending soft audience to my sweet design,
And credent soul to that strong-bonded oath
That shall prefer and undertake my troth."

' This said, his watery eyes he did dismount,
Whose sights till then were levell'd on my
    face ;
Each cheek a river running from a fount
With brinish current downward flow'd apace :
O, how the channel to the stream gave grace !
Who glazed with crystal gate the glowing
    roses
That flame through water which their hue en-
    closes.

' O father, what a hell of witchcraft lies
In the small orb of one particular tear !
But with the inundation of the eyes   290
What rocky heart to water will not wear ?
What breast so cold that is not warmed here ?
O cleft effect ! cold modesty, hot wrath,
Both fire from hence and chill extincture hath.

' For, lo, his passion, but an art of craft,
Even there resolved my reason into tears ;
There my white stole of chastity I daff'd,
Shook off my sober guards and civil fears ;
Appear to him, as he to me appears,
All melting ; though our drops this difference
    bore,   300
His poison'd me, and mine did him restore.

' In him a plenitude of subtle matter,
Applied to cautels, all strange forms receives,
Of burning blushes, or of weeping water,
Or swooning paleness ; and he takes and
    leaves,
In either's aptness, as it best deceives,
To blush at speeches rank to weep at woes,
Or to turn white and swoon at tragic shows.

' That not a heart which in his level came
Could 'scape the hail of his all-hurting aim,
Showing fair nature is both kind and tame ;
And, veil'd in them, did win whom he would
    maim :
Against the thing he sought he would ex-
    claim ;
When he most burn'd in heart-wish'd luxury,
He preach'd pure maid, and praised cold
    chastity.

'Thus merely with the garment of a Grace
The naked and concealed fiend he cover'd;
That th' unexperient gave the tempter place,
Which like a cherubin above them hover'd.
Who, young and simple, would not be so
     lover'd?   320
Ay me! I fell; and yet do question make
What I should do again for such a sake.

'O, that infected moisture of his eye,
O, that false fire which in his cheek so glow'd,
O, that forced thunder from his heart did fly,
O, that sad breath his spongy lungs bestow'd,
O, all that borrow'd motion seeming owed,
Would yet again betray the fore-betray'd,
And new pervert a reconciled maid!'   329

THE PHŒNIX AND THE TURTLE.

INTRODUCTION.

The Phœnix and the Turtle was printed as one of the additional poems to Chester's *Love's Martyr, or Rosalind's Complaint*, 1601, with Shakespeare's name appended. That it is his seems in a high degree doubtful ; Mr. Furnivall says, " it is no doubt spurious."

LET the bird of loudest lay,
On the sole Arabian tree,
Herald sad and trumpet be,
To whose sound chaste wings obey.

But thou shrieking harbinger,
Foul precurrer of the fiend,
Augur of the fever's end,
To this troop come thou not near !

From this session interdict
Every fowl of tyrant wing,   10
Save the eagle, feather'd king :
Keep the obsequy so strict.

Let the priest in surplice white,
That defunctive music can,
Be the death-divining swan,
Lest the requiem lack his right.

And thou treble-dated crow,
That thy sable gender makest
With the breath thou givest and takest,
'Mongst our mourners shalt thou go.   20

Here the anthem doth commence :
Love and constancy is dead ;
Phœnix and the turtle fled
In a mutual flame from hence.

So they loved, as love in twain
Had the essence but in one ;
Two distincts, division none :
Number there in love was slain.

Hearts remote, yet not asunder ;
Distance, and no space was seen   30
'Twixt the turtle and his queen :
But in them it were a wonder.

So between them love did shine,
That the turtle saw his right
Flaming in the phœnix' sight ;
Either was the other's mine.

Property was thus appalled,
That the self was not the same ;
Single nature's double name
Neither two nor one was called.   40

Reason, in itself confounded,
Saw division grow together,
To themselves yet either neither,
Simple were so well compounded,

That it cried, How true a twain
Seemeth this concordant one !
Love hath reason, reason none,
If what parts can so remain.

Whereupon it made this threne
To the phœnix and the dove,   50
Co-supremes and stars of love,
As chorus to their tragic scene.

THRENOS.

Beauty, truth, and rarity,
Grace in all simplicity,
Here enclosed in cinders lie.

Death is now the phœnix' nest ;
And the turtle's loyal breast
To eternity doth rest,

Leaving no posterity :
'Twas not their infirmity,   60
It was married chastity.

Truth may seem, but cannot be :
Beauty brag, but 'tis not she ;
Truth and beauty buried be.

To this urn let those repair
That are either true or fair ;
For these dead birds sigh a prayer.

GLOSSARY TO SHAKESPEARE'S WORKS.

ABATE, *v.t.* to shorten. M. N's Dr. III. 2. To cast down. Cor. III. 3. To blunt. R. III. v. 4.

Abatement, *sb.* diminution. Lear, I. 4.

Abide, *v.i.* to sojourn. Wint. Tale, IV. 3. *v.t.* to expiate (a corruption of 'Aby'). J. C. III. 1; Ibid. III. 2.

Able, *v.t.* to uphold. Lear, IV. 6.

Abridgment, *sb.* a short play. Ham. II. 2.

Abrook, *v.t.* to brook, abide. 2 H. VI. II. 4.

Absey-Book, *sb.* a primer. John, I. 1.

Absolute, *adj.* positive, certain. Cym. IV. 2; Ham. v. 2. Complete. Temp. I. 2.

Abuse, *v.t.* to deceive. Lear, IV. 7.

Abuse, *sb.* deception. M. for M. v. 1.

Aby, *v.t.* to expiate a fault. M. N's Dr. III. 2.

Abysm, *sb.* abyss. Temp. I. 2.

Accite, *v.t.* to cite, summon. 2 H. IV. v. 2.

Accuse, *sb.* accusation. 2 H. VI. III. 1.

Achieve, *v.* to obtain. H. V. IV. 3.

Acknown, *p.p.* 'to be acknown' is to acknowledge. Oth. III. 3.

Acquittance, *sb.* a receipt or discharge. Ham. IV. 2.

Action-taking, *adj.* litigious. Lear, II. 2.

Acture, *sb.* action. Lover's Com. 185.

Addition, *sb.* title, attribute. All's Well, II. 3; T. & Cr. I. 2.

Address, *v.r.* to prepare oneself. 2 H. VI. v. 2; Ham. I. 2.

Addressed, *part.* prepared. L's L's L. II. 1.

Advance, *v.t.* to prefer, promote to honor. Tim. I. 2.

Advertisement, *sb.* admonition. Much Ado, &c. v. 1.

Advertising, *pr. p.* attentive. M. for M. v. 1.

Advice, *sb.* consideration, discretion. Two Gent. II. 4; M. for M. v. 1.

Advise, *v.* sometimes *neuter,* sometimes *reflective,* to consider, reflect. Tw. N. IV. 2.

Advised, *p.p.* considerate. Com. of E. v. 1.

Advocation, *sb.* pleading, advocacy. Oth. III. 4.

Afeard, *adj.* afraid. Merry Wives, III. 4.

Affect, *v.t.* to love. Merry Wives, II. 1.

Affeered, *p.p.* assessed, confirmed. Mac. IV. 3.

Affy, *v.t.* to affiance. 2 H. VI. IV. 1. To trust. T. A. I. 1.

Afront, *adv.* in front. 1 H. IV. II. 4.

Agazed, *p.p.* looking in amazement. 1 H. VI. I. 1.

Aglet-baby, *sb.* the small figure engraved on a jewel. Tam. of S. I. 2.

Agnise, *v.t.* to acknowledge, confess. Oth. I. 3.

A-good, *adv.* a good deal, plenteously. Two Gent. IV. 4.

A-hold, *adj.* a sea-term. Temp. I. 1.

Aiery, *sb.* the nest of a bird of prey. R. III. I. 3.

Aim, *sb.* a guess. Two Gent. III. 1.

Alder-liefest, *adj.* most loved of all. 2 H. VI. I. 1.

Ale, *sb.* alehouse. Two Gent. II. 5.

Allow, *v.* to approve. Tw. N. I. 2.

Allowance, *sb.* approval. Cor. III. 2.

Ames-ace, *sb.* two aces, the lowest throw of the dice. All's Well, II. 3.

Amort, *adj.* dead, dejected. Tam. of S. IV. 3.

An, *conj.* if. Much Ado, I. 1.

Anchor, *sb.* an anchorite, hermit. Ham. III. 2.

Ancient, *sb.* an ensign-bearer. 1 H. IV. IV. 2.

Angel, *sb.* a coin, so called because it bore the image of an angel. Merry Wives, I. 3.

Anight, *adv.* by night. As you Like it, II. 4.

Answer, *sb.* retaliation. Cym. v. 3.

Anthropophaginian, *sb.* a cannibal. Merry Wives, IV. 5.

Antick, *sb.* the fool in the old plays. R. II. III. 2.

Antre, *sb.* a cave. Oth. I. 3.

Apparent, *sb.* heir-apparent. Wint. Tale, I. 2.

Appeal, *sb.* accusation. M. for M. v. 1.

Appeal, *v.t.* to accuse. R. II. I. 1.

Appeared, *p.p.* made apparent. Cor. IV. 3.

Apple-John, *sb.* a kind of apple. 1 H. IV. III. 3.

Appointment, *sb.* preparation. M. for M. III. 1.

Apprehension, *sb.* opinion. Much Ado, III. 4.

Apprehensive, *adj.* apt to apprehend or understand. J. C. III. 1.

Approbation, *sb.* probation. Cym. I. 5.

Approof, *sb.* approbation, proof. All's Well, I. 2; Temp. II. 5.

Approve, *v.t.* to prove. R. II. I. 3. To justify, make good. Lear, II. 4.

Approver, *sb.* one who proves or tries. Cym. II. 4.

Arch, *sb.* chief. Lear, II. 1.

Argal, a ridiculous word intended for the Latin ergo. Ham. v. 1.

Argentine, *adj.* silver. Per. v. 2.

Argier, *sb.* Algiers. Temp. I. 2.

Argosy, *sb.* originally a vessel of Ragusa or Ragosa, a Ragosine; hence any ship of burden. M. of V. I. 1.

Argument, *sb.* subject. Much Ado, II. 3.

Armigero, a mistake for Armiger, the Latin for Esquire. Merry Wives, I. 1.

Aroint, *v.r.* found only in the imperat. mood, get thee gone. Mac. I. 3; Lear, III. 4.

A-row, *adv.* in a row. Com. of E. v. 1.

Articulate, *v.i.* to enter into articles of agreement. Cor. I. 9. *v.t.* to exhibit in articles. 1 H. IV. v. 1.

Ask, *v.t.* to require. 2 H. VI. I. 2.

Aspect, *sb.* regard, looks. A. & C. I. 5.

Aspersion, *sb.* sprinkling; hence blessing, because before the Reformation benediction was generally accompanied by the sprinkling of holy water. Temp. III. 3.

Assay, *sb.* attempt. M. for M. III. 1.

Assay, *v.t.* to attempt, test, make proof of. Merry Wives, II. 1.

Assinego, *sb.* an ass. T. & Cr. II. 1.

Assubjugate, *v.t.* to subjugate. T. & Cr. II. 3.

Assurance, *sb.* deed of assurance. Tam. of S. IV. 2.

Assured, *p.p.* betrothed. Com. of E. III. 2.

Atomy, *sb.* an atom. As you Like it, III. 2. Used in contempt of a small person. 2 H. IV. v. 4.

Atone, *v.t.* to put people at one, to reconcile. R. II. I. 1. *v.i.* to agree. Cor. IV. 6.

Attach, *v.t.* to seize, lay hold on. Temp. III. 3 ; Com. of E. IV. 1.

Attasked, *p.p.* taken to task, reprehended. Lear, I. 4.

Attend, *v.t.* to listen to. Temp. I. 2 ; M. of V. v. 1.

Attent, *adj.* attentive. Ham. I. 2.

Attorney, *sb.* an agent. R. III. IV. 4.

Attorney, *v.t.* to employ as an agent. M. for M. v. 1. To perform by an agent. Wint. Tale, I. 1.

Audacious, *adj.* spirited, daring, but without any note of blame attached to it. L's L's L. v. 1.

Augur, *sb.* augury. Mac. III. 4.

Authentic, *adj.* clothed with authority. Merry Wives, II. 2.

Avaunt, *int.* be gone, a word of abhorrence. Com. of E. IV. 3.

Ave, *int.* the Latin for hail ; hence acclamation. M. for M. I. 1.

Ave-Mary, *sb.* the angelic salutation addressed to the B. Virgin Mary. 2 H. VI. I. 3.

Averring, *pr. p.* confirming. Cym. v. 5.

Awful, *adj.* worshipful. Two Gent. IV. 1.

Awkward, *adj.* contrary. 2 H. VI. III. 2.

Baccare, *int.* keep back. Tam. of S. II. 1.

Backward, *sb.* the hinder part ; hence, when applied to time, the past. Temp. I. 2.

Balked, *p.p.* heaped, as on a ridge. 1 H. IV. I. 1.

Ballow, *sb.* a cudgel. Lear, IV. 6.

Balm, *sb.* the oil of consecration. R. II. IV. 1 ; 3 H. VI. III. 1.

Ban, *v.t.* to curse. Lucr. 1460.

Bank, *v.t.* to sail by the banks. John, v. 2.

Barm, *sb.* yeast. M. N's Dr. II. 1.

Barn, *sb.* a child. 1 H. IV. II. 3.

Barnacle, *sb.* a shell-fish, supposed to produce the sea-bird of the same name. Temp. IV. 1.

Base, *sb.* a game, sometimes called Prisoners' base. Cym. v. 3.

Bases, *sb.* an embroidered mantle worn by knights on horseback, and reaching from the middle to below the knees. Per. II. 1.

Basilisk, *sb.* a kind of ordnance. 1 H. IV. v. 3.

Basta, *int.* (Italian), enough. Tam. of S. I. 1.

Bastard, *sb.* raisin wine. M. for M. III. 2.

Bate, *v.i.* to flutter, as a hawk. 1 H. IV. IV. 1.

Bate, *v.t.* to except. Temp. II. 1. To abate. Much Ado, II. 3.

Bat-fowling, *part.* catching birds with a clap-net by night. Temp. II. 1.

Batlet, *sb.* a small bat, used for beating clothes. As you Like it, II. 4.

Battle, *sb.* army. 1 H. IV. IV. 1.

Bavin, *sb.* used as an *adj.* a piece of waste wood, applied contemptuously to anything worthless. 1 H. IV. III. 2.

Bawcock, *sb.* a fine fellow. Tw. N. III. 4.

Bay, *sb.* the space between the main timbers of the roof. M. for M. II. 1.

Beadsman, *sb.* one who bids bedes, that is, prays prayers for another. Two Gent. I. 1.

Bearing-cloth, *sb.* a rich cloth in which children were wrapt at their christening. Wint. Tale, III. 3.

Beat, *v.i.* to flutter as a falcon, to meditate, consider earnestly. Temp. I. 2.

Beaver, *sb.* the lower part of a helmet. 1 H. IV. IV. 1.

Beetle, *sb.* a mallet. 2 H. IV. I. 2.

Being, *sb.* dwelling. Cym. I. 6.

Being, *conj.* since, inasmuch as. A. & C. III. 6.

Be-mete, *v.t.* to measure. Tam. of S. IV. 3.

Be-moiled, *p.p.* daubed with dirt. Tam. of S. IV. 1.

Bending, *pr. p.* stooping under a weight. H. V. v. Chorus.

Benvenuto, *sb.* (Italian), welcome. L's L's L. IV. 2.

Bergomask, *adj.* a rustic dance. M. N's Dr. v. 1.

Beshrew, *int.* evil befal. Com. of E. II. 1.

Bestraught, *p.p.* distraught, distracted. Induct. to Tam. of S.

Beteem, *v.t.* to pour out. M. N's Dr. I. 1.

Betid, *p.p.* happened. Temp. I. 2.

Bezonian, *sb.* a beggarly fellow. 2 H. IV. v. 3.

Biding, *sb.* abiding-place. Lear, IV. 6.

Biggen, *sb.* a night-cap. 2 H. IV. IV. 5.

Bilberry, *sb.* the whortleberry. Merry Wives, v. 5.

Bilbo, *sb.* a sword, from Bilboa, a town in Spain where they were made. Merry Wives, I. 1.

Bilboes, *sb.* fetters or stocks. Ham. v. 2.

Bill, *sb.* a bill-hook, a weapon. Much Ado, III. 3.

Bin=been, are. Cym. II. 3.

Bird-bolt, *sb.* a bolt to be shot from a cross-bow at birds. Much Ado, I. 1.

Birding, *part.* hawking at partridges. Merry Wives, III. 3.

Bisson, *adj.* blind. Cor. II. 1.

Blank, *sb.* the white mark in the middle of a target ; hence, metaphorically, that which is aimed at. Wint. Tale, II. 3.

Blench, *v.i.* to start aside, flinch. M. for M. IV. 5.

Blent, *p.p.* blended. M. of V. III. 2.

Blood-boltered, *part.* smeared with blood. Mac. IV. 1.

Blow, *v.t.* to inflate. Tw. N. II. 5.

Board, *v.t.* to accost. Tam. of S. I. 2.

Bob, *sb.* a blow, metaph. a sarcasm. As you Like it, II. 7.

Bob, *v.t.* to strike, metaph. to ridicule, or to obtain by raillery. T. & Cr. III. 1 ; Oth. v. 1.

Bodge, *v.* to botch, bungle. 3 H. VI. I. 4.

Bodikin, *sb.* a corrupt word used as an oath. 'Od's Bodikin, God's little Body. Ham. II. 2.

Boitier vert (French), green box. Merry Wives, I. 4.

Bold, *v.t.* to embolden. Lear, v. 1.

Bollen, *adj.* swollen. Lucr. 1417.

Bolted, *p.p.* sifted, refined. H. V. II. 2.

Bolter, *sb.* a sieve. 1 H. IV. III. 3.

Bolting-hutch, *sb.* a hutch in which meal was sifted. 1 H. IV. II. 4.

Bombard, *sb.* a barrel, a drunkard. Temp. II. 2.

Bombast, *sb.* padding. L's L's L. v. 2.

Bona-roba, *sb.* a harlot. 2 H. IV. III. 2.

Bond, *sb.* that to which one is bound. Lear, I. 1.

Book, *sb.* a paper of conditions. 1 H. IV. III. 1.

Boot, *sb.* help, use. Tam. of S. v. 2.

Boot, *v.t.* to help, to avail. Two Gent. I. 1.

Bootless, *adj.* without boot or advantage, useless. Temp. I. 2.

Boots, *sb.* bots, a kind of worm. Two Gent. I. 1.

Bore, *sb.* calibre of a gun ; hence, metaph. size, weight, importance. Ham. IV. 6.

Bosky, *adj.* covered with underwood. Temp. III. 3.

Bosom, *sb.* wish, heart's desire. M. for M. IV. 3.

Bots, *sb.* worms which infest horses. 1 H. IV. II. 1.

Bourn, *sb.* a boundary. Wint. Tale, I. 2. A brook. Lear, III. 6.

Brace, *sb.* armor for the arm, state of defence. Oth. I. 3 ; Per. II. 1.

Brach, *sb.* a hound bitch. Induc. to Tam. of S.

Braid, *adj.* deceitful. All's Well, IV. 2.

Brave, *adj.* handsome, well-dressed. Temp. I. 2.

Brave, *sb.* boast. John, v. 2.

Bravery, *sb.* finery. Tam. of S. IV. 3. Boastfulness. Ham. v. 2.

Brawl, *sb.* a kind of dance. L's L's L. III. 1.

Breast, *sb.* voice. Tw. N. II. 3.

Breathe, *v.t.* to exercise. All's Well, II. 3.

Breathing, *pr. p.* exercising. Ham. v. 2.

Breeching, *adj.* liable to be whipt. Tam. of S. III. 1.

Breed-bate, *sb.* a breeder of debate, a fomenter of quarrels. Merry Wives, I. 4.

Breese, *sb.* the gadfly. A. & C. III. 8.

Bribe-buck, *sb.* a buck given away in presents. Merry Wives, v. 5.

Bring, *v.t.* to attend one on a journey. M. for M. I. 1.

Brock, *sb.* a badger, a term of contempt. Tw. N. II. 5.

Broke, *v.i.* to act as a procurer. All's Well, III. 5.

Broken, *p.p.* having lost some teeth by age. All's Well, II. 3.

Broken music, the music of stringed instruments. T. & Cr. III. 1.

Broker, *sb.* an agent. Two Gent. I. 2.

Brotherhood, *sb.* trading company. T. & Cr. I. 3.

Brownist, *sb.* a sectary, a follower of Brown, the founder of the Independents. Tw. N. III. 2.

Bruit, *sb.* noise, report, rumor. 3 H. VI. IV. 7.

Bruit, *v.t.* to noise abroad. Mac. v. 7.

Brush, *sb.* rude assault. 2 H. VI. v. 3 ; Tim. IV. 3.

Buck, *sb.* suds or lye for washing clothes in. Merry Wives, III. 3 ; 2 H. VI. IV. 2.

Buck-basket, *sb.* the basket in which clothes are carried to the wash. Merry Wives, III. 5.

Bucking, *sb.* washing. Merry Wives, III. 3.

Buck-washing, *sb.* washing in lye. Merry Wives, III. 3.

Bug, *sb.* a bugbear, a spectre. 3 H. VI. v. 2 ; Cym. v. 3.

Bully-rook, *sb.* a bragging cheater. Merry Wives, I. 3.

Burgonet, *sb.* a kind of helmet. 2 H. VI. v. 1.

Burst, *v.t.* to break. Ind. to Tam. of S.

Busky, *adj.* bushy. 1 H. IV. v. 1.

Butt-shaft, *sb.* a light arrow for shooting at a butt. L's L's L. I. 2.

Buxom, *adj.* obedient. H. V. III. 3.

By'rlakin, *int.* by our little Lady : an oath. M. N's Dr. III. 1.

Caddis, *sb.* worsted galloon, so called because it resembles the caddis-worm. Wint. Tale, IV. 3.

Cade, *sb.* a cask or barrel. 2 H. VI. IV. 2.

Cage, *sb.* a prison. Cym. III. 3.

Cain-colored, *adj.* red (applied to hair). Merry Wives, I. 4.

Caitiff, *sb.* a captive, a slave ; hence, a witch. All's Well, III. 2.

Calculate, *v.t.* prophesy. J. C. I. 3.

Caliver, *sb.* a hand-gun. 1 H. IV. IV. 2.

Callet, *sb.* a trull. Oth. IV. 2.

Calling, *sb.* appellation. As you Like it, I. 2.

Calm, *adj.* qualm. 2 H. IV. II. 4.

Can, *v.t.* to know, be skilful in. Ham. IV. 7.

Canakin, *sb.* a little can. Oth. II. 3.

Canary, *sb.* a wine brought from the Canary Islands. Merry Wives, III. 2.

Candle-wasters, *sb.* persons who sit up all night to drink. Much Ado, v. 1.

Canker, *sb.* a caterpillar. Two Gent. I. 1. The dog-rose. Much Ado, I. 3.

Canstick, *sb.* a candlestick. 1 H. IV. III. 1.

Cantle, *sb.* a slice, corner. 1 H. IV. III. 1.

Canton, *sb.* a canto. Tw. N. I. 5.

Canvas, *v.t.* to sift ; hence, metaphorically, to prove. 2 H. IV. II. 4.

Capable, *adj.* subject to. John, III. 1. Intelligent. T. & Cr. III. 3. Capable of inheriting. Lear, II. 1. Ample, capacious. Oth. III. 3.

Capitulate, *v.i.* make head. 1 H. IV. III. 2.

Capocchia, *sb.* a simpleton. T. & Cr. IV. 2.

Capricio, *sb.* (Italian), caprice. All's Well, II. 3.

Capricious, *adj.* lascivious. As you Like it, III. 3.

Captious, *adj.* capacious. All's Well, I. 3.

Carack, *sb.* a large ship of burden. Com. of E. III. 2.

Carbonado, *sb.* meat scotched for broiling. 1 H. IV. v. 3.

Carbonado, *v.t.* to scotch for broiling. Lear, II. 2.

Card, *sb.* the taper on which the points of the compass are marked under the mariner's needle. Ham. v. 1.

Careire, *sb.* the curvetting of a horse. Merry Wives, I. 1.

Carkanet, *sb.* a necklace. Com. of E. III. 1.

Carl, *sb.* a churl. Cym. v. 2.

Carlot, *sb.* a churl. As you Like it, III. 5.

Castilian, *sb.* a native of Castile ; used as a cant term. Merry Wives, II. 3.

Castiliano vulgo, a cant term, meaning, apparently, to use discreet language. Tw. N. I. 3.

Cataian, *adj.* a native of Cathay, a cant word. Tw. N. II. 3.

Catling, *sb.* cat-gut. T. & Cr. III. 3.

Cautel, *sb.* deceit. Ham. I. 3.

Cautelous, *adj.* insidious. Cor. IV. 1.

Cavalero, *sb.* a cavalier, gentleman. 2 H. IV. v. 3.

Caviare, *sb.* the roe of sturgeon pickled ; metaph. a delicacy not appreciated by the vulgar. Ham. II. 2.

Cease, *sb.* decease. Ham. III. 3.

Cease, *p.p.* put off, made to cease. Tim. II. 1.

Censure, *sb.* judgment. 1 H. VI. II. 3.

Censure, *v.t.* to judge, criticise. Two Gent. I. 2.

Century, *sb.* a hundred of anything, whether men, prayers, or anything else. Cor. I. 7 ; Cym. IV. 2.

Ceremony, *sb.* a ceremonial vestment, religious rite, or anything ceremonial. J. C. I. 1 ; Mac. III. 4.

Certes, *adv.* certainly. Oth. I. 1.

Cess, *sb.* rate, reckoning. 1 H. IV. II. 1.

Chace, *sb.* a term at tennis. H. V. I. 2.

Chamber, *sb.* a species of great gun. 2 H. IV. II. 4.

Chamberer, *sb.* an effeminate man. Oth. III. 3.

Chanson, *sb.* a song. Ham. II. 2.

Charact, *sb.* affected quality. M. for M. V. 1.

Character, *sb.* a letter, handwriting. Lear, I. 2.

Character, *v.t.* to carve or engrave. Two Gent. II. 7 ; Ham. I. 3.

Charactery, *sb.* handwriting. Merry Wives, V. 5. That which is written. J. C. II. 1.

Chare, *sb.* a turn of work. A. & C. IV. 13.

Charge-house, *sb.* a free-school. L's L's L. V. 1.

Charles' wain, *sb.* the constellation called also Ursa Major, or the Great Bear. 1 H. IV. II. 1.

Charneco, *sb.* a species of sweet wine. 2 H. VI. II. 3.

Chaudron, *sb.* entrails. Mac. IV. 1.

Cheater, *sb.* for escheator, an officer who collected the fines to be paid into the Exchequer. Merry Wives, I. 3. A decoy. 2 H. IV. II. 3.

Check, *v.i.* a technical term in falconry ; when a falcon flies at a bird which is not her proper game she is said to check at it. Tw. N. II. 5.

Checks, *sb.* perhaps intended for ethics. Tam. of S. I. 1.

Cheer, *sb.* fortune, countenance. Temp. I. 1.

Cherry-pit, *sb.* a game played with cherry-stones. Tw. N. III. 4.

Cheveril, *sb.* kid leather. R. & J. II. 4.

Chewit, *sb.* cough. 1 H. IV. V. 1.

Childing, *adj.* pregnant. M. N's Dr. II. 2.

Ch'ill, vulgar for ' I will.' Lear, IV. 6.

Chirurgeonly, *adv.* in a manner becoming a surgeon. Temp. II. 1.

Chopin, *sb.* a high shoe or clog. Ham. II. 2.

Christendom, *sb.* the state of being a Christian. John, IV. 1. Name. All's Well, I. 1.

Christom, *adj.* clothed with a chrisom, the white garment which used to be put on newly-baptized children. H. V. II. 3.

Chuck, *sb.* chicken, a term of endearment. Mac. III. 2.

Chuff, *sb.* a coarse blunt clown. 1 H. IV. II. 2.

Cinque pace, *sb.* a kind of dance. Much Ado, II. 1.

Cipher, *v.t.* to decipher. Lucr. 811.

Circumstance, *sb.* an argument. Two Gent. I. 1 ; John, II. 1.

Cital, *sb.* recital. 1 H. IV. V. 2.

Cite, *v.* to incite. Two Gent. II. 4 ; 3 H. VI. II. 1.

Cittern, *sb.* a guitar. L's L's L. V. 2.

Clack-dish, *sb.* a beggar's dish. M. for M. III. 2.

Clap i' the clout, to shoot an arrow into the bull's eye of the target. 2 H. IV. III. 2.

Claw, *v.t.* to flatter. Much Ado, I. 3.

Clepe, *v.t.* to call. Ham. I. 4.

Cliff, *sb.* clef, the key in music. T. & Cr. V. 2.

Cling, *v.t.* to starve. Mac. V. 5.

Clinquant, *adj.* glittering. H. VIII. I. 1.

Clip, *v.t.* to embrace, enclose. 2 H. VI. IV. 1 ; Cor. I. 6 ; Oth. III. 3.

Clout, *sb.* the mark in the middle of a target. L's L's L. IV. 1.

Coast, *v.i.* to advance. V. & A. 870.

Cobloaf, *sb.* a big loaf. T. & Cr. II. 1.

Cock, *sb.* a cockboat. Lear, IV. 6.

Cock, *sb.* a euphemism for God. Tam. of S. IV. 1.

Cock-and-pie, an oath. Merry Wives, I. 1.

Cockle, *sb.* tares or darnel. L's L's L. IV. 3.

Cockney, *sb.* a cook. Lear, II. 4.

Cock-shut-time, *sb.* the twilight, when cocks and hens go to roost. R. III. V. 3.

Cog, *v.i.* to cheat, dissemble. Merry Wives, III. 3.

Cognizance, *sb.* badge, token. 1 H. VI. II. 4.

Coign, *sb.* projecting corner stone. Mac. I. 6.

Coil, *sb.* tumult, turmoil. Temp. I. 2.

Collection, *sb.* drawing a conclusion. Ham. IV. 5.

Collied, *p.p.* blackened. Oth. II. 3 ; M. N's Dr. I. 1.

Color, *sb.* pretence. L's L's L. IV. 2.

Colorable, *adj.* specious. Ibid.

Colt, *v.t.* to defraud, befool. 1 H. IV. II. 2.

Co-mart, *sb.* a joint bargain. Ham. I. 1.

Combinate, *p.p.* betrothed. M. for M. III. 1.

Combine, *v.t.* to bind. M. for M. IV. 3.

Commodity, *sb.* interest, profit. M. of V. III. 3.

Commonty, *sb.* used ludicrously for comedy. Induction to Tam. of S.

Compact, *p.p.* compacted, composed. M. N's Dr. V. 1.

Comparative, *adj.* drawing comparisons. 1 H. IV. I. 2.

Comparative, *sb.* rival. 1 H. IV. III. 2.

Compare, *sb.* comparison. T. & Cr. III. 2.

Compassionate, *adj.* moving comparison. R. II. I. 3.

Competitor, *sb.* one who seeks the same thing, an associate in any object. Two Gent. II. 6.

Complement, *sb.* accomplishment. L's L's L. I. 1.

Complexion, *sb.* passion. Ham. I. 4.

Compose, *v.i.* to agree. A. & C. II. 2.

Compostion, *sb.* composition. Tim. IV. 3.

Comptible, *adj.* tractable. Tw. N. I. 5.

Con, *v.t.* to learn by heart. M. N's Dr. I. 2. To acknowledge. All's Well, IV. 3.

Conceit, *sb.* conception, opinion, fancy. Two Gent. III. 2.

Concupy, *sb.* concubine. T. & Cr. V. 2.

Condition, *sb.* temper, quality. M. of V. I. 2 ; Lear, I. 1.

Condolement, *sb.* grief. Ham. I. 2.

Conduct, *sb.* escort. John, I. 1.

Confect, *v.* to make up into sweetmeats. Much Ado, IV. 1.

Confound, *v.t.* to consume, destroy. 1 H. IV. I. 3 ; Cor. I. 6 ; Cym. I. 5.

Conject, *sb.* conjecture. Oth. III. 3.

Consign, *v.* to sign a common bond, to confederate. 2 H. IV. IV. 1.

Consort, *sb.* company. Two Gent. IV. 1.

Consort, *v.t.* to accompany. L's L's L. II. 1.

Constancy, *sb.* consistency. M. N's Dr. V. 1.

Constant, *adj.* settled, determined. Temp. II. 2 ; Lear, V. 1.

Constantly, *adv.* firmly. M. for M. IV. 1.

Conster, *v.t.* to construe. Tw. N. I. 4.

Contemptible, *adj.* contemptuous. Much Ado, II. 3.

Continent, *sb.* that which contains anything. Lear, III. 2 ; M. N's Dr. II. 2. That which is contained. 2 H. IV. II. 4.

Continuate, *adj.* uninterrupted. Tim. I. 1.

Contraction, *sb.* the marriage contract. Ham. III. 4.

Contrary, *v.t.* to oppose. R. & J. I. 5.

Contrive, *v.i.* to conspire. J. C. II. 3. *v.t.* to wear away. Tam. of S. I. 2.

Control, *v.t.* to confute. Temp. I. 2.

Convent, *v.t.* to convene, summon. H. VIII. v. 1. *v.i.* to be convenient. Tw. N. v. 1.

Convert, *v.i.* to change. Tim. IV. 1.

Convertite, *sb.* a convert. As you Like it, v. 4.

Convey, *v.t.* to manage. Lear, I. 2. To filch. Merry Wives, I. 3.

Conveyance, *sb.* theft, fraud. 1 H. VI. I. 3.

Convict, *p.p.* convicted. R. III. I. 4.

Convicted, *p.p.* overpowered, vanquished. John, III. 4. A doubtful word.

Convince, *v.t.* to conquer, subdue. Cym. I. 5.

Convive, *v.i.* to feast together. T. & Cr. IV. 5.

Convoy, *sb.* escort. All's Well, IV. 3.

Cony-catch, *v.i.* to cheat. Tam. of S. v. 1.

Cony-catching, *pr. p.* poaching, pilfering. Merry Wives, I. 1.

Cooling card, *sb.* used metaphorically for an insurmountable obstacle. 1 H. VI. v. 3.

Copatain hat, a high-crowned hat. Tam. of S. v. 1.

Cope, *v.t.* to reward, to give in return. M. of V. IV. 1.

Copped, *p.p.* rising to a cop or head. Per. I. 1.

Copy, *sb.* theme. Com. of E. v. 1.

Coragio (Italian), *int.* courage! Temp. v. 1.

Coram, an ignorant mistake for Quorum. Merry Wives, I. 1.

Coranto, *sb.* a lively dance. H. V. III. 5.

Corinth, *sb.* a cant term for a brothel. Tim. II. 2.

Corinthian, *sb.* a wencher. 1 H. IV. II. 4.

Corky, *adj.* dry like cork. Lear, III. 7.

Cornuto (Italian), *sb.* a cuckold. Merry Wives, III. 5.

Corollary, *sb.* a surplus. Temp. IV. 1.

Corporal, *adj.* corporeal, bodily. M. for M. III. 1.

Corporal of the field, and aide-de-camp. L's L's L. III. 1.

Corrival, *sb.* rival. 1 H. IV. I. 3.

Costard, *sb.* the head. R. III. I. 4.

Coster-monger, *adj.* peddling, mercenary. 2 H. IV. I. 2.

Cote, *sb.* a cottage. As you Like it, III. 2.

Cote, *v.t.* to quote, instance. L's L's L. IV. 3.

Cote, *v.t.* to come alongside, overtake. Ham. II. 2.

Cot-quean, *sb.* an effeminate man, molly-coddle. R. & J. IV. 4.

Couchings, *sb.* crouchings. J. C. III. 1.

Count confect, *sb.* a nobleman composed of affectation. Much Ado, IV. 1.

Countenance, *sb.* fair shew. M. for M. v. 1.

Counterfeit, *sb.* portrait. M. of V. III. 2. A piece of base coin. 1 H. IV. II. 4.

Counterpoint, *sb.* a counterpane. Tam. of S. II. 1.

Countervail, *v.t.* to counterpoise, outweigh. R. & J. II. 6.

Country, *adj.* belonging to one's country. Oth. III. 3 ; Cym. I. 5.

County, *sb.* count, earl. R. & J. I. 3.

Couplement, *sb.* union. L's L's L. v. 2 ; Son. 19.

Court holy-water, *sb.* flattery. Lear, III. 2.

Covent, *sb.* a convent. M. for M. IV. 3.

Cover, *v.t.* to lay the table for dinner. M. of V. III. 5 ; As you Like it, II. 5.

Cowish, *adj.* cowardly. Lear, IV. 2.

Cowl-staff, *sb.* the staff on which a vessel is supported between two men. Merry Wives, III. 3.

Cox my passion, an oath, a euphemism for " God's Passion." All's Well, v. 2.

Coy, *v.t.* to stroke, fondle. M. N's Dr. IV. 1. *v.i.* to condescend with difficulty. Cor. v. 1.

Coystril, *sb.* a kestrel, a cowardly kind of hawk. Tw. N. I. 3.

Cozen, *v.t.* to cheat. M. of V. II. 9.

Cozenage, *sb.* cheating. Merry Wives, IV. 5.

Cozener, *sb.* a cheater. 1 H. IV. I. 3.

Cozier, *sb.* a tailor. Tw. N. II. 3.

Crack, *v.i.* to boast. L's L's L. IV. 3.

Crack, *sb.* a loud noise, clap. Mac. IV. 1. A forward boy. 2 H. IV. III. 2.

Cracker, *sb.* boaster. John, II. 1.

Crack-hemp, *sb.* a gallows-bird. Tam. of S. v. 1.

Crank, *sb.* a winding passage. Cor. I. 1.

Cranking, *pr. p.* winding. 1 H. IV. III. 1.

Crants, *sb.* garlands. Ham. v. 1. A doubtful word.

Crare, *sb.* a ship of burden. Cym. IV. 2.

Craven, *sb.* a dunghill cock. Tam. of S. II. 1.

Create, *p.p.* formed, compounded. H. V. II. 2.

Credent, *adj.* creditable. M. for M. IV. 4. Credible. Wint. Tale, I. 2. Credulous. Ham. I. 3.

Credit, *sb.* report. Tw. N. IV. 3.

Crescive, *adj.* increasing. H. V. I. 1.

Crestless, *adj.* not entitled to bear arms, low-born. 1 H. VI. II. 4.

Crisp, *adj.* curled, winding. Temp. IV. 1.

Cross, *sb.* a piece of money, so called because coin was formerly stamped with a cross. As you Like it, II. 4.

Crow-keeper, *sb.* one who scares crows. Lear, IV. 6.

Crowner, *sb.* a coroner. Ham. v. 1.

Crownet, *sb.* a coronet. A. & C. v. 2.

Cry, *sb.* the yelping of hounds. M. N's Dr. IV. 1. A pack of hounds. Ibid. IV. 1. A company, used contemptuously. Ham. III. 2.

Cry aim, *v.t.* to encourage. John, II. 1.

Cue, *sb.* the last words of an actor's speech, which is the signal for the next actor to begin. Lear, I. 2.

Cuisses, *sb.* pieces of armor to cover the thighs. 1 H. IV. IV. 1.

Cullion, *sb.* a base fellow. Tam. of S. IV. 2.

Cunning, *sb.* skill. Induction to Tam. of S.

Cunning, *adj.* skilful. Ibid.

Curb, *v.i.* to bend, truckle. Ham. III. 4.

Currents, *sb.* occurrences. 1 H. IV. II. 3.

Curst, *adj.* petulant, shrewish. Tam. of S. I. 2.

Curstness, *sb.* shrewishness. A. & C. II. 2.

Curtail, *sb.* a cur. Com. of E. III. 2.

Curtal, *sb.* a docked horse. All's Well, II. 3.

Curtal-axe, *sb.* a cutlass. As you Like it, I. 3.

Custalorum, a ludicrous mistake for Custos Rotulorum. Merry Wives, I. 1.

Custard-coffin, *sb.* the crust of a custard-pudding. Tam. of S. IV. 3.

Customer, *sb.* a common woman. Oth. IV. 1.

Cut, *sb.* a cheat. Tw. N. II. 3. ' To draw cuts ' is to draw lots. Com. of E. v. 1.

Cypress, *sb.* a kind of crape. Tw. N. III. 1.

Daff, *v.t.* to befool. Much Ado, IV. 1. To put off ; this seems to be a corruption of ' doff.' Ibid. II. 3.

Damn, *v.t.* to condemn. J. C. IV. 1.

Danger, *sb.* reach, control, power. M. of V. IV. 1.

Dansker, *sb.* a Dane. Ham. II. 1.

Dare, *v.t.* to challenge. 2 H. VI. III. 2.

Darkling, *adv.* in the dark. M. N's Dr. II. 2.

Darraign, *v.t.* to set in array. 3 H. VI. II. 2.

Daub, *v.t.* to disguise. Lear, IV. 1.

Daubery, *sb.* imposition. Merry Wives, IV. 2.

Day-woman, *sb.* a dairy-maid. L's L's L. I. 2.

Dear, *adj.* dire. Tim. V. 1. That which has to do with the affections. R. II. I. 1; R. & J. III. 3. Piteous. T. A. III. 1. Important. Lear, IV. 3.

Dearn, *adj.* lonely. Per. III. (Gower).

Deboshed, *p.p.* debauched, drunken. Temp. III. 2.

Deck, *v.t.* to bedew. This is probably a form of the verb ' to dag,' now a provincial word. Temp. I. 2.

Deck, *sb.* a pack of cards. 3 H. VI. V. 1.

Decline, *v.t.* to enumerate, as in going through the cases of a noun. T. & Cr. I. 3.

Declined, *p.p.* fallen. T. & Cr. III. 3.

Deem, *sb.* doom, judgment. T. & Cr. IV. 4.

Defeat, *v.t.* to undo, destroy. Oth. I. 3; IV. 2.

Defeat, *sb.* destruction. Much Ado, IV. 1.

Defeature, *sb.* disfigurement. Com. of E. II. 1.

Defence, *sb.* art of fencing. Tw. N. III. 4.

Defend, *v.t.* to forbid. Much Ado, II. 1.

Defensible, *adj.* having the power to defend. 2 H. IV. II. 3.

Deftly, *adv.* dexterously. Mac. IV. 1.

Defy, *v.t.* renounce. 1 H. IV. I. 3.

Degrees, *sb.* a step. J. C. II. 1.

Delay, *v.t.* to let slip by delaying. Cor. I. 6.

Demerit, *sb.* merit, desert. Oth. I. 2.

Demurely, *adv.* solemnly. A. & C. IV. 9.

Denay, *sb.* denial. Tw. N. II. 4.

Denier, *sb.* the 12th part of a French sol. R. III. I. 2.

Denotement, *sb.* marking. Oth. II. 3. Note or manifestation. Ibid. III. 3.

Deny, *v.t.* to refuse. Tim. III. 2.

Depart, *sb.* departure. 2 H. VI. I. 1.

Depart, *v.t.* to part. L's L's L. II. 1.

Departing, *sb.* parting, separation. 3 H. VI. II. 6.

Depend, *v.i.* to be in service. Lear, I. 4.

Derived, *p.p.* born, descended. Two Gent. V. 4.

Derogate, *p.p.* degraded. Lear, I. 4.

Descant, *sb.* a variation upon a melody, hence, metaphorically, a comment on a given theme. Two Gent. I. 2.

Design, *v.t.* to draw up articles. Ham. I. 1.

Despatch, *v.t.* to deprive, bereave. Ham. I. 5.

Desperate, *adj.* determined, bold. R. & J. III. 4.

Detect, *v.t.* to charge, blame. M. for M. III. 2.

Determine, *v.t.* to conclude. Cor. III. 3.

Dich, *v.i.* optative mood, perhaps contracted for ' do it.' Tim. I. 2.

Diet, *sb.* food regulated by the rules of medicine. Two Gent. II. 1.

Diet, *v.t.* to have one's food regulated by the rules of medicine. All's Well, IV. 3.

Diffused, *p.p.* confused. Merry Wives, IV. 4.

Digressing, *pr. p.* transgressing, going out of the right way. R. II. V. 3.

Digression, *sb.* transgression. L's L's L. I. 2.

Dig-you-good-den, *int.* give you good evening. L's L's L. IV. 1.

Dildo, *sb.* the chorus or burden of a song. Wint. Tale, IV. 3.

Dint, *sb.* stroke, J. C. III. 2.

Direction, *sb.* judgment, skill. R. III. V. 3.

Disable, *v.t.* to disparage. As you Like it, IV. 1.

Disappointed, *p.p.* unprepared. Ham. I. 5.

Discase, *v.r.* to undress. Wint. Tale, IV. 3.

Discontent, *sb.* a malcontent. A. & C. I. 4.

Discourse, *sb.* power of reasoning. Ham. IV. 4.

Disdained, *p.p.* disdainful. 1 H. IV. I. 3.

Dislimn, *v.t.* to disfigure, transform. A. & C. IV. 12.

Disme, *sb.* a tenth or tithe. T. & Cr. II. 2.

Dispark, *v.t.* to destroy a park. R. II. III. 1.

Disponge, *v.i.* to squeeze out as from a sponge. A. & C. IV. 9.

Dispose, *sb.* disposal. Two Gent. IV. 1.

Dispose, *v.i.* to conspire. A. & C. IV. 12.

Disposition, *sb.* maintenance. Oth. I. 3.

Disputable, *adj.* disputatious. As you Like it, II. 5.

Dispute, *v.t.* to argue, examine. Oth. I. 2.

Dissembly, *sb.* used ridiculously for assembly. Much Ado, IV. 2.

Distaste, *v.t.* to corrupt. T. & Cr. II. 2.

Distempered, *adj.* discontented. John, IV. 3.

Distraction, *sb.* a detached troop or company of soldiers. A. & C. III. 7.

Distraught, *p.p.* distracted, mad. R. III. III. 5.

Diverted, *p.p.* turned from the natural course. As you Like it, II. 3.

Division, *sb.* a phrase or passage in a melody. R. & J. III. 5.

Divulged, *p.p.* published, spoken of. Tw. N. I. 5.

Doff, *v.t.* to do off, strip. Tam. of S. III. 2. To put off with an excuse. Oth. IV. 2.

Doit, *sb.* a small Dutch coin. Temp. II. 2.

Dole, *sb.* portion dealt. Merry Wives, III. 4; 2 H. IV. I. 1. Grief, lamentation. M. N's Dr. V. 1.

Don, *v.t.* to do on, put on. T. A. I. 2; Ham. IV. 5.

Done, *p.p.* ' done to death,' put to death. 2 H. VI. III. 2.

Dotant, *sb.* one who dotes, a dotard. Cor. V. 2.

Dout, *v.t.* to do out, quench. Ham. I. 4.

Dowlas, *sb.* a kind of coarse sacking. 1 H. IV. III. 3.

Dowle, *sb.* the swirl of a feather. Temp. III. 3.

Down-gyved, *adj.* hanging down like gyves or fetters. Ham. II. 1.

Drab, *sb.* a harlot. Wint. Tale, IV. 2.

Drabbing, *pr. p.* whoring. Ham. II. 1.

Draught, *sb.* a privy. T. A. V. 1.

Drawn, *p.p.* having his sword drawn. Temp. II. 1.

Drawn, *p.p.* drunk, having taken a good draught. Ibid.

Dribbling, *adj.* weak. M. for M. I. 4.

Drive, *v.i.* to rush impetuously. T. A. II. 3.

Drollery, *sb.* a puppet-show. Temp. III. 3.

Drumble, *v.i.* to dawdle. Merry Wives, III. 3.

Dry, *adj.* thirsty. Temp. I. 2.

Duc-dame; perhaps the Latin duc-ad-me, bring him to me. As you Like it.

Dudgeon, *sb.* a dagger. Mac. II. 1.

Dull, *adj.* soothing. 2 H. IV. IV. 4.

Dullard, *sb.* a dull person. Cym. V. 5.

Dump, *sb.* complaint. Two Gent. III. 2.

Dup, *v.t.* to do up, lift up. Ham. IV. 5.

Eager, *adj.* sour. Ham. I. 5. Harsh. 3 H. VI. II. 6. Biting. Ham. I. 4.

Eanling, *sb.* a yeanling, a lamb. M. of V. I. 3.

Ear, *v.t.* to plough. All's Well, I. 3.

Eche, *v.t.* to eke out. Per. III. (Gower).

Ecstacy, *sb.* madness. Temp. III. 3.

Eft, *adj.* ready, convenient. Much Ado, IV. 2.

Eisel, *sb.* vinegar. Ham. V. 1 ; Son. 3.

Eld, *sb.* old age. M. for M. III. 1.

Embossed, *adj.* swollen into protuberances. As you Like it, II. 7. Covered with foam. A. & C. IV. 11.

Embowelled, *p.p.* disembowelled, emptied. All's Well, I. 3.

Embrasure, *sb.* embrace. T. & Cr. IV. 4.

Eminence, *sb.* exalted station. Mac. III. 2.

Empery, *sb.* empire. H. V. I. 2.

Emulation, *sb.* jealousy, mutiny. T. & Cr II. 2.

Emulous, *adj.* jealous. T. & Cr. IV. 1.

Encave, *v.r.* to place oneself in a cave. Oth. IV. 1.

End, *sb.* ' Still an end,' continually for ever. Two Gent. IV. 4.

Enfeoff, *v.t.* to place in possession in fee simple. 1 H. IV. III. 2.

Engine, *sb.* a machine of war. T. & Cr. II. 3.

Englut, *v.t.* to swallow speedily. Tim. II. 2.

Engross, *v.t.* to make gross or fat. R. III. III. 7.

Engrossment, *sb.* immoderate acquisition. 2 H. IV. IV. 4.

Enkindle, *v.t.* to make keen. Mac. I. 3.

Enmew, *v.t.* to shut up, as a hawk is shut up in a mew. M. for M. III. 1.

Ensconce, *v.t.* to cover as with a fort. Merry Wives, II. 2.

Enseamed, *p.p.* fat, rank. Ham. III. 4.

Enshield, *p.p.* hidden. M. for M. II. 4.

Entertain, *v.t.* encounter. H. V. I. 2. Experience. A. & C. II. 7.

Entertainment, *sb.* treatment. Temp. I. 2. A disposition to entertain a proposal. Merry Wives, I. 3. Service. All's Well, IV. 1.

Entreatments, *sb.* interviews. Ham. I. 3.

Ephesian, *sb.* a toper, a cant term. Merry Wives, IV. 5.

Equipage, *sb.* attendance. Merry Wives, II. 2.

Erewhile, *adv.* a short time since. As you Like it, II. 4.

Escot, *v.t.* to pay a man's reckoning, to maintain. Ham. II. 2.

Esperance, *sb.* hope, used as a war-cry. 1 H. IV. V. 2 ; T. & Cr. V. 2.

Espial, *sb.* a scout or spy. 1 H. VI. IV. 3.

Estimation, *sb.* conjecture. 1 H. IV. I. 3.

Estridge, *sb.* ostridge. 1 H. IV. IV. 1.

Eterne, *adj.* eternal. Mac. III. 2.

Even, *adj.* coequal. Ham. V. 1.

Even, *v.t.* to equal. All's Well, I. 3 ; Cym. III. 4.

Examine, *v.t.* to question. All's Well, III. 5.

Excrement, *sb.* that which grows outwardly from the body and has no sensation like the hair or nails. L's L's L. V. 1 ; Ham. III. 4. Any outward show. M. of V. III. 2 ; Wint. Tale, IV. 3.

Executor, *sb.* an executioner. H. V. I. 2.

Exempt, *adj.* excluded. 1 H. VI. II. 4.

Exercise, *sb.* a religious service. R. III. III. 2.

Exhale, *v.t.* to hale or draw out. R. III. I. 2 ; *v.i.* to draw the sword. H. V. II. 1.

Exhibition, *sb.* allowance, pension. Two Gent. I. 3.

Exigent, *sb.* death, ending. 1 H. VI. II. 5.

Exion, *sb.* ridiculously used for ' action.' 2 H. IV. II. 1.

Expect, *sb.* expectation. T. & Cr. I. 3.

Expedience, *sb.* expedition, undertaking. A. & C. I. 2. Haste. R. II. II. 1.

Expedient, *adj.* expeditious, swift. John, II. 1.

Expiate, *p.p.* completed. R. III. III. 3.

Expostulate, *v.t.* to expound, discuss. Ham. II. 2.

Exposture, *sb.* exposure. Cor. IV. 1.

Express, *v.t.* to reveal. Wint. Tale, III. 2.

Expulse, *v.t.* to expel. 1 H. VI. III. 3.

Exsufficate, *adj.* that which has been hissed off, contemptible. Tw. N. III. 3.

Extend, *v.t.* to seize. A. & C. I. 2.

Extent, *sb.* a seizure. As you Like it, III. 1.

Extern, *adj.* outward. Oth. I. 1.

Extirp, *v.t.* to extirpate. M. for M. III. 2.

Extracting, *adj.* distracting. Tw. N. V. 1.

Extraught, *part.* extracted, descended. 3 H. VI. II. 2.

Extravagant, *adj.* foreign, wandering. Oth. I. 1.

Extremes, *sb.* extravagance of conduct. Wint. Tale, IV. 3. Extremities. R. & J. IV. 1.

Eyas, *sb.* a nestling hawk. Ham. II. 2.

Eyas-musket, *sb.* a nestling of the musket or merlin, the smallest species of British hawk. Merry Wives, III. 3.

Eye, *sb.* a glance, œillad. Temp. I. 2.

Eye, *sb.* a shade of color, as in shot silk. Temp. II. 1.

Eyne, *sb. pl.* eyes. L's L's L. V. 2.

Facinorous, *adj.* wicked. All's Well, II. 3.

Fact, *sb.* guilt. Wint. Tale, III. 2.

Factious, *adj.* instant, importunate. J. C. I. 3.

Faculty, *sb.* essential virtue or power. H. V. I. 1.

Fadge, *v.i.* to suit. Tw. N. II. 2.

Fading, *sb.* a kind of ending to a song. Wint. Tale, IV. 3.

Fain, *adj.* glad. 2 H. VI. II. 1.

Fain, *adv.* gladly. Lear, I. 4.

Fair, *sb.* beauty. As you Like it, III. 2.

Faitor, *sb.* a traitor. 2 H. IV. II. 4.

Fall, *v.t.* to let fall. Temp. II. 1.

Fallow, *adj.* fawn-colored. Merry Wives, I. 1.

False, *sb.* falsehood. M. for M. II. 4.

Falsing, *adj.* deceptive. Com. of E. II. 2.

Familiar, *sb.* a familiar spirit. 2 H. VI. IV. 7.

Fancy, *sb.* All's Well, V. 3.

Fancy-free, *adj.* untouched by love. M. N's Dr. II. 2.

Fang, *v.t.* to seize in the teeth. Tim. IV. 3.

Fantastic, *sb.* a fantastical person. R. & J. II. 4.

Fap, *adj.* drunk. Merry Wives, I. 1.

Far, *adv.* farther. Wint. Tale, IV. 4.

Farced, *p.p.* stuffed. H. V. IV. 1.

Fardel, *sb.* a burden. Wint. Tale, IV. 4.

Fartuous, *adj.* used ridiculously for " virtuous." Merry Wives, II. 2.

Fast, *adv.* assuredly, unalterably. M. for M. I. 3 ; 2 H. VI. V. 2.

Fat, *adj.* dull. 1 H. IV. I. 2.

Favor, *sb.* countenance. M. for M. IV. 2. Complexion. T. & Cr. I. 2. Quality. Lear, I. 4.

Fear, *sb.* the object of fear. Ham. III. 3.

Fear, *v.t.* to affright. A. & C. II. 6.

Fearful, *adj.* subject to fear, timorous. Temp. I. 2.

Feat, *adj.* dexterous. Cym. V. 5.

Feat, *v.t.* to make fine. Cym. I. 1.

Feater, *adv. comp. degree*, more neatly. Temp. II. 1.

Featly, *adv.* nimbly, daintily. Temp. I. 2.

Feature, *sb.* beauty. Cym. V. 5.

Federary, *sb.* confederate. Wint. Tale, II. 1.

Feeder, *sb.* agent, servant. As you Like it, II. 4.

Fee-grief, *sb.* a grief held, as it were, in fee-simple, or the peculiar property of him who possesses it. Mac. IV. 3.

Feere, *sb.* a companion, husband. T. A. IV. 1.

Fehemently, *adv.* used ridiculously for "vehemently." Merry Wives, III. 1.

Fell, *sb.* the hide. As you Like it, III. 2.

Fence, *sb.* art or skill in defence. 2 H. VI. II. 1.

Feodary, *sb.* one who holds an estate by suit or service to a superior lord; hence one who acts under the direction of another. Cym. III. 2.

Fester, *v.i.* to rankle, grow virulent. Cor. I. 9.

Festinately, *adv.* quickly. L's L's L. III. 1.

Fet, *p.p.* fetched. H. V. III. 1.

Fico, *sb.* a fig. Merry Wives, I. 3.

Fielded, *adj.* in the field of battle. Cor. I. 4.

Fig, *v.t.* to insult. 2 H. IV. V. 3.

Fights, *sb.* clothes hung round a ship to conceal the men from the enemy. Merry Wives, II. 2.

File, *sb.* a list or catalogue. Mac. V. 2.

File, *v.t.* to defile. Mac. III. 1. To smooth or polish. L's L's L. To make even. H. VIII. III. 2.

Fill-horse, *sb.* shaft-horse. M. of V. II. 2.

Fills, *sb.* the shafts. T. & Cr. III. 2.

Filth, *sb.* a whore. Tim. IV. 1.

Fine, *sb.* end. Ham. V. 1.

Fine, *v.t.* to make fine or specious. H. V. I. 2.

Fineless, *adj.* endless. Oth. III. 3.

Firago, *sb.* ridiculously used for 'Virago.' Tw. N. III. 4.

Fire-drake, *sb.* Will o' the Wisp. H. VIII. V. 3.

Fire-new, *adj.* with the glitter of novelty on, like newly-forged metal. R. III. I. 3.

Firk, *v.t.* to chastise. H. V. IV. 4.

Fit, *sb.* a canto or division of a song. T. & Cr. III. 1. A trick or habit. H. VIII. I. 3.

Fitchew, *sb.* a polecat. Lear, IV. 6.

Fives, *sb.* a disease incident to horses. Tam. of S.

Flap-dragon, *sb.* raisins in burning brandy. L's L's L. V. 1.

Flap-jack, *sb.* a pan-cake. Per. II. 1.

Flat, *adj.* certain. 1 H. IV. IV. 2.

Flatness, *sb.* lowness, depth. Wint. Tale, III. 2.

Flaw, *sb.* a gust of wind. 2 H. IV. IV. 4. Metaph. sudden emotion, or the cause of it. Mac. III. 4; A. & C. III. 10.

Flaw, *v.t.* to make a flaw in, to break. H. VIII. I. 1.

Flecked, *p.p.* spotted, streaked. R. & J. II. 3.

Fleet, *v.i.* to float. A. & C. III. 11. To pass away. A. & C. I. 3. *v.t.* to pass the time. As you Like it, I. 1.

Fleeting, *pr. p.* inconstant. R. III. I. 4.

Fleshment, *sb.* the act of fleshing the sword, hence the first feat of arms. Lear, II. 2.

Flewed, *adj.* furnished with hanging lips, as hounds are. M. N's Dr. IV. 1.

Flight, *sb.* a particular mode of practising archery. Much Ado, I. 1.

Flirt-gill, *sb.* a light woman. R. & J. II. 4.

Flote, *sb.* wave, sea. Temp. I. 2.

Flourish, *sb.* an ornament. L's L's L. IV. 3.

Flourish, *v.t.* to ornament, disguise with ornament. M. for M. IV. 1.

Flush, *adj.* fresh, full of vigor. A. & C. I. 4.

Foil, *sb.* defeat, disadvantage. Temp. III. 1.

Foin, *v.i.* to fence, fight. Merry Wives, II. 3.

Foison, *sb.* plenty. Temp. II. 1.

Fond, *adj.* foolish, foolishly affectionate. Oth. I. 3; IV. 1.

Foot-cloth, *sb.* a saddle-cloth hanging down to the ground. 2 H. VI. IV. 7.

For, *conj.* for that, because. M. for M. II. 1.

Forbid, *p.p.* accursed, outlawed. Mac. I. 3.

Forbode, *p.p.* forbidden. Lover's Com. 164.

Force, *v.t.* to stuff, for 'farce.' T. & Cr. V. 5.

Forced, *p.p.* falsely attributed. Wint. Tale, II. 3.

Fordo, *v.t.* to kill, destroy. Lear, V. 3. To weary. M. N's Dr. V. 2.

Foreign, *adj.* obliged to live abroad. H. VIII. II. 2.

Forepast, *adj.* former. All's Well, V. 3.

Foreslow, *v.i.* to delay. 3 H. VI. II. 3.

Forfend, *v.t.* forbid. Wint. Tale, IV. 3.

Forgetive, *adj.* inventive. 2 H. IV. IV. 3.

Forked, *adj.* horned. Wint. Tale, I. 2; Oth. III. 3.

Formal, *adj.* regular, retaining its proper and essential characteristic. Com. of E. V. 1; A. & C. II. 5.

Forspeak, *v.t.* to speak against. A. & C. III. 7.

Forspent, *p.p.* exhausted, weary. 2 H. IV. I. 1.

Forthright, *sb.* a straight path; forthrights and meanders, straight paths and crooked ones. Temp. III. 3.

Forweary, *v.t.* to weary, exhaust. John, II. 1.

Fosset-seller, *sb.* one who sells the pipes inserted into a vessel to give vent to the liquor, and stopped by a spigot. Cor. II. 1.

Fox, *sb.* a sword; a cant word. H. V. IV. 4.

Fox-ship, *sb.* the cunning of the fox. Cor. IV. 2.

Frampold, *adj.* peevish, unquiet. Merry Wives, II. 2.

Frank, *sb.* the feeding place of swine. 2 H. IV. II. 2.

Franked, *p.p.* confined. R. III. I. 3.

Franklin, *sb.* a freeholder, a small squire. Cym. III. 2.

Fraught, *p.p.* freighted. M. of V. II. 8.

Fraughtage, *sb.* freight. Com. of E. IV. 1.

Fraughting, *pr. p. of v.* to fraught; loading or constituting the cargo of a ship. Temp. I. 2.

Fresh, *sb.* a spring of fresh water. Temp. III. 2.

Fret, *sb.* the stop of a guitar. Tam. of S. II. 1.

Fret, *v.t.* to wear away. R. II. III. 3; Lear, I. 4. To variegate. J. C. II. 1.

Friend, *v.t.* to befriend. H. VIII. I. 2.

Frippery, *sb.* an old-clothes shop. Temp. IV. 1.

From, *prep.* contrary to. Ham. III. 2.

Front, *v.t.* to affront, oppose. A. & C. II. 2.

Frontier, *sb.* opposition. 1 H. IV. I. 3.

Frontlet, *sb.* that which is worn on the forehead. Lear, I. 4.

Frush, *v.t.* to break or bruise. T. & Cr. V. 6.

Frustrate, *p.p.* frustrated. A. & C. V. 1.

Fub off, *v.t.* to put off. 2 H. IV. II. 1.

Fulfill, *v.t.* to fill full. Prol. to T. & Cr.

Full, *adj.* complete. Oth. II. 1.

Fullam, *sb.* a loaded die. Merry Wives, I. 3.

Fulsome, *adj.* lustful. M. of V. I. 3.

Furnished, *p.p.* equipped. Wint. Tale, IV. 3.

Furnitor, *sb.* furnitory, an herb. Lear, IV. 4.

Gaberdine, *sb.* a loose outer coat, or smock frock. Temp. II. 2; M. of V. I. 3.

Gad, *sb.* a pointed instrument, a goad. T. A. IV. 1. Upon the gad, with impetuous haste, upon the spur of the moment. Lear, I. 2.

Gain-giving, *sb.* misgiving. Ham. V. 2.

Gait, *sb.* going, steps. Tw. N. I. 4.

Galliard, *sb.* a kind of dance. Tw. N. I. 3.

Galliasse, *sb.* a kind of ship. Tam. of S. II. 1.

Gallimaufry, *sb.* a ridiculous medley. Wint. Tale, IV. 4.

Gallow, *v.t.* to scare. Lear, III. 2.

Gallowglass, *sb.* the irregular infantry of Ireland, and the Highlands of Scotland. Mac. I. 2.

Gamester, *sb.* a frolicsome person. H. VIII. I. 4. A loose woman. All's Well, V. 3.

Garboil, *sb.* disorder, uproar. A. & C. I. 3.

Garish, *adj.* gaudy, staring. R. III. IV. 4.

Garner, *v.t.* to lay by, as corn in a barn. Oth. IV. 2.

Gast, *p.p.* frightened. Lear, II. 1.

Gaudy, *adj.* festive. A. & C. III. 13.

Gaze, *sb.* an object of wonder. Mac. V. 7.

Gear, *sb.* matter of business of any kind. M. of V. II. 2.

Geck, *sb.* a fool. Cym. V. 4.

General, *sb.* the generality, common people. M. for M. II. 4.

Generations, *sb.* children. Wint. Tale, II. 1.

Generosity, *sb.* noble birth. Cor. I. 1.

Generous, *adj.* noble. M. for M. I. 1.

Gentility, *sb.* good manners. L's L's L. I. 1.

Gentle, *sb.* gentlefolk. L's L's L. IV. 1.

Gentle, *adj.* noble. Temp. I. 2.

Gentle, *v.t.* to ennoble. H. V. IV. 3.

Gentry, *sb.* complaisance, conduct becoming gentlefolk. Ham. II. 2.

German, *adj.* akin. Wint. Tale, IV. 4. Appropriate. Ham. V. 2.

Germen, *sb.* seed, embryo. Lear, III. 2.

Gest, *sb.* period. Wint. Tale, I. 2.

Gib, *sb.* a he-cat. Ham. III. 4.

Gifts, *sb.* talents, endowment. Merry Wives, I. 1.

Giglot, *sb.* a wanton girl. M. for M. V. 1.

Gilder, *sb.* a coin of the value of 1*s.* 6*d.* or 2*s.* Com. of E. IV. 1.

Gilt, *sb.* money. H. V. II. Ch. State of wealth. Tim. IV. 3.

Gimmal, *adj.* double. H. V. IV. 2.

Gimmor, *sb.* contrivance. 1 H. VI. I. 2.

Ging, *sb.* gang. Merry Wives, IV. 2.

Gird, *v.i.* to gibe. 2 H. IV. I. 2 ; Cor. I. 1.

Gird, *sb.* a sarcasm or gibe. Tam. of S. V. 2.

Gleek, *v.i.* to scoff. M. N's Dr. III. 1.

Gleek, *sb.* a scoff. 1 H. VI. III. 2.

Glose, *v.i.* to comment ; hence, to be garrulous. R. II. II. 1.

Glut, *v.* to swallow. Temp. I. 1.

Gnarl, *v.i.* to snarl. R. II. I. 3 ; 2 H. VI. III. 1.

Good-deed, *adv.* indeed. Wint. Tale, I. 2.

Good-den, *int.* good-evening, contracted from 'Good-even.' John, I. 1.

Good-year or Good-jer, *sb.* a corruption of the French goujere ; the venereal disease. Merry Wives, I. 1.

Gorbellied, *adj.* corpulent. 1 H. IV. II. 2.

Gourd, *sb.* a species of game of chance. Merry Wives, I. 3.

Gout, *sb.* a drop. Mac. II. 1.

Government, *sb.* discretion. 3 H. VI. I. 4.

Gracious, *adj.* abounding in grace Divine. Ham. I. 1.

Grained, *adj.* engrained. Ham. III. 4.

Gramercy, *int.* grand mercy, much thanks. M. of V. II. 2.

Grange, *sb.* the farmstead attached to a monastery, a solitary farm-house. Oth. I. 1.

Gratillity, *sb.* used ridiculously for 'gratuity.' Tw. N. II. 3.

Gratulate, *v.t.* to congratulate. T. A. I. 2.

Grave, *v.t.* to bury. Tim. IV. 3.

Greasily, *adv.* grossly. L's L's L. IV. 4.

Greek, *sb.* a bawd. Tw. N. IV. 1.

Green, *adj.* immature, fresh, unused. R. III. II. 2 ; Tam. of S. III. 2.

Greenly, *adv.* foolishly. Ham. IV. 5.

Greet, *v.i.* to weep. T. A. I. 2.

Grize, *sb.* a step. Tw. N. III. 1.

Grossly, *adv.* palpably. H. V. II. 2.

Groundling, *sb.* one who sits in the pit of a theatre. Ham. III. 2.

Growing, *pr. p.* accruing. Com. of E. IV. 1.

Guard, *sb.* decoration. M. for M. III. 1.

Guard, *v.t.* to decorate. M. of V. II. 2.

Guardage, *sb.* guardianship. Oth. I. 2.

Guinea-hen, *sb.* the pintado, a cant term. Oth. I. 3.

Gules, *adj.* red, a term in heraldry. Tim. IV. 3.

Gulf, *sb.* the throat. Mac. IV. 1.

Gun-stone, *sb.* a cannon ball.

Gust, *sb.* taste, relish. Tw. N. I. 3.

Gyve, *v.t.* to fetter. Oth. II. 1.

Hack, *v.i.* to become common. Merry Wives, II. 1.

Haggard, *sb.* a wild or unreclaimed hawk. Tam. of S. I. 1.

Hag-seed, *sb.* seed or offspring of a hag. Temp. I. 2.

Hair, *sb.* course, order, grain. Merry Wives, II. 3.

Halidom, *sb.* holiness, sanctification, Christian fellowship ; used as an oath, and analogous to 'By my faith.' Two Gent. IV. 2.

Hall, *sb.* an open space to dance in. R. & J. I. 5.

Hallowmas, *sb.* All Hallows' Day. Two Gent. II. 1.

Hap, *sb.* chance, fortune. Com. of E. I. 1.

Happily, *adv.* accidentally. Tam. of S. IV. 4.

Handsaw, *sb.* perhaps a corruption of Heron-shaw ; a hern. Ham. II. 2.

Hardiment, *sb.* defiance, brave deeds. 1 H. IV. I. 3.

Harlock, *sb.* charlock, wild mustard. Lear, IV. 4.

Harry, *v.t.* to annoy, harass. A. & C. III. 3.

Haught, *adj.* haughty. 3 H. VI. II. 1.

Haunt, *sb.* company. Ham. IV. 1.

Having, *sb.* property, fortune. Tw. N. III. 4.

Haviour, *sb.* behavior. Merry Wives, I. 3.

Hay, *sb.* a term in fencing. R. & J. II. 4.

Heady, *adj.* violent, headlong. Com. of E. V. 1.

Heat, *p.p. of v.t.* "to heat," heated. M. of V. I. 1.

Hebenon, *sb.* henbane. Ham. I. 5.

Heft, *sb.* a heaving. Wint. Tale, II. 1.

Heft, *p.p.* furnished with a handle : hence, metaphorically, finished off, delicately formed. Lear, II. 4.

Helm, *v.t.* to steer, manage. M. for M. III. 2.

Hence, *adv.* henceforward. 2 H. IV. V. 5.

Henchman, *sb.* a page or attendant. M. N's Dr. II. 2.

Hent, *v.t.* to seize, take. M. for M. iv. 6 ; Wint. Tale, iv. 2.

Hermit, *sb.* a beadsman, one bound to pray for another. Mac. i. 6.

Hest, *sb.* command. Temp. iii. 1.

High, *adv.* used in composition with adjectives to heighten or emphasize their signification, as, high-fantastical. Tw. N. i. 1.

Hight, *p.p.* called. L's L's L. i. 1.

Hild, *p.p.* held. Lucr. 1257.

Hilding, *sb.* a paltry fellow. Cym. ii. 3.

Hint, *sb.* suggestion. Temp. i. 2.

Hiren, *sb.* Qy. a prostitute, with a pun on the word " iron." 2 H. IV. ii. 4.

Hit, *v.i.* to agree. Lear, i. 1.

Hoise, *v.t.* to hoist, heave up on high. 2 H. VI. i. 1.

Hoist, *p.p.* hoisted. Ham. iii. 4.

Holp, *p.p.* of the *v.* to help ; helped. John, i. 1.

Home, *adv.* to the utmost. Cor. ii. 2 ; Cym. iii. 5 ; Lear, iii. 3.

Honest, *adj.* chaste. Oth. iv. 2.

Honesty, *sb.* chastity. As you Like it, iii. 3.

Honey-stalks, *sb.* the red clover. T. A. iv. 4.

Hoodman-blind, *sb.* the game now called blind-man's-buff. Ham. iii. 4.

Horn-mad, *adj.* probably, ' *harn*-mad,' that is, brain-mad. Merry Wives, i. 4.

Horologe, *sb.* a clock. Oth. ii. 3.

Hot-house, *sb.* a brothel. M. for M. ii. 1.

Hox, *v.t.* to hamstring. Wint. Tale, i. 2.

Hugger-mugger, *sb.* secresy. Ham. iv. 5.

Hull, *v.i.* to drift on the sea like a wrecked ship. H. VIII. ii. 4.

Humorous, *adj.* fitful, or, perhaps, hurried. R. & J. ii. 1.

Hunt-counter, *v.i.* to follow the scent the wrong way. 2 H. IV. i. 2.

Hunts-up, *sb.* a holla used in hunting when the game was on foot. R. & J. iii. 5.

Hurly, *sb.* noise, confusion. Tam. of S. iv. 1.

Hurtle, *v.i.* to clash. J. C. ii. 2.

Hurtling, *sb.* noise, confusion. As you Like it, iv. 3.

Husbandry, *sb.* frugality. Mac. ii. 1. Management. M. of V. iii. 4.

Huswife, *sb.* a jilt. Cor. i. 3.

Ice-brook, *sb.* an icy-cold brook. Oth. v. 2.

I'fecks, *int.* in faith, a euphemism. Wint. Tale, i. 2.

Ignomy, *sb.* ignominy. 1 H. IV. v. 4.

Image, *sb.* representation. Ham. iii. 2.

Imbare, *v.t.* to bare, lay open. H. V. i. 2.

Immediacy, *sb.* close connexion. Lear, v. 3.

Immoment, *adj.* unimportant. A. & C. v. 2.

Imp, *v.t.* to graft, to splice a falcon's broken feathers. R. II. ii. 1.

Imp, *sb.* a scion, a child. 2 H. IV. v. 5.

Impawn, *v.t.* to stake, compromise. H. V. i. 2.

Impeach, *v.t.* to bring into question. M. N's Dr. ii. 2.

Impeach, *sb.* impeachment. Com. of E. v. 1.

Impeachment, *sb.* cause of censure, hindrance. Two Gent. i. 3.

Imperceiverant, *adj.* dull of perception. Cym. iv. 1.

Impeticos, *v.t.* to pocket. Tw. N. ii. 3.

Importance, *sb.* importunity. Tw. N. v. 1.

Important, *adj.* importunate. Com. of E. v. 1 ; Lear, iv. 4.

Importing, *adj.* significant. All's Well, v. 3.

Impose, *sb.* imposition, meaning command or task imposed upon any one. Two Gent. iv. 3.

Imposition, *sb.* command. M. of V. i. 2.

Imprese, *sb.* a device with a motto. R. II. iii. 1.

Impress, *v.t.* to compel to serve. Mac. iv. 1.

Incapable, *adj.* unconscious. Ham. iv. 7.

Incarnadine, *v.t.* to dye red. Mac. ii. 2.

Incensed, *p.p.* incited, egged on. R. III. iii. 1.

Inch-meal, *sb.* by inch-meal, by portions of inches. Temp. ii. 2.

Inclining, *adj.* compliant. Oth. ii. 3.

Inclining, *sb.* inclination. Ham. ii. 2.

Inclip, *v.t.* to embrace. A. & C. ii. 7.

Include, *v.t.* conclude. Two Gent. v. 4.

Incony, *adj.* fine, delicate. L's L's L. iii. 1.

Incorrect, *adj.* ill-regulated. Ham. i. 2.

Ind, *sb.* India. Temp. ii. 2.

Indent, *v.i.* to compound or bargain. 1 H. IV. i. 3.

Index, *sb.* a preface. R. III. iv. 4 ; Ham. iii. 4.

Indifferent, *adj.* ordinary. Ham. ii. 2.

Indigest, *adj.* disordered. Son. 114.

Indite, *v.t.* to invite. R. & J. ii. 4. To convict. Ham. ii. 2.

Induction, *sb.* introduction, beginning. 1 H. IV. iii. 1.

Indurance, *sb.* delay. H. VIII. v. 1.

Infinite, *sb.* infinite power. Much Ado, ii. 3.

Ingraft, *part* of *v.* to engraff, engrafted. Oth. ii. 3.

Inhabitable, *adj.* uninhabitable. R. II. i. 1.

Inherit, *v.t.* to possess. Two Gent. iii. 2.

Inhooped, *p.p.* penned up in hoops. A. & C. ii. 3.

Inkhorn-mate, *sb.* a contemptuous term for an ecclesiastic, or man of learning. 1 H. VI. iii. 1.

Inkle, *sb.* a kind of narrow fillet or tape. Wint. Tale, iv. 3.

Inland, *adj.* civilized, well-educated. As you Like it, iii. 2.

Inly, *adj.* inward. Two Gent. ii. 7.

Inly, *adv.* inwardly. Temp. v. 1.

Inquisition, *sb.* enquiry. Temp. i. 2.

Insane, *adj.* that which causes insanity. Mac. i. 3.

Insconce, *v.t.* to arm, fortify. Com. of E. ii. 2.

Instance, *sb.* example. Tw. N. iv. 3. Information. 2 H. IV. iii. 1. Reason, proof. H. V. ii. 2 ; Merry Wives, ii. 2.

Intend, *v.i.* to pretend. Tam. of S. iv. 1.

Intending, *pr. p.* regarding. Tim. ii. 2.

Intendment, *sb.* intention. Oth. iv. 2.

Intentively, *adv.* attentively. Oth. i. 3.

Interessed, *p.p.* allied. Lear, i. 1.

Intermission, *sb.* pause, delay. Mac. iv. 3.

Intrenchment, *adj.* not capable of being cut. Mac. v. 7.

Intrinse, *adj.* intricate. Lear, ii. 2.

Intrinsicate, *adj.* intricate. A. & C. v. 2.

Invention, *sb.* imagination. Mac. iii. 1.

Inward, *sb.* an intimate friend. M. for M. iii. 2. *adj.* intimate. R. III. iii. 4.

Inwardness, *sb.* intimacy. Much Ado, iv. 1.

Irregulous, *adj.* lawless, licentious. Cym. iv. 2.

Iteration, *sb.* reiteration. 1 H. IV. i. 2.

Jack, *sb.* a mean fellow. R. III. i. 3.

Jack-a-lent, *sb.* a puppet thrown at in Lent. Merry Wives, v. 5.

Jack guardant, *sb.* a jack in office. Cor. v. 2.

Jade, *v.t.* to whip, to treat with contempt. H. VIII. iii. 2 ; A. & C. iii. 1.

Jar, *sb.* the ticking of a clock. Wint. Tale, I. 2.

Jar, *v.i.* to tick as a clock. R. II. v. 5.

Jaunce, *v.i.* to prance. R. II. v. 5.

Jess, *sb.* a strap of leather attached to the talons of a hawk, by which it is held on the fist. Oth. III. 3.

Jest, *v.i.* to tilt in a tournament. R. II. I. 3.

Jet, *v.i.* to strut. Tw. N. II. 5.

Journal, *adj.* daily. Cym. IV. 2.

Jovial, *adj.* appertaining to Jove. Cym. v. 4.

Judicious, *adj.* critical. Merry Wives, I. 3.

Jump, *v.i.* to agree. 1 H. IV. I. 2. *v.t.* to hazard. Cym. v. 4.

Jump, *sb.* hazard. A. & C. III. 8.

Jump, *adv.* exactly, nicely. Oth. III. 3.

Justicer, *sb.* a judge, magistrate. Lear, III. 6.

Jut, *v.i.* to encroach. R. III. II. 4.

Jutty, *sb.* a projection. Mac. I. 6.

Jutty, *v.i.* to jut out beyond. H. V. III. 1.

Juvenal, *sb.* youth, young man. L's L's L. I. 2.

Kam, *adj.* crooked. Cor. III. 1.

Kecksy, *sb.* hemlock. H. V. v. 2.

Keech, *sb.* a lump of tallow. H. VIII. I. 1.

Keel, *v.t.* to skim. L's L's L. v. 2.

Keep, *v.r.* to restrain. Two Gent. IV. 4.

Keisar, *sb.* Cæsar, Emperor. Merry Wives, I. 3.

Kern, *sb.* the rude foot soldiers of the Irish. Mac. I. 2.

Kibe, *sb.* a chilblain. Temp. II. 1.

Kickshaw, *sb.* a made dish. 2 H. IV. v. 1.

Kicksy wicksy, *sb.* a wife, used in disdain. All's Well, II. 3.

Kiln-hole, *sb.* the ash-hole under a kiln. Merry Wives, IV. 2.

Kind, *sb.* nature. A. & C. v. 2 ; T. A. II. 1.

Kindle, *v.i.* to bring forth young ; used only of beasts. As you Like it, III. 2.

Kindless, *adj.* unnatural. Ham. II. 2.

Kindly, *adj.* natural. Much Ado, IV. 1.

Kirtle, *sb.* a gown. 2 H. IV. II. 4.

Knap, *v.t.* to snap, crack. M. of V. III. 1.

Knave, *sb.* a boy. J. C. IV. 3. A serving-man. All's Well, II. 4.

Knot, *sb.* a figure in garden beds. R. II. III. 4.

Know, *v.t.* to acknowledge. Mac. II. 2.

Labras, *sb.* lips. Merry Wives, I. 1.

Laced-mutton, *sb.* a courtezan. Two Gent. I. 1.

Lag, *sb.* the lowest of the people. T. A. III. 6.

Lag, *adv.* late, behindhand. R. III. II. 1 ; Lear, I. 2.

Lakin, *n.* ladykin, little lady, an endearing term applied to the Virgin Mary in the oath, " By our lakin." Temp. III. 3.

Land-damn, *v.t.* perhaps to extirpate ; Hanmer thinks it means to kill by stopping the urine. Wint. Tale, II. 1.

Lapsed, *p.p.* taken, apprehended. Tw. N. III. 3.

Large, *adj.* licentious, free. Much Ado, IV. 1.

Largess, *sb.* a present. Tam. of S. I. 2.

Lass-lorn, *adj.* deserted by a mistress. Temp. IV. 1.

Latch, *v.t.* to smear. M. N's Dr. III. 2. To catch. Mac. IV. 3.

Lated, *p.p.* belated. A. & C. III. 9.

Latten, *adj.* made of brass. Merry Wives, I. 1.

Laund, *sb.* lawn. 3 H. VI. III. 1.

Lavolta, *sb.* a dance. H. V. III. 5.

Lay, *sb.* wager. Oth. II. 3.

League, *sb.* besieging army. All's Well, III. 6.

Leasing, *sb.* lying. Tw. N. I. 5.

Leather-coats, *sb.* a kind of apple. 2 H. IV. v. 3.

Leech, *sb.* a physician. T. A. v. 4.

Leer, *sb.* countenance, complexion. As you Like it, IV. 1 ; T. A. IV. 2.

Leet, *sb.* a manor court. Oth. III. 3.

Lege, *v.t.* to allege. Tam. of S. I. 2.

Legerity, *sb.* lightness. H. V. IV. 1.

Leiger, *sb.* an ambassador resident abroad. M. for M. II. 1 ; Cym. I. 6.

Leman, *sb.* a lover or mistress. 2 H. IV. v. 3.

Lenten, *adj.* meagre. Ham. II. 1. That which may be eaten in Lent. R. & J. II. 4.

L'envoy, *sb.* the farewell or moral at the end of a tale or poem. L's L's L. III. 1.

Let, *v.i.* to hinder. Tw. N. v. 1. *v.t.* to hinder. Ham. I. 2.

Let, *sb.* hindrance. H. V. v. 2.

Lethe, *sb.* death. J. C. III. 1.

Level, *v.i.* to aim. M. of V. I. 2 ; R. III. IV. 4.

Level, *sb.* that which is aimed at. H. VIII. I. 2.

Lewd, *adj.* ignorant, foolish. R. III. I. 3.

Lewdly, *adv.* wickedly. 2 H. VI. II. 1.

Lewdster, *sb.* a lewd person. Merry Wives, v. 3.

Libbard, *sb.* a leopard. L's L's L. v. 2.

Liberal, *adj.* licentious. Two Gent. III. 1 ; Oth. II. 1.

Liberty, *sb.* libertinism. T. A. IV. 1.

License, *sb.* licentiousness. M. for M. III. 2.

Lief, *adj.* dear. 2 H. VI. III. 1.

Lifter, *sb.* a thief. T. & Cr. I. 2.

Light o' love, *sb.* a tune so called. Two Gent. I. 2.

Lightly, *adv.* easily, generally. Com. of E. IV. 4 ; R. III. III. 1.

Like, *v.t.* to please. R. III. III. 4 ; Lear, II. 2.

Like, *v.t.* to liken, compare. 1 H. VI. IV. 6.

Like, *adj.* likely. M. for M. v. 1.

Likelihood, *sb.* promise, appearance. R. III. III. 4.

Liking, *sb.* condition. 1 H. IV. III. 3.

Limbeck, *sb.* an alembick, a still. Mac. I. 7.

Limbo, or Limbo patrum, *sb.* the place where good men under the Old Test. were believed to be imprisoned till released by Christ after his crucifixion. All's Well, v. 3 ; H. VIII. v. 3.

Lime, *sb.* bird-lime. Temp. IV. 1.

Lime, *v.t.* to entangle as with bird-lime. Tw. N. III. 4. To smear with bird-lime. 2 H. VI. I. 3. To mix lime with beer or other liquor. Merry Wives, I. 3.

Limn, *v.t.* to draw. As you Like it, II. 7.

Line, *v.t.* to cover on the inside. Cym. III. 3. To strengthen by inner works. 1 H. IV. II. 3 ; 2 H. IV. I. 3.

Linstock, *sb.* a staff with a match at the end of it used by gunners in firing cannon. H. V. III. Chorus.

List, *sb.* a margin, hence a bound or enclosure. Tw. N. III. 1 ; 1 H. IV. IV. 1.

Lither, *adj.* lazy. 1 H. VI. IV. 7.

Little, *sb.* miniature. Ham. II. 2.

Livelihood, *sb.* appearance of life. All's Well, I. 1.

Livery, *sb.* a law phrase, signifying the act of delivering a freehold into the possession of the heir or purchaser. R. II. II. 3.

Living, *adj.* lively, convincing. Oth. III. 3.

Loach, *sb.* a fish so called. 1 H. IV. II. 1.

Lob, *sb.* a looby. M. N's Dr. II. 1.

Lockram, *sb.* a sort of coarse linen. Cor. II. 1.

Lode-star, *sb.* the leading-star, pole-star. M. N's Dr. I. 1.

Loffe, *v.i.* to laugh. M. N's Dr. II. 1.

Loggats, *sb.* the game called nine-pins. Ham. v. 1.

Longly, *adv.* longingly. Tam. of S. I. 1.

Loof, *v.t.* to luff, bring a vessel up to the wind. A. & C. III. 8.

Loon, *sb.* a low contemptible fellow. Mac. v. 3.

Lot, *sb.* a prize in a lottery. Cor. v. 2.

Lottery, *sb.* that which falls to a man by lot. A. & C. II. 2.

Lowt, *sb.* a clown. Cor. III. 2.

Lowt, *v.t.* to treat one as a lowt, with contempt. 1 H. VI. IV. 3.

Lozel, *sb.* a spendthrift. Wint. Tale, II. 3.

Lubber, *sb.* a leopard. 2 H. IV. II. 1.

Luce, *n.* the pike or jack, a fresh-water fish. Merry Wives, I. 1.

Lumpish, *adj.* dull, dejected. Two Gent. III. 2.

Lunes, *sb.* fits of lunacy. Wint. Tale, II. 2.

Lurch, *v.t.* to defeat, to win. Cor. II. 2.

Lurch, *v.i.* to shift, to play tricks. Merry Wives, II. 2.

Lure, *sb.* a thing stuffed to resemble a bird with which the falconer allures a hawk. Tam. of S. IV. 1.

Lush, *adj.* juicy, luxuriant. Temp. II. 1.

Lustig, *adj.* lusty, cheerful. All's Well, II. 3.

Luxurious, *adj.* lascivious. Much Ado, IV. 1.

Luxury, *sb.* lust. Lear, IV. 6.

Lym, *sb.* a limer or slow hound. Lear, III. 6.

Made, *p.p.* having his fortune made. Tw. N. III. 4.

Magnifico, *sb.* the chief magistrate at Venice. Oth. I. 2.

Magot-pie, *sb.* a magpie, a pie which feeds on magots. Mac. III. 4.

Mailed, *p.p.* covered as with a coat of mail. 2 H. VI. II. 4.

Main-course, *sb.* a sea-term. Temp. I. 1.

Make, *v.t.* to do up, bar. Com. of E. III. 1. To do. L's L's L. IV. 3 ; R. III. I. 3.

Malkin, *sb.* a familiar name for Mary ; hence a servant wench. Cor. II. 1.

Mallecho, *sb.* mischief. Ham. III. 2.

Mammering, *pr. p.* hesitating. Oth. III. 3.

Mammets, *sb.* a woman's breasts. 1 H. IV. II. 3. A doll. R. & J. III. 5.

Mammock, *v.t.* to break, tear. Cor. I. 3.

Man, *v.t.* to tame a hawk. Tam. of S. IV. 1.

Manage, *sb.* management. Temp. I. 2.

Mandragora, *sb.* } a plant of soporiferous quality, supposed to resemble a man. Oth. III. 3 ; 2 H. IV. I. 2.

Mandrake, *sb.* }

Mankind, *adj.* having a masculine nature. Wint. Tale, II. 3.

Marches, *sb.* frontiers, borders. H. V. I. 2.

Marchpane, *sb.* a kind of sweet biscuit. R. & J. I. 5.

Margent, *sb.* margin. L's L's L. II. 1.

Marry trap, *int.* an oath. Merry Wives, I. 1.

Martlemas, *sb.* the Feast of St. Martin, which occurs on the 11th of Nov. when the fine weather generally ends ; hence applied to an old man. 2 H. IV. II. 2.

Match, *sb.* an appointment. 1 H. IV. I. 2.

Mate, *v.t.* to confound, dismay. Mac. v. 1.

Meacock, *adj.* tame, cowardly. Tam. of S. II. 1.

Mealed, *p.p.* mingled. M. for M. IV. 2.

Mean, *sb.* instrument used to promote an end. Two Gent. IV. 4.

Mean, *sb.* the tenor part in a harmony. Two Gent. I. 2.

Mean, *sb.* opportunity, power. H. VIII. v. 2.

Measure, *sb.* reach. Two Gent. v. 4. A stately dance. Much Ado, II. 1.

Meazel, *sb.* a leper, spoken in contempt of a mean person. Cor. III. 2.

Medal, *sb.* a portrait in a locket. Wint. Tale, I. 2.

Medicine, *sb.* a physician. All's Well, II. 1.

Meed, *sb.* reward, hire. Two Gent. II. 4. Merit. 3 H. VI. II. 1.

Mehercle, *int.* by Hercules. L's L's L. IV. 2.

Meiny, *sb.* retinue. Lear, II. 4.

Mell, *v.i.* to mix, to meddle. All's Well, IV. 3.

Memorize, *v.t.* to cause to be remembered. Mac. I. 2.

Mephistophilus, *sb.* the name of a familiar spirit. Merry Wives, I. 1.

Mercatante, *sb.* (Italian), a foreign trader. Tam. of S. IV. 2.

Merely, *adv.* simply, absolutely. Temp. I. 1.

Mess, *sb.* a company of four. L's L's L. IV. 3 ; v. 2.

Metaphysical, *adj.* supernatural. Mac. I. 5.

Mete-yard, *sb.* measuring-wand. Tam. of S. IV. 3.

Mew up, *v.t.* to confine. R. III. I. 1.

Micher, *sb.* a truant. 1 H. IV. II. 4.

Mickle, *adj.* much. Com. of E. III. 1.

Mill-sixpence, *sb.* a milled sixpence. Merry Wives, I. 1.

Mince, *v.t.* to do any thing affectedly. H. V. v. 2.

Mincing, *adj.* affected. 1 H. IV. III. 1.

Miscreate, *p.p.* illegitimate. H. V. I. 2.

Misdoubt, *v.t.* to suspect. 3 H. VI. v. 6.

Misery, *sb.* avarice. Cor. II. 2.

Misprise, *v.t.* to despise. As you Like it, I. 1. To mistake. M. N's Dr. III. 2.

Misprision, *sb.* mistake. Much Ado, IV. 1.

Missive, *sb.* messenger. A. & C. II. 2.

Mistempered, *adj.* angry. John, v. 1.

Misthink, *v.t.* to think ill of. 3 H. VI. 5.

Mistress, *sb.* the jack in bowling. T. & Cr. III. 2.

Mobled, *p.p.* muffled. Ham. II. 2.

Modern, *adj.* commonplace. John, III. 4.

Module, *sb.* a model, image. John, v. 7.

Moe, *adj.* and *adv.* more. Of frequent occurrence.

Moiety, *sb.* a portion. Lear, I. 1.

Mome, *sb.* a stupid person. Com. of E. III. 1.

Momentany, *adj.* momentary. M. N's Dr. I. 1.

Months-mind, *sb.* a monthly commemoration of the dead, but used ludicrously to mean a great mind or strong desire. Two Gent. I. 2.

Mood, *sb.* anger. Two Gent. IV. 1.

Moon-calf, *sb.* a nick-name applied to Caliban. Temp. II. 2 ; III. 2.

Moonish, *adj.* inconstant. As you Like it, III. 2.

Mop, *sb.* nod. Temp. III. 3.

Morisco, *sb.* a Moor. 2 H. VI. III. 1.

Morris-pike, *sb.* Moorish-pike. Com. of E. IV. 3.

Mort, *sb.* death, applied to animals of the chase. Wint. Tale, I. 2.

Mort-du-vinaigre, *int.* (French), a ridiculous oath. All's Well, II. 3.

Mortal, *adj.* fatal, deadly. Oth. v. 2. Murderous. Mac. I. 5.

Mortified, *p.p.* ascetic. Mac. v. 2.

Mose, *v.i.* a doubtful word, applied to some disease in a horse. Tam. of S. III. 2.

Motion, *sb.* solicitation. Com. of E. I. 1. Emotion. Oth. I. 2.

Motion, *sb.* a puppet. Two Gent. II. 1.

Motive, *sb.* one who moves. All's Well, IV. 4. That which moves. T. & Cr. IV. 5.

Motley, *adj.* used as *sb.* the many-colored coat of a fool. As you Like it, II. 7. A fool. Ibid. III. 3.

Motley-minded, *adj.* foolish. As you Like it, v. 4.

Mouse-hunt, *sb.* a weasel. R. & J. IV. 4.

Mow, *v.i.* to make grimaces. Temp. II. 2.

Moy, *sb.* a coin, probably a moidore. H. V. IV. 4.

Much, *int.* significant of contempt. 2 H. IV. II. 4.

Much, *adj.* used ironically. As you Like it, IV. 3.

Mure, *sb.* a wall. 2 H. IV. IV. 4.

Must, *sb.* a scramble. A. & C. III. 11.

Mutine, *v.i.* to mutiny. Ham. III. 4.

Mutine, *sb.* a mutineer. Ham. v. 2.

Napkin, *sb.* a handkerchief. As you Like it, IV. 3.

Natural, *sb.* an idiot. Temp. III. 2.

Nayward, *adv.* towards denial. Wint. Tale, II. 1.

Nayword, *sb.* a catch-word, by-word. Merry Wives, II. 2.

Neb, *sb.* the beak. Wint. Tale, I. 2.

Neeld, *sb.* a needle. M. N's Dr. III. 2.

Neif, *sb.* hand. M. N's Dr. IV. 1.

Nephew, *sb.* a grandson. Oth. I. 1.

Nether-stocks, *sb.* stockings. Lear, II. 4.

Next, *adj.* nearest. 1 H. IV. III. 1.

Nice, *adj.* foolish. Tam. of S. III. 1.

Nick, *sb.* score or reckoning. Two Gent. IV. 2.

Nick, *v.t.* to brand with folly. A. & C. III. 11.

Nighted, *p.p.* black as night. Ham. I. 2.

Night-rule, *sb.* nightly solemnity. M. N's Dr. III. 2.

Nine men's morris, *sb.* a place set apart for a Moorish dance by nine men. M. N's Dr. II. 2.

Ninny, *sb.* a fool, jester. Temp. III. 2.

Nobility, *sb.* nobleness. Ham. I. 2.

Noble, *sb.* a coin, worth 6*s.* 8*d.* R. II. I. 1.

Noddy, *sb.* a dolt. Two Gent. I. 1.

Nonce, *sb.* for the nonce, corrupted from 'for then once,' for the occasion. 1 H. IV. I. 2.

Nook-shotten, *adj.* indented with bays and creeks. H. V. III. 5.

Nourish, *sb.* a nurse. 1 H. VI. I. 1.

Novum, *sb.* a game at dice. L's L's L. v. 2.

Nowl, *sb.* head. M. N's Dr. III. 2.

Nuthook, *sb.* a hook for pulling down nuts, hence a thief. Merry Wives, I. 1.

O, *sb.* a circle. M. N's Dr. III. 2.

Oar, *v.t.* to row as with oars. Temp. II. 1.

Obsequious, *adj.* behaving as becomes one who attends funeral obsequies. Ham. I. 2.

Obsequiously, *adv.* funereally. R. III. I. 2.

Obstacle, *adj.* ridiculously used for 'obstinate.' 1 H. VI. v. 4.

Occupation, *sb.* persons occupied in business. Cor. IV. 6.

Occurent, *sb.* an incident. Ham. v. 2.

Od's body, *interj.* 1 H. IV.
II. 1.
Od's heartlings. Merry Wives, III. 4.
Od's pittikins. Cym. IV. 2.
Od's plessed will. Merry Wives, I. 1.
} 'Od's in these and all similar exclamations is a euphemism for 'God's.'

Oeilliad, *sb.* an amorous glance. Merry Wives, I. 3.

O'erparted, *p.p.* having too important a part to act. L's L's L. v. 2.

O'er-raught, *p.p.* overreached. Com. of E. I. 2. Overtasked. Ham. III. 1.

Offering, *p.p.* challenging. 1 H. IV. IV. 1.

Office, *sb.* benefit, kindness. All's Well, IV. 4; use, function. H. V. II. 2.

Old, *adj.* a cant term for great, as we say fine, or pretty. Merry Wives, I. 4; Mac. II. 3.

Once, *adv.* some time. Merry Wives, III. 4.

Oneyer, *sb.* a banker. 1 H. IV. II. 1. A doubtful word.

Ope, *adv.* open. Com. of E. III. 1.

Ope, *v.i.* to open. 3 H. VI. II. 3. *v.t.* to open. M. of V. I. 1.

Open, *adj.* plain. M. for M. II. 1. Public. H. VIII. II. 1.

Open, *v.i.* to give tongue as a hound. Merry Wives, IV. 2.

Operant, *adj.* active. Tim. IV. 3.

Opinioned, *p.p.* used ridiculously for pinioned. Much Ado, IV. 2.

Opposite, *sb.* adversary. Tw. N. III. 4.

Opposition, *sb.* combat. Cym. IV. 1.

Or, *adv.* before. Mac. IV. 3.

Order, *sb.* measures. Com. of E. v. 1; H. V. IV. 5.

Ordinance, *sb.* rank, order. Cor. III. 2.

Orgulous, *adj.* proud. Prol. to T. & Cr.

Ort, *sb.* leaving, refuse. Tim. IV. 3.

Ostent, *sb.* show, appearance. M. of V. II. 2.

Ostentation, *sb.* show, appearance. Much Ado, IV. 1; Cor. I. 6.

Ounce, *sb.* a beast of prey of the tiger kind. M. N's Dr. II. 3.

Ouphe, *sb.* a fairy. Merry Wives, IV. 4.

Ousel-cock, *sb.* the blackbird. M. N's Dr. III. 1.

Out, *adv.* all out, fully. Temp. I. 2.

Out-look, *v.t.* to face down. John, v. 2.

Outward, *adj.* not in the secret of affairs. All's Well, III. 1.

Outward, *sb.* outside. Cym. I. 1.

Owe, *v.t.* to own. Temp. I. 1.

Pack, *v.t.* to practice unlawful confederacy. Much Ado, v. 1; Tam. of S. v. 1.

Pack, *sb.* a number of people confederated. R. III. III. 3.

Paddock, *sb.* a toad. Mac. I. 1.

Paid, *p.p.* punished. Cym. v. 4.

Palabras, *sb.* words, a cant term, from the Spanish. Much Ado, III. 5.

Pale, *v.t.* to enclose. A. & C. II. 7; H. V. v. Ch.

Pall, *v.t.* to wrap as with a pall. Mac. I. 5.

Palled, *p.p.* impaired. A. & C. II. 7.

Palmer, *sb.* one who bears a palm-branch, in token of having made a pilgrimage to Palestine. R. & J. I. 5.

Palmy, *adj.* victorious. Ham. I. 1.

Parcelled, *p.p.* belonging to individuals. R. III. II. 2.

Pard, *sb.* the leopard. Temp. IV. 1.

Paritor, *sb.* an apparitor. L's L's L. III. 1.

Parle, *sb.* talk. Two Gent. I. 2.

Parlous, *adj.* perilous. As you Like it, III. 2 ; keen, shrewd. R. III. III. 1.

Parted, *p.p.* endowed, gifted. T. & Cr. III. 3.

Partizan, *sb.* a pike. R. & J. I. 1.

Pash, *sb.* the face. Wint. Tale, I. 2.

Pash, *v.t.* to strike violently, to bruise, crush. T. & Cr. II. 3.

Pass, *v.i.* to practice. Tw. N. III. 1 ; Lear, III. 7. To surpass expectation. Merry Wives, IV. 2.

Passant, *pr. p.* a term of heraldry, applied to animals represented on the shield as passing by at a trot. Merry Wives, I. 1.

Passing, *adv.* surpassingly, exceedingly. M. N's Dr. II. 1.

Passion, *v.i.* to have feelings. Temp. V. 1.

Passionate, *v.t.* to suffer. T. A. III. 2.

Passy-measure, *sb.* a kind of dance. Tw. N. V. 1.

Pastry, *sb.* the room where pastry was made. R. & J. IV. 4.

Patch, *sb.* a mean fellow. Temp. III. 2.

Patched, *p.p.* dressed in motley. M. N's Dr. IV. 1.

Patchery, *sb.* trickery. T. & Cr. II. 3.

Path, *v.i.* to walk. J. C. II. 1.

Pathetical, *adj.* affected, hypocritical. As you Like it, IV. 1.

Patient, *v.r.* to make patient, to compose. T. A. I. 2.

Patine, *sb.* the metal disc on which the bread is placed in the administration of the Eucharist. M. of V. V. 1.

Pattern, *v.t.* to give an example of. Wint. Tale, III. 2. Afford a pattern for. M. for M. II. 1.

Pauca verba, few words. Merry Wives, I. 1.

Paucas, *adj.* few, a cant word. Ind. to Tam. of S.

Pavin, *sb.* a dance. Tw. N. V. 1.

Pax, *sb.* a small image of Christ. H. V. III. 6.

Pay, *v.t.* to despatch. 1 H. IV. II. 4.

Peat, *sb.* a term of endearment for a child. Tam. of S. I. 1.

Pedascule, *sb.* a pedant, schoolmaster. Tam. of S. III. 1.

Peer, *v.i.* to peep out. R. & J. I. 1.

Peize, *v.t.* to balance, weigh down. John, II. 2 ; R. III. V. 3.

Pelting, *adj.* paltry. M. for M. II. 2.

Perdu, *adj.* lost. Lear, IV. 7.

Perdurable, *adj.* durable. H. V. IV. 5.

Perdy, *int.* a euphemism for Par Dieu. Com. of E. IV. 4.

Perfect, *adj.* certain. Wint. Tale, III. 3.

Perfect, *v.t.* to inform perfectly. M. for M. IV. 3.

Periapts, *sb.* charms worn round the neck. 1 H. VI. V. 3.

Perjure, *sb.* a perjured person. L's L's L. IV. 3.

Persever, *v.* to persevere. Two Gent. III. 2.

Perspective, *sb.* a telescope, or some sort of optical glass. Tw. N. V. 1.

Pew-fellow, *sb.* a comrade. R. III. IV. 4.

Pheeze, *v.t.* to comb, fleece, curry. Ind. to Tam. of S. ; T. & Cr. II. 3.

Pia-mater, *sb.* the membrane covering the brain, the brain itself. Tw. N. I. 5.

Pick, *v.t.* to pitch, throw. H. VIII. V. 3.

Picked, *adj.* chosen, selected. John, I. 1.

Pickers (and stealers), *sb.* the fingers, used ridiculously. Ham. III. 2.

Picking, *adj.* insignificant. 2 H. IV. I. 1.

Pickt-hatch, *sb.* a place noted for brothels. Merry Wives, II. 2.

Pied, *adj.* motley-coated, wearing the motley coat of a jester. Temp. III. 2.

Pieled, *p.p.* shaven. 1 H. VI. I. 3.

Pight, *p.p.* pitched. T. & Cr. V. 10.

Pilcher, *sb.* a scabbard. R. & J. III. 1.

Pill, *v.i.* to pillage. Tim. IV. 1.

Pin, *sb.* a malady of the eye. Lear, III. 4. The centre of a target. L's L's L. IV. 1 ; R. & J. II. 4.

Pinfold, *sb.* a pound, a place to confine lost cattle. Two Gent. I. 1.

Pioned, *p.p.* digged. Temp. III. 3.

Placket, *sb.* a petticoat-front. Wint. Tale, IV. 3.

Plain song, *sb.* a simple air. H. V. III. 2.

Plaited, *p.p.* intricate. Lear, I. 1.

Planched, *adj.* made of boards. M. for M. IV. 1.

Plantation, *sb.* colonizing, planting a colony. Temp. II. 1.

Plausive, *adj.* plausible. All's Well, I. 2.

Pleached, *adj.* interwoven. Much Ado, I. 2.

Point, *sb.* a lace furnished with a tag by which the breeches were held up. 1 H. IV. II. 4.

Point-de-vice, *adj.* derived from the French, faultless. Tw. N. II. 5.

Poise, *sb.* balance. M. for M. II. 4. Doubt. Lear, II. 1.

Polled, *p.p.* bare. Cor. IV. 5.

Pomander, *sb.* a perfumed ball. Wint. Tale, IV. 4.

Pomewater, *sb.* a kind of apple. L's L's L. IV. 2.

Poor-john, *sb.* a herring. Temp. II. 2.

Popinjay, *sb.* a parrot. 1 H. IV. I. 3.

Port, *sb.* pomp, state. Tam. of S. I. 1.

Port, *sb.* a gate. 2 H. IV. IV. 4.

Portable, *adj.* bearable. Mac. IV. 3.

Portance, *sb.* conduct, behavior. Cor. II. 3.

Possess, *v.t.* to inform. Tw. N. II. 3.

Potch, *v.i.* to push violently. Cor. I. 10.

Potent, *sb.* a potentate. John, II. 2.

Pouncet-box, *sb.* a box for holding perfumes. 1 H. IV. I. 3.

Power, *sb.* forces, army. 2 H. IV. I. 1.

Practice, *sb.* wicked stratagem. Tw. N. V. 1.

Practisant, *sb.* a confederate. 1 H. VI. III. 2.

Prank, *v.t.* to dress up. Wint. Tale, IV. 3 ; Cor. III. 1.

Precept, *sb.* a justice's summons. 2 H. IV. V. 1.

Preciously, *adv.* in business of great importance. Temp. I. 2.

Pregnancy, *sb.* fertility of invention. 2 H. IV. I. 2.

Pregnant, *adj.* fertile of invention. M. for M. I. 1. Ready. Ham. III. 2. Obvious. M. for M. II. 1.

Prenominate, *v.t.* to name beforehand, to prophesy. T. & Cr. IV. 5.

Pre-ordinance, *sb.* old-established law. J. C. III. 1.

Presence, *sb.* the presence-chamber. H. VIII. III. 1. High bearing. M. of V. III. 2.

Prest, *adj.* ready. M. of V. I. 1.

Pretence, *sb.* design. Wint. Tale, III. 2.

Pretend, *v.t.* to portend. 1 H. VI. IV. 1. To intend. Mac. II. 4.

Prevent, *v.t.* to anticipate. J. C. V. 1.

Prick, *sb.* the mark denoting the hour on a dial. R. & J. II. 4.

Prick, *v.t.* to incite. Tam. of S. III. 2. To choose by pricking a hole with a pin opposite the name. J. C. III. 1.

Prick-song, *sb.* music sung in parts by note. R. & J. II. 4.

Pricket, *sb.* a stag of two years. L's L's L. IV. 2.

Pride, *sb.* heat. Oth. III. 3.

Prig, *v.t.* to steal. Wint. Tale, IV. 2.

Prime, *adj.* rank, lecherous. Oth. III. 3.

Primer, *adj.* more-important. H. VIII. I. 2.

Primero, *sb.* a game at cards. H. VIII. V. 1.

Principality, *sb.* that which holds the highest place. Two Gent. II. 4.

Princox, *sb.* a coxcomb. R. & J. I. 5.

Priser, *sb.* a prize-fighter. As you Like it, II. 3.

Procure, *v.t.* to bring. R. & J. III. 5.

Proface, *interj.* much good may it do you. 2 H. IV. V. 3.

Profane, *adj.* outspoken. Oth. II. 1.

Progress, *sb.* a royal ceremonial journey. Ham. I. 3.

Project, *v.t.* to shape or contrive. A. & C. V. 2.

Prompture, *sb.* suggestion. M. for M. II. 4.

Prone, *adj.* ready, willing. Cym. V. 4 ; M. for M. I. 3.

Proof, *sb.* strength of manhood. Much Ado, IV. 1.

Propagate, *v.t.* to advance, to forward. Tim. I. 1.

Propagation, *sb.* obtaining. M. for M. I. 3.

Proper-false, *sb.* natural falsehood. Tw. N. II. 2.

Propertied, *p.p.* endowed with the properties of. A. & C. V. 2.

Properties, *sb.* scenes, dresses, &c. used in a theatre. Merry Wives, IV. 4.

Property, *v.t.* to take possession of. John, V. 2.

Propose, *v.t.* to suppose, for the sake of argument. 2 H. IV. V. 2. To converse. Much Ado, II. 1.

Propose, *sb.* conversation. Much Ado, III. 1.

Prorogue, *v.t.* to defer. R. & J. II. 2.

Provand, *sb.* provender. Cor. II. 1.

Provision, *sb.* forecast. Temp. I. 2.

Pucelle, *sb.* a virgin, the name given to Joan of Arc. 1 H. VI. V. 4.

Pudency, *sb.* modesty. Cym. II. 5.

Pugging, *adj.* thieving. Wint. Tale, IV. 2.

Pun, *v.t.* to pound. T. & Cr. II. 1.

Purchase, *v.t.* to acquire, win. As you Like it, III. 2.

Purchase, *sb.* gain, winnings. 1 H. IV. II. 1.

Put, *v.t.* to compel. M. for M. I. 1.

Putter-on, *sb.* an instigator. H. VIII. I. 2.

Putter-out, *sb.* one who lends money at interest. Temp. III. 3.

Putting-on, *sb.* instigation. M. for M. IV. 2.

Puttock, *sb.* a kite. Cym. I. 2.

Quail, *v.i.* to faint, be languid, be afraid. As you Like it, II. 2. *v.t.* to cause to quail. A. & C. V. 2.

Quaint, *adj.* curiously beautiful. Temp. I. 2.

Quake, *v.t.* to cause to quake or tremble. Cor. I. 9.

Qualify, *v.t.* to moderate. Much Ado, V. 4.

Quality, *sb.* those of the same nature. Temp. I. 2. Rank or condition. M. for M. II. 1 ; 2 H. IV. V. 2.

Quarrel, *sb.* a suit, cause. 2 H. VI. III. 2.

Quarry, *sb.* game, a heap of game. Ham. V. 2 ; Cor. I. 1.

Quart d'écu, *sb.* a quarter crown. All's Well, IV. 3.

Quarter, *sb.* the post allotted to a soldier. Tim. V. 5.

Quat, *sb.* a pimple ; used in contempt of a person. Oth. V. 1.

Queasy, *adj.* squeamish, unsettled. Much Ado, II. 1 ; Lear, II. 1.

Quell, *sb.* murder. Mac. I. 7.

Quench, *v.i.* to grow cool. Cym. I. 6.

Quern, *sb.* a hand-mill. M. N's Dr. II. 1.

Quest, *sb.* enquiry, search, inquest, jury. M. for M. IV. 1 ; R. III. I. 4 ; Ham. V. 1.

Questrist, *sb.* one who goes in search of another. Lear, III. 7.

Quick, *adj.* so far gone in pregnancy that the child is alive. L's L's L. V. 2.

Quicken, *v.i.* to come to life. Lear, III. 7.

Quiddit, } *sb.* a subtle question. Ham. V. 1 ;
Quiddity, } 1 H. IV. I. 2.

Quillet, *sb.* quidlibet, a subtle case in law. L's L's L. IV. 3.

Quintain, *sb.* a post for tilting at. As you Like it, I. 2.

Quip, *sb.* sharp jest, a taunt. Much Ado, II. 3.

Quire, *v.i.* to sing in concert. M. of V. v. 1.

Quit, *v.i.* to requite, respond. Lear, III. 7 ; Ham. V. 2.

Quit, *v.t.* past tense of the verb to quit, quitted. Cym. I. 1.

Quitance, *sb.* requital. H. V. II. 2.

Quiver, *adj.* active. 2 H. IV. III. 2.

Quote, *v.t.* to note. R. & J. I. 4.

Rabato, *sb.* a ruff. Much Ado, III. 4.

Rabbit-sucker, *sb.* a weasel. 1 H. IV. II. 4.

Race, *sb.* breed ; inherited nature. Temp. I. 2.

Rack, *sb.* wreck. Temp. IV. 1.

Rack, *v.t.* to enhance the price of anything. Much Ado, IV. 1 ; Cor. V. 1. *v.i.* to drive as clouds. 3 H. VI. II. 1.

Rag, *sb.* a term of contempt applied to persons. Tim. IV. 3.

Rake, *v.t.* to cover. Lear, IV. 6.

Rapt, *p.p.* transported with emotion. Mac. I. 3.

Rapture, *sb.* a fit. Cor. II. 1.

Rascal, *sb.* a lean deer. J. C. IV. 3.

Rash, *adj.* quick, violent. Wint. Tale, I. 2.

Rate, *sb.* opinion, judgment. Temp. II. 1.

Rate, *v.t.* to assign, to value. A. & C. III. 6 ; Cym. I. 5. To scold. M. of V. I. 3.

Ratolorum, a ludicrous mistake for Rotulorum. Merry Wives, I. 1.

Raught, past tense of *v.* to reach. H. V. IV. 6.

Ravin, *adj.* ravenous. All's Well, III. 2.

Ravin, *v.t.* to devour. Mac. II. 4.

Rawly, *adv.* inadequately. H. V. IV. 1.

Rawness, *sb.* unprovided state. Mac. IV. 3.

Rayed, *p.p.* arrayed, served. Tam. of S. IV. 1.

Razed, *p.p.* slashed. Ham. III. 2.

Rear-mouse, *sb.* the bat. M. N's Dr. II. 3.

Rebate, *v.t.* to deprive of keenness. M. for M. I. 5.

Rebeck, *sb.* a three-stringed fiddle. R. & J. IV. 5.

Receipt, *sb.* money received. R. II. I. 1.

Receiving, *sb.* capacity. Tw. N. III. 1.

Recheat, *sb.* a point of the chase to call back the hounds. Much Ado, I. 1.

Record, *v.t.* to sing. Two Gent. V. 4.

Recorder, *sb.* a flute. Ham. III. 2.

Recure, *v.t.* to cure, recover. R. III. III.

Red-lattice, *adj.* suitable to an ale-house, because ale-houses had commonly red lattices. Merry Wives, II. 2.

Red-plague, *sb.* erysipelas. Temp. I. 2.

Reduce, *v.t.* to bring back. R. III. v. 4.

Reechy, *adj.* smoky, dirty. Cor. II. 1.

Refell, *v.t.* to refute. M. for M. v. 1.

Refer, *v.r.* to reserve to. M. for M. III. 1.

Regiment, *sb.* government. A. & C. III. 6.

Regreet, *sb.* a salutation. M. of V. II. 9.

Regreet, *v.t.* to salute. R. II. I. 3.

Reguerdon, *sb.* requital. 1 H. VI. III. 1.

Relative, *adj.* applicable. Ham. II. 2.

Remember, *v.t.* to remind. Wint. Tale, III. 2 ; M. for M. II. 1.

Remorse, *sb.* pity. M. for M. v. 1.

Remorseful, *adj.* full of pity, compassionate. Two Gent. IV. 3.

Remotion, *sb.* removal. Tim. IV. 3.

Removed, *adj.* sequestered, remote. M. for M. I. 4 ; As you Like it, III. 2.

Render, *v.t.* to describe you. As you Like it, IV. 3.

Render, *sb.* account. Cym. IV. 4.

Renege, *v.t.* to renounce, to deny. A. & C. I. 1 ; Lear, II. 2.

Repair, *v.t.* to renovate, comfort. All's Well, I. 2.

Repeal, *v.t.* to reverse the sentence of exile. Two Gent. v. 4.

Reproof, *sb.* confutation. 1 H. IV. I. 2.

Repugn, *v.t.* to resist. 1 H. VI. IV. 1.

Requiem, *sb.* mass for the dead, so called because it begins with the words, Requiem eternam dona eis, Domine. Ham. v. 1.

Resolve, *v.t.* to satisfy. 3 H. VI. III. 2. To dissolve. Ham. I. 2.

Respect, *sb.* consideration. Much Ado, II. 3.

Respective, *adj.* respectful, thoughtful. M. of V. v. 1.

Respective, *adj.* corresponding. Two Gent. IV. 4.

Respectively, *adv.* respectfully. Tim. III. 1.

Retailed, *p.p.* handed down. R. III. III. 1.

Retire, *sb.* retreat. 1 H. IV. II. 3.

Retire, *v.t.* to draw back. R. II. II. 2.

Reverb, *v.t.* to echo. Lear, I. 1.

Revolt, *sb.* a rebel. John, v. 4.

Rib, *v.t.* to enclose as within ribs. M. of V. II. 7.

Rid, *v.t.* to destroy. Temp. I. 2.

Rift, *v.i.* to split. Wint. Tale, v. 1. *v.t.* to split. Temp. v. 1.

Rift, *sb.* a split. Temp. I. 2.

Riggish, *adj.* wanton. A. & C. II. 2.

Rigol, *sb.* a circle. 2 H. IV. IV. 4.

Ripe, *adj.* drunk. Temp. v. 1.

Rivage, *sb.* the shore. H. V. III. Chorus.

Rival, *sb.* a partner. Ham. I. 1.

Rivality, *sb.* equal rank. A. & C. III. 5.

Rive, *v.t.* to fire. 1 H. VI. IV. 2.

Road, *sb.* the high road, applied to a common woman (traviata). 2 H. IV. II. 2.

Roisting, *adj.* roistering, violent. T. & Cr. II. 2.

Romage, *sb.* unusual stir. Ham. I. 1.

Ronvon, *sb.* a term of contempt applied to a woman. Mac. I. 3.

Rood, *sb.* the crucifix. R. & J. I. 3.

Rook, *sb.* a cheater. Merry Wives, I. 3.

Ropery, *sb.* roguery. R. & J. II. 4.

Rope-tricks, *sb.* tricks such as are played by a rope-dancer. Tam. of S. I. 2.

Round, *v.i.* to whisper. Oth. I. 3. To become great with child. Wint. Tale, II. 1. *v.t.* to finish off. Temp. IV. 1.

Round, *sb.* a diadem. Mac. I. 5.

Round, *adj.* unceremonious. Mac. I. 5.

Roundel, *sb.* a dance or song. M. N's Dr. II. 3.

Roundure, *sb.* an enclosure. John, II. 1.

Rouse, *sb.* carousal. Ham. I. 4.

Roynish, *adj.* mangy. As you Like it, II. 2.

Rubious, *adj.* ruddy. Tw. N. I. 4.

Ruddock, *sb.* the redbreast. Cym. IV. 1.

Rush, *v.t.* to push. R. & J. III. 3.

Rushling, *adj.* rustling. Merry Wives, II. 2.

Sacrificial, *adj.* reverent, as words used in religious worship. Tim. I. 1.

Sacring-bell, *sb.* the little bell rung at mass to give notice that the elements are consecrated. H. VIII. III. 2.

Sad, *adj.* serious. Two Gent. I. 2.

Sadly, *adv.* seriously. Much Ado, II. 3.

Sadness, *sb.* seriousness. R. & J. I. 1.

Safe, *v.t.* to make safe. A. & C. IV. 6.

Sag, *v.i.* to hang down. Mac. v. 3.

Salt, *adj.* lascivious. Oth. II. 1 ; III. 3.

Salt, *sb.* taste. Merry Wives, II. 3.

Sanded, *adj.* marked with yellow spots. M. N's Dr. IV. 1.

Sans, *prep.* without. Temp. I. 2.

Saucy, *adj.* lascivious. All's Well, IV. 4.

Saw, *sb.* a moral saying. L's L's L. v. 2.

Say, *adj.* silken. 2 H. VI. IV. 7.

Say, *sb.* assay, taste, relish. Lear, v. 3.

Scaffoldage, *sb.* the gallery of a theatre. T. & Cr. I. 3.

Scald, *adj.* scurvy, scabby. Merry Wives, III. 1.

Scale, *v.t.* to weigh in scales. Cor. II. 3.

Scall, *sb.* a scab, a word of reproach. Merry Wives, III. 1.

Scamble, *v.i.* to scramble. H. V. I. 1.

Scamel, *sb.* probably a misprint for sea-mel, sea-mew. Temp. II. 2.

Scan, *v.t.* to examine subtly. Oth. III. 3.

Scant, *v.t.* to cut short, to spare. M. of V. III. 2.

Scant, *adj.* scanty, short. Ham. v. 2. *adv.* scarcely. R. & J. I. 2.

Scantling, *sb.* a small portion. T. & Cr. I. 3.

Scape, *v.t.* to escape. Much Ado, II. 1.

Scape, *sb.* a sally. M. for M. I. 1.

Scathe, *sb.* injury. 2 H. VI. II. 4.

Scathe, *v.t.* to injure. R. & J. I. 5.

Scathful, *adj.* destructive. Tw. N. v. 1.

Sconce, *sb.* the head. Ham. v. 1.

Scotch, *v.t.* to bruise or cut slightly. Mac. III. 2.

Scrimer, *sb.* a fencer. Ham. IV. 7.

Scroyle, *sb.* a scabby fellow. John, II. 3.

Scull, *sb.* a shoal of fish. T. & Cr. v. 5.

Scurvy, *adj.* scabby ; metaph. mean. Temp. II. 2.

Seal, *v.t.* to set one's seal to a deed ; hence, to confirm. Cor. II. 3.

Seam, *sb.* fat. T. & Cr. II. 3.

Seamy, *adj.* showing the seam or sewing. Oth. IV. 2.

Sear, *adj.* scorched, withered. Mac. v. 3.

Sear, *v.t.* to stigmatise. All's Well, II. 1.

Search, *v.t.* to probe ; hence, to apply a healing remedy. Two Gent. I. 2.

Seated, *adj.* fixed, confirmed. Mac. I. 3.

Sect, *sb.* a slip or scion. Oth. I. 3. A political party. Lear, v. 3.

Securely, *adv.* inconsiderately. T. & Cr. IV. 5.

Seel, *v.t.* to close. Oth. III. 3.

Seeling, *pr. p.* closing, blinding. Mac. III. 2.

Seeming, *adv.* seemly, becomingly. As you Like it, v. 4.

Seeming, *sb.* outward manner and appearance. Wint. Tale, IV. 4.

Seen, *adj.* versed, instructed. Tam. of S. I. 2.

Seld, *adv.* seldom. T. & Cr. IV. 5.

Self-bounty, *sb.* native goodness. Oth. III. 3.

Semblably, *adv.* alike. 1 H. IV. v. 3.

Seniory, *sb.* seniority. R. III. IV. 4.

Sennet, *sb.* a flourish of trumpets.

Sepulchre, *v.t.* to bury. Two Gent. IV. 2.

Sequestration, *sb.* separation. Oth. I. 3.

Sere, *adj.* dry. Com. of E. IV. 2.

Serjeant, *sb.* a bailiff. Ham. v. 2.

Serpigo, *sb.* a cutaneous disease. M. for M. III. 1.

Serviceable, *adj.* 'serviceable vows,' vows that you will do her service, or be her servant. Two Gent. III. 2.

Setebos, *sb.* the name of a fiend. Temp. I. 2.

Setter, *sb.* one who watches travellers to give information to thieves. 1 H. IV. II. 2.

Several, *sb.* land which is not common but appropriated. L's L's L. II. 1.

Shame, *v.i.* to be ashamed. Cor. II. 2.

Shame, *sb.* modesty. Com. of E. III. 2.

Shards, *sb.* shreds, broken fragments of pottery. Ham. v. 1.

Shards, *sb.* the wing cases of beetles; hence 'sharded.' Cym. III. 3; and 'shard-borne.' Mac. III. 2.

Sharked, *p.p.* snatched up, as a shark does his prey. Ham. I. 1.

Sheen, *sb.* brilliancy. M. N's Dr. II. 1.

Sheer, *adj.* pure. R. II. v. 3. Unmixed. Ind. to Tam. of S. 2.

Shent, *p.p.* rebuked, blamed. Cor. v. 2. Hurt. Ham. III. 3.

Sheriff's-post, *sb.* a post at the door of a sheriff, to which royal proclamations were fixed. Tw. N. I. 5.

Shive, *sb.* slice. T. A. II. 1.

Shot, *sb.* the reckoning at an ale-house. Two Gent. II. 5.

Shoughs, *sb.* shaggy dogs. Mac. III. 1.

Shouldered, *p.p.* a doubtful word. R. III. III. 7.

Shovel-board, *sb.* game played by sliding metal pieces along a board at a mark. Merry Wives, I. 1.

Shrewd, *adj.* mischievous. All's Well, III. 5.

Shrift, *sb.* confession. R. III. III. 4. Absolution. M. for M. IV. 2.

Shrive, *v.t.* to confess. M. of V. I. 2.

Shriving-time, *sb.* time for confession. Ham. v. 2.

Shroud, *v.r.* to enshroud oneself, cover oneself up. Temp. II. 2.

Side-sleeves, *sb.* loose hanging sleeves. Much Ado, III. 4.

Siege, *sb.* seat. M. for M. IV. 2. Stool. Temp. II. 2. Rank. Ham. IV. 7.

Sight, *sb.* an aperture in a helmet. 2 H. IV. IV. 1.

Sightless, *adj.* invisible. Mac. I. 5. Unsightly. John, III. 1.

Sign, *v.i.* to give an omen. A. & C. IV. 3.

Silly, *adj.* simple, rustic. Cym. v. 3.

Simular, *adj.* counterfeit, feigned. Cym. v. 5.

Single, *adj.* feeble. Mac. I. 3.

Sir, *sb.* a title applied to a bachelor of arts at the Universities. Tw. N. IV. 2.

Sith, *conj.* since. Two Gent. I. 2.

Sithence, *conj.* since. Cor. III. 1.

Sizes, *sb.* allowances. Lear, II. 4.

Skains-mates, *sb.* scapegraces. R. & J. II. 4.

Skill, *v.i.* to be of importance. Tam. of S. III. 2.

Skilless, *adj.* ignorant. Temp. III. 1.

Skimble-skamble, *adj.* rambling, disjointed. 1 H. IV. III. 1.

Skinker, *sb.* a drawer of liquor. 1 H. IV. II. 4.

Skirr, *v.i.* to scour. Mac. v. 3.

Slack, *v.t.* slacken. Oth. IV. 3.

Slave, *v.t.* to turn to slavish uses. Lear, IV. 1.

Sleave, *sb.* floss-silk. Mac. II. 2.

Sledded, *p.p.* sledged. Ham. I. 1.

Sleided, *p.p.* untwisted, raw, applied to silk. Per. IV. (Gower).

Sleights, *sb.* artifices. Mac. III. 5.

Slice, *int.* Merry Wives, I. 1.

Slipper, *adj.* slippery. Oth. II. 1.

Slips, *sb.* a kind of noose, or leash. H. V. III. 1. A piece of base money. R. & J. II. 4.

Sliver, *v.t.* to slice. Lear, IV. 2.

Sliver, *sb.* a slice. Ham. IV. 7.

Slops, *sb.* loose breeches. Much Ado, III. 2.

Slubber, *v.t.* to slur over. M. of V. II. 8.

Smirched, *p.p.* smeared, soiled. Much Ado, IV. 1.

Smooth, *v.t.* to flatter. Per. I. 2.

Smoothed, *p.p.* flattered, fawned upon. Tim. IV. 3.

Sneap, *sb.* taunt, sarcasm. 2 H. IV. II. 1.

Sneaped, *p.p.* pinched. Lucr. 333.

Sneaping, L's L's L. I. 1.

Sneck-up, *int.* go hang! Tw. N. II. 3.

Snuff, *sb.* anger. L's L's L. 'To take in snuff' is to take offence.

Softly, *adv.* gently. Wint. Tale, IV. 2; Ham. IV. 4.

Soil, *sb.* spot, taint. Ham. I. 3.

Solicit, *sb.* solicitation. Cym. II. 3.

Solidare, *sb.* a small coin. Tim. III. 1.

Solve, *sb.* solution. Son. 69.

Sometimes, *adv.* formerly. M. of V. I. 1.

Sooth, *sb.* truth. Wint. Tale, IV. 3. Conciliation. R. II. III. 3.

Sooth, *adj.* true. Mac. v. 5.

Sorel, *sb.* a buck of the third year. L's L's L. IV. 2.

Sorriest, *adj.* most sorrowful. Mac. III. 2.

Sorry, *adj.* sorrowful, dismal. Com. of E. v. 1.

Sort, *sb.* a company. M. N's Dr. III. 2. Rank, condition. R. II. IV. 1. Lot. T. & Cr. I. 3. 'In a sort,' in a manner. Temp. II. 1.

Sort, *v.t.* to choose. Two Gent. III. 2. *v.i.* to suit. Much Ado, v. 2. To consort. 2 H. IV. II. 4.

Sot, *sb.* fool. Cym. v. 5.

Soul-fearing, *adj.* soul-terrifying. John, II. 2.

Sowl, *v.t.* to lug, drag. Cor. IV. 5.

Sowter, *sb.* name of a dog. Tw. N. II. 5.

Specialty, *sb.* a special contract. Tam. of S. II. 1.

Sped, *p.p.* settled, done for. R. & J. III. 1.

Speed, *sb.* fortune. Wint. Tale, III. 2.

Sperr, *v.t.* to bolt, fasten. T. & Cr. Prol.

Spial, *sb.* spy. 1 H. VI. I. 4.

Spill, *v.t.* to destroy. Lear, II. 2.

Spilth, *sb.* spilling. Tim. II. 2.

Spleen, *sb.* violent haste. John, II. 2; v. 7. Used of the lightning flash. M. N's Dr. I. 1.

Sprag, *adj.* quick. Merry Wives, IV. 1.

Spring, *sb.* shoot, bud. V. & A. 656. Beginning. M. N's Dr. II. 2 ; 2 H. IV. IV. 4.

Springhalt, *sb.* stringhalt, a disease of horses. H. VIII. I. 3.

Sprited, *p.p.* haunted. Cym. II. 3.

Spurs, *sb.* roots of trees. Temp. V. 1 ; Cym. IV. 2.

Squandered, *p.p.* scattered. M. of V. I. 3.

Square, *v.t.* to quarrel. M. N's Dr. II. 1.

Square, *sb.* the front part of a woman's dress, stomacher. Wint. Tale, IV. 4.

Square, *adj.* equitable. Tim. V. 1.

Squarer, *sb.* quarreller. Much Ado, I. 1.

Squash, *sb.* an unripe peascod. Tw. N. I. 5.

Squier, *sb.* a square or rule. L's L's L. V. 2.

Squiny, *v.i.* to squint. Lear, IV. 6.

Staggers, *sb.* a disease in horses, attended with giddiness : hence any bewildering distress. Cym. V. 5.

Stain, *v.t.* to disfigure. Temp. I. 2.

Stale, *sb.* a decoy. Temp. IV. 1. A gull. Tam. of S. I. 1. A prostitute. Much Ado, II. 2.

Stale, *v.t.* to make stale, deprive anything of its freshness. T. & Cr. II. 3.

Stand upon, to be incumbent on. R. II. IV. 2.

Staniel, *sb.* an inferior kind of hawk. Tw. N. II. 5.

Stark, *adv.* stiff. Cym. IV. 2.

Starkly, *adv.* stiffly. M. for M. IV. 2.

State, *sb.* a canopied chair. Tw. N. II. 5.

Station, *sb.* attitude. Ham. III. 4. Act of standing. A. & C. III. 3.

Statist, *sb.* a statesman. Cym. II. 4.

Statua, *sb.* a statue. R. III. III. 7.

Statue, *sb.* image, picture. Two Gent. IV. 4.

Statute, *sb.* security, obligation. Son. 134.

Statute-caps, *sb.* woollen caps worn by citizens. L's L's L. V. 2.

Stay, *sb.* a check. John, II. 2.

Stead, *v.t.* to profit. Temp. I. 2.

Stelled, *p.p.* (a doubtful word) set or fixed. Lucr. 1444. Son. 24.

Sternage, *sb.* steerage, course. H. V. III. Chorus.

Stickler, *sb.* an arbitrator in combats. T. & Cr. V. 9.

Stigmatic, *sb.* a deformed person. 2 H. VI. V. 1.

Stigmatical, *adj.* deformed. Com. of E. IV. 2.

Still, *adj.* constant. T. A. III. 2.

Still, *adv.* constantly. Temp. I. 2.

Stilly, *adv.* softly. H. V. IV. Chorus.

Stint, *v.t.* to stop. H. VIII. I. 2. *v.i.* to stop. R. & J. I. 3.

Stithy, *sb.* a smith's forge. Ham. III. 2.

Stithy, *v.t.* to forge. T. & Cr. IV. 5.

Stoccado, *sb.* a stoccata, or thrust in fencing. Merry Wives, II. 1.

Stock, *sb.* a stocking. Tam. of S. III. 3.

Stomach, *sb.* courage, stubbornness. Temp. I. 2. Appetite, inclination. Temp. II. 1.

Stone-bow, *sb.* a cross-bow for throwing stones. Tw. N. II. 5.

Stoup, *sb.* a cup. Tw. N. II. 3.

Stout, *adj.* strong, healthy. Tim. IV. 3.

Stover, *sb.* fodder. Temp. III. 8.

Strachy, *sb.* A word of doubtful meaning. Tw. N. II. 5.

Straight, *adv.* immediately. Ham. V. 1.

Strain, *sb.* lineage. Much Ado, II. 1. Disposition. Merry Wives, II. 1.

Straited, *p.p.* straitened. Wint. Tale, IV. 4.

Strange, *adj.* foreign. L's L's L. IV. 2. Coy, reserved. R. & J. II. 2. Marvellous. Oth. V. 2.

Strangeness, *sb.* coyness, reserve. T. & Cr. III. 3.

Stranger, *sb.* foreigner. H. VIII. II. 3.

Strappado, *sb.* a kind of punishment. 1 H. IV. II. 4.

Stricture, *sb.* strictness. M. for M. I. 4.

Strossers, *sb.* trowsers. H. V. III. 7.

Stuck, *sb.* a thrust of a sword. Ham. IV. 7.

Stuck in, *sb.* corruption of stoccata. Tw. N. III. 4.

Stuff, *sb.* baggage. Com. of E. IV. 4. Material, substance. Oth. I. 1.

Stuffed, *p.p.* filled, stored. Much Ado, I. 1.

Sty, *v.t.* to lodge as in a sty. Temp. I. 2.

Subscribe, *v.t.* to yield. Lear, I. 2. *v.i.* to succumb. T. & Cr. IV. 5.

Success, *sb.* issue, consequence. Much Ado, I. 3. Succession. Wint. Tale, I. 2.

Successive, *adj.* succeeding. 2 H. VI. III. 1.

Successively, *adv.* in succession. 2 H. IV. IV. 4.

Sudden, *adj.* hasty, rash. As you Like it, II. 7.

Suddenly, *adv.* hastily. R. III. IV. 1.

Sufferance, *sb.* suffering. M. for M. III. 1.

Suggest, *v.t.* to tempt, entice. All's Well, IV. 5.

Suggestion, *sb.* temptation, enticement. Mac. I. 3.

Suited, *p.p.* dressed. All's Well, I. 1.

Sullen, *adj.* doleful, melancholy. John, I. 1.

Sumpter, *sb.* a horse that carries provisions on a journey. Lear, II. 4.

Suppose, *sb.* a trick, imposition. Tam. of S. V. 1.

Supposed, *p.p.* counterfeit. Tam. of S. II. 1.

Surcease, *v.i.* to cease. Cor. III. 2.

Surcease, *sb.* cessation, end. Mac. I. 7.

Surprise, *v.t.* to capture by surprise. 3 H. VI. IV. 2.

Sur-reined, *p.p.* over-worked. H. V. III. 5.

Suspect, *sb.* suspicion. R. III. I. 3.

Suspire, *v.i.* to breathe. 2 H. IV. IV. 4.

Swabber, *sb.* a sweeper of the deck of a ship. Temp. II. 2.

Swarth, *adj.* black. John, III. 1.

Swarth, *adj.* black. T. A. II. 3.

Swarth, *sb.* quantity of grass cut down by one sweep of the scythe. Tw. N. II. 3.

Swasher, *sb.* swaggerer. H. V. III. 2.

Swashing, *pr. p.* dashing, smashing. R. & J. I. 1.

Swath, *sb.* The same as ' swarth.' T. & Cr. V. 5.

Swathling, *adj.* swaddling. 1 H. IV. III. 2.

Sway, *v.i.* to move on. 2 H. IV. IV. 1.

Swear, *v.t.* to adjure. Lear, I. 1.

Swear over, *v.t.* to out-swear. Wint. Tale, I. 2.

Swift, *adj.* ready, quick. Much Ado, III. 1.

Swinge-buckler, *sb.* a bully. 2 H. IV. III. 2.

Table, *sb.* a tablet, note-book. Ham. I. 2.

Table-book, *sb.* note-book. Wint. Tale, IV. 3.

Tables, *sb.* the game of backgammon. L's L's L. V. 2. A note-book. Ham. I. 5.

Tabor, *sb.* a small side-drum. Temp. IV. 1.

Taborer, *sb.* a player on the tabor. Temp. III. 2.

Tabourine, *sb.* tambourine, drum. T. & Cr. IV. 5.

Tag, *sb.* the rabble. Cor. III. 1.

Taint, *p.p.* tainted. 1 H. VI. V. 3.

Tainture, *sb.* defilement. 2 H. VI. II. 1.

Take, *v.t.* to infect, blast, bewitch. Merry Wives, IV. 4 ; Ham. I. 1.

Take in, *v.t.* to conquer. A. & C. III. 7 ; Cor. I. 2.

Take out, *v.t.* to copy. Oth. III. 4.

Take up, *v.t.* to borrow money, or buy on credit. 2 H. VI. IV. 7. To make up a quarrel. As you Like it, v. 4.

Taking, *sb.* infection, malignant influence. Lear, III. 4.

Taking up, *sb.* buying on credit. 2 H. IV. I. 2.

Tale, *sb.* counting, reckoning. Mac. I. 3.

Tall, *adj.* strong, valiant. Tw. N. I. 3.

Tallow-catch, *sb.* a lump of tallow. 1 H. IV. II. 4.

Tang, *sb.* twang, sound. Temp. II. 2.

Tang, *v.t.* to sound. Tw. N. II. 5.

Tanling, *sb.* anything tanned by the sun. Cym. IV. 4.

Tarre, *v.t.* to excite, urge on. John, IV. 1.

Tarriance, *sb.* delay. Two Gent. II. 7.

Tartar, *sb.* Tartarus. H. V. II. 3.

Task, *v.t.* to tax. 1 H. IV. IV. 3. Challenge. R. II. IV. 1.

Tasking, *sb.* challenging. 1 H. IV. v. 2.

Taste, *v.t.* to try. Tw. N. III. 4.

Tawdry-lace, *sb.* a rustic necklace. Wint. Tale, IV. 3.

Taxation, *sb.* satire, sarcasm. As you Like it, I. 2.

Taxing, *sb.* satire. As you Like it, II. 7.

Teen, *sb.* grief. Temp. I. 2.

Tell, *v.t.* to count. Temp. II. 1.

Temper, *v.t.* to mix. Cym. v. 5.

Temperance, *sb.* temperature. Temp. II. 1.

Tempered, *p.p.* mixed. Ham. v. 2.

Tend, *v.t.* to attend to. 2 H. VI. I. 1.

Tender, *v.t.* to hold, to esteem. Temp. II. 1. To have consideration for. Two Gent. IV. 4.

Tent, *v.t.* to probe as a wound. Cor. III. 1.

Tent, *sb.* a probe for searching a wound. Cym. III. 4.

Tercel, *sb.* the male of the goshawk. T. & Cr. III. 2.

Termagant, *sb.* a ranting character in old plays. Ham. III. 2.

Tested, *p.p.* pure, assayed. M. for M. II. 2.

Testern, *v.t.* to reward with a tester, or sixpence. Two Gent. I. 1.

Tharborough, *sb.* (corrupted from 'third-borough') a constable. L's L's L. I. 1.

Theorick, *sb.* theory. All's Well, IV. 3.

Thewes, *sb.* sinews, muscles. 2 H. IV. III. 2.

Thick, *adv.* rapidly. 2 H. IV. II. 3 ; Cym. III. 2.

Thick-pleached, *p.p.* thickly intertwined. Much Ado, I. 2.

Third-borough, *sb.* a constable. Ind. to Tam. of S. 1.

Thought, *sb.* anxiety, grief. Ham. III. 1 ; A. & C. IV. 6. So 'to take thought' is to give way to grief. J. C. II. 1.

Thrasonical, *adj.* boastful. As you Like it, v. 2.

Three-man beetle, *sb.* a wooden mallet worked by three men. 2 H. IV. I. 2.

Three-man-song-men, *sb.* singers of glees in three parts. Wint. Tale, IV. 3.

Three-pile, *sb.* three-piled velvet. Wint. Tale, IV. 3.

Threne, *sb.* lament. Ph. & T. 49.

Thrid, *sb.* thread, fibre. Temp. IV. 1.

Throe, *v.t.* to put in agonies. Temp. II. 1.

Thrum, *sb.* the tufted end of a thread in weaving. M. N's Dr. v. 1.

Thrummed, *p.p.* made of coarse ends or tufts. Merry Wives, IV. 2.

Tickle, *adj.* ticklish. M. for M. I. 3.

Tight, *adj.* nimble, active. Tam. of S. II. 1 ; A. & C. IV. 4.

Tightly, *adv.* briskly, promptly. Merry Wives, I. 3 ; II. 3.

Tike, *sb.* a cur. H. V. II. 1.

Tilly-vally, *int.* an exclamation of contempt. Tw. N. II. 3.

Tilth, *sb.* tillage. Temp. II. 1.

Timeless, *adj.* untimely. R. II. IV. 1.

Tinct, *sb.* stain, dye. Ham. III. 4.

Tire, *sb.* attire, head-dress. Two Gent. IV. 4.

Tire, *v.i.* to tear as a bird of prey. 3 H. VI. I. 1. Hence, metaphorically, to feed. Cym. III. 4.

Tire, *v.t.* to attire, dress. Com. of E. II. 2.

Tod, *v.i.* to yield a tod of wool. Wint. Tale, IV. 3.

Tokened, *p.p.* marked with plague spots. A. & C. III. 8.

Tokens, *sb.* plague spots. L's L's L. v. 2.

Toll, *v.i.* to exact toll. 2 H. IV. IV. 4. To pay toll. All's Well, v. 3.

Too too, *adv.* excessively. Two Gent. I. 4 ; Ham. I. 2.

Topless, *adj.* supreme, without superior. T. & Cr. I. 3.

Touch, *sb.* touchstone for testing gold. R. III. IV. 2. Trait. As you Like it, III. 2. An acute feeling. Cym. I. 1.

Touched, *p.p.* pricked. T. A. IV. 4.

Touse, *v.t.* to pull, drag. M. for M. v. 1.

Toward, *adv.* nearly ready. M. N's Dr. III. 1.

Towards, *adv.* nearly ready. R. & J. I. 5.

Toys, *sb.* trifles, foolish tricks. 2 H. IV. IV. 4.

Trade, *sb.* beaten path. H. VIII. v. 1.

Tranect, *sb.* a ferry. M. of V. III. 4.

Translated, *p.p.* transformed. M. N's Dr. III. 1.

Trash, *v.t.* to check, as a huntsman his hounds. Temp. I. 2 ; Oth. II. 1.

Travail, *sb.* labor, toil. 1 H. VI. v. 4.

Tray-trip, *sb.* an old game played with dice. Tw. N. II. 5.

Treachers, *sb.* traitors. Lear, I. 2.

Treaties, *sb.* entreaties. A. & C. III. 9.

Trenched, *p.p.* carved. Two Gent. III. 2.

Trick, *sb.* technically, a copy of a coat of arms ; hence, any peculiarity which distinguishes voice or feature. Lear, IV. 6 ; Wint. Tale, II. 3.

Trick, *v.t.* to dress up. H. V. III. 6.

Tricked, *p.p.* blazoned. Ham. II. 2.

Tricking, *sb.* ornament. Merry Wives, IV. 4.

Tricksy, *adj.* elegantly quaint. Temp. v. 1.

Triple, *adj.* third. A. & C. I. 1.

Trojan, *sb.* a cant word for a thief. 1 H. IV. II. 1.

Trol-my-dames, *sb.* Fr. *trou-madame ;* the name of a game ; also called pigeon-holes. Wint. Tale, IV. 2.

Troth-plight, *adj.* betrothed. H. V. II. 1.

Trow, *v.i.* to trust, think. H. VIII. I. 1.

True, *adj.* honest. Cym. II. 3.

Trundle-tail, *sb.* a long-tailed dog. Lear, III. 6.

Tucket-sonance, *sb.* a flourish on the trumpet. H. V. IV. 2.

Tundish, *sb.* a funnel. M. for M. III. 2.

Turlygood, *sb.* a name adopted by bedlam-beggars. Lear, II. 3.

Turn, *v.t.* to modulate. As you Like it, II. 5.

Twangling, *pr. p.* twanging. Temp. III. 2.

Twiggen, *adj.* made of twigs, wicker. Oth. II. 3.

Twilled, *p.p.* Temp. III. 3. A doubtful word.

Twink, *sb.* a twinkling. Temp. III. 3.

Twire, *v.i.* to peep, twinkle. Son. 28.

Umbered, *p.p.* stained, dark, as with umber. H. V. IV. Chorus.

Unaneled, *p.p.* without extreme unction. Ham. I. 5.

Unavoided, *adj.* unavoidable. R. III. IV. 4.

Unbarbed, *p.p.* untrimmed. Cor. III. 2.

Unbated, *p.p.* unblunted. Ham. IV. 7.

Unbolt, *v.t.* to disclose. Tim. I. 1.

Unbolted, *p.p.* unsifted, unrefined. Lear, II. 2.

Unbreathed, *p.p.* unpractised. M. N's Dr. V. 1.

Uncape, *v.t.* to throw off the hounds. Merry Wives, III. 3.

Uncharged, *p.p.* undefended, applied to the gates of a city. Tim. V. 4.

Unclew, *v.t.* to unravel, undo. Tim. I. 1.

Uncoined, *p.p.* unalloyed, unfeigned. H. V. V. 7.

Undergo, *v.t.* to undertake. Tim. III. 5.

Undertaker, *sb.* one who takes up another's quarrel. Tw. N. III. 4.

Under-wrought, *p.p.* undermined. John, II. 1.

Uneath, *adv.* hardly. 2 H. VI. III. 4.

Unexpressive, *adj.* inexpressible. As you Like it, III. 2.

Unfair, *v.t.* to deprive of beauty. Son. 5.

Unhappily, *adv.* censoriously. H. VIII. I. 4.

Unhappy, *adj.* mischievous. All's Well, IV. 5.

Unhatched, *p.p.* undisclosed. Oth. III. 4.

Unhouseled, *p.p.* without receiving the sacrament. Ham. I. 5.

Unimproved, *p.p.* unreproved. Ham. I. 1.

Union, *sb.* a pearl. Ham. V. 2.

Unjust, *adj.* dishonest. 1 H. IV. IV. 2.

Unkind, *adj.* unnatural. Lear, III. 4.

Unlived, *adj.* bereft of life. Lucr. 1754.

Unmanned, *p.p.* untamed, applied to a hawk. R. & J. III. 2.

Unowed, *p.p.* unowned. John, IV. 3.

Unpregnant, *adj.* stupid. M. for M. IV. 4.

Unproper, *adj.* common to all. Oth. IV. 1.

Unquestionable, *adj.* not inquisitive. As you Like it, III. 2.

Unready, *adj.* undressed. 1 H. VI. II. 1.

Unrespective, *adj.* inconsiderate. R. III. IV. 2.

Unsisting, *adj.* unresting. M. for M. IV. 2.

Unstanched, *p.p.* incontinent. Temp. I. 1.

Untempering, *adj.* unsoftening. H. V. V. 2.

Untented, *adj.* unsearchable. Lear, I. 4.

Untraded, *adj.* unused, uncommon. T. & Cr. IV. 5.

Untrimmed, *p.p.* spoiled of grace or ornament. Son. 18.

Untrue, *sb.* untruth. Son. 113.

Unvalued, *adj.* invaluable. R. III. I. 4.

Upspring reel, *sb.* a boisterous dance. Ham. I. 4.

Urchin, *sb.* the hedge-hog. Temp. I. 2.

Usance, *sb.* usury. M. of V. I. 3.

Use, *sb.* interest. M. for M. I. 1.

Utis, *sb.* riotous merriment, which accompanied the eighth day of a festival. 2 H. IV. II. 4.

Utter, *v.t.* to expel, put forth. Much Ado, V. 3.

Utterance, *sb.* extremity. Mac. III. 1; Cym. III. 1.

Vade, *v.i.* to fade. P. P. 131, 170.

Vail, *v.t.* to lower. M. for M. V. 1.

Vailing, *pr. p.* lowering. M. of V. I. 1.

Vainness, *sb.* vanity. H. V. V. Chorus.

Valanced, *p.p.* adorned with a valance or fringe; applied to the beard. Ham. II. 2.

Validity, *sb.* value. All's Well, V. 3.

Vantage, *sb.* advantage. Two Gent. I. 3.

Vantbrace, *sb.* armor for the front of the arm. T. & Cr. I. 3.

Varlet, *sb.* a servant, valet. T. & Cr. I. 1.

Vast, *sb.* properly a waste-place, metaphorically, the dead of night. Temp. I. 2. A gulf. Wint. Tale, I. 1.

Vastidity, *sb.* immensity. M. for M. III. 1.

Vastly, *adv.* like a waste. Luc. 1740.

Vasty, *adj.* vast, waste. 1 H. IV. III. 1.

Vaunt, *sb.* the van, that which precedes. T. & Cr. Prol.

Vaunt-couriers, *sb.* forerunners. Lear, III. 2.

Vaward, *sb.* the van, vanguard, advanced guard of an army. H. V. IV. 3. Hence, metaphorically, the first of anything. M. N's Dr. IV. 1.

Vegetives, *sb.* herbs. Per. III. 2.

Velure, *sb.* velvet. Tam. of S. III. 2.

Velvet-guards, *sb.* literally, velvet trimmings; applied metaphorically to the citizens who wore them. 1 H. IV. III. 1.

Venew, *sb.* a bout in fencing, metaphorically applied to repartee and sallies of wit. L's L's L. V. 1.

Veney, *sb.* a bout at fencing. Merry Wives, I. 1.

Venge, *v.t.* to avenge. H. V. I. 2.

Ventages, *sb.* holes in a flute or flageolet. Ham. III. 2.

Verbal, *adj.* wordy. Cym. II. 3.

Very, *adj.* true, real. Two Gent. I. 1.

Via, *int.* off with you! Merry Wives, II. 2.

Vice, *v.t.* to screw. Wint. Tale, I. 2.

Vice, *sb.* the buffoon in the old morality plays. Ham. III. 4.

Vie, *v.i.* to challenge; a term at cards. A. & C. V. 2. To play as for a wager. Tam. of S. II. 1.

Viewless, *adj.* invisible. M. for M. III. 1.

Villain, *sb.* a lowborn man. As you Like it, I. 1.

Vinewed, *p.p.* mouldy. T. & Cr. II. 1.

Viol-de-gamboys, *sb.* a bass viol. Tw. N. I. 3.

Virginalling, *pr. p.* playing as on the virginals, a kind of a spinet. Wint. Tale, I. 2.

Virtue, *sb.* the essential excellence. Temp. I. 2. Valor. Lear, V. 3.

Virtuous, *adj.* excellent. M. N's Dr. III. 2. Endowed with virtues. As you Like it, I. 3.

Vizament, *sb.* advisement. Merry Wives, I. 1.

Voluble, *adj.* fickle. Oth. II. 1.

Voluntary, *sb.* volunteer. John, II. 1.

Votarist, *sb.* votary, one who has taken a vow. M. for M. I. 5.

Vulgar, *sb.* the common people. L's L's L. I. 2.

Vulgar, *adj.* common. John, II. 2.

Vulgarly, *adv.* publicly. M. for M. V. 1.

Waft, *v.t.* to wave, beckon. Ham. I. 4. To turn. Wint. Tale, I. 2.

Waftage, *sb.* passage. T. & Cr. III. 2.

Wafture, *sb.* waving, beckoning. J. C. II. 1.

Wage, *v.t.* to reward as with wages. Cor. v. 5.

Wailful, *adj.* lamentable. Two Gent. III. 2.

Waist, *sb.* the middle of a ship. Temp. I. 2.

Wannion, 'With a wannion ' = 'with a vengeance.' Per. II. 1.

Wappened, *p.p.* withered, overworn. Tim. IV. 3.

Ward, *sb.* guard. Temp. I. 2. Prison. 2 H. VI. v. 1.

Warden, *sb.* a large pear used for baking. Wint. Tale, IV. 2.

Warder, *sb.* truncheon. R. II. I. 3.

Warn, *v.t.* to summon. R. III. I. 3.

Wassail, *sb.* a drinking bout. A. & C. I. 4. Festivity. Ham. I. 4.

Wat, a familiar word for a hare. V. & A. 697.

Watch, *sb.* a watch light. R. III. v. 3.

Watch, *v.t.* to tame by keeping constantly awake. Oth. III. 3.

Water-gall, *sb.* a secondary rainbow. Lucr. 1588.

Water-rug, *sb.* a kind of dog. Mac. III. 1.

Water-work, *sb.* painting in distemper. 2 H. IV. II. 1.

Wax, *v.i.* to grow. H. V. v. 1.

Waxen, *v.i.* perhaps, to hiccough. M. N's Dr. II. 1.

Wealth, *sb.* weal, advantage. M. of V. v. 1.

Wear, *sb.* fashion. As you Like it, II. 7.

Weather-fend, *v.t.* to defend from the weather. Temp. v. 1.

Web and pin, *sb.* the cataract in the eye. Lear, III. 4 ; Wint. Tale, I. 2.

Wee, *adj.* small, tiny. Merry Wives, I. 4.

Wee, *v.i.* to think. 1 H. VI. II. 5.

Weed, *sb.* garment. Tw. N. v. 1.

Weet, *v.t.* to wit, know. A. & C. I. 1.

Weigh out, *v.t.* to outweigh. H. VIII. III. 1.

Welkin, *sb.* the sky. Merry Wives, I. 3.

Welkin, *adj.* sky-blue. Wint. Tale, I. 2.

Well-liking, *adj.* in good condition. L's L's L. v. 2.

Well said, *int.* well done ! 2 H. IV. III. 2.

Wend, *v.i.* to go. M. for M. IV. 3.

Wesand, *sb.* the wind-pipe. Temp. III. 2.

Whelk, *sb.* a weal. H. V. III. 6.

Whelked, *p.p.* marked with whelks or protuberances. Lear, IV. 6.

When, an exclamation of impatience. Tam. of S. IV. 1.

When as, *adv.* when. Son. 49.

Where, *adv.* whereas. 2 H. VI. III. 2 ; Lear, I. 2.

Where, *sb.* a place. Lear, I. 1.

Whiffler, *sb.* an officer who clears the way in processions. H. V. v. Chorus.

While-ere, *adv.* a little while ago. Temp. III. 2.

Whiles, *adv.* until. Tw. N. IV. 3.

Whip-stock, *sb.* handle of a whip. Tw. N. II. 3.

Whist, *adj.* hushed, silent. Temp. I. 2.

White, *sb.* the centre of an archery butt. Tam. of S. v. 2.

Whitely, *adj.* pale-faced. L's L's L. III. 1. A doubtful word.

Whiting-time, *sb.* bleaching time. Merry Wives, III. 3.

Whitster, *sb.* bleacher. Merry Wives, III. 3.

Whittle, *sb.* a clasp knife. Tim. v. 3.

Whoo-bub, *sb.* hubbub. Wint. Tale, IV. 4.

Whoop, *v.i.* to cry out with astonishment. H. V. II. 2. Comp. As you Like it, III. 2.

Wicked, *adj.* noisome, baneful. Temp. I. 2.

Widow, *v.t.* to give a jointure to. M. for M. v. 1.

Widowhood, *sb.* widow's jointure. Tam. of S. II. 1.

Wight, *sb.* person. Oth. II. 1.

Wild, *sb.* weald. 1 H. IV. II. 1.

Wilderness, *sb.* wildness. M. for M. III. 1.

Wimpled, *p.p.* veiled, hooded. L's L's L. III. 1.

Window-bars, *sb.* lattice-work across a woman's stomacher. Tim. IV. 3.

Windring, *pr. p.* winding. Temp. III. 3.

Winter-ground, *v.t.* to protect (a plant) from frost. Cym. IV. 2.

Wis, in the compound ' I wis,' certainly. R. III. I. 3.

Wish, *v.t.* to commend. Tam. of S. I. 1.

Wistly, *adv.* wistfully. R. II. v. 4.

Wit, *sb.* knowledge, wisdom. M. of V. II. 1 ; J. C. III. 2.

Without, *prep.* beyond. M. N's Dr. IV. 1.

Wits, five, the five senses. Much Ado, I. 1.

Wittol, *sb.* a contented cuckold. Merry Wives, II. 2.

Witty, *adj.* intelligent. 3 H. VI. I. 2.

Woman-tired, *adj.* hen-pecked. Wint. Tale, II. 3.

Wondered, *p.p.* marvellously gifted. Temp. IV. 2.

Wood, *adj.* mad. Two Gent. II. 3.

Woodcock, *sb.* a simpleton. Tam. of S. I. 2.

Woodman, *sb.* a forester, huntsman. Cym. III. 6. A cant term for a wencher. M. for M. IV. 3.

Woolward, *adj.* shirtless. L's L's L. v. 2.

Word, *v.t.* to flatter or put off with words. A. & C. v. 2. To repeat the words of a song. Cym. IV. 2.

World. 'To go to the *world* ' is to get married. Much Ado, II. 1. So ' a woman of the *world* ' is a married woman. As you Like it, v. 3.

Worm, *sb.* a serpent. M. for M. III. 1.

Worser, *adj.* worse. Temp. IV. 1.

Worship, *v.t.* to honor. H. V. I. 2.

Worth, *sb.* wealth, fortune. Tw. N. III. 3.

Worts, *sb.* cabbages. Merry Wives, I. 1.

Wot, *v.t.* to know. Two Gent. IV. 4.

Wound, *p.p.* twisted about. Temp. II. 2.

Wreak, *sb.* vengeance. Cor. IV. 5.

Wreak, *v.t.* to avenge. T. A. IV. 3.

Wreakful, *adj.* revengeful, avenging. Tim. IV. 3.

Wrest, *sb.* an instrument used for tuning a harp. T. & Cr. III. 3.

Writ, *sb.* gospel, truth. Per. II. (Gower).

Writhled, *p.p.* shrivelled. 1 H. VI. II. 3.

Wroth, *sb.* calamity, misfortune. M. of V. II. 9.

Wrung, *p.p.* twisted, strained. 1 H. IV. II. 1.

Wry, *v.i.* to swerve. Cym. v. 1.

Yare, *adj.* ready. Used as an *int.*, ' be ' being understood. Temp. I. 1.

Yarely, *adv.* readily. Temp. I. 1.

Y-clad, *p.p.* clad. 2 H. VI. I. 1.

Y-cleped, *p.p.* called, named. L's L's L. v. 2.

Yearn, *v.t.* to grieve, vex. Merry Wives, III. 5 ; R. II. v. 5.

Yellowness, *sb.* jealousy. Merry Wives, I. 3.

Yellows, *sb.* a disease of horses. Tam. of S. III. 2.

Yeoman, *sb.* a sheriff's officer. 2 H. IV. II. 1.

Yield, *v.t.* to reward. A. & C. IV. 2. To report. A. & C. II. 5.

Yond, *adj.* and *adv.* yonder. Temp. I. 2.

Zany, *sb.* a clown, gull. L's L's L. v. 2.